THE Litigation MANUAL

A PRIMER FOR TRIAL LAWYERS

SECOND EDITION

JOHN G. KOELTL, EDITOR

SECTION OF LITIGATION

AMERICAN BAR ASSOCIATION

The material contained herein represents the opinions of the authors and editors and should not be construed to be the action of either the American Bar Association or the Section of Litigation unless adopted pursuant to the By-laws of the Association.

© 1989 American Bar Association. All rights reserved.

Printed in the United States of America.

Library of Congress Catalog Card Number 88-83137

ISBN 0-89707-409-2

Discounts are available for books ordered in bulk. Special consideration is given to state bars, CLE programs, and other bar-related organizations. Inquire at Publications Planning & Marketing, American Bar Association, 750 North Lake Shore Drive, Chicago, Illinois 60611.

94 93 92 91 90 5 4 3 2 1

TABLE OF CONTENTS

III. DEPOSITIONS

IV. EXPERTS

VII. PREPARING AND EXAMINING WITNESSES AT TRIAL

VIII. EVIDENCE ISSUES

XI. SPECIAL PROBLEMS OF THE CRIMINAL CASE

FOREWORD

This is the second edition of *The Litigation Manual,* which was published first in 1983. This edition doubles the size of the original Manual, expanding many previous chapters, such as examination of witnesses and trial, and adding new chapters, such as initiating suit and special problems in civil litigation. The entire Manual is organized in the same chronological fashion as problems would be addressed in the course of a litigation. The Manual is intended to be a practical guide for litigation for all those involved in the process—whether neophytes or veterans.

All of the articles that appear in this edition of the Manual—like those that appeared in the first edition—originally appeared in *Litigation,* the quarterly journal of the Section of Litigation of the American Bar Association. *Litigation* was the brainchild of Charles H. Wilson, a former journalist and practicing lawyer in Washington, D.C., who was its first editor-in-chief. Charlie set the standards for *Litigation,* which have prevailed ever since—a readable, practical magazine which shuns footnotes, advertisements, and ponderous writing. *Litigation* concentrates on practical wisdom from those who have actually experienced litigation. The objectives for *Litigation* are reprinted in every issue:

> A serious journal does not have to be dull, and scholarship need not be presented with a long face. *Litigation* seeks to be practical and concrete, not abstract and theoretical, lively and readable, not sober and sesquipedalian. The editors want *Litigation* to come to a halt on its journey across the desks of busy lawyers and not to flow past like a leaf on a stream, unnoticed and untouched.

Each of the editors-in-chief who has followed Charlie has spent extraordinary time assuring that each issue of *Litigation* continues the standards of readability and practical wisdom that Charlie set. Like Charlie, each has been a practicing lawyer who has taken the time from his or her practice. Charlie was succeeded in order by Doug Connah of Baltimore, F. Wallace Pope, Jr., of Clearwater, myself, William Pannill of Houston, James McElhaney of Cleveland, Bart Schwartz of Los Angeles, and Jean Snyder of Chicago. Each has been helped by the great dedication of the editors and the editorial staff of the American Bar Association.

The success of *Litigation* has also depended on the judges and trial lawyers who have taken the time from their own schedules to share their experience with their co-venturers in this process. Finally, *Litigation* has been helped by the foresight and assistance of the leadership of the Litigation Section who have always supported the magazine and given it the editorial freedom that is essential for responsible journalism.

All of those who have been involved with *Litigation* for some or all of the past fifteen years dedicate this edition to Charlie Wilson, *Litigation*'s first editor-in-chief, for his commitment and continuing contributions.

John G. Koeltl
New York City
January 1989

PART I

Initiating
Suit

Federal Jurisdiction: Thrust and Parry

by Thomas E. Baker

Federal jurisdiction is a fencing match, a contest that has its own special art and form. For every jurisdictional issue there is a thrust and parry. How and when to make those moves is what this article is all about.

The object of our match is assumed: Storm the castle. Get into federal court and stay there. The problems in doing that lie in the very nature of federal courts and the federal government.

Even though some federal judges do not act that way, they all sit on courts of a *limited* sovereign. Limited sovereigns have limited power, and their courts have limited jurisdiction. That is the key to our subject.

Before a federal court may hear a case, it has to pass two tests. The case must fall within the scope of Article III of the Constitution *and* within the scope of some particular jurisdiction enabling act of Congress. If the case fails either test, the federal court does not have jurisdiction.

What is more, the presumption is against jurisdiction. The party invoking federal power must rebut that presumption. Not only can the other side resist jurisdiction, but the court also has the obligation to raise jurisdictional issues on its own motion. Even the party invoking federal jurisdiction can later challenge that jurisdiction when the result does not satisfy him. *See generally* C. WRIGHT, LAW OF FEDERAL COURTS, § 7 (4th ed. 1983).

In a system in which every actor must invoke the jurisdictional bar, is it any wonder that so many suits fail at the threshold?

So here we are at the castle gate, sword in hand. Whether we get in depends on the answer to two questions: Does the federal court have the power to hear the case? Should it exercise that power? Those are the

---

The author is Professor of Law at Texas Tech University in Lubbock, Texas.

questions, but our focus is going to be on the thrusts and parries involved in answering them.

THRUST: The plaintiff has no standing.

PARRY: Standing rarely becomes an issue in private litigation. The victim of some contract breach or tort brings suit, and his standing to raise the claim is obvious. In public law litigation, by contrast, when a plaintiff challenges some governmental action, whether the person bringing suit is more than a bystander is a difficult and important question. Public law standing doctrine separates taxpayer plaintiffs from those who are more closely connected with the controversy.

That does not mean taxpayers cannot have standing. They can, but it is difficult. A taxpayer has standing *as a taxpayer* if the federal action being challenged allegedly exceeds a specific constitutional limit on congressional spending power. The category is narrow and is controlled by constitutional principles, but it is there.

For example, a taxpayer can attack a program of federal religious school aid as a violation of the establishment clause but cannot challenge the same program under either the due process clause or the Tenth Amendment. Local plaintiffs, however, may claim standing more easily as taxpayers challenging local expenditures. This approach should not be overlooked.

A nontaxpayer challenging a government action can have standing if he shows an actual or threatened injury that can be redressed by a favorable decision. Injury, causation, and redressability are all that the Constitution requires. But nontaxpayer standing seems more difficult to establish these days. *See Valley Forge Christian College v. Americans United for Separation of Church and State, Inc.*, 454 U.S. 464 (1982).

Now distinguish the nonconstitutional, prudential principles of standing. They are frequently invoked (and almost as frequently excused). Because they are creatures of judicial restraint, a court feeling unrestrained may pay them only lip service. When they are the thrust, the parry may be either that they are satisfied or should be excused.

There are three prudential principles of standing:

First, the plaintiff's own concern must come within the zone of interest protected by the statute invoked in the case. The plaintiff can find this requirement in legislative intent or use the requirement's inherent ambiguity to make a bold assertion that the requirement is satisfied.

Second, courts will not hear generalized grievances commonly shared by everyone. The parry is to convince the court that the plaintiff's grievance is special.

Third, a prudential rule allows a plaintiff to assert only his own, and not some third party's, legal interests. The parry is the exception allowing representational standing—an exception of near-swallowing proportions. To say that the rule has been markedly relaxed may be an understatement. Any person involved in a relationship that is affected by the challenged government action most likely can proceed under the representational standing theory. Litigation surrogates also may be created, as when a not-for-profit corporation sues on behalf of its members.

(And now an important point that keeps popping up throughout federal jurisdiction: The exceptions to the rules have themselves become ways into federal court. A good proceduralist uses them to advantage.)

THRUST: The case is moot.

PARRY: The mootness doctrine is *not* a talisman requiring dismissal upon invocation. There is almost always room for the argument that something remains for a judgment to accomplish—there is a live case or controversy. If that does not work, a common exception allows an otherwise moot case to survive if the controversy is "capable of repetition, yet evading review." That means if the challenged action is of such brief duration as to be completed before the ordinary run of litigation and there is a reasonable likelihood that the plaintiff will suffer the same injury again, the case may go on.

THRUST: There is no personal jurisdiction over the defendant.

PARRY: Put aside the metaphysics of *in personam, in rem,* or *quasi in rem* jurisdiction. Forget for now about personal service, domicile, or consent and questions about state of incorporation, doing business, or presence. Those are all commonplace.

What about jurisdiction by *default?* There is always jurisdiction to determine jurisdiction. A federal court has the inherent power to consider whether there is jurisdiction over both subject matter and the person. Subject-matter jurisdiction is both constitutional and statutory and cannot be garnered by consent, waiver, or estoppel. But *in personam* jurisdiction is part and parcel of due process's liberty.

Entering a special appearance to contest personal jurisdiction permits that determination. However, the court may enter a discovery sanction order establishing personal jurisdiction over an obstreperous party who has frustrated discovery efforts to establish jurisdictional facts. Fed. R. Civ. P. 37(b)(2)(A); *Ins. Corp. of Ireland v. Compagnie des Bauxites de Guinee,* 456 U.S. 694 (1982). This strategy may be too much of a long shot for a plaintiff to pursue, but a defendant resisting jurisdiction and discovery should take care not to resist too much.

THRUST: There is no independent jurisdiction to support joining a particular claim or party.

PARRY: Once there is a federal jurisdictional anchor, you can append claims and parties without an independent basis under the related doctrines of ancillary jurisdiction and pendent jurisdiction. These doctrines are too complicated to discuss fully here. I mention them because they allow claims and parties into federal court that otherwise would never be permitted. The underlying policy is that if a federal court has *some* jurisdiction over part of a dispute, it can reach beyond its jurisdiction and decide related aspects over which there is no independent jurisdiction.

In short, the power to decide a case or controversy is the power to decide the *whole* dispute. Pendent jurisdiction and ancillary jurisdiction can apply in diversity and federal question cases and apply to claims and parties that neither jurisdiction reaches. Ancillary jurisdiction applies to claims and parties joined after the complaint by parties other than the plaintiff. Pendent jurisdiction applies to claims raised by the plaintiff in the complaint. C. WRIGHT, LAW OF FEDERAL COURTS, Secs. 9, 19 (4th Ed. 1983).

The liberal joinder provisions in the Federal Rules of Civil Procedure allow these two kinds of auxiliary jurisdiction. You do not need complete diversity for a compulsory counterclaim under Rule 13(a), even when additional parties are brought in under Rule 13(h), or in an intervention as of right under Rule 24(a), when a third party is impleaded under Rule 14 or when a cross-claim is asserted under Rule 13(g), as all such claims may fall under the ancillary power.

A federal court also can decide a pendent state law claim without independent jurisdiction, even after the federal claim is dismissed on the merits. And, at least when federal question jurisdiction is exclusive, a federal court may even allow joinder of a pendent party. An attorney who can get one foot in the federal courthouse door may get all the way in and even drag others along.

THRUST: The federal court should abstain.

PARRY: The abstention doctrine is really five more or less distinct categories in which the federal court declines to proceed even though there is jurisdiction:

First, the *Pullman* abstention doctrine allows a federal court to refrain from deciding a constitutional challenge to state conduct if there is an unsettled question of state law that may control and avoid the federal issue. *Railroad Comm'n v. Pullman Co.*, 312 U.S. 496 (1941).

Second, the *Burford* abstention doctrine generally allows the federal court to defer to a state's administration of state affairs and avoid unnecessary conflict. *Burford v. Sun Oil Co.*, 319 U.S. 315 (1943).

Third, the *Younger* doctrine (a variant of *Burford*) requires that a federal court abstain from granting declaratory or injunctive relief when a state criminal proceeding or its equivalent is pending against the federal plaintiff. *Younger v. Harris*, 401 U.S. 37 (1971).

Fourth, certification is when a federal court refers state law questions to the highest court of the state under some state statute or state court rule. *Clay v. Sun Ins. Office Ltd.*, 363 U.S. 207 (1960) is a good example.

Fifth, (a category of doubtful validity but mentioned for the sake of completeness) is the federal discretion to stay or dismiss a federal case simply because a parallel case is pending in state court.

It may be unfair to mention these doctrines and then weakly finesse my parry by observing that they are so subtle and full of nuance as not to be readily captured here. So I am unfair. A few observations, however, are in order.

The pending state court doctrine is invoked from time to time in wildcat fashion by lower courts. It must be of dubious validity considering recent Supreme Court opinions. *See Moses H. Cone Memorial Hosp. v. Mercury Constr. Corp.*, 460 U.S. 1 (1983).

Certification, the fourth variation, applies in diversity cases. It is a creature of the state rule and merely stays the federal proceeding while the state court answers the question.

Everything else remains federal. The first three doctrines—the *Pullman, Burford,* and *Younger* hybrids—can be costly in time and lost federal opportunity. Their application sounds in abstractions of constitutional law. The degree of certainty of the state law may control. The federal court may grant interim relief while you pursue state proceedings. Later federal proceedings, including Supreme Court review of state court decisions affecting federal rights, should be contemplated during the state court sojourn.

All right. That is enough to show that these doctrines are indeed complex—to the point of being downright metaphysical. That, however, is also their vulnerability.

(And that is another secret of much federal jurisdiction. Incantation and ritual can move the court to act or not to act. Steeped in their lore, a persuasive advocate often can convince the federal court to go on. My best, last advice is to research and reflect, never losing sight of the federalism concerns that undergird the area of abstention.)

THRUST: There is no diversity jurisdiction over domestic relations cases.

PARRY: For more than 100 years, that has been the announced rule. Traditionally, diversity plaintiffs have been denied a federal forum in domestic relations suits for divorce, property settlements, alimony, and child custody.

Nothing in the Constitution requires this approach. Instead, this has been a judge-made exception, which recently has shown signs of narrowing.

Recent cases have been inconsistent and unpredictable, in part because the courts do not seem willing to define the boundaries of the exception, or capable of doing so. An opportunistic proceduralist views this confusion as an opening into federal court. Some recent decisions have held that cases between family members, sounding in tort or contract, can be tried in federal court if the issues do not depend on familial relations and the suit is not a transparent effort at avoiding the rule.

If that sounds fuzzy, you are right. You cannot easily determine just when a claim is inside or outside the exception. One recent decision illustrates the wavering nature of the line. A man's tort action to recover

6

damages from his ex-wife for kidnapping their child was inside the diversity jurisdiction line, while his request for injunctive relief to enforce a child custody decree was outside and barred from federal court. *Bennett v. Bennett*, 682 F.2d 1039 (D.C. Cir. 1982).

THRUST: Federal courts may not hear probate matters.

PARRY: The analysis is like the one for domestic cases. Nothing in the Constitution or in the statute necessarily requires this second judge-made rule. There seems to be even more room for an exception here. Professor Wright says that the rule "is far from absolute" and depends on "unclear distinctions of the utmost subtlety." C. WRIGHT, LAW OF FEDERAL COURTS, Sec. 25 at 145 (4th Ed. 1983). Again, some recent decisions seem to be narrowing the bar to jurisdiction.

There is agreement that "pure" probate matters are outside federal diversity jurisdiction. A federal court may not take control of property in a state court's custody, may not invoke a general jurisdiction over the probate, and may not otherwise interfere with the state court's probate proceeding.

Once the suit may be characterized as not involving "pure" probate, the issue becomes whether the federal action will interfere unduly with the state probate proceedings. The courts have developed two ways to evaluate this interference. One approach focuses on the nature of the claim. If the plaintiff asks the federal court to rule on the validity of the will, there is interference, and the claim is barred. If the plaintiff admits the will's validity and merely claims a share in the distribution, there is no interference, and the federal court can hear the claim.

A second, more common, approach examines the procedures as if the federal claim had been brought in state court. If you could only try the claim in the state probate court, interference would be established, and the federal court would refuse to exercise jurisdiction. But if you could enforce the claim in a state court of general jurisdiction, the federal court would entertain the suit.

Either approach (or some combination) allows for significant federal jurisdiction despite the general rule. *See generally Rice v. Rice Found.*, 610 F.2d 471 (7th Cir. 1979).

THRUST: A state is not a citizen for purposes of diversity and may not be sued under that jurisdiction.

PARRY: That is the well-established rule. Also well established is that a state's political subdivision *is* a citizen of that state for diversity purposes unless it is the state's alter ego (the state is the real party in interest as determined by state law). A diversity suit may proceed against a state agency that is established to be independent, separate, and distinct from the state. Naming the state agency as a party may be the ticket into federal court.

THRUST: A party, "by assignment or otherwise, has been improperly or collusively made or joined to invoke the jurisdiction. . . ."

PARRY: In those words, 28 U.S.C. Sec. 1359 prohibits manufacturing diversity. When the transfer is absolute and the assignor retains no interest, however, the citizenship of the assignee controls, and there is no impropriety or collusion. *Kramer v. Caribbean Mills, Inc.*, 394 U.S. 823, 828 n. 9 (1969). A nondiverse assignor might sell a liquidated claim to a diverse assignee, but that strategy is limited to negotiable claims.

A party can change his own domicile to another state and gain jurisdiction, even if the move is motivated solely by a desire to create jurisdiction. *Morris v. Gilmer*, 129 U.S. 315 (1889). Most claims, however, are not so marketable and do not justify moving to another state.

Short of those strategies, the only way is to overcome Sec. 1359. Interestingly, Sec. 1359 is as effective in creating jurisdiction as it is in defeating it. The collusion issue commonly arises in cases started by nonresident fiduciaries, such as administrators or guardians. Two approaches have emerged. Some courts apply a motive or function test to the appointment and consider: (1) the relationship between the representative and the represented person; (2) the representative's powers and responsibilities; (3) whether the diverse representative is a logical choice; and (4) the nature of the suit.

Other courts apply a substantial stake test that deemphasizes motive and considers how much of an interest the representative has in the outcome of the suit. In courts following this second approach, the advocate might structure the assignment as to strengthen an anticipated claim of diversity.

THRUST: The Declaratory Judgment Act is not a grant of jurisdiction to the federal courts.

PARRY: I have no quarrel with that truism, but I suggest that invoking the court's discretion under the act can be an important part of an effective jurisdiction strategy. Generally, the declaratory judgment statute allows earlier access to federal court when neither party may yet be able to sue for a coercive remedy, so long as there exists a genuine case or controversy. The difficulty to be turned to advantage involves the rigid requirement that the federal question appear well-pleaded on the face of the complaint, a requirement that dates from the forms of action era. *See generally* C. WRIGHT, LAW OF FEDERAL COURTS, Sec. 18 (4th Ed. 1983).

When the plaintiff sues on an affirmative federal right, he obviously satisfies the well-pleaded complaint rule, as when an owner of a patent seeks a declaration of validity and infringement rather than suing the defendant for damages. But suppose that the request is for a declaration that the opposing party does *not* have a federal right. Before the creation of the declaratory remedy, that complaint only would have *anticipated* a federal question defense and would not have satisfied the well-pleaded complaint rule. Today, the defendant in the patent example can seek a declaration that he has not infringed or that the alleged owner does not hold a valid patent. This use of the act does allow some plaintiffs into federal court who otherwise could not get there.

Another creative use of the declaratory judgment involves a plaintiff asking the court to declare that federal law protects him from a non-federal claim by the defendant. Suppose one party to a contract asks for a declaration that a federal statute enacted after the contract excuses him from performing the contract and preempts any suit for breech by the other party.

As you have begun to expect, there are two approaches to the problem. The narrow approach requires dismissal. If the plaintiff in the declaratory judgment waited to be a defendant for breaching the contract, the federal question would be a defense to the case. And that would mean no federal question because it was not in the claim.

The broader (and seemingly viable) view would allow the artful pleading. Some cases suggest that a party who claims that federal law controls can institute a federal declaratory judgment action, even though a coercive suit by the party relying on state law could not be brought in or removed to federal court.

Strategy thus almost overtakes jurisdictional principles as the party claiming a federal preemption will seek to avoid an unsympathetic state forum by bringing a declaratory judgment action in federal court. *Compare Shaw v. Delta Air Lines, Inc.*, 463 U.S. 85, 96 n. 14 (1983) *with Franchise Tax Bd. v. Construction Laborers Vacation Trust*, 463 U.S. 1, 16-25 (1983). (And no one said federal jurisdiction could not get satisfyingly intricate.)

THRUST: Federal law creates a duty without expressly providing a remedy, and, consequently, there is no federal question.

PARRY: If a remedy may be implied, there is federal question jurisdiction. Such a remedy may be implied directly under the Constitution or under some relevant statute.

The important jurisdictional point is that the implied remedy simultaneously and necessarily creates federal question jurisdiction over the newly created private cause of action. While the constitutional category is somewhat limited to the text, in our highly regulated economic system there are many statutes from which to choose. Four factors generally indicate when a statute implies a remedy: (1) whether the plantiff is a member of the class sought to be protected by the statute; (2) whether there is any indication of legislative intent to create or deny a private remedy; (3) whether a private remedy would further the legislative purpose; (4) whether the cause of action is one traditional to state law, so that a federal implication would be inconsistent. *Cort v. Ash*, 422 U.S. 66, 78 (1975). *See also Davis v. Passman*, 442 U.S. 228 (1979) (Constitution).

Most important is divining a congressional intent to establish a private right of action from the entrails of legislative history. That is getting harder to do, since more recent Supreme Court decisions suggest a hardening of attitude against implying a private right from a public statute. The plaintiff should hope for a precedent from the earlier period of willingness to implicate, since new ones seem so hard to get. Nevertheless, implying a private cause of action is still possible, and some federal judges may be more willing than others to try it.

THRUST: There is no federal question arising under either the Constitution or any federal statute.

PARRY: If not the Constitution or a federal statute, then how about the federal common law?

That federal common law exists we may accept as an article of faith. What it is and when it applies are more difficult questions. Here are three possibilities for finding federal common law:

First, some situations require a federal common law to protect a uniquely federal interest when state law would be in conflict.

Second, federal statutes so dominate some situations that federal common law seems a necessary concomitant.

Third, there are some situations in which the federal and national concern is inherently superior, and federal law must control.

But what about jurisdiction? When federal common law does apply, federal jurisdiction follows necessarily. *City of Evansville v. Kentucky Liquid Recycling, Inc.*, 604 F.2d 1008 (7th Cir. 1979).

THRUST: There is no general federal question jurisdiction.

PARRY: Assuming that is so, the attorney should look over the menu of special federal question jurisdiction statutes. Between 1875 and 1980, the general federal question statute carried a jurisdictional amount requirement. Consequently, Congress enacted a plethora of special statutes without an amount requirement which are spread throughout Chapter 85 of Title 28 and beyond.

A partial list of examples from Title 28 discloses their breadth: Sec. 1333 (admiralty), Sec. 1337 (statutes regulating commerce), Sec. 1338 (patents), Sec. 1352 (federal bonds), and Sec. 1346 (United States as defendant). Additionally, specific grants of jurisdiction are sprinkled throughout the substantive statutes. Any of them can be a way into federal court.

THRUST: There is a statute depriving the federal court of jurisdiction.

PARRY: Argue that this case does not fall within the statutory prohibition.

Two provisions are commonly invoked. *See* C. WRIGHT, LAW OF FEDERAL COURTS, Sec. 51 (4th Ed. 1983). First, 28 U.S.C. Sec. 1342 deprives the district courts of jurisdiction to enjoin the effect of any order of a state agency affecting public utility rates if, *and only if:* (1) jurisdiction is based on diversity or a federal question arising under the Constitution; (2) the challenged rate order does not frustrate interstate commerce; (3) the rate order was preceded by a reasonable notice and hearing; (4) there is an effective remedy in state court. Second, 28 U.S.C. Sec. 1341 prohibits an injunction against the assessment or collection of any state tax if an effective remedy exists in state court.

The very strength of such provisions can be used against their application. Their particularity means that if any of the identified conditions is missing, the statute will not apply. Some research leavened with persuasion can show how the statute will not keep the case out of federal court.

What do we make of all these thrusts and parries?

Federal jurisdiction *is* complicated, sophisticated, and theoretical. We should expect that from a legal specialty that deals with such important issues of federalism. The litigator must be equal to that challenge. The crafty proceduralist uses that sophistication and complexity to advantage. In this, as in the rest of the trial arts, one must strive for mastery. One of Aesop's fables best describes what is at stake:

> A swallow hatched her brood under the eaves of a Court of Justice. Before her young could fly, a serpent crept out of his hole and ate all the nestlings. When the poor bird returned and found her nest empty, she began a pitiable wailing. Another swallow suggested, by way of comfort, that she was not the first bird who had lost her young.
>
> "True," she replied, "but it is not only for my little ones that I mourn, but that I should have been wronged in that very place where the injured fly for justice."

A lawyer looking to federal court may resemble our swallow. He brings his client's suit in federal court seeking a more just justice. Principles of federal jurisdiction, however, may play the role of the serpent. Sometimes, all is lost without even the opportunity to argue the merits of the cause. But there are some special ways to get in and to stay in federal court. Use them to help build your nest out of the serpent's reach.

The New Art of Forum Shopping

by Weyman I. Lundquist

Forum shopping may not be considered a topic to shape the fate of nations—although the current United States attempts to stay out of the World Court suggests otherwise. But forum shopping can affect the course of political events, as Harold Berliner just established.

Harold practices in Nevada County, California—in Nevada City to be exact—the old heart of California gold country. The most recent political campaign there produced at least as much heat as light. Harold's client, who aspired to be county supervisor, was the alleged offender. His opponent, the incumbent supervisor, brought suit charging that a mailing sent by Harold's client was misleading.

The dispute quickly found its way to court. The local judge, initially willing to act, on reflection came to the view that an out-of-county judge (not at all influenced by the local supervisor's interests in the court budget) might be a wise selection. The irate and allegedly maligned incumbent county supervisor was offended that the "judges we pay won't hear our cases." The more "eloquent" the supervisor, the more the judge was disposed to a different and distant forum. The judge prevailed.

The incumbent supervisor was concerned about campaign time lost and the need for quick, local justice. To convenience her, another county found an available jurist, a good friend of the local judge. This new judge was ready to do justice but loathe to travel to do it. There was, however, a right to a hearing in the county where the case was filed. It was demanded, and the visiting judge came to the county demanded by the plaintiffs.

Harold Berliner suggested to the out-of-county judge that Mr. Z's Bar,

The author, a member of the San Francisco firm of Heller, Ehrman, White & McAuliffe, is a former chairman of the Section of Litigation.

just over the Nevada County line, would be the most proximate forum for the visiting jurist. The visiting judge (from Placer County) agreed to come that far, but no farther. The hapless suing supervisor, having insisted on a forum despite one judge's opposition and another judge's reluctance to travel, found her case before an out-of-county judge at a neutral bar.

This is the end of the political forum-shopping adventure, except to report that the case was convened in Mr. Z's Bar. When the bailiff issued his first call for "Order," the response was "One rare hamburger."

"Order, order," the bailiff persisted, obtaining requests for "Two shots and a beer."

The supervisor lost the temporary restraining order, and the hearing on the preliminary injunction was held the following day. Local newspaper coverage indicated that "the Supervisor had a wimp of a case—judicially so determined—and that she had likely brought it for political purposes." The supervisor plaintiff had some harsh off-the-record remarks for the judge—who pleasantly informed her that "you are much better looking in person than your campaign posters indicate."

Despite the reality of this incident, there are some (law professors, legal writers, judges, and other aficionados of legal study) who believe that judge and forum shopping have seen their best days and now hold the status of a minor art. As often is the case with those expert at legal scholarship, their legal knowledge does not conform to legal fact.

To those involved in the messy business of representing clients, the real world of forum shopping and judge selecting has seldom presented greater opportunities and offered more challenges.

I hide the names and players in some of the incidents, but be assured that all that I disclose is not fancy.

With random assignments of cases in the federal courts and master calendar systems prevalent in most state courts, the ancient and once honorable practice of directly selecting a judge known for his or her wisdom and temperament (if not for direct predilection to your point of view) requires great skill. As with many things subtle, the process has new permutations. Interestingly, some of the new wrinkles in the process were produced by those very ones who were trying to abolish the market for forum choice.

For the sophisticated followers of the Litigation Art—presumably some of whom read this book—I need not deal at length with the obvious. If an automobile accident occurs in Solano County—where the jury has *not* delivered a $100,000 verdict—*ever*— it takes small wisdom to sue in the Los Angeles Superior Court, where the defendant auto manufacturer has a principal place of business. If a major antitrust action demands an efficient, well-directed bench with an established philosophy of damages guided by circuit court of appeals decisions, the sophisticated plaintiff's lawyer hauls out his handy select-a-forum guide (often a telephone list of companionable lawyers in appropriate cities) and seeks advice.

These are beginner steps. For other actions involving temporary restraining orders or needing quick preliminary injunctions, wait for Judge Curmudgeon's annual vacation before filing the case—thus eliminating a potential bad draw. Lawyers have been known to pass time in the clerk's office awaiting a file stamp showing that Judge Miserly has just drawn a case on the random selection list and then file on the statistically sound theory that seldom do the face of the dice repeat on the next roll.

But I turn to more sophisticated adventures—and their risks.

There is as always the minuet (the delicate dance) choice between suit in a federal or state forum. While the causes of actions at times are different, the underlying facts may be the same.

- A class action for land fraud—should it be brought under state or federal statutes?
- Consumer claims viable under state or federal law—where to go?
- Claims pendent to federal claims—should they tag along in federal court or take flight in a state court?
- Should a federal claim be backed up by filing a variation in state court? Filing the state claim might toll the statute of limitations but need not be served until one feels which way the federal wind blows.
- Is an alleged state claim really "artfully pleaded" to thwart removal to a federal court? *See Federated Dep't Stores v. Moitie*, 452 U.S. 394 (1981).

(By the way, I do not warrant the propriety of these devices; I merely point out that they are used.)

There have been learned discussions, articles, and treatises on whether claims are state or federal and whether they should be pursued as either or both. The point is that for the Learned Angler at Law, fishing for the right forum can be done in a number of ways. It may be wise to seek federal jurisdiction (good judge, fast track, ordered discovery). The state court, however, may be a sounder choice (home town, larger jury, better damage awards, you run your own case). What is certain is that it is naive—bordering on foolish—to fail to consider all options before filing suit.

Another forum-shopping gambit warrants attention. Your client carries a strong demand letter written by an out-of-state or out-of-county party. What to do? Consider at once the home court advantage. We will sue them in declaratory relief or whatever, right here at home.

> The objectives of the Federal Declaratory Judgment Act are to avoid accrual of avoidable damages to one not certain of his rights and to afford him an early adjudication without waiting until his adversary should see fit to begin suit after damages had accrued.

Travelers Ins. Co. v. Davis, 490 F.2d 536, 543 (3rd Cir. 1974), quoting *E. Edelman & Co. v. Triple-A Specialty Co.*, 88 F.2d 852, 854 (7th Cir. 1937).

Of course, there are some risks to forum shopping. And doing it by flaunting legal civility can create problems. In a recent case in the Federal District Court for the Northern District of California, *Capital Analysts v. Townsend* (N. D. Cal. No. C-83-1344—JPV), the defendants asked for sanctions under Rule 11 on the grounds that the plaintiff had filed his complaint for the improper purpose of depriving the defendants of their state court forum. The judge said:

> Plaintiff's action in this case cries out for sanctions. The court finds that plaintiff used defendants' good faith settlement efforts to rob the defendants of their chosen forum. The facts of this case strongly suggest that plaintiffs fictionalized their complaint in order to get a perceived tactical advantage. The court must impose sanctions.

The ground rules for forum shopping have some professional parameters.

On one occasion on behalf of an environmental group, we were comfortable with the jurisdiction. It was the District of the Great Lake Tahoe. We were most pleased with the judge we drew: sagacious, pleasant, concerned for the environment. But the judge immediately disqualified himself and, as presiding judge of that district, brought a visiting judge whose perspective of the environment must have been forged in a steel mill. Our case was a disaster because of his bias against preserving anything from developers.

Some time after the case started, the kindly, sagacious judge inquired about the case. I gave him a fulsome reply and finally blurted out, "We sure could have used you on that case; it cried out for your attention."

To which he replied, "I simply couldn't handle it. I was prejudiced against the developers, didn't you know?"

"Well, I suspected as much, but, when it comes right down to it, I'd rather have a judge who is prejudiced toward my client's case than against it, and that is what we have now." What is obviously the right forum can be not so obvious.

Litigation weariness, bad press for the usual judicial process, or perhaps good sense has led increasing numbers of courts to institute a forum within a forum. That is the ability to seek (and sometimes force) arbitration before trial. It is usually a defendant's gambit (quick, inexpensive, jury vagaries are out). It is a forum to shop. Consider the recent adventures of Attorney Eugene Rosenberg of San Francisco in the nearby Alameda County Superior Court.

Rosenberg's client had a rear-ender injury—a routine case. It was assigned by the court for mandatory arbitration, as the court felt the probable value was under $15,000. Rosenberg demanded $12,500 to settle.

The defendant said, "Only $8,500, or we'll choose arbitration."

"Arbitration it is," says Rosenberg. And arbitrate they did. Plaintiff received a $16,000 award. "Pay up," demands Rosenberg.

15

"Only $14,000," retorts the defendant. "Take it, or we'll go for a superior court jury trial *de novo.*"

"We accept the trial," says Rosenberg. The superior court became the new forum. The jury verdict—$84,000.

The lesson: Some forums cost more than others. Make certain you buy a ticket to the right event.

I have been discussing forum shopping practiced within the familiar arenas of courts and court processes. I suggest that, for the thoughtful lawyer, new horizons are emerging, particularly for commercial clients who want the latest fad.

Consider this scenario. Your client, CEO Corporation, comes with a claim against Macro Ego Incorporated. It comes reluctantly, for business people are ever embarrassed when their documentation has erred; their wonderous negotiating talent has been elusive. Then in-house counsel (for all their budget skills) say, "We'll have to go to our outside firm and discuss litigation." (No one discusses *suing*— such language is declasse.) You meet: CEO's president, general counsel, and you.

"Litigation—you want it?" you ask. "Sue Macro Ego? Do you think it is advisable? It will most assuredly be expensive."

CEO's president is impressed with such wisdom, especially coming from a lawyer. "What are our choices? I need to make my decision-tree analysis," he tells you.

You reply, "Well, there is federal court or state court, here or in New York, but, as you well know, courts and trials have their failings. Tell me about Macro Ego and your claims against it."

You soon learn that your client is into every aspect of his company's business and shares with his general counsel a certain paranoia about courts and lawyers (except the docile in-house variety). You also learn that the claim of CEO Corporation, while not rotten, does have some odor to it—which an astute judge might detect. And as with many things a trifle spoiled, time will not improve these claims.

A quick check indicates that Macro Ego has publicly committed itself to alternative dispute resolution. This option (nonviolent combat in the eyes of your client) is available. Instinctive courthouse logic tells you that when two companies are committed to resolving disputes alternatively, they do not want either side to go away mad. It leaves too many options for the lawyers—next time. And for a case that does not pass an early smell test, this could make sense.

"Or we could do a minitrial for you, Mr. CEO, and for Macro's president or the people you and he designate. Then you as businessmen could work it out, better than uninformed lawyers." Again leaving the ball in the client's court, and if the client can't hit it, there is always the lawyer's home ground—the courthouse—to resume play.

Mr. CEO is interested. "Anything else?"

"Well, we could rent a judge." (Now *that* is an attention-getter.) And the list goes on—arbitration, mediation, prefiling judicial conferences. The happy result is that you find a forum with a proclivity for middle-of-the-road decisions. Your client becomes directly involved. A bad case is lodged in a good forum—and outside counsel appears the wiser.

Yes, the horizons have widened. The skilled litigation communicator (formerly called a trial lawyer) will soon master this new terrain. Now it is not only avoiding Judge Curmudgeon, Judge Miserly, or the county courthouse, there is also the client's interest and personality, not to mention the merits of its disputes, your adversaries' disposition toward law, the nature of the claim, and a variety of forums, some maybe not even devised yet.

The more things change, the less change there may be for the astute forum shopper, ever looking for a good bargain.

Personal Jurisdiction: Leave Time for Trouble

by David D. Siegel

With long-arm jurisdiction, a plaintiff can try the case at home and make the defendant come to him. This is a blessing to plaintiffs, but many a plaintiff's lawyer has been so preoccupied with its beneficent side that he has been lulled into disregarding one of its darker prospects.

One of the darkest prospects for a plaintiff is the statute of limitations. It stops the plaintiff at the threshold, denying him even the satisfaction of having had a crack at the merits. The statute of limitations is a major part of this story, which revolves around a plaintiff who has prevailed on a jurisdictional objection at trial level and who—preoccupied with the nice outcome of this skirmish—loses the war.

It has to do with putting all of one's eggs into a single jurisdictional basket, only to learn that the basket is defective. It turns out that the chosen court lacks jurisdiction, and it is now too late to start the case somewhere else. The plaintiff picked the wrong forum, and it cost him his case. Having briefly described the final scene, we can now backtrack a bit and set the stage.

The choice of forum is important in litigation, not just for jurisdiction—as one need not tell trial lawyers. It can be a key element in a case that has no jurisdictional problems at all. One or two of these non-jurisdictional examples can aid as background.

Remember the United States Supreme Court's decision in *Allstate Ins. Co. v. Hague*, 449 U.S. 302 (1981)? It was a choice-of-law case, one of the Supreme Court's more recent pronouncements in that volatile realm. Hague (who worked in Minnesota) was killed while riding on the back of a motorcycle in Wisconsin. All the parties, including Hague, lived in Wisconsin. The others involved in the accident had no insurance.

Mr. Siegel is the McNiece Professor of Law at St. John's University, Jamaica, New York.

Hague had. He had three cars and an insurance policy covering all three of them. The policy had $15,000 uninsured-motorist coverage. Hague's widow maintained that the $15,000 coverage was for each of the three cars, so that she would be entitled to a total of $45,000 from Hague's insurer. This is called "stacking."

Wisconsin did not allow stacking, and, under its law, $15,000 would have been the amount due. But just next door, Minnesota did allow stacking, and, under its law, Mrs. Hague would have the entire $45,000. Wisconsin contracts predominated. Hague's job was the only connection with Minnesota. If suit were brought against the insurer in Wisconsin, it was a virtual certainty that Wisconsin would have applied its own law and restricted recovery to $15,000. And even if suit could be brought in Minnesota, there was no guarantee it would apply its own law to the case. But whatever chance there was for getting the Minnesota "stacking" rule applied was better in Minnesota than in Wisconsin. Mrs. Hague took that chance, sued in Minnesota, and won her point: Minnesota did apply its own rule allowing stacking.

(The U.S. Supreme Court found it constitutionally permissible for Minnesota to do so. Hague's job in Minnesota was the key. While the Wisconsin contacts predominated, they did not amount to so much as to keep Minnesota from applying its own law on its lesser but still significant contacts.)

Choice of forum carried the day in that choice-of-law case, just a recent example of many in which it has done so.

Choice of forum plays an equally important role when choice of law is not in issue. An example is in a diversity case, when the choice is between a state and federal court in the same state. Parties choose the forum based upon any number of factors, including the reputed generosity of the jury pools in the respective courts.

A favorite example of mine is *Schimansky v. Nelson*, 374 N.Y. Supp. 2d 771 (App. Div. 1975). The plaintiff's decedents were nonresidents killed in an accident in a rural New York county. They sued there, where verdicts were not terribly high, and only late in the case realized that federal diversity jurisdiction was available. And it was available in New York City, no less, where juries are not known to shrink from high verdicts.

What to do?

The plaintiff moved to discontinue the New York action, candidly confessing his tactical error and his wish to sue anew in the federal court so as possibly to get more money. One familiar with New York law would have thought that a discontinuance would be refused on such a ground. The plaintiff was made to pay costs, but the discontinuance was granted, and plaintiff permitted to go for federal jurisdiction.

This case gets us closer to one of the themes of this story. The original statute of limitations had to be alive in *Schimansky* before the second action—the one in federal court—would have worked. It apparently was. (Federal courts in diversity cases, by the way, apply the forum state's statute of limitations.)

The plaintiff in *Schimansky* who initially chose the wrong forum (which most lawyers do not), at least sued early enough to be sure that a new action would be timely when the first had to be undone. But most lawyers do not do that, either, so the *Schimansky* plaintiff compensated in diligence for what he had misgauged in tactics. He showed, on the peculiar facts of his case, how suing with a little time to spare can preserve options not thought about at the outset.

Suing with a little time to spare has a host of benefits, predictable and unpredictable. It has its greatest advantage, to my mind, when the earlier action meets an objection to personal jurisdiction, and the objection is sustained. This happens often enough to have generated quite a body of case law. A 1983 amendment of Federal Civil Rule 4, the main federal provision on process service and personal jurisdiction, expands this jurisdictional hazard in federal practice by introducing a time limit on summons service that did not exist before. See Commentary C4-35 in 28 U.S.C.A., Rule 4 [Pocket Part] and K. Gaines, *Rule 4: A Nightmare in Several Acts,* 11 LITIGATION No. 2 at 8 (Winter 1985).

If the action is dismissed for want of personal jurisdiction and there is still time to sue again, getting proper jurisdiction in the second round will make the dismissal count as just an inconvenience. But if the original statute of limitations has expired and under the applicable law there is no new period in which to start over, the plaintiff's case is dead. That is, it is dead as against the original defendants. The plaintiff may yet recover full damages—but in an action for malpractice against his lawyer for failing to take precautions against such a result.

This suggests the importance of the plaintiff's getting as early an adjudication as possible of any outstanding jurisdictional objection—so a new action may be started if the objection succeeds. It also suggests the importance of suing with enough time left under the original statute of limitations so there is time to start for a new action if need be. This entails research at the outset—before starting the first action—so as to have alternative routes timed and open before starting an action in the favored forum. Research postponed until after a dismissal is a tremulous affair that can have an adverse effect on actuarial statistics governing litigation lawyers.

First things first. How can a plaintiff accelerate a jurisdictional adjudication so as to have as much time as possible for alternatives should jurisdiction be found lacking? The defendant may have cooperated (inadvertently, to be sure) by moving to dismiss based on the want of personal jurisdiction. That will usually get the objection determined early.

But suppose the defendant is imaginative and has an eye on the calendar himself. He wants the action dismissed for want of jurisdiction but would like to put off the point until the plaintiff is out of time. What he may do is include his jurisdictional objection as a defense in the answer instead of using it in a motion to dismiss.

What is the plaintiff's remedy now? In states that have adopted the Federal Rules of Civil Procedure or their equivalent on this point, the plaintiff can move to strike the defense. Rule 12(f) of the FRCP supplies the motion. That will usually bring the point to early adjudication, and the plaintiff can pursue his options accordingly.

In either instance, if the jurisdictional objection is sustained and the plaintiff's action is dismissed, the plaintiff will need enough time under the applicable statute of limitations for a new action.

At this point, we must delve further into the nature of the jurisdictional objection. We know it concerns "personal jurisdiction," but that, too, requires subdividing. What was the defect:

- A want of proper service?
- Whether service was made at all?
- A want of jurisdictional basis, though method was okay, as where service was made outside the state on a long-arm basis?

Determining the specific category of jurisdictional objection is important in deciding what follow-up steps to take.

If only the method of service was the objection, a new action can be started in the same court with a little more attention to service in the second case. The same statute of limitations that governed in action one will govern in action two, and the plaintiff may only hope that it is still alive, either in its original length or perhaps with a little extension that local law might throw in to assist in such an instance. (In a state such as New York, the plaintiff's case is alive only if the original statute of limitations has not run. New York has no gift of additional time for a second action.)

But now suppose that it was not service but *basis* that grounded the jurisdictional dismissal. The plaintiff in action one relied on long-arm jurisdiction, serving the defendant by a proper method outside the state. Then the defendant got a dismissal on the grounds that his contacts in state one were not enough for long arm jurisdiction. In that case, the plaintiff would have to bring a second action in some other state—state two—that has personal jurisdiction over the defendant (the defendant's own state of domicile, for example, if no other is available). The statute of limitations would again loom as a factor but with an uncomfortable twist. It would now be state two's statute of limitations that the plaintiff must satisfy. Would he make it? Did he properly research state two's statute of limitations at the outset and prepare for the present contingency? If not, the plaintiff might be out of court altogether.

Whenever there is the slightest doubt about jurisdiction in state one, be ready to start a new action in state two in the time provided by state two's own statute of limitations. Thinking about that alternative should not be put off until after the court in state one has dismissed for want of jurisdiction.

Now suppose that the court in state one has not dismissed. It has denied defendant's motion to dismiss or granted plaintiff's motion to strike the jurisdictional defense. Either way, it has sustained jurisdiction. Now return to the paradox mentioned at the outset. The plaintiff's tendency may be to celebrate the moment, yet in retrospect the moment may become the plaintiff's undoing. It all has to do with the appellate process.

Where does the plaintiff stand if the defendant appeals the jurisdictional determination? An order sustaining jurisdiction is a nonfinal determination and as such is not separately appealable in federal practice or in states that follow the federal practice, except with a special certification (provided for in federal court by 28 U.S.C.A. Sec. 1292[b]). This means that it can be argued only as part of an appeal from a final judgment, which may be months or even years away. Even in states such as New York, which do allow the immediate and separate appeal of a jurisdiction-sustaining order, much time will pass while the case goes through the process.

Either way, if the appellate court determines that jurisdiction was improper, the intervening passage of time will make it all the more likely that the time for a new action has now expired.

The plaintiff allowed himself to be lulled into the assumption that, with the trial court sustaining jurisdiction, all was well. He failed to guard against the prospect of an appellate reversal on jurisdiction.

And now an important distinction. The prospect of reversal is not strong when the jurisdictional point turns on an issue of fact, such as when the defendant disputes the process server on the manner of service or contests that service was ever made at all. Appellate deference to the fact-findings of the trial court can ordinarily be expected.

But if the issue is one of law, as when the defendant concedes the fact of service by a given means and the only question is whether the means was authorized by law, the possibility of reversal expands. For that reason, it expands greatly when the issue is not service, but basis. The defendant, served outside the state based on a long-arm statute, maintains that the statute does not apply or, for want of adequate forum contacts, is unconstitutional if it does.

Does this happen?

Certainly. Long-arm inquiries proliferate and probably present more issues of law than issues of fact. Usually, the fact pattern is clear enough, perhaps even conceded by the parties. The question is whether the defendant's contacts with the forum justify extraterritorial jurisdiction. Appellate courts do not defer to trial courts on the law the way they do on the facts. Should the appellate court disagree on the law issue and reverse, the case may now be dead, made so by the passage of whatever time might have been left for a new action when the trial court first sustained jurisdiction.

Again it becomes necessary to pinpoint the objection. If only the method of service is defective, it may be possible for the appellate court to remand the case with instructions simply to quash the old service and permit new service within the same action—thus preserving it from the statute of limitations. But if basis is the defect, new service will not do. The case will be dismissed, and the plaintiff's only recourse will be an action somewhere else. In that situation, the statute of limitations will most likely have expired, along with the plaintiff's hopes.

What shall a plaintiff do, if he has won on the jurisdictional point at trial level and yet—cautious and thoughtful—still harbors some doubt about ultimate success on the point if it is appealed? One possibility, of course, is for the plaintiff to throw in the towel: Give up all hope of jurisdiction in the present forum and just bring the case where the defendant can be served without question.

Are there any midway options? Perhaps, but this entails thoughtful maneuvering. Can a precautionary action be begun in state two without giving up jurisdiction in state one? Maybe. It all depends on the combined procedural jurisprudence of state one and state two. Suppose state two is New York, which has a special rule permitting the dismissal of its action on the grounds that an earlier action is pending in state one. If the defendant moves to dismiss the state two action on those grounds, the plaintiff stands a good chance of defeating the motion, especially when the New York court learns the defendant plans to make (or has already made) an objection to personal jurisdiction in state one.

New York does not indulge lightly such a defendant, deeming this a kind of have-one's-cake-and-eat-it-too situation. *See, e.g., Clark v. Bilt-Rite Land Corp.*, 82 Misc. 2d 1026, 372 N.Y. Supp. 2d 466 (N.Y. Sup. Ct. 1975), where the court refused to dismiss the second action under these circumstances.

Instead of dismissing, the court can stay the second action, which is alive for statute-of-limitations purposes but quiescent unless the stay is vacated. If the state one case gets dismissed at some later time for want of jurisdiction, the plaintiff just moves the New York court to vacate the stay and revive the second action.

What another state will do when it is state two depends entirely on its own law, which needs initial research and conservative analysis. The statute of limitations tolerates no rosy assumptions. But when a plaintiff intent on state one jurisdiction is mindful of his jurisdictional and time dilemma, he must at least consider a precautionary second action in a forum with indisputable jurisdiction.

During all of this research into whether or not the plaintiff can file a "holding action" under state two's law, the plaintiff had also better see what state one thinks about all this. Perhaps there will be something in state one's procedural law that authorizes dismissing the first action when it is shown that a duplicate one has now been started somewhere else. If the court has some discretion in disposing of these matters, perhaps the best thing for the plaintiff to do is describe his dilemma and throw himself on the mercy of the court—prepared to fall back on plan B should the court have no mercy.

So far we have been talking about dismissing for lack of personal jurisdiction, including insufficient service. The objection is that it is not proper to bring *this defendant* before the court under these circumstances. In federal practice, incidentally—at least for purposes of making and preserving a jurisdictional objection—there are different subcategories of what we customarily call "personal jurisdiction." Federal Civil Rule 12(b) has three of them, numbered (2) "lack of jurisdiction over the person," (4) "insufficiency of process," and (5) "insufficiency of service of process." Some of the federal cases say that asserting one ground does not necessarily preserve another, so the defendant should be quite specific in designating his objection. (A want of long-arm jurisdiction falls under (2) "lack of jurisdiction over the person.")

Now suppose that the defect is a lack of subject-matter jurisdiction. The complaint is that the court lacks power over this kind of case. Dismissing for want of subject-matter jurisdiction is similar to dismissing for lack of personal jurisdiction in some respects. The dismissal is without prejudice to a later action that cures the objection. But there are differences between the two categories that are worth knowing.

One difference that might matter in our present scenario is that while an objection to personal jurisdiction (all categories) can be waived and is usually deemed waived when not raised by motion or answer, the general rule is that a defect in subject-matter jurisdiction cannot be waived and can be raised at any time, even by the court on its own motion. This is explicitly the rule in the federal courts under Federal Civil Rule 12(h)(3).

This issue of waiver can give the defendant quite a tactical advantage when the objection is subject matter rather than personal jurisdiction. A good example of a subject-matter defect is when jurisdiction in a federal court is based on diversity of citizenship and a party's citizenship is questioned. And a good example of the defendant's tactical advantage in making a late objection is *Knee v. Chemical Leaman Tank Lines, Inc.,* 293 F. Supp. 1094 (ED Pa. 1968).

Knee was an action against a corporation, which for diversity purposes is deemed a citizen of both its state of incorporation and the state in which it has its "principal place of business" (should the two differ, as they often do with large corporations). If the other side's citizenship is the same as either, down goes subject-matter jurisdiction. While place of incorporation is rarely an issue of fact, that is not true of the "principal place of business." Determining which of a large company's multiple offices is its "principal" one can present tough factual issues, with the corporation itself having an obvious advantage in assembling proof.

The plaintiff in the *Knee* case was a Pennsylvania citizen suing a corporation that was incorporated in Delaware. Plaintiff did not know that the defendant's principal office was in Pennsylvania and that there was therefore no diversity. The defendant knew but was not letting on.

The defendant served an answer with no jurisdictional objection, and only after the statute of limitations expired did the defendant point out its Pennsylvania citizenship with a motion to dismiss. The court granted the motion, citing the time-worn rule that subject-matter jurisdiction cannot be conferred by waiver, estoppel, consent, laches, or any other doctrine that might work in any other situation to avoid injustice. The result was a dismissal apparently too late to enable the plaintiff to start over again.

On this last point—the possibility of suing over—it is again important to determine in which state's court the second action is to be brought. If the only state courts available for the second action in *Knee* were Pennsylvania and Delaware, their own statutes of limitations would have determined the timeliness of a second action. Perhaps there would have been something in their procedural law that would have offered the second action a kind of reprieve with a little statute-of-limitations extension after this kind of first-action dismissal. Interestingly, New York would do just that under New York C.P.L.R. 205(a). The statute offers no extension to a case that was previously dismissed for a want of personal jurisdiction. But it distinguishes between personal and subject-matter jurisdiction dismissals in offering an extension. (This is hard to justify but is clearly the law.) New York does give a brief new time period to file a new action when the case was dismissed for lack of subject-matter jurisdiction. And—have I said this before?—the time to look into things like this is at the outset, before the first action is brought.

What can be said to help a plaintiff like the one in the *Knee* case, faced with an objection to subject-matter jurisdiction that turned on facts that he did not know and that the defendant deliberately concealed until the plaintiff could do nothing to protect himself?

The plaintiff cannot proceed upon any jurisdictional assumption without knowing the facts or educating himself about them with time to spare.

One thing he can do in a case like *Knee* is just forget about federal jurisdiction. Federal judicial hearts are not likely to break over the loss of a diversity case. If federal jurisdiction is doubtful and time is short, abstinence may be the plaintiff's best bet. (As Mark Twain said, there is nothing wrong with abstinence as long as it doesn't hurt anybody.) Suit in a state court will avoid the subject-matter jurisdiction problem.

But federal jurisdiction is no small gift. And a plaintiff who is after federal jurisdiction wants more than just the suggestion of abstinence. If he has any doubt at all about the defendant's citizenship, he can—as long as he has left some time for trouble—bring the federal action and promptly take the defendant's deposition about jurisdictional facts. He can get from his own mouth, under oath, all the facts relevant to citizenship. While the defendant may have been willing to play fast and loose by holding the jurisdictional ace up his sleeve until the most propitious moment—such doing high-handed but not false swearing—he is not likely to take chances when subject to the sanction of perjury.

With the facts in hand, the plaintiff can play his jurisdictional objections accordingly. It would even be permissible for the plaintiff himself to bring the issue of subject-matter jurisdiction to the court's attention for a prompt adjudication, now based on a fully developed set of jurisdictional facts. (Federal Civil Rule 12[h][3] says that the issue of subject-matter jurisdiction may be addressed by the court "whenever it appears by the suggestion of the parties or otherwise." A plaintiff should be able to qualify as either a "party" or an "otherwise" under that provision.)

If the court sustains jurisdiction, it will now be doing so on what amounts to a heavily fact-oriented foundation—the kind that invokes a higher degree of appellate deference and reduces the likelihood of reversal. But here, too, there is no certainty. No lawyer can have that.

The lawyer who comes closest to it is the one who prepares all the alternatives in advance. It is not an easy job, but it is always a good deal easier for a lawyer who has arranged to leave time for trouble. Leaving time for trouble is a salvation in any practice.

Federal Service Under Rule 4: A Nightmare in Several Acts

by Kenneth R. Gaines

Act I: The Office

Chicago. Mid-September. Friday afternoon, about an hour after lunch. You are sitting in your four-window office overlooking the lake, trying to catch up on the backlog of advance sheets and memos piled on your desk. You begin reading a particularly technical memo about the recent (for you at least) amendments to the Federal Rules of Civil Procedure. By Rule 4 you grow restive. You look out your window at Lake Michigan and try to see your new boat docked at the yacht club just a few minutes away. The day is too rare to miss. You decide to leave Rule 4 and enjoy an afternoon in the boat.

Rationalizations come easily. You have never been much interested in service of process. It is, after all, a routine matter normally handled by your paralegal or docketing department.

Besides, you already know the major changes brought by the 1983 amendments:

- Federal marshals are almost entirely removed from serving process;
- Mail has become the basic method for service;
- For the first time, Rule 4 contains an explicit time limit for service of summons—120 days after filing the complaint—except where "good cause" can be shown for the delay.

Nothing earth-shattering here, you say, as you prepare to leave for the marina.

But wait a minute. Suppose I were to tell you that the amendments to Rule 4, far from being mere housekeeping matters, are of great importance.

The author is a member of the Chicago law firm of Altheimer & Gray. The text was distributed in an earlier form by the Illinois Institute for Continuing Education.

The truth is, the new statutory scheme can complicate rather than simplify service of process, and the complications can be fatal.

Under the new amendments [Rule 4(j)], if a defendant has not been properly served within 120 days, the action can be dismissed. The dismissal is without prejudice; but if it occurs after the statute of limitations has run, the outcome is probably the same as if the plaintiff went to trial on the merits and lost.

All this is news to you. You make a mental note to save the memo for bedtime reading when you will have a chance to look at it carefully. You pull your captain's hat out of the drawer where you keep it and you are on your way.

Just as you get to the door, your secretary, Helen, buzzes you on the intercom to say that Jack Keifer, a former law school classmate turned businessman, has dropped by your office. Sensing the needs of an old friend (to say nothing of a potential client), you resign yourself to an afternoon of work. You remove your hat, take one last look at the lake, and listen.

Act II: The Case

On February 3, 1982, your classmate, Keifer, entered into an agreement with a Tulsa businessman, in which Keifer agreed to invest $250,000 in a limited partnership interest in a group of oil wells. Keifer later discovered that he had been seriously and intentionally misled by the sole general partner about the nature of his investment.

Keifer first asked his brother-in-law, a recent law school graduate, to get him his money back or his rightful piece of the action, whichever was more. The brother-in-law prepared a complaint alleging both state law claims and violations of the federal securities laws. The brother-in-law advised Keifer that, although Oklahoma law would govern many aspects of the case, the complaint could (and should) be filed in a federal district court in Chicago. The federal court had jurisdiction over the subject matter because of the federal claims, and over the defendant because of his presence in Chicago in connection with part of the transaction.

So, on August 1, 1984, your client's brother-in-law filed complaint No. 84-C-1221 in the Northern District of Illinois. He sent a copy of the summons and complaint with his clerk to the U.S. Marshal's office for service upon the defendant. The marshal's office turned the clerk away, telling him that under amended Rule 4, absent a court order, it no longer routinely served summonses and complaints. The clerk reported this to Keifer's brother-in-law, the lawyer, who reported it to Keifer. When Keifer learned of his brother-in-law's lack of familiarity with the service rules, he fired him.

After relating this story, your classmate asked whether *you* were familiar with Rule 4, to which you promptly responded ''yes.'' He then engaged you to represent him in connection with the case and paid you a $20,000 retainer which you immediately put down on a new Porsche.

Act III: You Go Into Action

As soon as your new client departed, you called your paralegal, briefly described the history of the case, and confirmed that Rule 4, as newly amended, provided for service of process by ordinary mail. Being a cheapskate by nature, you seized on this new rule and, two weeks later (on September 10, 1984), mailed a copy of the summons, complaint, and the appropriate notice and acknowledgment forms (called for by the rule and provided as Form 18-A), to the defendant at his business address in Tulsa. Having noted that service by mail must be accomplished within 20 days, you made a notation on your calendar for the date 20 days hence (September 30), and promptly left for your boat.

On September 30, 1984, however, you were in a local hospital recovering from the effects of failing to negotiate a hairpin turn late the previous night in your new Porsche. You finally returned to the office on October 15, 1984, and, several days later, saw the entry in your diary. That is when you found out that the defendant's acknowledgment form had not been returned by September 30.

Your paralegal was on vacation, so it was necessary for you to do a little independent legal research. You came upon the mail rule, Rule 4(c) (2) (C) (ii) which, you determined, took you back to Rule 4 (c) (2) (A) and Rule 4 (d) (1). You read those rules as permitting service on this defendant by any nonparty over the age of 18. Remembering that your client's former attorney was fired for failing to effect service, you decided to err on the side of caution. Not only did you send the appropriate documents to be served by a special process server in Tulsa, you also sent an additional set to your ne'er-do-well, out-of-work cousin who happened to be living in Tulsa. All of this was done on November 1, 1984.

In due course, you received the appropriate affidavits from both the process server and your cousin. The process server swore he served the defendant personally on November 15, 1984, and your cousin swore that he did likewise on December 8, 1984. The process server also swore that, while sitting in the defendant's office, he had seen your earlier mailed service on the defendant's desk, together with a letter, dated September 15, 1984, from the defendant's attorney advising him to ignore the summons.

On December 28, 1984, the defendant filed an appearance and an answer admitting every allegation in the complaint, but asserting two affirmative defenses: (a) that, as to the summons served by the special process server, service was defective because he had not been personally served; and (b) that as to the summons served by your cousin, service was ineffective because the date of service was more than 120 days after August 1, 1984, the date the complaint had been filed, and that there was no "good cause" for such service not having been made within 120 days.

On February 1, 1985, following a hearing on a motion relying on two of those defenses, the court dismissed the case, without prejudice, under Rule 4(j). Obviously you lost on both defenses. Service by the process server was stricken because the judge chose to believe the defendant's affidavit testimony (and that of his wife), which stated that on the day he was supposed to have been served in Tulsa, he was in fact in Dallas.

You learned an important lesson: using private process servers instead of federal marshals is likely to result in more factual disputes about whether service was made properly. When this happens, the process server's affidavit may not carry the same weight as a marshal's.

Service by your cousin was also stricken. You tried to show "good cause" for having failed to serve within 120 days by going through the litany of facts in the case and explaining your earlier attempts to serve the defendant, but the judge was not moved.

Consulting your calendar, you realized that under the applicable three-year statute of limitations, you now had exactly two days left to avoid disaster. Accordingly, the next day, February 2, 1985, you filed a new, identical action (85-C-803), obtained a new summons, and went out to get drunk to celebrate having escaped your narrow brush with malpractice. On February 4, 1985, after you sobered up, you flew to Tulsa, waited outside the defendant's office disguised as an Arab sheik, and laid the appropriate papers in his hand.

Twenty days later, the defendant filed an appearance and answer to your new complaint. The answer again admitted every allegation contained in the complaint. It also contained an affirmative defense—that all applicable statutes of limitation had expired. The next day both you and the defendant filed motions for summary judgment and, just to be safe, you also filed a motion for reconsideration of the court's dismissal of your first complaint. The decision was not long in coming.

If you were still in law school and this were a final exam, I suppose the question would be, how did the court resolve the pending motions? But since you are in the real world, I will attempt to supply one very plausible answer. If you suspect that you should be checking the deductible on your malpractice coverage and trying to sell your Porsche, you are right.

Act IV: Findings of Fact and Conclusions of Law

This case comes on for decision on the parties' cross motions for summary judgment in case number 85-C-803, and on plaintiff's motion for reconsideration of this court's granting of defendant's motion to dismiss in case number 84-C-1221. I will address the second complaint first.

Defendant admits all facts alleged in the new complaint but asserts that there is no genuine dispute as to any fact material to its affirmative defense—that all counts are time-barred under the applicable statutes of limitation. I agree.

The undisputed material facts show that on February 3, 1982, defendant violated numerous antifraud provisions of the federal securities acts and the common law in connection with an oil and gas deal. Since all common law claims arose in Oklahoma, the parties acknowledge that Oklahoma's statutes of limitation are applicable thereto.

The parties further agree that, as to the claims arising under the federal securities laws, none of which contain their own limitation periods, the applicable limitations periods are to be found in those Oklahoma statutes providing limitations periods for claims most closely analogous to the federal claims. Finally, the parties agree that, under the applicable Oklahoma law, all claims are governed by a three-year limitations period which began to run on the date of the transaction, February 3, 1982.

Plaintiff relies upon Rule 3 of the Federal Rules of Civil Procedure, which provides that a federal action is "commenced" upon the filing of the complaint. Plaintiff's argument, marvelous in its simplicity, is that: (1) the applicable limitations periods began to run on February 3, 1982; (2) "commencement" of an action stops the statute from running, and (3) Case No. 85-C-803 was filed on February 2, 1985. Therefore, plaintiff contends, the action was commenced within the three-year statute of limitations, and thus is not barred.

Defendant, however, says Rule 3 is inapplicable. He relies upon OKLA. STAT. TIT. 12 Sec. 97 (1971), which states the Oklahoma rule that an action is not commenced when the complaint is filed, but rather when the defendant is served. The defendant says the action was commenced on February 4, 1985, one day too late. Defendant argues that under *Walker v. Armco Steel Corp.*, 446 U.S. 740 (1980), the Oklahoma rules apply because they are an integral part of the Oklahoma statute of limitations.

Plaintiff, on the other hand, contends that the *Erie*-based analysis leading to this conclusion does not apply to cases on which there are federal claims and the companion state claims are in court under pendent jurisdiction.

Walker is not precisely on point. *Walker* involved no federal claim. The sole basis for federal subject matter jurisdiction there was diversity of citizenship, and the Supreme Court expressly reserved the question of whether Rule 3 would determine the commencement time of an action based on federal law. Defendant's arguments for the extension of the *Walker* rule are well founded, and I accordingly hold that Rule 3 only controls the commencement question for statute of limitations' purposes with respect to federal claims for which Congress has enunciated a limitations period.

Because Oklahoma law provides the limitation periods for all claims in the complaint, the Oklahoma commencement provision also applies.

Since summons was not served until February 4, 1985, the claims were not commenced until then and they are all, therefore, time-barred.

Plaintiff next asks for reconsideration of this court's prior ruling on defendant's motion for summary judgment in the earlier case.

Case 84-C-1221 was dismissed without prejudice because: (a) the court was persuaded by defendant's affidavit that he could not have been personally served in Tulsa on November 15, 1984, because he was in Dallas, and (b) service by plaintiff's counsel's cousin did not take place within 120 days, and plaintiff did not show ''good cause'' for this delay within the meaning of Rule 4(j). Plaintiff has advanced no reasons for the failure to serve the defendant within 120 days of August 1, 1984, other than the change of attorneys and the brief hospitalization of the attorney ultimately responsible for this case. This, in my opinion, is not good cause.

Moreover, I note that plaintiff could have easily protected himself simply by moving under Rule 6(b), within 120 days of August 1, 1984, for an extension of time to effect service. This court routinely grants these motions. Plaintiff failed to protect himself at his peril. *See, e.g., Coleman v. Greyhound Lines, Inc.,* 100 F.R.D. 476 (N.D. Ill. 1984).

Finally, plaintiff contends (and I agree) that the record shows the defendant in fact received the mail service sent by plaintiff's attorney on September 10, 1984, within the 20 days allowed in Rule 4 (c) (2) (C) (ii). Plaintiff correctly points out that the record also reflects that defendant willfully refused to return the acknowledgment form.

Plaintiff argues from these facts that the mail service was effective notwithstanding the defendant's failure to return the acknowledgment form, and relies upon *Bell v. London,* 580 F. Supp. 62 (S.D. N.Y. 1984). In that case, where the defendant undeniably received the mail service but failed to return the mail service acknowledgment form, the court held that the defendant did receive personal service within the statute of limitations.

To the extent that *Bell* is not distinguishable (and I believe that it is), I decline to follow the softhearted logic of my brother from New York. Rule 4 (c) (2) (C) (ii) states that if no acknowledgment is received by the plaintiff within 20 days of attempted mail service, ''service . . . *shall be made''* by the plaintiff in another way [emphasis added].

Moreover, Rule 4 (c) (2) (D) provides that the only sanction upon a defendant who fails to return an acknowledgment is the payment of costs for personal service. Because Rule 4 is a technical rule, it requires technical compliance. Attempted service by mail is not ''service,'' even if the defendant receives the papers, unless the defendant returns the acknowledgment form and does so within 20 days (I leave to deeper thinkers the intriguing question of when that ''20 days'' begins to run).

In addition, I have grave doubts about the propriety of mail service on nonresident defendants under Rule 4 where, as here, such service is arguably based upon a state long-arm statute. Rule 4 (a), of course, permits service on nonresident defendants to the full extent authorized by the law of the forum state; however, I do not read Rule 4 (a) to authorize the *manner* of service in such cases.

Rather, I believe that the manner of service upon such out-of-state defendants is controlled by the law of the forum state. Unlike Rule 4, as recently amended, Illinois (like most states) does not permit service by ordinary mail. Hence, my ultimate decision in Case 84-C-1221 might be the same even if the mail service sent on September 10, 1984, had been timely made and acknowledged. *See, e.g., Davis v. Musler*, 713 F.2d 907 (2d Cir. 1983). The foregoing analysis, of course, has no application to service on nonresidents under the federal securities act.

Accordingly, I find and hold:

1. That proper service in case 84-C-1221 was not made within 120 days from August 1, 1984, and the case was properly dismissed, without prejudice, under Rule 4 (j) because plaintiff failed to show good cause why service was not so effected.

2. That all claims in Case 85-C-803 became time-barred on February 3, 1985, because the action was not commenced by that date within the meaning of OKLA. STAT. TIT. 12 Sec. 97.

3. With respect to defendant's additional motion for its attorneys' fees under newly amended Rule 11, I:

    a. Grant the motion with respect to fees incurred by defendant in resisting plaintiff's motion for reconsideration of my prior ruling in 84-C-1221. That motion was frivolous in light of the clear language of Rule 4, the applicable law, and plaintiff's failure to assert any theories not raised in its response to defendant's prior motion for summary judgment.

    b. Order a further hearing to determine the amount of the fee award, which award will be assessed against plaintiff's counsel only, plaintiff having suffered enough.

BY ORDER OF THE COURT

Act V: The Office

You are in your office overlooking Lake Michigan two hours after you have read the court's opinion. You buzz Helen on the intercom. She answers.

"Helen, do you remember the name of the private brokerage service we used to sell the Porsche? Would you give them a call and find out if they can handle the sale of a boat? A thirty-foot sloop in top condition. Tell them it was new last spring, and it hasn't been used since September."

• • •

Anyone whose curiosity is aroused by this nightmare should read two comprehensive articles by Professor David D. Siegel, which are published at 96 F.R.D. 88-115 and in 28 U.S.C.A. Rule 4, at 18-63 (Supp. 1984).

Rule 11: Stop, Think, and Investigate

by Edwin A. Rothschild, Richard L. Fenton, and Sheila Hegy Swanson

The lawyer's signature is required on all pleadings, motions, and other papers in federal court. It is not an idle formality. Under amended Rule 11, Fed. R. Civ. P., that signature certifies that the lawyer has made a reasonable inquiry and determined that the filing is well grounded in fact and warranted by existing law (or a good faith argument for its extension, modification, or reversal) and is not interposed for delay, harassment, or some other improper purpose. It means there is an obligation for the lawyer to stop, think, and investigate.

The courts are encouraged—if not required—to impose costs, attorneys' fees, and other sanctions against the lawyer, the client, or both for unfounded pleadings, motions, and similar abuses of the judicial system.

In principle, the stop, think, and investigate concept is not revolutionary. Any conscientious lawyer does his homework before making factual assertions or taking legal positions in court. And the canons of ethics have long required legal positions to be supported by existing law or a good faith argument to extend, modify, or reverse existing law. *See* Code of Professional Responsibility, DR 7-102(A)(2) (ABA, 1969, as amended; see 1976 ed.), and Rule 3. 1, Model Rules of Professional Conduct (ABA, 1983).

Yet the new rules have provoked sharp debate and concern. Lawyers and judges are faced with some troubling questions:

- How much inquiry is required?
- Can a lawyer rely on his client's word or does reasonable inquiry require corroboration from independent sources?
- When is it appropriate to move for sanctions against one's opponent?

Mr. Rothschild is a partner and Mr. Fenton an associate in Sonnenschein, Carlin, Nath and Rosenthal, in Chicago. Ms. Swanson is Counselor for the U.S. Dept. of Health and Human Services in Chicago.

Before the amendments, Rule 11 did not require lawyers to look into either the factual or legal grounds of a pleading or motion. The lawyer's signature only meant he had read the pleading, believed that there was good ground to support it, and that the pleading was not interposed for delay. It was unclear whether these certification requirements also applied to motions governed by Rule 7. *See* 1983 Advisory Committee Notes to Rule 7, Fed. R. Civ. P.

The courts generally applied a subjective bad-faith standard in determining whether a lawyer had violated old Rule 11. *See, e.g., Badillo v. Cent. Steel & Wire Co.*, 717 F.2d 1160 (7th Cir. 1983). Although one court found that a lawyer had a duty of inquiry before starting suit based on unverified hearsay based on rumor, *Miller v. Schweickart*, 413 F. Supp. 1059 (S.D.N.Y. 1976), most courts found good faith where a reasonable lawyer "could have concluded that facts supporting the claim *might* be established" and where a complaint was not "entirely without color." *Nemeroff v. Abelson*, 620 F.2d 339, 348 (2d Cir. 1980).

Good faith is no longer enough. The requirement that the pleading, motion, or other paper be well-grounded in fact and warranted by existing law is far more stringent than the old rule. 1983 Advisory Committee Notes, Rule 11, Fed. R. Civ. P. and Rule 11 pleading standards are now expressly applicable to motions under amended Rule 7, Fed. R. Civ. P.

In addition, the new rules enhance the court's ability to punish violations. The court *shall* impose appropriate sanctions against lawyers, the client, or both. Sanctions may include reasonable attorneys' fees or other expenses. Rule 11, Fed R. Civ. P. (1983).

Shall suggests that courts are *required* to impose sanctions whenever a violation is found. But this is not the way the courts have administered Rule 37 where, despite similar mandatory language, severe sanctions have been applied sparingly in the enforcement of discovery orders. But at the least, new Rule 11 surely *encourages* judges to issue sanctions in appropriate cases.

The authority to assess attorneys' fees under Rule 11 is also new. Before the amendments, courts looked outside the federal rules for authority to deal with irresponsible litigators and litigants. Under an exception to the American rule that each party bear its own attorneys' fees, courts sometimes exercised their inherent power to shift fees to parties or lawyers who started frivolous suits or conducted litigation in an oppressive manner. *See Roadway Express, Inc. v. Piper*, 447 U.S. 752 (1980).

On occasion, the courts also punished the offending lawyer under 28 U.S.C. 1927, which allows courts to assess excess costs and fees against lawyers who unreasonably and vexatiously multiply proceedings. *See McCandless v. Great Atl. & Pac. Tea Co.*, 697 F.2d 198 (7th Cir. 1983). Rarely, a court awarded fees and costs for pleading violations when offenders were held in contempt. *See Schleper v. Ford Motor Co.*, 585 F.2d 1367 (8th Cir. 1978). But virtually no reported case imposed sanctions for anything less than willful and usually quite egregious conduct. *Deterring Dilatory Tactics in Litigation: Proposed Amendments to Rules 7 and 11 of the Federal Rules of Civil Procedure*, 26 St. Louis U. L. J. 895 (1982).

The basic question is: What is a reasonable inquiry?

The phrase is hardly self-defining. Like ''reasonable care,'' ''unreasonable restraint of trade,'' and ''beyond a reasonable doubt,'' ''reasonable inquiry'' needs interpretation. But those other phrases have a history of judicial meaning, and ''reasonable inquiry'' does not. Until it does, perhaps the best we can do is borrow Justice Stewart's famous phrase from *Jacobellis v. Ohio*, 378 U.S. 184 at 197, (1964), ''I know it when I see it.''

In general, the phrase requires you to be careful, skeptical, objective, and a judicious professional in all pleading and motion matters. On the other hand, your duty to your client requires you to be daring, innovative, imaginative, and a fierce partisan. With these clear guideposts you should have no problem—especially if you also know it when you see it.

The Advisory Committee Notes say that a reasonable inquiry is what is reasonable under the circumstances or what was reasonable to believe at the time the pleading or other paper was submitted. For example, the notes suggest that the extent of your investigation depends in part on how much time is available. When you are retained on the eve of some deadline, such as a statute of limitations expiration, or when you must ask for emergency relief, the time for inquiry is brief.

This does not relieve you of the duty of keeping abreast of subsequent developments; sanctions may be imposed for continuing to prosecute or defend after you knew (or should have known) that the facts or law no longer supported your position. *See Nemeroff v. Abelson*, 704 F.2d 652 (2d Cir. 1983) and *Steinberg v. Regis/Sheraton Hotel*, 34 FEP Cases 745 (S.D.N.Y. Mar. 30, 1984).

Assuming you have adequate time before filing, how thorough must your inquiry be? Can you rely solely on your client for the facts, or is outside verification required where it is available?

The committee notes say that one factor to be considered is whether a lawyer ''*had* to rely on a client for facts'' (emphasis added). One commentator says this means that a lawyer may never rely on the client's word alone where independent verification is available. Marcus, *Reducing Court Costs and Delay: The Potential Impact of the Proposed Amendments to the Federal Rules of Civil Procedure*, 66 JUDICATURE, No. 8 (Mar. 1983).

We disagree. We think the issue is whether it is *reasonable* to rely solely on the client.

You should consider the following factors:

1. Can your client's story be readily corroborated by information available from other sources?

2. Is the cost of seeking out other sources prohibitive—that is, is it disproportionate to factors like the amount at issue, the possible prejudice to the other side?
3. Does your client have actual knowledge of the facts or is his story based on hearsay or rumor?
4. How well do you know your client? If he is a client of longstanding, in whose credibility you have developed confidence, it may well be reasonable to rely on his word alone. Conversely, if you have had no previous experience with him, or if your experience leads you to question his candor, outside corroboration would be advisable.
5. Is the client's story plausible? If not, try to get independent verification.

Suppose that reasonable inquiry discloses that the client's story, although not inherently implausible, is contradicted by all the other witnesses, as well as by the relevant documents. The client nevertheless maintains that the other witnesses are mistaken (or lying), and that the documents are wrong or can be explained. It is his word against the world. Must you then desert him? Is it misconduct to represent him, to sign his pleading or his motion?

The answer depends largely on whether the client's proposed testimony is competent evidence. If his statements are inadmissible hearsay, a Rule 11 inquiry will probably require you to find other information that is either admissible or likely to lead to admissible evidence. If investigation does not bear out the client's assertions, it may be advisable to decline representation.

On the other hand, if the client's testimony is admissible, it should provide a sufficient basis for signing a pleading or a motion. This does not mean that you *must* sign it; no lawyer should sign his name to what he believes to be a lie. But if you are simply not sure, and there is competent and admissible evidence to support the claim, we think you can file the paper. After all, you are not the trier of fact. Rule 11 should not require you to weigh contradictory evidence or to resolve factual disputes against your client.

Can you make an allegation of fact without first having evidentiary support? That depends on the likelihood that you will ultimately be able to prove it. The new rules do not prohibit filing simply because your evidence is not yet in admissible form. On the other hand, a mere hunch that your client may have a cause of action is no longer enough to justify the filing of a complaint; you must have some reasonably reliable information that the plaintiff indeed has a claim. Furthermore, the bare existence of a claim does not justify exaggeration. *See Viola Sportswear Inc. v. Claude Clement Minum*, 574 F. Supp. 619 (E.D.N.Y. 1983), where the plaintiff's lawyer charged a nationwide trademark conspiracy because one pair of $10.00 counterfeit jeans had been discovered. The court said that the allegation of a nationwide conspiracy in those circumstances "can hardly be said to be well-grounded in fact."

You should also stop, think, and investigate before filing a complaint that joins more parties than may actually be implicated. You can no longer sue everyone who may have some conceivable involvement in the matter (however remote or tangential) on the assumption that you can always dismiss a defendant if you find that you should not have sued him in the first place. Rule 11 now requires a reasonable belief that there is actually a case against each defendant named. In a malpractice suit, for example, the once prevalent practice of including as defendants all doctors, nurses, and orderlies on call at the time of the event would now be likely to result in an award of attorneys' fees.

To what extent may you rely on cocounsel or forwarding counsel? The Advisory Committee Notes suggest that lawyers should not incur sanctions for the mistakes of other lawyers. *Cf. Colucci v. New York Times*, 533 F. Supp. 1011 (S.D.N.Y. 1982). Nonetheless, if you are asked to sign pleadings or motions prepared by other lawyers, you should at least investigate the other lawyers' "reasonable inquiry" and it would be better to make your own evaluation of the factual and legal positions which they took.

Despite the duty of reasonable inquiry, the courts are likely to be sympathetic to the plight of a lawyer who, acting in good faith, was misinformed or misled about the facts.

Misinformation about the law, however, is a different matter. A lawyer cannot blame his client for a misstatement or outright ignorance of the law; the responsibility is his own.

The Advisory Committee Notes say the courts should consider whether the pleading or motion is based on a plausible view of the law. Thus, you should not fear sanctions if there is some support for your position in law or logic. *See Perta, Inc. v. Comprehensive Serv. Co.*, No. 83-C-5518, slip op. (N.D. Ill. 1983). The amendments were not intended to overrule the American rule that each party bear its own costs of litigation. Awards of attorneys' fees are not appropriate just because one side turned out to be right and the other side turned out to be wrong.

Suppose you want to take a legal position that has been disapproved by every federal court of appeals that has considered it, including the circuit in which the court sits? Can you make your argument? In our view, yes, as long as you can advance a logical, cogent argument that the prior decisions are wrong or that they should not apply to the facts of the particular case. While you must be candid with the court about the existence of unfavorable prior law, just because an argument has been rejected in the past does not mean that it will never be accepted. Indeed, the argument *must* be advanced in the trial court to preserve it on appeal. The rules do not require that such arguments be suppressed.

The rules do require a good-faith showing why your position ought to be upheld. Cite the earlier cases, distinguish them if you can, or explain why you think they were wrongly decided. If you cannot do this in a way that carries conviction, then you should not certify that the pleading or motion meets the rule's legal standard. *See Rodgers v. Lincoln Towing Serv.*, 596 F. Supp. 13 (N.D. Ill. 1984), *aff'd*, 771 F.2d 194 (7th Cir. 1985), assessing fees against plaintiff's lawyer even though one claim of his multiclaim civil rights complaint "superficially ha[d] some of the earmarks of a claim for a denial of . . . due process."

Finally, what about enforcement? Most of us have seen opponents (never ourselves) who allege questionable facts and take unfounded legal positions. Suppose it happens to you. Should you suffer in silence? Should you wait for the judge to act *sua sponte?* Or should you bring your own motion for sanctions?

You should certainly act in a proper case. Rule 11 is not self-enforcing. It is the responsibility of both judges and members of the bar to see that sanctions are imposed when sanctions are deserved.

But it should be clear that sanctions *are* deserved. A motion for sanctions under Rule 11 should not be lightly made. It can reflect upon a lawyer's record. It can injure his reputation. It should not be used as a strategic ploy or a means of reprisal. Indeed, such a motion is itself subject to Rule 11; it requires reasonable inquiry and must be well grounded in fact and supported by law. Courts have imposed sanctions upon lawyers who have improperly sought sanctions against other lawyers. *Fisher Bros. v. Cambridge Lee Indus., Inc.*, 38 Fed. R. Serv. 2d (Callaghan), 1013 (E. D. Pa. 1983).

But when the violation is substantial, deliberately or irresponsibly committed, and particularly when the perpetrator is a seasoned litigator, you should move for sanctions. While most lawyers do not need the threat of sanctions to behave honorably or responsibly, there are always some who play close to the line and step over it if they can do so with impunity.

When this happens often enough and long enough, there is a general erosion of standards. No litigator wants his client to be hampered by scruples that his opponent does not share. A kind of Gresham's law affects professional conduct and we can see its results. Today, even the most respected lawyer will often allege more in his complaint than he thinks he can prove, while his equally esteemed adversary will answer by admitting much less than he knows to be true. In pleading and motion practice, as well as in discovery, tactical considerations usually prevail over all else.

To those who believe that "winning isn't everything; it's the only thing," the new restraints may seem irksome. But even professional football has its limits. Players do not mine their goal line or chloroform the opposing linemen. Even the minor forms of mayhem are less common when penalties are more sure and more severe. Winning is what we strive for, but not at all costs.

The real objective of the amendments is not to handicap the ingenious nor even to punish the wicked, but to elevate the standards of practice. When it becomes unthinkable for a reputable lawyer to make irresponsible allegations, we will have a better system of justice.

On the other hand, the rules must not be used to enforce orthodoxy. Ingenuity should not be penalized; the unusual, the unpopular, even the despised client should have his day in court. New concepts, new theories, new and even strange legal arguments should be listened to. As the Advisory Committee states, the rules are "not intended to chill a lawyer's enthusiasm or creativity in pursuing factual or legal theories."

Their purpose, in short, is to make lawyers responsible, not timid.

The Chill of Rule 11

by Jean Maclean Snyder

Rule 11 was amended to give judges more freedom in sanctioning lawyers who sign false or frivolous pleadings. Yet some judges are using this new power to punish lawyers who advance factual or legal theories that break new ground or legitimately challenge existing precedent. The decisions applying the rule this way may be personal, angry, and punitive. And because most lawyers assume that ingenuity in drafting a claim or defense should be cause for praise—not blame—the sanctions are unexpected as well.

New Rule 11 makes three important changes in the law:

First, signing a pleading certifies it is "well grounded in fact and is warranted by existing law or a good faith argument for the extension, modification, or reversal of existing law, and that it is not interposed for any improper purpose, such as to harass or to cause unnecessary delay or needless increase in the cost of litigation."

Second, if a pleading is signed in violation of Rule 11, the court "shall" impose sanctions—it need not wait for a motion from opposing counsel, but can act on its own initiative.

Third, sanctions can be imposed against the person who signed the pleading, or the party, or both and can include attorneys' fees and costs.

Courts are using Rule 11—quite correctly—to punish lawyers who have filed complaints before they have checked on the facts and the law, or have made false denials solely to forestall facing the facts. To date, most courts have imposed attorneys' fees, usually on the attorney.

But some judges are using Rule 11 a little differently. Here are three recent cases.

The author is a former editor-in-chief of LITIGATION, *and is with the Chicago firm D'Ancona & Pflaum, which represented the plaintiff in the second case discussed in this article.*

41

First consider *Rodgers v. Lincoln Towing Serv.*, 596 F. Supp. 13 (N.D. Ill. March 19, 1984), *aff'd*, 771 F.2d 194 (7th Cir. 1985). Rodgers brought a civil rights suit complaining that the Chicago police had conspired with Lincoln Towing Service to violate his civil rights. His complaint alleged these facts.

One evening in October 1982, Rodgers went to Lincoln Towing Service's depot to retrieve his car, which Lincoln had towed from a parking lot where it had been parked illegally. Rodgers paid the fee and drove his car home. At 1:00 o'clock in the morning Rodgers's phone rang and a voice said, ''This is the police, they're coming to your house for throwing paint on the building.''

Rodgers heard nothing more for a week. Then he got a call from a man who identified himself as Police Officer Philip Pagano. Pagano told Rodgers that the police had a witness who would identify Rodgers as ''the person who threw paint on the Lincoln Towing building.'' Officer Pagano said that if Rodgers would not come to the police station to answer charges, the police would issue a warrant for his arrest. Rodgers told Pagano he would come to the station and would bring bond money with him.

Rodgers arrived at the Nineteenth Police District Station in Chicago at 5:20 P.M. Pagano and several other police officers questioned Rodgers for an hour about throwing paint at the Lincoln Towing building. At no time during the questioning (or throughout his ordeal) did the police tell Rodgers that he could call a lawyer or could refuse to answer questions.

So Rodgers submitted to the questioning, steadfastly maintaining that he knew nothing about the paint throwing.

The manager of Lincoln Towing and another of its employees were present throughout Rodgers's interrogation. They pressed Officer Pagano to file charges against Rodgers. In his complaint, Rodgers alleged that the Lincoln Towing personnel were personal friends of Officer Pagano. According to Rodgers, this is the reason that Pagano eventually drew a complaint against Rodgers, although he and the other officers knew that Lincoln Towing's charges were false.

By now it was early evening. The police refused to tell Rodgers what charges had been brought against him, and refused his repeated requests to call an attorney, his wife, or a friend. At the same time, they would not let Rodgers make bail or post a bond, although he repeatedly told them he had the money to do this. Instead, they placed Rodgers in the lockup and held him at the station most of the night. Finally, at 5:00 o'clock the next morning—twelve hours after arriving at the station— Rodgers was released. He stood trial on the charges Lincoln Towing brought against him, and was found not guilty.

In his complaint in federal court, Rodgers alleged that Lincoln Towing and the officers of the Nineteenth Police District acted together in the hope of harassing him into paying for the damage to Lincoln Towing's building. Rodgers also alleged that what happened to him was part of a widespread practice of the police and Lincoln Towing to harass people who parked in the neighborhood.

In sum, Rodgers asserted that he had been unlawfully arrested, interrogated, and detained; that he had been forced to spend money defending a criminal charge the police knew was false; and that he had suffered mental anguish and damage to his reputation. He said that his civil rights had been violated and asked for monetary relief.

Did Rodgers's complaint state a cause of action under the federal civil rights laws?

The judge thought not. Moreover, he declared that Rodgers's lawyers should be sanctioned for suggesting that it did.

When several (but not all) of the defendants filed a motion to dismiss Rodgers's amended complaint, the judge dismissed it and denied leave to amend. In addition, acting on his own initiative, the judge assessed sanctions under Rule 11 for $858.43 (one-third of the defendants' total attorneys' fees and costs).

The judge faulted Rodgers's lawyers for inartful pleading and for mixing "worthless claims" with claims of possible merit. He said, "with even the modest research that is now required under Rule 11, any lawyer admitted to practice before this court quickly should have determined that this relatively minor incident did not amount to a federal case of constitutional dimension. At any rate, what would not have been done after proper research was what occurred here: the filing of a ponderous, extravagant, and overblown complaint that was largely devoid of a colorable legal basis. This was a clear-cut violation of Rule 11."

The parties' briefs and the court's two lengthy opinions (one denying a motion for reconsideration) show that the plaintiff filed claims under some legal theories that he could not or would not defend. It would be hard to quarrel with a finding that the lawyers had failed to satisfy Rule 11's requirement of a reasonable inquiry on the law and the facts as to those claims.

But that is not quite what the judge found. Instead he concluded that Rodgers's lawyers had violated Rule 11 by combining frivolous claims with claims that had possible merit.

As to this second group, cases cited by Rodgers's lawyers indicate that some of his claims could well have been found actionable under Section 1983 of the Civil Rights Act. *U.S. v. Black,* 675 F.2d 129 (7th Cir. 1982), cert. denied., 460 U.S. 1068 (1983); *Logan v. Zimmerman Brush Co.,* 455 U.S. 422 (1982).

But the court disagreed with Rodgers's lawyers about how these cases should be applied, and found other case law more compelling.

No amount of reasoning could have persuaded the judge that Rodgers's lawyers were not wasting his time. And no amount of research could have persuaded Rodgers's lawyers that their client was not entitled to his day in federal court.

43

It seems hard to avoid the conclusion that Rodgers's lawyers were punished, at least in part, because their view of the law differed from that of the judge.

The second case is also from Chicago. The complaint was brought by the employees and trustees of a retirement plan against the insurance company that had provided the plan's group annuity contract. Complaining that the defendant had wrongfully amended the contract without the plaintiffs' consent, the plaintiffs alleged that the defendant was a "fiduciary" under the Employment Retirement Income Security Act and had violated its fiduciary duties. The complaint also alleged breach of contract and violation of the Illinois Uniform Deceptive Trade Practices Act.

The court dismissed all three counts of the complaint. As to the count under the Employment Retirement Income Security Act, the court apparently felt that the complaint broke new ground better left unbroken.

The court held that the plan and the annuity contract did not make the insurance company a fiduciary under the Employment Retirement Income Security Act. The court went on to say that drafting the complaint based on this theory "cannot have been done in good conscience or mindful of counsel's responsibilities under Rule 11." *Chicago Bd. Options Exchange v. Conn. Gen. Life Ins.*, 553 F. Supp. 125, 130 (N.D. Ill. 1982). (The district court's opinion was drafted five months before the new Rule 11 went into effect, when the amendments were the subject of considerable favorable publicity.) The plaintiffs appealed, and the Seventh Circuit reversed the trial court. As if to avenge the chastised lawyers, the court held that "[d]espite the novelty of this issue, and the dearth of any definitive guidance," the complaint properly alleged the defendant insurance company to be a fiduciary under the Employment Retirement Income Security Act. *Chicago Bd. Options Exch. v. Connecticut Gen. Life Ins.*, 713 F.2d 254, 260 (7th Cir. 1983).

It is not unusual for a court of appeals and a district court to disagree about the meaning of a statute. But it is surprising that the plaintiff was threatened with sanctions for simply advancing a new interpretation of a statute.

The third case is from San Francisco. In June 1983, lawyers for a landscaping contractor filed a complaint against the contractor's employees' union and the multiemployer bargaining association that had negotiated a collective bargaining agreement with the union. Only one of the claims was based on federal law. The rest were joined on the theory of pendent jurisdiction.

After the complaint was filed, the judge held a series of status conferences that are memorialized in a joint statement of the plaintiff and the union that is part of the record on appeal pursuant to Fed. R. App. P. 10(c).

The record shows that at the first conference the judge said he did not

44

understand why the union had been included as a defendant in the lawsuit, and pointedly suggested that the plaintiff's lawyers read amended Rule 11. The judge reiterated his scepticism at later conferences. He repeatedly told the parties that they should settle the lawsuit and finally said that he did not want to see the case in his court again.

Faced with this hostility, the plaintiff decided to dismiss its complaint without prejudice and refile in state court. The multiemployer's bargaining association agreed to the dismissal, but the union did not. The union wanted a dismissal with prejudice, and it wanted attorneys' fees under Rule 11.

On hearing day, the union got what it asked for, and more than anyone expected. Waiting for the parties was the court's eight-page opinion. Here is what the judge did.

First, he held that he lacked subject matter jurisdiction over the lawsuit because the plaintiff's federal claim was "totally baseless." Then he held that he had no jurisdiction over the union, and that the state claim against it was "patently without merit." Despite finding that he had no jurisdiction, he dismissed the claim against the union with prejudice.

The judge did not stop there. He discussed the plaintiff's lawyers' conduct, and he was uncomplimentary. He concluded by saying, "Attorneys do not serve the interests of their clients, of the profession, or of society when they assert claims or defenses grounded on nothing but tactical or strategic expediency."

After dealing with their conduct, the judge turned to the lawyers themselves. He asserted that the law firm representing the plaintiff "holds itself out as preeminent in labor law." He added that the two lawyers signing the complaint "hold themselves out as specializing in labor law," and even stated how long each lawyer had been in practice. He concluded, "Given the claimed expertise and experience of these attorneys, a strong inference arises that their bringing an action such as this was for an improper purpose." He warned the lawyers that "the heaviest sanction they will suffer is the one they have inflicted on themselves—loss of the court's confidence in their probity."

Then the judge announced the court-inflicted sanctions. He awarded the union $5,625 in attorneys' fees (he based the amount on his estimate of counsel time spent on the case, but had to reduce the award to $3,406.25 after the parties submitted a stipulation of the actual hours spent).

He also awarded nonmonetary sanctions. He directed the law firm to certify promptly "that no part of this sum has been or will be charged to or paid, directly or indirectly, by the firm's client in this matter" and that a copy of this memorandum of opinion and order has been given to every partner and associate of the firm."

Finally, the judge decided to publish the opinion, making his attack a permanent part of the legal literature. *Huettig & Schromm Inc. v. Land-*

scape Contractors of Northern Cal., 582 F. Supp. 1519 (N.D. Cal. 1984), *aff'd*, 790 F.2d 1421 (9th Cir. 1986).

There is the punishment. Did it fit the lawyers' crime?

Remember that the plaintiff itself initiated a dismissal of the complaint seven months after filing suit. So even if the judge was correct in deciding that the suit was improper, it seems excessive to assess attorneys' fees and nonmonetary sanctions that include making the lawyers promise in writing that they had not used trickery to circumvent the order assessing attorneys' fees.

Equally disturbing, the joint statement on appeal—which the judge refused to sign—raises the possibility that the court unfairly distorted the plaintiff's case in his decision assessing sanctions. The statement suggests that the trial court used the threat of Rule 11 sanctions to attempt to force the parties to settle and, when the attempt failed, awarded sanctions in an opinion that mischaracterized the plaintiff's position.

These three cases are unfortunately not unique. Courts sometimes punish legal arguments made in good faith that Rule 11 was meant to protect.

Part of the problem comes from the language of the rule itself. The test for finding a violation of Rule 11 is not as precise as it may seem. Judges sanctioning legal arguments assume that a bright line divides legal theories that are warranted from those that should be sanctioned. But the line is not so clear. One lawyer's novel extension of the law is another's unwarranted abuse of the judicial system.

Whatever the cause, the problem is serious. Punishing a lawyer for the legal theory he pleads is a dangerous game. Certainly the punishment will discourage frivolous claims. But it will also stifle legitimate innovation—a result that the framers of Rule 11 never intended.

Thou Shalt Not Ignore Arbitration

by Marshall H. Tanick

If God had been an arbitrator instead of a lawyer, Moses might well have descended Sinai with the Ten Commandments of Arbitration, rather than the tablets we know.

With that kind of credibility from on High, arbitration could have replaced litigation altogether, and this article need not have been written.

Today arbitration is an unavoidable fact of life—and of legal practice. Commercial arbitrations have increased more than 33 percent in the past two years. Arbitrations for automobile accidents, various forms of personal injuries, construction cases, labor law, and other business disputes have grown similarly.

Face it: attorneys who insist on shunning arbitration will end up in a professional purgatory. To avoid that fate, here are some practical guidelines for using arbitration. Unlike the more established canons of professional practice, these principles are not cast in stone, but are intended to help those whose arbitral expertise rivals the climbing ability of Moses.

I. Thou Shalt Agree to Arbitrate

Arbitration generally is consensual; it does not occur unless the parties agree. Some arbitration is predetermined, particularly in adhesion contracts, insurance policies, and collective bargaining agreements. In some jurisdictions, statutes or local court rules require arbitrating certain kinds of disputes, such as medical malpractice or small damage claims.

Crafty attorneys generally channel potential disputes to arbitration before the conflict arises. In negotiating and drafting virtually all arm's-length transactions, an arbitration clause should be considered. Corpo-

The author is an associate editor of LITIGATION *and a member of the Minneapolis law firm Tanick & Heins.*

rate buy-sell arrangements, shareholders' agreements, real estate conveyances, and other business documents should be analyzed to determine the desirability of an arbitration clause.

The clause need not be omnipotent. The parties may elect to arbitrate only specific kinds of claims. By limiting arbitration to claims not exceeding $25,000, for example, the parties may achieve the benefits of arbitration—speed, economy, and confidentiality—without sacrificing, for larger claims, any of the traditional advantages of litigation: thorough preparation and discovery, established judicial procedures, and appellate opportunities.

Despite the desirability and flexibility of arbitration, the benefits of speed, informality, and confidentiality may conflict with a party's strategic position in a transaction. There may be legitimate reasons for the party with greater economic resources to refrain from proposing or to refuse to agree to an arbitration clause. Arbitration generally favors the party with less money or inferior bargaining power. Still, the stronger party usually can benefit from limited arbitration.

II. Thou Shalt Select Arbitrators Carefully

Choosing an arbitrator may be even more important than jury selection, because the final result of the arbitration depends on the decision of one or perhaps three arbitrators, with extremely limited right of appeal.

Of course there is no voir dire. But while an attorney cannot question the proposed arbitrators, he can investigate them. Lists of arbitrators are available from the American Arbitration Association and the Federal Mediation and Conciliation Service, as well as from other arbitral panels. Check with attorneys practicing in the particular subject area; usually they have a pretty good "book" on many arbitrators, including fellow lawyers who occasionally serve in that role. Also, review the prior decisions of prospective arbitrators, if available. Your familiarity with past decisions may be useful later, since arbitrators, like judges, relish having their prior decisions cited to them.

The question of *who* shall arbitrate is related to *how many* shall arbitrate. Some proceedings require one arbitrator; others dictate a panel of three. In rare cases, the parties have their choice of a single arbitrator or a panel.

The selection process varies. When using multiple arbitrators, each litigant usually designates one arbitrator, and the two designees then select a "neutral" third arbitrator. In single arbitration proceedings, the parties may agree on an arbitrator or, failing agreement, the organization conducting the proceedings will circulate a list, usually consisting of five or more candidates. The parties then select the arbitrators, either by alternate strikes or by numbering their preferences, so that the person with the top rank is selected.

A proceeding before a single arbitrator generally is swifter and cheaper. Three-arbitrator panels tend more towards compromise decisions. This tendency can help parties bringing money damage claims, who are less likely to be shut out where a compromise mentality exists.

III. Thou Shalt Consider the Judicial Forum

Even though a dispute is to be arbitrated, the arbitral forum does not oust the judiciary from a role in the controversy. Resort to the courts may be necessary before, during, and after the arbitration.

Prearbitral issues that are litigated include whether or not there is an agreement to arbitrate in the first instance, what issues are arbitrable, who will select the arbitrators when the parties are at an impasse, and how broad the scope of the proceedings shall be. The party seeking to move the arbitration forward generally will trigger the judicial process, usually to compel the other party to honor an arbitration agreement.

Sometimes a party antagonistic to arbitration can use the judicial forum as a tactical device. For example, an insurer may ask the court to determine that no coverage exists in a particular dispute subject to arbitration, thereby precluding the necessity of arbitrating liability and damages.

Both federal and state authorities permit, or at least condone, simultaneous proceedings in separate forums over the same dispute. For example, securities fraud disputes often are prosecuted in concurrent judicial and arbitral proceedings.

Those parallel proceedings raise difficult and delicate tactical considerations. The attorney must decide which proceeding has priority, and which should be placed on the back burner. Counsel in a securities fraud matter, for example, may simultaneously face a class action and arbitration under the Supreme Court's reasoning in *Dean Witter Reynolds v. Byrd*, 470 U.S. 213 (1985), holding that state common law fraud claims may be arbitrated while coextensive federal 10b-5 issues proceed through the judicial system. Rather than pursue the class action, which is costly, time-consuming, and full of technical pitfalls, the claimant's attorney may proceed with the arbitration on behalf of a single aggrieved individual or small group, achieve a successful result, and then try to invoke collateral estoppel to obtain an across-the-board victory without the rigors of drawn-out class litigation. The defense, however, may try to stay the arbitration while the litigation drags on, defeat any attempts at class certification, and then wear down the claimants through a series of individual arbitration hearings.

IV. Thou Shalt Honor Thy Arbitrator

The arbitrator reigns supreme in this forum, largely immune from judicial review or reversal. His power is virtually unlimited. Accordingly, arbitrators should be given all due deference.

This does not mean that counsel should refrain from insisting on the purity of the proceedings. Undue partiality is one of the few grounds for contesting an arbitrated decision. Possible bias or other improprieties should be noted and preserved as a basis for challenging an unfavorable result.

Under the Code of Ethics for Arbitrators in Commercial Disputes, an arbitrator must disclose any direct or indirect financial or personal interest in the outcome of the arbitration, as well as any financial, business, professional, family, or social relationships that may affect his impartiality. If requested to withdraw by all of the parties, the arbitrator must do so; if requested to withdraw by some, but not all, the arbitrator must still depart, unless that would create unfair delay or expense, or injustice, to any of the parties.

An attorney must, of course, tread lightly in challenging an arbitrator's ethics, at least before the result is determined. Like seeking to remove a judge, challenging an arbitrator on grounds of partiality is a two-edged sword: if you prevail, you gain a significant victory; but if you lose, you face a decision-maker who may be even more antagonistic than you first imagined.

Judges are aware of this unwritten dilemma. When presented with a strong challenge to the impartiality of an arbitrator, judges tend to relieve the party (and the arbitrator) of the problem by removing the arbitrator before the proceedings begin.

During the proceedings, however, a court is less likely to intervene. After the proceedings end, the chance of successfully challenging an arbitrator's ethics is even more remote. Therefore, find out as much as possible about an arbitrator before the proceedings, consider whether to challenge the arbitrator then, and if you decide to challenge, do so promptly.

Above all else, remember the cardinal rule of getting along with arbitrators: Pay their bills quickly. You never know when you may confront the same arbitrator again. An arbitrator whose fee is slow in coming definitely is not someone you want resolving your next dispute.

V. Thou Shalt Not Eschew Discovery

The widely held notion that arbitration precludes any discovery is a myth. Most arbitral proceedings do not allow for full-fledged discovery—with its attendant costs and delays—but selective discovery is likely to be available.

There are few formal rules. Subpoenas can be issued to witnesses, and requests to produce documents at the hearing usually are permitted. Otherwise, the federal arbitration statute, the Uniform Arbitration Act (in effect in 30 states), and other state arbitration laws generally limit prehearing discovery to deposing witnesses who cannot be subpoenaed or who cannot attend the hearing.

Some states, however, have versions of the Uniform Act, their own laws, or local rules that provide for much more discovery. In Texas, arbitrators can order depositions of adverse witnesses, as well as those who cannot testify in person or who are outside the reach of a subpoena. Kansas allows depositions of all witnesses in arbitration. The District of Columbia permits both interrogatories and document requests. Other states have varying forms of arbitral discovery, but none has anything like the extensive or formalized rules in most forms of civil litigation.

Even without statutory arbitral authority, the parties may achieve some discovery. In the original agreement, the parties may designate what can be discovered. Alternatively, counsel might agree, once the dispute develops, to engage in limited discovery. At a minimum, the attorneys might agree to identify all prospective witnesses, take depositions of at least the principals, identify documents to be used at the hearing, and stipulate to the documents' authenticity.

If these alternatives do not work, request discovery from the arbitrator. By showing need and justifiable circumstances, a party should be able to obtain at least some discovery. Prehearing information from the other side may also be secured through creative motion practice. For instance, a right to audit under an existing contract may be used as a basis to secure an arbitral order allowing review of the adversary's documents; or in an internal corporate business dispute between shareholders, a litigant may point to a state law granting a shareholder the right to inspect company records as grounds for allowing an arbitral order to produce those documents.

Failing dire need or creativity, counsel may appeal to the arbitrator's broad powers and sense of justice to secure discovery. Rule 43 of the ABA's Commercial Arbitration Rules empowers an arbitrator to make any rulings that are just and equitable." That offers a mountainous foundation for specific motions and requests to the arbitrator.

VI. Thou Shalt Not Escalate Costs

The war-of-attrition mentality, all too frequent in litigation, is even less well suited to arbitration. If arbitration is to work fairly, both parties should strive to keep costs down. The streamlined proceedings decrease the likelihood that one party can significantly outspend the other in a way that affects the result.

The cost of arbitration varies, depending on the length and complexity of the proceedings. Legal fees for arbitrating a dispute usually are substantially less than for litigating it, since arbitration is quicker, with less opportunity for discovery. Fees for arbitrating a dispute in the $25,000 to $50,000 range may amount to $5,000 or less.

Attorney fee arrangements can be adjusted to the arbitral forum. The usual arrangement is to set a per diem charge (with unlimited hours per day). Flat fees also may be appropriate, since an attorney's time commitment is usually more predictable (and smaller) in arbitration than in litigation. Even contingent fees may be used, but rates lower than the normal one-third often are appropriate.

The restrictions on discovery will limit the out-of-pocket costs of dispute resolution, including expert witness fees. The organization conducting the arbitration may charge a flat fee or an amount scaled to the size of the dispute. Generally, fees range from $150 to $1,000. The arbitrator's fees are extra. Arbitrators usually charge by the hour or the day (daily rates are likely to range from $300 to $500). Customarily, the arbitrator's fees are split between the parties.

One novel way to reduce the costs of arbitration is for the parties to agree in advance on the maximum amount they will spend. As intriguing as this may seem, it is done only rarely. Even if the lawyers are willing to cap their fees, the wealthier party is likely to be unwilling to agree, knowing that the arrangement will principally benefit the less affluent adversary. A stipulated fee ceiling is probably an idea whose time has yet to come.

VII. Thou Shalt Not be Inhospitable

"Your place or mine" is often supplanted by "my place or no place" as lawyers jockey with each other to have the arbitration conducted in their own offices. The fight for turf is not without reason, for there are home-court advantages to hosting a hearing. In the familiar surroundings of their own lawyer's facilities, the parties may feel more comfortable, and hence testify more easily. Also, an independent witness may perform better in the office of the lawyer who called him.

Sometimes an arbitration clause will have a home-court provision. Stockbrokers' customer agreements often provide for mandatory arbitration of disputes in New York City. This is convenient if the stock purchaser lives in Brooklyn and has enough money left to afford a subway token; but what if the customer happens to live outside the five boroughs, say in Honolulu?

The perceived home-court advantage occasionally backfires. I have attended a few arbitrations in lawyers' offices that were more conducive to packing sardines than to resolving legal disputes. In one case, a dozen participants were crammed into a lawyer's personal office that would have been crowded with just the lawyer and his secretary. In another unforgettable instance, nearly three dozen attorneys, parties, witnesses, and hangers-on were shoe-horned into a law firm's conference room designed for ten people at most. The situation resembled the Marx Brothers' stateroom in A *Night at the Opera.* In both these crowded affairs, the uncomfortable surroundings produced hostility, and the home-court lawyer lost. Deservedly so.

Battles over arbitral sites usually are silly and avoidable. Instead of fighting, the parties can use a neutral facility, like the offices of the American Arbitration Association, for hearings conducted under its auspices, or a courtroom for arbitral proceedings held as part of a judicial diversion program. The arbitrator may use his own facilities; I do so when I am the arbitrator simply to avoid tussles over turf. I even supply the coffee and sweet rolls (at no additional charge). When the proceedings include many participants, the parties can rent a hotel conference room or other public accommodation.

VIII. Thou Shalt Prepare Thoroughly

Testimony of witnesses is often more crucial in arbitration than in judicial proceedings for several reasons:

- Fact disputes usually predominate over legal disputes in arbitrations.
- The testimony is compacted into a shorter time than in litigation and, thus, is more easily remembered and carries greater impact.
- Arbitrations usually involve fewer witnesses than lawsuits do, and what each witness says is, therefore, magnified in importance.

Nonetheless, many litigators fail to prepare witnesses thoroughly for arbitration hearings. Some lawyers may think that the less structured arbitral setting merits less preparation. But winging it is not the way to win in arbitration.

The informality of arbitration allows intense witness preparation, because it is much easier to simulate an arbitration hearing and conduct a dress rehearsal of the testimony. Even in the relaxed setting, witnesses are likely to be intimidated. Thus, there is every reason to prepare the witness in great detail.

In addition to making the witnesses ready, be sure to prepare the arbitrator for what will be presented. Arbitrators often come to hearings remarkably unfamiliar with the facts or legal issues. Frequently, the only information available to them is in a skimpy official file, which identifies the parties and the nature of the dispute.

You might assume that most legal practitioners would leap at the opportunity to file prehearing briefs. But they do not. Perhaps they fear tipping their hand to the other side, a close-to-the-vest mentality that runs throughout the arbitral process. This fear is irrational and counterproductive. A short, focused pre-hearing brief can educate the arbitrator and frame the issues favorably. It also serves as a checklist during the arbitration.

On the other hand, the reluctance to file prehearing briefs may be prompted more by laziness than shrewd tactics. If so, that attitude is probably incurable.

The prehearing brief should concentrate on the facts. It should outline the dispute briefly, discuss the facts, identify the issues and state why they should be resolved in the client's favor, and clearly state the requested relief. The last is imperative because arbitrators have (or at least think they have) limited powers to award affirmative remedies, including equitable or declaratory-type relief.

Short post-hearing briefs also are helpful. They should focus on the principal legal issues, without reciting the underlying evidence. The combination of a factually based brief offered before the arbitration and a posthearing brief focused on legal issues cannot guarantee success, but, at a minimum, will establish the attorney's competence in representing his client.

By all means, keep the briefs short. Arbitrators do not have law clerks, and they generally charge by the hour.

IX. Thou Shalt Not Disregard the Rules of Evidence

Another myth is that rules of evidence do not exist in arbitration. It is true that the rules may be more lax in arbitral proceedings, but they do exist.

Most evidentiary battles are fought over hearsay. These skirmishes point up the biggest difference between lay arbitrators and attorney/arbitrators: most nonattorney/arbitrators do not understand the hearsay rules. By contrast, attorney/arbitrators think they do, but often demonstrate that they do not.

Here are the rules for hearsay in arbitration proceedings:
- You probably can count on introducing hearsay evidence, and having it presented against you, if the arbitrator (or panel) is not learned in the law.
- The likelihood of hearsay evidence being admitted is diminished if the arbitrator (or panel) is an attorney; and
- Hearsay evidence probably will not be admitted, regardless of who the arbitrator (or panel) is, if the hearsay involves significant facts and the other side complains vociferously.

The kind of evidence a party intends to introduce or anticipates that the other side will offer should be a factor in selecting the arbitrator or panel members. If the lawyer wants the leeway to offer evidence that might not be admitted in court, a lay arbitrator is preferable. If the case will be stronger with strict rules of evidence, choose an attorney/arbitrator.

X. Thou Shalt Not Stop at the End

The lawyer's work may continue after arbitration has ended. In most jurisdictions, the aggrieved party has 90 days to challenge the award. But the prevailing party need not rest on its laurels: force the other party's hand by moving for a judgment confirming the award as quickly as possible. By taking the initiative, the victor may even intimidate the other party into accepting the result of the arbitration.

Meanwhile, the party aggrieved by the decision must consider whether to challenge the award. In making its decision, the party must understand that the chance of a successful challenge is slight; most jurisdictions treat the arbitrator as final judge of both law and fact, subject only to an extremely narrow scope of judicial review.

Unlike an appellate tribunal reviewing a trial court, a court reviewing an arbitration award will correct only gross errors in process, not errors in substance. Thus, courts will refuse to upset an arbitration award even if clear factual or legal mistakes underlie the decision. Instead a party challenging an arbitration award must show that the decision is so flatly contrary to established precedent, or so out of line with the facts shown in the hearing, that the arbitrator exceeded his power. But this line of attack is strictly an uphill fight.

Corruption, fraud, or other undue means, exceedingly hard to prove, are the principal grounds for vacating an arbitration award. Only when an arbitrator has been guilty of blatant wrongdoing is a court likely to pass on the propriety of his conduct.

Proof problems in mounting a challenge are enormous. Establishing gross misconduct—for example, that the arbitrator accepted a bribe—is difficult. If the proceeding had only a single arbitrator, neither he nor the winning party is likely to come forward and admit malfeasance. When three arbitrators are used, the losing party is well advised to check with his designated arbitrator to ascertain whether any suspicious conduct occurred.

The nature of the arbitrators' relationship to the litigants is one basis for an appeal predicated on corruption, fraud, or partiality. Many jurisdictions require arbitrators to disclose prior and current personal, social, business, and professional relationships with the parties and with the lawyers. Failure to disclose a significant relationship, if later discovered, may form a basis for challenging an award.

But courts are reluctant to overturn an arbitral decision because of relatively innocuous preexisting relationships. One court has denied a challenge to an arbitrator's impartiality based on a claim that the arbitrator occasionally shopped at the retail store operated by one of the parties. In another case, the aggrieved party failed to vacate an arbitral award on the grounds that one of the three arbitrators was a distant relative of the winning party's ex-wife. Noting that the victor had been divorced for several years, the court rejected the challenge. The judge figured that if the party's former wife did not like him enough to stay married to him, it was doubtful that her second cousin would be contaminated in his favor.

Courts simply recognize that not every arbitrator has, or should be expected to have, the probity of a Felix Frankfurter, who recused himself in *Public Utilities Comm'n v. Pollak*, 343 U.S. 451 (1952), from ruling on the validity of the piped-in radio broadcasts in the Washington, D.C., transit system because, as a rider of the streetcars, he was a member of the "captive audience."

Ex parte communications can form a stronger basis for challenging an award than remote relationships between arbitrators and parties. Finding proof of the contacts is difficult, however. Once again, the best source for this kind of information, at least in three-arbitrator proceedings, may be the arbitrator selected by the losing party. But he rarely is privy to illicit contacts between his fellow arbitrators and the other party or counsel.

These Ten Commandments do not, of course, assure success, let alone salvation. But, for those who follow them religiously, arbitration can be a heavenly proceeding.

PART II

Discovery

Cutting Discovery Costs Through Interrogatories and Document Requests

by Robert Ehrenbard

As lawsuits multiply in number and complexity, lawyers and clients are becoming increasingly concerned about the cost of litigation. One focal point of this concern is the financial burden of discovery. With the advent of liberalized statutes and rules, discovery has become more extensive and correspondingly more expensive. And, since most cases are settled and seldom get beyond the discovery stage, the cost of discovery will be *the* cost of litigation.

Nevertheless, most discussions of discovery continue to emphasize the importance of taking the initiative and being aggressive. I suggest that the attorney has an obligation to be more discriminating in his approach. For example, while it may be heretical to suggest, why not forgo discovery altogether in some cases? There are certainly cases in which the other side will not necessarily seize the initiative if you do not. For example, some suits will simply languish if they are not prodded by discovery requests. Other suits are simply efforts to call attention to a problem which, once recognized, can be resolved without active litigation. In such cases, which concededly are in the minority, your client's interests are not served by rushing forward blindly with discovery.

Even in those cases in which the discovery process will inevitably or necessarily be invoked, a careful analysis of your discovery needs and available discovery tools can protect your client against undue expense. You should first ask yourself what you hope to achieve through discovery. Do you want to push the case to trial, or are you simply trying to force a settlement? How you answer that question will determine the scope and thrust of your discovery. You should also analyze carefully your information requirements. What type of information do you need

The author is the senior litigation partner in the New York firm of Kelley, Drye & Warren.

from the other side? Are there sources of that information other than your opposition? How will you use the information? How much will it cost to get the information?

It is significant that courts are beginning to provide an impetus for narrower and more limited discovery. When the federal rules of discovery were initially adopted, judges viewed them as a beneficial innovation to the conduct of litigation and encouraged liberal use of the rules. But, after being inundated with discovery and finding cases bogged down, judges have become more alert to the practical consequences of the discovery process and the financial burden it imposes. They have seen cases and parties overwhelmed by discovery requests, and they are rebuilding the floodgates with the controls in their hands.

Although the practice varies throughout the country, more judges are asking in advance for the details of discovery programs and supervising the process. Our judicial brethren in the Southern District of New York are beginning to say, "Before you start on ten depositions, pick the two most important witnesses on each side. Conduct their depositions first and then tell me if you really need more, and why."

No Resistance

The most obvious way to minimize the cost of collecting information is to draw upon sources that offer no resistance. Your client is always a valuable source of information and his files should be reviewed carefully. In addition, readily accessible files of government agencies may contain considerable information directly relevant to litigation. Finally, many business groups and trade associations publish statistics, maps, credit information and other data that can be useful to the litigator.

When those sources of information have been exhausted and you must resort to the discovery process, you can still protect your client against excessive costs by selecting your discovery tools carefully. Properly used, interrogatories can be the most inexpensive of the discovery alternatives available to you. For example, interrogatories are the obvious and best starting point when a plaintiff imagines that your client has done something wrong but neither you nor your client knows the basis for the plaintiff's assertions. Similarly, if you find yourself in a case where you do not know the identities of potential witnesses or relevant documents, interrogatories designed solely to establish that information are the logical way to initiate discovery.

Like other discovery devices, interrogatories have their limitations. At times they can be counterproductive and even harmful to your position. For example, if you have substantial knowledge of the facts of the case, you must consider whether interrogatories that go to the merits might be of more benefit to your opponent than to you. If the lawyer on the other side has not been pressing the litigation, he may well go to trial with very limited preparation. If you serve him with interrogatories that

59

require him to start digging, you may convert a lazy lawyer into a sophisticated and knowledgeable one.

Writing a Script

Moreover, there are categories of information that simply cannot be developed adequately through interrogatories. When you want to inquire into particular conversations or the recollections of eyewitnesses, interrogatories will work against you. You will eventually have to take the depositions of the persons who participated in the conversations or the eyewitnesses, and you will find the interrogatories have permitted the other side to write a script for those witnesses. The interrogatories will provide you only with a lawyer's carefully constructed version of an event rather than the spontaneous recollection of the witness. A witness who has been prepared for his testimony by previous answers to interrogatories will seldom deviate at deposition from those answers.

Despite these limitations, carefully honed interrogatories can significantly advance your information development. Where two corporations are in litigation, and each has a vast number of personnel and numerous contacts at various levels over a substantial period of time, nothing facilitates discovery more effectively than first establishing through interrogatories the dates, times and places of all oral communications. You can also learn whether the oral communications have been summarized in memoranda or other writings and identify those documents.

Sometimes interrogatories are the only practical means of getting certain information. There is nothing worse than taking depositions of corporate employees and hearing witness after witness say quite honestly, "I don't know." Through interrogatories, you can compel not only a "corporate" answer but an answer that reflects the knowledge of its lawyer. Sometimes the only person who knows the answers to particular questions is the other party's lawyer. Because of opposing counsel's investigations and interviews, he frequently will piece together the knowledge of many individuals in his client's employ or assemble from other sources information not within the client's knowledge. These answers are corporate answers that no individual at the corporation could readily furnish.

Interrogatories are frequently the ideal discovery tool in cases involving accounting data, complicated damages, technical information or statistical data. Many hours can be wasted in a deposition attempting in the first instance to obtain such material. Even when it can be obtained by that means, answers to interrogatories will usually provide it in much more intelligible and useful form so that it can be evaluated more easily by your client and experts and by the judge and jury at trial.

Interrogatories are also an important vehicle for discovering the identity of experts the other party intends to call at trial, the subject of the expert's testimony, the substance of the facts and opinions to which the expert will testify and a summary of the grounds for each opinion. Rule 26 of the Federal Rules of Civil Procedure designates interrogatories as the means for obtaining that information. Access to that information is indispensable when any aspect of the case will be based on expert testimony.

Effective interrogatories must be carefully drafted. Do not ask for too much or too little. You must also be careful that the interrogatories ask for what you need. If the interrogatories are phrased vaguely or imprecisely, you may get a yes or no answer that tells you nothing. By the same token, you do not want to draft plainly oppressive interrogatories and run the risk of sustained objections.

You can achieve clarity and precision—and avoid needless repetition—by preceding the interrogatories with a carefully drafted set of definitions and instructions. When you are inquiring into critical elements of the case, you must be certain that your interrogatories elicit all available information. You can do this by approaching the subject from several directions—which is sometimes called criss-crossing interrogatories.

You may also wish to issue several sets of interrogatories, with each set limited to specified areas of inquiry. For example, specific sets might pertain to the location of documents, the identity of witnesses, damages, or any other particular subject. When you take this approach, each set of interrogatories should be carefully labeled and each must cover completely the intended area of inquiry.

Deciding whether to object and how to answer your opponent's interrogatories requires the same careful attention as drafting your own interrogatories. You must read and analyze carefully interrogatories served on you to make sure you understand precisely what is required. Do not let your immediate reactions govern. A second close reading often reveals traps for the unwary. Conversely, the second reading may eliminate the demons and point to a simple way of answering. This process of analysis cannot be delayed, however. If you do not make timely objections to the interrogatories, you must answer them.

I have seen situations where the party was not ultimately able to answer the interrogatories and could not proceed with the case. As a practical matter, the obligation to answer interrogatories can force parties either to settle or drop the case. Your client may be unwilling or unable to supply the answers. In addition, inadequate answers may expose your client to summary judgment in favor of the other party. Sometimes answers to interrogatories require sophisticated technical information and cost of answering may bring your client to the reluctant conclusion that settlement is the preferred alternative to answering.

Confidential Information

Your adversary's interrogatories may seek information that is confidential or embarrassing. One way to avoid answering such interrogatories is to offer a stipulation limiting the case. An alternative is to negotiate a confidentiality agreement with your opponent or obtain a protective order from the court. Even with such protection, however, there is a risk of disclosure, and compliance with protective orders can create awkward situations in further proceedings and can be a serious problem at trial. Nevertheless, protective orders can avoid immediate difficulties for the client and, because so many cases are resolved before trial, protective orders may offer adequate safeguards.

Parties have sometimes decided that, rather than reveal certain aspects of their business activity, they would prefer limiting or even waiving a whole area of damages or a whole area of their case. In some cases, the party has made a claim, and must either back it up or withdraw it. If you can put the other side in that position, you have done your client a great service.

I had an antitrust case in which the other side claimed that the alleged antitrust violation had a nationwide impact. After we served interrogatories inquiring into the claimed impact, my opponents agreed to confine the case to a single metropolitan area. They abandoned the rest of the United States because they knew they could not answer the interrogatories.

You can create similar problems for yourself if you do not take advantage of available objections. Obtaining the information necessary to answer interrogatories may require searching files scattered throughout the country. You may be able to limit the burden and cost of such a search by objections or by negotiations. Under the federal rules, you can also offer your adversary the opportunity to conduct the file search himself. That is not a complete answer for him or for you, however. You will want to know what he has found in the files and what conclusions he may draw from what he has learned. You cannot avoid the problem of analyzing a large volume of documents you make available to your adversary. Indeed, if you let your adversary look at your records, you must know what is there before he gets to them, so he does not uncover information unknown to you that could change the course of your case or lead to entirely new or different claims.

When you receive an objectionable set of interrogatories, you may—and sometimes by local court rules must—sit down with your adversary and try to resolve the objections. Sometimes your adversary will have drawn burdensome interrogatories without realizing it. When this occurs, it is preferable to attempt to negotiate an appropriate limitation on the scope of the interrogatories rather than reflexively filing objections that may be soundly based. It almost always pays to negotiate first. However, when your opponent is determined to seek the information, no matter how burdensome or objectionable his inquiries, you might as well go to court.

When you respond to interrogatories, you should avoid the tactic of evading disclosure by providing "non-answer" answers. Your adversary will simply go to court and obtain an order compelling further answers. All you will have accomplished will be an increase in the costs of the litigation. A facetious answer may also be read to the jury at trial and you will pay a heavy price for cleverness.

You should also have a little humility in answering. A lawyer rarely knows all of the facts and he should not be overly positive in his answers. You should try to give an answer that reflects the situation as you know it but one that does not lock you into a position that turns out to be wrong. If you avoid absolutes and you find you have made a mistake, you can bow out gracefully.

Usually, the ideal person to verify answers to corporate interrogatories is the corporate secretary or someone in his office. Many answers to interrogatories involve knowledge that no single executive possesses. Since the answers often represent a collection of information from many corporate or other sources, someone in the secretary's office can properly verify them and, at the same time, be a person who will not be a witness in the case. There is no need to require key witnesses in a case to vouch for every answer or to go through a tedious deposition related to the answers.

A party may be faced with the problem of not being able to answer interrogatories. Many times the litigant may not be able to answer because the information is not available to him. A litigant in that situation may say he does not know and needs to conduct discovery. Indeed, he may be able to gain some sort of priority of discovery for this purpose. It is perfectly proper to use the lawsuit to get such information.

When your client is the only likely source of the information and he is unable to respond, you have a problem. A case sometimes comes to a practical end because a party cannot answer the interrogatories. Why can the party not admit he does not know? In some cases, the demand for particulars or the interrogatories go to matters pleaded by, and peculiarly within the knowledge of, that party. Either the party has the information or he does not. If he does not, he has no case.

In some cases, interrogatories will reveal noncompliance with Rule 11 of the Federal Rules of Civil Procedure and you will have a basis for summary judgment. Inquiry into the facts or information relied upon to support various allegations of a pleading will bring such a problem to light. A lawyer who has prepared that pleading and his client cannot say they have no basis for their allegations. They would be admitting, in effect, that Rule 11 was violated. When such a problem surfaces, you may wish to use the request for admissions procedure, a useful adjunct to interrogatories in pinning down some elements of a case.

The request for production of documents is a second low-cost discovery tool that can yield high dividends. Indeed, in complex litigation, document discovery can be the most critical aspect of trial preparation. In such cases, requests for document production are often the starting point for discovery. It is not possible, however, to lay down rigid rules for the order of your discovery priorities. For example, for your document discovery to be effective, you may have to issue interrogatories, or even take depositions, to identify the documents or categories of documents you wish to obtain from your adversary. But it is true that your trial preparation will never be complete until you obtain all documents in your adversary's possession that bear upon the issues in the case.

When I first started practicing law, I was told that attorneys in many outlying parts of New York know each other quite well. After the pleadings were filed, the attorneys would get together and literally exchange their files. Then, based on their review of the files, they would try to resolve their clients' differences without extensive litigation.

In New York City, and perhaps other parts of the country, lawyers do not have quite that much mutual trust and confidence in each other. There is more maneuvering, more motion practice and more steps in the pretrial process that I frankly doubt accomplish much at all in the long run. Sooner or later, you must get the real facts. If those facts are contained in readily accessible documents and you can agree to an informal exchange of those documents, you will have provided your client with the best and least expensive services.

I realize that my suggestion, taken literally and followed blindly, will not be acceptable to the proponents of the warfare theory of litigation. However, my suggestion is not intended to be an all-encompassing mandate but a proposal for a more practical, realistic and less expensive approach to resolving legal disputes. The longer I have practiced the more I have come to appreciate the practical value of prompt, frank discussions designed to confront the real problems in the dispute, and the more I have come to see a negative value in the impersonal jousting that takes place in so many cases.

When it is not possible to obtain documents through an informal exchange, the formal discovery process provides you with adequate access to your adversary's documents. Drafting subpoenas or requests for production of documents requires the same care and approach suggested for interrogatories. Too often, attorneys hastily scribble out the terms of a subpoena or notice and do not reflect on what they actually expect to get or the problems they are creating for the other side.

You do not want to ask for too much or too little. If you ask for too much, you may prompt an objection and get nothing, or you may be swamped with documents. You may be burdened to the point that you will beg your adversary to take the papers away and give you what you really want. But if you do not ask carefully enough for what you need, you may go through the litigation without obtaining important documents.

As with interrogatories, when you have been served with a broad request or subpoena, you should consider carefully the desirability of objections or motions to quash. The litigating lawyer and the house counsel who often handle document searches must understand what documents are being sought. Before your time to object or move expires, you must evaluate the consequences of production to your client—in terms of the size of the job, the effort to find and collect the documents, the prejudice that might result, and the possible disclosure of confidential, embarrassing or irrelevant material.

When you resolve the question of objections, you are left with the job of production. As litigation counsel, you cannot leave it to other people to know the contents of the documents you produce. You must know how the production request is framed, how the search was conducted, and what is in the material you are producing.

To comply with a broad request or subpoena that requires an exhaustive search of corporate files, you can organize a group within the corporation, generally supervised by the house counsel or someone on his staff. Give them a lecture on what is required and have them conduct the initial screening. Instruct them that, where there are questions of interpretation in terms of whether a document should or should not be produced, a lawyer should make the final decision. The lawyer who is consulted should prepare memoranda stating his interpretation of the request or subpoena and the reasons why certain documents or classes of documents were not produced. Many times there are perfectly sound reasons for not including certain documents. But, if no record is made, those reasons may get lost and the propriety of the decision may later be questioned.

After the documents to be produced are assembled, the next consideration is the method of production. A grand jury subpoena in an antitrust case may list ten categories of documents. You may wish to produce all of the documents collected without sorting them into categories. For example, some documents might apply to more than one category and classifying them according to categories may not be feasible. I prefer to supply documents without any elaborate classification. But, when I receive documents, I prefer that they be sorted so I can know which documents my adversary contends relate to particular points.

Important judgmental factors enter the decision of how to comply with a document production request. The problems can be illustrated by a grand jury subpoena. When your client is the target of an investigation, your goal is to avoid an indictment. In some cases, you may prefer to turn over a stack of documents and let the prosecutors and grand jurors laboriously work their way through the documents. In other cases, you may want to organize the documents meticulously and review them thoroughly and informally with the prosecutor to persuade him your client has done nothing wrong. You might even offer to submit witnesses to explain the materials more fully. In this way, you can reduce the risk of your client's indictment through a misunderstanding of the documents or the client's conduct. The more you can reason with your adversary, whether it be a prosecutor or an opposing attorney, the better off you will be.

Full Compliance

When you have received documents in response to your request for production or subpoena, you must satisfy yourself that there has been full compliance. You also want to determine whether any documents have been destroyed. If you are suspicious about the adequacy of the production of documents, or if you wish to establish proof of destruction, ascertain the identity of the persons involved in the search for the documents and take their depositions. You may be suspicious about the adequacy of production, for example, because a document that has been produced refers to a document not produced. Depositions are the only feasible method of resolving your suspicions.

On deposition, you should inquire into the kind of documents the opposing party maintains, its filing system and its document destruction practices. If the examination is conducted carefully and with a number of people, you can expect to uncover missing items or the reason they are missing. You may also find that the opposing lawyer was not responsible for the inadequate production and that he will take steps to obtain the missing documents. He will recognize that even innocent mistakes can result in unfortunate consequences for the person who failed to produce the document. The fact that a document has been withheld can be used during the trial in a way that can be more damaging than if the document is produced in the first place.

In the final analysis, discovery is no different from any other aspect of the lawyer's job. It calls for good sense, reasonableness, persistence and ingenuity. No set of precepts or guidelines can substitute for motivation, experience and judgment. With proper planning and effort, it should not be necessary to engage in saturation bombing or other wasteful and expensive maneuvering. It should be possible to strike at the heart of the opponent's case and bring about the disposition your client wants without shedding blood and without devastating your client financially.

Using and Abusing Interrogatories

by Timothy C. Klenk

Recently there has been a flood of criticism about the abuse of discovery in federal courts. A large part of that criticism is focused on the misuse of interrogatories.

It is true. Rule 33 of the Federal Rules of Civil Procedure is probably the most improperly, ineffectively, and inartfully used rule of discovery.

There are reasons for that, but they may not be what you think. Lawyers generally do not abuse Rule 33 simply to harass the opposing party. More often, lawyers misuse interrogatories because they spend too little time on them. Interrogatories are often prepared by people who are unfamiliar with the legal and factual issues in the case, who work from forms rather than from a thoroughly researched analysis of the case, and who are given little guidance by the lawyers who are familiar with the issues.

The result is interrogatories that are unnecessarily burdensome, unrelated to the real issues in the case, and that seek information that could more appropriately be obtained some other way.

One reason lawyers spend too little time on interrogatories is because they underestimate their value as a litigation tool. In the proper setting, interrogatories are one of the most efficient methods of discovery available:

- It takes a minimal amount of time to prepare a good set of interrogatories—much less than it takes to cover the same subject at a deposition.
- Unlike many questions asked at depositions, interrogatories can be carefully considered and phrased.
- You can use interrogatories to require your adversary to examine records and do a great deal of other factual research for you.

The author practices law with Pope, Ballard, Shepard & Fowle in Chicago.

- Interrogatories can be used to learn your opposing party's position about some key issues in the case—information which most deponents will not know.
- Interrogatories can be used to determine the facts and documents that form the basis for your opposing party's allegations, as well as the identity of the people who know those facts and have those documents—information that might take several depositions to unearth.
- When the parties are corporations, interrogatories may require them to gather and turn over the collective knowledge of *all* the employees about some facts.
- Best of all, the work your opposing party is required to do to get the information you ask for in your interrogatories usually costs you nothing more than the time to prepare the questions.

But do not let these advantages make you think that interrogatories do not have serious limitations:

- Interrogatories can only be served on parties in the case.
- Interrogatories educate the opposing lawyer.
- Interrogatories often result in carefully constructed, self-serving (and sometimes downright evasive) answers, rather than the spontaneous (and more enlightening) answers you might get at a deposition.
- Interrogatories do not work well when follow-up questions are required.
- Answers to interrogatories do not limit the proof at trial, as do admissions under Rule 36.

These limitations mean that interrogatories requiring long, narrative answers are counterproductive. Depositions are better suited for getting that kind of information. Avoiding interrogatories for such questions is a good way to keep from abusing discovery.

The best way to use interrogatories is to follow a carefully prepared discovery plan. This does not mean you should just think about what you do, but that you should actually outline a plan that is tailored to suit the individual case.

When I start work on a new case, I make a list of all the factual and legal issues involved. Then I try to figure out what information my opponent already has (or can reasonably find out through discovery). Not until then am I ready to develop a discovery plan that settles which kinds of discovery I intend to use and the order in which discovery should proceed.

In developing a discovery plan, I weigh the value and limitations of interrogatories as compared with other methods of discovery. Although this usually results in my use of interrogatories and document requests before depositions, I often serve only a limited set of interrogatories before taking the deposition of opposing parties, being careful to avoid asking about sensitive areas which I would prefer to cover first at a deposition.

Knowing when *not* to use interrogatories is important. In a recent case, the plaintiff alleged that he had signed a release under economic duress. Nevertheless, at his deposition he testified that he had discussed the release with his lawyer and signed it on his lawyer's advice. Even though he knew that the representations he made in the release were untrue, he said that he signed it because he knew that was the only way he could get the money he was being paid for signing it. He also identified notes that said he had been advised by his lawyer to take the money, put it in the bank, and then sue the defendant, claiming economic duress. Three days after the deposition, the plaintiff filed a notice of voluntary dismissal.

What would an interrogatory have done? It would have educated both the other party and his lawyer on how to keep the case alive.

Interrogatories can often get information that will resolve litigation during its early stages.

In one case, an aircraft manufacturer was sued by an aircraft owner on behalf of a class of all owners of his particular kind of airplane. The plaintiff alleged there was a dangerous defect in the airplanes that was expensive to repair and had caused a number of accidents.

It seemed unlikely that the plaintiff could meet the $10,000 jurisdictional amount required for each class member. So interrogatories asked him to identify each element of the damages he claimed, list the amount he claimed for each, tell how he calculated each amount, and identify the documents on which he based his calculations. His answers not only showed that his damages were speculative, but also that he did not even have a valid case for most of the damages he claimed.

In another case, a plaintiff brought a shareholder derivative action against a major corporation and its directors. The plaintiff alleged that the directors had improperly caused the corporation to enter into certain "interested director" transactions—to the benefit of the directors and the detriment of the corporation and its shareholders.

As required by Rule 23.1, the plaintiff verified his complaint. However, it seemed unlikely that the plaintiff had any knowledge of some of the essential facts he swore to in his complaint. Interrogatories showed that he had no basis for them, but simply hoped to establish them during discovery. His complaint was dismissed.

Even if interrogatories do not provide dispositive facts, they may encourage a quick settlement. Sometimes they will show you the value in your opponent's case; in others, your opponent may be forced to disclose his weaknesses. When the parties have to show their cards, the chance of settlement seems to increase.

By now you understand that the most important thing is when (and when not) to use interrogatories. Although the decision obviously depends on the individual case, here are some areas that are usually well-suited for interrogatories:

- The identity of documents.
- The identity of people who know the relevant facts.
- Facts supporting allegations. But be careful—this is an area that demands close analysis whether to use interrogatories, depositions, or informal discovery.
- Financial information such as income and sales. And do not forget to ask for the underlying documents.
- Damages.
- Information about experts. The deposition is the tool to get information from experts, but initial information *about* experts—required to be given to you by Rule 26 (b)(4)(A)(i)—can be obtained by interrogatory.
- Supplementary information. With a few exceptions, parties have no duty to supplement responses to interrogatories. So shortly before trial (or the discovery cut-off date, if there is one) serve an interrogatory asking your opponent to update the earlier answers to interrogatories.
- Information not admitted pursuant to Rule 36. This needs some explanation. Requests to admit are useful. The difficulty is, when a party refuses to make an admission under Rule 36, it helps for you to know why. So this interrogatory is one that should always be served with a request for admissions. It asks the opponent to explain the reason for denying the request, why he says it is untrue, and what he thinks the true facts are.

If you go back over this list, you will see that a little foresight saves a lot of going back and forth with questions and answers. Foresight also avoids a lot of confusion with numbers. Make it a habit to number all interrogatories sequentially, even when they are in more than one set. If your first set contains 11 questions, start your second set with number 12. That way all interrogatories can be referred to by number, without getting tangled in the different sets. Just as there are areas in which interrogatories do as well as (or better than) a deposition, there are some subjects for which interrogatories are the wrong choice:

- Information about conversations. On a number of occasions I have received interrogatories asking my client to list all conversations that took place concerning certain matters and to state what each person said during those conversations. Interrogatories like that invite a protective order from the court.
- "Why" questions that call for explanations. Long narrative answers, which will probably be prepared by counsel, are far better suited for depositions.
- Complex transactions or events. Depositions give you much greater flexibility, letting you follow up on unresponsive answers or answers that open up new areas of inquiry.
- Identity of trial witnesses. This almost never results in an informa-

tive answer, usually because at this stage the opponent has not yet decided which witnesses to call. In fact, some courts have held that this interrogatory is improper and does not require a response. In most cases, witness lists are exchanged when the parties file their pretrial memoranda or draft pretrial orders.

More times than I would like to count, I have slaved over interrogatories, served them on my opposing counsel, then a few weeks later, found myself answering the same interrogatories of their mirror image. The moral is that you should be careful what you put in the interrogatories served on the other guy. You may well be answering them yourself. That is when you will discover how difficult it is to object to your own written questions.

But turnaround is not the only limit on what you can do. Courts do not like lengthy definitions and instructions for answering interrogatories. One judge in the Northern District of Illinois has issued a notice saying that "boilerplate instructions" for answering interrogatories are not to be used in his court, and if used, "need not be considered in responding . . . "And in *Diversified Products Corp. v. Sports Center Co.*, 42 F.R.D. 3, 4 (D. Md. 1967), the court held that burdensome definitions in interrogatories (including instructions requiring the responding party to provide the substance of the statements contained in all documents identified) justified a blanket objection to all of the interrogatories and the imposition of sanctions.

Even so, short, carefully written instructions can help both sides. They can help avoid ambiguity and repetition as well as make the interrogatories shorter and easier to read.

Many federal district courts have adopted local rules governing interrogatories, and it is surprising how frequently they are ignored— perhaps one reason for the level of judicial hostility to discovery abuse.

Probably the most common local rule limits the number of interrogatories. In the Northern District of Illinois, the local rule allows 20. I recently received a set of 26 interrogatories, the first of which asked for the defendant's full name, the second whether the defendant used any aliases, the third asked for his address, and so on. Most of the substantive questions were after the limit of 20 was passed.

There is an argument that rules limiting the number of interrogatories may not be valid. The notes of the Advisory Committee concerning the 1946, 1970, and 1980 amendments to Rules 26 and 33 show that the committee specifically considered, but did not adopt, limitations on the number of interrogatories. It believed it was better for the courts to deal with the problem on a case-by-case basis. In the comments to the 1983 amendments to Rule 26(b), the committee said that courts may restrict the number of interrogatories "in an appropriate case," but must be careful not to deprive a party of discovery that is reasonably necessary to give it a fair opportunity to develop and prepare its case.

71

Nevertheless, local rules limiting the number of interrogatories are widespread and have been upheld in several cases. *See, e.g., Lykins v. Attorney General,* 86 F.R.D. 318, 319 (E.D. Va. 1980). In any event, it should seldom be necessary to challenge the rules. They are usually easy to comply with, and in the rare case where you need more, it can probably be worked out by agreement between counsel or an order permitting additional interrogatories.

Before the 1983 amendments to the Federal Rules of Civil Procedure, lawyers did not need to sign answers to interrogatories. Furthermore, their signatures on the interrogatories themselves and objections to them had limited significance.

No longer.

Under amended Rule 26(g), lawyers must sign interrogatories, objections, and answers. Signature certifies that the lawyer believes after a reasonable inquiry that the interrogatories or objections are consistent with the federal rules and are warranted by existing law or a good-faith argument for the extension, modification, or reversal of that law. This puts an obligation for factual and legal research on the lawyer. In addition, the rule requires the lawyer to certify that in light of the case, the interrogatories are not unduly burdensome, or expensive.

In some states, the failure to respond to interrogatories on time is of no great consequence. Where that is the law, interrogatories seldom seem to be answered or objected to within the time provided. Following that state-law practice in federal court is a mistake. Under Rule 33, a party waives the right to object to interrogatories if he fails to do so within 30 days of the date on which they were served.

But there are even more thorny problems for the unwary. One of them is in Rule 33(c). In 1970, Rule 33 was amended to give a party upon whom interrogatories are served the option of producing business records that contain the answers. This option exists when the burden of deriving the answers from the documents is substantially the same for both parties.

Answering interrogatories is often tedious and time consuming, especially when it requires reviewing and analyzing numerous documents. This is where Rule 33(c) can help. It is most useful when the interrogatories are accompanied by document requests that require producing the documents anyway.

But there are significant risks under Rule 33(c). First, you (or your client) may produce privileged documents or documents that are not called for by the interrogatories or document requests. The second risk is that by producing the documents you may be admitting the truth of their contents.

In re Japanese-Electronic Products Antitrust Litigation, 723 F.2d 238 (3d Cir. 1983), *rev'd on other grounds,* 475 U.S. 574 (1986), the court held that documents produced instead of answers were adoptive admissions by the party producing the documents, and were thereby exempted from the hearsay rule by Rule 801 (d)(2)(B), Fed. R. Evid.

Under this adoptive admission reasoning, it seems that the information vouched for by a party would be limited to information in the documents that responds to the interrogatories.

But notice that Rule 33(c) provides only for the production of "business records" instead of answers to interrogatories. So it might be argued that producing the documents is an admission that they are business records—admissible as an exception to the hearsay rule under Rule 803 (6), Fed. R. Evid. The district court in *In re Japanese-Electronic Products Antitrust Litigation*, 505 F. Supp 1190, 1236 (E.D. Pa. 1980), rejected this argument, but the court of appeals did not rule on it. The result is that the full scope of this rule is uncertain, and any party producing documents in place of answers needs to be particularly careful.

Rule 34: Controlling the Paper Avalanche

by Michael A. Pope

Lawyers who practice in the federal courts devote more time to Rule 34 than to any other Federal Rule of Civil Procedure. We spend time preparing extensive, carefully worded document requests, examining mounds of documents produced, and resolving disputes about the requests or the adequacy of the productions. Are the results worth the time and costs? The following highly publicized discovery disputes illustrate the problems:

- In April 1972, the State of Ohio sued the Arthur Anderson accounting firm to recover $8 million that was invested allegedly in reliance on financial statements audited by Andersen for a corporation that collapsed in 1971. To prove its case, Ohio sought almost 1,000 pages of documents relating to the bankrupt corporation's undisclosed dependence upon a single Swiss client. Andersen's refusal to produce the materials led to years of litigation on this one issue.

The fight involved hearings before a U.S. district judge in Denver, two appeals to the Court of Appeals for the Tenth Circuit, and an unsuccessful appeal to the Supreme Court. *Business Week* reported that by December 1976, Ohio had spent nearly $60,000 in the fight over document production, while the accounting firm spent more than $70,000. The District Court finally ordered Andersen to pay Ohio's legal costs and precluded the firm from contesting key assertions about what information it possessed.

- Berkey Photo won a $113 million antitrust jury verdict against Eastman Kodak in part due to the revelation that an attorney for Kodak lied when he stated he accidentally destroyed certain documents re-

The author, a partner in the Chicago law firm of Phelan, Pope & John, Ltd., expresses his thanks to Mitchell Frazen.

quested by Berkey. The documents were in fact located in the attorney's office. Berkey's judgment was reversed on appeal, but Kodak turned to another law firm for its appeal, and the attorney involved pleaded guilty to contempt and was sentenced to one month in prison.

- In an action between the publishers of *Penthouse* and *Playboy* magazines in which each alleged unfair competitive practices by the other, *Playboy* requested the production of *Penthouse's* advertising revenue projections. For almost four years *Penthouse* consistently denied the existence of these projections in responses to production requests, at pretrial conferences, and in open court. More than a month into the trial, however, *Penthouse* attorneys admitted they had found the documents, but would not produce them because of their commercial sensitivity. In March 1980, in response to *Playboy's* motion for discovery sanctions, the District Court dismissed *Penthouse's* complaint.
- The quintessential Rule 34 case, *United States v. IBM*, is now in its eleventh year. Lawyers produced over 64 million pages of documents during the first five years of discovery. One of many discovery disputes led to an appeal to the Court of Appeals for the Second Circuit, a simultaneous petition for a writ of mandamus, an attempted appeal to and a petition for a writ of certiorari from the Supreme Court, and a petition for an extraordinary writ. Almost a year and a half after the order was entered, IBM was found in contempt and assessed a fine of $150,000 per day until it produced the documents required by the pretrial order.

Discovery Abuse

These examples may make it appear that document production problems occur only in the so-called "big case." But discovery abuse occurs in "small" cases too. A "simple" case may produce a document request that requires days, or weeks, to review a client's files. A request for documents may evoke a response that requires the lawyer requesting the documents to sift through a paper haystack for a few helpful "needles."

Obstructionists may fail to comply with production requests, or produce documents only after interminable delays, objections, and piecemeal compliance.

Ironically, the two characteristics that make Rule 34 so useful make discovery abuse possible. Critics charge that the broad scope of the materials that must be produced upon request, while designed to eliminate surprises, has replaced "trial by ambush" with "trial by avalanche." Critics also attack the elimination of judicial management over discovery requests and compliance, intended to speed the discovery process and to make it more informal, charging that it permits rampant abuses, burdens and excessive delay. The 1980 Amendments to Federal Rules 26 through 37 continue the policy of permitting a broad scope of discoverable materials, but they signal a sharp reversal of past practice by requiring an increased judicial role in the discovery process.

Good Cause

The history of Rule 34 shows a continuing expansion of the scope of document discovery. The rule originally authorized a federal court, "upon motion of any party showing good cause therefor," to permit the inspection and copying of documents in the possession, custody or control of an opposing party, that were "material to any matter involved in the action." A 1946 amendment conformed Rule 34's scope to that of Rule 26(b), allowing discovery of "any matter, not privileged, which is relevant to the subject matter involved in the pending action."

The "good cause" requirement of Rule 34 continued to create confusion and uncertainty, however. While some courts equated it with "relevance," others required a showing of "special circumstances," while still others balanced the necessity and the burden of each request on an *ad hoc* basis. The drafters finally eliminated the "good cause" standard in 1970.

The courts have also read expansively the limitation of discovery to documents within the "possession, custody or control" of an adverse party. A party must produce documents even though it has no legal right to them, if the party or someone under its control has the means to obtain them. An example of this broad notion of "control" is its application to documents in the possession of former employees who receive retirement benefits from the party corporation. *In re Folding Carton Antitrust Litigation,* 76 F.R.D. 420 (N.D. Ill. 1977).

The 1970 Amendments to Rule 34 allow discovery of "data compilations from which information can be obtained, translated, if necessary, by the respondent through detection devices into reasonably usable form." In *Bell v. Automobile Club of Michigan,* 80 F.R.D. 228 (E.D. Mich. 1978), *appeal dismissed without opinion,* 601 F.2d 587 (6th Cir.), *cert. denied,* 442 U.S. 918 (1979), a Title VII action requiring the production and analysis of thousands of employment records, the trial court interpreted this provision to require the creation of a computer data bank through which the information requested by the plaintiffs could be produced, analyzed and presented. Another court required the production of input data, such as computer cards and tapes. *Adams v. Dan River Mills, Inc.,* 54 F.R.D. 220 (W.D. Va. 1972).

Some limitations remain. In a complex antitrust suit, one district court held that input information and alternative programs for the plaintiff's computerized market simulation was within Rule 26(b)(4)(B)'s protection of facts known "by an expert who has been retained in . . . preparation for trial" and required a showing of "exceptional circumstances" before allowing discovery. *Pearl Brewing Co. v. Joseph Schlitz Brewing Co.,*

415 F. Supp. 1122 (S.D. Tex. 1976). The Supreme Court concluded that Rule 34 could not be used to obtain from a defendant's computer the names of class members for a class action notice, since the names were not sought for any bearing they had on the issues in the case. *Oppenheimer Fund, Inc. v. Sanders*, 437 U.S. 340 (1978).

The 1970 amendments also require that data be produced in a "reasonably usable form." *Kozlowski v. Sears, Roebuck & Co.*, 73 F.R.D. 73 (D. Mass. 1976), illustrates the importance of this change. Kozlowski sought damages for injuries received when pajamas manufactured by the defendant caught fire. Sears refused to produce documents revealing prior complaints about the flammability of the pajamas. It argued that its long-standing practice of indexing claims and complaints alphabetically by the name of the claimant rather than according to the product involved made it unreasonably burdensome to locate the requested documents.

The court held that Sears could not excuse compliance "by utilizing a system of record-keeping which conceals rather than discloses relevant records." Kozlowski also refused the defendant's offer to transport the plaintiff's attorney to Chicago and allow him to peruse the massive files himself, labeling this "nothing more than a gigantic 'do-it-yourself' kit."

A party in another case produced approximately 50,000 requested documents—in Japanese. The court required that the company translate the documents, relying on the specific wording of Rule 34 requiring translation of data compilations, and noting *Kozlowski's* concern that parties might deliberately adopt such business methods in order to hinder discovery. *Mitsui & Co. (U.S.A.), Inc. v. Puerto Rico Water Resources Authority*, 26 F.R. Serv. 2d 377 (D.P.R. 1978).

There are, however, limits to the "reasonably usable form" requirement. The plaintiffs in an employment discrimination suit could not obtain compilations of raw data previously produced despite their argument that the compilations were needed to make the produced information useful. Noting that the compilations had not already been prepared, the court refused to shift the costs of trial preparation to the defendant absent a showing of circumstances" [approaching a] level of willful disregard for the interests of the public." *Webb v. Westinghouse Electric Corp.*, 81 F.R.D. 431, 436 (E.D. Pa. 1978).

The 1980 amendment to Rule 34 eliminated the "reasonably usable form" requirement. Rule 34 now requires that a party produce documents "as they are kept in the usual course of business or shall organize and label them to correspond with the categories in the request." The Advisory Committee Note states that the purpose of the amendment is to prevent mixing critical documents with unimportant ones in order to obscure their significance.

The rule as amended reaches such abuse where it is deliberate, but does not solve the more common problem of a party who produces huge amounts of paper acquired haphazardly in the usual course of business.

The manufacturer who files everything concerning a particular product into one drawer, for example, will still be allowed simply to produce the drawer's contents. Thus, if Sears delivered its entire alphabetical filing system in the *Kozlowski* case, it apparently would not have violated the amended rule, which now offers respondents a choice between a categorized response and a "course of business" organization.

The 1980 amendment to Rule 26 further attempts to reduce discovery abuse through the creation of the discovery conference under judicial control. Amendments to Rule 37 attempt the same goal through tougher sanctions to be employed against parties who abuse the federal rules.

The 1970 Advisory Committee believed that judicial time and effort could be spared if discovery matters were left to the parties. At that time, the Field Survey of Federal Pretrial Discovery showed that about half of all discovery motions were uncontested, and in almost all cases the party seeking production ultimately prevailed.

In the decade since that study was made, however, complex civil litigation in federal courts has increased enormously. Between 1970 and 1975, the number of securities cases nearly doubled and antitrust class action filings increased 60 percent. Employment discrimination, commercial products liability and construction litigation also increased in size and number. The greater use of discovery in these cases led to more frequent disputes that increasingly have to be resolved by the courts.

Faced with the criticism of discovery abuse, the Advisory Committee used the 1980 amendments to reintroduce a measure of judicial supervision of discovery while retaining the broad substantive scope of discovery. Amended Rule 26(f) allows the court to call a conference on discovery on its own motion, and requires such a conference when a party moves for it after "a reasonable effort to reach agreement with opposing attorneys" on discovery.

In order to obtain the conference, the party's motion must include a statement of issues and a proposed discovery schedule, along with proposed limits and orders. After the conference, the court must enter an order identifying the issues for discovery, setting limits and deciding other disputes.

Under Rule 37(g) as amended, parties who fail to participate in framing a discovery plan may be required to pay their opponents' costs and attorneys' fees. Disobedience of a conference order will also subject a party to the full range of Rule 37 sanctions. The discovery conference allows a party to obtain judicial control over discovery at the price of narrowing the case to manageable limits. It also allows the court to establish guidelines that may prevent later time-consuming disputes.

Increased Sanctions

This apparent shift from a wholly sanctions-oriented approach to a preventive approach to discovery abuse comes just as courts have begun to impose sanctions with increased frequency and severity. In *National Hockey League v. Metropolitan Hockey Club, Inc.*, 427 U.S. 639 (1976), the Supreme Court approved the dismissal of an antitrust action when the plaintiff failed to answer adequately the defendant's interrogatories after seventeen months and numerous extensions. The *per curiam* opinion concluded that the most severe Rule 37 sanction of dismissal was appropriate "not merely to penalize those whose conduct may be deemed to warrant such a sanction, but to deter those who might be tempted to such conduct in the absence of such a deterrent."

Roadway Express, Inc. v. Piper, 447 U.S. 752 (1980), also illustrates the Court's increased militancy concerning discovery abuse. A lower court ordered the plaintiffs' employment discrimination suit dismissed and over $17,000 in costs and attorneys' fees assessed against plaintiffs' counsel for their "deliberate inaction" in failing to answer interrogatories or provide one of the plaintiffs for a deposition.

The Supreme Court did not accept the district court's basis for granting attorneys' fees under 42 U.S.C. § 1927 (since amended to explicitly allow award of attorney fees), but it indicated the award would be proper under Rule 37. The Court noted the inherent power of federal courts to deal with abusive practices, and specifically expressed concern that "many actions are extended unnecessarily by lawyers who exploit or abuse judicial procedures, especially the liberal rules for pretrial discovery."

Lower courts have also imposed costs directly upon attorneys for their failure to comply with discovery, *e.g.*, *Stanziale v. First National City Bank*, 74 F.R.D. 557 (S.D.N.Y. 1977), or assessed costs against attorney and client jointly. *Chesa International, Ltd. v. Fashion Associates, Inc.*, 425 F. Supp. 234 (S.D.N.Y.), *aff'd*, 573 F.2d 1288 (2d Cir. 1977).

In *Associated Radio Service Company v. Page Airways, Inc.*, 73 F.R.D. 633, 634 (N.D. Tex. 1977), an action where District Judge Robert W. Porter noted that "[t]he Plaintiffs' allegations of antitrust have spilled over to the discovery process where nobody trusts anybody," the court ordered opposing attorneys to pay each other's costs. The court precluded indemnification or compensation by their clients. A 34-month study of reported federal cases recently concluded that "federal trial judges in general may be less reluctant than previously to exercise a literal application of Rule 37 sanctions." Werner, *Survey of Discovery Sanctions*, 1979 Ariz. St. L.J. 299, 316.

Other courts are beginning to implement Rule 37's broad range of sanctions. Orders include the conditional assessment of costs if production is not made and the imposition of daily fines until documents are produced. Failure to produce documents has resulted in the exclusion of the withheld documents or all evidence on issues to which they are relevant. *Admiral Theatre Corp. v. Douglas Theatre Co.*, 585 F.2d 877 (8th Cir. 1978); *Von Brimer v. Whirlpool Corp.*, 536 F.2d 838 (9th Cir. 1978).

It is too early to judge the effects of the discovery conference device on discovery abuse. Lawyers should note, however, that Justices Powell, Stewart and Rehnquist dissented to the promulgation of the 1980 amendments, arguing that the "tinkering changes" would only "create complacency and encourage inertia." They argued that the rules "invite discovery of such scope and duration that district judges often cannot keep the practice within bounds," resulting in delays, excessive expense, and the potential for abuse.

Greater judicial involvement combined with a willingness to impose sanctions for abuse may cure the document problems that burden discovery. If they do not, there will be increased pressures to restrict the substantive scope of discovery.

Rule 36:
In Praise of Requests
to Admit

by Edna Selan Epstein

Litigators file interrogatories in most substantial lawsuits. Few routinely file requests to admit. Yet answers to interrogatories are rarely as useful as the responses that must be made to well-framed requests to admit.

Requests are not useful tools for discovering the unknown. They are best used to establish the undisputed, relieving the parties of the need to prove such matters and shortening the trial. Formulating the request helps structure the case because the attorney must think through the basic elements and how he will prove them. The request to admit can also be used as the basis for a summary judgment motion. Here are ten reasons why a litigator should consider using requests to admit.

First, the request to admit can cover almost any issue, simple or complex. Anything discoverable pursuant to Rule 26(b) of the Federal Rules of Civil Procedure can be the subject of a request to admit under Rule 36. The requests can go beyond the "facts" of a case. They can relate "to statements or opinions of fact or of the application of the law to fact, including the genuineness of any documents described in the request."

Requests to admit can reach those legal theories that are at the heart of a dispute. Although you cannot ask an admission to an abstract proposition of law, if your request applies the law to the facts of your case it is permissible. Only privileged matters that are immune from discovery under Rule 26(b) are improper subjects for requests to admit.

Second, the recipient of the request to admit cannot avoid answering because he personally does not know the answer if the needed information is reasonably within his possession. Under Rule 36, the answering party can only avoid the admission if he "has made reasonable inquiry

---

The author is a partner in the Chicago law firm of Sidley & Austin.

and . . . the information known *or readily obtainable by him* is insufficient to enable him to admit or deny'' (emphasis added).

For example, the answering party need not prepare an elaborate computer program to answer a request. But if the facts sought to be established are available in an existing form, such as a computer tape, the information is "readily available." And the answering party cannot object that the request asks about a matter within the knowledge of the proponent of the request or a matter of public knowledge. The request is not a device to discover information, but to eliminate issues otherwise to be proven at trial.

Successive Sets

Third, while many jurisdictions stringently limit the number of interrogatories a party can pose without leave of court, no similar limitation exists for requests to admit. Indeed, in one patent case the court approved 704 separate requests to admit that took 114 legal-sized pages. *Photon, Inc. v. Harris Intertype, Inc.,* 28 F.R.D. 327 (D. Mass. 1961).

The rules recognize the value of requests to admit by not limiting their number. A party can serve multiple requests to admit as he learns more about his case and the facts. Courts do not treat successive sets of requests to admit as burdensome or oppressive in complex litigation. *United States v. Watchmakers of Switzerland Information Center, Inc.,* 2 Fed. R. Serv. 2d 605 (S.D.N.Y. 1959).

Fourth, a court and the parties can readily determine proper requests to admit. Rule 36 states that'' [e]ach matter of which an admission is requested shall be separately set forth.'' Requests to admit should be simple and direct statements of single propositions. Most judges can determine at a glance whether requests to admit are well-formulated and focus on the facts in dispute. While well-drafted requests to admit are likely to withstand objections, poorly drafted requests that are verbose, lengthy and compound will be struck. *Baldwin v. Hartford Accident & Idemnity Co.,* 15 F.R.D. 84 (D. Neb. 1953).

Fifth, requests to admit can be served upon the plaintiff *at any time* after the commencement of the lawsuit and upon any other party with or after the service of the summons and complaint upon that party. Nothing expedites discovery and brings the litigation to a head faster than filing requests to admit at the beginning of a lawsuit. You may not have to depose a witness at all if the facts that he knows are not in dispute. The recipient of the request must answer or object within 30 days, or within 45 days if the requests are served with the complaint. The court may lengthen or shorten the time allowed for answer.

Sixth, delaying answers to requests to admit without court approval is useless. The matter requested is deemed admitted if the recipient remains silent or does not deny the requested matter within the time allotted by the rule. If more time is needed, the recipient must ask the court for it.

Seventh, sweeping denials or evasive answers are ineffective if the proponent of the request presses the matter. Rule 36 provides:

> A denial shall fairly meet the substance of the requested admission, and when good faith requires that a party qualify his answer or deny only a part of the matter of which an admission is requested, he shall specify so much of it as is true and qualify or deny the remainder.

You can make evasion more difficult if you append an interrogatory to the request: "If you deny the request, set forth each fact upon which you base your denial." Answering the interrogatory may be more burdensome than admitting the request. This technique eliminates frivolous denials.

Eighth, although requests to admit are not self-enforcing, Rule 36 provides for court enforcement if the recipient of the request seeks to avoid answering by forbidden means. The proponent of the request may ask the court to rule on the sufficiency of an objection. If the reasons for not admitting the request are frivolous or inadequate, the court has several options: (1) the answers can be struck or taken to be admissions; (2) new answers can be ordered; (3) the answers can be taken as denials, permitting Rule 37(c) sanctions if the proponent is put to the burden of proving the matter requested to be admitted. *Bertha Building Corp. v. National Theatres Corp.,* 15 F.R.D. 339 (E.D.N.Y. 1954).

Evasive Answers

Indeed, courts have treated evasive answers or equivocal responses as admissions that will support motions for summary judgment and dismissals of the suit. *United States v. Jefferson Trust & Savings Bank,* 31 F.R.D. 137 (S.D. Ill. 1962). Courts have also said that no good reason exists to tolerate "straddling statements," such as a refusal to admit or deny, in response to requests to admit. *Princess Pat, Ltd. v. National Carloading Corp.,* 223 F.2d 916 (7th Cir. 1955).

Ninth, an admission conclusively establishes for the entire action the factual or legal proposition it sets out. It can be used in the pending litigation either in a motion for partial or full summary judgment or at a trial of the matter.

As an example, in one case an insurance company paid a bank on a claim that a bank officer made an illegal investment, although the coverage under the insurance policy was not clear. The insurance company felt confident that it could recoup its payment from the bank's accountants and brought a third-party claim against the accountants. After the insurance company spun elaborate but tenuous theories of liability and deposed 29 witnesses, the accountants served almost 200 requests to admit covering every factual aspect of the case. The accountants used the answers to these requests as the basis for a successful motion for summary judgment that was sustained upon appeal. *Rock River Savings and Loan Association v. American States Insurance Company*, 594 F.2d 633 (7th Cir. 1979).

Tenth, substantial sanctions are available against the party denying the request if the genuineness of the document or the truth of the matter is proved at trial. In that situation, Rule 37(c) of the Federal Rules of Civil Procedure provides that the court *shall* order the party making the denial to bear the reasonable expenses, including reasonable attorneys' fees, incurred in proving the denied matter. Take the party who denies a simple fact that is costly to prove, such as that delivery was made in many states. The costs of bringing witnesses from those states would be recoupable under Rule 37(c). No similar sanction exists for a recalcitrant failure to stipulate on the same issue.

Improper denials lay the groundwork for shifting the costs of proof. To avoid awarding expenses, the court must expressly find that one of four excuses applied: (1) the court must previously have found the request to admit to have been objectionable under Rule 36(a); (2) the admission must have been of no substantial importance; (3) the party failing to admit must have had reasonable grounds to believe that he might prevail on the matter; or (4) some other good reason must have existed for the failure to admit, such as a good faith lack of knowledge or that the requested matter was genuinely contested.

Requests to admit are one of the most effective tools for cutting litigation costs and narrowing the matters to be tried. But, they are used infrequently.

At a time when lawyers are criticized for the costly discovery they generate, the request to admit should be used more often.

Strategy Under the New Rules

by Thomas W. Evans

Recent amendments to the Federal Rules of Civil Procedure offer the hope of significant changes in trial strategy through admissions practice and the discovery conference. Taken individually, the changes are important. In combination, they represent an entirely new—and vastly improved—way to try a lawsuit.

In 1980 and 1983, the Advisory Committee directed its attention primarily to curbing abuses in discovery. Mr. Justice Powell's famous dissent to the 1980 amendments brought deserved focus to the problem—mere tinkering with the rules was not enough.

Although the various rules providing for heightened lawyer responsibility have probably drawn the most attention in the 1983 amendments, the revision in Rule 16, moving the pretrial conference to the beginning of the case (no later than 120 days after filing the complaint) from its customary place at the eve of trial, may represent the most important change from the standpoint of trial strategy.

The trend toward early judicial intervention had already been seen in the 1980 amendments (and, incidentally, in many state and local rules before that). Provision was made for a ''discovery conference'' under Rule 26(f). Indeed, many criticized the 1983 change as redundant, complaining that the discovery conference had not really been given a chance. But the emphasis was clear—bring the court in at the beginning. The era of the activist judge, the case manager, had arrived.

The first change, then, was one of timing. The pretrial conference had always been an occasion to address major strategic considerations: assessment of claims, detailed review of evidence, identification of witnesses, a court-directed attempt at settlement. And then to trial.

The author is a partner in the firm of Mudge Rose Guthrie Alexander & Ferdon, New York City.

Often the case had been allowed to drift for years to this point—from vague notice pleading, to waves of interrogatories, through production of countless volumes of documents, to taking of depositions of any witness who would come to mind. Discovery became increasingly a process of concealment and attrition. In those instances that discovery was conducted in good faith, lawyers became accustomed to deferring important strategic decisions to the eve of trial. And judges were generally not expected to get involved, to even become familiar with the case, until the last possible moment.

It would be a tragedy if the early pretrial conference was used simply as a scheduling event. But one faction in the bar wishes to make them so. Judith Resnick and others have raised the alarm—activist judges should not be allowed a roving commission to run roughshod over the adversary process. Committees at the district court level have proposed local rules intended to avoid "satellite litigation" in discovery conferences—often with the effect of deferring any consideration of the merits until a time with which the lawyers and judges are comfortable, the eve of trial.

Ironically, those who see the judge only as a scheduler frequently suggest a totally mechanistic approach. Allow one set of interrogatories, a certain number of depositions, just so many days for document production, regardless of the nature of the case. This thinking guarantees a continuation of the same kind of mindless discovery that has led to the cries for reform. It also ensures satellite litigation as lawyers apply for the inevitable continuances and expanded discovery. Most important, the mechanistic school completely ignores other changes in the rules that can provide the basis for an entirely new and promising approach to discovery and case management.

Modern discovery was introduced with the adoption of the Federal Rules of Civil Procedure in 1938. The heralded intention of the new procedure was the avoidance of surprise. The sporting theory of justice so decried by Dean Pound and others was laid to rest. But the simultaneous introduction of notice pleading virtually ensured that discovery would wander. The quest for information often became counterproductive, a process of attrition in which the truth was lost in mere bulk.

Reform is cyclical. Even the most striking innovations can become corrupted with time. Although we shall never return to common-law pleading—with its objective of distilling a controversy into a single concise issue of fact and law—the promise provided in the recent federal rules amendments does go directly to issue reduction and an attempt to eliminate the pursuit of unnecessary proof early in the case.

Rule 26(f) requires the party requesting a discovery conference to include in his application "a statement of the issues as they then appear." The principal objectives of the pretrial conference established under the amended Rule 16 are "the formulation and simplification of the issues,

86

including the elimination of frivolous claims and defenses . . . [and] the possibility of obtaining admissions of fact and of documents. . . ."

The net effect of modern discovery has been concealment. Although each lawyer is quick to disclaim his own complicity in this unsavory practice, there is widespread agreement among the bar that discovery has too often been abused.

This is not to say that documents are destroyed or witnesses encouraged to lie. But the production of documents in bulk, so that the incriminating paper may be extremely difficult to find, or the narrow answer in pleading, interrogatory, or deposition that effects a misleading appearance, do serve to defer a discovery of the facts. As the practice proliferates, discovery takes on a protracted life of its own. Often discovery makes a genuine determination on the issues so difficult that a party will abandon a meritorious claim rather than bear the expense of further pretrial proceedings.

If discovery is directed more toward issue formulation and reduction and less toward unbridled accumulation, the entire process can be made more productive. The assumption that "all facts must be in" before the court can deal with issues is not well-grounded. The members of the Advisory Committee must have believed that all facts need not be in or they never would have recommended that the time of the pretrial conference be moved up in the litigation continuum, while retaining the goal of formulating issues, obtaining admissions, and eliminating frivolous claims and defenses. The method by which the court can pursue this productive role at the *outset* of the cases is logical analysis.

The idea of using logic to discover true issues and to eliminate frivolous positions is not new. Both a law professor, Jerome Michael, and a logician, Mortimer Adler, published a classic series of articles on the subject in their article *The Trial of an Issue of Fact* (in the November and December 1934 issues of the Columbia Law Review), 34 COLUM. L. REV, 1224, 1462. But soon after their articles appeared, the Federal Rules of Civil Procedure were adopted, and with the arrival of notice pleading, the syllogism lost a crucial premise.

For lawsuits are, inescapably, syllogistic in form. "The major premise is the rule of law involved which is never explicitly stated," Professor Green points out in BASIC CIVIL PROCEDURE 91 (1972). "The minor premise consists of the facts which the pleader claims bring his case within the operation of the rule of law embodied in the major premise."

With the vagueness of notice pleading, and discovery limited only by an amorphous relevance to the subject matter in a pending action, the judge's job in the pretrial or discovery conference is difficult, but not impossible. The solution lies in use by the court of a powerful but generally ignored procedure which forces the lawyers to play a major role in the process.

In 1970, FED. R. CIV. P. 36 was amended to broaden the scope of requests for admission. Thereafter, matters of opinion and mixed questions of fact and law were included as appropriate subjects. Although the use of such requests has since increased fivefold, they are still among the least used of discovery devices. This is true even though substantial sanctions (including attorneys' fees) are provided. Rule 37(c).

Considered together, the recent amendments provide an opportunity for more exact assessment of a case at the outset. It is a rare methodology that permits logical analysis of legal arguments and their factual basis. As the case progresses, the role of admissions practice shifts from analytical tool to implement of proof.

Admissions practice is defined as "the use of successive requests for admission together with related enforcement provisions and pretrial and discovery conferences, to narrow issues and attendant requirements of proof in the course of litigation." See Evans, "Admissions Practice": Discovery Solution, NAT. L.J., May 23, 1983, at 15. This process can begin shortly after commencement of a suit, preferably after joinder of issue.

Court and counsel must rise to eliminate unnecessary claims, with attendant reduction of areas for discovery, at the beginning of an action. Although the customary placement of a pretrial conference has been the eve of trial, see 6 CYC. FED. PROC. § 19.27 (1981); 3 MOORE'S FEDERAL PRACTICE 16.07; (2d Ed.); WRIGHT, LAW OF FEDERAL COURTS § 91 (3d Ed. 1976), some courts have used early status or discovery conferences genuinely to consider issues and to shape discovery. See, e.g., the practice described by Chief Judge Robert F. Peckham of the Northern District of California in The Federal Judge as a Case Manager: The New Role in Guiding a Case from Filing to Disposition, 69 CAL. L. REV. 770 (1981). In complex litigation, periodic conferences have been the rule, but a predisposition for liberal discovery has encouraged deferral of a genuine narrowing of the issues until the later conferences. See MANUAL FOR COMPLEX LITIGATION § 1.20 (4th Ed. 1977). This same policy of substantive delay is included in the federal provision for contention interrogatories (in FED. R. CIV. P. 33 (b), where response can be postponed until a pretrial conference "or other later time."

If the early pretrial conference is to be more than just a scheduling event, there must be a basic change in trial strategy. Too often in recent years, the principal thrusts in discovery have been either defensive, with concealment and attrition as its hallmarks, or passively offensive, where the plaintiff has pursued a leisurely fishing expedition, not so much to prove his claims, but to wander through documents and witnesses until he discovers new claims, or accumulates enough time to support a large fee on settlement.

By exchanging requests for admission before the first pretrial conference, lawyers can eliminate areas of inquiry as they obtain admissions. In addition, by analyzing their adversaries' pleadings—their major premises, if you will—attorneys can draft their requests to ascertain whether a factual basis exists—the minor premise—for the claim or denial. As Michael T. Callahan and Barry B. Bramble point out in DISCOVERY IN CONSTRUCTION LITIGATION (1983) at § 5-3: "If counsel is uncertain as to whether a matter will be controverted, a request [for admission] may be stated in terms of application of law to fact. In other words, flag the issues to determine opposition counsel's position."

Requests for admission will enable the court to focus on the issues, as the parties see them, before conference. Discovery can then be tailored to an exploration of these issues. Callahan and Bramble provide a useful example from the construction field. If the defendant is not going to use defective workmanship as a basis for nonpayment for work done under a change order, the plaintiff can ascertain this through properly drawn requests to admit, and on that area will not have to be examined. On a major project, this can eliminate a vast area of discovery.

If a party forces the unnecessary pursuit of information by posing a false issue—or an issue where it is highly unlikely that factual support can be mustered—the court can later order the offending party to pay the costs, including attorneys' fees, involved in the fruitless search. Under admissions practice, wars of attrition will henceforth involve a considerable financial risk.

The conference format is essential to admissions practice. One of the reasons that requests for admission have been little used is the ease with which counsel could excuse response under the rules by filing a writing to the effect that he was unable to reply after making a reasonable inquiry in good faith. In a conference, such excuses can be subjected to closer, more persistent scrutiny by the court and in face-to-face colloquy with opposing counsel.

The scheduling order can be drafted to ensure immediate "reasonable inquiry" into the matter. Information which is not initially "readily obtainable" may be obtained after proper discovery. If the cost is burdensome, the court can require the requesting party to pay for it. After such inquiry, meaningful response will often be forthcoming and issues can be laid to rest.

Admissions practice requires periodic conferences, however, and continuing informed intercession by the court. The duty to supplement an earlier response varies from circuit to circuit, 10 FED. PRAC. L. ED. § 26:322, while the duty to amend an earlier incorrect prior response seems clear. 4 MOORE'S FED. PRAC. § 26.81 (2d Ed. 1983); *but see* Notes of Advisory Committee on the 1970 amendments to Rule 26 regarding the duty to review the accuracy of prior responses. Presumably, the periodic exchange of requests for admission will serve to inform the court, while retaining the traditional adversary process.

Throughout all of this, counsel will have a justification for failures to admit. FED. R. CIV. P. 37(c) excuses sanctions where a party has reasonable grounds to believe that he would prevail. Under a truly effective system of discovery, these are exactly the issues that should be preserved for trial.

The objectives of the new strategy—the reduction of issues and the admission of necessary facts—are enhanced by the recent redefinition of a lawyer's ethical and professional responsibility. The Federal Rules of Civil Procedure have been amended to require certification by counsel after a reasonable inquiry conducted in good faith. Rules 7, 11, 26(g). The new Model Rules of Professional Conduct prohibit concealment in Rule 3.4 (a). These changes should go far toward removing the traditional reluctance of courts to impose sanctions for discovery abuse. Although the duty of reasonable inquiry in good faith has long been a part of admissions practice, the new rules provide a useful reaffirmation.

Admissions practice establishes a favorable climate for settlement early in the case or for alternate procedures, such as mini-trials. The parties quickly gain a more realistic understanding of their positions. Fewer issues remain for trial (or mini-trial). And a venerable weapon for forcing unmeritorious settlements, the expense that protracted discovery adds to the prosecution or defense of a claim, is reduced or eliminated.

At least one commentator has observed that "forcing formal admissions of facts" can be "especially valuable . . . [in] laying the foundation for a motion for summary judgment." Green, Basic Civil Procedure 158 (2d Ed. 1979).

Recent concerns about the suitability of juries as triers of fact in a complex modern society are somewhat allayed by admissions practice. With fewer issues and a narrower ambit of proof, complex questions are more susceptible to jury determination. Moreover, if trials are less protracted, a larger pool of able people is available to sit on juries. In rare instances, special verdicts should be undertaken to ascribe responsibility for unnecessary proof, although this matter will probably be dealt with more often in a posttrial motion for costs.

Consideration of trial tactics, as distinguished from strategy, will be promoted as lawyers are able to deal with real issues and genuine requirements of proof. Lawyers can concentrate on such matters as the order of proof, the preparation of special exhibits, and the selection of the most persuasive expert.

Of course, if admissions practice has been fully pursued, the element of surprise will be reduced. That was what the original draftsmen of the Federal Rules of Civil Procedure intended long ago.

Rule 26(b)(3): Protecting Work Product

by Thomas McGanney and Selvyn Seidel

Protecting work product can generate vexing problems. Often an attorney must choose between the best way to preserve information and the best way to preserve confidentiality of his work product.

Consider these examples:

- An attorney for a client involved in litigation interviews a third-party witness and wishes to record the interview. The choices include: (a) a factual summary of the conversation; (b) a summary that includes the attorney's impressions of the witness and analysis of how the witness's testimony fits into the entire litigation strategy; (c) an attempted verbatim recital in question and answer form; (d) a shorthand transcription of a free-form recitation by the witness in response to the attorney's request to "tell me what happened"; (e) a tape-recorded interview. Can all of these documents be equally protected as work product?

What if the lawyer provides the witness with a copy of the document (in any of the versions above) to review? Does it make a difference if the witness makes changes? What if he keeps a copy? What if he signs the copy or swears to it before a notary?

What if litigation has not been started, but only threatened? Or what if the interview is conducted only because the client's general counsel is very cautious, but no one has yet written a threatening letter?

Assume that the witness is deposed a year later and is shown a copy of his previous interview report (in any of the versions above) before testifying. What if he testifies at trial?

- The same attorney wishes to interview several potential expert wit-

Mr. McGanney is a member of the New York City firm of White & Case. Mr. Seidel is a member of the New York City firm of Hale, Russell & Gray.

nesses and select the best one or two for trial. In order to get their views, he will interview them and provide them with relevant materials, in both respects disclosing his own views of the case. Can he protect against disclosure of these discussions or documents to the other side? If he works closely with the expert and together they produce a computer printout to be used at trial, can he protect it and related materials during the pretrial discovery phase of the litigation?

These questions and problems are illustrative. In some instances, the applicable principles are well defined; but in others, the answers vary from court to court and depend greatly on the particular circumstances involved.

Practical Principles

There are significant distinctions between the attorney-client privilege and work product protection. The former focuses primarily on the client and the right to confidential advice. The latter protects the lawyer's—principally the trial lawyer's—activities in preparing for trial. Unlike the attorney-client privilege, which is absolute once established, work product is a practical doctrine that will yield to a showing of necessity by the other side. In other respects, work product protection is broader than the attorney-client privilege. Work product can protect communications with persons other than the client and is not so easily waived.

Federal Civil Procedure Rule 26(b)(3) codifies the work product doctrine first announced in *Hickman v. Taylor*, 329 U.S. 495 (1947). *See also* Federal Criminal Procedure Rule 16. By its terms, Rule 26(b)(3) is sweeping; it protects any "document" or "thing," regardless of content and whether relating to fact or opinion, prepared by anyone at any time in anticipation of or preparation for litigation or trial. In *Upjohn Co. v. United States*, 499 U.S. 383 (1981), Supreme Court held that work product can be protected from an IRS summons, as well as typical federal court litigation.

When does the work product protection come into play? No lawsuit needs to have been filed to meet the "in anticipation of litigation" requirement of Rule 26(b)(3). *See Burlington Industries v. Exxon Corp.*, 65 F. R.D. 26, 42 (D. Md. 1974). Beyond that, the question is one for case-by-case determination, based on the degree of probability of litigation and the specificity of the asserted claim. In *Upjohn* the Court did not address this issue specifically. But it upheld application of the work product doctrine even though no proceedings had been threatened. This decision provides a broader scope to the protection than any previous case. Whatever protection applies continues until the litigation is concluded.

After the litigation has ended, the protection may or may not end. The most recent decisions favor extending the protection to a later unrelated litigation. *Duplan Corp. v. Moulinage et Retorderie de Chavanoz*, 487 F.2d 480, 484 (4th Cir. 1973).

What is protected? The rule by its terms safeguards only "documents" or "things." It does not protect oral communications, although some courts have. Facts contained in protected documents are not protected, only the documents themselves. Depositions, interrogatories, and requests for admissions can all be used to secure information to the extent it is discoverable and can be revealed without prejudicing protected material.

For example, a nonparty witness whose recollection of an occurrence has been recorded in an interview memorandum of one party, may be examined by the other party as to facts the witness knows, including facts in the memorandum, although the memorandum itself is beyond the reach of the examining party.

Rule 26(b) sets up a two-level standard of protection. The rule permits disclosure of documents and tangible things constituting "ordinary" [our word] work product—not including attorneys' "mental impressions" about the case—upon a showing of substantial need and inability to obtain the equivalent without undue hardship. But the rule goes on to provide that:

> In ordering discovery of such materials [*i.e.,* "ordinary" work product] when the required showing has been made, the court shall protect against disclosure of the mental impressions, conclusions, opinions or legal theories of an attorney or other representative of a party concerning the litigation.

One of the central unresolved issues regarding work product is whether this special protection for "mental impressions" is absolute. In *Upjohn*, the Supreme Court declined to pass explicitly on this issue. It did, however, reverse a determination ordering disclosure of documents containing mental impressions, holding that the lower court had applied too lenient a standard of need. 449 U.S. at 402.

There is a need to distinguish initially between mental impressions and factual reporting. *See Duplan Corp. v. Deering Milliken, Inc.,* 397 F. Supp. 1146, 1199 (D.S.C. 1974). Moreover, while the rule speaks of the mental impressions "of an attorney or other representative of a party concerning a litigation" without distinction, the courts have shown particular solicitude for the thoughts of trial counsel.

In the two cases in which courts have gone the farthest in ordering production of mental impressions, *Xerox Corp. v. IBM Corp.,* 64 F.R.D. 367 (S.D.N.Y. 1974) and *United States v. Brown,* 478 F.2d 1038 (7th Cir. 1973), the notes and memoranda ordered produced were not trial counsel's. In *Xerox*, the notes were interview notes of in-house counsel taken before litigation commenced. In *Brown*, involving enforcement of an IRS summons, outside counsel appears to have prepared the memo prior to commencement of the IRS investigation. The memo in Brown embodied "notes and legal judgments" prepared by an attorney acting as counselor, not as litigator.

In both of these cases, the requesting party demonstrated that it was not able to obtain admissible evidence in its opponent's files by any other means. In *Xerox*, the court ordered the production of the interview notes of the defendant's employees who could not recall crucial information at their depositions. Unlike *Hickman*, these were not notes of interviews with third parties, but with employees of the defendant. The court indicated that it would review the documents and excise, if feasible, the attorney's mental impressions; but:

> If such a distillation becomes impossible, however, then the entire contents of the document must be produced. This is especially true where one party has control over the information sought. A party should not be allowed to conceal critical, non-privileged, discoverable information, which is uniquely within the knowledge of the party and which is not obtainable from any other source, simply by imparting the information to its attorney and then attempting to hide behind the work product doctrine after the party fails to remember the information. 64 F.R.D. at 381–82.

This result conflicts with the Advisory Committee comments to Rule 26(b)(3) and with the statements of other courts, both apparently approved by the Supreme Court in *Upjohn*, that the prohibition against disclosure of mental impressions is absolute or close to it. *See, e.g., Duplan Corp. v. Moulinage et Retorderie de Chavanoz*, 509 F.2d 730 (4th Cir. 1974), *cert. denied*, 420 U.S. 997 (1975); *In re Murphy*, 560 F.2d 326, 336 (8th Cir. 1977).

Courts have gone beyond the limitations of the rule to "documents and tangible things" in protecting trial attorneys' thought processes. Thus, courts have held that a lawyer should not be called to testify to oral communications with witnesses concerning trial preparation. *E.g., In re Grand Jury Proceedings*, 473 F.2d 840 (8th Cir. 1973); *In re Terkeltoub*, 256 F. Supp. 683 (S.D.N.Y. 1966); *In re Rosenbaum*, 401 F. Supp. 807 (S.D.N.Y. 1975).

Use at Trial

The language of Rule 26(b)(3) does not distinguish between pretrial or trial protection. Work product protection at trial has not been litigated extensively. However, documents protected during discovery may be subject to production if they become evidentiary at trial under the Federal Rules of Evidence, such as Rule 612 (refreshing a witness's recollection) or by waiver.

In *United States v. Nobles*, 422 U.S. 225 (1975), the Court held that an investigator's notes of conversations with witnesses constituted work product, and that disclosure of an attorney's work product "at trial, as surely as disclosure during pretrial discovery, could disrupt the orderly development and presentation of his case." However, the work product protection was held to be waived when the investigator took the stand to testify to his conversations.

> What constitutes a waiver with respect to work product materials depends, of course, upon the circumstances. Counsel necessarily makes use throughout trial of the notes, documents and other internal materials prepared to present adequately his client's case, and often relies on them in examining witnesses. When so used, there normally is no waiver. But where, as here, counsel attempts to make a testimonial use of these materials, the normal rules of evidence come into play with respect to cross-examination and production of documents. *Id.* at 239, n.14.

Justice White, in a concurring opinion, suggested that at trial the court had the power to order the production of evidentiary material, including material useful for impeachment, whether or not work product. He did, however, suggest an exception for the classic *Hickman*-type document, the memorandum of the trial attorney recording the oral statements of a witness. Disclosure of those documents would tend to make the attorney a witness.

Insofar as disclosure of work product documents would "tend to disrupt the orderly development and presentation" of the case or make the lawyer a witness at trial, the policy of nondisclosure embodied in *Hickman v. Taylor* applies equally to the trial context. However, Federal Rules of Evidence 612, 613 and 705 permit the court to order production of work product material used by counsel to refresh the memory of a witness; or to examine a recalcitrant or forgetful witness; or which forms the basis for expert opinion.

The extent to which work product must be turned over at trial is thus, to a large extent, in counsel's hands. Trial counsel will have to decide in each case whether the use of work-product material carries a risk of waiver and, if so, whether the benefits outweigh the risks.

Certain practices can preserve the work product protection. The greater the involvement of trial counsel in the factual investigation, as distinguished from in-house or other nontrial counsel, or of a nonlawyer, the more likely the protection. It is easier to convince a court that legal theories are reflected in a document if in fact that document is written by an attorney, in contrast to a legal assistant or an employee of a party.

When trial counsel is not responsible for an analysis or study, at the least, he should record the fact that he asked for the work and that he is its intended recipient. The finished analysis should be addressed to trial counsel and should recite that it has been done in response to counsel's request, and under counsel's supervision. An employee's analysis, re-

95

quested by trial counsel, should not be headed "memo to the file" but should be directed to trial counsel. Similarly, in dealing with an expert witness, outside counsel should record by letter or memo to the file that he contacted the expert and make clear that it is done "in anticipation of litigation."

The best place to file analyses and reports, as well as communications with experts, is with counsel, not with the party, and certainly not in the party's general files.

Documents, such as factual analyses, should recite that they were done in anticipation of litigation or of trial. If a lawsuit has not yet been commenced but only threatened, the document should describe the particular facts that gave rise to the anticipation, and to the specific claims made.

The problem of whether a particular investigation has been done in anticipation of litigation, in contrast to that undertaken in the ordinary course of business, can arise both with respect to work done by outside and by inhouse counsel. See Diversified Industries, Inc. v. Meredith, 572 F.2d 596 (8th Cir. 1977). But it has arisen more frequently when done by house counsel. See Newell v. Capital Transit Co., 7 F.R.D. 732 (D.D.C. 1948); Galambus v. Consolidated Freightways Corp., 64 F.R.D. 468 (N.D. Ind. 1974). If the threat of litigation is strong enough to prompt the hiring of outside counsel, it is usually strong enough for the court to find that the work counsel did was done "in anticipation of litigation."

Mental Impressions

Any formal memorandum of a witness interview should include a description of the circumstances of its preparation, the manner in which it was prepared, and the nature of the lawyer's participation. The memorandum should reflect the lawyer's mental impressions and comment on his strategy. That record is important in litigating a discovery motion, which, in a complex case, might well be heard years after the document was prepared. The memorandum provides a readily available basis for advising the court of how and why the document was prepared. It also can be very helpful to have such a statement in the document itself if it is submitted for review in camera. It is helpful to label the memorandum "Attorney's Work Product," although the label itself is not determinative. The label can prevent inadvertent production.

The nature of the reporting in the memorandum is significant. The more purely factual the memorandum, the less showing the opponent has to make to compel disclosure. See Harper & Row Publishers, Inc. v. Decker, 423 F.2d 487, 492 (7th Cir. 1970), aff'd mem. by an equally divided court, 400 U.S. 348 (1971). On the other hand, if the court believes that a party deliberately has filled a memorandum with unnecessary comments about legal strategy as a ploy to avoid production, it may order disclosure of the entire document. See Xerox v. IBM, supra.

96

The work product protection permits an attorney to keep or discard notes of his investigations in accordance with normal work habits. Thus, if notes of interviews are used to prepare a formal file memo, there is ordinarily nothing wrong with destroying the raw notes and it is usually better practice to do so. However, the question becomes much more difficult when the notes are those of employees of the party who conducted a factual investigation under the attorney's direction. This is another reason for the attorney to conduct the investigation.

While a tape recording or stenographic record is a more accurate record of a witness interview, it cannot be as easily protected as work product as the lawyer's memorandum describing the interview. *See Wild v. Payson*, 7 F.R.D. 495 (S.D.N.Y. 1946). In *Upjohn*, the Court pointed out that the documents there went "beyond recording responses to interviews." The closer a memorandum is to a stenographic record of the interview, without the legal impressions of the lawyer, the more difficult it will be to protect.

If, after taking notes of an interview, the attorney either asks the witness to initial the handwritten notes, or after they are typed up, to acknowledge them, their protection as work product is impaired. First, a signed statement or affidavit by a third-party witness is obtainable by him from the questioning party under Rule 26(b)(3), and once obtained, would be available to be turned over to the adversary party if the witness chooses. Second, such a statement would generally be in the form of a factual narrative (without the attorney's comments and impressions), and thus less likely to enjoy immunity from production. *See Scourtes v. Fred W. Albrecht Grocery Co.*, 15 F.R.D. 55, 58 (N.D. Ohio, 1953). In *Goldberg v. United States*, 425 U.S. 94 (1976), the Court ordered production of initialed notes as constituting the "statement" of the witness, and thus producible under the Jencks Act. The Court also stated that if the initialed notes contained trial strategy or similar material, that could be excised.

Interviews of the opposing party prior to litigation but in anticipation of it follow the same general rules. Rule 26(b)(3) provides that a statement, including verbatim transcripts, taken of the opposite party must be provided to it. But courts will order production of unadopted interview notes and similar material only upon a showing of necessity. *Sharon Steel Corp. v. Travelers Indemnity Co.*, 26 F.R.D. 113 (N.D. Ohio 1960).

Work product protection, unlike the attorney-client privilege, is not lost automatically by disclosure to someone who is not the client. Attorneys representing clients with common interests can exchange work product materials. *Duplan Corp. v. Deering Milliken, Inc.*, 397 F. Supp. 1146, 1172 (D.S.C. 1974).

What a third-party witness recalls of an attorney's discussion with him is not "privileged." The witness, if he chooses, can relate the entire conversation including trial strategy and mental impressions to the adverse party or its counsel. However, if the witness does not make such disclosure voluntarily, the adverse party should not be able to obtain it through deposition questioning. *Ford v. Philips Electronics Instruments Co.*, 82 F.R.D. 359 (E.D. Pa. 1979).

Possible Pitfalls

Depositions present other possible pitfalls. If an attorney refreshes a witness's recollection before the deposition by showing him a memo of the attorney's prior interview, that memo might be ordered to be produced under Federal Rule of Evidence 612, "if the court in its discretion determines it is necessary in the interests of justice."

If a witness is examined at the deposition regarding his prior statement to his attorney—"whether written or not"—the court may order a written statement produced to opposing counsel under Federal Rule of Evidence 613(a).

Materials provided to experts create their own work product problems. Given the limits on expert discovery, these problems can be avoided in some cases. An expert who is not expected to be called as a witness is subject to discovery only upon a showing of exceptional circumstances. Rule 26(b)(4)(B). *See* Leval, *Discovery of Experts Under the Federal Rules*, 3 LITIGATION No. 1 at 1 (Fall 1976). Absent a motion, the proposed trial testimony of other expert witnesses can be obtained solely through interrogatories. Rule 26(b)(4)(A). The necessary showing to obtain depositions from experts differs among districts.

Even in a district where pretrial discovery of experts is normally limited to interrogatories, a transmittal letter to the expert should indicate that the material is being sent for purposes of litigation and that it reflects the attorney's thoughts about the case. If the attorney decides not to retain the expert after transmitting work product material, the material should be collected. If not, the attorney may find the material disclosed, if the adversary interviews the potential expert.

In complicated cases in all districts (and even in routine cases in some districts), pretrial discovery of experts beyond interrogatories is permitted. *See, e.g., Berkey Photo Inc. v. Eastman Kodak Co.*, 74 F.R.D. 613, 617 (S.D.N.Y. 1977). In such cases, Federal Rules of Evidence 612 (refreshing recollection) and 705 (which provides that an expert may be required to disclose the facts or data underlying his opinion upon cross-examination), may lead to pretrial disclosure of work product given to experts.

In one case, a magistrate invoked Rule 612 to require pretrial disclosure of an expert's report shown to a fact witness before his deposition. *Consolidated Edison Co. v. Westinghouse Electric Corp.*, No. 78 Civ. 1974 (S.D. N. Y., filed July 28, 1980). The court pointed out the "inherent tension" between Rule 612 and Federal Rule of Civil Procedure 26(b)(3) and

(4), and, in a case not involving attorneys' mental impressions, resolved the conflict in favor of disclosure.

Material prepared by the expert—including computer printouts and complex data—raises additional issues. If the attorney's involvement in providing data and consulting with the expert is substantial, a work product protection is possible.

However, if it appears that the computer-generated result is to be introduced at trial, the work product claims are overridden by the necessity of the opponent to test the validity of the proffered material before trial. *See Pearl Brewing Co. v. Joseph Schlitz Brewing Co.*, 415 F. Supp. 1122, 1138–39 (S.D. Tex. 1976); *United States v. Liebert*, 519 F.2d 542 (3d Cir.), *cert. denied*, 423 U.S. 985 (1975). These cases ultimately rest on considerations of convenience to the court in shortening the trial and of fairness based on the fact that work product protection will eventually be waived by use of the document at trial.

As confirmed recently and authoritatively in *Upjohn*, the work product doctrine plays a critical role in litigation. The protection available is substantial indeed and can be maintained, so long as lawyers use careful procedures and safeguards.

Preserving the Privilege

by Samuel R. Miller

Whether you successfully invoke the attorney-client privilege can make or break a case. The consequences of waiving the privilege may be serious in any case, and especially so in complex civil litigation and white-collar criminal proceedings. Despite much recent litigation on the scope and application of the privilege, the limits of the privilege remain unsettled, especially in the corporate context.

It is possible to bolster a claim of privilege for confidential communications between a client and counsel. It is also possible to waive the privilege without intending to do so. This article suggests how to protect confidential communications from compelled disclosure on the grounds that the privilege has been waived or does not apply.

The purpose of the attorney-client privilege is to promote freedom of consultation between a lawyer and his client and to encourage full discussion of the facts without the fear that disclosure can later be compelled from the lawyer without the client's consent. *See Upjohn Co. v. United States*, 449 U.S. 383, 389 (1981).

Dean Wigmore gives this definition of the attorney-client privilege, which has been adopted by federal courts:

> (1) Where legal advice of any kind is sought (2) from a professional legal adviser in his capacity as such, (3) the communications relating to that purpose, (4) made in confidence (5) by the client (6) are at his instance permanently protected (7) from disclosure by himself or by the legal adviser, (8) except the protection be waived.

8 WIGMORE, EVIDENCE § 2292 (McNaughton rev. 1961). In the *Upjohn* case, the United States Supreme Court discussed the scope of the attorney-client privilege in the context of corporations. Before that case,

The author is a partner in Morrison & Foerster in San Francisco.

two principal tests were applied by the federal courts to determine which corporate communications are within the attorney-client privilege.

Most widely accepted was the control-group test, under which a corporation could claim the privilege only when the corporate employee communicating with the lawyer was a member of management with authority to make decisions on the matter in question. *See, e.g., In re Grand Jury Investigation,* 599 F.2d 1224 (3rd Cir. 1979).

A more expansive statement of the attorney-client privilege in a corporation is the subject-matter test. Under this test, the application of the privilege extends to communications relating to the performance of the employee's duties made by a company employee at the direction of the employee's superiors. *See, e.g., Diversified Industries v. Meredith,* 572 F.2d 596 (8th Cir. 1978) *(en banc)*.

The *Upjohn* decision expressly rejected the control-group test as too narrow. Although the Court expressly declined to announce a general rule, it did uphold a claim of privilege on the facts before it. The court relied on these considerations:

1. The communications were made by corporate employees to corporate counsel on orders of superiors for the corporation to secure legal advice.
2. The information sought and communicated concerned matters within the scope of the employees' corporate duties.
3. The employees were aware that the communications with counsel were ordered so that the corporation could obtain legal advice.
4. The communications were ordered to be confidential, and they remained confidential.

The party asserting the privilege has the burden of establishing that it applies. By using the *Upjohn* decision for guidance, you may strengthen a claim that a communication between a client and a lawyer is privileged. Consider the steps that follow.

Counsel should direct investigations. Corporate employees often undertake investigations and make reports before the lawyer is notified of potential legal claims. There is a real risk that these reports will not be protected from disclosure. For example, courts have held:

- that a preliminary investigation, by management, of foreign payments alleged to be illegal was not privileged, even though the report was later forwarded to counsel. *In re Grand Jury Subpoena,* 599 F.2d 504 (2d Cir. 1979);
- that investigative reports prepared after a fire in a dormitory by the defendant university's security office and a committee appointed by a university officer were not protected work product, because the investigations were not under the direction of counsel and the reports were created in the ordinary course of business. *Janicker v. George Washington University,* 34 Fed. R. Serv. 2d 868 (D.D.C. 1982);

101

- that the report of an accounting firm hired by a bank to investigate a recently discovered embezzlement was not privileged under the work-product doctrine, because the accountants had been hired by management before a lawyer had been retained or a complaint filed. *Bank of the Orient v. Superior Court*, 67 Cal. App. 3d 588, 136 Cal. Rptr. 741 (1977).

The involvement of a lawyer is important not only to invoke the attorney-client privilege, but also to provide the independent protection of the work-product doctrine. As the Supreme Court recognized in the *Upjohn* case, the work-product doctrine may protect materials gathered or prepared by a lawyer "in anticipation of litigation," even if the attorney-client privilege does not apply.

Investigations may take place under the direction of in-house counsel as well as outside counsel. *In re LTV Securities Litigation*, 89 F.R.D. 595, 601 (N.D. Tex. 1982). But communications among in-house counsel may not be covered by the attorney-client privilege. *In re D. H. Overmeyer Telecasting Co.*, 470 F. Supp. 1250, 1255 (S.D.N.Y. 1979).

Especially with in-house counsel, a communication claimed to be privileged should be made to or by the lawyer acting in his capacity as legal counsel, not as a business adviser or a policymaker. *Securities Exchange Commission v. Gulf & Western Industries, Inc.*, 518 F. Supp. 675, 681–83 (D.C. Cir. 1981).

Experts, legal assistants, or investigators hired to assist in an investigation should be retained and supervised by a lawyer to ensure that communications between them and the client are either within the attorney-client privilege or constitute protected work product. *United States v. Cote*, 456 F.2d 142 (8th Cir. 1972).

The client should specifically request legal advice. Communications between lawyer and client are privileged only where the lawyer acts in a legal capacity. *See Securities Exchange Commission v. Gulf & Western Industries, Inc.*, 518 F. Supp. at 675, 681. Where possible, a corporate officer should make a specific request for legal advice in writing. The officer should be one authorized to retain counsel.

In the special case, the request could take place by a resolution of the client's board of directors. The request should specifically authorize a legal analysis, rather than a mere factual investigation. If appropriate, the request should include a specific reference to the likelihood of litigation, which will strengthen a claim to work-product protection.

In the *Upjohn* case and other cases, the existence of a written request has been considered an important indicium that the client was requesting legal advice and the counsel was acting as a legal adviser. In more routine cases, instruct company employees to make it clear in inquiries to an in-house legal department that they are requesting legal advice.

During an investigation, company employees should receive a directive advising them that they will be interviewed by a lawyer so that the company can obtain legal advice. The employees should be directed to cooperate with counsel in gathering information necessary to render the advice. In the *Upjohn* case, for example, the internal investigation included sending a questionnaire to certain company managers along with a letter signed by the chairman of the board. The letter described the legal nature of the inquiry. Such a written communication establishes the legal nature of the investigation and helps prevent misunderstanding by company employees about why they are being asked for information.

Never forget that the attorney-client privilege belongs to the company. The company may choose to waive the privilege and disclose the information gathered by counsel. In *In re Grand Jury Proceedings, Detroit, Michigan, August 1977*, 434 F. Supp. 648 (E.D. Mich. 1977), *aff'd per curiam*, 570 F.2d 562 (6th Cir. 1978), the corporation had waived the attorney-client privilege. A company officer could not block the grand-jury testimony of a company lawyer about his interview with the officer.

Some commentators have suggested that the company counsel should give *Miranda*-type warnings to company employees about the purpose of an interview and the use of information disclosed. They suggest that if a company employee begins to describe matters that make him vulnerable to criminal prosecution or disciplinary action, the lawyer should end the interview and give the employee a chance to retain counsel of his own.

Make the confidential nature of legal communications clear. Make and maintain the communications in confidence. In the *Upjohn* case, the Court emphasized that the chairman of the board had instructed that the communications were ''highly confidential,'' and the company kept them confidential. 449 U.S. at 395.

Inform employees interviewed in a legal investigation to treat the matter as confidential both within the corporation and with outsiders.

Documents claimed as privileged should be clearly designated to establish confidentiality. A corporate party claiming the attorney-client privilege must ''provide information about its own internal security practices which would support a finding of confidentiality.'' 2 J. WEINSTEIN & M. BERGER, WEINSTEIN'S EVIDENCE ¶ 503(b) [04] at 503–49. In the *Upjohn* case, the Supreme Court noted that the documents at issue had been treated as confidential and had not been disclosed to anyone except the company's counsel.

One way to designate privileged matter is to use a stamp or legend to identify attorney-client communications. All the same, inconsistent, indiscriminate, or inappropriate uses of stamps or legends can harm a claim of privilege.

A practical method of identifying privileged communications is to instruct company employees and lawyers to use legal titles in all correspondence and memoranda prepared by or addressed to lawyers. The company should maintain organization charts and directories of legal employees so that others do not forget the identities and responsibilities of company counsel when the issue of privilege is raised, which may occur years after the preparation and filing of the documents.

Documents of legal advice should relate only to legal subjects. They should not become memoranda of general business decisions. Although a lawyer may include nonlegal matters necessary for giving or receiving legal advice without destroying the privilege, documents that are reports of general corporate business decisions are not privileged. Documents relating to business matters, even if they include discussions with in-house counsel, are not privileged if the lawyer is acting in a business capacity.

Some courts have said that the privileged status of company documents may be lost if the documents are intermingled with other non-privileged, nonconfidential documents. However, in *James Julian, Inc. v. Raytheon Co.*, 93 F.R.D. 138 (D. Del. 1982), the court adopted a more pragmatic approach. It held that the placement of privileged documents in general corporate files did not waive the attorney-client privilege. The court notes that to hold otherwise would require the corporation to maintain at least two sets of files and to have a screening committee for special files. The court said the cases did not require such a system.

All the same, the authorities part on this question. It may be advisable to maintain privileged documents in separate "legal" files to which access is limited.

Control privileged documents. Many courts have held that disclosure of privileged materials to unnecessary third persons defeats a claim of privilege. For example, in *In re John Doe Corp.*, 675 F.2d 482 (2d Cir. 1982), a company's disclosure of a special investigative report to its underwriters and its outside auditors in a public securities offering waived the privilege for both the final report and prior drafts. In *Elgin Federal Credit Union v. Cantor, Fitzgerald Securities Corp.*, 91 F.R.D. 414, 418–19 (N.D. Ga. 1981), the company lost its privilege for board minutes because the minutes were made available to an accounting firm for audit.

The privilege may even be lost where the documents are recovered by the opposing party out of the garbage, unless meticulous care has been taken to preserve the privilege. *See Suburban Sew 'N Sweep, Inc. v. Swiss Bernina, Inc.*, 91 F.R.D. 254 (N.D. Ill. 1981).

Within a corporate client, distribution of legal advice should be limited to those persons who have a need to know or a reasonable degree of responsibility for the subject matter. Where legal advice is restated or discussed in internal memoranda, the legal advice should be attributed to counsel.

Instruct clients not to communicate legal opinions and advice to anyone outside the company without specific authorization of counsel. Advise clients to avoid disclosing privileged information in business negotiations. Advise them to consult before disclosing privileged matter even during settlement discussions, though some courts have held that no waiver occurs for disclosures in settlement negotiations.

Courts often hold that the disclosure of one privileged communication or document waives the privilege as to other communications on the same subject. Advise clients that what might seem like a harmless disclosure could result in a broad waiver of the privilege.

Here are some common situations in which courts have found the privilege waived.

Confidential materials to refresh recollection. The client may waive the attorney-client privilege or work-product protection by the use of privileged materials to refresh a witness's recollection before deposition or trial. In *James Julian, Inc.* v. *Raytheon Co.*, 93 F.R.D. 138 (D. Del. 1982), employees of the plaintiff corporation reviewed binders of relevant documents assembled by the lawyers before their depositions. The court held that the binders constituted work product, because the selection and ordering of a few documents out of thousands disclosed important aspects of the lawyer's understanding of the case of necessity. However, relying on FED. R. EVID. 612, the court held that the work-product protection was waived by allowing witnesses to review the binders before their depositions.

Other cases have also held that the disclosure of privileged material to a witness to refresh recollection waives any privilege. One court did find no waiver where a lawyer merely looked at his correspondence file before his deposition. *Jos. Schlitz Brewing Co.* v. *Muller & Phipps (Hawaii) Ltd.*, 85 F.R.D. 118 (W.D. Mo. 1980).

Inadvertent production of privileged material. A recurring issue in complex cases with large volumes of discovery is whether inadvertent production of privileged materials constitutes a waiver. A number of courts have held that it does, though there may be an exception in the context of an accelerated document production where good cause exists for the inadvertent disclosure.

A recent case addressing this issue was *Transamerica Computer Company, Inc.* v. *International Business Machines Corp.*, 573 F.2d 646 (9th Cir. 1978). In this case, the plaintiff moved to compel the production of IBM's privileged documents that had previously been disclosed in another suit. In the earlier litigation, the court had allowed the parties to claim the privilege for any documents inadvertently disclosed during accelerated discovery. *See Control Data Corp.* v. *International Business Machines Corp.*, 16 Fed. R.Serv. 2d 1233 (D. Minn. 1972).

IBM had inadvertently produced privileged documents in the *Control Data* litigation. The Ninth Circuit Court of Appeals avoided deciding whether inadvertent disclosure constitutes a waiver. The court held instead that the time limits of the *Control Data* discovery were so harsh that the production of a limited number of privileged documents was "compelled" by circumstances.

105

The *Control Data* documents were also sought by the government in its recent antitrust case against IBM. The government also claimed that the privilege had been waived by the prior disclosure. A panel of the Second Circuit Court of Appeals decided there had been no waiver. *International Business Machines v. United States*, 471 F.2d 507 (2d Cir. 1972), *rev'd on jurisdictional grounds*, 480 F.2d 293 (2d Cir. 1973) (en banc), *cert. denied*, 416 U.S. 979 (1974).

Thus courts have recognized that privileged documents may inevitably be produced in error during large-scale discovery. If reasonable precautions have been taken, and the party acts promptly to recover the privileged documents, a court may conclude that the privilege should not be lost. But if the screening has been less than careful, or if the party delays in repairing the disclosure, the privilege will be lost.

Disclosure to a government agency. The holdings conflict about whether disclosure of privileged communications to a government agency, such as the SEC, is a complete or a limited waiver. The limited waiver doctrine has been applied, for example, both to disclosure of a company's "questionable payments" to the SEC in a private investigation (the privileged material did not have to be disclosed to a private litigant in another suit) and to a disclosure of privileged materials to the SEC, the IRS, and a New York grand jury.

If you can stipulate to confidentiality or a protective order with the government agency, you may strengthen the claim of privilege in a later case. In *Teachers Insurance and Annuity Association of America v. Shamrock Broadcasting Company*, 521 F. Supp. 638, 644–46 (S.D.N.Y. 1981), the court considered disclosure to the SEC a complete waiver, unless the client specifically reserved the right to assert the privilege in later proceedings. If you submit confidential documents to a government agency, negotiate a protective order that reserves the right to assert the privilege later.

Injecting advice of counsel as an issue in litigation. A client may waive the attorney-client privilege by relying on "advice of counsel" as an affirmative defense in litigation. In *Handguards, Inc. v. Johnson & Johnson*, 413 F. Supp. 926 (N. D. Cal. 1976), the plaintiff claimed that the defendant had attempted to restrain trade by bringing patent-infringement actions in bad faith. The defendant intended to call the lawyers who had litigated the prior suits as witnesses. They would testify that the prior actions were brought in good faith and on the basis of competent legal advice.

The court held that the defendants had waived the privilege for communications and documents relating to the good-faith prosecution of the prior actions. The court further held that the defendants had waived the attorneys' work-product protection.

Another waiver occurred in *Garfinkle v. Arcata National Corp.*, 64 F.R.D. 688 (S.D.N.Y. 1974). The plaintiff alleged that the defendant corporation had failed to file a registration statement with the SEC. Arcata asserted, as one defense, the opinion of counsel that the plaintiff's shares could be sold without registration, and the plaintiff demanded any documents relating to the lawyer's opinion letter. The court held that, since the defendant had injected the opinion letter into the case, the plaintiff was entitled to probe the circumstances surrounding the issuance of the letter.

Waiver resulting from advice of counsel has also been found where a defendant relied on advice of counsel about legality of a merger, where a defendant intended to introduce evidence at trial relating to its good-faith prosecution of an administrative proceeding, and where a plaintiff alleged fraudulent concealment of a conspiracy for limitations purposes. On the other hand, the court in *Barr Marine Products Co. v. Borg-Warner Corp.*, 84 F.R.D. 631 (E.D. Pa. 1979), found that raising the affirmative defense of "meeting competition" did not waive the attorney-client privilege.

Consequences of a waiver. When a party discloses privileged communications, he may have waived the privilege for all communications between the same lawyer and the same client on the same subject. This does not mean, however, that the voluntary disclosure of confidential information waives the privilege for all conversations that may have taken place between a lawyer and a client.

In a number of cases, the scope of the waiver has been narrowly construed. The privilege has been held waived only if facts relevant to a particular, narrow subject matter have been disclosed in circumstances in which it would be unfair to deny the other party an opportunity to discover other relevant facts about that subject. *See Hercules, Inc. v. Exxon Corp.*, 434 F. Supp. 136, 156 (D. Del. 1977).

In *United States v. Aronoff*, 466 F. Supp. 855 (S. D. N. Y. 1979), the government sought a pretrial ruling that the defendant in a criminal case had waived the privilege for the substance of any communication with his former civil lawyer, Zielgelman, regarding a land transaction. One basis for the waiver alleged was the disclosure by the defendant's criminal lawyer in discussions with government lawyers that the defendant and Zielgelman had discussed aspects of the land transaction. The court held that the waiver extended only to the subjects disclosed to government counsel and not to all aspects of the land transaction. The legal effect of such disclosures was to let a whisker out of the bag, but not the whole cat.

In *Goldman Sachs & Co. v. Blondis*, 412 F. Supp. 286 (N.D. Ill. 1976), the court construed the scope of the waiver narrowly. This was an action by a stockbroker against a customer who refused to make delivery of stock certificates the broker had sold. During the owner's deposition, he related the substance of statements made by him to his attorney on a particular day regarding the stock sale. He also disclosed that he had had conversations regarding the stock transaction with his attorney on other days, but he did not relate the substance of them. The court held that the defendant's disclosure in his deposition waived the privilege only for "that specific subject during that particular conversation."

In *Status Time Corp. v. Sharp Electronics Corp.*, 33 Fed. R. Serv. 2d 1406 (S.D.N.Y. 1982), a patent-infringement action, the court found that the plaintiff corporation had waived the privilege for a specific letter from a patent lawyer to the president of the corporation. The letter had been disclosed to an officer of another company. But the court construed the waiver narrowly to apply only to the letter and not to all privileged documents bearing on the subject.

Even if a client does waive the privilege, you should argue that the scope of the waiver was limited. But with care, a company can avoid even limited waivers of these important protections.

Keeping Secrets Secret

by Dan Levitt

I know that's a secret, for it's whispered everywhere.

WILLIAM CONGREVE

In the pretrial excavation for nuggets of evidence, discovery digs up great volumes of facts, documents, and testimony, some of which are only remotely relevant to the case. Unfortunately, this process of strip mining by deposition and interrogatory also unearths secrets—sensitive information that witnesses or parties would prefer to keep buried, or at least out of sight.

Once litigation begins, both sides are likely to go after confidential information that is arguably relevant, but that can be used—by the parties or others—for purposes not directly related to the case. In personal-injury, matrimonial, and other noncommercial cases, discovery routinely trains its sights on private matters concerning a party's earnings, wealth, peccadilloes, or sexual habits.

That sort of thing also happens in commercial litigation. There, the parties—often competitors vying for business advantage—relentlessly pursue each other's trade secrets, technological know-how, customer lists, and marketing strategy.

In fact, businessmen sometimes sue each other, or invite suit, for the very purpose of compromising the confidentiality of sensitive commercial information. The inquisitive party may be more interested in the secrets than the relief. This is especially true in corporate-control contests, where intelligence about a target company's plans to sell off its "crown jewels," about the identity of a "white knight," or about an adversary's resources and banking connections may be as valuable to a party as Silicon Valley gossip is to the Russians.

The author is a partner in the New York City firm of Kramer, Levin, Nessen, Kamin & Frankel. He wishes to thank his colleague Lorraine Fields for her assistance with this article.

109

How great is the risk? Your client may think that secrets will be sold or appropriated for use in a competitor's business. The chairman of the corporation you represent may worry that company information will be passed on to government authorities to get them to block an important transaction. He may be concerned that the company's takeover plans, once leaked, might stir the corporate quarry to run for safer pastures. Or he may fear that "little transgressions" will be reported to the authorities, the newspapers, or the proxy solicitors.

Unless protective measures are taken, these nightmares can become realities: There are no automatic rules to prevent anyone from using information disclosed in civil discovery for anything. So what do you do?

Sometimes the best way to protect secrets is to forgo litigation altogether, or settle it quickly. The risks of exposing confidential information may outweigh the possible benefits of prosecuting or defending the lawsuit, as many a potential libel plaintiff or technology owner has reluctantly concluded. But most parties cannot so readily control their legal fortunes: Defendants do not choose to be sued, and parties cannot settle unilaterally.

When litigation seems unavoidable, consider some legal first aid to keep sensitive information private. If the lawsuit has not yet been filed, think about removing troublesome documents from your client's files. But proceed with caution.

Some statutes, like Title VII, impose an obligation to preserve documents even before a complaint is filed. Giving documents to outside counsel is generally no protection against discovery. And running the paper shredder all night before the complaint is filed can look incriminating. Such conduct may tilt the scales of justice against you. Specifically consider what unfavorable inferences the trier of fact might draw against your client simply because it has destroyed evidence.

Once the suit is filed, there are other protective measures short of a full-blown confidentiality agreement. Your client may be able to litigate under a pseudonym, especially if his right to anonymity is an issue in the case. Subject to Rule 11, you can also take tougher positions on relevance and other objections, as long as they are asserted in good faith.

If you must produce documents, you can redact sensitive but irrelevant information. But watch out: Like destruction, redaction can provoke fights and produce skepticism on the part of the judge or the jury. If your opponent complains too loudly, be prepared to show the judge in camera what you deleted.

Preliminary protections are also possible with evidence other than documents. Often, for example, you can get a stipulation that deposition transcripts and interrogatory answers will not be filed with the court, or will be filed only under seal. Or you can seek a narrow protective order concerning a specific document, witness, or subject.

But sometimes these intermediate measures are not enough. The only complete answer may be a general confidentiality agreement covering all forms of discovery.

Broad confidentiality agreements are common, and there is ample authority for entering them as court orders. For example, a federal judge may "for good cause shown . . . make any order which justice requires to protect a party or person from annoyance, embarrassment, oppression, or undue burden or expense." FED. R. CIV. P. 26(c). The rule lists eight examples of protective orders, ranging from a prohibition against discovery to the sealing of depositions and documents.

Until recently, the constitutionality of expansive confidentiality orders was open to question. Occasionally, serious questions were raised about whether discovery could be conducted in private. *In re Halkin*, 598 F.2d 176 (D.C. Cir. 1979), for example, called discovery protective orders "paradigmatic prior restraint" and subjected them to the first Amendment "strict scrutiny" test. Other courts also held that discovery must occur in public, except in the most special circumstances.

The Supreme Court's recent decision in *Seattle Times Co. v. Rhinehart*, 467 U.S. 20 (1984), has blown away much of this constitutional cloud. Observing that civil discovery is a matter of "legislative grace," the Court held that there is no constitutional right of unfettered access to private information made available only for litigation. It said that judges not only have the right to control access to and use of such information, but they also have an interest in preventing abuse of the litigation process.

In fact, the Court observed, compelled disclosure of information produced in discovery can itself violate litigants' privacy interests. Although *Seattle Times* involved other First Amendment issues and is not completely dispositive, it puts protective orders on a much firmer constitutional footing.

Rule 26 and *Seattle Times* mean that you can get a protective order if you can show good cause. But how do you do it?

The first step is to think ahead. Too often, a protective order is forged in the heat of a particular discovery dispute—a deponent's refusal to answer a question, a party's unwillingness to produce confidential documents, or one side's refusal to accede to expedited discovery. But handling the important matter of a protective order simply as a reaction to a specific discovery problem can have unfortunate side effects.

An order growing out of a particular dispute may fail to address more general confidentiality concerns. More than that, its terms may be largely the handiwork of a judge or magistrate with a limited understanding of the business and tactical nuances of the case.

A far better course is to negotiate a confidentiality order with your adversary. Do this at the beginning of a case, before problems arise, but after thoroughly thinking through the issues. Skeptical readers may doubt that parties embattled in litigation can often agree on protective orders. But it is easier than you might think.

The need for a protective order often comes up in litigation conducted under time pressure. The plaintiff may move for an injunction and the court may order expedited discovery. Because both sides usually have secrets to keep, they often have a common interest in keeping discovery materials out of the hands of third parties. To get discovery moving, the parties usually get together on some form of proposed order.

Each side's task is to draft an agreement that meets its needs without appearing too one-sided or onerous. If, despite your evenhanded draft agreement, your adversary unreasonably refuses to sign on the dotted line, you can simply submit it to the court for entry as an order. If the arrangement you propose is truly reasonable, the judge will probably adopt your proposal, even over opposition.

What should a proposed order say? Too much depends on the facts of each case to make a general form feasible. But most confidentiality orders have the same basic structure: They permit parties or others producing information—in the form of documents, interrogatory answers, or deposition testimony—to designate some or all of it as "confidential." This is usually subject to the qualification that the designation must be reasonable. The validity of such so-called umbrella orders has been upheld in such cases as *Cipollone v. Liggett Group, Inc.*, 785 F.2d 1108, 1121–23 (3d Cir. 1986).

The order usually provides that only certain "qualified" persons may see the designated confidential materials until the court either lifts the designation or modifies the restriction. The order also usually limits copying or distribution of confidential information, even by those qualified to see it.

Sometimes the order provides for parties to put information into ascending categories of protection—like "restricted," "sensitive," and "highly confidential." Smaller and smaller groups of people, subject to progressively stringent restrictions on distribution and copying, are allowed to see the increasingly "hot" material.

Another very common provision, and one of the easiest to sell to an adversary or a judge, allows all information obtained through discovery to be used "only in this litigation." That seems fairly innocuous, but it limits many common abuses, such as the use of discovered information in proxy solicitations or tender offers, disclosure to government agencies or the press, or improper business uses. Having agreed to use the information only in "this litigation," your adversary would find it desperately awkward to explain to you or a judge why he wants to use the material for unrelated purposes.

Besides including the usual provisions, consider some less common ones. For example, should the order cover pleadings, briefs, affidavits, and possibly even courtroom testimony and exhibits? That is a tough question.

It is one thing to restrict access to documents, interrogatory answers, and deposition testimony. After all, that information is exchanged in the privacy of lawyers' offices. It is quite another thing to try to control the availability of court filings, lawyers' arguments, or witnesses' courtroom testimony. That kind of restriction seems to impinge on what many, particularly in the press, believe is the public's right of access to all court proceedings.

Though it is sometimes possible to get secrecy orders covering normally public aspects of a case, compromises are usually easier. For example, the parties might agree to the confidentiality of designated items but permit one another to use arguably confidential information from those materials in pleadings, briefs, and other filings, subject to retrospective motions for sealing orders. That compromise avoids cumbersome sealing procedures, except in rare cases, and recognizes that whole documents are usually far more sensitive than the small bits or paraphrases that a lawyer is likely to use in argument.

Unfortunately, a compromise like that has its risks, and, in the Southern District of New York at least, it is simply no longer possible.

In litigation concerning the Trane Company, the parties negotiated the kind of compromise just described. After the court entered the resulting order, one of the parties filed papers containing arguably confidential discovery material, which would have been useful in a proxy contest that was then under consideration. Because the financial community pays close attention to such litigation, a reporting service copied the court papers from the public file and sent copies to its subscribers before any party sought relief. The sensitive information quickly appeared in *Barron's*.

Because of the ensuing controversy, the clerk's office in the Southern District of New York now requires that all confidentiality orders provide that "any pleadings, motions or other papers filed with the Court [and] disclosing any confidential information" shall be filed under seal. While the compromise may work in some jurisdictions—and should often be preferred for its practicality—the New York experience is fair warning that it may fail to provide the necessary protection, and that some courts may insist on complete sealing or nothing at all.

When necessary, even courtroom argument and testimony can sometimes be kept confidential. If there are no spectators, there is no problem. But, when asked, judges will sometimes enforce a confidentiality order by clearing the courtroom or moving a portion of the proceedings to the robing room or to chambers.

In a suit to preserve the anonymity of the plaintiff, who prosecuted the case under a pseudonym, one federal judge was persuaded to ask occasional spectators to find another trial to watch, and he sealed the entire hearing transcript. In rare cases, judges have even had the courtroom windows blacked out. Although conducting a hearing or trial in private is controversial, in appropriate circumstances some judges can be persuaded to take these extreme steps, particularly when they believe that one side is trying to use the courtroom to broadcast the other side's secrets.

Trying to close a trial raises some basic issues, particularly in class or derivative actions. In *Jay v. North*, 692 F.2d 880, 893–94 (2d Cir. 1982), *cert. denied*, 460 U.S. 1051 (1983), the court questioned whether a shareholder's derivative suit should be dismissed on the basis of ''secret documents.'' The court acknowledged that there might be a risk of abuse in disclosure of sensitive information, and said it might permit the sealing of discovery materials not crucial to the outcome of the case. But the court was unwilling to seal a highly sensitive report that was central to the district court's decision.

The emerging rule, which is likely unaffected by *Seattle Times*, seems to be that you can keep sensitive but unimportant information away from the public. Keeping dispositive material secret is much more difficult.

Deciding who can see sensitive material, and under what terms, is one of the most difficult and important aspects of drafting a confidentiality agreement. You particularly need to consider whether to limit a party's employees' and experts' access to confidential information.

Often discovery material is useless unless you can discuss it with your client, its technical or other expert personnel, or outside experts. But there will often be reasons not to let them see the material. Once a competitor learns its adversary's plans or costs, or a technical expert sees how the other side produces a chemical, it is hard to put the jinni back in the bottle.

Concerns like these often lead both sides to insist that materials turned over in discovery be analyzed only by experts outside the company who are retained specifically for the litigation. It is common to provide that only counsel and independent experts who sign confidentiality agreements may see certain highly sensitive information.

But beware. Such arrangements increase the cost of litigation. They can be unwieldy or just plain unworkable. You may even find, particularly in cases involving new or complex technology, that only your client's personnel have the expertise to assist you and the court. Though you may ultimately have no choice, you should not agree lightly to exclude your client's own employees from access to confidential information. In fact, often the only good reason for agreeing to a provision like that is to bind your opponent in the same way.

Sometimes you may want to prevent some other group from seeing discovery materials. The feared interlopers may be newspaper reporters, other potential litigants, parties in another action, or government agencies. Oral agreements not to let discovery materials fall into other hands are not much good. *See United States v. Davis*, 702 F.2d 418, 422–43 (2d Cir.), *cert. denied*, 463 U. S. 1215 (1983). If you want to exclude particular people or organizations, a provision that information may be used only "in this litigation" is also probably not good enough. You will have greater success in preventing access if the feared intermeddler is specifically identified in the original order.

By naming the party to be excluded, you set up the argument that, in reliance on protection from that very risk, your client has produced information. The excluded party will have the burden of persuading the court to modify an order that specifically contemplated his interest in the sensitive material.

A particularized exclusion often works. An extreme case is *Palmiere v. New York*, 779 F.2d 861 (2d Cir. 1985), which sustained a magistrate's refusal to grant the State of New York access to a settlement agreement and other documents when the magistrate believed that the case could not have been settled absent a provision specifically barring the state from seeing those documents.

Courts are usually reluctant to bar access by parties in consolidated or related litigation, especially when the result would simply be duplicative discovery. They are less solicitous, though, of potential litigants or parties in unrelated cases.

When the question is access by regulatory or law-enforcement agencies, the courts have tended to require agencies with their own discovery weapons—the Antitrust Division's civil investigative demands and prosecutor's grand juries, for example—to do their own discovery, while granting access to less well-equipped agencies.

In *Martindell v. IT&T Corp.*, 594 F.2d 291, 295–96 (2d Cir. 1979), the court approved the enforcement of a protective order against the federal government's informal request for access to depositions, observing that witnesses had relied on the order and that the government has its own "awesome" discovery tools. Conversely, in *Wilk v. AMA*, 635 F.2d 1295, 1299 (7th Cir. 1980), emphasizing the presumptive public right of access to "documents and information in [the court's] possession," the court granted the State of New York access to sensitive materials. The court observed that the state was a plaintiff in a similar antitrust suit, and that it does not have the discovery tools of the federal government.

Negotiating and drafting a confidentiality agreement is usually the hard part. Once you have jumped those hurdles, do not fail to take the next, easier step: Have the court enter the order.

An agreement between the parties that is not entered as a court order may give the parties enough comfort to begin expedited discovery. Absent overreaching, unfairness, or (occasionally) constitutional concerns, a court will enforce the agreement. But the court is much more likely to modify or lift a private agreement at the behest of an outsider. And breach of a private agreement is not contempt of court. So take the time to document why you need the agreement, and then ask the court to enter it as an order.

Once the court has entered a protective order, use it. More than that, rely on it.

When pressed to permit access to information covered by a confidentiality order, courts give great weight to whether someone has in fact relied on the order in producing documents. Take advantage of that propensity.

Scrupulously document your reliance. Each time you produce confidential data, make a record. Stamp each document with a legend like this: "Highly Confidential Material Produced in Reliance on and Subject to the Confidentiality Order in *Jones v. Smith,* C.A. No. 86-1002, N.D. Illinois." State in every response to discovery requests that you are producing in reliance on the order. And make your position explicit at depositions and in the courtroom.

Aside from relying on the order, also monitor compliance with it. Make sure you get what you bargained for. Trust no one. Assume that, inadvertently or otherwise, your adversary or its minions will file your confidential material in the public record, fail to designate which portions of deposition testimony are confidential, and otherwise mishandle sensitive materials. Members of your own team may do the same things. Accordingly, you should constantly remind your opponent, your client, and your colleagues of the order's existence. Frequently explain its requirements, regularly monitor what gets filed, and carefully police the handling of deposition transcripts.

That kind of careful monitoring will not ensure complete security; nothing can. But vigilance can minimize the number and size of the cracks that develop in the wall you have built. More than that, your efforts to ensure compliance will strengthen your position if someone launches an attack on the order, or if you seek sanctions for noncompliance. In addition, if you do not monitor compliance or, worse yet, tolerate breaches of the order, a court may conclude that you have waived its protection.

There is a final point to remember about protecting your client's secrets: Do not put all your faith in a protective order.

Even a carefully considered, adequately monitored order provides something less than foolproof protection. Secrets do tend to be "whispered everywhere." Accidental leaks occur, as do acts of unadulterated bad faith.

Even the best-drawn orders get modified or lifted, or become obsolete. It is often impossible to conduct litigation as a wholly private affair. Courthouses are, after all, public facilities. Parties remain free to disclose their own information or material not obtained through discovery. And that government agency or law-enforcement official you would like to keep away has powerful tools to get at your client's secrets.

So the prudent lawyer is not lulled into complacency by the existence of a confidentiality order. Even if you can get such an order, the better course may still be to forgo litigation or to settle fast. Likewise, an order does not eliminate the need to take tough positions on relevance and privilege questions, to redact irrelevant material, to arrange not to file deposition transcripts and interrogatory answers, to seek special relief on truly important matters, and to arrange for the destruction of sensitive materials once they are no longer needed. Keeping secrets secret is a full-time job in which perfection is impossible and diligence essential.

Civil Discovery and the Fifth Amendment

by Brian O'Neill

Civil lawyers and criminal lawyers are spending a lot of time these days looking at the same conduct. While white collar crime prosecutions for commercial activity proliferate, civil litigation under the Racketeering Influenced and Corrupt Organizations Act explodes. Whether someone faces a civil lawsuit or a criminal prosecution may depend on the mere accident of whether a private plaintiff or a public agency is the first to learn a set of facts. Often a person faces both actions.

To represent your client competently when one of the parties to a civil suit faces criminal prosecution, you must go beyond your usual routine and examine the implications of the criminal litigation. No, you do not need to retake that first year criminal procedure course that never sank in. But a few matters merit review.

When civil and criminal cases mix, the thorniest discovery problems come from the Fifth Amendment privilege against self-incrimination. The issue can arise whenever one of the parties is at risk in an imminent criminal case. While the history and wording of the Fifth Amendment privilege suggest that it applies only to criminal proceedings, a person may invoke it in any forum: *Lefkowitz v. Turley*, 414 U.S. 70 (1973).

Your client does not have to wait for the ultimate question, "Did you fix prices?" before invoking the privilege. Otherwise a clever questioner could extract enough pieces of information from the witness to construct a mosaic of his criminal liability. Recognizing this possibility, the Supreme Court held in *Hoffman v. United States*, 341 U.S. 479 (1951), that a witness can invoke the privilege in response to any question when the answer could provide a link in the chain of evidence leading to the witness's incrimination.

The author is a member of O'Neill & Lysaght in Santa Monica, California.

A reasonable fear of prosecution based upon the mere appearance of impropriety justifies invocation of the Fifth Amendment. In *Slochower v. Board of Education*, 350 U.S. 551, 557 (1956), the Court held:

[A] witness may have a reasonable fear of prosecution and yet be innocent of any wrongdoing. The privilege serves to protect the innocent who otherwise might be ensnared by ambiguous circumstances.

The client under criminal investigation not only *may* but *must* invoke the privilege when the answer sought might be incriminatory. Failure to do so waives the privilege, and the evidence in the civil case could then be used for criminal prosecution. *United States v. Kordel*, 397 U.S. 1 (1970).

A party invoking the privilege to oppose discovery bears the burden of demonstrating its propriety. But the party's attorney often cannot describe precisely the manner in which the privileged matter would tend to incriminate. The description itself could provide incriminating leads and defeat the purpose of the privilege. Nor could counsel make an *in camera* disclosure since that would run afoul of Disciplinary Rules 4-101(A) and 4-101(B) of the American Bar Association's Code of Professional Conduct which enjoin silence as to matters communicated in confidence by the client. Accordingly, an attorney can meet the burden of justifying opposition to discovery by representing that he has consulted with the client, assessed the circumstances, and concluded that the client's answers would tend to incriminate.

As a general rule, only a natural person can claim the privilege. Corporations, trusts, labor unions, and similar organizations, are not protected by the Fifth Amendment. However, courts have held the Fifth Amendment applicable to legal entities closely approximating a natural person, such as sole proprietorships, *Stuart v. United States*, 416 F.2d 459 (5th Cir. 1969).

Because the privilege is personal, it may not be invoked vicariously. A corporate officer may not claim his own privilege to resist the production of corporate documents, *United States v. Giordano*, 419 F.2d 564, 569 (8th Cir. 1969), *cert. denied*, 397 U.S. 1037 (1970), moreover, a corporation may not refuse to produce documents on the ground that they would incriminate corporate employees. *Flavorland Industries, Inc. v. United States*, 591 F.2d 524 (9th Cir. 1979).

Although documents may be incriminatory, the witness usually cannot resist production because he cannot claim that he was compelled to *prepare* them. However, if the act of production itself would be incriminatory—for example to authenticate the documents or to show that the witness was in possession of the documents—the witness may invoke the Fifth Amendment against disclosure. *United States v. Beattie*, 522 F.2d 267 (2d Cir. 1975), *vacated and remanded*, 425 U.S. 967 (1976).

How can you respond when your opponent invokes the privilege against self-incrimination to prevent discovery? Sanctions are unlikely. *Wehling v. Columbia Broadcasting System*, 608 F.2d 1084 (5th Cir. 1979), held that a court cannot default a party for validly exercising a constitutional right in refusing to provide discovery, although in *Lyons v. Johnson*, 415 F.2d 540 (9th Cir. 1969), *cert. denied*, 397 U.S. 1027 (1970), the court granted judgment against a plaintiff who refused to respond to *any* discovery requests while at the same time prosecuting his own claim.

Even less likely is an immunity order for the witness, prohibiting use of his deposition testimony in any criminal proceeding, so that the privilege against self-incrimination becomes inapplicable. Under the federal immunity statute, only the United States Attorney is empowered to seek such an order. 18 U.S.C. § 6003.

However, at least one state (California) allows a civil litigant to seek an immunity order for a witness who has invoked the Fifth Amendment privilege. *Daly v. Superior Court*, 19 Cal.3d 132 (1977). California procedure requires notification of both the District Attorney and United States Attorney. If neither objects, the California court will enter an immunity order compelling the witness to testify.

If a civil litigant has testified pursuant to a grant of immunity, the testimony is available for use in any civil or administrative proceeding, whether state or federal. *Patrick v. United States*, 524 F.2d 1109, 1120 (7th Cir. 1975). But a deponent who has previously testified pursuant to a grant of use immunity cannot be compelled to testify to the same matter in a deposition, unless he receives assurance of immunity for the deposition testimony because otherwise the deposition testimony could be used against him in a criminal prosecution. *Pillsbury Co. v. Conboy*, 103 S. Ct. 608 (1983).

A party in a civil suit who is also exposed to criminal prosecution may require greater protection than that provided solely by the privilege against self-incrimination. He should be spared the injustice of having to defend against both a civil and criminal action at one time, *see United States v. Amrep Corp.*, 405 F. Supp. 1053 (S.D.N.Y. 1976), and also should not have to disclose prematurely a defense that he will raise in the criminal proceedings. *United States v. Simon*, 262 F. Supp. 64 (S.D.N.Y. 1966), *rev'd*, 373 F.2d 649 (2d Cir. 1967), *vacated*, 389 U.S. 425 (1967).

There are several remedies available under both the Civil Rules and the Criminal Rules.

The most effective remedy, available under Rule 26(b) of the Federal Rules of Civil procedure, is an order enjoining discovery to protect the litigant's right to a fair criminal trial. The remedy of a stay of civil proceedings was suggested by the Supreme Court in *United States v. Kordel*, 397 U.S. at 9 (1970).

The party seeking a stay bears the burden of persuading the court that a stay should be granted under the particular circumstances of the case. The court must balance the criminal defendant's right to a fair trial against the right of a civil litigant to pursue a valid claim. Courts have both granted and denied stays and imposed stays conditioned upon events in the criminal case. Where the criminal defendant faces a substantial risk to his right to a fair trial, courts impose stay orders to protect his rights. But the stay will not go beyond what is necessary for that purpose. The civil litigant may ordinarily pursue the other aspects of his claim and is denied access only to the protected materials and only for a period necessary to protect the rights of the criminal defendant.

In the leading case of *Wehling v. Columbia Broadcasting System*, 608 F.2d 1084 (5th Cir. 1979), the plaintiff charged CBS with defamation for statements made in a news story about trade schools he operated. The plaintiff was then the subject of a grand jury investigation, having testified several times before the grand jury. When the plaintiff was asked at his deposition about the operations of the school, he invoked his Fifth Amendment privilege. The trial court dismissed the action when the plaintiff continued to assert his privilege. The Court of Appeals, however, reversed the trial court and directed entry of an order staying discovery for three years, the time remaining under the applicable criminal statute of limitations.

When the criminal proceedings are over or there is no substantial criminal exposure, the courts have denied relief. In *General Dynamics Corp. v. Selb Mfg. Co.*, 481 F.2d 1204, 1214 (8th Cir. 1973), *cert. denied*, 414 U.S. 1162 (1974), the defendant sought an indefinite stay of civil proceedings and asserted his right to resist discovery even after he had been convicted on criminal charges. He argued that the criminal matter was not terminated because a criminal appeal was pending. The court held that while the defendant's rights were substantial, further delay would jeopardize the plaintiff's rights, which had already suffered because of the death of one defendant and the departures of witnesses since the lawsuit had commenced.

If the court is not persuaded of the need for a stay, it can impose other conditions to protect the interests of the party facing criminal prosecution. In *D'Ippolito v. American Oil Co.*, 272 F. Supp. 310 (S.D.N.Y. 1967), the court refused a stay but ordered that depositions be taken under seal, preserved under seal, and not opened until completion of the parallel criminal trial.

An order sealing discovery is less satisfactory than a stay of discovery. Even when sealed, deposition testimony or answers to interrogatories can be dangerous to a person with potential criminal liability. The mere existence of that evidence may encourage litigants, private and governmental, to try to obtain it. Exactly that occurred in *Wilk v. American Medical Association*, 635 F.2d 1295 (7th Cir. 1980) and *Martindell v. ITT*, 594 F.2d 291 (2d Cir. 1979). In both instances the court protected the confidentiality of the material. But if the material were to leak out, it could be used by the prosecution in the criminal case.

A party may also invoke the power of the court where the criminal action is pending or which supervises the grand jury conducting the criminal investigation to protect against civil discovery that would jeopardize the rights of the criminal defendant. Rule 2 of the Federal Rules of Criminal Procedure provides that the rules "are intended to provide for the just determination of every criminal proceeding. They shall be construed to secure simplicity in procedure [and] fairness in administration. . . ." Supplementing Rule 2's broad charter is Rule 57(b), which provides, "If no procedure is specifically prescribed by rule, the court may proceed in any lawful manner not inconsistent with these rules or with any applicable statute." The district court also has inherent supervisory power over the administration of criminal justice. *McNabb v. United States*, 318 U.S. 332, 340 (1943).

There has been little litigation in this area. One court has held that Rules 2 and 57(b) and the inherent supervisory power authorize the criminal court to issue protective orders binding upon the parties as well as persons who are not party to the criminal action. *United States v. Simon*, 262 F. Supp. at 71. In *United States v. Birrell*, 276 F. Supp. 798 (S.D.N.Y. 1967), the district court noted that it had both the inherent power to supervise the administration of criminal justice and power under Rule 57(b) to enjoin civil proceedings involving the same facts as were involved in a criminal prosecution pending before the court. But it declined to exercise its power, because the evidence in the civil plaintiff's hands had already been the subject of a suppression order in the criminal case and thus could not harm the criminal defendant.

But protection from the criminal forum may be limited. Although a court supervising an investigative grand jury has inherent power to ensure fairness in the grand jury proceeding, it is unlikely that a party seeking protection against civil discovery could persuade a supervising court to intervene prior to an indictment.

Also, one court has urged that the preferable forum for remedial relief is the court where the civil case is pending, and that "it is only in exceptional circumstances that the district court in which the criminal case is pending should enjoin the taking of such a deposition." *D'Ippolito v. American Oil Co.*, 272 F. Supp. 310 (S.D.N.Y. 1967) (quoting *United States v. Simon*, 373 F.2d 649, 653 (2d Cir. 1967), *cert. granted sub nom. Simon v. Wharton*, 386 U. S. 1030 (1967)). But that proposition has not been developed further.

Parties who are the targets of criminal actions are not the only ones who may seek protective orders to prevent civil discovery from being used in criminal proceedings. The government too can seek a stay when a criminal defendant attempts to use the liberal civil discovery rules in a parallel civil action to avoid the severe limitations of criminal discovery.

In *Campbell v. Eastland*, 307 F.2d 478, 487 (5th Cir. 1962), *cert. denied*, 371 U.S. 955 (1963), a civil plaintiff seeking a refund against the Commissioner of Internal Revenue sought production of the IRS criminal investigative files. The court held that the trial court should review such requests to determine the effect civil discovery would have on a criminal proceeding that is pending or just about to be brought and if a party would gain an advantage in the criminal case by utilization of civil discovery, a stay should be ordered. The court stressed the importance of maintaining the integrity of the differing rules governing discovery in criminal and civil cases.

In *United States v. Mellon Bank N.A.*, 545 F.2d 869, 873 (3d Cir. 1976), the court granted a stay order to protect the government against the defendant's use of civil discovery to inquire into the government's evidence in a criminal case involving the same facts as the civil case.

A criminal investigation or prosecution of the opposing party in a civil suit does not produce only obstacles. The materials gathered by the investigative agency or the grand jury can be a rich resource for the civil litigant.

That is not to say that obtaining these materials is easy. Federal Rule of Criminal Procedure 6(e)(1) provides that matters occurring before a grand jury are to be secret and violations of secrecy are punishable by contempt. A private litigant seeking to obtain grand jury materials must demonstrate a "particularized, more discreet showing of need" to overcome the policy favoring grand jury secrecy. *United States v. Proctor & Gamble Co.*, 356 U.S. 677, 683 (1958).

There is a three-pronged test for determining whether that secrecy may be broken: "Parties seeking grand jury transcripts under Rule 6(e) must show that the material they seek is needed to avoid a possible injustice in another judicial proceeding, that the need for disclosure is greater than the need for continued secrecy, and that their request is structured to cover only materials so needed." *Douglas Oil Co. v. Petrol Stops Northwest*, 441 U.S. 211 at 222 (1979). When the criminal case has terminated and the grand jury material would not compromise the interests of innocent third parties, courts tend to grant Rule 6(e) orders to civil litigants able to show a need.

The authority for obtaining information from federal agencies, including criminal investigative files, is the Freedom of Information Act. The Act mandates disclosure of "agency records" to "any person" upon request (5 U.S.C. § 552(a) (3)), subject to certain statutory exemptions. Exemption No. 7 exempts from disclosure investigative records compiled for law enforcement purposes if disclosure would result in harm. To resist discovery, the government must show "that disclosure would either constitute an unwarranted invasion of personal privacy or disclose the identity of a confidential source. Unwarranted, in this context, means without justification or adequate reason." *Philadelphia Newspapers, Inc. v. U.S. Dep't. of Justice*, 405 F. Supp. 8, 12 (E.D. Pa. 1975). Where the criminal investigation has terminated and no privacy interests are implicated, criminal investigative materials should be provided under the Act.

When you seek information under the Freedom of Information Act, you may face serious resistance from the government. Resistance must be overcome by independent litigation. Nonetheless, as government investigative resources are almost always considerably greater than those of private litigants, the use of the Act to discover the government's investigative files is a device that deserves more attention. 14 AM. CRIM. L. REV. 73 (1976).

The greatest benefit in a civil case is the conviction of your opponent in a parallel criminal case. The conviction can even be dispositive of the civil litigation. The defendant may be collaterally estopped from retrying issues in a subsequent civil action if he had the opportunity to litigate those issues in the criminal case. That result has been most common in antitrust litigation, *United States v. National Association of Real Estate Boards*, 339 U.S. 485 (1950), but also has been applied to patent infringement actions. *Blonder-Tongue Laboratories, Inc. v. University of Illinois Foundation*, 402 U.S. 313 (1971), mail fraud, *United States v. Frank*, 494 F.2d 145, 160 (2d Cir. 1974), *cert. denied*, 419 U.S. 828 (1975), and RICO, *Anderson v. Javonich*, 543 F. Supp. 1124 (W.D. Wash. 1982).

If your client is the one facing criminal charges, these collateral civil consequences require careful attention in plea negotiations. Do your best to negotiate a plea to *limit* the defendant's civil exposure (negotiating on charges) or to *avoid* collateral liability (negotiating a nolo contendre plea).

Rule 37:
Sanctions for
Discovery Resistance

by David J. Krupp

Unjustified resistance to discovery increases the cost of legal services, delays the resolution of disputes, thwarts the purpose of discovery, and adds to the burdens of an overworked judiciary. As a result, judges seek to avoid discovery disputes by imposing sanctions, including dismissal and default, under Rule 37 of the Federal Rules of Civil Procedure.

National Hockey League v. Metropolitan Hockey Club, Inc., 427 U.S. 639 (1976), provides the impetus for more frequent use of sanctions to control discovery abuse. The plaintiff failed to answer crucial interrogatories over a seventeen-month period. Numerous warnings from the court went unheeded. The trial court finally dismissed the complaint, finding "flagrant bad faith" and a "callous disregard of responsibilities counsel owe to the Court and to their opponents."

The Supreme Court held that the trial court acted within its discretion in dismissing the complaint. It noted that severe sanctions were necessary, not only to penalize wrongdoers, but "to deter those who might be tempted to such conduct."

National Hockey League raises numerous questions. Does the record justify a particular sanction? Does withholding the information prejudice the party seeking it? Is disobedience to a court order an indispensable prerequisite to sanctions? What kind of record is necessary to sustain the imposition of any sanctions?

Rule 37 is deceptively simple. Rule 37(a) permits a party to obtain an order compelling a responding party to respond to a discovery request. Rule 37(b) authorizes such orders "as are just" for disobedience to a discovery order: establishment of facts, preclusion, the striking of pleadings in whole or in part, the staying of proceedings until there has been

---

The author practices law in Chicago.

compliance, dismissal, default, contempt and the imposition of costs, including attorneys' fees. Rule 37(d) provides that where there has been a total failure to respond to a proper discovery request, the court may impose any of the sanctions except contempt which is authorized only in cases of disobedience to a court order.

The overall framework of Rule 37 provides no sure guidelines for determining what constitutes a proper sanction. The question on appeal is one of abuse of discretion. But, the party seeking sanctions must make a record in the trial court that will support the sanctions.

In most instances, given the standard for review, protecting a given sanction on appeal will not be a heavy burden. The real problem is: How do you get a district judge to treat discovery resistance seriously and order sanctions?

The first step is to make certain your discovery request is clear, intelligible, seeks relevant information, and is not abusive, overreaching, untimely or otherwise objectionable. In most districts you may ask the other party in an interrogatory to state "all facts which support [his or her] contention that. . . ." Be careful not to use terms in your question that are so broad or vague that your adversary is compelled to speculate as to their meaning. In *Heritage Furniture, Inc. v. American Heritage, Inc.*, 28 F.R.D. 319 (D. Conn. 1961), the court held a reference in interrogatories to "early American furniture" to be "so indefinite and lacking in precision as to render them not susceptible of being intelligently answered."

Similarly, an interrogatory asking whether the defendant had "ever hired a white person with less experience than the men he is to supervise and placed the new white employee in charge of black employees 'of long tenure and experience' " required the defendant to draw too many opinions about too many employees. *Evans v. Local Union 2127, International Brotherhood of Electrical Workers*, 313 F. Supp. 1354, 1361 (N.D. Ga. 1969). A court compelled to "reconstruct" interrogatories to find them valid will usually deny costs to the party seeking discovery. *Ballard v. Allegheny Airlines, Inc.*, 54 F.R.D. 67, 70 (E.D. Pa. 1972).

Costs were denied in *In re Folding Carton Antitrust Litigation*, 83 F.R.D. 132 (N.D. Ill. 1979), where the court compelled some answers to deposition questions but found many questions had "lacked clarity and precision to the point of being misleading and argumentative." The court similarly refused to compel answers to questions that required a study and comparison of documents or asked a witness to testify about documents he had not seen prior to the deposition.

Objections to discovery must be timely or they are waived. Courts may nevertheless refuse to impose sanctions if the discovery sought is irrelevant or patently improper, even though the party resisting discovery failed to interpose a timely objection. *Shenker v. Sportelli*, 28 Fed. R. Serv. 2d 344 (E.D. Pa. 1979); *Williams v. Krieger*. 61 F.R.D. 142 (S.D.N.Y. 1973).

The second step is to demonstrate your own diligence by making follow-up demands *in writing* when your adversary is dilatory or evasive. A trial court is much less likely to be impressed by the adversary's allegation of "he said he didn't need that information" or "he agreed to wait until I finished my trial in another case," if the lawyer seeking sanctions shows that the discovery resister ignored repeated written demands for compliance.

The third step is to demonstrate that the discovery resistance has added to the costs of prosecution or defense, impeded trial preparation and otherwise prejudiced your client. Judges do not like to superintend discovery. You must give them reasons to become involved.

Until your adversary gives you the names of persons having knowledge of facts in issue, you cannot determine who must be interviewed or deposed. Without access to the other side's documents it is nearly impossible to take an effective deposition in business or property-related disputes. Unless your adversary supplies relevant information in the possession of his client, you may be compelled to involve third parties in the discovery process at great and needless expense. Groundless claims of privilege should not be used to shield material documents. Most judges, themselves former litigators, readily empathize with factors like these.

You must also comply with local rules that decree that no discovery motion will be entertained unless counsel advises the court in writing that "after personal consultation and sincere attempts to resolve differences" the parties are unable to reach an accord. *E.g.,* General Rule 12(d), (N.D. Ill.). This requirement is sometimes overlooked where the record shows that a conference would be futile, *Coates v. Johnson and Johnson,* 85 F.R.D. 731 (N.D. Ill. 1980), but in most instances it is an indispensable prerequisite to obtaining a hearing.

Finally, do not overreach in seeking sanctions. If all you are complaining about is a refusal to answer questions on one narrow issue or a failure to produce an expert's report, the court is unlikely to do more than strike part of a pleading, hold certain facts to be established, or preclude your opponent from using the expert as a witness. It probably will not dismiss or grant a default judgment. Unless you are able to suggest a sanction that is sensible under the circumstances, the judge may not bother to tailor one for you. The order may simply grant you costs on the motion and give your adversary an admonitory slap on the wrist.

Rule 37(a) affirmatively requires that the court award a successful movant his "reasonable expenses incurred in obtaining the order, including attorney's fees, unless the court finds that the opposition to the motion was substantially justified or that other circumstances make an award of expenses unjust." Some judges ignore the rule. Others assess an arbitrary amount that fails to compensate the moving party for actual expenses incurred. Fortunately, that view is changing. Judges are increasingly granting meaningful expenses for Rule 37(a) motions as well as the extreme sanctions available for motions brought under Rule 37(b) and (d).

Rule 37(f) does not permit an award of attorneys' fees against the federal government except to the extent, if any, permitted by statute. The courts do have the power to assess expenses and fees against a government lawyer personally and will do so in an egregious case. *United States v. Sumitomo Marine & Fire Ins. Co.*, 617 F.2d 1365, 1371 (9th Cir. 1980). *Compare E.E.O. C. v. Kenosha Unified School District No. 1*, 620 F.2d 1220, 1226–27 (7th Cir. 1980) (unless the government attorney has acted in bad faith, he will be entitled to reimbursement from the United States, and assessments against the government require explicit statutory authorization).

A trial judge's inherent power to prevent a fraud on the court may also justify expenses and attorneys' fees, not just for a sanctions motion, but for the defense of the entire action. *Roadway Express, Inc. v. Piper*, 447 U.S. 752 (1980); 28 U.S.C. § 1927. Few cases will warrant the imposition of attorneys' fees as an item of costs. But in cases involving bad faith and an attempt either to press a totally false claim or to inflate a minor one to enormous proportions, consider the possibility of obtaining reimbursement for the entire defense under the inherent power doctrine.

When is dismissal or default appropriate? These sanctions are generally ordered only when lawyers or parties act willfully, in bad faith, or with gross negligence. Parties choose lawyers and if their lawyers, through gross negligence or otherwise, engage in dilatory and obstructive tactics during discovery, their claim may be lawfully extinguished. *Cine Forty-Second Street Theatre Corp. v. Allied Artists Pictures Corp.*, 602 F.2d 1062, 1067 (2d Cir. 1979).

Dismissal is appropriate where the plaintiffs first deny the existence of documents and later attempt to explain their failure to comply by placing a strained construction on the language of an order requiring production. *G-K Properties v. Redevelopment Agency of San Jose*, 577 F.2d 645 (9th Cir. 1978). A "last-minute tender" of documents will not defeat dismissal. *Id.* at 647.

Class action plaintiffs have been dismissed for refusing to appear for depositions despite the absence of a prior order requiring them to appear where they previously failed to obey court orders requiring answers to interrogatories. The court relied upon the deterrence concept and noted a course of conduct that frustrated the fundamental purpose of the discovery rules. *Al Barnett & Son, Inc. v. Outboard Marine Corp.*, 611 F.2d 32, 36 (3d Cir. 1979). Another court affirmed a default judgment where the defendants repeatedly refused to produce documents, attend depositions, or answer interrogatories. *Haskins v. Lister*, 626 F.2d 42 (8th Cir. 1980).

Rule 37 contains a curious gap with respect to the discovery resistor who answers a request, but does so falsely. Rule 37(d) clearly authorizes dismissal against a party who fails to answer or gives an incomplete answer. "An evasive or incomplete answer is to be treated as a failure to answer." Rule 37(a)(3).

If your adversary answers, but does so falsely, sanctions generally have not been imposed. The problem is that a motion for sanctions under Rule 37(b)(2) lies only for violation of an order. In addition, *Societe Internationale v. Rogers*, 357 U.S. 197 (1958), holds that Rule 37 is the exclusive source of power to dismiss a complaint for noncompliance with an order to produce. However, the lawyer or party who lies by falsely denying, for example, the existence of relevant documents may prejudice the opposing party and frustrate justice at least as severely as the lawyer who fails to answer interrogatories.

A few courts have begun to rely upon the court's inherent power to avoid the illogic of failing to punish fake responses. In *Dependahl v. Falstaff Brewing Corp.*, 84 F.R.D. 416, 419 (E.D. Mo. 1979), *aff'd*, 653 F.2d 1208 (8th Cir. 1981), *cert. denied*, 454 U.S. 968 (1982), the court struck affirmative defenses and counterclaims as a sanction for the filing of evasive and incomplete answers even though there was no order outstanding to compel answers to interrogatories. Dismissal may also be ordered to redress a fraud upon the court. *Israel Aircraft Ind., Ltd. v. Standard Precision*, 559 F.2d 203 (2d Cir. 1977).

A trial court must clearly state its reasons for imposing sanctions. *Wilson v. Volkswagen of America, Inc.*, 561 F.2d 494, 505 (4th Cir. 1977), *cert. denied*, 434 U.S. 1020 (1978). *Wilson* and several other decisions of the Courts of Appeals for the Fourth Circuit and the District of Columbia also stress that where the sanction is dismissal or default, the reviewing court should carefully review the underlying discovery violation to make certain that the discovery withheld prejudiced the other side's case. Other courts of appeals appear to be more interested in the deterrence aspects of sanctions rather than in making the punishment fit the crime. *Compare Independent Investor Protective League v. Touche Ross & Co.*, 607 F.2d 530, 534 n.5 (2d Cir.), *cert denied*, 439 U.S. 895 (1978).

Discovery abuse has two aspects: excessive discovery and unjustified resistance to proper discovery. It is exceedingly difficult to legislate or make effective rules against overkill. Who is to say that two depositions or ten are excessive in the context of a given action? A case involving a relatively small amount may be very important to either of the parties because of its potential as precedent.

The answer to overdiscovery may be to provide that no party shall take more than "X" depositions except for good cause shown. That would require increased judicial supervision of the pretrial process and is unlikely to be welcomed by the bench.

Meanwhile, the remedies for discovery resistance are relatively clearcut and are being granted with increasing frequency. By pursuing those remedies in appropriate cases, we can spare our clients some of the expense associated with discovery abuse.

Pretrial Development in Major Corporate Litigation

by Edwin J. Wesely

My assumption in this article is that you have become involved in a big case and there is no easy way out. You have explained your future unavailability to your partners and you have lined up the associates, paraprofessionals and outside consultants who will help you. Most important of all, you have warned your family that you are at it again and to count you out of their lives in the foreseeable future, except for ceremonial occasions and family crises.

As we all know, the end of the road in the big case is frequently a negotiated peace, and occasionally a particular pre-trial skirmish may be geared to potential settlement. Nevertheless, it is essential that you plan and prepare fully for trial, and much, if not virtually all, of what must be done to prepare for trial is indispensable in the evaluation or proposal of the terms of settlement.

Your starting point is to know about your client everything there is to know that bears upon the litigation. One of your partners may be peculiarly knowledgeable in the affairs of the client, and he certainly is a primary source of information. So is the corporation's inside general counsel. In the lay management of the company, however, there may be executives who believe that what you think is germane is not really germane. When you encounter that attitude, the role of inside general counsel is critical. He must interpret your needs and desires to the top management and ensure their total support and cooperation. However, you and your staff bear the ultimate responsibility for learning everything the other side might know or come to know.

You may be dealing with a catastrophic situation for your client. For

Mr. Wesely is a member of the New York City firm of Winthrop, Stimson, Putnam & Roberts. Mr. Wesely acknowledges with appreciation the assistance of Eloise Morgan in preparing this article.

example, the reasonably based claims asserted against it may aggregate much more than the net worth of the company. In such a situation, it is frequently essential to restructure the management to meet the exigencies of the litigation. The litigation is the most important business of the corporation at that time, and it must be flexible enough to deal with it on that basis.

You must, therefore, establish a clear line of communication between you, the chief litigator, and the corporate executive designated to have principal corporate responsibility in the matter. There must be a similar liaison between your staff and the corporate legal and nonlegal staff. Where the magnitude of the case calls for it, you might also set up within the client a unit solely responsible for the case to deal exclusively with you and your staff. Complete and easy access to the client is crucial for prompt decisions on a variety of matters, ranging from the very important to the routine.

In major corporate litigation that lasts for months or years, an essential quality of the chief litigating counsel is that he be reasonable, not only in his relationships with the court but also in his relationships with his adversaries. I am not referring merely to an appearance of reasonableness—only the real thing will be effective over the long run.

Most lawyers will probably agree that reasonableness is an essential attribute of the litigator in his relationships with the court, particularly on pretrial discovery matters. But the litigator has considerably more exposure to his adversaries than to the court. Reasonableness, therefore, must be more than a courtroom stance.

An attitude of reasonableness is particularly important during pretrial discovery. Much of the litigator's time will be spent negotiating with his adversaries to work out the scope of document production and interrogatories and the conduct of depositions. Discovery applications, even in complex and protracted cases, tend to irritate busy judges. Where the case has not been assigned to a single judge for all purposes, rulings on discovery motions by judges not familiar with the complexities of the case may not help either side. Finally, no one is more familiar with your case than you. You can accomplish much more for your client by seeking sensible solutions to discovery disputes with your adversaries. You will also save your time and your client's money.

You face a delicate problem when, despite your efforts, your adversary has been unreasonable on discovery matters and you are forced to seek rulings from the court. Some judges will want to know whether you have been reasonable and whether you have made significant concessions. The prudent course is to keep all matters open until the negotiations have concluded, at which point all agreements are merged into the final agreement. It is best to have a preliminary understanding with your adversary that, if you cannot come to a complete and final agreement, whatever tentative concessions you may make in the negotiations are without prejudice to the position you may take in court and no reference may be made at the hearings to such concessions.

Seeking Sanctions

Whether you should seek sanctions against your adversary for his tactics, particularly at an early stage of the litigation, depends on the circumstances. Your client's interests usually are better served by obtaining substantive relief rather than sanctions against your adversary. A judge who believes a lawyer is abusing the discovery process is more likely to terminate or significantly limit the lawyer's discovery than to impose sanction.

The litigator will often find that pressure to force him to retreat from a position of reasonableness will come from his client. The reaction of a client who has been inundated by what he considers to be onerous and unduly expensive discovery requests from the other side will frequently be to encourage his attorney to retaliate in kind. The attorney who succumbs to those pressures may find that he has a satisfied client during the pendency of the litigation but that he has lost the leverage that a posture of reasonableness gives him with his adversary in long-term litigation. In the end, the client may be the victim rather than the victor in forcing his attorney to retreat from a posture of reasonableness.

In addition to reasonableness, the litigator's credibility is an indispensable ingredient in his relations with his adversaries and the court. Obviously the lawyer's credibility is substantially enhanced by being right on the facts and sound on the law. I do not mean that you must win every issue in dispute. But each position you take should have a sound basis. For example, if your adversary believes your objections to providing certain information or documents are motivated by the desire to hide something, his attitude will harden and your ability to protect your client's important interests will be diminished. You will also cause disputes that will waste your client's money.

The effect of reasonable and credible behavior is cumulative. By the time you reach serious settlement talks or the case is ready for trial, the reputation so hard-earned in the previous months or years will bring huge dividends.

Let me turn now to some important aspects of pretrial discovery. While this article bears my by-line, I thank twenty years of colleagues, adversaries, and judges for most of the contents of this article. Much of what follows is designed to illustrate the problems of major corporate litigation. For every general statement there are frequent exceptions demanded by the circumstances of particular cases. So consider what follows as rebuttable presumptions.

Interrogatories are more often abused than used properly. Nevertheless, both sides in major corporate litigation are likely to use them extensively. They require proportionately more work and expense for the return than any other discovery device. Yet, there are issues that can be developed most effectively through interrogatories, such as identifying persons and documents and obtaining statistical data, dates of employment and financial schedules. Interrogatories will also give you the "corporate answer" which no single witness may be able or willing to provide during depositions.

Upon receiving interrogatories, you should attempt first to negotiate limits on their scope. If you are defendant's counsel, you may find that, to obtain broader discovery, the complaint has been drawn beyond the necessary elements of the claims asserted. You should study the law and determine what appropriately should have been pleaded and whether you can negotiate out certain interrogatories that go beyond reasonable limits of the asserted claims.

Even if the complaint is narrowly drawn, your opponent may have included interrogatories on a highly expansive theory of what is reasonably calculated to lead to the discovery of admissible evidence. One example is information that goes back many years. Some practitioners purposely include such interrogatories expecting to give them up in later negotiations. They also want to have some interrogatories to trade away if a motion is filed. Regrettably, there are still judges who rule on interrogatories by giving one to you, one to the other side, one to you, one to the other side, and so on.

There is no more laborious, time-consuming and generally unproductive job than answering interrogatories. You should not permit that process to monopolize your time. I have found it particularly effective in dealing with an adversary's interrogatories, as well as his discovery generally, to use a two-platoon system. One platoon (or person, depending on the magnitude of the case) works on the answers to interrogatories and other discovery requests of your adversary, while the other platoon prepares your discovery. It is important not to permit your opponent's thrusts and sallies in discovery to deter you from preparing your discovery and your case.

Your adversary's answers to interrogatories are rarely satisfactory. They are prepared by lawyers to avoid making significant admissions. You should seek supplemental answers if you think no other discovery device will develop the information. You should be aware that Rule 26(e) of the Federal Rules of Civil Procedure specifically requires a party to supplement responses to discovery requests. Under that provision, a party must reasonably amend a response if new information makes the previous answer incorrect.

You should ask specifically for the name of each person who participated in preparing answers to your interrogatories. Those persons are prime candidates for depositions. You should also ask for each document used in preparing each answer, even though you might have had your document discovery. If your adversary thinks such requests are unreasonably burdensome, you should negotiate. Most courts look favorably upon providing that information, particularly if sought at an early stage of the litigation.

In most major corporate lawsuits, documents are the bedrock of the litigation. Because of the many persons who participate in corporate decisions, it is very difficult for a corporation to avoid creating documents reflecting actions taken. But while various echelons of the corporate hierarchy may participate in a matter, the decision is made at only one or a few levels. What may have been "decided" at one level may not have been adopted at another, or may have been adopted after significant modification.

Document Discovery

Your request for production of documents should be issued quickly. The rest of your discovery will be largely fashioned by the information you have obtained in documentary discovery.

A useful procedure in document discovery is to notice the deposition of the other party's custodian of documents exclusively to determine the type of documents kept by that company, the organization of its files, and similar matters. The notice should limit the deposition to those precise purposes. Generally, a deposition is more effective than interrogatories for determining the scope, type, and organization of an adverse party's files. Such depositions are proper even though the same person may be called again as a witness on substantive issues. You must, however, limit this initial deposition to its intended scope. If you touch on substantive issues, you will defeat the purpose of the deposition and provide your adversary with an opportunity to terminate the examination.

If the entity from which you are trying to obtain documents is required by law or regulation to maintain certain papers (*e.g.,* a brokerage firm, bank, or insurance company), your request should track the language of the specific regulation requiring those documents to be maintained.

Specify in your notice or subpoena that, if any documents are withheld pursuant to a claim of privilege, each document withheld and the privilege asserted must be identified. You should give formal notice that you expect those documents to be segregated for later judicial determination of the privilege.

You should consider working out an agreement with your adversary on privileged and work-product documents. As document discovery expands, inadvertent errors can occur even when the greatest care is exercised. You will want to ensure that, if a privileged document inadvertently slips through your document screening procedures, you have not waived the privilege. Most of the problems arising from the disclosure of privileged documents arise not from what the documents reveal, but from opening the entire subject matter raised in the disclosed documents. When both sides know they will be producing a large volume of documents, it should be possible to obtain a stipulation that privileged documents inadvertently turned over shall not be considered as having been produced.

You should also try to work out a confidentiality agreement where there are documents which the client considers sensitive or confidential but which are not privileged as a matter of law. Typically such an agreement will provide that documents produced may be used only for purposes of the litigation and not for any business or other use. In addition, the agreement can limit particularly sensitive documents to the eyes of counsel only. If such an agreement cannot be reached, you can seek a protective order under Rule 26(c)(7).

One method of handling confidentiality, or relevancy, problems with a document is to mask out the portions you wish to withhold from your adversary. An example is board minutes. Ten items may be covered at the directors' meeting but only one is germane to the controversy. In such a situation, you can mask out the nine items that are not relevant. If the other side is not prepared to take your word that masked-out portions are not relevant, you may allow opposing counsel to review them to verify the lack of relevance. However, if he does not agree, or if you think it unwise to allow him to review the masked-out portions, the court can review them.

There are, of course, risks to masking out portions of documents. You must weigh against the value of keeping certain information on a document from your opponent the impact that a masked-out document will have on the trier of facts, particularly a jury, when the document is exhibited at the trial.

Ordinarily, each document inspected—not just those actually turned over or copied—should be numbered by the producing party to avoid future disputes over whether it was made available. You should also copy whatever documents your adversary copies. At a minimum you should maintain a master chronological file and additional sub-files organized by subject matter and witnesses. You will want to integrate into your subject-matter files those portions of depositions or digests or summaries of depositions that relate to that subject. Documents you think relevant, but which your adversary did not copy, should also be integrated into the files, although they should be identified separately.

You should review the documents for ''holes''—that is, for documents that refer to other documents that you have not received. You may also find that questions are raised in interoffice memoranda but not answered. These ''holes'' should be noted during your document review. Depending upon the circumstances, you may want to seek the ''missing'' documents through a demand for further production, or you may want to make the inquiry through the deposition of the authors of the documents in question. You should also be aware that corporate employees—and their secretaries—often maintain "private files," including calendars and diaries, that will not always surface in response to production requests.

While several articles treat the subject of oral depositions, I would like to offer a few general observations to supplement those articles.

In significant corporate litigation it is important to bring the decision-makers directly to the firing line through depositions. Among other things, this facilitates ultimate settlement. Such depositions also permit you to take advantage of an interesting phenomenon of corporate litigation. While lawyers generally prepare witnesses very thoroughly prior to depositions, the chief executive officer and his principal aides may be less than fully prepared because their time is too valuable—or they consider it too valuable—to allow their lawyers to prepare them fully. As a result, you may get more accurate, or at least more spontaneous, answers from them than from officers in middle management.

I usually stipulate with my adversary that the depositions of my client's officers will be taken at my office and his client's officers at his office. Such an arrangement is generally most convenient for everyone. It is unwise to have a deposition taken in the client's office, not only because of the immediate availability of documents that may not have been produced, but also because of the availability of other persons in the company. You may want to be in the position of refusing to call upon an available person who appears capable of resolving some matter that has stalled the examination.

Possible Abuses

The opportunity to correct the transcript of the deposition is sometimes abused. Your adversary may have his witness "correct" a portion of his testimony so that its meaning is completely changed, gambling that the change will not occasion further examination by you. While you have the right to recall the witness, you may decide not to because of the pressure of events or other discovery. There may be more important depositions to take, or the judge may become impatient with what he considers an excessive amount of discovery. In any event, you can cross-examine the witness at trial on the changes made in his original testimony and invite the trier of facts to draw the appropriate conclusion.

Whether deposition transcripts should be filed depends on the status of the case. If you expect to rely on the transcript to support a motion for summary judgment, you should file it. If it appears that a settlement is possible, the transcript probably should not be filed. Some settlements provide for the return of all copies of the transcript to the party whose deposition has been taken so that it does not become public. Obviously, this purpose would be defeated if the transcript had been filed with the court.

It is often desirable to ask an adverse witness questions that elicit narrative answers. You should always remember that you are conducting a deposition to obtain admissions and information. A deposition is not a trial. If you limit yourself solely to specific matters suggested by the documents or other evidence you have, you may never obtain information not previously known to you and that can be elicited only by general questions. It is also desirable to get that information out as early as possible.

One very important function of a deposition is to "freeze" the witness's story. Achieving this result is particularly important when oral representations or other verbal statements are at issue. To "freeze" the story, you must cover every relevant moment and event. After you have the general story, turn to those specific conversations and events suggested by documents or other information you have. You should then ask about any conversations within specific, relatively short periods of time until all possible oral statements have been covered. This approach will minimize the possibility that the witness will recall a conversation at trial which "you never asked me about."

You should attempt to stipulate with your adversary for the return of the witness on a subsequent day after you have had an opportunity to review the transcript. If the day is coming to an end and you are at the end of your questions, such a stipulation is preferable to stringing out your questioning to carry the deposition over to another day. If your adversary will not so stipulate, however, you should pull out another file of documents and begin questioning the witness about them one by one.

In simple cases it is desirable, and in complex cases it is essential, to have the transcripts of depositions indexed by subject matter. In addition, there should be a master index by subject matter of all depositions that have been taken in the litigation with appropriate cross-references. Generally summaries and digests of deposition testimony are useful only for persons not directly involved. The lawyer on the firing line should review the Q. and A. so that he has the flavor of the examination and the full picture. In the preparation of indices, summaries, and digests, paraprofessionals can be helpful both in terms of efficiency and of keeping the costs of the litigation within reasonable limits.

In preparing your client for his deposition, you should be mindful of one possible pitfall that is a matter of some controversy. Some judges take the view that any document your client uses to refresh his recollection during the course of your private preparation must be produced if your opponent asks for it. You must guide the preparation of your own client accordingly. I will show my client only documents that have already been produced or other documents which, if called for by my adversary, would not be troublesome. The production requirement also applies to documents that are created for the purpose of aiding the witness's recollection, such as a chronology of events. If your client has that

137

chronology in front of him while he is testifying at the deposition, you can expect that your adversary will want access to it.

You should exercise great care in permitting others to participate in or be present during the preparation of your client. I generally believe you should prepare your witnesses separately, even though group preparation might sometimes be more efficient and less costly. In commercial cases at least, we may be reaching the point where the traditional resistance to group preparation should yield to the economies involved. However, individual preparation does avoid the argument by your adversary that the witnesses cooked up their testimony together to avoid inconsistencies or embarrassment to each other.

When the chief executive officer or other key person of your client is being deposed, you must consider issues beyond the deposition. For example, if what you are seeking is a settlement, you might permit your adversary rather free rein in his examination, perhaps even beyond what is ordinarily permitted. The president of the opposing company is likely to read the testimony of the president of your client, and you want the other side to believe that nothing was being held back. Particularly for lay people, information is more believable if it is obtained by their own lawyer's examination in the context of an adversary relationship than if it is developed during your examination.

If you are planning to move for summary judgment you will want to develop the evidence you expect to use for the motion during your client's deposition. While you can supplement the deposition with an affidavit, your adversary cannot argue that he did not have an opportunity to cross-examine on the matter if the information surfaced during the deposition.

Whether the examiner should try to obtain the trust of the witness he is examining or should try to dominate the witness is a matter of some dispute. Except when a disgruntled employee or an employee who tries to make himself look good at another's expense is being deposed, I think the approach you take to an adverse witness makes little difference. Such witnesses usually are well prepared and they view the examiner as their natural enemy.

However, the issue is of considerable importance with respect to third-party witnesses. There the examiner should strive to obtain the trust of the witness. The curse of the examiner is the answer, "I don't recall." But this is also the easiest truthful way out for the third-party witness, who has no motivation to do the homework necessary to refresh his recollection. In my view, a third-party witness is most likely to cooperate with the examiner if the witness has been treated courteously, if proper consideration has been given to his convenience, and if he understands that the examiner is a professional who is simply trying to ascertain the facts in the most skillful and expeditious way possible.

The rights of the attorney for the third-party witness are also the subject of considerable controversy. Some judges give the lawyer for such a witness virtually the same latitude for objections as the lawyer for the adverse party. Other judges appear to believe that the attorney for the third-party witness can raise only Fifth Amendment objections. That latter position is rather extreme. But even in that situation, the lawyer for the third-party witness can object to clarify the record and thus influence, if not control, the direction of the witness's testimony. There are instances where the independent rights of the third-party witness can be seriously jeopardized by his answering questions, such as where they would lead to the disclosure of the witness's confidential proprietary information. In those circumstances, the lawyer for the third-party witness must object and direct the witness not to answer.

The lawyer for the adverse party does not have the power to direct a third-party witness not to answer a question since the witness is not his client. He can, however, suggest that the witness need not answer the question. If there is a friendly relationship between the adverse party and the witness, the witness's lawyer may direct him not to answer. If he does not, your adversary's suggestion is not controlling on the witness and you should pursue your question immediately.

Little Attention

Judges are aware that some authority can be found somewhere to support almost any conceivable position on a discovery dispute. My experience is that judges pay little attention to prior opinions, except their own (and not always those) and those of judges they admire. You must know your judge's attitude, for he is the law on virtually every discovery issue. What will usually decide a discovery dispute is the essential reasonableness and equity of your position.

While the federal courts frown on the appointment of masters, some state courts increasingly are resorting to masters to facilitate and accelerate discovery. In the Southern District of New York and in some other federal districts, discovery matters are decided by a magistrate even though the case has been assigned to a specific judge. You can, of course, ask the judge to review the magistrate's decisions, but seeking that review can be a delicate exercise. You must be aware of the attitude of both the judge and the magistrate and understand the tensions created by their relationship.

Some discovery rulings are subject to appellate review. For example, questions relating to attorney-client privilege sometimes can be reviewed under the doctrine of *Cohen v. Beneficial Industrial Loan Corp.*, 337 U.S. 541 (1949). In addition, where an appeal does not lie under the *Cohen* doctrine, the Second Circuit, either on its own motion or pursuant to the suggestion of counsel, has treated the appeal as a petition for a writ of mandamus and reviewed it accordingly. *Industrial Prod. Corp. v. Koons*, 325 F.2d 403 (2d Cir. 1963). Many state courts provide a

139

broader scope of appellate review of discovery orders than the federal courts.

Why bother with the strains and tensions of the big case and the monopolizing effect it has on your time? Probably the principal satisfaction of the big case comes from being one of that rare—and perhaps crazy—breed willing to put up with significant sacrifices and demands in return for the intense excitement and satisfaction of being in the middle of a super-struggle.

Litigating the big case is the ultimate in civilized warfare. It is warfare—strategy and tactics are at least as important as the law and the facts. It is civilized—there is a resolution short of bloodshed and short of medieval trial by combat. Conducted the way it should be, the big case is also civil—with the camaraderie among colleagues gained through shared experiences in a hard-fought battle and the respect, if not friendship, of and for old foes and wise judges.

Informal Witness Investigation

by Brian Goodwin

Informal investigation is one way to learn the facts of a case. Sometimes it is the only way.

This was true when I assisted at an administrative hearing early in my career. The issue was whether our client, a large corporation that I will call Bosco Company, should be allowed to retain a multimillion dollar franchise to conduct a regulated business.

The state had ordered a hearing on whether the franchise should be canceled because Bosco Company's owners were allegedly morally unfit to conduct the business. There was no opportunity for any formal discovery.

The state began by introducing certain documents. Then, without warning, the attorney general called a state police investigator to the stand.

Suddenly a live witness was testifying to a recent meeting with a lawyer I will call Lake. According to the investigator, Lake had told him that some 20 years ago, he had bribed the governor at the direction of former officers of Bosco Company. Since Lake represented Bosco when the bribe allegedly took place, his confession to the police investigator was allowed in evidence as an admission of a party's agent.

In a confident but respectful tone, the investigator described his meeting with Lake. In exquisite detail, he outlined their conversation. If the hearing officers believed the investigator's story, Bosco Company's franchise was as good as gone.

When the prosecutor finished examining the police officer, I looked at the faces of the agency members. Their serene stares told the whole story. I shut my eyes and began listing the procedural issues we would argue on appeal.

The author is a member of the Phoenix law firm Lewis and Roca.

But the lead counsel, Alston Jennings of Little Rock, Arkansas, had something else in mind.

Jennings stood up and asked for a recess before beginning his cross-examination of the investigator. The members conferred and agreed that it would be a good time to adjourn for lunch.

Jennings's tasks seemed impossible. He was faced with cross-examining a handsome, articulate, and apparently thorough police investigator about out-of-court statements of a witness Jennings had never met. It was hard to imagine the police officer being anything but upright and honest. But Jennings had a hunch about Lake.

Jennings marshalled his trial team: his secretary, an employee of Bosco, and me. Jennings told us to call Lake's office, Bosco employees who had worked with Lake 20 years earlier, and anyone else we could find in the next hour who might know something about Lake. He also told us to find out about the club where Lake met the investigator.

Lake's secretary said she could not put Lake on the phone because he was not in his office. No, she could not tell us when Lake would return. She could not do this, she finally admitted, because she had not heard from Lake in five days.

Former friends and coworkers were helpful, too. When our team of three reported back to Jennings, we had pieced together a reliable picture of Lake. We reported that Lake was no longer actively practicing law, his appearance was disheveled, and he had a drinking problem.

When the hearing reconvened, Jennings was ready to cross-examine the police investigator.

Jennings began by getting the state investigator to admit that the "club" where the meeting took place was in fact a bar in a run-down section of town. Without ever having seen Lake, Jennings felt pretty sure that the investigator would admit, as he did, that Lake was unshaven, his clothes were wrinkled, and that in their brief time together he had had several drinks of straight whiskey. The investigator looked as if he thought he had been caught interviewing Lake.

When Jennings was done, the investigator had discredited Lake's testimony, and he knew it. In frustration he said, "You're trying to get me to describe Lake as a skid row bum." Jennings pressed further, and the investigator responded, "He was a cut above that." The faces of the agency members showed it—the out-of-court declarant had been thoroughly discredited.

The Lake investigation shows one way that talking to witnesses informally can be effective. There are others. Lawyers schooled in the rules of civil procedure sometimes forget them.

Normally what you learn from informal discovery need not be shared with your opponent. Of course, there are limits to the work-product doctrine, but generally the evidence that you, your staff, and your outside investigators gather in anticipation of trial is not discoverable.

Often, it is a strategic advantage to learn about evidence before your opponent does. Every time you send out a document request or subpoena a witness, you reveal something about your view of the case. Informal discovery allows you to keep some secrets and delay giving others away.

Informal discovery lets you put the witness at ease. We all know people who become intimidated by subpoenas and the formalities of a deposition. That nervousness may make the witness tight-lipped and uncooperative. It is hard to imagine Lake's secretary telling us her impressions of Lake's failure to keep on top of his legal practice and his drinking problems in a formal deposition with a lawyer at her side.

If a witness's story is helpful, you may want to preserve it by getting the witness to sign a statement or to testify at a formal deposition. Obviously, a deposition discloses the witness's story to your adversary. The statement you obtain after suit is filed, however, generally is not discoverable. Fed. R. Civ. P. 26(b)3. If the story is harmful, you will not get a statement, but having heard the story informally will prepare you for the witness's adverse testimony at trial. Learning the information ahead of time also will give you a more realistic appreciation of your client's position.

Even when a witness's testimony will be formally preserved, meeting with the witness informally beforehand can be helpful. If the witness is friendly, you may be able to build up his confidence or refresh his recollection. If he is hostile, you may be able to soften his anger.

Although formal discovery is sometimes the best way to commit a witness to a position, informal investigation has its advantages here, too. There can be no more effective impeachment of the nonparty witness whose testimony is critical and fairly simple than confrontation with a signed statement that the witness has long since forgotten.

Once you have decided to use informal investigation, which witnesses do you interview?

First, rule out the witnesses whom you should not contact without notice to your opponent. They are: the opposing party, unless he has appeared pro se; your opponent's experts (see Fed. R. Civ. P. 26(b)(3) and 35(b)); and employees of the opposing party. Persons in a privileged relationship with the opposing party, such as doctors, clergymen, and lawyers, ordinarily will not make themselves available to you without your opponent's consent, although you may be able to compel your opponent to consent to such an interview. See, for example, *Stempler v. Speidell*, 100 N.J. 368, 495 A.2d 857 (1985).

When the opposing party is a corporation, it is best to assume that the "no contact" rule applies to all employees, not just to key employees.

Rule 801(d)(2)(D) of the Federal Rules of Evidence treats as admissible against a party "a statement by his agent or *servant* concerning a matter within the scope of his agency or *employment* made during the existence of the relationship . . . " [emphasis added].

If a statement by any mere "servant" of a party can be admitted against that party, it follows that a lawyer for the employer's adversary should not contact that employee.

Yet there is support for the view that the prohibition should be narrower. The ABA's legal background memorandum to proposed Model Rule 4.2 of Professional Conduct says: "Where the opposing party is a corporation . . . an officer or other employee with the authority to commit the corporation is considered a 'party' for purposes of ABA's Model Code DR 7-104(A)(1), and presumably ABA Model Rule 4.2."

The comment to Rule 4.2 also would imply that the line should be drawn at a true agent, someone whose actions or words bind the adverse company. The comment says:

> In the case of an organization, the Rule prohibits communications by a lawyer for one party concerning the matter in representation with persons having a managerial responsibility on behalf of the organization, and with any other persons whose act or omission in connection with that matter may be imputed to the organization for purposes of civil or criminal liability or whose statement may constitute an admission on the part of the organization.

Despite this interpretation, it is safer to assume that all employees of your adversary are not proper subjects for informal discovery.

Once you have ruled out the people you cannot contact, think of witnesses you can contact who are likely to be helpful to your client. They include your opponent's ex-spouse, a disgruntled former employee, neighbors or coworkers who are not close friends, and officers ousted from control of a corporate adversary.

Having decided to contact a witness informally, you need to decide how to make the approach. Should you talk on the telephone or in person? Ordinarily, you should use the phone only to make a preliminary contact and to decide what kind of a meeting would make the person comfortable.

Be candid. You must say that you are a lawyer for a party to a lawsuit. Once you do that, most witnesses are on guard. Try to reassure the witness and anticipate his expectations, so that there are no surprises down the road. But do not mislead the witness into believing that if he meets with you he will not be bothered again. Some prospective witnesses are happy to be helpful and will agree to meet under any circumstances. Others resent the intrusion, and you must be careful to conserve their time and be as helpful as possible.

Pick a meeting place that you think will be comfortable for the person you are interviewing. A few people will enjoy coming to your office; others would be more comfortable in their own homes. Be accommodating. That way you are more likely to get results.

Remember that the interview you are about to conduct is not privileged. What you say to the witness and what he says to you can be repeated informally or in court. Lawyers who forget this may get burned.

Let us assume your interview is successful. The witness not only talks to you, but he says things that are helpful. Now what?

You need to pin down the witness's favorable story.

When you do this, it is important to avoid recording unnecessary details. Witnesses often want to show off their ability at recollection. Suppose you need to know what John Jones and his competitor were saying in a specific telephone conversation about the prices they would agree to charge for their identical widgets. Jones's ex-secretary may be willing to tell you what she overheard that day about the price agreement. She may also insist on explaining that Jones talked to the competitor every day for a solid month or that she is sure Jones was wearing his only gray pinstripe suit that morning.

Resist the temptation to include all details. If the competitor was in Europe during part of the month and no long-distance record links him to Jones, the secretary's credibility will be questioned. If Jones produces a receipt from a reweaver demonstrating that the suit was being repaired on the crucial day, the secretary's testimony is worthless. Listen to the secretary and get all the details so you can come to an independent judgment about her reliability. But when it comes to recording her story, use only crucial facts that the witness must remember at trial.

The form of the statement is often dictated by the witness's attitude, comfort, and preference. To some people, asking for a signed affidavit calls into question their truthfulness. To others, tape recording an interview makes them feel that their privacy has been invaded. We often use a statement in the form of a confirming letter like this:

Dear Mr. Smith:

Thank you for meeting with me on August 5, 1987. I want to be sure I have understood correctly what you told me at that time. Please understand that, while I am defending a lawsuit brought by your neighbor Mr. Jones against my client Mr. Callahan, I am only interested in learning the truth. If this letter accurately states what you told me, please sign the original in the space below and return it to me in the enclosed self-addressed, stamped envelope. If the letter is not correct, please do not sign it, but instead call me and let me know how it can be changed to be accurate.

It is my understanding from our conversation that the following is correct: that you live at 725 Oak Street directly across the street from 724 Oak Street; that you have lived at that address for more than three years; that you were living at that address during the entire summer of 1984; that the person living across the street from you is Robert Jones; that during the summer of 1984, you often saw Mr. Jones at his home at 724 Oak Street; that for at least a few weeks during the summer of 1984, you saw Mr. Jones remove boulders from a pickup truck, carry those boulders to the side and rear of his house, and mortar the boulders together to create a fence that now exists at 724 Oak Street; that the photographs attached to this letter accurately show the fence you observed Mr. Jones build; that you never heard Mr. Jones complain of any back pain before the summer of 1984; that after the fence was completed in about July, you went across the street to compliment Mr. Jones on the fence, and he said, "Thank you, it about broke my back to build that sucker. The boulders weighed between 50 and 100 pounds."

Again, if I have misunderstood anything you told me on August 5, 1987, please do not sign this letter. If correct, however, please sign and return the original as indicated. I have enclosed an extra copy of the letter for your records. Thank you once again for your kind cooperation.

Sincerely,
John Doe, Esq.

I have read the foregoing statement, and it is completely correct.

James Smith

Telling the witness in the letter that you want the statement to be truthful and that he should correct errors helps get an accurate statement. It also makes the letter more helpful in the rare case when the witness waivers from his story on the stand and you use the letter at trial. Usually, witnesses would rather give a written statement than submit to a deposition. But not always. One crucial witness we interviewed was disappointed to learn that we only wanted a written statement. He said he was looking forward to a deposition. We did not want to share his testimony with our opponent, but did want to pin him to a story. It turned out that what the witness liked about a "deposition" was having his words taken down by a court reporter, being sworn to tell the truth, and answering questions formally "just like in court." We invited the witness to the office, where we took a sworn statement in the presence of a court reporter. Our opponent never saw that statement until he called the same person as his witness, the witness waffled at trial, and we impeached him with his sworn statement. If our opponent had taken the witness's deposition and then requested production of any inconsistent statements, under at least one court's interpretation of Rule 26, the witness's sworn statement might have been discoverable. *Klaiber v. Orzel*, 148 Ariz. 320, 714 P.2d 813 (1986).

A lawyer must decide who should approach and interview witnesses. Ideally, the lawyer who will examine the witness at trial should be the one who interviews him. When this is not possible, other lawyers, legal assistants, or private investigators can conduct witness interviews.

Some investigations are like buckshot. You may need to hit entire neighborhoods, manufacturing plants, or university campuses, interviewing hundreds of persons on the chance that one or two will know something helpful. In these sorts of investigations, the lawyer needs assistance. Tell the investigator about the case and describe what kind of witnesses might help. If the investigator finds a witness who has useful information, you can outline an appropriate affidavit or written statement.

Key witnesses should be interviewed by the lawyer. They are more likely to respond favorably, and the lawyer will be able to assess them firsthand.

Once you have signed statements, you can use them as ammunition at trial. Ironically, witnesses may be able to retract deposition testimony more convincingly than they can disavow a properly drafted informal statement. This is because a witness is more likely to be prepared to explain prior inconsistent deposition testimony. After all, a lawyer attended the deposition, and, if they have prepared properly, the lawyer and the witness have reread the deposition transcript before trial. If there are inconsistencies, the witness has had time to think about them. There are standard excuses: "With all the lawyers in the room, I was so nervous I misunderstood the question."

In contrast, consider what happens when the witness on the stand acknowledges that the written statement bears his signature; that he had a copy of it since he signed it; that he received a letter with it asking him to tell the lawyer if any changes needed to be made; that he never requested any changes; that the statement was taken in the quiet of his home; that just above his signature are the words, "I have read the foregoing statement, and it is completely correct."

It is hard to imagine a better impeachment weapon.

One kind of informal witness investigation should be used cautiously. That is surveillance, the surreptitious observation of someone.

Jurors appreciate surveillance if it works; they resent it if it fails. No one likes a snoop; on the other hand, jurors do not like being lied to. So if you are going to present the fruits of surveillance, make sure that the evidence powerfully exposes your adversary's lack of truthfulness. When surveillance works, it is devastating, but the risks of failure are substantial.

Surveillance also is expensive. Do not use it unless you have good reason to believe that a party is making a false or exaggerated claim that you can expose. Before giving the go-ahead, make sure you have evidence from reliable records or from a reliable, unbiased witness strongly suggesting that your adversary is feigning or malingering. There is an additional concern. Surveillance is discoverable in some jurisdictions. If your surveillance proves the truthfulness of your adversary's claims and the jury learns that you hired investigators to keep tabs on your honest opponent, you will incur the jury's wrath.

147

Once you decide to use surveillance, you must choose the investigator carefully. Other lawyers may help you find an investigator who is competent and who will follow your instructions with care.

Surveillance is useful only if it demonstrates your adversary's false claim vividly. Rarely is it enough to have the investigator take the stand and testify to what he saw. You will need to support his testimony with videotapes, movies, photographs, or recordings of the person being exposed.

Be sure that the surveillance is directed to disproving actual claims of your opponent. You must show your opponent doing something he specifically said he could not do, at or near a time when he claimed he could not do it. A movie showing a plaintiff briskly walking down the street does not impeach his claim that he can no longer jog because jogging hurts his back. Deposition testimony in June 1983 by a man who says he had to give up his lifelong recreation of bicycle riding is not impeached effectively by a movie taken in January 1986 showing him riding a bike.

But if the surveillance testimony is on target, it can win the case, proving resoundingly the value of informal witness investigation.

Formal Discovery from Nonparties

by Jeffrey F. Liss

People do best what they do most often. Litigators—accustomed to out-maneuvering party opponents—are skilled in getting discovery from their adversaries. But there are valuable sources of information outside the party list.

Unfortunately, when contemplating discovery from nonparties, many lawyers get the shakes; subpoenas, motions to quash, and witness fees are often foreign concepts, and what is unfamiliar can be scary. Rule 45 of the Federal Rules of Civil Procedure—the principal means of third-party discovery—is uncharted territory for many. It does not have to be that way.

Rule 45 is a handy, flexible tool. Its requirements are easy to master. The first step is to understand some basics.

Rule 45 gives a party the opportunity to depose nonparties and, by doing so, to get documents as well. Unlike Rule 30, which covers party depositions, Rule 45 requires a subpoena to compel a nonparty's attendance at a deposition.

There are two types of Rule 45 deposition subpoenas: the subpoena *ad testificandum*, which merely requires the deponent to attend and give testimony, and the subpoena *duces tecum*, which also requires the witness to bring specified documents or other items.

Subpoenas are issued by the court clerk in the district where the deposition is to be taken. The party who wants a deposition subpoena must satisfy the clerk that a notice of the deposition has been served on all other parties to the case. A witness can be compelled to travel no more than 100 miles from his residence, workplace, or the place where he is served, unless the court orders that the deposition be taken at another convenient location.

Mr. Liss is a partner in the Washington, D.C., firm of Piper & Marbury.

In practice, then, the first step in taking a Rule 45 deposition is serving a notice of the deposition on all parties, in any manner authorized by Rule 30. Next, prepare a subpoena form and any necessary attachments, such as a schedule of documents, and take it to the clerk, along with a copy of the notice of deposition and a certificate of service. After receiving proof of service of the notice and usually taking a copy of the notice for filing, the clerk will issue the subpoena by affixing his official seal or stamp.

It is all pretty simple and only slightly more complicated if the deposition is to be taken outside the district where your case is pending. Say a case is pending in federal court in the district of Maryland and the witness lives in the district of Wyoming. First, you would serve the notice of deposition in Maryland. Next, if the local rules permit or require filing of discovery documents, you would file a copy of the notice and the accompanying certificate of service with the clerk in Maryland.

Then you would demonstrate to the clerk in Wyoming that the notice has been served in Maryland. You could do this by showing him a copy of the notice and either a duplicate original or a certified copy of the certificate of service. Find out in advance, either directly by telephone or through local counsel, what the clerk requires for the issuance of a subpoena. Some clerks demand an original certificate of service; for others, a copy is enough. Once you have given the clerk whatever papers he requires, he would issue a subpoena for service on the witness in Wyoming.

Being naturally inquisitive, most attorneys want more than just testimony. They thrive on paper, and they love any three-dimensional objects that might be evidence in the case. Since Rule 34 requests for production do not work with nonparties, it is necessary to use a subpoena *duces tecum*. This kind of subpoena must describe the documents or other things that the witness is supposed to bring to the deposition. There is a space on the subpoena form for this description, but because the space is small, the usual practice is to attach a schedule listing the requested items.

Once the subpoena has been issued, it must be served on the prospective witness. In addition to the subpoena and its attachments, the notice of deposition may be served, although that is not mandatory.

Subpoenas may be served by anyone who is 18 or older and not a party, and they must be be personally served on the witness. See Fed. R. Civ. P. 45(c).

The remaining basics mostly involve money. The federal rules reflect a concern for the fact that third parties—as strangers to a suit—may find discovery to be an imposition. To ease the pain, the server pays them. Thus, unless the party who wants the deposition is the United States, the server must tender one day's witness fees and mileage expenses along with the subpoena. The witness fee is $30 per day of testimony, including travel days. 21 U.S.C. § 1821(b). So $30 must be tendered at the outset; the remainder, if any, can be paid after the deposition.

Reckoning mileage money can be slightly more complicated. If the witness travels by common carrier, he gets the "most economical rate reasonably available," plus taxi fare to and from the terminal. If the witness travels by private car, he is entitled to the official government mileage allowance (currently 20.5 cents per mile), plus parking and tolls. 28 U.S.C. § 1821.

These are hardly precise guidelines. The party serving the subpoena usually has no idea how the witness intends to travel to the deposition, and so calculating mileage expenses is partly guesswork. Some lawyers deal with the problem by skipping the mileage money, with the intention of evening up after the deposition—if the witness asks. A better practice is to estimate the probable mileage expenses and to include that amount in the check tendered to the witness.

There is one final money matter. If a deponent must stay overnight, he is entitled to the government subsistence rate for food and lodging in the area where the deposition is to be taken. 28 U.S.C. § 1821(d). That can be paid after the deposition. Determine the amount owed by referring to 5 U.S.C. § 5702.

Rule 45 subpoenas may be served on corporations as well as individuals. The familiar provisions of Rule 30(b)(6) apply with full force under Rule 45, and so a subpoena may name a nonparty corporation, partnership, association, or government agency as the deponent, specifying "with reasonable particularity" the areas on which testimony is sought. The organization must then designate a witness to testify on its behalf.

The subpoena must inform the organization of its duty to designate a witness. Most subpoena forms have a printed notice designed to serve this purpose, but if the notice is inconspicuous or missing, make sure to include a special instruction. You can get documents and other things from an organization, as from an individual, under Rule 45(d)(1).

Every rule has its uncertainties, and Rule 45 is no exception. Some of the uncertainties arise in connection with taking discovery of corporations or other organizations.

What happens if you serve a subpoena on a firm at its field office in Texas, but it designates an employee at its headquarters in the District of Columbia? Can you make the employee come to Texas for the deposition? At least one court says no. See *Cates v. LTV Aerospace Corp.*, 480 F.2d 620, 623 (5th Cir. 1973). Similarly, if a deposition subpoena *duces tecum* is served on a corporation in Michigan, but the organization's responsive documents are located in the District of Columbia, does it have to produce them in Michigan? At least one court says yes. See *Ghandi v. Police Department*, 74 F.R.D. 115 (E.D. Mich. 1977), *aff'd in part and rev'd in part*, 747 F.2d 338 (6th Cir. 1984).

No discussion of Rule 45 would be complete without mentioning how to resist a subpoena. Rule 45 is a rich source of motion practice.

Again, some basics: If the witness does not object to the deposition itself but does object to bringing documents or other items requested, he may serve written objections to the *duces tecum* part of the subpoena within ten days of service or before compliance is required, whichever is sooner. The burden is then on the requesting party to move to compel production in the court that issued the subpoena.

If a witness wants to avoid a deposition altogether, though, or to limit it in some way, the obligation to act is his. He may make a motion in either the court for the district where the deposition is to be taken or the court in which the action is pending. Under Rule 45(b), a motion to quash or modify must be made ''promptly'' and, in any event, before the time for compliance.

Given a witness's duty to testify when served with process, few can avoid depositions altogether absent the most compelling of circumstances, such as failing health or a showing that the deposition is intended merely to harass. And given the broad scope of discovery under Rule 26, it is hard to prevail on a relevance objection to producing documents in response to a subpoena *duces tecum*. Despite this, any ground for limiting discovery under Rule 26(b) is also available under Rule 45.

A deposition subpoena may be quashed because the proposed discovery is unnecessarily duplicative or because it seems generally unreasonable after weighing the needs and importance of the case against the burden and expense of complying. Sometimes you also can get the court to limit the scope or length of the deposition or to change its time or place. Many judges will impose limitations to prevent personal embarrassment or wildly irrelevant questions or to protect confidential information, if the witness seeks the court's protection after the lawyers taking the discovery have refused to respect the witness's legitimate concerns.

A third-party deponent also may object to absorbing the excess cost of the deposition beyond the munificent sums that the statute provides. But Rule 45(b) suggests that additional expenses should be awarded only if the subpoena is ''unreasonable or oppressive.''

In practice, deposing parties often agree to pay a deponent's reasonable out-of-pocket costs, especially in connection with producing documents. Despite this common practice, witnesses have had a hard time getting cost awards in court. One case holds that costs should be awarded only when the expense to the deponent exceeds the reasonable burden he ought to shoulder as a citizen. See *SEC v. Arthur Young & Co.*, 584 F.2d 1018 (D.C. Cir.), *cert. denied* 439 U.S. 1071 (1978). But costs have been awarded when the witness had to compile information from his records, rather than just producing documents. *Miller v. Sun Chemical Corp.*, 12 F.R.D. 181 (D.N.J. 1952).

Those are the nuts and bolts of third-party discovery. Now consider the tactical issues.

The first is whether you need a deposition at all. Before you charge out and depose every nonparty witness in sight, stop and think. You really may not need all those depositions, and there may be pitfalls in your path.

There are, of course, good reasons for a deposition, whatever the affiliation of the witness. You may want to find out what he has to say about a material issue. You may want to pin down his story. You may want to assess his demeanor as a witness, to help you judge the strength of your case (or your opponent's, depending on who is likely to call the witness at trial).

A nonparty deposition can elicit information that is damaging to the other side. It can preserve the witness's testimony, a purpose that is particularly important if the witness is outside the subpoena power of the trial court. The deposition can be a show of strength, a way to impress the other side with particularly strong, and possibly surprising, testimony of a witness with no ax to grind. That could facilitate settlement. Or you may need the deposition to obtain and authenticate documents.

Now consider the disadvantages. First, and most obviously, a deposition costs money. Especially if the amount in controversy is modest, there will be a natural ceiling on the number of nonparty depositions you can take.

In addition, if the witness supports your opponent's case, you may, by deposing him, unintentionally prepare him for your cross-examination at trial. The deposition also could educate your adversary—a particularly acute danger of third-party depositions. And if the witness is likely to testify on your behalf at trial in any event, the deposition could make his testimony a less effective surprise than it otherwise might be. Another major risk is that you inadvertently might preserve adverse testimony, which may well be admissible at trial under Rule 32, especially if the witness is beyond the subpoena power of the trial court.

If any of these concerns looms large, the obvious alternative is an interview. Some lawyers make the mistake of noticing the deposition of every witness they can think of, forgetting that it can be much easier, less expensive, and more effective to pick up the telephone, set up an appointment, and talk to the witness.

Many of the purposes for taking a deposition—such as finding out what the witness has to say or assessing his demeanor—also can be accomplished in an interview. And an interview avoids some of the pitfalls, especially the education of your opponent and the risk of preserving adverse testimony. After an interview, you may conclude that it is important to preserve the witness's testimony; if so, a deposition can be scheduled. Most importantly, an interview can rarely hurt. It will at least give you a preview and eliminate surprises if you later take a deposition.

Talking to the witness informally first can have another benefit: It can establish a good working relationship between the two of you. Many lawyers do not consider that side of things, because they are accustomed to thinking of depositions as adversarial. With third-party deponents, though, good relations are important, and often possible.

So, if there is a chance that the nonparty witness is sympathetic, or at least disinterested, do *not* just serve a surprise subpoena on him. Talk to him first, either by telephone or, if possible, in person. Be nice to him. Advise him at an early stage that he may want a lawyer.

If the witness has a lawyer and you have decided to go ahead with the deposition, you may be able to get the lawyer to agree to an advance meeting among you, him, and the witness. If you have that meeting, explain to the witness how a deposition works, especially if he is a first-timer. Make him feel comfortable with the process and with you. Do not under any circumstances tell or suggest to him what to say at the deposition, but if it suits your purposes, explain the case and how his testimony fits into the overall picture. Emphasize that, while he should not speculate about something he does not know of his own knowledge, his first duty as a witness is to tell the truth.

When you interview a third-party witness, remember that what you say is discoverable. That is a reason to think not only about *what* you say in an interview, but also about *how* you say it. Unless you eliminate ambiguities, you may be surprised at a deposition by what the witness thought you said or—worse yet—what he thought you wanted *him* to say.

When you get to the deposition, do not try to hide the fact that you have met with the witness. In fact, you should probably bring that out during your examination. You may defuse its potential significance, and you might discourage your adversary from asking too many questions or trying to make too much of an issue of it.

If all you want from a third party are documents, again an informal talk is the best first step. If you get the documents without a subpoena, you are not obliged to disclose them to your opponent, unless he asks for them in discovery. Once you serve a subpoena, though, your opponent will know exactly what you are after and almost certainly will ask for copies.

Of course, you may need a deposition to authenticate the documents. If the witness is within the subpoena power of the trial court, a simple authenticating affidavit may do the job. Armed with it, you can be secure in the knowledge that if your opponent refuses to admit authenticity—something that only the most hard-nosed trial lawyers would do after seeing the affidavit—you always can subpoena the witness to testify at trial. And under Rule 37(c), you then will be in a position to recover the fees and expenses of proving authenticity.

Even if you have not contacted your deponent or his lawyer before serving the subpoena, get in touch with them to suggest that they produce any documents in advance. Although the witness is not required to produce documents before the deposition, you can explain that, if he agrees to do so, he will not have to sit there while you pore over the documents, one by one, at the deposition.

The same kind of informal approach is just as important if the prospective witness is a corporation. You may think you know who the corporation's key person is on a particular issue, but you also may be wrong. You may think you know who has important documents, but you could be mistaken.

To avoid unnecessary surprises, contact the corporation, usually through its lawyer. Arrange for an advance production of documents, and identify the officers or employees you really want to depose. If that is not possible, make liberal use of the provisions of Rule 30(b)(6) available through Rule 45. Take a 30(b)(6) deposition first, find out who the knowledgeable individuals are, get their relevant documents, and then subpoena and depose the really important employees or officials.

If, after informal discussions, you decide to go ahead with a deposition, do *not* neglect to serve the subpoena just because the witness has voluntarily agreed to attend. A subpoena protects you in case the witness has a change of heart. It also protects your pocketbook; if a nonparty witness fails to attend a deposition and you have not served a subpoena, you are liable for the expenses, including attorneys' fees, of the parties who do attend. See Fed. R. Civ. P. 30(g)(2). Also, witnesses sometimes want to be subpoenaed. It often makes it easier for them to get time off from work. Especially when others would prefer that they not testify, witnesses can fall back on the compulsion of the subpoena.

If there is to be a Rule 45 deposition, where should it take place? Lawyers traditionally notice depositions for their own offices if the deponent is not more than 100 miles away. And if the deponent is beyond the subpoena power of the trial court, they usually take the deposition at a friendly local counsel's office. Like other reflexes, these moves sometimes should be restrained.

Think first about the tone you want to set. If you want to awe or intimidate a difficult witness, your office (or local counsel's) is probably the right place. If you want to make sure that the witness is not distracted by his work, again the traditional choice is probably right. If you want to cultivate a friendly relationship with the witness, though, your best bet is to find out what suits his convenience. This will not always mean that you wind up taking the deposition at his office.

Some people like expense-paid out-of-town trips, especially if your city is an attractive one. Others might want to be deposed at home; be prepared to go there. But consider whether it is advisable to have the witness's files close at hand—especially if you suspect that he might otherwise leave important documents behind. In that case, take the deposition at his office.

If you are seeking documents with a subpoena *duces tecum,* think about more than location. Again, some spadework can pay dividends.

If you want documents from a corporation, it helps to contact its lawyer in advance to find out how the company's files are organized. Your request can be tailored accordingly. Try to avoid making the document list an exercise in kitchen-sink litigation. Blunderbuss subpoenas serve only to irritate; they are hard to understand and time-consuming to comply with. And they are more likely to provoke a motion for a protective order. Ask for what you reasonably need for your case—no more and no less.

Especially in Rule 45 depositions, think about whether your document request really requires page after page of definitions and instructions before the deponent ever gets to the list of documents. There are reasons to use the traditional mumbo jumbo, but there also are reasons not to.

If you suspect that your deponent or his lawyer might be less than forthcoming, hiding behind nit-picking linguistic ambiguities, use the mumbo jumbo (but make sure it really pins down, rather than obscures, what you want). That way, your deponent will not be able to say, ''But I didn't know that when you said 'document,' you meant my appointment book.'' Similarly, if the nonparty witness is hostile, use the mumbo jumbo. And if you suspect the subpoena will go straight to a lawyer in a big firm, use the mumbo jumbo.

But if the witness is friendly, forthright, and unrepresented, remember there is nothing like mumbo jumbo to send him straight to a lawyer. Five pages of definitions and four pages of instructions are likely to intimidate a lay witness. They will make him less cooperative. Concise instructions and a short list of documents written in plain English are more likely to make the witness feel comfortable with the process and therefore cooperative.

If you take an out-of-town Rule 45 deposition, do not try to be a hero. When in Rome, get Roman counsel.

When you take a deposition in another jurisdiction, get the relatively inexpensive and often invaluable assistance of local lawyers. They can help you to understand and deal with the peculiarities of practice there. They will be acquainted with the local clerk's office. They can help with issuance and service of the subpoena. And they can give you a base of operations on short notice.

A local lawyer can get you a capable court reporter. Should you run into problems mid-deposition, such as obdurate refusal to comply with a document demand or to answer a proper question, local counsel is more likely than you to be able to arrange a conference with the motions judge on short notice.

After adopting a sound strategy and complying with the rules, you finally will have to *take* the third-party deposition. In most ways, a Rule 45 deposition is like any other deposition. Have your outline in hand and your purposes clearly in mind. Even more than with a party deponent, you should avoid blather: Be concise, get to the point, and do not alienate a disinterested witness with a string of seemingly meaningless or marginally pertinent questions. Who cares where he went to school?

If the witness does not come with a lawyer, spend more time than usual "reading him his rights." Explain the deposition process on the record, ask him to tell you whenever he does not comprehend the question, explain the objections process, and generally make sure that he has no credible reason to say later, "I didn't understand."

Occasionally, especially when the witness is adverse, your opposing counsel may claim to represent him "for purposes of the deposition." This usually means the lawyer has prepared the witness and will protect him at the deposition. Be sure to explore the details and limits of this representation on the record. It may bear on the legitimacy of any assertions of attorney-client privilege during the deposition.

In most other respects, a nonparty deposition is like any other deposition. That is how it should be. If you understand Rule 45 and keep in mind the special problems associated with discovery of third parties, that kind of discovery will be a natural part of your approach to every case.

Discovery from Those at the Top

by Alan N. Salpeter, Richard A. Salomon, and Caryn Jacobs

While representing a corporate client in federal court, you receive a notice calling for the deposition of one of your client's highest-ranking officials. You think that the notice has been served solely to harass, and you begin to formulate ways to prevent the deposition from going forward. You are well aware, though, that federal judges generally do not look kindly on perceived attempts to ''thwart'' discovery (especially when such attempts wind up in court on motions to compel or for protective orders). The prospect of an unsuccessful discovery fight looms ahead.

A closer look at your dilemma, however, reveals that courts will not automatically order the deposition of a high-ranking corporate officer or government official. The deposition may be quashed; alternative means of discovery may be accepted. Further, the 1983 amendments to Rule 26 of the Federal Rules of Civil Procedure provide an impressive arsenal of defensive weapons if you decide to resist the deposition.

Whether to resist.—Before determining whether to resist a requested deposition of a high-ranking corporate or governmental official, the facts and needs of the particular case should be considered.

First, you should learn what the official knows about the relevant facts. Whether the deponent is the chief executive officer of a corporation or a cabinet-level official, if he has no involvement in the case and no firsthand knowledge of it, his deposition probably will not be permitted.

Next, you should examine the extent to which your response to the notice of deposition could hurt you later in the case. For example, do you

---

Alan N. Salpeter and Richard A. Salomon are partners in the law firm of Mayer, Brown & Platt in Chicago, and represented Chrysler Corporation in one of the cases discussed in this article. Caryn Jacobs is an associate in the same firm.

need to depose the opponent's chief executive officer? If so, can you distinguish between deposing your chief officer and your opponent?

Have you compiled your witness lineup for trial? Would resisting the deposition your opponent wants deprive you of the witness who can tell your client's story most effectively? If your officer's testimony is helpful, it may discourage your opponent, especially if the deposition is given early in the case.

Similarly, you should be aware of the dangers of allowing a premature deposition of a high-ranking official: The official might make harmful statements that would bind the client. For this reason, you might want to defer the deposition until you know enough about the case to prepare the official properly.

Tactically, delaying the deposition of a high-ranking official, especially one with little or no knowledge of the underlying facts, usually is wise. As discovery proceeds, it is easier to argue that the testimony of the official is not necessary, since it can add little or simply is inappropriate. With time, your opponent's desire to depose the official may subside. The lawyer may be satisfied that he has enough information, he may fear incurring sanctions by pressing for an unessential deposition, or he may be anxious to complete other important discovery before an impending discovery cutoff date. Beyond that, the case may settle, making the discovery moot.

On the other hand, if you decide not to contest the deposition, letting it go forward early in the case may offer certain advantages. The earlier the deposition occurs, the less likely it is that your opponent will know enough about the case to ask tough questions or confront the deponent with negative documents or testimony. Also, building a positive bulwark of your client's claims or defenses early sets the tone for the depositions that follow and sends a signal to the opponent that your client will prevail.

Finally, you should consider the extent to which the 1983 amendments to the federal discovery rules provide grounds for resisting abusive, duplicative, expensive, and unduly burdensome discovery. These amendments, designed to combat the assumption that "anything goes" in discovery, change the test of whether discovery may proceed. No longer is it enough for the party seeking discovery to say that the information sought "appears reasonably calculated to lead to the discovery of admissible evidence." Fed. R. Civ. P. 26(b)(1). The burden, expense, and proportionality of the deposition are especially important when the discovery being sought is the deposition of a high-ranking official.

New Rule 26.—Rule 26(b)(1) was amended in 1983 to provide that:

> [t]he frequency or extent of use of the discovery methods [outlined in Rule 26] . . . shall be limited by the court if it determines that . . . the discovery sought is unreasonably cumulative or duplicative, or is obtainable from some other source that is more convenient, less burdensome, or less expensive. . . .

The drafters of this amendment perceived an undue reluctance by district judges "to limit the use of discovery devices" if the information sought appeared to be "relevant." See 1983 Notes of Advisory Committee on Rules for Rule 26(b)(1). Relevance has had, and still has, a broad meaning under Rule 26. By amending Rule 26 in 1983, the drafters added a new requirement, namely that litigants employ, and courts foster, discovery that eliminates redundancy, minimizes costs, and produces requests proportionate to the size, complexity, and importance of each case.

The Advisory Committee notes also reveal that the amended rule was "intended to encourage judges to be more aggressive in identifying and discouraging discovery overuse." In particular, new Rule 26(b) was designed to "remind federal district judges of their broad powers—and . . . correlative responsibilities—under Rule 26" to limit unnecessary discovery of even relevant information. See *Marrese v. American Academy of Orthopedic Surgeons*, 726 F.2d 1150, 1162 (7th Cir. 1984) (en banc), *reversed on other grounds*, 470 U.S. 373 (1985).

Professor Arthur Miller, one of the principal drafters of the 1983 revisions, has pointed out that district courts now have a duty to enter a protective order if the party seeking discovery can obtain the information from some other source or at a lesser cost to the party against whom the discovery is sought. A. Miller, "The August 1983 Amendments to the Federal Rules of Civil Procedure: Promoting Effective Case Management and Lawyer Responsibility," 32–33 (Federal Judicial Center Workshop 1984). Professor Miller explains:

> Until last August [1983], the last sentence in Rule 26(a) said: 'Unless . . . the court orders otherwise, the frequency and use of discovery is not limited.'. . . . That sentence has been stricken and replaced, quite literally, by the reverse message, which you now find in Rule 26(b). Rule 26(b) now says that the frequency and extent of use of discovery shall be limited by the court if certain conditions become manifest. Just realize the 180-degree shift between the last sentence of the old Rule 26(a) and the new sentence. Judges now have the obligation to limit discovery if certain things become manifest. The things that are then listed in that paragraph are basically the evils of redundancy and disproportionality. Because one says that if discovery is unreasonably cumulative, or duplicative, or obtainable from some other source, that is redundancy. If you can get it more cheaply, or if you already have got it—stop asking the same questions.

Often there is no question that the information sought by the discovering party from a high-ranking official can be or has been obtained from "some other source . . . more cheaply." If that is true, the evils of redundancy and disproportionality are present, and that is what you should argue in opposing the deposition.

Another important amendment to Rule 26 is new subsection (g), which provides that an attorney's signature on a discovery request or response certifies that the request or response is consistent with the law, not interposed for any improper purpose, and "not unreasonable or unduly burdensome or expensive, given the needs of the case, the discovery already had in the case, the amount in controversy, and the importance of the issues at stake in the litigation." The Advisory Committee has explained that the new subsection is not meant to restrict "necessary and legitimate discovery," but ensures that lawyers conduct an objective "reasonable inquiry" into relevance *and* burden before requesting or responding to discovery.

A violation of Rule 26(g) allows a court, on a motion or *sua sponte*, to impose sanctions on the offending party, including any attorneys' fees and costs necessitated by the violation. Indeed, the subsection's use of the imperative "shall" appears to indicate that imposing such sanctions is nondiscretionary; See, for example, *Collins v. American Society For Testing and Materials*, LEXIS slip op. at 2, No. 83-3173 (E.D. Pa. May 20, 1985). The drafters of subsection (g)—by combining an objective standard of inquiry with the threat of sanctions—intentionally provided courts and lawyers with a potent weapon to combat discovery abuse.

Finally, subsections (b)(1) and (g) of Rule 26 should be read in tandem with subsections (c), (d), and (f). Rule 26(c) empowers the court to "make any order which justice requires to protect a party or person from annoyance, embarrassment, oppression, or undue burden or expense," including an order that "the discovery may be had only by a method of discovery other than that selected by the party seeking discovery." Rule 26(d) authorizes the court to control the sequence and timing of discovery. Rule 26(f) requires the court to convene a discovery conference on the filing of a proper motion by either party. Following the conference, the court "shall enter an order" identifying the issues for discovery and establishing the discovery plan and schedule.

These rules give powerful ammunition to the practitioner who wants to quash or reschedule the deposition of a high-ranking official or to substitute less intrusive discovery methods for an oral deposition. Your decision whether to attempt to prevent the discovery entirely or simply to limit its time, scope, or method must be based on the needs of your case and the extent of the deponent's knowledge of the facts.

Motion to quash.—When the goal is to prevent a deposition, a motion to quash or for a protective order should be pursued as the principal line of attack, particularly when the proposed deponent has no knowledge of the facts of the case. While taking some preliminary steps before making such a motion might prove helpful—such as suggesting that your opponent use interrogatories first or requesting a Rule 26(f) conference—you should not wait long to move for the protective order.

The strongest basis for quashing a deposition is that the deponent has no relevant knowledge. Before making that argument, of course, you must conduct a reasonable inquiry about the deponent's knowledge. See, for example, *Perkinson v. Houlihan's/D.C., Inc.*, 108 F.R.D. 667, 674 (D.D.C. 1986), where a lawyer responding to a document production request before having caused a search of the files was sanctioned pursuant to Rule 26(g). Having satisfied yourself on that point, a motion to quash typically is sufficient if it contains an affidavit executed by the official to be deposed demonstrating his lack of knowledge.

The United States district court for the eastern district of New York has even established requirements for taking the depositions of high-level officials. The rule recognizes that ''Often the chief executive officer of a company may know nothing regarding the subject matter but is noticed or subpoenaed for harassment purposes.'' Commentary to Standing Order 10 of the United States district court for the eastern district of New York. Standing Order 10 permits a putative deponent to submit an affidavit to the noticing party indicating that the deponent has no knowledge of the relevant matter and identifying a person within the corporation or government having such knowledge. Should the noticing party persist in taking the deposition, the order allows the deponent to seek a protective order. This rule provides sound advice for lawyers in other districts. Identifying alternative deponents skirmishing about which deposition should proceed first will demonstrate to the court that you are not trying to evade your discovery obligations.

If the potential deponent has no personal knowledge of the facts, the deposition is likely to be quashed. This was clear even before the 1983 rule changes. See, for example, *Amherst Leasing Corp. v. Emhart Corp.*, 65 F.R.D. 121, 123 (D. Conn. 1974). In *Armstrong Cork Co. v. Niagara Mohawk Power Corp.*, 16 F.R.D. 389, 390 (S.D.N.Y. 1954), the district court held that ''[i]n the absence of any reasonable belief that the persons have some knowledge of the facts concerning which their testimony is to be taken, there is no reason why they should be compelled to appear. . . .'' The court in *Armstrong* also observed that it must be ''alert to see that the liberal deposition procedure provided in the Federal Rules . . . is not used as a litigation tactic to harass the other side or cause it wasteful expense.'' Id. at 390–91.

Courts also have quashed depositions of government officials when the witness was unable to testify from personal knowledge about the material facts of the case. In *Community Federal Savings & Loan Association v. Federal Home Loan Bank Board*, 96 F.R.D. 619, 621–22 (D.D.C. 1983), for example, the district court held that the board members had no ''unique personal knowledge'' about the underlying facts of the case and therefore could not be deposed. Similarly, in *Cornejo v. Landon*, 524 F.Supp. 118, 122 (N.D.Ill. 1981), the district court held that the deposition of the acting commissioner of the Immigration and Naturalization Service was unnecessary because the information sought from him could be obtained through other means, including the depositions of other persons. (Depositions of governmental officials are also limited by special privileges and other consideration accorded to the government. See "Discovery from the Federal Government" at page 19.)

These cases offer strong arguments in support of quashing a deposition of an official who has no unique knowledge of relevant facts. Your opponent can anticipate these arguments by showing that (1) other discovery avenues have been exhausted, (2) other witnesses have not already answered the proposed questions, and (3) the official whose deposition is sought has some firsthand knowledge of the matters in the litigation. If your opponent does lay this foundation, a court is less likely to find that he is using the discovery to harass, in violation of new Rule 26. See *Digital Equipment Corporation v. System Industries, Inc.*, 108 F.R.D. 742, 744 (D. Mass. 1986).

Sometimes you will want to delay or prevent the deposition of a high-ranking official even when the official does have some knowledge about the case. In such a case, you will find that high rank alone is not a sufficient reason to suspend the deposition. See, for example, *CBS, Inc. v. Ahern*, 102 F.R.D. 820 (S.D.N.Y. 1984) (deposition allowed of president who had personal knowledge of contract in breach-of-contract action); *American Broadcasting Co. v. U.S. Information Agency*, 599 F. Supp. 765 (D.D.C. 1984) (deposition of U.S.I.A. director allowed because only he could answer proposed questions); *Union Savings Bank v. Saxon*, 209 F. Supp. 319 (D.D.C. 1962) (deposition of comptroller of the currency ordered because he personally was accused of committing a crime).

When the high-ranking official has knowledge of the case, your motion for a protective order should focus, when appropriate, on the evils of "redundancy" and "disproportionality," as described by Professor Miller. Redundancy is present if other witnesses already have testified to the matters that are to be the subject of the deposition or if those matters are uncontested. In this case, you should argue that the discovery is unreasonably cumulative and violates the express policies of Rule 26(b)(1) and (g) concerning duplication and expense in relation to the needs of the case. Disproportionality is present if other, more available witnesses have the same or greater familiarity with the relevant events or documents than the putative deponent. In this situation, emphasis should be given to the dictates of convenience and the avoidance of undue burden.

When you cannot in good faith argue that the proposed witness has no relevant knowledge, it is especially important to offer substitute discovery. Not only does this establish your good faith, it also avoids forcing the court to choose between denying your motion outright or depriving your opponent of all discovery on the disputed matter.

In your motion, therefore, it is important to offer a witness who can adequately replace the high-ranking official. If the witness has greater or more detailed knowledge of the relevant events or documents than does the proposed deponent, so much the better. Alternatively, you could propose that the high-ranking official first answer written interrogatories as a substitute for or a prelude to a deposition.

That tactic has succeeded in several cases. For example, in *Mulvey v. Chrysler Corporation*, 106 F.R.D. 364 (D.R.I. 1985), the plaintiffs, who had alleged injuries from a design defect in a Chrysler vehicle, noticed the deposition of Chrysler's chairman, Lee Iacocca. In a motion to quash the deposition, Chrysler relied on the language of new Rule 26(b)(1) and argued that, in lieu of Mr. Iacocca's deposition, there were other discovery methods available that were more convenient, less burdensome, and less expensive. Chrysler pointed out that depositions of its engineers or, if necessary, the use of written interrogatories could substitute for Mr. Iacocca's oral deposition.

Senior District Judge Raymond J. Pettine ordered that the deposition would not proceed until written interrogatories had been propounded to Mr. Iacocca and then only "if the answers to the interrogatories so warrant." In ruling, Judge Pettine commented, "[Mr. Iacocca] is a singularly unique and important individual who can be easily subjected to unwarranted harassment and abuse. He has a right to be protected, and the courts have a duty to recognize his vulnerability." See also *Mitchell v. American Tobacco Company*, 33 F.R.D. 262, 263 (M.D. Pa. 1963); *Community Federal Savings & Loan Association v. Federal Home Loan Bank Board*, 96 F.R.D. 619, 621–22 (D.D.C. 1983). Moreover, the *Manual for Complex Litigation 2d* § 21.452, p. 63, recommends increased use of "the rarely used procedures of Fed. R. Civ. P. 31, [providing] for depositions upon written questions, . . . [as a] very cost-effective means for obtaining evidence usable at trial."

After the written interrogatories are answered and other discovery is taken, the court may reexamine the question of whether the corporate executive's deposition should proceed and whether the executive has relevant evidence that cannot be obtained from another source. At this juncture, the party seeking the executive's deposition will have to demonstrate that (1) there is an independent justification for proceeding and (2) the deposition is not redundant or duplicative. As the court stated in *Colonial Capital Co. v. General Motors Corp.*, 29 F.R.D. 514, 518 (D. Conn. 1961), where the deposition of General Motors' chief executive officer was sought, the deposition of a high official should go forward only if the "answers to the interrogatories with regard to his participation in or knowledge of the matters forming the subject matter of this suit appear to the court to warrant it."

Another option available to the party resisting the deposition of the high-ranking official is to require that other discovery proceed first.

Again, the 1983 amendments explicitly support such a strategy by recognizing the factors of cost and redundancy. But courts long have held that in scheduling discovery, principles of expense and burden may be considered. In *Salter v. Upjohn Co.*, 593 F.2d 649, 651 (5th Cir. 1979), for example, the court emphasized the importance of controlling the timing of discovery when the witness was "extremely busy" and denied "direct knowledge of the facts." See also *Marrese v. American Academy of Orthopedic Surgeons*, 726 F.2d at 1161, which explains that Rule 26(d) should be used to "schedule the sensitive (and highly questionable) discovery last," and the *Manual For Complex Litigation 2d*, § 21.42, which stresses that every effort must be made to coordinate discovery—including discovery from related litigation—and to minimize discovery costs and burdens.

If you do contest your opponent's request for the deposition of a high-ranking official and the court rules against you, you may consider appellate review. Interlocutory appellate review of a discovery order is difficult, but not impossible, to obtain. See, for example, *Belcher v. Bassett Furniture Industries, Inc.*, 588 F.2d 904, 906 & n.4 (4th Cir. 1978). It even is possible to obtain a writ of mandamus, particularly if you can argue that the issue involves a new and recurring interpretation under a federal discovery rule. See *Schlagenhauf v. Holder*, 379 U.S. 104 (1964).

Rule 26(f) conference.—Besides a motion to quash or for a protective order, you can make your request to limit discovery by using Rule 26(f), which encourages the parties to agree during the course of the litigation on a discovery plan.

If reasonable efforts fail to produce such a plan, any party has the right, on filing a motion setting forth the issues and proposed plan, to have the court set a conference to order an appropriate discovery plan. Any party failing to participate in good faith in framing such a plan is subject to sanctions under Rule 37(d). This forces the parties to define the principal issues in the case and demonstrate the necessity of the requested discovery; ideally, it helps prevent abusive and inappropriate depositions. If the opponent's pleadings are vague or its intent to pursue certain claims is unclear, the conference may clarify these issues as well.

If your adversary fails to participate in framing a plan of discovery that puts reasonable limits on deposing your client's highest-ranking executives, you may petition the court to convene a Rule 26(f) conference. In such a conference, you can argue that discovery should proceed in an orderly fashion, starting with the most convenient witnesses with knowledge about the case and proceeding to the more burdensome and expensive discovery of high-ranking people only as the need for such discovery is shown. Moreover, if you want to depose your opponent's senior executive, you can draft a discovery plan that includes this deposition in exchange for a deposition of one of your senior executives.

A proper motion under Rule 26(f) should provide the court with the following: (1) a statement of the issues in the case as they then appear, (2) a proposed plan and schedule of discovery, and, most importantly for your purposes, (3) "any limitations proposed to be placed on discovery" (including requested protective orders and relief from abusive and inappropriate requests for depositions). The rule renders such a conference nondiscretionary; once a proper motion is filed, the court "shall" conduct a Rule 26(f) conference. Although few lawyers file Rule 26(f) motions, when they do they find that judges usually are receptive to narrowing the discovery issues.

In determining whether and how to resist the deposition of a high-ranking official, the particular facts and needs of each case will dictate your strategy. The amendments to Rule 26 make clear that relevance is no longer the sole test of whether a deposition may go forward; the needs of the case, the amount in controversy, the resources of the parties, and the relative importance of the issues must all be considered. By using these new provisions, you may succeed in preventing, deferring, or limiting oral depositions of your client's high-ranking officials.

Discovery from the Federal Government

by C. Coleman Bird

If you are in a case in which you have to seek discovery from the federal government, you should rely as much on George Orwell as you do on what the courts have said. If you only read cases like *United States v. International Business Machines Corp.*, 20 Fed. R. Serv. 2d 1082, 1086 (S.D.N.Y. 1975), you might think that "the Government, like any other litigant, is bound by the discovery provisions of the Federal Rules of Civil Procedure." But Orwell was closer to the mark in *Animal Farm:* "All animals are equal, but some animals are more equal than others."

In fact, the federal government benefits from many exemptions, loopholes, and exceptions that limit its discovery obligations. It may play according to the federal rules, but it does so with a deck somewhat stacked in its favor. You need to be aware of the limitations on discovery from the federal government, and you need to know practical ways of dealing with them if you want to have a reasonable chance of getting the discovery you need without undue delay or expense. This article provides such guidance. It focuses on discovery in litigation in United States district courts and ignores the peculiarities of discovery in proceedings before agencies and other courts such as the United States Claims Court.

It is important to understand why the government is "more equal" in discovery matters than others. The most commonly offered justification is that the government conducts important public business. Its ability to perform essential public functions should not be compromised by the need to comply with the burdensome discovery that sometimes afflicts private parties. Courts are more sensitive to discovery's interference

---

The author is a partner in the Washington, D.C., office of Pepper, Hamilton & Scheetz.

with the accomplishment of public goals than with private goals, and many times the courts' response is entirely justifiable.

There is another, rarely articulated but still powerful, consideration that sets the government apart. Many courts are concerned that the government may lack the resources needed to comply speedily or completely with discovery requests. Even before the Gramm-Rudman-Hollings era, many government agencies were regarded as underfunded and understaffed. Government counsel now can use evidence of continuing personnel cutbacks, program eliminations, and reorganizations to justify the claim that compliance with discovery requests would prevent the agency from meeting statutory deadlines or accomplishing important public purposes.

A private party arguing that complying with discovery would frustrate reaching important corporate goals usually will get little sympathy: Discovery burdens, the court will say, are a regrettable but necessary price of civilization or, if you like, the breaks of the game. But things are different with the government. Courts are far more likely to respond to claims of burden when advanced by a government agency, particularly when the agency is not a party to the litigation. You should bear this judicial leaning in mind when preparing any discovery efforts against the government.

It makes no difference whether you are persuaded by the ''important public business'' or ''lack of staff'' arguments—others have been, and that is what counts. As a result, not only judicial inclinations but also special laws, rules, and limitations affect the scope and means of discovery against the government, as well as the sanctions that can be imposed for unjustified failure to comply with discovery orders.

The scope of discovery against the government is narrowed by extra privileges. Of course, the government is entitled to the evidentiary and related privileges that are available to any private party, such as the attorney-client privilege and work-product protection. But the government also can take advantage of special evidentiary privileges.

Thus, if you want an otherwise discoverable tidbit of information, but the United States (and the court) thinks it is a state secret or touches on national security, you probably will not get it. *United States v. Reynolds*, 345 U.S. 1 (1953). Similarly, in most cases you cannot get discovery of opinions, recommendations, and advice given in government policy deliberations; those are protected by the government's ''deliberative privilege.'' *NLRB v. Sears, Roebuck & Co.*, 421 U.S. 132, 150–152 (1975).

Do you want the name of someone who gave information to law enforcement officials? Do not count on getting it; the ''informant's privilege'' will likely block the way. *Roviaro v. United States*, 353 U.S. 53 (1957). What about the investigative files of a law enforcement agency? A privilege protects them, too. *Black v. Sheraton Corp.*, 564 F.2d 531 (D.C. Cir. 1977). And—not surprisingly—a privilege protects from disclosure government "confidential reports." *Association for Women in Science v. Califano,* 566 F.2d 339 (D.C. Cir. 1977).

This is a formidable list, but not exhaustive. There are, for example, many specific statutory prohibitions on the disclosure by the government of certain kinds of information, such as tax return information (26 U.S.C. § 6103), census data (13 U.S.C. § 9), and material covered by the privacy Act (5 U.S.C. §§ 552a *et seq.*).

All this does not mean you should give up. The government's special privileges do not bar all discovery. And, as more than one administration has learned, the government's mere assertion of a privilege does not end the case. A judge may not agree that a report is or should be "confidential." He or she may not see the "national security" problems that the government does. The boundaries of governmental privileges are neither sharp nor self-defining. The government may be wrong in invoking a privilege. After litigation and, possibly, an in camera review of the material in question, you may get what you want.

Getting discovery from the government means being prepared to work within the framework of the government's various evidentiary and statutory privileges. It is especially important to know—and use—the procedural requirements for each type of privilege. For example, while the informant's and confidential reports privileges may be asserted simply by the government's counsel, certain other privileges such as those for state secrets, national security, deliberative, and law enforcement investigatory files can be asserted only by a formal claim of privilege by a department or agency head after actual personal consideration of the documents or information in question. In some cases, the difficulty of getting the agency head's time for the required personal review may force the government to abandon or reduce substantially its claim of privilege.

The means of discovery against the government, like the scope of discovery, are more limited than for private parties. For example, you cannot simply subpoena or notice the deposition of a cabinet officer or a department or agency head. Ordinarily these officials cannot be forced to testify at a deposition. *Kyle Engineering Co. v. Kleppe,* 600 F.2d 226, 231–32 (9th Cir. 1979). Two justifications are offered for this rule: First, unlimited depositions of these officials might interfere with them discharging their important duties to the detriment of the public interest. Second, in most cases it is the department or agency head's subordinates, not the officials themselves, who have the relevant knowledge or information anyway.

If you have represented a large corporation, these contentions may sound familiar. You probably have used them yourself to try to keep the chief executive officer of a Fortune 500 company from being deposed in a slip-and-fall case. But you may well have lost. Even though the heads of large private organizations are no more likely than high government officials to have relevant information or to be able to appear conveniently for depositions, they do not share such immunity from depositions. The supposed difference is that corporate executives' responsibilities are not public, but private. For private executives, the only remedy is a motion for protective order, with all the attendant costs and uncertainties and without the benefit of the rule ordinarily excusing such officials from deposition.

Does the difference make sense? Not very much. For guidance on this point, you need to go farther afield than George Orwell, to the ancient Roman who wrote, "What is allowed to Jupiter [the king of the gods] is not allowed to the cattle."

But department or agency heads are not completely exempt from depositions. They can be deposed if the discovering party can show that they alone have the necessary knowledge or information. This sometimes may be true when the administrative record is inadequate for effective judicial review of an agency's decision. See *Citizens to Preserve Overton Park v. Volpe,* 401 U.S. 402, 420 (1971) (examining the decision-makers themselves may be necessary when there are no contemporaneous written findings explaining the challenged agency action). Depositions of senior officials also have been permitted when the department or agency head's own actions were challenged as the unlawful product of ex parte contacts or favoritism to acquaintances. See *Community Federal Savings & Loan Ass'n. v. Federal Home Loan Bank Board,* 96 F.R.D. 619, 621 (D.D.C. 1983).

If you persuade the court to allow you to take the deposition of a senior government official, you still likely will be prevented from inquiring into the official's "mental processes," in reaching the decision. *United States v. Morgan,* 313 U.S. 409, 422 (1941). But you can avoid some of the sting of the *Morgan* rule by asking the right questions. Inquiries should concentrate on what materials the department or agency head reviewed and what facts the official was aware of when the decision was made. On the other hand, you should not ask questions like, "What made you think that the statutory requirements were satisfied in this case?"

Special care about the method of discovery is needed when the government is not a party to the litigation. In that case, the only way to get documents in discovery is through a subpoena *duces tecum* under Rule 45 of the Federal Rules of Civil Procedure. (A Freedom of Information Act request is useful only occasionally, as I will explain later.)

A careful litigator will not serve a subpoena on anyone, however, without first checking to see whether the agency has a "housekeeping" regulation. A housekeeping regulation normally gives the department or agency head legal custody of all department or agency records. It requires any subordinate employee served with a subpoena *duces tecum* to decline to produce anything without the approval of the department or agency head. Such regulations are designed to centralize decision mak-

170

ing on subpoena compliance; the government wants to be sure that lower-level subordinates are not coerced by the threat of contempt sanctions into producing documents that the department or agency head does not want produced. The regulations also promote consistency in an agency's approach to discovery. For a good example of such a regulation, see the Department of Justice's housekeeping regulation at 28 C.F.R. §§ 16.21 *et seq.* (1986).

Sanctions Are Limited

Housekeeping regulations do not, however, justify government stonewalling. The statute authorizing such regulations states that it "does not authorize withholding information from the public or limiting the availability of records to the public." 5 U.S.C. § 301. Instead, these regulations simply provide grounds on which a subordinate employee can successfully resist a subpoena *duces tecum.* Contempt convictions of subordinates who have relied on a housekeeping regulation to justify their refusal to produce subpoenaed documents have been reversed. See, for example, *United States ex rel. Touhy v. Ragen,* 340 U.S. 462 (1951); *Appeal of United States Securities and Exchange Commission,* 226 F.2d 501 (6th Cir. 1955).

One other significant effect of housekeeping regulations is inconvenience. Combined with the territorial limits on the district court's subpoena power, such a regulation can force you to take a document deposition in the judicial district where the department or agency head is amenable to service of a subpoena. Happily only for Washington lawyers, that district generally is in the Washington, D.C., area, even if the agency and the government officials involved have a local office in your city or somewhere a lot closer than Washington. See, for example, *Cates v. LTV Aerospace Corp.,* 480 F.2d 620 (5th Cir. 1973).

Just as the law restricts the scope and means of discovery against the government, it also limits the sanctions that may be imposed on the United States for failure to make discovery. Courts can be extremely lenient in imposing discovery burdens and deadlines on the government. This reluctance may be another symptom of the view that the government has inadequate resources to devote to discovery. It also may reflect judges' past uncertainty about what sanctions they could impose if the government refused to comply.

Contempt was once the only available sanction for the government's discovery derelictions. The sanction that the courts generally impose on a private party—an award of costs and attorneys' fees incurred in making the motion to compel—was not available for government discovery abuse. Until 1981, Rule 37(f) of the Federal Rules of Civil Procedure said that "except to the extent permitted by statute, expenses and fees [for failure to make discovery] may not be awarded against the United States under this rule [Rule 37]." But because there was no statute generally permitting such awards, the rule meant no expenses and fees could be awarded against the United States.

In 1981, the Equal Access to Justice Act repealed Rule 37(f) and provided for the first time that:

> The United States shall be liable for [reasonable fees and expenses of attorneys] to the same extent that any other party would be liable under the common law or under the terms of any statute which specifically provides for such an award.

28 U.S.C. § 2412(b).

The legislative history of this provision shows that Congress meant to permit the award of attorneys' fees and expenses against the United States for failing to satisfy discovery obligations. See, H. Rep. No. 96-1418, 96th Cong., 2d Sess. 19 (1980), reprinted in 1980 *U.S. Code Cong. & Ad. News* 4998. Yet courts have rarely used their new power to impose sanctions on the government. This may reflect a subconscious fidelity to the ways of the past or to the considerations once thought to justify limited sanctions. In any event, if the government now unreasonably fails to comply, you can successfully seek sanctions under Rule 37. You also can obtain sanctions against the government under Rule 26(g), which provides that signing a discovery request, response, or objection constitutes a certification that the attorney has read the document, that "to the best of his knowledge, information, and belief formed after a reasonable inquiry" the document is: (1) consistent with the federal rules and warranted by existing law or a good faith argument for the extension, modification, or reversal of existing law; (2) not filed for any improper purpose (like delay or harassment); and (3) not "unreasonably or unduly burdensome or expensive." See *National Association of Radiation Survivors v. Turnage*, 115 F.R.D. 543 (N.D.Cal. 1987) (monetary sanctions totaling $120,000 imposed on the Veterans Administration under Rules 26(g) and 37 for an alleged pattern of discovery abuse involving destruction of responsive documents and failure to produce other responsive documents).

In cases of extreme discovery intransigence, a court can award a default judgment against the disobedient party. Fed. R. Civ. P. 37(b)(2)(C). When the intransigent defendant is a government agency or officer, however, things are different: No default judgment can be entered against the government "unless the claimant establishes his claim or right to relief by evidence satisfactory to the court." Fed. R. Civ. P. 55(e). The reason for this rule is the view that the U.S. Treasury should not be depleted by a default judgment unless the plaintiff shows that he or she is entitled to the relief sought.

Rule 55(e) alone could be unfair. If a party could not establish the validity of his claim without obtaining the discovery the government wrongly has refused to provide, unjustified intransigence would be rewarded and a possibly valid claim extinguished. There is a way out of this problem, however: Rule 55(e) applies only to default judgments. It does not prevent the imposition of issue-related sanctions against the government under Rule 37(b)(2). Thus, government discovery disobedience can lead to preclusion orders or orders that certain facts be taken as established against the government. Such orders can be the basis for successful summary judgment motions, despite Rule 55(e). *Smith v. Schlesinger,* 513 F.2d 462, 466–67 (D.C. Cir. 1975). Therefore, it is important when you are confronted with the government's unjustified refusal to respond to discovery that you consider carefully what sanctions to seek.

Put Your Plan in Writing

Given the government's significant advantages in discovery, the resourceful lawyer needs to know more than the sometimes depressing details of the law on government discovery. Common sense, combined with an understanding of how government lawyers operate, is essential. To begin with, do not forget what you already know about taking discovery from private parties. Although the government plays the game of discovery with the benefit of some unique advantages, private discovery and government discovery have much in common. Many of the techniques that are successful in nongovernmental litigation also can be used effectively in taking discovery from the government.

Bureaucratic sloth is not unique to the government. In government discovery, you will need the same tenacity that you use in private litigation to ensure that your adversary exhausts all reasonable possibilities for locating responsive documents and information.

Even more than in private litigation, be sure to avoid discovery requests that can be made to appear too broad. Because, as noted, both the agencies and their lawyers may be seen as overworked and understaffed, courts can be quite sympathetic to the government's attempts to limit expansive discovery. To avoid squabbles over the breadth of discovery, you should try to agree with the government lawyers on a discovery plan in advance of taking discovery.

If you do reach a discovery agreement with the government, put it in writing. Because of the turnover in many government law offices, it is possible that you will later be dealing with a different government lawyer, one who might not be willing to accept your recollection of your oral agreement with his or her predecessor. Some agencies' personnel seem to believe that if it is not in writing and in the file, it never happened. So get the agreement in writing and file it.

But remember another principle of agreements with the government: If something is in writing, the government may insist it happened exactly as set forth in the written document, without regard to common sense or individual recollection to the contrary. An accurate written discovery agreement is essential, but it will not end all fights.

Even if you cannot secure a complete agreement, you can reach limited agreements to help you get the discovery you need first. You can reach an "agreement to disagree" in which government counsel, in response to discovery requests that the government believes are overly broad or unduly burdensome or seek privileged material, agrees to produce that which is clearly relevant, not privileged, and readily accessible, without prejudice to his or her objections and without any waiver of your right later to demand full compliance with the discovery requests. In this way, a lot of motion practice can be postponed or avoided. Another approach is to reach an agreement in which the government agrees to respond to discovery requests in stages. This can reduce the burden on the government, while getting you the discovery you need at an early point. Again, make sure all such agreements are confirmed in writing.

In negotiating agreements or framing discovery requests, try to understand the special difficulties the government may face—or say it faces—in responding. Most agencies have mountains of records. These records may be located at many places, such as individual offices, regional offices, agency headquarters, and government storage locations in Suitland, Maryland, and St. Louis, Missouri. As a consequence, the government frequently has difficulty completing a document search in what seems like a reasonable time. The key to insuring effective document discovery is persistence; follow up to make sure that all reasonable locations are searched thoroughly by employees who are capable of identifying responsive documents.

As in private litigation, you always should insist on the identification of any responsive documents that are withheld on the basis of any claim of privilege or other grounds. A privilege list should include the document's date, author, addressees, recipients of copies, title, subject matter, number of pages, and a description of the precise basis for its withholding. There is no better way to expose an agency's overly broad refusal to produce than by demanding such a list. In fact, the clerical and legal burden of compiling a privilege list may tip the balance in favor of producing documents when the agency's claim of privilege or burden is marginal at best.

You should tailor your discovery to the special circumstances of litigating with the government. For example, if an extensive administrative record has been developed at the agency level and you have a complete copy of it, your document request can exclude the documents contained in that record. As a precaution, you should get a list from the government of the entire contents of the administrative record to make sure you have the complete record.

If the case involves judicial review of agency action, the government is likely to resist all additional discovery on the basis that the validity of the challenged action must be judged only on the record compiled before the agency. This argument frequently succeeds because of the Supreme Court's teaching in *Camp v. Pitts*, 411 U.S. 138, 142 (1973), that ''the focal point for judicial review [of agency action under the Administrative Procedure Act] should be the administrative record already in existence, not some new record made initially in the reviewing court.'' The Supreme Court further held that, if the administrative record is inadequate for effective judicial review, the remedy is not unlimited discovery and de novo review in the district court, but instead allowing the agency to provide whatever additional explanation of its decision is necessary.

The government also frequently takes the position that no discovery should be permitted while a dispositive motion (such as a motion to dismiss or for summary judgment) is pending. Be prepared to respond with arguments showing that you will need discovery while the motion is pending, either because important documents or information is likely to be lost if discovery is delayed or because the discovery will be needed to resist the government's dispositive motion.

Be sure to consider the advantages and pitfalls of a Freedom of Information Act request (5 U.S.C. § 552) (FOIA) as an adjunct to formal discovery. Anyone can make a FOIA request, even litigators who want to use the requested records to prosecute or defend a case against the government. You can make a request before or after suit is filed. If you make your request after you file suit, however, do not be surprised if your litigation adversary acts as the agency's lawyer in responding to your request.

Once you file a request, the agency has to disclose the requested records, at your expense for search time and copying, unless one of the FOIA's specific exemptions allows it to withhold them. There is no limitation in FOIA—as there is in Rule 26(b)(1), Fed. R. Civ. P.—to documents that are ''relevant to the subject matter of the pending action.'' You cannot use a FOIA request to override the government's privilege claims, however. There is a specific FOIA exemption that allows agencies to withhold records that would not be available to a party in litigation with the agency. 5 U.S.C. § 552(b)(5).

In theory, a FOIA request should result in speedier access to records, because the act requires the agency to respond within ten business days. But theory and reality rarely coincide. In some agencies, the backlog of FOIA requests is too great to allow a response in ten weeks, much less ten days. When an agency responds by telling you, ''Take a number and your request will be answered in turn,'' there is little you can do. You can file a suit to compel a timely response to your request, but if you have requested the records for use in a pending suit or one that you intend to file shortly, it usually makes more sense to forget about FOIA and try to get the records in discovery.

It is important to try to understand how the government's litigators

175

are organized. Be conscious of the relationship between the agency, its in-house counsel, and the Department of Justice. In many cases, the Department of Justice, either through an attorney based in Washington, D.C., or through an assistant United States attorney (AUSA), will represent a government department or agency in litigation. Although the AUSA will enter an appearance on the government's behalf, frequently he or she will have limited knowledge of the case until the agency supplies a "litigation report." This report describes the proceedings before the agency and various possible claims and defenses. An AUSA usually will decline to discuss discovery matters until the litigation report is received.

Agency counsel and AUSAs frequently have different perspectives on a case. Agency counsel may feel bound to defend an agency position that the AUSA knows from bitter experience is a loser. An agency can be an extremely difficult client for the AUSA. Under the circumstances, some AUSAs may be less willing than their agency counsel counterparts to accept the agency's claims that responding to your discovery request in less than five years will bring the conduct of public business to a halt.

Because of these different perspectives, you should not feel foreclosed by agency counsel's previous refusal to make discovery; make your request anew to the AUSA. There is certainly no harm in asking. But be aware that the AUSA's independence cuts both ways: An AUSA may not feel bound by discovery agreements that you reach with agency counsel without the AUSA's participation. Once the AUSA has appeared for the government, you can exclude him or her from your discovery negotiations only at your peril.

A final point to remember in conducting discovery against the federal government is the considerable power of Rule 30(b)(6). This rule allows you to name as the deponent in your notice of deposition or subpoena "a public . . . corporation . . . or governmental agency and describe with reasonable particularity the matters on which examination is requested." Such a notice requires the government to "designate one or more officers, directors, or managing agents, or other persons who consent to testify on its behalf" on the matters described. The rule then requires the government's designated witnesses to testify not just from their personal knowledge, but "as to matters known or reasonably available to the organization."

Naming the Deponent

By putting the burden on the government, Rule 30(b)(6) provides a partial solution to one of the major frustrations of litigation with the government: the complexity and impersonality of its bureaucracy. Job titles may be misleading, and, for an outsider, identifying informed witnesses may be nearly impossible. With Rule 30(b)(6), you will not have to conduct a series of costly and time-consuming depositions at which each deponent passes the buck to someone else in the agency (an exercise that many government employees have perfected in their daily work). Instead, you can force the agency to designate one or more employees as "roving reporters" to find out all the information reasonably available to the agency on the matters you define and report it to you at the deposition.

Rule 30(b)(6) will not solve all your problems, however. Some agencies and their counsel do not always take it seriously. It cannot overcome the government's fundamental discovery edge: If you want to depose cabinet officers or agency heads, Rule 30(b)(6) is no help, and even at a 30(b)(6) deposition, the government's various privileges apply. Still, if a 30(b)(6) designee is not fully informed, you can work around the problem. At the deposition, you can ask what the designated deponent did to find out the required information and locate any required document: "Whom did you talk to? For how long? What files did you look at? What computerized records did you consult?" And so on. In this way, you can probably learn enough to name the key decision makers or most knowledgeable persons in your next deposition notice. Rule 30(b)(6) thus can be a wedge into the complex and sometimes resistant federal bureaucracy.

Perhaps the best description of the process of obtaining discovery from the federal government was provided by Mick Jagger and the Rolling Stones some years ago: "You can't always get what you want, but if you try, sometimes you just might find you get what you need."

Trial Lawyer or Litigator

by Weyman I. Lundquist

Discovery has become an instrument of abuse and oppression. It often fails to perform its original purpose as an essential tool in the search for truth. Lawyers have caused this transformation—lawyers who have lost sight of how to try cases and who instead have come to view discovery as an end in itself. Through clinical trial courses, rule changes, and other means, lawyers must refocus their efforts on the true ends of litigation: trial or settlement.

Discovery became fashionable in 1938 after the federal rules were changed to eliminate the high crime of "trial by ambush." The heart of the new approach was the phrase in Federal Rule of Civil Procedure 26 allowing discovery concerning all matters "relevant to the subject matter involved in the pending action." Through the broad discovery thus authorized, the adversary process was supposed to become a search for truth.

To state this proposition is to set a stage worthy of Don Quixote. The good adversary knight battles mightily for his client knowing that he must disclose the weaknesses of his own position just as he discovers his opponent's. Also, discovery reform was based on the assumption that truth consists of empirical facts, not abstract judgments.

In the annals of trial practice nothing has been as costly as this attack on "trial by ambush." Particularly after World War II the new enthusiasm for discovery was heightened by the development of large law firm practice. Litigation became a respectable part of commercial law practice, and the prosecution and defense of civil cases was undertaken on an hourly rate basis. The newly broadened scope of discovery and the

---

The author, a member in the San Francisco firm of Heller, Ehrman, White & McAuliffe, is a former chairman of the Section of Litigation.

growing respectability of litigation permitted, and many thought required, that law firms loose countless lawyers (now supported by hordes of paralegals) on unparalleled discovery efforts.

For many, effective professional representation seemed to demand that all possible discovery be undertaken to protect the client's best interests. With fees calculated by the hour, the more discovery the more the lawyer was paid. The client's best interests in litigation were in the lawyer's best economic interest. There is no more powerful coincidence than that of ethical responsibility and economic self-interest.

As litigation became respectable, more and more cases were filed. The courts became clogged. Judges came to dislike trials—and in federal courts, particularly jury trials—as an inefficient use of judicial time. Lawyers thus developed their efforts, attitudes, and tactics to use discovery as a tool for winning or losing cases by settlement rather than by trial.

Ever astute followers of legal economics, law schools concentrated on developing lawyers' interests in and talents for discovery. The focus of legal education was on discovery, not on trying cases. Increasingly, law professors lacked trial experience.

Malpractice Peril

Impelled by the broadened scope of discovery and the perceived need to leave no document unexamined and no witness undeposed—on peril of malpractice—lawyers developed a new ingenuity for limitless discovery. With this ingenuity came the new and now widely recognized problem of overdiscovery: warehouses of documents demanded and produced, depositions without end, and interrogatories word-processed with alacrity if not intelligence.

Because discovery operates between adversaries, ingenuity in discovery demands evoked ingenuity in discovery responses. So arose myriad motions to quash or limit, objections to interrogatories, instructions not to answer questions, and depositions filled with lawyers' colloquy—all of them paid for by the word, written or oral.

All of this comes at a high price in terms of increased delay, lost public respect, and higher client costs. Another price also has been paid: the erosion of the trial skills of judging how best to present a case, determining what evidence to use, directing that evidence and presenting it persuasively to win a favorable verdict.

Trial is a focused exercise requiring carefully selected evidence, presented on limited issues, so that the trier of fact can understand the case. Unless this approach is understood from the outset, discovery quickly exceeds reasonable bounds—and to little avail, for when forced to trial, litigators are poorly prepared. Having discovered everything, they now want to prove everything. Litigators often fail to recognize the difference between discovery for trial purposes and discovery for discovery-oriented litigation.

179

It is a vicious circle. Broadened discovery has eroded trial skills; lessened trial skills have led to discovery abuse. Fewer and fewer lawyers today try cases, particularly complex cases involving considerable discovery. Fewer lawyers understand how to try cases because discovery has replaced trial as the ultimate adversary weapon. Since they do not know how to try a case, more and more lawyers overuse discovery.

A popular anecdote has it that if employed to locate earthworms in a field after being told that they are usually found under moist rocks, and that the field is half moist and half dry, the litigator starts at the dry end, overturning every rock en route to the moist end. Faced with the same situation, the trial lawyer starts his worm hunt in the moist part of the field and stops overturning rocks when he has enough worms.

In many cases, particularly substantial personal injury cases, plaintiff's counsel knows 90 percent of his case by the time he files the complaint. Conversely, in such cases the defendant anticipates suit, and by factual investigation before or shortly after the time suit is filed, he too learns 90 percent of the important information about the case. The trial lawyer on either side will concentrate his discovery on the 10 percent not known. Not so the litigator. He will discover all the facts to obtain the 10 percent he does not know already.

As a result, discovery has replaced trial as the mechanism for resolving disputes. Litigators march forth from law firms flanked by junior partners, associates and paralegals much as fifteenth century Italian armies ventured from warring city-states. These armies left home and lived well off the land as they proceeded to confront the enemy. They avoided direct combat at all costs. The process leading to it was too rewarding, while battle itself was too risky. Thus does litigation proceed today.

Unbearably Expensive

Litigators no longer use discovery as an aid to trial, to focus or simplify the issues. To the contrary, discovery makes cases more complex. As more and more information is requested on more and more issues, discovery also makes litigation unbearably expensive. Discovery is used to wear opponents down, to confuse, to delay, to increase expense, to make complex—and ultimately to settle. Such settlements often have little to do with the merit of the case. Lacking trial experience, the lawyers have nothing against which to measure their cases or settlements.

Lawyers who seldom try cases fear trial as an unknown. They use extensive and expensive discovery to convince their own clients as well as the opponents that cases should be settled. They do so even when extensive discovery is not necessary. How often do litigators think of not deposing friendly and available third-party witnesses? How often do lawyers resist cross-examination during discovery when they should? "I did such a job on that expert they won't be able to use him at trial" really means "I just lost a priceless opportunity to impress the jury." How often do litigators ask interrogatories, then take depositions, then request production of documents and finally request admission of the same facts when one procedure would suffice?

All too many litigators depose three witnesses on the same subject when a little thought would make them choose only one. They turn paralegals loose on thousands of documents without having first scouted the terrain, found the most fruitful areas, and given the paralegals proper direction and advice. They eschew statistical samplings of documents and insist each page be examined. In return the paralegals all too often duplicate, microfilm or computerize thousands of documents that will never be looked at or used at trial. Forests disappear in this process but seldom is justice advanced. To paraphrase Colton's remark on civil jurisprudence and law:

> In "civil practice" it too often happens that there is so much "discovery" that there is no room for justice, and the claimant expires of wrong in the midst of right, as mariners die of thirst in the midst of water.

Lawyers find it easier to uncover new issue after new issue rather than to direct factual inquiries toward making the case intelligible. Instead of going for the jugular, it has become fashionable to bleed each capillary.

Today law is more complex and factual situations more varied, but in part this change is the result of broad-scale, overabundant discovery. The many who now say that cases are too complex for juries are really condemning lawyers for their increasing inability to present and explain complex legal causes simply in intelligible terms. It is a very sad development, for as Gilbert K. Chesterton has said:

> Our civilization has decided, and very justly decided, that determining the guilt or innocence of men is a thing too important to be trusted to trained men. If it wishes for light upon that awful matter, it asks men who know no more light than I know, but who can feel the things that I felt in the jury box. When it wants a library catalogued, or the solar system discovered, or any trifle of that kind, it uses up its specialists. But when it wishes anything done that is really serious, it collects twelve of the ordinary men standing about. The same thing was done, if I remember right, by the Founder of Christianity.

To break out of this vicious circle, we must find ways to give litigators more trial experience, to develop their trial skills. Our British brethren have long recognized this need and accordingly split their bar between barristers, who alone are permitted to practice in the high trial courts, and solicitors who have predominantly nontrial practices.

In this country the need for trial practice is also increasingly recognized. Trial practice courses are now given in many law schools, and more significantly there are a growing number of practical trial institutes where trial lawyers teach other lawyers how to try cases.

A leading light among these institutes is the Advanced Trial Advocacy Workshop, a National Program for Experienced Litigators, which is a joint venture of the American College of Trial Lawyers, the National Institute for Trial Advocacy, the ABA's Section of Litigation, the Trial Lawyers Section of the Florida Bar, and the University of Florida's College of Law. Each student in this workshop is a lawyer with 10 years of trial experience. Law firms, too, are joining the drive for more trial experience, developing in-house education programs and encouraging their litigators to attend workshops on how to try various types of cases.

Of course, even if all litigators were Clarence Darrows, discovery might still be abused. Many of our present discovery problems arise from the unresolved tension between a lawyer's role as a fearless advocate of his client's interest and the lawyer's duties as an officer of the court. If lawyers acted solely as officers of the court, they would produce in response to a simple general request their most important witnesses, the most pertinent documents, and the evidence most damaging to their cases. When lawyers act solely as advocates, they do not volunteer damaging evidence unless it is specifically asked for in a detailed narrow discovery request.

The tension generated by the lawyer's dual capacity is also apparent in his response to the problems of delay and cost. A rush to trial often will aid one party while the opponent wants delay. One party often can afford more discovery than the other. What is the lawyer's responsibility when he knows delaying trial a year or two will save his client or when he thinks the opponent will capitulate if confronted with a discovery blitz? There are no clear-cut answers to these questions. Judges place greater emphasis on the lawyer's role as an officer of the court. But clients expect militant defenses and unrestrained advocacy of their interests. Lawyers remain in the middle with substantial responsibilities to both sides.

There may be no final solution to this cause of overdiscovery, but an awareness of the problem at least will guard against the extremes of advocacy.

Whatever the present problems with discovery abuse, the trial bar's interest in reform is heartening. Change is seldom popular, particularly among lawyers, but most now recognize the need to deal with the problem of discovery abuse.

As an important first step in finding the needed solution, the ABA Litigation Section's Special Committee for the Study of Discovery Abuse has recommended changes in the Federal Rules of Civil Procedure governing discovery. These proposed changes seek to limit the scope of the issues on which discovery will be allowed, to make lawyers responsible for their discovery decisions, to make them weigh whether their discovery is necessary or redundant and to adopt new procedures to expedite and simplify discovery. Overall these changes aim at changing lawyers' attitudes so they no longer think the more discovery the better but instead carefully consider whether their discovery is directed to what their lawsuits are all about.

These changes could have repercussions for the litigation bar. Fewer people may be needed, but they should be better used and directed. Lawyers who can prepare cases for trial, and who can try them when necessary, will always be in demand. All of this will enhance public respect for litigation, win judges' approval, please cost-conscious clients and make litigation once more an interesting challenge.

PART III

Depositions

Taking Depositions

by Jerome P. Facher

In preparing for trial, depositions play an important and often crucial role. Tactics and strategy in planning, taking, and using depositions frequently determine the outcome of litigation and the trial lawyer cannot neglect or indiscriminately delegate this vital phase of his case. If he does so, he may discover to his regret that he has lost or wasted a valuable tactical opportunity which he may never regain.

Preparation of a case rarely fails to benefit from a deposition, and in general a decision to depose at least the adverse party should be the rule. Even in uncomplicated litigation, knowing the adversary's testimony, his legal contentions, his witnesses, and his documents and records is an incalculable advantage far superior to written interrogatories or private investigation on the same subjects. In addition, a deposition affords an early opportunity to evaluate the opposing party as a witness and to appraise the overall strengths and weaknesses of his case. Finally, depositions often include or are followed by settlement discussions and settlements are frequently reached at an earlier time than would ordinarily be the case.

Occasionally the argument is made that a deposition "educates" the adverse party, and should therefore be avoided. This is rarely, if ever, a sound tactical justification for not deposing a party who has information susceptible to oral discovery. While such a deponent may be exposed to some adverse facts and legal contentions, the usefulness of the informa-

Mr. Facher is a senior partner in the Boston firm of Hale & Dorr and a lecturer in trial practice at Harvard Law School. This article is abridged from a comprehensive treatment of deposition practice and tactics written for members of the Massachusetts Bar upon the Supreme Judicial Court's adoption of rules permitting discovery depositions in civil cases. References in the original text to the Massachusetts rules have been omitted or, where applicable, changed to the comparable Federal Rules of Civil Procedure. The article first appeared in the Massachusetts Law Quarterly *(Deposition Practice and Tactics, 52 MASS. L.Q. 5) and is excerpted here with permission.*

tion obtained by the examiner vastly outweighs this slight, and often illusory, disadvantage. Invariably, the "education" received will be far greater than any "education" given and the deposition will thus be worth taking. Moreover, in a skillfully conducted deposition, the adverse party may receive no "education" whatever, except a general awareness of the complexities of litigation and some familiarity with the examination process.

Tactically, the decision to depose a witness depends on the nature of his expected testimony, his availability and his willingness to testify at trial. Generally, a friendly or neutral witness is not deposed if he will be available to testify at the trial since, in this instance, the educational value to the opposing party outweighs the risk of not preserving the witness's testimony. With a hostile witness, counsel must decide (a) whether his adverse testimony at the trial will be sufficiently important to warrant preparing to refute it in advance or (b) independently of any adverse testimony, whether he has evidence or documents essential to counsel's affirmative case which may not otherwise be obtainable.

Practical Considerations

Frequently, practical considerations will dominate the decision to depose. If the testimony of the deponent—whether he is a witness or a party—is needed, and illness, age or distance indicate that he will not be available at the trial, there is little alternative but to take his deposition.

Since deposition testimony can affect the outcome of the trial, no competent trial counsel should consider taking or attending a deposition without thorough preparation. Not only examining counsel but deponent's counsel have important preparatory tasks if they are to represent their clients properly. If the examiner is unprepared, the deposition will likely be a tedious waste of time, effort and expense with little information to show for it. If deponent's counsel is unprepared, the consequences can be more serious since the deponent may unnecessarily provide or volunteer much damaging information.

Counsel should never permit his client or a witness over whom he has control to be deposed without adequate advance preparation. Not only must the deponent's testimony and documents be reviewed, but equally important, he must be prepared for the deposition process itself. A full explanation by counsel of the nature and mechanics of the forthcoming deposition is essential if the deponent is to understand his role.

Perhaps the most important consideration that counsel must emphasize is the difference between a deposition and a trial. He should explain the one-sided nature of a deposition, its broad scope, the absence of any judge to settle disputes, the purpose and type of objections, the general obligation to answer all questions, and the circumstances under which the deposition is usable at trial.

Above all, a party deponent must fully realize that the deposition is de-

187

signed to obtain as much information from him as possible, and that he cannot help his case by volunteering information, arguing with the examiner or explaining his answers. In simple terms he should be told that his deposition can be used against him but that, unless he dies, it is not likely to do him much good at trial. He must be instructed that the time for explanation and further testimony is in the courtroom and not the deposition room, and that when that time comes, his side of the case will be fully presented. In short, he must fully understand the nature of the deposition proceeding and the substantial dangers it may present for his case.

The limited role of deponent's counsel must also be explained and understood so that the deponent does not mistake a proper lack of active participation by his counsel for failure of representation. Without such understanding and explanation, deponent's counsel may tend to become active vocally for what appears to be no other purpose than to demonstrate his diligence to his client, perhaps on the theory that the client may mistake movement for action.

Once the nature of the deposition process is understood, the deponent's preparation on the merits should begin. A few general guidelines about deposition procedures and a short lecture on the virtues of brevity, responsiveness and truth are not adequate preparation for what may be a long and important examination. The client's testimony should be elicited in detail, the areas of possible examination reviewed and the documents scrutinized. In addition, he should be tested by cross-examination and asked the hard questions that are to be anticipated from opposing counsel.

The examiner's preparation for the deposition is no less essential or extensive than the deponent's. He not only must know his client's case but must learn as much as possible about his adversary's. Whether the deponent is a party or a witness, counsel should carefully investigate what part he has played in the case and the specific information, knowledge and evidence he possesses. At the same time counsel should review the existing documents and ascertain whether further documents are likely to be in existence and in the deponent's possession.

After obtaining the facts and documents, counsel should study the applicable law to learn what facts should be elicited at the deposition to support his overall legal theory or such specific legal conclusions as ''waiver,'' ''estoppel,'' ''wilful,'' ''knowingly.'' Thereafter, counsel should prepare a broad written outline of the general subjects to be covered as well as an event-by-event chronology of the case, noting each conversation, communication or incident. He should also prepare a detailed outline of his examination as a checklist to assure continuity, perspective and complete coverage. Without such a detailed guide, a deposition, which is peculiarly a proceeding where the subject matter can change frequently and fast, may tend to become disjointed and disorganized and its usefulness diminished.

Obtaining Stipulations

When the deposition convenes, the first practical and tactical situation generally facing counsel is that of stipulations. The most common stipulation waives the filing of the transcript and other related formalities and preserves to the time of trial all objections except as to form. Frequently signature is also waived and if they wish, the parties may broaden the stipulation to preserve all objections, even those of form, to the time of trial.

Without a stipulation, the deposition must be signed before the notary who took the testimony and the transcript must be sealed and filed in court. Objections as to form are waived unless made at the deposition, and no objections whose grounds could have been obviated at the deposition are preserved for trial. Rule 30(e)(6); Rule 32(d)(3)(A).

In considering a stipulation the tactical choices differ for each counsel. The examiner may prefer to have deponent's counsel make the required objections or lose them at trial. At the same time, he may wish to preserve until trial his own objections to the witness's answers. He may also want to avoid filing the transcript in court but may be unwilling to waive the necessity of the deponent's signing the deposition.

On the other hand, deponent's counsel may wish to waive signature on the theory that the deposition thereby becomes slightly less impeaching, but may insist on the transcript's being filed in court, based in part on the dubious ground of additional expense to the opposing party. He may also wish to preserve all objections to the time of trial so that he loses no rights in failing to object at the deposition.

Obviation Clause

Apart from the trouble-making obviation clause which does not preserve objections whose grounds are "obviable" [Rule 32(d)(3)(A)], Rule 32 itself would preserve to the time of trial all objections except as to form. The usual stipulation has the additional effect of rendering inoperative the obviation clause and thereby eliminating uncertainty at the deposition and controversy at trial. If counsel wishes to take the further step of eliminating any disputes about the distinction between form and substance, he may stipulate that *all* objections (not only those as to form) are preserved to the time of trial.

Where the deponent is a witness not represented by counsel the parties should be certain that he has been given a full and adequate explanation of the content and effect of any stipulation. Generally, the witness will have no objections to a stipulation in the usual form, including waiver of signature. It may be wise, however, for one party or the other to insist on signature, especially if the witness will not be available at trial and the deposition is to be offered in evidence.

Another preliminary matter which frequently arises concerns the attendance at the deposition of other witnesses, parties or potential deponents. Rule 26(c)(5) provides that the court may make an order "that discovery be conducted with no one present except persons designated by the court." [Although parties and counsel appear to have an absolute right to attend the deposition, *see* 8 Wright and Miller, Federal Practice and Procedure [S]2041, it is not altogether clear who is entitled to attend a deposition in the absence of a protective order limiting attendance. One court has held that neither the public nor the press has a right to attend a deposition, but that only "the principals" do. *Times Newspaper Ltd. (of Great Britain) v. McDonnell Douglas Corp..* 387 F. Supp. 189 (C.D. Cal. 1974).—*Ed.*] Therefore, if counsel wish to exclude other witnesses, application for such protection should be made in advance of the deposition.

Once the preliminary skirmishes about stipulations, attendance of spectators, and other matters have concluded, the witness can be sworn and the deposition begun. However, there are some depositions when long speeches of counsel "for the record" precede the commencement of testimony. These will denounce the scope of the notice or subpoena, challenge the designation of the deponent as managing agent or expound on some purported irregularity in the proceedings to that point. Most of such speeches accomplish no useful purpose, clutter the record and enrich the reporter. If counsel were genuinely concerned about such matters, some action prior to the deposition (or a simple objection noted for the record as to certain matters of procedure or form) would be the more meaningful and appropriate practice.

Although examining counsel will have his outlines, chronology and documents to guide his examination, perhaps the most important factors in the success of the deposition are his recognition and understanding of its purpose and an interrogation which reflects such purpose. Knowing the purposes of the deposition tells the examiner how to conduct the deposition. Unless counsel appreciates why and to what end he is interrogating, the examination may be not only meaningless, but harmful. Thus, his knowledge should include not merely a familiarity with the deponent's expected testimony, but how such testimony and the likely presence or absence of the deponent at trial affects his deposition tactics and fits into his overall trial strategy.

Examining counsel must first decide whether the deposition is primarily for discovery, for use as evidence at the trial, for later impeachment or contradiction at trial, for perpetuation as tactical insurance against age, illness or death, for securing admissions, narrowing issues or for some combination of these or other reasons. Usually there will be more than one purpose for the deposition, especially if the deponent is a party from whom both broad discovery and specific admissions will be sought and whom counsel may wish to impeach and contradict at trial.

The purpose of the deposition in general and of any specific question in particular largely dictates the form of question asked, and in turn, the form and substance of the answer received. If the purpose of the deposition is primarily for discovery, the examiner's questions will tend to be broad, the subjects far-reaching and the answers rambling and discursive. Such an examination is basically devoted to information-gathering with the examiner trying to discover what the deponent knows, without serious concern for the form in which the information is received or its later admissibility.

If the deposition is being conducted for the purpose of producing admissible evidence—whether documentary or testimonial—the form and substance of the questions and answers are crucially different since they must be admissible at trial in order to fulfill the examiner's purpose. Thus, the questions must be as sharp and precise, and the answers as complete and responsive, as if the deposition were in fact the trial. The examiner is primarily interested in usable evidence and not in gathering information. If the questions and answers are not in admissible form, the testimony becomes useless, the deposition will be excluded when offered at the trial and the necessary evidence lost.

When the purpose of the deposition is largely evidentiary, objections to the form of the question and answer become more significant. If not made at the deposition, such objections are waived both under Rule 32(d)(3)(B) and the usual stipulation. When they are made at the deposition, the examiner must decide whether to rephrase the question to meet the objection or allow the question to stand and thereby run the risk that it will be excluded at trial.

If the purpose of the deposition or of a line of questioning is to freeze the deponent's testimony so that it will not change at the time of trial, the questions must be directed to, and accomplish, that purpose. The subject matter must be sufficiently broad and the questions sufficiently specific so that the deponent is fairly committed to a version of the facts which he cannot change at trial.

Make Full Record

An examiner may be completely prepared for a deposition and fully understand its purposes and yet not achieve such purposes because of a lack of thoroughness in his interrogation, and a failure to make a full and complete record of the deponent's knowledge and information.

Attention to detail, in depositions as in other affairs, is the hallmark of a craftsman skilled in his art. Since the federal and many state rules permit, and indeed encourage, a latitude of questions in detail far wider than would be permitted at trial, the examiner should take full advantage of the opportunity. For each important conversation or transaction about which he inquires, he should be certain that he has obtained all that the deponent's memory can provide. When the deponent's memory is exhausted, the examiner should attempt to evoke further testi-

191

mony by refreshing his recollection or should establish for the record that it cannot be refreshed. The record should thus be clear that the deponent's version of a particular incident or conversation is complete so that at the trial the deponent will not be able to make changes or additions without risking impeachment. Frequently, an examiner fails to ask a deponent if he has given the substance of an entire conversation or conference. Thereafter, at trial the witness may give damaging testimony as to further conversation which would have been elicited on deposition if the examiner had pressed the point and insisted on complete information. Similarly, unless all of the witnesses to a given event are named, or all of the documents in a particular transaction identified, surprise witnesses and surprise documents may turn up to plague counsel at trial.

As to documents produced at the deposition, the examiner should make sure not only that they are made part of the record, but more importantly, that the questions and answers relating to them clearly identify the document or to words or phrases within a document, the examiner should make it clear precisely what language he is asking about and where it is to be found in the document. Vague references to "this letter" "that agreement" or "the report" may be clear to those attending the deposition but will be meaningless in the typed transcript.

Mark as Exhibit

Before the examiner asks any questions about a document, he should have it marked as an exhibit for identification so that he can then refer to it by exhibit number and make sure that the witness does the same. Assuming the usual stipulation is in effect, no objection need be made to a document's being marked as a deposition exhibit since the question of its admissibility is reserved by Rule 32(d)(3) until trial. However, if the obviation clause is operative, other objections such as lack of foundation or best evidence may be required in order to void the possibility of waiver.

Thoroughness in examination and attention to detail also include such basic and often crucial procedures as authenticating documents or photographs, laying a proper foundation for testimony, qualifying an expert, identifying and describing physical objects and other preliminary burdens required by the law of evidence before testimony or documents become admissible. Unless such matters are handled competently at the deposition, important evidence may be later excluded and the case seriously affected.

Once the purpose of the deposition and of a particular line of inquiry is fixed, the examiner should adopt the manner and method of examination which best serves that purpose. If the deposition is being taken to gather information, the witness should be encouraged to talk since the more he testifies the more the examiner knows. Counsel who takes a deposition for discovery and then prevents the witness from volunteering, bristles at self-serving statements, cuts off explanations and continually demands only yes-or-no answers, is neither hurting the witness nor helping the case.

Since the most important product of a discovery deposition is raw information, the examiner who prevents its emergence by such tactics not only defeats his own purpose, but may create a hostile atmosphere in which the witness is not likely to continue to be informative or cooperative.

Similarly, an examiner should never be reluctant to elicit unfavorable information at a discovery deposition. He should be as anxious to receive this information as the deponent will be to provide it. Although it should be the essence of the discovery procedure to learn adverse information early at a deposition rather than being surprised later at the trial, inexperienced examiners, allegedly seeking discovery, nonetheless avoid deposing on subjects which may yield statements and information damaging to their case. The damaging information will not disappear merely because counsel has not asked about it and sound tactics indicate that knowing the worst and preparing for it is far preferable to pretending that it does not exist.

If the purpose of the deposition is basically evidentiary, that is, for later introduction into evidence, the examiner's method and technique should closely resemble that used at trial. His questions should be in proper form and directed toward eliciting testimony which would be unobjectionable when offered at the trial. With this objective in mind he must carefully evaluate the answers received to assure himself that they are responsive and in proper form. An answer which is informative but inadmissible in form or substance serves no evidentiary purpose at the trial. Conversely, an answer improper in form may be admissible at the trial if the objection to form has not been made or preserved.

Some or all of the above considerations apply in varying degrees at every deposition. With a party, the examiner will ordinarily seek the broadest possible discovery, yet will also be concerned with obtaining usable admissions, laying the groundwork for possible later impeachment and obtaining any evidence necessary to his affirmative case. He must also consider that while the party deponent is limited to using his own deposition to rebut portions offered in evidence, his unavailability at trial may make the deposition usable as part of his affirmative case. As to a witness, the examiner may have less interest in broad discovery and more in fixing the witness's version of events or in putting the testimony in admissible form for use at trial.

With such considerations clearly in mind, the examiner must frequently switch the form and format of his questions depending on his purpose and whether the deponent is a party or a witness. Where the examiner wishes discovery, his questions will be broad, occasionally open-ended and may call for explanations or encourage the deponent to talk. For example, the "why" question which is usually avoided at trial by most cross-examiners as a foolhardy practice with an articulate hostile witness, may be a proper and logical question at a discovery deposition where information is the basic purpose served by the question. However, when the examiner comes upon a subject matter as to which he wishes to "freeze" the deponent's story, elicit an admission or put the testimony in admissible form for the trial, he must change both his tactics and his questions. To accomplish these purposes, he will switch from what has been essentially information-gathering by direct examination to the specifics of cross-examination, paying careful attention to the completeness of his examination and to the form and substance of both question and answer.

In short, a good examiner will, for part of his interrogation, sound as if he were conducting a direct examination of his own client and at other times, as if he were cross-examining the adverse party. Both techniques are dictated by the purposes which the deposition is to serve and by the constantly changing nature of information sought and the testimony received.

The examiner who habitually conducts his deposition as if he were in the courtroom overlooks the fact that he is not. The examiner who conducts his deposition without any thought of the courtroom is equally shortsighted and his results will be as haphazard and as limited. The "art" of deposing is the right mixture of discovery and cross-examination, information and evidence, broad inquiry and pointed question, useful knowledge and usable testimony, and of knowing when and how to get the information required in the form best suited to the needs of the case.

Not only can a deposition be rendered unproductive by lack of preparation or by a failure to understand its purposes, but the examiner's style and attitude can cause similar results. Particularly is this the case in examining the adverse party where discovery is usually part of the purpose to be served.

Unsound Attitude

Some examiners, long accustomed to flamboyant courtroom cross-examination, bring the same manner and mannerisms to the deposition without fully realizing that courtroom tactics differ substantially from deposition tactics. Their cross-examination is often marked by petty tests of credibility carried out in an atmosphere of open hostility and accompanied by insinuations of disbelief or expressions of incredulity. Such an attitude is usually unsound and impractical. Cross-examination designed to impress a jury should be saved for the jury. At a deposition no one is impressed by such tactics, except possibly the client, and contentiousness for his benefit is not a sound tactical justification for wasting valuable deposition time and money. Secondly, a hostile and overly aggressive attitude generally tends to defeat the examiner's purpose, by resulting in less, not more, information and by indoctrinating the witness early in the type of examination to expect in court. Such conduct can also create resentments and antagonism which will diminish the effectiveness of the examiner and thereafter plague the case, possibly preventing an early settlement.

As far as the examiner is concerned, there is little reason why the deposition should not be conducted in a friendly, or at least civil atmosphere. When cross-examination becomes necessary, a firm but polite manner is far superior to the slashing attack and will accomplish more. To be effective it need not degenerate into the quibbling and quarrelsomeness that often accompanies what passes for fierce courtroom cross-examination. The absence of any jury is precisely the reason why the examiner can concentrate on the major issues of the case, and on developing a broad base of discovery information which, by appropriate and selected examination techniques, he can narrow into admissible evidence when and if he chooses to do so.

For discovery purposes, there well may be much to gain and little to lose in the examiner's allowing the witness to volunteer information or make self-serving statements. However, at some point the examiner may need for the record a responsive answer in a form suitable for admission into evidence at the trial. A certain degree of tenacity is therefore required in rephrasing or repeating the question until a responsive answer is given.

While occasionally the deponent's answer remains wholly unresponsive, more frequently the examiner is faced with an answer part of which is responsive and part of which is not. In order to preserve his right to object at trial to the wholly non-responsive answer, or to have stricken the non-responsive portion of the otherwise responsive answer, the examiner may fear that he must do something further at the deposition—a fear based on the assumption that a non-responsive answer is either an obviable defect or one of form. The fear is illusory and the assumption is unsound since neither category is applicable.

Clearly, it is not within the examiner's control to obviate a non-responsive answer. Neither constant repetition of the question, long colloquies or the threat of sanctions can force a deponent to be responsive or produce an answer the deponent does not wish to give. To argue that such a result is an obviable defect is contrary to common sense and inconsistent with experience.

Nor is a plainly non-responsive answer or a non-responsive portion of an answer (which in most disputed cases includes self-serving assertions) a matter of form, but rather goes to the substance of the question and often to the merits of the case. If a witness were asked to identify his signature, and replied that the signature was his, but that his adversary had tricked him into signing, or if he were asked whether he knew the plaintiff and replied affirmatively, adding that the plaintiff was an alcoholic, the defects of such answers hardly go only to form. Such improper answers no more require that the examiner immediately echo the meaningless phrase "move to strike" than an irrelevant or immaterial deposition question requires an objection. If such were not the result, the jury, in the absence of such a "motion" in the transcript, would be entitled to consider the entire answer and give such evidentiary weight and effect as they wished to the plainly prejudicial material. This consequence would be highly unfair to the examiner and in turn would oblige him to clutter the record with repeated motions to strike, admonitions and suggestion of sanctions, although in the last analysis, he could do nothing to change the answer.

While the problem, if any, can be dealt with by broadening the stipulation to preserve all objections (both to the question and answer) to the time of trial, examining counsel should not be forced to seek such a stipulation at the risk that a clever deponent may create admissible evidence out of non-responsive and self-serving answers.

Best of Both Worlds

Although non-responsiveness is a matter of substance, there are defects in the form of answers to which the examiner should voice objections at the deposition. A familiar example would be the deponent's testifying with characterizations rather than facts. Subjective conclusions that the speaker "agreed," "pleaded" or "demanded" rather than testimony as to what he said are defects in the form of answer. Unless the matter has been covered by stipulation, counsel should note his objection and then either attempt to secure an answer in proper form or not as his tactics dictate.

In such a situation, the examiner has the best of both worlds. He has not only the information but the power to strike the defective answer at the trial should deponent's counsel attempt to offer it. On the other hand, deponent's counsel, recognizing this, may wish the testimony in admissible form and may seek to have the witness correct his testimony immediately or on cross-examination.

Although the deponent's counsel has a less vocal role to play at a deposition, it is no less important than the examiner's. At every stage of the examination, deponent's counsel must be alert for questions improper in form or considered outside the scope of the deposition, and must be prepared for any situation in which he is called upon to protect his client's interests. He may be obliged to make the hard decision instructing his client not to answer or to refuse production of documents, and ultimately he must decide whether to cross-examine and to what extent.

If the obviation clause has been rendered ineffective by stipulation and all objections except as to form have been preserved until the time of trial, deponent's counsel's principal concern will be identifying defects of form. Examples of such defects would be questions which are argumentative, ambiguous, multiple or leading, all of which can be cured by the examiner's rephrasing the question. When such a defect appears in a question, deponent's counsel need do no more than state his objection as to form. If he wishes, he may state the ground for his objection, which may be of some aid to the examiner (who may then decide to reframe his question) and perhaps to the witness. Often the examiner will suggest that deponent's counsel state the ground of objection so that the question can be rephrased.

Ambiguous Question

Occasionally, in lieu of making a formal objection, deponent's counsel will merely request a clarification to prevent the witness's being confused by an ambiguous question. Such participation, if not overdone, can be helpful in maintaining an accurate and non-misleading record. Occasionally however, whether a request for "clarification" more accurately represents advice to the witness than a genuine misunderstanding of the question becomes a matter of some debate.

Since the rules permit a broad scope of examination and generally require that all questions should be answered (with objections preserved until trial) counsel should rarely instruct his client to refuse to answer. *See* Rule 30(c). However, situations will arise when deponent's counsel must consider whether the examination so exceeds the permissible bounds that he is justified in running the risk of instructing his witness not to answer. His initial instinct should be against such an instruction if any other course is open, including asking that the question be reframed if its language is the source of difficulty. When all else fails and the subject is sufficiently important to the case (as opposed merely to a test of wills with opposing counsel), resort to a refusal to answer is not precluded by the rules. *But see Ralston Purina Co. v. McFarland,* 550 F.2d 967 (4th Cir. 1977).

Deponent's counsel should be aware that a refusal to answer gives the examiner the option to adjourn the deposition in order to obtain a court ruling. Rule 37(a) (2). Thus, the deposition may be halted and valuable time, effort and expense consumed in motion proceedings while the client awaits the result, often unable to attend to his business or to complete his deposition. When the motion is finally disposed of, the deposition will continue and the client may find that his inconvenience and expense were substantially increased by his own counsel.

Matters which are privileged are outside the scope of examination permitted under Rule 26(b) and questions concerning such matters need not be answered on appropriate objection and instruction by counsel. Occasionally, however, the privilege is prematurely asserted, since an examiner is entitled to know when, where, and to whom the deponent made the privileged communication in order to determine if the privilege applies.

Similarly, matters not relevant to the subject matter of the litigation are not within the scope of examination. However, since the broad concept of relevance as stated in Rule 26(b)(1) and in the decided cases clearly permits fishing expeditions, counsel takes some risk in using irrelevancy as a basis for a refusal to answer. Although the scope of relevant examination is not without limit, he may often have difficulty justifying the refusal if the question has any connection with the proceedings or can lead to any admissible evidence.

While disagreements as to relevancy are a common source of colloquy at depositions, a request of the examiner as to the relevance of his question will often elicit a satisfactory explanation that will eliminate a possible refusal to answer. Similarly, the examiner should not be reluctant to state the relevance of the question, not only to avoid controversy and obtain the information but also to make a clear record if, despite the explanation, the refusal to answer nonetheless persists.

While misleading, argumentative or ambiguous questions present, as a technical matter, only defects of form, often any response will provide misleading, argumentative or ambiguous information, or start the examiner on an improper and time-wasting line of examination. Since the examiner is presumably not deposing either to mislead or to argue with the witness, refusals to answer are probably easier to justify under these circumstances than others. Once again however, counsel can avoid friction, controversy, and eventual judicial intervention by seeking to reach agreement on the phraseology of the disputed question.

The form of interrogation, including endless repetition, overlong examination, overbearing behavior, unjustified preoccupation with minor matters for inordinate periods, and constant argumentativeness frequently result in refusals to answer. Such infringements by the examiner are matters of degree, and tactical judgments will differ as to whether it is simpler, faster and less wasteful for counsel to permit an answer than to advise a refusal.

Longer than at Trial

As to length of examination, the rules contemplate that a deposition examination, by its nature, will be longer than an examination at trial on the same subjects. Full discovery is one purpose of the rules and one of their chief benefits. Nonetheless there may well be a point at which a particular subject matter or the deponent's knowledge has been thoroughly exhausted or where the line between permissible and impermissible inquiry has been overstepped. At this point deponent's counsel may conclude that a refusal to answer is justified, although in so concluding, he must constantly be aware that the court may later draw the line differently and apply sanctions accordingly. *See* Rule 37(a).

In dealing with refusals to answer, both counsel should exercise restraint before taking rigid positions. Frequently, before giving any instruction not to answer, deponent's counsel should indicate his nonobjection to a certain line of questions if limited or clarified, or his willingness to continue with other areas of inquiry. If he finally decides to instruct the witness not to answer, it should be done with a minimum of speech-making, rancor or colloquy and, if possible, without encouraging a suspension of the deposition by the examiner.

Similarly, the examiner should usually not waste time and money in pointless argument and long "for the record" speeches since the relevance and propriety of a well-phrased question ought to be apparent from the question itself and from the prior record. However, the examiner may occasionally wish to explain such relevance and propriety in order either to resolve the objection and obtain the information or to call such matters to the court's attention when the transcript is read.

Although the examining party can suspend as of right when he is faced with a refusal, he should rarely do so but should try to complete the deposition on all other matters. Frequently, he will obtain the information with other questions and in connection with other subjects. If, on rare occasions, the attitude of deponent's counsel or the importance of the subject matter make it impossible for the deposition to continue, a judicial determination should be sought immediately and an effort made to see the nearest available judge as soon as possible.

In general, however, neither the examiner nor the deponent's counsel benefits greatly from refusals to answer. Much time can be consumed in colloquies and by motions concerning refusals on matters which later events prove irrelevant or unimportant or which were originally based on exaggerated fears. Further, in many instances, resort to judicial intervention never materializes either because other evidence provides the information or hindsight indicates it was not worth the effort. Finally, the information sought is often inadmissible in any event and its expected usefulness greatly overestimated. For such reasons, advising refusals to answer should be a last-resort measure for unusual situations and not a standard tactical procedure.

Unfortunately there are counsel who, far from seeking to avoid refusals to answer and infrequent resort to judicial intervention, appear to welcome, if not to precipitate, such circumstances. Thinking such conduct to be good tactics, they disrupt the continuity of the examination with constant objections and refusals together with challenges to the examiner to take up the matter with the court. Either these tactics mask an insecurity based on ignorance of the rules or their purpose is to prevent or hinder discovery.

Since the party deponent does not wish to provide his adversary with any more information than necessary consistent with giving responsive truthful answers, his counsel usually will not cross-examine him (or a favorable witness) if he will be available to testify at the trial. Exceptions to this general practice are often made to correct errors or to clarify misleading or ambiguous portions of the record in order to avoid the suspicion which attaches to last-minute changes or modifications of testimony at the trial.

Even if the party will be available to testify at trial, some counsel conduct a short cross-examination eliciting favorable testimony in general terms or denying the principal charges. It is argued that the possibility of the deponent's death or the possible introduction at trial of the cross-examination, if part of the deposition testimony is offered by opposing counsel, justifies this practice. The client's desire for equal time in order to present, in self-serving measure, his "side" of the case is also added as a minor justification. Although mortality is a fact of life, none of these considerations usually justifies more than a cursory cross-examination, if any. Such examination should probably do little more than indicate in broad outline that the party has a valid claim or has denied the allegations of the complaint.

The temptation to engage in extensive cross-examination, especially if the examiner has elicited some apparently damaging (but explainable) testimony, should be firmly resisted. Although the natural inclination of counsel and client may be to refute and rebut the examiner's case and to assert the righteousness of their own, the time for such presentation is normally not at the deposition but at trial. Counsel should ask himself what useful purpose will be served by trying to demonstrate to the examiner the worthlessness of his case and the validity of his adversary's. The examiner is not likely to be convinced and the attempt will provide him with valuable information and education. Absent some overriding consideration, deponent's counsel should save his efforts for the trial, but he should also make sure that his client understands why the deposition is not the appropriate place to explain and narrate his version of the facts.

A Warning Sign

If deponent's counsel embarks on extensive cross-examination of his own client or a favorable witness, it generally indicates that (1) the deponent's counsel is misinformed on deposition tactics (and is about to educate his adversary); (2) is excessively concerned about the possibility of death or unavailability; or (3) the deponent is likely to be unavailable at trial and thus must have his testimony perpetuated.

If the party taking the deposition concludes that the deponent's counsel is cross-examining in order to use the client's deposition at the trial, he must adjust his tactics accordingly. This will mean careful attention to the cross-examination to preserve objections of form and those which are obviable, and if necessary, conducting a redirect examination to obtain contradictions, admissions, or further testimony which can be introduced at the trial.

Counsel's judgment, intuition, and experience, and the form and substance of the questions are guides by which he can determine the purpose of cross-examination. If there is doubt, he should err on the side of assuming that the deponent's testimony is being preserved for use at trial and thereafter act accordingly.

Conducting the Oral Deposition

by Stuart A. Summit

The oral deposition can be the litigator's most useful tool when he enters the discovery phase of the big case. It is perhaps the most effective discovery device for developing the facts critical to the litigation. Properly conducted, depositions can affect the whole complexion of the action. Finally, oral depositions can play a significant role in settling the case. Since most civil actions are settled, the face-to-face confrontation of an important witness through the deposition can determine the extent and nature of the ultimate settlement.

Generalized advice for the conduct of a particular deposition is, of course, difficult to provide. However, one type of deposition—that of an important witness in a case where the facts are complex and the documents numerous—illustrates the many problems that are likely to arise in this form of discovery. Such depositions, which generally consume several days and can last for weeks, also require careful advance analysis and planning if they are to serve their intended purpose. It is that type of deposition that will be the model for my observations in this article.

Too many depositions are approached casually and conducted routinely. The examiner will ask the obvious questions suggested by the pleadings, perhaps pursuing some areas of inquiry in some depth, and he will consider that he has done his job. Too often the deposition is not preceded by careful planning, including a clear identification of the goals the examiner hopes to achieve through the deposition.

Is the deposition to be conducted simply to uncover facts? Are you honestly ignorant about certain areas of your case and will this witness supply the relevant information? Do you have serious doubts about the witness's view of the facts? If the deposition is needed principally to de-

The author is a member of the New York City firm of Summit, Rovins & Feldesman.

velop facts, you will want to isolate carefully the precise areas of factual inquiry for the witness.

However, oral depositions can serve other purposes. Would it be useful to have a full record of the witness's view of all possibly relevant facts, for example, to support a motion? Is it reasonable to expect that major factual disputes can be precluded by a careful examination of this witness on the entire case?

Or, perhaps the witness is in a position to encourage a settlement. Are there telling lines of inquiry that will suggest to the witness that settlement of the case should become a priority matter? Will a lengthy and exhaustive examination bring home to him the rigors of litigation and will he seek to avoid those rigors through settlement?

Perhaps the issues in the case have not yet been fully developed. The oral deposition can help you develop the issues favorable to your position. Can you emphasize certain lines of inquiry in a manner that will influence your adversary's thinking and thus influence the issues on which the case will be tried or settled? Particularly if the deposition will last for several days or weeks, the matters that assume importance during the deposition may be treated as important during the remainder of the action.

Setting Goals

If the examiner is fully conversant with the known facts of the case, and understands the witness and his role, he should be able to predict the reasonable result of the examination. There will be things that you cannot know in advance, but the likelihood that the witness has the missing information and the attitude he will probably take toward the relevant areas of inquiry should be predictable. Set your goals in advance and make them reasonable in light of what you do know.

It is also important that you know the witness as well as you can prior to the deposition. You should obtain as much background information on the witness as you can. The success of the oral deposition may depend on the extent to which the examiner understands the character, personality and temperament of the witness.

Is the witness a quick thinker? Is he accustomed to working in the early morning? In the evening? Is he controlled in speech or is he loquacious? Is he cheerful and composed? Is he used to pressure and does he accept pressure well? Will his composure suffer from long periods of questioning? Will he be substantially less controlled in the early morning or in the late afternoon? Does he have any personal or business problems that may affect his composure?

Personal background is helpful even when not directly related to the witness's probable conduct during the examination. You should attempt to learn the nature of his family life, and his community, church, recreation and social activities, and so forth.

Is he good at his job, respected by his fellow workers, subordinates and superiors? How does he prefer to be addressed? Does he resent any particular form of address? What is his attitude toward his work and his employer?

Such information enables you to visualize and understand the witness as a person as you prepare for his examination and will give added meaning to his answers at the deposition. Your sensitivity to him as a person when you are planning the deposition and when you are taking it will be invaluable.

Some may believe this kind of investigation is offensive, or interferes with the witness's "right of privacy," or constitutes gamesmanship. I disagree. If a particular witness may play an important role in the outcome of significant litigation, a careful review of his background and personal qualities is necessary and inevitable.

Next, you should identify precisely the witness's relationship to the case. You should not rely on your general knowledge of the witness's role. It is not enough to know that he is president of the adversary or that he had general responsibility for an activity at issue in the case. You should review all documents which he is known to have authored, all documents he is known to have received and all documents that he may have authored or received. You should also identify all documents which, in your understanding of his role, he logically should have authored or received but concerning which his role is not clear. Try to visualize what documents should exist, but apparently do not, which might affect his role. The documents frequently assume a pattern of their own, and you can spot events or subjects that should have been the subject of a writing, but apparently are not. Finally, you should attempt to distinguish between the "record" role and the actual role of the witness. There are instances of chief executives who insist on taking full responsibility but who, in fact, have little involvement in a given matter. Conversely, there are persons who prefer to remain in the background but who play a crucial role in a matter in dispute.

You should consider the possibility that the witness's attitude or motivations with respect to the case may not be the obvious ones. Ask yourself what his real attitudes or motivations might be. Try to think of him in relation to all of the other persons involved in the transaction. Was his role the natural one for him, given all the circumstances? Was he subordinate to persons he would resent? Was his role likely to have been resented by others? Might he have been overruled on some critical questions?

Getting Organized

Your next step should be to organize your materials. Your files should be well organized before you attempt to develop your actual method of questioning. Several methods of organization should be considered.

First, a full chronological memorandum is probably indispensable.

Such a memorandum should list, by date, every possibly relevant occurrence or communication. Each entry should be described sufficiently to enable you to recall quickly the witness's role in each transaction listed. The chronological memorandum must be updated as discovery progresses.

Second, you should isolate every topic you believe the witness can testify about and prepare a "fact sheet" for each of those topics. The fact sheet should contain itemized summaries of everything you know of the important facts relating to that topic and the witness's role with respect to it. Document references will be very helpful. For example:

January 23, 1973—
Smith was present at lengthy meeting—pricing structure discussed—see Jones' transcript, 11, 35; docs. # 23, 27, 29.

Important documents related to the witness's role can be annexed to the fact sheet.

Third, if you have a great deal of information available, you should compile a list of every "mention" of the witness by any person or in any document. If feasible, use actual quotations. Such a compilation may be of no help at all, but occasionally it will enable you to spot a pattern or otherwise give you a new insight into the witness's role or how he was viewed by others.

Finally, the relevant documents should be organized in as many different ways as you can conceive. A complete chronological file is indispensable. Each document should be related to as many topics as are at issue in the litigation and a copy of the document should be filed under each of those topics. Have a separate document file consisting only of documents the witness authored or which are addressed to him. The more places a relevant document can be found, the more likely it is that it will not be overlooked. Different juxtapositions of documents suggest different possible patterns of thought or conduct. You should read each different file in sequence, even though you are reading the same documents over and over.

The final step before the deposition is to prepare for the questioning. In most instances, you will want to avoid prepared questions. No matter how much you have prepared, you will not fully understand the witness and be able to predict how he will react until you are well into the deposition. Set patterns of questioning, which are usually the result of advance question preparation, make the examiner predictable and the witness comfortable. While this result may be desirable, you will not know in advance. It is simple to develop patterns that make the witness comfortable during the course of the examination if that turns out to be desirable.

The advantages of spontaneous questioning are overwhelming. If you compose your questions as you go, you will be much more alert to the nuances of each answer. You will not overlook a follow-up question. You will be able to determine on a continuing basis whether your method of questioning is producing the result you hope to achieve.

Most importantly, spontaneous questioning enables you to carry on a dialogue with the witness. The atmosphere that is created through that dialogue will necessarily affect the witness's answers. A question that is read invites greater care in the answer. It creates a cautious mood. Conversely, spontaneous questions, which demonstrate that you have total command of the facts, permit a fast pace. You want the witness to forget that he is in an adverse position to you, that he has a lawyer present and that a reporter is taking down every word he says. The witness must feel that he exists in a world in which there are only the two of you. Achieving this goal requires very hard work, good facility with questioning and a very fast pace.

Prepared Questions

There are occasions when you will have to prepare questions in advance. It may be that a particular line of questioning, with each question carefully worded, is necessary to force either an admission or the realization that evasion is futile. Also, where a number of documents must be referred to in the course of a single line of questions, some degree of advance question preparation may be necessary. Even so, your preparation should permit you to avoid the appearance of reading a line of questions. Prepare the questions in advance, review them thoroughly and keep the prepared questions in front of you. But you should attempt to maintain constant eye contact with the witness.

The extent to which questions are prepared in advance may also depend on your understanding of the witness. If he is a very controlled person who is likely to answer questions precisely and tersely, the questioning process will be slower and a greater degree of advance question preparation may be necessary.

One instance in which advance preparation of questions may be essential is when you anticipate an evasive or dishonest witness. You will want to prepare questions that will take advantage of the witness's dishonest and evasive tendencies and will lead him in a direction he is trying to avoid. An obvious example is where the witness wants to establish his ignorance of certain facts. If you attempt to establish that he is ignorant of certain insignificant facts, he may defend himself and show his total command of those facts. Having demonstrated that he is an astute perfectionist on these matters, he will be reluctant to claim ignorance of critical facts. Achieving this result requires careful advance wording of each successive question.

Whether you decide to make the entire examination spontaneous or prepare specific questions for certain areas of inquiry, you will need a checklist of the topics you intend to cover in the deposition. Such a checklist, combined with the "fact sheets" you have prepared for each topic, should assure a thorough and comprehensive inquiry.

With your preparation completed, you are ready to confront an important witness in the case. In such a deposition, as little as possible should be left to chance. Consider the room it will be held in. Consider how you want your papers arranged. Consider whether you want a colleague present to study the witness and advise you of the witness's reactions. Consider the timing of breaks and the lunch hour, and how such breaks will affect lines of inquiry. Consider whether you want to end the examination day with a dramatic flourish and whether you want to leave important lines of questioning open for consideration by the witness overnight.

You should have a reporter with whom you are familiar. There is nothing more frustrating than conducting an examination that has served your client well, only to find many days later that you have a garbled transcript. There is no sense in getting admissions that will never appear in print, and you cannot count on your adversary's good will when his choice is between a record of serious admissions or a garbled transcript.

You should face the witness directly. Put the reporter at the head of the table, with you and the witness occupying the seats adjacent to the reporter and across from each other. This forces adversary counsel to be out of the witness's line of sight and permits you to have direct eye contact with the witness.

Making a Record

In your preliminary questions, the witness should be made aware on the record of why he is being deposed and the nature of the litigation. You should also ask him how much notice he had of the examination. If the witness provides testimony favorable to your case which your adversary may wish to mitigate later, making a record of the extent of the witness's preparation may be important. You should determine what specific documents the witness reviewed in preparing for the examination. Objections of privilege may be raised to this line of inquiry. But you should be entitled to learn what the witness did, what the witness reviewed and how much time the witness spent in preparation, even if some of that time was spent in the company of counsel.

During your initial questions, you will want to determine the witness's role in the litigation process itself. Did he have a role in determining to sue? Did he assist in the drafting or review of a pleading? Was he instrumental in organizing information or documents after the transaction in issue was completed? Did he participate in interviews with others who may be witnesses? If he is familiar with the pleadings or other litigation documents, the first substantive line of questioning might be based on those documents. If he assisted in organizing documents for production or preparing answers to interrogatories, those activities will be fruitful areas for inquiry.

Depending on what you determine to be the extent of his preparation, you may wish to ease in to substantive questioning. If the witness seems to be very well prepared, you may have nothing to lose by starting at the beginning and taking him through the entire transaction chronologically. Some witnesses have a prepared story to tell and provide no useful testimony until they are permitted to tell that story. So you might as well get it out of the way promptly. If, however, you think the witness has not prepared adequately for the examination, he may need time to get comfortable and you may wish to plunge into a critical line of questioning before he relaxes. Properly done, nothing is more startling to an otherwise nervous witness than being asked a critical and difficult question just after he has given his name and address. If that method produces the answers you want, stay with it—jumping around from subject to subject to keep control of the witness.

In the important oral deposition, you can never obtain enough background information from the witness. You will frequently be unable to judge the candor of his answers unless you know a great deal of background. Do not hesitate to pursue lengthy lines of inquiry not directed to the immediate facts in dispute, if such inquiry will provide you with insight into the organization or persons who oppose you. This information should be obtained early, before your adversary's patience is strained.

You must at some point determine whether it is to your advantage to make the witness feel at ease. If the witness gives you the impression that he is trying to be candid and complete in his answers, you have nothing to gain by making him nervous. Indeed, if obtaining full and accurate testimony is your goal, you should make a deliberate effort to make the witness feel comfortable. If he is stumbling and you know of a document that will help him, offer it to him. Establish as much rapport as you can with the witness, in the hope that he will feel that he cannot in fairness be evasive or dishonest with you. If you are gratuitously nasty, the witness will view the deposition as a game in which his objective is to beat you out of whatever information you want.

A witness, however, must be taught to respect the examiner and to understand the dangers of being evasive. If you have treated the witness with courtesy and respect and he reciprocates with incomplete or evasive answers, you must quickly assert control and convince the witness his tactics are self-defeating. How you achieve that result necessarily varies with the circumstances. However, if justified by the witness's conduct, your questions should become sharper in tone and substance and your manner with him should become peremptory. You should ask and re-ask the same questions until the answers are satisfactory or until you are precluded from doing so. Your objective must be to convey to the witness that he is making his own job much more difficult.

Obtaining Admissions

If the deposition lasts more than one day, you should ask the witness at the beginning of the next day or next session what preparation he has done in the interval. The documents he will have reviewed or the persons, other than counsel, he has talked to between deposition sessions may be very meaningful. Presumably he has concentrated on areas that troubled him. If the witness has been candid with you, it may be advisable to ask whether he wishes to change or comment upon any testimony previously given. If he should make any such change or comment, you will want to know what has prompted it. Has someone pointed out to him that he made an error, or did something else indicate that his initial testimony was in error?

There can be no general advice for getting a witness to make admissions he does not want to make. The informality of the oral deposition generally works against you. But the witness will find it difficult to avoid admissions if he is confronted by objective facts or documents that he must concede. The pace of the examination also is critical to the possibility of procuring admissions. People will not knowingly and willingly make damaging admissions. The witness must become disoriented, losing all sense of the context of the questions, or he must feel that he has no choice but to make the admission. It is difficult to envision a slow-paced examination that will produce either result.

A witness whom you believe is lying presents a very different problem from the witness who is merely evasive. Often, it is best not to pursue the apparent lie immediately. You should first take stock. Analyze what led you to believe that the witness lied. If you have objective evidence, particularly documents, which virtually establish that the witness lied, you must decide first whether it is to your benefit to demonstrate promptly that he has lied or whether it would be better to save that demonstration for settlement discussions or the trial. If you conclude that the better course is to demonstrate the untruth during the course of the examination, be certain that your materials are well organized so that the attempt will not fall flat.

If, however, you find that you cannot establish the falsity objectively, you will have to expose, through your questions, the thought processes by which you concluded the witness had not been truthful. This frequently requires extensive questioning, and you will have to decide whether such an approach will accomplish anything. In the absence of objective evidence that the witness will have to accept, you may be able to do little more than embarrass him and you may not have a usable record for trial. Your appraisal of the degree to which the witness can control himself under tension should also be an important factor in determining whether you should attempt to demonstrate that he has lied during the deposition.

208

If you do decide to attempt to establish the untruth, you should wait until unrelated subjects have been covered. A witness who has lied will often have a strong consciousness of having done so and will be relieved when you move on to other subjects. He will also be all the more chagrined when you return to the critical subject. The witness's surprise and chagrin may assist you in demonstrating that he has perjured himself.

A common phenomenon is the witness who cannot recall matters of importance. The methods for dealing with that situation are not much different from those you use at trial, but the oral deposition offers you the opportunity to be more painstaking. You should first cover other matters that either took place within the same time period or are similar in nature. Then, in a single question if possible, accumulate all that he can recall during that period and ask him to explain the lapses in his recollection. Show him in rapid succession all of the documents that relate to the matter, or refer to events that took place at the same time, and ask him if these refresh his recollection. The object is to force him either to state his actual recollection (on the assumption that he has one) or to make his failure to recollect conspicuous and an embarrassment to him. He will then have an incentive to give an honest recollection, at least on other matters. If the witness persists in his inability to recall, and you do not believe him, move on. Come back to the subject later, from another direction, and use a different kind of question.

You should, however, keep clearly in mind your ultimate objectives. The witness's faulty memory might help you by limiting his testimonial usefulness at trial. If so, you will want to be sure that his failures of recollection are as many in number and importance as possible, and you will want to preclude the possibility of a credible recapture of recollection between the deposition and the trial. You should ask the witness whether he knows of any document or person that might assist his recollection. If he identifies a document, you should insist that he examine it immediately. If he identifies a person who may be able to assist his recollection, probe why he believes that person can help. When did he last see that person? When did they last discuss the matter involved? If the matter involved is critical, you may wish to take that person's deposition.

Under the practice in many states and in the federal courts, objections except as to the form of a question are reserved for trial. Lawyers, however, frequently object to the substance of questions and, indeed, instruct the witness not to answer. Your approach when this occurs must be guided by your assessment of the judge who will decide such disputes. You should at least attempt to force your adversary to state the grounds of his objection and remind him that objections as to substance are reserved. If he states the reasons for his objection, discuss them with him. Depending on the circumstances, you may be able at least to head off similar objections. You may also be able to imply to the witness that his lawyer is preventing a full and candid airing of the facts. If you have

209

been able to engage the witness in a dialogue with you, he might resent the intervention and believe that his lawyer does not respect him.

If the objection is that the question is misleading, point out that the witness does not seem to be easily misled. Ask the witness whether he understands the question as it was asked. Force his lawyer to acknowledge that he is not even allowing his witness to state whether he understands the question. Your specific approach should be governed by whether objections and instructions not to answer are being abused by your adversary.

In any event, you should not fight on weak ground. If you cannot adequately defend the question or its subject matter, why spread that fact on the record? But, if your adversary is truly obstreperous, develop an unambiguous record of his obstructive behavior and terminate the examination pending instructions from the court. There is little point to continuing an examination that is dominated by your adversary.

Rephrase the Question

You will not always want to rephrase a question when its form is objected to. First, you should determine if it matters to you that the answer will not be admissible at a trial. Often it is more important to keep the dialogue moving than it is to have an admissible answer to a particular question. Then determine whether the question is truly objectionable. While it is, of course, better to rephrase a question than to run the risk of nonadmissibility (if you care about admissibility), it is as important that your adversary come to realize that he cannot dominate or interfere with your examination. Your approach will often depend on the attitude your adversary is taking. It would be pointless to have a confrontation with a courteous and cooperative adversary over an occasional objection.

Witnesses occasionally will answer a question with a question. The examiner should not become involved with an explanation of the facts or of points he is trying to make. He should explain to the witness that it is not appropriate for the examiner to answer questions during the deposition and then re-ask or, if necessary, rephrase the question. Similarly, do not permit your adversary, through the device of objections or requests for qualification, to force you to state the point of significant questions. Any hope of an uncontrolled answer from the witness is lost the moment you are put on the defensive and forced to explain precisely what you are up to. If your adversary insists on an explanation of relevancy and you do not want to carry the argument further, discuss your question out of the hearing of the witness.

The measure of your success in the deposition of an important witness is, in the final analysis, whether it achieved your predetermined goals. That result will elude you, however, unless you engage in careful and painstaking preparation, keep your predetermined goals in mind as the deposition proceeds and maintain full control and initiative throughout the examination.

The Folklore
of Depositions

by Edward Bart Greene

The folklore of depositions has developed independently of the law of depositions. The folklore thrives on trial lawyers' (and judges') ignorance of the law governing depositions and their apparent indifference to it.

The two most universal folk practices that defy the law governing depositions are the exclusion of a nonparty from the deposition, though no protective order compels the exclusion, and an instruction to a deponent not to answer questions.

The folklore of depositions is that parties and their lawyers have the right to be present at any deposition taken in the case but that others may be excluded. Lawyers will insist, even to the point of refusing to proceed with the deposition, that all nonparties leave the room before the deposition begins. This is the deposition equivalent of "invoking the rule" that trial witnesses be sequestered upon the request of a party. The "rule" has its origin in the folklore of trials but has been legitimized in Rule 615 of the Federal Rules of Evidence and in case law.

The folklore rule that only parties and their lawyers may be present at depositions may have originated in a misreading of the rules. Wright and Miller state incorrectly that:

> Prior to 1970 the corresponding provision of what was then Rule 30(b) stated 'that the examination shall be held with no one present except the parties to the action and their officers or counsel.'

8 WRIGHT & MILLER, FEDERAL PRACTICE AND PROCEDURE: CIVIL § 2041 (1970). The pre-1970 Rule 30(b) of the Federal Rules of Civil Procedure did not state that. Instead, it authorized the court, "upon motion sea-

---

The author practices law in Miami, Florida. A version of this article appeared in the December 1984 issue of the FLORIDA BAR JOURNAL.

sonably made by any party or by the person to be examined" and "for good cause shown" to order "that the examination shall be held with no one present except the parties to the action and their officers or counsel." To say that the court may order sequestration is not to say that lawyers may insist on sequestration without a court order.

The substance of the pre-1970 Rule 30(b) is now Rule 26(c). Rule 26(c)(5) permits a party or the deponent to apply to the court for a protective order to exclude people from the deposition. Rule 26(c)(5) provides that, upon motion and for good cause shown, the court may order "that discovery be conducted with no one present except persons designated by the court." Rule 26(c), unlike former Rule 30(b), permits the court to exclude even parties from a deposition. *Galella v. Onassis*, 487 F. 2d 986, 997 (2d Cir. 1973).

At trial, a lawyer "invokes the rule" by an oral request to the court that witnesses be sequestered. This incantation and the court's inevitable acquiescence suffice to banish prospective witnesses from the courtroom. A pretrial request is not necessary. *Sperberg v. Goodyear Tire & Rubber Co.*, 519 F.2d 708 (6th Cir. 1975), *cert. denied*, 423 U.S. 987 (1975).

With depositions, the law is different. Rule 26(c)(5) is not self-executing. The lawyer who wants to sequester deposition witnesses must move for a protective order before the deposition. Without a protective order in hand, a lawyer has no right to insist that anyone, party or nonparty, be excluded from a deposition. On the contrary, "as a general proposition, pretrial discovery must take place in the public unless compelling reasons exist for denying the public access to the proceedings." *Am. Tel. & Tel. Co. v. Grady*, 594 F.2d 594, 596 (7th Cir. 1978), *cert. denied*, 440 U.S. 971 (1979). *But see Seattle Times Co. v. Rhinehart*, 467 U.S. 20, 32 (1984).

Rule 26(c)(5) requires a showing of "good cause." The cause may be to protect patents and trade secrets. It may be to protect the deponent from harassment, as when the trial judge excluded Jacqueline Onassis's tormentor, photographer Ron Galella, from her deposition in a lawsuit he brought against her. The court of appeal's opinion in that case establishes, contrary to the folklore, that even a party may be excluded from a deposition.

The most obvious reason to seek a protective order excluding people from the deposition is to prevent prospective witnesses from hearing the deponent's testimony before they themselves are deposed. Wigmore believed that "the expedient of sequestration is (next to cross-examination) one of the greatest inventions that the skill of man has invented for the detection of liars in a court of justice." 6 WIGMORE, EVIDENCE, § 1838, p. 354 (3d ed. 1984).

Wigmore was speaking of sequestration at trial. Sequestration will not detect liars who acquaint themselves with earlier depositions before they give their own. The rules of civil procedure do not prevent a prospective witness from reading depositions already taken in the case. Nor do they prevent lawyers or deponents from telling future deponents what testimony has already been given.

Unless a prospective witness's deposition is to be taken the same day as the deponent's or before the deponent's testimony will be transcribed, there is no practical reason to insist that the person be excluded from the deposition. The fight over who has a right to attend a deposition is usually a pointless ritual.

When the battle is worth waging, the appropriate weapon is a predeposition motion for an adequate protective order—one that not only excludes potential witnesses from depositions, but also forbids disclosure of deposition testimony to any person who is to be deposed in the future. *Beacon v. R.M. Jones Apartment Rentals,* 79 F.R.D. 141 (N.D. Ohio 1978). The prudent lawyer would also try to schedule depositions so that disclosure in violation of the protective order is impossible.

The practice of instructing deponents not to answer questions is so well entrenched that it has generated an elaborate set of rules. All of them are folklore, not law.

It is well settled in the folklore that a lawyer may instruct his own client not to answer a question. To silence a deponent who is not clearly his client, the lawyer must be inventive to expand the folklore.

While representing the plaintiff in a medical malpractice case against an anesthesiologist, a surgeon, and a hospital, I encountered the following examples of the folklore.

The lawyer who represented the hospital instructed a nurse-employee of the hospital, who was not a party, not to answer several questions. His rationale: "She's our nurse." He was on reasonably solid ground in the folklore of depositions. Next, the lawyer who represented the anesthesiologist instructed his client's partner, who was not a party, not to answer certain questions. That instruction was on much less solid ground. If pressed to justify it, the lawyer might have analogized his client's partnership with the deponent to marriage, invoking the unity of husband and wife at common law. Finally, the lawyer who represented the surgeon, after a predeposition conference with a physician-witness who was neither a party nor a party's partner, refused to allow the witness to be deposed at all. He argued that the deposition was improper because the doctor "might become a party" and he "ought to have a lawyer."

The Whole Truth

That cancellation of a deposition—the ultimate instruction not to answer—was improper even by the nebulous criteria of deposition folklore. The rationale that the deponent "ought to have a lawyer" reflects a belief widely held by trial lawyers that all information in a lawsuit should be filtered through lawyers.

Interrogatory answers are the purest form of facts filtered through lawyers. When drafted by a lawyer of even average ability, answers to interrogatories seeking information more complicated than names, addresses, and similar matters convey virtually nothing useful. But it is far more difficult to suppress information at a deposition. The deponent may give the whole truth, despite the lawyers' best efforts.

Though few lawyers will say so, almost all lawyers believe they have a right to censor a deponent's testimony. I once attended a deposition at which the deponent's lawyer, a puckish fellow of disarming candor, interrupted the reporter's administration of the oath to ask the lawyer who had noticed the deposition, "How can he promise to tell the truth? He doesn't know what you're going to ask him." Later in the deposition, the same lawyer instructed his client not to answer a question. He unabashedly stated his reason: He had not anticipated the question and had not prepared his client to answer it.

The folklore of depositions is that a lawyer has the right to censor the deponent's testimony by instructions not to answer. Censorship by the lawyer, regardless of his relationship to the deponent, is forbidden by the law of depositions.

The law is that a lawyer has no right to instruct a client or any other deponent not to answer a deposition question unless the question calls for privileged information. Fed. R. Civ. P. 30(c) provides that the reporter shall note all objections on the record and that "evidence objected to *shall be taken* subject to the objections." [Emphasis added.]

An attorney who objects to a question should state the objection for the record and then allow the question to be answered subject to the objection. *Ralston Purina Co. v. McFarland*, 550 F.2d 967 (4th Cir. 1977); *Coates v. Johnson and Johnson*, 85 F.R.D. 731 (N.D. Ill. 1980); *Lloyd v. Cessna Aircraft Co.*, 74 F.R.D. 518 (E.D. Tenn. 1977). If the court later sustains the objection, the objectionable testimony may be inadmissible at trial.

Although the cases cited state that a lawyer who objects to a deposition question should state the objection for the record, such a statement is not required to preserve the objection when responding to a later motion to compel. There is one important exception. When the ground for the objection can be obviated, removed, or cured if presented at the time, it must be stated at the deposition. FED. R. CIV. P. 32(d)(3). One example of this is an objection to the form of the question.

Courts that have commented on the practice of unjustifiably instructing witnesses not to answer questions have vehemently condemned it. The *Ralston Purina* court called it "highly improper" and "indefensible and utterly at variance with the discovery provisions of the Federal Rules of Civil Procedure." 550 F.2d at 973.

In *Shapiro v. Freeman*, 38 F.R.D. 308 (S.D.N.Y. 1965), the injured plaintiff claimed that she suffered permanent psychiatric shock when an airplane crashed into her parents' home. The defendants deposed witnesses from the injured plaintiff's school to learn about her pre-injury adjustment to everyday life. The defendants' lawyer asked many questions to bring out what the court characterized as "relevant and non-privileged facts." The plaintiffs' lawyer objected to nearly all the questions and instructed the deponents not to answer. One witness refused to answer 46 questions; another, 39.

The court appointed a special master to preside over future depositions and directed that the fees of the special master be paid by "plaintiffs' attorneys without reimbursement from their clients." In condemning the instructions not to answer, the court stated (at 311):

> It is not the prerogative of counsel, but of the court, to rule on objections. Indeed, if counsel were to rule on the propriety of questions, oral examinations would be quickly reduced to an exasperating cycle of answerless inquiries and court orders.

The court's use of the conditional tense misses the reality of depositions. In fact, lawyers daily presume to rule on the propriety of questions by instructing deponents not to answer. Many deposition transcripts contain more pages of lawyers' chatter than of testimony. Court reporters call transcripts of this verbal sparring "wall to wall" because the sparring runs from one side of the page to the other.

The rationale for requiring the deponent to answer despite the lawyer's objection is simple:

> The harm caused by being required to take additional depositions of a witness who fails to answer a question based on an improperly asserted objection far exceeds the mere inconvenience of a witness having to answer a question which may not be admissible at the trial of the action.

W.R. Grace & Co. v. Pullman Inc., 74 F.R.D. 80, 84 (W.D. Okla. 1977).

The folklore regards all irrelevant questions as improper, all objections to them as properly asserted, and all instructions not to answer them as justified. Yet the law is that an objection on the ground of irrelevance is improperly asserted at a deposition. The only objection that should be made at a deposition is one that can be cured, such as an objection to the form of the question. Ordinarily, the only proper basis for instructing not to answer is that the question seeks privileged matter.

A lawyer may and should instruct the deponent not to answer a question that calls for privileged matter. *International Union of Elec. Radio and Mach. Workers v. Westinghouse Elec. Corp.*, 91 F.R.D. 277 (D.D.C. 1981); *Perrignon v. Bergen Brunswig Corp.*, 77 F.R.D. 455 (N.D. Cal. 1978). After recognizing the general rule that deposition questions should be answered despite an objection, the *International Union* court stated at 279:

> [I]t is nonetheless clear that a firm application of the rule should not be followed in every case. For example, Rule 30(c) should not mandate disclosure of trade secrets or privileged information

merely because such information is sought through a question asked on deposition.

The failure to instruct the deponent not to answer a question seeking privileged information may constitute a waiver of the privilege. In *Perrignon v. Bergen Brunswig Corp.*, the deponent's lawyer objected to a question seeking disclosure of a privileged communication but did not instruct the deponent not to answer. The court held that by answering, the deponent had waived the privilege. The court listed the options available to the deponent's lawyer if he wished to preserve the privilege. First, he could have moved for a protective order before the deposition was taken. Second, when the question of privilege arose, he could have terminated the deposition and sought a protective order. Third, "at the very least," he should have advised the deponent not to answer the question.

Some cases suggest that the only proper way to resolve a question of privilege at a deposition is to terminate the deposition and apply for a ruling on the question. The rules furnish another option: to instruct the witness not to divulge the information claimed to be privileged and to allow the examination to continue on nonprivileged areas of inquiry.

Fed. R. Civ. P. 37(a)(2), which deals with motions to compel discovery, provides that "[w]hen taking a deposition on oral examination, the proponent of the question may complete or adjourn the examination before he applies for an order." This rule implies that a claim of privilege during a deposition is not waived if the deposition continues on other subjects. Unless those other subjects cannot be separated from the material claimed to be privileged, it is sensible to continue with the deposition. If the deposition is otherwise completed, it must be reconvened only if the court overrules the claim of privilege. But if the deposition is terminated when the question of privilege arises, and other subjects remain to be covered, the deposition must be reconvened no matter how the court rules on the objection.

Although it usually is improper to instruct a witness not to answer a question because it is irrelevant, there are times when doing that may be justified.

Grueling Examination

This is illustrated by *Eggleston v. Chicago Journeymen Plumbers Local Union No. 130*, 657 F.2d 890, 903 (7th Cir. 1981), *cert. denied*, 455 U.S. 1017 (1982), a class action civil rights suit against a plumbers' union alleging employment discrimination against blacks and Hispanics. The oral depositions of the plaintiffs lasted "about sixteen days before the whole process collapsed." There were 965 refusals of witnesses to answer questions and 127 conferences off the record between the plaintiffs and their counsel. One of the plaintiffs became ill and did not complete the deposition; he complained that he "collapsed from exhaustion" because of defense counsel's grueling examination. The trial court's response to the break-down in discovery was to dismiss the plaintiffs' claims with prejudice.

The court of appeals reversed, concluding that "there [was] more than enough fault for counsel on both sides to share." For example, one of the plaintiffs, obviously black, was asked: (a) the basis of his belief that his mother was a member of the Negro race; (b) whether any of his ancestors were Caucasian; and (c) his definition of an Hispanic. He was also asked, "Can you tell me what the difference is between a Negro with some Caucasian ancestors and a Caucasian with some Negro ancestors?" Another plaintiff (a plumber, not a lawyer) was asked if he knew whether Local 130 was "engaged in an industry affecting commerce" or if he knew whether Local 130 was "a labor organization within the meaning of 42 U.S.C. § 2000-D."

To support its conclusion that "some of the defendants' questions demonstrate a stubborn tendency to insist on valueless answers," the court quoted the following questions and answers at 899.

Q: When you discussed with Mr. Miner [one of plaintiffs' counsel] the facts known to him which gave rise to your allegations in the complaint, were you and Mr. Miner alone?

A: Yes.

Q: When you talked to him on the telephone, were there any other persons who were in on that telephone conversation?

A: Unless Mr. Miner has a party line, the answer would be no.

Q: Is your answer then that you don't know?

A: I said unless Mr. Miner has a party line, the answer is no.

Q: Does Mr. Miner have a party line?

A: You would have to ask Mr. Miner.

Q: Do you know whether Mr. Miner has a party line?

A: You would have to ask Mr. Miner. I don't pay his telephone bill. I don't know his installations.

Q: Do you know whether Mr. Miner has a party line?

A: I do not know whether Mr. Miner has a party line.

The court branded some of the defendant's questions as "argumentative and senseless" and others as "repetitious, or worse."

The court did not spare the plaintiffs' lawyers. It condemned the 965 refusals to answer "with only a limited number of those refusals being related to the excesses we have considered." It also condemned the 127 private, off-the-record conferences between the plaintiffs and their counsel at 902:

It is too late once the ball has been snapped for the coach to send in a different play. Sometimes plaintiffs' counsel would interrupt their client's answer and instruct that enough had been said.

After enumerating the discovery abuses, the court recognized the

217

general rule in the Northern District of Illinois, where the case arose, that it is improper to instruct a deponent not to answer except where there is a claim of privilege. The court noted, however, that 4A Moore's *Federal Practice* 37.02[2] (1981) states that it is proper to decline to answer when either privileged or irrelevant information is sought. The court also observed that the plaintiffs, in support of their refusal to answer, had supplied numerous affidavits of lawyers in the area who followed the same practice. The court did not endorse the practice of instructing witnesses not to answer *all* irrelevant questions. Instead, it recognized a distinction between two types of irrelevant questions at 903:

> Some questions of doubtful relevancy may be innocuous and nothing is lost in answering, subject to objection, except time. That is the general rule. Other irrelevant questions, however, may unnecessarily touch sensitive areas or go beyond reasonable limits as did some of the race questions propounded to Eggleston. In such an event, refusing to answer may be justified.

The distinction is between innocuous and obnoxious, irrelevant questions. The court did not condone "wholesale refusals" to answer even obnoxious questions. Instead, it counselled "thoughtful flexibility" in "limited instances." It left the definition of both phrases for another day.

In some states the folklore response to instructions not to answer deposition questions is the practice of "certifying questions." After one lawyer instructs the deponent not to answer, the questioner solemnly or angrily instructs the reporter to "certify the question." This does not mean, as the language implies, that the reporter will embellish the deposition transcript or any part of it with seals, stamps, or ribbons. It means that each question the deponent was instructed not to answer will be typed twice: where it belongs chronologically and in a list at the end of the deposition.

The young lawyer trying to divine some reason to certify questions might conclude that "certification" is what perfects his right to move to compel an answer. The theory proceeds by analogy to the requirement that objections to the form of the question must be voiced at the deposition if they are to be preserved. If a questioner merely *asks* a question, he may not feel strongly that it merits an answer. But when he *certifies* it, he gives formal notice that he is serious enough about wanting an answer to ask the court to compel it. Certification of the question gives the lawyer instructing the deponent not to answer a chance to reconsider his position, as objecting to the form of the question gives the questioner the chance to rephrase it.

While there may be states in which the law requires a procedure like certification, in other such diverse states as Florida, Illinois, and Texas, the rules of civil procedure do not refer to certification of deposition questions to perfect the right to move to compel an answer. As in the federal system, the only predicate for a motion to compel an answer to a deposition question is that the questioner ask the question and that the witness refuse to answer.

The folklore of depositions is the child of two disreputable parents, ignorance and indifference. To the extent the folklore is born of ignorance, awareness of the law will do away with it. But to the extent it is born of indifference, it will resist eradication and is a species of unethical conduct.

The folklore of depositions flourishes because those who break the rules have inertia and delay on their side. If a deponent fails to answer a deposition question, the questioner has a theoretical remedy—a motion to compel an answer. But motions to compel are usually futile unless a judge is available to rule during the deposition. A judge who hears a motion to compel the deposition will at best order the deposition to be reconvened and the question answered. By this time, the witness's answer will have lost its spontaneity. Or the court may order the deponent to answer but permit a written answer; this is guaranteed to be useless. At worst, the judge will deny the motion, knowing the folklore but not the law of depositions.

The discussion of the role of the deponent's lawyer in *American Jurisprudence Trials,* which purports to be an authoritative treatise on trial practice, illustrates (at 4 AM. JUR. TRIALS § 34) that the folklore of depositions is more than ignorance of the law. The author begins by defining the problem: The deponent is about to say something useful to the questioner.

> Deponent's counsel will sometimes be faced with a situation in which a question is asked his client that counsel, for one reason or another, does not desire to be answered.

The solution, offered as a legitimate tactic, is the folklore of depositions at its meanest:

> It is not uncommon for deponent's counsel to object to the question and instruct the witness to refuse to answer the question. This is done even though the reasons therefor are not contained within the objection to be asserted and no reservation is made. The hassle over whether or not the question should be answered thus serves the purpose, in many instances, of alerting the witness to the need of special care in answering the question.

Other tricks are available if needed:

> A like effect can result from deponent's counsel interrupting to ask that the question be repeated, or to ask whether the witness has understood the question. Alternatively, deponent's counsel may simply interrupt and point out an error in an answer.

The author describes the likely reaction:

219

In many instances, where deponent's counsel has interrupted in this fashion, opposing counsel may point out, facetiously or otherwise, that deponent's counsel is not being deposed. In such event deponent's counsel may counter by offering to be available for deposition.

This passes for wit in the folklore of depositions.

It is not surprising that the plaintiffs' lawyers in the *Eggleston* case were able to file "numerous affidavits" of lawyers who routinely instructed deponents not to answer. The folklore of depositions is better known than the law and influences trial lawyers more. It has flourished because discovery usually proceeds without judicial supervision or appellate review.

The law will supplant the folklore of depositions only if lawyers take the trouble to move to compel answers and ask for sanctions, and if judges have the fortitude to enforce the rules of civil procedure. Fed. R. Civ. P. 37 (a)(4) provides that the court "shall" require the party or deponent whose conduct necessitated the motion to compel "or the party or attorney advising such conduct or both of them" to pay the reasonable expenses incurred in obtaining the order, unless the court finds that the opposition to the motion was substantially justified. When the motion is based on folklore tactics, opposition to the motion is not justified. If obstructionist lawyers must pay for the delay and inconvenience they cause or explain to their clients why the clients have to pay, the folklore of depositions may begin to yield to the law.

The prognosis for that is poor. The discovery rules were designed for minimal judicial intervention. Many judges consider motions to compel an unwarranted imposition on their time. Like exasperated parents, they referee discovery disputes with the admonition that everyone behave. They do not read the specific questions to which answers are sought. Instead, they dispose of motions to compel with generalities: Do not be repetitious; answer all relevant questions. H.L. Mencken could have been talking about discovery when he said that the average American judge "converts the law into a series of rubber-stamps, and brings them down upon the scalped skulls of the just and unjust alike." THE VINTAGE MENCKEN (Vintage Books 1955), p. 195.

To protect his client in depositions, a lawyer must know the folklore: not to use it for obstruction but to recognize and challenge it when others use it. To prevail at motions for protective orders, motions to compel, and motions for sanctions, a lawyer must also know the law of depositions. The lawyers in the *Shapiro* case, ordered to pay their own money for a special master to preside over future depositions, discovered that the folklore and the law are not the same.

220

Deposition Traps and Tactics

by Thomas J. McNamara and Paul T. Sorensen

Deposition. Many of us never heard the word before law school. Some of us did not really understand the significance of the term, even *after* the civil procedure exam. And most of us had little idea of how to take one when we got our first file to handle.

Soon after we started in practice, though, the word became part of our everyday vocabulary. With a little experience, we learned how to ask sensible, concise questions in a conference room with a witness and his lawyer across the table and a court reporter taking it all down on one of those amazing little black machines with the quiet keys. Yet many trial lawyers still have problems using deposition transcripts effectively at trial, and occasionally they face the even more disconcerting problem of having transcripts of their own depositions used against them in unforeseen and devastating ways.

It is no secret that the deposition is one of the most productive discovery devices available. What is not so commonly appreciated are the creative and effective uses to which deposition transcripts can be put at trial.

The trick is knowing when and how to use a transcript to best advantage. The lawyer who recognizes that a "discovery" deposition can be a powerful weapon at trial will fit it into his overall strategy and take steps to stymie his opponent from later using the transcript against him.

- *A little law, like a little fasting, is good for the soul.* You cannot use depositions at all unless you follow the rules. Three of them apply: Rule 32 of the Federal Rules of Civil Procedure and Rules 801 and 804 of the Federal Rules of Evidence.

Civil Rule 32(a) sets forth the general circumstances under which a

Thomas J. McNamara and Paul T. Sorensen are partners in Warner, Norcross & Judd in Grand Rapids, Michigan.

deposition may be used at trial. Impeachment of a witness's trial testimony with a prior inconsistent deposition statement is the most common. Rule 32(a)(1) also provides that a deposition may be used "for any other purpose permitted by the Federal Rules of Evidence." That language (added in 1980) vastly broadens the use of depositions as a substitute for live testimony.

Evidence Rule 801(d) provides that neither a witness's prior inconsistent deposition testimony nor a previous admission by a party or his agent is hearsay. So, if deposition testimony is either at odds with what a witness says on the stand or is the testimony of a party or his agent, it may be offered *both* for impeachment and as substantive evidence.

A deposition of any witness may also be used as substantive evidence if the court finds that

(A) the deponent is dead;

(B) the deponent is more than 100 miles from the place of trial or out of the country (unless the party offering the deposition procured the witness's absence);

(C) the deponent is unable to testify because of age, illness, infirmity, or imprisonment;

(D) the party offering the deposition has been unable to procure the deponent's attendance by subpoena; or

(E) upon application and notice, such exceptional circumstances exist as to make it desirable, in the interest of justice, to allow the deposition to be used. FED. R. CIV. P. 32(a)(3).

While clauses (A) through (D) seem uncomplicated enough, the courts have had to answer a few lingering questions. For example, does the rule allow use of a deposition when the deponent is more than 100 miles away by the shortest land route but less than 100 miles away as the crow flies? No. *See SCM Corp. v. Xerox Corp.*, 76 F.R.D. 214 (D. Conn. 1977).

In *SCM*, the court also concluded that the 100-mile rule applied not only when the deposition was offered but at any time during the proponent's case when a subpoena could have been served. 77 F.R.D. 16.

If you intend to rely on clause (D), you had better introduce sworn testimony that you were unable to procure the deponent's attendance by subpoena. Bare assertions by counsel will not do. *State v. Keairns*, 9 Ohio St. 3d 228, 460 N.E.2d 245 (1984).

With the help of this judicial fine-tuning, clauses (A) through (D) have presented few problems. But what in the world does clause (E) mean? What (on application and notice) are the exceptional circumstances that also justify the use of a deposition at trial?

First, what is sufficient "application and notice"? This language probably requires that a party file a written request with the court, with copies to all counsel of record, for permission to use a deposition at trial. The application should set forth the reasons it is necessary to offer the deposition even though none of the specific conditions of Rule 32 have been satisfied.

Next how "exceptional" do the circumstances have to be for your opponent to read to the jury the transcript of the "discovery" deposition that you blithely sat through three years earlier? The short answer is, we are not sure. The rule does not define the term "exceptional circumstances," the committee notes are unenlightening, and the courts have given few guidelines.

One court held there are exceptional circumstances if a named defendant does not appear at trial notwithstanding her lawyer's pretrial assurances that she would be there. *Huff v. Marine Tank Testing Corp.*, 631 F.2d 1140, 1142–43 (4th Cir. 1980). Another court has suggested that exceptional circumstances might exist merely because a trial is long. *SCM Corp. v. Xerox Corp.*, 76 F.R.D. 214, 216 n. 2 (D. Conn. 1977).

The "exceptional circumstances" provision is obviously broad enough for a trial judge to justify the admission of almost *any* deposition transcript without abusing his discretion. From what we see and hear, though, there are a lot of judges out there who are as tough as Job, but not as patient. If none of the conditions of clauses (A) through (D) can be satisfied, your "exceptional circumstances" argument will have to be terse and overwhelming, as there is little telling precedent to hang your advocate's hat on.

Take another situation. What happens if your witness on the stand simply cannot remember the particular events about which you are questioning him? He remembered those events last year when you took his deposition.

You have the deposition transcript on the counsel table and would like to use it, but the witness is not dead, absent, old, sick, or in jail. He has simply drawn a blank, and nothing will refresh his recollection. You move for admission of the transcript under the "exceptional circumstances" clause, but the judge says the circumstances do not seem too exceptional to him, and besides, you did not make a pretrial application or give proper notice.

Even though that testimony is important to your case, you adjust the knot of your tie and move on to your next witness. Right? Not so fast.

Rule 804 of the Federal Rules of Evidence provides some additional grounds for admission of deposition testimony. The courts have recognized that Rule 804 is a proper basis, independent of Civil Rule 32, for using depositions at trial. *See United States v. I.B.M.*, 90 F.R.D. 377, 384 (S.D.N.Y. 1981).

Rule 804 deals with hearsay exceptions if the person whose out-of-court statement you want to introduce is unavailable as a witness. In Rule 804, unavailability is defined to include not only many of the same circumstances listed in Civil Rule 32(a)(3) but also situations in which the witness (a) claims to be exempt from testimony because of a privilege,

223

(b) refuses to testify despite a court order to do so, or (c) testifies to a lack of memory of the subject in question.

Lack of memory. There it is. Under Evidence Rule 804(b)(1), your witness is now "unavailable," and you can use his deposition as substantive evidence of the facts he cannot remember on the witness stand.

There is another way to do it that does not involve Rule 32 at all. The hearsay exception for past recollection recorded in the Federal Rules of Evidence, Rule 803(5), is broad enough to admit depositions. That is a big change from the common law, and here is how it works.

At common law, past recollection recorded required a writing made at or near the event, in addition to a failure of recollection on the witness stand. Obviously, "at or near the event" excludes all but the most unusual depositions. The result is we are not accustomed to thinking of depositions as past recollection recorded. But under Rule 803(5), the time requirement is relaxed. Now the writing need only be "shown to have been made or adopted by the witness when the matter was fresh in his memory and to reflect that knowledge correctly." Remembering accurately enough to swear to the testimony at a deposition ought to qualify as being "fresh in his memory." At least it is a good deal fresher than not remembering. And since past recollection recorded under the Federal Rules is only read to the jury (just as a deposition would be), it seems to fit depositions just fine.

If there is any basis for using deposition testimony at trial, then any party may use the transcript, not just the party who took the deposition. There is, however, one important ground for using a deposition transcript at trial that will, in the opening gambit at least, necessarily be available to one side but not the other.

Civil Procedure Rule 32(a)(2) permits *an adverse party* to use, for any purpose, the deposition of another party or of anyone who at the time of taking the deposition was an officer, director, or managing agent of a party. Either a plaintiff or a defendant, therefore, may introduce the deposition testimony of his opponent *even though that opponent is present at trial and has testified orally.* But co-plaintiffs or co-defendants may not use each other's deposition, unless they have adverse interests by reason of cross-claims or the deposition testimony is admissible on some other ground.

One final point about the rules. Say that you have satisfied one of the requirements for using a deposition transcript at trial but have no desire to offer the whole thing. You know that Rule 32 allows you to use all or part of a deposition, so you plan to offer only that portion of the testimony where your remarkably incisive interrogation got the deponent to concede a critical point.

After you introduce those crucial few pages, be ready for opposing counsel to demand that you also read, at the same time, "any other part which ought in fairness to be considered with the part introduced."

That is what Federal Procedure Rule 32(a)(4) and Federal Evidence Rule 106 both require.

Be alert to the possibility that your opponent's heavy-handed selection may bog down your neatly paced presentation and transport the jury to the state of judicial narcolepsy we all know and dread. "Long" is a great virtue in cigars and sailboats. It is no asset at trial.

- *The strategy of depositions: I'd rather see a sermon than hear one.* What good are rules without a contest? When you are sitting in your office hatching prediscovery strategy, the rules give no help in deciding how, when, or even whether to use the depositions that will mushroom during the course of discovery.

First, we will deal with pretrial strategy; then we will move on to the art of using deposition testimony at trial.

Interesting tactical problems arise during depositions. Sometimes lawyers forget that "discovery" depositions might well resurface as evidence at trial.

Unless a lawyer takes care to make a clean record at a deposition, the transcript will be unimpressive at trial. Asking imprecise questions, suffering harassing objections, and tolerating rambling answers can make the deposition virtually useless at trial, either for impeachment or as substantive evidence. But those problems can be minimized, if not avoided. *See* P. Kolczynski, *Depositions as Evidence,* 9 LITIGATION, No. 2 at 25 (Winter 1983).

It is important at the start of any deposition to make a record that the deponent understands what a deposition is and what you will be doing. Something like this works well:

Q: Mr. Jones, my name is Tom McNamara. I am the lawyer for the Essex Company in the lawsuit that Robert Emmett has brought against Essex. This deposition is an opportunity for the lawyers to ask you questions to learn more about what really happened. Do you understand that everything said in this room will be taken down by the court reporter?

A: Yes.

Q: If you do not hear one of my questions, please tell me and I will be glad to repeat it. If you do not understand one of my questions, let me know and I will rephrase it. Fair enough?

A: Fair enough.

Q: Do you understand that you have given an oath to tell the truth and that you should answer the questions here just as if you were sitting in court in front of a judge and jury?

A: I sure do.

Q: After we finish with the deposition, the court reporter will transcribe it, and you will have a chance to read it and correct any errors. You will then sign the transcript and return it to the reporter for filing with the court. Your signature means that the transcript, as corrected by you, accurately reflects your testimony today. Do you understand that?

A: Yes.

Why bother with this introduction? Because it makes the deposition a more potent weapon for impeachment.

When a witness at trial contradicts his deposition testimony, it is difficult for him to explain away the inconsistency if you remind him that (1) he said he understood the rules when he testified at the deposition, (2) he later had a chance to review and correct the transcript, and (3) he signed the transcript, confirming its accuracy. So go through the introduction. And do not waive reading and signing by the deponent, except for a very good reason.

The introduction is a useful way to reinforce impeachment. But what if there is no one to impeach because the witness does not appear at trial?

Instead, your opponent offers *your* "discovery" deposition against you at trial. Have you sharpened your sword only to sit on it inadvertently?

Say that your adversary can satisfy one of the conditions of Rule 32(a)(3), so the deposition can be used as substantive evidence. Now you have a problem. When you took the deposition, you assumed that it was just discovery. But, unless you are in a state where the rules specifically recognize the distinction, the courts have consistently concluded that discovery depositions (even if only exploratory in nature), can be used at trial if the requirements of Rule 32 or Rule 804 are satisfied.

In *Gill v. Westinghouse Electric Corp.*, 714 F.2d 1105, 1107 (11th Cir. 1983), for example, the plaintiffs' lawyer had taken the discovery deposition of the defendant's expert. The expert died before trial.

The defendant, now short an expert, offered the deposition transcript at trial. Plaintiffs' counsel objected on the grounds that he had taken the deposition only to discover what the expert had to say, not to challenge his opinions. Both the trial court and the court of appeals rejected that argument. In light of the witness's death, the requirements of both Rules 32 and 804 were met, and the deposition was admitted into evidence.

Early in the case, lawyers usually focus on uncovering the facts, not conducting a cross-examination to use at trial. But that "discovery" deposition you took a month after you got the complaint can come back to haunt you at trial. It is like the old Missouri proverb about appearances: "When a fellah makes a show of puttin' all his cards on the table, he probably ain't playing cards."

There are some circumstances to watch for. If the witness is:

- more than 100 miles from the courthouse or likely to be at the time of trial;

226

- beyond the subpoena power of the court or intending to be by the time of trial;
- elderly or very ill, you should be aware that your opponent could wind up using the deposition transcript against you at trial.

Then your standard discovery deposition technique should give way to a more structured, formal interrogation designed not only to elicit facts but also to score points as you would at trial. In this situation, you should consider taking the deposition later in the discovery period, after you have armed yourself with the facts and documents you need to cross-examine rather than just explore with the witness.

It is equally important to stay on the alert when your opponent notices the deposition of your elderly, infirm, foreign, or fleet-footed witness. If it is likely that either you will be unable to produce the witness at trial or that you will need the witness's testimony but might choose not to call him live, you should consider questioning him thoroughly at deposition. Your examination serves two purposes: to defuse any unfavorable testimony that your opponent elicits and to develop a coherent record to introduce as evidence at trial.

Sometimes your own interrogation can save your case. If the deponent is the only witness to key facts, conducting a thorough examination at the end of your opponent's discovery deposition will preserve the testimony for trial.

When you question your own client, there are few risks—if both of you are well prepared. If you take the time to get your client ready for the possibility that you may want to slam the door on a few points made by your artful opponent, the client will hardly ever surprise you with his testimony.

Remember: if, by answering a few additional questions, your client clears up some apparently damaging admission, you will be in a position to fight off your adversary's use of the deposition at trial. You will be able to read into the record those passages that take the sting out of the answers your adversary picks out, thus reminding the trier of fact that your adversary is selectively editing the transcript.

It is a different story if you are defending the deposition of an uncommitted, nonparty witness. Consider this scene: Your opponent has just questioned the witness. The lawyer has elicited a few facts that help his case, but nothing really devastating to your client. Because you know that the deposition transcript could show up at trial, you decide to ask a few questions to repair the damage done on direct.

As the witness answers your first question, you realize that you have made a big mistake. The witness is guessing, opining, and exaggerating, and you are to blame. You feel like someone explaining alternate-side parking to a cranberry.

You try to stop the debacle, but it is too late. What began as a harmless discovery deposition has ended in disaster. The moral? There are just two reasons for cross-examining in this situation: abysmal innocence and bottomless desperation. Neither is a sufficient justification for what inevitably follows.

The instinct to control the damage done on direct is a good one. But to avoid making a mess like the one in the example (if your unwholesome curiosity once again exceeds your self-control), you must prepare thoroughly beforehand. Be as ready for that deposition as you would be if you had to cross-examine the witness at trial without the benefit of a deposition.

Learn ahead of time what the witness knows. That information will dictate what questions (if any) you should ask. Without that kind of preparation, never assume that a neutral witness will help your case on cross simply because he did not devastate it on direct. Some witnesses listen very carefully to the questions, and maybe your opponent just asked the wrong ones.

- *Experts: the elegant lie sometimes prevails over the unintelligible truth.* Experts' depositions present unique problems. Because experts are scattered across the country, often their depositions are admissible at trial on the grounds that the witness lives more than 100 miles from the courthouse.

A lawyer deposing his opponent's expert faces some tough decisions. Certainly, he wants to discover the expert's opinion and the basis for it. But the last thing he wants is to set the stage for a replay of *Gill v. Westinghouse,* where the transcript of a foraging, nonconfrontational discovery deposition was introduced against the questioner.

Does all this mean that, when deposing an expert, you have to conduct a complete cross-examination right after you find out for the first time what his opinion is? That is an unappealing prospect.

It would be extremely difficult, if not impossible, to prepare adequately for a penetrating cross-examination without knowing in advance a lot about the expert's opinion. Even if you could prepare a good cross-examination, you might hesitate to pull out all the stops at the deposition because, if you did, you would reveal more than you cared to about your own strategy. If the expert later appeared at trial, he would be ready for every one of your questions.

There are several possible outs. For example, expert testimony will not be admitted at trial, either in person or by deposition, unless the expert's qualifications appear in the record. So when you take that discovery deposition of your opponent's expert, you do nothing but harm to your own case if you ask the typical series of questions about the witness's background and expertise. The answers often tell you little that you really need to know. Usually you already have the expert's curriculum vitae or can get it later. But your questions can do a nice job of qualifying the expert on the record.

Skip those questions. Move right into the meat of the deposition. If you do not qualify the witness, you will minimize the risk that the deposition will come back to bite you at trial. You will be able to discover what the expert has to say without having to cross-examine him at the same time.

Before you start to feel too smug, you should realize that your opponent can spoil your strategy. He can qualify the expert himself after you have completed your examination.

If this happens, then reserve the right to return and "complete" the expert's deposition another day, unless your opponent stipulates that he will not offer the deposition transcript as evidence at trial. If you have a co-party whose lawyer has not yet questioned the witness, urge him to make the same reservation. Alternatively, you could proceed to cross-examine the witness on the spot under the "innocence or desperation" rule discussed earlier, but you would probably regret it.

This quandary is as real as your opponent's willingness to dispense with the expert's live testimony at trial. You can make him show his hand if you skip a review of the expert's credentials. If he then fills in those credentials, you will have a better chance of avoiding the *Gill* trap if you have developed a contingency plan in advance.

Judges usually require lawyers to disclose at the final pretrial conference whether they intend to introduce depositions at trial. If so, transcripts must be reviewed and edited for reading to the jury.

The cleanup is not some sort of illicit editing. Its sole purpose is to make the deposition brief and comprehensible to the listener.

If you made objections during the deposition, decide whether to present them to the judge for decision. Cross out those that are carping or otherwise unmeritorious. The remaining objections should then be presented to the judge, together with any additional objections that were not made during the deposition but that are nonetheless preserved.

If the judge sustains an objection, the objection, question, and answer should be crossed out. Otherwise, the question and answer remain, but the objection is eliminated.

Follow the same process to eliminate motions to strike, colloquy, and extraneous remarks of counsel. In most cases, the deposition as read at trial will contain only the lawyers' questions and the witness's answers.

If you do not intend to introduce the entire transcript, you will have to designate which portions you are going to offer. Your opponent should then have an opportunity to identify any other portions that he believes you must, in fairness, also read. It is far better for both sides to resolve this issue before trial.

The lawyer against whose client the deposition is offered certainly wants a fair reading in context. The lawyer introducing a portion of a deposition wants to be as credible as possible to the jury, while avoiding an extended dramatic reading. His credibility would be undercut if he just read the favorable part of a deposition, only to have his opponent then stand up and demand: "Counsel, kindly also read pages 100 through 105, where the witness stated that he had misunderstood your previous question and then fully explained his answer."

Usually, it is not quite so obvious that some additional portion of the transcript should be introduced. If your opponent thinks you should read other passages along with the ones you have designated, and you disagree, get a ruling in advance. The risk of waiting until trial is far too great. If the jurors are convinced that you are trying to hide the "bad stuff" from them, they will ignore only two things about the rest of your presentation: the style and the content.

- *Using depositions: If you've only got one trick, you haven't got any tricks.* Some trial lawyers seem to assume that offering deposition testimony at trial runs a close second in captivating interest to reading the tax regulations.

You can tell it is not their favorite part of the trial from the way they announce it: "Your Honor, at this time I would like to read Mr. Smith's deposition into the record." And that is all they do—read it into the record. No persuasion. No pizzazz. Like a hunter with bad aim, they take whatever falls. And little does, except the jurors' eyelids.

Using depositions at trial does not have to be this grim. Sure, you miss the spontaneity of live interrogation, but there is still hope.

When you know that you are going to offer deposition testimony at trial, the first step is to let the jury in on it during voir dire. Something like this would work:

Ladies and gentlemen, during the trial, you will hear the testimony of John Smith. But Mr. Smith will not be here in the courtroom. Because he lives half-way across the country, Mr. Smith's testimony was taken in his hometown at a deposition, and that is what you will be hearing. Very briefly, a deposition is an official proceeding at which the witness and the lawyers for both sides appear. A court reporter gives the witness an oath to tell the truth, just like the one given in the courtroom. The lawyers then ask questions, and the witness answers. Either lawyer can object to questions just as he can here. The court reporter records the entire thing, word for word. Will any of you tend to give Mr. Smith's testimony less weight because he is not here in person? Can you commit to me that you will consider Mr. Smith's testimony the same as if he had testified from the witness stand?

This short piece of voir dire (whether done adroitly by you or less so by a time-conscious judge) accomplishes three things. First, it alerts the jurors that the deposition is coming and lets them know why it is being used. Second, it assures the jurors that the deposition process is just as serious as what they are about to see in court. Third, it gets as much of a commitment as possible that the jurors *will listen* to the testimony.

Listening. That is what you want. What else can you do to keep the jurors as interested in the deposition testimony as they are in the live witnesses?

You can turn the deposition into a live witness. Do not read the transcript all by yourself. Save the monologues for opening and closing. Get someone up on the witness stand to read the answers.

Make the exercise as realistic as possible. You want the jurors to look at the person on the witness stand and *believe* they are seeing the witness whose testimony they are hearing. You also want the jury to believe that witness's testimony. If the judge will let you select your reader, pick the most interesting, sincere person you can find—one who oozes credibility.

This "witness" must prepare before he appears at trial. The last thing you want him to do on the stand is stumble through because he is unfamiliar with the deponent's terminology or syntax. The witness should review the entire transcript carefully in advance. Bring him into your office as often as necessary before trial to rehearse, so he knows exactly how you intend to offer the testimony in the courtroom.

Some judges will not permit the lawyers to bring in a "ringer" to read the deponent's answers at trial. But most will allow you to use a colleague or a legal assistant. The same rules about preparation apply. Obviously, you should find out in advance what your particular judge's practice is.

The lawyer reading the questions should also review the transcript ahead of time. If you are going to introduce deposition testimony, know the questions well so that in court you do not sound as if you are reading. It is important for you to do the same things you would do if the deponent were testifying in person: modulate your voice, change the pace of your delivery, and show interest in the answers.

So much for using the deposition of an unavailable witness. How do you handle depositions of parties?

One of the most effective ways is to introduce the helpful admissions as part of your own case-in-chief. The tactic is particularly persuasive for a plaintiff, because he can fit the defendant's admissions into his case before the defendant has even had a chance to take the stand. By introducing the favorable deposition testimony as part of your own case, not only do you give the jury a longer time to think about it, but you also incorporate it neatly into your own presentation. Finally, if the defendant testifies differently later, then the plaintiff's lawyer can impeach him with the same deposition.

Medium v. Tedium: Video Depositions Come of Age

by David M. Balabanian

The medium has finally come to the courtroom. A lawyer can now record any deposition on videotape, if the other side agrees. In 1970 the Federal Rules of Civil Procedure were amended to permit electronic recording of depositions by stipulation. The change eliminates the requirement of a court order. FED. R. CIV. P. 30(b)(4). Even the criminal lawyer can now offer a videotaped defense. FED. R. CRIM. P. 15(d).

But you may want to check an impulse to record all your testimony for playback to the jury in color. Video depositions are a mixed bag, expensive and possibly misleading. And an alert opponent may not stipulate when the video deposition would do you the most good. Consider the following before you smear yourself with makeup.

A video record carries greater impact to a jury, and even a judge, than a cold transcript. A video deposition avoids the tedium that benumbs the mind on hearing large quantities of deposition transcripts. A video record may even entice judges in bench trials to watch rather than require that deposition testimony be submitted in writing.

A video record can capture the attention better than a transcript read by relays of dispirited lawyers. The new generation of jurors who receive their truth from the tube may prefer video to live testimony. But even for the print generation, video can be powerful.

- Video can show a witness's personal injuries in a manner that surpasses still photographs. Video can show limited motion or impaired function. Of course movies can also do this, but video can allow a distant witness to re-enact events or conduct experiments or demonstrations. But prepare yourself for disputes over the condi-

Mr. Balabanian is a member of McCutchen, Doyle, Brown & Enersen in San Francisco.

tions under which the deposition is taken, the nature of the demonstration or experiment, or even the camera angle.

- Video can record a terminally ill witness. Testimony from "beyond the grave" at trial could prove highly effective. In one recent case the court allowed a plaintiff to take his own deposition at the point of death despite the defendants' opposition. *Carson v. Burlington Northern, Inc.*, 52 F.R.D. 492 (D. Neb. 1971).
- Video can liberate doctors and other experts from the rigors of trial scheduling for their testimony.
- Video can yield an immediate record, unlike the reporter. In a fast-moving injunctive situation, this alone may dictate use of video. Of course, the necessary equipment and technical personnel must be easily available and the tape should not require editing or you may lose this advantage.
- Video can suppress obstreperous counsel. Lawyers on camera may forego their more obstructive practices. But they may also replace bombast with ham.
- Video can bring home to a nonchalant witness the seriousness of the proceeding.

There are many things that video cannot do. Video will not save money, despite the hopes of the Advisory Committee in the Notes to Rule 30(b)(4). If you want to save money, use an audio cassette recorder. Parties can stipulate that a deposition or interview will be recorded on tape and then use the tape or the transcript as the deposition. You will need no sophisticated equipment, although be sure to use an external microphone (usually provided with any cassette recorder) rather than the internal mike. Each party should bring its own recorder to the deposition and make simultaneous copies of the tape. This reproduces the tape and guards against doctoring.

Surreptitious Recording

Because of the unpleasant consequences of surreptitious recording under certain state laws (ranging from inadmissibility to felony penalties, for example, CAL. PENAL CODE § 632), have the witness acknowledge on the tape that he is aware of the recording. The questioner might also make occasional statements *on* the record that the conversation is being taped.

The cost of video will vary greatly with the number and type of cameras used, auxiliary equipment, and whether it is in color or black and white. Stenographic recording will almost always be cheaper. A hidden problem may be that the case will demand both methods of reporting. Counsel will rarely be able to do without a written transcript and will often require a certified transcript prepared by a reporter present at the deposition.

You will need a transcript (probably certified) if the witness's testimony is used in pretrial motions. You will need a transcript (probably not certified) for pretrial review of the testimony and preparation of the witness because reviewing a videotape is woefully inefficient. For example, comparison of different portions of testimony will be impossible without a transcript. You will need a transcript for presenting objections to the court in advance of trial. You will need a certified transcript if the deposition is used for impeachment.

Of course, a stenographer in your office can prepare a written transcript from the videotape (or a simultaneous audio tape), but this course may lead to inaccuracies. Extensive use of a written transcript, along with the inevitable disputes, suggests that you should obtain simultaneous official reporting and videotape.

Most courts concern themselves with preventing alterations in the video record. In fact, it is difficult to doctor a videotape. If the recorder uses a digital time-and-date generator, alteration becomes almost impossible. This device creates a digital record on the taped image, identifying date and time by minutes and seconds. This permits more accurate location of specific portions of testimony than does the footage meter. However, the videotape is invariably edited before trial. The tape played for the jury will have distracting gaps in the digital record. While the possibility of doctored tapes exists, it will not occur if the video operator is as qualified and respected as a court reporter.

Other video problems are not so easily solved.

People do not necessarily appear true to life propped in front of a television camera. A natural appearance can be achieved only with considerable effort. With some witnesses, it can never be achieved.

Counsel should not begin a video deposition without a rehearsal to check the appearance of the witness. During the deposition, a lawyer should look at a monitor from time to time while the camera rolls and check the tape during breaks in the deposition.

Where the appearance of the witness is particularly important, employ a professional consultant. Differences in camera angle, lighting, and other technical variables can change the entire effect of a deposition.

Pointers

Some practical considerations:
- Proper lighting is essential. Modern cameras can work with available light, but it must be properly balanced. Be alert for shadows that alter the witness's appearance. Light can turn a genial soul sinister.
- Color cameras are worth the extra expense. A natural look is hard to achieve in black and white.
- The best dress for a man will be a solid grey suit with a blue shirt. White "blooms" on television and black appears too dead. Checks and stripes are distracting.

- With women, prefer solid darker colors; avoid prints and checks.
- Women should use make-up and men a little talc or handkerchief action to keep down glow.
- Men should shave immediately before the deposition or at least use flesh-colored talc to cover stubble.
- Train the witness to look into the camera while testifying. Likewise, the witness should look at the questioner during accusatory questions or he will appear evasive.
- You must alter the conventional wisdom regarding witness behavior at depositions. A lawyer generally advises deponents to take all the time they need to formulate answers. But in a video deposition the camera grinds on through the delay and records expressions of confusion or dismay on the part of the witness. A witness must respond as promptly and confidently at a video deposition as at trial.
- The concentrated focus of the camera intensifies eccentricities or peculiarities of speech or manner. The witness's accents become more noticeable and mannerisms more distracting or offensive.
- Take care to muffle noise in the deposition room. Background noises such as air conditioning or traffic and the noises of shuffling documents or movements are intensified on television and will be distracting.
- Do not overlook camera angle. High shots produce pygmies. Low shots yield monoliths of the Citizen Kane type.

There are certain questions that frequently recur.

Do You Use Zoom Lenses? A zoom lens enables the cameraman to achieve close-ups of the witness or a particular anatomical feature. A witness who is having trouble with a question appears evasive and his discomfort more devious with zooming. We all remember the televised grilling. Some courts have required that the cameraman be independent or that the camera be aimed and then not moved. The use of independent operators may be an unnecessary expense, though a reasonable precaution, given the increasing availability of video equipment.

The model stipulation at the end of this article presents alternate solutions to the problem of camera control. Selection among them will depend on the trust between counsel and the funds available.

How Many Cameras? Both questioner and deponent should appear on camera when they speak. Otherwise the audience may ignore or downplay the unseen lawyer asking the questions. Panning the camera among the speakers will cure the problem but leaves viewers dizzy. Two cameras—the technique of television news reporting—will offer more relaxed shifting but is expensive. You will also have to rent mixing equipment and have an operator to switch back and forth from camera to camera to capture the current speaker. This will require great skill or it will become ragged. You could use a split-screen somewhat like the instant replay of a quarterback and receiver. But the audience will be frazzled after a few minutes of this technique.

Who "Notarizes" the Tape? In the usual deposition, the reporter, a notary, swears the witness. The Federal Rules suggest that the video operator should be the deposition officer.

But Rule 28(a) provides that "depositions shall be taken before an officer authorized to administer oaths by the laws of the United States or the place where the examination is held, or before a person appointed by the court in which the action is pending." This might require the presence of both a notary and the cameraman, unless you stumble across a video notary. The problem can be solved easily: Rule 29 authorizes the parties to provide by written stipulation that "depositions may be taken before any person. . . ."

Who Pays for the Deposition? Given the costs of video, disputes will arise over allocation of costs for creating the original tape, for taping cross-examination, for duplicate tapes, for blanking out objections, and for preparation of a transcript or stenographic record. Rule 30(b)(4) provides that even if there is a stipulation or order for the use of video, "a party may arrange to have a stenographic transcription made at his own expense." Think carefully about this problem before agreeing to a video deposition, especially if your client has limited means.

How Do You "Sign" a Video Deposition? As revised, Rule 30(b)(4) requires that a nonstenographic deposition be accompanied by a "writing" that sets forth any changes made by the witness and his signature identifying the deposition as his own or the statement of the officer if the witness does not sign. Presumably the witness will identify a videotape as containing his deposition and sign a writing to that effect before depositing it with the court. The suggested stipulation waives signature after an opportunity to review.

How Do You Handle Objections? One method for handling objections is to submit to the court before trial a written transcript of the testimony together with objections. After the court has ruled, an edited tape can be prepared. This is time-consuming and costly.

Another method, the "McCrystal Method," requires the court—equipped with a log that identifies the location on the tape of material to which objection has been made—to view the tape in advance of trial and note its rulings on objections. This technique may burden the court's time. Afterwards, an edited tape can be prepared.

Alternately, the technician who plays the tape at trial can suppress the audio during objectionable testimony. Although several authors recommend this latter practice, it sounds bizarre. How will a jury react to a videotape on which the witness mouths in silence? Jurors may become restive and annoyed with the party who shut off the sound.

One author suggests that jurors might lip-read and proposes that voir dire eliminate lip readers. *See* Kornblum & Short, *The Use of Videotape in*

Civil Trial Preparation and Discovery, 23 AM. JUR. TRIALS 95 (1976). That, too, seems bizarre. A better solution would be to suppress both audio and video during objectionable sequences.

Given the variety of questions and problems in a video deposition, the best results may be achieved by a stipulation rather than a court order. A number of courts have considered the cost and accuracy of video recording and issued widely varying orders covering techniques and procedures. *E.g.*, *Continental Federal Savings & Loan Ass'n v. Delta Corporation of America*, 71 F.R.D. 697 (W.D. Okla. 1976); *Matter of Daniels*, 69 F.R.D. 579 (N.D. Ga. 1975); *Wescott v. Neeman*, 55 F.R.D. 257 (D. Neb. 1972); *Kallen v. Nexus Corp.*, 54 F.R.D. 610 (N.D. Ill. 1972). The stipulation below represents an attempt to distill the best of these often conflicting rulings.

If agreement on a stipulation is not possible, video may still be available by court order. In *Colonial Times, Inc. v. Gasch*, 509 F.2d 517, 522 (D.C. Cir. 1975), the court ordered the trial court to grant a request for non-stenographic recordation. A different result was reached in *UAW v. National Caucus of Labor Committees*, 525 F.2d 323, 326 (2d Cir. 1975).

A number of states have adopted or are considering statutes or rules governing video depositions. Many of them follow Rule 30(b)(4) as it read before this current amendment. Read these rules before using this stipulation.

Televised testimony may bring life to the courtroom, but make sure you know what you are about before agreeing to try it. Video depositions could turn your client's tragedy into a soap opera and the opposing lawyer into Howard Cosell.

APPENDIX: Stipulation for a Video Deposition

It is hereby stipulated by and between _____ that the deposition of _____ (hereafter "deponent") in the above action shall be recorded on videotape in the following manner and upon the following conditions:

Time and Place

1. The deposition shall be taken at _____ on _____ commencing at _____. It shall continue thereafter from day to day, excluding weekends and holidays, until concluded.

Deposition Officer

2. The deposition shall be taken before _____, who is an employee of _____. He/she shall serve as deposition officer.

Video Equipment and Its Control

3. Except as otherwise provided herein, the deposition officer shall select and supply all equipment required to videotape the deposition and shall determine all matters of staging and technique, such as number and placement of cameras and microphones,

lighting, camera angle, and background. He/she shall determine these matters in a manner that accurately reproduces the appearance of the deponent and assures clear reproduction of both the deponent's testimony and the statements of counsel. The deponent, or any party to the action, may place upon the record any objection to the deposition officer's handling of any of these matters. Such objections shall be considered by the court in ruling on the admissibility of the video record. All such objections shall be deemed waived unless made promptly after the objector knows, or has reasonable grounds to know, of the basis of such objection.

Use of Day/Time Generator
4. There shall be employed at the deposition a day/time generator to create on the videotape a continuous record of the day and time.

Commencing the Deposition
5. The deposition officer shall commence the deposition by stating on the video record his/her name and business address; the name and business address of the officer's employer; the date, time and place; the name of deponent and the caption of the action; the identity of the party on whose behalf the deposition is being taken; and the names of all persons present in the deposition room. The deposition officer shall also swear, on the video record, that he/she will record the deposition accurately and in confidence and abide by all provisions of this stipulation. The deposition officer shall then swear the deponent on the video record. Such oath shall be effective without regard to whether the officer is otherwise authorized to administer oaths.

Going "Off Camera"
6. The deposition officer shall not stop the video recorder after the deposition commences until it concludes, except, however, that any party may request such cessation, which request will be honored unless another party objects. Each time the tape is stopped or started, the deposition officer shall announce the time on the record.

Changing Tapes
7. If the deposition requires the use of more than one tape, the end of each tape and the beginning of the next shall be announced orally on the video record by the deposition officer.

Availability of Monitor
8. There shall be available to counsel throughout the deposition a monitor on which they can view the video record as it is being made.

Camera on Speaker
9. The deposition officer shall endeavor, to the extent possible without creating undue distraction, to focus the camera (or the live camera if there is more than one) on the person who is currently speaking, whether it be the deponent or counsel.

Exhibitions and Demonstrations
10. Except by agreement of the parties or order of the court, the deponent shall not be required or permitted to exhibit personal injuries or limitation of movement, conduct demonstrations or experiments, or re-enact physical events.

Allocation of Costs
11. The costs of videotaping the depositions shall be borne [by the party who noticed the deposition] or [by all parties equally] or [by all parties who interrogate the deponent, in proportion to the length of their direct examination]. Such costs shall [not] be taxable costs in this proceeding. Any party may obtain at its own expense, a copy of the videotape or any portion thereof from the deposition officer.

Stenographic Reporting
12. [Any party may, at its own expense, have the deposition reported by stenographic means.] or
   [The deposition shall be reported by stenographic means in addition to video. The allocation and taxability of the costs of such stenographic reporting shall be governed by the provisions of paragraph 11, *supra.*]

Discrepancies between Video and Stenographic Records [If the latter is used]
13. In the event of any material discrepancy between the video record and the stenographic transcript, the parties shall stipulate or, if they are unable to agree, the court shall determine which record shall be submitted to the trier of fact.

Examination and Correction of Deposition Record
14. After completion of the deposition the deponent and all parties shall be given reasonable opportunity to review the videotape [and any stenographic transcript] of the deposition and to request in writing (or on the video record if it is still open) any changes or corrections in such record[s].

Waiver of Execution
15. Thirty days after notice to the deponent and all parties that the videotape is available for inspection as provided in paragraph 14, *supra,* the original of the videotape (together with all requests for changes or corrections theretofore received) may be filed with the court where it shall have the same force and effect as a duly executed stenographic transcript of the deponent's testimony.

239

Certification of the Video Record

16. [As soon as possible after expiration of the period prescribed in paragraph 15, *supra*] or [No later than ten days before trial] the deposition officer shall file the original videotape with the above court in a sealed envelope which shall identify the action, the deponent, and the date[s] of the deposition. To that envelope the deposition officer shall attach his/her sworn statement that the videotape is an accurate and complete record of the deposition and that he/she has complied with all provisions of this stipulation applicable to said officer.

Custody of the Tape

17. The deposition officer shall maintain custody of the original tape until it is filed with the court. Parties may view the tape while it is in the officer's custody, but only under conditions that make impossible the erasure or alteration of the tape.

Editing the Tape

18. A party who desires to offer any portion of the video record at trial for any purpose shall, no later than 60 days before trial, advise all other parties of the portions of the tape it wishes to offer. Any party who believes that the portions so designated contain objectionable material may, by motion, seek that court's ruling on its objections in advance of trial. An edited tape, eliminating material found by the court to be objectionable, shall be prepared (at the expense of the party responsible for the original inclusion of that material) unless the parties provide, or the court orders, another method for the suppression of the objectionable material.

Effect of Stipulation

19. This stipulation shall supplement and, to the extent permitted, supersede the provisions of any statute, rule, or regulation otherwise applicable to the taking of video depositions in this jurisdiction.

PART IV

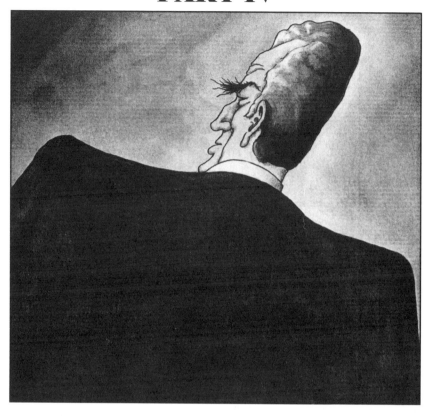

Experts

Experts:
A Few Fundamentals

by Peter I. Ostroff

In more and more business cases, juries and judges are being asked to believe "experts." For those lawyers who are not experts in this area, here is some basic advice on how to pick the right expert, how to set him to work for you, and how to prepare his trial testimony.

Under Federal Rule of Evidence 702 and the many similar state statutes and rules, lawyers have broad discretion in choosing their experts. To testify as an expert, a witness needs to be qualified only "by knowledge, skill, experience, training, or education." FED. R. EVID. 702. An early draft of Rule 702 would have required "special" knowledge, but the word "special" was deleted as too restrictive. An expert need not even have complete knowledge of his field of expertise or be certain of his opinion. *United States v. Spencer*, 439 F.2d 1047, 1049 (2d Cir. 1971); *Baerman v. Reisinger*, 363 F.2d 309, 310 (D.C. Cir. 1966).

The broad leeway you have in selecting an expert under these rules makes your decision all the more difficult and important. From the large number of persons who might qualify as an expert witness, whom should you choose?

First, choose a person who practices full time in the relevant field of expertise. In recent years, the increasing amount of litigation and use of experts has given rise to a number of firms and individuals who specialize in providing expert testimony. Shun both professional witnesses and litigation specialists.

A full-time practitioner will have more "knowledge, skill, [and] experience" about his field than someone who spends much of his time in court. The practitioner may also have more "training and education." And the more your expert knows, the better he can equip you to present your case.

The author is a partner in Sidley & Austin in Los Angeles, and is chairman of the Computer Litigation Committee of the Litigation Section.

"Professional witnesses" are often less credible; they appear to be hired guns, ready to render any helpful opinion so long as the pay is right. The natural skepticism with which many judges view expert testimony is most apparent with respect to such "professional witnesses." A full-time practitioner is not as subject to this criticism. Moreover, an expert is more convincing when he can testify about his own observations, experiments, and analysis rather than about conclusions he drew from others' work. The full-time practitioner who does every day what he is testifying about is more likely to be believed than one who testifies every day about what he seldom does.

Professional witnesses do have one advantage: often, they are more adept at communicating their knowledge to the jury. That skill is particularly important when the expert testimony will deal with abstruse, technical matters beyond the average juror's ken. Despite this advantage of professional witnesses, you should generally avoid them. You can usually teach communication skills to a full-time practitioner and, through videotaped practice sessions, mold his testimony into an understandable, persuasive presentation. But you cannot teach a professional witness his field of supposed expertise.

Technical Abilities

Second, involve your client in the search for an appropriate expert. Often your client will be involved in the same field or industry and, therefore, will be better able than you to judge the qualifications and technical abilities of potential experts. An expert consultant or witness is as much the client's representative as you are, and the expert may have an even greater role in the litigation's outcome. The client has a strong interest and a legitimate right to participate in choosing his expert.

Third, like a prudent driver, keep a spare. Select more experts than you will actually need, and designate all of them if you are required to designate expert witnesses before trial. While it is inappropriate and probably an abuse of discovery to name many more experts than you will actually use, it is appropriate and prudent to identify at least one "spare" for each type of expert you will need.

Why keep a spare? For the same reason the driver does: you cannot anticipate all the turns the road to trial will take; it is littered with potholes. To overcome those difficulties, you need the assurance of a spare. You do not want to start searching for a new expert if your expert goes flat or leaves you in a lurch far down the road to trial. And do not kid yourself, even the best experts sometimes fail. Their views may become incompatible with your trial strategy either because they reach the "wrong" conclusions or their opinions do not coincide with other witnesses' testimony. Their credibility or confidence may become irrevocably punctured during discovery. Or, they may go on vacation or sabbatical just as trial is finally reached. The road to trial is rough; you need a spare.

Engagement Letter

Once you have chosen and retained an expert, you must tell him what to do. It is crucial to define the expert's task well because that definition will control the expert's utility throughout the case. At the beginning of the expert's involvement in the case, define his job in an engagement memorandum or letter. That will diminish the possibility of confusion or misunderstanding and promote clarity in the definition itself.

The engagement letter will be discoverable if you later designate the expert as a probable witness. Therefore, draft it as though your opponent will read it. Work with your expert in drafting it. He can help you avoid ambiguities, focus on the right questions, and emphasize the proper points, thus lessening the chance you later will have to revise the letter or send a second one.

Frame the letter so that it does not suggest the answer you hope the expert will find from whatever studies, experiments, or analyses you ask him to perform. If you suggest the desired result, your opponent will use your letter to prove that your expert did not conduct true studies, experiments, or analyses, but, rather, that his efforts were shams designed to support your predetermined conclusion. Your letter should ask the expert for his opinion "respecting whether or not [certain facts and circumstances warrant a particular conclusion]" rather than asking him "to testify that [a particular conclusion follows from certain facts and circumstances]."

The same caution observed in drafting the engagement letter should govern all your communications with an expert unless you have firmly decided that you will never use him as a witness. If you ever decide to use the expert as a witness, all your written or oral communications with him may become discoverable, including the instructions you gave him, the background facts you described for him, and the documents you sent him to study. At a minimum, everything the expert witness reviewed and considered in reaching his conclusion or preparing his testimony will be discoverable.

Phrase all your communications with the expert in a manner consistent with the evidence and your theory of the case. Do not disclose facts or documents to the expert unless the opposition has already learned or seen them or you do not mind if the opposition does learn or see them.

Materials an expert witness generates are equally discoverable. Tell your expert this at the outset. While he may need to generate some documents as he pursues his studies, experiments, or analyses, caution him not to commit speculations or ill-considered conclusions to writing. Ill-considered writings can undercut subsequent, more carefully derived conclusions, rendering the expert useless as a witness. An expert should never write a report until he has first discussed his conclusions with you orally.

244

If you do decide to retain an expert solely as a consultant, be sure to insulate him from your expert witnesses so that your communications with the consultant and his work product will not be discoverable. Do not allow the expert witnesses to discuss the case or obtain information from your consultant; have all such communications funneled through you.

The first rule in preparing for a trial involving expert witnesses is to know the experts, both yours and the opposition's. Obtain and read every professional publication by each expert. Get as much information as you can about each expert's prior depositions and trial testimony. If the expert has extensive academic credentials, try to get transcripts of his grades as a student and obtain evaluations of him from his professors and peers.

Why all this work? The expert will almost always know more about his field than will trial counsel. Collateral or ad hominem attacks may be the only available avenue of cross-examination. If the expert has said something before on the same subject, you need to know it to point out any inconsistencies or to assure that his testimony is consistent. From time to time you may find the cross-examiner's dream—the expert who has written inconsistently about the subject of his testimony. If there is a blot somewhere on the expert's record, you need to know it to protect or attack the witness.

You cannot neglect the substance and underpinnings of the expert's testimony. You should depose the opposing experts, and then work with your own experts to devise the most effective cross-examination of the opposition.

You should carefully prepare your own experts, making them teachers who can simply and convincingly explain complex technical matters to the jury. Your experts should exude competence and credibility. This will come partly from careful preparation and thorough rehearsal of their testimony. It also will be telegraphed by their clothing and appearance. A clean, neat appearance is always desirable, but avoid dressing your experts in clothes inappropriate to their callings. Machine shop mechanics may be experts, but they should not appear in court in three-piece, pinstriped suits. Similarly, college professors should look the part, not like trial lawyers.

Give your experts the usual cautions about speaking simply, and never with condescension, arrogance, or pomposity. You should tell them that a good expert admits when he is uncertain, acknowledges he has erred in the past and doubtless will in the future, and concedes indisputable facts even when they are adverse. Point out that a good expert cannot be goaded into taking positions he has not considered carefully before assuming the witness stand.

Next, review the expert's testimony with him, finding out what he has to say, how it can best be phrased, and what questions you should ask to elicit that testimony. You should consider whether the expert's testimony can be enlivened or made more comprehensible with demonstrative evidence such as charts, graphs, or slides. If you decide to use such aids, the expert should prepare them or at least assist in their preparation.

The structure of the expert's testimony is very important. At the outset, of course, you must qualify the expert. In most jurisdictions this involves demonstrating that the subject matter of the testimony is an area in which the trier of fact will benefit by some assistance and that the expert has the training, skill, or experience to provide that assistance.

Unless the substance of the testimony will not be disputed or the expert's credentials are unimpressive, the expert's qualifications should be set before the jury or judge in loving (but also lively) detail. In view of the impact that such matters have on those who weigh credibility, do not surrender your opportunity to parade your expert's pedigree nor accept a stipulation as to qualifications unless the expert's credibility definitely will not be challenged.

Qualifications aside, the expert's testimony should be organized like an assault on Mt. Everest: first, climb the mountain; second, plant a flag at the top; and third, climb down. In climbing up, the expert should detail all the preparation, study, experimentation, rejection of alternative conclusions, and analysis that he has undertaken to formulate his conclusions or opinions. The flag at the pinnacle is the expert's statement of his opinion. In climbing down, the expert may explain the basis or reasons that support his conclusion. Taken in this order, the expert's testimony will be understandable and will lend credibility to his conclusion.

Once you have formulated the basic outlines of your expert's testimony, rehearse it with him. Rehearsal is particularly important if you use visual aids with the testimony. If the expert has mannerisms or speech patterns that may detract from his credibility, a videotape practice session is often helpful. You then can review the videotape with the witness to improve the presentation, and repeat the drill to refine the expert's testimony to a simple, persuasive performance. Similarly, you should try to anticipate cross-examination and prepare responses to predictable areas of inquiry.

Having followed all these fundamental guidelines, you and your expert should be well prepared for the rigors of trial. Your expert will be, as he should be, a convincing salesman for your position. And you will be equipped to deal with the opponent's experts as well. After a few trials with expert witnesses, you will be the expert.

Confessions of an Expert Witness

by Robert F. Hanley

I have two sources of expertise on experts. First, I have tried many cases in which the opposing party and I have used experts. But I would not be writing this article if I only knew what that experience taught. No, I value my second source of knowledge more; I recently testified as an expert myself.

Arguing that judges, not lawyers, should teach how to argue appeals, John W. Davis, the great American constitutional lawyer, once asked rhetorically, ''Who would listen to a fisherman's weary discourse on fly casting technique, if the fish himself could be induced to give *his* views on the most effective method of approach?'' I am a fish writing; I have been an expert witness. What I learned through that experience has greatly changed my approach to the experts I hire.

Before I was an expert witness myself, I used to prepare experts for their testimony by flying quickly through a laundry list of standard do's and don'ts.

I would tell the expert that a jury is smarter than the expert thinks it is. The jury's collective memory is absolutely breath-taking. The jury will understand if you talk to them simply and clearly. They are like students in a beginning course in some discipline new to them. They are bright enough; they are filled with fear; they are eager to learn; but they need a base of knowledge from which to build. If the expert dazzles them with his erudition, confuses them with technical buzz words and uses compound sentences with lots of modifiers, the expert might as well stay at home. I told experts and still tell them that the jury is sensitive; jurors resent and discount any expert who patronizes them.

My standard lecture to experts continued: You must use simple words

The author is a partner in the Denver firm of Morrison & Foerster; Adjunct Professor, Advanced Trial Advocacy, University of Colorado Law School; and a former chairman of the Section of Litigation.

in short sentences. Watch the jurors; when they look dazed, bring them back to life with an example, a metaphor, a story. Just treat everyone in the courtroom with courtesy. Be alert. Listen to the questions you are asked. Answer responsively. Just answer the question and stop. Do not argue; do not play lawyer. Let me do the arguing. Do not ask the judge for help. Do not lose your temper.

Then I would review the common techniques of cross-examining experts, often citing examples from James Brosnahan's *Trial Handbook*. The opposing lawyer, I would tell the expert, will try to do the following:

- Narrow the basis of your opinion to assumptions of questionable validity, taking your position to its illogical extreme. Be cautious, therefore, in answering casual questions which start a series leading to an illogical extreme. Develop a feeling for these questions in a series.
- Demonstrate that my client or I failed to give you important information or gave you inaccurate information.
- Show that you usually testify for one side in a case, have testified for me or my client in many cases, and have been paid a lot for doing so. I will take the sting out of those questions by my direct examination.
- Show errors in your computations—a technique especially effective against accountants. So go over your arithmetic. Do not leave it to assistants.
- Ridicule your being out of touch with "the real world." Above all, do not get angry; do not lose your poise when the opposing attorney suggests by his questioning that one ditch-digger from "the real world" is worth ten professors from "ivory towers."

I would end my peroration by assuring the expert he need not worry about these things. With his experience and intelligence, my opponent would be no match for him. My experts tended to agree with me, and that would be the end of it.

If things did not go well at trial, I would assume that my expert was an insensitive, unintelligent clod who had not listened closely enough to my instructions. After all, there is nothing to giving testimony in court. The expert knew more about his field than anyone else in the world, or so he said. All he had to do was sit up there and talk to the jury. There is nothing to it. That is what I used to think and say, but no longer.

I am chastised, purified, and humbled. I recently appeared as the plaintiff's expert in a lawyer malpractice case. Now I know firsthand what it is like to testify as an expert. It is not a piece of cake.

First Mistake

My first mistake was agreeing to testify at all. My second mistake was not learning enough about the case.

A lawyer friend called. He flattered the devil out of me and reminded me of all the favors I owed him.

"What do I have to testify to?" I asked. He replied, "I just want you to say that any lawyer who permits a default to be entered against his clients without going to the library, without making a thorough factual and legal investigation is negligent." I said, "Oh, that's a cinch. We cannot have people like that running loose in the profession."

Now, I knew better than to jump into a case like that. I know that effective expert witnesses insist on reviewing the documentary evidence themselves, reaching their own working hypothesis of fault before they talk to the lawyer and get his theories. But I agreed to testify before I knew anything about the case, and I accepted the lawyer's theory without thinking for myself.

If I ever testify as an expert again, I shall follow this rule: go over the file with a fine-tooth comb. Do whatever library work is required. Then, arrange for a preliminary interview to discuss my tentative conclusions and get the lawyer's theory to see whether I have the requisite expertise, interest, and ability to be an effective witness.

My third mistake was agreeing to testify outside the area of my true expertise. My friend, the lawyer, told me the malpractice defendant had accepted a retainer from the plaintiffs to handle a complicated mortgage foreclosure, the details of which I did not have to worry about. I know nothing about mortgage foreclosures. I should have stood my ground and paid my debts to my friend another day in another way.

But my friend said, "You need not know anything about real estate. You teach trial practice, you have handled cases for years. Without doing any research, the defendant decided that his clients had no defense. He just let them be defaulted; the foreclosure was entered; and the client lost his earnest money." My friend continued, "All I want you to say is that a lawyer who would permit a default to be entered without even going to the library is negligent." Foolishly, I agreed.

My fourth mistake was letting my friend define the area of my investigation. I knew better. In a previous building failure case, I had asked a fine engineer whether he would testify that it was malpractice for an architect-engineer to fail to supervise the retraction of a steel casing used to form a concrete caisson, part of the building's foundation. During the retraction of the casing, a 12-foot void had been left in the caisson. When the void was later discovered, 12 floors of structural steel had to be dismantled and all of the caissons cored and repaired.

My expert had said, "No. I will not testify on your theory—not on your life. I will make an independent review of the job and of all the documents. I will review the file and attempt to determine the actual cause of the caisson failure. Then I will review the architect-engineer's performance, and then I will tell you whether the defendant was negligent."

My expert did exhaustive work and found records that showed clearly that the defendant knew there was water between the steel casing and the surrounding dirt when the casing was retracted. My expert satisfied himself that hydrostatic pressure collapsed the casing and washed out the concrete. The water could and should have been drained. He was confident. It was his hypothesis, not mine, and he supported it. It was an opinion from the core of his expertise. My opponent could not shake my expert during his pretrial deposition, and the defendant settled, paying my client's entire loss.

That fine expert made it clear to me before he undertook the job that his reputation rode on his testimony. He expected to be paid for the time he spent investigating; if his investigation revealed no fault, he would tell me so and would not, of course, testify. I would probably settle the case quickly.

When I was an expert witness, I forgot the lesson I had learned in the caisson case. I let the lawyer establish my hypothesis: that the defendant was negligent in failing to research his case. Then I went to the library to support that hypothesis with appropriate canons of ethics and disciplinary rulings. I soon became convinced of the hypothesis I had started out to prove. And to help me along, the defendant admitted in his deposition that he had done no research.

Open and Shut

It never occurred to me or the lawyer who retained me that the mortgage foreclosure case could have been so open and shut that anyone really knowledgeable in the field would know the client had no defense and that it would be a needless expense to do any research. You can guess how the cross-examination went:

Q: Tell me, sir, how many mortgage foreclosures have you defended?

A: Now that you mention it, none.

Q: So it certainly would have been improper for you to advise a client about whether he had a defense to a mortgage foreclosure.

A: Absolutely, and I certainly would not have done that.

Q: You would have gone to the library, and you might have spent the whole day there.

A: Yes.

Q: You might have spent several days there.

A: Yes.

Q: It might have taken you a week.

A: It might have.

Q: It might have even taken more than a week.

A: Possibly.

Q: Then you would have written a memorandum.

A: Possibly.

Q: That would have taken a day or so.

A: Yes.

Q: Then you would have written an opinion letter, perhaps—another day?

A: Yes.

Q: If another client came along with the same problem a week after your opinion letter, you could have cut the time down substantially.

A: At least in half.

Q: As a matter of fact, you might not even have had to go to the library at all. That's why clients go to specialists. By the way, what is your hourly rate?

A: Do I have to answer that, Your Honor?

THE JUDGE. Yes.

Well, you can see what a wonderful impression I made. An expert cannot wear blinders. He has to have peripheral vision. He must not ignore his ignorance of connected, collateral, or overlapping areas of expertise.

My caisson expert had to know about the design of foundations, about plans and specifications for caissons; he had to know about subsurface soil conditions at the construction site, about the strength of the casing material, about the effect of water pressure, about pouring techniques, and about retracting techniques. He could not and did not put on blinders and say I am just an expert on the design of a foundation.

If I had done my homework, I might have found affirmative defenses to the foreclosure action. Or, if I found no defense available, then I would not have testified. Expertise on mortgage foreclosures was required. I should have determined whether I had or could acquire that expertise. I should have insisted that before testifying I had to have time to study and to confer with counsel, to be prepared to testify.

Preparation is essential—in-depth preparation including rehearsals of direct testimony and expected cross-examination. The expert needs to know what the lawyer is going to ask and how. He has to practice effective communication. The lawyer and his witness have to prepare each other with the facts. To be effective, they must go over and over their direct examination and anticipate and rehearse the cross-examination.

Too Aggressive

My fifth mistake as an expert witness was in being too aggressive, too one-sided. I had an excuse for this mistake. I had been burned so many times by experts who sounded like tigers in my office and turned into detached, disinterested, scientific pussy cats on the stand. I thought: ''I am not going to be a pussy cat when I take the stand. The jury will see I feel the righteousness of my client's cause. I will win this case. I am not an observer from Olympus. I am a partisan; my client's cause is my cause. I will show them.''

I showed them all right. I showed them that I had a lot to learn about judgment and perspective and that I should distinguish between the roles of advocate and witness. In my heart I could believe the plaintiff was poorly served by the defendant. I did and do. But it would have been so easy to appear straightforward, strong, sincere, and resolute without looking like Torquemada presiding over the local bar association grievance committee.

My sixth mistake was giving unclear testimony. It was unclear because it was not simple. To be simple one must be humble and sincere, qualities most well-known experts lack. The lawyer and his expert must talk simply to help the jury understand a subject that is new and strange to them.

The lawyer conducting my examination and I sounded like members of the profession discussing a technical and erudite point of professional responsibility. We spoke a secret language. If I had remembered how I felt the first day in law school, I would have empathized with the jurors as they listened to my testimony on the canons of ethics, disciplinary rulings, standards of professional responsibility, mortgagees and mortgagors—matters my friend, the lawyer, and I understood but not well enough to discuss simply in basic English. I failed to describe the fundamentals, to give the jury a common basis from which to understand the new ideas I was about to introduce.

Simplicity and clarity are essential, and they do not happen accidentally. The expert must know his material cold, and his testimony must be rehearsed.

One mistake I did not make as an expert witness was to try to anticipate the cross-examination and insert nice modifiers in every helpful statement I made on direct examination. I did not protect myself as experts usually do by modifying their opinions with such phrases as "in many cases," "usually," or "often," or with self-deprecating, mock-humble phrases as "of course that's only one man's opinion" or "there are, of course, those who would disagree."

These phrases water down helpful direct testimony and do not aid the expert on cross-examination. The cross-examining lawyer will just drop the modifiers; if the expert reasserts them he seems to be hedging, playing games, or not responding. An expert must defend his position. He does not have to be arrogant or to overstate the position, but once he takes a position, he cannot back away from it as I have seen so many experts do.

There were a few other mistakes I did not make because I did not have an opportunity to make them. I did not, for instance, fail to review my testimony in previous cases to see if I had ever taken an inconsistent view—I had not testified before. I did not forget about some inconsistent professional writing or speech I had given on the subject; I had never spoken or written on the subject.

To avoid the latter mistake with my own expert witnesses, I obtain, usually independently of my expert, a complete bibliography of my expert's writings. Graduate students often aid in preparing the bibliography and in helping me over technical hurdles as I read the expert's articles.

If nothing else, my painful example proves the importance of having an expert conduct an independent investigation to arrive at his own theory of the case. My example also shows that the lawyer must watch and hear his expert's testimony through the eyes and ears of the jury.

Being an expert witness is a difficult job, but it is not impossible. If the expert has a pleasant personality, if he can express himself in terms understandable to the jury and if he can and will defend his opinions, he has the game half won. He and you can win the rest by thorough preparation.

Modern Evidence and the Expert Witness

by Faust F. Rossi

In modern trials, the expert is as common as the lawyer. Case after case, civil or criminal, state or federal, turns on the testimony of one or more of many kinds of experts. Expert inflation is on the rise.

The causes are many. The growth of complex litigation, the explosion of technology and science, the increasing creativity of advocates—all play a role. But the main reason is the liberality with which modern evidence doctrine embraces courtroom experts.

The welcome mat was rolled out in 1975, when Congress enacted Federal Evidence Rules 702 through 705. These four provisions, comprising only eight sentences, confirmed the judicial trend toward expanded admissibility of expert testimony.

Dozens of state codifications have followed the federal lead. Decisions interpreting the rules of evidence within the last decade emphasize the presumption in favor of the admissibility of expert testimony. Long-standing doctrinal barriers have tumbled. As a result, the litigator's options in presenting expert testimony have increased manyfold.

A simple example makes the point.

Consider the medical expert in a personal-injury case arising out of a car crash. On the eve of trial, the plaintiff's lawyer hires a pediatric neurologist to testify on behalf of a seriously injured boy. The expert learns from the radiologist's X-ray report that the child suffered a skull fracture. Electroencephalograms (EEGs) reveal abnormal brain activity.

Reports from the treating physician record the parents' account that the child was unconscious for several hours after the accident and that he has since suffered several seizures. On reviewing these documents,

---

The author is the Samuel S. Leibowitz Professor of Trial Techniques at the Cornell Law School.

the expert is prepared to state that the child is suffering from traumatic epilepsy as a result of the injury.

Traditional evidence doctrine required a four-part courtroom presentation.

First, the doctor would state her qualifications. Second, during the direct examination, the doctor would lay out the bases for her opinion. She would explain her reliance on the X-ray evaluation, the EEG results, the history of unconsciousness, the seizures, and any other facts supporting her diagnosis and etiology. During this recital, opposing counsel would be all ears, since this information—the factual basis for the opinion—was the meat on which he would chew during cross-examination.

The third and most important requirement was that proof of all the facts underlying the opinion actually had to be received in evidence. Presumably, by the time the expert took the stand, this groundwork would have been laid. The X rays and EEGs would have been received and explained. Medical records or testimony of other witnesses would have established that the child had been unconscious and had experienced seizures.

Only after the facts supporting the opinion had been proved, the expert's qualifications laid out, and the bases for her conclusions explained could the expert take the fourth and final step: testifying to the opinion itself. Such was the presentation required in most jurisdictions as recently as 10 or 15 years ago.

What is necessary today under modern rules? Only two steps, the first and last, are required. The doctor must state her qualifications. Then she may give her opinion.

Much more is permitted. More may be expected. But no more is required as a condition to admissibility.

So modern evidence doctrine is a delight to the proponent of expert testimony, who now has a much easier time presenting expert opinions. At the same time, the new rules severely handicap the opponent of expert testimony.

To understand what an expert can say and how he can say it, trial lawyers should know the answers to three essential questions:

(1) About what can the expert testify?

(2) On what kinds of facts must the opinion be grounded?

(3) How, or in what form, can the opinion be given?

Under the modern rules, the answers to these three questions are far more permissive than they used to be. The test for determining what subject matter is appropriate for expert testimony has been liberalized. The permissible bases for expert opinion have been expanded. And traditional restrictions on how expert opinions must be presented have been eliminated.

Consider each of these developments in turn.

What subject matter is appropriate for expert testimony? Many years ago, Maguire described the boundaries of admissible expert opinion.

On one side, he said, is the great area of the commonplace, supposedly within the ken of every person of moderate intelligence; on the other side is the even greater area of the speculative and the uncertain. Expert testimony must lie somewhere in between.

Thus, the traditional requirements were two. The expertise had to encompass matters sufficiently complex to be beyond the ken of the ordinary lay person. Yet it could not be so novel or speculative that it was not generally accepted within its recognized scientific or professional sphere.

Modern evidence codes have relaxed both these limitations on the scope of expert testimony. The beyond-the-ken standard has all but disappeared. The criterion of general acceptance is fading fast.

Federal Rule 702, which governs when expert testimony is appropriate, does not require that the matter under consideration be beyond lay comprehension. Instead, helpfulness is the touchstone. If the expert's opinion ''will assist the trier of fact to understand the evidence or to determine a fact in issue,'' the expert testimony is appropriate.

Courts have interpreted Rule 702 liberally. Take, for example, *In re Japanese Electronic Products Antitrust Litigation,* 723 F.2d 238 (3d Cir. 1983) rev'd in part on other grounds, 475 U.S. 574 (1986), a massive antitrust action that Zenith Radio Corporation and other American companies brought against major Japanese manufacturers of consumer electronics products. One of the many evidentiary issues in that case was the admissibility of the expert testimony of the plaintiffs' economist.

Based largely on the plaintiffs' own litigation documents, the expert opined that the defendants had conspired to violate the antitrust laws. The district court concluded that the opinion did not depend on any special economic expertise.

The expert had done exactly what the jury is supposed to do—sift through the documentary evidence and decide whether the defendants had committed the violations alleged. Characterizing the expert as no more than an ''oath helper,'' the court excluded the opinion, stating that it added an unwarranted aura of scientific reliability and that it was not ''beyond the jury's sphere of knowledge.''

The court of appeals held that the district court had taken too narrow a view of the permissible scope of expert testimony: ''The requirement . . . that expert testimony be 'beyond the jury's sphere of knowledge' adopts a formulation which was rejected by drafters of Rule 702. While that formulation applied prior to the adoption of evidence rules, it no longer applies. 'Such a test is incompatible with the standard of helpfulness. . . .' '' 723 F.2d at 279.

Useful Knowledge

Citing cases favoring the admission, under Rule 702, of expert testimony, the court went on to adopt a ''presumption that expert testimony will be helpful.'' *Id.* at 280.

The point is that, even when jurors are well equipped to decide an issue based on their experience, an expert may still have specialized knowledge that can usefully be brought to bear on the same issue. Such an expert should be heard.

Trial judges now admit expert testimony that, before the enactment of the new evidence codes, would have been rebuffed as an invasion of the jury's province. *See, e.g., United States v. Roark*, 753 F.2d 991 (11th Cir. 1985) (the expert should have been permitted to opine that the defendant's confession was involuntary); *United States v. Barrett*, 703 F.2d 1076 (9th Cir. 1983) (a photographic expert was permitted to point out similarities between clothing shown in a surveillance photograph of a robber and clothing seized from the defendant); *Leonard v. Pitstick Dairy Lake & Park Inc.*, 124 Ill. App. 3d 580, 464 N.E.2d 644 (1984) (the expert should have been permitted to testify that, in his opinion, it was an unsafe practice for the defendant to permit youngsters to dive headfirst into the wading area of the defendant's lake).

With the abandonment of the traditional beyond-the-ken limitation, courts are increasingly receptive to expert testimony that does no more than sharpen the jury's common-sense evaluation of the evidence. Thus, within the last few years, courts have admitted expert opinions concerning:

- The unreliability of eyewitness testimony, *United States v. Smith*, 736 F.2d 1103 (6th Cir.), *cert. denied*, 469 U.S. 868 (1984).
- In homicide cases in which self defense was asserted, the behavior of women who claimed they were abused by husbands or lovers, *State v. Allery*, 101 Wash. 2d 591, 682 P.2d 312 (1984).
- Other kinds of psychological stress bearing on the voluntariness of conduct, *United States v. Winters*, 729 F.2d 602 (9th Cir. 1984).

If the beyond-the-ken hurdle has fallen with the advent of the evidence codes, another barrier still stands in many jurisdictions, although some courts are starting to give parties a boost to help them over it.

The American commitment to science and technology over the last generation has forced courts to rule on the admissibility of testimony based on many new discoveries and scientific applications. How should a court react when it is presented with a new form of expertise that has not yet been accepted as a proper subject for expert testimony? With caution is the traditional answer.

For many years, courts encountering novel scientific evidence applied the well-known *Frye* standard. Derived from language in *Frye v. United States*, 293 F. 1013, 1014 (D.C. Cir. 1923), the test is whether the process, system, or theory on which the evidence is based is "sufficiently established to have gained general acceptance in the particular field to which it belongs."

This standard, sometimes dubbed the "general acceptance" rule, has been applied to radar, public opinion surveys, breathalyzers, psycholinguistics, trace-metal detection, bite-mark comparisons, blood-splattering deductions, psychological-stress syndromes, and a variety of other studies, experiments, and tests. It has served at various times to exclude the polygraph, spectographic voice identification, voice-stress tests, and microphobic human-hair analysis.

Most recently, the *Frye* rule has condemned hypnosis as a tool for refreshing a witness's memory. *See, e.g., People v. Hughes,* 59 N.Y.2d 523, 466 N.Y.S.2d 255, 453 N.E.2d 484 (1983).

Its supporters view the *Frye* rule as a useful standard that ensures the trustworthiness of novel evidence. It leaves the reliability decision in the hands of experts, where it belongs.

Under the *Frye* rule, the scientific community becomes a kind of technical jury that must approve new scientific procedures before they can be put before the lay jury. The rule also protects litigants by ensuring that there will be a minimal reserve of experts who can critically examine novel scientific propositions advanced by their adversaries at trial and who can serve as rebuttal experts.

The *Frye* standard imposes special burdens on the proponent of scientific evidence. It is not enough that several expert witnesses are prepared to testify that a technique is valid. Nor is it sufficient for the court to believe that the evidence is helpful and reliable. The expert testimony will not be heard without a showing of general acceptance.

The *Frye* rule gives the scientific community a veto. Dispute or silence among the pundits bars courtroom testimony.

Does the restrictive general-acceptance test survive enactment of the Federal Rules of Evidence and its state counterparts? The answer is in dispute.

Rule 702 says nothing about general acceptance. As discussed above, it requires only that the expert testimony, whether scientific or not, "assist the trier of fact." The issue is not addressed in the Advisory Committee Notes. It was ignored in the congressional committee reports and floor debates.

Some commentators argue that silence signals repeal of *Frye.* Rule 401 defines relevant evidence quite liberally. Rule 402 states that all relevant evidence is admissible except as otherwise provided under the Constitution, a federal statute, or another rule.

Scientific evidence can be reliable and thus relevant under Rule 401 even if it is not generally accepted. None of the exceptions to Rule 402 apply. Therefore, in the absence of an express repeal or limitation of *Frye* in Rule 702, some commentators argue, the general-acceptance standard is no more. *See, e.g.,* 3 J. WEINSTEIN & M. BERGER, WEINSTEIN'S EVIDENCE ¶ 702[03] (1985).

A contrasting view is that silence means acceptance. The Federal Rules do not purport to be an exhaustive compilation of all evidentiary precedent. Since *Frye* represented the clear majority view when the Federal Rules of Evidence were enacted, one would expect that, if the Advisory Committee or Congress intended repudiation, the legislative history would say so. S. SALTZBURG & K. REDDEN, FEDERAL RULES OF EVIDENCE MANUAL 452 (3d ed. 1982 & Supp. II 1985).

The most accurate view is that silence means little. The drafters intended neither to accept nor to reject *Frye*. They simply did not think about the issue. Nevertheless, the enactment of the rules did affect the *Frye* rule by calling attention to its defects.

Some courts have relied on the omission of a general acceptance test in the rules to abandon the *Frye* standard. Other courts have rejected it simply on policy grounds.

Within the last decade, courts in more than 15 jurisdictions have rejected *Frye*. All that is required, say these courts, is a showing of sufficient reliability to satisfy the requirement of relevance.

In short, scientific evidence is treated like any other form of expert testimony. Under this approach, the general acceptance of novel techniques or applications is a factor for the judge or jury to consider. It is not a threshold requirement for admissibility.

Three decisions by the Second Circuit and the Supreme Courts of Maine and Ohio are prime examples of this approach. Although unrelated, all three decisions upheld voice prints and, coincidently, all three involved defendants named Williams.

In each case, the court refused to engage in scientific nose counting. It declined to adopt a special rule for scientific evidence. Expert testimony is admissible, without a survey of scientific opinion, so long as it is helpful to the trier of fact under Rule 702 and relevant under Rule 401, and its probative value is not substantially outweighed by the danger of unfair prejudice or confusion under Rule 403. *State v. Williams*, 4 Ohio St. 3d 53, 446 N.E.2d 444 (1983); *State v. Williams*, 388 A.2d 500 (Me. 1978); *United States v. Williams*, 583 F.2d 1194 (2d Cir. 1978) cert. denied, 439 U.S. 1117 (1979).

The movement away from *Frye* is not surprising. A test that requires the trial judge to determine if novel scientific evidence is generally accepted in the field in which it belongs raises a host of difficult questions.

Writers and courts alike describe *Frye* as "unclear," "imprecise," and "nebulous." *See, e.g.,* Giannelli, *The Admissibility of Novel Scientific Evidence: Frye v. United States, a Half Century Later,* 80 COLUM. L. REV. 1197, 1208–1223 (1980); *State v. Hall,* 297 N.W.2d 80 (Iowa 1980) cert. denied, 450 U.S. 927 (1981).

Perhaps *Frye* will survive this period of criticism and rejection. It is certainly a convenient label for courts that want to reject scientific evidence without engaging in a careful analysis of its reliability and relevance. Yet its survival seems unlikely. Too many courts in too many different jurisdictions have abandoned *Frye* in too short a time. The restrictive general-acceptance test is simply inconsistent with modern evidence concepts favoring admissibility of expert testimony.

Our first question is answered. What can an expert testify about? Almost anything helpful and relevant. Turn now to the second significant issue—the permissible foundation for expert testimony. On what kinds of facts must the opinion be grounded? What constitutes a proper basis for expert opinion?

Reasonably Reliable Basis

Here, too, changes wrought by the Federal Rules and modern state codes favor the expert witness. Federal Rule 703 and similar state provisions expressly expand the permissible basis for expert opinion.

Precodification law required that an expert's opinion be based upon one or both of two possible sources of information. One acceptable basis was the expert's firsthand observations. The treating physician, for example, having personally conducted tests and having examined the patient, might properly give an opinion based solely on his personal knowledge.

The other acceptable basis consisted of facts made known to the expert in court, usually by way of a hypothetical question. A physician hired solely to testify, with little firsthand knowledge of the case, might still venture an opinion after the lawyer asked him to assume the pertinent facts, based on the evidence introduced or to be introduced.

Rule 703 endorses these traditional foundations but adds a third acceptable basis for experts' opinions. It provides that an expert may base an opinion on facts presented to him before trial. It further states that, "[i]f of a type reasonably relied upon by experts in the particular field . . ., the facts or data need not be admissible in evidence."

Thus, the expert opinion may depend on data or documents that are inadmissible because they are hearsay or because they violate other evidentiary rules, as long as the expert's reliance on these sources of information is reasonable. Rule 703 shifts the emphasis from the *admissibility* of underlying data to its *reliability* as determined by the practice of experts when not in court.

Courts have readily accepted expert opinions based on inadmissible information.

For example, in *Mannino v. International Manufacturing Co.*, 650 F.2d 846 (6th Cir. 1981), a suit based on alleged defects in the design of a car seat for infants, plaintiff's experts' opinion was based, in part, on literature and information furnished by plaintiff's attorney, a seminar sponsored by General Motors, papers on automobile accidents prepared by the Society of Automotive Engineers, and "a whole body of literature in the area of bio-mechanics." 650 F.2d at 853 n.3. The trial court excluded the opinion, concluding that it had no proper basis.

The court of appeals reversed the decision excluding the opinion, since it was based on the sort of information that experts often rely on in forming opinions and since "great liberality is allowed the expert in determining the basis of his opinions under Rule 703.'' 650 F.2d at 853. *See also Bauman v. Centex Corp.*, 611 F.2d 1115, 1120 (5th Cir. 1980) (upholding a management consultant's opinion concerning the knowledge, intent, and financial condition of the defendant, even though the opinion was based, in part, on "research . . . done at the University of Houston library"); *Gregory v. South Hills Movers, Inc.*, 477 F. Supp. 484, 489 (W.D. Pa. 1979) (the defendant's doctor's opinion that the plaintiff's knee injury, similar to that sustained by many athletes, was curable was held to be admissible, even though it was based, in part, "upon published accounts of Mickey Mantle's knee injuries, subsequent surgery, and resumption of athletic activity").

If an expert may rely on media accounts, library research, and other inadmissible hearsay, what are the limits of reasonable reliance? If experts of a particular type normally and customarily rely on certain data in making determinations, is such reliance *per se* reasonable?

Take the case of *United States v. Roark*, 753 F.2d 991 (11th Cir. 1985). A psychologist was permitted to testify that the defendant's confession was involuntary.

Now let us add a hypothetical fact. Suppose that the psychologist's opinion was based, in part, on polygraph test results, which are inadmissible and considered unreliable for courtroom use in most jurisdictions.

But the psychologist testifies at length about the modern polygraph's widespread use in government and industry and its well-documented accuracy rate of more than 90 percent. And he says that "experts in my field regularly and customarily rely upon the polygraph in making psychological determinations." Assuming that the trial judge believes the assertion of regular and customary reliance, does the opinion now automatically pass the test of Rule 703?

The answer turns on another question. Who determines whether the expert's reliance is reasonable? Do we leave it to the expert, or does the judge have a say?

Some commentators would give the trial judge the final say. A finding that the expert and others in his field regularly depend on certain sources in their work is influential, but not binding on the court. The reliance may be customary, but it is for the judge to decide whether the custom is reasonable. J. McElhaney, *Expert Witnesses and the Federal Rules of Evidence*, 28 MERCER L. REV. 463, 486 (1977); M. Graham, Handbook of Federal Evidence § 703.1 (1981 & Supp. 1985).

This approach is consistent with the language of Rule 703, which speaks of data "reasonably," not "commonly," relied upon. *See Shatkin v. McDonnell Douglas Corp.*, 727 F.2d 202, 208 (2d Cir. 1984) (affirming the trial judge's "discretionary right under Fed. R. Evid. 703 to determine whether the expert acted reasonably in making assumptions of fact upon which he would base his testimony"); *Soden v. Freightliner Corp.*,

714 F.2d 498, 505 (5th Cir. 1983) (wide latitude is given to experts in deciding what sources to depend on, but "Rule 703 nonetheless requires courts to examine the reliability of those sources").

So, going back to our hypothetical, even if psychologists normally use polygraph tests in their work, the trial judge may still find such reliance unreasonable for purposes of litigation and therefore may exclude the expert's opinion on that basis. But what if the judge wants to receive the opinion in evidence?

If the polygraph itself is so untrustworthy that it may not be admitted in evidence, can an expert be said reasonably to rely on polygraph results in forming his opinion? Maybe so.

Information may not be reliable enough for jurors but may be sufficiently reliable for the expert to assess. See *United States v. Sims*, 514 F.2d 147, 149 (9th Cir.) *cert. denied*, 423 U.S. 845 (1975), which says that courts should "leave to the expert the assessment of the reliability of statements on which he bases his expert opinion. . . . Years of experience teach the expert to separate the wheat from chaff." That view is, after all, consistent with the thrust of Rule 703, which allows experts to rely on sources of information that are not admissible in their own right.

In fact, the assumption that Rule 703 requires application of a separate judicial standard to determine reasonable reliance has been criticized. 3 J. WEINSTEIN & M. BERGER, WEINSTEIN'S EVIDENCE ¶ 703[03] (1985). It has also been expressly rejected in the most recent pertinent decision.

In the massive, still-pending Japanese electronics antitrust litigation, the defendant manufacturers moved for summary judgment, arguing that much of the documentary evidence that the plaintiffs relied on to establish an alleged conspiracy was inadmissible. The trial court agreed that many of the documents were hearsay and insufficiently trustworthy to qualify as business or public records.

The court then turned its attention to the opinions of the plaintiffs' experts, who relied on many of the very materials that the court had already ruled to be inadmissible. Judge Becker excluded the opinions, concluding that experts could not reasonably rely on documents inadmissible because of untrustworthiness, and granted summary judgment for the defendants.

It made no difference that plaintiffs' experts swore, in uncontested affidavits, that the data on which they based their opinions were of a type generally relied upon by experts in their fields. Instead, the court applied its own standards for determining whether the experts' customary reliance was reasonable. *Zenith Radio Corp. v. Matsushita Electric Industrial Co.*, 505 F. Supp. 1190, 1325–1330 (E.D. Pa. 1980).

For three years, many scholars hailed the decision as a well-reasoned precedent on the role of the trial judge in controlling expert testimony. Then the Third Circuit reversed the decision of the trial court.

The court of appeals rejected the notion of an independent judicial test of reasonable reliance. "The proper inquiry is not what the court deems reliable, but what experts in the relevant discipline deem it to be. . . . In substituting its own opinion as to what constitutes reasonable reliance for that of the experts in the relevant fields the trial court misinterpreted Rule 703," the court held.

Once the district judge finds that the basis for the opinion is the sort of information that experts in the field rely on, the court concluded, the opinion is admissible; any concerns about trustworthiness may be explored on cross-examination. *In re Japanese Electronic Products Antitrust Litigation*, 723 F.2d 238, 276–278 (3d Cir. 1983) rev'd in part on other grounds, 475 U.S. 574 (1986).

But, you may ask, even if courts receive opinions based on otherwise inadmissible evidence, may the inadmissible supporting information itself also come in? May the expert who has reasonably relied on inadmissible hearsay, for instance, not only give his opinion but also go on, during his direct examination, to describe the hearsay basis for his opinion?

The Federal Rules of Evidence do not expressly address this issue. Common sense suggests that, if an expert gives an opinion, he should be allowed to explain how he arrived at it. A full explanation of the basis for the opinion allows the jury to assess the validity of the expert's conclusions.

One jurist has even suggested that judges should compel experts to reveal the basis for their opinions when the direct examination is too brief. G. Pratt, *A Judicial Perspective on Opinion Evidence Under the Federal Rules*, 39 WASH. & LEE L. REV. 313 (1982).

Explain the Reasons

In any event, most commentators agree that, as a general rule, a description of the data underlying an expert's opinion should be admissible on the expert's direct examination. *See, e.g.*, C. McCORMICK, MCCORMICK ON EVIDENCE § 324.2 (3d ed. 1984); S. SALTZBURG & R. REDDEN, FEDERAL RULES OF EVIDENCE MANUAL 467 (3d ed. 1982 & Supp. Il 1985); M. GRAHAM. HANDBOOK OF FEDERAL EVIDENCE § 703.1 (1981 & Supp. 1985). *But see* Carlson, *Collision Course in Expert Testimony: Limitations on Affirmative Introduction of Underlying Data*, 36 U. FLA L. REV. 234 (1984).

Most recent cases also approve disclosure of the basis for an expert's opinion on direct. There are a number of interesting examples. In *United States v. Ramos*, 725 F.2d 1322 (11th Cir. 1984), a fraud examiner was permitted to relate hearsay statements of other investigators in explaining the basis for her expert opinion. In *Paddack v. Dave Christensen, Inc.*, 745 F.2d 1254 (9th Cir. 1984), hearsay audit reports that were not admissible as business records or summaries were held admissible to show the basis for an accountant's expert testimony. In *American Universal Insurance Co. v. Falzone*, 644 F.2d 65 (1st Cir. 1981), a fire marshal was permitted to testify not only to his opinion about the origin of a fire but also to hearsay

263

statements that formed part of the basis for his opinion. And in *Bryan v. John Bean Division of FMC Corp.*, 566 F.2d 541, 545 (5th Cir. 1978), the court said, "Rules 703 and 705 codify the approach of this and other circuits that permits disclosure of otherwise hearsay evidence for the purpose of illustrating the basis for the expert witness' opinion."

In the personal injury area, *O'Gee v. Dobbs Houses, Inc.*, 570 F.2d 1084 (2d Cir. 1978), is one of the classics. The plaintiff did not call any of the physicians who had examined or treated her alleged back injury. Instead, she presented a doctor hired solely for the litigation. In forming his opinions, he had relied on the plaintiff's own statements about what other treating physicians had told her about her injury.

The testifying doctor gave his opinion. He was then permitted to explain the conclusions of other doctors as those conclusions had been stated in their reports and recounted by the plaintiff herself.

O'Gee is sometimes characterized as an exceptional case, but it does not stand alone. Similar results may be found in *Hernandez v. Faker*, 137 Ariz. 449, 671 P.2d 427 (1983), and *Ballenger v. Burris Industries, Inc.*, 311 S.E.2d 881 (N.C. App.) review denied, 315 S.E.2d 700 (1984), in which experts were permitted to describe the content of nontestifying doctors' reports on which they relied.

Perhaps the most dramatic example is *United States v. Madrid*, 673 F.2d 1114 (10th Cir.), *cert. denied*, 459 U.S. 843 (1982), a prosecution for bank robbery. The defense was insanity. The state's psychiatrist testified that he based his opinion that the defendant was sane in part on the fact that the accused "had committed armed robberies of stores prior to the offense in question in order to support a heroin addiction." 673 F.2d at 1118.

Since the only issue at the trial was the defendant's sanity, the testimony as to past crimes, standing alone, would be irrelevant and clearly excludable as character evidence under Federal Rules 403 and 404(b). The court of appeals conceded that, even as a basis for the expert's opinion, the probative value of the past-crimes evidence was questionable, and its prejudicial effect substantial. Nevertheless, the court of appeals upheld the admission of the testimony about the defendant's past crimes, since the expert "did state that Madrid's past robberies were an important part of the basis for his opinion." *Id.* at 1122.

In short, Rule 703 is, as many have phrased it, a "back-door exception" to the hearsay and other exclusionary rules.

Perhaps this overstates it a bit. So far, the decisions make clear that the hearsay or other inadmissible information is admitted only to explain the opinion and not as substantive evidence. There is no express hearsay exception authorizing receipt of "data underlying expert opinion." So courts generally admit such data for the limited purpose of supporting the expert's conclusion and not for their truth.

But the subtlety of this distinction is likely to escape triers of fact, especially jurors. The proponent who lays otherwise inadmissible facts before the jury is not likely to worry too much about a limiting instruction. Indeed, a skillful advocate may not have to tolerate even this limitation. There are, after all, good arguments for full, substantive admissibility of the hearsay basis for the expert's opinion.

There are guarantees of the reliability of such hearsay, since the experts in the field have relied on it. Moreover, the expert is present in court, subject to cross-examination and available to analyze and interpret the underlying data. Taken together, these circumstances may be sufficient to qualify the hearsay for admission under the residual hearsay exceptions embodied in Federal Rules of Evidence 803(24) and 804(b)(5).

Moreover, the distinction between data used to explain the opinion and data admissible for their truth is an artificial line usually not worth drawing. Because jurors are unlikely to perceive the difference between full and limited admission, some commentators urge that the hearsay basis should not be admitted for any purpose. *See, e.g.,* Carlson, *Collision Course in Expert Testimony: Limitations on Affirmative Introduction of Underlying Data,* 36 U. FLA. L. REV. 234, 246 (1984). However, the opposite approach—admission with an instruction that the jury is to consider the proof only for the allowable purpose—is more harmonious with modern evidence doctrine. *See* C. McCORMICK, McCORMICK ON EVIDENCE § 324.2 at 910 (3d ed. 1984). Granted, such an instruction may be ineffective. Where that occurs—when the distinction is too subtle—modern codes solve the problem not by exclusion but by providing full admissibility. Analogues leap to mind.

Statements of medical history made to a physician consulted solely for purposes of litigation used to be excluded as substantive evidence. Such statements were admissible, however, as part of the history or basis on which the doctor rested his opinion. Federal Evidence Rule 803(4) now provides for full substantive admissibility. Why? Because juries were unlikely to appreciate the distinction.

Traditionally, the prior inconsistent statement of a witness was admissible only to impeach, not for its truth. Partly because jurors were certain to ignore any limiting instruction, many jurisdictions today allow the prior inconsistent statement as full substantive evidence. Similar pragmatic reasons have led to full substantive admissibility of statements from learned treatises, under Federal Evidence Rule 803(18).

No one suggests that an expert should be able to recite the contents of otherwise inadmissible sources in every instance. There are, of course, extreme cases. In some situations, full exposition of the basis for an expert's opinion would excite sufficient prejudice to justify exclusion under Federal Rule 403.

People v. Robinson, 417 Mich. 661, 340 N.W.2d 631 (1983), is a good example. The state's psychiatrist testified that the accused was sane at the time of the alleged sex offense. The expert based his opinion in part on the defendant's criminal record. The opinion was properly received. The expert's reliance on the defendant's prior misconduct was reasonable and relevant to the psychiatrist's opinion.

Nevertheless, it was error to allow the expert to explain the basis for his opinion by testifying that the defendant had 32 prior convictions, including several for sexual offenses with children. This basis evidence was so obviously prejudicial that it was properly excluded under Rule 403. Aside from such extremes, though, the prevailing rule is one of admissibility.

The practical lesson is that Rule 703 is a tool that trial lawyers can use in several ways. It allows an expert to base his opinion on otherwise inadmissible but "reliable" data. It permits the jury to hear information that would normally be considered improper evidence. By allowing an expert to recite the sources on which he has relied, it enables his testimony to stand in for that of other witnesses or for documents.

Now comes our third and final question. How and in what form may the expert testify? Here again, the expert has been liberated.

A favorite limitation of the older cases was the well-known but frequently disregarded "ultimate opinion" rule. Years ago, courts prohibited an expert from testifying about his opinion on the ultimate issue in the case. The now discredited theory was that such testimony would invade the province of the jury.

Federal Rule 704 adopts the modern rule, providing that "[t]estimony in the form of an opinion or inference otherwise admissible is not objectionable because it embraces an ultimate issue to be decided by the trier of fact." Rule 704 allows the expert to give his most helpful testimony in a direct, straightforward manner. He need no longer engage in verbal gymnastics to avoid saying directly what his testimony communicates indirectly. Moreover, elimination of the ultimate-issue prohibition avoids inconsistent holdings arising from the inherent difficulty of defining what constitutes an ultimate issue.

Does this mean that an expert may now give a bold legal opinion on a matter that will decide the case? Not quite. The opinion must be "otherwise admissible," which means that, under Rule 702, it still must be helpful.

The Advisory Committee Note to Rule 704 illustrates the distinction between permissible and impermissible expert conclusions. Suppose the issue were whether a testator had the legal capacity to make a will. The expert could not say, "In my opinion, Tom the testator lacked capacity to make a will." That conclusion would not be helpful, since it does no more than tell the jury what result to reach. The Advisory Committee Note suggests exclusion of "opinions phrased in terms of inadequately explored legal criteria."

In contrast, the qualified expert could testify that "Tom the testator lacked sufficient mental capacity to know the nature and extent of his property and the natural objects of his bounty and to formulate a rational scheme of distribution.''

The distinction seems to be that, although opinions on ultimate issues of fact are permissible, opinions on questions of law are not. Therefore, the witness still may not testify that a particular legal standard has or has not been met. But many courts have ignored even this remaining limitation.

The distinction between ultimate issues of fact and issues of law is elusive. Therefore, in keeping with the modern tendency favoring expert testimony, many decisions seize upon Rule 704 to allow opinions phrased in terms of legal criteria. This is especially true when the expert is qualified to understand the legal standard about which his opinion is sought.

Imagine the following redirect examination of the government's expert in a securities fraud prosecution:

Q: Sir, after listening to all the testimony in this case and after examining the documents in this case and based upon your summary and analysis of all these records as you have testified, *do you have an opinion as to whether the bond money was obtained by fraud?*

DEFENSE COUNSEL: Objection!

THE COURT: Overruled! I believe under the new rules of federal evidence, the ultimate question may be put to the expert even though it is for the jury to decide.

You may answer.

A: There was fraud.

See United States v. Miller, 600 F.2d 498, 500 (5th Cir. 1979); *see also Tolliver v. Consolidated Rail Corp.,* 11 Ohio St.3d 56,463 N.E.2d 389, 391 (1984) (plaintiff's expert was allowed to testify, based on his research into the circumstances of the accident at issue, that the plaintiff ''had acted as a reasonable and prudent person given the circumstances of the accident'').

In *United States v. Young,* 745 F.2d 733 (2d Cir. 1984), *cert. denied,* 470 U.S. 1084 (1985), a drug-conspiracy prosecution, the narcotics agent who observed defendant's apparently ambiguous conduct was permitted to give his expert opinion that the accused was engaged in a narcotics transaction. Similarly, experts have been allowed to testify that age discrimination occurred in an age-discrimination case, *Davis v. Combustion Engineering, Inc.,* 742 F.2d 916 (6th Cir. 1984), and that certain sales were taxable under the Internal Revenue Code, *United States v. Garber,* 607 F.2d 92, 94–95 (5th Cir. 1979).

These decisions reflect the difficulty of distinguishing between impermissible ultimate legal opinions and testimony on ultimate issues of fact or issues of mixed fact and law. Rule 704, by expressly eliminating the ultimate issue objection, has encouraged courts to resolve doubts in fa-

267

vor of allowing expert testimony. This commendably simple rule was changed in October 1984, when Congress amended Rule 704 to forbid experts from testifying to the ultimate issue of the defendant's insanity in criminal cases.

Another old limitation on the form that expert testimony may take has gone by the boards. As recently as a decade ago, many jurisdictions required that every essential basis had to be specified during the direct examination before the opinion could be given. Typically, the expert would testify to the facts underlying the opinion, or the examiner would include them in a hypothetical question.

Federal Rule 705 abolishes this requirement. It permits the expert to testify without prior disclosure of the facts underlying the opinion. The hypothetical question is no longer necessary, not even when the expert bases his opinion on facts beyond his personal knowledge.

Under the Federal Rules, a trial lawyer could elicit an expert's opinion with just three questions:

What are your qualifications?

Do you have an opinion on issue x?

What is that opinion?

This examination would suffice for admissibility, but of course no trial lawyer interested in jury persuasion would cut his direct examination this short. A full exploration of the basis for the opinion is the usual courtroom practice.

What then is the practical value of Rule 705? It allows the advocate to streamline the expert testimony and to order his examination as he wishes.

Prior disclosure of the basis puts the opinion itself in the middle of the direct examination. Now the lawyer can get right to the point. Once qualified, the expert may state his opinion out front—when the jury is still wide awake. The explanation and basis may follow.

Moreover, the hypothetical question, when used, can be simple and straightforward. There will be no quibbles over its content. The advocate no longer need fear the once standard objection that facts included in the hypothetical question were insufficient to justify the opinion.

Under modern evidence codes and decisions, there is an unmistakable trend toward admitting expert testimony. The permissible scope, basis, and form of expert testimony all have been broadened. The trend reflects the lawmakers' confidence in juries and in the adversary system.

There is still concern over the unreliability of some expertise and over the false aura of infallibility that experts sometimes project. Nevertheless, the courts' growing tendency is to admit expert testimony, leaving exposure of its weaknesses to cross-examination and rebuttal testimony.

Discovery of Experts Under the Federal Rules

by Pierre N. Leval

Before the adoption of Rule 26(b)(4) in 1970, the subject of discovery of expert testimony in federal civil litigation was an unruly mess, without governing principle. It was commonplace for discovery of experts to be denied out of hand. Some courts awarded disclosure of the facts shown to, but not the opinions developed by, the expert. A few cases held that disclosure would be awarded only if it would be determinative in the litigation or if compelling circumstances were shown; and a few courts— very much in the minority—permitted discovery of experts and their testimony rather freely.

There was a widespread prejudice against discovery of experts rooted in the theory that the expert witness was the private property of the party employing him, and that notion survives to a degree in the terms of Rule 26(b)(4).

Although the rule now permits far greater discovery of expert testimony than before, it retains the principle that it is offensive to let one side gain relatively free insight and preparation from a source the other side has paid for, often dearly.

Rule 26(b)(4) was developed largely from two compromise cases in Maryland, *United States v. 23. 76 Acres*, 32 F.R.D. 593 (1963) and *Knighton v. Villian & Fassio*, 39 F.R.D. 11 (1965). The rule may be summarized as follows:

- If facts have been acquired or opinions developed by an expert in antic-ipation of litigation, and if that expert is to testify, the party (not the expert) must answer interrogatories about the expert's facts and opin-ions and their basis. Upon motion the court may order further discov-ery (but the rule gives no standards as to why, when, or how).

Pierre Leval is a United States District Judge for the Southern District of New York.

- An expert who will not testify but who has been retained or consulted specially in anticipation of litigation is not subject to any discovery unless, for exceptional reasons, the party seeking discovery cannot otherwise obtain the information it needs.
- Finally, a party who is authorized by order to make further discovery beyond the interrogatories may be ordered to pay for the expert's time spent in that discovery and may indeed be ordered to share a part of the expert's basic fee charged to the party that hired him.

This obviously is quite limited discovery: no discovery, in the ordinary course, of the expert himself; interrogatories answerable only by the party, making it hard to get what one really wants, particularly as to cross-examination material; a total shield for an expert informally consulted or one who will not be a witness, some cases holding you cannot even find out that expert's name.

The rule creates several status classifications, from which different discovery consequences follow. This raises such questions as: What discovery may be had of an expert if he falls in more than one classification, or none, or if he was a participant in the underlying transaction, or is named as a defendant?

How to Be Sure?

First of all, how can we be sure whether an expert witness comes within the application of the rule? The opening sentence of the rule announces that it concerns only facts and opinions "acquired or developed *in anticipation of litigation.*" If the information and expertise were developed otherwise than "in anticipation of litigation," the witness would fall outside the scope of the rule and would be fully subject to discovery.

A fascinating line of cases engendered by Judge Will in Chicago has created pitfalls as to the applicability of the rule's protection. *Thomas Organ Co. v. Jadranska Slobodna Plovidba,* 54 F.R.D. 367 (N.D. Ill. 1972), involved goods damaged while in transit at sea. The owner had filed a claim with the insurer who had hired marine surveyors to inspect the goods to determine the cause of the damage. The defendant (the carrier) sought to discover reports written by the surveyors. The plaintiff opposed discovery on the ground that the reports were the work of experts prepared in anticipation of litigation (and thus protected by both Rules 26(b)(4) and 26(b)(3), which utilizes the same "anticipation of litigation" standard to define the scope of protection for work product).

Judge Will, adopting a construction designed to favor the broadest possible discovery, ruled that unless the work is prepared under the direction of and at the request of an attorney acting in the role of "counsellor," it will not be deemed "in anticipation of litigation." The mere filing of an insurance claim does not sufficiently certify the anticipation of litigation. *See Spaulding v. Denton,* 68 F.R.D. 342 (D. Del. 1975).

A related line of reasoning further limits the applicability of the rule in accident cases. Courts have found it to be within the ordinary course of the business of a railroad, an aircraft manufacturer, or the like, to make investigations of the causes of accidents, regardless of the anticipation of litigation. In the "work product" context, several such investigations have been ruled discoverable. *Galambus v. Consol. Freightways Corp.*, 64 F. R.D. 468 (N.D. Ind. 1974), *Miles v. Bell Helicopter Co.*, 385 F. Supp. 1029 (N.D. Ga. 1974); *Teribery v. Norfolk & W. Ry.*, 68 F.R.D. 46 W.D. Pa., 1975).

The issue of a plural-status expert was explored imaginatively by Judge Gurfein in the Southern District of New York in *Inspiration Consol. Copper Company v. Lumbermen's Mutual Casualty Co.*, 60 F.R.D. 205 (1973). A copper mining company had bought and structured its production around a multimillion dollar piece of equipment, which broke down, putting substantial operations out of business. The company sued its insurer, which impleaded the manufacturer of the machine. The discovery issue arose with respect to the accountants for the plaintiff, who had prepared schedules of the losses suffered by the plaintiff.

The accountants were found by the judge to be wearing three hats: First, they were the company's regular auditors, and in that capacity had access to all of the plaintiff's books—not in anticipation of litigation but in the ordinary course of business. Second, the auditors had prepared an analysis of the damages as part of a settlement proposal but were not expected to testify about it. Third, they had prepared another analysis of the company's losses and were expected to testify about that schedule.

The court adopted a functional analysis, deciding that a single expert will be treated differently regarding each role he plays. The case was decided as if there were three distinct experts involved. Any information acquired by the accountant as the ordinary auditor was fully subject to discovery. The report on which he would not testify was not subject to discovery, and the report on which he would testify was subject to the interrogatory procedure set forth in the rule. The court rejected the notion that because the auditor had acquired knowledge of the company's financial data independent of the litigation he was totally disqualified from the protection of the rule.

Less Clear Analysis

Less clear is the analysis found in *In re Brown Company Securities Litigation*, 54 F.R.D. 384 (E.D. La. 1972). The plaintiffs, suing to set aside a merger, sought to take the deposition of an investment banker who, for dissemination in the proxy materials, had furnished an opinion that the merger was fair and equitable. The defendant argued that the protection of Rule 26(b)(4) was applicable because the investment banker was an "expert witness." The court rejected the contention: an expert who was to be examined on the role he had played in the underlying transaction is fully subject to discovery. But the court went on to add that the examination could not go into present opinions.

The reason for the latter limitation was not explained. The opportunity to cross-examine the investment banker as to the bases and *bona fides* of his opinion delivered in the proxy materials is substantially impaired if the examiner is not permitted to ask how the banker now assesses the facts. It is not stated whether the defendants anticipated calling the investment banker as an expert witness at trial to give his present opinion. If so, the court may have been making a "two-hats" analysis, comparable to the *Inspiration* case. But even if this were so, it does not seem appropriate that a party should be able to shield a witness from otherwise proper deposition by declaring an intention to make him an expert witness at trial.

Suppose the expert is a defendant? This arises frequently in medical malpractice cases. Of course, the defendant doctor is not protected from discovery by the fact that he is an "expert"; he is not functioning in the role of an expert witness in the litigation. But this raises an interesting question. What if a plaintiff deems it very important to obtain full discovery of his adversary's expert and to that end concocts a theory, amends his complaint and names the expert as a defendant? Then, having done so, he seeks full discovery of the expert "defendant." One might reason that the expert had obtained his information in anticipation of litigation and therefore was entitled to all the protection of Rule 26(b)(4). On the other hand, how can a defendant not be subject to broader discovery?

Litigants often are concerned about how they can shop for, select and prepare an expert for trial preserving the maximum protection from disclosure afforded by the rule. First of all, paragraph (B) of the rule provides a total screen of privacy to consult with a "specially employed [expert] . . . who is not expected to be called as a witness. . . ." In selecting the expert witness, to the extent that avoidance of disclosure is thought important, it is preferable to choose an expert who did not have prior knowledge of or access to the particular facts. When other factors dictate using an expert who was already acquainted with the facts (such as an in-house expert), some protection may be available if a clear showing can be made that his role as expert witness is entirely separate and distinct from his customary duties, *i. e.,* preserving the basis for a "two-hats" theory. The record will be clearer, especially as to the requirement of "anticipation of litigation," if the initial contacts with the prospective witness are made by the trial counsel (not house counsel) in writing referring specifically to the anticipation of litigation.

Since the rule does not require disclosure before the selection of an expert, a party may well be justified in answering an interrogatory merely by stating that there is no expert who is expected to testify. In such cases, the party must be diligent to update the response when an expert is selected. Rule 26(e)(1)(B) makes explicit the continuing duty to supplement prior responses as the party's expectations change. In two cases, dire consequences resulted from a failure to follow that practice. In *Weiss v. Chrysler Motors Corp.*, 515 F.2d 449 (2d Cir. 1975) a verdict in favor of defendant Chrysler was reversed on appeal because the defendant had sprung an expert on the plaintiff at trial without having previously disclosed him in answers to interrogatories. Similarly, in *Tabatchnick v. G.D. Searle & Co.*, 67 F.R.D. 49 (D. N.J. 1975), when plaintiff sought to call a previously unannounced expert, the trial court barred his testimony.

Regarding the timing of disclosure, the advisory committee's note states that neither party shall be required to disclose its experts until both parties are ready. One party, in other words, cannot hang back while sucking out discovery from the other. But the matter so glibly stated in the note (see 48 F.R.D. at 504) was not included in the rule itself, and there are cases on both sides. *Compare e.g., Kozar v. Chesapeake & O. Ry. Co.*, 320 F. Supp. 335 (W.D. Mich. 1970) and *United States v. John R. Piquette Corp.*, 52 F.R.D. 370 (E.D. Mich. 1971) with *Rupp v. Vock & Weidenhold, Inc.*, 52 F.R.D. 111 (N.D. Ohio 1971).

Another issue of contention may be the sufficiency of the substantive information furnished in the answers to interrogatories. The ingenuity of counsel is often devoted to the preparation of written answers which reveal nothing.

Here, for example, are some questions and answers from *Olmert v. Nelson*, 60 F.R.D. 369 (D.D.C. 1973), a medical malpractice case:

> For each expert state the subject matter on which he is expected to testify. For each expert please state the facts and opinions to which he is expected to testify. For each expert state the grounds of each opinion.

The answers:

> Dr. Wallace will testify about the nature and extent of any medical problems sustained by [plaintif]. I assume his testimony will be based upon office and hospital records. The grounds of his opinion will be based upon his knowledge of medicine and the true facts in this case.

More Answers Ordered

In that case, the court ordered further answers. But one wonders whether such ungenerous answers do not provide a perfect basis for demanding a deposition under the broad invitation in the last sentence of paragraph (A) of the rule.

Another weapon to bear in mind when an expert on the stand goes into explanations that have not been previewed in the interrogatories is to seek a ruling barring those areas of testimony, as in the *Tabatchnick* case, where the unannounced expert was barred altogether.

The old tendency to view the expert as the private property of the party employing him survives most explicitly in the provisions of the rule that authorize, and in some instances require, charging the other side for portions of the expert's fees if the expert is obliged to furnish additional disclosure. *See Herbst v. I. T. & T.*, 65 F.R.D. 588 (D. Conn. 1975); *Blyther v. Northern Lines, Inc.*, 61 F.R.D. 610 (E.D. Pa. 1973).

The advisory note explains in a somewhat moralistic tone that in deciding whether the fees will be shared by the party seeking discovery, the court must consider whether that party is merely preparing for cross-examination or trying to get some free expertise for his side of the case. But the rule itself states neither this standard nor any other.

It seems to me that more pertinent than these moral and proprietary admonitions is the potential, where one of the parties is at a financial disadvantage, for the other to use the high cost of experts to unfair advantage. A doctor will simply not agree to testify to a plaintiff's injuries if this will subject the doctor to endless days of depositions, especially without pay. A poor plaintiff would be unable to pay for so much of the doctor's time. On the other hand, a poor litigant should not be barred from making *reasonable* discovery of his adversary's experts by forcing him to bear prohibitive fees.

The rule deals with the dilemma by entrusting it, free of governing standards, to the judge's discretion and good sense.

Expert Witnesses and the Federal Rules

by James W. McElhaney

A casual reading of the rules pertaining to the examination of expert witnesses gives the impression that not much is changed by the new Federal Rules of Evidence, an impression which is wrong. Nearly everything is affected by Article 7 (Opinions and Expert Testimony) and some exceptions to the hearsay rule found in Article 8. Most of the departures from familiar practice were thoughtful measures which were proposed by the drafters and were unaltered in the long legislative process. They owe their deceptively simple appearance to the style with which they were written and to the rather complex set of common law rules concerning experts which must be thoroughly understood to follow what the Federal Rules accomplish. But not every change was advertent nor was every problem solved, with the result that some serious questions remain, including the applicability of some rules in diversity cases.

The easiest way to appreciate the scope of the changes made by the Federal Rules is to see how they will actually work in comparison with the customary method of examining witnesses, particularly medical experts. The problem is a simple one, with only a few twists to get as much out of it as possible.

A diversity action is brought in federal court for personal injuries to the plaintiff, Mr. Rockwell, who claims that he received a severe head injury as the result of the defendant's negligence. Shortly after the incident Mr. Rockwell consulted his family physician, Dr. Lombard, complaining of headaches and dizziness. Suspecting possible brain damage, Dr. Lombard referred the plaintiff to a specialist in neurology, Dr. Braun, sending him a review of Mr. Rockwell's worsening condition

The author is a former editor-in-chief of LITIGATION *and Joseph C. Hostetler Professor of Trial Practice and Advocacy at Case Western Reserve University School of Law in Clevelend.*

and the treatment thus far. Dr. Braun conducted a thorough neurological examination and also ordered an electroencephalogram, which was performed at a local hospital by a Dr. Willis who sent his findings back to Dr. Braun.

Being careful to cover all possibilities, particularly in view of the helpful but inconclusive electroencephalogram report, Dr. Braun referred Mr. Rockwell to a psychiatrist to rule out the possibility that the symptoms were psychological in origin, a distinct possibility in a number of apparent neurological disorders. The psychiatrist, Dr. Schulman, spent a number of hours with Mr. Rockwell and wrote Dr. Braun a complete psychiatric report, indicating that the plaintiff had essentially no psychiatric problems.

Armed with this information, Dr. Braun proceeded with his course of treatment which, unfortunately, was only partially successful. He was prepared to testify that Mr. Rockwell has indeed a serious brain injury that is difficult to treat. To add weight to the plaintiff's case, a nationally recognized expert, Dr. Brill, was consulted. He reviewed the case and would support Dr. Braun's conclusions in every respect.

But now, on the eve of trial, complications arise. Dr. Braun, the treating expert, dies, and Mr. Rockwell's new personal physician, while certainly competent, is a most unimpressive witness who is reluctant to testify. So, tactically, his role in the trial must be minimized, if not eliminated. Can Dr. Brill, the impressive expert, be called to supply the testimony that the late Dr. Braun might have given? In this sort of situation, the common law rules governing expert witnesses present a confusing maze, and while the case may be tried, it will be long and difficult, particularly against determined opposition.

Hearsay Problems

The first problem is that Dr. Brill is not a treating doctor. Almost everything he knows is hearsay for which he cannot prove the necessary foundations to establish whatever exceptions to the hearsay rule might be available. In addition, because he does not base his opinions on first-hand information, he will not be able to give his actual opinions. And because the usual role is that every essential fact in a hypothetical question must already be in evidence—or promised to be connected up later—the entire medical history will have to be proven by the testimony of the various other doctors, if they are available, or by hospital or business records, which may be extremely difficult because they contain not only factual data but also opinions and diagnoses.

Assuming these hurdles have been successfully overcome, Dr. Brill may be called to testify. After the plaintiff establishes his expertise (and resists the defendant's offer to stipulate to it), Dr. Brill is asked to assume a long list of facts. Finally he is asked with the familiar words, "Now, then, Dr. Brill, assuming all these facts to be true, would you have an opinion, based on a reasonable degree of medical probability (or certainty in some states) as to the nature of such a condition?" Then he responds, "Yes, I do." Then plaintiff asks, "What is that opinion?" At last Dr. Brill can testify—not about Mr. Rockwell himself but rather about some hypothetical person like him.

The difference between the necessary preliminary proof and ultimate questioning of Dr. Brill under the common law approach and what might be done under the new Federal Rules is startling. Not that it would necessarily be tactically sound to conduct the examination in this way, but here is how it might be done:

All of the preliminary medical proof may be omitted. After establishing that Dr. Brill is an appropriate expert, he may be simply asked, "Dr. Brill, are you familiar with Mr. Rockwell's medical history?" His answer is, "Yes, I am." Then he is asked, "Would you explain to the judge and jury, Dr. Brill, what condition he is suffering from?" "Certainly," he responds, and, without magic words or special form, he gives his opinion of Rockwell's injuries, their cause and the outlook for the future.

Rule 701 opens Article 7 with a simplification of the rule against opinions, and, instead of attempting to list the various opinions which lay witnesses are permitted to give, states that lay opinions are admissible if they are "rationally based on the perception of the witness and . . . helpful to a clear understanding of his testimony. . . ." Rule 702 (Testimony by Experts) performs a similar simplifying task for the recognition of experts, adopting Dean Wigmore's suggestion that the test ought to be whether this witness can help a jury on this subject. J. WIGMORE, EVIDENCE § 1923, Vol. 7 at p. 21 (3d ed. 1940). Rule 704 abolishes the irksome "ultimate issue" rule, which was a silly attempt by the common law to protect the province of the jury.

These rules, simple and straightforward, are the type one would expect. While they make the conduct of litigation easier, they were easily predictable progressions from the common law. Even Rule 706, which codifies the court's right to call its own expert witnesses and which raises a few troublesome questions, takes no giant steps.

Rather it is Rules 703 and 705, tucked in the middle of these unsurprising provisions, taken together with a short phrase in Rule 702 and a few exceptions to the hearsay rule found in Article 8, which offer such a complete alteration of the practice which was developed by the common law.

Rule 702 (Testimony by Experts) provides that an expert witness may testify "in the form of an opinion or otherwise." At first reading, this provision seems to track the common law rule completely. Close examination, however, raises an interesting question which is not entirely resolved by the legislative history or the Advisory Committee's notes. The problem is whether this language changes the usual practice of asking an expert witness whether he has an opinion to a reasonable degree of scientific certainty or probability.

Obvious Difficulty

The Advisory Committee's note is only somewhat helpful:

Most of the literature assumes that experts testify only in the form of opinions. The assumption is logically unfounded. The rule accordingly recognizes that an expert on the stand may give a dissertation or exposition of scientific or other principles relevant to the case, leaving the trier of fact to apply them to the facts.

It would seem logical that, if opinions are not the required form for testimony, when they are used no particular style need be followed in eliciting them. The difficulty is obvious. The common law developed a rather rigid method for obtaining expert testimony.

In some jurisdictions, for example, the question, "Doctor, do you have an opinion to a reasonable degree of medical probability as to the nature of this condition?" is considered to be foundational. That is, it must be answered in the affirmative before the opinion itself is admissible. If the reason for this requirement is a fear that juries are not capable of drawing inferences from opinions, Rule 702 as explained by the Advisory Committee logically alters that requirement, and the preliminary question need not be asked. That result follows because the rule was specifically drafted with the view that juries are capable of drawing their own inferences from expert testimony.

In a number of other jurisdictions, the traditional preliminary question, while it might in practice be put to experts in a variety of settings, is only required when the opinion is establishing causation in personal injury actions. See Musslewhite, *Medical Causation Testimony in Texas,* 23 SW. L.J. 622 (1969). Applying Rule 702 in these states would allow questioning the expert in any reasonable form without the usual magic words, but the degree of certainty or probability would still have to be established by the preliminary question or in some other manner, such as the totality of the expert's testimony. Such a requirement is imposed because the preliminary question is used in these states to insure that there is a sufficiency of the evidence to establish causation. Because sufficiency can be tested by means other than using a particular form question, it would seem that the *Erie* doctrine would not require displacing Rule 702 in diversity cases, where the rule of decision is provided by state law.

Bases for Expert Opinions

These considerations do not mean that litigators should use the liberality of Rule 702 to justify careless examination of experts. Judges are accustomed to hearing questions phrased in traditional ways. But it does free the careful lawyer from the procrustean bed of a stylized litany which conveys little meaning to the jury. Under Rule 702 the expert can be examined in any way that makes sense and that ultimately satisfies whatever rule that applies to the sufficiency of the evidence. So in the hypothetical Rockwell case, it was not necessary to ask Dr. Brill whether he had an opinion to a reasonable degree of medical certainty before asking his opinion. If that degree of certainty was not reasonably implicit as Dr. Brill developed his opinion for the jury, he could even be asked after the main body of his testimony how firmly he held the opinion. The result is a simpler, more comprehensible flow of expert testimony.

Rule 703 states:

> The facts or data in the particular case upon which an expert bases an opinion or inference may be those perceived by or made known to him at or before the hearing. If of a type reasonably relied upon by experts in the particular field in forming opinions or inferences upon the subject, the facts or data need not be admissible in evidence.

This rule starts with a recognition of current practice. If an expert is a fact witness, as well as one interpreting those facts, there is no change. Examination is only as complicated as the subject matter, since the traditional rules of evidence impose no hurdles other than the possible requirement of a foundation question relating to the certainty of the opinion. Having an expert listen to the testimony in the case to form an opinion is also permitted. Although the notes of the Advisory Committee give it no special emphasis, the rule seems to liberalize that procedure, since the rule does not contain the restriction some jurisdictions impose that the evidence on which the expert relies must be substantially undisputed. This limitation is actually one of formality. Since an expert responding to a hypothetical question gets his information from the question, it has always been possible for an expert to attend the trial and form his opinion based on what he learns there, whether or not the testimony is in dispute. But when the information on which he relies is not in dispute, many jurisdictions have permitted a shortening of the hypothetical question. Instead of reciting the entire basis for the opinion in the hypothetical question, the expert could merely be asked to assume that the testimony he heard was true. Rule 703 permits this practice even though the evidence is in dispute, a provision which matches a major change made by Rule 705.

Rule 703 makes another change which writers have been urging for years. The facts or data which an expert relies on in forming his opinion need not be admissible in evidence if they are of a type reasonably relied upon in the field. The Advisory Committee's argument for this provision seems attractive. Many experts, particularly doctors, make life and death decisions on information which is not admissible in evidence. If they carry out their professional responsibilities in that manner, why should they not be able to testify to the opinions they reach on the basis of such information, so long as it is reasonably reliable?

The logic of the common law in opposition to this position was a tightly closed syllogism. If an expert opinion was based on hearsay information, relating the opinion to the jury would be giving them hearsay in disguise. Since hearsay is considered unreliable unless it falls within one of the exceptions to the hearsay rule, the opinion was obviously fatally tainted.

In recent years, however, this rigid approach has been relaxed in many states, and most experts were permitted to base their opinions in part on information which was not admissible so long as it was the simple, mechanical type of hearsay, such as the results of a urinalysis or blood grouping, and those findings were not the central issue in the case. In other words, courts came to recognize that a doctor or other expert could still be a fact witness even though he did not personally perform all of the typical laboratory tests upon which he relied in reaching his opinion.

But Rule 703 goes much further. It has become virtually like a major exception to the hearsay rule. It is no longer necessary to prove independently the opinions and diagnoses of other experts upon which the opinion being introduced rests. Since all of the information that Dr. Brill, the non-treating expert witness in the Rockwell case, used was certainly reasonably reliable in the field of medicine, it would not be necessary to prove it independently—or at all.

Simplifying Trials

Rule 703, then, is a rule which, when properly understood, should ease and simplify complex trials. The central expert or the one who is the most effective witness and who is in position to give the essential opinion for a favorable finding can be called as the only expert witness. In the Rockwell case, Dr. Lombard (the general practitioner), Dr. Willis (who conducted the EEG), Dr. Schulman (the psychiatrist), and Mr. Rockwell's new physician may all be eliminated. Moreover, Dr. Braun's death no longer creates difficult problems of proof. While it would probably be helpful to have his findings and records admitted, they need not even qualify as business records for Dr. Brill, the testifying expert, to take them into account. In short, the case can be tried with one expert instead of four. The number of witnesses actually called will now depend on the importance of the issue to the trial and the economic value of the case rather than on rigid evidentiary rules.

One question which this discussion implicitly raises is whether the language of Rule 703, which permits opinions to be based on reasonably reliable facts or data, includes opinions, since evidence law usually distinguishes between facts and opinions. The Advisory Committee notes which say that facts or data includes opinions ought to settle the issue.

A final point on Rule 703 is who determines what is reasonably reliable in the field, the witness and the jury or the judge? The language of the rule suggests that the norms of the field of expertise control. On the other hand, the Advisory Committee notes suggest that "reasonably reliable" is a standard to be applied by the judge: "The language would not warrant admitting in evidence the opinion of an 'accidentologist' as to the point of impact in an automobile collision based on statements of bystanders, since this requirement is not satisfied."

But this hypothetical problem hardly puts the issue to rest. What about a policeman gathering information from bystanders from which he forms an opinion as to the speed of a moving vehicle, assuming his competence in the field? Would his apparent disinterest make his evaluation of bystanders' accounts any more reliable? Certainly policemen sometimes have to make life and death decisions on the information they gather from bystanders. The drafters relied on that rationale in dealing with medical doctors and their exchange of information and opinions.

If the example of the policeman does not seem close to the borderline, what about the emergency room doctor who acts on information from an ambulance driver? Such information would seem to be exactly the type the drafters contemplated as being within the rule. But what happens if the doctor's information comes from a policeman, or better yet a bystander?

The point is that what is reasonably reliable for emergency measures is probably the best information the expert can get at the time, a standard which has scant relationship to what is reliable for making a deliberate decision on contested facts in a subsequent trial. So while the desire of the drafters to free expert opinions from rigid common law restrictions is understandable, they chose a seductively simple appearing rule which may prove hard to administer. Moreover, it can provide a special set of problems because of what happens in Rule 705.

Logically, Rule 703 gives a hint of what is to come in Rule 705. Hypothetical questions are no longer required even for non-treating doctors or other experts who have no first-hand knowledge of the facts on which their opinions are based. This result fits with the provision of Rule 703 that the basis for an opinion need not be admissible in evidence. It would hardly make sense to permit that and then require that the expert assume the truth of those inadmissible facts, much less other facts already in the case.

It is interesting that Rule 705 eliminates the requirement for hypothetical questions without mentioning them. Instead, the rule rather cryptically provides:

> The expert may testify in terms of opinion or inference and give
> his reasons therefor without prior disclosure of the underlying

facts or data, unless the court requires otherwise. The expert may in any event be required to disclose the underlying facts or data on cross-examination.

Thus the casual reader must remember that the hypothetical question was a means for requiring that the bases for an opinion be stated in advance of the receipt of the opinion itself when the expert was merely interpreting data and was not also a fact witness to the bases of his opinion.

Hypothetical Questions

Obviously, Rule 705 does more than merely do away with the requirement for hypothetical questions. It also permits the direct examiner to omit having the fact witness-expert recite the information on which his opinion is based even when a hypothetical question was not required at common law. Rule 705 is a major change from familiar practice. While it does not abolish hypothetical questions, it makes them optional for the examining counsel, unless the trial court affirmatively requires that they be used.

Most litigators are aware that the hypothetical question has been under sustained attack by some evidence scholars for years. Following Wigmore's lead, they have argued that the hypothetical question is misleading to the jury and admits an opinion into evidence which might be far different from what the expert would say if he were to give his actual opinion on the facts as he knows them. And, one suspects, some writers have never been happy about a device which offers such a beautiful opportunity to make a succinct summary of the party's case in the middle of the trial.

For this very reason it is probable that Rule 705 will not get the attention it deserves. The chances are that most good trial lawyers who have developed the art of using hypothetical questions will simply ignore this rule which makes them unnecessary. Such an approach would probably be a mistake.

The common law requirement for an expert opinion was that every major basis for the opinion had to be testified to in advance of receiving the opinion. That requirement applied whether or not the hypothetical question was required. Certainly in the usual case, an expert opinion is far more persuasive if the jury can see that the expert has a good reason for entertaining it. So it makes sense to keep this part of the hypothetical question practice.

On the other hand, the strict requirement of the common law made hypothetical questions too long, even though trial courts were not always strict about enforcing the rule that every major basis of the opinion come in advance. Thus, the real advantage of Rule 705 is that it permits a streamlining of hypothetical questions. Now they do not need to be as stiff and stylized as before. And so long as they are not unfair or misleading, there is no reason why an examiner cannot be far more selective than previously in choosing the contents of the hypothetical questions he puts to a testifying expert.

It should be stressed that Rule 705 presents some problems. It makes it far more possible for the jury to hear an opinion which ultimately turns out to be inadmissible because it is based neither on admissible evidence nor on "reasonably reliable" information, as permitted under Rule 703. One effect of the common law rule was to screen expert opinions in advance of their receipt. Now, because of the procedure permitted under Rules 703 and 705, that screening process can be delayed until cross-examination. Such a result is not necessarily bad. After all, it is the method used for almost all other evidence except confessions and other exceptional matters, unless the opposing counsel takes some active steps in advance.

Expert Testimony

The lesson for the careful litigator, particularly defense counsel in personal injury cases, is to keep on his toes. Rules 703 and 705 do not "de-escalate discovery." They make it even more important. Furthermore, a number of cautious lawyers will probably make it a custom to ask for a *voir dire* examination of expert witnesses, perhaps outside the presence of the jury, because of the impossible task of "unringing the bell" with an instruction to disregard previous testimony. The other way to deal with the problem is for the trial court simply to insist on the use of hypothetical questions and the recitation of the bases for an opinion by fact witness-experts. Such a procedure, however, would merely undo the change permitted by Rule 705 and return to the long and confusing common law procedure.

Some provisions of the hearsay rules in Article 8 directly affect expert testimony. Under the common law, a statement of present bodily condition—no matter to whom it was made—is an exception to the hearsay rule. Rule 803(3) follows that doctrine without change. Closely associated with this familiar rule is the additional hearsay exception which admits statements of past bodily condition—medical history—which were made to a doctor consulted for the purpose of treatment. Federal Rule 803(4) follows this exception as well. But once again, a close reading of the rule and the Advisory Committee notes suggest that it goes much further, although such a result was not entirely understood by the drafters of the rules.

Under Rule 803(4) relevant medical histories are an exception to the hearsay rule if they are "made for the purposes of medical diagnosis or treatment." The most obvious effect of this language is to free this hearsay exception from the requirement that the statement be made directly to a treating doctor. As the Advisory Committee notes point out, the statement may be made to "hospital attendants, ambulance drivers, or even members of the family." Thus the test for admissibility under the new rule is merely the purpose for which the statement was made rather than to whom it was said. The Advisory Committee suggests that the reason for the rule which the common law evolved—that a person seeking medical treatment is likely to tell the truth because he wants to be cured—applies equally to statements of previous bodily condition which are not made directly to a doctor. All this seems to make perfectly good sense and is an entirely expected reform.

But there is an additional effect of this language. The rule says the statement may be made for the purpose of "medical diagnosis *or* treatment." (Emphasis added.) Does this mean that a medical history given to a nontreating doctor who is consulted for the purpose of diagnosis and *testimony*, rather than diagnosis and treatment, is also admissible under this exception to the hearsay rule? It does.

While it is perhaps unwarranted to read too much into a simple "or" without other evidence of the intention to make such a major change, the Advisory Committee notes help considerably.

> Conventional doctrine has excluded from the hearsay exception, as not within its guarantee of truthfulness, statements to a physician consulted only for the purpose of enabling him to testify. . . . The rule . . . rejects the limitation. This position is consistent with the provision of Rule 703 that the facts on which expert testimony is based need not be admissible in evidence if of a kind ordinarily relied upon by experts in the field.

The first point is clear enough. The non-treating doctor limitation on the medical history rule is abandoned. But the second statement makes little sense. Since under Rule 703 an opinion may be admitted even though the bases are not, that rule creates little need to make a medical history to a non-treating doctor admissible. Instead, it seems far more rational to defend this change on the basis of simplicity. Why make a distinction to exclude testimony which is not likely to be misleading to jurors, since they can see how motive in giving a medical history can affect its reliability?

Puzzling

Even more puzzling is the interpretation of the language by Dean Mason Ladd, one of the drafters, in his recent book, Ladd & Carlson, *Cases and Materials on Evidence* (1972). Discussing the identical language, he said at page 952: "Proposed Federal Rule 803(4) goes no further than the Model Code or Uniform Rules and limits statements given by a patient for diagnostic *and* treatment purposes." (Emphasis added.) Dean Ladd's interpretation seems unwarranted. While it could be argued that diagnosis should be construed to mean evaluation for the purpose of seeking treatment, the Advisory Committee notes are in disagreement. Moreover, the House Committee on the Judiciary assumed that statements made to non-treating physicians would be admissible under the rule: ''After giving particular attention to the question of physical examination made solely to enable a physician to testify, the Committee approved Rule 803(4) as submitted to Congress.''

The effect of this rule on the Rockwell case is impressive. If Dr. Brill merely examines Mr. Rockwell and listens to his medical history, he will be permitted to testify to what Mr. Rockwell tells him, so long as it is medically germane. In other words, Rule 803(4) will help the non-treating doctor be a far more effective witness. It will also encourage actual examination of a party by the testifying doctor, since if Dr. Brill merely got Mr. Rockwell's medical history from other doctors and medical files, he would be able to base his opinion on that information but could not testify to it since it would be double hearsay, only one part of which would be cured by a hearsay exception.

The business records exception, Rule 803(6) puts to rest a persistent problem with hospital records. While many early business records statutes were limited to ''acts or events,'' the new rule admits records of ''acts, events, conditions, opinions, or diagnoses.'' This overrules a substantial line of cases which excluded opinions in hospital records.

One of the most effective ways to impeach an expert witness is to confront him with a learned treatise which contradicts his opinion. So long as the language is understandable to the jury, the importance which average individuals attach to the printed word, particularly in books, makes this basis of impeachment a very powerful device.

But the common law practice has some difficulties. One of them is the minor annoyance that the treatise is not admissible for the purpose of proving the truth of the matter asserted, but only to impeach, requiring a limiting instruction of little meaning which can serve to break the spell created by a dramatic impeachment.

More troublesome is the requirement that the expert must have relied on the treatise in forming his opinion or at least acknowledge that it is authoritative in the field. This requirement has always meant that a wily and well-prepared expert witness is difficult to impeach with writings in his field. Rule 803(18) solves this very neatly. It makes learned treatises admissible in evidence as an exception to the hearsay rule. So long as some expert witness in the field establishes the treatise as a reliable authority, it can be used to impeach any expert during the course of the trial. If there is no other expert to validate the treatise, the court can even take judicial notice of its prominance and reliability.

Since the major effect of this rule is to deal with the means of cross-examination and impeachment of expert witnesses, it would have seemed appropriate to have it appear in Article 7 (Opinions and Expert Testimony) or Article 6 (Witnesses). But because the rule is framed as an exception to the hearsay rule, principally to eliminate the meaningless limiting instruction, it is tucked away in the middle of Article 8, awaiting discovery by the thorough reader.

The Federal Rules concerning expert witnesses change not only how witnesses are examined, but also what is admitted in evidence. That fact raises an interesting question concerning their applicability in diversity cases and other actions governed by state substantive law. Under the *Erie* doctrine, state cases are supposed to be decided by state law. As developed by *Guaranty Trust Co. v. York*, 326 U.S. 99 (1945), and *Byrd v. Blue Ridge Rural Electric Cooperative, Inc.*, 356 U.S. 525 (1958), federal procedural rules which definitely would affect the outcome of the case must yield to state law.

This apparently simple test was clouded when the Supreme Court decided *Hanna v. Plumer*, 380 U.S. 460 (1965). There the issue was whether the service of process permitted by Rule 4(d)(1) of the *Federal Rules of Civil Procedure* was applicable in a diversity case in which that service would not have been effective to initiate an action in state court. Faced with the specter of the *Federal Rules of Civil Procedure* being utterly inapplicable in all diversity cases, since most procedural rules are ultimately outcome determinative, the court took a fuzzy step back from a pure outcome test.

What about the rules of evidence? In *Monarch Insurance Co. v. Spach*, 281 F.2d 401 (5th Cir. 1960), the court wrestled with the problem. The action was against an insurer for a fire loss. The insurance company had taken the written statement of the plaintiff's president concerning the loss but did not give him a copy. Under a Florida statute, that omission made the document inadmissible. The Fifth Circuit held that the trial court's refusal to admit the document when the insurer attempted to use it to establish its defense was error. The court reasoned that, since there were unused procedures which had been available for admitting the document or its contents, it was not outcome determinative to admit it more directly—a somewhat tortured path to the conclusion that it was error to refuse to admit the document itself. The Fifth Circuit said that a court "must have the capacity to regulate the manner by which cases are to be tried and facts are to be presented." *Id.* at 411.

Strained Result

Because of the need to protect the integrity of the *Federal Rules of Evidence*—the policy implicit in *Hanna v. Plumer*—it is reasonable to anticipate that the Supreme Court will strain, as did the Fifth Circuit in the *Monarch Insurance* case, to find that challenged rules of evidence are not really outcome determinative.

But someday the case must arise when a party will be able to survive a motion for a directed verdict solely because of evidence which is admissible under the Federal Rules and is inadmissible under state law. It could happen in a number of variations of the hypothetical Rockwell case. Suppose, for example, that Mr. Rockwell died as a result of his injuries, and the only evidence available to establish that the defendant's actions were the cause of his injuries was a statement made to an ambulance driver, admissible under Rule 803(4) but clearly inadmissible under state law. What would happen then?

Many people are loath to predict. The drafters of the Federal Rules tried to avoid the problem. Rule 302 (Competency), Rule 501 (Privileges), and Rule 601 (Presumptions) all refer to state law for actions where there is "an element of a claim or defense as to which State law supplies the rule of decision." This deference to state law in rules promulgated by the Supreme Court suggests that, in instances when one of the Federal Rules of Evidence is in fact outcome determinative, the rule should not be applied.

But cases of that nature will be rare, leaving litigators with the expectation that the Federal Rules of Evidence will be available to modernize nearly every aspect of the examination of expert witnesses in federal courts.

How to Present Complex Economic Evidence to a Jury

by John L. Jeffers

The problem with complex economic evidence is that you must present to a jury of ordinary folk a mass of mathematical, tedious, and abstruse facts. The jurors will probably be people with no training in economics, finance, or even bookkeeping. Their personal finances consist year in and year out of wages earned and bills paid. On the other hand, they will have views about the economy, the value of money, the value of work, and good common sense. They are faced with evaluating expert economic testimony to determine issues worth perhaps millions of dollars. The lawyer's job is to serve as intermediary between his economic expert and the jury, to organize, simplify, and communicate with words and pictures.

Imparting the work and conclusions of an academic economist to jurors with little exposure to the dismal science is not likely to get easier. More and more cases involve economic issues. The courts encourage, and sometimes require, economic testimony on a large number of issues and demand great detail in the testimony. But there is no reason to believe that the juror will become more sophisticated in economic matters. In short, the problem of presenting economic evidence to juries will affect many trial lawyers.

Select your economic expert early. This rule applies especially to the plaintiff in a damage suit. The practice of pursuing discovery on liability for years until the case is set for trial and then casting about for an expert on damages may prove fatal to the proof of damages. The expert hired in this fashion may well need additional discovery that it will be too late to obtain. Put in this position, the expert may have to develop links in the damage model on the basis of surveys outside the discovery record or on

---

The author is a partner in the Houston firm of Baker & Botts.

logical assumptions grounded in economic theory. In other words, he may be forced to make assumptions that the jury or, later, the court will not accept. For this reason alone, the damage expert should be hired early.

The plaintiff in complex cases has no option but to select an expert witness for damages. It is doubtful whether the defendant should retain an expert witness to testify on damages in every case. Even on issues of liability, such as that of market definition in an antitrust case, the plaintiff may forego expert witnesses. Most trial lawyers opt for as few witnesses as possible in any type of case on the theory that less can go wrong. With issues other than damages, decide whether you can rely on industry witnesses without using experts. Industry witnesses have more credibility in this context. The jury may also reject an expert's economic conclusions about liability if the expert does not have a long, working association with the industry. On the other hand, the damage expert who has testified to certain profit projections based on an assumed sales volume can readily admit that he has no opinion on liability issues and has never been associated with the industry. The jury will likely think this is irrelevant to his testimony. They may take the expert's lack of knowledge as confirming his neutrality.

Agonizing Decisions

Deciding whether a defendant should use a damage expert in a jury trial can be agonizing. A defendant should always obtain an expert for counseling during discovery and trial. The expert can assist in drafting discovery requests, analyzing responses, and cross-examining the plaintiff's expert. But should you have him testify? In the first place, you must assume that what can go wrong, will. Your expert may be forced to admit valid points about the plaintiff's testimony. Even more serious, the very appearance of a defense expert may reinforce the damage issue in the jury's mind. Many lawyers argue that the defendant who calls a damage expert conveys to the jury that there is a question of the amount of damages to be decided. Thus the defendant places himself near the close of trial in the exact posture he wishes to avoid. All the points that the defendant will argue ought to be made on cross-examination of the plaintiff's expert, using the defendant's expert only to consult.

In many cases, able defense counsel have concluded that expert witnesses must be put on to make a record for post-trial motions and appeals. At this point the trial lawyer will find himself torn between the jury and the record. The nature of such decision making was perhaps best described by the great criminal lawyer Racehorse Haynes. When asked about his decision not to put the accused in a particular case on the stand, he said he had thought about it drunk and sober and had never been quite sure what to do. His client was acquitted. If the trial lawyer elects to go forward for the sake of the record, knowing that he is putting on more witnesses than he should and that they are likely to affect the jury in the wrong way, he must simply put the best face on it he can.

Sources

When an expert must be chosen from outside the industry in question to testify on matters like antitrust liability or market definition, he will almost certainly have to be a trained economist. Only an economist can bring economic theory to bear on data gleaned from the record of the case. Do not use an economist to testify on damages, however, unless finance was one of the major areas of his education and a subject about which he has taught and published extensively.

There are many sources of damage experts besides economists, including schools of accounting and accounting firms, schools of business administration, management consulting firms, and the research and analysis departments of brokerage houses. I prefer the accounting profession, and particularly professors of accounting and finance at universities. They combine the ability to construct a damage model with the ability to comprehend massive sets of books and records in a short time. Some of them can even communicate with skill and simplicity.

The selection of experts is often based on suggestions. For those who want professional advice, consider institutions such as National Economic Research Associates, the consulting firm in New York with which Peter Max is now associated. This firm provides witnesses based on the needs of the case, and also offers research tools and data. Another consultant is Lexecon Inc., a consulting firm in Chicago founded by Professor Richard Posner of the University of Chicago. This firm will also provide appropriate experts.

There are several rules to follow in hiring the expert. First, choose an expert from a school near the place of trial so that the jury will identify the school and not think the expert an alien highbinder. You can also work with him more easily if he is close to you. Second, avoid experts who are track weary with litigation experience. Third, while the prospective expert will usually agree to devote the time necessary to the case, the lawyer must be sure that the expert's schedule will actually fit the needs of the case. Fourth, the expert should be presentable to a jury; you should judge whether he can achieve a rapport with jurors. Most important, the expert must disclose in his interviews with you an ability to compose his testimony in the simplest possible manner and in a way that can hold the jury's attention. If the lawyer has to compose portions of the expert's testimony for him, the expert has failed.

There are brilliant experts who have difficulty talking clearly to people not trained in their field. Others do not take for granted that the listener understands technical terms or terms of art, have ready illustrations for abstruse points, and, above all, can express themselves simply. Hire that expert.

Once you have selected the expert, the next step is to work with him on preparing his testimony and exhibits. Do not write a script for testimony, though in the case of protracted testimony you might want to reduce the questions to writing for study. The real secret to preparing economic testimony for a jury is work followed by practice. Most of the work must be done by the expert himself, which is why choosing the right expert can make the case. The lawyer must help the expert understand what the case is about, what the likely order of proof will be, where the expert's testimony will fall in the trial, what the likely composition of the jury will be, and how to give testimony. The expert must assemble and analyze the data and outline his testimony.

Do not confine the expert's preparation to an examination of record materials. Encourage the client to talk with the expert so that the client assists in whatever economic theory the expert develops. Not only will the client's practical judgment about the industry assist the expert, but the lawyer will learn many points that the client must testify to as a predicate for the expert's conclusions. In the course of preparation, the expert should observe the client's plant and products. Then when the cross-examiner asks, "Isn't it true, Doctor, that you've never in your life been inside a Widget factory?" he will recoil in pain from the answer.

Once the expert has all the facts he needs and has outlined his testimony, lawyer and expert can work together to reduce the outline to questions and answers. These questions and answers should be practiced, rearranged, and refined repeatedly before the testimony is actually given.

The reason for repeated practicing of questions and answers in expert testimony is not just for the expert to refine and simplify his responses. The lawyer must understand exactly what it is the expert is saying at each moment so that there is synchronization between questions and answers. That way, if a point is left out in an answer, another question can be asked to pick it up. The jury should understand the question as well as the answer. In this way, the questions and answers will become a natural dialogue, and the communication with the jury will be from two persons rather than one. The jury will be more likely to follow this communication, particularly if both lawyer and expert maintain good eye contact. It will enhance communication if the lawyer, with a thorough understanding of the testimony, is able to do a little light leading. But do not lead so much as to take the initiative away from the expert or draw a rebuke from the trial judge.

The techniques of communication are important, but the substance of expert testimony must weave together a myriad of details and concepts. Organize the testimony as follows:

1. An elaborate statement of the expert's background and qualifications so that he will be well set for any voir dire.

291

2. A statement by the expert of his testimony's purpose and a dis-claimer about any substantive issues not being addressed.
3. A full description of the sources on which he has based his testi-mony.
4. An orderly statement of the expert's conclusions.
5. A step-by-step explanation of how the expert reached his conclu-sions, reviewing the work done and the calculations made.
6. A restatement of the conclusions.

In framing questions and answers, remember an excellent technique of teaching economics: explain a concept with illustrations using small numbers. Such illustrations reduce the points to the lowest common de-nominator and can be employed usefully in expert jury testimony.

With both lawyer and expert striving to communicate with the jury, the testimony can go beyond pat questions and answers and become a live demonstration of economic reality. To give full dimension to the tes-timony, use large, multi-colored charts prepared by a graphic artist. The expert should suggest or even draft the number and kinds of charts he thinks would be effective. Two warnings: allow ample time for prepara-tion, and check thoroughly for accuracy. Offer reduced copies in evi-dence during or at the close of the expert testimony, as the trial judge prefers. Place the charts themselves near the jury with both lawyer and expert moving to the charts for explanations as the testimony proceeds. Having the jurors follow these physical movements directs maximum attention to the charts pointed to by both lawyer and expert. You may not want to use charts in every case, but always consider them high pri-ority, because they can be of great help. Your reduced copies can lie in front of the jury as they deliberate, when the oral testimony will be only a memory.

Honest Expert

None of the jurors will comprehend fully what the expert says. Cer-tainly the jury will not understand the expert's concepts of accounting or economics. But it is vital for the jury to grasp the main points of the economic testimony; they should retain these points in their delibera-tions. If you achieve this object and convince the jury that the expert is honest and competent, then your job will have been done as well as can be. Concentrate on repeating and summarizing key points and conclu-sions in the testimony as much as the trial judge will permit.

Finally, do not have your expert explain every book entry underlying a total of costs or profits. Do not set forth every step in a complex calcula-tion. Smooth the flow of the presentation. You can omit the drudgery so long as you explain the essential steps leading to the conclusion. Your opponent must decide whether to challenge a particular conclusion or let it rest undisputed in the record. If he doubts the accuracy of a conclu-sion, let him cross-examine. You need not worry if he loses the attention of the jury on cross-examination. Moreover, an expert strong in accounting and finance will have the advantage over almost any cross-examining lawyer.

Defense counsel will watch the record as well as the jury. The case reporters are strewn with recent appellate reversals of jury awards based on some perceived inadequacy in the economic testimony. Defense counsel may sometimes make dull points on cross-examination for the record or put on additional witnesses and lose the jury's interest. The defendant may lose the battle with the jury and yet win with the trial judge, or lose in the trial court and win on appeal.

No Tomorrow

The plaintiff must persuade the jury, for there is no tomorrow. But he must also lay an ample basis in the record for appeal. Appellate reversal awaits expert testimony based on speculation or missing vital evidentiary links. You must ground expert testimony of damages firmly in the record; the testimony must be accurate and internally consistent. For this reason you should begin selecting an expert and preparing economic testimony with the filing of the lawsuit.

Despite all this tedium and hard work, expert economic testimony offers you the key to victory or defeat in a complex case.

I recall one antitrust suit in which we represented the corporate plaintiff. We had introduced upwards of 20 charts to the jury during the course of our case-in-chief, but there was one that encapsulated our damage model and summarized all the damages sought.

The chart had another nice feature. We were asking for a lot of money for a company that was very small and indeed almost out of business (we said because of the defendants' conduct). The argument was obviously that it was sheer fantasy to suggest that a company of our client's size and wherewithal could have made enough money to have been damaged in anywhere near the magnitude projected by our expert. To rebut this argument, this same chart had bar graphs in captivating colors depicting the amount of profit actually made by the defendant during the relevant time period as contrasted with the paltry sum that we sought.

This summary chart was placed before the jury during closing arguments. When the trial judge had completed his instructions and the jurors were rising to leave, I saw one of them, a longshoreman (who was to be elected foreman), take a quick glance at the bottom line of our chart. I said to myself what I remembered Augie Busch had said when his first World Series Championship was just an inning away, ''Oh boy . . . Oh boy . . . Oh boy.''

PART V

The Techniques
of Persuasion

Suggestions for Better Communication with the Jury

by John F. Grady

The job of a trial lawyer is to communicate persuasively with the trier of fact. He or she (hereafter the impersonal "he") does this by talking—by oral statements, arguments, and questions to witnesses. The talking done by the lawyers is the major percentage of the total talking done during the trial. The opportunity for persuasion is enormous. Lawyers say things that get in the way of their efforts to persuade. I will not mention individual idiosyncrasies, for that would be simply anecdotal and not instructive. Rather, I will point out some unfortunate speech and conduct patterns that the majority of trial lawyers have adopted. It is almost as though they were all bit by the same bug, or that they all attended the same ill-starred seminar.

The opportunity to make an opening statement in a jury trial, and sometimes even in a bench trial, is something a capable lawyer should regard as almost too good to be true. What greater head start could one ask than the opportunity to state his case clearly, concisely, and without interruption? While an opening statement must not be argumentative, only the naive would fail to recognize that it provides a significant opportunity for persuasion. Yet, it is the exceptional lawyer who avoids diluting the opportunity by the very first words he utters.

The typical opening statement in a jury case consists of three parts. The first part is an apology. The lawyer tells the jury that, because his case is going to be presented in a disjointed, disorganized fashion, the law gives him this opportunity to try to make it comprehensible in advance. Invariably, he follows this with one of two trite similes: The opening statement is like the picture on the jigsaw puzzle box; or an opening statement is like a table of contents to a book.

John F. Grady is Chief Judge in the Northern District of Illinois.

There are several things wrong with this part of the opening statement. First, it is not a very interesting way to start out. Second, it does not really say anything that is helpful to the jury. They know the purpose of an opening statement without being told. Third, it usually is not true. More often than not, the lawyer who tells the jury in his opening statement how his witnesses are going to be called out of logical sequence puts on his witnesses in a perfectly logical sequence, or at least in a sequence that confuses no one. Fourth, part one, with or without one of the similes, is just terribly trite. Juries hear it in every case, and by the time a juror is reaching the end of his term, each lawyer who uses the same routine probably depreciates himself in the eyes of that juror.

Habitual, Compulsive

Part two of the stereotyped opening statement is a disclaimer. The lawyer impresses upon the jury that nothing he says is evidence, and that if anything he says is contrary to the evidence, the jury should disregard it. He usually adds that the same thing goes for his opponent. Part two is not only habitual, it seems to be compulsive. I have on occasion introduced the opening statements by telling the jury that they are now about to hear the lawyers' opening statements, which are not evidence, but which are intended to acquaint the jury with what the lawyers expect the evidence will be. Invariably, the first lawyer will then begin his opening statement by saying, "Now, ladies and gentlemen, as the judge has told you. . . ." Jurors have smiled at me on those occasions, and I do not think they were just being friendly.

There are a couple of things wrong with part two. First, like part one, it simply is not necessary. For a lawyer to think that a jury might believe anything *he* says is evidence is overly optimistic, if not fatuous. For the lawyer to go further and suggest that he might say something contrary to the evidence does him no good, and may reinforce any suspicion that jurors already have. To suggest that one's opponent might be guilty of the same thing does not help matters.

There is a reason why part two is so popular. Lawyers really have no intention of misstating the evidence, nor do they usually expect their opponent to do so. Part two is simply a gambit to impress the jury with how *honest* the lawyer is, how extra careful he wants to be to see that he does not by inadvertence mislead the jury in any way. Some people may pull this off; I cannot prove they do not. But it is my definite impression that part two accomplishes nothing worthwhile in most instances and, in combination with part one, serves to get the lawyer off to a very sluggish and inauspicious start with the jury.

Part three is the lawyer's statement of what he expects the evidence to be. This may be well or poorly done, and a discussion of the technique is beyond the scope of this article. What I suggest is that trial lawyers scrap parts one and two, simply stand up and tell the jury what they expect the evidence to show, and then bring on the witnesses.

Asking questions of witnesses may be the most important means a lawyer has for communication with the trier of fact. His question is often as important as the answer the witness gives, and usually the answer can be no better than the question. Here are some common mistakes lawyers make in phrasing their questions.

Verbosity

Many lawyers forget the trier of fact does not know their case as well as they do. The judge and the jury are looking for cues. It is the job of the lawyer to direct their attention to the very specific things that are important to his case. One of the most effective ways of doing this is to ask questions that contain nothing extraneous and put the subject matter in clear focus. One of the most serious faults I notice in trial lawyers is the tendency to ask long, rambling questions that obscure the subject of the questions. One example is altogether typical:

> Mr. Jones, let me show you what has been marked for identification as plaintiff's exhibit 12; would you please tell the court and the ladies and gentlemen of the jury whether you have seen that document before.

The length of that question does not cause confusion, but certainly it causes tedium. Take another example that does both.

> Mr. Jones, now let me ask you this—and if you don't understand my question just say so and I will repeat it—now when did you— just give me your best recollection on this—last see the defendant, that is, before coming to court today?

Those two questions could be very simply put:

> Do you recognize plaintiff's exhibit 12?
> When did you last see the defendant?

Loves Own Voice

The causes of this kind of verbosity may occasionally be found in deep-seated personality problems but most of this is probably caused by one or both of two factors. One is intoxication with the sound of one's own voice, and the other is sloppiness. The remedy for the first is an awakening to the fact that juries and even judges are favorably impressed by clear and concise language and very unfavorably impressed by verbosity. The lawyer who is trying to make points by filling the air with words simply has to realize that he is hurting his case. The second factor, sloppiness, is eliminated by adequate preparation. Verbose and disorganized questions are far more common among older practitioners than they are among novice trial lawyers. The principal reason for this is that the novices generally write their questions out in advance. One simply would not include redundant and extraneous material in a written question. The older lawyer, confident of his abilities, has long since stopped writing his questions out and may just have an outline of subjects to cover with the witness—if even that. This is all right if the lawyer has the ability to ask concise questions from the hip, but unsatisfactory if he does not. Much of the hemming and hawing contained in the verbose question is simply temporizing by a lawyer who is groping for the right words.

Abstraction

Another common habit is to ask questions that are just slightly removed from what you really want to know. A phrase that has invaded the repertoire of almost everyone is the reference to an "occasion." Some lawyers who appear in my court include this phrase in almost every question put to almost every witness. I have gone so far as to call them to the sidebar and plead with them to stop it. This usually does no good, because it seems to be an obsession.

"Did you have occasion to see the defendant that day?" What the questioner really wants to know is whether the witness saw the defendant that day—not whether he had an *occasion* to see him. He may have had the occasion but did not see him. A variant is to ask the witness whether he had an "opportunity" to do something. "Did you have an opportunity to examine that document?" Presumably what the questioner wants to know is whether the witness looked at the document. He might have had opportunities galore but not taken advantage of them.

Another abstraction encountered often is the query whether "it would be fair to say" something. "Would it be fair to say that you were fifty feet away?" Perhaps it is a quibble to say that fairness is not the issue, and probably all witnesses understand what they are being asked. Still, it seems that the witness should simply be asked whether he was fifty feet away. Let somebody else worry about whether it is fair.

Abstraction is really a form of verbosity. It results from adding unnecessary words to what would otherwise be a clear question.

A final example is the "do you know whether or not" question. Sometimes, the examiner really wants to know whether the witness knows something, in which case this form of question is fine. But often it has already been established that the witness heard or saw or otherwise has full knowledge of an event and the examiner now wants to find out the particulars of what the witness knows. This is not the time to ask the witness whether he knows something. When the question is asked in this way, this is what usually happens:

Q: Do you know whether the train was on time?
A: No.

299

Q: (Awkward pause) Do you mean no, you don't know or "No, it wasn't on time"?

A: I mean it wasn't on time.

Double Questions

This troublesome creature comes in two forms, the conjunctive and the disjunctive:

Q: Did he arrive at about that time and tell you he had been with the defendant?

A: No.

The answer of the witness is ambiguous. It may be that he is denying only one of the two components of the question. An affirmative answer would be equally ambiguous.

The disjunctive form is no better:

Q: Did you stay or did you go?

A: Yes.

Here, the answer is not simply ambiguous, it is inscrutable. But the fault is not with the answer, it is with the question.

A third form of a double question is the ubiquitous, "Is that right?" appended to an otherwise understandable question.

Q: So you never left the city that day, is that correct?

A: No.

Is the witness saying that he did leave the city or that he did not leave the city? Some lawyers will recognize the ambiguity of the situation and ask a follow-up question:

Q: No, you did not leave the city or "No, that is not correct"?

How much simpler it would be simply to omit the "Is that correct?" or "Is that right?"

"Is that not true?"

The habitual use of "Is that right?" causes the problems noted above, but they are minor compared to the confusion resulting from the even more compulsive "Is that *not* right?" Almost always, the use of this and synonymous phrases (Is that not true, not correct, not a fact, not so) results in an ambiguous answer.

Q: Is it not true that you stayed home?

A: Yes.

An alternate form would be:

Q: You stayed home, is that not correct?

A: Yes.

In each of these instances, the witness probably means that he stayed home. In other words, he is agreeing with the proposition the lawyer intends to assert in the question. But what the witness has really said, as a literal and grammatical matter, is that he did not stay home—i.e., that it is *not true* that he stayed home. Substitute a "no" for a "yes" answer to these

300

same two questions and the ambiguity becomes worse. In fact, it is any-body's guess what a "no" would mean. Considering that the whole point of having a witness testify under oath is that he subjects himself to the risk of a perjury prosecution for untruthful testimony, it seems a shame to ask questions in a form that leaves the meaning of the answer in doubt.

The problem is aggravated when the questioner uses a double not, which, in fact, is the more usual form of this monstrosity. Here is a recent example that occurred in my court:

Q: Would I not be correct to state that you are not a tax expert? A "no" answer to this question would leave the matter in shambles. As it happened, the witness answered "yes," and from the context I think he meant that he was not a tax expert.

Another question and answer I heard while making notes for this article:

Q: So there is no interview sheet, is that not correct?

A: Yes.

The questioner then continued his examination on the assumption that there was no interview sheet, only to find out later that there was one and that the witness thought he had so stated.

These "is it not true" questions are usually asked on cross-examination, and they are motivated by the understandable desire of the cross-examiner to lead the witness. The problem is many lawyers simply do not know how to ask a leading question. It really is not complicated, and it is hard to understand how we got ourselves into this fix. All we have to do is avoid combining positive and negative elements in the same question and, of course, avoid double negatives. Assume that we want to lead the witness to say that he went home. There are various ways of doing this with clarity:

You went home, right?

You went home—is that true?

And then you went home?

Another means of avoiding ambiguous answers to leading questions is simply not to lead where it is not necessary. When the examiner has no reason to expect that the witness will deny going home, it should suffice simply to ask, "Did you go home?" Save the leading questions for those situations where you think the witness might be reluctant to give the answer you want.

Needless Conventions

Anything that serves only to interrupt the smooth flow of ideas is obviously an impediment to communication. There are a number of these useless distractions that most trial lawyers seem to regard as indispensable tools of their profession. I will mention the ones that are obvious to me. There are undoubtedly many others that have escaped my notice, probably because I regard them as indispensable.

301

One of the things that must puzzle jurors is our habit of saying to a witness after a recess, "Now, you are the same John Jones who testified here this morning, is that correct? You realize you are still under oath?" The jury can see it is the same John Jones, and certainly the court reporter's notes will indicate that it is the same John Jones, and I have never understood what purpose is served by this reaffirmation of his identity. As far as his still being under oath is concerned, I doubt that it would occur to anyone that the oath was vitiated by a recess.

Trivial Questions

There was a day when the parties to a lawsuit were each represented by one lawyer. When he finished examining a witness, he would simply announce that he had no more questions, and then his opponent would take over. Now, however, it is rare for a litigant to be represented by only one lawyer. Typically, there are two, sometimes three. The reasons for this are beyond the scope of this article, but the phenomenon is associated with the burgeoning ranks of the profession and the high cost of litigation. In any event, the fact that multiple lawyers are involved has given rise to another time-wasting convention. Invariably, the lawyer who has conducted the examination of a witness will, at the conclusion of his own efforts, turn to the court and say, "May I have a moment, Your Honor?" or "May I have the court's indulgence?" and then confer with his associates. My impression is that these conferences almost never result in any additional questions that are worth asking. The process is at best anticlimactic. I have seen lawyers end their cross-examination on a high note, only to dissipate the effect by asking a few more trivial questions after huddling with other counsel.

There are times when a conference with one's associates really is helpful, and the point is not that it should never occur. The point is that it should not occur with every witness. Some lawyers put a witness on for five or six questions, simply to identify a document, and then, through some reflex they are unable to control, ask for a moment to confer.

Asking the court reporter to read a question back is another nuisance that is usually unnecessary. The reporter has to search through his or her notes to find the question, and it is usually far simpler for counsel to ask the question again.

Finally, there are two common shortcomings in presenting documentary evidence. The first is the practice of having the court reporter mark exhibits in the presence of the jury. Some judges simply do not permit this, but most judges do. Try to put yourself in the place of a juror who has to sit and watch this boring process, sometimes involving scores of documents, and you will see the wisdom of marking your own exhibits before you get to court.

The second problem is the failure to let the jury know the contents of a complex document at the time a witness is being examined about it. It

302

may be difficult or impossible for the jury to understand the testimony without seeing the document. It is not practical to pass the document from juror to juror, because this would take too much time. The solution is to have a copy of the document for each juror, or else to show an enlargement of the document on a screen. No judge should refuse to allow either of these procedures when it is important for the jury to consider the document along with the testimony of the witness.

Jurors form opinions about the lawyers in the case at the same time they are forming opinions about the facts. Inevitably, the two things rub together. A lawyer who wins the respect of the jury will convince them of a doubtful proposition far more easily than a lawyer who generates doubt of his ability. The feedback I get from jurors convinces me that they have high expectations and a low tolerance for incompetence. They are not there by choice, and they want their time to be put to good use. They resent delay, confusion, and inefficiency. They have no patience with trivia, technicalities, and legal jargon, and they are critical of procedures whose purpose is not apparent. If jurors ever assumed that the judge and the lawyers know what they are doing, it was long before our time.

It is usually impossible to irritate and persuade at the same time. It is difficult to confuse and persuade at the same time. Neither effort should be necessary. Bad habits of the kind discussed here should not require much effort to break. It is an effort every trial lawyer should constantly make.

Persuading Judges
in Bench Trials

by Prentice H. Marshall

Imagine your shock. A juror—a meek-looking old man in the second row—interrupts your cross-examination of the other side's key witness.

"Counsel," he says, "I really don't know where you are going with this line of questioning. From your pleadings I had supposed your defense was contributory negligence. Now you seem to be suggesting that this accident never occurred. Just what is this all about?"

Cases where jurors pipe up and ask questions are rare enough to talk about for years to come. It is a violation of all the unspoken rules. The jurors are there to listen, not talk. They are not supposed to know anything about the case except what you tell them as the trial unfolds. They are there to find facts, not intrude on the trial.

And there you have the distinction between judge and jury trials. To be sure, the elements of advocacy are the same: candor, clarity and conciseness. So is the inclination of the decision maker to rule with the facts. Nevertheless, judge trials differ from jury trials in ways that real litigators never forget: In bench trials the fact-finder knows everything about the case from the time it was filed. Unlike the jury, the judge is a sophisticated person who has heard—or thinks he has heard—a hundred cases just like this one. And, unlike the jury, the judge is not just going to sit quietly throughout the trial. He is probably going to talk back.

A jury enters a case with a fresh and open mind. The law does everything practicable to keep it that way. But when a case comes to trial before a judge without a jury, it is all turned around. Now the fact-finder has been influenced by everything that has happened throughout its development.

Prentice H. Marshall is a United States District Judge for the Northern District of Illinois; Adjunct Professor of Law, Chicago Kent College of Law, Illinois Institute of Technology; and a team leader and Associate Director of the National Institute for Trial Advocacy.

Take the pleadings for example. What the judge sees at the very beginning has a real effect. Sloppy, ill-prepared pleadings and motions condition the judge to expect a sloppy, ill-prepared case on the merits. On the other hand, crisp, informative, well-organized, neat and grammatical pleadings promise a short, tight, well-tried case.

Good advocates never miss an opportunity to be persuasive with the court, either on the facts or on the law. Motions addressed to the pleadings should be accompanied by a brief memorandum of authorities that goes directly to the point. And the respondent on the motion should be ready to submit a memorandum in support of the challenged pleadings in time for it to really count when the motion is argued.

Then comes discovery, and with it another chance to impress or offend the decision maker. The unfortunate truth is that discovery has become too contentious. It was not meant to be that way, and contentiousness should be avoided, particularly in cases set for trial to the court. Judges become impatient with pettifogging over discovery, and the lawyer who expects the judge to put it out of mind when the case is tried simply expects too much.

If there must be controversy over discovery—and sometimes there must—it should be presented in a clear, succinct manner. Objections should be supported in a brief memorandum and the party seeking discovery should be ready to back up every demand on short notice.

Some things are easier in judge trials. Fact stipulations, for example, are sometimes too cryptic for juries to understand. This should not be true in bench trials. If the judge is competent, he should be able to understand the stipulated facts without a tedious in-court development. And judges, who are pressed for time with busy trial calendars, welcome counsel who have undertaken to dispense with the need for testimonial proof on facts that are really uncontested.

Exhibits offer another opportunity to win or lose the heart of the bench. They should be pre-marked and their foundations stipulated—even in criminal cases—except for items of legitimate controversy or materials to be used only for impeachment.

If one is faced with an adversary who refuses to stipulate, and a pretrial conference is not available for that purpose, then counsel should make a Rule 36 request to admit. Rid the case of unnecessary controversy and present the court with adversary proof only on the issues that really need to be tried.

After all this is done, is counsel ready for trial? Maybe not. Suppose for a moment that a lawyer has a case set for trial just a month away. Suppose that through the gift of prescience, a crystal ball or a magnificent system of jury selection, that lawyer knew a month in advance every juror who would sit on this case. Then suppose that it was perfectly proper to write a letter to every juror who would hear that case, explaining what it was all about, telling those jurors how the evidence would entitle that lawyer to a verdict. Can you imagine that any trial lawyer would let an opportunity like that slip by?

Once again, bench trials afford an opportunity for communication and persuasion that is never present with a jury: a pretrial statement of the case, the contemplated proof and the supporting legal arguments. It is the much-neglected trial brief.

Judges like them. They are helpful in jury trials and essential in bench trials. The trial brief should state the factual theory of the case; what the evidence will show, weaving in the stipulated and admitted facts; and the legal theories that will be urged for a favorable judgment. A section specifically devoted to anticipated controverted evidence questions is helpful. Finally, the brief should be accompanied by a list of witnesses (with a brief synopsis of their testimony) and photocopies of all documentary exhibits on which the judge can make notes.

The purpose of the trial brief is to give the judge a complete overview of the case. It should be delivered in advance of trial. Of course, the adversary must be served, and this causes some trial lawyers to hesitate. They feel that trial briefs disclose too much to their opponents. They forget that the first step toward persuasion is the audience's comprehension. The opportunity to communicate and persuade in advance of trial is one that should not be passed by.

Another frequent argument against trial briefs is that they will not be read. That notion is unfair to most trial judges. They are conscientious about their work and want help in arriving at a just decision. Furthermore, the brief that is not submitted can never be read. Present a trial brief.

Now the case is ready for trial. Some lawyers have the notion that they should dispense with an opening statement unless the court asks for one. That is a mistake. Do not waive opening statement unless you are directed to do so by the judge. This is true even if you have filed a trial brief and even if your opponent waives opening statement.

The fact is, some judges simply understand oral presentations better than written ones. Furthermore, the opening statement gives the judge a chance to ask questions about the case. As John W. Davis observed in his famous article, *The Argument of an Appeal*, 26 A.B.A.J. 895 (1940), reprinted in H. GOODRICH, R. CARSON AND J. DAVIS, A CASE ON APPEAL (ALI-ABA, Philadelphia, 1967), when the court asks questions, the advocate should "rejoice." Here is the value of the judge's talking back. The lawyer can see the workings of the judge's mind. Troublesome issues are ventilated, showing points that should be emphasized during the rest of the trial. While opening statements are not supposed to be argumentative, pity the poor advocate who cannot turn a question into an effective mini-argument.

Prepare the opening statement well. Rambling, discursive, stock opening statements should never be used in any trial—and certainly not when the advocate is making a presentation to a person who hears lawyers' speeches day in and day out. This audience knows a good performance from a bad one, and yours should be good.

The opening statement should be concise, structured and logical. It should define the contested issues, list the undisputed facts and state what the evidence will show about the disputed facts. In addition, it should develop the legal theories of the case.

Introducing evidence in bench trials is frequently more relaxed than in jury trials. The bounds of relevancy may be broader; the exceptions to the hearsay rule may be applied more liberally. But do not impose on the court by seeking to introduce clearly inadmissible proof or by failing to hold your opponent within reasonable limits.

Time is important to trial judges. Have I said that before? Well, it is. Of all the judicial functions—studying pleadings, motions and briefs and writing findings, opinions and judgments—there is one that can be done only in one place and during certain hours. That is trying a case. Other duties can be performed in evenings, on weekends or before or after normal court hours. But trial time is precious, and trial judges want their cases to move. Your job during trial—besides adducing the evidence in favor of your client—is to see to it that the trial moves.

This is particularly important when it comes to cross-examination. Judges squirm in jury trials when a pointless, rambling, repetitious cross-examination is conducted. Maybe it can be forgiven because the lawyer thinks some cross-examination (no matter what) is necessary just to impress the jury—a dubious rationale, I assure you. But in bench trials, before a trained observer, a pointless, rambling, repetitious cross-examination really detracts from the overall presentation of the case. Respect the court for what it is: a trained audience. Do not act as if this were the only case it will ever hear. Instead, try to make it the best.

When the evidence is all in, it is time for final argument. Closing argument in a bench trial is not appreciably different from that in a jury trial, with one exception. In a bench trial the decision maker can shape the law, while for the jury it remains fixed.

The closing argument should be the best-structured part of the trial. After all, that is what the advocate has been shaping the case for throughout its development. In preparing the final argument, take the time to develop a theme demonstrating that the fair result—the just result—is in your favor.

Many lawyers live by the old cliche that bench trials are preferred when the law is on their side, and jury trials are preferred when the facts are on their side. They forget that judges, like juries, are human. The simple fact is that in both bench trials and jury trials the result is frequently dictated according to who, in the eyes of the fact-finder, wears the white hat and who wears the black hat. Judges do not like to decide cases for the bad guys any more than juries do.

307

Because the judge is a lawyer and can shape the law to fit the facts, legal nuances are important in an argument to the bench. But never forget that facts win trials, and the emphasis in summation should be on the facts.

If the case has been long and the evidence complex, the effort should be to simplify it to support the basic theme of the argument. Demonstrative aids—photographs, models, enlargements of crucial documents—are just as important in communicating with the court as with a jury. This is true even though copies of the documents have been presented to the court for its use.

The personal trial habits of the court are important throughout the trial, particularly in summation. Watch what the judge does as the trial moves along so you can adjust your final argument. Does the judge take notes? Does he review these notes during the course of the trial? Has the court demonstrated a recollection of the testimony as the case unfolded? Knowing the answers to these questions can help determine how detailed you should be in reviewing the evidence. It is hard to know what a jury remembers during the course of a trial. But by the end of a bench trial you should know what interests or troubles the judge; that is the kind of knowledge a real advocate needs.

So we conclude where we started. In a jury trial the opportunity to persuade the fact-finder is limited to the time when the jury is in the box. When you try a case to the bench, persuasion begins when the case is filed. Never forget it.

The Language of Persuasion

by Theodore I. Koskoff

Hollow words, I deem, are the worst of ills.

AESCHYLUS

With daily transcripts of courtroom proceedings running to more than 150 pages, it looks as though many lawyers are out to corner the market on hollow words. It is easy enough to do, maybe just as easy to rationalize: Trials are intensive, demanding exercises in applied psychology. Lawyers have to be concerned with the total image they project to juries. They have to arrest and maintain the attention of the jury, influence and control their clients to present themselves as attractively as possible, and work, throughout the trial, to use the basic techniques of nonverbal communication in an effort to convince the jury that justice is on their side. How can they worry about the niceties of word selection and order, the techniques of dramatic attention or the beauty and compass of language?

Even with a case structured to maintain interest, the jury does not listen with unabated attention to what the lawyers say. Attention requires enormous concentration. While the average juror may be "listening," he is often not comprehending what is said. He is listening but not perceiving, because his thoughts are in some kind of stream of consciousness.

The housewife is thinking about the kids crossing the street, the banker is thinking about what is going on back at the bank, and the grandmother is wondering whether the pot roast is burning. You are lucky if you have a significant percentage of the jury following what you say at any given moment.

The author is a member of the law firm of Koskoff, Koskoff & Bieder in Bridgeport, Connecticut, and Chairman of the National Board of Trial Advocacy.

That should tell you that you have to develop effective ways to get attention with the words you speak, the order in which you say them and the timing you use.

Silence is one of the best ways to get attention. Suppose a lawyer is in the middle of final argument and notices a juror in the back row whose eyes start to flutter closed. Does he raise his voice, change the subject, or grab the jury rail and go on? No. He stops. Waits. Says nothing. The tension of the situation rises until all eyes are fixed on him unblinkingly.

At that moment the lawyer has the jury's total attention. The next thing he says or does will be remembered. It is a technique that is so effective it must be used with the restraint that only good taste can bring—once, twice, perhaps three times in the course of a long trial. It works so well that the lawyer who uses it must take special care that whatever follows justifies the expectation that was created.

Then, more than ever, the lawyer needs the power of the language of persuasion; words that carry impact, judiciously selected and in the right order, coupled with the use of effective nonverbal behavior that can communicate and persuade.

Choose Words Carefully

It starts with the choice of words. Carefully worded questions can influence both the answers and the way they are heard by the jury.

Dr. Elizabeth F. Loftus, a research psychologist at the University of Washington, makes the point: "I have found that the questions asked about an event influence the way a witness remembers what he saw. Changing even one word in a single question can systematically alter an eyewitness account." *Reconstructing Memory: The Incredible Eyewitness*, PSYCHOLOGY TODAY, Vol. 8, No. 1, p. 116 (1974).

Let me give you a few examples of both Dr. Loftus's and my own to illustrate the point. Suppose you ask, "Did you see the car with *the* broken headlight?" Phrasing the question that way will result in a significantly higher number of people who will say they saw a car with a broken headlight than if you simply ask, "Did you see the car with *a* broken headlight?"

It shows why plaintiff's lawyers should never use the word "accident." "What happened to you in the accident?" is a defense question. Plaintiff's lawyers should use "crash," "wreck," or "smash-up." Why? Just because it sounds more dramatic.

In an examination of responses to these questions, a significant number of people estimated higher speeds when the words "wreck" or "smash-up" were used than in response to the word "accident." The words you choose help to create a picture in the mind of the person being questioned and influence the range of answers they instinctively feel is plausible.

Think about simple automobile personal injury cases. In intersectional

310

collision cases, lawyers always tend to get tied up in what I call the numbers game. That goes something like this: "How far was car number one from the intersection before he saw car number two; and how far then was car number two. . . ." Intent on fixing the witnesses' estimates, the lawyers fail to act as advocates in framing their questions.

If you want the distance to be greater, use the words, "how far?" If you want the distance to be less, use the words, "how near?" It can make a difference.

In experiments on the accuracy of guessing measurements, people were asked to make an intelligent numerical guess to each question. Then they were asked either of two questions, such as, "How tall is the basketball player?" or "How short is the basketball player?"

The results were striking. On the average, subjects who were asked how tall the basketball player was guessed 79 inches. On the other hand, subjects who were asked how short he was guessed 69 inches—the difference of nearly a foot.

Perhaps you think this principle applies only to estimates based on casual, fleeting observation. Surprisingly, it works even on matters drawn directly from people's personal lives. Dr. Loftus once asked questions about headache products. One group of people was asked whether they had tried one, two, or three different headache products. A second group was asked whether they had tried one, five or ten different headache remedies. Once again, the results were impressive. The group that was asked whether they had tried one, two, or three headache remedies responded that they had tried, on the average, 3.3 different products. The one, five, ten group, on the other hand, claimed an average of 5.2 different remedies.

"How Often?"

"Do you get headaches frequently? If so, how often?" Or, "Do you get headaches occasionally? If so, how often?" The "frequently" subjects reported an average of 2.2 headaches a week. The "occasionally" group reported an average of only 0.7 a week.

The lesson could not be more clear. Completely neutral questions are rare indeed. Questions which will influence the answers—at least statistically—can be framed so they will not run afoul of the rule against leading. If the words in question are going to influence the answers, they should be carefully thought out in advance. If they cannot be put so they influence in your favor, at least they should not work against you.

Certainly if a witness is committed to a particular distance, weight or measure, the chances are that even if the direct or cross-examiner wants to change it by altering the words from far to near, the witness will hold his ground. But if you continue to use the word near, it has been my experience that you can usually get the witness to modify the figure to some extent.

311

The value of this technique does not end with the particular answer you get. How the question is framed also has an influence on how the jury views the answer. Asking how fast a car was travelling plants the idea, "fast," in the jury's mind. And that idea can continue to work for you throughout the trial. To put it another way, you can get double duty out of carefully worded questions.

Asking properly worded questions is not something that comes like a flash in the middle of trial. It takes a good deal of pre-courtroom cerebration. There are no geniuses in the courtroom—only drudges in the office.

Take this principle and apply it to jury voir dire. How you ask questions depends on what you are trying to accomplish. Jury selection has many functions, and the range of questions you will be permitted to ask depends not only on the state you are in and the judge you are before, but whether the case is civil or criminal or in state or federal court. So assume, for a moment, a criminal case in a jurisdiction that permits extensive jury voir dire. The lawyer may be trying to develop challenges for cause, discover which jurors to challenge peremptorily or predispose the jurors in his favor. If he goes about it well, he will be doing all three at some time during this voir dire examination.

If the lawyer asks, "You don't believe, do you, that just because a person is arrested, he is guilty of a crime?" the great bulk of jurors will answer, "No." This may be superficially reassuring, but does not really tell the lawyer anything about the juror.

Suppose he asks this instead: "What do you think it means if someone is arrested? Do you feel it means there is a good chance he is guilty of some crime?" That is the kind of question that does not signal to the juror what the official answer is supposed to be, and the lawyer is much more likely to find out something useful about the juror's attitudes.

Must Change Form

On the other hand, if the lawyer shifts gears, he must change the form of his questions as well. "Is there anyone here who would have any difficulty following the basic American belief that a man is innocent until proven guilty? I gather by your silence that you all agree with that. Do you all agree, then, that if the state fails to prove John Morgan guilty—fails to prove him guilty beyond a reasonable doubt—that you would return a verdict of 'not guilty'?" It is unlikely that such questions will reveal a juror who does not believe in the presumption of innocence, because they are designed to predispose the jury to that principle, to listen to the evidence with that thought in mind. And the lawyer learns nothing from the answer.

Persuasive language goes beyond the details of wording questions, a sort of micro-study of persuasive techniques; it extends to framing presentations such as opening statements and final arguments.

An opening statement that starts out, "The evidence will show this and the evidence will show that" will not do. Merely stringing facts together is not enough. More important is to create for the jury a picture of the case that emphasizes the things you want the jury to think about while listening to the evidence.

Suppose you have a case against a hospital. A man walked into the hospital with a pain in his shoulder. As a result of the claimed negligence he developed into a quadriplegic, and worse. An opening statement that would put the jury in the best frame of mind, from your point of view, would tell them the theme of the case. It would be a word picture that would focus their attention on the most critical part of your case. Here is how it might go:

> High on the eighth floor of St. Joseph's Hospital, in room 804, is Howard Neilson. In bed is Howard Neilson, my client. Every morning at eleven o'clock, a woman comes into the room, draws a chair up to the bed, kisses him on the forehead, but he doesn't feel her. She speaks to him, but he doesn't hear her. She smooths the covers over his body, she rubs his arm, she rubs his leg, but he doesn't feel it. She looks him in the eyes, and he sees her, but he doesn't perceive her. She sits down in the chair and reads to him for an hour, but he doesn't hear her. She gets up. She kisses him on the forehead again, and she walks out of the room.
>
> How did Howard Neilson get that way? What could have been done to prevent it?

When you begin your opening statement in that manner, you know the jurors are ready to listen to the evidence from your point of view. They will be critical of the evidence. They will want to know what happened and what could have been done to prevent it.

Criminal cases have themes, too—something criminal lawyers with stock opening statements that deal with vague generalities tend to forget.

Take a case with an alibi defense. The lawyer might say the evidence is going to show this and the evidence is going to show that, the evidence is even going to show that the defendant, Michael Straughn, could not be guilty because he was watching television with some friends when the crime took place. Not very effective.

But if the lawyer creates a warm, real word picture, here is how the opening statement might begin:

> Seventeen Bonnybrook Road. It was one of those exciting nights when the Celtics and the Knicks were at each others' throats. It was one of those frequent nights when Mr. Peck, Mr. Lawson, Mr. Fabriosi and Mr. Straughn were indulging in their favorite occupation—watching the gladiators of our time at it again on TV.

313

It was the weekly evening of good fellowship and beer. It was an evening with friends.

While this was going on, some distance away—at 1771 State Street—a tragedy was taking place. John Mullins was robbed; John Mullins was shot, and John Mullins was killed.

That is the kind of opening that would focus attention on the alibi. In a sense it removes this group of people from the crime which is charged. It means the alibi testimony will have to be good; but then, as you know, a bad alibi may be worse than none at all.

Impact Phrases

Persuasive language depends in part on what I call "impact phrases," memorable groups of words that touch our basic motivations.

The late Moe Levine, a master in the art of final argument, would sum up a wrongful death case with the words, "We are now engaged in the grisly audit of death." That is an impact phrase.

Or we might have the blond-haired child who speaks to us from the grave. If we speak of sympathy, there are tears of sympathy, cards of sympathy, visits of sympathy or wet pillows at night. In a wrongful death case, one might talk about a father who has been lost to a family of five. "There's a sixth chair at the dining room table that's always empty," or "Who will teach his boy how to ride a bike, throw a baseball or say his prayers?"

Impact phrases can be found everywhere. From politics, we have images such as Senator Jackson's response to President Ford's economic plan: "It is like moving chairs around on the Titanic," and the charge leveled at Ella Grasso when she ran for Governor of Connecticut: "Putting Ella Grasso in charge of the treasury in the State of Connecticut is like putting Dracula in charge of the blood bank."

The Bible is rich in images, such as these two that speak to the value of human life: "Her price is above the price of rubies," and "What is man that thou art mindful of him?"

Another way to help make language persuasive is to use the techniques that have been favored since time immemorial. Caesar's cadence is still commanding: "Veni, Vidi, Vici—I came, I saw, I conquered."

Churchill, a master of alliteration, used phrases such as, "We cannot fail or falter," "He was a man of light and learning," "Let us to the task, to the battle, to the toil." Those are words of persuasion.

Contrast can be arresting, as Dickens showed in the opening lines of *A Tale of Two Cities*. "It was the best of times, it was the worst of times, it was the age of foolishness, it was the epoch of belief. . . ."

Persuasive Cliches

Even cliches can be persuasive—"He had crumbled like an old ruin"—when not used to excess. It is the art of the familiar, the value of plagiarism. We need to remember the past. When someone said to Sir Isaac Newton, "Dr. Newton, how is it that you see things so clearly?" he responded, "I stand on the shoulders of men like Galileo." We all plagiarize from one another, we all learn from one another, and we can learn about the art of persuasion from both the classics and modern oration.

In 1965 Ossie Davis gave the oration at the funeral of Malcolm X.

> If you knew him, you know why we must honor him; Malcolm was our manhood! This was his meaning to his people, and, in honoring him, we honor the best in ourselves. However much we may have differed with him, or with each other about him, and his value as a man, let his going from us serve only to bring us together, now.
>
> Consigning these mortal remains to earth, the common mother of all, secure in the knowledge that what we place in the ground is no more now a man, but a seed, which after the winter of our discontent will come forth to lead us. And we will know him then for what he was and is, a prince, our own black shining prince who didn't hesitate to die.

I begin to weep every time I read it.

It was Robert Ingersoll who, perhaps for the first time, used the "I saw him" technique. At the tomb of Napoleon, Ingersoll said, "I saw him at Toulon, I saw him putting down the mob, I saw him at the head of the army, I saw him in Egypt, I saw him at Elba."

According to William Safire writing in *The New York Times,* it is a technique that has been used by politicians ". . . since at least the election of candidate James Blaine in 1876."

It can be used in many situations. In a personal injury case involving a child: "I saw this beautiful blond-haired child on her way to school. I saw her crossing the street. I saw her playing with her friends and laughing as they walked home. I saw . . ." It is a technique particularly adaptable to summation.

Suppose you have a case involving lawyers in which you need to dignify the role they play in society. See how the "I saw him" technique can be effective:

> It was the Fourth of July, 1976. As we saw the tall ships sail under the George Washington Bridge and our minds went back to the founding of our Republic, I thought of the great lawyers of the past. Lawyers, who, as Milton said of Shakespeare, "Thou hast created in thy wonder and astonishment a monument."
>
> I saw him so long ago, a Philadelphian in New York, the Philadelphia lawyer at the nation's first political trial, upholding John Peter Zenger's right to publish what he chose free from censorship or interference. His name was Andrew Hamilton, and he was a lawyer.

I saw him at the trial of Captain Preston, another political trial, the unpopular cause and client arising out of the Boston massacre. His name was John Adams. He was a lawyer.

I saw him at that miracle in Philadelphia, the Constitutional Convention of 1787 fighting for the Bill of Rights, the credo of American freedom not adopted until 1789. His name was James Madison. He was a lawyer.

I saw him presiding over the Supreme Court of our land, the architect of the real powers of the Supreme Court. His name was John Marshall. He was a lawyer.

I saw him exhorting the battle cry of the Republic, ''Give me Liberty, or give me Death.'' His name was Patrick Henry. He was a lawyer.

I saw him at Gettysburg with tears in his eyes, gaunt and morose, rededicating our country to the principle of equal justice for all. His name was Abraham Lincoln. And he was a lawyer.

And I saw him elemental man, fighting for one cause or another in Dayton, Tennessee, preaching the legitimacy of evolution. His name was Clarence Darrow. He was a lawyer.

I saw him speaking to us from his wheelchair, lifting our spirits, making us stronger with his inspirational philosophy, ''The only thing we have to fear is fear itself.'' His name was Franklin Delano Roosevelt. And he was a lawyer.

I saw him in the Senate hearing room in Washington, uttering his anguished cry for decency. His name was Joseph Welch. And he was a lawyer.

And I thought of the precious monuments they had left to their lives and of Milton's wonderful comment on Shakespeare, and I wondered what kind of monuments you and I will erect for the next hundred years. Not a monument of brick and mortar, but one that will live. For only a thought lives on. And finally I thought of that marvelous admonition of Holmes, when almost a hundred years ago, he said, ''I think that as life is action and passion, it is required of man that he should share the passion and action of his time at the peril of being judged not to have lived.''

Persuasive language means, in addition to everything else, a touch of eloquence. What a shame so many think that elegant speech is dead.

Lawyer Language

by Ronald Goldfarb

Lawyers always have been a prosperous and powerful group, and they always have been suspected by the public of fostering a selfish and secretive professional society. One cause of this bad image—critically worsened in the Watergate period—is the language we use. In our talk and in our writing, we unnecessarily mystify our work, baffle our clients, and alienate the public. We could change this, and we should.

Most lawyers must plead guilty to killing the English language. It is a paradox that a group that is so well educated and that relies so crucially on communication uses such bad language. Because lawyers speak the words and write the documents that define and govern our lives, a keen public interest in their skillfulness might be expected. Yet, legal language is little examined and rarely challenged.

In recent years, there have been increasing public complaints about the deficient education of youngsters graduating from elementary and high schools, and from colleges as well. Graduate school administrators say their candidates lack writing skills. In law schools, poorly trained students who do not write well get no help, and those who do write well are indoctrinated to write legalese. The models of legal writing that guide neophyte lawyers are poor ones. Law journals, judicial opinions, and legal textbooks are loaded with jargon, pomp, Latinisms—what Yale law professor Fred Rodell once called "high-class mumbo-jumbo." Rodell claimed decades ago in his iconoclastic book, WOE UNTO YOU LAWYERS, that though it deals with ordinary facts and occurrences of everyday business, government, and life—"the law is carried on in a foreign language."

Lawyers commit unnatural acts on language. All professions and spe-

Ronald Goldfarb, a trial lawyer and author, is senior partner in the Washington, D.C., firm of Goldfarb & Singer. During the Kennedy administration he was a special prosecutor in the Department of Justice. This article has been adapted from material that first appeared in The Washington Post.

cialized groups of people use linguistic shorthand; it is more of a public problem when lawyers do it.

Who would ever say to his wife, one Southern judge quipped to me, "Dear, my car keys are on the kitchen counter; would you please throw me said keys"? Who would write, "I was telling my secretary, hereinafter referred to as Cuddles . . ."? Rodell chides his brethren of the bar for converting a common street brawl into a tort, misdemeanor or felony—and for labeling a payoff a "consideration." And what balanced observer has not winced at some lawyer's "party of the first part" dealing with a "party of the second part." A Canadian judge told me about a colleague who once wrote: "This court has to be in another court this afternoon." This kind of stilted self-respect is common: lawyers and judges refer to each other as learned brethren, however inappropriate the flattering reference may be.

Love of Bombast

Lawyers love bombastic and antediluvian language, like this excerpt from a divorce decree composed by a lawyer and signed by a judge:

There should be a finality to litigation; all types of evils can arise from a situation where a party seeks a divorce, such party obtains their own independent counsel, such counsel prepares agreements and documents to consummate a divorce, such counsel presents the documents to the Court and the same are approved by the Court and made a part of the final decree and thereafter the party who initiated such divorce action and sought such counsel and had the same presented to the Court challenged such agreement of the parties that became part of the divorce decree, no matter what the grounds of challenge might be.

In reviewing a recent book about crime and punishment written by a group of prominent lawyers and law professors, I came across this dense, heavy-handed sentence:

It may be possible to delineate the limits on magnitude better than we have done, but the foregoing should suffice to illustrate the basic idea; in deciding the magnitude of the scale, deterrence may be considered within whatever leeway remains after the outer bounds set by a scale of a certain magnitude has been chosen, however, the internal composition of the scale should be determined by the principle of commensurate deserts.

I once reviewed a proposed Corporate Employees Profit Sharing Plan drafted for a client of mine by an eminent tax lawyer. The plan included one provision that I kept rejecting because I never understood it. Despite my objections, the clause survived prolonged negotiations and now governs the company's employees:

318

Should Pretax Profit fall short of any year's target, the bonus pool for the year will be reduced linearly to zero at sixty percent of the profit target.

Judged by standards of esthetics, efficiency, or accuracy, legal language is deplorable. According to U.C.L.A. law professor David Mellinkoff, the problem arises because legal language comes from an archaic melting pot. The etymological sources of legal language are Celtic, Saxon, Jute, Danish, German, French, and Latin. We still use Old English (manslaughter, ward), Latin (de minimis, arguendo), Gallic (descent, fee tail, cy-pres), and such combinations as breaking and entering, free and clear (Old English and French), peace and quiet, will and testament (Latin and Old English).

Archaic language leads to awkward jargon. Phrases like "assume arguendo" and "ipso facto" pepper lawyers' conversation and briefs. For members of the bar, a case under consideration is a matter "sub judice"; something unique is "sui generis" to the attorney "in the abovementioned matter." This fluff is habitual, and it is confused with erudition.

Lawyer language is pompous. We address ourselves to arguments rather than discuss them; we would rather utilize something than use it. Lawyers use what Rodell has called "the backhanded passive," encumbering their remarks with such phrases (hedges) as "it would seem" and "it is suggested." They love polysyllabic prose, preferring "notwithstanding" to "despite" or "however" and loading on all the "alleges," "hereinafters," and "thereupons" that will fit their forms.

Stomp on It

Lawyers are so careful they become clumsy and repetitive. They alone find the need to "cease" as well as "desist," to "give" as well as "bequeath and devise." An Arkansas judge once told of a contempt order that was reported to have been "reversed, vacated, and held null and void"; he suggested that the judge add "and stomped on."

A legitimate reason for using imprecise language exists in the area of developing constitutional law where flexibility is necessary. The words "reasonable," "freedom," "equal protection," and "due process of law" need constant redefinition in light of changing times and mores. The story is told that after Solon wrote the ancient Greek constitution he left the country for several years so that he would not be asked to say what he meant by this word and that. Interpretation of subjective concepts should be left to active decision makers and to the inspiration of the times.

This virtue, however, does not apply to statutory language or the language of documents, judicial opinions or public statements of policy.

Courtroom talk is more baffling than it needs to be. "I direct your attention to October 1975, and ask you if there came a time when . . .'' takes the place of "What happened in October 1975?"

U.C.L.A. professor Mellinkoff, in his book THE LANGUAGE OF THE LAW, made this comment about a judge's long-winded instruction to a jury:

> During the course of these instructions the term "burden of proof" will be used. By "burden of proof" is meant the duty resting upon the party having the affirmative of an issue to satisfy or convince the jury to a reasonable certainty of the truth of the contentions of that party. . . .
>
> By "preponderance of the evidence" is meant the evidence which possesses the greater weight or convincing power. It is not enough that the evidence of the party upon whom the burden of proof rests is of slightly greater weight or convincing power; it must go further and satisfy or convince the minds of the jury before the burden of proof is discharged.

Mellinkoffs comment: "What a letdown! The judge would have done his job much better telling the jury: 'Jones brought this case to court and it is his job to satisfy you that Smith hit him.' "

I recall a Kentucky judge telling a jury in one case I tried that he wished he did not have to give long-winded technical instructions. Instead, he said, he would prefer to tell them what Andrew Jackson told a jury when he was on the bench in Tennessee: "Go out and do right by these people."

The style of legal writing is bad enough to warrant alarm and reform. In addition, bad substance follows bad form. Then, the consequences become doubly serious. Poor language, even erroneous punctuation, has caused litigation and brought about unwanted results. Consider some examples.

Many lawyers use forms and canned legal lingo. One attorney added a set clause to a will, directing the executor "to pay all my just debts" before distributing the estate's proceeds. A New York court ruled that the addition of this clause (not requested by the hapless client) revived a debt that had been barred by the statute of limitations. The client probably moaned from the grave, thinking about what he got for the fee he paid.

Faulty punctuation can cause serious problems. The Kentucky Court of Appeals was asked to interpret a clause in a will that gave a large estate to nine different individuals and institutions. The clause enumerated equal shares but did not place a semicolon between the names of two of the recipients as it did between the other seven. The question was whether there were eight or nine shares—whether the two individuals within but not separated by semicolons got a full one-ninth share each or divided a one-eighth share between them. A lot of money was transferred on the basis of the court's interpretation of a missing semicolon.

An administrative law judge for the Federal Power Commission told me about one case that turned on his interpretation of the tenses of words used in a scientist's report about logging practices on a certain river. Here is how he dealt with the question in his opinion:

> He was, after all, obviously not reporting ancient events. He said logs *"have been* thrown . . . and floated,"* they *"have been* converted,"* the *"rise of the water *has* commonly *carried* them safely"* and their *"passage over the falls *has* often *been* witnessed"* (my emphasis). In good usage the present perfect tense does not denote an action that terminated in the distant past; correctly used, it refers to a just-completed or recently completed event, and we must assume that Dewey was familiar with proper usage. Therefore, even if he had not himself been an eye-witness, there would be less reason to question his report than if he had described a long-past occurrence.

An Alabama judge told me about a divorce trial he presided over where the issue was whether the husband had committed adultery. The wife's lawyer asked a woman witness whether she had had sexual relations with the husband. She replied that she had. After her testimony was completed and as she was leaving the courtroom, she stopped, turned and asked the judge: "Did you mean to ask whether I had intercourse with this guy?" When the judge replied that this indeed was the purpose of the question, she returned to the witness stand and testified that she never had "intercourse," only "sexual relations." The witness had been more precise in her language than the lawyer. Loose legal language had almost turned the trial around.

When lawyers become public officials and make and interpret the law as judges and legislators, they compound all these problems. I hold Bachelor of Law, Master of Law and Doctorate of Law degrees; and I drown in the quagmire of dense, turgid, confusing, prolix prose found in the sections of the Internal Revenue Code. In a recent speech, Fred Emery, Director of the *Federal Register,* cited this example of statutory language from an NLRB regulation:

> To the extent that portions of the systems of records described in notices of governmentwide systems of records published by the Civil Service Commission are identified by those notices as being subject to the management of an officer of this agency, or an officer of this agency is designated as the official to contact for information, access or contest of those records, individual requests for access to those records, requests for their amendment and review of denials of request for amendment shall be in accordance with the provisions of 5 C.F.R. 297 subpart A, § 297.101 of this Title et seq. as promulgated by the Civil Service Commission. Review of a refusal to inform an individual whether such a system of records con-

321

tains a record pertaining to that individual, and review of a refusal to grant an individual's request for access to a record in such a system may be obtained in accordance with the provisions of paragraph (j) of this section.

I wince at most judicial opinions; they commonly are full of thoughtless jargon, bumptious imprecision, faulty punctuation and grammar, clumsy structure, and stilted style.

Part of the judges' problem is that no one dares to question or challenge their writing styles. Columnist James J. Kilpatrick recently lamented about an afternoon he spent reading a batch of Supreme Court opinions without finding a simple, good sentence. He cited examples of writing that made him gasp: Justice Rehnquist's reference to "lacuna in a statute" and his question whether "the power of Congress may be thought to ex proprio vigore apply to the power . . ."; and Justice Marshall's comment that "none of the cases are to the contrary." Kilpatrick concluded with prickly but appropriate words:

> These birds are busy writing the supreme law of the land. They are dealing with the great gut issues of our country—racial tensions, sexual discrimination, employment, education, politics, religious freedom, criminal trials. Yes, they must try to write precisely. But do they have to write precisely turgidly? Can't they write precisely lucidly instead?

In the last several years, I have lectured frequently to trial and appellate judges on judicial writing. Most judges are bad writers, but they are both glad and quick to improve.

It is time we lawyers improved our language. Unfortunately, Rodell's dated and hyperbolic charge—that lawyers are "purveyors of pretentious poppycock" whose "writing style is unfit for the consumption of cultured men"—still hits uncomfortably close to home. Rodell once said that "there are two things wrong with legal writing. One is its style. The other is its content." The former problem is easy to tackle. We just have to acknowledge the problem, learn and relearn the fundamentals of good writing, and put these lessons into practice. We should do it.

The Risk of Non-Persuasion: An Irreverent View

by John L. Kane, Jr.

As every law student, whether boy or girl, man or woman, knows, there are some rules or concepts of law that are never understood or followed by the courts or by practitioners. I am reminded of the rather mediocre lawyer who once told his former professor, Thompson Marsh, that in the twenty years following graduation from law school he had never seen a Rule Against Perpetuities problem. Dr. Marsh replied, ''I believe it.''

Another frequently ignored fundamental concept is that the burden of proof never shifts. Yet, the reporter system is replete with shifting burdens of proof. They are about as transient as sand dunes. It is conceptually impossible to shift the burden of proof, but I think it is unfair to accuse appellate courts of sloppy thinking on that ground. After all, the appellate courts, we know, base their opinions on the record and, certainly, trial lawyers and trial judges are none too neat about the distinction between the burden of proof and the burden of going forward. I am sure that some of the lawyers who have appeared in my court would ask, ''What the hell is that?''

The distinction, of course, is best explained by what legal scholars call ''The risk of non-persuasion.'' Stated in its simplest terms, this fundamental rule of evidence is that the party who asserts the affirmative of an issue bears the burden of persuading the trier of fact that the assertion is proven, and that burden remains with that party until the termination of the action. The risk of not persuading is loss of the issue. The importance of this rule to the rest of this article cannot be understated.

Dean Wigmore explained the concept with his customary clarity:

> When the proponent has been able to adduce evidence which if believed would make it beyond reason to repudiate the proponent's

John L. Kane, Jr. is a United States District Judge for the District of Colorado.

claim, unless the opponent now offers evidence against the claim and thus changes the situation, the trier of facts should not be allowed to render a verdict against reason, i.e., against the evidence. And the stronger the prima facie case established by the plaintiff, the correspondingly more persuasive must be the evidence in rebuttal.

As I view the matter, the risk of non-persuasion is not limited to the cold record on appeal. It is truly the basis of the skill and the art of advocacy. (There are indeed more things in heaven and on earth, Horatio, than are dreamt of in your philosophy of evidence.) Human actions, motives and character, as well as the facts and circumstances of daily existence, are constantly brought into question. They are, by their very nature, only contingent and, at best, probable. Nothing of these things can be predicted with certainty nor can they be reduced to necessary laws. At most, human nature is only probable. Within this fog of the unexpected, the lawyer must persuade. He must be able to convince others that his perception of the probable is the correct one, the right one, the true one. The risk of non-persuasion is the failure to communicate; it is the absence of wit; it is the lack of precision and the lack of poignancy. The risk of non-persuasion is the acquired means by which lawyers lose lawsuits.

Fog of the Unexpected

I have been on the bench for only a very brief time, but in my short stay I have attempted to gather some of the choicer bits of non-persuading utterance in order to illustrate my observation.

For instance—(and I hasten to add that the following are actual comments made on the record—only the names have been omitted to protect the guilty)—we can begin with none more graphic than this gem in the diadem of rhetoric:

THE COURT: Are you ready for trial, Mr. Prosecutor?

ANSWER: Yes, your Honor.

THE COURT: Are you ready for trial, Mr. Defense Counsel?

ANSWER: In this matter, I did file a motion in this case. I would say that I would prefer it, and will formally move that the defendant be granted a trial continuance at this time. I have been in touch with the prosecutor. This case involves—well, without going into too much detail, we have had some relationship throughout this matter, this year, with the principal detective on the case. There have been negotiations, there have been—there's been some cooperation, there have been some disappointments. This case has involved this kind of relationship, this kind of activity, and I have been involved myself at the fringe of the discussion both with the defendant and the detective in regard to the kind of subject matter this case involves, and some further plans for activity from time to time, I might say. At this particular time I reasonably anticipated a disposition based on certain responses to the detective and, apparently it is not—it's not going to be disposed of. And I don't know whether the relationship, the productive relationship. . .

THE COURT: Let me ask you a question.

Direct Easiest?

I have heard some lawyers say that direct examination is the easiest part of the trial. Apparently, it is not. Try, for example, the following questions asked on various direct examinations:

• • •

Q: Did you keep that in your possession all the time that you had it?

Q: Generally speaking, sir, what were the specific instructions which you understood were given to her by you?

• • •

Q: Was this conversation reduced to writing?

A: No, it was oral.

Q: Where is it?

• • •

Q: And these pictures were—this is—these are not—one of these pictures reflects—were any of these—none of them reflect what the condition was on September 1st, is that correct?

• • •

Q: Well, the First Bank is not the first, is it? Actually the First was second or third—I can't remember which, but I do know that the First wasn't first—maybe it was First Federal. What was it?

• • •

Q: How was the agreement physically executed?

• • •

Q: Did you have any nonpersonal notice?

• • •

Q: Isn't it inferentially obvious?

• • •

Of course not all *bons mots* surface in the sea of direct examination. What tributes, what glories have not been paid to that greatest of all instruments—cross-examination! Masters of the art are heralded for centuries: Even prophets and seers are held in less esteem than a merely *good* cross-examiner. But, I submit, not enough attention is given to the

325

more pedestrian practitioners, who, in their own right, deserve at least a footnote on advocacy's page of history.

For example, we all know that a good cross-examiner never asks an open-ended question. But do we know why? Listen and learn!

Q: Well, just what do you suffer from?

A: I suffer from high blood pressure, nose bleeds, hypertension, diabetes, hernia, hemorrhoids, headaches, emphysema, prostate problems, arthritis, chemical burns from accidentally swallowing poisonous pills and from depression.

Q: I didn't ask you what caused the chemical burns. Just answer the question. Why are you depressed?

A: My high blood pressure causes nosebleeds which result in my missing work. I bleed all over the bricks and scaffold and I'm unable to stop the flow of blood. The diabetes causes me to be very tired so I cannot work very fast. My hernia keeps me from lifting heavy things and causes me to walk with difficulty. The hemorrhoids have the same effect as the hernia. My emphysema makes it difficult for me to breathe and results in my having dizzy spells and blacking out. The prostate problems cause a continuous burning and I have trouble urinating so it takes me longer to go to the bathroom. It takes me 20 or 30 minutes to urinate. My sinus trouble results in my not being able to breathe well and contributes to my headaches. Since I have to breathe through my mouth and breathe in the industrial dust my emphysema is worsened. My problems with my teeth including swollen jaws and abscessed gums contribute to my generally run-down condition. As a result of my arthritis my arms get numb and working together with my poor circulation causes my hands and arms to "go to sleep." As a result I lack mobility in my joints. These things make it difficult for me to function as well as I would like and that's why I'm depressed.

Q: You're not a psychiatrist, are you?

A: No, sir.

Q: Well, you just don't want to work for a living, do you?

A: I plan to return to work as a bricklayer just as soon as my health improves.

Gave Dog Away

Of course not all of these things happen in federal court. In a divorce case in the state court, an attorney was apparently cross-examining the defendant wife:

Q: You gave his dog away, didn't you?

A: Yes.

Q: Why?

A: Because he needed to be chained constantly, because he would go over the fence and neighbors threatened me with everything that you could possibly imagine if the dog ever got loose again. The dog was so strong he had to be chained with an automobile chain, not a dog chain. And even though he had that chain, he managed to get out of it several times. The chains cost $8 apiece, and I bought four of them. When he got loose, he ate fences, trees, shrubs, and patio carpeting. I left him in the house one day because I didn't have a chain and he took up the carpeting—it was an empty room, except it had a phone and carpeting—and he ate the phone to the point where the phone company charged me $13 for the phone because they said it was malicious damage.

Q: Who did you give the dog to?

A: The Police Department.

THE COURT: Did he consume the phone?

A: Yes. There was nothing left but the wires.

Q: And the radio, is that a fact?

A: Yes.

Q: Did he really eat the radio, too?

A: Yes, he really ate it.

Q: Okay.

THE COURT: Did he enjoy it?

A: I guess so. He kept doing it.

You may wonder whether judges ever listen to attorneys in oral argument. I must confess that, at first, I did not pay as much attention to this aspect of the trial as I did to others. Once my appetite was whetted, however, I became obsessed with listening to oral argument. Where else can you hear people with a minimum of seven years of higher education, specially trained in the art of logic, express themselves with such heated eloquence. Here is my favorite:

COUNSEL: Your honor, if you do that you will just unleash a can of worms.

THE COURT: Well, I certainly don't want to do that.

COUNSEL: I knew you'd see it my way.

THE COURT: The prospect is stupifying.

COUNSEL: Yes. Yes!

THE COURT: How would I ever leash them again?

COUNSEL: I beg your pardon?

Perhaps the following colloquy is more appropriate to a discussion of anthropology, but its elephantine characteristics suggest that I share it with you.

COUNSEL: Your honor, the rules require you to modify the pretrial order in order to prevent mammoth injustice.

THE COURT: They do?

COUNSEL: Rule 16 says so.

THE COURT: I didn't know that. What is mammoth injustice?

COUNSEL: It's great injustice.
THE COURT: I should think so. Is it anything like manifest injustice?
COUNSEL: Oh, yeah. It's the same thing.
THE COURT: Well then, we'll do our best to prevent it.

On another occasion, one of our most distinguished attorneys re-vealed the heretofore unknown connection between logic and nude sunbathers. In rebutting, as it were, the argument of defense counsel the learned gentleman said:
COUNSEL: Your honor, that argument is tan genital.
THE COURT: It is?
COUNSEL: It's tan genital; it doesn't even address the point.
THE COURT: What does it do?
COUNSEL: It goes out in left field somewhere. It just drops.
THE COURT: It doesn't drop in court, does it?
COUNSEL: Not even in this lawsuit.
THE COURT: I suppose that's why it's tan.

Not all arguments, of course, are addressed to or undressed for the court. Sometimes a budding Darrow will shatter a jury's sensibilities. Try this somewhat risky technique in your next closing argument:

> Ladies and Gentlemen of the jury, the prosecutor has made much of my client's stating that he can smell cops a mile away even though he admittedly spent three days in a station wagon with these four undercover agents. Well, they're not really cops— they're just as crooked as my client is.

We will have to leave for another time comment on lawyers' writing styles as an instrument of non-persuasion. For the moment suffice it to say that gibberish is not confined to oral presentations.

I wish to close by paying a small tribute to wit. Clearly, the time spent in writing or reading this article is more than justified if it does nothing more than encourage the use and development of wit. Surely wit is more than a mere weapon in the lawyer's arsenal. Its tactical employment is always devastating. But, more importantly, wit serves to place things in proper perspective. Wit is a virtue "devoutly to be wished." As Leon Harris said in his excellent book, THE FINE ART OF POLITICAL WIT:

> Wit may not be so noble as courage, nor so elevating as faith. How-ever, as it is given to man and not to other animals to know that he thinks and to laugh, so to men of wit is given that special felicitous perception of the comical, the ludicrous, and the absurd and that special insight which sees new associations between ideas and words not usually seen. So wit may lead (in law], as in other areas of human life, to wisdom and courage and perhaps even uphold if not lead to faith.

By the way, did you hear about the two lawyers. . . .

The Rhetorical Question and Other Forensic Speculations

by Jacob A. Stein

Some years ago, on a rainy evening in lonesome October and almost on impulse, I attended a lecture on the trial of cases given by James McArdle of Pittsburgh, Pennsylvania. Those who saw and heard Mr. McArdle during the years of his great courtroom accomplishments knew they were in the presence of a born advocate. What came naturally to Jim McArdle must be studied and practiced by the rest of us who are less fortunately endowed. I discovered that evening, as rain splashed against the window of the room we were in, his heavy reliance on a question-and-answer technique. He repeatedly asked questions of himself and then answered them. The dialogue gathered interest in a way that uninterrupted narrative cannot. Once I grasped the method, I found myself using it in both civil and criminal cases, in opening statements and in closing arguments.

The questions posed in such a dialogue parallel those that must certainly arise in the minds of judge and jury. These questions are the "who," "what," "where," "why" and "when" questions that journalists use in drafting news stories to gain quick interest and to inform. Not only must we gain quick interest and inform, we must also persuade. We can do this by asking the right questions and giving the right answers.

And now let us examine the use of the rhetorical question in the opening statement. I shall try to reproduce Jim McArdle's words in giving the illustrative statement he used in opening a simple traffic accident case for the plaintiff.

"Ladies and gentlemen of the jury, you must be asking yourselves

The author is a member of the Washington, D.C., law firm of Stein, Mitchell & Mezines; Adjunct Professor of Law, George Washington University Law School and Georgetown University Law School; and the author of LEGAL SPECTATOR (George Psalmanazer Press, Washington, D.C., 1976).

who is my client and what does he want. I represent Roger Fry. He is a young man. He is what is called a blue-collar worker. He works with his hands. He liked working long hours as a steamfitter. What does he want in this lawsuit? He wants to justify your decision to give money damages.

"Why does he think he's justified in bringing this case before you? The answer to this question takes us back to January 3, 1975. Why that day? Because on that day my client was a healthy, happy man driving through the intersection of Connecticut Avenue and L Street, Northwest in Washington, D.C. The defendant put an end to his happiness and his health by driving his big Chrysler through a red light and ramming Roger Fry's car. What injuries did Roger suffer when his car was rammed by the defendant's Chrysler? He hit his knee inside the car. The flesh, the ligaments and the knee cap were so badly twisted and torn that the doctors couldn't help him without a complicated operation.

"Were there any witnesses to this collision? Well, the police came to the scene and asked that same question. Frank Scott came forth. Who is Frank Scott? He is a young student. He had been in a nearby book store when he stepped outside and saw the defendant's car go right through the red light."

That is my recollection of the commencement of the opening statement Jim delivered accompanied by his dramatic gestures. Of course, there are differences in detail, but the style—the use of the question and answer scheme—is accurate.

Writing a Play

Asking the question—whom do I represent?—starts a line of inquiry that puts you in the role of a playwright. And just as a playwright, you must select those details from your client's background and personality that bring him to life in the minds of your audience, the judge and the jury. The important must be separated from the unimportant; then from the important must be selected the most important of all for your purposes. Much must be excluded. A touch here and a stroke there and a human being comes alive. What I describe can be illustrated by Thornton Wilder's handling of characterization in his moving play, *Our Town*. Here is the way Wilder chose to identify the cultural attitudes of the lives of the simple, hard-working people who live a small town life:

> LADY IN A BOX: Oh, Mr. Webb? Mr. Webb, is there any culture or love of beauty in Grovers' Corners?
>
> MR. WEBB: Well, ma'am, there ain't much—not in the sense you mean. Come to think of it, there's some girls that play the piano at High School Commencement; but they ain't happy

about it. No, ma'm, there isn't much culture; but maybe this is the place to tell you that we've got a lot of pleasures of a kind here: we like the sun comin' up over the mountain in the morning, and we all notice a good deal about the birds. We pay a lot of attention to them. And we watch the change of the seasons; yes, everybody knows about them. But those other things—you're right, ma'am,—there ain't much.—Robinson Crusoe and the Bible; and Handel's 'Largo,' we all know that; and Whistler's Mother—those are just about as far as we go.

We now know these people. We are interested in them and what happens to them.

David Napley in his book, THE TECHNIQUE OF PERSUASION, (London: Sweet & Maxwell, 1975), suggests that the opening statement in a bench trial should conclude with the statement, "Your honor, by my submission, the questions you will have to ask yourself when you have heard all the evidence are five in number, and are as follows. . . ." Napley says at that point the judge will realize you know your business and will write down the questions.

Now that we have found a way to put together an opening statement, let us look for the secret of closing arguments.

The secret of the closing argument is that there is no secret to it. No secret that was not well known eighteen or more centuries ago when the Greeks and Romans examined the problem.

If you read Cicero, you will be struck by how contemporaneous his comments are. In fact, you may even wonder if the translation is accurate.

If two thousand years have brought nothing much new about closing argument, why is the subject so frequently discussed and studied by lawyers in quest of novel insights and techniques? The answer may be found in the analogy that centuries have gone by and nothing new has been said on the art of lovemaking, but this inhibits no one from explaining what successes he has had through different techniques, and like lovemaking, the making of the closing argument is a talkative passion. It has another similarity to *ars amandi*. Everybody needs constant reassurance and supportive counseling.

Let it be understood that a good closing may not win the case. You have given bad ones and won. You have watched and heard some of the worst ever given, while you gave one of the best that was ever given, and you received absolutely nothing from the jury. In most cases, what precedes the closing argument determines the effects that are possible.

Therefore, let us give attention to the general pattern of a jury trial. If thoughtfully arranged, the trial may parallel a morality play. This art form arose in England in the 1500s. It has continued in one way or another ever since. The conception is quite fundamental. Each character in the morality play took the name of the vice or virtue he was to personify. The play divided itself into three parts: first the prologue, then the play itself, and finally the epilogue. You see the similarity to the pattern of the jury trial. You tell them what you are going to do. You do it. You then tell them that you did it.

The prologue states how vice is overcome by virtue. Then the play itself takes place and virtue does overcome vice.

In the epilogue, the narrator comes on stage and announces that vice has been overcome by virtue.

Victory Insured

If the trial takes that course, everything has been done to insure victory. Vice threatens to win because of the unscrupulous tactics of the defendant, and then suddenly virtue is able to overcome his cunning. If you can bring such a thing off, you have participated in an art form with a long and great tradition.

Turning from the production of the play, let us look at the auditors, the jury. Every rhetorical effect must take into consideration the audience. What changes overcome people when they become jurors? First of all, a jury room is the perfect setting for an outcropping of hypocrisy. Here are twelve people with the fate of another in their hands. The situation has a moral tone. The jurors are convened to examine the morality of another.

Take a case where the plaintiff is with somebody else's wife. There is a rear-end collision. Mrs. Somebody Else's Wife flees. The plaintiff is standing there with his hand on his neck. The policeman asks, ''Who was that who ran from the car?'' The person who struck the car in the rear in most cases does not know that Mrs. Somebody Else's Wife was involved, so along the lines of relevance that would have little to do with the lawsuit. But as the case comes to trial, it is the dominant problem in the plaintiff's lawyer's mind.

Should it be met head-on? Should it be disguised?

If you decide to confront it, how would it best be done? If success can be drawn from such a situation, it can be extracted by reminding each juror that he took an oath to ignore and repel attempts to mislead him, and draw him away from the evidence.

I once heard an elderly lawyer say in a case of this kind that to exploit a situation such as this requires a certain amount of cruelty when you are the beneficiary of it, and the beneficiary is going to be the defendant's lawyer. There may be people on the jury who are cruel, and one will vote for a defendant's verdict. On the other hand, there may be people on the jury who will respect their oath courageously. If they are not cruel they may ultimately prevail. I was not there when the jury returned its verdict so I do not know whether the technique of confrontation worked.

The worst closing argument is one that takes a case you would have won if you had not made the argument and turns it into a loser. Unfortunately, that happens.

So how can this be avoided? If your argument is an attempt to be objective and sincere, you will not lose a case because of your closing argument; you may even win one. Objectivity, then, is important.

How is objectivity demonstrated? First of all, you must admit to the jury that you will overstep the bounds of objectivity. It is likely that having the responsibility for the plaintiff's case, having known the plaintiff, having heard for a period of time his troubles, you will probably be too enthusiastic, and may overstate the case. That is all right. You are an advocate.

You can go on to explain that the responsibility of the jury is to correct any of your overzealousness. This approach creates a threshold credibility.

But if you say thereafter that even though there was no property damage and the plaintiff was not treated for six months after the accident, you are still entitled to $40,000, then you have destroyed whatever credibility you had.

A feeling exists on the part of some who have tried few cases but written much that there is room for a great deal of innovation within the framework of a closing argument. That probably is not true. It is dangerous to depart from the orthodox.

This may be so because speaking and writing are such different projects. When you write, you can be imaginative and introduce new principles. If the person who is reading what you have written does not understand it, you can hope he will come back and review it. That is not true in speaking. You speak once and for all, and the person either gets it or he does not.

Lloyd George, who was a powerful speaker, and who, by the way, gave Winston Churchill many of his turns of phrase, said the art of public speaking was the art of saying the same thing in many different ways. So it is with closing argument. You cannot go far beyond the platitudes. If you do, you are beyond your peers. If you try an entirely different technique, the audience is baffled.

The jury expects the use of words that have a legal ring. They are prepared to hear argument in moral terms. They will be disturbed if your argument sounds too different from the judge's charge.

If your voice has the ring of objectivity like the judge's should, if your tone draws off enmity which builds up like static electricity during a trial, I suspect the jury would identify you with the judge.

All I have said is summed up in a verse I like:

Begin slow,

Speak low,
Take fire,
Rise higher.
When most impressed,
Be self-possessed.
Give a bit of new thought
   but always to an old tune;
Then you end
   unexpectedly soon.

Basic Values and Techniques of Persuasion

by Craig Spangenberg

I learned to ride a bicycle the way most kids do, I suppose. I got on, wobbled and fell, remounted and fell. I finally began to move slowly and erratically, fighting for balance. Eventually I thought I had learned how to ride and how to go faster. Inevitably I miscalculated the traction of the tires on a hard turn, and the bike skidded and went down. The result was torn pants and a bleeding, skinned knee. After several falls, torn pants and skinned knees, I finally had some competence in riding a two-wheeler. You can learn to make a final argument in much the same way, the difference being that the scars will be on your client instead of you.

For about the first ten years of practice I took some pride—entirely misplaced—in never repeating a line of argument or an analogy. When my inventive talent ran out, I began to cull over those that had worked and those that had not, to repeat the ones that worked, and to select those that worked best. In time, I became curious to know why they worked. After many hours of reading in psychology and reviewing effective arguments, I came to some conclusions about why an argument works and why it does not—or, by analogy, how you can ride a bicycle with effective control.

The general principles of final argument can be applied not only to jury arguments, but to any argument to any court and, indeed, to a debate with your friends. In trials, however, the argument occupies a special place. After the argument comes the verdict. To me that is the starting place to plan the trial.

You know what verdict you want. The verdict is preceded by the jury deliberation, which you hope to have influenced by the whole trial. Cer-

The author is a partner in the Cleveland firm of Spangenberg, Shibley, Traci & Lancione. This article is based on a speech videotaped by the Association of Trial Lawyers of America.

tainly it is influenced by the judge's charge. The final argument, which precedes the charge, must relate to that charge. It must reinforce what is the judge's final argument to the jury. The argument should both follow the evidence and anticipate the court's charge by showing the jury how the instructions will apply to the facts it finds from the evidence. The evidence, in turn, follows the opening statement, which is designed to highlight the strongest evidence. The opening statement itself should anticipate the final argument.

In one sense, at least, the opening statement is more important than final argument. If the task were to achieve liability, and I could make only one argument to the jury, I would certainly make the opening statement. But if the object is to generate a substantial award of money damages, then final argument is more important. As a result, my opening statement is largely about liability. I confine the discussion of damages to a review of the injury and a general statement that we will ask for a substantial award of money damages. The final argument comes after the jury has achieved some emotional rapport with the case and has some understanding of the gravity of the injuries. At that point the jury is more receptive to an argument on how much money it should take to compensate for those injuries.

Four-Part Structure

The structure of final argument consists of four parts: the introduction, the argument on liability, the argument on damages, and the summation. The introduction is not to be viewed lightly. It must be designed to lift the jurors out of their everyday context—to make them aware that they are more than just people who are sitting there, doing something mundane. It must lift them to the very highest levels of the value systems of our society.

What are those values? They are all familiar. You might call them the standard corn. But do not negate corn. It has as much validity as folk-myth. Fundamental beliefs of our people, I think, are that every individual should be respected; that all people should be treated justly and fairly; that truth is admirable, falsehood despicable; that hard work, industry and thrift are the proper way to success; and that sloth and shoddy workmanship should not be tolerated. I think that Americans generally revere the Declaration of Independence and the Constitution. We also revere the underdog. It is a great thing when he overcomes the obstacles and wins. But of these and other value systems, certainly the highest value is placed on the concept of justice. It has been rightly said that justice is the greatest concern of all government and that the search for justice is one of the noblest aspirations of all mankind.

It follows that if the lawyer can equate the award of a large verdict with the dispensation of great justice he is much more likely to get that award than if he asks the jury for a handout. Of course, charity has a place in the value system, too. It is a good thing. But it ranks very low on the scale and is likely to be considered an obligation of conscience that can be dispensed with on a fairly penurious level. Proof? When the Salvation Army worker on the corner rings her Christmas bell beside the iron kettle, it is rare that a man of wealth puts in a twenty-dollar bill. He feels impelled to give something, but he soothes his conscience quite easily with a quarter.

The introductory appeal to a jury, then, should be designed not to generate feelings that it ought to be charitable, ought to be sympathetic, ought to give the plaintiff something, but rather to impress the jury with the importance of its part in the search for truth and justice. The introduction also must satisfy the needs of the jurors as human beings.

We all have very basic needs, indeed. They include the need to be appreciated, the need for self-esteem, the need for self-realization, the need to feel we have some control over the events around us. Every juror would like to feel he has some power to shape the world, to control his own destiny and, in a small way, that of others as well. Your argument will certainly be more appealing if the jurors feel they can take pride in the verdict you want them to reach and can exercise some great power to right a fundamental wrong.

This general tone should help shape the argument without letting it become condescending. I should hardly waste time by telling you *not to* talk down to the jury, the common admonition to young lawyers. The reason for that warning is simply this: talking down to anyone attacks his self-esteem. To persuade the person with whom you discuss a proposition, you must treat him with respect. You must treat him with words, tone, and manner as your full intellectual equal and fortify his own sense of worth.

Exalted Sense

What, then, does one bring together to start a final argument? In the opening of the argument, in about a paragraph, counsel should weave together the power of the jury, Divine Providence, the Declaration of Independence if not the Constitution, and the search for truth and justice, and literally leave the jury with a sense of exaltation. This will not take long; but though short, it sets the tone and is of primary importance.

Having finished the introduction, you must turn your attention to the body of the argument. Now there is another question. Should you argue liability? I realize I have said you control liability with the opening statement. You remember the Chicago jury studies, which said that 80 percent of the jurors made up their minds irrevocably on opening statement and never changed them, no matter what the evidence was. That leaves 20 percent still to be persuaded, and I think one needs to fortify the 80 percent. Should you argue the liability issues? Certainly. In great detail?

Probably not, unless a particular detail is conclusive. You can often argue many points quite simply by quick reference to some striking piece of testimony.

Next, how should you organize your argument on liability? You may, for example, have four excellent reasons why you believe your client should win the verdict, but these are of varying strengths and cogencies. Do you start with the weaker ones, build up to a crescendo and give the crushing hammer blow last? Or start with the strongest argument, then descend in rank to the weakest? To psychologists, the question is whether to argue "climax to anticlimax" or "anticlimax to climax." A good many tests have been run on this point. Generally, the more persuasive arguments follow the pattern of "climax-anticlimax"—they use the strongest argument first. It certainly has been the more successful approach for me.

But there is another reason for using this pattern. The idea a person holds often becomes a part of his personality. If you attack the idea, you insult the person. The plaintiff's lawyer has the opening argument, and he must use his most powerful argument to convince the jury that his side is right. He will not only have the juror's mind fixed in that direction, but will also have this advantage: the defense attorney who attacks that opinion will often be insulting the juror who has already reached that opinion. Psychologists differ on how many people are subject to this pattern of personality extension, but a common estimate is that about half the population exhibits the phenomenon in varying degrees. It all means that whether you start strong or end strong it is a mistake to save your best argument for rebuttal, deliberately risking a hostile reaction.

Should you anticipate the defense arguments? Here I give an unqualified yes. It is more persuasive to weaken a counterargument in advance than to try to answer it later. And, by the time you reach final argument, you should know from the defense lawyer's opening statement and his line of questions what he is thinking about.

There is another important point. The judge will finish the case with his charge, and the jury will then indulge in its own argument in the jury room. In normal human behavior, many of the beliefs we hold or the opinions we reach are based on an emotional reaction, a "feeling," that seems to rise from the lower abdomen. However, human beings take great pride in their powers of intelligence and reasoning. Even though our opinions may come from "feelings," they must be supported by an apparently intelligent reason. So, reasons are invented by the brain to justify the "feelings."

If you have done your job throughout the trial, when the jury retires you will have some friend on it ready to take up your cause. It is essential that your friend in the jury room not be forced to say, "I think the plaintiff ought to win because he ought to win." Instead, he must be able to say, "I think the plaintiff should win because: point one, point two, point three."

Certainly you ought to be able to give him better arguments than he can think up himself. That is what lawyers are trained to do. Therefore, give supportive arguments for your position so that your friend may use them in the jury room. This leads to the next question: To what extent do you appeal to the juror's emotions?

Appeal to Reason

Again, psychological testing has been done on this point with results lawyers probably will not believe. Appeals to reason are better than appeals to emotion. They are more important and more lasting. Very strong emotion somehow blocks the mind so completely that it cannot reason. If a person is caught up in an emotional storm, he will have very little memory of what was going on. He will have a strong memory of his feeling, but he will not be able to reason. On the other hand, dry appeals to pure intellect with no emotional content are not very persuasive, either. They seem to have little power to penetrate. A good argument, therefore, is more reasonable than emotional, but some emotional content is necessary. The proof comes from the high school football coach at halftime who tells his team to "win this one for the Gipper." He knows he can whip up his adolescent boys so they charge out of the locker room with tears streaming down their cheeks. For five minutes they will be supermen. After that, disaster. Emotion does not last long.

Suppose you give the jurors a rousing emotional speech and bring tears to their eyes. If they could decide the verdict right then, you might win. But they are not going to do that. They are going to be cooled off for an hour or more by a judge reading a long charge. They will go to lunch, then pick a foreman, start to debate, and come back the next morning. By this time they will hate you because you made them cry in public. Indeed they will. That is a breach of manners. If you make them take off the social mask, they will not forgive you the next day.

Do Not Make Them Cry

I have the ability to make juries cry; in fact as a *tour de force* I have made court reporters and lawyers cry in mock trials. It is not all that big a trick. But I do not make a jury cry. When I see their eyes get a little misty, I stop the emotional appeal, back off, go to something else, and then perhaps get them misty again. We want a little emotion, but not an overt display.

Emotional content comes not so much from words as from the voice and manner, from the techniques of nonverbal communication. I am very much impressed with the work of men like Professor Ray Birdwhistell, who insists that more than 50 percent of all communication between human beings is done nonverbally—that is, by eyebrow, ear, shoulders, set, movement, tone. His observations are true. Because they are true, a lawyer cannot fake his way through a case and con a jury into a verdict he does not believe in himself. The jurors will know they are being conned; they will resent being thought of as such easy marks. A sure way to lose is to think you are smart enough to win a case you should not win. The sincerity of a lawyer who knows that his client is entitled to win and that justice demands a verdict for him is the greatest part of final argument. It does not matter *how* you achieve this conviction, but you cannot make a successful argument unless you have it.

What other emotions do you reach for? A big question for the lawyer is deciding between love and hate. Should you go into a savage attack on the defendant and his counsel? Should you try to convince the jury to hate the defendant for what he has done, or for the false defense he has tried to raise? Cases where one should do that are rare indeed. While people may think hate is the most powerful emotion, it is not. Love is. Witness the Christian religion for some proof of that. And the appeal to love—love for fellow man, love for the plaintiff, love even for the fellow lawyer who does not deserve it—is much more moving to the jury than an attack on another person. In fact, attack is very likely to make the jury feel uncomfortable. When an argument occurs on a sidewalk and voices are raised, notice how people will circle at great distance to avoid it. They do not want to be confronted with it.

Similarly, one may approach damages in two ways: first, as a fine or punishment to be levied on the defendant for what he did; second, as the payment of an obligation. In the value system of American society, we do not cotton very much to punishment, but we do believe people should keep their word, pay their obligations, and pay them on time. A friend of mine who had access to credit records kept track of his juries for three or four years to see who were the best plaintiff's jurors. He found that the best had "double A" credit ratings. They paid their bills before they were due. To these people, paying a debt is an important part of their lives. So arguments that approach damages as the way to make the person whole, to restore what has been taken away, arguments, in short, that ask the defendant to pay his debt are more effective than arguments that seek punishment.

How does one balance his time between opening and closing for the plaintiff? The defendant has no choice; he makes one argument. The plaintiff may split. My own answer is that the opening argument should be complete, as if it were the only statement you were permitted to make. When you are through, you should have covered every element of the case. You should not sandbag, saving your best points for last. Put up your first argument for opposing counsel to shoot at. If it is good enough, he will not shoot it down, and in closing, you can remind the jury that he has not.

In my practice, rebuttal argument is very short, usually breathless, hasty, running through points. The argument has already been made.

If I have convinced the jurors in my opening argument that I am right, the defendant may shake them a little, and a short rebuttal should bring them back. But if I make a weak opening and leave the jury with unresolved questions, I allow the defendant to make up their minds in his favor with a powerful argument. Then I will not change their minds on closing, no matter what I say.

Double Damages

When you come to damages, how much should you ask for? That is easy: twice as much as you want. Not one-and-a-half times, not five times, twice as much. The Chicago jury studies showed that jury after jury started its discussion at the halfway point. The lawyer asked for fifty thousand and tried to justify it. The first suggestion on the damage deliberations was: "What would you think of twenty-five thousand?" The higher the figure asked for, the higher the result, until the amount asked for looked greedy, overreaching, grasping. Then there would sometimes be a verdict for the defense in punishment for the grasping, greedy, overreaching lawyer. So although counsel must ask for enough, one does not want to ask for too much. If what is really wanted from the jury—and what a reasonable verdict would be—is five thousand, then ask for ten. If you think it is a hundred and fifty thousand, ask for three hundred. But justify that amount of money with some logic.

The "Rousements"

After the defense has argued and you rise to rebut, you can show a little more emotion. This is what we call fondly the "rousements." Here you can use scorn, ridicule, and vehemence, but it is important to show that the object of your anger or ridicule is the argument or the ideas of opposing counsel or the testimony of the defendant. Do not look in a juror's eyes and roar at him over something the defense lawyer said. It will only make the jury uncomfortable, particularly if you are so excited that streams of saliva spread over the jury. If you are going to declaim and carry on and pound and shout, aim it all toward your opponent: "Why do you insult the minds of this jury? Why demean their intelligence with this concocted story that you were only going forty miles an hour and at forty skidded 260 feet and hit another car so hard it was airborne for twenty feet?" When you say this, look at the fellow who said it. When the jury knows the assertion is ridiculous, you can give voice to its belief. You can show scorn and anger when you sense the jury wants you to. Here you follow the jurors instead of leading them.

All of these techniques are important. But there is one device I think is more valuable than the others. The greatest weapon in the arsenal of persuasion is the analogy, the story, the simple comparison to a familiar subject. Nothing can move the jurors more convincingly than an apt comparison to something they know from their own experience is true.

It is worth some real effort to develop analogies to use in final argument. But a word of caution. Before you use one, test it against all the ways it might be turned around and used against you. Here are some stories that have worked for me. The first helps explain circumstantial evidence:

This reminds me of my father reading *Robinson Crusoe* to me when I was a little boy. Remember when Robinson Crusoe was on the island for such a long time all alone? One morning he went down to the beach and there was a footprint in the sand. Knowing that someone else was on the island, he was so overcome with emotion, he fainted.

And why did he faint? Did he see a man? He woke to find Friday standing beside him, who was to be his friend on the island, but he didn't see Friday. Did he see a foot? No. He saw a footprint. That is, he saw marks in the sand, the kind of marks that are made by a human foot. He saw circumstantial evidence. But it was true, it was valid, it was compelling, as it would be to all of you. We live with it all our lives. So let's look at the facts of this case for those tracks that prove the truth.

Here is another argument, this one on the point that what is ordinary care depends upon the circumstances:

If you were loading potatoes into a wagon in the field, you'd pick them up on the fork and heave them toward the wagon. You wouldn't be much concerned if one potato fell off, would you? One potato isn't worth much, and if it fell off, it wouldn't hurt anyone. But suppose you were loading nitroglycerin. Then how carefully, how gingerly you would carry it and place it in someone else's hands, wrapped in foam or cotton and protected against vibration. Both acts would be done with ordinary care; ordinary care in handling great danger, nitroglycerin, and ordinary care in handling nondangerous potatoes.

In this case the defendant was handling that silent assassin, electricity. With what care should he handle it? Ordinary care, his honor will tell you, but care dependent upon the circumstances. Where the danger is great, care that is ordinary in degree must be great in amount.

Another story concerns latent defects. In this case, the negligence occurred years before when the car was designed and built. Seven years afterward the part failed because of the built-in hazard of fatigue. The comparison here is almost obvious:

They produced a bomb. Day after day, month after month, the bomb ticked, waiting, waiting for its time to explode. All that was really uncertain was the identity of the unfortunate human being who would be killed. Fate answered that. She chose to lay her hand on my widow's husband. But what was always certain was that the bomb would explode and someone would be killed.

Negligence *per se* can be a very helpful instruction, if you can get it. When you do, you need to explain it simply and forcefully:

> Negligence *per se* is something else the judge is going to tell you about. *"Per se"* is Latin and means "in and of itself." "Negligence *per se*" means negligence in and of itself. The court will tell you in its charge that if this defendant was driving sixty miles an hour in this zone, he was guilty of negligence *per se*.
>
> All that means is there's no way to break the law carefully. There's no way to make rain fall up. There's no way to eat raw celery without a lot of noise. There is no way to drive legally at an illegal speed. If he was driving sixty, and you know he was from the evidence, he was not exercising ordinary care.

If contributory negligence is an issue, you must argue it. It cannot be ignored. But how do you argue it? We argue it first with instructions (but this is not the essay for that). The instruction will allow us to say:

> Contributory negligence, members of the jury, consists of two totally different ideas. One has to do with cause, or causation. The word that says cause is "contributory." It must contribute to the cause of the injury. The other concept is fault, or negligence—that is, the failure to exercise reasonable care. You have to have both. The defendant must prove both to establish this defense of contributory negligence. Now let's look at the facts with the principle in mind that the key word is *negligence*, not conduct. The plaintiff doesn't win just by showing that the plaintiff did something that caused the accident. He got up that day, that's contributory conduct. He got his car and drove on that road. His conduct on the road was contributory conduct. The question is: Was he guilty of *careless* conduct that caused the accident?
>
> The defense says he should have hit the ditch when he suddenly was confronted with a car roaring at him over the centerline, on his side of the road, head on. Now was his conduct reasonable? Well, he was driving where he had a right to drive and where he ought to drive, between the berm and the centerline. He was driving at a legal, proper rate of speed. He was driving carefully. His failure to hit the ditch cannot be considered contributory negligence unless you think the ordinary driver hits the ditch whenever he has any threat to his well-being, and unless you think the ordinary careful driver can throw away years of training that he should drive on his side of the road. In two terrifying seconds, faced with this sudden emergency of someone coming at him, the human reaction is to hit

the brake. My client hit the brake. The skidmarks prove it. That's the ordinary conduct of the ordinary driver using ordinary care. And, although his failure to get out of the way might be considered contributory conduct, it cannot be considered contributory negligence.

What do we mean by ordinary care anyway? Your little boy comes home from school with his arithmetic test. He got a 98. What do you say, "Son, A-plus, that's great!" Or do you say, "What's the matter, stupid, you missed it by 2 percent. You were not perfect." Remember, the test is ordinary care, average care. In an arithmetic test, that's 70. If you get 71 or 72, you've passed with an average grade of C. You may have missed by 28 or 29 percent, but you've exercised ordinary average care when you've passed. So, the defendant's burden here is to give my plaintiff 68 percent and say he flunked. He can't do it. I'll grant him 5 percent, and give my plaintiff an A. And, if you feel that way about it, too, then you'll find that the defense of contributory negligence is not established.

My favorite story is the analogy of the farmer's pickup, because it has so many variations. Originally, it had to do with aggravated arthritis. It was a standard defense argument that the plaintiff's pain was caused by the old condition. The accident probably would not have hurt a stronger, healthier man, yet it hurt the weakened plaintiff. The problem was to persuade the jury to accept the legal principle that the test of damages is the actual hurt suffered by the actual man. Here is the story:

We have come to damages and a difficult field of decision. I wish it could be a simpler case, oh, like a farmer driving his pickup truck along the highway, when someone crashes to a stop sign and hits him and turns him over. He is not injured, just the truck is. Windshield out, dented fenders. And if you, as a jury, were asked what's fair compensation, I do not think you would have much problem. You would give him the kind of truck that he had. He is not entitled to a new truck, because he did not have one. But he should not have to drive a wrecked truck with mashed fenders and no windshield, because he did not have that either. So a fair result, a fair compensation, would be the cost of putting the fender back in the condition that it was in and replacing the windshield. You would have no problem with it, and I am sure my learned brother on the defense would accept that.

Well, suppose the farmer was a poultry farmer, and he was taking eggs to market. And he had a hundred dozen grade A eggs in the back of his pickup truck. After it is turned over, there are a hundred dozen grade A fresh eggs all over the highway, with the broken yolks and whites running over the pavement. What is fair compensation? Those were his eggs. They were marketable. His property has been taken away. His income has been taken away. What is fair compensation? Ninety cents a dozen retail? No. He was not going to sell them retail. He was going to sell them wholesale, and the wholesale market prices reported in the newspaper were forty-six cents a dozen. So he is entitled to forty-six cents times a hundred dozen. Forty-six dollars. Now in that situation, wouldn't you think a defense lawyer was completely out of his mind if he said, "Don't give him forty-six dollars for those eggs! Why, if they had been golf balls, not a one would have been broken."

I don't mean my client was an egg, but he was like an egg. He was fragile. But he was still useful and marketable. He could sell what strength he had in the marketplace of labor. He was certainly not a golf ball and he didn't bounce. But fair compensation is to restore the loss that has actually been inflicted upon the actual man. And when you break an actual egg, fair compensation is paying the value.

That story can go on:

Suppose it wasn't an egg. It was a horse. What is the value of the horse? What kind of horse? An old plow horse worth fifty dollars? Or was it Nashua, the day after he was sold to the Syndicate for one million, two hundred thousand dollars as the first million-dollar horse? There have been many since. Well, if it was Nashua, Nashua was worth one million, two hundred thousand dollars. No man that I know of is worth as much as a horse, but that's not so surprising. Men are not as productive, generally, as horses. A horse races for hundred-thousand-dollar purses. Men don't, even though they race the same mile and a quarter. Then a horse, a great sire, gets about ten thousand dollars for each service at stud, and I don't know any man who was ever worth that, either. So you say the horse was more productive than the man and that's why you pay a high price for the horse.

But what about, say, a painting? Rembrandt's *Aristotle Contemplating the Bust of Homer* was sold at auction for two million, three hundred thousand dollars. A copy of it might be worth fifty. But what did you destroy, the copy or the original? And why should the original be worth so much? It isn't productive of anything. Well, it's valuable because Rembrandt is dead, and was unique and talented, and no man will ever lay pigment on a canvas with a brush again the way he did. No one will ever again paint light coming out of the background the way he did.

So his painting is unique. And you members of the jury know that God will never make another human arm quite like the arm Joe Wilson had. It was unique to him. It had value, great value. I'm

345

going to ask you for one hundred and twenty-five thousand dollars for that arm. I know that kind of money doesn't grow on raspberry bushes, but a good right arm doesn't grow on a raspberry bush either.

Useful Story

I close with an old story, told to me by a senior partner long ago, which has been useful over the decades. It is particularly apropos in rebuttal when the defense lawyer has been uncommonly verbose and inaccurate in restating evidence.

It seems that when Abe Lincoln was a young trial lawyer in Sangamon County, Illinois, he was arguing a case with a lawyer whose version of the facts came more from his imagination than the testimony. Lincoln, in his argument, turned on him and said, "Tell me, sir, how many legs has a sheep got?" "Why, four, of course," the fellow answered. "And if I called his tail a leg, then how many legs would that sheep have?" Lincoln asked. The answer came, "Then he'd have five." "No!" Lincoln roared, pounding the jury rail, "he'd still have just *four* legs. *Calling* his tail a leg won't make it a leg. Now let's look at the actual testimony and see how many tails you've been calling legs."

Perhaps that story might be applicable to this whole article. The principles given here are not necessarily true just because I believe them to be true. But, whether tails or legs, they have served well in the practical test of experience.

PART VI

Trial

The Last Thirty Days

by Robert F. Hanley

The final strategy is formed, the pieces have been collected. What do experienced lawyers do in preparation for trial those last 30 days? We are really not well informed about how lawyers prepare their cases. It is not a subject generally covered in continuing education courses. I am going to set out as candidly as I can how I approach those last 30 days.

Candidly—I enter into a state of complete and total misery. There is no time to prepare, there is undiscovered discovery I wish I had discovered. The client is confused about the basic issues of the case, although I have explained them a hundred times. The other side and the judge are pressing for an unsound settlement. My *other* clients do not understand why I am not answering their phone calls. They don't understand why I must spend every breathing moment on the case set for trial. They do not share the intensity of my feeling about the outcome of the case.

All of these things come together. Happily, my wife is used to the process and ignores me as I pace up and down and look vaguely out the window at 4:00 A.M thinking about my case. This is the miserable time of total commitment. It is the time you think, breathe, and live the case every second.

I have been deposing witnesses in this case for years. I have a computer full of deposition and document abstracts. I have files full of legal memoranda. Despite tremendous judicial arm-wrenching for settlement, it looks as if this one is going to trial. The judge at the last pretrial conference cut off discovery, asked for suggested drafts of a final pretrial order, and set the case for trial 30 days hence.

The case has been investigated and discovered pursuant to a well-

The author is a partner in the Denver firm of Morrison & Foerster; Adjunct Professor, Advanced Trial Advocacy, University of Colorado Law School; and a former chairman of the Section of Litigation.

planned program. I have all the raw material I need to win. The problem is how to put all the pieces together. How to organize and simplify my proof. How am I going to spend this last month?

The first thing I really want to do is organize the facts for the final time. I do not just start reading depositions and exhibits. First, I prepare a sequence of events—the year, the month, the day, and sometimes even the hours that events occurred. Then I read the deposition summaries and exhibits with reference to that sequence.

I want to be sure I have a cohesive, coherent, simple, consistent theory of my case. I want to get rid of confusing, inconsistent claims and defenses. This is the moment of truth. This is the time to cut out the claims or defenses I pleaded to be on the safe side. This is the time I want to make sure that I have a logical framework on which to hang my version of the facts. Is it consistent? Is it simple? Can I stand up and tell the jury that this is what really happened?

I look to my draft of the jury instructions and ask: Do they give me a *legal* framework that will permit me to present the facts in a persuasive manner? This is the time to dismiss that count under Section 1 of the Sherman Act if I cannot prove a conspiracy.

Drop the Losers

I will look at my trial chart and see what evidence I have to support each claim and the evidence I anticipate my opponent will introduce. And I drop the losers. I create a theme. What am I really going to be able to prove? I develop my theory of the case. Then I order my proof. I usually start with the closing argument I want to make—the argument I believe to be most persuasive. Then I go back to ensure that I have evidence to support that closing argument.

When I am convinced that I have the evidence to support my closing argument, I prepare my opening statement, my introduction to the case. I find that preparing my opening is a great way to fight that old ogre, confusion. Good grief. Four weeks until trial—150 depositions have been taken, 120,000 documents exchanged, 25 witnesses to call. Where am I? What do I do first? Well, I sit down and draft an opening statement. That's right—I write it out verbatim. I will not read it at trial, but I find this is the way to get out the cobwebs—to ensure that I have a coherent theory of my case.

I believe that the opening statement is extremely important, and I am convinced that most of us don't give our openings sufficient time or attention.

The jury studies by Kalvin and Zeisel at the University of Chicago established that by the end of the opening statements, 80 percent of the jurors had made up their minds on liability and that their opinions could not be changed later. These studies showed that if, in his opening statement, the lawyer said that something could be proved and said it boldly and forcefully, the jurors would insist that the lawyer's statement was evidence. That happened even though in the trial they heard, the evidence had been removed and all they heard was the lawyer's statement. When the jurors were asked who gave the evidence, they said they did not remember who said it, but they knew that some witness had testified to it.

I believe in the psychological principle of primacy, which teaches that the thing a human first believes about a subject he believes most deeply, retains most strongly, and resists *changing* most frequently. I, therefore, like to make a strong introductory statement in my opening. I try to set the theme of my case in the opening sentences.

> May it please the Court and you, ladies and gentlemen of the jury. My name is Bob Hanley and I represent John Jones, a local contractor, who puts up homes in Denver. John is suing Stonebuilt Products Company and Readymix Cement Co. for damages that he suffered when Stonebuilt and Readymix got together and fixed prices of cement blocks here in Denver.
>
> At this point in the trial it is my duty, my responsibility, my privilege to tell you what we expect the evidence to show and to tell you what this case is all about.
>
> This case is about how the two defendant companies acting together in a mutual understanding raised the price of concrete building blocks, which John Jones needs in his construction business, and cost John hundreds of thousands of dollars. We will show that the defendant companies raised prices and John had no alternative but to pay those fixed prices.

I try to establish the theme of my case in my opening and to keep playing it to the jury through my witnesses throughout the trial.

Dull Testimony

I do not spend ten minutes, as so many lawyers do, explaining to the jury what an opening statement is. I do not tell them it is an unadorned Christmas tree or whatever the analogies are that are being used today in trial practice courses. I certainly do not tell them that opening statements are not evidence. That would be like telling them to stick their fingers in their ears and think about Raquel Welch while I tell them about concrete building blocks.

I also try to remember that it is hard for a jury to accept an emotional argument from someone they do not know. I have learned that I have to earn the right to share a jury's emotions. The jurors have to trust me before I can get them to believe I am being sincere when I am emotional. I usually try to save the fireworks for the closing argument.

I also do not give a detailed account of the testimony of each of my witnesses. The testimony of most antitrust witnesses will be dull

350

enough when the jury hears it the first time. I believe in letting the jury believe that they discover facts for themselves. I try to lead them just short of the ultimate issue and let them discover it for themselves.

I do try in my opening statement to teach them the technology they will need to understand my case. To do that I use charts, diagrams, overhead projections, movies, and other kinds of visual guides. I try to use examples, similes, and metaphors. I try to be a good storyteller.

I try to make the jurors the heroes of their breakfast tables. They are going to be hearing about electrical distribution systems or telecommunication systems or the manufacture of cement blocks for weeks, even months. They will feel happily disposed toward the lawyer who makes them an expert, lets them answer the question, "Daddy, how does a telephone call go from Grandma's house in California to us in Denver?"

When I have completed my opening and have checked it against my trial chart and have become convinced that I have admissible evidence to support every factual assertion I have made, I rehearse it. I call in my trial team and videotape operator and give my opening. Then I look at the tape and listen to the critique. Boy. There is nothing those arrogant young lawyers like better than those sessions when they can really lay it on the old man. Then I pull my ego together, revise the opening, and present it again.

In the case of *MCI v. AT&T* in Chicago several years ago, my team and my wife got tired of hearing my opening, so I had Victor DeGrazia, who conducted our jury survey, bring in panels of people who had answered our questionnaire. We had them listen to the opening. Then I had one of our best and brightest team members make our opponent's best arguments, and I watched the jury deliberations through one way mirrors.

Just like President Nixon, the jurors soon forgot that they were being listened to, and I learned a great deal. I found the areas of confusion. I found our strengths and weaknesses. We brought in three different panels and presented opening statements to each panel—revising each statement on the basis of what we learned during each deliberation session. I plan to repeat that operation in every large jury case I try. It was extremely helpful.

When I have an opening that I am satisfied with, I find it pretty well answers the question of the order of my proof. I fit my witnesses and exhibits to the story I have told in my opening. I will have interviewed my witnesses and know what their testimony will be. I have not given them their final preparation—that comes almost last. But I know what they will testify to, and this is the time I call witnesses. Most of us call far too many witnesses. You bore the jury and take the chance of building in inconsistencies. If you can make the point with one witness, just call one.

I arrange my witnesses in the order of my opening—an order that will logically and forcefully present my evidence to the jury. If possible, I want to begin and end with a strong witness. I try to hide in the middle of the case the few adverse witnesses I must call, but I do not follow the rule of calling the strong witnesses first and last. I also ignore the old rule to put on my strongest witnesses in the morning when the jury is awake. I prefer an order that tells the story in the most logical order. The testimony should follow my clear, concise, orderly opening statement.

In that last month before trial, I give a great deal of thought to the kind of jurors I want, and even more to those I do not want. We all know that jury selection is a negative process. If you like a juror a lot, your opponent will probably strike him. What kind of people do I not want? I do not want those whose occupations, ages, social background, marital status, education, and experience will lead them to identify with my opponent and his position in the case.

I remember that jurors usually react in ways consistent with their backgrounds. I try to figure out what is the gut issue in the case. If it is whether or not there should be competition in a regulated industry and I am a plaintiff against a utility, I need to know what kind of person usually favors competition. Then, by questions put to prospective jurors in voir dire examination, I need to determine into which category they fall. I have found that jury surveys are helpful in deciding what kind of people will probably react in favor of and which against my side.

I would not leave the jury survey until the last month before trial. I would take the survey when I had a pretty good idea of what my theme was going to be, but not too late to change the theme.

There are some good experts to help you with your jury survey. You need experienced people to help in constructing a questionnaire. And I stress *help*. They can help you phrase the questions of the questionnaire in an unambiguous form, but you are the one who knows the issues in your case.

You need experts to train and supervise the interviewers, the coders, the keypunching operation, the computer programming, and the analysis of the data.

The cheapest method of conducting the interview is by telephone. You should attempt to select the same pool from which your interviewees are selected as those people who could be selected to serve as jurors. If your jurors are selected from the voters in the county or district, your sample should be drawn from that same group.

The experts tell us that a minimum of 600 interviews will be needed for a jury selection survey. Maybe so, if you are trying to have a survey admitted in evidence in a trademark infringement case. But for a jury survey to assist you in jury selection, I believe 300 to 400 is enough.

The excellent treatise *Jurywork: Systematic Techniques* (published by the National Jury Project in cooperation with the National Lawyers Guild and National Conference of Black Lawyers) says that a well-designed sample provides an efficient and economical way to discover the attitudes and characteristics of the population. You should use a random sample. By random, I mean one that is unbiased in the sense that all people in the universe have an equal chance of being interviewed. In our hypothetical jurisdiction, jurors are selected from voter registration lists. So, your sample should be drawn in such a way that all voters have an opportunity of being drawn into the sample. Computer-generated sampling grids can be used to assure random sampling and your experts can tell you how they work.

If your client can afford it, face-to-face interviews are quite desirable. They are usually longer and more searching than telephone interviews, and a great deal more expensive.

According to the authors of *Jurywork: Systematic Techniques,* most questionnaires have five parts: an introduction, screening questions, general attitude questions, specific questions about the case, and demographic or background questions.

The introductory part introduces the interviewer to the respondent and tells the general subject of the interview. The introduction usually anticipates some resistance on the part of the respondent and provides the interviewer with methods of overcoming the resistance by giving assurances concerning confidentiality and the importance of the project. The screening part ensures that only eligible respondents are interviewed, so you would ask if the respondent is a registered voter.

The general-attitude part usually includes questions about the respondents' attitudes toward the system of justice and other relevant attitudes. In the case I mentioned, we would ask a number of questions about attitudes toward competition among the utility monopolies.

The specific questions about the case are the ones the trial lawyer will have to have a heavy hand in. This part of the questionnaire may include a description of a hypothetical case modeled on your case. The description of the case will be followed by questions about the respondent's opinions on the facts and issues presented.

These questions should be designed to present, evenhandedly, your client's strongest arguments and your opponent's strongest arguments. The last part of the interview will consist of personal questions about the respondent's background. This section of the interview presents personal questions about the respondent's background—the demographics.

Assume we have conducted a jury survey and have a nice clear profile of the best and worst type of juror for our case. What do you do to ensure that you do not wind up with the worst?

All of the trial texts tell us that conducting a successful voir dire examination of prospective jurors is one of the most important steps to a favorable verdict. We all know that Clarence Darrow thought that once the jury was selected the trial was over.

But in most federal trial courts, the judges have about taken away this, the lawyers' favorite method of ensuring a jury unprejudiced against his client, of preconditioning the jury, and ingratiating himself to the jury. Many judges will permit you to supplement their oral voir dire questions only with written questions. During the final weeks before the trial, I do prepare questions designed to identify the demographic characteristics of the jurors I do not want.

If the judge permits me to participate in the oral questioning of the jurors, I am all set. If he does not, I can submit my questions to him to put to the jurors.

I really spend time designing questions to ferret out bias against my client and to reflect the background characteristics I look for. I have little luck trying to condition, educate, or brainwash the jury about the substance of my case these days, so I have stopped trying. I try to do that in my opening statement. In the voir dire I try to elicit information. I put myself in the role of a salesman who has been told he can question potential customers. He is going to make a sales pitch to them later, and to do it successfully, he wants to know as much about them as he can. So, in addition to learning what I can about the jurors to see how they fit my survey profiles, I want to know as much as I can about those who will remain on the panel. I go back over the transcript of the voir dire if time permits, before my opening statement, and always before my closing statement.

I learn the most when I use open-ended questions:

> Mrs. Jones, to what newspapers and magazines do you subscribe?
> Mrs. Jones, what did you read in the paper or see on TV about this case?

I have found a technique used by Judge John Grady in Chicago and Judge Jim Carrigan in Denver to be salutary. They establish a nice, warm, casual atmosphere and then say:

> Folks, these lawyers and their clients have been working on this case a long time. It is an important case and, I believe, the trial will be extremely interesting. Now, instead of asking you a bunch of questions to learn whether you are qualified to sit as jurors on this important case, I'd like you to just stand up and tell us about yourself and where you live, and tell us about your family—what do you do for a living and, if you are married, what your spouse does, and what you like to do in your spare time.

In a complex case before Judge Grady, each juror stood up and gave a revealing biographical picture of himself or herself. The subjects each picked and the order in which the prospective juror presented them were illuminating.

The judge gently prodded the more introverted jurors with supplemental questions. When he finished, he gave us an opportunity to supplement. I asked few questions, yet I have never exercised my peremptory challenges with greater confidence.

Before calling in my witnesses for final preparation, I get my charts, diagrams, photographs, slides, and exhibits ready. I want my demonstrative evidence ready so that the witnesses who will use it become familiar with the exhibits and rehearse their use in the exact form in which they will be used at trial.

In preparing charts and slides, I have had good luck using television advertising firms and public-relations firms. They are expensive, but they know how to make a visual impact. They do it every day, every minute on television.

We and our expert witnesses take the advertising people through the technical aspects of the case and prepare rough sketches. Then the advertising people make drawings, or slides, and present them to us. My team and I check them out for clarity. We may even try them out on our rehearsal juries.

I am becoming a real believer in the use of the overhead projector and the expert making diagrams from the witness stand. But I want him to rehearse it in the office during my witness preparation.

I use slides, charts, enlarged photographs, movies, and models. I use anything that will explain my case to the jury, and I use my visual-arts experts to tell me the most effective medium to use to explain each aspect of the case.

The *MCI v. AT&T* case was one in which the jury had to be made to understand that, for a company to survive in the inter-city telephone market, it had to have access to the local distribution equipment of the operating companies of American Telephone & Telegraph Corporation. The jury had to understand why that equipment was essential, and why the refusal of AT&T to lease the equipment over which it had monopoly control, on reasonable terms and conditions, kept MCI from obtaining its fair share of the market. The jury had to be made to understand that lost profits could be projected without speculation. The jury also had to know to follow the testimony of an economic expert. We knew that we would have to do a job of simplifying, of explaining, of clarifying.

I decided that this was one case in which I would have to put to work everything I had ever learned about illustrative or demonstrative evidence from every good trial lawyer against whom I had ever tried a case. We really had to make a visual impact. Most of the charts, slides, photographs, and other visual aids I had used (and seen used) in court had created, not diminished, jury confusion, in my opinion.

I realized that the charts that the economists loved so much became meaningful to me only after the third or fourth run-through. The jury would have one run-through. It suddenly became clear to me that I had a great thing going. As a person easily confused by charts and diagrams, if I could understand one when I saw it for the first time, a jury would understand it.

Where to get such a chart? Who best knew what the public could and would understand? Obviously, the people who make their daily bread communicating with the public. That meant the advertising people who must present their clients' wares to the public in a meaningful and effective way. It meant someone who has a line on the artists, film directors, producers, photographers, and other talent, as well as a knowledge of the current state of the art in visual presentations.

We made a series of charts and slides and even a movie to illustrate our client's growth. Obviously, we did not wait until the last 30 days in the *MCI* case to prepare our demonstrative evidence, but we did spend a good deal of final preparation time rehearsing the use of that evidence.

Perhaps the most important use of the last 30 days before trial is the final preparation of the witnesses. I do everything I can to bring them into the office, and I have our conference room set up to resemble a courtroom with a bench, a witness stand, and a podium. I also use a videotape camera and recorder. I have one of our team act as my opponent and one act as judge.

I put the witness through direct examination. Then we play it back. The great thing about videotape is you cannot talk back to it. I'm certain that you all have learned, as I have, that there is a reverse correlation between a man's position in a corporate hierarchy and his willingness to accept criticism. Well, with videotape you do not have to say a thing. You don't have to say, "Listen B.G., you sound like the most arrogant, abrasive s.o.b. in the world; you aren't being responsive, you sound defensive." No, all you have to do is turn on the monitor and watch him squirm as he sees himself as an arrogant, abrasive, unresponsive, defensive s.o.b.

Two Notebooks

In the critique, you and your team will, of course, stop the tape and show the witness where he was being unclear, unresponsive, or unpersuasive. You can point out distracting mannerisms. But mainly you let the witness watch himself.

Then you go back and run through the testimony again and again until everyone is comfortable with it. You turn the witness over to your assistant for cross-examination and you critique that examination. I find that, in a case where you have been working with a witness for years, a relationship of mutual trust develops and it hurts the relationship to assume suddenly the role of inquisitor. Have another lawyer prepare the cross. When you are finished, you will have a confident witness, one who will pay you the ultimate compliment when he steps down from the stand at trial, "Bob, I didn't hear a question I didn't hear first in your office."

Some critics of this tough rehearsal program say the sessions will make the witnesses sound stilted and rehearsed. My experience is that a real live judge, six or twelve jurors, and an actual opposing lawyer at trial infuse enough adrenalin into the witness's system to keep the examinations fresh. I will take my chances on staleness. I want my witnesses prepared.

With my witnesses prepared, I put my trial notebook in final shape. Everyone has his own way of organizing a trial book. I use two large loose-leaf notebooks with tabs. They are organized so that I can find anything I need in 30 seconds. In the courtroom, you should be able to find any document or deposition testimony within 30 seconds for the very good reason that, if you cannot, the opportunity to use what you are looking for will have passed.

In one notebook, I put the materials of the case and in the other the outline of my proof. In the material notebook, I include a consolidated pleading. This document alternates an allegation of the complaint with the answer to it.

I include a section covering all admissions of my opponent during discovery, whether by interrogatory answer, deposition testimony, or admissions in documents produced.

In the materials notebook, I have a cross-index of exhibits and depositions by subject, but I arrange the exhibits in individual manila files in filing cabinets, if the court permits. If not, I place them in file transfer cases and keep them under the counsel table.

Jury Profile

In each of the exhibit files, I place a sufficient number of copies for the judge, each juror, and my opponent. I also attach to my copy a colored sheet that states the relevance of the document, anticipates my opponent's objection, and contains a one or two-line argument and authorities to support the document's admissibility.

My materials notebook also has short legal memoranda covering the critical legal issues of the case. It also contains important pretrial motions and orders. It contains a witness list containing the names, addresses, and telephone numbers of each witness with a checklist showing whether a subpoena has been issued and whether the witness has been interviewed. It also contains a list of the names, addresses, and home telephone numbers of the members of the trial team, including paralegal assistants. Finally, it will contain a to-do list. By the day of trial, I hope that section will be blank.

The other notebook, which is the trial notebook, will contain my demographic profiles of the best and worst jurors, my supplementary voir dire questions, and a chart of the jury box for notes I take during voir dire. The notebook contains a list of the grounds of challenges for cause. It will also contain my notes for my opening statement. Each direct examination outline has its separate tab. Of course, I include in the outline the exhibits that I will refer to with the witness.

I have an exhibit list, arranged in the order in which I intend to introduce the exhibits. On the document column, the list shows whether I introduced the document and whether the judge admitted it, sustained an objection to it, or deferred ruling on it.

My trial notebook will also have outlines of my expected cross-examination, which will include verbatim excerpts from the witnesses' depositions and exhibits. The trial book contains anticipated trial motions and my drafts of jury instructions. It also contains my outline of my final argument.

I use three-ring notebook paper to take my notes during trial and have a section called "Notes During Trial."

With my notebooks all set in apple-pie order, I go into court with confidence. All that terrible planning and preparation is behind me. I am ready to do battle.

I am ready to do that fantastic thing that makes all the awful preparation and organization worth it—to be able to speak with authority and confidence in court for a fellow man. What a fantastic responsibility. What a wonderful way to make a living.

How to Try a Jury Case: A Judge's View

by Patrick E. Higginbotham

The longer I am a judge, the more difficult it is to distinguish between those mistakes I made while in the pit and the mistakes I now see lawyers making. The word "mistake" is admittedly an arbitrary term for things lawyers do that I have come to believe are not helpful to their case. But there are some themes to these things called mistakes. These themes are related and occasionally overlapping, but they are sufficiently distinct to merit separate discussion.

1. *Scout the terrain.* Worse than not having tried many cases is giving the appearance that you have not. If you can give the impression to everyone that you are very experienced, then you are. On the other hand, no matter how experienced you are, if your conduct gives the appearance of inexperience (when it is not helpful to do so) then you are inexperienced.

As you mentally run the film of the anticipated trial and attempt to see the case as it will unfold, have a clear picture of the trial scene in mind. This mental preparation requires visits to the courtroom, both when the court is in session and when it is not.

You should learn exactly where you can place your demonstrative exhibits and not block the judge's view of the jury or opposing counsel's view of the court. There are usually one or two favorite spots where such exhibits can be placed, keeping the blockage to a minimum. Knowing where that is will later give the appearance that you have indeed been there before. It may even give you the opportunity to assist your opponent in locating his exhibits properly (in the presence of the jury, of course).

You can also learn how the sound system is arranged and how loud

---

Patrick E. Higginbotham is a member of the United States Court of Appeals for the Fifth Circuit.

you must speak to carry your voice properly to the last juror. Trivial, perhaps, but the ultimate law of evidence is that the unheard statement was never said.

The trial scene itself will reflect the idiosyncrasies of the particular judge before whom you are trying your jury case. Scouting the courtroom terrain means gaining familiarity with the court's preference for a host of little details. For example, the court's practice with regard to counsel approaching the witness—is it the custom to request permission of the court to approach the witness? Is counsel expected to stand while interrogating or to remain seated at counsel table? Does the court expect the use of a lectern for opening statements, or will he allow a little stump speaking?

You must be familiar with the judge's practice in conducting voir dire. Most experienced lawyers who come into my court for the first time do not hesitate to request detail as to how I conduct voir dire, such as whether counsel is expected to conduct the interrogation of the panel, whether I want questions from him to submit to the panel or simply allow him to supplement my questioning. Does the court require the list to be struck in open court or will you be allowed to retire and discuss the list with co-counsel? When you have struck the jury list, to whom do you hand the strike list?

Questions Abound

Possible questions abound: Does the court use the pretrial order in the interrogation of the jury panel or will he refer to other pleadings? Does the trial judge instruct the jury preliminarily, and, if so, what does he customarily tell them? The law clerk, courtroom deputy, or court reporter will usually give you a copy of the court's "standard instructions." In mine-run cases, trial judges will seldom deviate from their usual practices, creatures of habit that they are.

Remember that this is usually the jurors' first trip to the courtroom, but they fully expect that the lawyers have been there before. Frequently, however, the jurors have more experience than the lawyers—at least in that judge's court. This is true even though the attorney may be a very experienced trial lawyer. Putting to one side the effect of knowledge upon your gastrointestinal tract, the point is that those little awkward moments that creep into the beginnings of trials telegraph to the jury in loud and clear language that this lawyer is not very experienced in this court. I have had lawyers in the presence of the jury upon commencing interrogation of the first witness turn to me and say, "Judge, do you prefer that I sit or stand?" The translation is, "Ladies and gentlemen of the jury, I've never been before this judge." The same translation follows: "Your Honor, do you wish the strike list, or do I give the strike list to this lady here," or "Judge, do you prefer that I use the lectern?"

Opening statements also reveal the failure to scout the terrain, where in nine cases out of ten, the lawyer begins with, "Ladies and gentlemen of the jury—now what I am about to tell you does not constitute evidence." This happens in my court although I have just told the jury the same thing in preliminary instructions. The immediate reaction of the jury is, "You dummy, the judge just told me that."

2. *Do not act like "a horse's rear."* Reading this will not be helpful to those thoroughbreds who are simply born and raised as horses' rears. There may be help for those persons who are ordinarily pleasant people, easy to get along with, but for some reason become obnoxious when they enter the courtroom. This often happens out of nervousness and a misconception of the image desired or the image projected, or both.

The person I am talking about is petty. He has no sense of humor. He sits at counsel table and would not smile if Bob Hope were presiding. He will not laugh at the judge's jokes even when cued by loyal assistant United States marshals—the judicial straight men.

Seizes Technicalities

The horse's rear will seize on technicalities to inconvenience his opposing counsel. He will wait until counsel is halfway to the witness box with a document to be shown to a witness before demanding to see the instrument in a whiney voice, although he has seen it and studied it carefully before trial. The horse's rear abuses witnesses. He is simply unfair.

I recall one wrongful death case where a young man's surviving widow appeared at trial with her handsome young son. The cross-examination pointedly developed the short time between the dates of the widow's marriage and her son's date of birth, all with knowing glances at the jury. Actually, the glances were not very knowing. Those questions cost his client approximately $25,000 each; at least, that's my rough approximation of how they contributed to a substantial verdict.

All the trial books and all the studies of the rules of evidence will not protect you against the reverberations of such unfairness. Yet, a word of caution. I believe it is very difficult to feign fairness, particularly in longer trials. If you are really a thoroughbred horse's rear, it will out. Unfairness by counsel, such as counsel's comments about witnesses or questions to witnesses, do not escape a jury's attention. My only advice is to be aware that you are one. If so, waive a jury and pray that the judge is cut from similar cloth so that your personality is lost beside his.

3. *Do not succumb to jury amnesia.* In mine-run cases, jury selection is oversold. The judge usually conducts a substantial part of the voir dire examination. In federal court you have only three persons in an ordinary civil case that you may peremptorily strike from the panel. Strikes for cause are uncommon.

A simple look at the odds shows that you have very little control over the selection of jurors. Your real concern ought not be so much with selection as with understanding what you drew.

Some lawyers take voluminous notes as the panel is voir dired and pore over them intently as they strike their list. Then the trial proceeds for three, four, or five days, at the end of which the lawyers cannot identify the occupation of any more than two members of a twelve-person jury. They may have had a hundred opportunities to drive home a point by questions framed in a particular way if they had been sensitive to the make-up of the jury.

Accurate Clerks

My law clerks and I play a game where we each try to predict the jury foreman as well as the verdict. At the end of a year's clerkship, the clerks are usually accurate in the foreman selection and hit jury verdicts much more accurately than the lawyers.

In the midst of its deliberation, a jury will often send out a note stating, "Judge, we would like to recess because Mrs. Jones is not feeling well." In my consultation with the lawyers, the usual question is, "Which one is Mrs. Jones?" No wonder Mrs. Jones is ill.

4. *Develop jury empathy.* Assuming that you know the background of the jury hearing your case and have reflected on its significance, there are two mistakes that occur most often. Both reflect a lack of empathy for the jury.

The first is talking down to the jury. Lawyers startle me by opening statements that begin (either literally or by implication), "Ladies and gentlemen of the jury, this case is very complicated. I'll try to state it in a way that even you can understand." All the same, lawyers should not go to the other extreme. Most trial manuals and courses in trial advocacy teach lawyers to be aware of the problem. Lawyers will go to the extreme of prefacing questions with, "Doctor, please explain to me how electro-convulsive treatment affects the cellular structure of the brain, although some jurors already know that."

A second manifestation of no empathy is the repetitious lawyer. It usually happens when a lawyer has mapped out the points of proof, witness-by-witness. With witness No. 1 he unexpectedly develops points he planned to cover with witness No. 2. Although the matters may no longer be disputed, the lawyer persists in covering the same terrain with witness No. 2, and then again with other witnesses.

There is a common myth among trial lawyers that important points need to be repeated and repeated so that they will not be lost on the jury. This technique may have been sound in earlier years or in more rural areas where the education of jurors had been poor. Very little is ever missed now by a jury of twelve persons.

I try to visit with each jury panel when excused. One of the questions jurors ask most frequently is, "Judge, why do the lawyers go over and over the same points?'' One lady juror confessed to me that she had counted every tile in the ceiling to avoid screaming at a lawyer that she had heard that point ten times already. In retrospect, the scream might have been helpful. I found that her tile count coincided with mine.

Interminable Examination

Closely related is the interminable examination. A witness that may take five minutes if the critical points are succinctly made will often take 25 to 30 minutes while counsel laboriously asks questions ''for the record.'' The longer the witness is in the box, the more interest in his testimony will wane. If the witness is yours, make your important points as quickly and as up-front as possible. If you are cross-examining, follow this maxim with even greater loyalty.

5. *Be sensitive to the ties between judge and jury.* You are an advocate, as is your opposing counsel. The jury is right in distrusting both of you. The one professional observer in the courtroom in whom the jury is most likely to have confidence will be the judge. Whatever else they may think of the judge, they know that with rare exception he is trying to be fair. More likely than not, the judge is a substantial, well-known figure in the community.

The very trial structure itself creates and builds the bond between jury and judge. In longer trials, it can become a syndrome of ''us versus them.'' I usually eat quite well at coffee breaks during lengthy trials because the distaff members of the jury persist in bringing me cookies and cakes. They knit me doilies and bring me pictures of their grandchildren.

It is beyond me how, in the face of this reality, lawyers do other than treat judges with reverence in the presence of the jury. While I think that lawyers should be courteous to judges out of respect for the law, my point is the very practical one that you must do so to be successful.

Juries are quick to sense petulance in lawyers. The manner in which an objection is stated, and more critically, the manner in which a ruling of the judge is accepted, is a frequent transmission line of this respect between lawyer and jury. The lawyer who frowns when an objection is sustained or otherwise discloses his annoyance, by pencil dropping or more subtle responses, creates an enormous hurdle to persuasion.

True, there may be the rare case where a trial judge is so unfair that jury sympathy will swing in a different direction. But in such a case, that unfairness will be so apparent that the lawyer need do nothing to communicate it to the jury. Indeed, the appearance of the courteous lawyer, long-suffering, may do much to take care of the trial judge who acts like a horse's rear.

Occasional Bad Days

Putting to one side the occasional bad days all judges have, most judges are warm people; sometimes, by their own perception of the office, a little distant. Sensitivity to the relationship of judge and juror teaches the lawyer that both his opening statement and his closing argument should build on the court's charge. The jury takes the court's charge as gospel, as properly it should, and wise advocates are aware of this circumstance in their arguments. A good summation will use catch-phrases of the court's charge so that when the court delivers the charge, the lawyer's earlier argument is reinforced and strengthened.

One of the great trial lawyers of the southwest was Henry Strasburger. He had a tendency in closing statements to tell the jury, while thanking them for their services, that he was blessed to appear before one of the greatest trial judges in the United States. While that caused me to bite my tongue (as a lawyer, not as a judge), I never saw a trial judge who doubted for one moment that the statement was true. But unless you have the instincts of that trial genius, I suggest that you might tone down that technique a bit.

6. *Do not sandbag.* Your chances of reversing an adverse verdict because you have clearly implanted error are slim and none. Despite this, many lawyers persist in making objections, trying hard to keep error in the record.

At its best, this consists of making hypertechnical objections to matters that are most harmful. At its worst, it borders on deliberate injection of error.

I give to counsel a written copy of my proposed charge and review it with them page by page to ensure that they understand the proposed charge and, most importantly, that I understand the errors that the draft usually contains. The second part of the conference consists of the taking of objections to those parts of the charge that the counsel believe to be in error.

It is extremely irritating to listen to dictated objections to parts of the charge never mentioned earlier. It is still more irritating to listen to objections by counsel to parts of the charge for which they were responsible. I seldom see any genuine conflict between a lawyer's duty to his client and his responsibilities as an officer of the court. The duty to his client does not include misleading the court.

At the more practical level, the lawyer who tends to get the most attention is the lawyer who makes few but meaningful objections. Judges know those lawyers and know that when they object they have a serious question. On the other hand, it requires an iron will to find the meritorious objection when a whole covey is flushed by any piece of evidence remotely harmful to a lawyer's case.

Once when carrying water for Henry Strasburger, I asked why he had not pressed on with a line of questions in order to preserve the "record." Without breaking stride, he replied, "Lawyers who try cases with their eyes on appeal usually have to."

7. *Avoid trial fumbles.* Apart from those few trial lawyers who thrive on

studied disorganization, I have found persuasive lawyers to be extremely well organized in court. They are not only organized, they give the appearance to the jury of being well organized. That organizational skill becomes a strong persuasive tool because the jury senses the lawyer's thoroughness.

Some areas bear particular emphasis because they control the actual in-court scene. The first is that the lawyer must control his documents.

I have seen elaborate organizational schemes and retrieval systems collapse in court when after a few days in trial the lawyers are totally unable to locate an exhibit previously received into evidence. Recently in a large criminal case I warned the government counsel, who intended to offer thousands of exhibits into evidence, that they not only had to organize their exhibits to be offered, but had to generate a system for locating exhibits once *into* evidence. The system devised was simple. As exhibits were introduced, they came from file cabinets behind the counsel table and moved to desk-level file cabinets in front of the bench. The same organizational system for the documents before offer was retained for the documents after their receipt into evidence.

Even in cases with fewer than 100 exhibits, some simple organizational scheme is important. Even metal dividers where exhibits are grouped by subject or number is helpful; it prevents the morass of stacked papers on the courtroom deputy's desk. This problem is aggravated by the fact that many district judges no longer keep their courtroom deputy in the courtroom during trial. The court reporter is the only person available to collate exhibits. He is usually busy with other things.

The second area that invites fumbling is depositions. Put to the side that far too much client money is wasted in taking depositions. Even important depositions do not receive their full effectiveness unless they have been indexed, cross-referenced, or otherwise organized in a fashion the lawyer can use.

Pungent Statement

My practice always included an indexing of depositions by subject matter. If the question concerned the speed of the vehicle, every mention of speed was placed by number reference under the subject "speed." The same index was followed with each of the testifying witnesses. Where a particularly pungent statement with regard to speed had been made, the reference point would include a quote of that statement.

There is no magic to any particular system. The system must enable the lawyer to find the witness's prior statement immediately. The well-prepared lawyer can bring an errant witness quickly to heel by a couple of accurate references to prior testimony. This immediately communicates to the witness (and to the jury) that the lawyer knows precisely what this witness had said previously and will not tolerate deviations.

365

The lawyer doing the examining should personally index the deposition. In many enormously complex cases, this is not practical. Paralegals must do the work. However, it is not a waste of client money for the lawyer who is actually trying the case to index at least the critical depositions of persons he will cross-examine. No one can delegate the ultimate task of cross-examination, nor its preparation. It is also helpful to record in a trial notebook following the indexed deposition a list of every exhibit that was pertinent to that particular witness's testimony.

8. *Shoot with rifles, not with shotguns.* While lawyers must work hard to prepare their cases as thoroughly as possible, they must not offer into evidence every thing they have learned about the case. The point of learning all you can about the case is to sort out those matters that are important. Insistence upon dealing with minutiae loses many a lawsuit.

Of course there are situations where intricate detail is essential. The jury will know in those cases that the detail is important. But a lawyer should not spend an hour developing a point whose marginal contribution to the case would justify no more than 30 seconds.

The general wisdom is that opening and closing statements should be as brief as possible. It is commonly said that "no souls are saved after the first 30 minutes." I endorse that principle. But apply it in the development of evidence itself. Indeed, the soporific effect of too much detail is used by some highly skilled lawyers for the very purpose of dulling the evidentiary antennae of the jury.

I sometimes think that all of us in the trial business have overdone the emphasis upon specific techniques and devices for winning. There may be a germ of truth to the statement that "trying jury cases is like making love—either you got it or you ain't." But there are certain practices to avoid. Even the artist must learn to select the best brush and paint.

The most common traits of the lawyers who have proved to be successful in my court, and those successful lawyers I have opposed at counsel table, are that in their dealings with the court they are: impeccably honest, scrupulously fair, respectful of the court as an institution, and hardworking in preparing the case.

I tell Henry Strasburger stories because I am still waiting to meet another trial genius. They all seem to be on the lecture circuit.

Henry Strasburger never was. Come to think of it, neither was Percy Foreman.

Trying a Case to a Jury

by Newell Edenfield

Being shy by nature, my audacity in even pretending to write on this subject astounds me. I am a federal trial judge; but before that I was, and at heart still am, a lawyer; and, I hope, a trial lawyer. But I have learned from a philosopher (I cannot remember who he was) that if one, however humble, does not speak his own words of wisdom he is ultimately put to the embarrassment of hearing them spoken by someone else. Reassured by that truism (but not too much) I have become bold enough to try.

To an aspiring trial lawyer there is no such thing as an unimportant trial, or an insignificant hearing. The stakes may or may not be high; but remember, like every struggling actor who finally stars, you must build your lifelong reputation, one pleasing, effective appearance at a time. You do not always have to win, but you do have to improve your image constantly.

Each trial, if one becomes necessary, is, and must be, a separate work of art, and, like a play, its reception depends on many things beyond your control: the lighting in which your production will be done; the features, visible and otherwise, of your subject; the setting or background against which your client must be posed; the dialogue which you must plan and try to control; the critics (that is, the jury) to whom your work will be presented and by whom it will be once and forever judged, and the judge who, though neutral, carries a terrible swift sword. You must start considering all these things from the moment your client walks in the door for they will become very real when the curtain goes up for your performance.

The author, now deceased, was a United States District Judge for the Northern District of Georgia. This article was adapted from a series of columns written by the author for the Georgia State Bar Journal. *Reprinted with permission.*

I have never known a trial lawyer who did not agree that selecting the jury is one of the most important steps in a trial, and I have never seen two who could completely agree on the criteria to be applied in making the selection. There are a few things, however, about which all agree: if you can, obtain a list of the names, addresses, and employments of the panel in advance of trial and find out everything you can about each one before the trial begins.

Leave no stone unturned. If you have a friend who lives near the prospective juror, call him. If you know someone who works at the same place, call him. If you know someone who goes to the same church, call him. Of course you should keep your inquiries confidential. Besides, you do not wish to know the juror, you only want to know all *about* him or her. What are his loves, hates and hobbies? To what "isms" does he subscribe? How is his employment history likely to affect his feelings toward your client or his business?

If all these efforts fail and you are forced to strike in the blind, I know of no better rule of thumb than that advocated by the great, and now infirm, A. Walton Nall: Try to pick jurors from the same social and economic background as your client, hoping that, coming from the same strata of society, they can better understand, approve of, and appreciate the hopes, motives and fears that caused your client to act as he did.

Mass Psychology

With the opening statement to the jury you are about to begin the public part of your performance; and before you do so there is one collateral subject that you must understand and remain constantly aware of: psychology, and particularly mass or crowd psychology. Not that you will rely on mass psychology in every situation or in every case, like a crutch, but in every situation and in every case you must be conscious of its potential and understand at least the rudiments of how feelings and attitudes can be generated, manipulated, and controlled. Mass psychology begins with creation and generation within the audience of undivided and enthusiastic attention.

I got my first lessons in applied mass psychology from two experiences in my youth, far removed from the dignified settings of a courtroom. I was raised on a farm and, as with all farmers, Saturday afternoon was our time to go to town. Frequently there was a traveling medicine show in town. All farmers, including my sedate, conservative father, loved to go. It was usually set up on a vacant lot with the back of the truck serving as a stage.

The show started with music to attract the crowd. Then came dancing, and finally the huckster with a rapid series of appropriate jokes. By that time the lot was full, and the crowd hanging on, and straining to hear, every word. Suddenly, while they were still hanging, the show stopped and in no more than two minutes the huckster completed his pitch about the tonic he was selling. Suddenly salesmen appeared among the crowd offering the elixir in question, saying that, just for today, you could get two bottles for the price of one.

No matter what it was, my father always bought. I used to ride back home in a buggy and wonder to myself what had happened. I knew that not a man in that crowd would have bought that stuff from any local merchant for one dollar a barrel; yet the huckster had sold a lot of medicine, and at a much higher price. I could not really understand it.

Later in life, when I was in college, I was on the debate team. Once or twice every year a British debate team came to our campus to debate our local team. They always won, even with local judges, and I began to analyze their operation. Suddenly I realized that it was the old medicine show act all over again, only on a more intellectual plane. In the arguments our boys would get up and pedantically and in dead seriousness hammer away at the assigned question, enumerating one logical conclusion after another.

Then the Briton would casually stroll to the lectern and for the first thirteen of his allotted fifteen minutes the audience would not even know why he was there. In his inimitable and impeccable British accent he would extol the glories of our country, express his pleasure at being here, recount some of his interesting experiences, and then go into a series of appropriate British-American jokes. Just as his time was about to expire, and while you sat there hoping it would, he hit the subject of the debate. By then, of course, the crowd was completely charmed and every one was sitting on the edge of his seat. In about four well chosen sentences he then proceeded to annihilate our team's ponderous, studied argument. Then he sat down. He had won, and in your heart you knew he had won—from the applause, if nothing else. In both cases it was applied mass psychology.

Move Mountains

· If you want to sell your case to the jury, you must, in some way, generate within the jurors excitement and pleasure at what you have said and an enthusiastic desire for more; and when you get them hanging on every word, you had better make your message short, clear, and sweet. If you are one of those few who can enlist the lightning of mass psychology on your side you can win cases, and you can also move mountains, one handful of dirt and rocks at a time. How else, within a single generation, did three charismatic, mesmerizing phrase-makers, Hitler, Churchill, and Roosevelt, charm and arm the whole world and destroy its complacency for all time to come?

In presenting your opening statement be relaxed, calm, and casual. Act like you did it every day for a living, as indeed you do. But keep it moving; never lose the attention of the jury.

You begin, then, with the knowledge that an opening statement to the jury should be fairly short. It should reveal some things, but not too much. It should leave something to the imagination and arouse interest and curiosity about the evidence to come. Like everything else in the trial, the opening statement must be planned. If you represent a plaintiff, then from either your opening statement or your first witness the jury must be sufficiently informed about the setting and background to know what the case is about.

Simple Language

However this background is conveyed, it must be presented in such simple terms and simple language that any lay juror can understand. In one sense the whole function and value of lawyers, in society and in every phase of practice, is their ability to take esoteric and complicated problems and subjects such as laws and lawsuits and reduce them to simple problems in simple terms so the lay public can understand and deal with them. In talking to juries, discard your "legalese."

If you represent the plaintiff, you have already planned the presentation of your case, and your opening statement should obviously dovetail with this plan. The first question this presents is the order of your presentation. Who will be your first witness? Is he sufficiently pleasant and articulate to permit you to lead him through the factual background of the case by questions and answers, or should you not count on him and do it yourself in the opening statement? This is important—you want it done right. The way the problem is stated can sometimes suggest the answer.

If you represent the defendant, the jury will have already heard the opening statement of the plaintiff. You may wish to adopt it, reject it, or amend it. If the disparity between the plaintiff's version of what occurred is vastly different from yours, you may wish simply to start over from the beginning. Unless I could think of a more interesting or exciting way, I always tried to outline my version of the facts in the order in which they occurred. This gives you a "built-in" plan and makes it easier for the jury to follow.

You will have to exercise your judgment on these matters, depending on the facts and the developments in your particular case; but from this opening point all the way to final verdict, keep one thing always in the back of your mind: some lawyers put jurors to sleep, others keep them enthralled. Ask yourself this question: If the outcome hangs in doubt, which of these lawyers is more likely to get the verdict?

Much of what I have said about the opening statement also applies to the presentation of direct testimony. The manner in which you proceed with your direct case must again necessarily depend in some measure on whether you represent a plaintiff or a defendant. If you represent a defendant, the background of the case will already have been covered by the plaintiff and by the opening statements, though you may want at the outset to supply any vital omissions in the background or to correct and refute by your first witness any false or incorrect statements about the background suggested by the witnesses of the plaintiff. If the discrepancies about the background are great, you may wish to start over and have your witness paint an entirely new or different background more in keeping with your theories of the case.

If you represent a plaintiff you start the presentation of evidence laboring under one distinct disadvantage: you have to go first. Remember the old saw that "figures don't lie but liars do figure." While you are questioning your client on direct, your opponent and his lawyer are sitting there listening to everything he says and busily adjusting their tactics and position to capitalize on every advantage revealed. In many situations it is a distinct advantage for your opponent to have to take a position first. Frequently there is nothing you can do about this and in some cases it makes little difference, but there are also many cases in which you should consider completely reversing this advantage by calling the opposite party as your first witness for purposes of cross-examination.

This is particularly true where the testimony of your client will contain surprises your opponent may not know about. In such a situation first pin down your opponent by cross-examination and then hit him with the surprise. Sometimes this can produce pleasing results. Of course if you plan to follow this strategy you will first have to outline the background of the case in your opening statement in order to put your cross-examination in context.

In any event, from this point on, whether representing a plaintiff or defendant, I would also again try, as nearly as possible, to present my case chronologically; that is, to present each successive event in the direct order in which it occurred, saving questions on which special emphasis is needed for last.

Score Points

Before you cross-examine any witness you must answer for yourself a critical question: Did this witness really hurt your case in his direct examination? If your answer is no, then your decision about cross-examination should always be the same: don't. Some lawyers would make an exception to this rule when the witness is friendly or at least not hostile. But how can you be sure he is not hostile? You must decide for yourself, but I warn you: If you make a practice of trying to score points by cross-examining witnesses called by the other side who have not hurt you on direct, sooner or later you will get burned. More cases are lost during trial by risky cross-examination, or too much cross-examination, than in any other way.

Personally, I would also forego cross-examination where the witness in question *has* hurt my case but the damage involves something I already know I must admit or explain away. The most dangerous notion in the world for a trial lawyer is the idea that he has to cross-examine every witness in order to be a good lawyer.

Young lawyers seem to think the jurors expect it and that to decline is a sign of weakness. Along with this, young lawyers also conjure up another vain and very dangerous hope: that somehow they will succeed in breaking down the hostile witness and so produce a miraculous victory.

Disabuse yourself of such notions except in very, very rare cases or when your case is already so badly lost that more harm is impossible. Otherwise, if your determination to say something becomes overwhelming, try this: "Your honor, I have no quarrel with the testimony of this witness and no questions on cross-examination. Mr. Witness, you may step down." That avoids the risk and at least explains to the jury why you didn't cross-examine.

We come then to the critical witness who has really hurt your case and whom you must cross-examine. How do you begin? By this time you are keenly aware of the areas of your case in which the witness has hurt you most. Having hurt you there once, he would probably like to do so again, so that is where he would like for you to start. Be sure you do not give him the chance, unless you have other positive proof that he is either lying or in error.

If you disbelieve his damaging testimony, he must have some reason—some interest, connection, bias or prejudice—that has caused him to want to crucify your client and to testify as he has. He is also likely to be conscious of this reason for his hostility and would prefer not to have his motives examined. Since this examination is not what he wants, that is precisely where you should begin. This is where your pre-trial preparation should come in handy. If he is a crucial witness, as his testimony would indicate, you should already know something about him. Is he related to the other party? Have they ever worked together? Owed each other money? Fished or golfed together? Gone to the same church or club? Have they ever served on the same bureaus, boards or committees? Have they ever visited in each other's home? Has he or anyone in his family ever had any difficulty with your client or been involved in a similar suit or situation?

I do not suggest that in every case you ask all of these questions. Your advance knowledge and investigation of the witness should suggest the most promising place to start. Once you find a connection, bore in. Maybe the witness will get mad. Good: "Whom the gods would destroy they first make mad." That is how Clarence Darrow broke down William Jennings Bryan in the famous Scopes trial.

In cross-examining a crucial witness I *always* wrote out most of my critical questions in advance, setting pitfalls every few questions for him to fall into, since he can not know what the next question will be. In every litigated transaction there must always be a few indisputable circumstances that tend to favor your version of the occurrence. If you can lead the hostile witness to deny an indisputable fact or claim an impossible one, you are making progress.

Sometimes a witness will entrap himself before you even ask a question. Suppose, for example, you are defending against a railroad crossing injury. A witness for the plaintiff swears positively that the crossing sign was completely invisible, being hidden by bushes or covered with kudzu. Suppose further that you happen to have a photograph, taken immediately after the accident, showing the naked sign, clearly visible from 100 yards away. Show him the photograph and confront him with the impossibility or incredibility of his testimony.

At this point you will have to bifurcate your future questions into two lines of questioning, depending on his answers. If he persists in his obviously erroneous answer you will have to proceed one way, for which written questions should be already prepared, whereas if he admits his error, you will have to pursue another tack for which written questions should also be prepared. In spite of these clever little traps he may escape your snare. If so, go on to the next circumstance indisputably favorable to you and see if you can get him to take an indefensible stand about that.

In all of this there is another rule that is supremely important: Do not ever ask the witness a general question that will allow him to repeat his recital of the damaging testimony given on direct. Ask nothing but narrow and very specific questions confined to and designed to bring out only the specific detail about which you inquired. To keep the questions narrow and precise you will have to ask leading questions. You are allowed to do this on cross-examination, so ask no other kind. This is one important reason why I would write out my questions in advance.

The ability to direct a question to a narrow issue is one you must acquire. As we said of the great Reuben Arnold: "In asking a question he could split a hair between northeast and north." Having asked a narrow question, do not let the witness respond with a general answer. If so, he will invariably repeat and embellish his prior damaging testimony. If he starts that, stop him and ask the court to require him to respond only to the narrow question asked.

Lean on Crutch

You should *never*, I repeat *never*, write out *all* of your cross-examination questions. Otherwise, secure in the knowledge that your next question is already written down, you will tend to lean on them as a crutch, and are apt to lose the attitude of being constantly alert for opportunities to pose new questions which may suddenly develop from the interrogation.

I know of no activity in life that requires more in the way of absolute concentration and quick reaction than cross-examination. The cross-examiner must be poised at every second to thrust for the jugular vein the instant it is inadvertently exposed. In a trial I might also jot down other areas of inquiry that I wish to cover, but notes should not become a substitute for complete awareness of everything that goes on. Nothing should dull the ability to seize instantly upon every opportunity the moment it is presented.

There is another rule that, in my book, should always be observed in conducting cross-examination: Never, never ask a hostile witness "why" he did or did not do a certain thing. The simple reason for this is that the question invites, and will usually make admissible, any outrageous and prejudicial reason the witness can dream up.

The most flagrant example I ever witnessed occurred in defending the husband in a divorce case. In that case, opposing counsel called my client as his first witness for purposes of cross-examination, seeking to show that on a previous weekend he had traveled to Miami to consort with a young lady alleged by plaintiff to be the "other woman." When my client denied he had gone to Miami for this purpose, opposing counsel, in an insulting and disbelieving fashion, said: "Well, then tell the jury why you did go to Miami that weekend." Without batting an eye my client said, "Mr. X, I had to go. I discovered that you had been to Miami ahead of me and talked to some of my friends there while wearing a concealed microphone. You told them you were my lawyer and sought to record any incriminating statements they might make. Upon learning of this, I went to Miami to tell my friends you were not my lawyer but instead were a liar and a cheat and a disgrace to the Atlanta Bar, which you are!" Amidst screaming objections and motions for a mistrial, the trial judge let the answer stand. Opposing counsel never recovered and was in fact discharged by his client at the end of the day.

On the other hand, there is one thing you should always try to do, and when you have done it, sit down: Always try to end your cross-examination on a high note. If you succeed in getting a telling and damaging admission from a hostile witness, my advice is to stop right there with the admission ringing in the jury's ears. Even if you have other questions, let them go, at least for the time being. Otherwise you run a grave risk of committing the most devastating and frequent sin of all cross-examiners: asking one question too many.

The preparation and delivery of your closing argument presents anew the same challenge to your resourcefulness and imagination that the whole trial process presented in the first place, only more so. This is the last this jury will ever see of you and the last impression of things tends to become permanent.

You must, of course, have a plan. Whatever your plan, let it be fresh and resourceful, calculated to rekindle and stimulate the jurors' interest and excitement about their function. In many, if not most, cases, by the time of closing argument the jurors are bored and numb after hearing the lawyers thrust and parry, strain and quibble over details that must often appear, to them, to be trivialities and technicalities. Your argument should therefore be deliberately calculated to wake them up, to present something new, or at the very least to present the issues and the evidence in a new and more interesting light.

One of the poorest arguments I can imagine, though it is frequently used, is to review by name, and one by one, each witness who has testified, restating what each has said. At worst, this kind of argument can deepen a juror's existing boredom and cause him, in his heart, to curse all lawyers for wasting his time. At best, it can only jog, for a moment, their jaded memories. If you win your case this way it is usually done in spite of your argument, not because of it.

The very best arguments, in my experience, are those in which you are able to analogize and compare your case or position to some experience or occurrence in life, in nature, or in the animal kingdom with which the jurors are already familiar or which they will immediately recognize or accept and understand. If your analogy has a tinge of humor or irony, so much the better.

One of the most difficult arguments I ever had to meet was given in Augusta, where I was representing an elderly lady as plaintiff in a damage suit. Disdaining even to discuss liability, my opponent, John Hardin, told the jury: "Gentlemen of the jury, there is not a thing wrong with Edenfield's client that my mother-in-law hasn't had for twenty years."

You will of course have to refer in your argument to those bits of testimony that favor your version of what occurred, but do so not by repeating them in sequence like a parrot, but by fitting them into appropriate places to buttress your analogy.

In your argument never try to make water run uphill. If you have a fact in your case that hurts, but which you know to be true, admit it. The jury will not accept your denial anyway, and to deny it not only insults their intelligence, it may cause them to reject other parts of your argument that they might otherwise accept.

At some time during your closing argument you will have to "clear out the underbrush": that is, you will have to deal with and dispose of all of the numerous fallacies, details, irrelevancies and "red herrings" you know your opponent will parade, or has paraded, before the jury. You will have to exercise your judgment as to when and how to do this, but unless some other dramatic opening presented itself I always liked to do it first; this saves your best and most convincing argument on the real issues for the last, so that, again, you can end on a high note.

Another excellent way to begin an argument and gain the full attention of your jury is to begin with a joke or an anecdote, if you can find one that is truly humorous and that can be made applicable to some aspect of your case; otherwise, forget it. Some lawyers, during the course of their practice, develop little idiosyncrasies, phrases, and mannerisms

375

that are pleasing to jurors and that become virtual trademarks. If you have developed one, and have proved it before previous juries, work it into your act.

Professional Thing

When the verdict is returned, *always,* in every case and regardless of the outcome, be the first to rush to opposing counsel and congratulate him, either upon his victory or his presentation. There are several reasons for this, all sound. In the first place, it is the gentlemanly and professional thing to do; second, on reflection, it will please opposing counsel, if for no other reason because it gives him a boost with his client who is usually nearby; third, it will smooth your relations with him in future cases.

Finally, there is a less altruistic reason: chances are that the client hired your opponent not because he was the best lawyer in town but because he was the best lawyer the client knew in town. Now he knows another one. If you have done your job well he may hire you the next time for the same reason.

How to Try a
Non-Jury Case

by Simon H. Rifkind

The trial of any case involves a philosophy of proof, a science of legal proof, and an art of presentation of proof. I shall deal only with the third.

The art or craft of trying a case, and especially a non-jury case, embraces pleadings, proof, and persuasion. I shall emphasize only the last of these.

The method of persuasion used in the trial of causes has been treated by speakers in a variety of ways, most popular being the recitation of anecdotes, of brilliant examination, or disastrous cross-examination, and on rare occasions, by the exhibition of samples of ripe wisdom, dry and heartwarming like old wine, which fell from the lips of sage judges.

I will tell no such anecdotes. To me these smell more often of the midnight oil of the study than of the dust of the courtroom.

It may nevertheless be worth your while to hear the observations of a trial judge on the courtroom activity of lawyers. So much of what the trial judge does, especially in the federal court, is beyond recall and beyond reproof. Indeed, of about 1,400 decisions of all kinds that I rendered in my first seven and one-half years on the bench, only 85 ever reached the Court of Appeals and only seven the United States Supreme Court. Your fate is so often in the hands of the trial judge that you may as well hearken to the reaction of one member of this fatal tribe.

What do I mean by a non-jury trial? I do not refer only to cases that are traditionally so tried. I mean to include any case that is, in fact, so tried. Such a case may be a criminal case, a bankruptcy case, an admiralty case, a case in equity, or an action for negligence.

I cannot prove but I do believe and hold a conviction that many cases

The author, now a partner in the New York City firm of Paul, Weiss, Rifkind, Wharton & Garrison, served as a United States district judge in New York City during the 1940s. This article was adapted from a speech he delivered to the Association of the Bar of the City of New York in 1949.

are lost that could be won and vice versa. Mind you that I say could, not should. A good example is the case of *Harlot v. Harlot,* reported in Scripture as having been decided by Solomon, J. You may recall that when the evidence was first presented, the judge had ordered that the child be cut in twain. "Bring me a sword," he commanded.

Let us assume for a moment that the parties had rested at that time. Can you imagine the reputation of Solomon, J., had his initial judgment been executed? What saved his reputation was an impetuous woman who had not learned that one is not supposed to address the court after the judge has ruled. It was she who said, "Give her the living child and in no wise slay it."

Had Harlot No. 2 kept her mouth shut at that point the inference would have been inescapable that Harlot No. 1 was a spurious claimant who stopped short of murder. But, as usual, the other had to take the stand and add, "Let it be neither mine nor thine but divide it."

After that, of course, the resolution of the controversy was inevitable. And thus was the King's reputation as a great judge established for all times.

The judge, of course, likes to believe that in every case justice has prevailed. He is nourished in that illusion by his hearing glowing reports about his wisdom. That springs from the victorious lawyers, who spread the report of his sagacity. The losers do not like to talk about their misfortune. But only the naive and the credulous are victims of such self delusion. The fact is inescapable that the lawyer's skill and craftsmanship had much to do with the result.

That such is the case with jury trials is generally credited. Indeed, with respect to jury trials, that belief has become tinged with cynicism. What is frequently overlooked is that nonjury cases are tried to a one-man jury, that the juror-in-robes, like the juror-in-the-box, is made of human material, possessed of the common virtues and common frailties. He, too, has to be kept interested. If he is sleeping he has to be aroused. He has to be persuaded. Your knowledge must become his knowledge, your inferences must be made his inferences. If you fail in these primary objectives, you might as well keep your client at home and save the subpoena fees of your witnesses.

Time after time, I have noticed a lawyer go through the elaborate ritual of proving the signature, the delivery, and the receipt of a paper, exhibiting it to his adversary, arguing admissibility, and, finally, marking it in evidence. No sooner is the sacred symbol affixed by the clerk than the paper is calmly deposited in the lawyer's briefcase. The exhibit is in the record, but alas, its presence is unfelt in the judge's mind. Perhaps the lawyer is under the illusion that the judge's law clerk will decide the case and that therefore getting the paper into the record is all that is required. I suggest to you that such a gamble is not worth the risk.

A few basic propositions:

1. I think it would be useful to acknowledge that a trial is not an agency for the exploration of facts. It is not a fact finding instrument except in the peculiar meaning that fact finding has for lawyers. Whatever may once have been the practice, today, with the liberal provisions for pretrial discovery, we can declare with certainty that the trial is neither the time nor the place for the lawyer to discover the facts of his case. It is both the time and the place for the exhibition and demonstration of his case to public view.

   If I were to use the language of science, I would say that the trial is the verification of an hypothesis by experiment. A trial, by dictionary definition, is a test. In the courtroom the lawyer's hypothesis is tested. The object of the trial is to reduce two contradictory hypotheses to one, to a single "given" to which a rule of law can be applied.

2. Lawyers sometimes labor under the illusion that the trial is a means for the ascertainment of the truth. Professional readers I am sure will understand when I say that such a proposition is only partially true. Service of truth is not the exclusive concern of the law. The parol evidence rule, the hearsay rule, the statute of frauds, the attorney's privilege, the physician's and clergyman's privileges, the privilege against self-incrimination, all serve public policies that may parallel or run counter to the interests of the truth.

   I mention this fact because all too often have I seen lawyers fluttering around like trapped butterflies, struggling with a case as it exists in their minds instead of with the case as it is developed in the courtroom.

3. Within the limitations I have mentioned, there can be no difference of opinion over the proposition that the chief and predominant concern of the trial lawyer is and ought to be with the facts, broadly conceived, rather than the law. For that there are a number of reasons:

   - You can get another chance to argue your view of the law before the same judge or before an appellate court but the facts, except in rare instances, remain as found by the trial judge. In the federal courts the facts stand unless "clearly erroneous."
   - The facts set up emotional or cardiac reactions in the judicial mind and heart. The judge's reaction is either, the plaintiff ought to win, let me see if the law permits such a result, or, the defendant ought to win if the law will allow it.

The law being what it is, living and fluid, you can generally find what you are looking for. The function of the trial lawyer, in part, consists in persuading the judge to look for the helpful rule of law. I remember Judge Joseph Proskauer saying to a court, "My defense is the statute of limitations and now, if you will allow it, I shall spend the rest of my allotted time in persuading you to apply it."

How does one go about trying a non-jury case? A number of propositions have become clear to me.

1. One never learns how to try a case by listening to lecturers any more than one can learn to ride a bicycle that way.
2. After you have tried a case it may be desirable for you to get audience reaction to your performance.
3. Every controversy sufficiently significant to warrant the employment of counsel and court is bottomed on a story, and every story that involves conflict has the elements of drama.

I maintain that every trial is theatre and every trial lawyer is a producer of a good, bad, or indifferent play. The purpose of every play is to persuade, to cause the audience to identify itself with the hero.

The hero may be a saint, in which case he must not arouse the sense of sanctimoniousness. He may be a villain, but if so, he must be a lovable villain. If you will think of your case as the raw material of a play, your imagination will suggest a hundred relevant lines to pursue that otherwise you would neglect.

I always observe with amazement the lawyer who looks around the courtroom to call whichever of his witnesses happens to be there. No playwright behaves so quixotically. Is it any wonder that the judge's mind wanders from the case, that he reads a brief while such a lawyer is trying his case. It has always been my view that if a judge falls asleep, it is the lawyer's fault. Certainly, that rule prevails in the theatre and I see no reason why the same rule should not also apply in the courtroom. It is your task to arouse his attention. It is your job to build your case. Let it develop with all the arts of the stage called into play. You may present it chronologically or logically, that is by developing different elements of the case. You could even use what the motion pictures call the flashback. But always build it to a climax.

I know that some lawyers believe that such methods are useful in a jury trial but that it is an unnecessary art to display in a non-jury case. I disagree. A judge is not a grinding machine into which you dump a group of ingredients in any kind of order.

My conviction is that the judge is a one-man audience. True, he is a sophisticated playgoer. Perhaps, like many a critic, he may be a weary playgoer. All the more reason why your artistry must be more subtle, less corny, more intriguing. After all, your one-man juror awards the Pulitzer Prize.

It is safe to assume that the judge, like most people, is responsive to the tugs of fair and foul play, to sportsmanship or its absence, to courage or timidity, to kindness or ill will, to charity or malice. It is safe to assume that even a conscientious judge would rather listen because he is interested than because he is a slave to duty. If you have succeeded in identifying your client's cause with the ends of justice, generally speaking the law will follow, fawning.

Since I suggested dramatic treatment of a case, it follows that every piece of stage business that interrupts the development should, wherever possible, be avoided. When a character on the stage tears open a letter and reads it, the audience normally supplies the evidence of sending, of authority, of authenticity. At the trial, we generally pause while the tedious proof is put in—frequently when no genuine issue is presented.

Once, that may have been excusable. Today, it is a sign of carelessness. The pretrial rules provide ample means for the elimination of such interruptions, either by admissions, interrogatories, depositions, or stipulations.

It has been my experience that few lawyers make adequate use of such simple aids as blackboards, charts, graphs, photographs, and models. Recently, I had an experience that brought it forcefully to my attention. The subject matter was a fire on board a large freighter. One witness, a surveyor, with the aid of notes, recited a long chain of facts, including dimensions, storage in each hold, areas of fire damages, and so on. It all left a blur on my mind.

Another came up with a large scale drawing of the vessel showing hold dimensions, storage arrangements, and some red paint indicating fire. The intensity of the color varied with the extent of the damage. It left a vivid impression, it became a constant source of reference by other witnesses. It got across the footlights.

Cross-examination has only three possible purposes. One, discredit the witness's story by showing it could not have happened. Two, discredit the witness by showing that he did not see or hear, that he does not remember what he saw or heard, that he did not accurately report what he remembered, that he is biased, that he is interested, that he is unworthy of belief. Three, make him your witness. Generally, these are mutually exclusive, although not all the time. Therefore, it is important that you should know before you start which of these objectives you will pursue. If the answer is that you will pursue none of these objectives, then you should not cross-examine. The gravest mistake is to guess.

There are a few specific suggestions that I should take the liberty to offer. *One,* employ that style of presentation in which you find yourself most at ease. There are as many sound ways of proceeding as there are sound lawyers. My advice is, be yourself. You are more likely to succeed than by trying to imitate a personality unlike yourself.

Two, present your material dramatically, but do not be theatrical. The difference is that which obtains between an actor and a ham.

Three, know what you want to do. You may have to yield to the judge's preference, but often you will not. On numerous occasions I have been asked whether I cared for an opening. Schubert might as well step up in front of the curtain and inquire whether the audience wished

381

to see the prologue. Generally, my answer was no, because I assumed that if the lawyer felt he could get along without it, there was no reason why I should waste my time. I never, however, refused an opening to a lawyer who offered to make one.

Four, the opening to a judge serves a different purpose from a jury opening and should be differently constructed. "This is an action for rescission of a policy of life insurance," tells the judge a great deal more than similar words would convey to a jury.

I find it useful to have the plaintiff's attorney tell the judge in his opening what elements he must prove for his prima facie case. To illustrate, if the action is one for deceit, I should like to be told that the elements are (1) a misrepresentation of facts, (2) intentionally made, (3) with intent to induce reliance thereon, (4) which does induce reliance, (5) to the damage of the person to whom the representations are tendered.

Another example: the elements of a preference are (1) a transfer, (2) of a debtor's property, (3) to or for the benefit of a creditor, (4) on account of an antecedent debt, (5) made while the debtor is insolvent, (6) within four months before the filing of the petition of bankruptcy, (7) the effect of which will be to give the creditor a greater percentage of his debts than another creditor of the same class.

If any of these elements has been admitted by answer or concession, the lawyer should state it then and there. An experienced judge checks these elements off in his mind as the case goes along. He is ready with his decision on the defendant's motion at the end of the plaintiff's case as soon as it is made. If you have done so, you may be able to omit recitation even of the skeleton of the plaintiff's case when the motion to dismiss is made, unless, for reasons beyond your control, the evidence has been received in disorganized array.

A sentence or two to fix the color of your case is all that is required to conclude your opening. To do more is unnecessary and hazardous. More than once have I seriously considered dismissing a complaint on the opening alone.

Five, at the close of your case, please do not commit this cardinal sin: Please do not say to the judge, "I am ready to rest unless your Honor wants more evidence." First, it is an admission that you don't know your own case, that you have not evaluated the weight of your proof. Second, you are asking help from one who knows far less of your case than you do. Third, you might suffer a serious misadventure if the court should call for more evidence not at your disposal. Finally, you run the risk that the judge will take over the trial of your case and lose it for you.

Six, a good summation will seal victory upon a good case. It gives you a fighting chance with a poor case. For reasons beyond my comprehension, I have seen many lawyers throw away this opportunity when trying a case without a jury. An effective summation should do two things. One, it should complete the process of persuasion by showing the logical superiority of the inference from the evidence which you are advocating. Two, it should, in effect, tender to the judge an opinion in your favor which, if he is persuaded to follow, he could sign. By that I mean that you must fabricate before him a complete chain, coherent, consistent, and articulated in all its parts, which leads inevitably to victory for your client.

If you let the judge get off the bench without having caused him to say to himself that he will work on the case on the hypothesis that you are right, you have not done all you should have done. Except for very complicated cases, it ought not to be necessary for a lawyer to wind up his case with a request that he be allowed two weeks for a brief.

Seven, I suppose most lawyers, but especially New York lawyers, are parochial. They assume that the law of New York is the law of the universe. Not in one case in ten do lawyers so much as suggest which law governs the case.

I suppose that in the state courts, conflict of law questions are not as abundant as in the federal courts. Let me make a confession that in a number of cases, after finding nothing but New York law cited on a problem manifestly governed by the law of a sister state, I have had counsel stipulate that the New York law is the same as the applicable law. I found that my independent adventures to discover the law of Massachusetts or Nebraska were too great a drain on my time. I was confronted by that problem at least six times during the last few months of my service.

Eight, a minor detail—but one that should be mastered from the very beginning of a trial career—that is, to learn to handle your papers and other props. The lawyer who cannot find his pleadings, his exhibits, his depositions, who is always fumbling around, whose courtroom table looks like a rummage sale, does not impress a trial judge. He wastes time. He slows down his story. I remember the admiration with which I watched the mechanical perfection with which papers were handled in one of the Russian cases I tried for many weeks. Hundreds of exhibits were handled without a hitch, without lost motion, and without boredom.

A final suggestion: There used to be circulated a cynical aphorism that success comes to some lawyers from knowing the law, to others from knowing the judge. My own recommendation is: know the facts of your case. Without that, victory is highly improbable. With it, you have a chance. And a chance is all any good lawyer really wants.

McGarry's Illustrated Forms of Jury Trial for Beginners

by Mark R. McGarry, Jr.

All the advice herein was not dreamed up or devised originally by me. This material reflects what the very best lawyers do on their good days. Beginners probably won't pay any attention to all this, but if they have any talent and are lucky enough to have two trials a week for two full years, they will have learned everything called for herein the hard way.

If the beginners are not lucky enough to have two trials a week for two years—just a few now and then—but read and try to follow the framework of these sketches, they might still look like pros.

Those who are beginners and choose to ignore all this and only have a few cases a year will always look like beginners and should stay. . .

out

of

the

courtroom.

M. R. McGarry, Jr.

Er . . . ahem . . . ah . . .

Let me say this . . . some of the very best lawyers, bless 'em, never go near a courtroom. This is for those who want to and do.

It is urged that this material be read at least once before every jury trial with the idea that the sole purpose of these notes is to help you clear the garbage and meaningless persiflage out of your presentation. You will feel better about it all and you may very well look like a real pro long before you get to be one.

Voir Dire

So you want to look like a pro?

The author is Circuit Judge for the 6th Judicial Circuit Court of Florida, Pinellas County.

Well then. . . . The very first word out of your mouth as you stand before the jury must be a proper voir dire question.

However, if you feel compelled to say something else, you may go down behind the building in the vicinity of the dumpster and say the following, or something similar:

> Well, good morning prospective members of the jury. How are you? My name is Running Mouth. I am an assistant state's attorney working for the people of Florida and this is my opportunity to ask you a number of questions touching upon your qualifications to be a juror in a case such as this. This is the only opportunity we'll have to talk to one another during this trial. After I finish my questions, the other side will have an opportunity to ask questions of you and these questions will probably be similar to the ones I ask. It is necessary these questions be asked so we find out something about you.
>
> I want to thank you in advance for the attention that I know you are willing to pay to this trial and for the sacrifices that you have made in being here. I know this is a great imposition upon your time. However, I want each of you to know that I appreciate it, the state's attorney appreciates it, and the people throughout the state of Florida (or wherever) appreciate it.
>
> This case, of course, is a criminal case and it is my job to prove this case beyond and to the exclusion of a reasonable doubt.

To this paragraph you may want to add your own personal witticisms or other gems that you think reflect your personality and your skill and ability and to show what a fine fellow you are. I suggest you work this statement up ahead of time and have it ready for trial, have it neatly typed, or better yet, memorized so that you will not falter or stammer. Then, as you lean over the dumpster, speak in loud, clear tones so that every corner of the dumpster may hear exactly what you have to say.

Having thus refreshed yourself and cleared all of that gunk out of your system, you may return to the courtroom, stand before the jury, open your mouth . . . and ask a proper voir dire question.

Whenever asking voir dire questions, always strive to ask a question that does not—and I say again—does not result in a yes or no answer. The question, ''Have you any friends in law enforcement?'' may well yield a yes or no answer. However, if phrased, ''Will you tell me of your contact with any friends or acquaintances that you have in law enforcement?'', the juror addressed will be required to speak and as long as he or she is talking, you will be gaining some information and insight into that juror. And remember, your role in voir dire is not to give the jurors poop, but to glean information from them.

Proper voir dire may include, but not necessarily be limited to, the following questions.

Tell me of your . . .
1. Friends in law enforcement.
2. Participation in civil or criminal litigation.
3. Age, occupation of children and husband or wife, as the case may be.
4. Hobbies, social and professional organizations, and offices held now or in the past.
5. Special training (medicine–accounting–law–insurance).
6. Being a victim of a crime.
7. Health or physical problems.
8. Probation or guidance-counseling experience.
9. Prior jury service.
10. Sensitivity in religious or moral areas.
11. Being under medication that would affect thinking or sitting.
12. Reading of this case in the press.
13. Belief in the death penalty. (Not ''Do you favor. . .?'') (Yes or no is best here.)
14. Church group work or other group work.

Only ask questions that will provide information to help *you* evaluate this juror. Don't expect a juror to evaluate himself. For example, do not ask:

- Will you follow the law?
- Can you be fair?
- Can you pay attention?

It is a rare juror indeed who will tell you that he breaks the law, cheats at cards, or daydreams.

Do not question jurors about possible instructions.

Do not attempt to adjust the attitudes of jurors because you will fail, and in this regard, it is ordinarily not proper to explain the case (and your theories) on voir dire. On rare occasion it may be permissible to give a short synopsis about the case, but clear it with the judge and opposing counsel beforehand, and you will thus avoid the embarrassment of being corrected in front of the jury.

Cut out the garbage. For example:
1. My name is . . .
2. I work for . . .
3. This is my opportunity to . . .
4. I want to thank you for . . .
5. Can you assure me that . . .
6. You won't hold it against me if . . .
7. We are just trying to get to the truth.
8. Can you understand . . .
9. Now, I have just a few questions.

This is not intended to single out state's attorneys. This all applies to defense lawyers and blackstocking civil lawyers as well.

Opening Statements

It is not necessary to curtsy or fawn. It most certainly is not necessary to explain what an opening statement is. It is not a game plan or a road map or anything of the sort. It is a short, succinct, simple, and understandable statement of the case, the number of witnesses, and a synopsis of what each will say.

Get to work, dammit. Don't stammer, shuffle, or babble. Don't waste words or time. Be brisk and to the point and professional. Put yourself in the place of a juror. How would you like to sit there and be told by some young pup what an opening statement is?

You will always do your best if you think and talk of something you know a lot about. For example:

Defense in a criminal case:

When you hear the instructions given by the court at the end of this trial, you will hear the words, "reasonable doubt" about 19 or 20 times. My role in the proceedings will be to point out that the evidence in this case is shot through with reasonable doubt, inaccuracies, errors, wretched talk from wretched people, and just plain garbage.

Prosecution in a criminal case:

The peace and dignity of the state of Florida has been abused by that man and the state of Florida is going to prove that he is guilty as charged. The testimony of five witnesses will show you without any doubt that on the night of _____ the Defendant _____, the sum total of which. . . .

Plaintiff in a civil case:

On the _____ day of _____, 19_____, an accident occurred wherein the Plaintiff, Lowe Bhakpayne, was injured severely. The Defendant caused this accident by virtue of negligent driving accompanied by intoxication. The injuries thus caused were treated at _____ Hospital by Drs. _____ and _____ and thereafter on an outpatient basis by Drs. _____ and _____. Pain has been considerable and disabling and expensive. The disability is permanent and the loss of ability to earn is shocking. The medical testimony will demonstrate the extent of the injuries and treatment and prognosis for future improvement (or in the alternative, deterioration). Other witnesses will tell you of _____. At the conclusion of the testimony you will find it perfectly proper for Mr. Bhakpayne to seek monetary damages.

Defense in a civil case:

We agree that there was an accident and that Mr. Bhakpayne was

387

injured. Our purpose in participating in this proceeding is to inform you of certain facts, which will clearly show:

1. Mr. Wheelie, the Defendant, was not at fault and the Plaintiff, Mr. Bhakpayne, was solely responsible for his own injuries.
2. We will show you through the testimony of Drs. _____ and _____ that Mr. Bhakpayne's injuries are minimal or nonexistent.
3. If after all the testimony there does appear to be some slight injury for which Mr. Wheelie is responsible, the defense hopes to be of assistance in providing information that will make it easy for you to render a proper verdict . . . a verdict that reflects sanity, common sense, sound reasoning, and justice.

Presenting Evidence and Testimony

Here is where your preparation shows up, and happily, most lawyers are quite good at it. After all, you have lived with the evidence for a while and studied it and are comfortable with this area of the trial.

There are a few dumpster areas, however:

1. Now, Mr. Witness, I have a few questions, et cetera.
2. How are you, Mr. Witness?

Try not to tell the witness you have a few questions, because sure as blazes some of the jurors will start counting.

Don't ask a witness how he is, because he just might say something you do not want to hear. Example:

I was fine until you two-bit shysters hauled me in here off my job to help you try to cheat the insurance company out of some bread.

The most abused area of presenting testimony is overkill. By that I mean endless questions and minuscule detail. Example:

Q: Mr. Witness, how far was the table from the wall?
A: About 4 feet.
Q: Could it have been 4 feet, 6 inches?
A: Yeah, could've been.
Q: Well, which was it—4 feet or 4 feet, 6 inches?
A: Yeah, well, uh, something like that.
Q: Well, that's not very specific, Mr. Witness—try to be more specific. Could it have been 4 feet, $1^1/_{16}$ inches?
A: Couldabeen, I guess.

And on and on and on.

You are better off by far to place a bare-bones case before the jury, an interesting, bare-bones case. You can be sure your idiot opponent will fill in the bones on his cross-examination. If he doesn't, the jury will do so in their minds, and you can put some more flesh on with redirect.

If you try to smother the jury with endless trivia, they will become bored with you *and* with your case, and you will lose their attention.

Give the jury something to think about and remember; most people who are bored are not inclined to be alert.

There are three basic rules that may prove helpful when the average new attorney considers the matter of cross-examination.

Rule No. 1: Don't.

Rule No. 2: Don't.

Rule No. 3: Don't.

Almost without exception, cross-examination will accomplish the following:

1. It will allow the testimony of the witness to be heard by the jury at least three times (on direct, on cross, and on redirect).
2. It will fill in any gaps or oversights in the witness's testimony on direct.
3. It will give opposing counsel a splendid chance to recall what he has forgotten to ask on direct.
4. It will give you an opportunity to ask a question that will ruin the case for you.

The mere fact of your opponent's calling this witness should give you your first clue. He wants him there, and he wants him talking. Your opponent will stop his direct examination only when he can't think of anything else to say. He frequently will have forgotten much that he would like to ask under the stress of it all. So don't you come along and solve his problems for him.

It takes guts, but you know you have the intelligence to say, "No questions." You may want to embellish that statement somewhat, such as, "Judge, sir, the defense doesn't feel it necessary to dignify the absurdities of that testimony with any questions at all."

It must be said that very few new attorneys (almost none) have the skills necessary to succeed at cross-examination. Many (almost all) erroneously think they do, however, and will vigorously cross-examine the most innocuous witness, hurling questions until one or more of the above-numbered results have been achieved.

Don't conclude that lawyers' intellect is lacking. Not so. By dang, witnesses are hard to shake. Witnesses are psychologically geared to defend their story, and the more they are pressed on cross-examination, the more they will remember (and some of it true).

Jurors want to believe a witness and frequently resent withering cross-examination, especially if it's unproductive.

You just can't improve your case with your opponent's witness. Now, doesn't that make sense?

The longer your opponent's witness is on the stand, the more you will be hurt. Your task is to get the witness off the stand, out of the courtroom, and slam away from the courthouse as soon as possible.

Your cross gives your opponent another shot at his witness, doesn't it? And by this time he will have had time to reflect and may have his wits about him and will probably do a better job on redirect than he did with his first opportunity.

So, if you feel you must consider cross-examination, if you have searched your soul and if you have properly prepared your case, then at least one day before trial, prepare your cross and the answers you know for sure that you can expect in writing and don't allow yourself to deviate in the heat of battle.

Never ask a witness to clarify some of his testimony. How many times have you heard the question, "Now, Mr. Witness, I'm a little confused by your testimony." (And so on.) By the time your confusion is all cleared up, it will feel like a kick in the tail with a frozen gum boot. For heaven's sake, talk about the confusing testimony on final argument.

Keeping in mind your written questions and your expected answers (which you better be able to back up), you may ask questions touching upon . . .

- inconsistent prior statements;
- conviction of crime;
- reputation;
- inconsistent testimony of other witnesses; or
- some false testimony.

Sound familiar? See your Criminal Instructions on Impeachment.

Most people don't perform with peak mental efficiency when they are under stress. This is particularly true of attorneys under the strain of a jury trial. (There are few more stressful situations.) Add to that a lack of vast trial experience and natural self-consciousness and you have a mixture that will render a person incapable of calm reflection.

Yes, yes, of course you can handle it. Why, sitting in your air-conditioned office with your witty colleagues, you know absolutely and positively that you can handle any situation on cross-examination.

Make no mistake . . . You can't do it under stress. You just can't.

But . . . trust your stupidity because you can rely on it. And rest comfortably in the knowledge that if you do something on cross, you will probably do it wrong.

As lawyers attain that field of vast experience with a reputation for skill and success, their need to cross-examine diminishes considerably. What little there is, is short and never repeats the facts brought out on direct.

Never.

No, never.

A good rule of thumb: If the witness hasn't really hurt you, don't give him a chance to hurt you, and if the witness has hurt you, don't give him a chance to kill you.

If by any chance your client gets restless and urges you to cross-examine, show him these notes and comfort him by pointing out that on the average, you will get better results by questioning your own friendly witness.

On some rare occasions you will find a witness who is such an outrageous and bald-faced liar that he needs cross-examination and you can have a good time with him. Do it quietly and with a delicate touch. If the jury has any sense at all (and remember . . . you picked 'em), they'll know. The loud bulldozer attack may cause the jury to resent you both.

Closing Argument

Well, here we are. Here is your chance to look either like a pro or like a loser on a freshman debating club. It is fortunate for all of us that very few cases turn on the closing argument. However, your rating as a player will surely be affected by how controlled you are in getting in your last licks.

So how do you do it right?

First off, don't stand there like a jerk and thank the jury for the attention they have given.

Don't say one word that strays away from the parameters of the case, not one single word. You only have a few minutes to summarize all your efforts. That, coupled with the reasonable certainty that the jury is probably at its collective wits' end, should be all you need to inspire you to be (1) succinct, (2) interesting, and (3) above all, quick, for God's sake.

I know it will be practically impossible for you to do, but try to forget that you are the most charming, skillful, best-looking, best-dressed cat in town. Not one juror in ten will tumble to your charms, but almost all of them are interested in something you both know something about—the case at bar—so stick to it. You will be more comfortable and so will the jury.

Don't be cute or fawn or dance. The very first words out of your mouth should be something to the effect of:

> We said at opening statement that we are going to prove . . . and that is exactly what we have done.

Since you have sensibly decided to stick to the facts and evidence, now what? Never try to tell a jury what a witness said. Each one will remember it a little differently and that puts you on the line. Tell the jury what that witness's testimony means—editorialize on it. It's a lot easier that way. Now, let me say that again. On closing, never try to recall testimony verbatim, comment on the effect of it. Tell the jury what it means. Following are some examples:

Closing for the prosecution:
Members of the jury, the cumulative effect of the evidence in this case proves beyond and to the exclusion of a reasonable doubt that

the Defendant, Dungy Skumbag, is guilty as charged. Witness No. 1 saw him enter the back window. Witness No. 2 saw him leave the front door. Witness No. 3, the victim, saw him with his hands in the safe. Witness No. 4 found his fingerprints on the safe. And so on.

Closing for the plaintiff:

Members of the jury, the preponderance of the evidence in this case shows that my client, Jane Myklient, was injured while operating her auto at the intersection of 4th Street and 4th Avenue and her injuries and all the damages that followed were caused by the negligence of the Defendant, Mary Badriver. Witness No. 1 said Miss Myklient had a green light and Mrs. Badriver had a red one. Witness No. 2 said that Mrs. Badriver did not even slow down at the intersection and that, yes, the light was red for her. Witness No. 3 said that Miss Myklient suffered terribly in the hospital for 30 days. Witness No. 4, Dr. Seeit Myway, gave graphic testimony as to the extent of her injuries and he says she is permanently disabled over 20 percent of her body. And so on. And finally after all this it is clear that Miss Myklient certainly has nothing to be ashamed of in asking for damages in the amount of [you name it].

Closing for the defense (criminal):

The state's case is a shambles—it is shot through with reasonable doubt. Reasonable doubt is what this case is founded on, nothing else. For instance, the fourth witness called by the State said there were *no*—I say again, NO fingerprints. Now, if that isn't reasonable doubt, what in the blue-eyed world is it? Witness No. 6 for the State said that no gun was found—no gun. I can't believe the State would bring a witness whose testimony shows no gun was found. Once again, reasonable doubt. As a matter of fact, that goes beyond reasonable doubt all the way to positive doubt. The State has quoted three of their witnesses verbatim—and that ain't the way I heard the testimony, folks, and I don't think you heard it that way either, and so on.

Closing for the defense (civil):

Civil defense lawyers are all perfect.

Now, what you should not do (among other things) on closing. You should not attack your opposing attorney. You should not attack your opposing attorney's tactics. You should not in fact pay any attention at all to your opponent on closing argument. To mention your opponent, to allude to him, to criticize him, to acknowledge his existence gives him nothing but credence and wastes your valuable time.

Remain Unruffled

Ignore your opponent. You will save time, your feathers will remain unruffled, and you will be better able to concentrate on your own affairs. Cooperate with your opponent as necessary to present the case in an orderly and efficient way. But on closing, ignore him.

For the dumpster:

1. Members of the jury, I want to thank you . . .
2. This is my opportunity to . . .
3. This is my only opportunity to speak, after which my *opponent* will have an opportunity . . .
4. Evolution of our system of laws and trials began with . . .
5. Don't hold it against my client. . . .

And so on. In case you missed the point, do not use any word, phrase, sentence, paragraph, chapter, or verse, any wheeze, gasp, snort, or sigh that does not verbally inform the jury of the merits of your case.

Only say it once. Say it right—but say it once. Nothing is more amateurish than repeating yourself. Everybody (jurors included) can conclude that someone who has very little to say usually says the same thing several times.

Now, remember, it takes practice. Like tennis or golf or football or typing, or any skill, much practice equals more skill (in most cases).

Walter Cronkite gets right down to business. He doesn't fawn or thank you or say anything unnecessary. You may not believe him or like him, but he looks like a pro.

And so can you.

Jury Research: Spotting Jurors Who Can Hurt

by Farrald G. Belote

Lawyers who try cases know that every one has its own special risks. When they try to estimate them for their clients, they may say something like, ''I think we have about a 70 percent chance of getting a good verdict,'' or maybe, ''I am afraid this one is going to be a toss-up,'' meaning that they think the chances are about 50-50.

This kind of estimate—when it is made at all—is usually based on experience with similar cases or some kind of impressionistic evaluation of what is likely to happen when the case is tried. Usually there is very little scientific information behind it.

But there is some reliable information that can be gathered about any case—information that lends a measure of scientific precision to estimating the outcome of a case; information that is important in selecting jurors; information that helps develop case strategy, strengthen key issues, and even decide when to settle and when to fight.

Jury research uses social science methods to get information about the risks that different cases present. One of the most obvious places to put this kind of knowledge to work is in picking a jury. If we know the attitudes, beliefs, and demographic makeup of potentially damaging jurors, we can use this information in jury voir dire. We then stand a better chance of getting a jury that, if not sympathetic, will at least be free of strong prejudice against us or of bias in favor of the other side.

Jury research does more than just help pick a jury. It can uncover issues that are likely to be important to jurors—issues on which they will base their verdict. With this information, a trial lawyer can develop a more effective presentation of his case.

To demonstrate how jury research works, let us examine an actual case:

The author is an attorney with Litigation Sciences in Los Angeles.

The plaintiff was a mother whose child was born with heartrending deformities. She claimed her daughter's birth defects were caused by contact with some highly toxic products while she was pregnant and working in a chemical manufacturing plant. The defendant was her employer.

The defendant thought there was not enough evidence to establish a conclusive link between the child's birth defects and the substances with which the woman had worked. Although it was arguable that exposure to some of the chemicals that were in her workplace could have caused the child's birth defects, there was no evidence that they had done so. There were other causes—entirely unrelated to the mother's work—that could have been responsible for the child's condition.

The defense thought that this was exactly the kind of case in which compelling damages might cause a jury to overlook the holes in the plaintiff's case on liability.

Now suppose you are conducting the defense in this case. After years of depositions, briefs, and motions, it is time to pick the jury. Who will you challenge? What are the chances of using your peremptory strikes wisely? What elements in a juror's background will identify this person as a juror who can cost you the case and your client a good deal of money?

Take a good look at them. Among the jurors in the pool are some upper-middle-class, conservative, white, elderly males, as well as some young, liberal, Hispanic females. Obviously, these are widely different sorts of people. Faced with choosing between a member of one or the other group, who would be preferable? What is the probability that people in the first group will hurt you and that those in the second group will be on your side?

Remember, to find for the plaintiff in this case, a juror must be able to conclude that there was a link between the birth defects and exposure to the defendant's chemicals, and from a factual standpoint, there is no strong supporting evidence. Is this the sort of determination that the jurors' backgrounds will affect?

Absolutely. Research has shown that when there is a lack of specific evidence linking cause and effect, jurors are likely to decide the issue on the basis of attitudes and beliefs that are firmly in place at the beginning of the trial. Even in the presence of strong factual evidence, people rely on their attitudes and beliefs and use them to interpret the facts and evaluate their importance.

To determine what kinds of juror would be most dangerous to the defense in this case and how they could be identified, we did some empirical research. This involved conducting telephone interviews with 600 randomly selected people who were qualified for jury service in the area where the case would be tried. Using this group as a test population, we explored people's attitudes toward the issues in the case. Each person in the sample was telephoned and read a scenario that provided the essential elements of the case. The survey respondents were asked to render a verdict and to give us some opinions about the case.

First, we discovered that 27.5 percent of those surveyed favored the plaintiff and would probably support the plaintiff's claims. This meant that in any group of ten prospective jurors, three of them would probably fall into the category of those who would hurt the defense. Identifying those people with measurable, objective characteristics became the primary task of further analysis.

One of the advantages of using a large sample of people, such as the 600 in this case, is that it allows us to draw statistically significant conclusions about subgroups within the larger sample. Using a small group as a basis for understanding a larger group to which it is related gives us valuable information about which jurors are likely to be hostile to our case. Even if you cannot keep them off the jury, the survey findings will let you understand their reasoning processes so that you can present the case to them more effectively.

Potentially hostile jurors in this case become evident as soon as you look at jurors by age, race, and sex. Remember, in the population of potential jurors as a whole, about 27.5 percent favor the plaintiff.

Subgroups by Age

	Under 25	25-39	40-59	60 and over
Percent of subgroup favoring plaintiff	38.7%	27.5%	21.9%	23.9%

The "Under 25" group sticks out because they are substantially more likely to favor the plaintiff than any other. Notice that in this case, people over 40 tend to be more defense-oriented. That is not always true.

This demonstrates one of the basic ideas underlying juror attitude surveys: What is the chance that a person's membership in a subgroup of the population makes that person more likely to be a hostile juror than anyone chosen at random from the total population?

Let us look at another set of demographic subgroups. This time the respondents were grouped by race. But a word of warning before we go on: These statistics only fit the peculiar facts of this particular case and the areas in which the people were surveyed.

Subgroups by Race

	Caucasian	Asian	Black	Hispanic
Percent of subgroup favoring plaintiff	24.7%	33.4%	33.8%	45.0%

Recall that there is a 27.5 percent chance of a member of the population as a whole being in favor of the plaintiff. Examining subgroups by race, one group deviates considerably from the population as a whole. Among Hispanics, there is a 45 percent chance that a member of this subgroup will favor the plaintiff. When statistical tests are applied to the other three racial subgroups, it is discovered that although they all differ from the norm of 27.5 percent in favor of the plaintiff, none differs enough to be statistically significant. In other words, these differences are small enough to be accounted for by chance factors arising out of the sampling process.

It is important to be careful whenever statistical inferences are made. For example, in this case we know that people under the age of 25 have a much greater chance of becoming problem jurors for the defense than do members of other age groups. Does our finding about Hispanics add anything to this? Suppose the Hispanics in our sample are mostly 25 and under. Then we would not know whether their plaintiff orientation was related to their age or ancestry. But in this case, further analysis shows that the Hispanics in our survey are represented in the age groups in about the same proportion as all the other races. Our finding about race is a new and independent factor.

So far we have two demographic variables—race and age. What about sex? Here is the verdict preference by sex among Hispanics:

Plaintiff Jurors Among Hispanics by Sex

	Male	Female
Percent of subgroup favoring plaintiff	43.8%	45.8%

In the subgroup of male Hispanics, 43.8 percent favor the plaintiff; among female Hispanics, the proportion is 45.8 percent. Among Hispanics as a whole, the figure is, as we have seen, 45 percent. Among Hispanics, the difference by sex is not significant.

This case shows how demographic information like age, race, and sex may relate to verdict tendencies. When it does, subgroup membership can be used to help determine which jurors to strike and which to keep.

But contrary to conventional wisdom, demographic characteristics such as race, age, and sex rarely differentiate between plaintiff's and defendant's jurors. Instead, it has been found that people's attitudes, beliefs, and behaviors are far more effective in differentiating juror types. We have to go beyond demographics to uncover how people's attitudes and life styles relate to the issues in the case. We need to know something about a potential juror's attitudes, beliefs, and behaviors. While these may not be the direct cause of verdict preference, they are at least indicators of whatever it is that causes verdict preference. This information can be the basis for more sophisticated approaches to identifying prospective jurors.

397

The birth defect case is one in which the jurors' pretrial attitudes were particularly important. First look at some commonly held attitudes toward political issues by the respondents in our sample. We might suppose that in a case of this type where an injured plaintiff is pitted against a large corporation that an individual's political position would be related to verdict preference. Here are some data for political attitudes in this case:

Subgroups by Political Orientation

	Conservative	Moderate	Liberal
Percent of subgroup favoring plaintiff	24.5%	25.0%	33.1%

Political orientation does not matter as much as we might have supposed. Liberals are more plaintiff-oriented than conservatives, but the difference is barely significant from a statistical standpoint. However, further analysis might reveal that political orientation was an important variable. Its effect may be hidden by another variable. By examining beliefs more closely related to the specific case issues, we might be able to discover this.

Analysis of the survey data showed that it was useful to discover whether or not prospective jurors thought they knew what caused this particular birth defect. General questions were asked about the causes and frequency of birth defects, and a number of people revealed that they thought they knew the causes of birth defects in this case. These people were designated the "can tell" group. On the other hand, others in the sample said they could not tell or did not know what caused the birth defects, placing themselves in a "can't tell" group. We then wondered whether or not membership in one of these groups or the other constituted a tendency to favor the plaintiff more than the 27.5 percent chance of being plaintiff-oriented in the total population. Here are the splits for plaintiff and defendant in the two groups:

Verdict Preference for Subgroups
"Can Tell" and "Can't Tell"

	Can Tell	Can't Tell
Plaintiff jurors	41.0%	21.1%
Defense jurors	59.0%	78.9%

The difference between the percentage of those in the "can tell" subgroup who favor the plaintiff and the percentage of those in the "can't tell" subgroup is significant. If a respondent believes that he can tell what caused the birth defect in this case, there is a better than four in ten chance that he will favor the plaintiff. But in the "can't tell" subgroup, the probability is only slightly better than two in ten. In other words, there is twice the probability that the members of the "can tell" subgroup will favor the plaintiff than will members of the "can't tell" group.

To use this information in connection with what we already know about jurors who can hurt the defendant, let us look at the subgroups of conservatives and liberals under 25 years old. We already know that being under 25 gives one a greater chance of being plaintiff-oriented than people over 25.

Percentage of Plaintiff Jurors in Subgroups under 25 Determined by Dimensions of Political Orientation and "Can Tell" and "Can't Tell" Cause of Birth Defect

	Conservative	Liberal
Percent in Total Political Subgroup under 25	32.7%	44.7%
Percent in "Can Tell" Subgroup under 25	46.2%	52.4%
Percent in "Can't Tell" Subgroup under 25	29.7%	35.3%

Here we see that there is a difference in the probability of being plaintiff-oriented among conservatives and liberals under the age of 25 when the distinction "can tell" and "can't tell" is superimposed. In fact, this latter distinction is a much more powerful discriminator than either age or political orientation alone. Under 25, whether conservative or liberal, the distinction between "can tell" and "can't tell" is potent. Among liberals under the age of 25 who say they can tell what caused the birth defect, over half are in favor of the plaintiff, as opposed to a little more than a third in the "can't tell" group. Among conservatives the same relationship exists, although it is slightly less pronounced.

If you want to know more about these people, you are on the right track. Who are these "can tells," and what do they believe?

If we go back to our total sample of more than 600 people and examine the two main subgroups, "can tell" and "can't tell," we can begin to identify what the "can tell" subgroup members believe will be relevant to this case. If we are unable to keep them off the jury, we can at least have some idea of their thought processes. Here are some measures and five key beliefs held by members of the "can tell" and "can't tell" groups:

Subgroups "Can Tell" and "Can't Tell"
Percent Yes Answers

	Can Tell	Can't Tell
Cough medicine unsafe for pregnant women	52.8%	39.7%
Contact with yellow 5 dye unsafe for pregnant women	62.78%	52.3%
Contact with phenylalanine unsafe for pregnant women	73.8%	61.1%
Frequency of birth defects greater than 1 in 50 births	58.4%	43.7%
Company's safety procedures inadequate	50.0%	29.3%

There are the figures; now what do they mean?

Overall, the sample of more than 600 divides into a proportion of 69.2 percent in the "can't tell" subgroup and 30.8 percent in the "can tell" subgroup. This is very close to the proportion of defense- versus plaintiff-oriented jurors. When we look at the percentage of subgroup members who hold certain key beliefs, we discover that the "can tell" subgroup believes that more things are dangerous to pregnant women than the members of the "can't tell" group believe. They believe that birth defects are more frequent than the "can't tell" group and that the company's research in this case was less adequate than the "can't tell" group believes it to be. It is exactly the kind of information a good trial lawyer can use to help identify problem jurors without tipping his hand.

Another attitudinal factor concerns how frequent a juror thinks birth defects are in the general population. Let us examine two subgroups, those who think birth defects are frequent and those who think they are infrequent.

Plaintiff Preference by Estimated
Frequency of Birth Defects

	Frequent	Not Frequent
Percent of subgroup favoring plaintiff	30.4%	24.3%

By itself, this distinction does not tell us a great deal: Those who think birth defects are frequent are slightly more plaintiff-oriented than those who do not.

If, however, we combine this information with the "can tell"—"can't tell'' distinction, something more interesting emerges. ''Can't tell'' jurors are more likely to consider birth defects to be frequent. Among those who maintain they can tell what caused this birth defect, there is a marked tendency to suppose such defects are not frequent. When we look at these subgroups based on combining the ''can tell''—''can't tell'' variable with the frequent-infrequent variable, we discover some interesting effects:

Percent Plaintiff Verdict by Estimate of Birth Defect Frequency and ''Can Tell''—''Can't Tell'' Cause

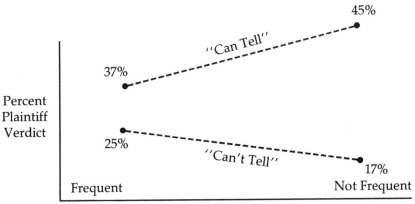

Here we see an inverse relationship between believing that birth defects are frequent and being plaintiff-oriented in the ''can tell'' group. Among those who are in the ''can tell'' group are people more likely to be plaintiff-oriented when they think birth defects are infrequent. The reasoning seems to be that since birth defects do not occur very often, we stand a pretty good chance of knowing what causes them.

In the ''can't tell'' group, the situation is reversed. There are more plaintiff-oriented jurors among those who believe that birth defects are frequent. Here it would seem that a different psychological mechanism is at play. Apparently these people reason that they do not know what caused this birth defect, but they may still react to tales of corporate misconduct, finding for the plaintiff solely on those grounds.

In practice, jury research is usually somewhat more complicated. Our purpose here has been to give the flavor of what jury research can do.

The kind of information jury research develops can be valuable in voir dire. What can be done with it depends in part on how the court treats jury selection. When the judge asks all the questions, its value is reduced, even though it still leads to more intelligent peremptory challenges than does guesswork.

When you can have the jurors fill out detailed questionnaires, jury research can be used with real sophistication. To be sure, the questions cannot appear to be so far afield from issues in the case that the court will find them irrelevant. Neither should the questions provide too much information to opposing counsel. But careful wording coupled with the knowledge of the connection between demographics, attitudes, and juror verdict preferences can yield excellent results.

The value of jury research extends beyond voir dire. Case strategy, the issues to be emphasized, and whether or not to pursue settlement, can be illuminated by behavioral insights into the jurors. It lets us position the presentation of case material effectively. We can support jurors whose attitudes are for our side and work to change the minds of jurors who are against us. Just remember, each piece of litigation requires its own research. Generalizing about jurors from case to case is not just inadvisable, it is downright hazardous.

A View from the Jury Box

by M. Michael Cramer

Lawyers are obsessed with how a jury reacts to them. Does a jury respond to an eager or aggressive manner and resent strong or frequent objections? Does a jury appreciate a highly skilled professional approach, or sympathize with the disadvantaged lawyer? Is it advisable to patronize the jury? How does the lawyer's interaction with the judge affect the jury? What reaction is likely to derive from the use of drama, such as the appearance of surprise or disbelief? Is it advisable to disparage the opponent or his case?

Despite this obsessive interest, there are surprisingly few studies of jury reactions to the lawyer in the case. This prompted me to seek permission to interview jurors in the courthouse at the completion of their term of service.

The interviews took place over three years in three disparate, Maryland jurisdictions ranging from semirural to industrial-urban. I interviewed approximately 1200 jurors after their service in both criminal and civil cases. Jurors spoke freely and were eager to relate their many observations about the lawyers who appeared before them. The results of the survey were made available to the bar as part of various continuing legal education programs. The response has been such that wider circulation is merited.

A few preliminary, general observations are helpful. Most often, jurors noticed the ineptness rather than the proficiency of counsel. No single facet of the lawyer's presentation caused him to stand out. Jurors' comments related mostly to the manner of presentation of evidence and overall thoroughness of approach. Most jurors recalled in surprising detail almost all phases of counsel's demeanor. There appeared to be little

The author practices law in Washington, D.C., and Maryland.

difference between the way jurors perceived lawyers or the cases at the beginning or toward the end of their term of service. Jurors were genuinely interested in arriving at a logical and fair verdict. The jurors were remarkably consistent in their reactions, so generalizations are possible.

Jurors identified with those lawyers whom they regarded as ''professional.'' This word is stated because it was so often used by the jurors. ''Professionalism'' was perceived as careful preparation of the evidence and authoritative presentation. Jurors were favorably impressed with those lawyers who used obvious care by preparing their questions in a manner designed to inform and who brought on witnesses who testified responsively to those questions. Compliments were given to those lawyers who had their questions written out.

The lawyer who had his witnesses readily available and ''kept the trial moving,'' was considered to be the lawyer in command. Jurors were sensitive to the tidiness of counsel's papers and exhibits. Momentary confusion about names of witnesses, dates or events was considered unprofessional. A confident presence in the courtroom and incisiveness of presentation inspired the jury's confidence and respect both for the lawyer and his case. A careful and deliberate approach to every aspect of the trial tended to give a favorable bias on the part of the jury.

Dependable Elements

The lawyer was expected to be able to give immediate reference to the page of a deposition, or the number of an exhibit. A professional did not waste time groping for the evidence. Jurors gave especial consideration to documentary evidence. They were cognizant of the documents marked as exhibits but not subsequently introduced into evidence. Jurors often attributed this breakdown to the lawyer's inability to manage the trial. Litigation is often tumultuous, and exhibits are the dependable elements. Careful management of documentary evidence promotes jury confidence. Christiansen, *A Judge's Observations on Managing Exhibits*, 3 LITIGATION No. 2 at 5 (1977).

Jurors expected the lawyer to act appropriately respectful to all witnesses, even those who were obviously biased or untruthful. Jurors were favorably impressed by vigorous and thorough cross-examination. However, a loud or overbearing approach to the witness was often seen as intimidating, which might have precluded the witness from ''telling the entire story.'' Jurors anticipated that lawyers would use language appropriate to the dignity of the courtroom and they were disappointed by the use of slang, jargon, or informal phrases.

Jurors believed that the cases they heard were not entirely translucent, and a lawyer's full preparedness suggested a creditable case. Many seemed to think that a good lawyer must have a good case because good lawyers can be selective in their choice of cases. This tendency seemed to prevail over sympathy for the disadvantaged litigant.

A well-known jury study, KALVEN & ZEISEL, THE AMERICAN JURY at 376 (1966), indicated that in many instances there existed sympathy for the inexperienced lawyer or sentimentality for the aged lawyer in the declining phase of his career. That survey concluded that this consideration produced a reversed impact and turned weakness into strength. I observed no such charitable examples, and my impression was that sympathy for counsel was rarely of any benefit. Likewise, there was no general tendency to give mercy to litigants because they were disadvantaged by inept counsel.

Professionalism was not synonymous with a reserved, passive approach. Jurors were favorably influenced by a lawyer who was demonstrably enthusiastic for his client, and the lawyer's fervor had a marked influence upon most verdicts. Several jurors said: "If the lawyer doesn't show us that he believes his client, why should we?" Jurors wanted the lawyer to act as if this were his only case. They criticized the lawyer who distracted by interruption for other matters, such as when court clerks or others took their attention or gave counsel messages that obviously involved a different case. Lawyers who read newspapers or other extraneous material, even during recess, were criticized for lack of commitment. Unfortunately, friendliness with opposing counsel, demonstrated either inside or out of the courtroom, evoked negative comments. This observation was made by jurors who acknowledged that they expected lawyers to be friendly, but would not like their own lawyer to be friendly with the opposition.

Surprisingly, only in exceptional cases did jurors criticize lawyers for persistent objections. Jurors often saw vigorous objections as a desirable demonstration of allegiance to the client. Other studies also have found that juror tolerance to objections was high and that jurors were often disappointed by the paucity of objections. Broeder, *The Impact of the Lawyers: An Informal Appraisal*, 1 VAL. L. REV. 40 (1966). However, as one might expect, jurors were disturbed by picayune or excessive objections to the same type of evidence, especially when the objections were not sustained. Because admitted evidence in significant areas of the case was often highlighted by objections preceding it, trial lawyers should consider greater use of motions in limine.

Dramatic Gestures

Dramatic gestures were well-received when natural and authentic, but damaging when strained. They also could be dangerous. As previously noted, jurors paid careful attention to counsel's demeanor. One reaction in particular devastated many cases. This was the appearance of surprise. To a marked degree, jurors consistently regarded counsel's surprise, genuine or feigned, as an indication of an obscure but significant weakness in the case. Others who have studied juror reactions report on this phenomenon. Broeder, *supra* at 4. Their personal interviews led them to conclude that jurors reason that the lawyer is surprised because the client has failed to disclose all of the facts to him. And, a client who does not make full disclosure is more likely to be hiding the truth. Another explanation is that counsel's surprise indicates his unprofessional oversight of important facts.

Numerous commentators have remarked about the singular impact that the opening statement has upon jurors. Marshall, *The Telling Opening Statement*, 19 THE PRACTICAL LAWYER No. 6 (1973). But many lawyers apparently do not appreciate the importance of this phase of the trial. Jurors too often remarked that they would have appreciated more detailed opening statements. They needed this guide to facts and trial proceedings that were entirely new. Jurors stressed that they tended to be more alert and give weight to evidence identified in the opening statement. Jurors frequently stated that they expected the lawyer to use the opening statement to explain his objections and state the relief he wanted from the jury. From this observation, one may conclude that the bar has assumed too much about the juror's knowledge of his function. In this regard it appears obvious that many trials would be facilitated by giving partial jury instructions at the beginning of the trial. Counsel should consider suggesting to the court this practice, which is permitted by the rules.

All jurors related that they had not reached a conclusion until after the closing arguments. Contrary to conventional wisdom, closing arguments were frequently considered too brief and lacking of sufficient detail. Jurors criticized lawyers for not reviewing the important testimony, witness by witness. Many jurors remarked that they forgot evidence and relied on the lawyers to remind them. Illustratively, in an eminent domain case jurors knowledgeable in business matters criticized counsel for not reviewing the prices in several offers made to buy the property. There, counsel wrongfully assumed that the jurors would be bored with the review of testimony with which they were obviously thoroughly familiar. But the jurors were disappointed by what they perceived as counsel's oversight.

The lawyer whose closing statements were repetitive or irrelevant came under criticism. Jurors disparaged as a waste of their time closing arguments that contained a string of platitudes. Remarks requesting jurors to "give close attention" to the argument were considered demeaning. Lawyers who thanked juries for their service to the community or for their attentiveness were considered patronizing, and those lawyers were in danger of being criticized either for not observing that certain jurors were in fact not giving full attention, or for insincerity in overlooking that fact.

Lawyers who admonish jurors about their responsibilities, like, "This is the most important decision you will ever make," were in danger of being regarded as presumptuous. Obviously, certain comments about the jurors' functions or the approach they should take, were well received when made by the court, but were considered unseemly when given by counsel. Disparagement of opposing counsel invariably proved to be an egregious tactical error. Disparagement of the opponent's case, with such general comments as, "This is the weakest case I ever defended against," also produced unfavorable comments. Juror criticism was commonly given to those lawyers who "strayed from the facts of the case," or who "were unable to get right down to discussing the evidence in the case."

Personal comments about incidents in the lawyer's life, or about private philosophies, were rarely well-received and often damaging. Attempts by counsel in closing argument to explain scientific principles or other esoteric subjects without evidence from an expert witness frequently caused jury antagonism. For example, jurors became antagonistic when a lawyer cited and applied a reasonably sophisticated principle of science to explain the issues in the case on trial without explanation by a scientific witness.

Attempts to explain strategy or tactics, like explanations of why certain persons were called to testify, or were not called, or the reasons particular questions were or were not asked, evoked the suspicion that the lawyer was simply playing a game. On the other hand, jurors commended reasonable explanations for not presenting corroborating evidence, a subject often contemplated by jurors.

The use of similes, metaphors, and analogous references sometimes distracted and confused the jurors. "The plaintiff's lawyer was doing a fine job of explaining his client's disability, but I got lost when suddenly he compared the plaintiff to a broken factory machine," said one juror. It is difficult to predict what associations might be conceived by reference to analogy. There are reports of too many incidents of inadvertent affront engendered by well intentioned similes. As a general rule, counsel is less exposed to danger when his closing argument focuses only on the facts of his case.

Commentators Theorize

Some commentators have theorized that emphasis on the court's jury instructions was the single most important factor in modern jury trial technique. Kennelly, *Closing Argument: Instructions Are the Key*, Trial Lawyer's Guide 52 (1962). The results of the present survey support that belief. Jurors evinced a substantial appreciation for the legal principles given to them by the court. Jurors commented on the ability, or lack thereof, of counsel to structure their case within the context of the instructions. Some lawyers effectively repeated in closing arguments those several instructions that favored their position. Closing arguments that integrated and analyzed the evidence in connection with the court's jury instructions were commended.

It should come as no surprise that jurors manifest the same degree of antipathy about lawyers as do others. Report of Hollander, Cohen Associates to The Maryland State Bar Association: *The Law Profession as Perceived by Marylanders* (1978). They often voiced a preoccupation with the disturbing prospect of the large fee, especially the contingent fee. Certain phrases seemed to raise this sensitivity. Reading the obviously inflated *ad damnum* clause caused jurors to focus on the fee. However, the jurors felt benefited by arguments that sought to justify reasonable sums of money. Most jurors wanted damage amounts to be argued. But, the words, ''win'' and ''award,'' suggested the lawyer's interest more than the client's, as did the phrase, ''this case is worth.''

The conclusions derived from the jury survey should be encouraging to the industrious lawyer. Trial attorneys with no more than normal talents were able consistently to achieve excellent results. Rarely did jurors acclaim a lawyer's ability deftly to cross-examine, to present argument without reference to notes, or to incite emotion. Instead, the prototype lawyer who inspired confidence and influenced decisions was meticulous, incisive, and demonstrated allegiance and zeal for his client's cause.

Voir Dire: Preparation and Execution

by Windle Turley

Too little is known about the strategy and scientific method for selecting juries. Judges foster this ignorance by imposing constraints on voir dire examination or conducting it themselves. What can lawyers do to obtain a reasonably fair and unbiased jury for their clients?

There are three steps to selecting a jury that will help your case. First, understand what type of juror is likely to have a preconceived bias regarding the facts of your case. Second, acquire information about particular prospective jurors. Third, apply the information to select the jury that will hear your client's case.

You should begin preparing your voir dire examination early. Your trial notebook should include a tabbed section on voir dire examination. As you prepare for trial, file specific questions and general procedural thoughts for voir dire in the trial notebook.

Lawyers unfamiliar with the community where the case is pending must also hire local counsel to assist throughout the jury selection process. This should be done well in advance of trial.

Decide whether to hire special consultants for jury selection. Large cases may justify hiring an expanded jury selection team that will analyze exhaustively prospective jurors and conduct socioeconomic studies of the community. The forensic psychologist or forensic juror consultant is particularly helpful in developing the "ideal juror profile." This person also may be very helpful in observing the responses of prospective jurors and in analyzing their responses to questions.

The author practices law in Dallas, Texas.

Lawyers who wait until the morning of trial to consider the impact of voir dire rulings cannot hope to influence the kind of jury that will sit in their case. Effective jury selection includes well-prepared pretrial motions brought well before trial. These motions should cover all procedural issues, from the number of jurors that will hear the case to the kind of questions that can be asked or excluded.

The first issue is the number of jurors that will hear the case, as well as the number of alternate jurors. Some federal districts use 12-member juries exclusively, while other districts use only six jurors. Different courts within a single federal district may use either 12- or six-person juries. The number of jurors may also vary with the nature of the case. The court's use of a six-person jury does not violate the Seventh Amendment. *Colgrove v. Battin*, 413 U. S. 149 (1973). Thus, an attorney who wants a six-person jury instead of 12, or vice versa, should seek such a jury with appropriate motions and briefs well in advance of trial.

The pretrial motion should also seek the maximum number of peremptory challenges the court will allow in the case. In federal court, all parties are entitled to a minimum of three peremptory challenges in any civil case. But the court has discretion to treat several defendants or plaintiffs as a single party or to allow additional peremptory challenges to be exercised separately or jointly. 28 U.S.C. [§] 1870.

Equitable Adjustments

Where there are multiple defendants, the plaintiff's lawyer should seek an adjustment in the number of strikes or challenges the court allows. The court may make equitable adjustments in challenges for joint defendants with less than total adverse interests. Conversely, a co-defendant's lawyer needs to be certain that he or she will be allowed separate challenges and to know the number of challenges permitted his opponent.

A motion to establish the rotation order by which the party will examine the jury panel can have a far-reaching impact. In some multiple party cases, the order of presenting proof and witnesses among the parties will influence the outcome of the case. The order of the voir dire examination will probably be followed by the court during the remainder of the case. Lawyers should attempt to seize a favorable rotation rather than leaving the matter to a last minute decision by the court.

Your motion should always ask for the right to examine the jury panel. The court has wide discretion in electing to conduct the entire examination of prospective jurors. Rule 47(a), FED. R. CIV. P. According to a 1977 survey conducted by the Federal Judicial Center, 49 percent of the federal judges conduct the entire voir dire examination and use all of their own questions. *Judicature*, Vol. 61, Aug. 1977, p. 73. Another 19 percent of the judges conduct their own voir dire examination but ask some questions submitted by the parties. Sixteen percent of the judges conduct a preliminary examination and then allow the lawyers to examine the veniremen. Only 5 percent of the federal judges polled permitted the lawyers to conduct the entire examination.

These statistics indicate the importance of filing a motion to conduct at least part of the voir dire. Proponents of judge-controlled voir dire argue that it is quicker and avoids indoctrination by the attorneys. But the attorney is more familiar with facts, issues, and methods of proof likely to be used in the case. The attorney is also better able to elicit candid answers and establish preexisting bias through direct and personal communication. Unfortunately, many judges either do not know how to ask, or will not take the time to ask, probing open-ended questions. A judge's leading question, ''Can you be fair and impartial?'' is unlikely to uncover any preexisting bias and probably does not satisfy the minimum inquiry requirement. *United States v. Lewin*, 467 F.2d 775 (3d Cir. 1965).

Louis Nizer set forth the trial advocate's need to face the jury in *My Life in Court*, pp. 35–36 (1961):

> By speaking individually to each juror, one can get behind the face's mask. Sometimes a hard face lights up in a warm smile, or a kindly face becomes forbidding as the lips curve during an answer. The voice and diction are always revealing. During personal questioning, one may sense a sympathetic bond or, conversely, resistance. All the psychological arts can be employed to evaluate the juror's leanings. But when a number of jurors merely shake their collective heads in answer to the Judge's formal questions, observation gives very limited clues.

Your motion to examine the prospective jurors should outline the areas of inquiry, the reasons requiring the questioning, and the authorities, if any, compelling it. In difficult circumstances, you can agree to some restraints such as the following:

- that the lawyers will not ''argue'' the case during voir dire;
- that the lawyers will not engage in efforts to indoctrinate or educate the jury about the case beyond that which is necessary to uncover any existing bias;
- that the lawyers will not make special efforts to establish a ''rapport'' with the jury;
- that areas of inquiry will be defined in advance and particular limits be applied concerning anticipated instructions or theories of the law; and
- that questions will be directed when possible to the entire panel and not to individual jurors.

While most lawyers would rather avoid these restraints, they are better than a court-conducted jury examination.

The pretrial voir dire motion may also include a request for an expanded voir dire examination on particularly troublesome or critical issues such as pretrial publicity. The motion also should seek to limit voir dire discussion on inappropriate and potentially prejudicial matters that you do not want your opponent to mention.

If you are permitted to question the prospective jurors, submit to the court for advance approval questions that are close to the line and to which your opponent may object. Examples are questions involving insurance and experience as insurance claims adjusters.

If the judge is going to conduct the examination, submit proposed questions directly relevant to the inquiry and tailored to the particular case. A judge is more likely to ask a few well-selected questions than a laundry list of barely relevant questions. Attempt to obtain an advance ruling on the questions the court intends to ask. If you are denied the right to question the prospective jurors, you also should file a second motion asking permission to submit supplemental questions to the court following the court's initial examination of the panel.

Some courts use juror information sheets filled out by jurors in advance of the voir dire examination. The information is limited in scope, and lawyers often are not given adequate time to study and assimilate the data before the voir dire examination. Accordingly, the pretrial voir dire motion also should seek adequate time to use the information sheets.

Extensive Questionnaire

The juror information sheet will be more useful if it is comprehensive and tailored to the particular case. Ask the court to submit this more extensive questionnaire to prospective jurors. Lawyers often must guess at numerous facts that they need to know but cannot ask about because of time limitations or potential embarrassment to jurors. This is true for questions about divorce, religion, politics, or the extent of a juror's education. A detailed questionnaire can develop this information which is helpful in identifying preexisting bias.

If the clerk of the court has available the complete jury list in advance of trial and refuses to provide it, your motion also should seek a copy of the list. Finally, you should assure yourself that you will have adequate time to exercise your challenges in jurisdictions where the peremptory challenges are acted on by ''striking'' a list following the entire voir dire examination.

Many courts routinely will provide most of these safeguards to an orderly voir dire. Nevertheless, you should always call these matters to the attention of the court in the form of a motion heard at least several days before the trial begins.

You can determine other procedural matters by discussing them with the court or local counsel in advance of trial. Lawyers who try cases outside their home jurisdiction quickly learn that not all districts or states conduct voir dire examinations in the same manner. Some courts examine one prospective juror at a time and require you to exercise peremptory challenges on each juror after examination until a panel is secured. In other courts, you may be asked to exercise your peremptory challenges on six or 12 prospective jurors at a time. In some jurisdictions, such as Texas, the entire panel is examined. The court then dismisses prospects for cause and the attorneys proceed to strike from the remaining list their allocated peremptory challenges. The first six or 12 jurors remaining on the list become the jury.

General Idea

Before filing proposed questions for the jury, consider what kind of juror you want and what kind you do not want. While the profile may be similar in like cases, it is rarely identical. Simply having a general idea of what you want in a potential juror is not adequate. You must take the time in advance of jury selection to write down the ideal juror profile. In almost every case, it should include a studied determination of characteristics relating to:

- occupation;
- sex;
- race, nationality, and ethnic background;
- marital and family status;
- extent of education; and
- age.

You also need to know characteristics peculiar to your particular case. For example, the plaintiff's lawyer in a products liability case will determine that persons with precise technical backgrounds, farmers, and others such as police officers and medical personnel, who by training or experience have developed some immunity to pain and suffering, will not fit the ideal juror profile.

Study the jurors before they are questioned. Always get to the courtroom early to observe and prepare notes on physical items such as race, demeanor, age, physical infirmities, how the prospective jurors respond to people around them, their reading materials, and whether they are wearing buttons, lapel pins, or identifying jewelry. Do they appear alert or dull? Have they dignified the event by wearing a tie and jacket when they might not otherwise do so? Do they carry tools of their trade such as pens, pencils, briefcases, work from the office?

Observation is a two-way street. While you watch the prospective jurors, they watch you. The all-important first impression is being created. Your first impression should show the jury that you are organized, businesslike, serious, busy, warm, and in calm command.

Unfortunately, in many instances, this is the time when you first learn the identity and preliminary information about the prospective jurors. You then must quickly study the preliminary questionnaires to develop

413

necessary follow-up questions. If you are doing your job correctly, this should be a very busy time.

The questions to be submitted to the prospective jurors depend on the particular case. But there are fundamental questions that should be developed in almost any jury examination. In addition to the basics of the ideal juror profile, determine the following:

- *residence,* including whether the juror has always lived in the same rural or urban environment;
- *prior jury service,* including the nature of the case and how recent the service might have been;
- *prior litigation involvement,* including whether the prospective juror has ever testified as a witness, or acted as an investigator or claims adjuster;
- *prior accidental injuries or parties to unfulfilled contractual agreements*—the crucial point is whether the prospective juror pursued any rights he may have had as a result of accidental injury or breach of contract. Why a person does or does not prosecute their rights may reveal how they will treat the litigants' rights in your case;
- *acquaintance with any of the lawyers,* witnesses, or litigants in the case;
- *any special training in medicine,* law, or other technical matters that may appear in the case;
- *how employed in occupation*—merely identifying an occupation does not necessarily indicate what the person does or the nature of his responsibilities. An engineer, for example, may have worked in corporate management for many years. Whether a prospective juror owns a business or has always worked for another is meaningful in almost every case;
- *knowledge of this case* or personal experience with similar cases; and
- *occupations of adult children* or parents of prospective jurors.

You should find out the answers to these questions in almost every case. The following questions are very important in particular cases, but are less likely to apply in every instance:

First, does the prospective juror have any essential beliefs, whether religious, political, or personal that might interfere with his adhering completely to the court's instructions? For example, some religious groups in this country believe it is wrong to sue your fellow man for any reason. Other people have such strong personal feelings toward physicians that any medical malpractice case would be counter to their convictions. Some citizens have these same beliefs concerning suits against their government.

Second, if the case is expected to take more than one week to try, then it is essential to discover whether the length of trial may result in prejudice against any party in the case. This question must be handled carefully. It is better asked individually, out of the presence of the remainder of the panel, and should be asked by the judge, who can handle the responses with a firm hand. This question must be submitted.

Third, in large damage cases, whether commercial or personal injury, there may be some prospective jurors who simply cannot, irrespective of the law or evidence, return a substantial damage award. Simply asking the jurors if they can follow the court's instructions and award damages as indicated by the evidence is not likely to identify persons who have already established artificial barriers to large damages. Ask the panel if there is anyone who could not award one million dollars in damages, or two million, or five million, or ten million. Additional hands are likely to appear as the increment of damages increases substantially.

Fourth, disclose serious problems in your case. While these areas of inquiry must be handled with care to avoid going on the defensive early in the case, there are some circumstances that must be exposed to prospective jurors to determine serious underlying bias.

Trial lawyers know never to embarrass a prospective juror. Yet it happens, and when it does it embarrasses all counsel, the court, and often the entire jury panel. You are in danger of embarrassing the prospective juror when you probe too deeply into occupations or employment of which they may not be particularly proud. Some member of the panel will be embarrassed if you ask whether they believe in God or attend church regularly, if you ask the extent of his college education, or probe too deeply into his marital status. Any question that a juror has difficulty understanding or answering is a potential source of embarrassment to that juror and the entire panel.

While you cannot carry on a running dialogue with every prospective juror, key questions should be open-ended. Few jurors will admit that they cannot be fair and impartial, or admit to prejudice, bias, or that they are incapable of following the court's instructions. If, for example, you ask prospective jurors if they bear any prejudice against motorcycle riders, you will most likely get no response. Ask instead, "What do you think about motorcycles and people who ride them?"

Remember that only a limited portion of communication is through oral response. You must study the inflections and the voices, the facial expressions, the body movements, and all of the physical indicators that supplement the oral response. Numerous studies and many authorities have evaluated body movements and other subjective indications used in jury selection. The literature today considers everything from crossed legs and folded arms, to eye pupil size.

One of the greatest opportunities to put your opponent at a disadvantage and improve your own position is through challenges for cause.

These are the jurors who, because of their experiences, beliefs, exposure to the case, or various other reasons, indicate that they cannot be fair and impartial. Your goal is to save your favorable jurors from dismissal for cause, thus forcing your opponent to exercise his peremptory challenges on them, while at the same time dismissing for cause as many of the unfavorable jurors as possible. This will influence the way your opponent must exercise his strikes, while maintaining full discretion in the exercise of your own.

Favorable Juror

The first problem is to save the favorable juror from challenge for cause. An overstatement of your case during early voir dire, particularly if you are representing the plaintiff, can result in some jurors becoming so outraged or convinced that they will freely admit that they can no longer be fair to your opponent.

It is generally near the end of voir dire when the court or counsel asks the common question, ''Do you know of any reason why you should not serve on the jury based on what you have heard about the case?'' Plaintiff's counsel sinks as he sees the older woman who has been smiling warmly and who perfectly fits his ''ideal juror profile,'' raise her hand. She tells the court that based upon all the suffering and anguish the plaintiff has gone through in this case and the great damages the plaintiff has suffered (which defendant does not contest), she really does not see how she can be fair and impartial to the defendant.

This woman was never going to serve on that jury. The defendant would certainly exercise a peremptory challenge on her. If he can have her dismissed for cause, then he has saved a challenge to exercise against you. Your task is to save this person from dismissal for cause. The rescue might proceed along the following lines:

Q: Mrs. Jones, when you came here this morning, you did not have any preconceived prejudice against the defendant, did you?

Q: We all have natural sympathies toward anyone who is seriously injured, don't we?

Q: You would listen to all of the evidence, wouldn't you?

Q: You would consider all of the evidence that you hear fairly and impartially, wouldn't you?

Q: You are not hiding anything that would cause you to be unfair to either side in this case, are you?

Q: Aside from natural sympathies that everyone in the courtroom shares for a seriously injured person, you would not be unduly and improperly influenced by such sympathy or prejudice, would you?

Q: You would vote your true convictions fairly and solely on the basis of the evidence you hear from the witness stand, would you not?

416

The discussion is out of the jury's presence, either at the bench or with the prospective juror's examination taking place apart from the remainder of the panel, with the entire dialogue put on the record.

In some instances your opponent may challenge for cause a juror who is not wholly acceptable to you. Instead of simply agreeing to dismiss the juror, consider rehabilitation in order to force the opposing lawyer to use a peremptory challenge.

Sense of Fairness

You should, when possible, construct a successful challenge for cause to unfavorable jurors, thereby salvaging a peremptory strike to be used against another juror. Appeal to the juror's sense of fairness. Simply asking the potential juror if he or she can be fair will seldom yield a meaningful response. On the other hand, consider the example of a juror whose husband is a professional taxicab driver. She is now called in a case where the defendant is a local bus company driver. Explain to the prospective juror:

1. As evidence is heard there will be criticism, some of it severe criticism, of the way this professional driver operated his vehicle.
2. There will probably be moments when you may feel uncomfortable having the other jurors know that your husband is also a professional driver.
3. Isn't it possible that this uneasiness toward the other jurors and their uneasiness toward you might prevent you from considering all the evidence and deliberating totally unaffected, because your husband is a professional driver just as the accused defendant is a professional driver?
4. In view of this, do you think you might be more comfortable having an opportunity to serve on another jury where you have no relationship whatsoever to the facts of the case as you do with this one?

You should make a particular effort to challenge for cause those jurors who have personality traits that can constitute a dangerous influence on any jury. These are the superextroverts, the hyper and sometimes not fully coherent prospects and those who are not emotionally ready for the case at hand. Very often your opponent will share your apprehension towards such "ringers," and will not contest your motion to dismiss for cause. Thus, again you may have preserved a peremptory challenge.

Using the information and data developed during voir dire should not stop once the jury has been seated. Prepare a seating chart on each selected juror and alternate that includes a physical description, the essential information regarding that juror's background, and physical communications that may subsequently appear from that juror during the course of the trial.

417

Study this information and use it during the remainder of the trial. It may have a direct bearing on your tactics. If, for example, in a products liability case you have both lay and highly trained technical experts on the same issue, you may elect to present one or both of these experts depending on the nature of the jury. The manner in which you present factual evidence, the exactness of the proof, and the extent to which it must be demonstrative should be greatly influenced by the background and experience of the jurors selected.

This jury information should be shared with key witnesses and particularly with forensic witnesses, such as engineers, economists, and physicians. It is important that these key witnesses understand the nature of the people with whom they are communicating. The character of the jury should influence the particular examples and illustrations used to communicate technical matters to them.

A close study of the jurors may cause you to omit marginal evidence that may possibly be offensive to one or more of the jurors. Finally, you should structure the closing argument to the collective character and personality of the jury.

The jury selection process should be well planned and orchestrated from early preparation through closing arguments. Despite the moans of my trial advocate colleagues, I believe the chances of obtaining an impartial jury are equally as good, if not superior, when a fair, well-planned examination is conducted exclusively by the court, as opposed to an unplanned examination by the attorneys.

Irrespective of whether the court or the lawyers ask the questions, the attorney who aggressively pursues voir dire planning can enhance his chances of obtaining a reasonably fair and unbiased jury.

Voir Dire: The View from the Jury Box

by Robert F. Hanley

There were 72 of us. We were prospective jurors in a heavily publicized criminal case. We participated in a three-day voir dire examination. When the ordeal was over, we were angry. We were upset with the legal establishment—the lawyers, the judge, the court attendants who spoke their own language, who herded us around from one room to another, were rude if any one of us were a few minutes late and then let us sit in silence with no explanation as to why we were kept waiting.

I am a trial lawyer. I have been trying jury cases for 36 years. In my newly adopted state, Colorado, lawyers are not exempt from jury service.

I shared my fellow prospective jurors' anger, and I had a much better idea than they did about what was going on. I have spent more than half my life in and around courts, and I may have learned more about jurors' reactions to jury selection in those three days than I have in the past 36 years.

I knew the judge was discussing procedural matters with the lawyers, was hearing argument on pretrial motions and taking care of the usual preliminary matters before we would be ushered into the courtroom. But I could not understand why they did not tell us why we were kept waiting. Why did we have to sit and wait with no idea of how long it would be until we would get into the courtroom and get the case started, so that it might end and we could return to our jobs and other pursuits?

Finally we were herded into the corridor by an attendant who seemed to be in a perpetual state of annoyance. She was curt with anyone brave enough to question her about the procedure to be followed.

The author is a partner in the Denver firm of Morrison & Foerster; Adjunct Professor, Advanced Trial Advocacy, University of Colorado Law School; and a former chairman of the Section of Litigation.

419

She led us into the courtroom, a room designed to make everyone but the judge feel insignificant. There it was, the altar; the high priest was not on the bench as we entered the temple. There was a collective jury gulp. This was indeed a strange place. Few of the jurors had been in a courtroom before. No one explained the room to us—where the witness would sit, where the lawyers sat, where the court reporter sat, or even what the reporter did. We were not told who the attendants were and what their roles were. We were just shunted into rows of backbreakingly hard benches—to wait once more. We felt like outsiders—involuntary spectators.

Our first view of the attorneys was troubling. What turned out to be the defendant was standing near counsel table laughing wildly at something one of his lawyers had said and his other lawyer joined in the levity.

The two young prosecutors were sitting at the table making notes in their yellow pads in a most professional manner. The prosecutors made a fine first impression; the defense team appeared to be taking the proceedings as a joke. My impression as a juror was vivid: one set of lawyers was not taking this trial seriously. They were acting in a manner inconsistent with the almost church-like atmosphere of the courtroom.

I learned, as I was to learn again and again, how perceptive the jurors were and how they noticed everything, just as our children do when we take them to the zoo for the first time. The prospective juror sitting next to me had been the foreman in a federal court case in which a good friend of mine had successfully defended a national company. "He was one fine lawyer," my fellow venireman told me, "but we knew he was from out of town."

"How did you know that? The judge didn't tell you?"

"Oh, no, and I'm sure the judge would have really jumped on the other lawyers if they'd brought it up. But we knew."

"How?"

"He was a good dresser. He wore beautiful suits but, in a three-week trial, he wore the same pair of shoes every day. We knew he was from out of town."

Observant? You bet.

The judge ascended the bench, and we all stood in silent obsequiousness. The clerk announced the name of the case. The judge mumbled the names of the lawyers and gave us a cursory and unhelpful introduction to the case. Our surly bailiff took 12 of us and put us in the jury box. The judge had a list of demographic subjects on a chart, and he told each prospective juror to stand in turn and, using the subjects on the chart, recite his biography. A visible tremor went through the venire.

I had seen a great trial judge in Chicago use a similar procedure with great effect. That judge, John Grady, spent a good deal of time settling the jury down. He told them that the case was an important one, a case the lawyers had been preparing for many months, and that the lawyers and their clients had a right to a fair trial—to a jury without the kind of bias human beings acquire because of their family background, their employment, their interests.

"Folks," Judge Grady had said in a pleasant, quiet voice, "instead of me or the lawyers asking you a bunch of questions touching on your qualifications to sit as jurors in this case, why don't you just stand up and tell us about yourself, what you do for a living, what your spouse does. Tell us about your family and how you like to spend your time. Tell us what interests you."

In that Chicago trial, each juror stood and unself-consciously gave the lawyers a startlingly effective picture of himself. No list of subjects was used, and the order of the subjects they selected was as illuminating as the substance of their statements. The judge sensitively supplemented their accounts by asking good questions. The atmosphere was warm and comfortable. The judge did everything he could to make the jury feel at ease and an important part of an important proceeding. Judge Jim Carrigan of the Federal District Court in Denver and many other judges have adopted this method of jury selection. When properly handled, it is extremely helpful to lawyers seeking to learn as much as possible about the folks in the box.

But, in the case in which I was a prospective juror, the judge did not condition or prepare the jury. Suddenly, every eye in the courtroom was riveted on the juror in seat number one. Good grief! You could almost hear her say, "I have to speak. I have to make a speech. Let me get through this as fast as possible." She started to mumble an embarrassed statement following the list of subjects with minimal content. She sounded like a tobacco auctioneer.

The judge quite firmly told her to speak up. That really threw her. She whipped through the list in a desultory manner and sat down, greatly relieved. She set the standard. Each of the other 11 people in the box followed her presentation in kind. The judge did not ask any supplementary questions. I noticed that neither set of lawyers was taking many notes and did not seem to be paying very close attention to what the prospective jurors were saying.

When the biographical statements were concluded, the judge turned the questioning over to the lawyers, and I learned why the lawyers had not taken many notes. They did not care much about who these jurors were. They asked almost no questions about the jurors' qualifications. They asked the jurors almost no questions about themselves. They spent their time trying to brainwash us.

What a mistake.

We trial lawyers have lost our right to question jurors in most federal courts, and here were lawyers given the opportunity to learn about the jurors, squandering their time with silly, leading questions. We have lost the opportunity as salesmen to learn about our customers and, when some judge gives us a chance to ask questions, what did we do? "Mrs. Jones, you understand my client is entitled to a fair trial and that the State has to prove my client guilty beyond a reasonable doubt. Now, Mrs. Jones, you will give my client a fair trial, won't you?"

At the first recess, did I get an earful from Mrs. Jones! "What kind of nonsense were those lawyers asking? I know nothing whatsoever about the case, and they are asking me how I'd react to it. Can I be fair? What kind of a question is that? I'm a fair minded person, but by the time they finished asking their stupid questions, I'm not sure I could be fair to either of them."

How those lawyers droned on with their leading questions trying to establish an agreement with each juror that he would decide the case fairly—"fairly" clearly meaning consistent with their client's position. Here they were, trying to persuade prospective jurors to abandon their biases—a real uphill battle in the first place—without attempting to learn what their biases were.

I resolved to spend whatever time judges granted me for oral questioning in my future practice learning what I could about the folks behind the jury railing. I know jurors decide cases on the basis of biases they have adopted by reason of their background, neighborhood, employment, sex, religion, reading, TV, movies, friends, and political affiliation. And I know it is futile to try to persuade them to ignore their biases. But Lordy, it is my job to find out what biases they probably have and to decide whether those biases will make them antagonistic toward me, my client, my witnesses, and my case.

I want to know if this man is the kind of person who is apt to believe my client's story. How will this woman react to my witnesses? Is this the kind of person who will most likely hold it against my client if he fails to take the stand? Will this person understand my complex defense? Is this a person who will buy a technical argument? Is this the kind of person who will react positively to an emotional appeal? How will this sentimental type respond to my case—to my theme—to me? How will this rather cold, taciturn person with no children and a boring job view my case?

In the case in which I was a prospective juror, I did not see any attempt by the lawyers to try to figure out what kind of people we were. We were just the subjects of their ineffectual attempted brainwash.

When they finally got to me, I was excused for cause because one of the prosecutors had worked briefly for the law firm with which I am now associated. He left the firm before I ever joined it. I had never heard his name.

The defense lawyer agreed without argument that it was appropriate to excuse me for cause. I am not certain that I would have so readily agreed to the challenge had I been the defendant's attorney. I would have at least tried to find out where I was coming from.

The case was well-publicized and my reading left me with the impression that the newspapers were out to hang the defendant. My going-in feeling was that he was being unfairly treated. I was somewhat sympathetic toward him. I also firmly hold constitutional due process as a personal religion. The prosecutors would certainly have had to prove their case beyond a reasonable doubt.

And I am a sucker for a technical defense. I admire innovative lawyering. As an experienced trial lawyer, I have to think that I would have been thrust into a leadership role in the jury's deliberations.

I am not certain that I would have left me on the jury were I the defendant's lawyer, but I am certain I would have asked a lot of questions before I would agree to a challenge for cause.

I did not know the prosecutor. I did not know why he left our firm. I had no personal feeling about him. Had I been the defense lawyer, I would have tried to make the prosecutor use one of his precious peremptory challenges.

I was tossed off the jury before either side had any idea what kind of a person I was or what my biases were.

I learned later that the prosecutor recognized me in the jury box the first day of the three-day voir dire but decided to let me sit for three days rather than seek to excuse me at once. I would certainly tell that young prosecutor to excuse me if I appear on any of his future jury panels.

I realized that I was experiencing an extremely valuable exercise, and I used it to learn everything I could about the impressions of the other prospective jurors. My questions to them revealed that they were angry, bored, and generally out of sorts with the lawyers, judges, and with the system.

They were not being treated as partners in the system. They were relegated to bleacher status. They were confused by much of the procedure and could have gained a great deal from a short introductory statement explaining why we were going to be required to spend a good deal of waiting time, why the lawyers and judge whispered to each other from time to time so we could not hear them, and something more about the case initially than they could glean from a mumbled reading of the indictment. We did all see a movie on jury service. It was fairly well done but did not answer the jurors' specific questions.

My fellow veniremen wanted to know: Why didn't the lawyers listen to my answers to their questions?

Why wasn't this the fulfilling experience friends of mine told me it had been for them?

Why am I being treated as an ignorant outsider and not as an important part of the process?

Why do they start asking me my reaction to their case before I know anything about the case?

Why wasn't I warned in advance that I'd have to get up and make a

423

speech so that I could have thought about what I wanted to say and could have avoided making an ass of myself?

Judge Jim Carrigan has experimented successfully with having the entire venire hear the opening statements before the voir dire examination. The venire then knows what the case is about, and the prospective jurors can then be examined about their initial reactions to the case with some hope of discovering their biases.

I learned from my experience:

- To use whatever time I am given to learn as much about each juror as I can by careful, sensitive questions;
- To ask questions for which I really want and need answers;
- To listen to the answers to my and the judge's questions and to watch the telltale body language;
- To avoid side-bar conferences like the plague;
- To realize that every second I am in the jury's presence, the jurors are watching and evaluating me;
- That the jury as a panel is extraordinarily perceptive; and
- To do everything I can to include the jury in the process, and perhaps suggest diplomatically that the judge keep the jury apprised of everything that is happening and why it is happening.

I would have enjoyed sitting on that jury. As a matter of fact, I would give a fair amount to be permitted to sit as a juror. What an education for a trial lawyer. I understand that some lawyers have sat as jurors throughout a trial. What a fantastic experience that must have been for them. They were probably tax lawyers.

Lordy, what a waste!

Advocacy in Opening Statements

by Weyman I. Lundquist

Opening statements determine the outcome of trials more than 50 percent of the time. Indeed, respectable studies indicate that it may be as much as 85 percent of the time. While other parts of the trial confirm it, opening statements give the jury a basic feeling for who is right and why, who has the better facts, what is the logical result. This first impression is not often changed. Why is that? First, under the doctrine of "primacy" first impressions are made when people are most aware, most interested, and most receptive. Thus first impressions count and first impressions become lasting impressions.

There are other reasons for the critical role of opening statements. They give the trial lawyer an opportunity to present the facts in the most logical, comprehensible, compelling manner; to indicate how these facts lead to the solution that produces the correct result—a trial victory.

Opening statements are personalized. They differ from lawyer to lawyer, and it is often easier to know by instinct what must be done than to describe how to do it. But there are some general principles that should guide opening statements. Consider the following simple rules.

1. Let the Facts Argue Your Case

An opening statement should tell the jury not only how they should decide the case, but why. That is the essence of advocacy in the opening. There is a proper way to argue in the opening. It is to analyze, marshal, and present the facts in such a manner that there is only one logical conclusion, the one you are advancing. And if the facts are so marshalled, there is no need to argue what the jury must find, what they must con-

---

The author, a member of the San Francisco firm of Heller, Ehrman, White & McAuliffe, is a former chairman of the Section of Litigation.

clude, or what verdict they must deliver. The facts can speak for themselves. It is enough that the lawyer tell the story, presenting the facts logically so that the jury knows what the right answer is.

2. Be Prepared

Whether you draft a closing argument when the complaint is filed or await major discovery developments to prepare for the trial or whether you follow a more usual middle-ground approach, you should know your case when the trial begins. But that knowledge alone is not preparation for the opening. Opening preparation requires reviewing your case to think about its logic, to determine what story the evidence can tell through witnesses, documents, and other demonstrative exhibits, and above all how you can make this most comprehensible to the jury.

In doing this you will determine how your case should be staged: what witnesses best explain what documents, when witnesses should be called, and what experts are required. Having thought this through, it is your responsibility in opening—when you are in control of the courtroom—to describe what will follow so the jury understands it.

3. Introduce Yourself

While voir dire will give you some opportunity, at least in most state courts, to have the jury "get to know you," the opportunity usually has been sketchy. Opening is the best chance to have the jury meet you. What you wear is obviously important. Where you stand (assuming the judge permits movement) can promote your rapport with the jury. At the time of opening, jurors are reluctant to have lawyers approach the jury box, their domain; they prefer to be addressed from afar. Size and voice dimension can change this, but, generally speaking, jurors become more comfortable with lawyers close to them as the trial progresses.

The sort of person you are will inevitably make itself known, but you should put your best foot forward. Being comfortable in the jury's presence combined with an ability to explain to them what the case is about gives you credibility. There is no one way to learn this; it comes with practice, with experience, and with a sense of self. It is what differentiates the good trial lawyer from the humdrum. It is not guile, supersalesmanship, or aggressive forcefulness. It is being believable.

How do you make yourself credible in an opening statement? First, you tell what the case will be about in a manner that the jury can understand. It is hard to believe what one does not understand. Be candid with the jury. If you are going to present evidence that is foundational, such as statistics as a basis for an economist's opinion, tell them that part of the trial will not be the most interesting. When it is not, they will believe you. Conversely, they will remember you told them that the expert testimony it supports is important. They will believe that because you have been honest about the dull evidence. Tell them also some of the factual problems in your case, explaining that there will be testimony that allows more than one conclusion, that different people saw things differently. In doing this, be careful not to make admissions but to indicate that there is a logical solution—the one you seek.

4. Be Helpful to the Jury

The most important role a trial lawyer can assume in a courtroom is working with the jury to find the facts that will let the jury make the right decision. A good trial lawyer is one who identifies with the jury and insists that the focus of the trial is to help them understand. I have seen Philip Corboy fight and badger his own witnesses to assure that they spoke to the jury in a manner the jury understood. How do you do this? One good starting point is to explain to the jury why they are there.

Nine out of ten times neither the trial judge nor opposing counsel will have explained to the jury what a trial is all about—that there is the voir dire, the process by which jurors are evaluated so that they can "seek the truth"; that an opening statement *explains* what is to follow, that it is not evidence; that the evidence comes thereafter, perhaps not as logically as one would like, but for the jury to receive and understand. The presentation of evidence is followed by the judge informing the lawyers about what law will apply. With this law the lawyers can argue from the facts presented about the appropriate conclusion. They can draw inferences; they can explain to the jury why they argue for certain conclusions. Then, of course, the judge instructs the jury on the law.

This basic explanation assists the jurors in understanding what their role is and what the trial is all about, and it gives them a sense of ease and comfort in the courtroom. They understand that the lawyer who will help them in this respect will help them in other respects. But do not limit yourself to explaining the trial process. If there are to be depositions, tell them what a deposition is and why it is going to be used rather than having a witness there. If there are to be charts or difficult exhibits to be explained by several experts, have the exhibits there so you can explain them to the jury clearly. When the evidence comes in through experts, what you have told them is reinforced and will be more intelligible.

Explain to the jury that while you can tell the story of the case in a chronological or sequential fashion, this may not be the case at trial. Witnesses will appear out of order; testimony will come in a fragmented fashion. Some witnesses will be foundational to others. Explain all of this as you explain what the trial is about, because to help the jury understand what is happening in the courtroom is to help them understand the result you advocate.

5. Educate the Jury

A jury wants to know what the trial processes are. Jurors want to understand the trial. You can do this best by explaining your case fully in the opening, reinforcing this explanation by presenting evidence skill-fully, and then tying it all together with an argument that reinforces your view of the evidence.

Opening is the best time to achieve this. It is the time to deal with diffi-cult terms, to spell them out, to explain what it means in lay terms, to deal with diagrams and exhibits, and to explain what is to come. It is the opportunity to tell how the witnesses interact, what they will say, and what it means. You are not likely to be hampered with objections, and you can explain your case naturally with words and visual aids.

The opening will also educate the trial judge, even if it is a jury trial. It is the time to explain to the judge how the evidence ties together and what will be relevant. This assists the judge in seeing the total picture and may help you to introduce more evidence as relevant than would be the case if no explanations were offered. It is also the time to commit counsel to what the course of trial will be. It is usually a time not to be conservative, particularly for plaintiffs.

6. Set a Theme

One of the founders of my firm, the late Jerome White, gave one of the best demonstrations of setting a theme. White represented the head of a major corporation, the son of the distinguished founder of the com-pany. The client was a dilettante, given to excesses. He was charged with a rather obvious crime: forging documents. White, heavyset, silver-haired, and eloquent, addressed the jury:

"Gentlemen of the jury, *my client is a fool*. We will show that he knows not what he does nor how to do it nor that he could intend anything." And so the theme was set. I do not commend such a courageous ap-proach, at least not often, but the "my client is a fool" theme set the stage for what followed.

Usually a theme is easier to conceive for a plaintiff. "We will present evidence about a boy injured when he was four and a half years old who will never walk again. His will be a life in a wheelchair, always assisted by others. He will live for 64 years this way. Let me explain the evidence in greater detail and his medical injuries. . . ." The opening proceeds from there.

For the defense at a minimum there is a theme which begins, "There are two sides to all stories, and you have indicated from the outset of this trial you want to hear both. Let me now explain to your open minds what the evidence on behalf of the defendant is. . . ." But in my view, it is better to set a more specific theme: "In the lives of all of us—big, little, corporate, and individual—things happen which are the fault of no one and sometimes the fault of the person injured. Indeed that is the way Jones, an engineer, conducted the experiment which gave rise to this lawsuit—in violation of company policy, of safety rules, and, worst of all, in a manner that injured two other people. You've agreed that there

428

are two sides to every story and that you will hold your minds open until our side is in. Let me explain to you some of the evidence overlooked by plaintiff's counsel in his explanation of what happened. It is as follows.''

7. Settle Preliminary Issues Before the Opening Statement

If you are going to use exhibits, charts, or pictures in the opening statement, tell the other counsel and obtain judicial approval to do so. Nothing is more likely to produce a mistrial than waiving documents or demonstrative evidence that will be excluded as trial evidence. Apart from its prejudicial effect, it greatly discredits the lawyer who said he will introduce certain evidence that the judge then excludes. It is also advisable to review briefly with opposing counsel and the court the outline chart that will be an aid to your extemporaneous explanation of the trial.

A caveat about this. While it is well not to run the risk of objections made and sustained during opening argument, it is sometimes advisable not to ask the judge to make too many in-chambers rulings. All too often the judge himself needs the opening to understand the case. In the opening statement it is often necessary to educate the judge as to how the trial will proceed. He or she will thus understand what evidence is foundational, why it is relevant, why it is probative, and why it should be admitted. A verbal explanation of critical testimony may achieve greater results than seeking the judge's advance ruling before the case is fully laid out. You may not want to show specific exhibits to the jury, because you do not want to seek preliminary rulings, but you can whet the jury's appetite by explaining the exhibit, and a momentum toward admitting the evidence builds with the court and jury.

8. Be Persuasive

Do not read the opening statement. Even if still a novice, do not even tempt yourself with a prepared written opening statement—maybe an outline, maybe a simple list, and certainly a list of exhibits and documents for reference. Indeed, reading from critical exhibits and documents that will be admitted assists your explanation, but it must not be rote. To say this is easier than to do it. Lawyers, despite a reputation for articulateness, can be notoriously stumble-mouthed or ponderously pedantic in the courtroom. They speak in terms and phrases unknown to locales except the courtroom. To avoid this, outline the significant parts of your opening statement. Then have that list on the rostrum where you can easily refer to it. To aid yourself, you may even want to back up your outline with a detailed list of important points to cover. This you can walk over to peruse just before concluding your opening and then advise the jury that there is ''one more thing you want to talk about before you sit down'' or, if all is covered, ''I think I have covered it all.'' Then sit down.

429

But there is another, and for me, better way. That is, to use a pre-prepared flip chart, a chart which in essence is your opening outline but is not used as an outline. It is an aid to you and to the jury. It enables you to combine an oral and visual presentation to the jury. A great double-header. What should such an outline contain? It ought to cover the important stages of the trial, such as, in a simple case, what happened, to whom it happened, and the consequences. You may want to list the witnesses, introduce the name of the witness who will testify as to what happened, and how it happened. When explaining to whom it happened and what the consequences were, you will again want to refer to the people involved, how they were involved, and what consequences befell them.

Such a chart can be an even more elaborate aid. It can contain important terms, spelled out—words that the jury should become familiar with, words that experts will be using and explaining as the trial progresses.

9. Handle Objections During Opening Statement Delicately

Of course there are permissible objections. Argument is impermissible. *See Lafrenz v. Stoddard,* 50 Cal. App. 2d 1, 122 P.2d 374 (1942). There must be a good faith reliance that evidence will be admissible. *Hawk v. Superior Court,* 42 Cal. App. 3d 108, 121, 116 Cal. Rptr. 713, 721 (1974), *cert. denied,* 421 U.S. 1012 (1975). But the real difficulty is how to raise objections. The problem can be even more difficult if the plaintiff's lawyer has proceeded through his opening without objection and now the plaintiff's counsel believes it is necessary to object during the defense opening.

Whatever the event, objections during opening need to be handled carefully. They are delicate because the lawyers are making first impressions with the jury. If the judge starts to overrule these objections, the lawyer making them has in effect penalized himself. The court has said that you are wrong, early on. This impression is likely to carry throughout the trial, particularly a shorter trial.

How can this sort of judicial stigma be avoided? One way is to raise certain matters *in limine,* to discuss with the judge what his views of a proper opening are and to obtain his admonitions about certain matters—for instance, punitive damages before a *prima facie* case has been established, or unnecessary prejudicial references concerning evidence, for example, referring to a substance as cancer-producing when cancer is not involved in the injury in question. When the opposing lawyer approaches these limits, perhaps direct objection is not the best course.

John Shepherd approached the problem something like this: Rising at the counsel table, he obtained the attention of the court and the opposing lawyer. The court: "Yes, Mr. Shepherd?" John Shepherd: "Your

Honor, I was wondering if this portion of the opening goes beyond some of the early rulings made by the court?'' The court: ''It does not.'' John Shepherd: ''I thought not, but I just wanted to be sure.'' Or if the court retorts, ''It does.'' John Shepherd: ''I thought so, and I thought perhaps I should call it to the attention of plaintiff's counsel by making an objection at this time, because it is not at all likely that this evidence can be admitted because it would prejudice the jurors on matters unrelated to my client.''

There is another aspect to objections during opening which should be considered. As long as there is a valid basis, there are times when objections should be made because the jury is so mesmerized by the opposing attorney's opening that it may be better to break the trance by objecting than to permit the hypnotic process of an overly effective opening.

10. Concluding Thoughts About Opening Statements

Never put your own credibility before the jury. Do not, for example, argue: ''I promise you that we will present evidence as follows . . . and I ask that you evaluate my promise at the time this trial concludes.'' There are enough problems in the trial of a case—explanations, witness credibility, opposing counsel, contradictory evidence—that the burden of putting your own credibility in issue should be avoided.

Opening statements are usually recorded. It can be helpful for an attorney to have his own opening statement transcribed so that he can use it in his closing argument to reinforce his view of the case. For example: ''I indicated in the opening statement as follows. . . . You've heard evidence about this, now let me tie it all together in my closing argument to show you why the defendant is correct in this case.''

Or if the lawyer has overstepped permissible bounds in the opening, the transcript can be helpful support to point this out: ''Plaintiff's counsel indicated in his opening statement that there would be evidence that this accident occurred as follows—indeed he said before you in his opening statement exactly the following. . . . Now let me review with you how exact that description was. You will recall that police officer Jones said. . .''

• • •

Finally, in *lay* parlance an ''opening'' is an opportunity, a chance to get ahead. In lawyer parlance, it is all that and more. It is a means to shape the jurors' views of the evidence and the entire case. In a case I recently tried involving punitive damages, the plaintiff attempted to have the jury judge my client's conduct over a 30-to-40 year period by today's standards. My objective in talking about the case and the evidence was to impress on the jury that what was done was reasonable in light of the times when it was done. The ultimate accolade was to hear from the jurors after the trial that they approached their deliberations in the way I had outlined in the opening statement.

Persuasion and the Opening Statement

by Abraham P. Ordover

The paper pushing is over. The motions, interrogatories, and briefs are behind you. The jury is sworn and waiting. You have rehearsed with partners, friends, spouse. You cannot be too long or too short, too detailed or too simple, too argumentative or too understated. You know that the opening statement determines the rhythm of the trial and, often, its outcome.

Persuasion is an art practiced in its most subtle form in the opening. With the first words to the jury, the art begins. You have only a few moments to present your theory of the case, demonstrate your mastery of the facts, show your leadership and honesty, convince each juror your client's position is fair. All of the trial—the direct, the cross, and summation—flows from the opening.

The rule of primacy teaches that what is believed first tends to be most difficult to dislodge. So the opening sets the stage. Primacy means the plaintiff or prosecution has a great advantage in going first. If the narrative is clear and compelling, the defendant must immediately neutralize the impact of his adversary's remarks. To delay leaves the jury with only one view of the case and no reason to withhold judgment. The process of persuasion has begun.

First, the plaintiff must attract the jury's attention. A thematic opening paragraph that discloses his overall position in capsule form is best. An example is a civil action that involves whether arson or accident caused the fire that destroyed a building.

Counsel for the owner of the ruined business has a thematic opening paragraph:

Members of the jury: The case you will hear and decide involves

Abraham P. Ordover is the L. Q. C. Lamar Professor of Law at Emory University School of Law.

the refusal of an insurance company to live up to its promise. Mr. Jones entered into an agreement with that company, paid his premiums to purchase insurance to protect him from this very type of loss. He faithfully paid his premiums for some ten years. Now that his plant, all that he has worked for these ten years, has been destroyed in a horrible accidental fire, the insurance company has refused to honor its promise.

A narrative story will follow this opening salvo about the hardworking Mr. Jones and the accidental and dreadful loss of his building.

The insurer, who has refused to pay, has its theme, too. Members of the jury: This case is not about contracts, it's about arson. The deliberate burning of a building for the purpose of collecting the proceeds of an insurance policy. The only question is whether that man deliberately fired his plant. We contend that he did, and we will offer evidence to prove it.

This thematic start, which rivets the jury's attention, is followed by a narrative of the evidence that supports the theme. Counsel will tell a coherent story with a beginning, a middle, and an end.

Grab Attention

Do not engage in a lifeless, dull recitation of each witness's testimony. The jury is not ready to be buried in evidentiary detail. That which is important will be lost in a morass of minutiae. Vacant stares will greet a litany of what each witness will say. Moreover, the joy of discovery will be removed from the jury. Narrative allows the relevant connections to be made because they will occur naturally during the storytelling. Who will testify to what fact is not necessary. Where one witness's testimony is of major significance, however, it is wise to mention it.

Lawyers and jurors share the common heritage of learning from stories. It began in childhood. If we would persuade, we must first grab the jury's attention. This is done not by a recitation of dry, unconnected facts, but rather through a simple story that contains the facts that support the theory of the case. The remainder—the details that lend credibility to the theory—will come out during the trial and be highlighted in summation. In this way, what you promise in opening is delivered in closing.

In addition to avoiding undue detail, the story should be couched in real, human drama. All trials involve human beings and the mistakes, disagreements, miscalculations, frailties, emotions, and other failings to which humans are prone. Witnesses will testify to these failings. The opening is interesting and credible if it reveals both parties' feet of clay. While you should not dwell on the weaknesses of your case, the jury should hear about them from you, not from your opponent.

If the evidence will include blood and gore, let the jury know. To be sure, the shock value of such evidence is reduced.

Do not engage in obvious argument. The opening is not the time to argue the meaning of particular pieces of evidence or to draw inferences from the disparate facts.

If we return to the arson scenario, counsel for the insurer will, in his story, tell the jury that the plaintiffs business was suffering large losses, that the market for plaintiff's product was disappearing, and that plaintiff had said he was desperate over his plight. This is what the witnesses will say. This is what the documents will prove. Argument is not necessary.

With plaintiffs plight described, defense counsel will continue with information about the hiring of the unsavory Mr. X just before the fire. Finally, the jury will be told of the highlights of the arson investigation. Neither "argument" nor drawing of inferences is required. The selection of facts and the order in which they unfold suggest the desired conclusion quite dramatically. You need not argue; let the facts argue for you. They need no conclusory language from the lawyers. And if counsel cannot resist drawing inferences for the jury, he should do so in quiet tones and in an understated manner. To the judge, argument is frequently defined more by tone than content. How something is said may be more important than what is said.

That raises the question. What is argument?

Argument has been so loosely defined in judicial decisions that its precise parameters are hazy. The trial judge has wide discretion in regulating the opening. Moreover, objections during the opening are mercifully few—probably for fear of antagonizing the jury. The law of opening statements, then, is essentially what individual lawyers actually do in courtrooms—usually with the forbearance of their adversaries—and bears little relation to the boundaries set by appellate decisions.

These decisions describe undue argument as:

1. The assertion of material, which counsel knows or should know, is inadmissible at trial;
2. The assertion of "facts" for which no proof will be offered;
3. The injection of personal opinion as to the merits of the case or the credibility of witnesses;
4. The drawing of inferences from the facts;
5. Blatant appeals to prejudice—the so-called "Poison-the-mind-of-the-jury" rule;
6. Undue argument of the law; and
7. Vehement or angry comments.

Reversals Are Infrequent

The first three areas have nothing to do with argument. They are as improper in summation as in opening. Counsel is never permitted to argue from inadmissible evidence or "facts" for which no proof has been presented. Opinion of counsel is universally condemned as unethical, though reversals on this ground are infrequent.

The last four items on the list are most frequently encountered and involve judgment calls by court and counsel.

Drawing inferences from the facts is generally reserved for final argument. Indeed, that is the purpose of summation. The proper opening will present the facts in a narrative that requires no comment until summation.

Blatant appeals to prejudice are easily identified. When a prosecutor detailed some 80 or 90 indicted crimes allegedly committed by the defendant, the court condemned his opening as character assassination designed to poison the minds of the jurors. Fair enough. The real test is in drawing the line between persuasion—a proper attempt to have impact on the minds of the jurors—and prejudice. If we define prejudice in the same manner used for evidentiary purposes, then we can find the line.

In one sense, all evidence is prejudicial to your adversary's case, or you would not bother offering it. But legal prejudice is different. Legal prejudice involves trying to obtain a verdict on facts not in evidence or on passion, anger, or confusion of the issues. Proper persuasion in an opening statement is simply the skillful use of narrative so that the admissible evidence is compelling. Improper argument involves matters outside the record and appeals to outrage or sympathy.

Permissible argument of the law is a matter of local custom. Where counsel are allowed to argue the law, the actual argument is reserved for closing. The law that governs the case may, however, be adverted to in the opening. How much is too much usually involves attempts by the lawyers to explain and apply the law at the outset. Judges see this as an invasion of their province.

Excerpts from two prosecution opening statements will help illustrate the line between a proper narrative where the facts argue the case and an improper statement filled with inadmissible evidence and conclusions of counsel. To be sure, even the "proper narrative" contains some arguably improper material—that is the nature of this beast.

The prosecutor's opening in Case One:

On an afternoon in August 1975, two men got up from a table at Jones's Restaurant in New York and went into the men's room. After looking around to be sure that no one else was there, one man reached into his pocket and handed the other man a white envelope containing $15,000 in brand-new $100 bills.

The man who was handed the envelope was the president of the Brown Corporation, one of the largest stevedoring companies in the United States.

435

The man who received that white envelope with $15,000 in cash is the defendant.

That event, one incident from the testimony that you are going to hear in this case, tells you in a nutshell the story of what this case is about.

It is a story of corruption, it is a story of greed, it is a story of a powerful labor leader who, despite receiving a salary of $140,000 a year from his union, demanded and received over $300,000 in cash, illegal payoffs from companies doing business on the waterfront.

From the first minute, the jury knows the nature of the case and the power with which it will be presented. This narrative contains facts that speak for themselves.

Are "corruption" and "greed" argumentative because they are conclusions, or are they facts to be introduced by the government? Should we conclude that "corruption" and "greed" are improper because no witness will testify that defendants were corrupt or greedy? Such simplistic reasoning has the merit of ease of application. It has no other merit. The story is, after all, one of a powerful leader who received a salary of $140,000 per year and, in addition, obtained substantial monies from others.

For the true flavor of argument, consider Case Two:

We will prove to you beyond any reasonable doubt how these conspirators operated in league together to systematically enforce their will to corruptly, venally exact tribute from those who sought to do business in Atlantic City, New Jersey. Their greed could never be satiated. . . .

These defendants ruled Atlantic City, New Jersey, as if it was their private kingdom. They enforced a total feudal system of corruption upon that society, and they acted as the lords of corruption.

We will prove beyond any reasonable doubt that these defendants knew what they were doing was wrong, that they knew what they were doing was immoral, and that they knew what they were doing was against the laws of the United States. . . .

Certain he would never be caught, never be brought to justice, this defendant, Arthur Jones, was brazen and arrogant in his dealings while publicly representing himself to be acting in the best interest of Atlantic City, New Jersey. This charlatan lied whenever it pleased him, and secretly collected tens of thousands of dollars for himself and the other members of the conspiracy.

(Interestingly, the convictions in this case were affirmed despite the court's view that the portion of the opening statement quoted above was an improper attempt to poison the minds of the jury.)

436

The prosecution's burden is essentially to lay out a *prima facie* case in the opening. It must deal with facts. Indeed, in a few states, the failure of the prosecution to detail a *prima facie* case in its opening may result in the granting of a motion to dismiss.

A more difficult problem arises with some defense openings in criminal cases. There are many criminal cases in which the defense opening can consist of the same type of narrative used by the prosecution. And in civil cases, both sides can use the storytelling approach. But what does defense counsel do when his defense is an argument that the government's charges cannot be proved and that the prosecution's witnesses are incredible?

There are a number of cases in which trial judges have sustained objections to defense opening statements that rely on reasonable doubt, question whether the charges were brought in good faith, or urge the jurors to use their common sense as they listen to the witnesses.

Fortunately, most judges permit the defense wide latitude where no affirmative defense is urged, and the primary defense is an attack on the people's evidence. But when judges seek to restrict defense counsel to "just tell us what you intend to prove," it raises several problems.

First, that approach fails to recognize the essential differences in what the people must accomplish compared to what the defense must do. The defense may be an argument that seeks to neutralize the prosecution opening. Indeed, the defense need not open at all—a permissible but dangerous tactic.

Moreover, rigid application of the "just tell us what you intend to prove" approach gives the court too much power. The lawyer is at the mercy of the court and reduced from an advocate to a mere functionary.

Defense Should Always Open

In practice, defense lawyers customarily caution jurors to pay close attention to the prosecutor's promises and to listen to the cross-examination of the people's witnesses as well as the direct. They also talk about the presumption of innocence and the burden of proof.

The defense should make an opening statement. To be sure, there are always exceptions. It may be that the case will be tried in a day, and that the defense has been permitted to conduct a voir dire of the jury. In such a situation, the jury selection may contain what counsel would do in an "argumentative" opening.

Generally, however, defense counsel must be aware that the rule of primacy, the order in which a trial unfolds, and the presumption of guilt hurt the defendant. Stated differently, many jurors will enter the courtroom believing that the defendant is probably guilty. After all, they reason, the police arrested him, the district attorney decided to prosecute, and the grand jury indicted. If we now add a good, strong prosecution opening, the process of belief will take hold. The rule of primacy instructs that this belief will be difficult to dislodge. If the defense does not open or reserves its opening until after the people's case, the jurors will be captured by the prosecution, especially if the court has conducted the voir dire. By the time the defense presents its case, it will be too late.

Even if the defense has conducted voir dire, it should open anyway. Prosecution's opening will be sandwiched between the defense voir dire and opening, giving the defendant his only procedural advantage.

The voir dire should set up the defense opening. For instance, the voir dire can alert jurors to the unsavory background of the people's witnesses, circumstantial evidence, problems with eyewitness identification, and the like. The opening is, however, the better forum for the defense theory of the case and for the use of narrative.

During the opening, counsel must establish his credibility, leadership, and fundamental fairness. This is acutely necessary when the court has conducted jury selection. A number of standard phrases widely used in opening statements tend to defeat these goals. For instance, leadership cannot be found in counsel's apology for taking the valuable time of the jury to listen to this tedious case. How many lawyers seek the obsequious route to ingratiating themselves with the jury? "Sorry you folks have to sit in a gloomy courtroom on such a glorious day," they say. This will hardly lead to an image of leadership or honesty. The jurors are well aware of the glorious day. They would all prefer to be elsewhere, but they are trapped in the box. Do not remind them of their unhappiness.

Another ploy is for counsel to admit that what he says is not evidence in the case, but only intended as a guide or road map to what will follow. This says that what counsel is doing is not very important. Lawyers should not undercut the significance of their role or their words. If the court wishes to instruct the jury that counsel's remarks are not evidence, so be it; the effect will be quite different. Defense counsel, however, may want to remind the jury that what his adversary says is not evidence. Indeed, that warning usually responds to some overstatement of plaintiff's case.

Leadership and credibility also depend upon the image of the lawyer. The advocate who delivers his opening without notes will seem to be well prepared and conversant with the facts. He will have eye contact with each juror. He will not be trapped behind the podium. There will be no barriers between him and the jury.

The lawyer who is stuck to his notes cannot establish the same rapport with the jury. His delivery will be to the podium. He will not establish good eye contact, nor will he seem as well prepared. The reader tends to move too quickly. Impact will be lost; barriers erected.

Recognition of leadership will not be awarded for discourtesy. Courtesy to the jury, court, and colleagues is important. Yet the number of lawyers who alienate their juries by rank discourtesy is unpleasantly large. But should the attorney thank the jurors for doing their civic duty, wrap them in the flag, and explain the trial? The answers to these questions depend on the particular jurisdiction and on who conducted the voir dire.

If counsel conducts the voir dire, the "thank you" can be delivered. Wrapping jurors in the flag and giving civics lessons usually results in talking down to the jury and should, in most instances, be avoided. Many courts now show all prospective jurors a movie about jury service just before selection. All trial lawyers should see the film. It likely will save the effort of the civics lesson and permit counsel to use his opening for the merits of his case.

Freed of these impediments, counsel can launch into his thematic opening, go on to the narrative, and sit down having accomplished his objective—starting to persuade the jury.

Documents: Keeping Judge and Jury Awake

by Janeen Kerper

You are preparing for trial. You have just reviewed two cartons of correspondence and sixteen cartons of filings with the FTC, SEC, EEOC, DOE, ACLU, and ASPCA. You are understandably glassy-eyed. You can guess how the jury will look. From past experience you know that the judge will be snoring audibly. How do you cope with this mess?

The first rule for effective use of documents is to start early. Before discovery even begins, develop a discipline and a program for weeding out unimportant documents.

This is a difficult assignment. Law students and lawyers are trained to be defensive, over-inclusive, to be conversant with every detail, envision every possible situation, and have five fallback positions. We panic if we have not covered every last angle. We think we have to get into evidence every document that has anything whatsoever to do with the case.

But judges and juries have no patience for such nonsense. The challenge is to do exactly the opposite of everything we were taught. Be under-inclusive, not over-inclusive. Distinguish essential documents from just plain documents.

You can do this only if you have a coherent plan of your case. This means deciding from the outset what the case is all about. Interview the client, review his documents, and research the issues of the case. Before discovery begins, write out in simple language your version of the jury instructions. After all, this is the pitch you will be making to the jury throughout the trial, especially at closing argument.

In most jurisdictions the judge's instructions will be the last thing the jury hears. In all jurisdictions they are the last thing the jury will hear

Ms. Kerper practices law in San Diego, California.

from a supposedly neutral source. In all but a few courtrooms, the judge is the authority. His word carries far more weight than that of any attorney. The most effective documents are those that relate to the judge's instructions. If you formulate those instructions before discovery begins, you can distinguish essential documents from unimportant ones.

One means of handling documents is to distinguish "documents" from "potential exhibits." "Documents" are pieces of paper that may be relevant to the case. Number "documents" to indicate their source and date of discovery, tersely summarize them by groups, index and store them. If you need them, they can be retrieved.

Two Questions

The only documents that qualify as "potential exhibits" are the essential documents for the case. You can distinguish a potential exhibit from a mere document by asking two questions:

- Does the document provide essential support to a jury instruction?
- Does the document have sufficient collateral importance such that it will be useful to bring it to the jury's attention?

If the answer to either question is yes, the document is a potential exhibit. An opponent's document is a potential exhibit for the opponent's case if it is used in a deposition or as an exhibit to any significant pretrial motion, or if it provides significant support for an aspect of the opponent's case.

Potential exhibits should receive special treatment. A potential exhibit should have the same exhibit number throughout the discovery process and, if opposing counsel agrees, throughout trial. There are few things more exasperating than to prepare for trial only to find that a key exhibit has separate numbers for several depositions. You can eliminate the preparation of elaborate cross-indexes and a great deal of jury confusion by stipulating at the outset to a uniform numbering system for all purposes, including discovery, pretrial motions and trial.

Lawyers frequently object to this system because they are concerned that once a document becomes a potential exhibit, there is a tacit concession that it is admissible in evidence. You can handle this problem by filing a stipulation and order that recites that the uniform numbering system is solely for purposes of identification and does not constitute an admission by any party of the authenticity or admissibility of the documents.

Lawyers also object to a uniform numbering system because they fear it may force them to disclose prematurely material favorable to their case. Lawyers can overcome this hurdle by assigning each party a block of potential exhibit numbers. The potential exhibit only obtains a number when it first surfaces publicly in a deposition, motion or other pretrial proceeding. Under this approach, documents that are not revealed

441

during pretrial discovery can be withheld and not assigned a potential exhibit number until shortly before trial.

When you identify a document as a potential exhibit, place it in a separate exhibit folder. As discovery progresses, add the necessary backup material, such as a list of witnesses who can authenticate the document, digests of important witness testimony about the document, notations about any amending or supplementing documents, and brief memoranda concerning possible evidentiary objections to the exhibit and how to overcome them.

Bricks and Mortar

In complex cases, one means to keep track of potential exhibits is to digest them in duplicate on index cards. The digest describes the potential exhibit by date, title, author, recipient and number, and contains a summary of the document. Then arrange the cards by subject matter and chronologically.

If you discipline yourself early in the discovery process, you will find that even in the most complex business case there are only about two or three hundred documents that are really potential exhibits. And of those, only about ten or twenty really matter.

Charles J. Alexander, Special Litigation Counsel for the Tax Fraud Division of the Department of Justice, in his lectures on the use of documentary evidence, emphasizes the difference between "mortar" and "brick" exhibits. Mortar exhibits are the glue of your case. They are the unexciting documents that are the framework on which everything else depends. If it is a contract case and the instructions require the jury to find a written contract, you must introduce the contract. But no one ever admired a brick wall for its mortar—it is the bricks and their arrangement that matter. Every case has its "hot" documents and those are the ones to exploit at trial.

In cases that involve numerous documents, Mr. Alexander recommends that you tell the jury from the outset: "Ladies and gentlemen, this case involves a lot of paper. From time to time you will see the attorneys and the clerk and the witnesses handing papers back and forth to each other, and you are going to wonder what is going on."

Mr. Alexander reassures the jury that they will see some of the documents during the testimony and that experts will summarize others. At the end of the trial, they will have the opportunity to look at those papers and think about them quietly in the jury room. You can also state that in closing argument you will tell them something about how those pieces of paper fit together and why they are important to the case.

In civil cases, you may use documents extensively in opening statements. Although it is rarely done, you can place a blow-up of a document in front of a jury or use an overhead projector during opening. The

442

only stricture in using a document or blow-up in the opening statement is that it must be plainly admissible in evidence.

Attempt to obtain a stipulation from your opponent that such material can be used in opening. Stipulations are particularly likely when the document at issue is also important to your opponent's case, such as the partnership agreement whose meaning everyone is fighting about. If a stipulation is not possible, bring the question before the trial judge and obtain the court's permission before using the potential exhibits themselves in opening.

Once past opening statement, how can you move the trial along and reduce the document boredom factor?

First, wherever possible, seek and give stipulations that documents are authentic and, where appropriate, business records. Reserve all other objections: relevance, materiality, privilege. There are very few forged documents in this world. Few things are more deadly than a parade of clerks and custodians testifying in monotones that "yes, these records were kept in the regular course of business" and "yes, they were intended to be accurate."

Stipulations can avoid the need to call numerous witnesses and drive the judge and jury crazy. "Mortar" documents that are not subject to objection can be introduced as a group in a few seconds. The judge will smile at you and admire your efficiency.

Use Stipulations

If you do not stipulate, watch out. The lawyer who refuses to stipulate will discover at trial that the judge and opposing counsel paint him as an obstructionist. Any self-respecting juror will resent the lawyer who, by insisting on "technicalities," drags out the trial with dull testimony about lifeless bits of paper.

If your opponent fails to stipulate on authenticity and business records, use this stubbornness aggressively. Consider a recent ACLU class action challenging the conditions in a county jail. Shortly before trial, plaintiffs' counsel attempted to arrange a meeting with the attorney for the county to premark exhibits and stipulate to authenticity—to no avail. During the trial, the plaintiffs called the sheriff as an adverse witness in their case-in-chief.

The afternoon that the sheriff was to testify, the courthouse buzzed with activity. The courtroom was jammed with reporters and high level administrators from the sheriff's department. The sheriff knew that county counsel would give him the opportunity to make a public statement in defense of the conditions at the jail as soon as he completed the adverse direct testimony.

Lead counsel for the ACLU began the adverse examination. He asked 20 or so well-placed questions that extracted several highly quotable concessions about the conditions in the jail. Thereafter, the ACLU attor-

443

ney began asking the sheriff to authenticate documents authored by various members of his department. By 2:00 P.M., there was a stunned silence in the courtroom. By 3:00 P.M., there were soft snores from the rear. By 3:30 P.M., the press was gone. They never came back. By the time the sheriff gave his speech, the courtroom was empty.

Second, use charts and summaries extensively. Federal Rule of Evidence 1006 and similar rules in most states expressly permit the use of charts and summaries to present the contents of voluminous documents that cannot be conveniently examined in court without great loss of time. The records from which the summaries are prepared must be admissible in evidence.

The federal rule requires that you make available for inspection or copying at a reasonable time and place the originals or copies of the summarized documents. FED. R. EVID. 1006. Some state rules provide merely that the court in its discretion can order the production of the underlying documents. *E.g.*, CAL. EVID. CODE § 1509. The creative use of summaries can prevent many hours of jury somnolence.

Third, be selective in choosing the exhibits you intend to publish to the jury. Bring most "mortar" documents into evidence quickly with as little fanfare as possible. You should not place these documents on the overhead projector, pass them out to the jury, or read them aloud. You should ask few, if any, questions about such documents. Place them in evidence efficiently and refer to them in passing in closing argument.

Fourth, be as creative as possible by publishing your really good documents to the jury. Many lawyers make the mistake of treating all exhibits alike. They lob them into evidence after asking the witness whether he recognizes the signature. He asks no further questions about the document, which is neither read nor shown to the jury.

The document just hangs there like a big question mark. Suddenly at the end of trial during closing argument, the lawyer springs on the jury that exhibit 94 is the most vital piece of evidence in the whole case.

Exploit Good Documents

If a document is really important, it deserves to be published to the jury immediately after it is introduced into evidence. There are many ways to do this. Important documents can be read aloud by counsel, individual copies can be handed to each juror, or the document can be blown up to small billboard size. Exhibits can be photographed, made into slides, and placed on screens by opaque or overhead projector. They can be filmed or videotaped.

The overhead projector is an excellent method for publishing an important exhibit. For a few pennies, you can reproduce the document onto a transparent piece of plastic that is projected onto a screen. Both the jury and the witness watch the screen as the document is discussed. You can ask questions to highlight the key phrases in the document.

"When you read in this letter that Mr. Lubell wanted the goods shipped 'as per our usual agreement' [pointing to the key language], did you check the file to determine what that agreement was?" When it is time for closing argument, you can talk about the exhibit and its important language and the jury will understand the argument.

Use documents in your closing statement sparingly. Mortar documents should be stitched into your story and referred to only in passing. For example: "It was Big Company's uniform custom and practice to do business this way—it's reflected on every single invoice between the parties—all of which are in evidence. If you have any doubts about this, you can take a look at them in the jury room."

If you have published a document effectively to the jury during the trial, you generally will not have to republish it completely during closing argument. Use only your best charts and two or three overhead transparencies of whole exhibits in closing. Rather than projecting an entire page of an exhibit, project only the key phrases or portions of the document. Whenever possible, tie the document excerpt to a jury instruction.

A very powerful way to use documents in argument is to create a two-column transparency that pairs the opponent's contentions or allegations in one column with a directly contradictory quote from an exhibit in the other column. It takes only a few examples to discredit an opponent's entire case.

Juries will trust a document far more readily than any witness's memory. But most jurors (and many judges) are not readers. They are especially unlikely to read any document if they feel they have to read 500.

As a trial lawyer, you must assume that most exhibits will never be read. To use documents effectively, you must convince yourself and the trier of fact that there are very few documents in the case that are really worth reading. That is the key to the successful use of documents in the courtroom.

445

Effective Final Argument for the Plaintiff

by James Touhy

The last seven times Philip H. Corboy had been before juries his clients had received at least a million dollars, but the smart money said this time it would be different. His clients would be lucky if they received a million cents. Ten thousand dollars seemed more than they had coming to them and so did the $100,000 they were asking.

Corboy's clients this time out were not maimed or paralyzed, run down by trains, or smashed by automobiles. They had merely been bumped, and then only figuratively.

His clients were Thomas E. and Melanie Kluczynski, he a retired Illinois Supreme Court judge, she a member of the Chicago Public Library Board; he was the brother of the late Congressman John C. Kluczynski, a man so powerful he had a federal building named after him. Mrs. Kluczynski herself had run for Congress but lost.

The Kluczynskis had been heading, in February of 1976, for a social weekend in Florida but had been bumped from the flight at O'Hare Airport. Now, in October 1981, as Philip Corboy waited to begin his closing argument, they were in the Circuit Court of Cook County, Illinois, suing Delta Airlines for $100,000 because of the inconvenience they had suffered that weekend five years before. It was not a case that appeared likely to launch a jury of regular citizens to the rescue of the Kluczynskis, who were not exactly Ma and Pa Have-not.

"Even if there is a good case against the airline for the bumping, he's got the wrong plaintiffs," whispered one lawyer who had squeezed onto one of the six benches of Judge Irving R. Norman's courtroom on the 24th floor of the Daley Civic Center. Most of the other lawyers who

---

James Touhy is a free-lance reporter in Chicago. This article is edited and reproduced from the Chicago Lawyer *with the permission of the author.*

had packed the courtroom every day to watch Corboy in action agreed.

So did the defense counsel for Delta, Cornelius P. Callahan, who had implied, whenever an opportunity presented itself in the two-week trial, that this was not so much a case of a ruined weekend as it was of a damaged ego. The Kluczynskis, it was brought out, had been on their way to Ocala, Florida, for a weekend party to watch the birth of a foal, the property of Leonard Lavin, head of Alberto-Culver Company, the hair-care people.

When it was discovered that there were not two seats for the judge and his wife on Delta's Flight 253, the airline offered to book them on a flight leaving an hour and 55 minutes later. Delta also would give them their round trip fare back—$443—plus one half the fare, a routine offer for those passengers with confirmed reservations who somehow get bumped.

The Kluczynskis refused the offer. Instead, they argued with the representatives of the airline. Kluczynski threatened to sue, according to witnesses. Mrs. Kluczynski, according to her husband's testimony, was "aggravated, disappointed, disillusioned and disturbed." He said she became "extremely nervous, loudly protesting . . . and not easy to manage" and had to take vitamin B to calm her nerves.

To make matters worse, said the plaintiffs, in the midst of their distress and humiliation, they were told they lost their seats because they had arrived late. Then along came Albert E. Jenner, Jr., of Jenner & Block, who was allowed on the flight. Even later than Jenner came a man in a dark coat and a Cossack-style fur cap. He too was allowed on board.

Never Made It

The Kluczynskis were so aggravated by all this that they never made it down to Florida to see the birth of the foal. However, the defense suggested that missing the birth of a little horse was not all that damaging to the Kluczynskis.

"By the way, Mrs. Kluczynski," Callahan had said when he had her on the stand, "did you ever find out if the foal was born?"

Mrs. Kluczynski hesitated and then said, "No."

One of the key points of the defense was that Delta had done nothing illegal in overbooking the Kluczynskis. A Delta vice president testified that it was common knowledge that airlines overbook, that they had to offset no-shows and prevent planes from taking off half filled. This policy kept air fares down and only occasionally caused an inconvenience such as the Kluczynskis experienced. Delta's records showed that 300,000 persons every month make flight reservations and then never show up.

The defense said that airlines in general and Delta in particular acted in good faith, that they did the best they could for everyone, and that they could not be assessed damages. All the Kluczynskis really had coming to them was their $443, they said. What was this crazy talk about

447

$100,000? The Kluczynskis, by refusing the airline's offer of a later flight, had ruined their own weekend and probably that of the Lavins as well.

Through all this, Philip Corboy chiseled the form of his case: that Delta unquestionably had overbooked intentionally and quietly. To the vice president's claim that overbookings were public knowledge, Corboy put Flight 253's gate attendant on the stand and he said *he* did not know about overbooking. Then Corboy put on the travel agent who sold the Kluczynskis their tickets and she said *she* did not know about it either. And although the Delta executive could readily cite the statistics for 300,000 no-shows a month, Corboy got him to admit that there were no records of the number of overbookings a month.

"Conceivably there could be 10 million a year?" Corboy asked.

"Yes, that's conceivable," said the man from Delta.

Still, until the last day of trial, Corboy was the betting underdog. "Mr. Corboy," said the judge, "you may proceed."

Mr. Corboy proceeded. When he was done proceeding, the jury awarded Thomas and Melanie Kluczynski, victims of a "ruined weekend," an astonishing $208,000 in damages.

Corboy almost immediately led the eight-woman, four-man jury to the fact that his clients apparently were not in an empathy-arousing plight.

"[Y]ou might say to yourself . . . 'We don't think it is seemly to use our time at $16 a day to settle this dispute. . . . If this big-shot judge thinks he is going to use our talents, the twelve of us, as his stick to bring Delta down to size, he's got another thought coming. Just because he was on the Supreme Court of the state of Illinois doesn't mean he should use the processes of this court to soothe his feelings and soothe his ego. Sure, Melanie Kluczynski got terribly upset. . . . That's not unusual for somebody when they want to go on a vacation. But she could have had $600 right then and there. Why use us five years later, and waste our time?'"

Corboy answered that question. Referring to the jurors as "officers of the court," he told them that "this is a legitimate dispute, a principle that has to be determined by bus drivers and students and secretaries and nurses and housewives and people who work for cemeteries and people who come from all walks of life.

"You were brought in and asked to accept that responsibility. We know—and I think for one of the few times in this lawsuit these gentlemen [the opposing lawyers] would agree with me—we know you are going to do just that. Why? Because you said you would. . . . Under oath you said you would follow the law . . . and if under the law my client was entitled to a fine determined by you against this corporation, you would have no hesitancy in assessing that fine."

Corboy paced slowly in the small area between the jury box and the two tables where the lawyers sat. Corboy said the fact that the Kluczynskis and four others were overbooked on Flight 253 was uncontested and that this was no isolated case.

''. . . Delta had a designed, specific, planned, secret, intentional method of overbooking for their passengers,'' said Corboy. ''The policy was, 'We want to control the seats. We want to sell more seats than there are on this plane.' Inherent in a policy such as this is the potential of somebody being bumped. . . . We know it was intentional. But we know it was secret. Mr. Crivolio didn't even know about the policy and he is the man at the gate. . . .

''Now, there is a legitimate purpose for overbooking: making money. And in a society like ours, making money is a legitimate function. But if you make money at the expense of people, I respectfully suggest, ye shall suffer the wrath of your peers.''

Corboy pointed out that even with a policy of overbooking, the airlines have, according to their own admission, the obligation to notify the affected passengers by telephone, which they did not do in the case of the Kluczynskis. Then he went back to the matter of money.

''There is nothing wrong with making money,'' he said. ''As a matter of fact, this company has been doing pretty well. In 1976 they were worth $500 million. In 1981, five years later, through the use of various policies, they are worth $1 billion. Their overbooking policies are apparently successful.''

Corboy referred to the testimony of a Delta sales representative at O'Hare, a troubleshooter to whom passengers are sent if problems arise.

''He said to Judge Kluczynski, 'Judge, we have a slight problem'. . . . Now I am not complaining about the choice of language. I think it starts on high. I think to the airlines this is a 'slight problem.' Inconveniencing passengers—overbooking, overselling—is a 'slight problem' to this airline if the overbooking policy is successful. . . .''

What's the Difference?

''It would be nice if the transportation companies on the ground would be able to say, 'Let's overbook so we keep our buses filled.' That's what they do in the air. This airline, starting at the top, is so calloused, so noncaring, so oblivious to the rights of passengers that whether there are two seats left, one seat, or no seat, it doesn't make any difference. . . . What difference does it make? It is only a 'slight problem.'

''It only means that either one or two, in this case six, people were overbooked. But what difference does it make? We fill the airplane. And if you have 135 people on that plane instead of 134, you are making $92 more than you would if there were 134.''

Corboy sarcastically referred to Delta's ''Denied Boarding Compensation Plan,'' under which the offer of more than $600 to the Kluczynskis was made:

"Most people jump at that. Most people say, 'Why not? This kind, courteous airline.' The people don't know about overbooking. They don't know about this intention to get 135 seats as often as they can and to hell with the public. So they take the 600 bucks on the spot. What does the 600 bucks mean [to the airline]? The other passengers keeping that plane full are paying for it. The public is paying for their 'Denied Boarding' policy."

With the steadiness of a metronome, but with an increasingly intense beat, Corboy was about to take the case away from Thomas and Melanie Kluczynski and their small irritations and move it into the realm of a class action.

"Ladies and gentlemen, the Kluczynskis were party to an agreement. They entered into an agreement to go to Orlando, Florida. . . . They could have been neurosurgeons going down to operate on somebody's head that had to be there at a certain time. They could have been going down to get married and miss the church. They could have been somebody working for the government, very important, who didn't want to fly in a government plane because he would be seen, who wanted to take a commercial plane because it was important to his government.

"None of those people could get on that plane under these circumstances. Fortunately for the Kluczynskis all they missed was the delivering of a foal, hardly anything to get excited about. . . . But, the point is they made an agreement.

"You know, it is like being an employee in a union. When you make an agreement with the management, whether you work for a public utility, whether you work for a transportation company, whether you work for a school, whether you are a college student, whether you are a secretary, whether you are a nurse, if you make an agreement with somebody and then they say to you, 'Well, things are tough, let's change the agreement,' you are a little reluctant to change the agreement."

Corboy admitted the actual damage incurred by the Kluczynskis probably wasn't much, a "limousine ride out there and cab fare home, 25 bucks, practically nothing." And, if one looked at it a certain way, "their outrage and humiliation might not be worth too much either," said Corboy.

"Delta put a price tag on it," he said. "They said $600. You can bet your boots it is worth a little more than that or they wouldn't have been offering $600 at the scene of the occurrence.

"Maybe it is worth a thousand, maybe two, I don't know. Whatever it is, it is certainly not worth your time or the constituents' or the responsibilities of our judicial system to grant these people a couple thousand dollars because they were outraged, because they were humiliated as we get humiliated every day in our lives. Trying to go through this world is not easy, putting up with the incompetence of government at the top and the neighbor next door at the bottom. Nobody understands us. We as people are certainly not important to corporations whose function it is to make money at the expense of us.

"So, what's all this ado about nothing? What is this judge coming in here for and using our time? Why have we been taken from all walks of life to grant this 78-year-old man one hundred or six hundred or one thousand or two thousand, whatever this small amount of money might be?"

Corboy would tell them why. He would tell them they were there for much more important matters, things of a nature so broad in their scope that they affected all of us consumers. And the man who was bringing these important issues to public scrutiny was Judge Kluczynski, whom Corboy likened to "the Good Samaritan of the Bible."

"Judge Kluczynski at the age of 73 . . . filed a lawsuit, I respectfully suggest because an injustice was done. He doesn't need this five years of waiting. His career needs no assuagement. He doesn't have to be told he is a great man. People have told him that all his life. He has been serving the people of this community since 1940. And you or your fathers and mothers elected him to the Supreme Court in 1966. Now if they can do this to him, what can they do to the rest of us? Maybe they wouldn't offer the rest of us even 600 bucks."

It was important, Corboy said, important to all consumers, that Kluczynski stood his ground at the airport.

"Because if he had been like most people, his outrage could have been assuaged right at the scene. We would have regarded him as an oversold passenger and gotten him out of there, and then the airline would go on and fill that plane up and fill the next plane, fill it up the next day, and fill it up the next day. As long as there are people who will be humiliated, as long as people don't mind spending five, 25 bucks for cabs, as long as you can get over it, this system will go on. And the temporary outrage will be forgotten. And the temporary excitedness will disappear. And the people who get the brunt of overbooking will go back to their lives and miss their marriages or miss the funeral of their parents or miss an important meeting or just miss an hour, two, three of their time. And this corporation can keep on and do it and do it. Just grant Judge and Mrs. Kluczynski $600 or $800, a couple thousand apiece and forget about it. That's what they [the defense] would love you to do."

Corboy paused. The jurors were staring at him. The spectators were staring at him. There was no sound in the courtroom. The betting odds had just shifted.

Corboy next led the jurors through the four counts in the complaint and moved to the matter of punishment for an airline that carelessly and disdainfully pushes people around.

"Why punish them?" he asked.

"So that others in the same business, so that those people in the airline business, so that Delta Airlines [which is] here, at your sanction—

you the people, you give them the right to fly in the sky, you as the people in this community supply them with the corporate entity by which they can sell and overbook—and if you believe that giving punitive damages against them will deter . . .''

He wrote on his big pad on the easel, and orally spelled out ''DETER.''

''[Y]ou as judges now, you as judges, shall fine this company that amount of dollars and punish them in that amount of dollars which you believe they are entitled. And that's what this lawsuit is all about.''

Before Corboy brought up the subject of money again, he wanted once more to emphasize that there was a larger principle involved and the jury should be aware of its importance and therefore of their own.

It was a case, he said, involving the civil rights of the ''passengers of this community, the fare-paying people who believe when they pay for a ticket they have got a right'' to get to their destinations. Kluczynski, in this action, was representing those people, Corboy said.

''Now, is that silly? Is that a waste of your time? Is that an imposition on you, the citizens of this community? If it is, grant them no punitive damages. Tell the airlines they can keep this overbooking practice. Tell the airlines . . . they can overbook as much as they want. And tell them that by showing no punitive damages should be assessed against them. Tell them that it is an absolute waste of Kluczynski's time and your time and the court's time and award them nothing. Or you can follow the law.''

It was now time to move onto money, and Corboy began. He said that the net worth of a corporation should be taken into account in determining punitive damages.

''You may say, 'That's unfair. Just because a company is big and got a lot of dough, we shouldn't sock it to them. Just because a company has assets of $1 billion doesn't mean we should take some award from them because a couple people got bumped.' ''

But to put a stop to overbooking, Corboy said, the jury must do its duty and consider the assets of Delta because ''big business recognizes money. Chairmen of the boards of corporations recognize money. Presidents of corporations recognize money. Shareholders of a corporation recognize money.''

He stood before an easel with a big grease pencil.

''Now, how do you determine what dollars will impress the president of this company and the chairman of the board of this company and the shareholders of this company?

''You start in 1976. They had five hundred million dollars. This overbooking practice is apparently working. They have kept their planes full. They are now worth one billion dollars, which is a thousand million dollars. . . .''

Corboy, printing quickly on his big white pad, spelled out a ''THOUSAND MILLION.''

"Astronomic, beyond even recognition. That's why I've spelled it out. There are nine zeros in a billion dollars."

He wrote nine zeros.

"There are eight zeros in five hundred million. Well, if you were to take 10 percent of their one billion dollars, that would mean you would fine them a hundred million dollars. Absurd? Of course it is absurd. Sure, the president of the company would recognize it. And maybe this company would get rid of its overbooking policy . . . but I think that would be outlandish and ridiculous.

"So instead of a hundred million dollars, maybe you suggest, instead of 10 percent, 1 percent. One percent of a billion dollars is ten million. Would that impress them? Of course it would. But I think it is too much money."

"I respectfully suggest even if you took one-tenth of one percent, instead of being ten million it would be one million. Maybe one million dollars, you are beginning to say, maybe that's what we ought to fine them. It would certainly stop them, certainly deter them in the future. But a million dollars is an awful lot of money to fine anybody."

Corboy continued to write down figures as he talked.

"So, what about one-one/hundredth of one percent of their net assets. One-one/hundredth of one percent of their bottom line figure. One-one/hundredth of one percent of their wealth? And that's one-one/hundredth of one percent. . . . That's a hundred thousand dollars. A hundred thousand dollars may be an appropriate figure and it may not. Let's look at what a hundred thousand dollars is.

"To somebody that's got a billion dollars, one-one/ hundredth of one percent is a hundred thousand dollars. Some people spend all their lives saving ten thousand bucks. One-one/hundredth of one percent of ten thousand dollars is a dollar. Somebody has got ten thousand dollars in the bank and they are fined or punished one one/hundredth of one percent of that ten thousand dollars in the bank. If somebody has got a billion dollars in the bank, one-one/hundredth of one percent is a hundred thousand dollars. So if you fine this company, and you punish this company to the extent of one hundred thousand dollars, it is the same as fining somebody or punishing somebody, for the purpose of deterring them from acting in the future, by one dollar."

One Dollar Bill

Corboy reached into his pocket and pulled out a one dollar bill, straightened it and held it before the jury by both hands.

"Will the president of this company and the chairman of the board accept a one-dollar fine because you said so? My guess is they will be mad about it. But it will certainly make them think that, 'Maybe we should get rid of our overbooking policy.' And it may make them think that for spending one dollar that it is a punishment and they may think about policies."

The jury was out five hours. When it returned, it had awarded $4,000 dollars each in actual damages to Thomas and Melanie Kluczynski, and $200,000 in punitive damages.

Two of those little one dollar bills.

Editor's Postscript: On February 19, 1982, trial judge Irving Norman reduced the award to $7,000—$2,500 each for punitive damages and $1,000 each for compensatory damages. Judge Norman found that the evidence warranted the punitive and compensatory awards, but said that the amounts were grossly excessive. On March 18, the Kluczynskis filed a consent to the remittitur. On April 16, Delta agreed to pay the reduced award of $7,000, and, subsequently, the judgment was satisfied.

Nondefensive Final Argument for the Defense

by Frank Cicero

The trial lawyer must persuade the jury that his client should win. Every moment the jury is present, from the time the panel first enters the courtroom for jury selection until the verdict is returned, the lawyer should be persuading the jury.

The closing argument is the crowning point of this process. It is your only opportunity to describe to the jury in detail your view of the case and to tell the jury what they should do and why.

Effective final argument has several characteristics. First, and most important, it is *argument.* Closing argument is not just a review of the trial evidence. It is that, but it is much more. It is your opportunity to explain the significance of the evidence, to offer reasons in support of conclusions and inferences. It is also the time to discuss credibility, the law, and the right verdict.

Second, effective final argument presents a positive theory of the case, explicitly, logically, and not defensively. Your theory should be simple and understandable, and should incorporate the same themes emphasized from the opening statement throughout the trial.

Third, final argument is sincere, plain, and forceful. Elaborate oratory and high-blown rhetorical devices are generally insincere and inappropriate.

Fourth, effective final argument tells the jury what to do. It lets the jury understand the issues they should resolve and how to resolve them. It explains the case and answers the questions that are likely to trouble the jury in reaching a verdict.

Preparation for final argument begins when you first get the case. Your objective from the beginning of legal research and factual investi-

The author is a partner in Kirkland & Ellis in Chicago.

gation is to develop the theory for final argument. The theory becomes the framework on which the rest of trial preparation takes place.

An effective way to focus on the applicable law is to prepare, very early, draft jury instructions on the legal issues that will be central in the case. Drafting instructions demonstrates where the argument theme must be altered to conform to the law. It assures that there is a proper legal foundation for the arguments to be made at the conclusion of trial.

At this stage, you also should prepare a final argument outline. The outline makes the factual preparation throughout the pretrial proceedings more efficient arid focused. It is a checklist to assure that you develop necessary evidence and avoid unnecessary discovery.

Using the outline enables you, for example, to examine deposition witnesses to develop the evidence needed to support your themes, and to avoid developing evidence that may contradict or refute your argument. Similarly, you can focus interrogatories, requests to admit, and other discovery devices to develop the material necessary to support the argument themes while avoiding extraneous or contradictory matter.

As the trial approaches you will want to take several specific steps to prepare for it and your closing argument.

First, review the final argument themes and outline. Make them as simple and straightforward as possible.

Second, organize the factual proof into two categories. One consists of the facts that will definitely be proved at trial. You should list not only ultimate facts, but also the precise testimony, documentary evidence, admissions, or other evidence that will support those ultimate facts.

The second category of facts that may be proved at trial includes testimony from witnesses who may not be called, facts to be developed on cross-examination, or evidence that must await rulings concerning admissibility.

Third, prepare the outline for the opening statement to conform to the theories and specific points you expect to argue at the end of the case. In most cases, the facts I discuss at the beginning of the case correspond to the points I expect to argue at the end.

Finally, of course, preparation for final argument continues through the trial itself. The trial lawyer views the entire trial as the vehicle to develop the material for final argument. "How can I use this in final argument?" is a useful standard for analyzing everything that occurs in a trial, whether referring to the evidence, the witnesses' demeanor, impeachment, comments by the court or counsel, or anything else that occurs before the jury.

Effective final argument for the defense should include these common elements.

1. *Introduce the argument positively.* A defendant's closing argument should never be defensive. Begin positively. The first impression must

show your confidence in your case and change the focus from the plaintiff's argument.

The way to start the argument depends in part on the way the plaintiff's argument ended and whether there was a recess for the jury to relax before the defense begins. If the plaintiff ended on a strong and perhaps emotional chord, and especially if there was no recess before beginning the defense argument, the defense lawyer must change the jury's mood promptly and redirect the jury's attention positively to the defendant's case.

Thanking the jury and patriotic platitudes about jury service are almost universally invoked. But if they are extensive or insincere, they are awkward, beside the point, and a waste of defensive time. If used, they should be short, simple, and sincere. Very briefly, simply say that of course you and your client thank the jury for their service and appreciate their attention.

Then launch promptly into the task of changing the jury's focus. One way to do this is to confront directly the mood the plaintiff created and assure the jury that the true facts are somewhat different. For example, you can say, "Now you have just heard a very emotional, impassioned presentation by Mr. Jones. Of course, that is his side of the story and what he would like you to believe. But let's now look at what the facts really are."

Begin by reminding the jury of your opening statement and what you intended to prove. Reiterate positively and explicitly a short conclusory statement of your theory and the ultimate facts supporting your theory. Then state that you will now discuss how you have proved what you said you would prove.

All of this can be done in a simple and understated way. This allows the jury to sit back and adjust from the climax of the plaintiff's case. At the same time, in just a few brief sentences, you have turned their attention smoothly and positively to your theory, the facts of the case as you wish to argue them, and your confidence that the plaintiff's rhetoric is easily refuted by the facts.

2. *Argue the facts.* Facts persuade the jury. Argue them. Refer to facts specifically, and argue them by explaining their significance with explicit reference to the issues to which they apply.

Many final arguments are far too general in discussing the facts. Whether from lack of disciplined preparation and organization, or other reasons, often the factual discussion is conclusory and unconvincing.

Express your factual conclusions. Then amplify on those conclusions by reviewing and analyzing the facts developed during the trial. Do so specifically. Remind the jury of specific bits of evidence by detailed reference to the fact and the source. Finally, explain the significance of the fact for the ultimate issues.

3. *Use exhibits.* In arguing the facts use those documents and other ex-

457

hibits that support or demonstrate the facts you are arguing. Quote from the documents. Show them to the jury. If the document was emphasized during the trial, remind the jury when and by whom.

For example, if exhibits were passed among the jury or read to the jury during the trial, use those same documents again, but remind the jury how they were used before. If the documents were displayed during the trial, with an overhead projector, for example, remind the jury of that fact in using the specific document again.

4. *Use demonstrative aids.* Demonstrative aids are very effective during final argument. If you used such aids during the trial, like enlargements of documents, an overhead projector, charts, or photographic projections, use them again during final argument to reemphasize evidence from the trial. If you did not use these aids during the trial, use them during the final argument to emphasize particular exhibits or portions of exhibits.

A large artist's tablet is useful during trial to make calculations, summaries, drawings, diagrams, or present other materials for the jury's view. Successive sheets of the tablet can be used with successive witnesses; the witnesses themselves may make entries on the sheets displayed. The tablet is then available for use during final argument. Turning to the pages used by the witnesses, you can remind the jury how a specific witness made the particular entry that appears on the tablet.

I prefer to avoid using a blackboard during trial and final argument. Used during trial, blackboard entries are too difficult to preserve. Used during final argument, the blackboard is too readily altered by opposing counsel as part of his argument.

5. *Be specific in referring to witnesses.* In arguing the facts, remind the jury what was said by particular witnesses. Remind the jury who the witness was. Particularly in a long trial, jurors may be unable to recall and distinguish particular witnesses. Describe the witness—his or her name, employment or function, and how the witness looked.

Refer to what the witness said, and how the witness said it—"directly," "reluctantly," "forthrightly," "hesitantly," or "nervously."

Argue the witness's credibility or lack of credibility. Explain what credibility is, perhaps by explaining the instructions the jury will receive from the judge. Review the importance of demeanor or impeachment in judging credibility. After explaining the principles involved in the court's instructions about credibility, discuss the witnesses specifically in terms of those principles.

For example, remind the jury of the witness's demeanor:

Remember Mr. Ryan. He was the plaintiff's executive vice president who testified here about two weeks ago, the very tall man wearing horn-rim glasses and a blue suit. Remember how, when

458

[plaintiff's counsel] questioned him and led him through his planned direct examination, Mr. Ryan confidently turned and looked at you after each question. Remember how he spoke at length in his deep, resonant voice trying to reassure you and convince you.

Then remember what happened when I began to cross-examine him. He no longer looked at you. He no longer spoke in those confident, resonant tones. His answers became short. They became clipped. They became sarcastic. They became evasive. In fact, you remember how his honor, the judge, had to tell him to be responsive and simply to answer the question.

Remember in particular how evasive he became when I showed him that letter he wrote back on December 7, 1978, to my client, Mr. Right. He wouldn't answer my simple, direct question about the letter. He kept . . .

Refer specifically to the facts to show impeachment. Explain what impeachment is. Then discuss the facts. Show the jury how the witness made one statement in court to them under oath, but how on a prior occasion the witness's sworn testimony had been different. Finally, explain the significance of that difference in testimony, using the court's instructions as a backdrop.

On the other hand, if your witness stood up well to vigorous cross-examination, remind the jury of that in arguing your witness's credibility:

Remember Ms. Sharp, Mr. Right's secretary, whom we called to the stand. She was obviously very nervous about having to be here to testify on a matter like this, which is understandable, of course.

She told you what Mr. Ryan said that day he called Mr. Right before sending those letters. [Discuss what she said in her testimony, then continue.] Remember how Mr. [plaintiff's counsel] tried to shake her testimony on cross-examination. Over and over again he asked her the same questions, repeatedly trying to shake her story. Remember how she sat there and patiently explained time and again exactly what she had originally told you.

In numerous other ways the witness's demeanor can be argued by reminding the jury how the witness testified. If the witness was embarrassed, pompous, argumentative, or evasive, if the witness had particular mannerisms, recall those to the jury's attention, and, in an understated way, explain the significance of that demeanor to credibility.

These principles apply with particular force to the testimony of experts. Help the jury to understand how the other side's experts were little more than actors trying to sell them a story. Do this by pointing out the devices the expert used to attempt to convince the jury. For example, in one recent case an accounting expert with considerable experience in testifying asked the judge's permission on several occasions to leave the stand in order to step down directly in front of the jury and talk to them from charts he had prepared. He stood confidently a few feet in front of the jury box, looking the jurors in the eye, talking directly to them, persuasively speaking to them about his charts.

On cross-examination, however, his demeanor became substantially different. During final argument I simply reminded the jury of the way he had acted. I reminded them first that he was an experienced trial witness, by his own account having given expert testimony in numerous trials. He was being paid a high fee to appear, and it was understandable he could command such a large fee for he was obviously an accomplished witness. I reminded the jury how he had confidently stood in front of them, speaking directly to them, and pointed out to them the various devices he had used, like an actor practicing his craft. I contrasted that practiced conduct on direct with his demeanor and way of handling questions on cross-examination.

Similarly, in another recent trial a document expert testified for one and one-half days on direct about the examination conducted on various documents. Armed with a pointer, using photographs and slides, the expert spoke at length about styles of type, spacing, placement of commas, alignment of lines, sizes of margins, staple holes, and numerous other aspects of the documents.

Virtually all of these matters could be ascertained by anyone who bothered to take the time to look closely at the documents. Nevertheless, the expert gave a virtuoso performance at reciting the obvious in an authoritative manner, armed with pointer, photographs, and slides.

Much of cross-examination consisted of having the expert acknowledge that each of these matters was one which was observable by the layman—indeed by each juror, if he bothered to take the time to look at the particular matter. The jury began to realize that much of the expert's testimony was nothing more than a show.

During final argument I repeated the entire exercise. I reminded the jury how the expert had acted during direct examination by reviewing the specific observations made and how they had been discussed in an authoritative way, suggesting to the jury the expert was dealing with arcane matters beyond the understanding of mortal folk. My focus on the expert's demeanor undermined the significance of his testimony and, reinforced by several admissions made during cross-examination, his effectiveness was nullified.

Recreate the mood of the courtroom during a witness's testimony if that will help your argument. If there were tears or moments of embarrassment, temper, nervousness, or tension, recreate those matters.

Thus, in one recent trial a stockbroker who was a key witness for the plaintiff was reluctant during cross-examination to answer questions directly and simply, preferring to launch into long, unrequested explanations. At my request, the witness was admonished by the judge several times to answer the question and not digress into nonresponsive discourses. Finally, the witness slipped, and began to argue with the judge about the judge's admonition concerning a nonresponsive answer. The witness caught himself quickly, but not before a few awkward moments when he, the jury, and most observers were embarrassed by his remonstration to the court.

While he may have already destroyed his credibility, I specifically reminded the jury in final argument how his answers had been nonresponsive, how he had argued and evaded my questions, and how he had even argued with the judge! It was apparent as I discussed the incident that the jury was reliving the embarrassment of that occasion, to the witness's detriment.

To prepare for this kind of detailed and specific final argument, during trial I make notes on a daily basis of items that I may wish to use. For example, if a witness has contradicted himself, been impeached, argued with the judge, been admonished to give responsive answers, or in some other way done something relating to his or her credibility, a marginal note made at the time will preserve the matter for final argument.

After court or early the next morning, I dictate notes for final argument drawn from the prior day's trial session. These notes may refer to matters such as demeanor and credibility; to specific exhibits or other items of evidence; to admissions, impeachment, or other material developed on cross-examination; or quote specific questions and answers. Transcribed by a typist each day, these notes are a lode of material for final argument.

6. *Argue the instructions and the law.* In most jurisdictions, the lawyers know the court's instructions before final argument begins. Use them in your argument. Referring to particular instructions reinforces the theme you have developed for the case, provides a framework for arguing the relevance of your facts, and also suggests that the law supports your side of the case.

Weave the instructions into your argument. Use the court's instruction on a particular point either as an introduction to your factual discussion on the issue, as a summary and conclusion, or both. The relation between the two demonstrates how the law and the facts combine to support your position.

If the law is particularly favorable to your position but may appear to be contrary to the equities in the case, refer to the instruction and explain why the law makes sense. Remind the jury in a positive way that they are not to be governed or influenced by sympathy but are bound by an oath to uphold the law and follow the instructions to be given them by the court.

7. *Do not be defensive about the burden of proof.* Effective final argument

461

stresses from the outset a positive theory of the case and demonstrates that the defense has proved what it said it would in its opening. That approach can be undercut by defensive argument about the burden of proof, particularly by arguments in a civil case that the plaintiff has failed to prove its case by a preponderance of the evidence. Preponderance is a tenuous concept; appearing to concede that your adversary has proved points of its case but not by a sufficient quantity of evidence is dangerous.

It is far better to show the jury positively how you have proven your theory. Begin by reminding the jury that, of course, the plaintiff has the burden of proof. Then state simply that the plaintiff has failed to meet that burden and, to the contrary, the preponderance of the evidence shows that your view of the case is correct. As you subsequently argue the facts and the law, reiterate how they show that the preponderance of the evidence supports your position.

The problem of burden of proof is somewhat different in criminal cases. The defendant may not be in a position to enunciate and support, particularly by the defendant's own evidence, a positive theory of the case. It may be much more appropriate therefore for the criminal defendant to stress the prosecution's burden and its failure to meet that burden. Again, however, that argument should be made in a positive way to show the jury affirmatively why the prosecution has not met its heavy burden.

8. *Anticipate your opponent's closing.* In most jurisdictions, the plaintiff has the opportunity to open and close the argument. On behalf of the defendant you must not only argue your case but also anticipate what may be argued by your opponent in rebuttal. Explain to the jury that the plaintiff gets the opportunity to reply and that you will not have another opportunity to speak. Assure the jury that you are confident that you could reply to points made by the plaintiff if you had the opportunity, but that the evidence and the jury's recollection will have to speak for you. If you know opposing counsel has habitual ways of arguing in rebuttal, anticipate those and warn the jury about them.

9. *Tell the jury what you want them to do.* Effective argument explains the case. It assists the jury to understand the case and causes the jury to believe it is arriving on its own at the conclusion you want. It is critical, however, that the jury understand what you want them to do. I have been amazed to hear arguments in which lawyers did not make it clear what they expected from the jury.

Explain the verdict form to the jury if the jury will decide a general verdict for your client. In many jurisdictions, special interrogatories or special verdicts are used, sometimes in great numbers. Explain to the jury how they should answer each question. Look for some rhetorical device to assist them in remembering the way you want them to answer the questions. If the verdict form calls for answers to detailed interrogatories, deal with the questions in a logical sequence, referring to the evidence and the law as they bear on each question. Warn the jury about any peculiarities in wording of the verdicts that may cause confusion or error.

10. *Limit discussion of damages.* Damages are usually not a defense issue. I seldom discuss damages at all or discuss them only very briefly, playing them down as immaterial because the plaintiff is not entitled to prevail. This approach is best taken early in the argument as an introduction to the strongest defense points on liability.

Thus, early in the argument the defense lawyer can point out how the plaintiff's counsel spent much of his argument time talking about damages and, perhaps, asking for very large amounts of money. Point out that the plaintiff wants the jury to begin to think in big figures to avoid discussing the fact that the law and the evidence make clear that the plaintiff is not entitled to recover at all. Then move into the strongest parts of argument showing why the plaintiff is not entitled to prevail on liability issues.

Arguing the amount of damages is always dangerous, and it risks appearing inconsistent with assertions that the plaintiff is not entitled to recover anything. There are, of course, cases—hopefully rare—in which the defendant must recognize the likelihood of liability and direct its efforts to holding down the damages. In such cases it may be necessary tacitly to concede certain damages by concentrating the argument against other elements, particularly if very large, such as intangibles or unliquidated amounts. This argument does, however, undercut the liability defense and is likely to result in a damage award.

Effective final argument is simple, specific, and explanatory. Make your theories and your points simple. Discuss the facts and the law specifically and in detail. Explain the significance of the facts and law in relation to the questions the jury must decide. Show the jury you want them to understand the case and the significance of everything that happened in the trial because it all supports your position.

PART VII

Preparing
and Examining
Witnesses at Trial

Preparing Witnesses

by David H. Berg

A Texas tort lawyer recently won an $8.5 million verdict for the owner of a deceased stud bull, felled midstream of an enviable career by cruel circumstance and an apparently lethal pesticide. When I inquired of the attorney how he had persuaded the jury to return such a large award, his answer seemed particularly germane to the topic of preparing witnesses. He draped his arm over my shoulder, kicked the dirt with his pointy-toe boots, and said, apparently without embarassment, "Well, boy, I just humanized the bull."

Little of what we do as trial lawyers raises profound moral issues. Voir dire, opening statement, cross-examination, and closing argument seldom involve unsettling ethical problems, unless we strive to ferret out philosophy from under every legal rock—an exercise better left to monasteries than to courthouses.

It is in the privacy of our offices, preparing parties and witnesses to testify under oath, that we can affect the integrity of the judicial system. There we find our raison d'etre: winning, and the lengths to which we will go to win.

The problem is perjury. A state court judge cogently wrote in 1913, "The prevalence of perjury is a serious menace to the administration of justice, to prevent which no means have as yet been satisfactorily devised." It is easy to treat a trial as a blank slate upon which to write the dialogue, and in courthouses across the country there are lawyers known for doing just that.

All of us swear eternal hostility to perjury, but it is facile to dismiss the subject without examining its causes and determining if we contribute to its occurrence.

The author practices law in Houston, specializing in criminal litigation.

Let me be clear: I do not condone tampering with testimony or mean to imply that many of our colleagues do.

But I do suggest that, sooner or later, most of us trim the sail of the testifying client a bit too much. It is one thing to say, "No perjury," and yet another to avoid it always or to encourage it never. In neither case do we necessarily suborn the lie. For instance, who among us has not warned the client, "Before you tell me your side of the story, let me tell you what the law is in this area," or, "If you say that, you'll lose." Or who, wincing at his client's explanation, has not reminded the client, "Well, that's not how your boss remembers it," or, "Aren't you really telling me. . . ."

It is at those moments, draped with the mantle of the Canons of Ethics and its injunction to represent the client's position zealously, that we are on the edge.

By most standards the law lags 50 years behind the rest of society. To urge that ours is a conservative profession understates the case. The lawyer who exhibits creativity, the basic right-brain personality who occasionally sings his closing argument or claims television caused his client's criminal behavior, is back to pipefitting, or worse, remains in the profession. Cross-examination is hardly a science lab, and one rarely hears a closing argument described as a breakthrough. But in preparing witnesses for trial, we are on the cutting edge, where we are forced to consider questions with profound implications for all society.

My conclusion—based solely on experience—is that we do not do badly, and not necessarily because of our sterling moral fiber. Practicalities help to keep us from pushing too far. In the first place, you can get, well, caught.

The criminal law is filled with instances of the convicted client who is visited at the Federal Hotel by agents of the Federal Bureau of Investigation and asked, did his lawyer do anything wrong, like trying to get him to lie on the stand? When turning on the lawyer becomes the fast track to parole, you should sooner rely on the kindness of strangers than on the loyalty of the jailed client. Nor will you be saved by handling only civil cases. Increasingly there are instances, especially in actions brought under the Racketeer Influenced and Corrupt Organizations Act, where judges ship deposition testimony to the U.S. Attorney's office for investigation of all manner of crime, including perjury.

Another consideration in not eliciting this sort of testimony is that it can be exposed. Cross-examination often leaves false testimony in shards, like a pane of glass dropped from a third-story window. Moreover, jurors frequently knock off the lies, if not from the facts, simply from the feel of the case. Juries hate liars, and the liar's side, once exposed, is going to lose.

So the integrity of trial law rests both on the common sense and on the ethical standards of its practitioners. Now there's a chilling thought.

467

Isn't the law practiced by human beings? Didn't Shakespeare first raise the issue in *The Merchant of Venice* when he asked, "Hath not a lawyer eyes? Hath not a lawyer hands, organs, dimensions; and incredible overhead?" The point is that the overall admirable behavior of trial lawyers can be understood fully only if you consider that the penalty for getting caught is indictment and possibly loss of your license.

The American Bar Association's Canons of Ethics are clear. Ethical Consideration 7-26 codifies an answer to what has to be one of the most difficult moral issues faced by any profession:

> The law and Disciplinary Rules prohibit the use of fraudulent, false, or perjured testimony or evidence. A lawyer who knowingly participates in introduction of such testimony or evidence is subject to discipline. A lawyer should, however, present any admissible evidence his client desires to have presented unless he knows, or from facts within his knowledge should know, that such testimony or evidence is false, fraudulent, or perjured.

The bright light of this Ethical Consideration grows dim in the office as you stare across your desk at the client, listening to him pour out what may be a completely fabricated account of the facts of the case. This problem is acknowledged in other, less wholly idealistic sections of the Canons. For instance, Ethical Consideration 7-6 discusses the perplexing problem of developing and preserving evidence related to the client's state of mind and intent. When the lawyer is not certain about the state of mind, "he should resolve reasonable doubts in favor of his client."

Here Are the Questions

The questions that arise from this rule are endless. Is judging the client the proper role of the advocate? What do we do if we disbelieve the client? And what if we cannot disprove that which we do not believe? What if the untruth is unarguably irrelevant? How much of our soul do we owe the client in resolving that "reasonable doubt"? Are we to withdraw from representation based on a hunch? What if the client has already paid the fee? What if the doubt develops the day before trial? And what do we do about the lawyer on the other side whose definition of reasonable doubt may be far different from our own? Or about the lawyer on the other side who we know will tell his client to lie?

Your client may get on the stand and start lying. If he does, the next step is dictated by an American Bar Association procedure outlined years ago and recently reaffirmed in a Supreme Court decision, *Nix v. Whiteside,* 475 U.S. 157, 106 S. Ct. 988 (1986). The lawyer is to go to chambers, explain the dilemma to the judge, and ask leave to withdraw, which may or may not be granted. Being forced to sit there while a client lies or, worse, being incorrect about whether he is lying are only two of a parade of infinite horribles that immediately suggest themselves. There is also the dread possibility that the client is president of your most lucrative client. But that is irrelevant, isn't it?

Only those who consistently stake out a superior moral position can resolve these issues easily. That is why, with little guidance but our own godly nature, we should all be grateful to my friend the Texas tort lawyer. Seldom is the Gordian knot so easily undone, rarely is the thorny philosophic issue so quickly unravelled as in his synthesis: Our job is to humanize the bull.

This is not to imply that the trial lawyer should avoid answering these questions because they are difficult. It is to say, however, that much of what creates philosophical dilemmas is taken from the hands of the lawyer who follows the rules, and not just those found in the Canons of Ethics. While no one would argue that the Canons were drafted with the intent to suborn perjury, they nonetheless grant us wide latitude in putting together our cases. In essence, they urge us to leave justice to judges, to represent our clients vigorously, and to win cases. It is easy to rationalize questionable trial behavior if you drag down the Canons at 2:00 A.M. and read them through the enlightening haze of brown whiskey. The possibility that a trial will reveal the truth or something that closely resembles it results, not from a course in professional responsibility, though that helps, but primarily from the ethical beliefs of the lawyer and his willingness to live them out.

There are lawyers who refuse to woodshed witnesses at all, who just throw them up there on the stand and let them tell their story. Their clients most often are referred to as "appellants."

It is axiomatic. Everyone who testifies has to be woodshedded. It is probably unethical to fail to prepare a witness, and it is undoubtedly cruel to subject anyone to cross-examination without preparation. The unrehearsed witness can deal a lethal blow to an otherwise winnable case.

But sooner or later we all risk putting a client on the stand without sufficient preparation. Here I share the rarest of lawyer anecdotes, a story about a case I lost.

The trial had seemed unwinnable from the start. My client, an addicted physician, was accused of three hand-to-hand sales of cocaine; several eyewitnesses would testify about the sales. In defense of myself and the ultimate verdict, the client was no, er, gem. In addition to his having shown up in court with a telltale trace of white powdery substance dangling from his iridescent nose, proof was offered that he once had fallen asleep on a patient while taking the patient's pulse.

We worked on his testimony for hours and, surprisingly, he turned out to be a pretty good witness during the guilt/innocence phase of the trial. The jury almost deadlocked before finally convicting him. I had some hope that they would grant him a probated sentence during the punishment phase of the bifurcated trial. My only advice, given his earlier, stellar performance, was to answer "No," and nothing more when I asked him if he had ever been convicted of a felony in this or any other jurisdiction. That was the way to establish his eligibility for probation.

Here is the colloquy that followed:

Q: Have you ever been convicted of a felony in this or any other jurisdiction?

A: Mr. Berg, I have never been in trouble in my life.

I have a fairly decent reputation for truth and veracity, nothing to write home about, but believe me when I say that I tried to stage a heart attack, in fact, fervently prayed for one at that moment. The prosecutor was scarcely able to conceal his ecstasy during cross-examination.

Q: Never been in trouble? Didn't you turn a 14-year-old girl on to cocaine?

A: Sir, that is a lie! She was 16.

Exit here, stage left, for the Texas Department of Corrections, to return in five years.

Currently on appeal, that case haunts me. The client had come within inches of the only success he could possibly have enjoyed. Absent my misplaced faith in his intelligence, he might have gotten probation. Thus, I drew a lesson. Especially in criminal cases, always remember that the client got this far because of his own intelligence. During trial, rely on your own.

The first rule, then, is to woodshed in every instance, rehearsing both direct and cross examination. Almost invariably, the properly prepared witness warms to the task when finally placed under oath. Direct becomes more concise and vivid; cross is seldom as bad as anticipated.

There is an important, if obvious, caveat for this sort of pretrial preparation. Know when to stop. Over-rehearsing robs testimony of credibility; nothing is more devastating than memorized answers delivered in an emotionless monotone.

Nor should the lawyer whose client is superb in the office on Saturday before trial, blubbering out his remorse over what he has done or outlining in exquisite detail the ways in which he has been defrauded, be entirely sanguine that the same compelling performance will be repeated in the courtroom. It often happens that the client clams up or, all too frequently, that he takes tranquilizers and testifies like a zombie when he gets on the stand.

There are other general ground rules, none of which is etched in stone. Ideally the rehearsal should take place a few days before deposition or trial. This creates a more relaxed learning environment for witnesses, who are generally unfamiliar with courtroom procedures and justifiably concerned about how they will perform. As you go over the case, bear in mind how a judge or jury will react, and bear down on the ultimate issues.

Most important: Forget what the client has at stake and remember that your reputation is on the line here. Some creep from another law firm is trying to beat you personally, ruin your career, and molest your children. More than any other single factor, what you have going for the client is your own Swiss-cheese super ego, your own inestimable opinion of yourself, and an insatiable desire to win. None of this hurts the client; it just looks a little odd in print.

Therefore: Take command immediately. You know more than clients do. Caution them that what they say is frequently less important than how they say it, and if they lose their temper, they lose, period. Instruct them that after they are passed to opposing counsel their tone of voice should remain the same; it is ''Yes, Sir'' and ''No, Sir'' to both sides.

Warn them that appearances are vital to the jury, that they must dress unpretentiously and leave expensive jewelry at home. Remind them that their decorum will be monitored by the judge and jury in the courtroom and during recess and that a trial must be conducted in a sober atmosphere if they want to create the right impression. Tell him to get a haircut or her to get her hair done, and if you want, dictate the style. (Buy yourself a David Boies $125 polyester suit. You heard me: polyester.) Tell them not to tranquilize, speed up, or otherwise medicate themselves during trial. Gum chewing, smoking, and candy sucking are better left to the cafeteria. If they object on grounds of superficiality, invite them to hire a philosopher.

Your most important instruction to the client is to listen to each question carefully and answer only what is asked. There is an old trick designed to teach the uninitiated how to answer directly. After cautioning the client to answer only the question asked, nonchalantly ask if he has a watch. Ninety percent of the time you will get the answer, ''Sure, it's 3:15.'' At that point the gifted practitioner, asserting his superiority, pounds on the desk and screams, ''Listen here, buddy, I didn't ask for the time of day. I asked if you have a watch.'' Usually the client suffers an immediate epiphany; the answers become progressively less expansive. Thereafter, each time the client slips up and begins to talk too much, slam your hand down on the desk. Once the actual deposition or trial testimony begins, the client will be gun-shy, hearing the echo of the irate attorney's fist as it slams into the desk. It really works.

The general rule then is to impress on the witness not to volunteer an extra word to opposing counsel during cross-examination. I warn my criminal clients that for each extra word they utter they can add a year to their sentence, if they are convicted. The civil plaintiff need only be told that each extra utterance costs $100,000 out of the verdict.

As with virtually every other inviolate rule of trial work, there are exceptions to this minimalist credo. The first comes when it is absolutely necessary to explain an answer. The lawyer and client should establish in advance those areas that need to be expanded upon, especially when a simple answer would be misleading or harmful. However, clients sometimes be-

471

come so anxious to explain their position that they forget the simple preface of "yes" or "no" that allows for the fuller testimony. Warn them that their failure to answer the question directly before the explanation can lead to an admonition by the judge to be responsive, and that if the warning is repeated, the jury will think the witness is hiding something.

The second exception occurs when the door is opened by opposing counsel. This exception is especially valuable when key testimony is excluded by a motion in limine or other adverse ruling. Often opposing counsel will open the door to the evidence by careless cross-examination. Once the question is asked, you have two choices. You may develop the exposed issue or redirect, or, preferably, the witness may "spontaneously" get into testimony you have wanted to bring out all along.

In 1979, I defended a case in which a wife was accused of shooting and then dismembering her husband after he held her hostage for three days, threatening her life and the lives of her children. The judge granted the prosecution's motion in limine and excluded expert psychiatric testimony about the battered-wife syndrome. His theory was that the evidence of the beatings spoke for itself and that no psychiatric testimony was admissible because we did not rely on insanity as a defense. The psychiatrist's testimony was central to our defense because of the particularly heinous nature of the crime and the accused's apparent failure to retreat before the shooting, a legal prerequisite for a claim of self-defense. The psychiatrist was prepared to testify that my client, like all battered women, had developed a kind of psychological bondage that would not allow her to leave under any circumstance.

It was during the defendant's testimony that the prosecutor blundered. After fighting for hours to keep the psychiatrist off the stand, he asked these questions.

Q: Let's see. You first shot him, then cut his body into five pieces, put them into the trunk of your car, and drove him all the way to your parents' home in California. Is that correct?

A: Yes, sir.

Q: He kept you in your house for three days and nights prior to this killing?

A: Yes. And he threatened to kill my children.

Q: You have a telephone there, I presume?

A: Yes, of course.

Q: And in three days and nights in which you claim you were tortured and beaten it never occurred to you to pick up the phone and call the police?

A: Of course it occurred to me . . .

Caveats for Preparation

Emboldened by her failure to have capitalized on his first open-ended question, he then moved closer to her, shouting and waving a picture of her husband's body: "You didn't leave because you didn't want to, did you? You enjoyed every minute of what you did, didn't you? It was far easier than getting a divorce, wasn't it?"

He turned to his seat, not really expecting an answer. The client simply said, "It's not fair for me to try to answer this by myself. I know I was chained to that man, just like the abused child goes to the parent who beats him. The only person who can fully explain this answer is my psychiatrist, and if you really want the answer to the question, you ought to let him testify instead of objecting."

The judge agreed, called the testimony invited, and let the psychiatrist take the stand. The jury acquitted in less than two hours. My client and I had rehearsed the answer the night before; I had told her to wait for a legitimate opening and to hope it would come.

There are countless other caveats about effective preparation of witnesses. One is that the pretrial work never ends, even when the trial begins. For example, parties and those witnesses who are allowed to sit in the courtroom should profit from what they hear. During recesses and at night, go over the main areas of concern in light of the testimony elicited. Another caveat is to make the client aware of what is going to happen after you announce "ready," even to the point of outlining legal arguments you expect and their significance.

A friend in Washington, lawyer Liebman, counsels his clients to anticipate where the attorney is headed with his questions. This is good advice so long as the witness does not try to prove he is smarter than the attorney. He probably is, but the courtroom is not his forum, especially if the attorney is prepared. Conversely, the lawyer who senses that he is not establishing any momentum on cross because the witness is anticipating his questions accurately can regain the advantage simply by skipping around. The person on the stand must be warned ahead of time that the interrogation may not be chronological or even organized and that the apparent confusion should not be mistaken for ignorance on the part of the lawyer.

It is also helpful to reassure clients that you will protect them from irrelevant or bullying questions when they take the stand, at least insofar as the judge will sustain your objections.

These are the general rules for successfully preparing witnesses for testimony, whether during deposition or during trial. All of them are designed to leave clients and witnesses better prepared and more relaxed when they finally have to testify. Your own experience will allow you to modify, alter, or ignore much of this advice.

One kind of lawyer—the public prosecutor—is a special case. Ethical Consideration 7-13 provides:

> The responsibility of a public prosecutor differs from that of the usual advocate; his duty is to seek justice, not merely to

473

convict . . . With respect to evidence and witnesses, the prosecutor has responsibilities different from those of a lawyer in private practice: the prosecutor should make timely disclosure to the defense of available evidence, known to him, that tends to negate the guilt of the accused, mitigate the degree of the offense, or reduce the punishment. Further, a prosecutor should not intentionally avoid pursuit of evidence merely because he believes it will damage the prosecution's case or aid the accused.

The prosecutor carries more power in his briefcase on a single day than most of us will know in a lifetime. Frequently his role determines the future life of a fellow human being. Given the extraordinary support prosecutors currently receive from courts and juries alike, they should exercise extraordinary restraint not to yield to the temptation of convicting at any cost.

The following exchange occurred during a recent federal perjury and false swearing case in which I represented a man accused of lying about his ownership of an airplane in documents he submitted to United States Customs authorities and in testimony before the grand jury. Customs recovered the plane on a Carolina beach after a forced landing. It was filled with marijuana. My client claimed that the plane had been sold by his corporation on a conditional sales contract and that, since he had received only the down payment, he was entitled to return of the plane. There was no implication that he had been involved in the drug transaction, only that he had been opportunistic in trying to get the plane back.

The government's position was explained by its first witness, a postal inspector. He had testified on direct examination that my client, the defendant, had never mentioned in his initial interview that he had sold the plane on a conditional sales agreement. The agent concluded that the defendant had made up the story and supporting documents after the fact, in order to get his plane back. That, he explained, was why he and Customs agents had taken the case to the assistant United States attorney and gotten my client indicted.

On cross I asked if the inspector had filed a case agent report, standard operating procedure, and he replied that he had. The prosecutor handed it to me. The typewritten document did not mention the terms of sale of the airplane, just as the agents had testified.

Q: Who prepared this document?
A: A secretary at the agency.
Q: From what source? Did you dictate to her or what?
A: I don't recall what her source was. Maybe I dictated it.
Q: What about notes? Did you take notes?
A: Yes, sir, I did.

He then produced a document from his briefcase, a crumpled handwritten memo of his first meeting with my client.

Q: Why didn't you tell me about these notes when I asked you what your secretary used to prepare the typewritten document?

A: Because I don't know what she used.

Q: Is there another reason you didn't offer these notes to me at the first opportunity?

A: No, sir.

Q: You said that if my client had told you about the conditional sales agreement during that first meeting in his office you would never have had him indicted?

A: Yes, sir.

Q: Well, tell me, sir, what these last few lines on the handwritten notes say.

At that point he read a few numbers, and I drew them on a chart so that the judge and jury could read: "250 d. p., with 240 over 12 mos." It was immediately apparent that the inspector had been told about the terms of the sale. My client had been paid $250,000 down, and the balance of $240,000 was to be paid over 12 months, exactly as he later reflected in his correspondence with Customs, the documentation he supplied, and his testimony before the grand jury.

At my client's prompting, I reminded the inspector that during the interview, the defendant had swung around in his chair, totalled some numbers on the adding machine, and handed him the tape. I asked if he remembered that my client had then begged off, saying he was busy but promising to deliver the necessary documents at a later date. The inspector remembered nothing of that, since it was not reflected in the notes; but he was stuck with the numbers. The case was over for the government, although the prosecution plodded on. The not-guilty verdict was a belated announcement of what had happened with the government's first witness.

Months later, as I jogged in the park, the cross-examination got even better. In my fantasy the government witness admits he had been instructed not to turn over the notes unless I asked specifically for them and then, in a fit of remorse, asks the prosecutor to dismiss the case. The applause from the spectators grows deafening as I return, slowly and with great care, to my client, now a free man.

Double Standards

It was far more difficult to wrest those notes from the inspector than space allows me to develop. I cannot prove that the inspector was instructed to resist turning them over to me, but I have my suspicions. While it is well within the rules for a defense lawyer to instruct his client not to offer anything to opposing counsel unless he asks for it, it is not acceptable for a prosecutor to tell that to a state's witness. This double standard is acceptable only if we agree with the Canons and their obvious mandate. Prosecutors enjoy a huge advantage of manpower and

475

money over their less powerful opposition. The implications of their conduct are overwhelming and far more important than the outcome of a civil suit.

Alone in their offices, prosecutors must make the most difficult decisions of all, not only when they may have to compromise their will to win, but when they must decide in favor of a defendant they may hate.

Kingman Brewster, while president of Yale, remarked that the best minds of each generation go into the law. He did not say what happened to us next, and probably with good reason. We soon discover that this nation reserves a special loathing for its lawyers. While we should acknowledge the frailties of our profession that lead to low regard, we should not do so with unrelenting self-abuse. In reality we probably mirror what society wants us to be. Clients do not choose their attorneys because of a reputation for fair play and Christian benevolence. They expect us to do the gunslinger's work, preferably by ambush. They generally give little thought to means; they want us to win. Given these imperatives, the fragile structure of the adversary system is tested each time we put a witness on the stand. That is why the hard choices about the conduct of a case are left to the lawyers. And that is how it should be.

Working the Witness Puzzle

by Robert F. Hanley

We trial lawyers have an impossible job. We do not have a nice, anesthetized patient lying under a sterile sheet passively waiting for the surgeon's knife. We must operate on a wiggling, frightened witness who perceived little of what he saw, recalls little of what he perceived, and has great difficulty expressing what he recalls.

As you stand at the end of the jury box, or at the lectern, or wherever the judge requires counsel to stand, you look at your terrified, not overly bright witness and you realize it is your job to bring forth from his mouth an account of a complex or involved incident or transaction in such a way that six or twelve untrained jurors will understand and accept it. No wonder we so often resort to leading questions and everything short of a semaphore in an attempt to control the situation and minimize the chance of a real disaster.

That witness is usually not of our choosing. We may be able to avoid calling one or two of the least gifted witnesses to whatever happened, and we can establish the order in which we call the witnesses, but generally we must rely upon those who witnessed the event or participated in the transaction. Our freedom in presenting our client's story is further limited by complicated and far from consistent rules of evidence. The human factor and the laws of evidence conspire to present us, the American trial lawyers, with an extraordinarily difficult task.

Our success or failure rests largely in the manner in which we prepare and present those witnesses. The following observations dealing with those processes have been arranged in the following order: (1) the preparation and presentation of lay witnesses; (2) the order of presentation;

The author is a partner in the Denver firm of Morrison & Foerster; Adjunct Professor, Advanced Trial Advocacy, University of Colorado Law School; and a former chairman of the Section of Litigation.

(3) preparing lay witnesses for your opponent's cross-examination; (4) preparing for cross-examination of your opponent's witnesses; and (5) the preparation, presentation and cross-examination of the expert witness.

Most cases will be won or lost on the basis of witnesses' knowledge, recollection, and perception and their ability to describe the events at issue. As a trial lawyer, you must take the witnesses you find, train them in simple exposition and teach them how to communicate, simply, clearly and accurately. You must become a teacher in effective communication. You must teach the witness to use simple words and short sentences. You must introduce him to the eloquence of brevity. You must teach him to listen.

Not Very Alert

You must also become something of a psychologist. The witness is often a person who has seen an event or been through a transaction he was probably not anticipating. He undoubtedly was not expecting to be called upon to recount what he saw. He was, therefore, no more alert than usual, and that usually is not particularly alert.

Because the witness has only a hazy recollection of the details of the event, he will tend to substitute "logical" guesses for recollection. The trial lawyer knows that those logical guesses will provide his opponent with outstanding demolition material. The human mind does not stop with the facts it has perceived; it transforms those facts and supplements them.

Most witnesses suffer perception and communication difficulties. We must somehow overcome or at least mitigate the damaging effect of those shortcomings. We realize that witnesses are inattentive to details, generally have poor memories, and tend to oversimplify. A witness tends to modify his story to please the questioner, even on cross-examination.

Knowing the effect of these human weaknesses, what can we do about them? The witness must be shown the effect of this kind of testimony. A good starting point for preparing a witness is to run him through a rehearsal of his direct and cross-examination on a tape recorder and play it back to him while you provide a running commentary. You might have prepared yourself with a good college textbook on public speaking. One excellent example is GUIDE TO GOOD SPEECH by Ernest Wrage and James McBurney.

In presenting a witness on direct examination, I like to let the jury know immediately why I have called him. What, in a sentence, will they hear from this witness? If the witness did not participate directly in the drama, I let the jurors know immediately so they won't be disappointed later.

Q: When did you first visit the site?

A: The day after they poured the concrete slab.

Q: What did you do?

A: I took measurements and photographs.

Then I like to set the scene.

It is not only objectionable but unwise to have a witness tell a narrative until the jury is looking at the event or transaction through the witness's eyes. Don't have the witness ''tell the court and jury please in your own words what transpired'' until the court and jury know where, when and with whom the event about which you want him to testify took place.

If your witness gets off the track during his direct examination, bring him back with an apology. ''Sorry, Mr. Jones, I didn't follow you there. Now where were you standing in relation to the red tractor?''

Don't repeat a question when you are especially pleased with the answer. How many times have you repeated a question for emphasis and had the witness change or blur his previous answer in the hope of pleasing you? A nice pregnant pause to let the answer sink in is much more effective and much less dangerous.

We all know that it is usually a good idea to steal the march and bring out the damaging portions of the witness's story ourselves rather than wait and have our opponents bring them out on cross-examination. A word of caution: Many of us give our opponents far too much credit. We bring out every little negative aspect of the case. But doing so confuses the jury and makes for a terribly ineffective account. Often your opponent will not have thought of it, and you will have unnecessarily diminished the value of your witness's testimony.

Honest Witness

You will, from time to time, find an absolutely truthful witness. He will have told everything accurately—without flourishes, exaggeration or ambiguity. One tactic suggested by Wellman in his ART OF CROSS EXAMINATION (and used by Abraham Lincoln with success) is to ask this extremely honest witness about some aspect of the case about which you are certain he knows little or nothing. His answer, ''I'm sorry, sir, I don't know enough about that to swear to it,'' is an excellent way to corroborate his credibility.

Another technique used by advocates for at least a century is to omit on direct examination a portion of the story with which the witness had considerable trouble at his deposition. You will have prepared him carefully in the trouble area and together you will have solved or mitigated the problems encountered on deposition. You will sit back smugly through your opponent's ineffective cross-examination of your well-prepared witness.

I think most of us over-try our cases. We put on too many witnesses. The testimony becomes repetitive and dull. Even our own witnesses often hurt our case. Don't call witnesses you really don't need.

479

Psychologists tell us that people remember what they hear first and last. Usually you should start with the witness who will tell the story most effectively. If you have one who can tell all or most of the story, put him on immediately.

I don't like to start with an adverse witness. Some lawyers start with adverse witnesses as part of their standard operating procedure. But adverse witnesses are up there with one thought in mind: to kill my client and me. I put them on only if I really need their admissions. Even then, I carefully control them with a deposition in one hand, pretty much as a lion tamer uses a whip and chair. Every time that adverse witness strays from his deposition, I let him feel the whip: "Mr. Witness, you do recall coming to my office last month? You recall that your lawyer was with you and that you were sworn to tell the truth and at that time and place, I asked you this question and you made this answer. Question: 'Did you see the bus?' Answer: 'No.' Were you asked that question and did you make that answer?"

Hold him in. Ask questions in the same form they were asked on the deposition—it enhances the effect of the impeachment and keeps him from destroying your case and usually forces out of him the admission you need. On adverse examination, control is the key. Get your admission and run.

I bury the adverse witnesses in the middle of my case. If one hurts me, I can still take some sting out of it by the testimony of friendly witnesses. Where possible, I have reserved someone who can re-establish the fact a bad witness has blurred or demolished.

Save a good witness for last. Usually I like to finish with a good strong expert, and I use a hypothetical question as a mini-closing argument. I like a final witness who I am relatively sure will hold up on cross-examination.

In preparing your lay witnesses for your opponent's cross-examination, you actually should conduct a practice cross and put your witness through what you anticipate will be the cross-examination. A trial lawyer does not want to give the witness the impression that there is anything improper about preparing him to testify. The witness should be told the difference between preparation to make certain that he can clearly present his story and the unethical coaching of a witness, where a lawyer gives him a story to recite.

It is malpractice not to prepare a witness. It is not only unethical but idiotic to provide him with your version of what must have happened. As soon as the witness wanders off your script (as he must), he will be at the mercy of the cross-examiner.

When going over a witness's story with him, stop him whenever he uses defensive-sounding words such as "to tell you the truth," "honestly," or "you know." Try to get him to purge his vocabulary of those words. Also get rid of the qualifiers that make his testimony sound speculative—"I guess," "everyone knows that," "I think," "I felt," and "I always thought."

Caution him to use his, not your, vocabulary. It is amazing how fast witnesses start sounding like not very bright law students. Have him listen to a police officer in traffic court: "I was proceeding north on South State on the date and time in question when the subject was observed vacating the premises at 2714 South State all in the City of Chicago, County of Cook and State of Illinois." Your witness will soon see how much more effective he is when he uses his own vocabulary and a simple sentence structure.

Take him to court early. Explain where he will be testifying; where you will sit; where the jury sits. Give him a route to follow to the stand. Talk him through the trial—tell him how the jury is selected, the purposes and method of making an opening statement, the order of proof, what you expect your opponent to do. Tell him about the judge's charges and the closing arguments. Take the mystery out of the proceedings in which he will soon participate.

Think Carefully

Tell him about objections and to stop his answer when there is an objection. Tell him only to answer if the objection is overruled. On cross-examination, make sure that before he answers he thinks carefully about the question. This will insure that he does not answer a question that has not been asked. It will also give you an opportunity to interpose an objection.

Even tell him something about the rules of evidence so he won't be too surprised or disturbed by objections and will know he can't talk about what someone else said unless you ask.

At your last conference, tell your witnesses that although the story has become old and tired to them, to the jury it will be brand new. Tell them to tell it as they would tell their favorite story to some new friends. Tell them to speak to the jury, not you. Tell them to make the jury understand and to teach the jury the facts. Tell them to watch the jury and to help you help them clarify their testimony when they see that the jury has failed to follow it.

Keep making them strive for clarity, crispness and conviction. Those are the hallmarks of good testimony. Then let them know that you are happy with them, and your confidence in them will become contagious.

Many books and articles on cross-examination start out with something resembling a beatitude: Blessed are those who do not cross-examine a witness at all, for they shall inherit the verdict. If you do not cross-examine a witness, you are at once wise, courageous and brilliant. You are counseled not to cross-examine if the witness has failed to hurt your case or if the witness has hurt your case beyond repair. I don't know about your opponents, but mine usually don't bother calling a witness unless he will hurt my case. By a carefully planned and executed cross-examination, I can usually raise at least a slight question about the accuracy of that witness's story, or question his motives or impartiality.

I believe that many inexperienced lawyers, fearing cross-examination, follow the beatitude and fail to utilize that instrument, which is the basis of the Anglo-American jury trial.

When a witness has demolished your case, you have no choice. You have to cross-examine him. Maybe you can do no more than conduct an apparent or ghost cross-examination, but that is better than no cross-examination. You will bring out the fact that the witness was not subpoenaed and is appearing voluntarily to help his friend. Perhaps he is being paid for his time away from the job. It is old hat to you that he talked to your opponent before he testified—it is brand new to the jury. Jurors generally believe, thanks to television, that trial lawyers have mystic power they sprinkle over the witnesses. If a witness has talked to your opponent but refused to discuss his story with you, the jury may be offended and suspicious of his story. These tangential areas are worth developing. A failure on your part to ask any questions on cross-examination concedes that the witness and his story are impervious to attack.

The human machine is a poor communicator, and with the aid of the discovery devices available to the cross-examiner, he should be able to produce a cross-examination that will make either the witness or his story sound a bit incredible. We all know that in real life we don't expect to win Perry Mason victories on cross. No person in the back of the courtroom is going to be so shaken by the magnetic force of your personality that he will dash forward sobbing, shaking and confessing the guilt of the crime with which your client is charged. With proper preparation, however, and some practice, you should be able to increase the improbability of the witness's story by showing that he was not really in a place where he could see what he said he saw, heard what he said he heard, touched what he said he touched or remembered what he said he remembered. No human being perceives everything. No human being remembers everything. You should be able to find some way to weaken his version of what happened. I do not forget for a moment that cross-examination is a two-edged sword and that many cases are lost by poor cross-examinations. I do know, however, that I won't win many cases if I fail to cross-examine witnesses who have seriously hurt my case. It is a dangerous weapon and it should be used, not as a sledgehammer, but as a sabre, or even better, a foil. Although there are few absolute rules of trial practice, one rule I consider an absolute is that you must control a witness on cross with leading questions. The second absolute is to stop after you obtain the admission or the impeaching answer.

Identifies with Witness

The jury identifies with the witness, not with you and your magic power. It sits there during your cross-examination just waiting for the witness to score a point. It is amazing how clever even the most unsophisticated witness can be when he is cornered. Little victories for the witness are magnified. Your victories had better be big ones. Jurors will continue to empathize with the witness until you show them he is not worthy of their trust and sympathy.

Be brief on cross-examination: examine only in areas where you are fairly certain to do some damage or secure admissions. It is usually a mistake to inquire in more than two or three areas. It is important not to try to do too much with a witness and not to lose control. You keep that control with short leading questions made up of plain, honest words spoken crisply and authoritatively. You should never permit the witness to explain anything on cross-examination. During your first few years in practice, you may have to seek judicial intercession to keep the witness on track. After a few years, you will probably have such mastery over the witness and yourself that the witness is compelled to answer with a "yes" or a "no."

Many of the old pros eschew that advice—often with horrible consequences. I shall always remember one English example of a horrible consequence. Five other American trial lawyers and I were watching a barrister—we'll call him Percy—at work defending a man charged with murder. Sir Percy was Queen's Counsel.

The High Court Judge was resplendent in his crimson robe. His wig seemed six feet long. The ancient wooden walls of Old Bailey shined. We Americans were poleaxed.

The Q.C. was magnificent. He was well over six feet tall. His features were craggy. His wig was down on his forehead, his glasses down over his nose. He did marvelous swirling things with his robe and gestured menacingly with his glasses as he relentlessly cross-examined the prosecution's chief witness.

The witness was the manager of the company that had employed both the defendant and the victim. During his direct testimony, he had created a fairly strong circumstantial chain leading to the conclusion that Sir Percy's client had surreptitiously done in his fellow employee in the manager's office.

Percy whaled away:

Q: Now, Quigley, you admit that my client, Jacob Jones, was not the only employee with a key to your office.

A: That's quite right, Sir Percy.

Q: And my client wasn't the only employee who had expressed a strong dislike for the deceased, Smyth, was he?

A: No, Sir Percy, Smyth wasn't very well liked at all.

Q: And my client wasn't the only driver who returned his lorry late on the night of Smyth's death, was he?

A: No, Sir Percy, there were several others.

Q: And my client wasn't the only employee who went on holiday the day after Smyth's death.

A: No, Sir Percy, there were others. (Pause)

Fine job—every juror followed the cross-examination. They were beginning to have that wonderful questioning look all defendants' lawyers find so comforting. We waited for Percy to sit down triumphantly. Then we heard something we could not believe . . .

Well, sir, then how in the name of heaven can you possibly contend that my client Jacob Jones murdered Samuel Smyth?

We winced as one. Maybe these fellows in England did have a magic power. Maybe Percy had so brainwashed the witness that he would admit that his belief in the guilt of the defendant had been shaken by Percy's masterly cross-examination. That would never happen in Chicago. As it turned out it would never happen in London. The answer came out just about as it would have in less impressive courthouses in New York, Grand Rapids, Chicago or Los Angeles:

Sir Percy, I can answer your question in seven parts:

First, Jones told me and everyone within earshot that he would kill Smyth if Smyth didn't stop playing around with his daughter.

Second. . . .

He reached point four after about fifteen minutes. We left on five—after the judge had admonished Percy for the third time to refrain from interrupting the witness. We just could not stand another minute.

It was reassuring to learn that with all the magnificent trappings of Old Bailey, the beautifully articulate, magnificently skilled barristers get destroyed when they ask foolish questions on cross-examination, just as we do in New York, Grand Rapids, Chicago and Los Angeles. Wherever you practice, you should take "how" and "why" and "how do you explain" out of your cross-examination vocabulary.

We are told never to ask a question the answer to which we do not know. We are told that the trial is a poor place to seek discovery. Sometimes poor preparation makes you violate this rule. Usually you'll wish you had not. When you go off script, remember to take steps and leave yourself an escape route. First, just a little step—if the witness agrees, a second slightly longer and more dangerous step. If he balks, you may have to take a small step back or laterally to an alternative and safer area.

It is important to distinguish between cross-examination and closing argument. Save your ultimate point for your closing. Don't try to get the witness to admit that he was mistaken or was lying. He will invariably take something away from the victory you won. During your closing argument when his mouth is closed, you can remind the jurors of the difference between the witness's version of the story during direct and cross and counsel them that when a person lies about one thing he is certain to lie about other things.

484

I like to try to close my cross-examination on an upbeat. It is surprising how often lawyers sit down after a witness has made a telling point against them or after their opponent's objection to a question has been sustained. If you have properly prepared your cross, you will have saved your best line of questions till the end and will sit down hearing that nice little rustle that always follows an effective cross-examination.

We are all increasing our reliance upon expert opinion. The types of expert witnesses used are varied: economists; actuaries and other wage and damage experts; structural engineers; architects; foundation experts; real estate appraisers; accountants; individuals with a wide range of marketing experience in various industries; psychologists; the expert who has made a life study of people's buying habits and who knows how to design and conduct a public opinion poll, market surveys or consumer reaction tests. It is a rare case today that does not include some opinion testimony. Some think it is being overdone. I have not experienced over-utilization of expert testimony, but I have seen much misuse of it.

Flatter Him

Sometimes it is hard to persuade a qualified expert to testify. Flatter him. You can often convince him that a great injustice would be perpetrated if he, the world's only living expert on Middle English tapestry, does not take the stand against the charlatans who would try to convince the jury that a shoddy, poor copy woven across a saggy warp was authentic. You are an advocate. Use the skills you have to persuade the witness you need him to testify for you, for your client, for art.

You must assure the expert at the outset of your first conversation that you do not expect *him* to become an adversary. Tell him that you only want him to recount in a clear, humble, straightforward manner his qualifications, his opinion and the basis for his opinion. Often if you settle for a reasonable degree of scientific certainty, rather than absolute certainty, his reluctance to testify will dissolve.

Insist on and pay for a "consultation"—before an expert's deposition is taken. Arrange for enough time to permit a complete exploration and simplification of the scientific aspects of the case. Start from scratch. Make no assumptions. Have your expert define each term and explain each step he takes in reaching his opinion. Let the expert (especially one who has had no courtroom experience) know that the consultation is to prevent embarrassment to him as well as to you. Review every piece of technical data upon which he will rely. Make certain that you understand it and are in agreement as to its significance. Explain the theory of your case, and he will help you find the places where you are vulnerable and buttress them.

Most trial lawyers are excited about new technology. We enjoy obtaining at least a superficial look at new fields of knowledge. We generally enjoy talking to the experts. We like to show off our newly acquired expertise in conversations with our expert witnesses.

The trouble is that some of us never stop showing off. We continue to carry on mysterious conversations with our experts during the trial. We sound right out of medical or engineering school symposia. Jurors probably think, "Here are a couple of extremely smart fellows. I wish I knew what in the world the two of them are talking about." The mystery hour won't help much when the jury retires to deliberate. You and your expert have a teaching job to do. It can usually best be done in short steps. You both watch the jury for the telltale sign of imperception—the lost look of the walleyed pike.

Those twelve people have not shared your exciting new educational experience. You and your expert must get through to them. That means taking that overqualified, overpriced, fancy-talking professor and making him into an English-speaking human being. Teach him to speak simply and to draw simple, understandable sketches and diagrams.

Encourage him to explain his testimony—first to you, ultimately to the jury—by using charts, diagrams, maps, drawings, or in the case of doctors, by x-rays, skeletons or medical drawings of the parts of the body involved. Make him be specific. Forget fancy projections. Most jurors can't read a blueprint—most of them did not take a course in engineering drawing. Use drawings they will recognize from their experience. Make your expert tell it to you and then to the jury as if he were reviewing a book on his subject for a bright bunch of fifth graders. Not cloying, not patronizing, but very, very clear and well-organized.

Q: What is a caisson, professor?

A: Caissons are supports for buildings. They are used to support tall buildings.

Q: What kinds of caissons are there used today in construction in Chicago?

A: Mainly two types. Both are made of concrete. One goes right down to bedrock, and the other goes to hard clay or hardpan and is belled like sailors' trousers. Both hold up and act as part of the foundation of the building.

Q: With the court's permission, would you leave the witness stand, and using the blackboard, describe for the court and jury how the caissons support the building.

A: Now these columns I have marked A, B, and C are columns of concrete running from the surface of the ground down 125 feet to bedrock. This is the way it would look to you if you could slice off a piece of earth and look at the caissons from the side. Sort of the view you get of ants working in their dirt hills on one of those glass-enclosed ant farms they sell in pet stores.

In your preparation, make your expert interrupt himself and define every technical word he uses. Interrupt him in practice sessions until he

486

does it automatically or at least at the slightest cough from you. Try to avoid having to interrupt him constantly during his testimony to define terms. If he forgets and your coughs don't help, you should take the blame: "Sorry, doctor, I'm afraid you lost me there—what were you referring to when you used the term 'annular space'?"

Figures of Speech

Get your expert to use similes and examples. Make him watch the jurors as he would a class of students. Do they understand? Are they following him, or has he lost them? Make your expert as jury-aware as you are.

Go through your direct examination outline with him carefully. It is as important to insure effective communication by repetition of your examination with an expert as it is with a lay witness.

Take your time in qualifying your expert. Try in pretrial conferences to instill patience in the judge. Ask him not to push you through your examination of your expert's qualifications. The judge may have heard a thousand orthopedic surgeons qualified. The jury has not. Do not, of course, accept your opponent's offer to dispense with a recital of your expert's qualifications by stipulating that he is qualified. You might express your appreciation for the recognition of your witness's qualifications, but since the qualifications go to the weight to be afforded the testimony as well as to the admissibility of the opinion, you believe that the jury is entitled to hear the qualifications in detail.

Take your expert carefully through the cross you anticipate. Use leading questions and warn him how your opponent might use them unfairly. Tell him to say so if it would be misleading or inaccurate to give an unqualified answer. Warn him of pitfalls. Tell him to listen to questions very carefully and not to supply missing parts with assumed facts. He should be told not to change his manner during his cross. He should certainly be careful but not evasive or hostile. He should only answer the question asked and stop. He should never argue with counsel and never, never exaggerate.

Most Fertile Areas

Be sure to let your expert know that he will be given an opportunity to clarify, amplify or correct his testimony on redirect examination and that he is not required to straighten out your opponent by argumentative answers. Advise him not to be afraid to change his testimony immediately if he realizes he has made a mistake.

Point out the most fertile areas of cross-examination: textbooks, his own writings, other possible causes, inexactness of the science, possibility of errors of fact in the hypothetical question. Tell him that on redirect examination you will ask him if he took into consideration the other *possible* causes before he reached his opinion.

487

Obtain a written bibliography of his professional writings and accomplishments (curriculum vitae) and skim them for embarrassing or inconsistent opinions. Ask him to help you ferret out seeming inconsistencies. Often they disappear.

Do everything you can to present him to the jury as an honest, fair, sincere, friendly man of science who has done his homework and knows his subject. And God bless him if he is a little humble. The meek may not inherit the earth, but they can certainly help you to persuade the jury you are on the right side of the case.

The successful cross-examination of your opponent's expert usually requires much thought and preparation; you must shake some of the gloss from him and from his harmful opinion. Usually, if he is well-qualified and has expressed an opinion recognized by your expert to be honest and sound but at variance with your expert's opinion, you may be well-advised to obtain an admission that the question is the subject of professional debate. You probably are wise if you establish *your* theory with *your* expert and conduct an apparent or ghost cross-examination of your opponent's expert. His financial arrangement with your opponent may be of interest to the jury. The number of times he has testified for your opponent or for your opponent's side of cases may seem terribly shopworn to you, but it will be new to the jury.

Occasionally your opponent will have come up with a witness of the highest competence in his field, but his field isn't *specifically* related to the subject in issue. His qualifications may be adequate enough to get him over the admissibility hurdle, but his experience and training have been general and not specifically directed to the issue in your case. You may not want to attack the plaintiff's expert directly, but you can show indirectly and comparatively that he has general knowledge, where your expert has specific, detailed knowledge.

You may be able to have the expert testify that there are alternative explanations. Your expert tells you that such alternatives are certainly possible. You have not lost much of anything if the plaintiff's expert denies the probability since your expert will support your theory and if your expert is more persuasive, he may shake the jury's confidence in your opponent's expert. There is always the hope that you will gain an admission of an alternative probability. You won't have much of a problem if you took a good deposition. You know how the expert will testify. You will undoubtedly have had to pay his witness fee, but it is usually money well spent.

At the expert's deposition, look for and try to develop uncertainties and qualifications in his theory. Most experts will admit there is a possibility that there is another explanation and even that he has occasionally been wrong. Use caution in probing for qualified opinions on cross at trial if you have not developed the qualification in the deposition. Experts have a way of becoming convinced of the certainty of their opinions when they are attacked. It is usually unwise to insist on a yes or no answer from an expert. Let him qualify and then use his qualifications during your closing argument to show his uncertainty and unresponsiveness.

Skipped Steps

Use your expert to help you prepare for cross-examination of your opponent's expert. Have him show you where to probe for weaknesses in the procedure and methodology adopted by the expert in reaching his opinion. Perhaps the expert skipped some steps in a known process or failed to perform recognized tests. Get him to point them out and have your opponent's expert admit these omissions.

If your opponent's expert is testifying strictly on the basis of a hypothetical question, bring out the fact that he has no personal knowledge of the facts. Vary the hypothetical and ask the witness how the change would affect his opinion. This is excellent as a method of testing the expert's knowledge and fairness and as a preface for your expert's testimony. It is effective if you can isolate each factor the witness has stated as supporting his opinion and then inquire hypothetically whether the removal of that factor would affect his opinion. Find a weak link, one piece in the puzzle, and you have the basis for some effective argument during your closing argument. Always try to gain an admission that a contradicting source is well known.

Witnesses are human beings, and they are most unusual if their testimony is unbiased, disinterested and completely honest. It is usually colored and partisan. As an advocate, you must educate them and make them put aside their partisanship. John A. Wilson closed an excellent paper on common sense in advocacy as follows:

> No one is more conscious than I that I have been giving rather freely, much advice on a very old and most difficult subject. And, therefore, let me conclude on a note of caution and admonition both to myself as well as to you: As a noted woman advocate, Portia in *The Merchant of Venice*, put it:
> "If to do were as easy to know what were good to do, chapels had been churches and poor men's cottages princes' palaces."

It is certainly easier to discuss methods of presenting witnesses effectively than to present witnesses quietly, smoothly, clearly, pervasively and elegantly, but the difficulty does not excuse the effort.

489

Counseling the Client: Refreshing Recollection or Prompting Perjury?

by Monroe H. Freedman

Experienced litigating attorneys are well aware of the vital importance of eliciting all relevant facts from the client and helping the client—who, typically, is not skilled at articulation—to marshall and to express his or her case as persuasively as possible. The poorly educated day laborer who has suffered an injury, and who can only say, "It hurts bad," must be helped to articulate what the pain is like, when it is present, and how it interferes with work, sleep, family life, and recreation. Also, the statement, "I hurt myself while I was working," will not be enough. The relevant details must be elicited through skilled questioning, and the witness must then be sufficiently rehearsed to assure that no important evidence will be overlooked in testimony at trial, where leading questions will not be permitted.

Numerous books and articles have been written and innumerable lectures have been given about effective interviewing and preparation techniques. What has not been adequately considered, however, is the extent to which proper preparation crosses the line of ethical conduct and becomes a violation of Disciplinary Rule 7-102(A), which, among other things, forbids a lawyer to participate in the creation of false evidence. In short, when is a lawyer refreshing recollection, and when is he or she prompting perjury?

The "best legal thought" regarding proper interview and preparation techniques has been set forth in *Selected Writings on the Law of Evidence and Trial* (W. Fryer ed. 1957), which was compiled under the sponsorship of the Association of American Law Schools by a committee of the nation's leading authorities on the law of evidence. In one of the se-

The author is Professor of Law and former Dean of Hofstra Law School, and Counsel to Orenstein, Snitow & Sutak in New York City.

lected articles, Harry S. Bodin notes that it is generally advisable to let the client tell his or her own story while the lawyer just listens. If the attorney insists upon getting only answers to specific questions, important points may be screened out because a lawyer cannot possibly anticipate all the facts in every case. Having gotten the client's story in narrative fashion, the lawyer must then seek additional facts that may have been omitted. That is done by asking questions and by explaining to the client how important the additional information may be to the case. "If the client can be made to understand your thoughts," Mr. Bodin writes, "he may tell you facts which otherwise would have been inadvertently overlooked or consciously and erroneously discarded by him as immaterial."

Subconscious Suppression

At the same time it is recognized that the client's story will be affected by a "subconscious suppression, psychologically induced by the wish to put one's best foot forward or by nature's trick of inducing forgetfulness of what one does not like to remember." That is, people will, in perfectly good faith, relate past events in a way that they believe (rightly or wrongly) to be consistent with their own interests. Necessarily, therefore, in pressing the client for additional information, and in explaining the relevance and importance of that information, the lawyer will be affecting the ultimate testimony. As emphasized by Professor Edward W. Cleary in another of the selected articles, although it is improper to prompt or suggest an answer to one's witness during the actual testimony, the interview "affords full play to suggestion . . . and evokes in advance of trial a complete verbalization, the importance of which cannot be overlooked."

The process of preparing or coaching the witness, of course, goes far beyond the initial eliciting of facts. In the course of polishing the client's testimony, eminent author Lloyd Paul Stryker recommends as many as fifty full rehearsals of direct and cross-examination. During those rehearsals, the testimony is developed in a variety of ways. The witness is vigorously cross-examined, and then the attorney points out where the witness has been "tripped" and how the testimony can be restructured to avoid that result. The attorney may also take the role of witness and be cross-examined by an associate. The attorney's "failures" in simulated testimony are then discussed, and the attorney then may conduct a mock cross-examination of the associate. In that way, "new ideas are developed while all the time the client is looking on and listening. He probably is saying, 'Let me try again.' And you will then go through the whole process once more." By that time, as one might expect, the client "does far better." In fact, after many weeks of preparation, "perhaps on the very eve of trial," the client may come up with a new fact that "may perhaps make a difference between victory and defeat."

491

Nowhere in those three selections relating to preparation of witnesses is there any analysis of the ethical implications of the model practices that are set forth. Mr. Stryker does say that, in repeatedly going over the "hard spots" and the "awkward places" and in showing the client how to "surmount his difficulties," the witness is "still staying well within the truth, the whole truth, and nothing but the truth." Saying that, however, does not make it so. If people do respond to suggestion, and if the lawyer helps the client to "fill in the gaps" and to avoid being "tripped," by developing "new ideas" in the course of repeated rehearsals, it is reasonably clear that the testimony that ultimately is presented in court will have been significantly affected by the lawyer's prompting and by the client's self-interest. Whether the end product is "well within the truth, the whole truth and nothing but the truth" is therefore subject to considerable doubt.

In fact, one finds in the three selections an astonishing disregard of the ethical implications of the preparation of testimony. It is difficult to believe that one with Stryker's experience and sophistication is unaware of the impact of suggestion, which is recognized in the article by Cleary. Similarly, Cleary concerns himself only with the problem of how rules of evidence—but not the rules of legal ethics—might be reformed to take into account the psychological realities that he discusses. Bodin also recognizes the "psychologically induced" inclination to remember or forget in a way consistent with one's own interests. However, he ignores the implications of that fact when he discusses how important it is for the lawyer to make the client aware of the importance and significance of information that may have been left out of the client's original narrative.

In addition, the Bodin article (unlike Cleary's) reflects the general ignorance within the legal profession of psychological learning regarding memory. For example, Bodin says, "Experienced trial lawyers have learned that even an honest and rational client, who will not *invent* 'facts,' may nevertheless *suppress* facts." Experiments by psychologists, however, indicate that those experienced trial lawyers (whoever they may be) are wrong: Invention is no less common than suppression. Bodin also states, "Of first importance in any action are the *facts*—the *exact* facts and *all* the facts." He then explains how the lawyer must seek to elicit "all the important facts" by probing the client's memory with "detailed questioning." What Bodin does not seem to realize is that the effort to obtain "*all* the facts" is virtually certain to result in obtaining something very different from "the *exact* facts."

One of the most common misconceptions about memory is that it is a process of recollection or reproduction of impressions, closely analogous to the functioning of a phonograph record or tape recorder. In that respect, legal thinking is centuries out of date, proceeding as if highly relevant experiments in behavioral psychology had never taken place. In fact, perceiving is itself active and constructive, and memory is much more a process of reconstruction than one of recollection or recall. More-over, the process is a highly creative one, affecting what is "remem-bered" as much as what is "forgotten."

Subjective Accuracy

Thus, contrary to Bodin's assertion, an honest and rational client will invent facts as readily as suppress them. Indeed, even before the pro-cess of remembering begins, what goes into the supposed "mental storehouse" is significantly influenced by the personality and previous experiences of the observer. As noted by F.C. Bartlett, who is probably the leading experimental psychologist concerned with memory, "tem-perament, interests, and attitudes often direct the course and determine the content of perceiving." Nor is any dishonesty involved in that pro-cess. "[One] may do this without being in the least aware that he is ei-ther supplementing or falsifying the data of perception. Yet, in almost all cases, he is certainly doing the first, and in many cases he is demon-strably doing the second." According to another expert, the "vast ma-jority" of testimonial errors are those of the "average, normal honest man," errors "unknown to the witness and wholly unintentional." Such testimony has been described as "*subjectively* accurate but *objec-tively* false."

An interesting illustration of the tendency to eliminate situational am-biguities in remembering was provided in the Senate Watergate hear-ings. John Dean was testifying regarding a meeting with Herbert Kalm-bach. Dean had no incentive whatsoever to lie about that particular incident. In fact, it was extremely important to him to state the facts with as much exactness as possible. He testified that he had met Kalmbach in the coffee shop of the Mayflower Hotel in Washington, D.C., and that they had gone directly upstairs to Kalmbach's room in the same hotel. Dean was pressed several times on that point, in a way that implied that his questioners had reason to believe that he was lying as to whether the meeting had taken place at all. Each time, Dean confidently reaffirmed his clear recollection about the incident. Finally, it was revealed that the register of the Mayflower Hotel indicated that Kalmbach had not been staying at the hotel at the time in question. Dean nevertheless remained certain of the occurrence, putting forth the unlikely theory that Kalm-bach had been using an alias. The difficulty was cleared up when some-one realized that there is a Mayflower Doughnut Coffee Shop in the Statler Hilton Hotel in Washington—and Kalmbach was found to have been registered there, under his own name, on the day in question. Thus, Dean's basic story was confirmed. Without realizing it, however, Dean had inaccurately resolved the ambiguity created by the coinci-dence of the two names by confidently "remembering" the wrong ho-tel, and by inventing the use of an alias by Kalmbach, despite the fact that he had had every incentive to report those details correctly and had

493

come close to being seriously discredited because of his unconscious error.

Questioning is, of course, an essential part of interviewing and preparing a witness for trial. It is particularly noteworthy, therefore, that questions, even "straightforward questions of fact," may play a very strong part in inducing "importation of detail" into the process of remembering, and that leading questions, when purposefully used to induce error, succeed in doing so to a startling degree. A recent study by Elizabeth Loftus showed that witnesses' estimates of the speed of an automobile involved in an accident will vary with the verb used by the questioner in describing the impact: "smashed" (40.8 mph), "collided" (39.3 mph), "bumped" (38.1 mph), "hit" (34.0 mph), and "contacted" (31.8 mph). In addition, twice as many witnesses reported seeing non-existent broken glass on the ground when the questioner used the word "smashed" instead of "hit." Dr. Loftus concluded that "memory itself undergoes a change" as a result of the type of question asked.

Moreover, memory in general, and responses to questions in particular, will be affected by "preferential psychological reactions." As Bartlett notes, there is a natural and honest tendency to remember-reconstruct in ways that are "strongly determined by an active subjective bias of the nature of interest."

To sum up, the process of remembering is not one dependent upon "memory traces," which can be played back as if by placing a stylus into the groove of a phonograph record. Rather, the process is one of active, creative reconstruction which begins at the moment of perception. The reconstructive process is significantly affected by the form of the questions asked and by what we understand to be in our own interest—even though, on a conscious level, we are responding as honestly as we possibly can.

Those conclusions might seem to suggest that the conscientious lawyer should avoid giving a client or other witness an understanding of what is relevant and important and should rely only upon narrative statements unassisted by questions that seek to elicit critical facts. However, anyone who has conducted interviews will immediately recognize that such a procedure would be highly impractical. An untrained and perhaps inarticulate person cannot be expected to relate all that is relevant without a substantial amount of direction. That is why one of the most important functions of the lawyer is to provide an awareness of what is legally relevant. Moreover, the same psychological authorities support the necessity of prompting to maximize recall. What prompting can do is to trigger recognition, which is a less complex process than remembering. Bartlett notes, for example, that in any experimental series, "only a relatively small portion of the material that can be recognized can, as a rule, be recalled." Another authority observes similarly that narrative is "the most accurate" but "the least complete" of all forms of recall. That is, if we rely only upon unprompted narrative, many important facts will be omitted, facts which can be accurately reported if memory is prompted by recognition, such as through leading questions.

Dilemma

Obviously, therefore, we are faced with another dilemma. On the one hand, we know that by telling the client that a particular fact is important, and why it is important, we may induce the client to "remember" the fact even if it did not occur. On the other hand, important facts can truly be lost if we fail to provide the client with every possible aid to memory. Furthermore, since the client's memory will inevitably be affected by reconstruction consistent with self-interest, a client who has a misunderstanding of his or her own legal interest could be psychologically inclined to remember in a way that is not only inconsistent with the client's case, but also inaccurate.

The Code of Professional Responsibility is ambiguous on the general question of whether the attorney may give advice that might induce perjury. The applicable Disciplinary Rule provides only that the lawyer should not "participate in the creation" of evidence when the lawyer knows or it is obvious that the evidence is false. The relevant Ethical Considerations are of only limited assistance, in part because they are intended to be only "aspirational," and do not have the binding force of disciplinary rules. Ethical Consideration 7-5 provides that a lawyer should not "knowingly assist the client to engage in illegal conduct," and that a lawyer should never "encourage or aid" the client to commit criminal acts or "counsel his client on how to violate the law and avoid punishment therefor." However, the footnote to the Code at that point suggests the extreme situation in which the lawyer is representing "a syndicate notoriously engaged in the violation of the law for the purpose of advising the members how to break the law and at the same time escape it." Ethical Consideration 7-6 says that the lawyer may properly assist the client in "developing and preserving evidence of existing motive, intent, or desire," but adds that, "obviously," he may not do "anything" furthering the creation or preservation of false evidence. That last proscription is extremely broad. The same Ethical Consideration also notes, however, that in many cases a lawyer may not be "certain" as to the client's state of mind, and holds that in those situations the lawyer "should resolve reasonable doubts in favor of the client."

Close Case

A situation that I consider to be close to the ethical line is the following. Assume that Jurisdictions X and Y are adjacent to each other and that many lawyers practice in both jurisdictions. In Jurisdiction X, there are a large number of workmen's compensation cases in which workers strain themselves while lifting, and recover compensation. In Jurisdic-

495

tion Y there is an equivalent number of such cases, but in all of them the workers who strain themselves while lifting also slip or trip on something in the process. That coincidence is fortunate, because in Jurisdiction X it is sufficient for compensation simply that the strain be work-related, while in Jurisdiction Y the applicable law requires that the injury be received in the course of an "accident," such as a slip or a trip. Obviously, the same lawyers whose clients are not slipping or tripping in Jurisdiction X are prompting their clients to recall a slip or trip when the injury is received in Jurisdiction Y.

In those cases, there are no issues of intent or of judgment, but only of objective fact. Nevertheless, even if the client's initial narrative of the incident should omit any reference to slipping or tripping, I believe that the lawyer's obligation is to explain to the client in Jurisdiction Y that one of the legal requirements for recovery is an accident, such as a trip or slip. As we have seen in the earlier discussions of experiments by behavioral psychologists, a factual detail of that sort might very well be omitted in a narrative of the incident. Moreover, the narrator's understanding (whether accurate or inaccurate) of his or her own self-interest will affect the remembering-reconstruction of the incident entirely apart from any conscious dishonesty. Thus, the client who incorrectly assumes that tripping or slipping might preclude recovery (perhaps because it might imply carelessness) might unconsciously screen out that fact. Despite the risk, therefore, that a dishonest client might consciously invent a trip or slip to meet the needs of the occasion, the attorney is obligated to prod the client's remembering-reconstruction by explaining the relevance and importance of that factual element.

To sum up, the attorney who is interviewing and preparing a witness must take into account the psychological realities of the situation. That means, at least at the earlier stages of eliciting the witness's story, that the attorney should assume a skeptical attitude, and that the attorney should give the client legal advice that might help in drawing out useful information that the client, consciously or unconsciously, might be withholding. At the same time, there will inevitably come a point at which the lawyer knows, to a moral certainty, that the client's ability to reconstruct in good faith has been fully tapped. It is at that point, I believe, that the attorney who continues to seek the desired testimony crosses the ethical line and enters upon active participation in the creation of perjury.

496

The Witness Needs Help

by Stuart A. Summit

The important witness has the most difficult role in litigation. The subjective pressures on any witness—whether a party or not—make testifying a frightening prospect. Few lawyers perceive the difficulty of the witness's job, and that may explain why lawyers are supposedly among the worst witnesses.

The least we can do is help the poor fellow. By ''help'' I do not mean the casual run-through that suffices for many. A witness is entitled to substantial assistance not only on the subject-matter of his testimony, but also on the special problems of being a witness.

The important witness in civil litigation will be examined twice—at the oral deposition and at trial—and his role in each phase is different. The preparation should be different, too. One startling fact is true in both phases: being a witness is a highly artificial business for which there is no adequate background or experience. Preparation of an important witness must start from scratch, whoever the witness and whatever the case.

Testifying at an oral deposition is the most artificial process of all. The witness will think he is participating in an essentially oral event—he will be questioned and must answer. That impression is dangerous. A deposition is a process by which a document is prepared, and nothing else. *All that matters is the transcript.* Somehow you must convince the witness that his job is to dictate a very important document.

Think of it! A lawyer or business executive faced with having to prepare an important writing will consider what he wants to say and will draft and edit until he is satisfied. He may seek the opinion of others before he permits the document to be made final. In the real world we treat documents of potential importance with respect.

The author is a member of the New York City firm of Summit, Rovins & Feldesman.

But the witness at the deposition is given no such opportunity. No matter how much he prepares before he enters the deposition room, he cannot know what questions will be asked, and he cannot prepare answers in advance. His opportunity to change answers is limited. He must account for changes. It will not be enough for him to say, as we sometimes do of an early draft of a legal document, that its only deficiency is that it can be improved. The witness will not be permitted, without peril, to improve his answers.

There are a number of ways to help keep the witness aware throughout the deposition that he is dictating an important document. The most important principle is that the witness should take his time. No less than five seconds should elapse between the last word of the question and the first word of the answer. The witness should be drilled to know what five seconds are, and to stay perfectly quiet for at least that long. (Five seconds is a very long time indeed when everyone in the room is staring expectantly.) The witness must be taught that this long pause before answering is *invariable*—once he has given his name and address, that must be his pattern. If he answers some questions quickly, he will be unable to sustain the pattern, and may warn the examiner of areas of concern.

During the long pause between question and answer, the witness should make sure he understands the question, say so if he does not, and compose his answer. He should not begin to talk until he knows the last word he is going to say. If the question is so open-ended that the answer cannot be composed wholly in advance, at least he should make notes of the thoughts to be included in the answer.

Talk to Stenographer

The witness should face the examiner until he is ready to answer the question, then turn and speak to the stenographer. Facing the stenographer will remind him he is dictating. The witness should talk in sentences. He should be as concise as the question permits. That does not mean stretching to give a yes or no answer, but using as few words as completeness permits.

The witness should be taught that it is the examiner's job to ask a question so that it can be intelligently answered. It is the lawyer's role to argue with the examiner if argument is necessary, but never the witness's. Unless instructed by you to the contrary, he is to answer as best he can all questions he understands. He should ask that a question be repeated or rephrased until he understands it. He does not ask the examiner any questions, he does not state gratuitously the cause of his need for rephrasing; in sum, he does not assist the examiner. The deposition is the adversary's inning, and it is no part of the witness's burden to make points. He is to answer questions, and nothing more. His general attitude should be that of the bystander, who has no interest in the outcome.

From the outset, the witness should be informed, precisely and repetitively, of the differences between knowledge, hearsay, and surmise. He must never answer a question by suggesting he knows something he does not. The jingle that begins "I don't know, but I've been told" makes the distinction neatly. The witness only testifies to what he has been told if he is asked what he has been told—otherwise, he does not know something he has merely been told.

Witnesses make mistakes. Point out how normal that is, so he will not become flustered or worse. He should correct errors as quickly as he realizes them—interrupting if necessary. If it is a matter of importance and he has any doubt, he should confer with you first. Many witnesses attempt to defend error, but it cannot successfully be done. "Don't try—correct the error quickly, and don't build a story around it." On the other hand, he should be suspicious of recollections newly found while testifying, and you should test these before they become a matter of record.

Before your first briefing meeting, you should have reviewed all that you know about the witness's role in the events in suit. Separate the documents he wrote from the documents he saw and the ones he neither wrote nor saw. It is important to remind the witness of what he did not know during the events in suit, because he may have learned much after the fact.

Relaxed First Session

The first briefing session should be relaxed, and neither lawyer nor witness should be subject to time pressures or interruptions. At this early stage you must get to know the witness as a person, to understand his perspective on the events in suit, and to start identifying the areas where he needs the most help. It is best to start by giving your over-all picture of the case, generally including his involvement. Then ask him to tell of his involvement in his own words, without reference to documents or notes. In particular, ask him to comment on your description of his role. This is no time for close questioning; let him tell his story as he sees it.

Be particularly alert as the witness tells his story for the first time. The nuances in his first narration can be considerable. Facts glossed over, omitted or unduly emphasized are clues to possibly troublesome areas.

Unless the witness is your individual client, do not be certain he views you as an ally. An employee of a large concern, for example, may well view the company's lawyer as a source of potential danger. It is critical that you find common ground and that he comes to trust and rely on you. (A sensitive task, but it must be done.)

Should the witness's spontaneous recital of his role contain any surprises, attempt to clarify, but be gentle. Assuming you have received no major surprises, you have probably accomplished as much as you

499

should at the first briefing conference. At this point, assign homework and schedule a second meeting. As a minimum, give him a package containing copies of all the original documents with which he should be familiar, and a brief chronological recital of the major events surrounding the case. If there are interrogatory answers or transcripts of prior witnesses bearing on his anticipated testimony, he usually should have these also.

The hard work begins at the second briefing conference. Ask the witness whether he sees any problem with the role you expect him to play in the litigation, and see if his homework has produced any questions. Before going further, re-establish or redefine the common ground; the witness will resent a failure to do so. He must be satisfied that he can properly and truthfully do what is expected of him. In the course of re-establishing or redefining the witness's role, carefully identify his areas of knowledge and those where he lacks knowledge. Then, remind him of your instructions about how to answer questions and take him through a casual examination covering his entire knowledge. By a casual examination, I mean one that may be interrupted for questions and comments. Give him a running critique on his answers, and he may seek advice too.

After the subject-matter is covered through casual questioning, you should take the witness through a serious examination under laboratory conditions. This should not take place in particularly comfortable surroundings, beverages should not be served, there should be no interruptions, and the conditions under which the deposition will be held should be duplicated. Another lawyer should be present, if possible, to get a cold evaluation. During a serious examination there are no comments or questions from either the lawyer or the witness; these are saved.

Do not spare the witness at this point. Let him see, through your questioning, where a gratuitous comment can lead. If he says he cannot answer without a document, produce the document. Show him the dangers of evasion. Use your knowledge of the whole case to try to have him claim knowledge he does not have. Try to make him look foolish for every ''I don't know.'' If he claims not to understand a question, ask him what he does not understand. Do all the things you know how to do to make a witness err.

When you are done, you may need to re-establish that you really are on the witness's side. Do not overlook this. No matter how poorly he performs, reassure him, pointing out that the object of preparation is to avoid the problems that were just illustrated. If he performs well, however, do not permit complacency.

Whether to conduct any further questioning at this time should turn on whether the witness seems ready for more. If he seems anxious to show he can do better, go ahead. In either event, at the end of this meeting, schedule the next. Three full practice examinations are the minimum for a witness who has an important role, and make sure you leave enough time for at least that amount. The last practice examination should be scheduled just before the deposition, and intermediate examinations should be scheduled a few days apart. The object of leaving intervening days between practice examinations is to test the witness's memory. Unless he seems hopeless, ask him to do no homework for his last practice examination, so you may see how he will do on that basis.

Use Another Lawyer

If another lawyer familiar with the case is available, you may wish to have him take the witness through the second serious examination, so that the witness does not get so used to you that you can no longer test him. This will give you the opportunity to watch and evaluate.

In the course of observing the witness under laboratory conditions, you must make decisions about the conduct of the deposition. You may detect that the witness cannot keep details in his mind that he should be able to testify about. "I don't know" at the deposition may limit the witness's usefulness at the trial. In that event, you will want the witness to have in front of him at the deposition whatever is necessary to assist his memory. He may have notes or a document collection to refresh his recollection. Because the examiner will be able to see them, the witness should not use privileged documents or notes that contain work product. Conversely, a witness who has a good recollection without notes or documents is probably better off without them. If he needs anything, your files at the deposition should be organized so that you can quickly supply it.

A deposition witness prepared enough times by these methods should be able to handle the unique and difficult role assigned to him without the need for you to intervene at the deposition. That is the ideal.

Often a deposition witness will resist making available the time necessary for proper preparation. Lawyers, doctors, senior executives and public officials particularly make this mistake. The prospect of a trial is awesome enough to frighten a witness into acquiescence, but a deposition in a lawyer's office may not impress him. This is simply untenable and, somehow you must communicate the seriousness of the risk. This is no time to be deferential—you will not be thanked for it when things go awry.

It is best if there is a long period between deposition and trial, since the witness's role will be quite different, and he must shake some of the habits you instilled for the deposition.

The witness's role at trial bears little relationship to that at the deposition. The trial is almost exclusively an oral event. While the trial transcript may become important, this will be purely as a record of what took place, in contrast with the deposition transcript, the making of which is

501

all that took place. Thus, many things that were unimportant at the deposition become of great importance for the trial.

Critical Chore

Your first critical chore is to visualize the witness on the stand. What will he be like? You should (or must come to) know him and his patterns of speech and thought well enough to make that judgment. Think through his strengths and weaknesses. Is he brash? Ponderous? Does he think slowly and talk quickly, or think quickly and talk slowly (the ideal)? Does he have nervous mannerisms? Does he tend to use large words, or too many?

Videotaping should be excellent for this purpose. A lot could be learned from watching a videotape of the witness being questioned at length.

One of the greatest dangers is that the witness will react differently on the witness stand than in the deposition room or your office. If he is not a seasoned witness, take him to an empty courtroom and have him sit on the witness stand. Point out how things will look at the actual trial. Take him to a trial in progress. (If it is permitted, he should watch prior witnesses testify at the trial itself.)

To prepare him for the substance of answering questions, you should start all over again even if he was extensively prepared for a deposition. Be sure that you do not make the witness's role any harder than it has to be. Before you start to prepare him for trial decide precisely what areas he needs to cover on direct examination and what areas he must know for cross-examination. You will have the deposition transcripts, and while you may give him summaries, he should read the transcripts of his own deposition, word for word. As to the deposition transcripts of other witnesses, do not expose him to information he cannot testify about. He should see, however, what other witnesses have said about areas of overlapping knowledge. He should again be given a collection of the documents and interrogatory answers that relate to him.

By now you should have identified every problem area for the witness. Areas where he and other witnesses disagree should be discussed at length. While somewhat different recollections may not undercut an entire case, the witness should not be in the position of disagreeing with others without knowing it and being certain about his own recollection. This is true whether the witnesses with whom he may disagree are friendly or unfriendly.

The witness must be prepared for both direct and cross-examination, and the emphasis should be balanced between the two. It is a frequent spectacle to see a witness tell much about the events covered on direct examination, and grow vague on cross. He appears to be purposely withholding information from the cross-examiner. This is often unfair; the fault may be the lawyer's failure to be sure the witness is as prepared for cross-examination as for direct. Conversely, some lawyers enjoy practicing their cross-examination techniques to the point that their witness is ready for anything a hostile questioner may ask but cannot tell a straightforward story.

For direct examination, I find it helpful to prepare a short narrative statement of everything I need the witness to say, prepared as if he were writing a high school essay. While he must understand, of course, that he will not be given the chance to state his story so neatly from the witness stand, it still helps the witness to see it in this fashion.

I do not give a witness the precise questions that I will ask. He is made familiar during the practice examinations with the areas that will be covered in his direct examination, but no more. Scripts are to be avoided. A witness should not be permitted to become comfortable with a particular way of asking a question, and your examination will be of limited effectiveness if you have to read the questions. You must be free to extemporize. Cross-examination will not be conducted from a script, so the witness must be prepared on the whole subject-matter, no matter how the question is asked.

Witnesses have difficulty understanding the limitations of direct examination. It pays to educate them, so that they will appreciate the limitations under which you are operating in questioning them. Do not use leading questions when you are conducting a practice direct examination.

It may help to divide the practice examinations, direct and cross, between two or more lawyers. If others are available, ask them to prepare a cross-examination of the witness as if they were his adversary. Ask them to determine what areas they would concentrate on, and to do so. (It can be enlightening to ask the witness what he would ask if he were responsible for his own cross-examination. This is a good way of determining what is worrying him most.)

The object, obviously, is for your witness to be as plausible on the stand as he can be. You cannot rebuild a personality. Instead, you must take the personality and mannerisms that you find and work with them. If the witness is a fast talker, you may get him to slow down somewhat, but you cannot count on it. Instead, you must make certain he is so full of information and so aware of the nuances, that you can live with his speed. If he is ponderous, perhaps that mannerism can be converted to concern and thoughtfulness. That kind of maximization of the witness's own traits is the most that can be accomplished. A self-conscious witness is almost invariably a bad one.

For the trial even more than the deposition, the more practice the better. I know of no disadvantage to repeated rigorous examination, and you must stay with it until you are satisfied.

Depending on the importance of the case and the witness, there is almost no limit to the number of sessions or hours that can be constructively devoted to practice. At the beginning, concentrate on direct, and take your witness through the full direct, under laboratory conditions, with the critique following. The witness will be better able to cope with rigorous cross-examination after he is confident of his direct testimony. Then, after achieving a reasonable performance on cross-examination, alternate between direct and cross, with discussion saved for the conclusion of a full examination. Do not permit the practice examinations to become a ritual. You or the lawyers helping you prepare the witness must vary your routines and should exchange roles as well. These examinations must be rigorous or the witness will receive a false sense of security.

On the other hand, you do not dare destroy the witness's confidence just before he gets on the stand. It can be fatal to delay your initial final preparation to the last minute, so that the difficult side of cross-examination and critique must take place within a few days or hours of the actual testimony. If you start early enough, the more brutal aspects of the process can be covered, and the last few practice sessions can be utilized to give or restore to the witness a sense of confidence.

I prefer that the witness use no notes or documents in testifying unless a question specifically calls for it. However, this must depend on the witness. If he has a bad memory and no amount of practice and homework can cure it, you are much better off if he does take notes or files to the witness stand. Some witnesses will never be comfortable without such props.

If the adversary examining the witness at the deposition will be the same as at the trial, it is easier for the witness. If they will be different, you should familiarize the witness with the examiner's methods. If the witness will not be able to watch the adversary examiner during the trial, try to arrange for him to do so in advance. If that is not possible, then you should describe to the witness in as much detail as possible the nature of the examiner and his methods.

Be sure to warn the witness that he may be under scrutiny the whole time he is in the courthouse. The judge or jury may observe him in the corridors or sitting in the back row. It is old-fashioned to dwell on clothes and grooming, but I believe a witness is entitled to know that unusual clothes look much more unusual from the witness stand. While the witness must be comfortable, the judge and jury must find him plausible, and if his clothes or manner are, to their perception, grossly inconsistent with the role he verbally portrays, plausibility is undermined.

I have not dealt with the difficult ethical questions that can arise in preparing a witness for deposition and trial. In his article, *Counseling the Client: Refreshing Recollection or Prompting Perjury?*, Dean Monroe Freedman notes the difficulty of being certain that the witness understands the impact of what he says, while avoiding the encouragement of false recollection, or worse. See page 490, *infra*. A good trial lawyer knows what rings true, at least by the time of trial, and the ethical lawyer (the practical one, too) will naturally (and gently, assuming good faith) guide his client toward the avoidance of incorrect recollection and characterization. There are many situations, however, where the lawyer's instinct will be of no help, and the dilemma posed by Dean Freedman remains such.

The elaborate suggestions I have made may smack of theatrical staging. If so, it is not the methods suggested for preparing the witness that are the cause, but the discovery and trial processes themselves. It is not the function of this article to ponder whether adequate preparation of a witness, and other such lawyer's techniques, assist or deter the search for truth. Again others have done so (for example, see *The Search for Truth—An Umpireal View*, by District Judge Marvin E. Frankel, 30 Record N.Y.C.B.A. 14 (1975)). The oral deposition and trial are artificial events, and it is not a public service to rebel against that fact at the expense of a particular witness or client. The witness deserves, and desperately needs, the exercise of the lawyer's highest skills.

Direct Examination

by J. Patrick Hazel

It is a very busy day in your office. A lawyer from Argentina has brought you a big case that will have to be tried in this country. Fortunately, the lawyer speaks English. Because his system is inquisitorial rather than adversarial, he has only heard of jury trials. He would like to see one. You ask your paralegal to take him to the courthouse and slip him into a courtroom where a jury trial is proceeding.

Later that day the two of you are having drinks together. The lawyer remarks, ''At one point the judge went to sleep. What part of the trial was that?'' You answer that it could be almost any part. ''But,'' he says, ''at one time everyone went to sleep!'' Ah, you know what that was: DIRECT EXAMINATION.

Many direct examinations are boring and some have other equally undesirable characteristics. Far too many are just plain bad. Often the witness is unbelievable. At other times the examination is incomplete. Oh, it is plenty long, but it leaves out elements critical to proving the case—elements that this or another witness could provide.

You do not have to have any of these problems in your direct examinations. Yours can be different. Maybe not exciting, but at least interesting enough to hold the jury's attention. If the jury does not believe your witnesses, all is lost. If you do not present evidence during your direct examination on every element of proof, you are subject to a directed verdict either on the entire case or on some important aspect of it.

These problems evoke some principles. The first, although not the most exciting rule of direct examination, is that direct must cover all the

The author is the Director, Tiny Gooch Centennial Professorship in Trial Practice, and of counsel to the law firm of Spivey, Grigg, Kelly and Knisely, Austin, Texas.

elements of proof for your case. Second, the testimony *must* be believable. Third, the jury has to listen to it.

Effective direct examination (like every other part of a successful trial) begins long before you go into the courtroom. Some lawyers do not want to hear that you need to know the law to be a good trial lawyer. Most agree on the importance of knowing the rules of evidence and, maybe, even procedure. But substantive law? Too many cases—good cases—have been lost because the lawyer did not know the substantive law. The lawyer did not know what needed to be proved in order to win at trial and maintain the victory on appeal.

A simple and effective way to be certain you know the substantive law in your case is to prepare a court's charge. Whether your jurisdiction uses a general verdict or a special verdict, that charge will have all the substantive law essential for the case. Prepare the charge early and use it throughout your preparation and during the trial. Let it be your bible, your road map, or whatever other solemn designation you give it while you marshal evidence, work on voir dire, draft opening statement and closing argument, and plan direct and cross-examination. You can avoid running down a lot of endless rabbit trails in search of the inconsequential and you will know that you are doing what needs to be done. Break the charge down into the elements of proof. Every piece of evidence and testimony in the trial ought to be related to these elements in some way to establish them, to make them believable, and to enhance interest in them.

The beginning of self-preparation is planning your case. The target is your entire case, not just direct examination. Most lawyers try early on to develop a theory or theme for their case. While it may change a dozen times, a theme helps you focus on the highlights and helps the jury evaluate the evidence, put it in perspective, and remember it. There is, however, a danger to developing a theme. It cannot be all inclusive for if it is, it is too broad. It necessarily leaves out many of the elements of your case, elements you must remember. Preparing a court's charge will help you focus on these other elements.

Once you know what you need to prove, you must find out what evidence is available to do so. Although discovery is important, preparation begins with thorough investigation. The lawyer who neglects investigation and tries to substitute discovery in its stead begs for trouble. Investigation remains critical even after you assemble the available evidence. Some elements of your case will be weaker than others. Then you need to decide how to fill those gaps. Eyewitnesses or witnesses with personal knowledge of the facts and documents directly on point frequently cannot establish every element satisfactorily. Then you need to consider circumstantial evidence and experts. Investigation provides the answers. Investigation (and, later, discovery) also must consider the other side's case and its available evidence. This, too, is important for

507

your direct examination and not solely for cross-examination.

In presenting evidence during direct examination, you often have little or no choice of potential witnesses; you must use the ones who know the facts. The axiom that ''a good client can make the case and a bad one break it'' equally holds true for other witnesses. As part of your preparation you must determine what important facts, yours and theirs, can be shown by what witnesses. You are fortunate when several witnesses can testify to the same facts. Then you can evaluate the potential witnesses' impact on the jury before choosing among them. Those who will testify also require decisions to be discussed later: preparation, placement, and timing. But you must make other determinations based on your evaluation. Will the witness be available? If not, a deposition, perhaps videotaped, may be necessary. Similar decisions are required of those who will be available. If the witness will not make a good live witness, you should consider a deposition presentation. Will the witness appear voluntarily and, if not, how do you handle a subpoena without making the witness hostile?

You need a description of each witness that includes your evaluation. You should list the essential elements of your case about which each witness can testify. What is there about each witness personally that will add to or detract from general credibility? What further facts will be available from each witness that will enhance believing the essential facts?

The considerations are myriad. The point is that you need to make those decisions about each witness. I suggest doing it systematically and in writing.

Using exhibits also will influence your choice of witnesses. Exhibits range from the essential—the dope in a narcotics prosecution, to the illustrative—a model of a spine in a sore back case. This is not the place to discuss the value and importance of exhibits: If you do not already know that, you had better learn it. But you must decide what exhibits will prove or help prove each element of your case and then you must choose what witness to use for introducing each exhibit. It is not enough just to get the exhibit into evidence. You must plan how you will use the exhibit, including what witnesses will testify about it.

Before trial, anticipate problems with evidence and witnesses. Your time will not be wasted, for preparation can avoid many problems and overcome others. For example, suppose you represent the plaintiff in a motorcycle-car accident. Your client claims to have been stopped behind a car on his motorcycle when the defendant rear-ended him. The defendant claims your client was not stopped, but darted in front of him from a side road. The driver of the car behind which your client was stopped says she saw him stopped some four or five feet behind her with his left foot on the ground. She saw this out of her rearview mirror. Problem: Could she see a foot on the ground out of a rearview mirror when your client was that close? If not, the driver must be mistaken about the distance, and that mistake needs correcting. But, if she insists on the distance, perhaps the *side* mirror is the one she means. This problem needs to be handled in advance.

Exhibits, too, can be problematic. Even one that generally meets the business records exception may still have items in it that help or hurt. Those that help may be subject to another objection. You must plan how to overcome it. Those that hurt may yet be excludable. That, too, must be determined. There are enough unforeseen problems and objections that will arise during trial. Those that can be anticipated need pretrial preparation.

Like everything else in life, direct examination has a beginning, a middle, and an end. With direct examination, each must be prepared.

Most lawyers start by accrediting the witness. This means introducing the witness to the jury, humanizing him or her, and easing the witness's tension. It is more important than most of us think. Jurors tend to be very attentive when a witness first takes the stand. How you accredit your witness can keep the jury awake and interested or drive it into a coma.

"Please state your name for the record" is the invariable opening of direct examination on television. Unfortunately, the phrase is heard in real courtrooms, too. It is not the record that will decide your case; it is the jury! "Tell us your name" would be better. With clients and critical witnesses, "Introduce yourself to the jury" is a good way to start.

Witnesses are not machines under oath; they are people. Let the jury know that. Let them feel it. There is something unique and fascinating about each person. But you cannot communicate those qualities to the jury unless you have already discovered it—another part of your preparation.

Unless the witness is a professional testifier, terror is likely the witness's dominant emotion. Ask a few questions to ease that feeling. Ask things that cannot be challenged by the opposing lawyer and the jury. "Where do you live?" "Where do you work?" "Are you married?" "Do you have any children?" "Where do your children go to school?" are a few such questions. Even if the witness goofs in answering these questions, no one else will know.

But beware of getting too detailed. I recall a father who, after being asked if he had any children, was asked to give their ages and dates of birth. The terror did not subside, it increased! Who will believe a witness who cannot remember the ages of his own children?

Beware, too, of spending too much time on this accreditation. You do not want to lose the jurors to their own daydreams or to sleep.

A juror's attention can be maintained only as long as the rear end can endure. This rule of thumb ought to guide you. Keep your direct examination short and get to the important matters early. While reading this article, you may get tired and decide to stop and pick it up later. Jurors cannot stop trials. They hear each witness once and that is it. If you bury the important elements in a mass of testimony, they will be missed easily.

To keep the important elements at the front, you need a well-thought-out approach. I recommend a determined combination of the chronological and topical. You want to re-create something for the jury that can be recalled easily. Since you cannot re-create it as it actually happened, try to do it the way people naturally recall events. Usually one or two happenings dominate and are recalled first, before we put the event together chronologically. The chronology puts the dominant happenings in a context for us to evaluate. I believe we get confused when we try to combine too many events at once. For organizing a direct examination, the events are the topics, the dominant happenings are the critical elements of these topics, and the chronology is the context.

I submit, then, that the best direct examination will begin topically. Many witnesses are going to testify only about one topic or event. Others may testify about several. Approach each topic or event separately. Announce to the witness and the jury what the topic is. This is not so much a question as it is the foundation or predicate for the question. Once you are into the topic, bring out the dominant happenings; then go back to the chronological context.

For example, take the same motorcycle-car wreck mentioned earlier.

(Announcement of the Topic)

    Q: Mr. Jones, I would now like you to take us to August 30, 1985, at about 5:10 P.M. Would you do that for us?

    A: Yes.

(Dominant Happenings)

    Q: Would you briefly tell us what happened to you then?

    A: Yes, sir. I was hit from the rear by an automobile.

    Q: What were you doing just before you were hit?

    A: I was stopped on my motorcycle behind a car waiting to turn left.

    Q: How can you be sure you were stopped?

    A: Well, I had my left foot on the ground to balance my bike.

(Contextual or Chronological Portion)

    Q: Where had you been before this happened?

    A: I had been at work.

    Q: Where were you working?

    A: Travis State School.

    Q: What time did you get off?

    A: 5:00 P.M.

    Q: What did you do after you got off work that day?

    A: I went to the parking lot to get my motorcycle.

    Q: Where were you going?

    A: Home—my parents' home—to have dinner.

Q: What route did you take?

A: Well, the exit to the school comes into the south side of Webberville Road. I was going to turn right at the exit, go onto Webberville Road, and then turn left onto Decker Lane. Decker Lane takes me to my parents' house.

Q: Did you do that?

A: I never got to turn onto Decker Lane.

Q: Let's go step by step and tell us what you did do and what happened.

Now, go back to the parking lot, get him on his motorcycle, onto the exit road, and the like.

After completing one topic or event, move onto the next with an announcement. Some call the announcement a transitional statement. Whether you call it a dog or a canine, you still have to feed it and housebreak it.

Each element of a trial—be it direct, cross, or argument—needs a strong ending. Keep in mind that the end of direct examination is not the end of the witness's testimony. Cross-examination will follow, so try to end your direct on a point that is difficult to attack on cross-examination. For example, in the case mentioned before, you could end the direct examination of one of your witnesses this way:

Q: By the way, did you ever get near the defendant, Mr. Johnson?

A: Yes, I did.

Q: Did you notice anything unusual?

A: Yes.

Q: What was that?

A: I smelled alcohol on his breath.

Q: Pass the witness.

Note: When you "pass the witness" don't ever say, "I have no further questions"; you might be held to it!

Some cross-examiners will take the bait and plunge into this quagmire. Most will not. If your witness has even more to say about this, you should be able to develop it thoroughly on redirect. Even if it is outside the scope of the cross, most judges will allow it; but you need to have some advance idea of the judge's habits. You could get burned if the judge does not let you go back to the subject, or if there is no cross-examination.

Another strong ending is to throw the cross-examiner a bone he cannot afford to bite but cannot easily leave untouched. For example, in a case where your client is suing for fire insurance proceeds and the defendant claims your client burned his building, consider the following as an ending:

Q: Mr. Smith, do you know the insurance company's defense?

A: Yes, they claim I burned my own building.

Q: Did you?

511

A: No, I did not.

Q: They claim you had a motive?

A: Yes.

Q: Do you know of anyone else who had a motive to burn your building?

A: Yes, I do.

Q: Pass the witness.

This should leave the jury with one big question: "Who?"

If you asked that question, you would draw an objection. Even if it is not sustained, the objection alone would detract from your ending. But if you leave the jury with that question, only the most foolish cross-examiner would ask, "Who?" Most likely the examiner will have to hesitate before beginning cross. The silence can be thunderous. The cross-examiner who goes to a new topic—not you—will be blamed for not getting them the answer to the question. You, however, can return to the question on redirect and either satisfy the jurors' longing or draw an objection that now should add to your case.

Even neophytes realize they must prepare for direct examination. But what about redirect; don't you wait until the cross has been completed to prepare? How can you decide what to ask before that?

The answer is easy when you consider what was said earlier: You need to end strongly. Redirect is the end of direct, so it must be strong. If all your time during redirect is spent patching up after cross, you conclude with the witness on the defensive. That is weak at best, so you must prepare for redirect examination.

First, there are certain things from your direct you want to reemphasize. You can plan these easily. Yes, they are cumulative, but if they are important to your case, it is likely they will be attacked on cross and are fair game for redirect. If not, it takes an objection to stop you and the judge may overrule it. But be certain you do not broadcast what you are doing with phrases such as "Once again," "Tell us again," "Repeat for us," and the like. Not only will these invite an objection, they will assure its being sustained.

Second, and closely related to reemphasizing, you should be able to anticipate some of the cross-examination. By doing this you help yourself prepare for redirect.

It may be clever to save a particularly strong point for redirect by not bringing it out on direct. But, it is dangerous! If after your direct the opposing lawyer says, "No questions," you are sunk. Also, an objection is very likely to come and be sustained to new matter on redirect.

Frequently, there is a letdown by your opponent after cross. Some lawyers are so happy to survive cross-examination that lethargy sets in. So you may be able to lead the witness on redirect. This is especially important for the "patchup" work. You need to let the witness know the problem. For example, on direct the witness says the light was green; on cross he says it was red. If you simply ask on redirect, "What color was the light?" you may well get the wrong answer. But instead you can ask, "In response to the plaintiff's lawyer you said the light was red. Is that correct or was it green?" With luck the witness will get the message. Remember, you know the witness made a mistake on cross but often the witness does not know it.

Finally, be prepared not to conduct a redirect. If your opponent's cross does no damage, stop! The recross may do the damage.

The main evidentiary rule regarding direct is no leading questions. The witness is to supply the answer, and the lawyer is not to suggest it. There is an even better tactical reason than the evidentiary one for non-leading questions. When the answer is supplied in the words and phrasing of the witness, credibility is enhanced. Merely agreeing or disagreeing with the lawyer does little for the believability of the witness.

Nonleading questions tend to be vague. At times witnesses have difficulty knowing what is being asked. For example, when a lawyer asks, "Where were you going?" the witness may answer, "To the parking lot," "To my motorcycle," or "To the exit." But the answer the lawyer wanted was "To my parents' home."

The best way to avoid this problem is to prepare the witness properly. At times, however, even preparation does not help. So, if the witness answered, "To the parking lot," you may find it necessary to lead a bit to get back on track.

Objections are seldom made to leading questions on background and preliminary matters. If made, they usually are overruled; but do not be lulled into thinking you can or should conduct your entire direct with leading questions. Not only is it a weak way to present your case, but you can become derailed by a sustained objection and never be able to establish the essential elements of your case. You and your witness must be prepared to carry out the entire direct without leading questions, because you may be required to do it that way.

It takes time, practice, and experience to become adept at fashioning good nonleading questions without reading them. Force yourself to do it from the very beginning.

Preparation for direct includes preparing the questions—partly to avoid leading. You need to write them out. There is nothing wrong—and much right—about writing out your questions. The wrong lies in doing the wrong thing with them.

Do not read them! If you do, the direct becomes stilted and causes you not to listen to the answers. You must listen. If you fail to get the answer you need, you cannot just go to the next question. You must ask another question until you get the answer you need.

But even before you write out any questions, you should write out the answers you want and need from this witness—at least the critical ones. Then, write the questions to elicit those answers. This reverse method

513

will aid you in communicating with the witness. You can measure the worth of the question by its ability to elicit the correct answer.

Make a list of topics to cover and answers that are needed. Use the list as your trial guide during direct. Check off topics when they are covered.

Your questions on direct examination should communicate with the witness and with the jury. There are certain "lawyer-like" words and phrases to avoid. Make your questions short and simple. Eschew words like "eschew." Do not ask if the witness has "had the occasion" to do thus and so. An honest answer might be "Yes, but I never did it!" Even if you think "prior" and "subsequent" are okay in legal documents, say "before" and "after" in front of jurors.

Examine a recent deposition to analyze your questions. You will be amazed at the amount of useless verbiage. "I see," "Uh-huh," "Okay," and "All right" will appear in abundance. You probably shadowed the answer many times. See how often you have said something like, "There is another thing I would like to ask you." Perhaps we fear silence, but more likely, these are just nervous habits. Still, the habits are distracting and should be avoided. Jurors may begin counting the number of "all rights" rather than listening to the answers, since your direct examination questions often mirror those in deposition.

At some point in your career you will be tempted to get someone else to prepare your witnesses. Resist the temptation. Preparing witnesses is not fun, but the time spent with the witness is valuable for you, and it sends the message that you think the witness is important. The success of your examination will be directly proportional to the amount of time you spend preparing the witness.

It is important to let the witness know the questions you will ask to elicit the critical responses. If you have written down the key answers you need from the witness and the questions to go with the answers, this job ought to be easy. Of course, this method assumes you already know what critical answers this witness has to offer. Be careful, however, not to feed witnesses answers of your making. You want to help witnesses make a clear presentation, not to put words in their mouths. If you do, the results will be stilted and credibility will suffer.

You want to make the witness familiar with the courtroom atmosphere. The easiest place to prepare a witness is in your office—but for the uninitiated witness this setting may be too relaxed. The witness needs to be in an atmosphere similar to the courtroom. At least have the witness sit in a straight chair away from you, as if alone on the stand. The real courtroom or a simulated one is ideal. It will be uncomfortable at the time, but the comfort at trial makes it worthwhile.

Some people are very positive about testimony in your office but become tentative on the witness stand. Perhaps they begin to realize that they could be wrong. Who couldn't be? For example, the woman in the car ahead of the plaintiff who stopped on his motorcycle will tell you she saw him stopped with his left foot on the ground. Yet in the courtroom she may say she "thinks" he was stopped and "believes" his left foot was on the ground. She is just as sure as when she was in your office, but she throws in the qualifiers and sounds tentative.

So you need to caution her not to do this, and to practice with her. At the same time, do not let her go to the other extreme. There is something unbelievable about people who are too sure.

Never use a witness to introduce an exhibit without going through the steps first. I know a lawyer who failed to do this. The father of a young man killed in an accident took photographs of the scene where his son was killed. The lawyer attempted to introduce the photographs during trial. When the lawyer asked the witness, "Can you identify Plaintiff's Exhibit One?" the witness answered, "No."

Remember, we become very familiar with foundational questions; witnesses do not. It is your job to make sure the witnesses know what is coming.

If the neophyte witness is terrified of direct examination, the fear of cross-examination is even greater. You must help your witness get over that fear.

When you are preparing for direct, ask yourself how you would cross-examine this witness. What are the weak points in the testimony? Are you familiar with the style of the opposing lawyer? Go through a realistic anticipated cross-examination. This will do more for the confidence of your witnesses than anything else.

Your own familiarity with the courtroom, however little it may be, tends to make you forget some simple matters. Help the witness decide how to dress for court: Colors, jewelry, and styles all can be important. A laborer may feel strangled in a coat and tie. Yet if the court requires them, the best preparation you can offer is to have the witness come for preparation so dressed.

The story is told of the service station attendant who had gone out in a wrecker and collided with another car, injuring the driver. The claim was that the attendant was speeding. In preparing the witness for trial, the lawyer suggested that he wear his Texaco uniform, one that was washed and pressed but not new—the lawyer wanted some old oil stains and dirt on the clothing. Because the trial started on a cold day, the witness came to court with a coat over his uniform. When the coat was removed, beneath the Texaco star was his nickname: "Speedy." A quick change was in order.

In your preparation, help the witness get used to speaking loudly. Practice having the witness look at you while talking. If the judge allows, stand near the jury; that way, the witness will look at the jury as well as you when answering. During cross-examination, it is also important for the witness to look at the questioner; otherwise, the jury may suspect fear or shame as the reason for the avoidance. You might ask the witness to direct his or her answer to the jury occasionally.

Logistics are important, too. Be prepared for your client to want to know answers to the following questions: Where do I go? Where do I park? When should I be there? Will someone meet me? What do I do when I get there? Have answers, or a practical solution, to these questions.

Of course you want the witness to tell the truth. But does the witness know that? From what witnesses have heard of lawyers, they might think you do not. Be certain you tell every witness: "Tell the truth!" If that is not what you want, then for the sake of the profession, get another job.

In some jurisdictions lawyers are allowed to move freely about the courtroom. In Texas, where we are known for flamboyance, most state courts require lawyers to be seated when they examine a witness. In federal courts you frequently are trapped behind a podium. The more your movement is restricted, the more important are the few movements you make. Not purposeless movement, however. Some activity is required to awaken the jury, even with the most interesting subject matter.

Introducing exhibits and using exhibits while questioning the witness are excellent times for this movement. When the testimony becomes tedious, introduce an exhibit or refer to one already in evidence. Large exhibits can be approached by the witness and, at times, by the examiner as well. When both of you are at an exhibit, however, be careful not to hold a private conversation. Project your questions and have the witness project the answers to the jury.

Many examiners use direct examination to take the sting out of cross. They bring up the weak points before the cross-examiner does. For example, suppose you are examining your client's brother:

    Q: Mr. Jones, you are the brother of Rick Jones who brought this suit, are you not? (Do not worry about objections to leading questions. You can always rephrase the question, and the objection will make it appear that the other side is trying to keep the evidence out.)

    A: Yes, I am.

    Q: So, can we trust you to tell us the truth or are you fudging to help your brother?

    A: No, I am telling the simple truth.

    Q: How can we be sure of that?

    A: [Make sure the witness has a good—not schmaltzy—explanation.]

Here is an example with an expert:

    Q: Doctor, have you ever examined Mr. Jones?

    A: No.

    Q: Have you ever met him?

    A: No.

    Q: Then, isn't it strange that you can give us a believable opinion about his medical condition?

A: No, I don't think so.

Q: Why not?

A: [The witness should be prepared to give a persuasive reason.]

Doing all that you need to do for a perfectly prepared direct examination may overwhelm you. "I don't have time to do all that," you may think, and that may be the fact. If you do not have time to do it all, do as much as you can. It is not malpractice not to do it all. It would be malpractice to do none of it. But you must guide yourself and decide, based upon the time you have and the nature of the case, just how much of this you can do. The more you do, the better your direct examination will be. Ideally it will be complete, believable, *and* interesting.

Cross-Examination

by David Berg

Professor Wigmore wrote that cross-examination is the greatest engine ever invented for the discovery of truth. But truth is rarely what a trial lawyer is after.

Truth is for engineers, who reduce their problems to mathematical certainty: What is the pressure per square inch as the fuel passes through the pipe? How much stress can the pipe withstand? Truth is for doctors, who search for the cause of illness: Where is the pain? How badly does it hurt? Truth is for probate lawyers, their issues decided by precise bequests: To whom have you left your estate? In what proportion to each?

The trial lawyer exists to win. But how do we win when the truth is against us? When an honest witness relates the events as they occurred, events that devastate our client, is it our job to rise dramatically, compliment the witness on an excellent memory, and sit back down?

Our role is to search for the weakness in the witness's testimony and use it to win the case. Since the moral imperative of our profession is to represent the client zealously—then, in the "is" and "ought" of things—we ought to create the impression that the witness's testimony, no matter how honestly given, is either immaterial or unworthy of belief.

For example, few trial lawyers would forgo the opportunity to impeach a witness who had threatened to testify against their client unless the witness was paid. Who among us would be deterred by the fact that the witness had told the unvarnished truth to the jury?

The ability to cross-examine effectively when all the facts are against us probably will not get us canonized, and—in my darker moments, I

The author practices in Houston, specializing in criminal law.

fear—may disqualify us from heaven altogether. But what the hell, where else can you get someone to pay you serious dollars to be hostile?

The goal of cross-examination, then, is to damage the credibility of the adverse witness, even if the witness is telling the absolute truth. There are a number of ways to do this, including the presentation of negative character witnesses, rebuttal witnesses, and impeaching documents. Of these methods, none is as effective as the use of a witness's prior statement that contradicts the testimony on the stand.

This is the moment you wait for in a trial. It is never enough just to impeach the witness. Be relentless. Dramatize the lie. Make certain the witness's credibility is shredded before you let the witness off the hook. No better opportunity will present itself to win the case.

Consider what Richard "Racehorse" Haynes did in this re-creation of testimony a few years ago in a case based on the Racketeer Influenced and Corrupt Organizations Act. Haynes's firm and mine represented two members of a Gulf Coast family accused of outfitting their midstream fueling barges with a small valve below deck that secretly drained a portion of each fuel delivery back into the main cargo tank. Haynes represented the man who ran the fueling operations and I represented his brother-in-law, who was in charge of their shipyard.

This is Texas. The amount of fuel allegedly drained back was about $70 million.

One of the witnesses, a former employee (we will call him R. J. Johnson), claimed that he had stolen fuel from our clients' midstream fueling customers, but admitted that he had pocketed the money himself.

The Lawyer Is a Teacher

Haynes believes that the lawyer is a teacher and the jury is the class. Questions should be asked carefully and slowly, each answer explained by the witness until the least among the jurors understands it clearly. My corollary to the Haynes Rule, with which he would surely agree, is that the lawyer is the actor and the jury is the audience. Each opportunity to make a serious point has to be milked the way Richard Burton milked lines in Hamlet.

Q: Sir, you have previously given testimony in this case, have you not?

A: Yes, sir, I gave a deposition.

Q: And prior to the taking of the deposition you swore that you would tell the truth?

A: Yes, I believe so.

Q: Well, let me refresh your memory [approaching the witness]. Here it is, at page one, 'The witness was duly sworn.' Do you remember swearing to tell the truth, the whole truth, and nothing but the truth, so help you God?

A: Yes, sir.

Q: That's the same oath you have taken here today, isn't it?

A: Yes.

Q: Do you recognize this transcript as a copy of the deposition you gave on March 5, 1985?

A: If you say that's it, then it is.

Q: Wait a minute and let's satisfy you. Look at this signature: 'R. J. Johnson.' That is your signature, isn't it?

A: Yes.

Q: And you signed your name to this document after you had reviewed the deposition for errors in your testimony?

A: I don't remember.

Q: Will you agree with me that just above your name is the notation, 'I have read this deposition and there are no errors in my testimony.'

A: I see it.

Q: And your name is below that entry.

A: Don't mean I read the deposition.

There is nothing to be gained by lingering on this point, so Haynes pauses, peers over the top of his glasses, and pinches his lips as though he has smelled something noxious in the courtroom. Then he speaks softly and the jury leans forward to hear what he says next:

Q: Follow me as I read, at page 19, line 25, where the lawyer asks you: 'Mr. Johnson, did you ever steal money or anything of value from your employers?' And you answer, at page 20, 'Never, I'd never do that.' You did say that, didn't you?

A: That's what it says.

Q: And yet, here today, before this court [pause] and this jury [pause], you have told us that you in fact stole money from these accused citizens [never 'defendants'], didn't you?

A: Yes, sir, I did.

Q: In fact, during Mr. Berg's [brilliant] cross-examination, you admitted to having stolen upwards of 20,000 gallons of fuel at a time, didn't you? [Certain editorial comments are added for accuracy.]

A: I ain't no thief. Everybody was doing it. Including your clients.

Q: Perhaps it was my question, and if so, I apologize. Let me ask it again. Did you tell Mr. Berg on cross-examination only minutes ago that you had stolen for your own personal account up to 20,000 gallons of diesel fuel in one fueling?

A: Yes, I said that.

Q: One of these statements is not correct, then, Mr. Johnson?

A: Is that a question?

Q: Perhaps the way I worded it, the question confused you, Mr. Johnson, and I apologize. Let me ask it this way. Which is the lie: The statement you swore to under oath on deposition—that you did not steal from your bosses, from your company—or the one you

520

swore to today, in front of this jury, that you in fact committed
thievery on the job, by stealing thousands of gallons of diesel fuel?
A: My testimony today is the truth.
Q: So that when you swore to tell the whole truth when you gave
your deposition, you did not see fit to honor your oath to God? [In
Texas, this is pronounced "Gawd." This is not the southern district of New York.]
A: I guess I lied back then.
Q: And didn't you volunteer to this jury that 'Everyone was doing it,
that your employers were stealing too,' to try to minimize your
own theft from your own employer?

Everything Haynes did had purpose. A careful examination of this exchange reveals rules that apply not only to the use of a prior sworn deposition, but to all cross-examination.

For example, the subject matter of cross-examination must always be
placed in context. Haynes first demonstrated that the witness had taken
an oath before he gave the deposition, something we understand is
standard procedure, but the jury may not. Then he emphasized the solemnity of deposition testimony by demonstrating that the same oath
was administered at the deposition as was given in front of the jury.
Finally, he repeated the oath in its entirety, probably because the jurors
had taken an oath imposing a similarly serious obligation on them, and
they presumably would not treat theirs as cavalierly as the witness had.

The same thinking—that the subject matter must be placed in context
so the jury can follow your questions—applies if you cross-examine
about quantum mechanics or a real estate contract. In the latter case, the
proper protocol is to identify the contract by exhibit number and subject
matter, such as, "Mr. Witness, I hold in my hand plaintiff's exhibit
number six, your contract to purchase a 1.23 acre tract of land from the
defendant . . . ." And with each question, remind the jury where you
are in the document and what part of the transaction you are talking
about.

Haynes read the page and line numbers of the testimony he intended
to read to avoid giving the prosecutor an opportunity to lodge the legitimate and distracting objection that he could not follow because he did
not know where Haynes was in the deposition. Then Haynes read the
offending testimony himself. If you ever allow a witness to read it back,
he can change the pace of cross, and take all the drama, even the sting,
out of the impeachment.

When the witness was unresponsive to the question concerning his
own theft of fuel, Haynes politely apologized and asked the question
again. This is an effective device to control the witness who will not give
a straight answer. With each evasive response Haynes will repeat very
politely, "I apologize, sir, it must have been my question. Let me repeat
it for you." By the third or fourth time he says that and the third or

fourth time the witness has been forced to be responsive, the jury knows he is avoiding the questions and Haynes's "polite" comment becomes a searing indictment. The remark is especially effective when the answer is obviously unresponsive and the structure of his question clearly was not the reason.

> Q: How much money did you receive as a result of having stolen fuel from your employers and sold it for your own use and benefit?
>
> A: I only took it to help my family . . .
>
> Q: I apologize. And I do not doubt that. Perhaps it was my question. . . .

If you happen to have a pretty good judge, do not hesitate to ask the judge to instruct the witness to answer the questions and the jury to disregard the witness's prior answer. A properly peeved judge can be more devastating to a witness's credibility than the finest cross-examination.

And do not let a witness get away with a volunteered statement calculated to slam dunk your client, such as Johnson's comment that everyone was stealing, including the employers. This is a common problem in cross, to which there are two reasonable avenues of response, neither of which is to ignore the comment. You can take him on as Haynes did, asking a question designed to lay bare that which some of the jurors instinctively may suspect: His gratuitous testimony is designed to deflect from his own criminality. Or you can ask the judge to instruct the witness to answer the questions and the jury to disregard the witness's unresponsive answer. In both instances, plodding ahead with cross or asking the judge to instruct, there is an inherent risk that probably has to be taken, that you are calling attention to the testimony.

In this example, the previous statement taken from the deposition was the lie. When the witness has lied in front of the jury, the other side can say good-bye to its chances. In either case, force the witness to identify which of the statements is a lie or, at least, which one is "incorrect."

Haynes's cross-examination is a vivid example of the recognized relationship between good lawyering and good drama. The consummate lawyer should be a consummate actor, able to use the dramatic pause, the disbelieving scowl, the hushed or angry voice, and the power that being in control of one's own emotions gives you.

Listen, Analyze, and Think about what the witness said in response to your questions. The acronym is LAT. Wear it for signposts upon thy forehead. Focus on the witness. If expansive answers give you more fodder for cross-examination, dissect what the witness tells you, even if you have to pause to assimilate what is said or wonder aloud about its meaning. Always stay involved in what you are asking, or you will sound flat and lose your audience.

Finally, cross-examination should never sound like direct. Cross-examine with a purpose—drive toward a particular point—but never wander aimlessly through the mire of the witness's most devastating testimony against your client. ("What did you say my client said after he shot your grandmother?" "Really? My client said that? How droll! What happened next?")

The Johnson testimony offered at least five fertile areas of cross, which Haynes ultimately explored, but not until he had clearly made his first point: The witness lied under oath about a material matter in the case.

Great trial lawyers have a genius, a feel for the part of a witness's testimony that is the truth, and the part that is a lie, and what the witness can be coerced into saying that is beneficial to the client. The common denominator of effective cross-examination is not, however, genius. It is a combination of preparation and an instinct for the jugular that allows even the journeyman attorney to appear inspired.

It is imperative that trial lawyers know as much as possible before trial. In criminal litigation where formal discovery is limited, this will mean interviewing as many adverse witnesses as possible before trial. That sneak preview will give conscientious attorneys an opportunity to prepare significant areas of cross-examination in the relative calm of their offices. Sometimes, because of the interview, opposing counsel will no longer have the courage to put the witness on the stand because the lawyer may not know what you have been told. There is almost always an area the witness knows about that opposing counsel did not want you to discover. It is also possible that your interview may reveal sufficient weakness in the testimony so that a properly prepared motion *in limine* may eviscerate the testimony or keep it out entirely.

For example, in the previously mentioned prosecution based on the Racketeer Influenced and Corrupt Organizations Act, a witness was prepared to testify that he had gotten orders from my client to open a valve and drain fuel back into the "main" cargo hold. Yet in his grand jury testimony, the witness had said only that he "received those orders" from my client, a statement worth examining closely. After interviewing him on the morning of his scheduled appearance, I filed a written motion *in limine* alleging that his testimony would be speculative. The judge, out of the presence of the jury, allowed me to develop this contention:

Q: Mr. Smith [not his name], it is correct that you are here because you got a subpoena from the government?

A: Mr. Berg [actual name], I wouldn't have come if they didn't send it.

Q: We talked this morning for the first time, did we not?

A: Yes sir. In the prosecutor's office.

Q: And you told me that you had received orders to open the valve and steal fuel, did you not?

A: Yes, I did.

Q: And you told me that those orders came from the main office.

A: That's right. From your client, Mr. Jones. [Not his real name; be-

523

fore you say anything about the names, lawyers are not supposed to be creative. In fact, we have a rule against creativity in my firm.]

Q: You assumed that Mr. Jones gave those orders?

A: Well, they came through the chain of command.

Q: I understand that. You are telling me you received your orders from your immediate supervisor. Correct?

A: Yes, from the manager of the dock.

Q: And earlier you told me, did you not, that you assumed the order started with Mr. Jones?

A: Well, I put an assumption to it.

Q: You also told me you had never received a direct order from Mr. Jones, didn't you?

A: I never talked to him personal about this, no. But I know he must have been behind it. Who else would have been able to authorize me to steal the fuel? You're using my own words against me.

Q: They are your words, aren't they?

The judge disallowed the testimony, but had I been forced to conduct the same cross-examination in front of the jury, they would have concluded, incorrectly, that my client was involved in the alleged theft. Based on other pretrial statements taken from government witnesses, I filed two more successful motions in limine regarding two other key witnesses against my client. A fourth witness had a massive stroke prior to testifying, a fortuitous circumstance for which I can claim no particular credit. The case against my client was dismissed.

The object of the exercise during direct and cross is to listen, analyze, and think, and then cross-examine for maximum benefit to your cause. Listen to what the witness says. Practice listening when you are not in trial, as superfluous as that may sound. Witnesses may not say exactly what they want to say or what you expect to hear. Analyze what you have heard. Has the witness hurt your client on a material issue? If not, do not ask any questions or you risk letting the witness say something that might do damage. If the testimony was helpful to you, be careful before examining for elaboration—the witness may be hostile to both sides. If the witness has killed you and you have no way to rebut through that witness, why go over the testimony again? All you will do is bolster the testimony. Restrict your cross to those areas in which you are certain you can do some damage.

Decorum can make a difference, too. Tell everyone at your table to write notes if they want to say something to you, and if anyone grabs your arm to tell you to ask a particular question, do not hesitate to pull out a .357 Magnum and kill him. Stride to the podium and exude confidence, even if there is a chance that the high school dropout on the stand is going to make you look like an idiot. Take command of the courtroom. Once you begin, do not grope for questions, shuffle through papers, or take breaks to confer with co-counsel. Let the jury know that you are prepared, that you do not need anyone's advice, and that you care about the case. This is the most important rule, because if you don't care, the jurors won't care.

Witnesses presented by opposing counsel will not always be hostile, so do not cross-examine all witnesses as if they were pederasts. You can make your case with a few admissions gently coaxed from a supposedly adverse witness.

Size Up the Witness

Your attitude toward the witness should be defined to some degree by the way the witness appears on direct. Try to see who the jury sees. Is this witness actually hostile? Is he really angry at my client? Is he likely to defend his position? Has he become an advocate? If the answer to these questions is yes, be certain to keep the witness in check from the start. Almost always avoid asking open-ended questions, but especially be careful not to do so with an explosive witness. Begin by telling the witness that you will be asking questions that should require only a "yes" or "no" answer and that you will never ask a question that calls for a hearsay response. "I only want to know what you know, never what someone else has said." This will help, to the extent possible, to secure the loose cannon to the deck.

Ease into the examination. Jurors sympathize with witnesses until there is significant impeachment. Unless you have some bulletproof impeachment, avoid leaping into hard questions immediately. Introduce yourself and explain to the jury your relationship, or lack of one, to the witness: "Mr. Johnson, my name is David Berg. I represent Mr. Smith, and I believe, sir, that we've never met. Is that correct?" or "We met last Tuesday, did we not, in your office?" and "While there, we discussed what you had told the insurance company lawyers that you would say on the stand." To avoid accusations of impropriety, try something like, "Wouldn't you agree with me that our meeting was businesslike and proper?"

Gerry Spence seems to start his cross with a statement that capsulizes the weakness of the direct. A lawyer friend tried this approach in a recent trial against an oil company. With the oil company's expert on the stand, the lawyer sought to illustrate that the opposition was hiding key material from the jury.

Q: Mr. Expert, you've been reading for two days now, in response to questions from those fine lawyers over there, from the oil company's manual of operations.

A: Yes. That's right. It's their company bible.

Q: Well, then, it's fair to say that for the last two days, you've been singing only the hymns their lawyers have selected, haven't you? And none that would harm the company that hired you and those lawyers.

525

A: That's not so.

Q: Then turn to page 24 and sing along with me for a while.

Always ask if the witness has given any prior oral or written statements recorded on paper, in tape recordings, or on videotape or if the witness made any reports or kept any notes, diary, or memoranda related to the events in question. If any such material exists, get it. It is great fodder for cross-examination. If you have been given a prior statement such as grand jury testimony, confirm the total number of appearances made. And always develop in detail the number of meetings the witness has had with the opposing lawyer, especially if the witness has spent little or no time with you or refused to meet with you.

Never answer a question from the witness, unless it is a request to clarify your question. And never allow the witness to get away with unresponsive answers. If you keep control, the witness will stop embellishing answers. When the witness strays, cut off the testimony immediately, as in the Haynes example, or ask the judge to do it. The rule is, never ask a witness a question when you do not know the answer. But every once in a while hubris grabs us by the briefcase so that we break the rule and elicit a devastating answer. When that happens, act as if ye had faith. Remain implacable. Try something like this: "Exactly, Mr. Schmidlapp, and I'm glad you brought it up." To respond "Oh, yeah" or "Just say that again" is probably, well, bad form.

Do not get blown away from an important area of inquiry because an objection has been sustained or because the judge has ordered you to "move along." Press on, ask the question differently, do what you have to, but do not give up. If you must give up, make sure you protect the record. Ask whether the judge is restricting your cross-examination and ordering you not to proceed into that area. If so, make a proffer of the evidence that you would expect to adduce if you were allowed to continue your line of questioning. Judges, too, can be bullied out of their position, especially if they sense you know how to protect your record.

Perhaps the most important maxim of all is that you should not laminate your cross-examination. Do not get so wed to a line of questions that you cannot ask about matters you never contemplated or cannot abandon cross altogether.

There are other admonitions about cross-examination that cannot be fully developed here, but are worth mentioning.

Nail down every detail so that the witness cannot back out of the trap when you finally ask the most significant question. Squeeze all the beneficial answers you can get from a witness before impeaching him. Once you have the answer you want, move away from it so that the witness cannot repair the damage. Timing is everything. If you get an answer that really helps make your case, quit—even at the expense of potentially valuable cross-examination.

Witnesses and parties frequently are warned to answer only that which is asked, so frame your questions to cover all bases. It is not enough to ask "Have you sent a letter to Mr. Smith?" Neither a "yes" nor a "no" tells you what you need to know. Try something like this: "Have you communicated in any manner with Mr. Smith?" "Did you send anything to him in the mail?" "Have you talked to him at all in the last two years?"

Analyze every aspect of cross-examination until you develop your own approach and can instinctively respond to the most difficult situations. Think about cross, talk about it. Do not be embarrassed to watch the good lawyers do it, even if only for the satisfaction of saying you could have done it better, which, oddly enough, is always my response. Except for when I listen to lawyer Haynes.

Few lawyers take the time necessary to cross-examine witnesses thoroughly. Examining in detail generally produces unexpected avenues of examination and discovery that can provide the edge in winning your case. Question doggedly, and the judge and opposing counsel will soon grow tired of it. You will be besieged with objections and orders to "move it along, counsel." Co-counsel will write you notes saying the judge is getting mad, and for God's sake, stop! Ninety percent of the time the only people you are likely to impress by relentless questioning is the jury. They will think you care a lot about the witness's testimony.

A few years ago, I tried a murder case in a small, neo-Nazi community (the chamber of commerce there would more likely describe it as a German settlement) just outside Houston. On my way to the courthouse on the first day of trial, I drove into the Fina gas station and, as the attendant filled up my car, he said, "You're the lawyer, ain'cha? Well, I tell you what, ol' buddy. If I were you, I'd turn it around and head right back to Houston."

I did not turn tail—the fee was paid—and before the trial was over, I was able to make a strong case that a major state witness, the victim's widower, was at least as likely to be the killer as my client, the victim's ex-husband. All I knew about the witness at the start of trial was that during a brief marriage, he had been designated the only beneficiary in his wife's will; that the wife's estate was considerable; and the witness already was involved with another woman. When the witness came into court, he was shaking.

Q: You fairly shook with rage when you came into this court and saw Mr. Jones, my client?

A: Yes.

Q: You glowered at him; that is a fair statement, isn't it?

A: Yes.

Q: And you hate Mr. Jones, because you believe he killed your wife?

A: Yes.

Q: And because you were able to live together as man and wife for only a brief period of time?

527

A: Yes. A year, a month, and two weeks.

Q: And I take it you are bereaved?

A: Yes.

Q: And that you deeply loved your wife?

A: Yes.

Q: Tell the jury who Billy Faye is.

A: Billy Faye?

Q: Billy Faye.

A: My fiancee.

Q: And where does Billy Faye Baxter live?

A: She lives on my farm, with me.

Q: Your farm? The farm you inherited from your deceased wife?

A: That's right. My farm.

Q: Her daughter, and Mr. Jones's daughter, did not inherit a single inch of land, did she?

A: We discussed it, me and my wife. And I will take care of the child.

Q: Perhaps it was the way I asked the question. Mr. Jones's daughter didn't inherit a square inch of land, did she?

A: No sir.

Q: How much time elapsed after the death of your wife before Billy Faye moved in with you at your farm?

A: I first laid eyes on Billy Faye—

Q: Perhaps it was my question, and I apologize. How long was it, after the death of your wife, that Billy Faye Baxter moved in with you on that farm of yours?

A: Six months.

Q: You were pretty wracked with grief, were you? When did you recover—How many day's after your wife's death did it take for you to be interested in another woman?

A: I'm still not over it.

Q: All right. Tell me where you met Ms. Billy Faye Baxter.

A: At the Continental Trailways Station on November 5.

Q: When did she move into your house with you?

A: The first week in December, I believe.

Q: So, you would say roughly a month passed in this romance before the two of you decided to move in together?

A: That's right. If you want to know, it was 14 days.

Q: And you claim to this jury that you never met Billy Faye Baxter before you ran into her at a bus station?

A: I didn't run into her at a bus station. It was a planned meeting.

Q: Okay, tell the jury how it was planned.

A: She is a mail-order bride. She met me through an advertisement I placed in *Mother Earth News*. We corresponded for approximately a month to six weeks. We phoned each other. I have some $150 in telephone bills.

Q: Well, you could certainly pay those, given what you inherited from your deceased wife?

A: [Inaudible response.]

Q: Wait a minute. Did you say *Mother Earth News?*

A: Yes.

Q: And your wife was killed June 23rd, only three or four months before the ad appeared?

A: Yes.

Q: Let me ask you, are you quite certain that ad was in October?

A: I will bring the magazine if you like.

Q: I would like that and you can bring it back tomorrow. Incidently, how many responses for a wife did you get from the ad in *Mother Earth News?*

A: Between 20 and 30. It was not for a wife.

Q: It was not for what?

A: Not for a wife.

Q: For a pen pal?

A: Whatever.

Q: You did call her a mail-order bride.

A: Yes, sir.

Q: What did the ad say?

A: 'Rural violin maker seeks slim Mother Earth Type'—to the best of my memory, now. I will produce the document.

Q: Seeks—Did you say slim?

A: Yes.

Q: Pretty creative ad for a guy wracked with grief, isn't it? [Objection] Let me ask you this. Did you have something else in mind other than a pen pal?

A: I had hopes. My wife was dead. I hoped that something would develop a year or two down the road.

Q: Your overweight wife was dead, right? [Objection] And I guess things just developed with your girlfriend a lot faster than you hoped?

A: That's right.

Q: Let me suggest that it is only for convenience that you now tell the jury that you placed that ad with the idea that something would develop down the road, so that it would appear to them that you had a proper mourning period.

A: No, it is the truth.

He returned the next morning with the October issue of *Mother Earth News.*

Q: Now, according to this, in order to have your ad in this issue, the September-October issue, you had to have your ad in before July 11, isn't that correct?

A: That is what it says.

Q: Now, your wife died on June 23, 1983, did she not?

A: She was killed.

Q: She was killed, yes. No one disputes that. It is who killed her we are after here. Now, sir, was the date of her death June 23?

A: Yes.

Q: Did you pay for this ad?

A: I did.

Q: And you paid by July 11, only 14 days after the death of your wife. . . .

A: Yes.

Q: Isn't it a fair statement, isn't it safe to say, that you were thinking about having another woman there living with you at your farm very shortly after the death of your wife?

A: No.

Q: Maybe before her death you longed for a 'slim Mother Earth type.'

A: Sir, that is a lie.

Q: Yet, you placed this ad?

A: Yes.

Q: Then let me ask again. Weren't you looking for another woman, a 'slim Mother Earth type' to move in with you?

A: May I amplify?

COURT: You can answer the question.

A: During that period I was crazy, insane with grief. I was under the care of a psychologist. I will not accept rational responsibility for any of my actions during that time.

Q: So, you would tell this jury that you were just too crazy to be responsible for what you did?

A: Yes.

Q: I understand. And you are a man of great sensitivity?

A: Yes.

Q: And that you are not the kind of man who would have the kind of anger it takes to kill. Please take your time and answer calmly, and I see you are shaking again.

A: Yes, I have that kind of anger. I will tell you true.

Q: You could kill, is that what you're telling us?

A: Yes, I could kill.

I might have gone on with this, but I knew by now he was a Vietnam vet and I assumed he would claim he would only kill the enemy, or some such thing. The point was made and I moved on.

The widower admitted also that he had "happened" on the scene of the murder at 3:00 P.M. on his way to work, that he lived only 15 minutes away from work, and that he was not due there until four (records from his current job showed that he had never gotten to work more than five minutes early in the year he had worked there), and that when he arrived at the murder scene the police did not question him, nor did they

530

ever execute a search warrant at his house or for his automobile.

So the man in mourning who, despite his brief marriage, was heir to a sizable estate under a will that excluded the deceased's natural daughter, happened on the scene of the murder uninvited at a time he would not ordinarily pass that location. Within days of his wife's demise, he was busily writing away for a "mail-order bride."

Now it was clear that the widower had the motive—the inheritance; the opportunity—he lived a few blocks from the scene of the crime; and the means—he owned a weapon similar to that used to kill his wife. All of this in a case where there was virtually no evidence that could be offered on behalf of the defendant, who was placed at the scene only a few moments before her death. Only cross-examination could have saved the accused from a long prison term.

Professor Wigmore's assessment of cross-examination is not wrong, just a bit naive. In fact, a judge or jury will arrive at the truth, or, in my view, a close approximation thereof, by observing witnesses subjected to cross-examination. But the variable in the search for a proper verdict based on the facts as they really occurred is the talent of the respective lawyers in the art of cross-examination. And the lawyer who knows how to cross-examine, no matter how egregious the facts inherited from the client, will amass a winning record.

Whether that has much to do with truth, as Aristotle sought it, is arguable. On the other hand, no one ever claimed Aristotle could cross-examine.

Cicero on
Cross-Examination

Translated and Edited by Irving Younger

The world lost a good part of the literature of Greece when the library at Alexandria burned. Julius Caesar was unperturbed, however. Told that "what is burning there is the memory of mankind," he replied, "A shameful memory. Let it burn." (G.B. Shaw, *Caesar and Cleopatra*, Act II) His equanimity has about it something of the smugness of the patriot. The *logos* of Athens may have been going up in smoke; the *virtus* of Rome was not. Alexandria's library contained but little Latin literature. For one thing, the Egyptian chrestomaths devoted themselves single-mindedly to Greek. For another, most of Latin literature had yet to be written.

Busily writing some of it in the very year of the library's destruction was Marcus Tullius Cicero, whose eminence in affairs as politician and trial lawyer is the gossip of posterity. Between tenures of public office and appearances before the jury box, Cicero produced poetry, history, oratory, and philosophy, enough to fill thirty-one quarto volumes. With time and energy left over, he wrote letters. Eight hundred and thirty-five survive, among them 416 to his lifelong friend, Titus Pomponius Atticus. To these must be added a 417th, copied in a crabbed scribal hand on both sides of a yellowed sheet of papyrus, handed to me as wrapping by a Neapolitan fruiterer from whom I had purchased a dozen cherries, and now, rescued from the obscurity of the twenty centuries since Cicero wrote it, published for the first time. Modern lawyers may find in it an interest not entirely antiquarian.

• • •

The gods know, dear Titus, that nothing an advocate does is simple, but of all the things an advocate must do, by far the most difficult, the

The author, now deceased, was a member of the Washington, D.C., firm of Williams & Connolly, and lectured and wrote extensively on trial practice.

most complex, and the most subtle is cross-examination. I had better say at once what it is I mean to signify by the word "cross-examination." I do not refer to friendly cross-examination, in which the advocate questions a witness who, though called to testify by the adversary, supports the advocate's side of the controversy. Nor do I refer to cross-examination of a witness who takes no position between the litigants but who possesses information which the advocate, through his cross-examination, wishes to lay before the jury. I refer, rather, to impeachment, cross-examination to discredit, cross-examination the purpose of which is to persuade the jury or the judge that the witness is not worth believing. That is the kind of cross-examination most commonly encountered and the kind most difficult to do competently.

To do it better than competently, to do it superbly, requires the convergence in one cross-examiner of three qualities.

The first quality is experience. Advocacy is not a phenomenon of infancy. A competent advocate must have behind him at least twenty-five jury trials. When he has tried his twenty-five, he begins to know what to do.

The second quality is talent. More about it later. It is the third quality of which I wish to speak just now.

No advocate ever cures his stage-fright. From first to last, when he stands up to cross-examine, panic beats on his chest and prostration lurks nearby. Two questions fill the advocate's mind. One is, "What shall I ask?" The other is, "How shall I ask it?" And those two questions, dear Titus, find their answer in the third quality, a thorough grasp of both the rules of evidence and the principles of advocacy, which for ease I shall call technical mastery. Do you want an answer to the first question, "What shall I ask?" The rules of evidence supply it, in ways about which I shall write you after the Senate adjourns. Do you want an answer to the other question, "How shall I ask it?" It is furnished by the principles of advocacy.

The chief, the central principle of advocacy, in all its parts and in every aspect, is preparation. Preparation. Preparation. Whether he has one week, one month, or one year to prepare, the advocate concentrates upon his case to the exclusion of everything else. The case is uninterruptedly in his mind when he is awake and forms the matter of his dream when he sleeps. To what end? That nothing come as a surprise. Everything at trial must be planned. Everything must be anticipated. Because if it is not, it will go wrong. The courtroom is the most intricate of institutions. So much happens, there is so much for the advocate to do, to know, to sense, that none of it can be done *ex tempore.*

What follows is that the summation must be worked up in advance. Indeed it must. Before the trial starts, the advocate knows what he will say to the jury when it is over. He should be able to say it at home to an amanuensis whose transcript can be compared with the summation actually delivered in the courtroom. The two must be within 90 percent of each other. I allow 10 percent for the disappointments of existence. If the surprises amount to more than 10 percent of the trial, if the summation delivered at home is not within 90 percent of the summation delivered in the courtroom, the advocate has prepared poorly.

Since the summation is worked up in advance, then the part of it that deals with the credibility of the adversary's witnesses is also worked up in advance. Yes, before the trial starts, the advocate knows what he will say to the jury at its conclusion about the credibility of the opposing witnesses.

There, dear Titus, there is the secret of cross-examination. The advocate will cross-examine *only* to the extent necessary to obtain the information he needs to support the argument he has planned in advance to make in his summation about the credibility of the cross-examined witness. And once he has obtained that information, he will stop. Stop. S-t-o-p. That four-letter word is the most important in the advocate's vocabulary. When things are going well, what should he do? Stop. When things are going badly? Stop. When he doesn't know what to do? Stop. When he is ahead? Stop. When he has blundered? Stop.

Stop.

Stop.

But not yet I, Titus, for I wrote above that the principles of advocacy tell the trial lawyer how to ask the questions on cross-examination. I must now set forth those principles, artlessly and without embellishment.

Do you recollect the conversation of the rabbi we met once while strolling in the Forum? It suits my fancy to call these principles of cross-examination commandments and to number them from one to ten. Here, then, are the ten commandments of cross-examination.

I. Be Brief

The cross-examiner's purpose, always remember, is to obtain the information necessary to support an argument in summation about the credibility of the witness. Well, never more than three such arguments. Two better than three. One best of all. So obvious is the reason for this commandment that it is often overlooked. No matter how simple a case may be to the advocates, to the jurors it is always confusing. They have not studied it in advance: they learn about it for the first time in the courtroom, and what's more, they learn about it, not by reading, which is how we are accustomed to learn, but by listening, which we are not at all accustomed to do. There is a very low limit on the capacity of the juror to absorb information by ear. Once that limit is reached, he can absorb no more. Ask him to do so by dragging out the cross-examination and he becomes bored and sullen. The interminable advocate, in short, is rarely the victorious advocate.

II. Short Questions, Plain Words

For some reason, many lawyers think that the sign of a lawyer is the habitual use of fancy words, long sentences, and elaborate syntax. Why don't lawyers understand, as do practitioners of all other arts, sciences, and mysteries, that simplicity marks the master? Simple words and simple sentences are not only good style; they are also good sense. The jury probably includes two or three simple folk, and the advocate must talk to them as well as to the learned. He cannot talk to them if his tongue drops only tangled clumps of twisting polysyllables.

III. Ask Only Leading Questions

The law of evidence contains a single rule about the form of questions on direct examination. Leading questions are forbidden. They are forbidden because they suggest the desired answer, because they put words in the witness's mouth. Therein lies the vice of the leading question on direct examination, and therein lies its utility on cross-examination. On cross-examination, an advocate never asks anything but a leading question. Every question on cross-examination should put words in the witness's mouth: all the witness need do is reply, in strict rhythm, "Yes," "No," or "I don't know." That is how a clever advocate controls a witness, and controlling the witness, making him say only what the advocate wants him to say, is the whole idea of cross-examination. Isn't it?

IV. Never Ask a Question to Which You Do Not Already Know the Answer

Cross-examination is not an examination before trial. It is hardly the occasion for discovering what the case is all about. If a lawyer doesn't already know what the case is all about, he shouldn't be trying it. This fourth commandment is a direct corollary of what I said earlier concerning the secret of cross-examination. Knowing before the trial starts what he will argue in summation about a witness' credibility, the advocate also knows the information he needs to support that argument; and in cross-examination he will seek nothing else. Hence the advocate always knows the answer to the question before he asks it. If he doesn't know the answer, he won't ask it. Two qualifications are necessary here. First, even though he does not know the answer, a good cross-examiner may ask a question when he does not care what the answer is. Second, it is possible not to know the answer to a particular question at the start of the cross-examination, but to discover the answer by cunning use of preliminary questions to which the answer is either known or unimportant. The advocate closes doors, he eliminates possible explanations, and gradually escalates himself to the point where he does know the answer. He has learned it in the course of the cross-examination, and so he may now ask the question.

V. Listen to the Answer

From time to time, a witness will say something extraordinary. It is contradicted by other testimony; it is contrary to human experience; it is inconsistent with the way the universe is organized. Yet the cross-examiner goes heedlessly on, as if somehow he hadn't heard the answer. Correct. He hasn't heard the answer, and the reason he hasn't heard it is that he wasn't listening, and the reason he wasn't listening is that he was so immersed in his own fright that he had left no reserve of attention for listening to the witness. Now, fright is natural, but if the lawyer wishes to be a true advocate, he must train himself to overcome it. Not that fright ever disappears. It does not. It must be mastered, however, controlled, limited, so that the cross-examiner can turn from himself and listen to the witness.

VI. Do Not Quarrel with the Witness

It is only human for the cross-examiner to be tempted to respond to the witness's absurd or patently false answer with "How dare you say that?" or "Do you really expect the jury to believe such bilge?" Resist the temptation. To quarrel with the witness is unurbane. It infallibly elicits a sustained objection on the ground that the question is argumentative. And it serves to permit the witness to rationalize an absurd or patently false answer, diminishing or altogether avoiding its adverse impact on the jury. Better, should the witness give such an answer, for the advocate simply to s-t-o-p.

VII. Do Not Permit the Witness to Explain

The good advocate asks leading questions only, as required by the third commandment, questions to which he already knows the answer, as required by the fourth commandment, and questions which do not quarrel with the witness, as required by the sixth commandment. He gets his "yes" or "no" or "I don't know," and briskly moves on. He does not permit the witness to explain an answer, for that would be to hand control of the cross-examination to the witness, and the good advocate allows no one but himself to control the cross-examination. Of course, the judge may interrupt and give the witness an opportunity to explain. That is one of life's misfortunes. And, of course, the proponent of the witness may come back on redirect examination to elicit an explanation. Let him. Do not do it for him. Possibly he will neglect to do it, and in any event, to the jury the explanation that comes later always has the false ring of an afterthought.

VIII. Do Not Ask the Witness to Repeat the Testimony He Gave on Direct Examination

If the jurors hear something once, they may believe it or they may not. If they hear it twice, they will probably believe it. And if they hear it three times, they will certainly believe it. Thus, when a lawyer asks a witness on cross-examination merely to repeat his direct testimony, all he accomplishes is elevation of the witness' credibility. What had been a perhaps becomes a doubtless. That, dear Titus, is not the purpose of cross-examination. And has it struck you that the law of evidence makes it easy to obey this commandment? It specifies many subjects into which a lawyer may inquire to discredit a witness without ever permitting the witness to repeat his direct testimony. But more on this in the letter I will write you after the Senate adjourns.

IX. Avoid One Question Too Many

After a while, the advocate develops an instinct for this commandment. He cross-examines; he asks an especially good question; he gets an especially good answer; and he stops. Without this instinct, he will not stop. He pursues the point with a question following up on the especially good question. Sometimes, as he asks it, the cross-examiner says to himself, "I just know I shouldn't ask this." But too late. The question has been asked. It cannot be recalled. And invariably it turns out to be one question too many.

X. Save the Explanation for Summation

Assume this case: a lawyer has conceived in advance of trial an unanswerable argument to make to the jury in summation about the credibility of an opposing witness. The argument rests upon information the lawyer can obtain by cross-examining in scrupulous compliance with these commandments. The only difficulty is that the argument is so profound, the cross-examination so masterful, that the jury will not then and there, while the cross-examiner is cross-examining, grasp the point of the cross-examination. The lawyer now feels the desire to draw out the cross-examination so that the jury comprehends at once the nature of the questioning and the brilliance of the questioner. Should he succumb, he is lost. In drawing out the cross-examination, it is inevitable that the lawyer will violate one or more of these commandments and thereby dissipate the force of the cross-examination. All the better for the lawyer that the jury not understand. There is no keener state of mind, none better calculated to help the jury concentrate and remember, than unsatisfied curiosity. Let the jurors wait. In summation, the lawyer will recall the puzzling cross-examination and at last make everything clear. The jurors' relish of satisfied curiosity will render the lawyer's argument irresistible and a favorable verdict inevitable. All this because the cross-examiner saved the explanation for summation.

I remind you, dear Titus, that the second quality which goes to make a superb cross-examiner is talent, and that I said I would return to it. I now do.

The talent to cross-examine is a rare commodity. No more than three lawyers in all of Rome have it, and sometimes I wonder whether I myself am one of them. If an advocate has this talent, he should offer daily thanks. And if he lacks it, there is no way for him to acquire it. Alas, he will never be a superb cross-examiner. Should he flee the courts and take up farming? No, my dear Titus. For though a man be missing the second quality, it is within his power to acquire experience and technical mastery. With those first and third qualities, he can be a reasonably competent cross-examiner, and to be a reasonably competent cross-examiner is to be one lawyer out of ten thousand.

With much affection,
M. TULLIUS CICERO

Systematic Cross-Examination

by William D. Snapp

Every lawyer who is or wants to be a trial lawyer knows that effective cross-examination is both important and frighteningly difficult. An effective cross-examiner must ask every necessary question but not one question too many. An effective cross-examiner must control the witness but not bully him. An effective cross-examiner must drive a point home but not gild the lily.

Because most trial lawyers want to improve their cross-examination techniques, there has been a great demand for and supply of books and articles on cross-examination. Although many are valuable, most of these books and articles treat cross-examination as if it were a skill like riding a bicycle. The authors seem to suggest that if only you learn the rules of the road, overcome your fear of falling, and manage to keep your balance, you will be able to ride any bike with the best of them. Then, to demonstrate the truth and wisdom of their advice, the authors typically recount their personal experiences of riding without any hands while leaping through a ring of fire to the resounding ovation, or better yet, stunned silence of a jury of 12 admirers.

In fact, cross-examination is not like riding a bicycle. To be sure, effective cross-examination requires skill, but it is much more akin to the skill needed by a demolition expert who is ''deconstructing'' a building with dynamite. Although skill is necessary, skill alone will not get the job done effectively. Indeed, skill without care will not even keep an expert from self-destructing in the middle of a building demolition or a cross-examination.

Of all the prerequisites to effective cross-examination, meticulous preparation is by far the most important, and the one the average trial

---

The author is a partner in Jenner & Block in Chicago.

attorney can do the most to improve. That observation is often over-looked by readers of perhaps the best known recent article on cross-examination, Irving Younger's *"The Art of Cross-Examination,"* (ABA Litigation Monograph Series No. 1, 1976); *see also,* Younger, A *Letter in Which Cicero Lays Down the Ten Commandments of Cross-Examination,* 3 LIT-IGATION, No. 2 at 18 (Winter 1977). That article is widely known for set-ting forth, as the ten commandments of cross-examination, advice con-cerning the techniques to be used in examination. But note what Younger says about preparation:

> Whether he has one week, one month, or one year to prepare, the advocate concentrates upon his case to the exclusion of everything else. . . . To what end? That nothing come as a surprise. Every-thing at trial must be planned. Everything must be anticipated. Be-cause if it is not, it will go wrong.

Id. at 18. Thus, though questioning techniques may be the ten com-mandments, it is preparation that constitutes the golden rule of cross-examination.

Younger's ten commandments are an insightful guide to effective questioning techniques. But they are neither a sufficient nor a necessary guide to effective cross-examination. Consider recent examples of mar-velous cross-examinations by Frank Oliver and Gerry Spence. Oliver, *Witness for the Prosecution,* 10 LITIGATION, No. 4 at 10 (Summer 1984); Spence, *Questioning the Adverse Witness,* 10 LITIGATION, No. 2 at 13 (Win-ter 1984). Oliver's cross-examination of a government informant in a criminal trial and Spence's cross-examination of a newspaper reporter in a libel trial were masterpieces, yet each repeatedly violated Younger's ten commandments. Part of the reason these lawyers were effective while violating the ten commandments is that they have tremendous skill. But their cross-examinations share one common ingredient: ex-haustive preparation. Even the most skilled trial attorney must be thor-oughly prepared to conduct an effective cross-examination. You can vio-late Younger's ten commandments, but violating the golden rule of preparation is always a mortal sin.

Although preparation is the key to effective cross-examination, few articles have been written on how to prepare for cross-examination. That may be because many attorneys think "preparation" means the same thing as "hard work." It does not. Preparation for cross-examination requires hard work, but it also requires that the hard work be conducted in an orderly fashion. The more complex the trial, the more important it is that your preparation for cross-examination pro-ceed in an orderly manner. If your preparation is not organized, you will not only waste your client's money, but also a trial lawyer's most pre-cious commodity: time.

So how does a trial lawyer prepare to conduct effective cross-

540

examination? The degree and manner of organization varies with the complexity of the trial and the availability of discovery. For purposes of this discussion, let's assume that the case is quite complex, that your opposing counsel is expected to present numerous witnesses, and that you have adequate discovery concerning the expected testimony of all of those witnesses.

The first step in preparing your cross-examinations does not require that you frame a leading question or control an unruly witness. The first step is to prepare a theory of your case—the simpler the better. To prepare the optimum theory of your case, you must have discovered all the relevant facts. But make no mistake, a theory is more than merely a neutral recounting of provable facts. It is a persuasive explanation of the events at issue in your case. Just as a houseboat can be described either as a house with a rudder or as a boat with a roof, the same set of provable facts are subject to numerous formulations, not all of which will lead to the same result at trial.

Not all facts are equally provable. Obviously, you would not be preparing for trial if there were not a genuine issue as to one or more material facts. Moreover, your discovery almost certainly will reveal that the witnesses have numerous disagreements about nonmaterial, subsidiary facts that may, but will not necessarily, be the subject of testimony at trial.

As a general rule, you should construct a theory that depends, as much as possible, on uncontested facts. Moreover, although many uncontested facts may be irrelevant to your theory, your theory must be consistent with *all* of the uncontested facts.

To the extent that you must rely on contested facts, identify those on which you are most likely to prevail. If possible, construct a theory that uses those relatively safe contested facts as transitions between, and therefore internally consistent with, uncontested facts.

After you have developed a simple theory of your case, make another one. Keep making more until you are satisfied that you have found the best one.

After you are satisfied with your theory, develop a theme: a one-sentence summary of your theory. The theme may be hokey, and you may never actually articulate it at trial. But if you can distill your case to a single sentence, you can truly focus your preparation efforts.

If you doubt that experienced trial attorneys really expend time and effort distilling a case to a single sentence or that such distillation has any impact on their cross-examinations, re-read the masterful cross-examinations by Frank Oliver and Gerry Spence. Oliver used his theme as the last line of his closing argument: "[Y]ou cannot accomplish anything good by the employment of evil." Oliver, *Witness for the Prosecution*, 10 LITIGATION, No. 4 at 69 (Summer 1984). The theme of Spence's case is revealed in his next-to-last question to the newspaper reporter.

Spence's theme was that freedom of the press must not be abused so as to injure an innocent man. Spence, *Questioning the Adverse Witness*, 10 LITIGATION, No. 2 at 67 (Winter 1984).

Are you now ready to decide what facts to bring out on cross-examination? No. Instead, with your theory and theme in mind, you are now ready to prepare your closing argument.

Your closing argument has three purposes:

1. to explain your theory of the case;
2. to persuade the jury to accept your theory; and
3. to persuade the jury to reject your opponent's theory.

How to do all that in closing argument is a topic for another day. For now it is enough to say that a good closing argument has all the elements of a good story. After the characters are introduced, they interact in a plot that consists of conflict, suspense, climax, and denouement. Of course, you can structure the argument to make the jury part of the story, in which case they will supply the denouement in the form of a verdict.

Finally, and most importantly, find an argument that you really believe. You cannot sell that which you would not buy.

After you have added the last creative flourish to your closing argument, dissect it to identify every factual component of that argument. Then identify every possible evidentiary source for each fact reflected in your closing argument.

You should also determine which facts in your closing argument should be charged with emotional impact. That emotional element may influence your choice of when and how to establish certain facts during the trial.

Now decide which fact sources you will actually use at trial. There are no hard-and-fast rules for these decisions, but, all things being equal, you should consider the following six guidelines:

First, if you can establish a fact (contested or uncontested) through a written document, do it. If it is in writing, juries (and judges, too) believe it.

Second, use direct examination rather than cross-examination to establish constructive facts. By constructive facts, I mean those facts that concern the underlying events rather than the credibility of witnesses. It is particularly important to fully develop contested facts through direct examination, because you can control the reinforcement of details and nuances that will make your version of these facts believable. In addition, control over the details and nuances of critical contested facts is important to foreshadow the emotional impact you want from these facts in closing argument.

Third, establish uncontested facts through cross-examination only if you have no other source. If you must use cross-examination to establish uncontested facts, use the easiest witness possible. Remember, juries do not award bonus points based on the degree of difficulty of the cross-examination. If you have to struggle to obtain admissions, you may even lose points.

Fourth, cross-examination may be used to corroborate contested facts. But be careful. Opposing counsel will have prepared the witness to resist and, if possible, humiliate you unless you stick strictly to the letter of previously obtained admissions.

Fifth, if absolutely necessary, cross-examination may be used as the sole source of a contested fact. But if you find you must rely on cross-examination as the sole source of a contested fact, consider opening settlement negotiations.

Sixth, the principal use of cross-examination is the development of destructive facts that undercut the credibility of your opponent's witnesses.

For each cross-examination witness, prepare a short list of constructive facts that you need to elicit from that witness to make your closing argument. This is a mandatory list for your cross-examination. For each cross-examination witness, also prepare an exhaustive list of every possible destructive fact that could be elicited from the witness to enhance your closing argument. This second list will contain some mandatory facts and many optional ones.

After you have prepared a short list of all the constructive facts that you must establish and a long list of all the destructive facts that you may establish in each cross-examination, you are ready to prepare the first draft outline of each cross-examination.

First, determine your last line of questioning and, preferably, the precise wording of your last question. Your last question should be absolutely, totally safe. You should know that, if necessary, you can force the witness into an admission or impeach the witness.

Your last line of questioning should also be genuinely significant. It need not be your best set of questions, but it must be a good one. If your best line of safe questioning concerns constructive facts, you should consider the possibility of eliminating your destructive cross-examination entirely. If you are in the uncomfortable position of having no safe questions, consider ending with a question that forcefully states your client's position even though the witness will disagree.

Having planned the end, go to the beginning. Determine your first line of questioning. If you are going to establish any constructive facts on cross-examination, your first line of questioning must concern one of those constructive facts. Like your last line of questioning, your first line should be genuinely significant. However, although your first line should be relatively safe, it need not be perfectly safe.

Now you are ready to organize the rest of your examination. Establish all of your constructive facts before beginning to ask any questions designed to attack the witness's credibility. This order is essential for two

543

reasons. First, the witness will be more cooperative before you have attacked his credibility. Second, his affirmative admissions will be given more weight if obtained before you have attacked his credibility.

Organize your questions in a logical sequence so that the jury or judge can more readily understand the points you are trying to establish. Admittedly, there are some attorneys who intentionally use a disorganized approach to cross-examination because it keeps the witness confused. But disorganization also confuses the finder of fact. Thus, admissions will have less impact, if they are noticed at all. For purposes of trial practice, a tree that falls when the jury is not paying attention does not make any noise.

Use of a logical sequence in cross-examination does not mean that you need to adopt the same sequence as the witness's direct examination. On the contrary, you should use a logical sequence that differs from the one you expect opposing counsel to use in direct examination. Typically, you should avoid the use of a chronologically ordered cross-examination.

The first draft outline of your cross-examination begins on a strong point; ends on a strong, absolutely safe point; and progresses from beginning to end in a logical sequence. Now, revise the outline so that the cross-examination tells a story.

A trial should consist of one big story, which the lawyer gets to tell in closing argument, and a series of mini-stories told by each witness. The organization of testimony into a mini-story helps the jury to remember fully the witness's testimony.

Chronologically organized direct examinations generally need little revision to constitute a memorable story. By contrast, nonchronologically sequenced cross-examinations emerge as a story only by carefully relating established information to new information being elicited through leading questions. The decision of whether to use or discard various items from your optional destructive cross-examination list is dictated, in large measure, by whether those items fit into your story line. For a description of the function and technique of storytelling in cross-examination, see McElhaney, *Trial Notebook, The Story Line in Cross-Examination,* 9 LITIGATION, No. 1 at 45 (Fall 1982); Spence, *Questioning the Adverse Witness,* 10 LITIGATION, No. 2 at 13 (Winter 1984).

Allow yourself some creative freedom in developing an effective story for a particular cross-examination. You must not limit yourself either to the analysis that led to the first draft outline of that cross-examination or to your traditional notions as to the expected sequence of a cross-examination.

The story you choose to tell depends not only on the facts to which the witness will be testifying, but also on the personality and character of the witness and the examiner. As an obvious example, a rape victim can be subjected to a far more aggressive cross-examination by a no-

nonsense woman than by any man. But not every example is so obvious. You need to be keenly aware of how you are perceived by others in order to be consistently effective in your cross-examinations. Remember that perceptions at trial are as likely to be based on stereotypes as on the real nature of your personality. You may truly be a gentle, patient, wonderful human being who is justly angry at your opponent's milquetoast expert witness because he is lying through his teeth. But if you are a large man whose voice booms through the courtroom, you must move slowly in exposing the lies, or you will be perceived as an overbearing ogre.

As a result of your revisions, some of your cross-examination outlines will have no questions. You should review those outlines once again. For some witnesses—usually those who are testifying to undisputed facts—the best cross-examination is no cross-examination. You are now properly prepared to say "no questions."

For other witnesses, usually those who are testifying to disputed facts but who cannot be impeached, you will want to prepare an apparent cross-examination. An apparent cross-examination usually consists of questions that merely reaffirm undisputed facts. The apparent cross-examination is used in an effort to avoid the appearance that you have accepted all of the witness's testimony as true. One alternative to an apparent cross-examination is the use of body language and intonation that make it clear that "no questions" does not mean, "I believe you," or worse, "I surrender."

After you have revised the outlines of your cross-examinations, you should give individualized consideration to the issue of witness control. The preparation that you have already done will provide you with all you need to control most witnesses. Nevertheless, you should look for opportunities to insert witness-control questions at the beginning of each new line of cross-examination.

Basically, witness-control questions are those that inform the witness that you know the subject at hand as well as he does, so he should not try to quibble with you. These questions also let the jury know you have done your homework, and help your credibility with them.

A Light Touch

Witness-control questions can be particularly important for the cross-examination of expert witnesses. But effective witness-control questions for an expert may be so esoteric that they are not useful devices to enhance your credibility with the jury. To keep from distracting the jury, find questions that are short, and pose them with a light touch.

At trial you need not use your witness-control questions if all is going well. Moreover, these questions will not save you if you have totally lost control of the witness. They are intended to maintain rather than to regain control.

To a great extent, controlling uncooperative witnesses requires on-the-spot application of questioning skills. For a description of witness-control techniques, see Walter, *Controlling the Witness on Cross-Examination,* 7 LITIGATION, No. 1 at 36 (Fall 1980); McElhaney, *Trial Notebook, Witness Control,* 5 LITIGATION, No. 4 at 47 (Summer 1979). But proper preparation may help you anticipate and avoid witness-control problems.

After you have inserted witness-control notations into the outlines of your cross-examinations, you should plan for your use of documents and other exhibits. This planning depends, in part, on the physical arrangements in the courtroom. It also depends on whether the parties have exchanged premarked exhibits. You must plan your presentation so that it proceeds smoothly, so that everyone can see, and so that you have no legitimate interference from opposing counsel.

At the beginning of most cross-examinations, you should give the witness copies of all the documents he will need. Obviously, there are times when you want to withhold documents because you do not want the witness to anticipate the direction of the cross-examination. But too often, for no good reason, an attorney turns himself into a messenger boy by carrying one document after another to the witness.

Your own copies of the cross-examination documents should be placed in order of presentation where they can be reached easily. They should be annotated to remind you of each point in your cross-examination of this witness. The absence of an annotation will remind you that, in preparation, you decided *not* to pursue a line of questioning that, in the heat of battle, seems irresistible. At trial, it may not be necessary to resist, but the absence of annotation will force you to think twice before continuing into uncharted waters.

Choreograph the use of large demonstrative exhibits or slide shows. Demonstrative evidence loses its impact if it is handled awkwardly or is difficult to see. Find a system that allows you full, facile control over the exhibits without the need for any assistants. This puts you in total control of the pace of the cross-examination and avoids the distractions that necessarily result when you put additional actors on the stage.

On cross-examination, you should not plan to ask a witness to assist you with an exhibit. More important, never put a marker in the witness's hand. If you want to mark the exhibit, make the witness tell you where the mark should be placed. If your jurisdiction does not permit that technique, then do not plan to put any marks on the exhibit during cross-examination.

Next come deposition transcripts. Preparing for destructive cross-examination based on depositions presents some unique problems. Nearly every experienced trial attorney agrees that cross-examination questions should not be read from a written script. But cross-examination from a topical outline frequently results in the embarrassment of a false impeachment. A false impeachment happens when the deposition testimony does not actually contradict the witness's testimony at trial. Even if the attorney sees what is happening and does not actually try to complete the false impeachment, the cross-examination loses its effectiveness whenever the examining attorney opens the deposition transcript in obvious but unfounded anticipation of finding impeaching testimony. You can almost feel the jury thinking, ''Whoops!'' Jury ''whoops'' should be reserved for witnesses, not attorneys.

One messy but effective technique for avoiding false impeachments is to cut and paste excerpts from a photocopy of the deposition transcript onto your cross-examination outline. The resulting outline is bulky, but very useful at trial. The problem of bulkiness can be overcome if you reduce the size of the photo copies or if your deposition transcripts are on computer so that excerpts can be printed in a space-saving format.

The annotated outline is useful at trial because, as you formulate your questions, you can quickly glance at the precise wording of the testimony that caused you to believe that you could force a useful admission. Then you will be able to phrase the question so that the witness will admit the contested fact or, even better, will be impeached by his deposition testimony.

The annotated outline is particularly useful for lengthy cross-examinations. In lengthy examinations, there is time to shape the witness's responses through principles of behavior modification. With the annotated outline, you can proceed with assurance that you have the witness nailed on each point. That permits you to punish the witness every time he deviates from your leading questions. If it is consistent with the attitude you wish to display to this witness, you may also give social rewards, such as a reassuring smile when the witness responds affirmatively to leading questions.

Once you have trained the witness to seek rewards rather than punishment, you can carefully stretch some of the deposition admissions, so long as you leave yourself an easy transition back to the precise language in the deposition. Thus, for example, deposition testimony that ''I do not recall locking the door'' becomes the basis for the following cross-examination question: ''You did not lock the door, did you?'' The possible answers and suggested responses are as follows:

Answer	Response
No, I did not.	Reward the witness. You got exactly the answer you wanted.
I do not recall locking the door.	Reward the witness. Pretend you got exactly the answer you wanted.
I am not sure.	Follow up with questions to establish that locking the door is important and that the witness does

547

	not recall locking the door. (This sequence is nearly as good as an outright admission to the initial question. It is decidedly better than the unembellished deposition record.) Now, reward the witness for giving you exactly the answer you wanted.
Yes, I did.	Follow up with a question establishing that the witness now claims to recall locking the door. Punish the witness by impeaching him with the deposition transcript.

Properly handled, the witness will accede to most of the stretched admissions and will never realize that he avoided your efforts to stretch other admissions.

Theoretically, you are ready for trial. You started with a theory and have now arranged a harmonious group of facts that, put together, support that theory.

Before you walk into court, however, you should mentally rehearse the entire trial from beginning to end. There are two purposes to this exercise. First, the mental rehearsal constitutes a holistic inspection of your trial strategy and preparation. You may decide to revise certain examinations to simplify and streamline the presentation of your case.

Second, the mental rehearsal allows you to feel yourself successfully cross-examining each witness. If necessary, you can make a conscious decision to change the way you will feel and thus the image you will project in conducting various direct examinations and cross-examinations.

In making your revisions, you should consider four of Younger's ten commandments:

Be brief.

Do not ask a question unless you know the answer.

Do not let the witness repeat what he said on direct examination.

Save your ultimate point for summation.

As a result of your mental rehearsal, not only are you prepared, but you know you are prepared. That knowledge will serve you well when unexpected developments arise during trial.

Be Ready to Adjust

You should be prepared to conduct every cross-examination before the trial begins. But there is at least some element of reality to the image that a cross-examination is conducted in response to the direct examination. You must be ready to make adjustments to your prepared cross-examination based on the direct examination.

Generally, the content of the direct examination should come as no surprise to you. Even if it does, avoid taking copious notes during direct examination. If you are well prepared, a few sketchy notes will remind you of the surprising testimony. Instead, focus your efforts on watching the witness, watching the interaction between the witness and opposing counsel, and watching the jury react to the witness.

It is the demeanor of the witness and your assessment of the witness's credibility that will cause you to make significant adjustments in your cross-examination.

Now it is time to conduct the cross-examination for which you have so carefully prepared. Unless you are a grand master, you should religiously apply these six of Younger's ten commandments:

Use plain words.

Use only leading questions.

Listen to the witness's answers.

Do not quarrel with the witness.

Do not allow the witness to explain anything.

Do not ask one question too many.

If you apply both the golden rule of preparation and Younger's ten commandments, you will never lose a case you should have won, and you may win some cases that you should have lost. That's as good as it gets for a trial lawyer.

Controlling the Witness on Cross-Examination

by Michael J. Walter

Professor Irving Younger's lecture on "The Ten Commandments of Cross-Examination" is a classic. The commandments provide rules for lawyers to avoid embarrassment and defeat on cross-examination.

1. Be brief.
2. Short questions, plain words.
3. Always ask leading questions.
4. Don't ask a question, the answer to which you do not know in advance.
5. Listen to the witness's answers.
6. Don't quarrel with the witness.
7. Don't allow the witness to repeat his direct testimony.
8. Don't permit the witness to explain his answers.
9. Don't ask the "one question too many."
10. Save the ultimate point of your cross for summation.

But the commandments command without telling us how to obey. What are short questions? How can you avoid quarreling with the witness or asking the one question too many?

The commandments can be summed up in a single phrase: control the witness. Several basic principles that the cross-examiner should follow to control the witness will lead to obedience of Younger's ten commandments.

To satisfy the second and third commandments, each question should be short and contain a "leading phrase." There are two ways to accomplish this and to control the witness. First, do not ask any question that contains more than one new fact. Second, do not ask any question that

---

The author is General Counsel for the Computerland Corporation in Hayward, California. This article is based on a lecture by Irving Younger, see p. 532.

contains more than five words per question, excluding the leading phrase and connecting words.

A leading phrase is like a spoon to put the castor oil of unpleasant facts into a witness's mouth. For example, you want the witness to say: "The light was red." That is the castor oil. To convey those words to the witness's mouth, there are a variety of spoons such as: *"Isn't it a fact that* the light was red?" or "The light was red, *isn't that correct?"* or "The light was red, *was it not?"* The witness does not answer the statement "the light was red" but the leading phrase: "Isn't it a fact that. . . ."

Limiting questions to one new fact allows them to be brief while still leading. For example, you want the witness to testify that when he saw that the light was red, he was sitting in his car listening to the radio while parked next to the curb. A long question might be: "Isn't it a fact that you were sitting in your car parked by the curb with the radio on when you noticed that the light was red?" He may answer "yes." However, he may seize the opportunity to disagree with the order of the facts in the question and deny the statement, even though it is otherwise true. But, notice what happens with short or one new fact questions:

Q: You were in your car, were you not?
A: Yes.
Q: You were, at that time, seated, were you not?
A: Yes.
Q: And your car was then parked, was it not?
A: Yes.
Q: Parked next to the curb, isn't that a fact?
A: Yes.
Q: The radio was on, was it not?
A: Yes.
Q: And while sitting in your car which was parked next to the curb with the radio on, you noticed the light, did you not?
A: Yes.
Q: And the light was red, was it not?
A: Yes.

Wait a minute, you say. The sixth question contained more than one fact. Indeed it did, but all the others contained only one fact and this question contained only one new fact—"you noticed the light." The witness had already conceded all of the other facts in the question.

Review the seven questions above. The first question contains five words and a leading phrase. The second question contains three—"you were seated" plus a connecting phrase, "at that time," plus a leading phrase, "were you not?" The third question contains four words: "Your car was parked," the connectors, "and" and "then," and a leading phrase, "was it not?"

Short questions control the witness. By obtaining his concession to each new fact, you close off avenues of retreat that the witness could use to defeat a line of cross. examination.

Remember, you rely almost exclusively on the jurors' ears. A juror might miss the details of a long question. Short questions paint a word picture that even the least attentive juror can receive and store in the mind's eye. Final argument that relies on facts established by these short questions triggers the jurors' recall of the word pictures. One picture is worth a thousand words.

To become a Picasso of the courtroom and to gain further control over the witness, familiarize yourself with the use and artistry of plain words. Plain words are the speech of the common person. One of the top Nielsen-rated shows is a situation comedy about two women who work in a Milwaukee brewery, "Laverne and Shirley." Before choosing a word for a question in cross, ask yourself: Would Laverne say this to Shirley? If the answer is "no," do not use it, Avoid legalese, terms of art, and multi-syllable words that are uncommon and that the witness and jury may not understand. The simpler the word, the less the opportunity for the witness to take some semantic exception to your intended meaning and give you a "no" when your plan required he answer "yes." Bear in mind that the witness asks no questions. The choice of words is solely yours. Be precise in your choice, and you will exercise power over the witness and control his testimony. The jury must understand each word exactly as you intend. Otherwise, the picture the jury sees might fall far short of the one you were attempting to paint.

Commandments four, six, seven, and eight address some of the ways a witness gets out of control. When this happens, the lawyer begins to feel frustrated and embarrassed. The lawyer then quarrels with the witness and asks questions without knowing the answers. How does the witness get out of control?

Lose Control

A lawyer can lose control by long questions or nonleading questions. He can also lose it if he uses phrases such as "you testified on direct examination that. . . ." Avoid such phrases at all cost.

A cross-examiner likes things neat. He wants to set the witness up for a devastating inconsistency with the witness's direct testimony. But what the witness said during direct is never relevant. What is relevant is the fact described by the witness during direct examination. Almost every time a lawyer has prefaced a cross-examination question with the words, "You testified on direct examination that . . . " the response from the witness has invariably been: "That wasn't my testimony"; "I don't recall saying that"; "You're trying to put words in my mouth"; or some such complaint. A "no" answer, where a "yes" was expected, is another frequent reply. The expected "yes" almost never occurs.

There are other reasons why you should never use those phrases. You ask the witness to repeat his direct testimony which violates command-ment seven. Since the witness has focused on the offensive statement he made on direct examination, you invite him to explain it away: "Oh yes, but what I really meant to say was . . . " This violates the eighth com-mandment: "Don't permit the witness to explain his answers." Finally, if you are afraid the jury will not recall the statement made on direct ex-amination by the witness, then you probably do not have a basis for an effective cross-examination on that statement. If you are sure the jury will recall the statement, then there is no need to repeat it.

If the witness says he did not testify to the statement or claims he can-not recall it, you could ask the court to have the reporter read it back. But, that is surely one of the most boring, time-consuming, and ineffec-tive approaches to cross-examination.

Every time a witness is able to escape a "yes" answer by claiming he does not recall or is able to force you to start a time-consuming search for the precise words he used on direct, that witness is out of control. You may also be in the middle of a quarrel with the witness and his attorney over what the witness said.

The cross-examiner is also sure to provoke arguments when he inserts a modifier or generalization even in short, leading questions.

Consider these questions asked on cross:

Q: The radio played *loudly*, did it not?

Q: You saw him *very clearly*, did you not?

Q: You *always* apply your brakes, do you not?

Q: You made a *careful* investigation, isn't that a fact?

In the first question, the word "loudly" modifies the phrase "the ra-dio played." Using the modifier provides an escape hatch for the wit-ness.

Q: The radio played loudly, did it not?

A: Oh, I wouldn't say loudly.

or

A: What do you mean by loudly?

or

A: That depends.

or

A: As a matter of fact, I could barely hear it.

If the cross-examiner had asked himself: What fact or facts make up the descriptive word "loud," he might have restructured his cross:

Q: The radio was on, was it not?

A: Yes.

Q: Had you turned it on? (Nonleading, because the answer literally doesn't matter.)

A: Yes.

Q: You turned it on to listen to it, did you not?

A: I turned it on for background music.

553

Q: You turned it on to hear it in the background, did you not?
A: Yes.
Q: And you could hear it, could you not?
A: Yes.
Q: It was loud enough to hear, was it not?
A: Yes.
Q: Louder than the street noise, wasn't it?
A: Yes.
Q: Because you could hear it, could you not?
A: Yes.
Q: Above the noise of the traffic, did you not?
A: Yes.
Q: Above the noise of the people on the street, isn't that a fact?
A: Yes.
Q: It was loud enough to hear above the traffic and the people, was it not?

Now, the jury has a word picture that the radio was playing loudly. The witness is still under control, where he belongs.

The witness on cross-examination is primed to resist giving the examiner the answer sought. The witness will invariably seize any opening to escape. Using modifiers and generalizations, before cutting off the paths of retreat, enables him to take issue with the descriptions. It also telegraphs what it is we want the witness to say. When a resistant witness knows this, he will try to say the opposite. When this happens, quarrels result. The witness is out of control and a carefully planned cross is lost.

The only time that modifiers and generalizations may be used in cross-examination is when, with short questions and plain words, the examiner has already committed the witness. At that point a jury would view a "no" answer to the question: "Isn't it fair to say then that you could see him *clearly?*" as an obvious, stubborn refusal to speak the truth.

The ninth and tenth commandments address a similar problem—trying to get too much from the witness, whether by the "one question too many" or getting him to testify to the ultimate point. How can it be avoided?

"You Testified . . ."

The "one question too many" often begins with the phrase, "You testified on direct that . . .", which should not be used. Sometimes, it uses a modifier or generalization before the examiner has pinned the witness down. But there are other times when the lawyer rushes headlong into the "one question too many." Like the twenty-game winner who knows, as soon as the pitch leaves his hand, he has just thrown a home run pitch, we shout to ourselves, "Please, let me have that one back!" Why do we do this to ourselves?

554

A cross-examiner is like a baseball pitcher. He tosses a question at the witness. If the witness gives a "yes" or other expected answer, the examiner has pitched a strike. A series of such strikes and the witness strikes out. A few bad pitches and the cross fails or, worse yet, the witness hits a home run.

A witness is like a batter facing a premier pitcher. He is powerless, and he knows it. His only hope lies in the chance that the cross-examiner will become over-confident and toss the witness a bad pitch. The cross-examiner has all the power until, motivated by his subconscious desire to show the jury just how powerful he is, he abuses it. As soon as that happens, watch out for a late-inning rally by the witness. How do you avoid abusing power?

First, recognize the problem. You can watch for signs of abuse of power when you realize the potential for abuse. Second, plan each cross-examination to evoke a "Eureka!" response from the jury—not from the witness. A "Eureka!" response is the satisfying glow when you are able to put all the pieces of the puzzle together.

We are more likely to defend vigorously any conclusion we reach ourselves. When others tell us their conclusions, we may resist and dispute the accuracy of the conclusions. It is easier and more powerful to persuade the listener with his own conclusions. Cross-examination should lead the jury to a conclusion, not confront it with one. You can avoid asking the "one question too many" by allowing the jury to reach the ultimate conclusion.

Obeying the fifth commandment by listening to the witness may lead to a "Eureka!" response in a cross-examiner. The witness, struggling to avoid a trap may say something that is better than expected.

The examiner is sometimes so involved in the cross-examination, thinking of the next question, that he misses the opportunity. Many lawyers also do not know how to handle an answer that does not fit their expectations.

Consider a cross-examination at a recent NITA Regional. The witness is Henry Fordyce, a young forest ranger who is suing two other men for having assaulted him outside a bar. The cross-examiner knows that Fordyce has been arrested twice for drunk and disorderly conduct. He hopes to show that Fordyce was so intoxicated the night of the assault that his identification of the defendants is unworthy of belief.

Q: You were with Miss Long that night, weren't you?
A: Yes.
Q: Before you picked up Miss Long, you were at Fenster's bar?
A: Yes.
Q: You were drinking at Fenster's, weren't you?
A: I don't know what you mean by "drinking."
Q: How many is more than one?
A: I don't understand your question.

Q: You had some drinks, didn't you?

A: No. I had two drinks.

Q: So you were pretty high, weren't you?

A: High, counselor? No, to the contrary.

Q: You had a lot of drinks, hadn't you?

A: If you consider two a lot.

The examiner did not apply some control techniques. But, perhaps most importantly, he did not listen when the witness handed him a golden opportunity.

Q: You were drinking at Fenster's, weren't you?

A: I don't know what you mean by "drinking."

Q: You don't know what I mean by drinking, do you?

A: No.

Q: But you know what drinking means, do you not?

A: Yes.

Q: And you knew what drinking meant in March of 1978, did you not?

A: Yes.

Q: And you were drunk and disorderly in March of 1978, were you not?

A: No.

Q: You do know what drunk means, do you not?

A: Yes.

Q: And disorderly, you know what that means, do you not?

A: Yes.

Q: And you knew the meaning of both those words on January 1, 1979, did you not?

A: Yes.

Q: And you were drunk and disorderly on that date, too, were you not?

A: I don't recall.

Q: You don't recall, do you?

A: No.

Q: But, you do recall Fenster's, do you not?

A: Yes.

Q: You recall being there, isn't that right?

A: Yes.

Q: And you recall having a drink at Fenster's, do you not?

A: Yes.

Q: In fact, you had more than one drink, did you not?

A: Yes.

Q: Now, you understand that you were drinking at Fenster's, do you not?

A: Yes.

Q: And when a person drinks, he sometimes gets drunk, does he not?

A: Yes.

Q: And sometimes disorderly as well as drunk, true?

A: Yes.

Q: And sometimes he gets so drunk, he can't *recall* being drunk and disorderly, isn't that a fact?

A: No. (The answer doesn't really matter, does it?)

In the second examination, the examiner controlled the witness throughout. He turned the witness's words about not understanding the word "drinking" against him. He got the answer he originally wanted and more. How did he accomplish this? Look at the second question. The examiner took the words the witness used in the answer which preceded it and made those words into the next question. By doing this, the examiner forced the witness to answer "yes." At the same time, he pinned the witness down to an indefensible position. Every time a witness gives an answer other than the expected "yes" or "no," he is trying to avoid being trapped. If the witness senses what it is you want him to say, he will, in all likelihood, equivocate. Whenever he does, he hands the examiner a perfect opening for just such an examination. This technique of using the witness's answer as the next question, takes away the fear of not knowing how to deal with the unexpected answer. In every instance, the witness's answer will become the next question. You no longer have to be overly concerned with the problem of thinking about what the next question will be. If you do not listen to the witness, you will not hear his exact answer. Without that, you cannot use this technique effectively.

Professor Younger says that every time a trial lawyer disobeys one of his commandments, that lawyer wishes the courtroom floor would open beneath his feet, swallow him, and hide him forever from further embarrassment. I hope that these suggestions will help keep you from that fate.

Getting More Than You Asked For: The Non-Responsive Answer

by Steven C. Day

The defendant is on trial accused of robbing and beating an old woman. Having only recently been expelled from the Hell's Angels for antisocial conduct, the defendant's usual personal appearance includes unkempt hair and a beard, a motorcycle jacket with a skull and crossbones, and steel-toed boots. Following his attorney's advice, however, today he appears in court clean shaven in a three-piece suit, looking so squeaky clean respectable that he might be confused with a life insurance agent.

The prosecution calls to the stand its star witness, the 80-year-old white-haired victim, and begins the direct examination:

Q: Mrs. White, please state your full name for the record.

A: My name is Maggy White; the same Maggy White that dirty, rotten ex-con over there beat to a pulp, kicked when she was down, and spat on. I tell you that bum has been terrorizing my neighborhood for years, and if this jury doesn't have enough guts to send him up this time, I'm going to get my gun and take care of him myself.

DEFENSE COUNSEL: Objection, your honor, move to strike the answer as nonresponsive to the question.

COURT: Objection overruled.

After deliberating for 10.2 seconds, the jury returns a verdict of guilty on all counts. Waiving the presentence report, the judge sentences the defendant to life plus 300 years at hard labor. The defendant appeals.

Assuming there is no other trial error, the conviction probably will be affirmed and the defense lawyer will end up with egg on his face.

The problem with the appeal is that the defense lawyer, who did not place the question, had no standing to ask that the answer be stricken as

The author is a member of the law firm Woodard, Blaylock, Hernandez, Pilgreen & Roth in Wichita, Kansas.

unresponsive. Worse yet, by relying exclusively on nonresponsiveness as a basis for objection, all other grounds were waived. The defendant is left to argue the generally unrewarding plain error doctrine.

To avoid this problem, the lawyer needs to understand how to deal with the nonresponsive witness.

No definition of "nonresponsive" can be any clearer than the word itself. Nevertheless, the following formal definition is available: "In evidence, an answer to a question which is irrelevant to the question asked." *Black's Law Dictionary*, 5th Ed. In practice, the issue of whether testimony is responsive is, in essence, one of fairness: Is the answer a fair attempt to meet the question? Obviously, that depends on the particular question and answer.

For example, a lengthy explanation given by a witness in response to a strict "yes or no" question would seem, at first glance, clearly unresponsive. But if the question does not fairly allow a yes or no answer, a reasonable explanation is deemed responsive. See *Saputo v. Fatla*, 25 Ill. App. 3d 775, 324 N.E.2d 34, 41-42 (1st Dist. 1975).

By the same token, of course, if the question can fairly be answered with a yes or no, an explanation should be held unresponsive. Unfortunately, this point is often overlooked by trial judges.

Whether an answer is a fair attempt to meet the question depends then in part on the fairness of the question. A straight question deserves a straight answer. An argumentative question may justify an argumentative response. See, for example, *Saputo*, at 41.

Responsiveness also is to be determined by the actual question asked, not by the question the interrogator wanted to ask. The lawyer who places a poorly worded or far-reaching question will receive no sympathy when stung by the witness. *State v. Worrey*, 322 A.2d 73, 78-79 (Maine 1974).

Determining whether particular testimony is unresponsive is, of course, only the first step; there remains the question of what to do about it. In particular, when may a lawyer have testimony stricken from the record solely because it is nonresponsive?

There is some dispute about whether even the party questioning the witness has the right to have nonresponsive testimony stricken.

One view, advocated by Wigmore, holds that nonresponsiveness standing by itself is not a ground for objection by anyone. Under this rule, where a witness gives relevant and otherwise proper testimony, it is admissible, even though not specifically asked for. If the unsolicited information contains inadmissible facts or opinions, they may be stricken and the jury instructed to disregard them; otherwise the testimony stands.

The justification offered for this rule is that to strike relevant evidence is to suppress the truth. In Wigmore's words: "No party is owner of facts in his private right. No party can impose silence on the witness called by Justice." III *Wigmore Evidence,* § 785, p. 201. (Chadbourn rev. 1970).

Unquestionably, this view has a certain poetic truth. Nevertheless, the practical business of running an adversarial trial would seem to demand a tighter rule. A frequently quoted statement of the problem appears in *United States v. Schneiderman,* 106 F. Supp. 892, 905 (S.D. Cal. 1952), where the court noted:

> While it is true that neither side has the right to suppress the truth, it is an obvious requisite of orderly procedures that each side have a voice in determining the order in which the truth shall be told. If the questioning attorney attempts to suppress the truth, opposing counsel can bring it out on the cross or re-direct examination. But to deny the questioning attorney the privilege of having non-responsive answers stricken would make the course of direct examination infinitely more difficult and render cross examination virtually useless.

Falling under the weight of such arguments, the Wigmore view has been rejected in most modern cases. Most courts hold that nonresponsive testimony should be stricken on motion by the questioning party. See *McCormick on Evidence,* § 52 at 127, n.6 (3d Ed. 1984); *Beeck v. Aquaslide 'N' Dive Corp.,* 350 N.W.2d 149, 170 (Iowa 1984); *State v. Beam,* 45 N.C. App. 82, 262 S.E.2d 350, 351-52 (1980).

It is difficult to see how this rule can do injustice. An order striking testimony as nonresponsive does not prevent the opposing lawyer from eliciting the same information in later questions; nothing need be kept from the jury permanently.

At the same time, permitting unresponsive testimony to stand hinders a party in the orderly presentation of its case. The clearest problems come in examining uncooperative or hostile witnesses.

For example, watch what happens when the defense lawyer attempts to cross-examine this arresting officer:

Q: Officer, you did not personally see who broke into the store, did you?

A: No, but I did see the defendant at 2 A.M. carrying a T.V. set and running away . . .

Q: (Interrupting) Now wait a minute, officer . . .

PROSECUTOR: Your honor, he is interrupting the witness.

COURT: Yes, the witness may explain his answer. You may continue, officer.

A: (Continuing) Yes, well, as I was saying, he ran down an alley when he saw me coming.

DEFENSE COUNSEL: Your honor, I move to strike the answer as nonresponsive.

COURT: Overruled, it was relevant.

> Q: Officer, my client told you he ran because he thought you were trying to rob him, did he not?
> A: Yes, he told me a lot of things; he told me he had a receipt for that T.V. that he never came up with.
> DEFENSE COUNSEL: Move to strike as nonresponsive.
> COURT: Overruled.

All of the unresponsive testimony was relevant. The net effect, however, was to foil any meaningful cross-examination. The defendant was effectively denied the right to confront his accuser.

Another problem with allowing unsolicited testimony to stand is the likelihood that a chronically nonresponsive witness will eventually say something prejudicial. In *Hobbs v. State*, 650 S.W.2d 449 (Tex. App. 1982), the defendant was charged with promoting obscene material. During the trial, the state's key witness, Officer Hugo, gave many unresponsive answers. Of particular concern to the appellate court was the following exchange, which occurred during cross-examination by the defense lawyer.

> Q: Diner's News, 240 Westheimer; adult book store, sells sexually explicit adult oriented literature?
> A: I've made numerous cases in there also, yes.
> Q: Kirby Street Newsstand, twenty-four hour adult newsstand, 3115 Kirby Drive. This store sells sexually explicit adult oriented literature; is that true?
> A: Yes, we arrested many people in there for homosexual acts. . . .

In reversing the defendant's conviction, the appellate court concluded that the statement tying homosexuality to adult bookstores was so prejudicial it could not be cured by the judge's instruction to the jury to disregard it. The court admonished the trial judge, in the event of a retrial, to restrain the officer's statements: "Unresponsive comments by witnesses have no place in the courtroom and tend to militate against an atmosphere which is favorable to a fair trial for an accused." *Hobbs* at 453.

Not all unresponsive answers are unfavorable to the party posing the question. For example:

> PLAINTIFF'S COUNSEL: Mrs. Brown, did you see what color the light was when the defendant's car entered the intersection?
> A: Yes, the light was red; but the defendant couldn't see it, because his view was blocked by the big whisky bottle he was drinking out of.

It is unlikely that the plaintiff's lawyer will move to strike the unresponsive portions of the answer. Can defense counsel have it stricken?

The undisputed answer is no. Only the questioner may move to strike testimony on the sole ground it is unresponsive; the opposing party lacks standing to do so. See *McCormick on Evidence,* § 52 at 127, n. 6 (3d Ed. 1984); *State v. Beam,* 45 N.C. App. 82, 262 S.E. 2d 350, 351-352 (1980); *Cardenas v. Peterson Bean Co.,* 180 Neb. 605, 144 N.W.2d 154, 158 (1966).

The requirement that witnesses be responsive is, after all, chiefly designed to protect the procedural rights of the interrogator. To allow opposing counsel to attack an answer on the basis of nonresponsiveness would undermine the rights of the interrogator by interfering with the examination.

If the nonresponsive testimony is also incompetent (for example, if it constitutes hearsay, opinion, or prior crimes), it must, of course, be stricken on motion of any aggrieved party, regardless of who placed the question. Likewise, a statement that a witness volunteers with no question pending should be stricken on the motion of any party, or even by the court on its own motion. See *Cardenas v. Peterson Bean Co.,* 180 Neb. 605, 144 N.W.2d 154, 158 (1966).

But the issue of whether an otherwise proper answer is strictly responsive to a pending question is solely one for the questioner.

Note that we are dealing here only with the right to strike testimony. Even a noninterrogating party is free to ask the court to admonish a persistently nonresponsive witness to be responsive in the future. Unquestionably, a trial judge's broad discretion over the manner in which testimony is received extends to requiring a witness to be responsive, even absent an objection. Thus a nonquestioning party is not without remedy against an uncontrolled witness.

When an improper answer is given to a proper question, the motion to strike provides the remedy. *State v. Childs,* 198 Kan. 4, 422 P.2d 898, 905 (1967). In theory, when the judge sustains the motion and instructs the jury to disregard the offensive testimony, all error is cured. See 4 *Jones on Evidence,* Chap. 28.5 p. 285 (6th Ed. 1972).

Practice is something else, however, and most trial lawyers believe that prejudice often remains despite the court's admonition. Nevertheless, once a nonresponsive comment is made, an order striking it from the record is the only remedy possible, except in the rare instances when a mistrial is justified.

This is not to say that a motion to strike should be advanced every time a witness's answer is unresponsive. Tactical as well as legal considerations come into play.

Whenever the interrogating lawyer moves to strike an answer, the flow of the examination is interrupted. The opposing lawyer is given an opportunity to speak and perhaps to key the witness. Too, some judges are extremely tolerant of nonresponsive witnesses and may overrule the motion. If this happens, the witness will be even harder to control.

Consideration also must be given to the jury's reaction. Purely technical motions to strike may be perceived as being harassing and as generating sympathy for an adverse witness.

As a practical matter, it is better to save the formal motion to strike for testimony that is prejudicial. Garden variety nonresponsiveness usually can be handled without seeking help from the court but instead by politely but firmly requesting the witness not to volunteer information and to answer only the questions asked. If the unresponsiveness continues, then consider a formal motion.

Although tactical considerations are important, they must not prevent the lawyer from moving to strike when necessary. Remember that unresponsive comments, no matter how improper, will remain in evidence, insulated from appellate review, unless the motion is made.

In addition, the questioner who fails to have a nonresponsive answer stricken will be held accountable for the answer to the same extent as if it had been responsive. For example, if the nonresponsive testimony opens up an area of inquiry otherwise foreclosed, the opposing lawyer is free to explore the new area. See *Moschetti v. City of Tucson*, 9 Ariz. App. 108, 449 P.2d 945, 950 (1969).

Assume, for example, that a wrongful death action is being tried. The plaintiff is a 55-year-old businessman whose wife of 30 years was killed in a car wreck. Just three months after his wife's death, the plaintiff was remarried to an attractive young heiress.

For obvious reasons, the plaintiff's lawyer would prefer that the jury not be told of the new wife, and the law supports this result, since most courts hold that evidence of the surviving spouse's remarriage is inadmissible in a wrongful death case when offered in mitigation of damages.

But evidence inadmissible for one purpose may become admissible for another. Thus, when the plaintiff calls his brother to give testimony about damages, this is what happens:

> PLAINTIFF'S COUNSEL: Sir, tell the jury how your brother reacted when he heard the news of his wife's death.
>
> A: He was crushed. He never got over it. To this very day, he is a lost and empty man, totally alone.

This testimony will probably have the effect of opening the door to evidence of the plaintiff's remarriage. Very likely the defense will be allowed to cross-examine the plaintiff's brother about the new marriage—not to show mitigation of damages, but to impeach his testimony about the extent of the plaintiff's present loneliness.

But the plaintiff's lawyer has a remedy. Because the brother's comments were nonresponsive, they will be stricken if the lawyer immediately makes a motion. Once the comments are stricken, the record will be clear of any basis for impeachment, and the defendant again will be precluded from mentioning the new wife.

In making a motion to strike, a few procedural rules should be kept strictly in mind. First, the words ''move to strike'' should be treated as if they were magic. Some courts have held that merely objecting to an answer without making a specific motion is insufficient to preserve any issue for appeal. See, for example, *State v. Chatman*, 308 N.C. 169, 301 S.E.2d 71, 77 (1983). The better rule allows a party to appeal prejudicial testimony that has been objected to, however the objection is phrased. *McCormick on Evidence*, § 52 at 127. Still, the safer practice is to use the proper form.

The motion to strike, like an objection, must be particularized. When only part of the answer is nonresponsive, the motion to strike should be directed only against the nonresponsive portion of the answer. If the motion attacks the entire answer when only a portion is objectionable, the motion properly may be overruled. See, for example, *State v. Pope*, 287 N.C. 505, 215 S.E.2d 139, 144 (1975). All substantive grounds for objecting also must be particularized in the motion. Moving simply to strike an answer as nonresponsive will not, by itself, preserve for appeal any other specific complaint. *State v. Griffin*, 438 A.2d 1283, 1284 (Me. 1982). If the answer contains nonresponsive hearsay, the motion to strike should be based both on nonresponsiveness and on hearsay. If the hearsay is overlooked, it will be lost as a basis for appeal, subject only to the unforgiving plain error doctrine.

Cross-Examination: Torching the Calendar

by Daniel H. Skerritt

I recently reviewed a transcript of a trial to assist our appellate lawyers in brief preparation. As I read the transcript of the opponent's cross-examination of the first and most important witness, I noted that all the right techniques were in place: short leading questions, lawyer in control, snappy give-and-take.

But while this cross-examination was technically correct, the first ten minutes were a monument to insignificance. They were wasted on preliminaries.

I puzzled for a moment about why this lawyer—an otherwise experienced and able advocate—fell into this trap. The answer came quickly. The cross-examination was organized to track the chronology of the complex business dispute we were trying.

A complex case demands extraordinary organization. But even for less complex cases, chronology is a seductive approach to organizing the files. The exhibits are often arranged by date. Discovery deposition questions are often organized to cover each event as it unravels. A legal assistant or associate usually has summarized those depositions, and they become the starting point for pretrial preparation for witness cross-examination.

The other side usually adds to this seductive appeal by having the witness on direct present the facts in a logical, organized fashion—in other words, chronologically.

In business cases, the parties normally start out as friends or at least as suitors. Both sides expect and want to profit from dealing with the other. The lawsuit arises because friction develops later in the relationship.

Following this chronology is a mistake. Cross-examination should al-

---

The author is a partner in Lindsay, Hart, Neil & Weigler in Portland, Oregon.

ways be organized by themes. It should *never* be driven by the calendar or mere sequence. The reasons are somewhat obvious, but experience teaches that we need constant reminders of some basic points. Here are some of the avoidable problems caused by chronological cross-examination.

- Preliminary events seldom involve key issues in a case. An important witness has just completed direct. The jury is anxious for cross to begin. The witness is nervous. The lawyer clears his throat and asks, ''When did you say you first met the defendant?''

Thud.

Lawyers often fail to realize that the direct testimony has already established the foundation for cross-examination. The trial lawyer is free to make the first 30 seconds of cross-examination count—and failure to do so is a major sin.

- Preliminary events are remote in time. Even good issues are difficult to use effectively against a witness who is schooled to remind you (and the jury), ''You are asking me about something that took place five years ago.'' Never forget that witnesses follow the coaching of their lawyers most carefully at the beginning of their testimony. If the point is unimportant, the bad memory of the witness will be excused. On major subjects, by contrast, the jury will expect the witness to give a more forthright answer. The trial lawyer can ensure that the excuse of fading memory is unconvincing for the first line of questions by selecting a significant topic.
- The witness reinforces damaging testimony. Any examination that is time-structured leads to one of the great sins in cross-examination—the witness is allowed to restate damaging testimony. Although this danger always exists, it seems pointless to invite trouble by cross that tracks the same outline your opponent used in direct testimony.
- Zingers get buried. Jury service can be a numbing experience. Lawyers forget that the jurors must suffer through a great deal of dead time during jury selection or court hearings on motions. As a result, the jurors are anxious for some action, and they are programmed to expect it to come at once upon the shift from direct to cross. Do not disappoint them.

  Unless examination is done by themes—rather than sequence—the judge and jury will be anesthetized by the time a telling issue surfaces. If you grab the jurors' attention at once, they will continue to pay attention, hoping for a little more excitement. At the same time, once the jurors lose interest in your examination, you may never regain their attention.
- Ending on a low note. In the typical business case, the final phases of a transaction often will be as noncritical as the initial events. The serious problems that led to the lawsuit may have festered for

some time before the plaintiff became sufficiently angry to take action. Even more likely, the relationship may have ended with a whimper rather than a pivotal confrontation. Just because an event was the last episode in a business transaction does not make it worthy of selection as the final matter to cover in your cross-examination. The last question always should play to an important theme. Otherwise, the witness gains the advantage: the lawyer appears to end flat or pester the witness about an event the jury regards as unimportant.

- Witness control suffers. Even the most seasoned or articulate witness has a small anxiety attack at the onset of cross-examination. At this point a witness is vulnerable, and the trial lawyer should exploit this vulnerability. Speaking from experience, I was surprised to find that I was nervous when cross-examined as a witness in a recent trial. Yet, I had the opportunity to settle down before any significant issues surfaced.

A preliminary or foundation question cedes the initial psychological advantage to the witness. The witness returns to familiar turf—the place where his or her own lawyer began. The opportunity to at once challenge the witness with a difficult question is lost.

An example from a recent trial demonstrates the good fortune that may result from an immediate frontal attack. An issue in the case was whether plaintiff, Powers Medical Systems, had funded research work of another company, EMIT, which was run by a Mr. Yukl. This was the very first exchange:

Q: Mr. Katz, I'm not sure I heard you right. Did you testify that Powers Medical Systems did not fund or provide any research and development funding for EMIT in 1981?

A: That's the way I testified. I'm not sure whether they did or not. I don't believe they did. I may be wrong on that point, but that's my belief.

Q: Well, isn't it a fact that the [EMIT] facility that Mr. Yukl had that you visited in June was in fact leased by and paid for by Powers Medical Systems as a tenant?

A: That may be. I don't know that.

Q: Isn't it a fact that Mr. Yukl and his assistant, Mr. Vineyard, were on the payroll of Powers Medical Systems through all of that period?

A: That may well be.

A witness who gets stung at the very outset like this tends to give up more than he or she should in the remaining examination. The same witness would be damaged less, both as to credibility and self-confidence, had this exchange occurred even shortly after answering several unimportant questions.

There is a way to prepare for cross-examination that helps avoid the

567

time trap. Develop each examination based on issues or themes, and place the examination outline in three-ring binders. The key is to start with a new page for each separate topic. That page then begins with a statement of the point to be established, followed by suggested questions with annotations for impeachment from depositions or exhibits.

The theme approach allows the lawyer to refer to sequential documents or prior deposition summaries during initial pretrial preparation. The themes then may be shifted and reorganized several times, even at the last minute. This system provides a strong basis for comparing the strength of various issues. After a few run-throughs, the two best themes for cross-examination usually become obvious. Regardless of your organization, one of these themes should be used immediately when your opponent completes direct examination. The other should be saved as your exit for the witness.

Ending cross-examination with an insignificant exchange with a witness is a sure sign of poor organization, but your trial will suffer even worse results if you end on a high note for the adverse witness.

Any experienced trial lawyer has war stories of cross-examination gone awry. Even with good organization and thorough discovery, real live witnesses often wound the cross-examiner. The lawyer, however, should never lose the very last exchange with a witness. There are two ways to end at the right spot. The first—and most difficult to enforce—is to stop, even with more questions in hand, if you have great success. Do not give the opposition a free round after a knockout punch so the witness can regain the jury's respect. Indeed, it is wise to end with an even less than spectacular result (not great, but good) if your remaining salvos will yield no better results.

In most trials, the witness is rarely destroyed by a clever lawyer. Yet even the most difficult witness should be maneuvered to the losing end of a final confrontation.

The second way to ensure a proper exit point from cross-examination is to organize for a fail-safe completion. Locate the best point you can use against a witness from a prior deposition or an exhibit, and press the question. The witness is left in a no-win situation for the conclusion of the examination. Forcefully repeat your final point in that last leading question. If the final premise is admitted, you can say, ''Thank you, that's all I have,'' in a way that lets the jury know you just scored a point for the good guys. If the witness denies your point, then your final thrust will be to restate the favorable evidence from the deposition or exhibit. As an added benefit, you also will remind the jury through your impeachment that this witness lacks credibility.

One final point—when reshuffling the witness notebook during the final preparation for examination, toss out the less important items. Even when chronology is jilted as the wrong approach for organization, and cross is organized by themes, the zingers in the middle still get buried if the jury must wait too long between the initial challenge and the final thrust.

Forget chronology on cross-examination. Start strong. End stronger. And in the middle, limit your time to important themes that help your case.

Cross-Examination: Using Depositions at Trial

by Lansing R. Palmer

A corporate director is on the witness stand. He and his fellow directors voted in favor of making a successful tender offer for a company that turned out to be worthless. They are now defendants in an action by their shareholders, who assert that the tender offer resulted in a waste of corporate assets. The witness is trying to show that his vote to acquire the target company was reasonable. He has testified that before voting he examined the target company's financial statements. The plaintiffs' lawyer is now cross-examining:

Q: Are you testifying today that you saw financial statements of the target company prior to your vote on September 4, 1974?

A: Yes.

Q: Sir, do you recall your deposition being taken in this case on March 10, 1975 at my office?

A: Yes.

Q: You were asked certain questions under oath at that time, were you not?

A: Yes, sir.

Q: You were represented by counsel at that deposition, were you not?

A: Yes.

Q: Now, sir, I am going to read to you beginning at line 4 on page 38 of your deposition:

'Q: The records of the corporation reflect that it acquired 70 percent of the stock. Do you recall if prior to the acquisition of that stock you received any financial statements of the target corporation?

The author practices law in New York City.

'A: I personally did not.

'Q: Do you recall if any were made available to you?

'A: Not to me.

'Q: Did you have any knowledge of the worth, the financial worth of this company at the time the Board voted to acquire its stock?

'A: No, I had no knowledge of that.'

Q: Now, sir, is this a reflection of what your recollection was as of March 10, 1975?

A: That is correct.

Q: Isn't it a fact that you did not even look at any of the financial statements of this company before you voted approval to acquire its stock?

A: Look, I reviewed all these things. I was asked questions cold at that time and I, as I have told you here, I glanced at them. I did not review them or analyze them.

Plaintiffs' counsel has destroyed the witness's credibility by demonstrating that he said one thing at his deposition and the opposite at trial. Neither statement has been elicited to prove whether or not the defendant examined the target company's financial statements. The mere fact that of the two statements one must have been incorrect is sufficient.

A Valuable Aid

Deposition testimony can be a valuable aid to the cross-examiner at trial, both to impeach the testimony of a witness and to prove the cross-examiner's case. Rule 32(a)(1) of the Federal Rules of Civil Procedure permits a deposition to be used to contradict or impeach the testimony of a witness. Confronting a witness with an inconsistent statement contained in a deposition weakens his credibility in the mind of the jury or judge and highlights contradictory statements that would otherwise be buried in the trial record. It can also raise doubts about the witness's testimony on other matters and may upset him and lead to additional contradictions or admissions.

In some cases, a plaintiff's witnesses may consist entirely of parties who are defendants, each of whom can be examined—actually cross-examined—as an adverse witness under Rule 611(c) of the Federal Rules of Evidence. Suppose some or all of the defendants have been deposed at least once and that the transcripts contained inconsistent statements and admissions. At trial, the plaintiffs lawyer could use deposition testimony both to impeach the defendants' testimony and as evidence of his case-in-chief. It might also develop that material in a defendant's deposition could be more favorable to the plaintiffs case than the contradictory testimony given at trial. When that occurs, the plaintiff can introduce the more favorable deposition testimony under Rule 32(a)(2) of the Federal Rules of Civil Procedure.

Multiple Uses

Also, the deposition testimony of defendant A could be used to impeach A's testimony at trial and also as substantive evidence against A under Rule 801(d)(1)(A) of the Federal Rules of Evidence. In addition, A's deposition testimony could be used on the cross-examination of defendants B, C and D to impeach their credibility by confronting them with statements made by A that contradicted their trial testimony.

Such effective use of depositions at trial depends on thorough preparation, which must begin before the pretrial deposition itself. When you are struggling to learn facts during the early stages of a case, it is easy to overlook that your questions and his answers may be read back to a witness in a courtroom before a jury many years later. Depositions of a party are particularly important, since every word a party utters not only may be used to impeach his trial testimony but also may qualify as an admission, defined in Rule 802(d)(2) of the Federal Rules of Evidence as a statement "offered against a party [as] his own statement, in either his individual or representative capacity. . . ." As defined in this rule, these statements are not hearsay, and one must not underestimate the rule's importance.

From the outset of discovery, you should consider the effect on the jury of the presence or lack of a subpoena for a deposition—the lack perhaps suggesting undue cooperation by the witness with examining counsel. More importantly, you should not waive the requirement that the witness sign his deposition. If he has had an opportunity to review the transcript to correct errors and has signed his deposition, he can hardly be heard at trial to complain that the stenographer misheard his prior statements.

It is important to prepare for the examination of a witness at a deposition as thoroughly and orderly as for trial. Prepare an outline of the areas about which you will examine the witness. Ask clear questions that require clear answers. Remember that your questions and the witness's answers may become part of a trial record. If the deposition transcript is confusing, the effect of confronting a witness on cross-examination at trial may be completely lost on the jury.

Upon learning the witness's version of the facts, make sure he commits himself to that position. If the transcript is full of equivocation, it cannot help you at trial and may harm your case. If, in a rambling deposition transcript, you find a nugget with which to confront the witness at trial, be sure he has been consistent on the point within the deposition itself. If not, your opponent will use Rule 106 of the Federal Rules of Evidence to force you to introduce any part of the deposition that would eliminate the contradiction you sought to raise.

Decide on Use

You must decide before trial which portions of deposition testimony to use as evidence for your case-in-chief and which portions to reserve

572

for cross-examination. Sometimes an admission made by a party opponent at his deposition is the only evidence available to establish an essential element of your case. When this is true, you must introduce the admission into evidence as part of your proof. Often, however, you will have other evidence to establish your case and can reserve some deposition material for impeachment on cross-examination.

Creating a system to put your hands instantly on prior inconsistent statements contained in deposition testimony is another essential part of pretrial preparation. In a case with relatively simple issues and facts, an index to deposition testimony may be sufficient. In a complex case you should prepare summaries of the depositions as well as an index to the testimony. These digests will serve as valuable pretrial aids and will be useful reference sources during the trial itself, when you may only have a lunch break to dig out contradictory testimony. In recent years, the computer has become a valuable aid in large cases for indexing deposition testimony and for document retrieval. Vendors of computer systems estimate that the need to store 15,000 to 20,000 pages may be considered an economic threshold for use of a computer-based system. Whatever method you prefer, you must have available at trial the resources to find prior inconsistent testimony with a minimum of time and effort. Few things impress a jury less than having to wait while trial counsel thumbs through deposition transcripts looking for testimony, and of course this gives the witness valuable time to consider his answers and recall his prior testimony.

If a witness has been properly prepared for trial, he will have reviewed the testimony given at any pretrial deposition. While this reduces the chance of surprising him with a contradictory statement at trial, it increases the damage to his credibility if an inconsistent statement can be used.

If you think you might be able to impeach a witness's testimony, you must get him to take a firm position on the issue at trial. Lead him into an unequivocal position with no room to explain away his prior inconsistent testimony. This may require that you postpone the confrontation during your cross-examination until you are as certain as you can be that the witness's position at trial is clear to the jury. You should balance the need to pin down the witness against the risk that an alert witness might equivocate if he thinks you are trying to commit him unalterably to a position. Once he is so committed that he cannot easily change his testimony without impairing his credibility, confront him with his prior inconsistent statement.

Successful impeachment can be illustrated by the hypothetical case against the company directors referred to at the beginning of this article. At issue is the acquisition (for an allegedly grossly inflated price) of a company in which one of the defendants had a direct and indirect financial interest. At trial, the directors argue that the acquisition price was

573

reasonable and that there had been full disclosure to the board of the acquiring company of the director's interest in the transaction. It is crucial to the defendant's case that they obtained full disclosure. Otherwise, they could not avail themselves of a defense that they exercised due care in making a business judgment to take over the company. One of the directors testifies on cross-examination:

Q: Did you know that the X partnership was a vendor to the corporation with respect to a portion of the shares which were to be purchased by the corporation?

A: I knew at that time.

Q: Did you also know that your fellow director, Mr. Y, was an investor and limited partner of X?

A: I was told so.

Q: Now, I am going to call your attention to the deposition you gave on April 26, 1974 and specifically to line 16 on page 39 and thereafter. Page 39, line 16:

'Q: Did you know that one of the parties that sold a significant portion of the company's stock to your corporation was the X partnership?

'A: No, I did not know that.

'Q: Did you know that Mr. Y had a financial interest in the X partnership?

'A: No I did not. I am learning all kinds of interesting things.

'Q: Did you know that prior to my telling you this at this time?

'A: No, I did not know that.

'Q: To your knowledge, there were no representations made to you which indicated that Mr. Y indeed had an interest in the X partership?

'A: No.'

Q: Now, is your testimony today correct under oath or was your testimony correct in April of 1974?

A: I knew at that time. I had forgotten it.

Q: Why did you give contrary testimony under oath April 26, 1974?

A: Sir, I gave you the best testimony I could at that time, and I am doing the best I can today.

Devastating Tool

This exchange illustrates how prior inconsistent statements taken under oath, with proper preparation and use, can be a devastating tool in impairing a witness's credibility. Sometimes witnesses forget, and sometimes they lie. Successful impeachment can support either inference.

At an appropriate point, you must impress the jurors with the solemnity of a deposition. They may be vaguely aware that it is a written statement of questions and answers, but not that it was taken under oath, that all parties had a right to be present, that the deponent's counsel had the right to cross-examine or that the witness had the opportunity to review and correct the transcript of his deposition before testifying at trial. You may not want to interrupt the flow or dull the impact of cross-examination to explain these facts to the jury before you use the witness's deposition. To avoid this, you may prefer to impeach the witness first, then inform the jury of the circumstances surrounding the taking of the deposition. I prefer to use a series of questions and answers to avoid an objection that counsel is giving a lecture to the jury and to establish a pattern of questions to which the witness must respond by saying yes:

Q: Was your deposition taken in this case on May 12, 1976?
A: Yes.
Q: Were you represented by counsel at that deposition?
A: Yes.
Q: Was your testimony given under oath at that deposition?
A: Yes.

If the witness has made corrections in his deposition transcript or has signed it, I might also ask:

Q: Were you given the opportunity to read the transcript of your deposition and to make corrections?
A: Yes.
Q: Did you read it?
A: Yes.
Q: Did you make any corrections in your testimony?
A: Yes.
Q: Did you sign your deposition before a notary public?
A: Yes.

There are at least two ways to confront the witness with his prior contradictory statement. If you believe the witness is being dishonest, it is usually advisable to make the confrontation dramatic. But if the witness is honest but confused or forgetful, it is better to use the prior statement to help him reconstruct his testimony to help your case. Dramatically confronting the confused witness only alienates a jury and will tend to alienate and further confuse the witness.

One principal advantage of impeaching with depositions, rather than other forms of inconsistent statements, is the ease with which a foundation can be laid. The deposition was taken as part of the trial preparation and it has been available to opposing counsel. In addition, the witness need not have a copy before him during the cross-examination. The Fifth Circuit, perhaps presaging the adoption of the Federal Rules of Evidence, held in *Wright Root Beer of New Orleans v. Dr. Pepper Co.*, 414 F.2d 887, 891 (5th Cir. 1969) that among other things it was reversible error to force the cross-examiner to permit the witness to have a copy of his deposition during the cross-examination. Now, Rule 613(a) of the Federal Rules of Evidence provides:

In examining a witness concerning a prior statement made by him, whether written or not, the statement need not be shown nor its contents disclosed to him at that time, but on request the same shall be shown or disclosed to opposing counsel.

The first object of using a prior inconsistent statement to impeach the credibility of a witness's testimony is to destroy it. The cross-examiner normally does not care if the jury disbelieves both versions of fact, as long as it determines that the testimony is not credible. There will be times, however, when you will want the jury to consider an impeaching statement as proof of the facts to which the witness testified in the deposition. As already noted, this poses little problem when the statement sought to be admitted is that of a party. Traditionally, the out-of-court statements of non-party witnesses have been considered hearsay and thus not admissible to prove the truth of the matters contained in the statement. See, e.g., *E.L. Cheeney Co. v. Gates,* 346 F.2d 197, 204 (5th Cir. 1965); J. MOORE, FEDERAL PRACTICE § 32.03 (2d ed. 1975).

The orthodox rule rejects these statements as substantive evidence "because their value depends on the credit of a declarant who was not under oath . . . and exposed to cross-examination at the time he made his statement." 4 WEINSTEIN'S EVIDENCE § 801(d)(1)[01] (1975). In a deposition, however, the prior inconsistent statement is made under oath and the right of contemporaneous cross-examination is available. As the Supreme Court has recognized, prior testimony "under oath and signed . . . would have afforded protection against mistakes in hearing, mistakes in memory, mistakes in transcription. Statements made under those conditions would have an important safeguard—the fear of prosecution for perjury." *Bridges v. Wixon,* 326 U.S. 135, 153 (1954).

This exception is now codified in the Federal Rules of Evidence. Rule 801(d)(1) provides that a prior statement is not hearsay if

[t]he declarant testified at the trial or hearing and is subject to cross-examination concerning the statement, and the statement is (A) inconsistent with his testimony, and was given under oath subject to the penalty of perjury at a . . . deposition . . .

Accordingly, the use of deposition on cross-examination at trial is not limited to aiding counsel in dramatically confronting a witness with prior testimony to shatter his credibility. Depositions may also contain essential statements of facts that may be admissible as substantive proof of key portions of the cross-examiner's case. This use is often overlooked by plaintiffs and defendants, especially during the early, pretrial stages of a case. As with so many other elements of trial practice, the lawyer who is better prepared in this respect will often have an advantage over his adversary. A pretrial deposition can be an invaluable tool for the trial lawyer on cross-examination, and like all tools, it must be fashioned adequately to do the job.

576

Questioning
the Adverse Witness

by Gerry Spence

At the Section's annual meeting in Chicago in November 1982, Gerry Spence, of Wyoming, conducted a mock trial. In the problem, a newspaper was sued for libeling a public official through false accusations of kickbacks. Mr. Spence, representing the defamed official, examined the newspaper reporter who wrote the libelous story and explained the purpose of his examination.

SUMMARY OF FACTS

The case of *Morton Winslow v. Owenville Herald Examiner and Richard Sweitzer,* filed by the mayor of Owenville, arises out of an article printed by the *Herald Examiner* in October 1980. The article was published before the mayoral election. The pertinent portion of the article was as follows:

MAYOR CHARGED IN KICKBACK SCHEME

The re-election aspirations of Mayor Winslow have been harmed by widely circulated rumors that all was not right with the bidding procedures to begin construction last year of the new city hall. Although no official action has been taken, the *Herald Examiner* has learned that at least one witness has told the district attorney's office that Winslow solicited and received payments from contractors who were ultimately awarded the subcontracts for construction work on the city hall.

According to one source, Winslow was seen at his lake cabin receiving $20,000 in cash from one mechanical contractor and $15,000 from a representative of another company. According to the source, the money was later deposited into a bank account us-

---

The author is a member of the Jackson, Wyoming, firm of Spence, Moriarty & Schuster.

ing an alias name and has been drawn out periodically to pay campaign expenses for Mayor Winslow.

The source maintains that the mayor gave to contractors information regarding other bids on the job and agreed to seek approval of later overruns from the contractors, thus increasing actual costs to the city.

The spokesman for the mayor's office denied the allegations, stating that the denial was "official" but Mayor Winslow refused to comment on the charges, stating that he "would not dignify them with a response." However, the *Herald Examiner* source stated in part that "I heard Mayor Winslow tell his chief deputy that one of the contractors was too cheap to pay more than $15,000 and that it would cost him when time came for cost overruns." The mayor's chief deputy, Kevin Pillizio, was out of the country on vacation and was unavailable for comment.

Mayor Winslow also presented the newspaper with a statement from the district attorney's office, saying that the district attorney did not intend to present charges to the grand jury. The *Herald Examiner* printed another story two days later stating that the mayor "had been accused" of taking kickbacks and that the mayor had denied the charges. Winslow was reelected and subsequently brought suit.

Discovery disclosed that, in fact, the only source for the story was Brenda Hazelton, a resident of Owenville who had approached the newspaper two weeks before the election and volunteered that she had information "that the public should know about the mayor." Mr. Sweitzer, the reporter, interviewed Miss Hazelton on two occasions. She provided Mr. Sweitzer with a written statement.

Miss Hazelton was the jilted girlfriend of the mayor. Her motive for the false statement to the reporter was to get even with the mayor. Mr. Sweitzer admitted in his deposition that he "was not able to do as thorough a job of checking as he would have liked," but he stated that he "had no reason to doubt the veracity of Miss Hazelton." He did verify that Miss Hazelton had been on the city payroll from February 1979 to May 1980 as an administrative assistant to the mayor. Sweitzer had also called the district attorney's office to attempt to see if Miss Hazelton had made a statement to them but had been told by the district attorney's secretary that the office "could not, as a matter of policy, comment on whether any matter not presented to a grand jury was being investigated."

From public records available through the city, the plaintiff presented evidence at trial to show that there were in fact no claims for construction cost overruns from the mechanical contractor or from any cement contractor or subcontractor on the city hall, which was completed in December 1979.

STATEMENT OF BRENDA HAZELTON

My name is Brenda Hazelton and I am making this statement to Mr. Sweitzer and to the *Owenville Herald Examiner* of my own free will and with full knowledge of the facts given to the newspaper. I believe that it is important that the public know the truth about Mayor Winslow and the people with whom he is involved at city hall. I was personal secretary to Mayor Winslow for a period of 16 months during 1979 and 1980, ending in May 1980. On several occasions, I observed Mayor Winslow with expensive items of jewelry or stereo equipment, which he jokingly told me ''not to talk about or the Internal Revenue Service would wonder how he was able to afford them on his salary.''

I know that in the summer of 1979, the mayor met with at least two subcontractors on the city hall construction job at his lake house outside of the city. On each occasion, I was at the lake house working with the mayor and was told to go to another part of the house when the mayor met with the visitor. However, I did recognize one of the contractors as the cement contractor on the city hall job, and the other gentleman, who I did not recognize, arrived at the lake house in a pickup truck marked ''Western Mechanical Contractors.''

Following one of the meetings, I was given an envelope by the mayor and asked to take the envelope to the mayor's house and to place it in the safe in his study. While out of the mayor's presence, I opened that envelope and saw that it contained $20,000 in cash. Although I did not see any money on the other occasion, I overheard the mayor tell his deputy that the contractor had only paid $15,000, instead of $20,000, and that this wouldn't help him get the overruns he wanted on the jobs.

Both of the meetings occurred before the awarding of bids for the city hall construction. Both men who met with the mayor were awarded construction jobs on the city hall project. I reported this matter to the district attorney's office in June 1980 and gave them a statement as to what happened.

I certify to the *Herald Examiner* that the statements contained herein are true and that I have no reason to harm Mayor Winslow or to make false statements about him.

/S/ BRENDA HAZELTON

EXAMINATION OF RICHARD SWEITZER

MR. SPENCE: A good cross-examination should have a beginning and an end, should have a purpose, should have a direction, should tell a story. Let me briefly show you the story I would tell with this witness up to the point where we start. Let's believe that we had asked him this series of questions, that you're a journalist? Yes. You believe in freedom of

579

speech? Yes. It's an important right? Yes. It's guaranteed to us under the Constitution? Yes. Why is it an important right? Because democracy requires it. Democracy can't work without a free press, can it? No. People of the press think it's one of the most important rights of all. Is that true? Yes. It's as important as freedom of religion? Yes. It's as important as not having to testify against yourself? Yes. And you belong to a whole series of organizations, don't you, Mr. Reporter, that protect that First Amendment right? Yes. Your organization hires lawyers? Yes it does. These lawyers file briefs in the courts and the greatest courts in this country and the Supreme Court of the United States to protect that right, isn't that true? Yes.

My point is that you need to lay a foundation as to what we're talking about, what makes this right important, why we're all upset about freedom of the press. The next question is that you agree that no right can exist without a corresponding duty. If you have a right, do you think you may also have a duty? We have a right, for example, to drive down a street and you agree that we have a duty not to run over people carelessly? Yes. We have a duty not to be reckless? Yes. These ideas of what he knows, what he understands to be his duty before we ever get to dealing with the issue at hand, I think, are important. So it isn't enough to say I have a right. I must also say I have a duty not to exercise that right recklessly to injure someone. You would agree with that, wouldn't you? Yes.

Now when people of the press preach the right to freedom of the press—and you do preach the right to freedom of the press, don't you? and he says yes—then you would also say, well, do you also preach what your duty is? Do you know what your duty was on October, whenever the date was, 1980, when you wrote the mayor's kickback story? What exactly did you think your duty was to the mayor when you wrote that story?

Now that's the first open-ended question that I have asked. Please note that my questions tell a story, tell the defense or the plaintiff's side of the story. They are properly leading and it really doesn't make too damn much difference how he answers the questions, so you are not afraid. You've written them all down. You feel nice and cocky, like I feel, because the questions are all there.

Now we turn to the facts. You had a duty not to be reckless when you wrote a story that could destroy a man, isn't that true? You had a duty not to be reckless, didn't you? And you knew that the reckless story might destroy a man, didn't you? You have attended seminars, workshops, in which this matter was discussed, haven't you? And your editors have talked to you about being careful not to destroy innocent people, isn't that true? You can understand that you can kill a man with words, in effect—kill his heart, kill his reputation, destroy his pride with words just as easy as you can kill a man with a gun. You would agree that next to life there is nothing more valuable to an honorable man than his reputation? You knew that at the time, didn't you? You knew on October 20 you couldn't be reckless with your right to a free press any more than anyone can be reckless with a gun?

Now we're starting to develop a picture. It's all right if there are objections. What we want to do is to create word pictures, word images, because of what this thing is all about—the power of the press—as powerful as it is to shoot somebody with a gun. Did you ever hold a public office? Do you recognize that? Or do you believe that all politicians are dishonest, and therefore open game and that you can therefore say anything that you want to say about them?

Do you know that on October 20, 1980, Mayor Winslow's reputation may have been his most cherished possession? He'll say, "Well, I didn't know." Well, then, could you make room for that possibility—that there is a man on this earth whose reputation may be his most cherished possession? You don't have much respect for gossip and rumormongers, do you? Objection. Overruled. Now, Mr. Sweitzer, if I came to you with a rumor about your editor-in-chief, saying he was a crook and he took nasty payoffs from the opponents of Mayor Winslow to write a false, libelous story about Mayor Winslow, you wouldn't put that in the paper, would you? You would use your discretion, you would use your judgment? It's true you have to use your discretion, your judgment, and so forth? You have a duty not to print groundless rumors.

So when Miss Hazelton came to you with this infamous and dastardly story, she handed you, so to speak, a loaded gun, isn't that true? She handed you what you could use to destroy a man, isn't that true? And you knew that and understood that, didn't you? Now you had the choice, didn't you, Mr. Reporter, of either pointing this loaded gun and firing at Mayor Winslow, or not? The choice was up to you, and you chose to write the story. You chose to point the gun. You chose to pull the trigger, didn't you?

That is the kind of background that I would have constructed. With objections it might have taken all morning. But with objections, by the time that we worked through it, a question at a time, an objection at a time, the story would have gotten fully and completely told. Not once but twenty times, so that by the time you get to this point, the basic ideas and ideals and the propositions that are involved have been well established. It becomes, I think, the tactic of the defendant at this point to decide whether he is going to engage me all morning and get that story fully told or whether he is going to say let's get it told as quickly as possible. That takes us to the examination on the facts.

MR. SPENCE: Mr. Witness, you agree, don't you, that you had a duty to be fair?

REPORTER: Yes.

Q: And you had a duty not to make false implications, didn't you?

First of all, you knew that the only source you had was Miss Hazelton, isn't that right?

A: I had other information.

Q: The only source. You understand the word source. The only source you had was Miss Hazelton. Isn't that true?

A: Yes.

Q: And you didn't know her, did you?

A: I knew of her.

Q: You didn't know her, did you?

A: I knew of her.

Q: You hadn't met her before, had you?

A: No.

Q: And when she came in, and she said I have some information and my name is Miss Hazelton, did you say well, Miss Hazelton, before we take stories that are going to be published to thousands, tens of thousands of people in our paper, we need to verify some things? Could you first of all give me a little identification? Did you do that?

A: No.

Q: And you know, even when you are stopped by an officer just for driving 25 miles an-hour in a 20-mile-an hour zone, first thing he asks for is a driver's license, doesn't he?

A: Yes.

Q: The officer makes ordinary reasonable efforts to see who he's dealing with on a little simple traffic ticket, doesn't he?

A: Yes.

Q: You didn't ask her for anything, did you?

A: No.

Q: You know right now that she did lie to you, don't you?

A: I know that now, yes.

Q: And of course, you never checked out this lady in any other way. Didn't you have any clue at all that she was not telling you the truth?

A: I had two conversations with her on two separate occasions.

Q: I didn't ask you how many conversations you had. I asked you did you have any clue. Do you understand the question?

A: I had, based on the conversations I had with her, I made a determination that what she said—made an overall determination that what she said was correct.

Q: Yes, but my question was a simple one. Did you have any clues that she was telling you a lie, yes or no?

A: Based on my overall determination that she was telling the truth, there were no suggestions or clues.

Q: Do you have trouble with the words yes or no? They are easy words. Did you have any clue, yes or no, that she was telling you a

582

lie? You either had clues or you didn't. I want to know, and the jury wants to know.

A: I had some suggestion that she was not totally credible, just as I had some suggestion that what she was saying was substantive.

Q: Then you are saying that you had some clue that she wasn't telling you the truth?

A: Well, early on in our discussions—

Q: Is that right?

A: I can't answer that question yes or no.

Q: Well, will you just, I just want to understand what you are saying. You said, "I had some clues that she wasn't telling me the truth." Did I hear you correctly?

A: During our conversations, there were some suspicions that were aroused, which were satisfied to my knowledge. I always have suspicions when I begin to conduct an interview that perhaps someone is not telling the truth.

Q: Did you have some clues here that the witness wasn't telling the truth? Yes or no.

A: I had suspicions. I don't think I understand the word. I don't think I understand your question.

Q: Do you know what a clue is? I mean, you are an investigative reporter, aren't you?

A: Well, I don't think we deal with that word in my business.

Q: You mean you're out trying to get a Pulitzer Prize, aren't you?

A: No.

Q: You know what a clue is, don't you? You know, some evidence that maybe something is or isn't true. That's what a clue is. Did you have any clue that this woman was or wasn't telling you the truth?

MR. SPENCE: Let me talk. The reason I am stopping is because something happened in that cross-examination that is important. The rattling attack between me and the witness on just the use of the word starts to create the impression that the witness is evading, that he is afraid to tell you the truth, to give you a straightforward answer. Sometimes in the course of cross-examination I will pray, please give me an evading witness. I have got one now. All right, so let's go on.

Q: She told you she was the personal secretary to the mayor?

A: That is correct.

Q: And she told you as the personal secretary to the mayor that she was at the mayor's house.

A: That is correct.

Q: And she said, as the personal secretary she often went to the boss's house, didn't she?

A: I'm not sure I would use the word "often." She said, "on occasion."

Q: So you knew that the information that you were receiving came to you from her as a personal secretary, isn't that true?

A: That's true.

Q: Now before you published this, you found out what her real title was, didn't you?

A: Yes.

Q: And you found out that her real title was not personal secretary at all, but her real title was administrative assistant, isn't that true?

A: In my mind, those two jobs could have been the same thing.

Q: I didn't ask you that. I asked if you knew that her real title was administrative assistant?

A: The title on the payroll was administrative assistant.

Q: Judge, would you tell the witness to answer.

JUDGE WOLFSON: Try the best you can to respond to the question asked.

A: The title on the payroll records was administrative assistant.

Q: You knew that?

A: Yes, sir.

Q: And you knew that before you published the matter in the paper, didn't you?

A: Yes.

Q: And don't you think that—didn't you think that she would know the difference? You know that this little open-faced girl that just walked in here—just happened to tell you a story for no reason at all—don't you think that little girl knew the difference between being a personal secretary and a mere administrative assistant. Don't you think she knew that?

A: As I said before, I think that the job title—

Q: I didn't ask you what you thought.

A: Could you repeat the question please?

Q: Yes. (Question read back.)

A: She was apparently not aware of the difference.

Q: You knew that the mayor's office told you that the story was false.

A: The mayor's office denied the story.

Q: Well, you knew that the mayor demanded a retraction.

A: Subsequent to the story's publication.

Q: Well, that's right. It's hard to demand a retraction before you publish it, isn't it? And so the mayor was saying that it was false and Lady Hazelton was saying it was true. That was the situation before you published. Isn't that right?

A: That's correct.

Q: And so you chose to publish this rot when you yourself didn't know the truth, did you?

A: I published what I believed to be true.

Q: Would you instruct the witness to answer the question?

OBJECTION, your honor, with a question like that, I think that was an appropriate answer.

JUDGE WOLFSON: The answer may stand.

MR. SPENCE: I just made a mistake. You don't turn to the court and ask for help. First of all, they don't like to help you as a general rule. Secondly, merely that you turned to the court and asked for help establishes for the jury that somehow you can't control the witness yourself.

Q: Let me restate it. You didn't know the truth when you published this, did you?

A: I published what I believed to have been true at the time.

Q: Here is a good time to move the blackboard up here. I'm going to grab a piece of chalk and write the word "know" on the blackboard. See it?

A: Yes.

Q: Your eyes on the word. You didn't know the truth when you published that article, did you?

A: Not necessarily.

Q: Don't you think that it's reckless to publish something about a man, about him having committed a crime, about having received kickbacks. Don't you think that it's reckless for a man to publish such things without knowing the truth?

A: (No answer.)

MR. SPENCE: Now, Mr. Witness, you will see that I'm going to choose to just go on to the next question without an answer, because the silence from a failure to answer within a reasonable time is better than demanding an answer that isn't going to be helpful anyway.

Q: Don't you think, Mr. Witness, that if you were guilty of making a false story worse than it really was, that you might be guilty of malice under those circumstances?

OBJECTION: That's a hypothetical, speculatory—

JUDGE WOLFSON: Could you be a bit more specific?

MR. SPENCE: Yes, thank you, Your Honor. There is a headline here that reads as follows: "Mayor Winslow Charged with a Kickback Scheme." Do you see that in the paper? (And at this point you want to hold up the paper, the big headline there. Hold it up to the jury.)

Q: That's in the paper, isn't it? We can both see that.

A: Yes.

Q: No doubt about that, is there?

A: No.

Q: You know the word "charged." When John Doe is prosecuted for murder or rape, you use the word charged, isn't that right?

A: It could be, yes.

Q: John Doe charged with child abuse, huh?

A: It could be read that way, yes.

585

Q: (Reading): "Mayor Winslow charged with kickbacks." That follows the same connotation, isn't that right?

A: Not necessarily.

Q: Who made the decision to use the word "charged?" Did Miss Hazelton tell you to put that in the paper that way?

A: No, she did not.

Q: Well, I guess then that somebody at the paper decided that. Right?

A: Yes.

Q: It wasn't you, was it?

A: No.

Q: It must have been an editor of the paper, right?

A: Yes.

Q: And so the paper, which is also a defendant in this case, decided they were going to expose this false story themselves by using the word "charged." Isn't that true?

A: Yes.

MR. SPENCE: That's the time you have got to look at the jury. You see, there is no law about looking at the jury. There is no canon against looking at the jury. You have a right to look at your jury as long as you don't wink at them.

Q: Now, Mayor Winslow wasn't charged with any criminal complaint, was he?

A: No.

Q: And you knew he was not charged with any criminal complaint, didn't you? At the time you published the article, you knew that, didn't you?

A: The article did not say he was.

Q: Well, wait a minute. You knew that wasn't true, didn't you?

A: I knew that he had not been charged and did not write that he had been charged.

Q: We have already showed the paper to the ladies and gentlemen of the jury, what the headline was. Now you're not denying that headline, are you? The word "charge." Now wait a minute, you are not denying the headline, are you?

A: No.

MR. SPENCE: Thank you.

You see, you have to make him answer the questions correctly, and if you don't, you shouldn't cross-examine. If you can't make him respond to the questions correctly, you shouldn't cross-examine at all.

Q: You know that many people read the headlines, don't you?

A: Yes.

Q: Did Miss Hazelton ever say to you that the mayor had taken a kickback? Did she ever use the word "kickback"?

A: No.

Q: That was your word, then, I guess, Huh?

A: Yes.

Q: And so, would you agree that if somebody makes a bad story worse than it really is by choosing a word that implies criminal conduct and does so intentionally, that the jury might conclude that such a person was malicious?

A: No.

Q: The only source of the rumor of kickback that you could pin on the mayor was the statement of Miss Hazelton. Isn't that true?

A: Yes.

Q: And yet you used the words ''widely circulated.'' Let's read that nice little, cute little paragraph, the first one in the article.

A: ''The re-election aspirations of Mayor Winslow have been harmed by widely circulated rumors—''

Q: Let's stop and write the words up here (on the blackboard) ''widely circulated.'' Did you write those words?

A: I wrote those words.

Q: Did those words come out of your little mind?

A: Yes, they did.

Q: The only source to the rumor of kickbacks that you could pin down to the mayor was the statement of Miss Hazelton. Isn't that right?

A: Yes.

Q: And yet it was you who used the words ''widely circulated.'' Isn't that right?

A: Yes.

Q: And so the person who really widely circulated the rumor was you, wasn't it, Mr. Witness?

A: No, I don't think that's correct.

Q: How many people read your paper every day?

A: A million.

Q: A million people? Did you say a million people?

A: That's correct.

Q: That's a lot of power, isn't it?

OBJECTION: Your Honor. A lot of readers.

JUDGE WOLFSON: Objection sustained.

Q: Do you think it would be malicious to state that something was widely circulated, until a million people read it, when the only thing that you had in your file was one statement by Miss Hazelton. Do you think that's evidence of maliciousness?

A: No. I do not.

Q: All right. Now when you printed, ''At least one witness told the district attorney's office,'' et cetera. Read that.

A: ''At least one witness has told the district attorney's office that Winslow solicited and received payments from contractors who

587

were ultimately awarded subcontracts for construction work on the city hall.''

MR. SPENCE: What I think you should do when dealing with something like this is have this thing on an overhead projector against the wall over here so this jury and everybody can see it.

Q: Now when you say at least one witness, that suggests, doesn't it, that there were others, or possibly others?

A: Yes, it does.

Q: Yes. And Miss Hazelton didn't tell you that there were possibly other people that saw anything like that, did she?

A: No, she did not.

Q: And you didn't have any basis for any implication that there was anybody but Miss Hazelton?

A: Based on Miss Hazelton's statement, there was at least the possibility of one other person who had possibly witnessed these transactions.

Q: Well, but you said that at least one person had talked to the county or the prosecuting attorney. That suggests that the prosecuting attorney told you that, doesn't it?

A: I don't believe so, no.

Q: The prosecuting attorney wasn't the source for you, was he?

A: No, he was not.

Q: You say, ''According to one source, Winslow was seen . . . receiving $20,000 in cash from one mechanical contractor and $15,000 from a representative of another company.'' Now, you made that up, didn't you?

A: No, I did not. I based that on Brenda Hazelton's statement.

Q: Miss Hazelton's statement is in your hands. Let's just read it to the jury again. With the court's permission, I would like to read it to the jury. Come on up here. Now, it says here, ''I was at the lake house working with the mayor and was told,'' read right along here if there's any question about it, ''and was told to go to another part of the house when the mayor met with the visitor.'' I'll just go on reading this. Just read it quietly to yourself. ''However, I did recognize one of the contractors as the cement contractor on the city hall job. . . .'' Write up here (on the blackboard) ''cement contractor.''[A]nd the other gentleman, who I did not recognize, arrived at the lake house in a pickup truck marked Western Mechanical Contractors.'' Now, did you know who—did she tell you who was in that truck marked mechanical contractor? I mean, it doesn't say who that person was, it just said it was a truck, isn't that true?

A: It doesn't mention.

Q: It doesn't. And so we will write up here Miss Hazelton didn't know who was in the Western Mechanical Contractors' truck. And you didn't ask her, did you?

A: No.

Q: (Reading): "Following one of the meetings, I was given an envelope by the mayor and asked to take the envelope to the mayor's house and to place it in the safe in his study." Now, it doesn't say that she knew or saw anybody give the mayor an envelope, does it?

A: Not in her statement, no.

Q: And it doesn't say that she got anything—that she saw anybody take an envelope from a mechanical contractor. It doesn't say that at all, does it?

A: Not in her statement, no.

Q: No. And you have heard her testify here earlier today under her oath that she never made any such statement to you in her statement or otherwise. "While" [reading] "out of the mayor's presence, I opened that envelope and saw that it contained $20,000 in cash. Although I did not see any money on the other occasion, I overheard the mayor tell his deputy that the contractor had only paid $15,000, instead of $20,000."—Doesn't say which contractor and that this was the allegation. Now that's what she told you, isn't this right, that you wanted her to certify this. Isn't that true?

A: Yes, I think it was true.

Q: You wanted that so that you could rely on the statement. Isn't that right?

A: That's correct.

Q: Yes. Now, you have to admit to the ladies and gentlemen of the jury that Miss Hazelton didn't tell you in that statement that you asked her to certify that a mechanical contractor gave the mayor $20,000. You made that up, didn't you?

A: She did not say it in the statement. No.

MR. SPENCE: I'll tell you the rest of the cross-examination. The next cross-examination that we would fight through and the questions that we would ask and demand answers to are: When you make up things that can destroy a man, don't you think that's malicious? And you knew you had no basis for claiming a mechanical contractor gave $20,000 to the mayor? If he wants to argue about that, it's all right, because Miss Hazelton's already testified [in the mock trial]. You have heard her testimony [omitted here]. She only said she once saw a cement contractor, and so forth, so he knew that the source didn't tell him that.

And you know it's malicious to publish libelous falsehoods intentionally? You knew when you wrote, "According to one source, Winslow was seen . . . receiving . . . $15,000 from a representative of another company," that you were the source for that. You were the one who said that and made it up and published it and you were the only source.

589

You knew that, didn't you? And even Miss Hazelton never told you that.

So we come to the finale, the conclusion that, you've lied to a million people. It doesn't make any difference what his answers are. There is a foundation factually now for me to make those statements. The court can't really do much with my demand that he answer those questions.

You published information that you personally knew to be false and refused to publish information that you personally knew to be true, isn't that true? The personal information that he knew to be true was that no charges had been presented to and none had been contemplated by the grand jury.

Now here is the conclusion of the cross-examination with these questions. It doesn't make any difference if the court sustains an objection to it or not, you have concluded with a statement that ties it in with the opening:

Q: So if the jury finds you abused this sacred right of ours in this free country to freedom of the press—abused it, hid behind it, and used it to injure an innocent man, then wouldn't you agree that both you and your paper should be punished?

Q: And don't you agree that you not only recklessly pointed a loaded gun at Mayor Winslow, but that you aimed it at him intentionally and purposely and maliciously pulled the trigger?

He says objection and the judge says, sustained. You say: Thank you, I have no further questions.

Former Employees as Witnesses

by Kennedy P. Richardson

Your client is a corporation. The lawsuit is based on events dating back several years. As luck would have it—and frequently does—your key witness has left the company. Where does that leave you?

Does the attorney-client privilege shield communications between you and the former employee? Can you represent both the corporation and the former employee? Should you? Can your adversary take the former employee's deposition without a subpoena, and can it be admitted into evidence regardless of his availability for trial?

These are some of the questions that are likely to arise as you prepare your case for trial. I have a few answers to offer and, where there are no clear answers, some thoughts on what the answers should be and why.

Obviously you cannot conclude much about the application of the attorney-client privilege to former employees if you do not know how the privilege applies to employees still working for a corporation.

Until recently the courts disagreed over which of a corporation's employees came within the corporation's privilege. Many, including a majority of the lower federal courts, followed the control-group test, which extends the privilege to any employee who can control or substantially participate in a decision made on the advice of counsel. *E.g.*, *City of Philadelphia v. Westinghouse Electric Corp.*, 210 F. Supp. 483, 485 (E.D. Pa. 1962). Others allowed the corporation's lawyer to gather information in confidence from all corporate employees who, in the course of their employment, were involved in the transaction being lit-

The author is a partner in Thelen, Marrin, Johnson & Bridges in Oakland, California. He gratefully acknowledges the research assistance of his associate, Arne D. Wagner.

igated. *E.g., Harper & Row Publishers, Inc. v. Decker,* 423 F.2d 487, 491-492 (7th Cir. 1970), *aff'd per curiam,* 400 U.S. 348 (1971). The United States Supreme Court recently endorsed this broader view for actions under federal law. *Upjohn Company v. United States,* 449 U.S. 383 (1981).

Although the Supreme Court declined to express a hard-and-fast rule, it held that the privilege extends to communications that are:

1. between any employee and the corporation's lawyer;
2. occurring at the direction of management;
3. concerning matters within the scope of the employee's corporate duties; and
4. to assist lawyers in giving legal advice to the corporation.

Extending the Privilege

Though the holding in the *Upjohn* case, as in earlier cases adopting a similar rule, is limited to current employees, Chief Justice Burger suggested in a separate concurring opinion that the rule protects communications with former employees as well. The Court of Appeals for the Ninth Circuit recently applied the privilege to former employees. *In Re Coordinated Pretrial Proceedings in Petroleum Products Antitrust Litigation,* 658 F.2d 1355, 1361 n. 7 (9th Cir.), *cert. denied,* 455 U.S. 990 (1982). *But see In Re Grand Jury Subpoena,* 478 F. Supp. 368, 374 (E.D. Wis. 1979) (dictum).

The court of appeals' conclusion is correct because the interests served by the corporation's attorney-client privilege are more important than the former employee's contractual independence from the corporation. A former employee may have the best—or even the only—living memory of what the corporation thought and did during the disputed events. The confidence guarded by the privilege facilitates a free and full exchange of information and advice between attorney and client. A company, which operates through human actors, cannot maintain this confidence unless the privilege encompasses all employees involved in the transaction being litigated, including former employees.

The extension of the corporate attorney-client privilege to former employees undoubtedly increases the risk that the former employee's recollection and testimony will be influenced by the corporate lawyers' partisan perspective. The same risk applies to current employees under the *Upjohn* privilege. Any such bias can be disclosed by able cross-examination, including inquiry concerning the occurrence of the privileged communication and other matters that establish the witness's affinity with the corporate party, and by the right to inspect and cross-examine the witness about documents used to refresh his recollection.

Circumvention Strategies

Applying the corporate attorney-client privilege to confidential communications with former employees is more forthright than some of the strategems that have been employed in efforts to extend the attorney-client privilege to former employees. One such strategem is to reemploy the former employee. Besides wasting corporate money, this strategy sets up a sham.

Another strategy is to have the corporation's lawyer represent the former employee as well as the corporation. The district court in the *Petroleum Products* case condemned dual representation as a device that would allow the corporation's attorney to bias former employees and would keep the adversary's attorney from communicating directly with them.

Although it did not decide whether a corporation's lawyer can represent two clients, the opinion of the Ninth Circuit Court of Appeals suggested that dual representation is acceptable. The court's position is unfortunate, however, because a corporation lawyer's claim to represent a former employee is usually a pretense that serves no legitimate purpose. The former employee is neither a named nor a potential party to most civil actions. He has no real reason to retain counsel. In most cases, the corporate lawyer's only allegiance is to the corporation. His claim to represent the former employee is also a sham.

It makes more sense to apply the corporate attorney-client privilege to confidential communications with former employees. As the holder of the privilege, the corporation may then prevent the former employee from disclosing any privileged communications. *See, e.g., Perrignon v. Bergen Brunswick Corp.,* 77 F.R.D. 455 (N.D. Cal. 1978). And any unauthorized disclosures by former employees are not admissible at trial. *See, e.g.,* CALIF. EVIDENCE CODE §§ 912, 916-19, 954; MCCORMICK ON EVIDENCE § 2 (E. Cleary 1972).

Dual representation also works an unnecessary hardship on the opposing lawyer. Once he has received notice of the dual representation, he is apparently prohibited by professional ethics from attempting to communicate directly with the former employee. *See* ANNOTATED CODE OF PROFESSIONAL RESPONSIBILITY, EC 718 and DR 7-104 and comments at 331-36 (1979). The former employee in turn will be more apt to follow the corporate lawyer's warning against talking to the opposing lawyer after the corporate lawyer graciously agrees to represent the former employee free of charge.

The insulating effect of dual representation is more than a frustrating inconvenience. A former employee may have relevant knowledge that is outside the corporate attorney-client privilege. An informal interview is a far cheaper and often more effective means of tapping this knowledge than a deposition.

Many former employees will refuse to submit to an interview with the opposing lawyer out of a sense of loyalty to their ex-employer, regardless of whether dual representation is provided. However, there are undoubtedly many former employees who would not refuse from a strong sense of independence, a desire to see justice done, or the hope of avoiding a deposition.

Where the former employee has a personal stake in the litigation, dual representation is proper unless a conflict of interest requires separate representation. *See* ANNOTATED CODE OF PROFESSIONAL RESPONSIBILITY, Canon 5 and EC 5-14 to 5-20 (1979).

Taking a Deposition

The deposition of a former employee cannot be taken merely on notice to the corporation. This is the prevailing and more persuasive view, though there is contrary authority. *See Annot.,* 98 A.L.R. 2d 622, at 629-30 (1962).

Since the corporation usually has no contractual power over the former employee, there is no sense in subjecting the corporation to sanctions for not producing the former employee. In some cases, the former employee will appear voluntarily. If the adversary is unable to subpoena a recalcitrant former employee, the court should bar the former employee from testifying on behalf of the corporation at trial.

If the corporation's lawyer does not represent the former employee, he cannot instruct him not to answer questions at his deposition. But the inability to instruct does not render the corporation's counsel helpless in the face of objectionable questions.

Where communications are privileged, the corporation's lawyer will be justified in restricting the former employee's deposition. The proper procedure was explained in *Perrignon v. Bergen Brunswick Corp.,* 77 F.R.D. 455 (N.D. Cal. 1978). There, a former president of a company was asked questions at his deposition concerning a conversation he had had with the company's inside counsel during his employment.

At the deposition, both the lawyer for the company and the former president's personal lawyer objected on the basis of the company's attorney-client privilege. On the advice of the personal lawyer, the former president answered the questions after the objections were made. The company's lawyer gave no advice.

The court held that the company's lawyer waived the attorney-client privilege by failing to take further action to prevent the former president from answering the objectionable questions. The court pointed out that the proper tactic would have been for the company's lawyer to have adjourned the deposition and to have applied for a protective order under FED. R. CIV. P. 30(d). A less disruptive approach would be for the lawyers to stipulate that the company can seek a protective order after the examining lawyer has deposed the former employee on the matters outside the claimed privilege.

Under Rule 32(a)(2), the deposition of a party or of anyone who is an officer, director, or managing agent may be used by an adverse party for any purpose. Similar rules have been enacted in many states.

594

This rule says nothing about former employees. Does it require that a former managerial employee's deposition be treated as that of an ordinary witness? If this interpretation is followed, the deposition could be admitted only where the former employee was unavailable for trial under the usual criteria. *See* FED. R. CIV. P. 32(a)(3).

If a former managerial employee is sufficiently identified with the corporate party to come within the corporation's attorney-client privilege, there is little reason to forbid the use of his deposition as a party admission. The courts should presume the admissibility of the deposition if the former executive conferred before the deposition with the corporation's attorney behind the shield of the corporate privilege.

The rules of evidence with regard to party admissions provide adequate authority for admitting the former executive's deposition. Thus, FED. R. EVID. 801(d)(2) excludes from the hearsay rule ''a statement by a person authorized by [the party] to make a statement concerning the subject.'' The deposition of a former executive who has been warmed up in confidence by the corporation's lawyer ought to come within the scope of this exception. Evidence that the former executive is hostile or otherwise adverse to the corporation should rebut the presumption that the corporation authorized his deposition testimony.

FED. R. EVID. 611(c) authorizes cross-examination by leading questions for witnesses ''identified with an adverse party.'' Former managerial employees, and probably former nonmanagerial employees as well, meet this standard. *E.g.*, FED. R. EVID. 611 (c), *Advisory Committee's Note, Lowry v. Black Hills Agency*, 509 F.2d 1311, 1314 (8th Cir. 1975); *Sanford Bros. Boats, Inc. v. Vidrine*, 412 F. 2d 958, 969 (5th Cir. 1969); 3 J. WEINSTEIN & M. BERGER, WEINSTEIN'S EVIDENCE § 611[05] (1982). The former employee's presumed alliance with the corporation is rebuttable. If the former employee is shown to be hostile or otherwise adverse to the corporation, the opposing party should be required to examine the former employee without leading questions.

To sum up, there is now good authority as well as good reason for applying the corporate attorney-client privilege to communications with former employees whose employment coincided with the events being litigated. Beyond this, the rules are not clear. My own conclusions are:

- Without special circumstances, the corporation's counsel should not act as a former employee's lawyer.
- Opposing lawyers should be allowed to try to interview the former employee.
- The deposition of a former managerial employee can be compelled only by subpoena.
- Although the corporation's lawyer lacks the power to instruct a former employee not to answer deposition questions, he may nonetheless prevent questioning about privileged matters.

- The deposition of a former managerial employee whose predeposition conference with corporate counsel is claimed to have been privileged should be admissible without regard to the former employee's availability for trial.
- The opposing lawyer should be entitled to examine a former employee by leading questions.

Cross-Examining the Accomplice Witness

by Stacey J. Moritz and Marcy Ressler Harris

As a group, the seven accomplice witnesses in the racketeering trial of reputed mobster John Gotti and six codefendants could not have been more reprehensible. Collectively, these career criminals had been convicted of nearly 70 different crimes, ranging from bank robbery and car theft to drug trafficking and murder. On cross-examination, each confessed to a life of crime, to lying and cheating when it suited some criminal purpose.

The accomplices' testimony against the *Gotti* defendants was devastating, and painted a picture of heinous and violent crime. Nevertheless, in a verdict that stunned seasoned court watchers, the jury acquitted all defendants of all counts. Many believe that the government's witnesses were simply too tainted by crime to be credited.

While the acquittals in the *Gotti* case were unusual, the government's choice of witnesses was not. Convictions in criminal cases often are based, at least in substantial part, on the testimony of accomplice witnesses—admitted criminals who participated in the crimes alleged and who, when caught, opted to testify against other defendants in exchange for money and promises of leniency.

Without question, a prosecutor would prefer to establish the government's case from documentary evidence, tape or video recordings, and the testimony of respectable citizens. The fact of the matter, however, is that this evidence usually is unavailable. As a rule, criminals do not detail their schemes in lengthy written contracts; they do not divulge their criminal lives in gilt-edged personal diaries; and they do not consult their law-abiding neighbors for advice on criminal activity.

For lack of alternate sources of information, the government must turn

---

Ms. Moritz is a partner and Ms. Harris is an associate in the firm of Schulte Roth & Zabel in New York City.

to criminal insiders to uncover and prove criminal behavior. Generally, the closer the insider is to the criminal decision making, the greater his value to the prosecution's case. The close insider can provide the smoking gun needed to prosecute the rest of the group.

But building a case upon the testimony of turncoats is a risky proposition. Skillful cross-examination can turn the government's greatest witness into its greatest liability, by exposing the accomplice as a liar, a traitor, and a bought and paid-for snitch. Moreover, while the use of accomplices is an appropriate law enforcement technique, in the eyes of many jurors, the government's association with such sordid types can taint the credibility of the whole prosecution and even the prosecutors themselves. In short, the cross-examination of an accomplice witness can determine the outcome of the entire case.

Having emphasized the critical importance of impeaching turncoat witnesses, we must admit that there is no magic formula for cross-examining these rogues. As with any trial technique, success depends on a combination of good ideas, quick reflexes, hard work, and more hard work. The goal of any cross-examination is to establish facts from which to argue your client's case on summation. But certain lines of inquiry are particularly effective when cross-examining an accomplice. In addition, the style can be more aggressive and more hostile—even righteously indignant.

For instance, in a typical civil case, waging a full-scale attack on a witness's character is risky business, likely to provoke the jury's sympathy for the witness, rather than its disdain. A character attack may at times be necessary, but kid gloves should be used with this maneuver.

Take Your Gloves Off

On the other hand, the gloves can and should come off when cross-examining an accomplice. Consider that the witness usually is someone who on direct examination has admitted to at least two key vulnerabilities: He is a criminal, and he has struck a deal to testify for the government to save himself from prosecution or a long prison term. In addition, the traitor often is a documented liar as well. Thus, the cross-examiner may aggressively attack the witness's character and elicit his motives for testifying, his interest in the outcome, his prior criminal conduct, and his past lies, all with little risk of engaging the jury's sympathy for the accomplice.

Yet destroying the witness in the jury's eyes may not be the cross-examiner's only goal. The accomplice also can provide evidence in support of the defense. It is rare that a defendant in a criminal trial will testify. Thus, an accomplice who admits to having participated in the crimes alleged is in a singular position to help the defense establish facts critical to its theory of the case. Introducing evidence through the accomplice may, indeed, be the only way to prove the defendant's version of the facts.

For example, take a multidefendant bank robbery conspiracy case in which the defense theory is that a particular defendant did not conspire to commit the crime but was merely present in an escape vehicle. There, the cross-examiner might ask:

Q: Isn't it a fact that my client was not at the planning meeting?

Q: Isn't it also true that you never saw my client in any of the cars that were driven over to the bank?

Q: In fact, you never saw my client before the robbery or during the robbery, did you?

Q: Even according to your story, isn't it true that you never laid eyes on my client or spoke to him or heard of him until after the robbery when you got into a car outside the bank, and saw him behind the wheel?

Even if the accomplice also testified that the defendant drove the robbers from the bank and attended the division of spoils, some of the accomplice's testimony can aid the defense.

While a careful defense lawyer should always consider the beneficial uses of the turncoat's testimony, carrying out both constructive and destructive cross-examination of the same witness obviously is a tricky maneuver. Logic dictates that you perform the constructive examination first.

Once you have torn a witness to shreds, he is unlikely to be cooperative in answering constructive questions. And even if he responds to a sudden overture of friendship, the jury may not—and may instead resent the technique as gamesmanship. In any case, and perhaps most importantly, if the destructive cross-examination has been effective, the jury will be more suspicious of the witness's later testimony, including the testimony that supports the defense case. Finally, since both the witness and the jury probably will be expecting you to reveal your fangs from the start, beginning with a series of nonthreatening questions will impress the jury as being fair and reasonable, which also may redound to your client's benefit.

It also is important to make a smooth transition from constructive to destructive questioning to avoid the appearance of hypocrisy. An abrupt change may suggest to the jury that you do not believe a word of the witness's testimony, regardless of the good the testimony has done for your case. One way to make this transition is to turn to the witness's deal with the government. In federal cases, immunity is conferred by statute or by agreement. Statutory immunity under 18 U.S.C. § 6001 *et seq.*, also known as "use" immunity, provides that a witness's statements cannot be used against him either directly or indirectly through evidence that is developed from his statements. Since the prosecution would have the heavy burden of establishing that no evidence used in a later prosecution derived from immunized testimony, use immunity effectively guarantees the accomplice a walk for his crimes.

While statutory use immunity can be conferred without the witness's cooperation, the witness also can explicitly negotiate to inform on others for his own advantage. In negotiated immunity agreements, a witness may receive transactional immunity—immunity for the whole "transaction" about which he is testifying—from the federal district in which he is testifying, together with the government's representation that the witness's cooperation will be brought to the attention of other law enforcement agencies or prosecutors' offices as well. Alternatively, the witness may receive only partial immunity and be required to plead guilty to certain offenses, albeit far fewer than the number he might otherwise face. The government may even be paying the witness for his testimony, either directly as an informant or through a subsistence allowance.

Grist for the Mill

These immunity and cooperation agreements are obviously grist for the cross-examiner's mill, especially since the typical accomplice witness receives his sentence only after testifying at trial. His fate thus is psychologically, if not actually, tied to the convictions achieved through his testimony. The witness's deal, his self-interest in testifying against others, his hope for leniency, and his perceived need to please the prosecutor, all undermine his objectivity and credibility. Eliciting these facts on cross-examination lets you argue in summation that the turncoat will say anything, regardless of its truth, if it will benefit him or win his freedom.

For instance, in the cross-examination excerpted below, which was conducted in a recent trial, the examiner used the witness's earlier statements and grand jury testimony to force him to concede that to get immunity he had to change his prior testimony.

Q: When you worked out your—or your attorneys worked out your deal with the government for immunity, did you expect that the government thought you were going to go into . . . this trial room and repeat exactly what you had said in Chicago and New York; did you believe that was what was expected of you?

A: No, I did not . . .

Q: You did not?

A: I did not.

Q: And so, I can take it that you believed that it was the government's position that what you had said in Chicago and New York was untrue; is that right?

A: That sounds more right.

Q: And to ask the final question here, didn't you believe, sir, that if you continued to give here the testimony that you gave in the grand juries in Chicago and New York, that you never would have gotten immunity from the United States government; didn't you believe that?

600

A: I had to tell the truth here.

Q: Well, didn't you believe that if you continued to give the testimony you gave in Chicago and New York, you wouldn't have gotten immunity from the United States government; didn't you believe that? Is that a fair statement?

A: That testimony was false. I had to tell the truth.

Q: And so you believed that if you continued to give that testimony you wouldn't have gotten immunity; is that a fair statement?

A: Since that was false—

THE COURT: Yes?

THE WITNESS: Yes.

Q: Will you say yes?

A: Yes.

Q: It's not that hard. Thank you.

As you begin the destructive portion of your cross-examination, keep in mind that much depends on the rapport among the players. Consciously or not, the jury will evaluate your courtroom demeanor as well as the testimony you elicit. And while the jury will not hold you to the Golden Rule, it will be more receptive to your arguments if your manner toward the witness is warranted by what the jury has seen and heard.

The key, of course, is to appear fair and reasonable, while at the same time maintaining total witness control. If the task is difficult with the typical witness, it is even harder with an accomplice, who is likely to be especially defensive. Moreover, many accomplices delight in appearing obstreperous and cocky. Your goal, then, is to turn the witness's posturing to your own advantage. Ask sharp and hostile questions, but save your arguments for summation. The jury will appreciate your restraint and may resent the witness's belligerence.

A particularly effective way to undermine the accomplice's testimony is to point out ways that it is inconsistent with the witness's prior testimony or statements. The witness's testimony on direct examination can be the most theatric source for such impeachment. The jurors saw and heard the witness swear to tell the truth and then heard his statements on direct. No matter how much they know of the accomplice's prior deceit, they will feel personally betrayed when they learn the witness lied to them. The dramatic effect is heightened if the witness tries to escape the inconsistency.

Consider the following exchange, in which the examiner tries to establish that a man we have called Mr. Smith paid for the witness's dinner.

Q: On direct examination you told us about dinners that—or lunches that Mr. Smith paid for. Do you recall that?

A: I'm sorry.

Q: Didn't you tell us on direct examination last week that that was an example of Mr. Smith buying a meal for you?

601

A: I recall saying that Mr. Smith bought dinner for me in Gordon's Restaurant in Amagansett.

Q: Now you say you don't know whether he was the one who paid; it could have been the other couple; is that right?

A: When you asked me the question, I said to you I didn't recall.

Q: You don't recall. And when you testified last week, you just said it because it would help the prosecution; is that right?

A: No, that's not true.

Q: In any event, when you said it last week, you really didn't recall; is that right?

A: No, that's not true. I did recall.

Q: Last week but not this week?

A: That's correct.

Q: You lost it over the weekend?

A: No. You asked me the question whether or not Mr. Smith paid or the other couple paid. I think Smith paid, but I don't have it crystal clear in my mind. It was many years ago.

Q: You had no problem saying on direct examination that he did; isn't that right?

As is clear from this example, the witness's evasiveness becomes a key issue of credibility. After a point, his actual answers are irrelevant.

Direct testimony is not the only source of prior inconsistent statements. Statements made outside the courtroom, and even before trial, can and should be used for impeachment.

There are several ways to get these statements. For instance, under the rule of *Brady v. Maryland*, 373 U.S. 83 (1963), and its progeny, the government must disclose upon request any evidence that either exculpates a defendant or that the defendant can use for impeachment. The existence and nature of any cooperation arrangements with accomplices, as well as accomplices' prior conviction records, fall into this latter category. Additionally, Rule 26.2, FED. R. CRIM. P., and the Jencks Act, Title 18 U.S.C. § 3500, both require the government to disclose upon motion the witness's prior statements, including those made before the grand jury, which relate to his direct testimony.

Brady and Jencks Act material usually are disclosed in response to a simple letter request. Although the government is not required to give Jencks Act material to the defense until direct examination is finished, many federal judges urge pretrial disclosure to avoid midtrial delays. Even where the material is delivered at the last possible moment, the value of this material to the cross-examiner far outweighs the inconvenience of its delivery.

The debriefing of an accomplice witness generally is accomplished over many hours. While agents and prosecutors ask questions and take notes, the accomplice details his version of events. Often, he follows his own disclosure agenda and only gradually comes clean with the government. On cross-examination, the defense lawyer can use the notes to trace the course of the witness's disclosures and to show that the accomplice withheld critical information until the very last minute, even until the trial itself. From the witness's gradual progression of candor, the defense can argue that the later-disclosed incriminating information has been fabricated to please the prosecutors or to get a better deal.

By showing how long it took the government's star witness to arrive at his final version of the facts in the prosecution of reputed crime boss Paul Castellano and nine others, the defense was able to argue in summation that the witness had lied to the grand jury and had breached his cooperation agreement. The accomplice, whose agreement to testify saved him a possible prison sentence of 70 years to life, had waited until the week before the start of jury selection to link Castellano to the major crimes alleged. By then, the witness had been cooperating with the government for more than two years and had undergone more than 200 hours of interrogation.

In another case, where the accomplice had been debriefed over weeks and only gradually told his trial-time version of the facts, a defense lawyer asked as to each debriefing session, "So you lied to the agents on this date?"—to which the accomplice answered, "Yes." For every day the witness had lied, the cross-examiner asked him to mark a black "L" on a huge calendar the lawyer had set up. At the end, the picture of 25 "Ls" out of 30-odd days of interviews was a striking visual image of the witness's propensity for guile.

Keeping in mind that many accomplice witnesses are experienced con artists, it also can pay off to request as *Brady* information and to explore on cross-examination the lengths the government has gone to keep its star performers happy. It is not unheard of for prosecutors to have arranged, in their own offices, conjugal visits between imprisoned witnesses and their spouses or mates, or to have helped arrange housing for the witness's family members. Prosecutors even have arranged for special treatment within the prison itself, such as food, uncensored mail, alcohol, drugs, and even cosmetic surgery.

Delving into the witness's prior criminal record also makes for successful impeachment, as long as the crimes are admissible. For example, in the *Gotti* trial, the defense team created a large, striking chart laying out the various accomplices' past crimes and convictions. The jury was impressed. In general, prior felony convictions or convictions involving dishonesty or false statements are admissible under Rule 609, FED. R. EVID., provided that the convictions were handed down within ten years of the trial. The admissibility of prior convictions is often decided in advance in an *in limine* ruling, to avoid unfair surprise. If the government knows in advance that an accomplice's prior convictions will come in, it will likely raise them on direct, to minimize their impact on the jury. Even so, reviewing the witness's convictions again on cross-examination can be damaging to the witness; repetition of this type makes its mark on the jury.

Tone also is important. For example, a little sarcasm can go a long way toward discrediting the witness's promise of reform, as the following colloquy shows:

Q: I just want to review for a moment with you some testimony you've given. Between 1960 and 1968, I don't think there's any doubt, is there, that you committed certain frauds with Mr. Jones. No doubt about that, is there?

A: That's correct.

Q: And then between '68 and '74, you committed frauds pretty much on your own; is that right? You became your own man, so to speak; is that right?

A: That's correct.

Q: And then you went into retirement for a few years—between '74 and '76, '77, you were out of work?

A: That's correct.

Q: Then you went over to [your next job], correct, a little bit after that, '78 to '84?

A: '85, that's correct.

Q: And you started to commit further frauds and deceptions for [that job]; correct?

A: That's correct.

Q: So now, really, you actually are celebrating a quarter of a century of committing frauds and deception; correct?

A: That's correct.

Q: Now, you met the FBI in 1986?

A: '85.

Q: The end of '85, the very end of '85?

A: That's correct.

Q: You're now about to start a new life; right? You're going to come clean; right? Is that a fair statement?

A: I did cooperate, yes.

Q: They got you; correct?

Q: That's correct.

Q: And you're going to turn over a new leaf; right?

A: I agreed to cooperate, yes.

Q: And that means you're going to tell the government everything; isn't that right?

A: That's correct.

Q: No more the old [conduct]; right?

A: I agreed to cooperate fully with the government.

Q: This is [your] come clean [behavior]; correct?

Regardless of the witness's answers, the examiner has made the point to the jury.

In fact, this example raises another key point. Keep in mind the image of "death by a thousand cuts." Why cut the witness down in a single blow? It is far more effective to prolong your attack and for the jury to register each blow. The following testimony shows how effective this technique can be.

Q: Now, you testified earlier that you helped secure a couple of diplomas from a place called Philathea College.

A: That's correct.

Q: In fact, at one point you were a member of the faculty of Philathea College, weren't you?

A: Well . . . I never taught any courses.

Q: You were on the faculty as a professor of psychology; is that correct?

A: That's correct.

Q: Philathea published a catalog and in the catalog it listed you as a professor of psychology; is that correct?

A: That's correct.

Q: And it listed your mother as an associate professor of natural sciences; is that correct?

A: I believe so.

Q: And it listed your mother's husband as an associate professor of natural sciences; is that correct?

A: I believe so.

Q: It listed your lawyer as an instructor. He was on the faculty, too, wasn't he?

A: I believe so.

Q: Also, at one point, [John Doe] was awarded a degree from Philathea College; is that correct?

A: Yes.

Q: 1966 is the year that you received your doctor's in church history; is that correct?

A: I believe.

Q: First by forgery, you also received a doctorate in churches?

A: I believe so.

Q: The same year that [Richard Roe] received a doctorate in church history?

A: I believe so.

Q: The same year that Mr. Roe's wife—

Clearly, the examiner here could have established in a question or two that the witness obtained phony degrees for himself, his family, and his friends. Yet the cumulative effect of eliciting this testimony through a series of damaging answers has a greater impact.

Although cross-examining the accomplice witness can be crucial to the outcome of a trial, there may be times when the most effective cross is no cross. You may represent a client in a multidefendant case, for instance, in which the witness on direct has said nothing damaging about your client. Then you can make the point quite well by asking the witness two or three questions such as "You don't even know my client, do you?" and "You certainly have no knowledge that he was involved in any conspiracy, isn't that correct?"

If the witness's testimony has been harmful to your client, but you have no substantive evidence with which to discredit it, you may, at the least, develop that the witness has rehearsed his testimony or coordinated it with others. Even if the witness does not remember the exact number of times he went over his testimony with the prosecutors, persistence in this line of inquiry may pay off, as the following example demonstrates.

Q: Is is fair to say that between March 6th and now you met with government agents more than a hundred times; yes or no?
A: I can't answer that.
Q: Would it be fair to say it's more than 50 times; yes or no?
A: I can't answer it that way.
Q: Would it be fair to say it's more than 25 times; yes or no?
A: I can't answer it that way.
Q: You can't answer that. How about more than five times; yes or no?
A: Yes.
Q: More than ten?
THE COURT: Oh, come on.
Q: Your Honor, I think it indicates the reluctance on the part of the witness.
PROSECUTOR: I object.
THE COURT: Sustained. It's perfectly obvious he was debriefed by the government, talked to by the government, and gone over this by the government ad nauseum. That's perfectly obvious.

You cannot always count on this type of help from the court, of course. Even so, the judge is likely to allow you to explore the degree to which the witness has been rehearsed. Finally, the judge may become your ally in the end, with a helpful instruction on the value of accomplice testimony. The Eleventh Circuit's Pattern Instruction No. 1.1, among the more favorable to the defense, provides as follows:

The testimony of some witnesses must be considered with more caution than the testimony of other witnesses.

For example, a paid informer, or a witness who has been promised that he or she will not be charged or prosecuted, or a witness who hopes to gain more favorable treatment in his or her own case, may have a reason to make a false statement because he wants to strike a good bargain with the Government.

So, while a witness of that kind may be entirely truthful when

606

testifying, you should consider that testimony with more caution than the testimony of other witnesses.

Whenever a criminal insider testifies, defense counsel should request an instruction along these lines. The judge's failure to grant some form of cautionary instruction, even a diluted one, is reversible error in most jurisdictions.

Obviously, these ideas and examples are just clues that must be adapted to your own temperament and style, the facts of the case, and any circumstances that will affect the jury. Nonetheless, the goal does not change. The more crucial the accomplice's testimony, the more important it is to conduct a cross-examination that allows you to sum up, in the words of one prominent defense attorney, "Ladies and gentlemen, the government's witness is walking reasonable doubt."

Cross-Examining the Sympathetic Witness

by Leonard M. Ring

When LITIGATION asked me to write an article on cross-examining sympathetic witnesses, the idea seemed most challenging—and challenging it turned out to be. It is one thing to do the cross-examination, quite another to write about how to do it. Cross-examination, after all, is a "do it" art, best analogized to mother's chicken soup: a mix of experience, instinct, talent, and individual style—blended with the right amount of preparation.

We all have read and heard the teachings of the masters that good cross-examination is exclusively the product of preparation. For some it may well be. I once belonged to this camp, or at times preached its theories. Certainly, even the most skillful master of the art cannot cross-examine a technical witness without knowing the science involved. But after reflecting on the scores of cases from which I wear scars, I have come to realize that cross-examination is more art than science, more instinct than study, more intuition than plan. The best cross-examination I ever witnessed was of a close friend by his wife about where he had spent the previous night—and she wasn't even a lawyer.

Although intonation, demeanor, stance, and other body language that project the style and technique of others are instructive—and, *where adaptable*, they are something the student of the art should study—they only go so far. As is true with every other aspect of the art of advocacy, sincerity is the hallmark of truth. An approach well worn by another is not guaranteed to be as good a fit for you; you must feel comfortable in the role.

With that sermon behind us, let me turn to some illustrations of cross-examining sympathetic or appealing witnesses.

Leonard M. Ring is a Chicago attorney who specializes in representing plaintiffs in personal injury suits.

The child witness is the most difficult to cross-examine. Whether it be eyewitness testimony of an injury to a playmate or fond memories of a deceased parent killed in an air crash or auto accident, the impact is the same. The competency of a child to take the stand is, of course, a matter for the court. But assume your *in limine* motions have been denied, and you come face to face with a tot of tender years and a sympathetic and approving jury—and what jury isn't partial to a small child?

I learned the technique the hard way.

The witness, an eight-year-old, had been playing with her younger brother in an abandoned auto in the back yard of the apartment building where their family lived. Her brother fell from the car window and cut his eye on shattered glass. The little girl, only four at the time, immediately ran to tell her mother.

We sued the landlord for failing to remedy an attractive nuisance on his property. I tried to get the child's account of the incident in through the mother's testimony, but it was excluded as hearsay. With no alternative, I put the child on the stand.

On direct examination the girl was wonderful. Cutely dressed and shy, she was the epitome of the sympathetic witness in a most sympathetic case. The little tyke related the scene and the event very clearly, and she very positively explained the crucial point: Her little brother fell on the broken pieces of glass, and that is how he cut his eye.

The lawyer for the defendant-building owner, an attorney with years of experience at the bar, stood to cross-examine. Did he attack the details of her story to show inconsistencies? Did he set her up for an impeachment by attempting to reveal mistakes, uncertainty, or confusion?

I sat there praying he would.

But no, he did none of the things a competent defense lawyer is supposed to do. He was old enough to be the girl's grandfather, and even though his appearance did not project that image, the image came through just the same.

He asked her, very softly and politely: "Honey, could you tell us again exactly what you saw?" She told it exactly as she had on my direct. I felt relieved.

But he wasn't through. "Honey, would you mind telling again what you saw?" She did, again exactly as she had before.

He still wasn't satisfied. "Would you do it once more?" She did. She repeated, again, the same story—the same way, in the same words. By that time even I got the message. The child had been rehearsed by her mother the same way she had been taught "Mary Had a Little Lamb."

I won the case, but it was a very small verdict.

Sometimes the least likely witness will turn out to be sympathetic. One such witness was a physician who, while a hospital resident, had ordered an endotracheal, or breathing, tube removed prematurely (the technical term for such removal is extubation). At the time, the patient had been in the recovery room after neurosurgery. Removing the breathing tube caused an obstruction of the patient's airway and, ultimately, a stroke that left the patient without the use of her right arm or leg.

I was representing the patient in a suit against the hospital, which was the doctor's employer at the time. Our legal theory, of course, was *respondeat superior*.

The first thing you might ask is: What made the doctor a sympathetic witness?

Nothing, as far as I could see in the course of trial preparation. I was all prepared to engage the fellow head-on and lay him bare before the jury as a villain. But when he took the stand, he was not the arrogant, self-righteous witness he had been on deposition. He slumped over in the witness stand, scared and pitiful—the very image of a remorseful young man. Everything about his appearance and demeanor showed that he was sorry for the frightful mistake he had made while still an apprentice in the art of healing.

Whether he was playing a role written for him by my opponent did not matter. He was eliciting sympathy from the jury, and I saw that I could not afford to humiliate him on cross without antagonizing the jurors and risking the case.

Gut instinct told me to throw the script away.

As I rose to the dare, "You may cross-examine," the doctor looked as if he were ready to die. I took a few steps toward the stand and said, as casually as I could: "Hey, it's okay, we all make mistakes, doctor." At the same time, I gestured downward with both palms, to reinforce the suggestion that the doctor should relax. Though I did not look at them, I could sense the jurors' relief as the doctor leaned back in the witness box, visibly calmed.

The Usual Rules Fail

I admit one could make a forceful argument that my prefatory statement to the witness was improper. But at the moment of confrontation, you cannot always match instinct and experience against a textbook on cross-examination. Instinct told me that I had to defuse the situation. (It also told me that defense counsel was in no position to object.)

Having now "forgiven" the doctor, I proceeded with a more conventional cross. But I took pains never to raise my voice, never to attack the doctor, and to content myself with establishing the basic evidentiary links regarding the doctor's negligence and the hospital's liability as his principal and employer. The criticism could come later, if necessary, in closing argument:

Q: Doctor, you were at the time a fourth-year resident?

A: Yes.

Q: I believe that's called 'fellow'?

A: Yes.

Q: And as a fellow you were in charge of the other residents and interns caring for Ms. Patient?

A: Yes.

Q: The decision to remove the endotracheal tube was a group decision?

A: Yes.

Q: Of you and the other residents working on the case?

A: Yes.

Q: And you were employed by whom?

A: Metropolitan Hospital.

Q: And who was Dr. Smith, the next senior resident, employed by?

A: Metropolitan Hospital.

Q: And Dr. Jones [another resident on the shift]?

A: Metropolitan Hospital.

Q: All right. Now insofar as the day-to-day care, you're the one that made the rounds, you're the one that examined the patient, and you're the one that worked with the other service, the neurological service; is that right?

A: I made rounds. I made decisions always in conjunction with the attending physician.

Q: In this case, the decision you made after consulting with your fellow resident was reduced by you to a long note in the chart; is that right?

A: Yes.

Q: I take it this note was rather important, wasn't it?

A: Yes.

Q: Because just above it is the note, 'In my opinion, the endotracheal tube should be left in place for at least another couple of days. E. Knifeblade.'

A: Yes, that's a note by the attending neurosurgeon.

Q: He wrote that himself?

A: Yes, he did.

Q: He didn't assign it to a resident? He wrote that note himself?

A: Yes.

Q: Orders are usually written by residents at teaching hospitals like Metropolitan, as part of their training; isn't that true?

A: Yes.

Q: So, when a physician, such as the neurosurgeon in this case, personally makes such an entry, it's something for you to take note of, isn't it?

A: Yes.

Q: He's, in effect, expressing what he thinks ought to be done?

A: He's expressing his opinion.

Under normal circumstances, I suppose I would have jumped on such

611

an obvious attempt to evade the question. But in that particular situation, I let it pass.

Q: Okay. Now, then, following that note—could you read this from where you're at?

A: Yes, I can.
'Respiratory care fellow. Events of last night discussed with Drs. Able, Baker, Charlie, and Dog.'

Q: Could you tell us who they are?

A: Dr. Able was the respiratory care physician who reintubated the patient [that is, reinserted her breathing tube] that previous evening.

Q: He was a resident under you?

A: Yes, he was.

Q: All right.

A: Drs. Baker, Charlie, and Dog were all residents on the neurological—Dr. Knifeblade's service.
'Have discussed with the neurological service, Dr. Baker. Plan to extubate this morning with close observation of arterial blood gases and parameters.'

Q: Now, Doctor, you had reviewed, as you note, the prior events that had occurred with this patient?

A: Yes.

Q: And you knew that she had been extubated twice before?

A: That's correct.

Q: And had to be reintubated?

A: Yes.

Q: And you knew that after each extubation, she had become obstructed?

A: Yes.

Q: And you knew that the last time, at 1:45 in the morning, she had to be reintubated?

A: Yes.

Q: And notwithstanding that and Dr. Knifeblade's note in the chart to leave the tube in place, you went ahead and extubated her?

A: [No response.]

After a short pause, I said, "Thank you," and sat down. On the crucial issues of agency and negligence, the point had been made. And it had been made without humiliating the young doctor and, more importantly, without offending and losing the jury.

By the way, we won the case, and the verdict against the hospital was more than $15 million.

Some witnesses are sympathetic only in contrast to those on the other side. The story I am about to tell—which comes not from one of my own examinations, but from that of a colleague and friend who has taught me an occasional trick—is a good example.

Hearing the facts, you might think that the witness, the plaintiff in the case, would be an easy target. But you had to be there. The problem was that the defendant, my friend's client, was the unappealing sort who sometimes inspires juries to vote the death penalty—in civil cases.

The witness, a young American model, sued for false arrest after being apprehended by the Paris police on complaint of the defendant. It seems the defendant, who had paid the young lady's way to Paris, was angered when she left without kissing him good-bye, and with his entire bankroll.

The plaintiff had wholesome, girl-next-door looks and a likable manner—the kind that wins Miss America contests. Her testimony was forthright and credible and gave a plausible explanation for her conduct. She had flown to Paris with the defendant, she said, only after he had led her to believe that she was to participate in a beauty contest there. Her agency had sent her and several other models to try out for a series of commercials being produced for a large and successful company run by the defendant's family. The defendant told her that she had won the tryouts, but that she would have to win the contest in Paris to appear in the commercials.

On arrival at the *Georges V*, one of Paris's plushest hotels, the plaintiff discovered to her horror that the defendant had booked her with him in the same room, which had only one bed. She escaped at the first opportunity. She took the defendant's money, she said, so she could buy herself a plane ticket home. Also, she expected the defendant to pursue her, and she hoped that a lack of ready cash would slow him down.

What made this all so believable was the defendant himself. Exceptionally homely, his mien both shifty and possessive, he had the air of a man who was not above unscrupulous conduct in pursuit of romance. And, in fact, before luring the plaintiff to Paris, he had plied her with gifts in a vain attempt to win her affections.

The Low-Key Approach

The plaintiff's lawyer must have thought he had a terrific case. No doubt when he prepared his client for deposition, he advised her to expect a vicious attack on her character and morals—relishing all the while the expectation that such savagery would merely increase the sympathy for his client, who was now being abused by both the defendant and his lawyer.

My friend, however, refused to play that role. Instead, his tone was searching, low-key, even quizzical. And his questions stuck pretty closely to the facts of the case:

Q: Ms. Wholesome, how long had you known my client before making the trip?

A: Three months.

Q: Where did you meet him?

613

A: At the club where I worked.

Q: How long before your trip to Paris?

A: About six weeks.

Q: Had you dated him before?

A: Him! Absolutely not.

Q: You would not go out with him?

A: No. He was definitely not my type.

Q: Someone you wanted to have nothing to do with?

A: Oh, definitely.

Q: But he was a regular customer at the club?

A: Yes.

Q: Every night?

A: Well, almost every night.

Q: So you wanted to please him?

A: No more than anyone else.

Q: Well, you knew he liked you?

A: I suppose.

Q: In fact, he gave you gifts, didn't he?

A: Uh huh.

Q: What did he give you?

A: Well, he gave me a small replica of an oriental shrine.

Q: What was it made of?

A: I don't know.

Q: Well, it was ivory, wasn't it?

A: That's what I was told.

Q: By an appraiser?

A: No, by a friend—who was an art collector.

Q: And what did he appraise it at?

A: Well, he thought it was worth 15 to 20,000.

Q: Dollars?

A: Yes.

Q: He also gave you another present, didn't he?

A: Well, I didn't want to take it.

Q: But you took it?

A: Yes.

Q: What was it?

A: A bracelet.

Q: Diamond bracelet?

A: Uh huh.

Q: What did your appraiser tell you that one was worth?

A: 15,000 more or less.

Q: Same appraiser?

A: No, this was a friend—a friend in the jewelry business I happened to date.

Q: Just to be clear, you did take the gifts?

A: Well, I didn't want to—but he insisted.

Q: And he being a good customer, you didn't want to hurt his feelings?

A: [No response.]

Q: But you still wouldn't go out with him?

A: Definitely not.

Q: Now getting back to the Paris trip, when did you first decide to go to Paris with Mr. Devious?

A: When I found out his family was the customer my modeling agency was working with.

Q: When was that?

A: The night before we left for Paris. The four runners-up were feted at a dinner to select the winner.

Q: And you won?

A: Yes.

Q: You knew how you won?

A: Well, not exactly, I thought it was my looks, you know.

Q: So you agreed to go to Paris with him?

A: Yes, but only to take photographs.

Q: You knew he was booked on the same plane and he had the seat next to you?

A: Well, yes, but not that he also planned to stay with me in Paris.

Q: Well, didn't you ask where he was staying in Paris?

A: No, I didn't even know where I would be staying. He had made all the arrangements.

Q: What did you talk about on the plane?

A: Small talk, you know, he told me how his family owned the company that was promoting the contest.

Q: Now, when you got to the hotel in Paris, you found you were both registered in one room?

A: A suite—one-bedroom suite.

Q: And you went into the room?

A: Well, I didn't want to, but Mr. Devious and, yes, the man at the desk said that that was the only room in the house, something about a big convention in town.

Q: How many beds were there?

A: One—and I didn't like that either.

Q: Well, you didn't run out?

A: No, but I got into a big argument with him about it—and he left to go downstairs to the bar for a drink.

Q: Before he left did he say anything?

A: Nothing I want to repeat.

Q: Well, did he say anything about money?

A: Oh, that—well, he said he had brought a lot of money with him which was in his blue suit in his large suitcase, and for me not to let anyone in.

Q: By the way, how much money was there?
A: $12,000.
Q: And after he went down to the bar you decided to go back to the States?
A: Yes. I thought that definitely this was not for me.
Q: And to protect the money you decided to take it with you?
A: Well, I couldn't just leave it there.
Q: So you took it to protect it?
A: Yes, I took it—to protect it.
Q: Thank you.

Thus my friend accomplished his purpose. He had simply pressed the plaintiff for further explanations of her conduct until she was revealed as far less gullible and unsophisticated than she first appeared—indeed, as a worthy match for the hapless defendant, who, after all, had been the loser between them.

After the deposition, Ms. Wholesome's lawyer approached my friend to discuss settlement.

The next witness I will call Dr. Brainstem. He was a renowned, retired neurosurgeon, who was testifying for the defense in a medical malpractice case against a hospital, an internist, and another neurosurgeon.

To understand what follows, you will have to bear with me while I explain a few medical terms. My client had suffered brain damage (technically, nerve palsies) after surgery to remove what is known as an acoustic brain tumor; the name indicates that the tumor had developed in cranial nerve number 8 (there are 12 in all), which conducts auditory impulses from the inner ear. The operation left my client with extensive neurological damage, in large part because a questionable surgical technique had permitted a post-operative infection to develop in the "cranial ventricles." The ventricles are nothing more than tubes through which spinal fluid flows around the brain and into the spinal canal. In the days following the operation, the neurosurgeon had tried to treat the infection by repeatedly draining ("tapping") the infected fluid from the patient's head with a hypodermic syringe.

Dr. Brainstem was called as an expert witness by the neurosurgeon's lawyer, whom I will call Mr. Earnest. Mr. Earnest had saved the good doctor until the very end of the case, on the venerable theory that you should always close with a strong witness.

Dr. Brainstem seemed an ideal choice. He was near 80, or even past it, with more than half a century of experience in his field. His credentials, had they all been read to the jury, would have consumed more than an hour. As it was, Mr. Earnest spent some 15 minutes qualifying him. To me, sitting there helplessly, knowing full well the magnitude of Dr. Brainstem's qualifications, the time seemed an eternity. It took all my inner strength to look nonchalant and to restrain myself from jumping up and shouting, "No contest!"

After more than three hours on the stand, Dr. Brainstem had won the jury, heart and soul.

As expected, he exonerated the defendant-neurosurgeon. But he did it so persuasively that he pulled the other two defendants along as well. By the end of his testimony, it appeared that no one was liable.

As I studied the jurors' faces, I could not miss their serious expressions. All of them were turned intently toward Dr. Brainstem; not one of them was looking at me—definitely not a good sign! To make matters worse, my adversary drew out his direct (deliberately, I am sure) to conclude just at the morning recess, so the jury could ruminate on it over lunch.

But I had a letter, a smoking gun letter. It had been produced in discovery. The question was how and when to use it. My gloomy young associates, who had watched Dr. Brainstem perform in the morning, voted during lunch to lead him on during cross with a number of questionable points in his direct testimony, then spring the letter on him toward the end.

I saw it differently. The longer that witness remained on the stand unsoiled, the more impressed with him the jury would be. No, I had to destroy him with the first blow!

> Q: Dr. Brainstem, my name is Ring. I guess you know I represent the plaintiff?
>
> A: Yes.
>
> Q: I listened to you for several hours this morning, doctor, and in summary I take it that it's your testimony that nobody did anything wrong; is that right?
>
> A: What I said was that whatever was done was within the standard of practice, the physicians and hospital were confronted with a hopeless situation—impossible to cure.
>
> Q: So, no one did anything wrong?
>
> A: Yes, I think so.

I moved a touch closer.

> Q: Doctor, you haven't always felt that way, have you?
>
> A: What do you mean?
>
> Q: Do you remember the letter you wrote to your lawyer, Mr. Earnest, on July 27, 1983, Doctor?
>
> A: Yes.
>
> Q: Would you read it for us?
>
> A: You want me to read the whole thing?
>
> Q: Yeah, would you mind?

On cue, one of my associates moved toward a projector we had set up, and prepared to show a blow-up of Dr. Brainstem's letter on a screen for the jury to follow along.

Mr. Earnest, who was no dummy, objected and asked for a conference at sidebar.

MR. EARNEST: It's highly improper to attempt to impeach a witness

617

in this fashion. If the witness has made a statement and he's going to be impeached, [it] can be read from a document. But Mr. Ring hasn't—is not doing that. This document is no different than a deposition. . . . [I]n addition, I don't see any reason to put the letter on the screen, as Mr. Ring's associate was doing, and have the double impact, so to speak.

THE COURT: Can I see the letter?

MR. RING: Sure.

MR. EARNEST: The only reason I bring it to the court's attention is that this should not be done any differently than any witness who [is] going to be contradicted, or impeached . . . and to throw the letter up on the screen for the jury and then ask the witness to read it is a double stroke.

I must confess that defense counsel was right to object, although maybe not for the reasons he gave in the heat of battle. According to the scriptures, impeachment requires that you first establish a prior inconsistent statement, which the witness gets a chance to admit, deny, or explain away. Then you argue to the jury that the witness is not to be believed because he has spoken out of both sides of his mouth. By asking Dr. Brainstem whether he had "always felt that way"—a question that really went to his state of mind—I was leaping ahead to my closing argument and trying to make Dr. Brainstem agree with it in advance.

But then, the classical approach is often a very, very dull way to make a point—and I was in a critical spot. Besides, this is an area of discretion, and no one can foretell what the judge's rulings will be. At worst, if I lost the gamble, the jury had already been alerted to be prepared for something hot.

As it happened, I lucked out.

MR. RING: This is cross-examination. The witness's last answer was that the plaintiff's entire problem is a result of a large tumor, and everything just followed from it, and nobody did anything wrong. And I think I have a right to show that he changed his opinion from what he had held earlier.

THE COURT: Well, I think the first paragraph [of the letter] is impeaching. I will allow him to read the first paragraph, and he can read the third sentence of the third paragraph, which seems overall to be directly contradictory to what he said on the witness stand today.

The court was not so generous with my attempt to flash the letter simultaneously on the screen before the jury, even after I offered to block out the inadmissible portions. As defense counsel had surmised, I wanted two bites at the apple: one, to let the jurors *hear* the damaging statement, and two, to let them *see* it and follow along while Dr. Brainstem read aloud. This was worth trying for, because statistically, after three days, jurors will recall 65 percent of what they see, but only 10 percent of what they hear. Obviously, my opponent had read those statistics or, like me, had observed the same phenomenon in practice.

After we left the sidebar, the cross-examination continued:

Q: Doctor, this letter that I have handed you is your response to a request by Mr. Earnest to review the records in this case in connection with the suit pending against Dr. Knifeblade, right?

A: This is in response to a letter from Mr. Earnest asking me to go over the records, yes.

Q: Doctor, was that your first knowledge of this case?

A: Yes.

Q: Do you have the letter that he sent you?

A: I don't have it anymore. I gave it to your representative at my deposition.

Q: Okay. But you wrote back to Mr. Earnest in response to his letter; is that right?

A: Yes.

Q: And that's the letter I handed you, right?

A: Yes.

Q: Doctor, would you please read for us the first paragraph of your letter?

A: 'Dear Mr. Earnest:
The situation with acoustic tumors is the smaller the tumor, the more successful is its removal. To have multiple cranial nerve palsies—'

Q: Excuse me, doctor, it has medical terms, so would you mind reading it a bit slower—so we can follow it?

If I could not have my projector and screen, I could at least force the witness to focus the jury's attention on the damning parts of the letter!

A: 'To have multiple cranial nerve palsies after removal of a tumor of, say, five centimeters' diameter is not unheard of. They are, however, rare. I have had one patient in my 50-year career who had 5, 6, 7, and 8 cranial nerves damaged. I have not had 9, 10, 11, 12 damaged. To lose 7 and 8 completely is commonplace. To lose 5 through 12 is, I think, beyond my experience.'

Q: Doctor, would you read the last sentence?

A: 'I think the surgeon would have to give a reasonable explanation of what might have gone wrong.'

Q: Doctor, would you next read the first sentence of the last paragraph beginning with, 'Repeated'? Do you see it, sir?

A: Yes.
'Repeated tapping of the wound in the face of infection of the ventricles would not be in accord with common practice.'

I paused for a moment to let that sink in.

Q: And would you read the last sentence?

A: Overall, the impression I have is that this would be difficult to defend.'

Although the letter did not use terms like negligence or malpractice, it
was clear from my tone, mixed with appropriate pauses, that Dr. Brainstem had earlier told Mr. Earnest, albeit in a carefully-guarded fashion,
that the defendant-neurosurgeon's treatment had deviated from the
proper standard of care. For that reason, the case would be ''difficult to
defend.''

With that, I had achieved my goal of discrediting this otherwise impeccable witness. The way was now clear for further impeachment on
other portions of Dr. Brainstem's direct where he had stretched the
truth—points that would have seemed mere quibbles if the jury's sense
of him had remained what it was when I first stood to cross-examine.

It bears repeating: This type of witness must be demolished with the
first salvo. Later may be too late.

No Questions

But what do you do if you do not have a smoking gun? And what
about the kind of witness who just cannot be impeached? Take, for example, the severely brain-damaged quadriplegic who faces the jury not
from the witness stand, but from his wheelchair, accompanied at all
times by a nurse. Or the mother of a teenager killed or maimed, who
relates her child's educational ambitions and love of sports. Or the nun
who shows up as the representative of a hospital sued for malpractice.

I have had them all.

Others may offer different advice. For me it is easy. Half rise in your
seat and say, very, very respectfully: No questions, your honor.

Crossing the Star

by Scott Turow

It may be the plaintiff in a personal injury case or the defendant mounting the stand to testify in a criminal prosecution. It may be the chief executive officer of a company involved in an acquisition struggle; a former employee who is complaining about the circumstances of his job termination; or a co-conspirator who has made a deal to testify for the state. Virtually every trial has its central players, the star witnesses whose critical position in the litigation makes the cross-examination a special crossroad for opposing counsel.

Obviously, all of the classic pointers for cross-examination apply to these confrontations. Start and end on a high note. Make a limited number of points and emphasize them. Err on the side of brevity. Avoid opening doors. Think about the redirect and avoid points that may prove to be merely rhetorical achievements which, when refuted, will diminish your credibility with the finder of fact.

But the star witness's cross-examination also has special imperatives. The main principles are not revolutionary or numerous; they come down to two words: planning and caution. The central witness's cross requires a carefully calibrated sense of what you need to accomplish. Such an examination also is enhanced by recognizing that the star's presence magnifies the potential for gain or loss.

The following observations amplify those two themes. The suggestions, however, are far from statutory, and, like any other rules of trial advocacy, they no doubt are proved by their exceptions. Still, they have enough currency to bear repeating.

First, figure out what you must accomplish. There are times you get up to

---

The author is a partner in the Chicago law firm of Sonnenschein Carlin Nath & Rosenthal. He is the author of two novels.

cross-examine a witness while smothering the inexpressible feeling that comes from having no idea of what to ask. That happens when the witness has appeared as a surprise—a tangential player who was somehow invited into the courtroom by the course of the trial itself. But it should not happen when you confront your opponent's star. The rule here is to plan and prepare with a single focus: What do I need to accomplish?

Of the countless cross-examinations I have heard, not one of them equaled what I saw every week as a child on Perry Mason. In real courtrooms, witnesses do not break down and confess on the stand, the alibi witness never admits that the defendant was not really with him, and the chief accuser does not grow weak and uneasily confess that his testimony was made up. Instead, the success of a cross-examination can be measured by a witness's occasional self-contradictions, his evasions, and the cross-examiner's skill in eliciting facts favorable to his client—facts that mitigate a damaging direct examination or otherwise support the cross-examiner's theory of the case.

It is tempting to come to a critical cross-examination thinking that you have to slay the witness. Lawyers may adopt this guerilla warfare mentality on their own, or they may be urged on by clients whose differences with their opponents become even more intense during the fury of trial. But it is wise to consider whether you really need to blast with both barrels during cross.

Even if your opponent's case rests substantially on the star witness's testimony, you are not required to engage in a snarling confrontation. For one thing, it is hard to remain well liked once you have displayed your worst side. More importantly, doing so may make it difficult to succeed. The heated and intense cross-examination assailing a witness's credibility on all fronts is a high-risk undertaking. In making it, you often communicate the unmistakable impression that you think the witness's direct testimony is so devastating to your case that you will lose if the witness is believed.

Of course, sometimes that is true. Criminal defense work, especially, is likely to present situations where a no-holds-barred cross-examination of the government's chief witnesses is indispensable. If a co-conspirator says that your client masterminded the crime, there is little place for subtlety or nuance on cross-examination. Either you slay the dragon or he slays you.

But before beginning your cross, consider whether there is some alternative to the junkyard dog approach. Again, what do you need to accomplish?

Listen to a senior prosecutor about to cross-examine a defendant who had flatly denied the testimony of six government witnesses. When asked, "What are you going to do with him on cross?" the prosecutor replied, "Very little." He explained, "Nobody is going to believe him anyway."

622

Six people had come before the jury, sworn to God to tell the truth, and directly contradicted the defendant. Engaging in an extensive attack on the defendant's testimony was unnecessary and may even have given credence to the defendant's story.

In civil cases, especially, the case may come down to interpreting events that are substantially undisputed. Were statements made with the intention of entering into a binding agreement or were they merely hopeful projections? Were the acts that harmed the plaintiff the result of negligence or bad luck?

When these are the issues, your summation will not be substantially changed by the star witness's testimony. Your case depends on developing certain favorable facts whose persuasive influence you hope will ultimately prevail over whatever your opponent can offer. Your goal on cross is only to gain some small edge that can be used to buttress the convictions of jurors already disinclined to accept the star's testimony. With your points made, you should sit down. Trying to win a confession may only give the opponent the chance to refute your case again, detail by detail. Your attack on the star is your case as a whole, not a devastating cross-examination, and the best time to explain why that is so may be closing argument, when the star is gone and no longer can offer a rebuttal.

Sometimes you want to create the impression that the star witness has not said anything that hurts your case. That tack is not consistent with a spirited cross-examination. Instead, a polite, even welcoming, cross may be called for. Sometimes you will focus your cross on a concession you know from depositions that you can obtain. In that case get it, gild it, and get out.

In the end, you have to know your evidence and your theory of the case. No matter how tempting the chance to play Perry Mason, ask yourself if the game is worth the risk.

The other side's star also can help you develop your case. The star stands before the jury as the opposition's spokesperson. Whether the witness is an executive of one of the parties, a co-schemer, or another witness critical to the transaction, the star witness is somebody who is presented as having unique knowledge of contested facts.

The first inclination is to use cross-examination to undermine the witness's credibility, whether by contradiction or by exposing bias, motive to fabricate, or failed recollection. But sometimes the best examiners exploit an important witness so that, to one degree or another, they make the witness their own. Rather than trying to assail the opponent's contentions, you may instead advance your own case through the cross-examination of a supposed antagonist.

As a prosecutor, I lost a bribery case when the defense attorney asked the immunized public official we claimed had been paid off, ''Isn't it true that the defendant always told you not to do anything wrong when-

623

ever he gave you money?'' The witness stared at the ceiling for 30 seconds and finally answered, ''Yes.''

Rarely will your opponent's star deal a blow as devastating as that to his own side; but usually the witness has some helpful information. Consider the key points of your case and see how many of them the other side's star can confirm.

Often the other side's star cannot deny contentions fundamental to your case. Suppose you represent an employee in a lawsuit against his employer. The company is never going to minimize the importance of its own mission or, a fortiori, of the employee's responsibilities—whatever the employer thinks about the way your client carried out those responsibilities. ''Now even though it's the bottom of the organizational ladder, the mail room has an important function in your company, does it not, Mr. Jones? Your company can't function without the smooth flow of information, can it? And the folks who work in the mail room are, in a very real sense, part of an important, even indispensable, operation, aren't they?''

While I was an assistant United States attorney, I was involved in a series of prosecutions at the Cook County Board of Appeals, a local real estate tax reviewing agency where some lawyers had made it a practice to pay off decision-making officials. The investigation moved in waves. First, officials were convicted; then they were turned against lawyers who, after their convictions, implicated a new round of officials. More than a dozen trials took place, with some of the government's chief witnesses testifying half a dozen times about conduct that varied little from case to case.

Over time, our witnesses had developed a demeanor of quiet confidence that kept them from being cowed by the harsh denunciations of defense counsel. That made the standard direct confrontation an especially difficult technique on cross-examination. One attorney did an especially good job of coping by making the prosecution's witness his own. His client was a deputy board commissioner. The lawyer's theory, announced in the opening argument, was that his client had taken some (but not all) of the money the government's witnesses claimed they had paid him, but that the deputy commissioner regarded the payments as gifts motived by friendship. Thus, the witnesses had enlarged these occasional kindnesses into a procession of bribes in their attempt to please the government.

This theory allowed the defense to avoid direct confrontation with the government's strongest witnesses. The defense lawyer cross-examined the most contrite of the government's convicted lawyer-witnesses for 45 minutes. He never challenged the witness's contention that there had been six payments instead of two, as the deputy commissioner contended. Instead the lawyer spent the full 45 minutes eliciting a succession of details about the warm friendship between his client and the witness. On redirect examination, we could do little to dispute our own witness.

Although the jury ultimately rejected the defense, the strategy had dealt as effectively as possible with damaging prosecution testimony. The story makes an important point: The opponent's star may be converted to your own cause; in fact, he may be very useful to you in that capacity. In approaching a focal cross-examination, no matter how you disdain the witness, you should consider what he can do for you.

Whatever your strategy on cross-examination, you need to do your best not to get hurt. The cross-examination of a pivotal witness presents opportunities not only for gain, but also for disaster. What is merely imprudent with a less significant witness can be magnified into a blunder of the first order with the star.

Demeanor is foremost. You must know in advance how you intend to react to the witness. It is important to show disbelief towards a witness whose credibility you mean to assail. I remember one veteran prosecutor who would demonstrate a cross-examination that consisted of nothing more than advancing on the defendant with a wagging finger, while repeating the defendant's direct testimony in a scornful tone.

Usually, though, a witness should be challenged with an approach that is firm but not openly contemptuous. The star witness is a pivotal player whom the jury knows a lot about. His point of view likely commands some sympathy—otherwise, the case would not be on trial. The cross-examiner who examines so hard that he alienates the jury takes an enormous risk. Going for broke and missing is likely to cost you more than just a loss of ground in proving facts. Even if you score points, a cross-examination that appears overzealous can devastate a lawyer's credibility.

Criminal defense lawyers should be careful that they do not get caught up in trying to satisfy their client's desire to see the government's cooperating witness bloodied. In post-trial interviews, I have heard more than one juror say that what appeared to be a devastating cross-examination had left the witness's credibility largely unaffected. The witness may have contradicted himself and often seemed unsure, yet the jurors found the cross-examination so bullying and protracted that they felt they would have admitted anything themselves, just as the witness did, in order to end the examination.

The point is to beware of having too much of a good thing on cross-examination. Occasionally in criminal trials, witnesses will acknowledge such contemptible conduct in such unsympathetic circumstances that they can be brutalized freely by cross-examiners. But by and large, witnesses have understandable reasons for having behaved as they did, and the fact finder seldom welcomes a protracted display of discourtesy.

Behaving courteously can keep you from getting hurt and, in the process, smooth the path for the win. Recently I appeared in an administrative proceeding on the west coast involving two large companies in a heated contest for control of a third. The chief executive officer of my client's rival was a charming older man, well known to the commission. I was a younger lawyer from "the East" with a fistful of devastating documents. The documents proved very handy indeed, but the cross-examination was conducted with a politesse appropriate to a drawing room. I smiled to show I was not mean-spirited. The chief executive officer smiled to show he was not beaten. The commissioners smiled to show their gratitude that everybody was being so nice. And my client won big.

A corollary to not getting hurt on cross-examination is to learn to control the star witness. This may not be easy, because the pivotal personalities frequently are strong personalities as well. Unresponsive witnesses often are disliked by juries, but star witnesses may proceed under different rules. The fact finder is eager to hear what they have to say, and the court often will grant them wide latitude to expand on answers or even to make an occasional aside. Once a young lawyer asked an older lawyer, "How can a young lawyer control a witness?" The answer: "Get older."

But there are other ways. You might begin the star's examination in areas where control is easier to establish. For example, you might begin with questions about the contents of documents. Essentially you are asking a witness to agree with you about various numbers or words that appear on a printed page. In a civil case, you might begin by reading a string of deposition answers; this likewise will have the effect of anchoring the witness and preventing him from straying. Once you and the witness know you have established control, you can work toward more difficult parts of the examination.

As a prosecutor I cross-examined Judge Reginald Holzer, on trial for extortion, racketeering, and mail fraud. Holzer was 20 years my senior and, at the time, a sitting judge of the chancery division of the circuit court of Cook County. The government's case had emphasized the authority of this position to explain Holzer's consistent extortion of various financial favors from lawyers who had cases pending in his courtroom. It would have been inconsistent with this theory, and personally unbecoming for me, to upbraid the defendant. On the other hand, it was essential that Holzer, a commanding personality, not be allowed to dominate the courtroom—and, thus, the jury.

I began my cross-examination with one of the defendant's own exhibits. Holzer had prepared a list to dispute the government's contention that he had in essence sold receiverships in his courtroom in exchange for financial benefits. His list showed that of the 17 receiverships in his courtroom that had netted fees of more than $5,000, only one third had gone to the two government witnesses who had testified that they provided benefits to the judge. My plan was to start cross-examination by confronting Holzer with other financial records showing that all but 2 of those 17 receivers had provided financial benefits of some kind—cash, unrepaid loans, assistance in obtaining bank loans, or the purchase of insurance from Holzer's wife.

For most of the first two hours of the cross-examination, Judge Holzer refused to answer questions directly; instead he temporized, he qualified, and he reacted with considerable hauteur. But the procession of documents allowed me to meet each evasion and to make Holzer appear obstreperous and even dishonest. The papers let me take control.

Finally, you must remember the rule against asking questions to which you do not know the answers. The rule is better phrased as not asking such questions when you cannot adjust to the wrong answer. But however framed, nowhere is the rule more important than on these pivotal cross-examinations. Whatever hazards you are willing to run with a minor witness, you invite devastation with a star. Tame the impulse of adrenalized courtroom excitement, and do your best to hold your tongue when you are not prepared to handle any possible response.

627

PART VIII

Evidence Issues

A Quick Review of the Federal Rules

by James W. McElhaney

The very idea that there would be Federal Rules of Evidence was exciting. Evidence suddenly became more important—not just a loosely knit group of ideas that federal courts casually adopted from the locals (and which necessarily varied from state to state). Federal Rules could bring reform, simplicity, and uniformity.

They could provide inspiration—a standard the states could look to for guidance in preparing for the year 2000 and beyond. It was in this spirit that the Supreme Court turned to the proposed rules to give definition to the requirements of the Fourteenth Amendment in *Chambers v. Mississippi*, 410 U.S. 284 (1973).

New rules of evidence suggested an opportunity for rethinking old ideas; creating new intellectual models that would not only cause us to reexamine an entire subject, but would let us borrow the new ideas for an exciting sort of legal cross-fertilization.

Some of that—but not nearly enough of any of it—turned out to be true.

Working with the rules has made us lower our expectations. The Federal Rules of Evidence are not a code. They are not self-sufficient. Many of the rules only make sense against a detailed understanding of the common law. A number of the provisions are fragmentary, leaving the gaps to whatever was already in place or to subsequent judicial development. Moreover, some areas were simply left out.

Do not let that give you the wrong impression. It is a worthwhile contribution to write a restatement of evidence that covers most of the main points. The Federal Rules do that and more.

The author is former editor-in-chief of Litigation *and Joseph C. Hostetler Professor of Trial Practice and Advocacy at Case Western Reserve University School of Law in Cleveland.*

Nowhere in the Federal Rules has there been a great conceptual departure from the common law, but some rules, such as expert witnesses and the best evidence rule, have been significant steps forward, while some of the tricky parts have been taken out of character evidence.

It is not a great reformation, yet the rules set the new standard for the admissibility of prior convictions used to impeach witnesses—especially defendants in criminal cases.

In the seven years since their adoption, trial lawyers have not only lowered their expectations for the rules, they have changed their attitude toward them somewhat. What once looked intriguing may now appear to be a wrinkle or a wart, while some blemishes have seemed to fade. The following catalogue discusses some of the warts and gleams of the Federal Rules:

1. Hearsay Definition

Consistency may be an overrated virtue, but inconsistency can be a genuine vice.

Rule 801 defines hearsay as a "statement, other than one made by the declarant while testifying at the trial or hearing offered in evidence to prove the truth of the matter asserted."

It is—for a set of rules—decently short and clear. Two things are required: 1) an out-of-court statement 2) that is offered for its truth. The authors of the rules successfully avoided the more arcane academic pronouncements about hearsay and used the working definition that most trial lawyers prefer instead.

That was commendable. The next step was not.

Faced with a definition of hearsay, most lawyers would think that if evidence fits the definition it should be called hearsay, and that to be admissible it should have to qualify as an exception to the hearsay rule. That simple pattern is the approach of the common law, one that is easy to apply in the pressure of a trial.

But consistency ran out. Instead, Rule 801 contains—as part of the definition of what is hearsay—a number of important exceptions to the hearsay rule. Why did the drafters do that when there were two rules specifically set aside for hearsay exceptions?

There is an answer, but it is not a very good one.

Admissions are a common-law exception to the hearsay rule. But in the Federal Rules they are called "nonhearsay." In the Advisory Committee notes, the drafters say that admissions are "excluded from the category of hearsay on the theory that their admissibility in evidence is the result of the adversary system rather than satisfaction of the conditions of the hearsay rule."

It is not very compelling logic. Admissions are out-of-court statements. We admit them for their truth. In other words, they fit the definition of hearsay in the Federal Rules. That they do not share the

631

unreliability of other hearsay is reason enough to make admissions admissible in evidence. That there may be different good reasons for admitting them that are not shared by other hearsay exceptions does not mean they should be called "nonhearsay."

Not content with admissions, the authors also declared that some prior consistent and inconsistent statements are non-hearsay as well— but admissible for their truth. They gave statements of prior identification the same treatment—admissible for their truth, but non-hearsay. They also chose the definition of what is hearsay as the place to put the foundation for prior consistent statements. The foundation for prior *inconsistent* statements, however, is in Article Six, Witnesses.

In short, the drafters did not stick with their definition, but garnished it with rules of admissibility and exclusion that belong in other parts of the hearsay section or in entirely different articles.

Should that matter? The result is the same—the evidence is either admissible because it is non-hearsay or admissible because it is an exception to the hearsay rule. What difference does it make where it is located, especially if its location satisfies some deep-felt academic need?

Major exceptions to the hearsay rule—especially ones that have been recognized for hundreds of years—do not belong in a rule that defines hearsay. It makes the organization harder to use and gives no genuine reward in return.

Like the medieval scholar who stayed up too late, the definition of hearsay in the Federal Rules smells of the lamp. And what pleases the scholar at night may frustrate the lawyer during the day as he tries to find the right rule in the middle of trial. A system of organization is not much help if you have to know where the rule is before you start to look for it. That may not bother lawyers who use the rules every day, but it is a trap for those who only get occasional trials.

Having seen the practical annoyance caused by the Federal Rules, New York did something different in its proposed code of evidence. It took admissions, prior identification, and prior statements back out of Rule 801 and made them exceptions to the hearsay rule. That is a sensible improvement.

2. Privileges

Some of the most important work done by the drafters of the Federal Rules was in the field of privileges. But in the early 1970s, privileges— particularly *governmental* and *executive* privileges—suddenly became unpopular. The specific rules were dropped and a general provision was enacted instead. It says that federal courts should be "governed by the principles of the common law as they may be interpreted by the courts of the United States in the light of reason and experience." To avoid forum-shopping problems, the rule defers to state law "with respect to an element of a claim or defense as to which State law supplies the rule of decision."

It was an understandable accommodation to the times. But Watergate is over, and we still do not have any real section on privileges in the Federal Rules.

The gap has not been unnoticed. The Supreme Court recently took advantage of it nearly to destroy the familiar rule that let a defendant in a criminal case keep his spouse from testifying against him unless that spouse was the victim of the crime. In *Trammel v. United States,* 445 U.S. 40 (1980), the Court held that the privilege no longer belonged to the defendant, but only to the spouse who had been called as a witness.

3. Other Crimes or Wrongs

The theory is easy to state. Only evidence tending to show that a defendant is guilty of the crime charged is supposed to be admissible in evidence. If a defendant in a criminal case has committed other crimes, they are not admissible to show that he is guilty of the one he is charged with now.

This is not because the evidence has no probative value. On the contrary. Experience is one of our few guides to the future. Other acts do have probative value. Failure to pay attention to the other acts of a person can easily constitute negligence. The driving record that would be inadmissible against the operator of a car can be offered against the owner to establish negligent entrustment. *Guedon v. Rooney,* 160 Ore. 621, 87 P.2d 209, 120 A.L.R. 1298 (1939).

So when evidence of prior acts is offered against the defendant in a criminal case, it is not excluded because it lacks probative value, but because the danger of misuse by the jury is too great. In the language of evidence, its probative value is outweighed by its prejudicial effect.

But do not conclude that evidence of other crimes or wrongs is completely inadmissible. It may not be admitted to show that the defendant is the sort of person who would commit this crime. But if evidence of other crimes or wrongs is relevant to prove something else, it is admissible.

That is the starting point for understanding what the Federal Rules do with other crimes and wrongs. Rule 404(b) gives a decently accurate restatement of the common law. It provides:

> Evidence of other crimes, wrongs, or acts is not admissible to prove the character of a person in order to show that he acted in conformity therewith. It may, however, be admissible for other purposes, such as proof of motive, opportunity, intent, preparation, plan, knowledge, identity, or absence of mistake or accident.

The similarity between this rule and the common law is perhaps its biggest problem. A few examples should show why that is so.

In the first, the defendant is charged with robbing a federally insured bank. Because it is a federal crime, he is being tried in federal court. Stealing a car that is not taken across state lines is not a federal offense.

633

But evidence that the defendant stole a car to serve as a getaway vehicle would be admissible because it showed "preparation" or "plan."

That is how the rule is supposed to work. Evidence of other crimes is admissible when it is relevant for some purpose other than poisoning the well. But now consider this second case:

The defendant is charged with the burglary of a woman's apartment. He is acquitted, then charged with another burglary. Evidence tending to show he was guilty of the crime for which he had been acquitted was offered in the second trial on the issue of "intent."

Just to make sure you have it straight, the two burglaries were not similar enough to be evidence of identity, nor did one provide the motive for the other. The only excuse for offering the evidence is that buglary is a crime of intent.

As it is. But intent was not really in issue. The only real question was identity, but this evidence did not go to that point.

Would a prosecutor attempt such a transparent way around the general rule?

Certainly. Could both a trial and an appellate court accept the evidence without critical injury?

Without a doubt. *See People v. Massey*, 196 Cal. App. 2d 230, 16 Cal. Rptr. 402 (1961). The case is representative of the way in which many courts treat evidence of other crimes or wrongs—the principle is often stated but seldom honored.

The drafters of the Federal Rules had an opportunity to attack this problem, but did not. Professor Kenneth W. Graham's reaction sums it up:'' [T]his is a topic deserving of some statutory ordering. Lamentably, the Advisory Committee chose to leave the law in its messy state; Rule 404(b) does nothing to clarify the issues, and may in some respects have muddied the waters even more.'' 22 C. WRIGHT & K. GRAHAM, FEDERAL PRACTICE AND PROCEDURE: EVIDENCE § 5239 (1978).

4. Subsequent Remedial Measures

The tenant falls through the front steps and sues the landlord for his injuries. After the fall (but before the suit), the landlord fixes the steps. Now the landlord claims that he was not negligent in the way he maintained the steps, so the tenant wants to use evidence of the repair as an admission of the defective condition.

Enter the rules of relevance.

It used to be thought that subsequent remedial measures had no probative value—that is, they did not raise a valid inference that there had been any negligence. *Columbia and Puget Sound R. R. Co. v. Hawthorne*, 144 U.S. 202 (1892). Later we came to realize that the more sensible reason for the rule is that we want to encourage remedial measures—or at least we do not want to discourage them. The result is that we do not permit evidence of repairs to prove fault.

But because it is a rule of evidence, it is riddled with exceptions. Subsequent repairs are admissible to show almost anything except negligence. Once again, the Federal Rules restate the law. Rule 407 provides:

> When, after an event, measures are taken which, if taken previously, would have made the event less likely to occur, evidence of the subsequent measures is not admissible to prove negligence or culpable conduct in connection with the event. This rule does not require the exclusion of evidence of subsequent measures when offered for another purpose, such as proving ownership, control, or feasibility of precautionary measures, if controverted, or impeachment.

So if our landlord argued that he had no obligation to repair the steps, or that they could not have been made safer than they were, the repairs would be admissible.

There it is—a judge-made rule enacted by Congress as part of the Federal Rules of Evidence. Perhaps that is its difficulty. To understand why, we turn to a recent California case, *Ault v. International Harvester Co.*, 13 Cal. 3d 113, 528 P.2d 1148, 117 Cal. Rptr. 812 (1974).

In the *Ault* case, two men were riding in an International Harvester Scout. Suddenly it went out of control and plunged to the bottom of a 500-foot cliff. Both of them developed retrograde amnesia about the accident. In the wreckage it was found that the steering gearbox—the housing that holds the gears that transmit control from the steering wheel to the front wheels—was broken. The box was made out of an aluminum alloy.

The plaintiffs claimed that a defect in the box caused the Scout to go out of control and plunge down the cliff. International Harvester, on the other hand, claimed that the fall to the bottom of the cliff broke the steering gearbox.

To prove their point, the plaintiffs wanted to introduce evidence that International Harvester had stopped making steering gearboxes out of aluminum alloy and had gone back to what other auto manufacturers used, malleable iron.

It turned out to be important evidence. The case was tried twice. In the first trial, the judge excluded the evidence and there was a hung jury. In the second trial, the evidence was admitted and the jury found for the plaintiff.

On appeal, the Supreme Court of California had to interpret a statute nearly identical to Federal Rule 407. It held that in products liability cases, proof of subsequent remedial measures was admissible to prove a defective condition—on the dubious notion that making a defective product was not "culpable conduct." In other words, evidence of the switch back to malleable iron in manufacturing was admissible even though it did not fit any exception to the basic rule.

Some jurisdictions have followed the *Ault* holding, while others have rejected it. Lawyers who have thought about the problem tend to line up depending on the interests they usually represent.

Perhaps the most interesting aspect of the controversy is the stunted role played by the Federal Rules. Because Rule 407 was written before the *Ault* case was decided but was enacted by Congress a year afterward, the rules have provided no real guidance for dealing with the competing interests. But that does not mean that Rule 407 has not played a part.

There is the real possibility that Rule 407—the rule about subsequent remedial measures—is based on a false notion of human behavior. Perhaps landlords are going to repair their steps whether or not the evidence is admissible. If that is the case, then we are sacrificing relevant evidence and getting nothing in return. But there is little that federal judges can do about that now. Making the rules of evidence an act of Congress has limited judicial action to tinkering with definitions—like the Supreme Court of California did in the *Ault* case.

5. Business and Public Records

One of the astonishing things about the history of hearsay is that the business records exception was created by statute only about 50 years ago. Before that, commercial litigation had to struggle along under the old "shopbook rule." *See* McCORMICK ON EVIDENCE, 2d Ed., 717–19 (E. Cleary, ed. 1972).

For the most part, the Federal Rules version, Rule 803 (6), tracks the ideas—if not the language—of the early business records statutes. *See* Read, *The Business Records Exception: Something Less Than Revolutionary*, 2 LITIGATION, No. 1, at 25 (Fall 1975).

Like most state business records statutes, the federal rule is intended to have broad application. Rule 803 defines business as "business, institution, association, profession, occupation, and calling of every kind, whether or not conducted for profit." That definition is broad enough to include governmental activities of any sort.

The problem is that the Federal Rules also have a "public records" exception, Rule 803(8). And it overlaps with the business records exception. The public records exception has an important limitation, intended to protect defendants in criminal cases. Rule 803(8)(B) provides that "matters observed by police officers and other law enforcement personnel" are not admissible against the defendant in a criminal action.

The question is whether a prosecutor can avoid the protection given criminal defendants by choosing the business records rule rather than the public records exception. In *United States v. Oates*, 560 F.2d 45 (2d Cir. 1977), the court said no.

6. Prior Convictions

Anytime a witness takes the stand to testify, his credibility becomes an issue. That suggests a number of important things.

One of them is the right to attack the witness's credibility with prior convictions. The typical way to proceed is to confront the witness with the conviction on cross-examination. If he denies the conviction, it can be shown by extrinsic evidence—ordinarily by introducing a certified copy of the conviction.

This is the practice that most jurisdictions follow. Some of them permit a witness to make a brief "explanation" of the conviction on re-direct examination, while some states do not permit a witness to deny guilt. A few states apparently permit the explanation to be avoided by permitting the impeachment with documentary evidence after the witness has left the stand.

Instead of seeking uniformity on such minor problems, the authors of the Federal Rules concentrated on more important matters. Unfortunately, they did not get all of those, either. Yet what they accomplished was considerable.

Under the common law in most states, a witness could be impeached with a conviction for any felony or for a misdemeanor of "moral turpitude." Some states imposed the "moral turpitude" limitation on felonies as well, but only a few jurisdictions had a prohibition against using old convictions to impeach.

Rule 609 makes a significant change in this practice. It permits impeachment with any felony or misdemeanor of dishonesty or false statement. Other convictions can be used only if they are felonies and the trial court specifically determines that the probative value of the conviction outweighs the prejudicial effect to the defendant, a test adopted from *Luck v. United States*, 348 F.2d 763 (D.C. Cir. 1965). The other major change is the ten-year limit on convictions that may be used. Time is calculated from the date of conviction or release from confinement, whichever is later.

These are valuable changes, to be sure—yet they leave out something important. To understand just how important, you must picture yourself in preparation for trial in a criminal case. The person you are representing has two prior convictions—both less than ten years old—and neither involving dishonesty or false statement. Your defendant tells you he is not guilty and says he wants to testify on his own behalf.

Now you see the problem. What do you tell the defendant? Your entire strategy is determined by whether he testifies. And your advice on whether he should take the stand will hinge on the admissibility of the convictions. The difficulty is that the situation falls in the gray area in which the judge weighs probative value against prejudicial effect, so the trial judge might decide either way. What you need is a ruling before trial.

Rule 104(c) offers a little help, but not enough. It says that when the accused is a witness, he has the right to a hearing on preliminary matters outside the presence of the jury. That is fine for the middle of trial, but does nothing to help advance planning. You can make a motion to suppress in advance of trial, but the rules do not require the judge to hear it.

637

Instead of leaving it to the whim of the particular trial judge, New York's proposed evidence code makes pretrial determination of the admissibility of convictions a matter of right for a criminal defendant.

7. Learned Treatises

Experienced trial lawyers know that impeaching expert witnesses with learned treatises is difficult. If the expert is properly prepared, it will be difficult to get an agreement that a particular treatise was relied on in forming the opinion—or is even regarded as authoritative in the field.

The Federal Rules make that unnecessary. In addition to the testimony of the witness, the treatise can be established as authoritative by the testimony of another expert or even judicial notice.

One would expect a rule like that in Article Six, Witnesses, or perhaps in Article Seven, Experts. But it is not in either place. It is part of Rule 803(18), that makes learned treatises an exception to the hearsay rule. The common law rules in most jurisdictions did not admit learned treatises for their truth, but just to impeach. Rule 803(18) changes that and makes them admissible for their truth, but there are limitations. Not only must the treatise be recognized as authoritative, it is only admissible "[t]o the extent called to the attention of an expert witness on cross-examination or relied upon by him in direct examination. . . ."

8. No Privity Admissions

One of the consequences of squeezing major exceptions to the hearsay rule into the hearsay definition is that something is likely to be overlooked. That is apparently what happened to "privity admissions"—statements made by a predecessor in interest that were considered admissions at common law. A perfect example is provided by a recent case.

The plaintiff, Mrs. Huff, brought an action for wrongful death of her husband, who had been fatally injured driving a truck manufactured by the defendant, White Motor Corporation. While her husband was in the hospital before he died, he told a witness how the accident took place. The defendant offered the evidence as an admission, or alternatively under the catchall exceptions to the hearsay rule. The trial court excluded it.

The court of appeals reversed, holding that privity admissions could be admissible under Federal Rules 803(24) and 804(b)(5)—the catchall exceptions. *Huff v. White Motor Corp.*, 609 F.2d 286 (7th Cir. 1979). While the result makes sense, the difficulty the court goes through to reach a decision does not. It would be unfair to create a derivative cause of action that could be freed of the derivative admissions that might accompany it. Privity admissions make sense, and a court should not have to treat each one as an original question under an exception to the hearsay rule that was intended for unusual cases.

9. Two Identical Hearsay Exceptions

When the proposed Federal Rules of Evidence went to Congress, there were two different catchall exceptions—one in Rule 803 and the other in Rule 804. The exceptions in Rule 803 are admissible in evidence whether or not the declarant is available as a witness. The exceptions in Rule 804, on the other hand, require that the declarant be unavailable. As originally drafted, there were some minor differences between the two catchall exceptions in addition to the availability of the declarant.

But not after Congress had finished. In a master stroke of legislative equality, Congress made the two exceptions identical. The result is that now the only difference between them is that one requires a showing that the declarant is unavailable, while the other does not. And if you talk to those who watched the rules go through Congress, they will admit in private that it makes no sense to have both.

But there are some who think the emperor is well dressed. They insist there is an advantage to having the same catchall in two separate lists of hearsay exceptions.

Some of the states that have adopted the rules have been fooled as well. Ohio was not. It refused to adopt either one, apparently on the idea that judges had no rightful place in the continuing development of judge-made rules.

New York, on the other hand, saw the value of the catchall exception, but realized it needed only one. It kept the one in Rule 804, with some modifications. The result requires a showing of nonavailability of a declarant before catchall hearsay is admissible. In view of the general policy favoring live testimony, that makes good sense.

The Silent Revolution

by Faust F. Rossi

The Federal Rules of Evidence have brought about a quiet revolution. They are destroying many traditional barriers to proof.

Three words describe the direction in which the Federal Rules of Evidence have taken us: *discretion, creativity,* and *admissibility.* The codes give abundant discretionary power to the trial courts. The judges add a sizable measure of interpretive creativity. Greater admissibility has resulted.

The federal rules bristle with language granting discretion to the trial judge. Rule 102 invites judicial construction to promote the "growth and development of the law of evidence." The relevance standard of Rule 403 allows exclusion of even relevant evidence if the court finds its probative value substantially outweighed by the danger of prejudice, confusion, or undue delay. Rule 609 authorizes impeachment by proof of certain felonies if the court determines that the probative value outweighs the prejudice.

Rules 701 and 702 deem lay and expert opinions appropriate if the opinions are "helpful" or "will assist the trier of fact." Hearsay, not otherwise admissible, may be received if the judge determines (among other things) that "the general purposes of these rules and the interests of justice will best be served by admission of the statement into evidence." So say the residual hearsay exceptions embodied in Rule 803(24) and 804(b)(5).

The judge's power to determine foundation questions that underlie admissibility provides him additional discretion. Trial judges react differently to the inviting language of the rules. Some are restrained, but most enthusiastically grasp the opportunity to make changes. A review of the last seven years shows that judicial activism has carried the day.

What an irony. Not everyone favored Federal Rules of Evidence.

The author is the Samuel S. Liebowitz Professor of Trial Techniques at the Cornell Law School. He presented a speech based on this article at the November 1982 meeting of the Section of Litigation.

Many feared that rules would produce rigidity. Some believed that only case-by-case adjudication permitted principles of evidence to mesh with the facts and needs of individual cases. These critics argued that the clarity and uniformity of a code might not be worth the danger. Codification threatened to give us wooden rules that would stifle judicial enterprise and that could not cover unforeseen circumstances.

There was no need to worry. Judicial ingenuity has been stimulated, not stifled. When necessary (and sometimes when not), the courts have stretched or even disregarded the language of the rules and the intent of Congress. We have flexibility aplenty.

The result has been greater admissibility of evidence. That is the fundamental lesson of the federal rules. Many have sensed the trend, but few appreciate its scope or the pace at which the barriers are falling.

Free Admissibility

The once-restrictive best evidence rule is rendered obsolete by the creation of "duplicates" under Rules 1001 and 1003. Rule 902 abandons the formality of a foundation for a broad category of documents deemed "self-authenticating." Rules 702 to 705 eliminate traditional limitations on expert testimony. Once he has shown relevance, the articulate proponent faces few obstacles.

It is not much of an exaggeration to say that Rule 403, governing general relevance, is the only rule of exclusion that counts. Of course, Article IV prohibits evidence about subsequent repairs, liability insurance, and the like, and there are privileges in Article V to contend with. But aside from these exclusions based on a policy, little else excludes evidence. Today, the courts will likely admit any evidence probative enough to withstand attacks about prejudice, confusion, or delay so long as the proponent properly labels and packages the evidence.

What of the rule against hearsay, you may ask? The out-of-court statement or document may prove something. It may pass the relevance test of Rule 403. Nevertheless, if offered for its own truth, Rule 802 excludes this hearsay unless it fits an exception. Rule 802 does say that, but the ban on hearsay is now almost a fiction.

The judicial commitment to admissibility under the federal rules is clearest in hearsay. The prohibition against hearsay, a keystone of the law of evidence, faces extinction. The decisions of the last seven years about hearsay have created theories and precedents to admit almost all probative hearsay.

Judges and lawyers still talk about hearsay, so the labels, the objections, and the ability to cite exceptions remain important for now. But in reality, important hearsay is seldom excluded under the Federal Rules of Evidence. That is true even if the hearsay seems to fit none of the express exceptions. The lawyer who proffers hearsay should no longer ask, "Can I get it in?" but "How do I get it in?"

Consider four favorite avenues to admit hearsay, all fashioned by recent liberal interpretations of the federal rules. The first concerns hearsay received as the basis for an expert opinion. The second and third concern expansion of the exceptions for states of mind and for public records. The fourth concerns the flood of decisions accepting hearsay under the catchall exceptions of Rules 803(24) and 804(b)(5).

Take, first, the use of expert testimony as a means for placing hearsay before the jury. Rule 703 has been called the "back-door exception to the rule against hearsay" for good reason.

Traditionally, the expert's opinion had to be based on facts the expert knew from his own observation or facts presented in evidence at the trial and submitted to the expert. That usually occurred in a hypothetical question. Rule 703 allows a third basis for the expert's opinion. It provides that

> The facts or data in the particular case upon which an expert bases
> an opinion or inference may be those . . . made known to him . . .
> before the hearing. If of a type reasonably relied upon by experts in
> the particular field in forming opinions or inferences upon the subject, the facts or data need not be admissible in evidence.

In other words, the expert may now base his opinion on information presented to him out of court, even though the information is not within his personal knowledge. That is true even though the underlying facts would not be admissible even if offered at trial.

In short, the expert may base his opinion on inadmissible hearsay. Suppose he does. What happens next? May the expert explain his opinion by describing the underlying data? Does the basis—the otherwise inadmissible hearsay—come in?

The cases answer yes. The point is treated in a series of decisions within the last several years. In *American Universal Insurance Co. v. Falzone*, 644 F.2d 65 (1st Cir. 1981), the fire marshal testified that the fire was of human origin. He based his opinion in part upon statements by his co-workers that they had found no difficulties with an oil burner on the premises. During the marshal's direct examination, he not only gave his opinion, he recited the basis for it and, over objection, described his conversations with his colleagues. The Court of Appeals found no fault with this procedure. The same conclusion was reached by the Fifth Circuit Court of Appeals when it said, "Rules 703 and 705 codify the approach of this and other circuits that permits disclosure of otherwise hearsay evidence for the purpose of illustrating the basis for the expert witness's opinion." *Bryan v. John Bean Division of FMC Corp.*, 566 F.2d 541 (5th Cir. 1978).

Perhaps the most striking exposition comes in *United States v. Madrid*, 673 F.2d 1114 (10th Cir.), *cert. denied*, 459 U.S. 843 (1982), a prosecution for bank robbery. The defense was insanity. The state's psychiatrist testified that the defendant was sane. He based his opinion partly on the accused's having committed armed robberies of stores before the offense in question to support his heroin addiction.

Since the only issue at trial was the defendant's sanity, testimony about past crimes would ordinarily be irrelevant and clearly excludable under Rules 403 and 404(b) as character evidence.

The court questioned the probative value of the evidence of past crimes. It found the prejudice substantial. Nevertheless, the court declined to find error because the expert "did state that Madrid's past robberies were an important part of the basis for his opinion."

True, most decisions admit the hearsay and other data that is not evidence only to explain the opinion. The hearsay does not come in as substantive evidence. But the subtlety of this distinction is lost on juries. And an advocate can contest even this limitation.

After all, the underlying data does have some reliability. The expert opinion must be based on hearsay of a type reasonably relied on by the expert's profession. If the expert's profession relies on the hearsay out of court, the argument goes, then it must be reliable enough to fit under the residual hearsay exception at least. That would render the hearsay substantively admissible for its truth.

The lesson for the trial lawyer is that Rule 703 provides a convenient additional exception to the rule against hearsay. You have hearsay data. Perhaps the facts you would like to establish are incorporated in writings and records. These documents by themselves fail to qualify for admission if offered directly. What can you do? Consult your expert—an accountant, an economist, or a member of some other appropriate field. Perhaps he can give an opinion that relies on these documents. If so, he will accomplish two things. He will give his opinion, and then he will support the opinion by expanding on the data he relied on. Through the expert's opinion, inadmissible hearsay can be received.

Mental State

Now consider hearsay admitted as evidence of the declarant's mental state. Trial lawyers know from experience that the expression "state of mind" works well as a response to hearsay objections; it is almost as good as "not offered for its truth." "State of mind" is one of the most conceptual and complicated exceptions. Because its boundaries are blurred, the exception gives the knowledgeable advocate an advantage in seeking to admit hearsay. The scope of the exception, and hence the advantage, have been enlarged by decisions under the Federal Rules of Evidence.

Rule 803(3), although stated in one sentence, combines a variety of state-of-mind utterances and bodily condition utterances into one exception. For example, take the statement of intention offered to show subsequent acts of declarant. In this instance a two-step process is in-

643

volved: (1) The statement of the declarant is admitted to show his intent at the time. (2) From this intent, the trier of fact may infer that the intended act was carried out.

The latter step is a matter of relevancy, rather than a concern of the hearsay rule. For example, parents seek damages for the wrongful death of their daughter in a plane crash. The airline seeks to reduce its damages by proving that the daughter had abandoned her parents. In rebuttal, the parents offer a postcard the daughter wrote to others stating her intention to return home. This hearsay declaration may be received under 803(3). These statements of intent may be admitted under the decision in *Mutual Life Insurance Co. v. Hillmon,* 145 U.S. 285 (1892).

It is one thing to say that the declarant's profession of intent may form the basis of the inference that he *later* carried out his intent. It is another matter altogether if the state of mind is the memory of a past act. To allow out-of-court statements of memory or belief to show some prior event or condition would destroy the rule against hearsay. So the courts exclude out-of-court statements of memory or belief if offered to prove the assertions they contain. Thus Rule 803(3) excludes "[A] statement of memory or belief to prove the fact remembered or believed. . . ." This is the limitation expressed in *Shepard v. United States,* 290 U.S. 96 (1933).

That is the theory. In reality, the judges frequently smudge the line between admissible statements that look forward and inadmissible declarations that look backward.

Mixed Statement

There is the problem of the mixed statement. What is the court to do with a statement that combines intent with memory? It looks both forward and backward, and both the fact intended and the fact remembered may be relevant. Many courts have followed the lead of *United States v. Annunziato,* 293 F.2d 373 (2d Cir. 1961), *cert. denied,* 368 U.S. 919 (1961), and admitted the entirety of combined statements.

There is also the principle of "continuity of states of mind." A statement of an existing state of mind may not be used to reflect upon a prior act. But it may be used to look backward to a prior state of mind. The theory is that the declarant's state of mind was likely the same in the not-too-distant past. An example is *In re Anderson's Estate,* 185 Cal. 1700, 198 P. 407 (Cal. 1921), where the testatrix's declaration of fear was held to relate back to the execution of her will some months earlier to establish undue influence.

The newest expansion of this principle comes in the use of declarations of existing intent to prove the acts of others in cooperation with the declarant. If those cooperative actions are themselves at issue, there is a significant danger that the jury will use the declarant's statements as proof not only of the declarant's actions but also of the actions of another.

644

As long as this exception is used to show the intent of the author of the statement, it is justified. If, however, the declarant's statement of intent is admitted to prove the intent or cooperative action of another, then it exceeds the rationale of the exception.

For example, the declarant's statement that he intended to meet with another may seem to fall within the framework of 803(3). But if the evidence is offered to show that the other person was present at the meeting, it is no longer a declaration that looks forward. It is a statement describing a past event—the arrangement of a meeting.

This statement carries the usual risks of faulty memory and is excludable as a "statement of memory or belief to prove a fact remembered or believed." For this reason, the report of the House Judiciary Committee approved 803(3) with the admonition that the rule be construed "so as to render statement of intent by a declarant admissible only to prove his future conduct, not the future conduct of another person." Yet courts of appeals for three circuits have now approved the use of the declarant's statement of intent for the sole purpose of showing the subsequent conduct of another.

The case of *United States v. Pheaster*, 544 F.2d 353 (9th Cir.), *cert. denied*, 429 U.S. 1099 (1976), involved a prosecution for conspiracy to kidnap. The court allowed testimony that the victim told friends shortly before he disappeared that he was going to meet the defendant. The court of appeals frankly admitted that the victim's declaration of intent had been used to prove the future conduct of the defendant. The court conceded the "theoretical awkwardness" of its ruling, but approved admissibility of the statements. The *Pheaster* case was followed by *United States v. Jenkins*, 579 F.2d 840 (4th Cir.), *cert. denied*, 439 U.S. 967 (1978), and *United States v. Moore*, 571 F.2d 76 (2d Cir. 1978).

The list of hearsay loopholes includes the public records exception. In modern litigation, hearsay comes embodied in documents, sometimes layers of it. The proponent's traditional weapon has been the business records exception.

But one important limitation to the exception for business records has been the doctrine of *Johnson v. Lutz*, 253 N.Y. 124, 170 N.E. 517 (1930). That case requires that the person with personal knowledge of the record information have a business duty to transmit it. That means that the entry must be based upon information transmitted by someone with both firsthand knowledge and a business responsibility to report the information. If the record is based upon statements from outsiders and witnesses not under a duty to report, it is not admissible as a business entry.

The public records exception once added little to the proponent's arsenal. Public records were routinely admissible as business records. But the courts often imposed the restriction of *Johnson v. Lutz* on official documents.

Now Federal Rule 803(8)(C), as interpreted in recent years, has changed the official records exception into a potent force for hearsay. No longer does *Johnson v. Lutz* restrict the receipt of multiple levels of statements made outside court.

Rule 803(8)(C) now admits evaluative reports of official investigative agencies. The rule allows the admissibility in civil cases of "factual findings" resulting from an investigation made pursuant to law. What does this phrase "factual findings" mean? The House Judiciary Committee approved subdivision (C) intending that "that the phrase 'factual findings' be strictly construed and that evaluations or opinions contained in public reports shall not be admissible under this Rule." The Senate Committee, on the other hand, took "strong exception to this limited understanding." So what's admissible?

Almost everything. The phrase "factual findings" now includes the investigator's conclusions and opinions, even those based on statements of third parties not testifying in court. For example, consider the classic instance of a police report assigning responsibility for an accident. Is that report admissible in a personal injury case? Courts would not usually admit such a report as a business record. But what if offered as factual findings in public records?

Factual Findings

The Sixth Circuit Court of Appeals holds the report admissible. A negligence action followed a collision at an intersection where there was a traffic light in *Baker v. Elcona Homes Corp.*, 588 F.2d 551 (6th Cir.), *cert. denied*, 441 U.S. 933 (1978). The defendant offered the report of the policeman who arrived after the accident.

The report stated the policeman's opinion that the plaintiff's automobile had run a red light. The report also quoted the driver of the defendant's truck, whose statement formed part of the basis.

The Court of Appeals held the accident report admissible in its entirety under Rule 803(8). The policeman's conclusion the court received under Rule 803(8)(C). The court read "factual findings" to include reports like this one. The court held that the onus of showing unreliability is on the opponent of the evidence, and that the plaintiff had failed to carry the burden of showing lack of trustworthiness.

The court considered the timeliness of the investigation and the skill of the investigator. The court decided the policeman had no motive to falsify the facts. Thus the court found the police report reliable enough to admit into evidence.

This case makes two things clear. First, a court will usually admit official evaluations and conclusions as factual findings. Second, the reported conclusion need not come from the official's firsthand knowledge. The conclusion may be based on information supplied by others.

Other cases support this expansive view. In *Sage v. Rockwell Interna-*

tional Corp., 477 F. Supp. 1205 (D.N.H. 1979), a lawyer offered reports on the cause of a plane crash as evidence. As the court stated, ''the reports are replete with hearsay evidence or statements including military sources and nonmilitary sources such as the Sheriff's Department . . . doctors and an eyewitness.'' The court also questioned the skill and experience of the investigators. All the same, the court admitted the reports. The opponent did not offer enough evidence to impugn the trustworthiness of the records. The court decided that the official's lack of skill or experience went to the weight of his conclusion, but did not justify exclusion of his report.

In civil cases, Rule 803(8)(C) has relaxed the hearsay policy. ''Under the aegis of 803(8)(C),'' one judge has written, ''materials representing the distillation of a process that may have involved years of investigation and the taking of thousands of pages of testimony may be presented to the trier of fact in one fell swoop.'' *Zenith Radio Corp. v. Matsushita Electric Industrial Co.*, 505 F. Supp. 1125, 1143 (E.D. Pa. 1980).

Naturally, the court can exclude the official record or report if the court deems it untrustworthy, but the court will not presume the report untrustworthy merely because the official author lacked personal knowledge. Nor will the court presume a report that embodies multiple hearsay untrustworthy.

Rule 803(8)(C) supposes the evidence admissible. To exclude the evidence, the court will probably look to nothing more than the basic criterion of relevance in Rule 403. Even a report based on multiple hearsay, the cases seem to tell us, the court will exclude only when so unreliable that the report's probative value is ''substantially outweighed by the danger of unfair prejudice, confusion of issues, or misleading the jury.''

The avenues of admissibility discussed so far have concerned the expanded use of traditional evidence. Otherwise inadmissible hearsay seeps in as expert testimony or as creative constructions of class exceptions, such as state of mind or public records. The next avenue dwarfs the prior discussion. Under the catchall loophole, hearsay does not seep in. It floods in.

This is the most striking aspect of the Federal Rules of Evidence—the use by the courts of the so-called residual or catchall clauses to admit hearsay that fits no traditional exception. More hearsay has been admitted through these clauses in the last seven years than in the preceding generation. Since 1975, the application of the catchall rules—803(24) and 804(b)(5)—has marked a dramatic departure from precodification restraint. Moreover, the judges have been disposed to ignore the clear efforts of Congress to curtail liberal use of the residual exceptions.

This judicial activism came as a surprise. Unlike the Federal Rules of Civil Procedure, the Rules of Evidence show extensive Congressional revision. The purpose of many of the Congressional changes was to exclude evidence that would have been admissible under the rules as submitted by the Supreme Court. This legislative intent was particularly clear in hearsay. In fact, Congress enacted Rules 803(24) and 804(b)(5) only reluctantly, to provide flexibility in the rare instances when highly reliable and necessary hearsay could not fit within the precise confines of a specified class exception. Congress intended to keep the hearsay exclusion intact and operating along traditional lines.

Residual Exceptions

The residual exceptions transmitted to Congress in 1972 provided simply for the receipt of statements "not specifically covered by any of the foregoing exceptions but having comparable circumstantial guarantees of trustworthiness." As finally enacted, the requirement of "equivalent circumstantial guarantees of trustworthiness" became just one of five conditions. In addition, the statement had to be "offered as evidence of a material fact." It had to be "more probative on the point for which it is offered than any other evidence which proponent can procure through reasonable efforts." Admission had to serve "the general purposes of these rules and the interests of justice." Finally, Congress required the proponent to give notice before trial that he intended to offer the statement, along with particulars, including the name and address of declarant.

The legislative history discloses the limited role envisioned for the residual exceptions. The House Committee deleted the exceptions entirely as "injecting too much uncertainty into the law of evidence." Congress adopted the Senate version, with its restrictions. The Senate Committee on the Judiciary stated:

> [i]t is intended that the residual hearsay exceptions will be used very rarely, and only in exceptional circumstances. The Committee does not intend to establish a broad license for trial judges to admit hearsay statements that do not fall within one of the other exceptions contained in Rules 803 and 804(b). The residual exceptions are not meant to authorize major judicial revisions of the hearsay rule. . . .

Congress declined to reform other areas of hearsay law. It refused general use of prior inconsistent statements, which California, New Jersey, and a dozen other jurisdictions have allowed. Congress authorized substantive use only if the statement was "given under oath subject to penalty of perjury at a trial, hearing or other proceeding or in a deposition." *See* Blakey, *Liars, Turncoats, and Hearsay*, p. 38 *infra*. Congress limited the Supreme Court's proposals to expand admissibility for former testimony, statements against penal interest, and public records containing official reports of the police. Congress also rejected proposals to admit statements against social interest and statements of recent perception by a declarant who was unavailable. In short, no one expected in

1975 that the federal rules would threaten the traditional doctrine of hearsay.

The academics believed that the rules had presented the opportunity for reform but none had occurred. The language and history of the rules led the commentators to predict that the residual exceptions were unimportant. Professor Laurence Tribe complained that, ''while the British have seen fit to virtually abandon the hearsay rule in civil cases, progress in the United States has been exceedingly slow.'' In 1975 Professor Jon R. Waltz predicted in the pages of this magazine that federal judges would recognize that the residual exceptions ''are reserved for those instances of 'great' hearsay so rare as never to have inspired exceptions all their own.'' Waltz, *Present Sense Impressions and the Residual Exceptions: A New Day for "Great" Hearsay?* 2 LITIGATION, No. 1 at 22 (Fall 1975). The cases have proved otherwise.

Judicial enthusiasm for the residual exceptions mocks the caution of Congress. Indeed, the original and more liberal Supreme Court version of the hearsay article more accurately expresses the current law than the rules as enacted. Today the courts almost always admit hearsay that fits exceptions that Congress rejected. The courts use Rules 803(24) and 804(b)(5) routinely to admit almost any out-of-court statement that passes the relevancy standard of Rule 403.

Consider, for example, the statements of prior witnesses. Congress declined to admit generally the statements of declarants, even when the author was present at trial and available for cross-examination. Thus Congress rendered admissible an out-of-court statement consistent with the declarant's trial testimony only in limited circumstances to rebut charges of recent fabrication.

Yet one of the earliest and most significant cases under the federal rules was *United States v. Ioconetti,* 540 F.2d 574 (2d Cir. 1976), *cert. denied,* 429 U.S. 1041 (1977). This decision approved receipt of two prior consistent statements under Rule 803(24). These statements were reliable, because they had been made closer in time to the event and their author was in court subject to cross-examination and observation by the jury. But of course this is always true of prior consistent statements. The *Ioconetti* case opens the door to most such statements.

What of prior inconsistent statements? They are admissible to impeach, of course. But the federal rules permit substantive use only if the inconsistent statement was given under oath at some kind of formal hearing or proceeding. In *United States v. Leslie.* 542 F.2d 285 (5th Cir. 1976), witnesses alleged to be accomplices testified at trial to facts clearing the defendant. Prior unsworn statements of these witnesses accusing the defendant were then admitted as substantive evidence under Rule 803(24).

The witnesses were alleged to have made their statements, after their arrest, to the F.B.I. The statements were neither under oath nor given at a formal hearing. The witnesses repudiated their statements at trial as having been given in the hope of more favorable treatment. The Fifth Circuit Court of Appeals held the statements reliable because the witnesses were available for cross-examination and their out-of-court statements had been made close in time to the events.

These are sound arguments that apply generally to prior inconsistent statements. These points and others the advisory committee made to Congress. Yet Congress expressly rejected this class of evidence. The conference report stated:

> The rule now requires that the prior inconsistent statement be given under oath subject to penalty of perjury at a trial, hearing or other proceeding or in a deposition.

By contrast, a federal judge recently said:

> Courts have been particularly prone to rely on Rule 803(24) to admit hearsay when the declarant is available and subject to cross-examination and the statement in question poses no special danger that the trier is likely to mis-evaluate.

United States v. Muscato, 534 F. Supp. 969, 978 (E.D. N.Y. 1982). The *Leslie* case admits what Congress sought to prohibit.

Prior Testimony

The courts have also ignored Congress's refusal to expand the exception for former testimony. The Supreme Court sought to relax the requirement of an identity of parties. It proposed to admit former testimony against anyone with an interest in cross-examination similar to that of the party against whom the live testimony was originally given. In other words, testimony could become evidence against a new party not in privity to the prior action. Congress rejected this rule. The House Judiciary Committee said that, "it is generally unfair to impose upon the party against whom hearsay evidence is being offered responsibility for the manner in which the witness was previously handled by another party."

Thus the final version of Rule 804(b)(1) accepts former testimony only if originally given against the same party or a "predecessor in interest." But some courts have avoided the congressional limitation by reading "predecessor in interest" to include anyone with a similar motive and interest. *Lloyd v. American Export Lines*, 580 F.2d 1179 (3d Cir.), *cert. denied*, 439 U.S. 969 (1978); *In re Master Key Antitrust Litigation*, 72 F. R. D. 108 (D. Conn.), *aff'd*, 551 F.2d 300 (2d Cir. 1976). The result has been to apply Rule 804(b)(1) as the Supreme Court proposed it rather than as Congress enacted it.

The residual exception accomplishes the result more easily. For example, *In re Screws Antitrust Litigation*, 526 F. Supp. 1316 (D. Mass. 1981), is

650

instructive. The United States brought criminal antitrust actions against certain screw manufacturers. NL Industries, one of the original defendants, pled *nolo contendere*. Thus NL Industries avoided standing trial with the remaining manufacturers.

At the criminal trial of the other manufacturers, one Martin testified for the government. The distributors then brought a civil antitrust action against NL Industries. Martin was no longer available, but the plaintiffs offered as evidence a transcript of Martin's former criminal trial testimony.

To admit this testimony under Rule 804(b)(1), the court would have had to find that the criminal defendants in the first trial were predecessors in interest of NL Industries. The court declined, observing that

> No court . . . has gone so far as to find such a relationship between defendants in a criminal action and different defendants in a subsequent civil action arising out of the same facts. 526 F. Supp. at 1319.

The Court did not apply the former-testimony exception. But that made no difference, because the court held Martin's prior testimony admissible under the residual exception of Rule 804(b)(5).

Can you prove facts given to the grand jury by introducing the grand-jury testimony of a witness now unavailable? In 1975, few would have said yes. The grand jury is an exparte proceeding largely under the control of the prosecutor. Witnesses appearing in this closed setting may feel pressured to testify. They frequently respond to leading questions, and there is no opportunity for cross-examination. Except for the oath, a grand jury statement has no special reliability.

Congress made no provision for this kind of evidence. Given its importance, this possible exception could hardly have been overlooked. In fact, Congress rejected a more liberal exception for former testimony because it was concerned with rights of cross-examination. Congress also declined to admit statements about recent perceptions even when made "not in contemplation of pending or anticipated litigation."

For purposes of litigation, grand-jury testimony presents no real opportunity for cross-examination by anyone and is given at the instance of the prosecutor. Yet within the last several years, several courts have admitted grand-jury testimony against the accused in criminal cases.

The most recent decision is *United States v. Boulahanis*, 677 F.2d 586 (7th Cir.), *cert. denied*, 459 U.S. 1016 (1982). The court admitted the grand-jury testimony of a prosecution witness who refused to testify at trial. The court found the testimony reliable because the declarant had been a disinterested bystander. He had testified under oath, and parts of his testimony had been corroborated by other evidence. The Seventh Circuit Court of Appeals conceded that the prosecution did not need the grand-jury testimony. All the same, said the court, Rule 804 does not

651

require that hearsay evidence be essential in order that it be admissible.

Seven years ago it would have been difficult to find any significant decision allowing hearsay like this against the accused in a criminal case. Today, the *Boulahanis* case is but one of many such decisions.

Grand-jury testimony is given under oath. So is an affidavit. Can the affidavit of an unavailable witness meet the test of the residual exception? The First Circuit Court of Appeals said yes in *Furtado v. Bishop*, 604 F.2d 80, *cert. denied*, 444 U.S. 1035 (1979). Inmates at a state prison sued prison officials for deprivation of civil rights. The plaintiffs offered as evidence the affidavit of a deceased lawyer. The affidavit told of damaging admissions by one of the defendants and the lawyer. The lawyer had not been retained by the parties to the litigation.

The court held the affidavit admissible under 804(b)(5). The court said that, as a lawyer, the declarant "could not have failed to appreciate the significance of the oath he took in executing the affidavit and, as such, was not a person likely to make a cavalier accusation against a prison official."

Unsworn Statements

So far, my examples of hearsay admitted through the residual exception have been situations where either the declarant was on the witness stand (as in the case of prior testimony) or where at least the extrajudicial statement was given under oath. What about the ordinary unsworn statement? Is it admissible?

Many decisions say yes. In the case of *United States v. AT&T*, 516 F. Supp. 1237 (D. D.C. 1981), *aff'd sub nom. Maryland v. United States*, 460 U.S. 1001 (1983), the defendant raised the issue of admissibility of third-party documents. The defendants offered documents composed by employees or agents of competitive companies. The companies were not parties, so the out-of-court utterances could not be admissions. The court said that the residual exception has a "substantial vitality of its own" and admitted writings, diaries, and correspondence as evidence under Rule 803(24).

A self-serving written statement was admitted in *Turbyfill v. International Harvester Co.*, 486 F. Supp. 232 (E.D. Mich. 1980). An employer had been sued over an accident. A former employee had denied responsibility in an unsworn statement. The court received the statement under Rule 804(b)(5).

Some statements have even been oral. In *United States v. Ward*, 552 F.2d 1080 (5th Cir.), *cert. denied*, 434 U.S. 850 (1977), the question was whether the vehicle had been stolen from interstate commerce. The driver from whom the truck had been stolen was later arrested on unrelated charges, escaped jail, and was a fugitive unavailable at trial. The court allowed an F.B.I. agent who had spoken to the fugitive to repeat his account of the theft. The fugitive certainly had reason to lie to avoid the blame for the loss of his truck. The court admitted the hearsay anyway as specially reliable under Rule 804(b)(5). The court said the content of the hearsay was corroborated by other evidence in the case.

The court admitted oral unsworn statements of a complainant in *United States v. Van Lufkins*, 676 F.2d 1189 (8th Cir. 1982). The accused was charged with assault. The victim described his version of the fight in conversations with his sister and later with an F.B.I. agent. At trial the victim was unavailable. The government called the sister and the agent as witnesses, and each repeated the victim's description of the fight. The Eighth Circuit Court of Appeals held the testimony admissible. The Court said "The district court has wide discretion in determining the trustworthiness of a statement for purposes of Rule 804(b)(5)." 676 F.2d at 1192.

The court admitted a statement of a decedent in *Robinson v. Shapiro*, 646 F.2d 734 (2d Cir. 1981). The survivors had brought an action against the owner of an apartment building for the wrongful death of a workman, who had been killed when a rooftop gate gave way. The trial court allowed a co-worker to repeat an oral statement by the dead man. The dead man had repeated a conversation with the superintendent of the building. This kind of statement might have been admissible as a "statement of recent perception" under the proposed Rule 802(b)(2) in the Supreme Court draft, but Congress deleted that exception. The Second Circuit Court of Appeals admitted the dead man's statements under Rule 804(b)(5).

Multiple hearsay was admitted in *United States v. Medico*, 557 F.2d 309 (2d Cir.), *cert. denied*, 434 U.S. 986 (1977). Five minutes after a bank robbery, a bank employee was locking the entrance door when a customer told him the license number and description of the getaway car. The customer was himself repeating what a bystander had just told him. The employee jotted down the information.

Neither the customer nor the bystander were ever identified or produced. At trial, the employee testified to what the customer reported that the bystander said. This was hearsay upon hearsay. The court received the evidence under Rule 804(b)(5). The court said the two reports had been near enough to the event to assure their accuracy.

This litany of cases suggests a rapid erosion of the doctrine of hearsay. An energetic judiciary is accomplishing the change under the rubric of the Federal Rules of Evidence by using plausible arguments and the full range of discretion available to the courts.

State Codes

This is not to say that all courts accept all hearsay. Many decisions have rejected use of the residual exceptions. But more often than not, the hearsay excluded proved little and seemed unreliable. Published decisions represent a small sample of all the decisions about evidence. It is dangerous to assess how the courts apply the rules on this limited data.

But these cases are what we have. They are what the judges read. Published appellate decisions may not be a fair sampling, but they are the precedents that influence the other courts. It is impossible to read the decisions of the last few years and still take seriously Congress's suggestion that the courts use the residual exceptions only rarely, in exceptional circumstances.

The states have noticed the willingness of federal judges to admit hearsay. The movement for a code of evidence continues in most states, but the states have begun to depart substantially from the federal model. Colorado, Florida, Ohio, and Washington have codified their rules within the last three years. All four declined to enact the residual hearsay exceptions. The proposed New York code permits residual hearsay only if the court makes ''specific findings of the facts and circumstances supporting the substantial guarantees of trustworthiness and the exceptional need for receipt of the statement.'' Whether these efforts to legislate control over judicial discretion will succeed is problematical.

In the meantime, the revolution in the law of evidence carries a message for judge, lawyer, and scholar. The trial judge can no longer take refuge behind mechanical rules of thumb. Specific exceptions have been subordinated to probativeness and reliability. The judge must exercise discretion, which requires time and thought—both sparse commodities in the courtroom setting. The trial lawyer should no longer presume that hearsay is inadmissible. It is wise to assume the contrary unless the evidence is really unreliable. The absence of cross-examination will not, by itself, indicate unreliability. This is the only way to make sense of the decisions. The academic should abandon the usual analysis and refining of the theory of hearsay. Alas, it has been refined to the point of extinction.

Reformers yearn for the day when the myriad rules of exclusion will disappear. They wish for a single basic principle, a rule like 403: relevant evidence would be admissible unless considerations of unfair prejudice, confusion of issues, or waste of time outweigh its probative value. This general rule would contain some specific exclusions for reasons of policy. But all relevant evidence would be presumed to be admissible.

Hearsay would be received unless its opponent could show it unreliable. The opponent would have to prove that the sources of the evidence or the circumstances were not trustworthy. Cross-examination would be a consideration, but not a fetish. The trial judge, a worthy and reasonable scholar, would have a wide discretion in weighing the value of the evidence against its prejudice, or its unreliability.

That is the reformer's dream. Seven years' experience of the Federal Rules of Evidence suggests the dream is close to reality.

Objections

by John J. Curtin, Jr.

Experienced trial lawyers, particularly those singed by past errors, often warn young lawyers to be careful of objections. The reason is that lawyers who seem to be hiding something cause jurors to lose confidence in them and their case. Many of us can recall interviewing a juror who complained about the lawyer who tried to prevent disclosure of the facts.

The sages warn neophytes that objections frequently fail and that the impact of damaging evidence is heightened by an objection that rivets attention to the evidence. Remember the cartoon depicting a blasé judge, a disturbed lawyer, a self-satisfied witness, and 12 jurors with their hair standing straight up and saucers for eyes. The caption reads, ''The jury is instructed to disregard that testimony.''

I view objections from a different perspective. The experienced chief judge of the federal district court in Massachusetts takes the position that the chief deficiency of lawyers in federal trials before him is that they often fail to object when they should object. The question is, when should you object?

I think of myself like a baseball player. When a question is asked in a courtroom, I think of it like a pitch. I may not want to swing even though it is a strike the same way that a batter need not swing at every pitch. Often there are good reasons for not swinging, yet the batter does not have much time to make up his mind. He should be up there looking to hit if he can, and not take the pitch because a key hit gives his team momentum or disrupts the pitcher's momentum. But you have to swing to get a hit.

In the same way, I believe in objecting—at least sometimes. But remember that objecting is an art and not a science.

The author is a partner in Bingham, Dana & Gould in Boston and a former chairman of the Section of Litigation.

Know the Basic Law and Lore

Without further explanation, the admonition to know the law does not help much. There are two general categories of objections: objections to the substance of the evidence offered and objections to the form of the question.

Objections going to the substance of the evidence involve the entire law of evidence. In federal courts, you are assisted by the codification contained in the Federal Rules of Evidence. The evidence rules of many states are based on the federal mode. You can look them up.

Read the rules, the statutes, and the relevant case law from the perspective of basing an objection on them. For example, FED. R. EVID. 408 precludes questions designed to elicit evidence of conduct or statements made in compromise negotiations. On the other hand, you will find the needle in the haystack more easily than finding rules that define the proper form of a question. Most jurisdictions would probably accept the principle of FED. R. EVID. 611(a), which gives the judge the power to "exercise reasonable control over the mode and order of interrogating witnesses and presenting evidence as to (1) make the interrogation and presentation effective for the ascertainment of the truth, (2) avoid needless consumption of time, and (3) protect witnesses from harassment or undue embarrassment.

The language of this rule is not recommended for courtroom use. An objection that counsel's question is ineffective for ascertaining truth might puzzle some judges, even federal judges. "Time-consuming" begins to sound more familiar. We know the objection, "He is harassing the witness, Your Honor." The governing principle is that the judge can exercise reasonable control over trial testimony, but the form in which you object arises from the common lore, and you will learn it only through experience.

State rules, statutes, and court decisions will be of limited help in supplying appropriate guides to the proper form of objections. Trial manuals will be more useful. For example, read Judge Keeton's book, *Trial Tactics and Methods.*

Frequently, important types of objections to the form of a question are contained in the lore rather than the law of your jurisdiction. A question may be leading, argumentative, compound, asked and answered, overly broad, or ambiguous. It may state the evidence or assume facts not in evidence. These are common objections but are unlikely to be analyzed in the cases. If you sit in the back of a courtroom, you will hear most of the objections as to form.

Check your law and lore to learn all the possible kinds of objections. Particularly remember that you can object to opening statements and closing arguments.

A common objection to an opening statement is that the proponent is arguing his case rather than stating what he intends to prove. There is no bright red line dividing a statement of the expected evidence from an argument. Knowledge of the judge's views is crucial, particularly because overruling the objection may create an early, unfavorable impression with the jury. Other possible objections are that the opening refers to facts that had been excluded by prior rulings or contains a misstatement of the law.

Common objections to closing argument include that it misstates the evidence, refers to matters excluded at trial, contains inflammatory remarks, or includes statements of the personal belief of counsel.

Do not forget that objections, particularly as to form, are important in depositions. Depositions are frequently taken without stipulation or under a stipulation that does not preserve the right to object as to form at trial. If you don't know what questions are objectionable for improper form at the time the deposition is taken, you lose rights at the trial. FED. R. CIV. P. 32(d)(3)(B) (which is loosely incorporated into the "usual stipulation") requires seasonable objections to be made to certain errors and irregularities in the form. In depositions you can ignore most of countervailing reasons for not objecting. In general, therefore, you should keep open your trial options by objecting at deposition. Other tactical benefits may follow at deposition, including interrupting the rhythm of a poorly prepared questioner and preventing the lawyer taking the deposition from running away with the witness.

Know How to Preserve Your Rights on Appeal

If you are going to object, do it right. Having learned all possible objections, you need to know how to make them effectively. While very few cases are reversed on grounds that the trial judge erred in admitting evidence, that is no reason to throw away your right to raise evidentiary issues on appeal.

You may have heard the terms "general" and "specific" objection. If you do not state the ground for your objection, you have made a general objection at common law. To adapt a famous example: In a trial of Mr. Sparrow for the murder of one Robin, a policeman is asked the following question:

PROSECUTOR: Who killed Cock Robin?

DEFENSE: Objection.

That is a general objection. In the example, the lawyer may have objected on the ground that the answer by the policeman would be hearsay or perhaps opinion, or even that the answer should be suppressed because of a failure to give the defendant his Miranda warning, or at least that the question lacks foundation.

If you pick one of those grounds and state it, you have changed your objection to a special objection. If the answer is admissible for any purpose, even though objectionable on many grounds, the trial judge will be upheld if he allows the question. Of course, if he sustains the objection, he will be upheld on appeal because there is at least one ground to support the objection. The proponent of the question then has the burden of making a limited offer for a proper purpose.

At common law, if the court sustained an objection based on the wrong ground, it was upheld if there was any ground to exclude the evidence. If the court overruled a specific objection, the court was upheld on appeal unless the lawyer picked the right ground and demonstrated prejudice.

Most jurisdictions have a rule similar to FED. R. EVID. 103 that requires a timely objection stating the specific ground if otherwise not apparent. In most jurisdictions, statement of the ground is necessary to preserve the right to argue on appeal that the court erred in ruling on an objection.

Logic dictates that you should be able to stand up and say, for example, "Objection. Leading," or, "Objection. Hearsay."

Federal courts will almost always permit you to state briefly the ground of your objection. Some state courts, even those such as Massachusetts that adopted the mandatory language of FED. R. CIV. P. 46, have been more picky. They may limit you to shouting, "Objection!" without any grounds. You can shout the word as loudly as you wish, but you may not say anything else.

This approach may seem arbitrary but was adopted by our wise ancestors for entirely practical reasons. We all know that lawyers can use objections as an excuse to make an argument—sometimes an extensive one. Judges like to hear arguments on their terms and sometimes do not want to hear any argument at all. In response, some jurisdictions, such as Massachusetts, developed a practice of limiting the lawyer to the single word "objection." The practice developed at a time when an objection was merely a preliminary warning to the judge.

At common law, an exception to the judge's ruling was necessary to preserve rights on appeal. Exceptions are now unnecessary to perfect an objection under the federal rules and in most jurisdictions, but the practice of denying a lawyer the right to state the ground for an objection may survive. In Massachusetts, even after exceptions were abolished, some good trial judges refused to permit a lawyer to say more than the word "objection" unless the judge specifically asked for a statement of grounds. A specific rule was needed to permit attorneys to state the ground of their objection at the time of its making, even though Massachusetts had adopted a rule similar to FED. R. CIV. P. 46. Check the practice in your jurisdiction, as well as the rules.

One important technical point. If you wait until the answer, it is too late. You must object when the question is asked unless the answer is too quick for normal response. Then you must move to strike the answer.

In some instances, you may not care about preserving your rights on appeal. On some occasions your instinct tells you that the question is objectionable, but you do not have the ground on the tip of your tongue. This puts you in something of a dilemma. A general objection asserted with confidence may be sustained. On the other hand, if you shout, "Objection," the judge may ask your ground. If you stumble and mumble, you create a poor impression on the judge and a worse impression on the jury. Some of you may be quick enough on your feet that you can think of the right ground as you stand. Most of us are not so quick. For this and other reasons, you should know what the judge is likely to do.

Know Your Judge

Evidentiary rulings are seldom the basis for reversal on appeal. Even an objection to the substance of evidence is usually meaningful only in the trial court. In jurisdictions following the federal rules, a judge may exclude even relevant evidence on the ground that its admission is outweighed by prejudice, confusion, or waste of time—handy language to remember. If the trial judge has the final say on objections to the form of questions and most objections to substance, you should concentrate in the short run on the trial judge and the jury, not the appeals court.

Knowing the judge involves knowing his attitude toward procedure and substance. Politeness is always a good starting point. Allow the question to be completed before objecting unless completing the question will itself be prejudicial. Never address your opponent directly. Object to the judge. If the judge is irritated by argument, limit your objections to a succinct statement of your ground in understandable language.

Know whether he permits a continuing objection. A continuing objection is useful where the judge has overruled your objection to a question that begins a series of questions developing the same topic. To preserve your rights, you would have to object to every single question asked about that topic. You can avoid constant interruption of the witness and irritation of everyone else if the court will permit a continuing objection to the entire line of questioning.

Sometimes the judge will permit you to anticipate important evidentiary issues by objecting in advance, briefing them, and arguing when the jury is not present. Such an objection is styled *in limine*—a motion made "at the threshold." Many judges appreciate early warning even on less crucial matters and can be persuaded to listen to brief argument at the start of a session. The key is to find out what the judge in your case usually does. Ask the clerk. Ask other lawyers. Sit in the back of the courtroom. Even if you want to persuade the judge to handle your matter a little differently, you have to know the judge.

The judge has such broad discretion that you may encounter directly contrary rulings from different judges on many objections, particularly

659

those as to form. This should not be unexpected. Umpires have varying ideas about strike zones. You only ask that each judge be consistent.

You want to know in advance whether he calls the low strike. For example, judges take different views of leading questions—not only as to what is leading but whether the question should be allowed under one of the many exceptions to the rule prohibiting leading questions. The argumentative objection often depends on the judge's viewpoint. Some judges think that this question is argumentative: "You don't know any reason why Mr. Smith (the 'important' fact witness) would lie, do you?" Others might allow it.

The wisdom of the objection turns on what the judge will do and its effect on the jury. If he simply grunts, "Sustained," the jury may feel cheated. If he adds, "That would be true of any witness," the jury may feel the question was offensive.

Be Aware of the Jury

In a jury case, your audience expands. The judge remains the key to whether you win or lose any single objection but your overriding objective is to persuade the jury. Objection strategy and techniques become part of the impression that you make on the jury concerning the credibility of your case. The jury's reaction to your objection must be weighed and considered as part of the tactical decision to object.

If you object, you want to minimize the adverse effect on the jury. The skillful objection educates the jury to the reasonableness of excluding the other side's evidence. The jurors' natural reaction is annoyance because the objection seems to keep evidence from them. Often succinct legal grounds are not really understood by the jury. The judge, who understandably wants to move the case along, will not permit extensive explanation in front of the jury. The art is to explain briefly the objection so that the jury will believe that your opponent is being unfair, without irritating the judge. "Objection—leading," becomes, "Objection. He is putting words in the witness's mouth." Instead of "Objection—compound," you might try the simpler, "He is asking more than one question." You may be able to add to the phrase, "Objection—hearsay," the following: "The jury can't evaluate the credibility of the person who told the witness because that person is not on the witness stand." That phrase is a little long and may not sit well with some judges.

Even if you minimize the adverse effect, the risk of alienating the jury remains. There is no satisfactory way to evaluate an adverse effect. Much depends on the entire trial context. You certainly do not want to object for objection's sake. Never object because you do not like the evidence. If an objection is likely to result in only temporary delay of the evidence, do not object. Carefully consider the effect on your credibility of a series of unsuccessful objections. You may, with wisdom, choose not to object even though it will be sustained. If the witness is doing well under cross-examination and the jury seems impressed, do not intrude. Only object if the unfairness of the question will be obvious to the jury.

Know Your Opponent

It is, of course, unethical to object solely to upset your opponent or to prevent him from eliciting testimony in a smooth fashion. Nonetheless, such considerations may bear on whether it is tactically wise to make an otherwise valid objection, particularly as to form.

You should also consider the resourcefulness of the opposing lawyer. Can he frame a proper question if pressed? A frequent objection to the form of evidence is that the question is ambiguous. Some lawyers say that you should never permit an ambiguous question to stand without objection. My experience is that a rephrased question following objection frequently results in more persuasive testimony than if no objection were made.

Similarly, sometimes a successful objection on best-evidence grounds may be counterproductive. The proponent produces the underlying document, which becomes an exhibit that the jury can read and touch and take into the jury room for examination during deliberations. Consider whether your opponent can meet your objection and better his case.

On the other hand, if your opponent is easily rattled, you may choose to make more objections as to form in the hopes of permanently excluding the evidence. Even if the opponent is resourceful, you may wish to make a valid objection to slow his momentum on direct.

Know Your Witness

How does the witness handle himself? Does he need the assistance of every valid objection that you could make? For example, your expert is supposed to be able to turn the tables on a lawyer who is putting words into his mouth. His impact on the jury will be increased if he can fend for himself. He can turn an ambiguous question into a closing argument.

Parties and employees of parties can be prepared at greater length. You may know their likely reactions better than the disinterested witness. Witnesses may need to be treated differently at different times in their testimony. Your clients or experts may be given more room early in their testimony when they are fresh. You may know some areas to be more dangerous than others because of your preparation. An otherwise valid objection may warn the witness of danger and keep him from becoming confused. The more you know about the witness, the better you can judge whether to object.

Know Your Case

Object for the right reason. There should be a strategic and a tactical advantage. Even if there appears to be a tactical advantage with this witness this time, be sure that any objection is consistent with your general

661

strategy and, above all, with your overall theory of the case. Will admission of the evidence open up other unfavorable evidence from this or other witnesses? Could the judge's ruling sustaining your objection be used against you by your adversary when you seek to introduce testimony? Be consistent in your objections throughout the case. Know what is important. Some lawyers object to a question because they believe the answer will hurt their case—even a little. Do not compound a little damage by an objection that emphasizes evidence that will probably be admitted. Sometimes silence is a better weapon.

You probably cannot ignore the key piece of evidence, also known as the smoking gun. If this evidence is crucial, you may have to ignore all the negative aspects of an objection. Do not forget the excessive prejudice objection. FED. R. EVID. 403 expressly authorizes an objection to otherwise relevant evidence where, on balance, the benefit to the proponent of the evidence is outweighed by the unfair prejudice to your client.

Know What You Intend to Do in Advance

The time to object is short. Objections are likely to be better if you anticipate them.

Analyze your opponent's case. Think about the witnesses through whom objectionable evidence may be offered. Anticipation gives you an edge in objecting.

Be alert in the courtroom. One of the techniques of a good direct examiner is to move so quickly through certain parts of his examination that his momentum deters objections. To counter this technique you will have to be prepared.

The objection is an important tool. Do not abandon it. Think before you object, but object when appropriate. An objection in proper form and for a good reason can provide important tactical and strategic benefits and greatly improve your effectiveness as an advocate.

Trial Objections

by John C. Conti

It is your second jury trial. Standing accused of medical malpractice is your client, Dr. Detroit, a well-respected, middle-aged surgeon. He is alleged to have allowed a small sponge to remain in the plaintiff's abdomen after performing an emergency appendectomy. Called by the plaintiff for cross-examination, Dr. Detroit nervously takes the stand. After some background questions, the doctor is asked where he was at 2:00 P.M. on the afternoon of June 17, 1982, when he was called by his answering service to rush to the hospital and attend the plaintiff. "At the Ritz Carlton" comes his uneasy reply.

Next question: Who were you with and what were you doing there?

Your antennae have been exquisitely tuned. Before a response is uttered, you leap to your feet and, out of blind reverence for the rules of evidence, proclaim loudly, "Who my client was with and what he was doing at that hotel are completely irrelevant to the issues of this case. I object!"

Her Honor sustains the objection. Even though Dr. Detroit was at the hotel having an innocent luncheon with members of the local United Way, the jury confidently concludes that he is an alcoholic, a philanderer, or both. They rabidly await the commencement of deliberations.

Now it is your 52nd jury trial. You have learned much. This time you represent an obstetrician alleged to have improperly monitored the fetal heartbeat during labor, resulting in brain damage to the infant. In the courtroom are the parents and the pathetic three-and-one-half-year old child, who is blind and severely retarded.

Plaintiffs' counsel is attempting to place in evidence a number of special toys and learning devices on the ground that the child will need

The author is a member of the Pittsburgh law firm Weis & Weis.

them to achieve even a minimally normal lifestyle. One of those items is a chess set made specifically for the blind.

The lawyer moves for their admission. Your mind whirls with the precision of a rocket scientist's. Rising slowly, you swagger to the center of the courtroom, thumbs tugging at your suspenders, ready to impress. "Your Honor, I must object to the introduction of the chess set. There is no evidence that this child will ever attain the intellectual capacity required to play chess." Like the sharp thwack of a bullet passing through your foot, the judge blurts, "Sustained." You cast a furtive glance to the jury and observe that each member is smiling; in unison they are mentally moving the decimal point of their contemplated verdict one place to the right.

Mastering trial objections seems an easy proposition. Obviously you must be conversant with the rules of evidence. Then all you do is sit at counsel table, your ears scanning the courtroom like radar, getting a fix on the evidence being hurled through the air by the opposing lawyers and their witnesses. When a violation is detected, you launch an objection and take smug comfort when the judge barks, "Sustained," effectively pronouncing the target destroyed.

We approach trial objections in that manner because law school has taught us to. Such an approach, of course, is nonsense; but all too many trial lawyers are oblivious to the folly of bringing law school methodology into the courtroom.

As an example, consider torts. Law school examinations were graded in large part on the basis of the sheer number of theories of liability the student could conjure up and the number of possible defendants the student could implicate. True, when a complaint is being prepared, you must consider all options and you may decide to sue many defendants. But all too often the academic baggage of "many defendants/many theories" is carted into a courtroom and placed before the common-sense scrutiny of a jury. Instead of proceeding against the target defendant with a strong, clean case, the plaintiff's counsel assails four or five defendants, attempting to sway the jury to the unlikely notion that all were negligent, each in a variety of ways. The trial becomes unfocused and tedious. The plaintiff's claim either becomes diluted beyond recognition or terminally wounded by the loss of credibility.

Not to be outdone, defense lawyers all too often raise technically valid but suicidal defenses. Consider the following:

Hysterical parents arrive at their pediatrician's office with their two-year-old son who had begun to have seizures 20 minutes earlier. Suspecting meningitis, the pediatrician directs the family to take the child to the nearest university-affiliated children's hospital instead of the small community hospital nearby. The child reaches the hospital after a 35-minute car ride, but it is too late.

The parents sue, claiming, among other things, that the pediatrician should have made arrangements to transport the child by ambulance or helicopter. In response, the defendant physicians assert contributory negligence on the part of the parents for not taking the quickest route to the children's hospital. That creative tactic may have gotten the defense lawyers an A in the classroom, but it gets them flambéed in the courtroom.

So it is with trial objections. The simplistic notion that an objection must be raised to every technical violation of the rules of evidence should be discarded. Instead, we must appreciate that recognizing a violation of the rules is only the first step. The attorney then must decide whether to object and, after that, how to object—in open court or in a sidebar.

To make those decisions, the lawyer must consider the overall effect that the proffered evidence and the potential objection will have on the judge, the jury, and the appellate record. This must be done in a split second. Is it possible? Yes, but only if you consider beforehand what trial objections are all about.

Now, suppose you are in the final stages of preparation for trial. You are young, but you know a few things about trial objections. First, there is the appellate record. If you fail to object, the point will not be preserved for appeal.

You need not make the objection immediately, however, since that often serves only to emphasize the point and to cause severe embarrassment if the objection is overruled. For example, when a witness unexpectedly and improperly mentions insurance, the worst thing you can do is to object in open court. You also get into trouble by objecting during opening and closing arguments, since many trial judges will openly admonish such an objection. Thus, when an objection in open court might be counterproductive, simply make the objection at the first opportunity at a sidebar or in chambers. Then the judge can order the evidence stricken, issue a curative instruction, or grant a mistrial.

Once a trial begins, judges like to move things along. Some objections will make them become irritated or even hostile. These include hypertechnical objections (for example, objecting to leading questions when the witness is being interrogated on matters not in dispute) and sloppy objections (for example, "Your Honor, that question is misleading and prejudicial!"). Repetitive objections are annoying when a single objection to a line of questioning or a continuing objection would suffice. The ire of the court also can be raised when a lawyer makes a relatively complex objection (for example, one based on the Dead Man's Act) and cannot cite any legal support for the objection.

Then there is the jury. Almost invariably they want out of the courtroom as quickly as possible. Whining, repetitive objections serve, at best, to interrupt the flow of evidence. At worst, they signal to the jury that you are attempting to conceal harmful evidence. Jurors grow especially suspicious if you continually ask for sidebars when sensitive subjects are mentioned. At the same time, the jury can be favorably impressed by the lawyer whose crisp, well-stated objections are continually sustained.

Some judges run their courtrooms with no less adherence to the rules of evidence than one would expect from Professor McCormick. Other judges view a trial as a New England town-hall meeting: If a witness is concerned enough to show up willing to say something, then the heck with all this nonsense about hearsay objections. You are not worried, though, because you have done your homework, and you know the predilections of this judge.

Provide the judge and your opponent with a trial brief outlining your position on significant evidentiary issues that are likely to arise. Although you should try to anticipate all your opponent's objections, you do not want to include anything in your trial brief that might tip off your opponent to something that otherwise might have been overlooked.

Your adversary may attempt to introduce evidence that your client has a criminal record and was drinking before the accident. Recognizing that the case is lost if the jury gets even a whiff of those allegations, you will argue a motion *in limine* to preclude reference to such matters. If the motion is denied, you nonetheless have acquainted the judge with your position. When the witness with the objectionable testimony is called to the stand, you will ask for a sidebar, request an offer of proof, and, if appropriate, reassert the objection.

Preliminary matters are finished, and trial is about to begin. His Honor is not known for keeping a tight reign on trial counsel. Your opponent appears to have slunk only that morning from the primordial ooze. You know this lawyer will not feel constrained by the rules of evidence, the trial court's rulings, or, for that matter, the code of professional responsibility. Therefore, in your opening statement, you tell the jury about objections and sidebar conferences, explaining that they are necessary to save time and to smooth the journey toward the sacred objective of trial, a search for truth. You explain that rules of evidence have evolved over hundreds of years in an effort to make the search expeditious and fair. You explain your obligation to make sure the other side plays by the rules.

If you anticipate objections in a certain area, you also may wish to explain the rationale for the applicable rule. If the area is hearsay, you will say that a trial is the search for truth, and cross-examination is the most efficient implement to uncover the truth. Since there can be no cross-examination of a hearsay statement, there is no way to judge its veracity. Therefore, an objection must be voiced.

Once the trial has begun, determine how much latitude the judge will permit. If the other lawyer is unusually fond of leading questions, do not object the first time, but wait for a particularly improper question. Stand and state the objection firmly and clearly. When you prevail, you have started on the right foot; later objections will receive fair consideration. If instead your objection is overruled, at least you know the judge's position. Do not bother repeating the objection unless, of course, the evidence is of such significance that you need to preserve the point for appeal. Even then, the objection should be made at a sidebar or in chambers.

Now the trial is in full stride. Do not make objections when the evidence is harmless. Remember the lesson you should have learned when you objected to the question asked of Dr. Detroit—if the objection is sustained, the neutral evidence may be transformed into a negative inference.

Likewise, remember what you learned after objecting to evidence of the chess set being used against your client, the obstetrician, and do not be lured into making a technical objection when doing so forces you to concede a crucial factual point. Object in open court only when you have weighed the benefit of excluding the evidence against the risks of making the objection.

Some lawyers object only so that they can make a speech to the jury. The speech is technically improper, and it may infuriate opposing counsel and the court. Nonetheless, there are times when you must do more than simply object. For example, if your adversary persists in asking leading questions, you may want to request the court to admonish the lawyer to stop asking leading questions, "so that we can hear from the witness."

Another strategic reason for making an objection is to rescue the floundering witness. If your adversary's cross-examination is making your witness confused, you may object that the questions are misleading and may even make a short statement that allows your witness to clear his head.

If your witness is an auto mechanic who is being questioned about the physics involved in accident reconstruction, you may want to object to the questions on the basis of competency. When you do so, however, be careful what you say. You do not want to announce to the jury that the questions are improper because your witness is incompetent; instead, say that the questions are beyond the witness's area of expertise.

Trial objections are much more than a means of recording a perceived violation of the rules of evidence. Objections provide opportunities to enhance your likelihood of success (or to guarantee failure). As with all aspects of litigation, the key is preparation. If you consider all significant points of evidence before trial, you can integrate your trial objections into your strategy. You may even make tactical use of your opponent's anticipated objections. This final example will show what I mean.

You are defending an insurance company in a suit filed by the estate of a young man killed in an automobile accident. The lawyer for the estate claims that the insurance company acted in bad faith when it denied coverage to the person whose negligence caused the accident. Your defense will be that the attorney representing the estate orchestrated a fraudulent insurance claim by inducing various witnesses to change their testimony. Through discovery you have obtained copies of letters from the attorney to the witnesses establishing the fraudulent conspiracy. The letters are blown up to poster size and, as you begin your opening statement, they rest against the counsel table, wrapped in plain brown paper.

You explain your theory that the plaintiff's lawyer induced the witnesses to change their testimony. You have the jury's attention, not to mention your adversary's.

Now you walk over to counsel table and pick up the enlargements of the letters. You tell the jury that you will prove the fraudulent scheme through a series of letters written by the plaintiff's lawyer, as well as by third party testimony. As you say this, you carry the enlargements across the courtroom and rest them against the jury rail.

The tension proves too much for the plaintiff's lawyer. The lawyer rises and shrieks "Objection! Counsel is not permitted to show those letters to the jury in his opening." With that objection, the plaintiff's lawyer has effectively erased any doubt you had about convincing the jury that the letters are important. The lawyer has committed the fatal error of making an objection that is technically correct but serves only to enhance the credibility of the evidence it seeks to exclude.

Objectionable Objections

by Joseph M. McLaughlin

As a trial judge, I hear countless objections that range from the outrageous ("Your Honor, he is a liar.") to the hilarious ("Your Honor, he can't do that.") to the close-but-no-cigar ("I object. The statement was made in the absence of my client.") to the simply obscure ("I object. It's irrelevant, immaterial, and incompetent.").

Arguments over the admissibility of evidence often leave the darkness unobscured. For example, "Your Honor, it's admissible as part of the res gestae." Much of this is due to the logorrhea to which our profession is particularly susceptible. And the rest of it is due to bad habits that have dulled the edges of evidentiary distinctions so carefully honed in law school.

This article will sweep into one pile most of the sillier objections. I will then sift through the pile to determine whether any ideas lie at the bottom of the heap.

Why should the trust and estates lawyer merely *give* property in a will when, with little effort, one can "give, devise, and bequeath" the same property? And why should a trial lawyer object that evidence is hearsay, when he can just as easily fulminate that it is "incompetent, immaterial, and irrelevant?" The answer is that the words are not fungible. They mean different things.

Evidence is never incompetent. People are. Properly used, the term "incompetent" means that a witness who proposes to testify lacks the minimal testimonial qualities to make his testimony acceptable.

The author is a United States district judge in the Eastern District of New York.

Typically, the witness suffers from some physical or mental impairment that makes his testimony worthless. Another illustration is the Dead Man's Statute, which makes people who are interested in the outcome of a lawsuit incompetent to testify to a transaction with a decedent. The same evidence coming from the mouth of another witness, however, would be admissible. Accordingly, it is sloppy usage to object that the testimony is incompetent. Rather, the objection should be that the witness is incompetent.

Immateriality means that under the pleadings and the substantive law, the proposed evidence does not address an issue in the case. Thus, for example, in a worker's compensation case, it is no defense that the plaintiff employee was guilty of contributory negligence. Accordingly, evidence that the plaintiff was chattering idly with a fellow employee when the plaintiff's hand went into the printing press is inadmissible in an action against the employer, not because it is irrelevant or incompetent, but because it is immaterial.

Relevancy, unlike materiality and competence, is not a legal notion at all. Rather, it is a logical concept. Under FED. R. EVID. 401, evidence is relevant if it has "any tendency to make the existence of" a material fact "more probable or less probable than it would be without the evidence." In a personal injury action arising out of a car accident, for example, evidence that the plaintiff was sexually promiscuous would be irrelevant to the material issue of pain and suffering.

Hearsay

Most lawyers have mastered the distinction between hearsay and nonhearsay, which is the use of words to prove the truth of what the words say as distinct from merely proving that the words were uttered. Nevertheless, when it comes to invoking the twenty-five or thirty exceptions to the hearsay rule, lawyers often fuse two or three exceptions into one with a consequent loss of clarity.

1. *Res gestae.* Res gestae has become to the modern trial lawyer what limbo was to the medieval theologian—a place to isolate miscellaneous exceptions to the hearsay rule that do not fit neatly under any other exception. The term should be avoided.

Res gestae has at least five distinct usages. Only one is correct. Properly used, the term refers to words that are uttered as part of a legal transaction and impart legal coloration to the transaction. We know, for example, that if a person unintentionally destroys his will, the will is not revoked. On the other hand, if he rips up the will and says at the same time, "I hereby revoke my will," the words become part of the act; and just as a witness may testify to what he *saw*, he may also testify to the contemporaneous words that he *heard*.

Unfortunately, the notion has arisen that words uttered as part of any transaction somehow become part of that transaction and may thus be testified to. In criminal cases, for example, I have heard countless defense lawyers ask the arresting officer:

Q: "And, sir, what did the defendant say when you arrested him?"

The answer sought is the defendant's statement:

A: "I'm innocent."

The argument is often made that the defendant's exculpatory statement is admissible as part of the res gestae. It is not.

A statement by the defendant when he is arrested is not a part of the legal transaction in the same sense as a statement by a testator when he revokes the will. Accordingly, the defendant's exculpatory statement, if admissible at all, must come in either as an exception to the hearsay rule or as nonhearsay.

Only in an unusual situation is there a hearsay exception to admit an exculpatory statement when offered by the defendant. It is not an admission for the simple reason that it is consistent with the defendant's position in court. Obviously, it is not a declaration against the defendant's interest. Occasionally the statement will qualify as an excited utterance or as a declaration of present state of mind. *See United States v. Di-Maria,* 727 F.2d 265 (2d Cir. 1984).

When offered by the defendant, the exculpatory statement cannot be viewed as nonhearsay. It is offered to prove the truth of the matter asserted, which is to say, that the defendant is innocent. It may be worth noting, in passing, that the prosecution might be entitled to use the exculpatory statement as nonhearsay if it were offered as false exculpatory evidence, indicating a consciousness of guilt. In any event, it does not advance the argument one whit to cast it in terms of res gestae.

In an earlier era, res gestae was used to describe a spontaneous declaration or, as it is more commonly known now, an excited utterance. FED. R. EVID. 803 (2) deals with this exception to the hearsay rule. Again, applying the term res gestae simply creates confusion.

Another older usage of the term refers to statements by a person about his bodily condition ("My back hurts") or mental condition ("I hate Del Vermo"), and these too are expressly dealt with in FED. R. EVID. 803(3)(4). They should not be clouded by references to res gestae.

2. *Admissions and declarations against interest.* There is no such thing as an "admission against interest." There are admissions, and then there are declarations against interest.

An admission is an out-of-court statement by a party that is inconsistent with the position he later takes in court. It need not have been against his interest when made. For example, when a person files his income tax in April, he may believe it in his interest to understate his income. Nevertheless, if he later brings a personal-injury suit and seeks to recover lost income, his tax return would be admissible against him if he asserts that he lost more income than he reported on his tax return.

A declaration against interest is an out-of-court statement, almost invariably made by a nonparty, which statement was known by him to be against his interest when made. Thus, a statement by Brown that he shot Del Vermo might be admissible in Smith's behalf if Smith were prosecuted for the murder of Del Vermo. The rationale, of course, is that normal people do not go around admitting murders unless they are, in fact, murderers.

Since an admission is made by a party (or his agent), the rules of evidence permit statements like these to be used even though the party is available to testify. A declaration against interest, on the other hand, since it is made by a stranger, may be used only if the stranger is not available to be called as a witness.

3. *Self-serving.* One of the more dissonant chords in the symphony of a trial is the objection that evidence is "self-serving." Since the whole purpose of a lawsuit is to serve self, it must be at once apparent that there is no rule of evidence excluding self-serving statements.

Writings, when offered to prove the truth of the matter contained in them, are hearsay. If the writing does not fall within any exception to the hearsay rule, then the writing is inadmissible, not because it is self-serving, but because it is hearsay. On the other hand, if the writing falls within an exception, then the writing is admissible even if it happens to be self-serving.

Most business records, for example, are self-serving. Yet they are perfectly admissible. Appellate courts occasionally become impaled on this distinction when they are dealing with accident reports. Indeed, the United States Supreme Court, in *Palmer v. Hoffman*, 318 U.S. 109 (1943), stumbled awkwardly over the self-serving aspects of a railroad accident report. The Court held that such a report did not qualify as a business record. Modern courts, however, reject this and hold that if the accident report is kept in the regular course of business and otherwise qualifies, its self-serving nature does not affect admissibility. *See, e.g., Toll v. State,* 32 A.D. 2d 47, 299 N.Y.S.2d 589 (N.Y. App. Div. 1969).

4. *Presence of Client.* One of the hardiest weeds in the field of evidence is the assumption that if a statement is made in the presence of a party, that statement is admissible. In an action by Fielder against Parker for breach of contract, for example, Fielder produces Jones to testify that Jones was in a barroom one night and heard the bartender say that Parker had not kept his part of the bargain. The judge asks: "Was Parker present in the bar that night?" The parties agree that Parker was, and the judge then admits the bartender's statement through the lips of Jones. Is this error? Yes.

It is difficult to trace the origin of this heresy. As with every heresy, there is a grain of truth in it. The "presence-of-the-client" rule is probably the illegitimate offspring of the rule that the party's silence may, in certain circumstances, constitute an admission. Under well-defined, narrow conditions, where an accusation is leveled at a party, and he has an opportunity to deny it, and every normal human instinct would suggest that he would deny it, then a court may construe the party's silence as acquiescence in the truth of the charge. It is rare that all the conditions can be met to invoke this doctrine.

In the barroom hypothetical, I cannot imagine anyone ruling that Parker should have denied a patron's charge that the party had breached a contract. It most assuredly is not the rule that any statement made in the presence of a party may be offered against him in evidence.

Cross-Examination

In criminal cases, it is not uncommon for the prosecutor to cross-examine the defendant by repeating the prosecution testimony (often from a policeman) and then to ask the defendant: "Is that testimony a lie?" This technique is pure rhetoric. If the testimony is contrary to the defendant's testimony, which it always is, the answer is obvious. The prosecution testimony is either mistaken or an outright lie. In either case, the question is one for the jury and not for the defendant to answer on cross-examination.

In the same vein, it is improper to pose questions in a manner that requires the defendant to characterize the prosecution's witnesses as liars. Leaving aside that this line of cross-examination wastes everyone's time, the defendant's belief that other witnesses are lying is simply irrelevant.

There are several objections that run the gamut from well-founded but ineptly articulated to just plain silly. It is amazing how often they are heard.

1. *Calls for operation of the witness's mind.* The question put to the witness is: "Was the car going fast or slowly?" The objection: "Your Honor, I object. The question calls for the operation of the witness's mind." Heaven forbid! The judge should rule the question proper, and permit the witness to answer.

What the objector probably intends to raise is that the question calls upon a lay witness to express a conclusion. Under FED. R. EVID. 701, however, even a lay witness may express his opinion on the speed of a moving vehicle. In any event, if the objection is under Rule 701, it should be stated in terms of an objection to conclusions rather than to the "operation of the witness's mind."

2. *Nonresponsive answer.* The question is: "As the defendant approached the intersection, what color was the traffic light?" The answer is: "The defendant was driving fast and. . . ." The objection is: "Your Honor, I move to strike the answer on the ground that it is nonresponsive." The judge should deny the motion and permit the answer to stand.

Nonresponsiveness is a problem between the questioner and the witness. It is none of the adversary's business. In other words, the only per-

673

son who can move to strike a nonresponsive answer is the person who put the question.

A moment's reflection suggests the reason. If the nonresponsive answer is independently admissible (and the speed of a moving vehicle is), it would serve no purpose to strike it. The questioner would only have to ask the question directly. If the nonresponsive answer is inadmissible, then the adversary should move to strike on whatever ground makes it inadmissible, e.g., it is hearsay, a conclusion of the witness, and so on.

3. *Asked and answered.* There is no rule of evidence that bars the asking of the same question twice. If the question is crucial, or if there is good reason to repeat it (perhaps Juror No. 4 was asleep the first time), a party should be permitted to re-ask the question. Analytically, the motion is one under FED. R. EVID. 403 to move the trial along because the questioner is propounding cumulative questions. It is the rare judge who will sustain an objection to a question as asked and answered, and more time is usually wasted over the objection than permitting the repetition of the question.

4. *Argumentative.* The question is: "Did you intend to make a gift?" The objection is: "I object. The question is argumentative." The objection should be overruled, and the witness should be permitted to answer.

Whatever the question may be, it certainly is not argumentative. An argumentative question is one that seeks to frame as a question matter that properly belongs in a summation. For example, the question, "How can you remember the events of five years ago, when you cannot even remember what dress you wore yesterday?" does not really seek an answer. Rather, it seeks to embarrass the witness and pick a fight with her. This should be left to summation.

The question, "Did you intend to make a gift?" is proper since any witness is competent to testify about his own state of mind. That the ultimate question in the case may be whether a gift was intended does not bar the question, because FED. R. EVID. 704 expressly sanctions opinion testimony even on "an ultimate issue to be decided by the trier of fact."

5. *Calls for a narrative.* The question is, "Tell us what happened on June 3, 1980." The objection is, "I object. The question calls for a narrative." Whether the objection should be sustained rests in the discretion of the court.

There is no rule of evidence that forbids narratives. The rules forbid only inadmissible testimony. Accordingly, if there is substantial assurance that an uninterrupted narrative by a witness will not result in a flood of inadmissible statements, the court may permit such testimony.

Some witnesses have had more time in the trial pit than many lawyers. Policemen and experts come readily to mind. If reasonably intelligent and well-prepared, these witnesses may be given their head and may be permitted to testify without the jerks and jounces of the lawyer's questions. It is a judgment call by the trial judge for which he is rarely second-guessed.

6. *Ex parte considerations.* In a criminal case, the prosecutor surrenders to the defendant a statement made before trial by the key prosecution witness. The statement has been redacted to eliminate several paragraphs. The defendant says, "Your Honor, may I request that you review the original document ex parte?" The statement is meaningless.

There are three terms that lawyers persist in confusing, perhaps because two of them are in Latin: off-the-record, ex parte, and in camera.

An off-the-record discussion is one that is not recorded by the court reporter. It is a useful device to take care of housekeeping details of the trial without cluttering up the record. It is important to remember, however, that evidence off the record cannot be considered by an appellate court even to reverse a judgment of conviction. If, therefore, in an off-the-record discussion, something of importance develops, it should be dictated into the record to preserve it for appellate purposes.

An ex parte communication is one between the court and a party without notice to the adversary. It may or may not be on the record, but in any event, it is frowned upon.

In camera is Latin for in chambers. It means that the trial judge will look at some piece of evidence or perhaps even conduct a part of the trial in the privacy of his chambers. A record should always be made of what occurred, and both sides should be present.

7. *Offer of proof.* I am surprised at how few offers of proof are made. It is my experience that when an objection is sustained, most lawyers simply grumble something like, "May I have an exception?" and let the matter drop. This can be dangerous.

In the first place, few jurisdictions require a formal exception to a ruling on evidence. When a party has made an objection and it has been ruled on, there is no need to make a formal exception.

In the second place, the party who proffered the evidence is playing Russian roulette if he does not make an offer of proof. Suppose he was right and the trial judge was wrong. How can an appellate court that agrees with him determine whether the error is reversible or harmless? Unless the answer that would have been given is clear from the record, the trial judge must be affirmed in the absence of an offer of proof.

An offer of proof may be made in one of two ways. Most judges prefer that it be done at sidebar or during a recess by having the lawyer simply dictate into the record what he *knows* (not believes) the witness would have said in response to the question. If the proffered testimony is crucial, an alternative and more precise way to make an offer of proof is to get the objectionable answers on the record. This can be done by dismissing the jury while the lawyer asks the questions that the judge has already ruled to be objectionable.

675

Techniques of Objection

An objection, besides being clear, must be timely. It should be made at the first available opportunity, which normally means the moment the objectionable question is put.

If the question is proper, but the answer is objectionable, then the correct procedure is a motion to strike, rather than an objection. The trial lawyer is entitled to more than "motion granted" from the judge. An instruction should be given to the jury to disregard the answer. Incidentally, it is worth noting that if the question is improper, but this is not noticed until after the answer is given, it is technically too late to move to strike at that point, although the judge has discretion to grant such a motion.

When an objection is made, the ground may usually be stated in a word or two without the encumbrance of having to conduct a sidebar conference. For example, it is sufficient to say:

"I object—hearsay."

"I object—it's not a business record."

"I object on the ground that it is irrelevant."

If further elaboration is required, then a sidebar conference is unavoidable, although judges—and more importantly, juries—hate them.

Apropos timely objections, perhaps the single most commonly overlooked objection is that of variance. Where the plaintiff proves one theory, and then offers evidence of another, if the defendant does not make timely objections to evidence supporting the second theory (on the ground of materiality), most judges will deny a later motion to strike all the testimony on the second theory.

In a recent malpractice case, for example, the complaint alleged that the defendant doctor had performed an operation negligently. While I had, of course, read the pleadings, I did not intrude when the plaintiff began an extensive direct examination of his own client about the risks involved in the operation of which he had been advised by the doctor. This, of course, represented a change of theory from simple malpractice to lack of informed consent. However, I did not conceive it to be my duty, in the absence of an objection, to intervene, and, extensive testimony came out concerning the doctor's failure to warn the plaintiff about the risks of the operation. Later in the case, the defendant moved to strike all testimony concerning the lack of informed consent, and the plaintiff cross-moved to amend the pleadings to conform to the proof.

In denying the motion to strike and granting the plaintiff's motion to conform, it was clear to me that all the evidence on the point had been developed on the record, and that the jury was in position to decide that question. Nothing could be gained by taking that question from them at the last minute. On the other hand, if the defendant had been alert to object to the variance the moment the irrelevant questions were put, I undoubtedly would have sustained the objection.

Objections serve two purposes. They keep impermissible evidence from being heard by the jury and, perhaps more importantly, they preserve for appellate review whatever error was committed in the trial court. Occasionally, these purposes are at cross-purposes. A short-tempered jury may quickly conclude that a lawyer who continues to object is a pettifogger with something to hide. Yet if error is allowed to be sown in the record without objection, it will escape appellate review. The art of the trial lawyer is to know every moment which of the two purposes is more important.

The objection must be timely, should be crisp, and at all times should be clear. The blunderbuss objection (irrelevant, incompetent, and immaterial) should be avoided at all costs because it irritates everyone within hearing distance and will probably not preserve the error for appellate review.

Finally, there are few experiences as frustrating as putting a series of questions only to have an objection to each question sustained without explanation. If the objecting party has not stated a ground, and the trial judge has sustained the objection, and the questioner is befuddled, it was common years ago for trial judges to grumble something like, "Move on to another subject. I'm not here to teach you the law of evidence."

Happily, most judges today are less dyspeptic, and a request for a sidebar will usually be granted. There, an olive branch question like, "Your Honor, may I have some guidance?" will, more often than not, receive a benign response. Indeed, appellate courts have urged trial judges to remember that they, too, were once humble lawyers. *See United States v. Dwyer*, 539 F.2d 924 (2d Cir. 1976).

Invoking and Applying Rules of Evidence

by Philip W. Tone

Like rules of practice and procedure, rules of evidence are merely the tools by which those who work in the system of justice render issues ready for decision. In any well ordered system of justice, these rules should be capable of being correctly applied by the people working in the system with a reasonable degree of consistency. The opportunities for errors that will cause reversals on appeal and retrials should be minimized. The procedural rules restated in Article I of the Federal Rules of Evidence have been developed over the years to help achieve this condition.

As Dean Mason Ladd has said, the rules of admission and exclusion of evidence are not self-operating. They depend for their successful operation on knowledgeable trial counsel who must be alert to invoke the rules to obtain their benefits. This requires knowing not only the exclusionary rules, but also those procedural rules of evidence which govern admitting and excluding evidence and preserving objections.

Rule 103 deals with what lawyers frequently speak of as "making the record"—laying the necessary groundwork for challenging the trial court's ruling on evidence if the case is appealed. Rule 103 is written from this perspective, for it speaks to when error may be predicated on a ruling which admits or excludes evidence.

I suggest that it is useful to think of this matter in a different way: What should be done to make counsel's position known to the trial judge so he can avoid error? In other words, how can the trial judge be made aware that there is a question on which he is supposed to rule and which rules

The author is a partner in the Chicago law firm of Jenner & Block. This article was developed from talks given at the Evidence Seminar sponsored by the College of Law of the University of Iowa, held in Las Vegas, Nevada, November 25–27, 1974 and a special conference, "How to Practice Under the New Federal Rules of Evidence," sponsored by the NEW YORK LAW JOURNAL in Vail, Colorado, July 16–18, 1975.

of evidence he is being asked to apply? If you think of the rules in this way, you will have a better understanding of their purpose and therefore their proper application.

Before examining Rule 103 from the standpoint I have suggested, let us briefly consider the opening clause of the rule, which says that error may not be predicated on an evidence ruling unless a substantial right of a party is affected. This well-settled principle will not be paramount in the mind of the trial judge, for the parties are entitled to a correct ruling on any question presented. Lawyers cannot always tell in the heat of battle whether a substantial right will be affected, but they can avoid trivial objections to evidence which could not conceivably affect the outcome.

Good Judgment

Elihu Root is quoted by Wigmore as saying that, according to his observation, "there are about twenty objections to the admission of evidence in a trial in an American court to one in an English court." 1 J. Wigmore, *Evidence*, p. 269 (3d ed. 1940). I cannot accurately update Root's ratio, but I would guess it has changed very little. One of the earliest stated objectives of the proposed Federal Rules of Evidence was to remedy the excessive number of objections. Clarity in the rules of evidence will help toward that goal, but substantial progress depends on the trial lawyers' good judgment and sense of responsibility to the court.

The tactics of objecting are discussed in an excellent article by Dean Mason Ladd:

> There is much inadmissible evidence which can do no harm. In fact, it is good practice for counsel to object as little as possible, because constant objections may lead the jury to believe that counsel is attempting to withhold important evidence from them, when it may actually be of little value. Upon close questions of admissibility, in which the damage from the evidence cannot be great, counsel may regard it advisable not to risk an adverse ruling which sometimes causes the jury to give the evidence, when admitted, much more attention than it would have otherwise received. If the damage of the anticipated answer to a question appears to be substantial, then the question must be analyzed to discover the exact point of attack and to select the specific rule of evidence to invoke. The use of the objections, therefore, requires a sense of evaluation and the exercise of careful judgment, as well as a knowledge of the rules and the methods of applying them.

Ladd, "Objections, Motions, and Foundation Testimony," 43 *Cornell L.Q.* 543 (1958).

The lawyer offering the evidence must often share the blame for the excessive number of objections that is commonplace in American courts. Slovenly examination of witnesses, leading when it is unnecessary, and failing to lay foundations when they are obviously required, invite objections which slow the trial and distract the jury's attention from what is important in the case.

Let us turn now to what lawyers must do to apprise the trial judge that there is a question on which he is being asked to rule and what that question is.

It is fundamental that a rule of evidence is waived unless asserted. There is no prohibition against consideration by the trier of fact of hearsay or any other evidence which is subject to a rule of exclusion, unless the party against whom the evidence is offered specifically invokes the rule of exclusion.

Accordingly, if the lawyer wishes to object to the admission of evidence, he must, as Rule 103(a)(1) provides, make a timely objection or move to strike, stating the specific ground of objection if that ground is not apparent from the context. Although the rule speaks of the motion to strike as an alternative to an objection, the word "timely" before "objection" preserves, I take it, the existing practice.

Timely Objections

Ordinarily an objection, to be timely, must be made before the witness answers. The lawyer may not gamble on the answer and then object if he is disappointed. It is only when he does not have an opportunity to object before the witness answers that he may obtain relief through a motion to strike. This may occur because (1) the witness answered quickly before the lawyer had time to object, (2) an apparently proper foundation is later discovered to be faulty, or (3) the witness's answer is unresponsive in whole or in part, so that the basis for the objection did not appear from the question itself. In any of these situations, the lawyer may move to strike. He must first state his ground for the motion, explaining why he did not object before the answer came in, and then give the specific ground of objection to the answer.

The unresponsive answer often provokes what is probably the most frequently recurring blunder made by lawyers who attempt to try cases. Except for the situation I have just described, the objection that the witness's answer is unresponsive belongs to the examining counsel, not to opposing counsel. You, as opposing counsel, have no right to object to an answer to your opponent's question merely because it is unresponsive. The lawyer examining the witness is entitled to accept the answer if he wishes. Unresponsiveness, so far as the opposing lawyer is concerned, is only an excuse for not having objected before the answer came in. A motion to strike based on unresponsiveness must be accompanied by an objection stating why the answer is inadmissible under the rules of evidence.

The examining counsel, on the other hand, is entitled to move to strike an answer of the witness he is examining simply because it is unresponsive. This is because, while he is conducting the questioning, he is entitled to control the matters on which the witness testifies. Without this right, the effectiveness of adverse examination is hampered. The motion to strike an answer for unresponsiveness is the most effective means of forcing the witness to answer a question and focusing the witness's attention on the specific question. Some trial judges do not appreciate this. I think it is important.

The same rules apply to depositions read in evidence. If circumstances permit, it is desirable to obtain rulings in advance on objections to material in depositions, so they need not be dealt with in the presence of the jury and the introduction of the deposition may be expedited.

The rules are less complicated with respect to documentary evidence. When a document is offered, the court will ordinarily inquire of opposing counsel or look at him to give him a chance to object. If he has an objection, he should say so and state the grounds. Counsel may ask the judge to defer ruling if he wants to cross-examine concerning the foundation or if the admissibility is conditioned on the offering of other evidence. In that event, the court may admit the evidence subject to its being "connected up," upon a representation of the proponent that the other evidence will be offered later. If the remaining foundation is not offered later, the objecting counsel must move to strike the evidence which was conditionally admitted. Failure to do so waives the right to have the evidence stricken. In other words, the judge has no obligation to review on his own initiative the conditional rulings made earlier in the trial.

Sometimes opposing counsel wants to cross-examine the witness about the document before deciding whether to object or which objection to make, but the proponent may need the document admitted to complete his direct examination concerning it. In that event, opposing counsel will be allowed a *voir dire* examination limited to the foundation for the document so the court can rule on its admissibility before the end of the witness's direct examination.

The requirement in Rule 103(a)(1) that counsel must state "the specific ground of objection, if the specific ground was not apparent from the context" is based on the principle that a rule of evidence not invoked is waived. It is nevertheless a requirement which is often ignored, even by experienced trial lawyers. Observing the rule of specificity is essential to the proper operation of the trial system and to the protection of the client's interests. There are at least three justifications for the rule:

(1) A timely objection permits correction of inadvertent omissions.

(2) Even if the evidence could not be made admissible, a timely objection would prevent the error or allow the trial court to correct it, making a new trial unnecessary.

(3) A party should not be permitted to gamble on what the evidence

and its effect will be and then have the power to annul the verdict if he loses his gamble.

While specific objections are required, there are some cases holding that merely saying "I object" raises the so-called general objection, "incompetent, irrelevant and immaterial." To make a general objection is slovenly practice, however, unless the ground is perfectly obvious from the situation, as when it follows an immediately prior specific objection to similar evidence, or when the objection is so plainly justified that the judge rules in your favor even as you say your first words. But the need for specificity is not when the judge rules in your favor but rather when he rules against you. It is then that specificity is essential.

Ambiguous Word

If you mean to raise relevance or materiality, which is really a specific objection, say so. The term "material" is not used in the Federal Rules of Evidence. Instead of that "loosely used and ambiguous word," as the Committee's Note to Rule 401 calls it, the words "any fact that is of consequence to the determination of the action" are included in the definition of relevant evidence. Rule 401, in defining relevant evidence, makes materiality a necessary element of relevancy. Thus, "immaterial" adds nothing to the objection for which irrelevance has been specified as a ground. The word, "incompetent" in most instances adds little or nothing. While the word has a precise meaning with respect to some evidence, such as testimony from a person barred from testifying by the terms of a dead man's statute, its use is meaningless in most instances and almost never satisfies the requirement that the specific ground of the objection be stated.

While the rule excuses stating a specific ground for an objection when the basis is "apparent from the context," I would advise you not to rely on that exception, which I am sure was not intended to gobble up the rule's requirement that the objection be specifically stated. It is not reasonable to expect that this rule will have the same limitations as it did at common law. As you might expect, the following rules of appellate review favor the trial judge:

(1) If no ground is stated, and the trial judge overrules the objection, his ruling will ordinarily not be disturbed on appeal. A general objection at most preserves a challenge to relevance and materiality.

(2) If no grounds are stated but the judge sustains the objection, his ruling will be affirmed if any grounds exist for excluding it. It would be useless to reverse, because counsel would presumably state the correct specific objection if the case were retried.

(3) If a specific objection is overruled, the ruling will be affirmed if that objection was not well founded, even though other unstated valid grounds of objection exist. It will be inferred that the other grounds are waived.

(4) If a specific objection is sustained, the ruling will be affirmed even if that objection is invalid if any other grounds for objection exist which could not have been obviated. Again it would be useless to send the case back to the trial court because counsel would presumably state the correct objection the next time.

There are a number of cases which hold that if a proper objection has been urged and overruled, counsel need not reiterate that objection when the same or similar evidence is offered again later in the trial. Most lawyers will, however, ask that their objection be permitted to stand for that possible future evidence as well, probably a wise precaution to avoid any possibility of an implied waiver of a later objection.

The need to move to strike conditionally admitted evidence which has not been connected up has already been mentioned. Similarly, when an objection is properly overruled at the time it was made, but it later appears that the evidence was inadmissible, as when it subsequently develops that a witness's earlier answer was based on hearsay, a motion to strike the earlier testimony must be made.

The rules governing offers of proof are based on the same considerations as those related to objections. Under Rule 103(a)(2), a party offering evidence is required to make its substance known to the court unless it is apparent from the context. The rule is necessary not only to give the trial judge a chance to determine the relevance and competence of the proffered evidence, but also to enable the reviewing court to determine whether a substantial right was affected by the exclusion.

If an objection is sustained to a question on cross-examination, it will ordinarily be unnecessary to make an offer of proof, because the cross-examiner can hardly be expected to know what a hostile witness would say. The possibilities the question would open up are usually sufficiently apparent to permit the court to rule intelligently without an offer of proof. Counsel will often be wise, however, to advise the court, out of the presence of the jury, what he is attempting to bring out and his theory of admissibility. Not only will this procedure preserve the matter for appeal, it may also result in the trial judge changing his ruling.

Some state courts are very strict about the form of an offer of proof. Rule 103(c) is more flexible. It permits, but does not require, the court to direct offers of proof to be made in question and answer form. Depending on the nature of the proffered evidence, it is often wise to take the time to make the offer in testimonial form. That enables admissible evidence to be separated from any which is inadmissible and insures that the witness will in fact testify as represented.

Narrative Offer

On the other hand, the point may be adequately dealt with by a narrative offer from counsel if the facts are simple and the only dispute is admissibility. The rule also allows the judge to add a summary of the evidence problem presented and his ruling to facilitate review.

Quite properly, the rule requires that problems of admissibility be handled so that inadmissible evidence is not suggested to the jury by questions, offers of proof or colloquies in their presence. At the same time, frequent sidebar conferences and sessions while the jury waits in the jury room are undesirable. Problems that can be anticipated should be raised either before trial or at some point during trial when as little of the jury's time as possible will be wasted.

The final paragraph of Rule 103 is a plain-error provision, drawn from Rule 52(b) of the Federal Rules of Criminal Procedure. The provision applies to civil as well as criminal actions, although it is less likely to be invoked in a civil case. While the provision is addressed to the court of appeals, the trial lawyer should always be aware of it. When a problem which may provoke a finding of plain error is not brought to the attention of the trial judge, the party benefiting from the error risks reversal.

I must, however, point out the conflict that exists between the plain error doctrine, which permits an issue to be raised for the first time on appeal, and the old and fundamental principle that a rule of evidence not invoked is waived. The sound policy grounds for the latter principle are especially compelling in these days of overcrowded courts. When a litigant gets a fair allotment of time to present his claim or defense, he has had his due and should not ordinarily be allowed to usurp the time to which other waiting litigants are entitled in their turn. He should be held to a duty to prevent the waste of precious courtroom time. I suggest, therefore, that the plain-error doctrine in the rules of evidence should be applied only under the most extraordinary circumstances in a civil case. In a criminal case, particularly where the defendant is represented by counsel not of his choosing, or a new development in the law justifies the failure to have raised a point at trial, the situation is different.

One final matter: If the reason for the trial court's ruling on any evidence point is not apparent from the context, which includes the ground for the objection stated by counsel, the lawyer against whom the ruling is made is entitled to a statement by the court of the reason for the ruling. It is error for the judge to refuse to give a reason and if prejudice results from the refusal—as it would if the basis for the ruling would show that there was some problem which could be cured—the error is a ground for reversal. So if you do not know the reason for the ruling against you, you may ask and are entitled to an answer.

Motions in Limine—
A Primer

by Edna Selan Epstein

Mention that you are about to make a motion *in limine*—even to an experienced trial lawyer—and you may get a blank stare and a question: "What is a motion *in limine?*" Once you translate the Latin and explain that it refers to a motion at the threshold of a trial to obtain a ruling on the admissibility of specific evidence, you are still unlikely to be overwhelmed with war stories. But a motion *in limine* can be the critical weapon in an individual case.

The uses of motions *in limine* are as varied as the evidence for the case. A lawyer's analytic skill and strategic ingenuity alone limit the issues that can be brought before the trial judge on such a motion.

Evidence that is potentially damaging because it is inflammatory, prejudicial, or likely to evoke sympathy without being probative, can be excluded by a motion *in limine*. So can irrelevant evidence or other matters that would be excluded after a proper objection. More rarely, you can use the motion to establish the admissibility of evidence that is usually excluded. A motion *in limine* often serves the same purpose in a civil case as a motion to suppress in a criminal case except that it is usually rooted in evidentiary rather than constitutional principles.

Good candidates for a motion *in limine* include: the pretty young widow plaintiff with four small children has remarried; the defendant has received a congressional medal of honor; a plot of land adjacent to another plot taken by eminent domain has increased in value; the defendant in an eviction proceeding actually tendered the rent even though belatedly; or a junior employee of an antitrust defendant suggested that a potential strategy for meeting competition was to "crush the competition."

The author is a partner in the Chicago law firm of Sidley & Austin.

Judges know that in ruling on a motion *in limine* to exclude evidence they must walk a fine line. They can bar specific evidence that is inflammatory or irrelevant, but they cannot foreclose an entire claim or defense as a result of their ruling. Thus, where a child is the plaintiff in a negligence action, a motion can bar any evidence that the parents were guilty of contributory negligence. *Lapasinkas v. Quick,* 17 Mich. App. 733, 170 N. W. 2d 318 (1969). Similarly, a trial court in a strict liability action properly banned any reference to the fact that the decedent failed to wear rubber gloves and shoes as a contributory cause of his electrocution. *Good v. A.B. Chance Co.,* 565 P.2d 217 (Colo. App. 1977).

On the other hand, a motion *in limine* that successfully prevented an insurance company from referring to arson in a suit on a fire insurance policy improperly foreclosed an entire defense. *Lewis v. Buena Vista Mut. Ins. Assoc.,* 183 N.W.2d 198 (Iowa, 1971).

Admitting Evidence

Motions *in limine* may also seek admission of evidence. Will the jury be permitted to view the site, thereby avoiding charts, drawings, and photographs that otherwise would have to be prepared? Will a motion picture or videotape depicting some physical aspect of the case be received? Will documents produced in the course of discovery be admissible? Motions *in limine* that seek the inclusion of evidence usually help to arrange the details for advance planning rather than to help strategic planning.

Plaintiffs' lawyers developed the motion *in limine* in personal injury jury trials. Its primary use is still to avoid any risk of tainting the jury by the introduction of evidence that is inflammatory, likely to evoke undue sympathy or prejudice, or legally irrelevant. The first reported appeal from a denial of a motion *in limine* occurred when a lawyer sought to exclude any reference to the plaintiff's morals and character in a personal injury case. That early attempt to obtain an *in limine* ruling was rejected as an unwarranted judicial intrusion into an attorney's right to try his case as he saw fit. *Bradford v. Birmingham Electric Co.,* 227 Ala. 285, 149 So. 729 (Ala. 1933).

Courts no longer react as the Alabama court did. They now welcome such motions. In complex litigation elaborate motions *in limine,* particularly concerning documents, can consume enormous time and effort. The motions in *Zenith Radio Corp. v. Matsushita Electric Industrial Co.* should be in the *Guinness Book of Records.* In *Zenith v. Matsushita,* a complex antitrust case, a hearing on motions *in limine* to exclude and to include extensive documentary evidence dragged on for over a month and generated several opinions that read like an advanced treatise on the Federal Rules of Evidence. 505 F. Supp. 1125; 505 F. Supp. 1190 (E.D. Pa. 1980); 505 F. Supp. 1313 (E.D. Pa. 1981), *aff'd in part and rev'd in part,* 723 F.2d 238 (3d Cir. 1983), *rev'd on other grounds,* 475 U.S. 574 (1986).

Motions *in limine* are not limited to determining the use of evidence before juries. In the *Zenith v. Matsushita* case they formed the basis for summary judgment motions. Summary judgment can only be entered on admissible evidence. The *in limine* motions decided what evidence was admissible. Even in bench trials the evidentiary motion *in limine* can educate the trial judge and focus the judge's attention on critical issues of proof. Moreover, some trial judges, recognizing that they, like other people, may be influenced by the prejudicial impact of certain evidence, may refer motions *in limine* relating to a bench trial to a fellow judge.

There are many advantages to the motion *in limine*. It reduces the risk of exposing the jury to inadmissible, inflammatory, or irrelevant evidence. It avoids repeated objections or sidebar conferences. The jury may view these devices as obfuscating tactics designed to hide the truth. It avoids cautionary instructions to the jury which, rather than erasing the evidence from a jury's mind, may imprint it all the more indelibly. Motions *in limine* also permit lawyers to plan strategy and foresee necessary rebuttal testimony with far greater certainty.

The motion *in limine* places the party who opposed it unsuccessfully at a severe disadvantage. The attorney has been ordered not to introduce certain matters. He must be constantly on guard so that the ruling is not violated by a remark in the opening statement, by questions put to witnesses, or by answers volunteered by witnesses. Witnesses must be instructed explicitly not to refer to the excluded evidence while the jury is present. A lawyer may be hamstrung from presenting the case in the most effective way. Even if the judge eventually reverses an *in limine* ruling, the opening statement will be history, the case will have proceeded, and it may have proceeded in less than the best way.

The benefit of an *in limine* ruling admitting rather than excluding evidence is that it saves the unnecessary expense of preparing special exhibits or producing distant witnesses for trial. Where there is a genuine question whether certain evidence is admissible, an *in limine* ruling may also help a lawyer to avoid interjecting unnecessary reversible error into the trial.

Before you rush off to file a motion *in limine* to exclude evidence, consider the disadvantages. If you lose, you will have educated your opponent about the Achilles' heel of your case. Is the evidence so damaging that its introduction must be forestalled if at all possible? By all means bring a motion *in limine* to exclude the evidence. Is the evidence only marginally damaging? You may be better off with the risk that your opponent will not have discovered that damaging fact or will have failed to analyze correctly its sting.

From the judge's perspective, motions *in limine* may encourage an eleventh hour reappraisal and settlement. Those motions also streamline a trial by removing irrelevant evidentiary issues. Indeed, complex lawsuits may not be triable responsibly without extensive evidentiary motions *in limine*.

A judge may still not be eager to see a motion *in limine* because it may require hearings more complex and time consuming than necessary when the evidentiary question arises during trial. Motions *in limine* may also encourage piecemeal, repetitive, and uneconomical evidentiary proceedings. A complex case may require the judge to reevaluate and possibly reverse his initial ruling. Nevertheless, motions *in limine* help to focus the judge's attention on crucial evidentiary issues at the onset of the trial.

No statute or rule expressly authorizes motions *in limine* in the federal courts. By implication, Rule 16 of the Federal Rules of Civil Procedure, which governs the pretrial conference, gives the judge authority to make preliminary evidentiary rulings. Similarly, state procedural rules and statutes seldom expressly permit such motions. No express authority is necessary. Motions *in limine* are a proper extension of the trial judge's authority to rule on the evidence and to administer the conduct of a trial.

Where court administration is divided into pretrial and trial calendars, bring the motion *in limine* before the judge who will actually try the case. A pretrial judge, who supervises the discovery process but does not try the case, will rarely be willing to bind another judge on matters that traditionally are within the trial judge's province.

When should you bring the motion *in limine*? After discovery is complete and as close to the start of the trial as possible. Why alert your opponent to your trial strategy too far in advance? Moreover, judges' memories are fallible, and their own rulings may not seem so important if there is significant time between the motion and trial.

Always try to bring the motion before the jury venire is actually called into the courtroom. Juries do not relish waiting while lawyers argue about unexplained matters. In addition, motions *in limine* may seek to permit or to preclude counsel from alerting or "conditioning" the jury on a specific issue during the *voir dire*.

Above all, the motion should be made before the trial begins to prevent your opponent from referring to the evidence in his opening statement.

Many courts allow oral motions *in limine*. It is generally better, however, to present a written motion setting forth clearly the evidence sought to be excluded and the reasons for exclusion. Written motions and briefs are vital where the evidentiary issues are multiple and complex. But even in the simple case, ignoring this procedure may jeopardize your record on appeal.

In one case a lawyer sought, unsuccessfully, to exclude any mention that one defendant had settled. The appellate court sustained the denial of the motion on the ground that the nature, purpose, and scope of the proposed ruling were unclear. The court said that the motion should have been in writing, setting forth the evidence to be excluded more clearly and giving reasons for the requested exclusion. *Bridges v. Richardson,* 349 S.W.2d 644 (Tex. Civ. App. 1961), writ of error refused, n.r.e., 354 S.W. 2d 366 (Tex. 1962). A written motion is also more likely to avoid the pitfalls of overbreadth or vagueness that make enforcement of even a successful motion difficult at trial and vulnerable on appeal.

Another advantage of the written motion, particularly in bench trials, is that the judge may adopt the reasoning of the motion in his memorandum opinion and in his other substantive rulings. Even if the motion is denied, its rationale may be clearer after the evidence is heard and it may continue to influence the judge.

Do not overreach in seeking an *in limine* ruling. You want a ruling that is clear, simple, and straightforward. It is dangerous to win too much. A ruling that is overbroad or too complicated may be difficult even for well-intentioned lawyers to obey. If so, the ruling will probably not withstand the scrutiny of a reviewing court. And any sanction for violation of the ruling will be vulnerable to reversal on appeal.

In one case the judge excluded any mention of what the defendant's car was doing some miles from the accident. That ruling was grounds for reversing the judgment and vacating the finding that the lawyer who tried the case was in contempt for violating the exclusion order. *Reidelberger v. Highland Body Shop, Inc.,* 416 N.E.2d 268 (Ill. Sup. Ct. 1981). If you win a motion *in limine,* consider preparing a draft-written order especially if the ruling is complex.

Assume the motion *in limine* has been lost or the ruling has been reserved for trial. You should still raise specific objections to the actual evidence when it is presented at trial. Indeed, by failing to object, you waive your objection. Rulings *in limine* are interlocutory by their very nature; the trial judge is free to reconsider, revise, and reverse the ruling at any time during the course of the trial.

Offer of Proof

If the motion *in limine* to exclude evidence has been granted, and you want to introduce the evidence, make an offer of proof outside the presence of the jury when the evidence would ordinarily have been introduced. You may also make the offer at the end of the day after the jury is excused, but before the trial judge's patience has run out. Reviewing courts often want to see the evidentiary issue clearly and squarely presented. Note, however, that if the evidence is merely ''inflammatory'' and not substantially relevant to a broader issue, an elaborate offer of proof is not likely to get you anything more than a very angry judge.

Like all evidentiary rulings, the ruling on a motion *in limine* is largely discretionary. It is unlikely to be reversed unless patently erroneous. Judges are reversed less frequently when they deny a motion *in limine* than when they grant one. Nonetheless, denying an *in limine* motion may be the basis for reversal. In a personal injury action, it was reversible error when the trial court refused to prevent defense suggestions that the plaintiff was an alcoholic and a drug abuser. *Doyle v. New York,* 281 App. Div. 821, 119 N.Y.S.2d 71 (1st Dep't 1953). It was also error when a trial court denied the state's motion *in limine* to exclude evidence of possible future flooding of the land taken by eminent domain. *Sacramento & San Joaquin Drainage District v. Reed,* 215 Cal. App. 2d 60, 29 Cal. Rptr. 847, *modified,* 217 Cal. App. 2d 611, 31 Cal. Rptr. 754 (1963).

Evidence excluded *in limine* may well become admissible if a witness or opposing counsel opens the door. For example, conversations between an attorney and a client seeking advice on some legal matter are clearly privileged. Ordinarily they should be ruled inadmissible *in limine.* If, however, a witness claims in the course of testimony that his conduct was undertaken upon ''advice of counsel,'' the attorney-client conversations are put into issue and lose whatever privilege they were accorded before trial.

Similarly, a defendant and his lawyer, in a civil personal injury action arising out of an automobile accident, opened the door to the introduction of evidence that a criminal charge of assault had initially been lodged against the defendant. The evidence originally was barred by a successful motion *in limine.* The defendant insisted on cross-examination that his speed had been less than 25 to 30 miles per hour. Asked if he had ever said he had gone 25 to 30 miles per hour, the witness proved foolishly recalcitrant. His attorney sprang to the rescue. He challenged the cross-examiner to produce the impeaching statement. The attorney did. The statement was an affidavit given to the police in the criminal case. *Montgomery v. Vinzant,* 297 S.W.2d 350 (Tex. Civ. App. 1956).

If an *in limine* ruling excluding evidence is violated, various sanctions are available. These range from civil contempt to a reversal on appeal of a favorable judgment won by the offending party. Unless the violation is repeated or clearly deliberate, contempt is rarely appropriate. Even where granted, it does not cure the harm done or undo a verdict won in violation of court order.

The grant of a mistrial during or at the conclusion of the trial is also available. Granting a mistrial, however, has dubious value. The time and money expended on retrial may penalize the party seeking the mistrial more than the party that violated the order.

A more severe sanction is to permit the case to go to the jury and to reverse the jury's verdict if it is in favor of the offending party. Thus, a jury verdict on behalf of the defendant insurance company in a personal injury action was reversed where the defendant's attorney alluded repeatedly to misdemeanors of which the plaintiff had been accused and to the plaintiff's multiple remarriages. A motion *in limine* had successfully barred the introduction of those facts. *McClintock v. Travelers Ins. Co.,* 393 S.W.2d 421 (Tex. Civ. App. 1965), writ of error refused, n.r.e. (Tex. 1965).

The same principle applies in criminal proceedings. An improper attempt to prejudice the jury, in violation of an *in limine* ruling barring certain evidence, will result in a reversal of a conviction. When the prosecution alluded to the defendant's dishonorable discharge from the Marine Corps in a prosecution for an assault, the conviction was reversed. *State v. Smith*, 189 Wash. 422, 65 P.2d 1075 (1937).

Another sanction is to direct a finding on the issue of liability against the party willfully violating the *in limine* order. The rationale for this severe sanction is that a party should not have to try a case twice to enforce an evidentiary ruling *in limine* in its favor that has been deliberately violated.

The evidence that may be subject to a motion *in limine* is as complex, manifold, and varied as the facts of a case. All the evidence in the case should be examined with an eye to making appropriate motions *in limine* regardless of whether the case is tried to a jury or to the court.

Bibliography

Motions to Exclude Prejudicial Evidence, 63 A.L.R.3d 311; *Motion in Limine Practice*, 20 AM. JUR. TRIALS 441; Davis, *Motions in Limine*, 15 CLEV.—MAR. L. REV. 225 (1966); Davis, *The Motion in Limine—A Neglected Trial Technique*, 5 WASHBURN L.J. 232 (1966); Comment, *The Evidence Ruling at Pretrial in the Federal Courts*, 54 CALIF. L. REV. 1016 (1966); Note, *Pretrial Exclusionary Evidence Rulings*, 1967 Wis. L. REV. 738 (1967); *The Motion in Limine: Pretrial Trump Card in Civil Litigation*, 27 U. FLA. L. REV. 531 (Winter 1975); Trasta, *Protecting Your Client with the Motion in Limine*, 22 TRIAL L. GUIDE 147(Summer 1978).

Tactics of the Motion in Limine

by Stephen A. Saltzburg

Mayor Portash and his lawyers wanted to find out whether he could testify in his own behalf at his trial for misconduct in office and extortion without having his prior grand jury testimony used to impeach him. The mayor had testified before a state grand jury after receiving use immunity.

The defense lawyers requested the court to rule on this issue before trial, and the trial court ruled against them. Faced with this ruling, Portash chose not to testify. The jury convicted him on both counts.

How should a court of appeals review this kind of pretrial ruling? As motions in limine become more commonplace, the question of how to analyze a party's claim that his trial strategy was significantly altered by a pretrial ruling on an evidence issue will arise more frequently. Although the motion in limine is not a new weapon in the trial lawyer's arsenal, several developments in federal law have increased its popularity in federal courts. *See* Epstein, *Motions in Limine—A Primer, supra* at 685.

In criminal cases, for example, lawyers have become used to the need under FED. R. CRIM. P. 12 to present various motions to suppress in advance of trial. It is equally convenient for the lawyers and the judge now to include in these pretrial hearings other evidence issues that are not strictly based on a constitutional claim that evidence should be suppressed. The adoption of the Federal Rules of Evidence may have encouraged judges to be more actively involved in pretrial proceedings while outfitting them with a convenient compilation of the law of evidence they will need to apply. Trial judges who are willing and sometimes even anxious to expedite litigation, to streamline cases as much as

---

The author is a professor of law at the University of Virginia School of Law.

possible, and to promote settlements find it helpful to require the parties to focus on issues that truly divide them, including important questions of evidence.

The Federal Rules of Evidence do not mention rulings in limine, but the existence of a set of evidence rules makes the law of evidence more accessible to both judges and trial lawyers. It is easier to raise evidence questions and to answer them now that everyone has a set of rules. Everyone benefits from an in limine ruling, because the parties learn what evidence will be heard at trial. If evidence is to be admitted, the proponent may not need to gather further evidence. The opponent, in turn, learns that he must be prepared to respond to this evidence.

If the judge excludes the evidence, the proponent knows he must find some other way to prove his case. Discovery is designed to eliminate trial by surprise. A pretrial evidence ruling may eliminate surprise by the court itself.

Trial preparation is much easier if the parties know in advance what evidence can be presented. Thus prepared, the lawyers also may prevent inadmissible evidence from creeping into the trial and causing a costly mistrial despite the judge's best efforts to instruct jurors that the evidence must be disregarded. The parties even may be better able to discuss settlement once they know the court's ruling on important evidence questions.

Tedious Process

The trial judge also benefits from resolving these issues before the trial starts. He can take the time necessary for independent and careful consideration of evidentiary disputes. He can request written briefs to aid his deliberations. The result should be rulings that are more deliberate, dispassionate, and learned than those made in the heat of trial, when there is little, if any, time for the judge to reflect on his options and to consult relevant legal authorities.

Even jurors are helped by these rulings in advance of trial, for it saves them the tedious process of retiring from the courtroom while the lawyers argue evidence issues to the court. These interruptions waste the jury's time, interfere with the orderly presentation of evidence, and leave the jury wondering about what has happened while they were sequestered in the jury room.

Although trial lawyers too often fail to think about what kind of record they are creating for possible appellate review, motions in limine are helpful in this respect as well. The record that is made in an in limine proceeding is more likely to indicate clearly the respective arguments of the parties about the evidence than is a trial transcript. Trial judges do not welcome lengthy objections or offers of proof during trial, and they are unlikely to spend much time stating reasons for rulings during the course of a trial. Before trial, or during appropriate breaks in the midst of

693

a trial, there is time and there is often more judicial patience. Patience may not be a sufficient condition for a good appellate record, but it is often a necessary one.

Despite the advantages of advance evidence rulings, a good trial lawyer should recognize when it is unwise to use a motion in limine. In many instances, to rule wisely the trial judge would need to know more about a case than he can feasibly learn during pretrial proceedings. For example, a trial judge who is asked to exclude evidence as being cumulative under FED. R. EVID. 403 might well need to see how the proof develops at trial before acting on the request. Or, a judge who is asked to rule on the admissibility of other act evidence offered under FED. R. EVID. 404(b) to prove intent may want to reserve judgment to see whether intent actually is disputed during the trial.

Sometimes a motion in limine gives the opponent too much of a preview of the deficiencies in an adversary's proposed evidence. For example, it may be true that there is an insufficient foundation for certain evidence that the adversary intends to offer. If an advance ruling is sought to exclude this evidence, the motion usually discloses the deficiencies in the foundation. There will still be time before trial for the proponent of the evidence to take those deficiencies into account and develop a proper foundation. Then the evidence might be retendered. If instead, the objection is saved until the adversary attempts to introduce the evidence in the course of the trial, there may be insufficient time for creative thinking in the heat of battle to enable the lawyer to realize how he can cure the problems in his evidence through another witness or through further examination of the witness on the stand.

Once the trial court has ruled on a motion in limine, what should a court of appeals do in situations such as Mayor Portash's? Mayor Portash's lawyers argued on appeal that his entire trial strategy was altered by the pretrial ruling. The Supreme Court's opinion in *New Jersey v. Portash,* 440 U.S. 450 (1979), reversed the mayor's conviction.

For rulings on constitutional questions of trial evidence, the Court's reasoning may give a party who loses a pretrial ruling an unwarranted advantage on appeal. That is, without knowing whether or not the proffered evidence would have affected the outcome of the trial at all, the losing party has the opportunity to argue on appeal that something much different (and presumably much more favorable to him) would have occurred at trial but for the advance ruling. A similar unwarranted advantage may have been given to the defendant in the decision of the United States Court of Appeals for the Ninth Circuit in *United States v. Cook,* 608 F.2d 1175 (9th Cir. 1979) (en banc), *cert. denied,* 444 U.S. 1034 (1980).

Writing for the majority in the *Portash* case, Justice Stewart first addressed the state's contention that, since Portash had never testified, the appeal presented an abstract and hypothetical question. The majority decided to proceed on the merits. The trial judge had ruled on the impeachment issue and the state appellate court had held that the claim had been properly presented. All the same, the concurring justices (Justices Powell and Rehnquist) suggested that the preferred method for raising a claim like Portash's would be for the defendant to take the stand and appeal a subsequent conviction if, after asserting his claim of immunity, the prosecutor was still permitted to use the immunized testimony to impeach him.

The dissenting justices (Chief Justice Burger and Justice Blackmun) argued that Portash had presented the Court a remote and speculative claim of injury to his federally protected right and that this was not sufficient to support Supreme Court jurisdiction. To them, because Portash never took the witness stand, he was never in fact incriminated through testimony he had previously supplied under a grant of immunity. Thus it was difficult to ascertain what federal right had been infringed by the trial court's advance ruling that such impeachment would be allowed in the event Portash chose to testify. The dissenters believed that requiring Portash actually to take the witness stand and present his claim was necessary to prevent a defendant from manufacturing a constitutional challenge when he in fact had no intention whatever of testifying in his own behalf.

The decision in *United States v. Cook,* decided slightly more than three months after the *Portash* ruling, shows the extent to which lower courts have taken the *Portash* decision as a sign that appeals are proper following in limine rulings about impeachment evidence that go against a defendant—even though the defendant, based upon that ruling, had elected not to testify. In the *Cook* case, the defendant wanted to exclude evidence of prior convictions for armed robbery if he took the stand in his own defense. The case involved a bank robbery in which there had been a shootout between four robbers and the police. The district court ruled that any robbery convictions that had occurred within the ten years specified under FED. R. EVID. 609 could be used for impeachment purposes if Cook testified. With this ruling in hand, Cook chose not to testify. He was convicted but appealed, relying in part on the evidence ruling.

In the en banc decision, five of the judges refused to find any waiver of the defendant's opportunity to appeal from the adverse evidence ruling, even though he did not testify. These five judges found it unnecessary to decide the appropriate timing for a motion in limine, but they did outline a procedure that a defendant should follow to preserve a claim like Cook's for review:

> [A] defendant must at least, by a statement of his attorney: (1) Establish on the record that he will in fact take the stand and testify if his challenged prior convictions are excluded; (2) sufficiently outline the nature of his testimony so that the trial court, and the re-

695

viewing court, can do the necessary balancing contemplated in Rule 609.

The majority reached the merits and affirmed the trial judge's ruling. In a concurring opinion, a sixth judge emphasized that the defendant has the burden to prove prejudice from a ruling by the trial judge.

Another two judges agreed that a failure to take the stand in a criminal case should not be deemed a waiver of the right to complain about an erroneous decision to admit prior convictions. These judges also would require some kind of offer of proof to preserve the record for appeal. On the facts presented to them, these two judges declined to join the majority in affirming the trial judge's original evidence ruling. Five dissenting judges believed that the majority's approach would complicate trials and offer defendants a chance to manufacture erroneous rulings. These judges feared that a defendant who decides to remain silent after an advance ruling he seeks on an evidence question could be in a better position than a defendant in a case in which the trial court decides to defer the decision until after the defendant has given his direct testimony.

It would be a mistake to dismiss the *Portash* and *Cook* cases as having no significance in civil litigation. In limine rulings occur as often in civil as in criminal trials. In fact, the more elaborate discovery permitted in civil cases makes it likely that civil lawyers know more about evidence disputes than criminal lawyers before trial. That increases the attraction of an advance hearing to resolve these disputes.

For example, if the parties have exchanged experts' reports before trial and then one moves for an order barring the other's expert from relying on certain facts or data under FED. R. EVID. 703, a procedural question similar to that of the *Portash* and *Cook* cases may be posed to a court of appeals. Say the party offering the expert decides not to call him once the court grants his opponent's motion. After losing on the merits, that party then appeals from the pretrial ruling. The court must again decide whether a party may respond to a pretrial ruling by deciding not to call a witness and later arguing on appeal that the witness was not called because the judge ruled incorrectly in advance on the evidence.

When the Supreme Court divides on the appropriateness of appellate review of a trial judge's ruling and a court of appeals finds itself in disarray *en banc* on the same question, one plainly correct answer to this question may be elusive. The analysis offered thus far by federal appellate courts could be improved if the courts would separate five different concepts: prematurity, deviousness, predictability, harmless error, and irrelevant error. Each is important to a full understanding of the costs and benefits of in limine rulings, but only the last two shed light on the appropriateness of appellate review in cases like the *Portash* and *Cook* cases.

The first concept, prematurity, relates to a general problem with in limine rulings: Does the trial judge have sufficient information to make an informed decision when he is asked to rule? The *Portash* case is the best example of one in which prematurity is never likely to be a concern. The Supreme Court held that a person who has been immunized simply may not be impeached with the immunized testimony. Since this ruling would not depend on additional facts, there would be no reason to delay it.

The *Cook* case is different, however. The trial judge had to balance the probative value of a prior conviction offered for impeachment against its prejudicial effect. Such a decision may turn, at least in part, on the importance of the defendant's testimony, the other available impeachment evidence, the extent to which other witnesses are impeached, and other considerations not known before trial.

Similarly, in the hypothetical civil case involving an expert witness, the trial judge may be wary about ruling on the scope of expert testimony before the details of the case have been disclosed and before the judge understands the importance of the expert and the bases for his opinion. A trial judge may generally postpone a final decision on a motion in limine. Indeed, in most instances, a trial judge can refuse to make a ruling in advance of trial or in advance of a witness's taking the stand.

The best protection against premature decision making is the sound exercise of judicial discretion to hear, to postpone, or to reject requests for rulings in limine. Questions about appellate review of advance evidence rulings only arise once the trial judge rules. The problems of prematurity and appellate review in reality are distinct.

Conditioned Rulings

The second concept, deviousness, means the possibility that one party may successfully seek an in limine ruling and turn around and attempt to take unfair advantage of it. For example, a defendant who manages to exclude prior convictions may attempt to convey to a jury an impression of a clean personal history. Or a party who succeeds in preventing an expert from disclosing data to a jury might imply that there was no data.

The trial judge can handle this by conditioning his ruling—that is, stating that it is only binding as long as a party does not attempt to use it unfairly against an opponent. The judge should state the scope or fair use. The problem of deviousness is associated with an in limine victory that is abused. The problem of appellate review is quite different. It is associated with loss of the motion in limine.

Thus, while concerns about prematurity and deviousness obviously bear on whether there should be advance rulings at all, they shed no light on when a party who loses an in limine point should be able to appeal the ruling following an adverse judgment. Nor does the third concept, predictability, help to answer the question. One of the most important advantages of advance rulings is that they inform the parties of the proof that will be accepted at trial so that they will not be surprised by the judge's rulings. A judge who refuses to rule in limine increases the uncertainty of the parties over evidence disputes. Once the pretrial ruling is made, however, predictability is achieved no matter how the question about appellate review is resolved.

The final two concepts are the ones that really should be considered in deciding when appellate review is appropriate. The concept of harmless error is usually applied when a mistake is made at trial, but an appellate court concludes that it had so little impact on the outcome that reversal is not required. Understandably, a majority of the judges in the *Cook* case did not want a party to be able to obtain a reversal as a result of an in limine ruling that would have been deemed harmless error had it been made during the trial. They insisted, therefore, that to preserve for appellate review an advance ruling concerning the scope of impeachment of a witness who does not testify, the party who loses the in limine ruling must make an offer of proof that demonstrates the harm resulting from the ruling.

This procedure may still leave the losing party in a better position than the party appealing from a ruling made during the trial, and it is this possibility that is disturbing to the *Cook* dissenters. To understand their concern, it is necessary to consider the final concept, irrelevant error.

In the most familiar version of irrelevant error, the trial judge makes a mistake on an evidence ruling but the injured party nevertheless receives the judgment he requested. In a *Portash* or *Cook* case, for example, the defendant might testify and be acquitted. Or, in the hypothetical civil case, the expert might testify and fully persuade the jury, even without elaborating on various facts and data. When the party who should have won an evidence point wins the trial, he has no need to appeal. Thus, any evidentiary error is no longer relevant to the prevailing party.

The usual rule in American courts is that appeals on evidence and other non-final decisions must await a final judgment. One of the most powerful arguments for the rule is that many issues disappear (or become irrelevant) once a judgment is rendered. If, for example, the trial judge improperly excludes impeachment evidence that might have demonstrated the bias of a witness, the mistake becomes inconsequential if there is a judgment for the cross-examining party. Or, if the trial judge admits evidence of subsequent measures in a negligence case in the mistaken belief that feasibility is disputed, the jury may still find for the defendant, thereby eliminating any need for an appeal on the evidence point.

Hypothetical Issues

In the first example, the impeaching party is expected to attempt to discredit the witness within the evidentiary limits set by the court. If he is successful, the jury will discount the witness' testimony. The examination might not be as telling as if the court had ruled properly, but it still might be effective. Rarely, if ever, has a cross-examiner been permitted to respond to an evidence ruling on a single point by not cross-examining at all and later complaining that he did not want to cross-examine at all if he could not do it exactly the way he wanted.

In the second example, the party is expected to attempt to persuade the jury that there was no negligence and that negligence, not feasibility of repair, is at issue. If he succeeds, he is likely to obtain a favorable judgment. If he does not make the attempt, he is likely to convince an appellate court that the trial judge was correct. In both cases an appellate court will be concerned about the effect of the error on the judgment below only if the party injured by the error loses.

Had Portash and Cook been called to testify, juries might have believed them regardless of the impeaching evidence offered by the government. They claimed on appeal that their testimony was important to their defenses, but they chose at trial to shun the witness stand instead of testifying and attempting to persuade the jury of the truth of their testimony. Should the courts have sanctioned this approach?

Justice Blackmun and Chief Justice Burger in the *Portash* case and five judges in the *Cook* case offer one troubling reason why the defendants may not have testified: in truth, they might have never wanted to testify, regardless of how the trial judges ruled on their in limine requests. These appellate judges were concerned that litigants could create hypothetical evidence issues in an effort to bolster chances of winning on appeal without suffering any real harm at trial. A majority of the *Cook* court responded by adopting a procedure that purports to limit appeals to only those defendants who sincerely want to testify. Presumably, a similar rule could be employed to cover the expert witness in our hypothetical civil case. It will be difficult, however, to decide whether a defendant is sincere in professing a desire to take the stand, or whether a civil litigant really wants to call a particular expert witness.

Assume that this decision can be made. Assume that only defendants who sincerely want to testify may complain about impeachment rulings, that Portash and Cook were such defendants, and that they abandoned their sincere desire to testify because they did not want to be impeached. Is sincerity sufficient, or should there be some actual testimony to justify an appeal about the permissible scope of that testimony or of cross-examination?

The argument that a defendant must take the stand and be impeached before appealing a ruling permitting the impeachment rests on the relationship between harmless and irrelevant error. Most lawyers would agree that even well-intentioned and careful courts sometimes err. Although it is impossible to prevent all mistakes, it may be possible to design evidence and procedural rules that minimize the consequences of error.

A rule that a defendant is required actually to testify before attacking an in limine ruling concerning his own impeachment might reduce the costs of error. It would give the defendant an incentive to mitigate the adverse consequences of an evidence ruling. For example, he could explain away impeachment evidence, he could give a strong performance on the stand, he could corroborate his trial testimony, and so on.

Failure to mitigate increases the likelihood of an adverse judgment, since the impeachment evidence will be before the jury. The harder a defendant works to minimize the adverse effects of the judge's error, the more likely it is that he will win and that any error will be rendered irrelevant. And if the defendant loses, his efforts at mitigation may be so successful that a new trial will be unnecessary because the error will appear harmless by the end of trial.

It may be harmless because the impeachment is neutralized or because the impeachment is less significant than other parts of the trial. Portash, for example, might have faltered so badly while testifying that the judge's in limine ruling would have been considered a harmless mistake. Or Cook might have been so effectively cross-examined or contradicted once he testified that his prior convictions would not have seemed important in the context of his testimony. Thus a requirement that a defendant actually testify and risk impeachment before he may complain about the trial judge's ruling on the scope of impeachment would reduce the number of unnecessary retrials by recognizing harmless and irrelevant errors. Such a rule would assure that a court that orders a new trial can be confident of the significance of a trial error.

The most powerful argument in favor of appellate review in the *Portash* and *Cook* cases is that a defendant who is hurt by an erroneous evidence ruling should be encouraged to pursue the litigation strategy that is most likely to be effective. By doing so he increases the likelihood that the error will become irrelevant when he emerges victorious. If the best strategy is to avoid impeachment, the defendant should be encouraged to choose that strategy.

The problem with this argument is that it is not plain that the *Portash* and *Cook* cases provide an incentive for the defendant to do everything possible to win at trial despite a trial judge's error. Once the trial judge makes a pretrial decision that the defendant may be impeached if he testifies, the defendant has two available strategies: he can take the stand, suffer impeachment, and fight back; or he can refrain from testifying. The first choice may be more likely to produce victory, but it also is more likely to render the in limine evidence mistake harmless. Thus a defendant might choose not to testify—even though this diminishes his chances of winning at trial—if not testifying increases the probability that he will prevail on appeal.

The defendant's chances of convincing an appellate court that the error was prejudicial may increase if he does not testify. The appellate court will have to assume that he can do what he claims in his offer of proof. It will take a second trial to determine whether the first error was actually harmful.

It is possible that a defendant may think he will lose and, in fact, is prepared to use the first trial as a discovery mechanism to help him prepare for a better second trial. Evidence rules may not completely prevent such tactics from being used, but they should be designed to discourage them. To require a defendant to testify as a condition of appellate review of impeachment rulings cannot completely deter the defendant from planning to lose to improve his chances on appeal. But it may make it more likely that an appellate court will not reverse a trial judgment even if it finds error.

To require the defendant to testify gives him the incentive to attempt to win at trial. The problem with the *Portash* and *Cook* cases is that they may take away this incentive.

The wisdom of appellate review is questionable in the *Portash* and *Cook* cases even assuming that in limine motions are always made in good faith. Denying review in such cases would only require acceptance of the proposition that a party cannot complain about a ruling admitting impeachment evidence until he has been impeached. Until then, he cannot show that he has been hurt by the judge's ruling. Put another way, any harm that follows an in limine ruling should be considered hypothetical until the witness who is affected by the evidence ruling testifies.

There is another reason to question the *Portash* and *Cook* results. Judges probably cannot effectively differentiate sincere from insincere litigants. It will often be difficult to evaluate a defendant's reasons for not testifying or a plaintiff's reasons for not calling an expert witness. How can the judge tell whether the defendant or expert would have testified had the trial judge made a different in limine ruling?

The *Cook* case assumes that a defendant's promise to testify if successful on the motion, accompanied by a summary of his proposed testimony, is enough to permit an assessment of sincerity. This is questionable. Defendants who succeed with their motions in limine may change their minds about testifying. If they do, it is hard to see what penalty judges would or could impose upon them.

And when rulings are unfavorable to a defendant and he does not testify, any summary of his foregone testimony will be cast in the light most favorable to the defendant. It will be difficult to know how well he would have done had he actually testified. In a civil case a summary of an expert witness's testimony will be cast to favor the party who says he wants the expert to testify. Again, it will be difficult to know how effective the expert would have been on the stand.

In the civil case, the judge might permit full examination and cross-examination of the expert outside the jury's presence or allow a deposition to be admitted as an offer of proof, but these options may not always

701

be attractive. The deposition is often a discovery deposition in which the proponent of the expert's testimony chose not to fully develop his testimony. Full examination and cross-examination are likely to be time-consuming and might require the judge to rule on other aspects of a witness's testimony, when the judge knows that the witness is not going to take the stand no matter how he rules. Such a process would burden courts to the point where in limine rulings might be thought to be more trouble than they are worth.

In criminal cases, constitutional questions will be raised if the court attempts to force a defendant to take the stand and be questioned in advance of a ruling on an in limine point to preserve a record for appeal. And constitutional questions aside, the burdens of such a procedure on the court would be as great in criminal as in civil cases.

The majority in the *Cook* case suggested that if the government thinks that a defendant is not sincere in seeking an in limine ruling, the government should agree to the defendant's request and remove the evidence issue from the case. That ignores the legitimate concern of the government. As long as the government believes that a defendant is subject to impeachment if he testifies, it wishes to assert that position. The government can never be sure whether the defendant will ultimately take the stand. It wants to protect its legitimate interests if he does testify.

Thus the government may oppose an in limine motion without knowing whether or not it is sincere. In fact, the government may be indifferent about whether the defendant takes the stand. That the government wants protection if something happens does not mean that it believes that it will happen.

Despite all these problems with the *Portash* and *Cook* rulings, there is undeniably something attractive about giving a litigant the right to respond to a trial judge's mistake by changing strategy in an effort to win despite the error. Yet it is difficult to recognize that right without also providing opportunities for the kind of tactical maneuvering that permits litigants to preserve issues for appeal that might become harmless or irrelevant but for the maneuvering.

There is no one right answer to the question of how much appellate review ought to follow in limine rulings. In an uncertain world, the strongest argument against review in the *Portash* and *Cook* cases may be that they open a can of worms. If a party cannot obtain appellate review of a ruling concerning impeachment or the scope of testimony of a witness who never testifies, in limine motions surely would continue to be made and ruled upon.

In fact, judges who now fear that such motions may be made by insincere litigants might be more willing to make advance rulings. Litigants could use such motions to avoid surprise and to achieve the beneficial results described at the beginning of this article. The motion in limine would be treated just like a ruling at trial, only it would come earlier, for the benefit of the parties' planning. Appellate rights flowing from in limine rulings would be identical to those provided for trial rulings, so that litigants equally disadvantaged by judicial error would receive equal treatment, regardless of whether the error was made before or during trial. All of the problems with appellate review in cases like the *Portash* and *Cook* cases would disappear.

A number of courts have chosen to permit defendants who plead guilty to preserve certain preplea rulings for appeal. The Supreme Court has approved an amendment to FED. R. CRIM. P. 11 to permit such pleas. These pleas make it unnecessary for a defendant to go to trial to preserve one or two pretrial rulings for appeal.

Postplea appellate review avoids litigation. The *Portash* and *Cook* cases are different in that they permit litigation while also permitting appellate review.

In the future, appellate courts would provide a great service if they were to identify the benefits they see flowing from appellate review in these cases. Of course, there may be substantial benefits that outweigh all of the costs associated with appellate review suggested here. By articulating the rationale for appellate review of rulings about witnesses who never testify, the appellate courts might cause reconsideration of some of the current limitations on interlocutory orders. If some issues are central to the trial of a case, it may be better to permit early appellate review than to invite tactical wrangling.

The *Portash* and *Cook* cases are well-intentioned rulings. They may be more right than wrong. But they raise important problems. Those problems warrant the most careful consideration as courts continue to seek ways to make the trial of cases more efficient while maintaining fairness for all.

Rule 801:
More Than a Definition

by William E. McDaniels

Fresh from law school evidence, I tried my first cases in Philadelphia. Colloquies such as the following would occur. In a trial for burglary, the state would have its police officer witness on the stand.

Q: Officer Jones, did you return to the scene of the burglary with the defendant after you arrested him?

A: Yes.

Q: Did any conversation ensue?

A: Yes.

Q: What was that conversation?

DEFENSE COUNSEL: Objection, Your Honor, hearsay.

THE COURT: Was the defendant present?

THE PROSECUTOR: Yes, sir.

THE COURT: Objection overruled.

A: The owner of the premises stated that the defendant was wearing the same type of clothing as the man who had broken into the building.

Since this ruling defied my primitive knowledge of the hearsay rule, I consulted with more experienced colleagues and was informed that I had just been exposed to the Philadelphia exception to the hearsay rule: anything said in the defendant's presence is admissible against the defendant. Having since had the privilege of trying many more cases in Philadelphia and elsewhere, I have found that no jurisdiction has an exclusive corner on unique hearsay exceptions. Some even claim the ''Philadelphia'' exception as their own.

As with many unique exceptions, this one is not without some basis.

The author is a member of the Washington, D.C., firm of Williams & Connolly. He is also an Adjunct Professor of Law at Georgetown University Law Center, where he teaches evidence.

The defendant's presence can be an important factor in making a number of out-of-court statements by third persons admissible over a hearsay objection. For example, if the statement is being introduced not for the truth of the matter asserted but to show the effect of the statement on the defendant-hearer, the statement is not hearsay and not excludable on that ground. Even if the statement is being offered for the truth of the matter, and is therefore hearsay, the defendant's presence may be integral to the operation of a hearsay exception. The most pertinent exception, the tacit admission doctrine, holds that, if a statement calling for denial is made within the hearing of the person who should deny it and no denial is forthcoming, the silence of the person is admissible as a circumstantial fact and, to give meaning to the silence, the accusatory statement is also admissible.

While it is obvious that the presence of the defendant is important to each of these theories of admissibility, something more than his presence is required. The court must inquire into the relevant purpose for which the statement is offered to determine if it is a non-hearsay use of the statement. If it is hearsay and the prosecution is relying on some exception, such as the tacit admission doctrine, the court must look beyond the defendant's presence to ascertain whether the qualifying factors for the exception are present, such as a statement naturally calling for denial.

Specific Guidelines

One result of the Federal Rules of Evidence should be the elimination of automatic responses to hearsay problems which do not reflect a reasoned application of the hearsay rule. Counsel now has specific guidelines articulating the scope of the hearsay rule and its exceptions, an arsenal by no means assured at all times during the framing of the rules by the Advisory Committee. The Advisory Committee took a fresh look at the hearsay rule and its rationale to determine the most appropriate way to legislate the common law doctrine and considered (1) the abolition of the hearsay rule in its entirety, (2) an in-between step of abandoning specific hearsay exceptions in favor of a case-by-case consideration of each offer of hearsay, and (3) a system of rules which would enshrine the common law procedure and its numerous exceptions.

The hearsay rule expresses the preference of the adversary system that proof in lawsuits be elicited under ideal conditions—the physical presence of the witness before the trier of facts, under oath and subject to cross-examination by the party against whom the proof is being admitted. Observance of these ideal conditions permits the litigant affected to test before the trier of fact the factors determining the trustworthiness of a witness' testimony, which include the witness' perception, memory, narration and, more generally, his sincerity—is he telling the truth? The hearsay rule grew out of the conviction that proof not elicited under these ideal conditions lacked sufficient trustworthiness.

The common law generally proscribed as hearsay any statement made out of court when offered for the truth of the matter asserted and thus resting for its testimonial value on the credibility of the out-of-court declarant. It quickly became apparent that not all out-of-court statements were so suspect as to justify their exclusion, particularly in such situations as when there is no other evidence on the point. Thus, despite the reduced trustworthiness of testimony elicited under less than ideal conditions, courts developed exceptions to the rule of exclusion if an adequate need, combined with sufficient guarantees of trustworthiness, made exclusion of the testimony more damaging to ascertaining truth than its admission.

Middle Ground

Admissibility of statements under these exceptions, plus several categories of non-hearsay statements (statements not admitted for their truth), became so pervasive that they threatened to engulf the rule of exclusion. Despite the resultant impetus for reform of the common law approach to a rule of exclusion and a plethora of exceptions, the Advisory Committee rejected abolition of the hearsay rule. It also refused to adopt the alternative of leaving the decision to the trial judge based on a relevancy standard—weighing the probative value of the evidence against the possibility of prejudice, waste of time and the availability of more satisfactory evidence. The Advisory Committee instead selected the approach of the common law while making numerous changes in the common law.

Rule 801, innocently entitled "Definitions," was the first of six rules dealing with hearsay and is the source of some of the changes. Rule 802 proscribes hearsay—hearsay is not admissible except as provided by these rules or by other rules prescribed by the Supreme Court under statutory authority or by act of Congress. Rules 803 and 804 establish the exceptions to the proscription under two headings. Rule 803 lists the exceptions applicable when the availability of the declarant is immaterial. Rule 804 contains the exceptions applicable when unavailability of the declarant is required. Rules 803 and 804 have 27 specific exceptions and each has a catchall exception, a carryover of the considerable support among the rulemakers for a case-by-case determination of hearsay by the relevancy approach. Rule 805 recognizes the common law rule, most frequently encountered under the exception for business records, that hearsay within hearsay will not be admissible unless each part of the combined statement conforms with an exception to the hearsay rule. Rule 806 provides for attacking and supporting the credibility of the declarant of a hearsay statement, incorporating by reference the impeachment tools of Article VI and authorizing the party against whom a hearsay statement has been admitted to call the declarant as his witness and examine him on the statement as if under cross-examination.

Misunderstood Concept

Rule 801(c) defines hearsay as "a statement, other than one made by the declarant while testifying at the trial or hearing, offered in evidence to prove the truth of the matter asserted"—the generally accepted common law definition of hearsay. The definition also highlights the often misunderstood concept that, even though the declarant is present in court, the statements he has made out of court are nevertheless hearsay and excludable despite his presence at the trial or hearing for cross-examination. In 801 (d), discussed below, the rulemakers made some significant inroads into this concept by carving out of the proscription of hearsay certain statements offered for the truth of the matter when the declarant is at trial.

By its terms 801(c) preserves the admissibility of a category of out-of-court statements which are nonhearsay because they are not offered for the truth of the matter asserted but are offered for an evidentiary purpose not dependent on the truth. This well-established category includes statements offered as operative facts (verbal conduct to which the law attaches duties and liabilities, such as the words of offer and acceptance in a contract), statements offered to show the effect on the hearer (to show the defendant's fear because he was told that the victim had knifed three people in the last year), statements evidencing knowledge, and statements evidencing insanity (the classic "I am the Pope" utterance). Although these out-of-court statements are sometimes criticized for sharing as many of the hearsay dangers as statements offered for their truth, the rulemakers made no changes in this area.

Rule 801(b) merely defines the "declarant" as the person who makes the "statement." But Rule 801(a), by its definition of the meaning of "statement," addresses one of the thorniest academic questions of the common law of hearsay—non-assertive conduct. "Statement" is defined as an oral or written assertion or non-verbal conduct of a person intended by him as an assertion. Thus, the rule limits the application of the hearsay rule to strictly assertive conduct—for example, the witness who, when asked who did it to him, points his finger instead of shouting, "There is the man."

The common law had been split on whether non-assertive conduct was inadmissible under the rationale of the hearsay rule. The older decisions excluded it while a few recent cases have gone the other way. One leading case which had found it inadmissible contains examples which clarify what non-assertive conduct is. *Wright v. Doe D. Tatham*, 7 Ad. & E1. 313, 112 Eng. R. 488 (1834, 1836, 1837). Assume the issue in a lawsuit is the seaworthiness of a vessel. The party seeking to establish seaworthiness offers the testimony that a famous sea captain inspected the ship and thereafter set out on a trans-oceanic voyage on the ship with his wife and family. Does this circumstantial evidence violate the hearsay rule? Courts answering "yes" considered the relevant purpose of the evidence was to prove seaworthiness, translated the actions of the sea captain into a statement that the vessel was seaworthy and then excluded evidence of his conduct on the theory that it constituted hearsay. The reason for exclusion was that the relevancy of the conduct depended upon the perception and judgment of the out-of-court individual. The conclusion of seaworthiness depends on the captain having diligently inspected the vessel while possessing sufficient expertise to determine seaworthiness. Thus the hearsay dangers are present and cross-examination of the out-of-court actor is necessary to protect the party against whom the evidence is to be admitted.

Weak Argument

The weakness of this argument is that, since the person engaging in the conduct is neither making an assertion nor perceiving its possible use as a circumstantial fact in a later lawsuit, the hearsay danger of insincerity is remote. This is particularly true when the person is acting in reliance on his conduct and sailing on the ship with his family. Accordingly, it should be weighed as any other circumstantial fact—by the standards of relevancy. The rulemakers favored the latter view and, if any of us in the next hundred years or so runs into an instance of non-assertive conduct that we recognize as such, it is admissible if relevant.

Rule 801(d) was one of the most controversial provisions of the rules as they progressed through Congress, particularly the section dealing with the use of prior inconsistent statements. The section is entitled "Statements Which Are Not Hearsay" and should not be confused with the non-hearsay provisions of Rule 801(c). Non-hearsay is admissible if relevant because it is not being offered for the truth of the matter but merely because it was said. Statements which are made "not hearsay" by Rule 801(d) are statements offered for the truth of the matter but which the rulemakers have chosen to make admissible—not as exceptions to the hearsay rule, but as a new theoretical category of "not hearsay." One category of 801(d) statements—admissions—formerly was admissible as an exception. The other—certain prior statements by a witness who is present at trial—was not admissible and thus is where the greatest change occurs.

The reason these categories of statements are labeled by rulemakers as not hearsay, as opposed to exceptions to the hearsay rule, is conceptual. The exceptions to the hearsay rule generally exist because the statement was made under circumstances indicating it is substantially trustworthy or because there are varying degrees of need for the statement, or because of a combination of both factors. The justifications for admitting the "not hearsay" statements are different. The prior statement of a presently testifying witness is admissible largely because he is present at trial and the opportunity for cross-examination is considered a sufficient justification for admitting certain classes of prior statements. An admission by a party-opponent is a creature of the adversary system and is admissible on the theory that the party against whom the evidence is offered cannot complain about the inability to cross-examine the declarant, since that party or his representative is the declarant.

Admissions by a party-opponent are made not hearsay by Rule 801(d)(2). Statements included in that category are (1) those by a party in his individual or representative capacity, or (2) a statement of which he has manifested his adoption or belief in its truth (adoptive or tacit admission), or (3) a statement by a person authorized by him to make a statement concerning the subject (admission by an agent), or (4) a statement by his agent or servant concerning a matter within the scope of his agency or employment made during the existence of the relationship (admission by an agent expanded), or (5) a statement by a co-conspirator of a party during the course and in furtherance of the conspiracy (co-conspirator exception). The rule makes one significant expansion of the common law. The common law exception as to admissions by an agent required that the principal confer authority on his agent to speak for him. Rule 801(d)(2) recognizes that qualification, but Rule 801(d)(3) expands the rule to make admissible statements by an agent who may or may not have been authorized to speak by his principal as long as the agent is speaking about the subject matter of his agency during the existence of the agency relationship.

Under Rule 801(d)(1)(A), the prior inconsistent statement of a witness which was given under oath at a trial, hearing or other proceeding or at a deposition is admissible for the truth of the matter asserted when the declarant testifies at the present trial or hearing and is cross-examined concerning the statement. As originally drafted by the Advisory Committee, this rule would have gone much farther to authorize admissibility of all prior inconsistent statements when the declarant is present, irrespective of the conditions under which the prior statements were made. Although the Supreme Court has held such a rule does not violate the right to confront witnesses preserved by the Sixth Amendment, it was the distinct minority position in state jurisdictions and without precedent in the federal courts. Even as narrowed by Congress, the rule still represents a clear minority of state jurisdictions and finds prior precedent in federal courts solely in the Second Circuit. See *United States v. De Sisto*, 329 F.2d 929 (2d Cir. 1964), *cert. denied*, 377 U. S. 979 (1964); *United States v. Cunningham*, 446 F.2d 194 (2d Cir.), *cert. denied*, 404 U.S. 950 (1971).

The rule that emerged from the Conference Report did not narrow the prior inconsistent statements to the extent that the House Committee on the Judiciary would have. The House Committee not only would have required the prior inconsistent statements to have been made under oath at a prior trial or hearing or at a deposition, but also to have been made while the declarant was subject to cross-examination. The Senate Committee on the Judiciary rejected the House's limitations entirely and reinstated the Advisory Committee version. In the spirit of compromise, the Conference Report preserved the oath requirement of the House version but eliminated the cross-examination requirement. The chief result of the compromise is to permit substantive use of grand jury testimony by the government in a criminal prosecution.

The practical consequences of the changes wrought by Rule 801 (d)(1)(A) cannot be lightly dismissed. There can be no question that the prime stimulus for this change was the recalcitrant witness in a criminal case. Thus, Brown, eyewitness to a murder, identifies the defendant Smith to the police as the assailant. He so testifies before the grand jury. At the time of trial, for whatever reason, Brown retracts his earlier statements and testifies that Smith did not do the shooting. In strict common law jurisdictions, absent a valid claim of surprise, the prosecutor must watch the core of his prosecution disappear. Since he has called the witness, the voucher rule prohibiting a party from impeaching witnesses he has called precludes the government from bringing to the attention of the jury the witness's prior statement identifying Smith.

Even assuming that, because of a valid claim of surprise or the elimination of the voucher rule, the prosecutor is able to cross-examine his witness, the prevailing common law rule sharply inhibits his full use of a prior inconsistent statement. Under traditional common law doctrine, the prior statement is not admissible for the truth of the matter asserted because it is hearsay; it is admissible solely to assist the jury in evaluating whether the statement made at trial that Smith was not the killer constitutes the truth. And limiting instructions would be administered to the jurors to preclude them from considering the prior inconsistent statement for its truth. Putting aside whether the jury can ever follow such instructions, the prosecutor has been severely limited, for if the matter contained in the prior inconsistent statement is essential to his *prima facie* case, his case will never be submitted to the jury for decision.

The new rules remove most of these restrictions on the government. The voucher rule is eliminated so that any party may impeach any witness by prior inconsistent statement, including his own witness. No claim of surprise is required. A prior inconsistent statement under oath used to impeach is admissible substantively and therefore contributes to the government's *prima facie* case. Under the new rules, the prosecutor could impeach Brown with both of his prior statements, but only the one before the grand jury will be admissible substantively.

The proponents of this change argued that the old rule limiting the prior inconsistent statement to impeachment purposes made little sense, not only because jurors would not heed the traditional cautionary instructions and would merely select which of the two statements they believed, but also because present cross-examination more than adequately protected the party against whom the statement is admitted. Detractors of the new rule claim it will permit convictions to be made in the privacy of the grand jury room and merely be presented to the trial court for endorsement. The prosecutor with the undeniable advantage of the *ex parte* grand jury proceeding can, once a record is made in the grand jury, always present such statements for the truth of the matter as long as it calls the declarant, whether or not the declarant affirms or denies the statements.

The concern over convictions being made *ex parte* in the grand jury gave rise to one lingering limitation on the prosecutor's full use of prior inconsistent statements. A footnote appears in the legislative history to the Conference Report which states that 801(d)(1)(A) ''is not addressed to the sufficiency of evidence to send the case to the trial but merely to its admissibility. Factual circumstances can well arise where, if this were the sole evidence, dismissal would be appropriate.'' Thus, the Conference Report is saying that, while a prior inconsistent statement comes in for the truth of the matter asserted and while the testimony of a single witness traditionally has been sufficient to convict, where the testimony is in the form of a prior inconsistent statement admitted substantively under Rule 801(d)(1)(A), the prosecutor might not have presented a sufficient case. The footnote seems to suggest that statements introduced substantively under 801(d)(1)(A) will nevertheless carry less than full testimonial force at the stage the burden of production is tested. Precedent for such a distinction exists. For example, when tacit admissions were admissible in criminal cases as evidence against the accused, some decisions recognizing the tenuous theory of admissibility refused to allow conviction of an accused based solely on evidence contained in a tacit admission. *See, e.g., Commonwealth v. Karmendi.* 195 Atl. 62 (Pa. 1937).

Incentive for Reform

One result of 801(d)(1)(A) may be further incentive for reform of the grand jury process. This stage becomes critical to an accused if testimony elicited before the grand jury may later be introduced substantively. Can the grand jury remain an *ex parte* proceeding with no representative of either the defendant or the testifying witness present? Consideration should be given to an ombudsman representing persons possibly affected by the grand jury to preserve on the record matters which may be essential to a later evaluation of a given witness's grand jury testimony. A witness who testifies differently at trial than before the grand jury will often explain away his grand jury testimony by stating alternatively: I was sick; I was on drugs; the prosecutor or police threatened me; I was given a prepared script to testify from; I was held incommunicado for days before my testimony; I asked to see a lawyer, my wife, my friend. As soon as this testimony is given, the prosecutor will respond with investigative officers or prosecuting attorneys, or both, to contradict the witness's assertions. The result will be a swearing contest between government officials and witnesses which is not only unseemly but also unfair to the accused, who is unlikely to prevail in any such factual controversy.

In an analogous context, lineup identifications, the Supreme Court required counsel for the accused, a holding later modified to require counsel only at post-indictment lineups. The ombudsman would not be counsel for any one person. He would be an individual not aligned with the prosecution who could testify about the conditions under which grand jury testimony was given. It is not enough to say that the oath and recording proves without possibility of contradiction that the statement was made and is therefore sufficient protection for the accused. The circumstances of making the statement may be vital to combatting its admission. The ombudsman could make a record of these circumstances and avoid the swearing contest between prosecuting officials and citizens.

The practical effect of 801(d)(1)(A) in civil cases is to expand the already loose prior recorded testimony exception. No *ex parte* proceeding analogous to the grand jury exists to raise a problem unless the phrase "other proceeding" receives an overly broad interpretation. From the history of the section and the placement of the words in the section, the "other proceeding" must be an official judicial or quasi-judicial hearing. The rule-makers emphasized the official nature of the hearing process and the solemnity of the oath. Also, the phrasing "trial, hearing, or other proceeding or in a deposition," suggests that, except for depositions, the testimony must occur before a tribunal of some kind. Given the ingenuity spawned by the adversary process, however, one can foresee insurance investigators, policemen or counsel conducting an *ex parte* "proceeding" in the privacy of their offices where a stenographer records a statement made by a sworn deponent. This "proceeding" should not qualify to make statements elicited admissible under 801(d)(1)(A).

Rule 801(d)(1)(B) provides the second category of statements by a declarant present in court which are not hearsay. These are statements which are consistent with the declarant's trial testimony and are offered to rebut an express or implied charge against him of recent fabrication or improper influence or motive. Under traditional common law principles, prior consistent statements were inadmissible except to rebut a charge of recent fabrication and, under those circumstances, such statements were not admissible for the truth of the matter asserted. The change to allow these statements to be considered substantively is of little practical consequence, since the jury was probably unable to follow the admonition which accompanied the common law rule. Elevating the use of such statements to substantive levels is not a great change since presumably the witness has already produced substantive evidence to the same effect during his direct testimony. Accordingly, there is no limitation, as in Rule 801(d)(1)(A), that the prior statements be under oath. Any prior consistent statement will qualify.

As originally proposed, Rule 801 (d)(1) relating to prior statements by a testifying witness had an additional category, subsection (C), which made admissible for the truth of the matter asserted statements identifying a person made after perceiving him. Extra-judicial identifications by a presently testifying witness are hearsay. Although there was a split among the states, a substantial body of authority supported the admissibility of extra-judicial identification under a hearsay exception. These decisions recognized that identifications made relatively contemporaneous with the events are generally of more value than later identifications made in court. Subsection (C) survived the House Judiciary Committee but was opposed in and eliminated by the Senate. In this instance, a growing body of state decisions recognizing the wisdom of an exception to the hearsay rule favoring admissibility was rejected. It is doubtful, given this legislative history, that statements of prior identification will be allowed in under the catchall hearsay exceptions alluded to above. Admissibility will only be achieved through amendment.

Interestingly, the reason that the Senate rejected subsection (C) was a concern that a person could be convicted solely upon evidence of an identification admissible under that exception. Unlike its action with respect to the House's change in prior inconsistent statements prompted by the same concern, the Conferees did not overrule the Senate's deletion of subsection (C) with a note that (C) made no statement as to sufficiency of the evidence. The interplay between the history of subsections (A) and (C) raises an interesting question when applied to the Smith-Brown example cited previously. There the prior inconsistent statement admitted substantively was one of identification. Given the history of subsection (C), are such prior inconsistent statements definitely within the type of "factual circumstances" envisioned by the Conferees in their footnote, where if the prior inconsistent statement was the sole evidence, "dismissal would be appropriate"?

The Federal Rules of Evidence, reflecting the consideration by an Advisory Committee and both Houses of Congress separately and in conference, have a rich legislative history for interpretation. No rules, no matter how tightly drawn, can remain inflexible in the face of the unending variations of adversarial contexts. Since Rule 801 (d)(1)(A) represents the compromise of a clash between two fundamentally opposing views, its interpretation will be particularly difficult. Support for each side exists in the record—those who tilt the balance toward an unrestricted right to confront one's accuser under ideal testimonial conditions and those who view the non-substantive use of prior inconsistent statements as extracting too large a price for ascertaining the truth. Only experience in the rule's operation can determine the appropriate balance.

713

Catch (24): Residual Hearsay

by Jo Ann Harris

It is probably safe now to confess that, when the Federal Rules of Evidence were first enacted into law in 1975, you were too busy trying cases to notice—or care. From time to time, of course, some callow young lawyer on the other side would try to impress a venerable district court judge by uttering a number to identify one of those new-fangled rules.

"Objection. 801(c)," he would say.

And you would join in the guffaws of judge, jury, and court buffs, united in a shared eyes-to-the-heavens expression.

All of this is to say—with due apologies to those scholars and lawyers who labored long in this vineyard—that some of us did not pay a whole lot of attention to the rules when they were first enacted.

"Not offered for the truth, judge" or "state of mind, your honor" continued to be more than sufficient to get you through the ordinary case.

I vaguely remember that I knew that somewhere in the hearsay exceptions was the preposterous concept that, if a hearsay statement does not fit any exception, the judge can let it in anyway, in the interests of justice, or something like that. "Fat chance," thought I, and promptly ignored the whole idea. My casual attitude was reinforced when Jon Waltz assured me, in these very pages, that there was not "A New Day for 'Great' Hearsay." 2 LITIGATION, No. 1 at 22 (Fall 1975).

I remained in that state of near oblivion until Faust Rossi (again in these pages) described "The Silent Revolution." 9 LITIGATION, No. 2 at 13 (Winter 1983). If the sky was not falling, at least the horse was out of the barn, we were over the brink, and the floodgates had opened. The residual exceptions to the rules against hearsay had, according to the

The author practices law in New York City.

eminent evidence professor, snuck up on us and virtually gobbled the rule.

It was this gloomy forecast that finally sent me to the books to figure out how to beat the new-rule mongers, and, if I could not, to join them. What follows, then are the practical observations of a reprobate who would rather be doing almost anything but researching the hearsay rule in the local law library.

If it even crossed your mind, before 1983, to use the residual rules, this may be a bit basic for you. It is aimed at fellow sloths who secretly, if not publicly, share a sordid history of inattention to such important matters.

The first thing to understand is that Rule 801(c) of the Federal Rules of Evidence tells you what you already know: "Hearsay is a statement, other than one made by the declarant while testifying at the trial or hearing, offered in evidence to prove the truth of the matter asserted," and that Rule 802 makes hearsay inadmissible except as provided by the grace of Congress. (Congress? Yes, Congress. Congress makes and unmakes these rules, not the Court.)

Comfortable old Shoe

The specific exceptions to the hearsay rule are itemized in Rules 803(1) to (23) and 804(b) (1) to (4). Rule 803 deals with exceptions for certain kinds of statements, most of which are familiar old reliables, that are admissible even if the declarant is available. Gathered under Rule 804 are those few exceptions that you may invoke only if you demonstrate that the declarant is absent, unreachable by process or other reasonable means, or exempt by reason of privilege, or that he has refused to testify, suffered a failure of memory, a physical or mental illness—or is dead.

So far, so good. Comfortable as an old shoe. But at the end of each of these rules, our lawmakers added a section. These sections have come to be known as the residual exceptions, the catchall exceptions, or the expansion exceptions to the hearsay rule. The language of each of Rules 803(24) and 804(b)(5) is exactly the same and it bears repeating here:

> Other exceptions. A statement not specifically covered by any of the foregoing exceptions but having equivalent circumstantial guarantees of trustworthiness, if the court determines that (A) the statement is offered as evidence of a material fact; (B) the statement is more probative on the point for which it is offered than any other evidence which the proponent can procure through reasonable efforts; and (C) the general purposes of these rules and the interests of justice will best be served by admission of the statement into evidence. However, a statement may not be admitted under this exception unless the proponent of it makes known to the adverse party sufficiently in advance of the trial or hearing to provide the

715

adverse party with a fair opportunity to prepare to meet it, his intention to offer the statement and the particulars of it, including the name and address of the declarant.

Truth in the Flotsam

Why Congress saw fit to provide us with this new tool has been the subject of much learned discussion, but basically it comes down to this: The professorial types have believed, probably forever, that justice is best served by letting the kitchen sink into evidence and relying on the fact finders to wallow around until they find the truth among the flotsam.

Naturally, the hearsay rule long has been a target of this elite group of thinkers. When it became evident that there was actually going to be a federal code of evidence, the scholars feared that, without some device to permit the future growth of exceptions to the hearsay rule, codification would stultify this search for truth.

Many trial lawyers and judges were reluctant to include an open-ended invitation to untested hearsay. They had visions of trial-by-out-of-court declaration; we would never again see a live witness cringe under the withering fire of cross-examination, no longer treasure the god-given abilities to parse and ply the common law rules.

More important, the practitioners feared the real loss of pretrial predictability. How could you prepare for trial or, for that matter, make rational settlement decisions, if lurking about the case was a spicy piece of absolutely inadmissible hearsay that some judge might willy-nilly let into evidence. In Judge Henry J. Friendly's words, the proposed residual provision permitting judges to exercise case-by-case discretion, with no real standards to guide them, would thrust the "chancellor's foot with a vengeance" into our courtrooms. *Proposed Federal Rules of Evidence: Hearings on H.R. 5463 Before the Special Subcomm. on Reform of Federal Criminal Laws of the House Comm. on the Judiciary*, 93d Cong., 1st Sess., Vol. 1 at 252, 264 (1973).

A congressional compromise resolved the matter. The professors got their residual sections to encourage continued development of hearsay exceptions; Judge Friendly got standards requiring a measure of trustworthiness to discourage unbridled discretion and legislative history unambiguously proclaiming that the residual rules should be used "very rarely and only in exceptional circumstances"; and the Rumpoles of this world were supposed to get pretrial notice when their adversaries planned to offer some otherwise inadmissible hearsay into evidence.

Thus, to invoke either of the catchall rules, the proponent is required to (1) give enough pretrial notice to the other side, including the name and address of the declarant, to provide a fair opportunity to meet the hearsay; (2) demonstrate that the proffered statement is likely to be as trustworthy as anything that comes in under any of the other exceptions set forth in Rule 803 or 804; and (3) convince the judge that the proffered statement is the most probative evidence, on the point for which it is offered, that can be obtained with reasonable efforts.

The other provisions in the catchall exceptions boil down to a redundant requirement of materiality (already mandated by common law, if not common sense, but not by Rules 401, 402, and 403, which speak only of relevance) and an entreaty to observe the spirit of the rules and the interests of justice.

One of the problems in trying to assess the present status of the catchalls is that many courts are paying no more than lip service to any of the requirements. Courts are simply not treating the residual rules as something special requiring careful analysis and articulated findings.

A busy district court judge is unlikely to take the time, midtrial, to parse out the bases for evidentiary rulings. In criminal cases, when the government unsuccessfully invokes the catchall rules (or the defendant does so successfully), chances are the decision will never hit the books because there will be no appeal on the issue and thus no incentive for the lower courts to make a record.

Even some appellate courts are ducking the hard analysis and intoning bromides, such as: "It is sufficient to observe that in admitting these documents the district court properly found that the requirements of FED. R. EVID. 803(24) were satisfied." *United States v. Marsh,* 747 F.2d 7, 14 (1st Cir. 1984). Worse yet is the case in which it is unnecessary to mention the catchall rules at all, but the court does, suggesting, for example, with no reasoning whatsoever, that the evidence in question might have been admissible under the residual rules. *See, e.g., Gryder v. Comm'r,* 705 F.2d 336 (8th Cir.), *cert. denied,* 464 U.S. 1008 (1983). Other courts are using the catchall rules for pretrial *in terrorem* effect, encouraging parties to settle or to stipulate or to run for the hills.

In short, it is hard to generalize with confidence about what is really happening in the trenches with these catchall rules. But it appears that, although they did not free vast hordes of hearsay-rule haters from judicial closets, a lot more hearsay is coming into evidence these days because of the open invitation of Rules 803(24) and 804(b)(5).

There is one area in which the use of the catchalls has gotten entirely out of hand. Many courts are admitting as substantive evidence grand jury testimony of the class of co-conspirators loosely known in the parlance of the trade as "cooperating individuals." These folks have a habit of flipping when arrested and cutting their own sweeter deals, deals that often require them to testify against their former colleagues in crime.

Cooperating individuals usually testify before the grand jury. That is pretty easy. But, as a group, they do not like to testify at trial. Instead, they leave or suffer contempt. And in case after case, district courts are finding them unavailable (with justification) and letting the prosecutor read their grand jury testimony to the petit jury under Rule 804(b)(5).

Not only does this practice raise serious confrontation-clause issues; courts are also using the residual rules for this purpose without seriously analyzing, or even addressing, whether their requirements have been met.

At one time, a minority of Supreme Court justices wanted to review this issue. *Garner v. United States*, 439 U.S. 936 (1978) (dissent from denial of *certiorari*). But *certiorari* was denied in a recent case, on worse facts, without a murmur. *United States v. Thomas*, 705 F.2d 709 (4th Cir.), *cert. denied*, 464 U.S. 890 (1983).

In *Thomas*, the government's entire case rested on the testimony of two co-conspirators, both long gone by the time of trial. The government got its conviction by reading their grand jury testimony to the petit jury. The Fourth Circuit's affirmance was utterly perfunctory.

The other problems for the trial lawyer that have come up under the catchall rules are not as horrifying. They are more in the nature of Catch-22's that the experienced practitioner, forearmed, can cope with. Here are some of those catches:

No notice may be good notice.

If there is anything explicit in Rules 803(24) and 804(b)(5), it is the requirement that the proponent give the other side pretrial notice of the intention to offer a hearsay statement under those rules and disclose the particulars of the statement, including the name and address of the speaker. Nothing about the residual hearsay rules has been more frequently ignored.

It all started with *United States v. Iaconetti*, 406 F. Supp. 554 (E.D.N.Y. 1976). United States District Judge Jack Weinstein presided over the trial. Judge Weinstein is, of course, widely regarded as a liberal prime mover in the world of evidence.

As luck would have it, in *Iaconetti*, the government had not given the defense pretrial notice of the hearsay it offered to rebut the defendant's exculpatory version of the facts. Undeterred, Judge Weinstein found that the government could not have known before trial that it would need the hearsay.

Claiming to heed the spirit of the rule, the judge offered the defense a continuance to prepare to meet the hearsay (the defense turned down the offer, unwisely), and then he admitted the prior consistent statements of the government's key witness as substantive evidence under Rule 803(24). The defendant was convicted. The court of appeals affirmed, agreeing that the late notice satisfied the notice provision of the residual hearsay rules, so long as the defendant had an opportunity to deal with the hearsay after it was offered. 540 F.2d 574 (2d Cir. 1976), *cert. denied*, 429 U.S. 1041 (1977).

Good Hearsay

Reasonable people might agree with this reading of the notice requirement if the legislative intent had been to get all good hearsay into the record. But that simply was not why Congress adopted the residual hearsay rules.

Instead, it seems that the strict notice requirement was the linchpin in the congressional compromise that finally fielded the catchall exceptions and that the notice provision was added not only in the name of fairness to the opposition but as a very real limit on the type of hearsay that would be admitted under the new rules. In short, it seems more than likely, given the legislative history, that Congress intended the residual hearsay loophole to be just big enough to admit needed hearsay that the proponent knows about before trial, for example, hearsay offered to authenticate a foreign bank account number because witnesses are beyond the reach of process and foreign depositions are too expensive.

In any event, in 1977, the Second Circuit saw the light and, without a breath of shame or any mention of its *Iaconetti* decision, shifted positions, requiring strict adherence to the notice requirements. *See United States v. Oates,* 560 F.2d 45, 72–73 n.30 (2d Cir. 1977).

Too late. Several circuits had already followed *Iaconetti. See, e.g., United States v. Carlson,* 547 F.2d 1346 (8th Cir. 1976), *cert. denied,* 431 U.S. 914 (1977); *United States v. Leslie,* 542 F.2d 285 (5th Cir. 1976). Only the Fifth Circuit has now turned around and joined the Second Circuit in requiring strict notice. *See United States v. Atkins,* 618 F.2d 366 (5th Cir. 1980).

A recent case explicitly holds that failure to comply with the notice requirement is not dispositive if the defendant has not been harmed and has had a fair opportunity to meet the proffered hearsay. *United States v. Parker,* 749 F.2d 628 (11th Cir. 1984).

The hearsay in *Parker* was an American executive's testimony about telephone conversations with a business associate in Scotland who described business practices of a Scottish company. There is no reason why the proponent cannot anticipate the need for this type of testimony and give his adversary pretrial notice of his intent to use it, but many courts continue to apply a harmless-error standard, instead of heeding the plain words of the rules.

Given the uncertain prospect that the notice requirement will protect you from surprise (trust the Second and Fifth Circuits at your peril), what can you do by way of self-help?

After you have analyzed the case, your facts, your opponent's facts, his theory, and your theory, you will know whether there is, on the face of the record, some hearsay the other side is thirsting to offer into evidence under the residual rules.

If there is, you have a choice.

You can lie in the weeds and, if you do not get notice, hope that your adversary (a) has forgotten about it or (b) is convinced he will never get it in and so won't try or (c) will try but will fail for lack of notice. Or you can demand to know whether he intends to offer anything under the residual rules. A demand will alert your adversary to the possibilities, but it will also fortify your defensive position considerably if he tries to spring something at trial without prior notice.

If your opponent responds to your demand with notice of his intent to offer some piece of hearsay under the residual exception, you can then make a pretrial motion *in limine*. If the judge rules before trial that he will receive the hearsay statement in evidence, the ruling will at least enable you to prepare for trial unencumbered by fanciful theories that, in the event, could be shot to shreds with one well-aimed hearsay statement.

The criminal defense lawyer has a special problem because of the courts' increasing tendency to receive as substantive evidence transcripts of the grand jury testimony of convicted co-defendants, even when there has been no pretrial notice because, for example, the witness disappears or changes his stripes just before he is scheduled to testify at trial. In anticipation of this problem, the savvy (and gutsy) practitioner might routinely seek material witness arrest warrants about a month before trial in those jurisdictions where otherwise the government can use the led, uncross-examined, sometimes intimidated, and often biased grand jury testimony of "unavailable" witnesses.

If you are confronted in midtrial with sudden notice of your adversary's intention to offer residual hearsay, do not—repeat: *do not*— decline the judge's offer of a continuance to meet the surprise evidence. If you do, you will have waived any objection based on the lack of notice.

Indeed, do not wait for the judge to offer. Ask for a continuance before the judge rules on the admissibility of the proffered statement. If you appear to be dead serious about the need for a 12-day continuance in the middle of a jury trial, chances are the judge will discover and apply the notice provisions to keep the trial going.

Be prepared to meet the argument that you should have known that this evidence might be offered under the residual exceptions. You could play dumb, but the more effective response is probably the common-sense one: If the evidence is so obvious that you should have known, how much more obvious should it have been to your adversary, whose evidence it is?

The lawyer representing a party in a civil case, or the prosecution in a criminal case, will, of course, before trial have completely mastered the facts and the evidence available to both sides. An informed judgment about the need for hearsay evidence, and about whether the other side knows about your hearsay, should come easily.

If you figure that your adversary knows about your hearsay, then there is every reason to give notice. Indeed, overdo it. It will drive him nuts. If you do not want to give him chapter and verse of the hearsay, a more general notice may do the trick. *See United States v. Evans*, 572 F.2d 455, 489 (5th Cir.), *cert. denied*, 439 U.S. 870 (1978).

If you reckon that your adversary does not know about your hearsay, then you have a bigger problem. You will want to take the up-to-the-minute pulse of your circuit on the notice question before you decide to sandbag your opponent and proceed without notice until it becomes crystal clear at trial that you need the evidence.

Give Them Nothing

There are lots of reasons why a criminal defense lawyer does not want to give the prosecution notice of anything. Sometimes there is simply nothing to give. But even if there is, whether the occasion to use it will materialize depends entirely on the development of the government's case.

The criminal defendant's predilection to wait and see is, in a very real sense, constitutionally based. But even as a purely practical matter, there is no theory so fixed in a criminal defense to warrant identifying your best witness and thus inviting the intimidating (however unintentionally so) visit from the FBI. In at least one circuit, though, the notice requirement has been enforced against criminal defendants. *See United States v. Rodriquez*, 706 F.2d 31 (2d Cir. 1983).

The wary criminal defense lawyer might be well advised to try an *in camera, ex parte* submission to the court. A protective order may be another way to handle defense counsel's quandary.

A long shot may be better than a near miss.

Some courts have invoked the so-called near-miss doctrine to exclude hearsay offered under the catchall rules. Under the near-miss doctrine, the residual exceptions may not be used to admit hearsay that almost fits within one of the specific exceptions enumerated in Rules 803 and 804(b).

The idea has some surface appeal. Courts and lawyers labored long and hard to develop the exceptions to the hearsay rules that are now embodied in Rules 803(1)-(23) and 804(b)(1)-(4). The circumstantial guarantees of trustworthiness on which those exceptions hinge are the result of decades of thought.

Surely Congress did not intend for Rules 803(24) and 804(b)(5) to be used to weasel around the well-settled exceptions with their carefully thought-through indicia of reliability? The short answer is "yes," according to some courts. *See, e.g., United States v. McPartlin*, 595 F.2d 1321 (7th Cir. 1979), *cert. denied*, 444 U.S. 833 (1980). And "no," according to others. *See, e.g., United States v. Love*, 592 F.2d 1022 (8th Cir. 1979).

Cutting Intellectual Knots

The Second Circuit has approached the matter more sensibly than many others. *Robinson v. Shapiro,* 646 F.2d 734, 742-43 (2d Cir. 1981), captures the essential spirit of the rules. Each piece of proffered evidence must be analyzed on its own. If it comes close to fitting one of the traditional exceptions but just misses—for instance, because it is a narrative describing an event that occurred several hours before it was written and therefore does not qualify as a present-sense impression under Rule 803(1)—then the analysis turns to other indicia of trustworthiness to substitute for the ones on which the just-missed exception depends (like immediacy). So, for example, the disinterestedness of the declarant may substitute for the spontaneity of the statement.

Actually, it is entirely possible that the near-miss doctrine, as a doctrine, is dead. Its strongest and most analytic support came from *Zenith Radio Corp. v. Matsushita Electric Industrial Co.,* 505 F. Supp., 1190, 1263 (E.D. Pa. 1980), *aff'd in part, rev'd and remanded in part,* 723 F.2d 238 (3d Cir. 1983). There, the district court reasoned that the near-miss doctrine should be applied only to the most specific exceptions—like Rules 803(18) (learned treatises), 803(22) (previous convictions), and 804(b)(1) (former testimony of an unavailable declarant). To apply the near-miss doctrine to the more ''amorphous'' exceptions—like Rules 803(1) (present-sense impression) or 803(6) (business records)—would effectively do away with the residual exceptions altogether, the court reasoned.

On appeal, the Third Circuit rejected the district court's finely parsed application of the near-miss doctrine. Cutting through the intellectual knots the district court had tied, the court of appeals observed that

> the residual exceptions cannot be explained by a theory that makes
> sense for only a few of the 27 other [itemized] exceptions. . . .
> Plainly stated, the theory puts the federal evidence rules back into
> the straight jacket from which the residual exceptions were in-
> tended to free them.

723 F.2d at 302, *rev'd on other grounds,* 475 U.S. 574 (1986).

The astute practitioner should nonetheless beware of certain rules that may preclude near-miss hearsay for different reasons. For instance, no amount of trustworthiness can make admissible, under Rule 803(24) or 804(b)(5), a government report offered against a defendant in a criminal case. This is because Rule 803(8)(c) simply will not permit it. *United States v. Pinto-Mejia,* 720 F.2d 248 (2d Cir. 1983), *modified on other grounds,* 728 F.2d 142 (1984). Similarly, do not hold out a whole lot of hope for getting in, under Rule 804(b)(5), a statement against penal interest if you cannot come up with the corroboration that Rule 804(b)(3) specifically requires.

In short, before you get carried away, it pays to sit down, identify any explicit conditions in the rules, and figure out how to satisfy them.

If you can get it, don't flaunt it.

At first glance, Rule 803(24) seems to apply whether or not the declarant is available. Your fertile mind will instantly grasp the possibilities.

The sleaziest looking snake you have ever thought about calling to the witness stand made a great statement on the day of the accident to the single most credible looking truth-sayer you have encountered. The statement bears all the circumstantial guarantees of trustworthiness of a present sense-impression, except that it was made several hours after the accident. What a tactic! Give the other side Rule 803(24) pretrial notice, and introduce the rank hearsay through the terrific witness.

Look again. Rule 803(24) has a built-in requirement of unavailability. It is in the provision that the hearsay you offer must be the most probative evidence, on the point for which it is offered, that you can get your hands on with reasonable efforts. Most courts will rule that a live witness is more probative than a hearsay statement and force you to call the snake if you want his evidence.

In this connection, there is a story that bears telling. Once there was a very famous plaintiff's antitrust lawyer who took the position that, rather than call a lot of available witnesses from Japan, he would rely on Rule 803(24) to get into evidence snippets of notes that the defendants' officers wrote and that sounded pretty incriminating in their raw, cryptic form. Indeed, the lawyer talked up his position time and again in the district court.

The trial judge observed that the plaintiff's strategy seemed to suggest that full explanations from the note writers might well undermine the plaintiff's case. Plaintiff's counsel stuck to his guns—and to Rule 803(24)—and went down in a blaze of glory as the district court excluded the key evidence and granted summary judgment for the defendants. *See In re Japanese Electronic Products Antitrust Litigation,* 513 F. Supp. 1100 (E.D. Pa. 1981); *see also id.,* 505 F. Supp. 1190 (1980).

The Third Circuit—while reversing and remanding on other matters, including the near-miss question—agreed with the district court that the "most probative" language of Rule 803(24) is to be strictly construed. The trial judge, the court of appeals said, was right to hold that the plaintiffs had failed to establish that the documents were more probative on the point for which they were offered than any other evidence that the proponent could procure with reasonable efforts. 723 F.2d at 301–02.

The lesson is, if the witness is available out there somewhere, do not flaunt it. Sometimes you can persuade a judge that hearsay is more reliable and more probative than a live, available witness, but not often.

Shudders of Apprehension

Indeed, as the novelty of Rules 803(24) and 804(b)(5) wears off, it is this point that most often brings judges back into the fold. They are holding frequently that when a witness is in fact available, his out-of-court statement is *not* the most probative evidence, and so they are excluding the hearsay, however trustworthy it appears to be.

The most recent example is one that must have sent shudders of apprehension (or desire) through faint hearts throughout the legal profession.

In a complex, multidistrict case, 41 private law firms and state attorneys filed a claim for legal fees amounting to $21 million, out of a total class-action settlement of $50 million. A group of class members objected and hired another big law firm to investigate the claim.

In the course of 73 hours of hearings on the claim, over 41 days, the trial judge took under advisement a proffer by the objectors to the fee award of three volumes containing 1,053 pages of documents, letters, memoranda, and notes. The claimants objected.

After the hearings were closed, the trial judge—without specifying a basis—admitted the documents in evidence and issued a 189-page opinion slashing the fees and expenses to a total of $5.4 million. *See In re Fine Paper Antitrust Litigation,* 98 F.R.D. 48 (E.D. Pa. 1983).

Not surprisingly, the claimants appealed. Their opponents intoned "803(24)" in support of the admission of many of the documents in the three volumes.

The court of appeals was not impressed. "We place no reliance," the court wrote, "on Rule 803(24) . . . because since the authors of the correspondence could have been called as witnesses, the statements cannot be found to be 'more probative on the point for which [they are] offered' than any other evidence. . . . FED. R. EVID. 803(24)(B). For the same reason, we place no reliance on Rule 804." *In re Fine Paper Litigation,* 751 F.2d 562 (3rd Cir. 1984). This glitch, among others, resulted in a remand to the heroic district court for, one presumes, even more hearings, and, of course, more legal fees, at least for the objector's attorneys.

Now the corroboration dilemma.

You have a great piece of hearsay. There are no notice problems; it is not a near miss; your declarant is genuinely unavailable, and you can prove it; and you can demonstrate that it is "probative on the point for which it is offered."

Have you negotiated the mine field? Not yet. The hearsay must have "equivalent circumstantial guarantees of trustworthiness."

Some courts have held that trustworthiness must be measured by looking at the circumstances in which the out-of-court statement was made. *See, e.g., Huff v. White Motor Corp.,* 609 F.2d 286 (7th Cir. 1979); *see also Karme v. Commissioner,* 673 F.2d 1062 (9th Cir. 1982). In other words, you look to the facts bearing on the declarant's credibility when he made the statement, not at the time of the trial when someone else repeats the statement from the witness stand. You repair to the tried-and-true tests of credibility: the declarant's ability to observe and to communicate and his interests and biases when he made the statement. Fair enough.

But it is important to proceed cautiously. There are crosscurrents in other circuits. For instance, in spite of the seeming necessity to establish the declarant's unavailability to demonstrate that your hearsay is the most probative evidence on the point, some courts have, from time to time, given trustworthiness credits because the declarant was available. *See, e.g., Calhoun v. Bailar*, 626 F.2d 145, 149 (9th Cir. 1980), *cert. denied*, 452 U.S. 906 (1981); *United States v. McPartlin*, 595 F.2d 1321, 1350–51 (7th Cir.), *cert. denied*, 444 U.S. 833 (1979). Never mind that some of those same courts may use the declarant's availability against you at another point in the analysis.

Some courts read the trustworthiness requirement as mandating, or at least permitting, corroboration by other admissible evidence of the facts that the out-of-court statement is offered to prove. *See, e.g., United States v. Barnes*, 586 F.2d 1052 (5th Cir. 1978); *United States v. Garner*, 574 F.2d 1141 (4th Cir.), *cert. denied*, 439 U.S. 936 (1978). But therein lies another dilemma. For every judge who gives trustworthiness points for corroborating evidence, there is another judge who views corroboration as proof that the hearsay statement is *not* the most probative evidence on the point and who will therefore decide that you do not need it at all.

Picky Courts

As you carefully work your way through this maze, it is probably wise to focus the judge's attention on the language of the rule and argue that what may be viewed as equally probative evidence does not really prove the precise point for which the hearsay is offered but merely corroborates the trustworthiness of the out-of-court statement. You may very well decide to limit your hearsay offer, depending upon the venue in which you find yourself in this conceptual thicket.

Looking at the hazards of unreliability inherent in hearsay, you would think that courts would have been especially demanding about the trustworthiness of *really* important hearsay, like hearsay that is the sole proof of an essential element of the case.

Some courts are very picky indeed. As the importance of the hearsay increases, the standard of trustworthiness becomes more exacting. *See, e.g., United States v. Ward*, 552 F.2d 46 (5th Cir.), *cert. denied*, 434 U.S. 850 (1977).

By contrast, in other jurisdictions, the more important the hearsay is, the *fewer* indicia of trustworthiness are required. *See, e.g., United States v. Medico*, 557 F.2d 309 (2d Cir.), *cert. denied*, 434 U.S. 986 (1977). The logical, but absurd, extension of this principle is the proposition that if your hearsay is *really, really* important, it need not be trustworthy at all.

Because the courts of appeals do not suffer foolish ideas gladly, it is probably safe to assume that another view will prevail. It holds that the importance of the evidence should not have anything to do with the re-

725

quired degree of trustworthiness. *See United States* v. *West,* 574 F.2d 1131 (4th Cir. 1978). Before assuming the vitality of that seemingly healthy proposition, though, you had better check the latest cases in the circuit.

Some experts have suggested that Rules 803(24) and 804(b)(5) are identical and thus redundant. Not necessarily so. Maybe it helps to have two rules. You should at least be sensitive to the language in each catch-all rule explicitly requiring guarantees of trustworthiness equivalent to the "foregoing exceptions." There is a difference between the guarantees of trustworthiness inherent in, say, records of regularly conducted activities—which are admissible under Rule 803(6)—and statements against penal interest—which are admissible under Rule 804(b)(3). The latter are simply a lot less reliable.

This means it would be wrong to borrow the catchall from Rule 804 and apply it to situations that miss qualifying under Rule 803. An example will help. If you have a document like a business record that does not quite measure up to Rule 803(6) standards, do not get the idea that it is admissible under Rule 804(b)(5). At least, do not be over-confident.

There are some courts, though, that do not seem to care. They have admitted affidavits and testimony of unavailable witnesses into evidence under Rule 803(24), even though the most analogous exception seems to be Rule 804(b)(1)'s exception for prior testimony. *See, e.g., Herdman v. Smith,* 707 F.2d 839 (5th Cir. 1983).

What all this means is that, at the least, you should think about which residual exception you are going to invoke. There may be a court out there that sees a difference.

Use your common sense to marshal indicia of trustworthiness. In Judge Friendly's words:

> [T]he scheme of the federal rules of evidence excludes certain hearsay statements with a high degree of trustworthiness and admits certain statements with a low one. This evil was doubtless thought preferable to requiring preliminary determinations of the judge with respect to trustworthiness, with attendant possibilities of delay, prejudgment and encroachment on the province of the jury.

United States v. Di Maria, 727 F.2d 265, 272 (2d Cir. 1984).

Yet, as Judge Friendly recognized in *Di Maria,* the residual rules have put judges in the business of deciding, in the process of making preliminary rulings, essentially whether they believe the hearsay statement. And, in turn, the residual rules have put trial lawyers in the business of persuading judges on matters of credibility, a subject generally held dear between us and the jury.

So, when all the other elements of the residual rules are shifting and shaking, it is of some comfort to know that you can leap to solid ground as you argue the trustworthiness of the statement. You will find a helpful checklist of indicia of trustworthiness, culled from the cases, in

Sonenshein, *The Residual Exceptions to the Federal Hearsay Rule: Two Exceptions in Search of a Rule,* 57 N.Y.U.L. REV. 867 (1982). The article provides the following taxonomy:

Indicia of Trustworthiness
  Short time-lapse.
  Made voluntarily.
  Would implicate declarant in a crime.
  Under oath.
  Based on personal knowledge.
  Made to government.
  Made to disinterested person.
  Rich in detail.
  Availability of witness to written hearsay.
  Written statement corrected, edited by maker.
  No motive to falsify.

Indicia of Untrustworthiness
  Trying to get good plea or to curry favor with authorities.
  Statement recanted.
  Statements made by political enemies.
  Made in hurley-burley of legislative politics.
  Prepared for litigation purposes.
  Declarant had a personal relationship with a party.
  Made by declarant in fear of physical harm.

Sound familiar? Of course. It is a list you have worked with for years.

In sum, to live with the residual rules, you must do what trial lawyers have always been superbly equipped to do: watch your flanks, use common sense, and adapt what you know best.

No longer can you rely on just saying, ''Objection, Your Honor, the jury can't tell whether some casual bystander this witness overheard was telling the truth.'' J. MCELHANEY, TRIAL NOTEBOOK 95 (1981). The trial judge may find that the bystander's statement was indeed trustworthy and absolutely needed by your opponent, and he may cheerfully tell you so over your objection, even, to your chagrin, in front of the jury.

Face it, you have got to come to grips with these catchall exceptions. Some whippersnapper, maybe tomorrow, is going to stand up and spout: ''803(24).'' And this time the judge will be listening.

Uncharged Misconduct

by Edward J. Imwinkelried

The prosecution of Wayne Williams in Atlanta is one of the most publicized cases of our time. Williams was *formally* charged with only two murders, the killings of Nathaniel Cater and Jimmy Ray Payne. For all practical purposes, though, Williams was tried for 12 murders.

One of the turning points in the Williams trial was the judge's decision to admit evidence of 10 other slayings that Williams was supposedly connected to. *Williams v. State*, 251 Ga. 749, 312 S.E.2d 40 (1984). The testimony about the 10 other homicides undoubtedly hit home with the jury.

All the studies to date—research by the Chicago Jury Project, the London School of Economics, and the National Science Foundation—confirm that proof of a criminal defendant's uncharged crimes is among the most damaging weapons in a prosecutor's arsenal. Evidence of uncharged misconduct can portray the defendant as a vile fiend and predispose the jury to convict.

The Wayne Williams case has civil counterparts. For example, a plaintiff sues Proctor & Gamble Company, the manufacturer of Rely tampons, claiming that the tampons cause toxic shock syndrome and constitute an unreasonably dangerous product. *Wolf v. Proctor & Gamble Co.*, 555 F. Supp. 613 (D.N.J. 1982). To strengthen her case, the plaintiff offers evidence of other customers' complaints about the tampon. Testimony about other accidents allegedly involving the same product may convince the jury that the product is hazardous.

The rules governing evidence of a party's uncharged torts or crimes boil down to two basic propositions. First, evidence of a person's "other crimes, wrongs, or acts is not admissible to prove [his] character . . . in

---

The author is a professor of law at University of California, Davis School of Law.

order to show that he acted in conformity therewith." FED. R. EVID. 404(b). Therefore, a prosecutor or plaintiff may not offer evidence of a defendant's uncharged misconduct to prove the defendant's bad character as circumstantial evidence that the defendant committed the crime or tort of which he stands accused.

Second, although uncharged-misconduct evidence is inadmissible to prove bad character, this type of evidence may be admitted if it has "independent" logical relevance. *United States v. Forgione*, 487 F.2d 364, 366 (1st Cir. 1973), *cert. denied*, 415 U.S. 976 (1974). For instance, in *Williams*, after reviewing the fiber and hair evidence connecting the 12 killings, the Georgia Supreme Court concluded that all the crimes followed a peculiar pattern tending to show that Williams was the killer.

Similarly, the plaintiff in the Proctor & Gamble case, who sued for punitive damages, could offer evidence of earlier toxic shock syndrome cases involving the Rely tampon. In many jurisdictions, proof of a civil defendant's recklessness allows the recovery of exemplary damages, and earlier accidents involving the same product are relevant to show that the defendant had notice of the hazard but continued to manufacture the dangerous product and failed to warn consumers. *Soden v. Freightliner Corp.*, 714 F.2d 498, 508 (5th Cir. 1983). One recent study of jury behavior indicates that if a civil plaintiff succeeds in introducing evidence of the defendant's uncharged misconduct during the trial, the plaintiff can expect a verdict approximately nine percent larger than normal.

The past decade has seen dramatic changes in the law governing uncharged-misconduct evidence. It is now easier for a prosecutor or plaintiff to introduce evidence of a defendant's other crimes and torts. At the same time, though, the courts have imposed new procedural restrictions on the admission of uncharged-misconduct evidence—special requirements for pretrial notice, out-of-court hearings, and limiting instructions.

At first blush, these evidentiary and procedural trends may seem contradictory. But the two trends are really consistent. They spring from the courts' growing realization that uncharged-misconduct evidence can be uniquely probative *and* prejudicial.

Under the so-called exclusionary approach to uncharged misconduct evidence—an approach that, at one time, three-fifths of the states and the majority of the federal circuits had adopted—evidence of other bad acts is excluded unless it falls within one of a few recognized exceptions, such as proof of the defendant's motive, intent, or identity, as in the *Williams* case. The undesirable result of this approach is the mechanical exclusion of evidence falling outside the traditional exceptions, even when the evidence is relevant under a noncharacter theory.

The opinion in one of the most celebrated modern uncharged-misconduct cases, *United States v. Woods*, 484 F.2d 127 (4th Cir. 1973),

729

cert. denied, 415 U.S. 979 (1974), highlights the weaknesses of the exclusionary approach. Woods was charged with killing her foster son. The son died as a result of cyanosis, a condition caused by lack of oxygen. The defendant claimed that the death was accidental. The prosecution offered evidence that nine children in the defendant's custody had suffered 20 incidents of cyanosis. Seven of those nine children had died. Woods was convicted and appealed, challenging the admission of the evidence.

The court of appeals held that the evidence was admissible, but the case divided the panel. The dissent pointed out that uncharged-misconduct evidence had been admitted before in the Fourth Circuit only under a "limited" number of "circumscribed" exceptions and that evidence showing that a death was intentional, rather than accidental, was not a recognized exception. *Id.* at 140.

The majority rejected the dissent's textbook application of the exclusionary approach as arbitrary "pigeonholing." The majority held that "evidence of other offenses may be received, if relevant, for any purpose other than to show a mere propensity or disposition on the part of the defendant to commit the crime. . . ." *Id.* at 134. They said the evidence was admissible, both to show the cause of death of the child in the crime charged and the identity of the defendant as the wrongdoer.

The *Woods* rule has come to be known as the inclusionary approach. It is codified in the second sentence of Federal Rule of Evidence 404(b): Evidence of the defendant's uncharged misconduct "may . . . be admissible for other purposes, such as proof of motive, opportunity, intent, preparation, plan, knowledge, identity, or absence of mistake or accident."

Eight circuits have already concluded that the phrase "such as" in Rule 404(b) commits the federal courts to the inclusionary approach. Reed, *Admission of Other Criminal Act After Adoption of the Federal Rules of Evidence*, 53 U. CIN. L. REV. 113, 159–60 (1984); *United States v. Boroni*, 758 F.2d 222 (7th Cir. 1985). There is a marked trend toward the adoption of the inclusionary approach among state courts and the legislatures of the 28 states that have enacted versions of the Federal Rules.

Nor is the trend toward admissibility of uncharged misconduct evidence restricted to criminal cases. Until recently, many courts applied the exclusionary approach in civil cases. There was a general rule barring evidence of the defendant's other torts, and there were only limited exceptions to the rule, such as proof of causation or of a product's hazardous character. *See* 1A. L. R. FRUMER & M. I. FRIEDMAN, PRODUCTS LIABILITY § 12.01[2] (1983).

Evidence of uncharged torts was routinely excluded unless it fit neatly within a recognized exception. Connolly, *Evidentiary Problems in Products Cases*, 11 PRODUCT LIABILITY: LAW, PRACTICE, SCIENCE 46 (1967).

Now support for the exclusionary approach in civil cases is eroding.

An ever-increasing number of courts have applied Rule 404(b) to evidence of the civil defendant's other torts, and the application of the rule has hastened the emergence of the inclusionary approach in civil cases. Annot., 64 A.L.R. Fed. 648 (1983); Note, 61 Wash. U. L. Q. 799 (1983).

Not only is evidence of uncharged misconduct now admitted in evidence more freely in many jurisdictions; it is also getting easier to prove the uncharged misdeed.

Because uncharged misconduct can be highly prejudicial, traditionally courts required very convincing proof of the defendant's commission of the uncharged act. Some of the older decisions in criminal cases required the prosecutor to establish the defendant's commission of an uncharged crime by proof beyond a reasonable doubt. The prevailing modern view, though, has been that the proponent must demonstrate the defendant's identity as the perpetrator of the other bad act by clear and convincing evidence (or some similar standard).

Recently, the standard of proof has become even more relaxed. In the jurisdictions that have adopted the Federal Rules, the proponents of uncharged-misconduct evidence cite Rule 104(b), which reads: "When the relevancy of evidence depends upon the fulfillment of a condition of fact, the court shall admit it upon, or subject to, the introduction of evidence sufficient to support a finding of the fulfillment of the condition."

The relevance of uncharged-misconduct evidence depends upon proof that the defendant committed the other crime or tort. Demonstrating that the defendant was the perpetrator is "the fulfillment of a condition of fact" under Rule 104(b). On that premise, the standard for proof of the defendant's identity as the person who committed the other bad act is "evidence sufficient to support a finding of the fulfillment of the condition."

Under Rule 104(b), the judge does not pass on the credibility of the evidence. He asks only whether, on its face, the foundational evidence has sufficient probative value to support a permissive inference that the defendant committed the other bad act.

Several courts have already accepted this application of Rule 104(b). *See, e.g., United States v. Beechum,* 582 F.2d 898, 912–13 (5th Cir. 1978), *cert. denied,* 440 U.S. 920 (1979). This interpretation tumbles one of the biggest barriers to the introduction of evidence of the defendant's uncharged misconduct.

In another way, too, it is getting easier to introduce uncharged-misconduct evidence. More often, courts are holding that other uncharged misdeeds are legally relevant to the case on trial.

To be admissible, evidence must be both logically and legally relevant. The concept of logical relevance deals only with the probative value of the evidence, while the legal relevance doctrine involves a balancing of the probative value of the evidence against the dangers of its admission, such as potential prejudice and undue consumption of court time. If the judge concludes that the dangers of the evidence outweigh its probative value, he may exclude the evidence as legally irrelevant.

Under the old cases, the proponent of uncharged misconduct evidence had the burden of persuading the judge that its probative value outweighed its potential to excite prejudice. Appellate courts repeatedly said that trial judges should resolve any doubt about the proper balance in favor of the defendant and against the admission of the evidence.

The common-law rules on the burden of demonstrating legal relevance may not have survived the adoption of the Federal Rules of Evidence. Rule 404(b), the basic provision on uncharged-misconduct evidence, is silent on the issue. But the accompanying Advisory Committee Note says that "The determination must be made whether the danger of undue prejudice outweighs the probative value of the evidence in view of the availability of . . . other facts appropriate for making decisions of this kind under Rule 403."

Rule 403, in turn, provides:

> Although [logically] relevant, evidence may be excluded if its probative value is substantially outweighed by the danger of unfair prejudice, confusion of the issues, or misleading the jury, or by considerations of undue delay, waste of time, or needless presentation of cumulative evidence.

The "substantially outweighed" language of the rule has prompted several courts to hold that Rule 403 tips the scales in favor of the admissibility of uncharged-misconduct evidence. In the view of these courts, judges should exercise their Rule 403 exclusionary power sparingly, and doubts should be resolved in favor of admissibility. *United States v. King,* 713 F.2d 627, 631 (11th Cir. 1983), *cert. denied sub. nom. McGlocklin v. United States,* 466 U.S. 942 (1984); *United States v. Cole,* 670 F.2d 35, 36 (5th Cir. 1982).

If this becomes the accepted interpretation of Rule 403 and Rule 404(b), the Federal Rules will diminish the legal relevance restrictions on uncharged-misconduct evidence. The proponent will no longer have the burden of persuading the judge that the probative value of the evidence outweighs its potential for prejudice.

Instead, the opponent of the evidence will have the onerous burden of convincing the court that the dangers of admitting the evidence "substantially" outweigh its probative value. Together with the inclusionary approach and the liberal Rule 104(b) standard for proving that the defendant did the misdeed, Rule 403 should make it much easier for the proponent of uncharged-misconduct evidence to overcome relevance objections.

The apparent paradox in this area of the law is that, even while the evidentiary barriers to proof of uncharged misconduct have been falling, the courts have been erecting new procedural hurdles.

In the early 1970s, a student comment called for the adoption of special procedural safeguards on the admission of uncharged-misconduct evidence. Comment, *Developments in Evidence of Other Crimes*, 7 U. MICH. J. L. REF. 535 (1974). At the time, the call for special procedures was a novel proposal.

Today, special procedures for the admission of uncharged-misconduct evidence are in place in more than a quarter of the states—including leading jurisdictions such as New York, California, and Michigan—and in several federal circuits. E. J. IMWINKELRIED, UNCHARGED MISCONDUCT EVIDENCE § 9:01 (1984); Berger, *The Federal Rules of Evidence: Defining and Redefining the Goals of Codification*, 12 HOFSTRA L. REV. 255, 268–69 (1984).

A number of jurisdictions have departed from tradition by requiring prosecutors to give defendants pretrial notice of any uncharged-misconduct evidence that they intend to offer. Connecticut, Florida, Louisiana, Minnesota, Montana, and Oklahoma have adopted this rule. E. J. IMWINKELRIED, UNCHARGED MISCONDUCT EVIDENCE § 9:09 (1984). *See, e.g., United States v. Foskey*, 636 F.2d 517, 526 n.8 (D.C. Cir. 1980). In some of these jurisdictions, the requirement is statutory; in others, it is judge-made.

Some states have another new rule for the admission of uncharged-misconduct evidence in criminal trials. They require the prosecutor to make an offer of proof spelling out why the evidence is logically relevant.

A trial lawyer normally does not have to specify the logical relevance of the evidence he offers. The proponent must state a theory of relevance only when an offer of proof is necessary. Federal Rule of Evidence 103(a)(2) requires an offer of proof to predicate error on a ruling excluding evidence if the import of the evidence is not apparent from the context.

As a practical matter, the proponent ordinarily states a theory of relevance at trial only after his opponent has objected and the judge has shown an inclination to sustain the objection. Even after the proponent discloses the evidence he intends to offer, the trial judge normally does not force him to identify the specific theory of relevance that he is relying on.

A handful of states, including Michigan and Minnesota, now insist that the prosecutor specify a theory of relevance when he offers uncharged-misconduct evidence. The prosecutor must identify the theory in a pretrial notice or at the time of the proffer at trial. This requirement forces the prosecutor to think through the logical relevance of the uncharged-misconduct evidence before trial.

So far, the requirements of giving pretrial notice and explicitly stating a theory of relevance have been confined to criminal cases. But other procedural requirements for the admission of uncharged-misconduct evidence have been applied in both criminal and civil cases.

Traditionally, in the judge's discretion, the admissibility of uncharged-misconduct evidence could be argued in the jury's presence. Federal Rule of Evidence 104(c) generally preserves the judge's discretion to hear argument in front of the jury on the admissibility of uncharged-misconduct evidence, as on most other evidentiary issues.

The rule requires a hearing out of the jury's presence only when the defense is challenging "the admissibility of confessions" or "when an accused is a witness, if he so requests." In all other situations, the judge has discretion to determine whether "the interests of justice" necessitate an out-of-court hearing. (Of course, it is improper to suggest in front of the jury, either in argument or in an offer of proof, what the evidence in question is before the judge rules on its admissibility. FED. R. EVID. 103(c).)

Now, though, two federal courts of appeal and state courts in California, Kansas, New York, and Tennessee have ruled that the admissibility of uncharged-misconduct evidence must be argued and determined outside the jury's presence. E. J. IMWINKELRIED, UNCHARGED MISCONDUCT EVIDENCE § 9:46 (1984). Notwithstanding Rule 104(c), the preference for hearings outside the jury's presence is spreading to civil trials, too. *See, e.g., Rexrode v. American Laundry Press Co.,* 674 F.2d 826, 830 (10th Cir.), *cert. denied,* 459 U.S. 862 (1982).

Another procedural constraint on the admission of uncharged-misconduct evidence is the requirement that the judge give an instruction admonishing the jurors that they may consider the evidence only for a limited purpose. Under Federal Rule of Evidence 105 and its state-law counterparts, at the defendant's request, judges routinely give limiting instructions when they admit evidence of uncharged misconduct.

A few jurisdictions now require the judge to give the limiting instruction *sua sponte,* even absent a defense request. Also, in several states trial judges are no longer permitted to give shotgun instructions that mention all recognized theories for admitting uncharged-misconduct evidence, including motive, opportunity, intent, identity, and knowledge. Instead, appellate courts are beginning to insist that trial judges single out the very purpose for which the evidence is admitted.

In other jurisdictions, the judge must read the limiting instruction twice—once when the evidence is admitted and again during the final jury charge. *See* Colo. Rev. Stat. § 16-10-301 (1978). This practice is becoming popular in both criminal and civil cases. Dooley, *Some Observations About Products Liability Litigation,* TRIAL LAW. GUIDE 233, 250 (1973).

The new refinements of the law on limiting instructions not only give the jury better guidance; they also give the trial judge an incentive to scrutinize more critically the profferred uncharged-misconduct evidence.

The judge can no longer hide behind a multifaceted instruction and gamble that the appellate court will find a proper purpose somewhere in the laundry list. He knows that, sooner or later, he must specify the precise purpose for which the evidence is admissible.

Uncharged-misconduct evidence is one of the most damaging weapons that a trial lawyer can lay his hands on. It is not surprising that Federal Rule 404(b) has generated more reported cases than any other section of the rules.

In most states, alleged errors in the admission of uncharged-misconduct evidence are the most common grounds for appeal in criminal cases. In many states, errors in the admission of this type of evidence are also the most frequent grounds for reversal in criminal cases.

Yet independently relevant uncharged-misconduct evidence can be highly probative. If a criminal uses a distinctive *modus operandi,* proof that he committed another crime with the identical *modus* is persuasive evidence that he perpetrated the crime of which he stands accused. In a civil case in which the question is whether a design defect caused the accident at issue, proof of a similar accident involving the same product may be cogent evidence of causation. The other accident involving the defendant's product may be the only evidence of the product's hazardous character, and if the judge excludes the evidence, the plaintiff may suffer a directed verdict. *See, e.g., Holbrook v. Koehring Co.,* 75 Mich. App. 592, 255 N.W.2d 698 (1977).

Congress evidently concluded that the courts had too often excluded probative uncharged-misconduct evidence and that courts should place "greater emphasis" on such evidence. *See United States v. Czarnecki,* 552 F.2d 698, 702 (6th Cir.), *cert. denied,* 431 U.S. 939 (1977). That conclusion explains the widespread trend toward the relaxation of evidentiary barriers to proof of uncharged misconduct in federal courts and the courts of those states that have adopted some version of the Federal Rules of Evidence.

It is equally clear, though, that many of the same courts believe that the balance tips in favor of admission of uncharged-misconduct evidence only when it is both reliable and used only for an independently relevant purpose. This belief accounts for the new procedural safeguards.

Pretrial notice, the specification of a theory of independent relevance, and the refinement of limiting instructions are all designed to allow or force the proponent, opponent, and judge to analyze uncharged-misconduct issues more precisely. These procedures help to guarantee that any uncharged-misconduct evidence admitted is relevant on a noncharacter theory. The new, more precise limiting instructions help jurors to understand the noncharacter theory. The new procedures hold out the promise of improved administration of the rules governing proof of uncharged misconduct.

Planning
Demonstrative Proof

by George P. Haldeman and S. Allan Adelman

The call from Matt's father came three days after the accident. Even with what little information Mr. Roger was able to give us, we knew we were facing a major personal injury case.

Matt Roger, a 16-year-old high school sophomore, had been returning to classes after lunch. He had the green light as he approached an intersection, as did the tractor-trailer coming from the opposite direction. But then suddenly the tractor-trailer made a left turn in front of Matt, and the right front corner of the truck struck the left front side of Matt's car.

Although Matt was pinned in his car, only his head was injured. He had a relatively minor scalp laceration, but was unconscious.

Three days later, he was still in a deep coma. X rays and CAT scans showed a large hematoma—a collection of blood—in the right frontal lobe of his brain. Every indication was that Matt would have severe brain damage.

Everything about the case seemed overwhelming—liability, assets, and damages. In fact, the very size of the case created problems.

Because of the amount of money involved, we could expect that every effort would be made to challenge liability and minimize damages. Furthermore, we were certain we would not see the defendant's best offer until shortly before trial. That outlook allowed us to condition ourselves to accept the work ahead and avoid distracting thoughts of a quick and easy settlement. We filed suit right away to get in line for a trial date.

We began our preparation of the case with two mistakes. We assumed that because more than three days had passed since the accident, all traces of it at the scene would have been obliterated. Our assumption was correct, but we still should have had an independent investigator

The authors are partners in Adelman & Haldeman in Rockville, Maryland.

document and photograph the scene as soon as possible. You never know what physical features at the scene may become significant, as you will see.

Our second mistake involved trying to get a taped telephone interview with the truck driver before he could be coached by an insurance adjuster or defense attorney. Because time was short, we made the call ourselves, and one of us spoke with the driver on the telephone. We got an excellent statement in which the driver candidly described the accident and his failure to see Matt's car as it approached.

But now we risked disqualification as trial counsel if it became necessary for either of us to testify to the conversation. This did not happen because in his deposition, the driver repeated everything he said in the taped interview. Perhaps the very existence of the tape helped hold him to his original story. But we learned our lesson. The interview should have been conducted by an independent person who could be called as a witness if necessary to put the driver's statement in evidence. Still, no investigator will ever conduct the interview as well as the lawyer in the case.

Expecting a vigorous defense, we assumed that the defendants might try to blame the accident on a defect in Matt's car. We employed an independent accident reconstruction expert. He photographed and documented the damage to the car. The information he obtained included the condition of the braking and steering systems, measurements of the depth and width of the crush damage, and documentation of the marks on the car to determine at what angle and by what parts of the truck they had been inflicted. Those measurements were invaluable later when questions about the relative speed and angle of the vehicles became issues to be resolved by computer reconstruction.

Three weeks after the accident, Matt had still not come out of his coma, although his condition had stabilized. Reports from his parents were tinted with either optimism or depression as they struggled with the enormity of Matt's injuries. We wanted to begin assembling demonstrative evidence that would show Matt's condition in these early stages. However, we did not feel we could approach Matt's parents about photographing him until a month after the injury.

Still photographs were inadequate to convey Matt's condition because they lacked the movement and sounds essential to understanding his limitations. Motion pictures cost too much, require too much technical expertise, and are difficult to edit. Videotape became the obvious choice. The tapes were inexpensive, so we could shoot as much footage as we wanted. And they were easy to review, edit, and duplicate.

Initially we hired a local service to accompany us to the hospital to tape Matt. After only a few sessions, it became apparent that the technical expertise required to take good videotape pictures was minimal, and the cost of the equipment was relatively low. A decent video recorder and camera, along with the necessary accessories, can be acquired for less than $1,500. Because we expected to get a great deal of use from the videotape equipment, we decided to buy our own, which turned out to be one of the best investments we made in the case.

We began a long series of videotape sessions showing Matt's torturous progress through various levels of coma, cognitive recovery, and physical rehabilitation. The videotape sessions every few weeks lasted only 15 to 20 minutes each, but over the months they accumulated into a series of windows into his changing condition and treatment. The candid audio and visual confirmation of his pain and suffering was powerful beyond words.

The videotaping continued through Matt's 60-day confinement at the local hospital and his transfer to a hospital in nearby Virginia for more specialized treatment of brain-injured adolescents. After another 60 days, the video camera followed him to a facility in Pennsylvania where he remained for eight months. During his stay in Pennsylvania, about 300 miles from home, the videotapes also served to carry messages between Matt and his family and friends in Maryland.

As Matt was progressing, so was his pending case. Our expectations of an intense defense were right. Defense attention soon focused on the skid marks created by Matt's car. They were too long, and that suggested a possibility of excessive speed. Because Maryland does not have comparative negligence, any contributory negligence by Matt—no matter how slight—would deny recovery. Photographs had been taken at the accident scene by the police. But their poor quality created as many questions as they answered about where the skid marks actually began. The investigating police officer measured the skid marks. Because they did not start abruptly, but rather faded in, there was a serious question as to the point from which the officer had measured. Nevertheless, the photographs showed enough to justify our obtaining the negatives from the police department and having a commercial developer prepare better enlargements.

We videotaped the intersection from every possible angle, including from vehicles moving in the same direction and at the same speed as we thought the car and truck had been at the time of the accident. We filed a request for inspection of the truck and asked that it be produced at the scene of the accident so that it could be videotaped there. Not only did the defense comply with that request, but we were able to get the driver to drive the truck through the intersection several times in the same way he had at the time of the accident. We were able to videotape the truck's movement from inside and outside the cab. The tape showed that as the driver approached the intersection, he had a completely unobstructed view of oncoming traffic for more than a quarter of a mile. There was no reason for failing to see Matt other than inattention.

We had aerial photographs of the intersection taken to show the accident scene, and also to help prepare a large diagram which measured $2^1/2$ by 7 feet. We wanted to have a large display of the scene, so witnesses could show the paths of the vehicles and also show the jury where the witnesses were located when they saw the accident. Although aerial photographs are helpful in setting the stage, they are expensive to enlarge to poster size. Besides, they contained distracting clutter-like vegetation, signs, and power lines—things that can be left off a diagram. Another advantage of the diagram is that scale models or cutouts of vehicles permit witnesses to place the vehicles and trace their movements.

As the case progressed, the defendants retained an accident reconstruction expert who had used a computer program known as CRASH3—Calspan Reconstruction of Accident Speeds on the Highway, Third Edition. He used it to determine the speed of Matt's car before the accident. We obtained the expert's report before his deposition and learned that his initial computer runs put the speed of Matt's car before he applied his brakes between 50 and 70 MPH in a 40-MPH zone. We were most concerned about the 50-MPH figure because we felt that the amount of damage to the car and the lack of substantial bodily injury to Matt would refute any claim of a 70-MPH speed.

The first thing we did after learning of the computer program was to get a copy of the user's manual. Although these manuals may seem too technical for someone without a great deal of training, once you overcome the initial intimidation, they are generally understandable. Our review of the manual produced several startling discoveries—not the least of which was an explicit statement that the program could not be used for accidents involving trucks. After reviewing the purpose, uses, and limitations of the computer program as stated in the manual, we were ready to take the expert's deposition.

At the deposition, the expert was forced to contradict many of the statements in the manual concerning the program and its uses. So as the time for trial drew nearer, we had the key pages of the manual reproduced and blown up into 2-by-3-foot posters for display to the jury.

The defense expert had prepared copious notes of his observations and findings, including the data he had used to generate each of the computer runs. In reviewing those notes, we found that some figures had been juggled to affect the outcome. We felt these notes would be extremely effective in cross-examining the witness and wanted to display them to the jury. Because we already had a number of expensive blow-ups, we decided to use transparencies of the notes and show them with an overhead projector. The transparencies are easy to make in many dry copiers. The plastic sheets are simply put in the copier instead of paper. In addition to being inexpensive and easy to prepare, transparencies may be marked with a felt-tip pen to highlight information. Although using a pointer may be helpful, there is nothing like a big, red circle around an item to focus the jury's attention.

739

Even with the manual on our side, we could not help being concerned about the effect the computer-generated evidence would have. Even though computers generate $75,000 telephone bills to homeowners and $150,000 tax refunds to the unemployed, computers enjoy a reputation for accuracy and impartiality. This means you should never miss an opportunity to have any fact presented through computer-generated or verified evidence in the form of a graph, drawing, or printout that can be marked and handed to the jury.

Judges are still struggling with the ground rules for admitting computer-generated data as evidence but will undoubtedly continue to err on the side of allowing the evidence in through an expert and treating objections as going to weight rather than admissibility.

Although we felt confident that we could challenge the defendants' expert effectively, we were nevertheless on the defensive. We concluded that only one thing would be more effective than the program manual in refuting the expert's findings—the individual who wrote the manual. We found him, and after several telephone calls and a trip to his place of business in North Carolina, we had a witness who could fight printout with printout.

The author of the manual verified our conclusions that the program was being used incorrectly. Equally important, he was able to direct us to a more sophisticated computer program known as SMAC— Simulation Model of Automobile Collisions—which produced a computer-generated diagram (in multiple colors, no less) showing the route the car had travelled, the manner in which it had rotated, and the relative position of the two vehicles immediately before and after impact.

Cranked into the new program, all of the data boiled down to a conclusion by the computer that Matt Roger was going between 37 and 45 MPH immediately before he applied his brakes. We now had our client possibly going under the speed limit and certainly not going over it enough to cause any jury to deny him recovery on the basis of contributory negligence.

As we grappled with the problem of proving the speed of Matt's car, we found we were missing two items of physical evidence that we could have obtained from a prompt investigation of the accident scene. Our experts felt that there was an area in the intersection over which cars did not normally pass, and in which dirt, gravel, and other debris accumulated. Matt's car had skidded through that exact area where the dirt and gravel would cause him to skid further than he would have on a clean surface. Unfortunately, by the time we discovered this possibility, it was winter, when an inspection of the scene could have easily been challenged because of the additional accumulation from the road crews spreading cinders to combat ice and snow.

A second piece of missing information was the actual measured coefficient of friction at the intersection at the time of the accident. We measured it more than a year after the accident. By then, some minor repairs had been made to the road, so the figures were not as reliable as they would have been with a more prompt measurement.

Neither of these issues were ones we anticipated immediately after the accident. The lesson is basic. Thoroughly document the condition of an accident scene even if you do not know at that time why you will need it.

After we acquired the videotape equipment, we had much of the taping done by Matt's father. That was a deliberate decision made partly as a matter of convenience and partly because we felt that Mr. Roger would be the most effective individual to place the tapes in evidence. We anticipated that at trial we would ask Mr. Roger to narrate the tapes for the jury, pointing out Matt's improvements and limitations. A significant aspect of the case was not only the problems Matt would have to live with for the rest of his life but also what he had endured during the first 18 months after his injury.

Twelve months after the crash, Matt was still improving, although the changes were becoming less and less significant. The defendants' doctors examined Matt and contended that he would experience substantial improvement well into the future and would ultimately recover far beyond what our experts were projecting. We sought a way to demonstrate that the defense prognosis was overly optimistic. The videotapes provided the perfect medium. By editing brief segments from tapes taken over a 14-month period, it became apparent that Matt had made real progress early in his recovery but had essentially reached a plateau about 12 months after the injury. It was obvious that any future gains would be small and painful.

We also used this condensation of tapes to provide a medical history for the doctors who got involved in Matt's case later on. Matt's physiatrist and neurosurgeon both found the tapes extremely helpful in understanding the problems Matt had in the past and the course of his recovery. This helped them deal with his current problems and project his future recovery. That both doctors would testify that the tapes were helpful in evaluating and treating Matt would lay an even stronger foundation for admitting them in evidence.

While the tapes taken during Matt's recovery were an excellent record of what he had suffered, they did not give a complete picture of the impact his injuries had on his daily living. We decided to prepare a ''day in the life of'' Matt. We delayed shooting this tape so it would show Matt's lifestyle at the time of trial. By the time we were ready to begin that project, we had become experienced with the video equipment and were producing pretty good footage. We had interviewed several firms that produce these films professionally. After viewing several products, we concluded that the quality of the tapes was dictated more by good subject matter selection than by expertise with camera angles, lighting, or

741

professional techniques. Moreover, the price of professional tapes was high (generally around $2,500), and there were difficulties in scheduling, editing, and related matters. We finally decided to produce the film ourselves, using Matt's father as the cameraman and ourselves as producers, editors, and directors.

That decision had a significant by-product. By accompanying Matt through an entire day, we gained an insight and an understanding of the magnitude of his problems that we could not have gotten in any other way. Every lawyer expecting to try a personal injury case that uses a "day in the life of" film should actually accompany the handicapped person for a typical day. From 7:00 A.M., when Matt arose for breakfast and home tutoring, through a half-day session at a busy high school and cafeteria, a long rehabilitation session at a local treatment center, an evening with the family, shower and bedtime activity, the daily life of a wheelchair-bound or otherwise handicapped person must be observed directly, in its entirety, to be understood.

We acquired two video recorders to edit the more than two hours of videotape we had into a 20-to 30-minute segment. We felt that anything longer would begin to wear on the jury. The difficult part of the editing was selecting the material, not any mechanical problems in running the recorders. Although there are companies that will produce a finished product, we are convinced that the editing should be done by the trial attorney. Often the tape was significantly affected by shortening or extending segments by mere seconds.

We were dealing with an injury that had no visible signs other than its effect on Matt Roger. The absence of scars or broken bones, coupled with our argument that the impact occurred at a relatively low speed, made us worry that the jury might give some credibility to the defense position that the injury was not as severe as we maintained, and Matt would ultimately have a substantial recovery. We needed something tangible to demonstrate the actual injury.

We obtained copies of Matt's CAT scans, which showed a porencephalic cyst about the size of a golf ball in the center of his brain. That cyst was an area where the brain tissue had been destroyed by hemorrhaging and had been replaced with spinal fluid. It was now simply a liquid-filled cavity in his brain.

Then we employed a medical artist who worked with Matt's neurosurgeon to prepare drawings of cutaway sections of the brain that illustrated—in color—the size, location, and configuration of the cyst. The anatomical portions of the brain and the functions they controlled were labeled. Then we had all these medical illustrations put on slides.

Because CAT films are small and hard to see, we had them made into slides, as well. We planned to have the neurosurgeon display the slides of the CAT scans and the medical illustrations side by side when he explained exactly what had taken place in Matt's brain.

Many of Matt's limitations involved physical handicaps, such as the inability to stand and walk unassisted and the loss of some motor control in his arms and hands. It is often difficult for doctors to describe effectively the conditions they find in patients. The language is too technical for the jury, and hearing the symptoms recited in medical terminology is far less dramatic than actually seeing them. Talking about a 30-percent reduction in range of motion is much less effective than seeing someone unable to straighten his arm.

We did not want to have Matt actually exhibit his deficiencies in the courtroom, because it would embarrass him, and the jury might interpret it as showboating. To overcome this problem, we arranged to videotape one of Matt's regular examinations in the doctor's office. He was checked for strength, range of motion, balance, motor control, dexterity, and all the other physical attributes that are better understood when seen.

We planned to have the examining doctor narrate the videotape in court and explain what tests he was conducting, what he was looking for, and the significance of his findings. The tape was not only an effective means of presenting this aspect of the case, but it also insured that nothing would be overlooked during the doctor's testimony.

There was more tangible evidence of Matt's limitations in the files of his neuropsychologist. In the course of testing Matt's neurological status and motor skills, the psychologist had obtained samples of his handwriting and drawings showing his attempts to connect dots, draw straight lines and circles, and perform other mechanical skills. Blowups of handwriting samples from before and after the accident were an eloquent illustration of Matt's struggle in attempting to perform even the simplest manual tasks.

We discussed the merits of preparing enlargements of the photographs showing the damage to the car (there was no visible damage to the truck). The damage to the car appeared extensive and would support our position that Matt had sustained a violent blow to his head resulting in severe brain damage. However, to minimize the impact and reduce the speed of the car at the time of collision, our experts were explaining that most of the damage was to the soft sheet metal portions of the car and not to the heavier structural members. After weighing the conflicting messages that the pictures conveyed, we decided not to enlarge those photographs, but to use them only to support the testimony of our experts concerning the angle and degree of crush damage to the car. Although we were caught up in preparing demonstrative evidence, we had to keep in mind that demonstrative evidence for its own sake might not help our case but could actually hurt it.

In the course of his treatment, Matt was fitted with various braces, casts, and appliances to give him support and to combat the tendency of his extremities to go into spasm and become rigid and flexed. We decided not to introduce any of the appliances in evidence. Our videotapes of Matt's progress showed practically all of these devices in place and in use at one time or another. We felt that in this case the actual presentation of these items to the jury would be too showy.

Oddly enough, by the time we had completed our preparation for trial, we had used videotapes for everything except the one purpose they most commonly serve—depositions. We had considered videotaping some of the doctors for trial but felt that if we used any more videotape we would probably bore or annoy the jury. We concluded that videotape used in small or moderate quantities can highlight or enhance information presented to a jury while an excess of tape can become dull and uninteresting. The treating doctors we intended to use as witnesses were articulate and persuasive; we felt they would have a much greater impact on the jury by testifying in person.

By now we had amassed 17 groups of demonstrative evidence:

Accident Scene Videotape,
"Day in the Life" Videotape,
Physician Examination Videotape,
Compilation of Recovery Videotapes,
Videotape of Truck Driving through Intersection,
Large Scene Diagram—2½ by 7 feet,
CRASH3 User's Manual Blowups,
SMAC Diagrams and Printouts,
Photographs of Automobile,
Handwriting Sample Blowups,
Psychological Testing Blowups,
Enlarged Police Photographs,
CAT Scan Films and Slides,
Slide of Medical Illustration of Brain Cyst,
Overhead Transparencies of Expert's Notes,
Aerial Photographs, and
Matt's Appearance in the Courtroom.

We now looked at various problems of procedure, admissibility, and trial tactics. Approximately two months before trial, we gave the defendants a copy of the videotape excerpts we had prepared for the doctors to review the course of Matt's recovery. Although we had not made a settlement demand at that point, we wanted to begin educating the defense as to the magnitude of the case and the state of our preparation (or the state of the case and the magnitude of our preparation). Later, when the tape of the "Day in the Life of Matt Roger" was ready, we gave a copy to the defense. About a month before trial, we offered the defense the opportunity to view all of the raw tapes, which at this point consisted of probably 20 to 25 hours of videotape.

We did not believe that the court would require us to turn over the raw tapes. But we felt we had not taken anything out of context unfairly and

744

therefore had nothing to risk by giving them to the defense. We wanted to blunt any objection at trial that the defense had to review all of the tapes before the edited selections could be admitted. We also invited the defendants to give us any objections they had to the edited tapes in advance, so that we could make any necessary changes before trial. Turning the tapes over early would make it hard for the defense to object for the first time at trial when re-editing was impossible.

We planned to present each tape with a witness who could vouch for its authenticity and accuracy and also explain what the tape showed. The tapes had all been made with sound, but in most cases we would turn down the sound and have the witness give the commentary at trial. The few exceptions would be to show deficiencies in Matt's speaking abilities at various times through his recovery.

We planned to have Matt in the courtroom only at the very close of the plaintiffs' case. We wanted the sense of drama to build as all of the evidence was presented. No matter how effectively we prepared our videotapes and other demonstrative evidence, nothing would make the same impression as Matt Roger in person. Matt was to be our last witness, and his testimony would consist primarily of attempting to leave his wheelchair and take the witness stand.

To prepare Matt and his family, we made arrangements to take them to an empty courtroom a few days before the trial. We had Matt transfer from his wheelchair to the witness chair to make sure he could do it. While we wanted the jury to see Matt's struggle, the last thing we needed was for him to fall and be embarrassed, if not injured.

As we surveyed the evidence, we became concerned that we were going to overtry the case. While it might seem difficult to overtry a case of this size, we thought we were reaching that point. We arranged the evidence and the witnesses to break up the monotony of the case. We planned to alternate witnesses who would merely testify, who would use still photographs, who would refer to diagrams, who would use videotapes, who would use blowups, and who would use slides.

Preparing the jury for what it would see was even more important than the order in which we presented the witnesses and evidence. We planned to use our opening statement to tell the jury exactly what we were going to do and how we were going to do it. We would tell the jury that it was our job to convey in a few days the nature and extent of the problems Matt Roger had encountered in the past 18 months and would experience for the rest of his life. We would then briefly touch on each item of demonstrative evidence, telling what it was, why we were using it, and what it would show.

We had filed suit within 60 days after the accident without any effort at settlement because we knew it would not be productive. The first trial date was scheduled 15 months later. The obligatory (it seems) defense motion for a continuance was made and granted, which moved the trial

745

back another three months. Our first settlement demand was not made until about a month before the first trial date. The case was continued shortly after that, and so we had no meaningful settlement discussions at that time.

Then, about a month before the second trial date, settlement negotiations began in earnest. The discussions revolved around a structured settlement. The trial was scheduled to begin on a Monday morning, and on Sunday evening we reached agreement on a structured settlement that would bring Matt benefits for the rest of his life—well into eight figures.

We may not have another case that will justify the massive use of demonstrative evidence to the same extent as Matt Roger's case. But it is easy to see how all of the techniques can be scaled down and adapted to other situations. It is hard now to imagine a case that does not lend itself to demonstrative evidence.

Computer Printouts in Evidence: Ten Objections and How to Overcome Them

by Irving Younger

A lawyer (call him the "proponent") wants to put into evidence a computer printout of voluminous and complex information, after which he proposes to have an expert witness state his opinion based in whole or in part on the printout. The adversary is staunch in opposition. He concedes nothing but relevance and materiality, which are beyond argument.

A witness has testified about the computer, the program, and the way in which the program was run. He has identified Exhibit 1 as the computer printout. The proponent now offers the exhibit in evidence, and the adversary rises to make his objections. There are at least ten.

First

ADVERSARY: To receive this printout in evidence would violate the rule against hearsay. Hearsay is an out-of-court statement offered to prove the truth of the matter asserted in the statement. The printout is an out-of-court statement. It is being offered to prove the truth of the matter asserted in it. Thus it is hearsay, and the rule against hearsay has it that hearsay is inadmissible.

PROPONENT: It is hearsay, to be sure, but admissible nevertheless because it falls within an exception to the rule. Had the printout been made by the adversary's client, I might argue that it is admissible as an admission. Since it was not, the exception in point is the business records exception.

COURT: Objection overruled.

Second

ADVERSARY: The business records exception contemplates a book or record with entries on it, such as an accountant's ledger. This computer

The author, now deceased, was a member of the Washington, D.C. firm of Williams & Connolly, and lectured and wrote extensively on trial practice.

printout is no such thing and therefore is inadmissible.

PROPONENT: The typical business records statute extends the exception beyond the accountant's ledger to any writing or record, whether in the form of an entry in a book or otherwise. *E.g.*, Fla. Stat. Ann. tit. 7, ch. 92.36(2) (Supp. 1972); N.Y.C.P.L.R. § 4518(a); Rev. Stat. Canada E-10, § 30.(12) (1970). And even where the statute doesn't, the cases do. *E. g., Transport Indemnity Co. v. Seib,* 178 Neb. 253, 258-59, 132 N.W.2d 871, 875 (1965).

COURT: Objection overruled.

ADVERSARY: Ah, your Honor, we haven't finished. A record is admissible under the business records exception only if the transactions reflected in it occurred in the regular course of business and the record was made in the regular course of business at or near the time when the transactions occurred. This foundation requirement comes down to four elements:

(1) the enterprise making the record must be a business;

(2) the transactions reflected in the record must have occurred in the regular course of business;

(3) the record must have been made in the regular course of business; and

(4) the record must have been made at or near the time when the transactions occurred.

These four elements underlie my next four objections.

Third

ADVERSARY: I object on the ground that the proponent's client is not a business.

PROPONENT: For purposes of the business records exception, "business" means business, profession, occupation, or calling of any kind. *E.g.*, Federal Evidence Rule 803(6); N.Y.C.P.L.R. § 4518(a). So broad is the definition that it is hard to imagine an enterprise which uses a computer yet is not engaged in business of some sort.

COURT: Objection overruled.

Fourth

ADVERSARY: I object on the ground that the transactions reflected in the printout did not occur in the regular course of business.

PROPONENT: The transactions did occur in the regular course of business. I could not say this were my client engaged in activities outside the regular course of business solely to generate a computer printout for use in litigation. In that case, I would concede the objection. *Compare Palmer v. Hoffman,* 318 U.S. 109 (1943). But in all other cases, which means virtually all cases, and certainly in this case, the transactions occurred in the regular course of business.

COURT: Objection overruled.

Fifth

ADVERSARY: Even though the transactions may have occurred in the regular course of business, I object on the ground that the printout was not made in the regular course of business. Now, it will usually happen that the printout is made in the course of an enterprise's business activity. If that were so here, I would expect the court to overrule my objection. Occasionally, however, the transactions occur in the regular course of business, but the enterprise makes no printout because it needs none. That is the case at bar. The need arose when this lawsuit came along, and that's when the printout was made—not for use in business, but for use in litigation. Hence it is not a record made in the regular course of business, and my objection should be sustained.

PROPONENT: If the court is content merely to skate on the surface of words, then the printout was not made in the regular course of business and is not admissible. But if the court's concern is a deeper one—to admit evidence on the ground of reliability, tested by the willingness of serious people going about the serious affairs of everyday life to accept the record as trustworthy—the court will come to a different conclusion. For example, in *Transport Indemnity Co. v. Seib, supra,* the plaintiff sued for insurance premiums which had been determined retroactively on the basis of the claims experience of the insured, and, to prove the amount of those premiums, offered a computer printout. The defendant objected on some of the grounds the adversary raises here. No, said the court, these objections exalt form over substance and will be permitted only as arguments going to the weight of the evidence, not its admissibility. The purpose of the business records statute is "to bring the realities of business and professional practice into the courtroom and the statute should not be interpreted narrowly to destroy its obvious usefulness." *Id.* at 259, 132 N.W.2d at 875.

COURT: Objection overruled.

Sixth

ADVERSARY: The fourth element of the foundation for the business records exception is that the record be made at or near the time when the transactions occurred. The proponent would have satisfied this element had the printout been run off promptly after the data was fed into the computer. Since it was not, since data was fed into the computer and the printout made weeks or months later, the fourth element of the foundation is lacking and my objection must be sustained.

PROPONENT: First, I argue that the printout is not really the record. The record is the glob of electrons in the computer's memory, and the glob of electrons was put there at or near the time when the transactions occurred.

ADVERSARY: If that is your position, you've met my objection but

749

played into my hands on a later objection (the eighth).

PROPONENT: Second, I argue, as I did in connection with the fifth objection, that the test should not be mechanical compliance with the elements of the business records exception; rather, it should be reliability.

COURT: On either argument, objection overruled.

Seventh

ADVERSARY: Undismayed, I reach into my objection bag and pull out yet another. For shorthand, I will call it the "personal knowledge" issue. Some authorities say the witness who testifies about the record-making process must have personal knowledge of the transactions reflected in the record. See 5 Wigmore, *Evidence* § 1530 (3d ed. 1940). Others say that the witness need not have such personal knowledge, but the person who made the record must. *E.g., Arnold D. Karmen & Co. v. Young,* 466 S.W.2d 381 (Ct. Civ. App. Tex. 1971), writ of error refused n.r.e. (Tex. 1971). In this case, the proponent satisfies neither requirement.

PROPONENT: The requirement of first-hand knowledge either in the foundation witness or in the maker of the record is outmoded and ought to be rejected by this sophisticated court as it has been by so many others. *E.g., King v. State ex rel. Murdock Acceptance Corp.,* 222 So. 2d 393 (Miss. 1969). A better rule is that the maker's lack of personal knowledge is irrelevant so long as the information contained in the record comes from someone who has personal knowledge and is under a duty to report such information to the maker; or, where the information comes to the maker from someone with no personal knowledge or under no duty to report, another exception to the hearsay rule independently authorizes receipt of the information contained in the report. This is the argument resting upon *Johnson v. Lutz,* 253 N.Y. 124, 170 N.E. 517 (1930), and *Kelly v. Wasserman,* 5 N.Y.2d 425, 158 N.E.2d 241 (1959), and crystallized in Federal Evidence Rules 803(6) and 805.

COURT: Objection overruled.

Eighth

ADVERSARY: Return with me for a moment to the sixth objection. I urged that the printout was inadmissible because it was not made at or near the time when the transactions occurred. The proponent responded with two arguments, of which the first was that the glob of electrons was really the record and that the glob was placed in the computer's memory at or near the time when the transactions occurred. I said that this played into my hands on a later objection. It did, and I now make it.

If the glob of electrons is really the record, I object on the ground of the best evidence rule. That rule requires a party proving a document to offer the original of the document. *E.g., Harned v. Credit Bureau of Gillette,*

513 P.2d 650 (Wyo. 1973). It follows that the printout—not being the glob of electrons—is not the best evidence and therefore is not admissible.

PROPONENT: The best evidence rule requires that the original of a document be offered only when it is feasible to do so. McCormick, *Evidence* § 230 *et seq.* (2d ed. 1972). It is not feasible to offer a glob of electrons in evidence. Secondary evidence—the printout—is consequently admissible. And looking to the common sense of the situation, a printout should be regarded as the original. This is the approach taken by Federal Evidence Rule 1001(3). Moreover, the best evidence rule is an historical anachronism better suited to the 1820s than to the 1970s. The rule should be adapted to modern times as follows:

> A mechanically produced copy will be admissible as if it were the original unless the adversary raises a bona fide question with respect to the accuracy or authenticity of the copy. This is the approach taken by Federal Evidence Rule 1003.

COURT: Objection overruled.

Ninth

ADVERSARY: The proponent's expert witness has taken the stand, and I have a few more objections to make. In addition to those available whenever an expert testifies, there are two specifically applicable to the expert who bases his opinion in whole or in part on a computer printout.

The prevailing rule is that an expert's opinion must rest exclusively upon evidence in the case. If it does not—if it rests upon information not in evidence—it is immaterial. *Sirico v. Cotto*, 67 Misc. 2d 636, 324 N.Y.S.2d 483 (Civ. Ct., N.Y. Co. 1971). For example, the issue is one of medical diagnosis. The expert is a specialist in internal medicine. He customarily bases his diagnosis not only on what he discovers when he examines the patient, but also upon the reports of other specialists, such as roentgenologists, hemotologists, and neurologists. Assume that the reports of the roentgenologist, hemotologist, and neurologist have been fed into a computer, which is programmed to print out a physical profile of the patient. The diagnostician's opinion rests in part upon the printout. The difficulty is that the roentgenologist, hemotologist, and neurologist have not testified, and their reports are inadmissible as naked hearsay. The diagnostician will not be permitted to give his opinion. Accordingly, since the expert in this case bases his opinion on the computer printout, and since the computer printout includes information not in evidence, I object.

PROPONENT: Federal Rule of Evidence 704 takes a more liberal view:

> The facts or data in the particular case upon which an expert bases an opinion or inference may be those perceived by or made known to him at or before the hearing. If of a type reasonably relied upon by experts in the particular field in forming opinions or infer-

751

ences upon the subject, the facts or data need not be admissible in evidence.

The test under Rule 704, then, is whether the expert reasonably (which I take to mean customarily) relies upon such data. If he does, he may base his opinion on it even though it is not admissible in evidence.

COURT: Objection overruled.

Tenth

ADVERSARY: A huge mass of data lies dormant in the computer. The issues in this lawsuit have made it necessary to analyze the data in a new way, and a new program was devised to generate the desired analysis. The general nature of the computer and of computer programming is well known, but this particular program is not well known. It was invented just now, for use in connection with this case. The printout based on the new program is therefore inadmissible under a settled rule.

PROPONENT: The new program is a technical device. It has produced certain results which I am offering in evidence. The settled rule to which the adversary refers is this: For the results to be admissible, the reliability of the device must be generally accepted by the scientists concerned with such matters. *State v. Cary*, 99 N.J. Super. 323, A.2d 680 (1968), *aff'd*, 56 N.J. 16, 264 A.2d 209 (1970). So it is that radar readings in speeding cases are admitted. All engineers accept the reliability of radar. Electronic voice-print graphs are sometimes admitted and sometimes not, because some judges are persuaded that the voice-print device is generally accepted as reliable and others not. Polygraph results are not admissible because the polygraph's reliability is not generally accepted.

Back to our new computer program. It was invented for this lawsuit. Then it cannot possibly be accepted as generally reliable by the community of computer engineers, simply because they've never heard of it. Still, there's more to be said.

In *Coppolino v. State*, 223 So. 2d 68 (Fla. 1969), *cert. denied*, 399 U.S. 927 (1970), the issue was what caused Mrs. Coppolino to die. The prosecution contended that it was an injection of succinylcholine chloride. But the presence of that drug cannot be determined on autopsy. All that Dr. Milton Helpern found when he examined Mrs. Coppolino's remains was a needle track in the left buttock. What he needed was a test to determine whether the tissue around the needle track contained succinylcholine chloride. Alas, such a test was unknown to biochemistry. Undaunted, Dr. Helpern turned to his colleague, Dr. Umberger, a toxicologist, and told him to invent a test. Dr. Umberger did. He used it to analyze the tissue, and found succinylcholine chloride. Defense counsel argued that since the test was brand new, it could not command the general scientific acceptance, which is the prerequisite of admissibility. The judge overruled the defense objection and permitted the jury to hear the evidence. Dr. Coppolino was convicted. On appeal, he urged that it was error to admit the results of this brand new test. The Florida court stated the general rule by quoting from an earlier case about lie detectors:

> We think the [polygraph] has not yet gained such standing and scientific recognition among physiological and psychological authorities as would justify the courts in admitting expert testimony deduced from the discovery, development, and experiments thus far made. *Id.* at 70.

But then the court went on as follows:

> However, it is also a rule in Florida that the trial judge enjoys wide discretion in areas concerning the admission of evidence and that his ruling on admissibility of evidence will not be disturbed unless an abuse of discretion is shown. . . . On appeal it is incumbent for defendant to show that the trial judge abused his discretion. This the defendant has failed to do. *Id.* at 70–71.

Hence Dr. Coppolino's conviction was affirmed. While the opinion lacks something of force and eloquence, I think it should be followed. If the new computer program was devised by a technician with substantial professional credentials, and if the technician testifies persuasively that the program is coherent and logical, the printout will be admitted.

COURT: Objection overruled.

ADVERSARY: Your Honor, the law of evidence is nothing if not flexible. It's therefore hardly surprising that, from the authorities as they stand, the court has somehow extracted guidelines for decision. I can't help wondering, though, whether this proliferation of objections, arguments, and doctrine is wise. Since computer-generated evidence will be offered more and more frequently in the years ahead, might it not be better to have clear and definite rules specifically formulated to resolve the issues raised by such evidence? I think it would. And the way to get those rules is to write them into a statute. So far as I know, no American jurisdiction has enacted a comprehensive statute on computer evidence. England has, English Civil Evidence Act of 1968, sec. 5, and so has Australia. South Australia Evidence Act Amendment Act of 1972, sec. 14. Perhaps the Section of Litigation of the American Bar Association will put a committee to work on the problem. Using these English and Australian statutes as a starting point, the committee might draft a model act for submission to our legislatures. It seems to me to be a job worth doing.

COURT: I agree.

ADVERSARY: A long time ago, your Honor, I learned that when your objection is overruled, the thing to do is smile, say thank you, and sit down. I've made ten objections. You've overruled every one of them. And so now I smile, say thank you, and sit down.

753

Computer Evidence

by Michael B. Keating

You represent the plaintiff class in a lawsuit against a major airline. A plane carrying passengers from various states crashed just miles from its destination, killing all aboard. You allege negligence. The company denies it.

You have simulated the crash by feeding into a specially programmed computer data on the plane and the weather conditions. Your computer printout describes what must have happened in the air: The pilot was negligent. If this simulation is received in evidence, a victory is all but assured. But will the judge let it in?

You have also calculated each plaintiff's damages based on the decedent's earnings. A series of computer printouts shows the wages and other benefits the passengers earned over the past 20 years. Will the judge let these in?

Computer-generated evidence is still not regularly used at trial, so it is often difficult to predict how receptive a judge may be to admitting this type of evidence. More and more, though, litigators are offering computer evidence.

A number of recent cases, together with the Federal Rules of Evidence, provide some clues on how to get your computer-generated evidence in over your adversary's objection. Here are four guidelines that should enhance your chances of getting computer-generated evidence admitted at trial.

Step One: Know Your Evidence

A computer simulation of an airline crash might fall under the heading "special computer preparations," that is, evidence prepared by com-

The author is a litigation partner in the firm of Foley, Hoag & Eliot in Boston. Babetta R. Gray, an associate in the same firm, assisted him in preparing this article.

puter for use at trial. More common than special preparations are computer-generated business records. Since these two types of computer evidence present different problems under the Federal Rules, it is important to know which animal you are dealing with.

A host of computer printouts of business-related data are business records. These include, for example, the printouts of the payroll and benefit records for the deceased passengers in the airplane-crash case. The data have been regularly fed into the computer and later printed out in the ordinary course of business. Another example of this type of evidence is a monthly computerized bank statement.

Sometimes data are electronically stored in the ordinary course of business but are printed out in full or summary form only when the litigation comes along. Take, for example, computerized bank records printed out not monthly or on some other regular basis but instead specifically for use at trial. This is another kind of computerized business record.

Unlike computerized business records, special computer preparations are generated by applying specially designed programs and models to selected data to create evidence for trial. One example is a computer simulation of a physical event, like the airplane crash. Another example is a computer analysis of when a defendant would have exhausted his inventory, had he not concealed his assets. *See, e.g., United States v. Dioguardi*, 428 F.2d 1033 (2d Cir.), *cert. denied*, 400 U.S. 825 (1970).

You must distinguish among the types of computer-generated evidence to know what evidentiary problems you are likely to face. As with all evidence, to get computer-generated evidence admitted, you must establish that it is (1) authentic, (2) relevant, and (3) otherwise admissible. The third requirement means that, among other things, you must comply with—or sidestep—the hearsay and best-evidence rules. The first step is always to identify what type of computer-generated evidence you have.

Step Two: Lay a Solid Foundation

Demonstrate that the computerized information is authentic. The authenticity requirement applies to both special computer preparations and computer-generated business records.

Rule 901(a) of the Federal Rules of Evidence sets forth the minimum requirement for authenticity: The proponent must present "evidence sufficient to support a finding that the matter in question is what [he] claims."

Rule 901(b)(9) specifically addresses the requirememt of authenticity for a document whose accuracy depends upon the process or system that produced it. FED. R. EVID. 901(b)(9) Advisory Committee Note. This rule is central to the admissibility of computer-generated evidence. Rule 901(b)(9) says that the product of a process or system will be deemed authentic if the proponent produces evidence (1) describing the process or system and (2) showing that the process or system produces an accurate result.

There are also a number of other ways to authenticate a computer printout. If, for example, a computer printout is a public record, evidence that it "is from the public office where items of this nature are kept" will suffice. FED. R. EVID. 901(b)(7). This means that the proponent must show that the printout came from the office that is its proper legal custodian.

The traditional but not the only way to establish custodianship is to call the public officer who keeps the record. Another possibility is to have the appropriate public office certify it. A certified printout, if it is also an official record, is self-authenticating under Rule 902(4), and is admissible without additional proof. *United States v. Farris*, 517 F.2d 226, 228–229 (7th Cir.), *cert. denied*, 423 U.S. 892 (1975).

Rule 901(b)(8) offers yet another (but less frequently useful) way for a lawyer to authenticate computerized evidence. This rule, governing ancient documents and data compilations, says that a document will be presumed authentic if (1) it is regular on its face; (2) it was found in a place where it would likely be, if authentic; and (3) it is at least 20 years old. FED. R. EVID. 901(b)(8).

It is more than a little odd to think of computer printouts as ancient documents, but the rule is not limited to yellowed deeds in the bottom of an old trunk. As 20-year-old computer records become more commonplace, the rule will be increasingly helpful in authenticating computer-generated evidence.

A final way to lay a foundation for computerized evidence is to convince the judge to take judicial notice of the accuracy of the computer process. One commentator has suggested that this method should be used for the printouts of organizations, such as the Internal Revenue Service, that have a history of computerized record keeping. *Guidelines for the Admissibility of Evidence Generated by Computer for Purposes of Litigation*, 15 U. C. D. L. REV. 951, 955 n.14 (1982). In those circumstances, since the accuracy of the computer system and its records is generally accepted, judicial notice seems appropriate, and it may be worth making that pitch to the judge before taking the time to put on testimony to prove authenticity.

Assume, however, that the computer printout is neither a public record nor 20 years old and that the court refuses to take judicial notice of the accuracy of the computer process. Now we must return to the general guidelines of Rule 901(b)(9). Since this is probably the most frequent situation, the trial lawyer with computer evidence to offer should know how to have a witness describe the computer system and establish that its product is accurate.

Courts are divided over what kind of proof they require. Because of the unique aspects of computer technology, some courts have demanded much more information than is usually necessary to authenticate ordinary business records. *See, e.g., United States v. Scholle,* 553 F.2d 1109, 1125 (8th Cir.), *cert. denied,* 434 U.S. 940 (1977).

But other courts have been more easily satisfied, requiring only the kind of evidence necessary to authenticate ordinary business records. In these jurisdictions, the proponent need not establish, for example, that the computer was in proper working order to prove that the printout is authentic. *See, e.g., United States v. Vela,* 673 F.2d 86, 90 (5th Cir. 1982).

If there is no firm rule in the jurisdiction, the careful lawyer should build a complete foundation. It does little good to establish that the computer-generated evidence is relevant and that it satisfies some exception to the hearsay rule if the judge is likely to exclude it because he doubts its authenticity.

What type of authentication is required? According to those courts that require a strong foundation for computer evidence, the lawyer should prove that (1) the procedures used to feed the data into the computer were reliable; (2) someone checked the accuracy of the data and the computer's operations; and (3) the computer record was generated and relied on in the ordinary course of business. *United States v. Weatherspoon,* 581 F.2d 595, 598 (7th Cir. 1978); *United States v. Russo,* 480 F.2d 1228, 1241 (6th Cir. 1973), *cert. denied,* 414 U.S. 1157 (1974).

The "ordinary course of business" requirement actually goes not only to authenticity but also to a second condition of admissibility: the requirement that the computerized records qualify under an exception to the hearsay rule. Nevertheless, the courts have invariably discussed this last factor, along with the first two, in ruling on authenticity.

What evidence will satisfy the first two requirements? Evidence of the source of the data and the input procedures will show the court that the data are accurate and were properly fed into the machine. Someone should be prepared to testify that no errors were made when the data were keypunched or otherwise converted into a computer-readable form.

In describing the input procedures, the witness should also identify who has access to the terminal and the program and who is responsible for feeding the data into the computer. It is important to identify the responsible employees to establish that the data were not altered.

Finally, the witness should testify that both the machine and the program used to generate the printout were in working order, and he should explain how they were checked for defects. *Guidelines for the Admissibility of Evidence Generated by Computer for Purposes of Litigation,* 15 U. C. D. L. REV. 951, 956 nn. 19–20 (1982).

Because jurisdictions vary in their approaches, a particular court may not require such a detailed description of the computer system to authenticate the computer-generated evidence. Still, laying a stronger foundation than is absolutely necessary is often beneficial. First, it will make your computer-generated evidence more credible. Second, a complete foundation allows you, rather than your opponent, to expose any cracks in your evidentiary edifice. That may limit the damage that your opponent can inflict on cross-examination.

When a computerized business record is printed out solely for the purpose of litigation, a solid evidentiary foundation may require additional proof. The proponent of a printout generated for litigation should prove that the computer retrieved the information in an unaltered form. This showing may be doubly helpful. Not only will it help establish authenticity, but it may later help meet a second requirement of admissibility: compliance with the hearsay rule. More on this point later.

For special computer preparations, it is more difficult to generalize about the standards for authenticity. The courts have simply not yet addressed the issue.

Under Rule 901(b)(9), simulations and analyses prepared for litigation, like computerized business records, can be authenticated with evidence that describes the computer process and shows that the results are accurate. Whether evidence of the input procedures and the tests used to assure the accuracy and reliability of the computer and the data will meet this requirement remains to be seen.

At least one commentator has suggested that this is all that courts should require to authenticate special computer preparations. *See Guidelines for the Admissibility of Evidence Generated by Computer for Purposes of Litigation*, 15 U. C. D. L. REV. 951, 956 (1982). But, absent any cases on point, it is hard to tell.

Once the lawyer who has computer evidence to offer decides what proof of authenticity is necessary, he must find a witness to present it. The data processor? The comptroller? Another financial officer?

The courts uniformly hold that the authenticating witness need not be the custodian of the records or even have personal knowledge of the data plugged into the computer or the preparation of the printout. Still, the witness must be able to attest to the authenticity of the printout. In practice, this means that the witness must be familiar with the printout and know how it was prepared.

How much the witness has had to do with the preparation and storage of the records will affect the credibility, if not the admissibility, of his testimony and the computer evidence. So it is usually best to put the evidence in through its custodian or someone closely involved in its preparation.

To complete the foundation for computer-generated evidence, you must show that you have made the requisite pretrial disclosure. Courts have required that before trial a lawyer must tell his opponent about any computer-generated evidence he plans to use and must turn over the computer program and all other important material. *See* MANUAL FOR COMPLEX LITIGATION § 2.70 (5th ed. 1982).

Courts have not, however, always enforced these requirements. At least one court has found that the programmer's proprietary interests outweighed the need for disclosure of the program. *Perma Research & Development v. Singer Co.*, 542 F.2d 111, 115 (2d Cir.), *cert. denied*, 429 U.S. 987 (1976).

Another court did not require disclosure of a program that was so simple that the cross-examiner was not unfairly prejudiced when he learned of it for the first time at trial. *United States v. M. Cepeda Penes*, 577 F.2d 754, 761 (1st Cir. 1978).

Of course, lawyers with computer evidence are wise to disclose it before trial. No matter what some of the cases say, a good way to get your computer evidence excluded is to spring it on your adversary at trial. Under Rule 403, the judge may exclude relevant evidence that is unduly prejudicial, and your adversary will have a good argument that a computer analysis he has not seen until shortly before he has to cross-examine a witness about it is unduly prejudicial.

If what you have is a computer-generated summary of computerized records, the foundation requirements also include a showing that you have complied with Federal Rule of Evidence 1006. That rule allows trial lawyers to present summaries of the contents of voluminous records that cannot be conveniently examined in court, provided that the original records are made available to the other parties.

In accordance with the rule, some courts have required lawyers who want to present computerized summaries at trial first to turn over the underlying records to opposing counsel. Other courts have required lawyers offering computerized summaries first to establish the admissibility of the underlying records. *See, e.g., United States v. Johnson*, 594 F.2d 1253, 1255–1257 (9th Cir.), *cert. denied*, 444 U.S. 964 (1979).

Step Three: Comply with the Hearsay Rule (or Duck It)

Unless an out-of-court statement offered for its truth falls within some exception, the hearsay rule generally prohibits its admission in evidence. FED. R. EVID. 801. If a computer printout is offered to prove the information it contains, it must qualify as one of the exceptions to the hearsay rule.

In many instances, computer-generated business records will qualify for the business-records exception to the hearsay rule. This exception applies to "data compilations, in any form" that are generated in the regular course of business. FED. R. EVID. 803(b).

To invoke this exception, the trial lawyer must show that: (1) the record was made at or near the time of the event in question; (2) the record was kept in the course of a regularly conducted business activity; and (3) it was the regular course of business to keep such a record. FED. R. EVID. 803(6).

When a lawyer invokes the business-records exception to introduce a

759

printout of computerized records generated for use at trial and not for business purposes, he should be prepared to face two likely arguments. First, the printout was not made at or near the time of the data entry but just before trial. Second, the printout was not prepared in the ordinary course of business but instead for trial.

The first argument is not too much of a problem. Most judges will be satisfied if the data were stored at or near the time of the event, even if the printout was generated later on. Otherwise, the admissibility of computer-generated evidence would be too severely restricted. *United States v. Russo*, 480 F.2d at 1240.

The second argument raises the concern that a printout generated for litigation is not as reliable as one generated for business purposes. To meet this argument, the foundational evidence that the computer retrieved the stored information in an unaltered form can be helpful. If the data are unaltered, there is really no difference between a printout generated for litigation and a printout of the same data generated for business purposes, except, of course, the time at which the printout was made. If this is so, the printout generated for litigation should be as reliable as one prepared in the ordinary course of business, and it should qualify for the business-records exception.

Even without evidence that the computer retrieved the data in an unaltered form, though, the printout should qualify for the business-records exception. The reason is that the printout carries the traditional guarantees of reliability that underlie the exception. The user relied on the electronically stored data and the computer program in the ordinary course of business, even if there was no printout, and this reliance is circumstantial evidence that the data are trustworthy. *See United States v. Sanders*, 749 F.2d 195 (5th Cir. 1984).

If the printout comes not from a business but from a government agency, it may qualify for the public-records exception to the hearsay rule. Under Rule 803(8), printouts that contain data describing either the activities of a public office, matters observed pursuant to public duty, or the factual findings of a government investigation are admissible.

Also, if an entry is missing from a computerized public record and that entry would be in the record if a certain event had occurred, then the record is admissible under Rule 803(10) to prove the nonoccurrence of the event. *United States v. M. Cepedu Penes*, 577 F.2d at 760–761. A similar exception to the hearsay rule is available under Rule 803(7) for computerized business records.

The court has discretion to exclude either public records or business records if the source of information or the circumstances of their preparation indicate a lack of trustworthiness. FED. R. EVID. 803(6), (8). Again, a good foundation should help avoid any inference of untrustworthiness that might lead a judge to exclude otherwise admissible public or business records.

There may also be other exceptions to the hearsay rule for a computer printout. For example, if the printout contains data reported to a public office concerning births, deaths, or marriages, it is admissible under the vital-statistics exception in Rule 803(9).

Under one of the familiar exceptions to the hearsay rule, computerized business or public records will usually slide right into evidence. But how about special computer preparations—computer simulations or computer analyses that would not exist but for the litigation? Here the traditional exceptions will not work. Only the residual exception of Rule 803(24) offers a glimmer of hope, and none too bright a glimmer at that.

To invoke the residual exception, the trial lawyer must meet a number of requirements. Most important, there must be circumstantial guarantees of trustworthiness equivalent to those of the other hearsay exceptions. For special computer preparations, this is a problem.

For business and public records, there are apparent guarantees of reliability, namely reliance in the ordinary course of business or preparation pursuant to a legal duty. But there are no such guarantees for computer simulations and analyses prepared for litigation.

On top of that, many courts have taken a restrictive view of Rule 803(24), applying it only in exceptional circumstances. Although the courts have had little to say about the admissibility of computer printouts under the residual exception, at least one court has held that the exception could not be used to introduce a printout of a sophisticated and reliable technological device—a telex message summarizing bank records. *United States v. Kim,* 595 F.2d 755, 765 (D.C. Cir. 1979). If *Kim* is any guide—and it is about the only guide around—the chances that a computer printout of a special litigation analysis will be admitted under the residual exception seem pretty slim.

If your computer evidence does not fit into one of the exceptions to the hearsay rule, you may have to dodge the rule altogether by using a computer-generated simulation or analysis as the basis for expert testimony. Rule 703 allows an expert to base his testimony on facts and data that "need not be admissible in evidence." FED. R. EVID. 703.

So a lawyer might call an expert to the stand and ask whether, in his opinion, based on the results of the computer simulation, the defendant's negligence caused the airplane crash. The expert's answer will come into evidence; the computer simulation as a whole need not. It probably won't make a whole lot of difference.

In one case the court upheld this use of a computer simulation. The plaintiff claimed that the defendant had breached a contractual obligation to use its best efforts to perfect, manufacture, and market an automotive anti-skid device covered by a patent that the plaintiff had assigned to the defendant.

To counter the defendant's assertion that the device had uncorrectable defects, the plaintiff called two experts who testified, based on a

761

computer simulation, that the device was indeed perfectible. *Perma Research & Development v. Singer Co.*, 542 F.2d at 113, 115.

The facts and data on which the expert's opinion is based need not be admissible in evidence if they are "of a type reasonably relied upon by experts in the particular field." FED. R. EVID. 703. Might this qualification bar an expert opinion based on a computer simulation? Ordinarily, it should not.

Experts in computers and in other fields routinely rely on simulations. Notwithstanding certain widely acknowledged shortcomings, computer simulations are widely regarded as useful tools in a variety of circumstances. The lawyer probably needs to show only that the simulation is as reliable as current technology permits. *Guidelines for the Admissibility of Evidence Generated by Computer for Purposes of Litigation*, 15 U. C. D. L. REV. 951, 968–969 (1982).

Rather than just describing the simulation, the expert can bring the computer to court and re-create the simulation on the stand, so that it is no longer an out-of-court statement. Aside from the possibility of avoiding the hearsay rule in this manner, the jurors' seeing the simulation might help them to understand the expert's testimony.

With the proper foundation, the in-court simulation can come in as independent evidence. Failing that, with the judge's permission, it can be used as an aid to help the jury understand the expert's testimony.

If an expert is to testify about otherwise inadmissible special computer preparations on which he bases his opinion, must the lawyer turn over the computer program and the underlying data to opposing counsel before trial? For the expert's testimony to be admissible, the rules do not require pretrial disclosure (although the other side can obtain some discovery through interrogatories under Civil Procedure Rule 26(b)(4)). FED. R. EVID. 705.

One court has suggested, though, that the underlying data and the theorems should be disclosed. *Perma Research & Development v. Singer Co.*, 542 F.2d at 115. Another court has not required it. *United States v. Bastanipour*, 697 F.2d 170, 177 (7th Cir. 1982), *cert. denied*, 460 U.S. 1091 (1983).

Again, unless the relevant jurisdiction has a settled rule that pretrial disclosure is unnecessary, it is probably advisable to turn over the pertinent material. No one can claim surprise when he has had a fair chance to prepare for cross-examination.

Step Four: Be Ready to Beat Back a Best-Evidence Objection

The best-evidence rule generally requires that the original of a writing or recording be produced to prove its contents. FED. R. EVID. 1002. Since the rules broadly define writing and recording to include data compilations, computer-generated evidence may encounter a best-evidence objection.

Is the computer printout an "original"? Although a printout is in some sense a copy of the original record stored within the computer, under Rule 1001(3) a printout is itself an "original."

However, if the printout is a summary, rather than a complete record of the data stored by the computer, it is arguably not an original. Nevertheless, the printout should still be admissible: it is a summary of voluminous recordings that cannot be presented conveniently in court. To get this evidence in as a summary, the trial lawyer must make the underlying records available to opposing counsel for examination or copying at a reasonable time and place. FED. R. EVID. 1006.

As in most other fields, the role of the computer in trial law is expanding rapidly. Undoubtedly, the rules on the admissibility of computer evidence will gel as courts get more experience. Meanwhile, proponents of such evidence would do well to make adequate pretrial disclosure and a convincing showing of the reliability of the computer process and the underlying data.

A Primer on the Use of Tape-Recorded Evidence

by Gary S. Jacobson and Sharon T. Jacobson

White-collar crime is usually verbal crime. Because "intent" more often is derived from language and nuance than inferred from violent actions, activities that are white-collar crimes are by themselves often ordinary and unremarkable. Proof may depend upon evidence of the intent of a phrase rather than a smoking gun. Prosecutors, therefore, find white-collar crimes ideally suited for the use of tape-recorded evidence.

There is little substitute for a tape recording's impact upon the jury. Hearing a tape recording, the jury becomes a witness to the acts in question. No longer must it rely on an intermediary who has his own interpretation of the event. No longer can counsel exploit the witness's courtroom demeanor, appearance, intelligence, memory, truthfulness, and past activities to shape the jury's understanding of the story he relates.

Nor is it simple, where tape-recorded evidence is presented, for a defendant to remain comfortably silent before a jury and to rely on the usual testimony from distinguished witnesses about his reputation for truth, veracity, and clean living. In all probability, the defendant's own biases, indiscretions, and other unguarded behavior will be heard plainly in his own voice. In a recording, a defendant often speaks of his previous criminal acts in a way that is inseparable from the evidence in the case in chief, raising the spectre of self-prejudice.

Conscientious defense counsel, therefore, carefully examine tape recordings before trial and move expeditiously for deletion of references to the defendant's prior criminal acts. Evidence might be presented to show that the taped statements were the result of coercion. Nevertheless, other traditional defenses, such as alibi and mistaken eyewitness

Sharon T. Jacobson currently practices in Summit, New Jersey. Gary S. Jacobson is a partner in the firm of Kleinberg, Moroney, Masterson & Schachter in Milburn, New Jersey, and was formerly a Special Assistant Attorney General with the law office investigating the New York City criminal justice system.

identification to remove the defendant from the scene, may be negated by tape-recorded evidence. Attack on the prosecution's motivation by alleging fabrication of its case also can be blunted by a recording of the conduct in question.

Because of the impact of recorded evidence, defense counsel must try before trial to prevent its introduction. At trial, faced with tape recordings, the defense probably will have fewer alternative strategies than a prosecutor who is forced to forego the use of his tape recordings. Resolution of the admissibility of the recording is crucial to plea negotiation and the decision to go to trial.

Was There Consent?

In evaluating the admissibility of tape-recorded evidence, the first question is whether the recording was made with the consent of one or more parties to the conversation. As the Supreme Court stated in *Katz v. United States*, 389 U.S. 347 (1967), the Fourth Amendment protects people, not places. The scope of the Fourth Amendment's protection is the individual's legitimate expectation of privacy. Thus, a tape recording made with the consent of one party to the conversation is constitutionally valid without prior judicial authorization or probable cause. The Federal Wiretap Statute, 18 U.S.C. § 2511(2)(c) and (d), permits such surveillance, and the Supreme Court, in *United States v. White*, 401 U.S. 745 (1971), upheld its constitutionality. Some states, however, have statutory restrictions upon the making of consent recordings by private citizens or by law enforcement authorities without prior judicial or administrative authorization. *See, e.g.*, N.J.S.A. 2A:156A-4 (1978); Pa. Stat. Ann. tit. 18 § 5703(a)(1) (Purdon 1978).

Consent tape recordings may be made by a number of means, including placing a recording device at one end of a telephone conversation, wearing a concealed tape recorder, or wearing a miniature radio transmitter whose signal is recorded at the receiver. Placing a hidden recording device in the proximity of the consenting party, such as in a room or automobile, should be constitutionally permissible, if what is recorded is within earshot of the party who consents to the recording, and does not intrude into the nonconsenting party's reasonable expectation of privacy. *Cf.*, 18 U.S.C. § 2510(2) (1968); *United States v. Padilla*, 520 F.2d 526 (1st Cir. 1975).

On the other hand, interception of a conversation without the consent of any of its participants invokes the protection of the Fourth Amendment against unreasonable searches and seizures. *Berger v. New York*, 388 U.S. 41 (1967), states the minimum requirements for satisfying these constitutional standards:

- an initial showing of probable cause that a particular crime has been or is being committed;

- particularization of the person and places to be "searched" by the eavesdropping;
- limitation on the length and scope of interception necessary to obtain the objectives of the eavesdropping;
- continued proof of probable cause to extend interception; and
- notice to the subject of the warrant, and its return to the issuing court.

Shortly after *Berger*, Congress enacted Title III of the Omnibus Crime Control and Safe Street Act of 1968 (18 U.S.C. § 2510 *et seq.*), which established stringent federal standards both for judicial approval of eavesdropping warrants and for their execution by law enforcement officials. Title III is directed to nonconsensual eavesdropping where the participants to a conversation have a reasonable expectation of privacy. While the provisions of Title III bind the states as well, they are free to impose even more restrictive provisions.

Under Title III, eavesdropped conversations must be recorded whenever possible. 18 U.S.C. § 2510(8)(a). This deters prosecutorial misconduct and better enables a defendant to determine if there has been compliance with the statute and eavesdropping warrant.

Discovery of eavesdropping recordings is provided defendants under 18 U.S.C. § 2510(8)(a) and Rule 16 of the Federal Rules of Criminal Procedure. Additionally, Title III requires that notice be given within 90 days of the termination of interception to all named parties whose conversations have been intercepted. The persons notified can apply to the court for inspection of the eavesdropping application and order. Any party against whom eavesdropping evidence is to be offered must be served with the eavesdropping application and order at least 10 days before the proceeding commences. Some states require more prompt notice. New York, for example, requires that notice be given within 15 days after arraignment. N.Y. CRIM. PROC. L. § 700.70 (McKinney's Supp. 1978). In practice, pretrial disclosure of conversations to defendants often is made informally. Disclosure of possible electronic surveillance to parties not named in the warrant is left to the discretion of the court.

Since consensual recordings are not governed by the Fourth Amendment, defense counsel has little pretrial recourse about them other than their discovery as evidence of prior statements by the defendant. Nonconsensual, eavesdropped conversations, however, provide several constitutional and statutory grounds for a suppression motion.

A suppression motion must be made before trial. 18 U.S.C. § 2518(10)(a). Since the Federal Wiretapping Statute establishes no special procedural requirements, the applicable procedure is that in Federal Rules of Criminal Procedure 12 and 41(e) governing the suppression of evidence generally. Of course, state legislation or rules may dictate specific procedures or time limitations for motions to suppress eavesdropping evidence. *E.g.*, N.Y. CRIM. PROC. L. § 710.20(2) (McKinney's Supp. 1978).

Discovery of the content of the eavesdropping should precede a suppression motion so that the manner of execution may be scrutinized with the warrant itself. A well-drafted motion should clearly and succinctly state its bases of attack, with reference to the statutory provisions governing each issue and to particular flaws in the warrant or its results. This is more likely to succeed than broad allegations of misconduct. Specificity also is essential to show that the issues asserted require a factual hearing.

Title III (at 18 U.S.C. § 2518(10)(a)) sets forth three bases for suppression:

- the communication was unlawfully intercepted (no warrant);
- the order under which it was intercepted is insufficient on its face; or
- the interception was not made in conformity with the order of authorization or approval.

In addition, 18 U.S.C. § 2515 provides a blanket prohibition against the introduction, as evidence, of portions of fruits of conversations where disclosure would violate any of the provisions of Title III. *See generally* CARR, THE LAW OF ELECTRONIC SURVEILLANCE (Clark Boardman 1977) § 6:02[3].

Failure to comply with any term of the order or governing statute, even if technical or ministerial, may justify suppression of the tape-recorded evidence and its fruits. *See, e.g., United States v. Sklaroff*, 506 F.2d 837 (5th Cir.), *cert. denied*, 423 U.S. 874 (1975). And a hearing on the motion to suppress may provide a pretrial opportunity to cross-examine the informant or undercover agent whose sworn statements provided the basis for the eavesdropping warrant.

Among the major grounds for overturning an eavesdropping warrant are:

- inaccuracy of the factual allegations upon which it was based;
- unreliability of the informant, if named;
- insufficient description of the conversations for which interception is authorized;
- nonspecificity of the designated location of the bug or telephone line; and
- failure to prove, as required, that conventional investigative techniques, short of eavesdropping, were unsuccessful or too dangerous.

Both probable cause to issue the warrant and its statutory sufficiency also can be explored.

While not likely to be as factually revealing as motions controverting the warrant itself, motions that attack its execution may be more successful in preventing the introduction of tape-recorded evidence under the exclusionary rule of 18 U.S.C. § 2515. Title III establishes a number of exacting technical and administrative requirements which have been construed quite strictly by the courts. Among the areas of execution that may be attacked are:

- minimizing the overhearing and recording of conversations not pertinent to the objects of the warrant and not authorized by it;
- possible overhearing of conversations without recording them;
- failure to observe court-ordered limitations on the length of interception;
- noncompliance with court-ordered progress reports to the supervising judge during the term of interception;
- failure to amend the eavesdropping warrant to include evidence of a new crime if it emerges during the course of an authorized interception;
- custody of tapes after recording;
- failure to seal the original tape recordings promptly under court supervision as required by statute; and
- failure to comply with Title III notice of interception requirements.

A hearing on challenges to the technical execution of the wiretap order also offers an opportunity to discover the strategy of the investigation. Questioning the investigators who conducted the wiretap may reveal the extent to which the court's directives were conveyed by the supervising prosecutors and their superior officers. Knowing which telephone numbers and individuals the investigators were instructed to record may reveal strengths and weaknesses in the prosecution's underlying case.

Close Scrutiny

Close scrutiny of the eavesdropping warrant and comparison with the requirements of the statute are essential. If the evidence obtained through recording passes pretrial muster, to be introduced at trial, the eavesdropped conversation still must comply with the rules of evidence. This, of course, also applies to consent recordings.

In the court's discretion, many of the evidentiary challenges to the use of tape recordings, consensual or eavesdropped, may be heard before trial. Where the existence of a tape recording is known, a motion for a pretrial ruling on the admissibility of the recording should be included in any omnibus pretrial motion. Inclusion of a general demand for discovery of all tape-recorded evidence also is advisable. The motion should emphasize the potential significance of the tape-recorded evidence at trial, and the convenience both to the parties and to the court from an expedited ruling. A pretrial ruling is particularly desirable where the admissibility of an entire conversation is in question, and where that recording appears to play a significant role in the prosecution's case.

As Watergate demonstrated, surreptitious tape recordings do not always yield clear, unambiguous conversations. While telephone taps are relatively free from overpowering background noises, microphones that are secreted in rooms, automobiles, or hidden on one's body are plagued by fading, sounds of traffic, background music, banging dishes, and ruffling paper and clothing. Crucial parts of conversations can be obliterated as an automobile drives over a metal bridge grating or after a stranger puts a coin into a jukebox.

In general, tape-recorded evidence is admissible unless the inaudible portions or omissions are so substantial to render the recording untrustworthy as a whole. *See, e.g., United States v. Clements,* 848 F.2d 928 (5th Cir. 1973), *cert. denied,* 415 U.S. 991 (1974); *see generally* Annot., 57 A.L.R.3d 746 (1974). The partial omissions or inaudibility have been compared to the absence of a witness from a portion of a conversation. *Monroe v. United States,* 234 F.2d 49, 55 (D.C. Cir.), *cert. denied,* 352 U.S. 873 (1956). Nevertheless, courts have recognized that juries may speculate about the content of the inaudible or missing portions of a recorded conversation. Irrelevant conversations or portions also can be prejudicial. By resolving these issues before trial, both parties are spared disruption and surprise. Moreover, if the inaudibility or irrelevancies are found to be prejudicial to the defense, an edited version of the tape can be prepared for submission at trial with appropriate instructions.

Closely related to the issue of audibility is the use of transcripts of tape-recorded evidence. Particularly where there are numerous conversations, transcripts are indispensable in trial preparation and management. Tapes are unwieldy to use and difficult to retrieve and index. A listener may not recognize all voices on a tape, and his perception of what is said may vary from that of other listeners. Reading a transcript while listening to the tape improves one's comprehension of the tape.

Obviously, preparation of a transcript invites interpretation and choice where ambiguities occur. If a transcript is prepared by the undercover investigator or informant, his familiarity with the speaker or recollection of events may color his interpretation of mumbled or interjected phrases and his identification of the speaker. A stranger to the investigation, however, may misinterpret a conversation, particularly in transcribing names and places.

The proponent of a transcript sometimes will offer it in evidence in conjunction with the recording. More often, it is only marked for identification and offered to the jury as an aid to understanding. In either instance, a foundation must be laid to establish that the transcript is an accurate reproduction of the recording.

A defense attorney should be wary of stipulating to the accuracy of a tape transcript and should listen to the tape before trial while reading the transcript. Cross-examination of its proponent often can undermine the sanctity of the prosecution's transcript of a poor recording. This may reveal various drafts, with changes, as the tape was listened to repeatedly, perhaps by different persons. Introduction of the transcript generally will not be blocked if its proponent testifies that it is a fair and accurate rendition of the conversation he heard, but a judge may instruct the jury that it alone will determine what is on the tape, and not allow the transcript to be used during deliberation. *See United States v. Koska, supra; but see United States v. Carson,* 464 F.2d 424 (2d Cir.), *cert. denied,* 409 U. S. 949 (1972). Vigorous cross-examination about the transcript also may encourage individual jurors to express their own interpretation in the jury room.

Lengthy, Costly, Painstaking

Preparation of transcripts is a lengthy, costly, painstaking process. If counsel for both sides prefer to have a single transcript made available to the jury—reserving the opponent's right to impeach its preparation—it is advisable to litigate this issue before trial.

Tape recordings do not fit neatly into the traditional categories of the law of evidence. They are not the testimony of witnesses who can be cross-examined; yet they usually contain out-of-court statements by both witnesses and nonwitnesses at trial. Often, the statements contained on the tape recordings constitute the act at issue, or contemporaneous reactions to the act by parties or witnesses, in the nature of res gestae. The tape itself is physical evidence, subject to alteration.

The contents of the tape recording are subject to evidentiary objection. *United States v. McKeever,* 169 F. Supp. 426 (S.D.N.Y. 1958); *rev'd on other grounds,* 271 F.2d 669 (2d Cir. 1959), sets forth the most frequently cited foundation requirements for the use of tape-recorded evidence. After indictment, one of the defendants conversed with prosecution witnesses and recorded the conversations. Offering these tapes at trial, defendant claimed that the only foundation necessary for their introduction was the witness's recollection that the conversation had taken place. In rejecting this, the court stated:

> [B]efore a sound recording is admitted into evidence, a foundation must be established by showing the following facts:
> 1. That the recording device was capable of taping the conversation now offered in evidence;
> 2. That the operator of the device was competent to operate the device;
> 3. That the recording is authentic and correct;
> 4. That changes, additions or deletions have not been made in the recording;
> 5. That the recording has been preserved in a manner that is shown to the court;
> 6. That the speakers are identified;
> 7. That the conversation elicited was made voluntarily and in good faith, without any kind of inducement.

As tape recorders have become common household items, the first two requirements have been relaxed considerably. Generally, with the emphasis in the Federal Rules of Evidence on tests of reliability and need, the foundation for recorded evidence has become less technical. Federal Rules 106, 901(b) and 100 reflect a policy that treats electronic recording like written recordings and photography.

The critical foundation bases now are clear and convincing proof of the authenticity and accuracy of the recording. *United States v. Fuentes*, 563 F.2d 427 (2d Cir.), *cert. denied*, 435 U.S. 525 (1977). In *Fuentes*, the court admitted tape recordings between a defendant and an informant, where no witness to the conversation testified at trial. One of the recordings was made on a concealed, body tape recorder. Testimony was given by the government agent who had placed the recorder on the informant, and had maintained custody of the tape after it was removed. The other tape admitted was a recording of a conversation sent by a transmitter on the informant's body to a receiver operated by the agent.

Thus, there are two acceptable foundations for tape-recorded evidence. One is similar to the authentication of a photograph, where a witness to the conversation testifies that he has listened to the recording and that it is a fair and accurate representation of the conversation he heard. If this is challenged, the alternate proof essentially is the chain of custody of the tape to establish that everything said was recorded and that nothing has been altered.

Even if the recording's authenticity and accuracy are demonstrated, the admissibility of the tape's contents still must be established. A claim of hearsay may be made. Usually, the conversation contains admissions of a party to the litigation, with statements of others permitted as forming the context of those admissions. Other hearsay exceptions under which taped conversations often are admitted into evidence include statements of co-conspirators, res gestae, and excited utterances. While it is not an exception to the hearsay rule, argument that the recording is corroboration of admissible testimony often is successful. *See generally* Annot., 58 A.L.R.3d 598, 606–12 (1974).

Occasionally, an objection will be based on "best evidence" grounds. This objection usually has been overruled where the original recording has been lost or destroyed, or where there is no question about the accuracy of the duplicate. The issue also may be that the live testimony of a witness is the best evidence of a conversation or, conversely, that a tape recording (rather than a witness's testimony) is the best evidence. Where either recordings or testimony have been claimed to be "best evidence" to the exclusion of the other, courts generally have held both to be admissible.

Voice Identification

Identification of the speakers generally may be made by anyone familiar with the speaker's voice. Voice identification is more of a problem in wiretapping and eavesdropping situations than it is with consent recordings, since all participants in the eavesdropped conversation may not be known. Voice identification of defendants or known conspirators is somewhat less difficult because the prosecution can compel voice exemplars by subpoena without violating the right against self-incrimination. While still sharply divided over the admissibility of voice spectrograms as a means of identification, many courts now acknowledge the scientific acceptance and reliability of such devices. *See* Annot., 49 A.L.R.3d 915 (1973). Whether voice identification is accomplished by lay or expert testimony, the standard instruction is that the voice identity is a question for the jury to decide.

The use of tape-recorded evidence provides substantial challenges for both sides of the criminal case. When electronic eavesdropping is involved, counsel is confronted with one of the most technical areas of trial practice. A prosecutor obtaining and executing an eavesdropping warrant and diligent defense counsel litigating a tape's admissibility both need to act with precision. Tape recordings require a proper foundation and grounds for admissibility at trial. When counsel knows the rules of evidence, admission of these recordings is not automatic.

PART IX

Appeal

Appellate Advocacy, Modern Style

by Murray I. Gurfein

Some appellate courts are "hot"; some are "cold." Some advocates like them hot and some like them cold. On a cold court the judges generally have not read the briefs and the relevant parts of the appendix before argument. The worst bench—and this must be the rare exception—is one on which at least one but not all the judges have studied the appeal before argument. A court should not blow hot and cold because that is unfair to the advocate who is sidetracked by giving answers that the other judges already know. The good advocate will be ready for all the vagaries of individual judicial idiosyncrasies.

Even Jupiter may nod on occasion. Taft once related that he said to Holmes, "But do you think it was right or fair to leave *that* fact out of consideration?" Holmes replied, "I'm sorry; I didn't read that far in the record."

Oral argument today is not the structured, cohesive oration it once was. There are as many variations among courts as there are among panels and even individual judges. Some judges shoot the first question before the advocate has cleared his throat. Others hold their fire until the argument is well under way. And still others ask no questions at all. The maxim for the advocate must be *Semper Paratus*. He must be prepared to be told that the panel needs no oral recitation of the facts, to have his argument taken over completely by questions from the bench, or to find that he delivers an entire argument without a single question.

This does not mean that felicity and clarity of speech are no longer required. The worst vice for appellate lawyers is to be inarticulate. Remember that by the time judges get to an appellate bench they are, on the whole, no longer young. And while not deaf, they tend to be some-

---

Murray I. Gurfein, now deceased, was a member of the United States Court of Appeals for the Second Circuit.

what hard of hearing and without benefit of lipreading courses. When there is a microphone in the courtroom, speak directly into it, but do not shout. Adjust it to your mouth level before you begin and do not move your head from side to side. And just as judges groan when the lawyer hems and haws, so they despair when the lawyer simply talks too fast, when his words come too trippingly off the tongue. The worst offenders in this regard seem to be young lawyers who are so bright that they cannot restrain their train of thought to a reasonable speed limit. You are not trying to hear yourself think. You are trying to get the judges to understand what you are saying and to think along with you. Hence, do not exceed a proper intellectual cruising speed.

Since you cannot foretell how thick and fast the questions will come, it is well to prepare for a full-scale uninterrupted argument. Fritz Wiener in his excellent book, *Briefing and Arguing Federal Appeals* (BNA, 1961), advises practicing the argument aloud to hone the rough edges and acquire a sense of timing. This is still a good idea. It helps a lawyer to recover after a series of questions, picking up the argument at a place that provides a chance to finish the main points.

Practice will also help to improve the manner of presentation. I would emphasize measured speech, clearly articulated, spoken in a confident but unpatronizing manner. An appellate advocate is a salesman. His skill in advocacy is shown by how well he "sells" his wares. Assurance and belief in his cause are important ingredients. And even dress may play a part. While I doubt that many of us still own what used to be called a "Court of Appeals suit"—striped trousers and morning coat—I would hardly recommend as proper apparel dungarees or T-shirts.

As important as expository preparation is, an advocate must be prepared for a dialogue with the court. It is the advocate's only chance to insinuate himself into the voting conference. A good answer to a hard question may make the difference in the decision. This means that in appellate advocacy, as in trial preparation, it is important not only to scout the other side but to give adequate weight to the strongest counterarguments. An overconfident team is often a losing team.

Search out the difficulties in your case. They cannot be wished away. Appellate judges generally are people of first-rate legal minds. Do not underestimate either their learning or acuity. Assume that they will go for the jugular. If the hard point is not raised at argument, be assured that they will find it before an opinion is filed.

This could lead to the generalization that there is no generalization for planning an oral argument. It depends on the subject of the appeal. But some generalizations are still in order. In some respects an appellate argument is an obstacle race for the appellant's counsel. To be particularly pitied is the lawyer who did not try the case below and comes to the appellate bar with fresh ideas and a veritable key that should give him a reversal.

In gambler's parlance, the cards are stacked against him. In federal civil cases he will run into the obstacle that the finding of the trial court must be sustained unless it is "clearly erroneous." And the verdict of a jury is quite sacrosanct. If he turns to attack the charge to the jury and no objection was made below he must show "plain error." In criminal cases, the nemesis is "harmless error." Even when there has been a constitutional violation, the defendant will not prevail on appeal if the appellate court thinks the error was "harmless beyond a reasonable doubt." Another impediment is that motions addressed to the indictment even for constitutional deficiency may not have been timely made before trial.

Appellate judges are, by and large, self-limiting toward the scope of their review, and self-deprecating in matching skills with trial judges. One must approach quite gingerly, yet firmly, the proposition that a respected trial judge has "abused his discretion." This pejorative word, probably grounded originally on the opportunity of the trial judge to measure the credibility of witnesses, now carries a distinct weight of its own on the balancing scale.

The appellee's lawyer, including a prosecutor, will be wise to stress these "technicalities," for they will, more often than not, bring him a relatively easy affirmance. The appellant's lawyer, on the other hand, cannot afford to disregard these obstacles. They will surely prove his undoing if he does.

Unless there is a paramount error of law that can be relied on as the sole point, the appellant must often take the hard road of attempting to show that a crucial finding was "clearly erroneous," that a ruling constituted "plain error," or that the judge "abused his discretion."

The success or failure of such an attempt may well turn on whether the advocate can convince the court that his client may be innocent or that it is grossly unfair to mulct his client in damages under the circumstances of the case, or that the dismissal of the complaint was a denial of justice. If appellant's counsel can find some legitimate way to convince the court of the intrinsic unfairness of the judgment below, he should press the point with cultivated vigor. For, while it is the fashion to deprecate decisions that are "result-oriented," Holmes was probably exaggerating when he told Learned Hand that "we do not do justice; we simply apply the law." It is still the mystery of the appellate process that a result is reached in an opinion on thoroughly logical and precedential grounds while it was first approached as the right and fair thing to do. If there is any legitimate way to argue the equities, it should be done, though not in the style of a jury summation. As Karl Llewellyn put it, "The very reason that appellate courts exist is that there is doubt, that skilled men do not agree about the outcome."

It is here that the doctrine of *stare decisis* becomes a roadblock. In federal courts of appeal where the judges sit in panels of three, the vote of two judges can effectively make "the law of the circuit," which binds as many as fifteen other judges. Succeeding panels are bound by the decision of the panel that first got the question the week before. Reading the advance sheets to see whether your issue has been written about is essential. There is nothing more devastating than a pronouncement from the bench that it is bound by a case that came down last month, when counsel has not read the opinion and is not prepared to distinguish it.

Some lawyers try to argue that the decision of a particular panel is aberrant or simply wrong. Unless the advocate can distinguish the decision on the facts, he will find that the entire court is bound to follow it. Here a skill in dialectic is a useful tool. It is sometimes said of one of my colleagues that he can find a distinguishing feature for any precedent because of his scholarship and dialectic skill.

Despite the importance of precedent, however, it is generally a poor advocate who cites a number of cases in oral argument and compounds his error by reading quotations. The judges read the briefs and that is where the citation of authority to support the points belongs.

There is an exception, of course, when one or possibly two cases may be the key to the decision. In that event the advocate faces the difficult choice of directly distinguishing or asserting the authority of the particular decision or lying in wait for what may be the inevitable question from the bench. Some great advocates prefer the latter technique. I recall that when United States Attorney George Z. Medalie was preparing to argue the McGovern contempt case in the Second Circuit in 1933, each of us noted that the basic issue would turn on whether McGovern had been given adequate notice and opportunity to defend. As a neophyte assistant, I suggested that he open his argument with a direct statement of the facts showing that the prosecution had afforded adequate due process. "No," said Medalie. "The point is so vital that they are bound to ask about it. It will be more effective if I give our position in answer to a question." That is precisely what happened. Judge Learned Hand asked, "What about due process?" Medalie responded, "If your Honors will look at page so-and-so of the appendix you will see how far we went." The judges looked at the reference. Judge Hand slammed the book shut and we had won the appeal.

There will be occasions when a judge will imply that the answer given is not good enough. Here the advocate must stand his ground with dignity and assurance but without overt antagonism. There are other judges on the panel who may remain convinced, and there is always hope of leading the questioning judge to a better appreciation of your point of view. If you have thought your case through in advance, you may have devised a pithy comment to cover the circumstance. And sometimes it is easy to summon a countervailing approach to that urged by your questioner. For example, if the matter deals with statutory interpretation you will find ample authority for strict construction, for liberal construction, for a literal reading or for a reading that makes more sense in context. Preparation will enable you to remind the court that decision by maxim or by canons of interpretation is likely to be no more acceptable than in-depth analysis of the coverage of the statute. On the other hand, if you are on the other side, be ready with maxim and canon to bolster your argument that the court is not at liberty to stray too far afield.

The advocate should also be prepared to identify apparent trends in Supreme Court doctrine. He must be prepared to argue either that the most recent case goes no further than its facts or that it spells a new era of jurisprudential thinking. Either approach is legitimate, and the court will be grateful for your reasoned help in solving the problem. I say "reasoned help," for the mere assertion of a position without more can only serve to irritate. Courts do not accept *ex cathedra* judgments from lawyers. In short, it is not safe to assume that a recent decision of the Supreme Court establishes "new" doctrine as the wave of the future. Judge-made law proceeds, as it always has, on a case-by-case basis.

This raises the question of how to argue a hard case that may make bad law—a variation of the problem of the guilty defendant who has been convicted by an allegedly unfair process.

The federal courts of appeal are reviewing courts of first instance as well as courts of last resort in most cases, given the limited number of cases that reach the Supreme Court by certiorari. As courts of first instance review, they have a responsibility to the litigants that, for the most part, is limited to reversal only for egregious error. On the other hand, the responsibility for fashioning the general law of the circuit will sometimes aid a particular unworthy litigant or, perhaps as often, deprive an objectively worthy litigant of success because of the need to preserve uniformity of decision or to avoid recognizing a doctrine that would not be in the broader interests of the law.

This is where the able advocate recognizes the common problem of appellate judges and tries to help them to move along "his way." A sharp appellate advocate will not falter at recognizing the equivocal position nor will he ignore discussing it. Perhaps some cases in point are the application of an exclusionary rule, a doctrine of suppression of evidence, or dotting the i's and crossing the t's in a wiretapping order and its implementation. A defense lawyer should measure the boundaries of rational interpretation or precedential compulsion and try to explain why the challenged conduct was beyond the extreme limit. The prosecutor, on his part, should not rely on a literal reading alone but should muster arguments of policy with adequate reference (without boring detail) to cases in his favor that he suggests are controlling precedent.

If the trend of the authorities is against you, you must try to show why, on the facts, a distinguishing decision will not disrupt the trend unwisely. Sometimes you can do this by stressing that the result in your case is so far different from the ordinary that it deserves special treatment. Perhaps you can argue that, contrary to the outcome in the cases cited, the result in your case is harsh and unwarranted.

This approach is particularly significant in criminal appeals involving business crimes where intent, smothered in swaddling clothes, shows its head only on intermittent occasions or is wholly circumstantial in proof. Judges, we may assume, are unanimously against sin, but there may be room for doubt that particular business conduct bears the stamp of illegitimacy, or that the practices of the appellants so far deviate from the morals of the marketplace as to be held criminal. In those cases, since the appellant is faced with a jury verdict against him, he should bolster his argument on the insufficiency of the evidence with an attack, where legitimately possible, on the instructions to the jury and the reception or exclusion of evidence. Sometimes the whole turns out to be greater than the sum of its parts.

The prosecutor of course should not assume the role of an avenging angel, though a few well-chosen words on the evil of the practices found criminal are in order. He should stress the salient facts pointing to criminal intent, not with the calm dispassionate approach of a law professor, but without the undignified exhortation of a soapbox orator. He must, above all, be prepared to answer the harder questions that a good appellant's argument will prompt the court to ask. In those cases, rehearsal with a colleague who knows the record well enough to ask the hard questions will be useful.

An important appellate argument demands as much random reflection as the concentrated thought given to it while the clock is running. The opening gambit may come to the lawyer on a quiet walk or while he is sleeping lightly. The synthesis of the argument, sometimes its reduction to simplicity, may not come except through thinking that is not trammeled by a time clock. I heard John W. Davis on several occasions come to a point in his argument where he would say, "After all, Your Honors, this is quite a simple case" and then follow with a pithy sentence going to the essence. I have a sneaking suspicion that sometimes the *tour de force* did not come to him while he was sitting at his desk.

While every lawyer likes to be associated with an extraordinary case, the appellee generally has nothing to gain by noting that the case is one of first impression, for he has the judgment below. The appellant, on the other hand, may whet the appetite of the court for an intellectual challenge if he stresses the importance of the case as one of first impression. He may do this, however, only if he is able to distinguish earlier case law or if the statute has not been interpreted before.

On the civil side, subject-matter jurisdiction of the federal court, and recently "standing," are often issues upon which the appeal will turn. It should be routine for the advocate to check jurisdiction, standing and appealability in any case where such questions may fairly arise. Familiarity with the case law is essential.

779

The oldest advice is still the best. Know your case thoroughly and deal openly and fairly with the court. We recently had before us a lawyer for an appellant in a criminal case whom we had never seen before. The presiding judge asked him, ''Did you come here *pro hac vice?*'' to which he responded, ''No, I came by taxicab.'' The moral, I suppose, is: if you cannot penetrate a Latin fog do not be ashamed to ask what it means.

Some Nuts and Bolts of Appellate Advocacy

by Jim R. Carrigan

While the rules governing briefs and oral argument in state courts of last resort differ substantially, the tactics, skills, and techniques of persuasion are universal. Yet even with the most arduous research, law books will not produce many workable pointers in this field. Some practical hints on appellate advocacy from a recently "benched" trial lawyer might, therefore, be helpful. My views are based on personal observations from "the other side of the bench."

A newly appointed appellate judge soon learns that friends and former colleagues approach him with awkwardness when greeting him "off the bench." Some who have always been on a "first name" basis suddenly begin using titles like "Your Honor." The problem for the lawyer is how to walk the line between stiff formality on the one hand and obsequious servility on the other. He should not be overly friendly, yet not disrespectful. There are a few judges who have a taste for ermine and would prefer to be called "Your Worship," but, generally speaking, the best course is to do what comes most naturally and not worry about it.

What then is the proper attitude, frame of mind, and tone of communication for a lawyer to cultivate in arguing to an appellate court? For some lawyers, especially the young, arguing before a state supreme court is a fearful experience calculated to humble, mortify, and confuse. The very setting—with the lawyers down in the pit before several black-robed "wise men"—is awe-inspiring. The atmosphere is not a congenial setting for communicating ideas.

Jim R. Carrigan is a United States District Judge for the District of Colorado. When he wrote this column, he was a Justice of the Colorado Supreme Court in Denver. A similar version of the article originally appeared in THE COLORADO LAWYER. *The article is reprinted by permission of* THE COLORADO LAWYER *from Vol. 8, No. 5 (1979).* © *The Colorado Bar Association, 1979. All rights reserved.*

The persuader should begin with a mind-set that will facilitate concentration on the ideas involved in the argument without being distracted by the personalities present or their elevated status. One highly successful Colorado lawyer says that as he stands to begin his oral argument, he visualizes all the justices sitting on the bench in red "long johns." Thus, he pierces the barrier of dignified pomposity and gets down to telling these other lawyers—who happen to be wearing black robes—about his case.

Civility, Respect

By whatever means, the lawyer's attitude must be to seek to *communicate*. This entails concentrating on the *content* of the legal issues involved in his presentation, in his opponent's argument, and in questions raised by the court. The demeanor most likely to facilitate communication is one of mutual respect and civility due to coprofessionals working together to solve a problem.

The question frequently arises: Who should handle the case on appeal—the lawyer who tried it, or an appellate specialist? In an earlier era there was perhaps more specialization in appellate advocacy, and there are still many lawyers who follow this specialty. Some of the best briefs and oral arguments are the work of specialists in the appellate divisions of the public defender's office and the attorney general's office. But, by and large, there are many advantages to having the same lawyer who tried the case write the brief and argue the appeal.

Obviously there are substantial savings for the client in *not* familiarizing a new attorney with the vast detail of the trial record. The lawyer who tried the case has lived intimately with it—its facts and law—its bone and marrow—for a year or two. The issues on appeal must have been raised at trial. The lawyer who lived with the case in the lower courts can explain it better—give more life to those issues and their complexities. Very often a justice will ask a specific question about something that occurred at trial—and it is frustrating for everyone in the courtroom when the response is, "I don't know, I didn't try the case."

Moreover, the lawyer who tried the case is less likely to misstate the record accidentally. Misstating the record is a cardinal sin that raises the hackles of the justices and totally undermines the credibility of counsel. There is just no way to know for sure whether such a misstatement of the record is blameless, negligent, or intentional.

One less obvious aspect cannot be overlooked. The attorney who tried the case is certainly more likely to be able to communicate—nonverbally—that critical sense of injustice that makes appellate courts scrutinize cases closely. Arguing an appeal of someone else's trial must be, emotionally, a little like kissing your sister.

A caveat must be kept in mind. The appellate lawyer's function is primarily intellectual. Too much emotionalism can be counterproductive, in bad taste, and downright offensive. Therefore, if the attorney who tried the case cannot overcome and put aside any *hostility* toward the trial judge and *bad* feelings toward opposing counsel that the trial may have generated, it is probably better for the attorney who tried the case not to brief and argue the appeal.

Brief means what it says. Court rules regarding the number of pages allowed in briefs set *maximums* not minimums. Lawyers should not feel that they have to use all the pages allowed. Briefs are not graded by length or weight, as we sometimes suspected in law school.

Anyone acquainted with the case load problems in most appellate courts must realize that as briefs grow in girth, the chances of their being read decrease. For example, our court typically hears six or seven cases on each oral argument day. In each case, assuming only one party on each side and no amici curiae, we have to read at least one opening brief, one answer brief and one reply brief. Often, multiple parties and amici file extra briefs. Thus, each justice is expected to read and digest at *least* three briefs for each case. In the seven cases set for each oral argument day, each justice must plow through at least 21 briefs. Our court hears cases four days during the week of each month that we devote to oral argument. This means about 84 briefs (plus amici and extra party briefs) must be read in preparing for oral argument week. In addition many courts have their law clerks or staff attorneys prepare, and circulate in advance of oral argument, memoranda highlighting the points raised in the briefs.

Simple Point

The point is simple. To be persuasive, a brief must be read. Its chances of being read and assimilated are in inverse proportion to its length. Briefs should be edited and "boiled down" to eliminate repetition and surplusage.

Points or issues to be covered in the briefs, and on oral argument, should be carefully selected. The fewer points raised, the greater will be the court's concentration on each. The rifle shot, rather than the scatter-gun, is likely to hit the bull's-eye—or at least the judge's eye.

Similarly, oral argument should concentrate only on the strongest points raised. Oral argument time is far too precious to be spread thinly over many issues. The weaker points should be submitted on the briefs. As Mr. Justice Jackson said, "The mind of an appellate judge is habitually receptive to the suggestion that a lower court committed an error. But receptiveness declines as the number of assigned errors increases. . . ."

If I were to advise attorneys when to waive oral argument, my advice could be stated in one word: Never! Waiving oral argument inescapably carries the implication that counsel feels the case is not important enough to justify argument. Even worse, waiver may cause some judges to infer that counsel feels the arguments set out in the brief are so weak or doubtful that counsel is embarrassed to appear personally to express them. Waiver thus marks the case, in the minds of some judges, as a *pro forma* appeal of a hopeless cause that the lawyer is processing because the client demanded an appeal or because he has a sense of duty to exhaust all possible avenues of relief.

Oral argument is far too important to be waived. Impersonal persuasion—or selling of ideas—through a brief is useful. But its efficacy compared to a vigorous, personalized argument is much like that of a salesman's letter compared to his personal sales call to present his pitch to the prospect.

In today's busy, overscheduled courts, oral argument is critical to assist the judges in focusing on the really important issues. Moreover, a scheduled oral argument date acts as a deadline to stimulate the judges to read the briefs. In many courts, oral arguments are tape-recorded and any judge may play back any part or all of the argument.

Oral argument is usually followed immediately the same day by a brief conference at which each argued case is discussed and a tentative vote taken. All the justices who heard the argument participate fully.

By contrast, a case submitted on the briefs without oral argument may be assigned to one judge. His job is to study the briefs, then write and circulate to his colleagues a proposed opinion. Such a decision, and opinion, tends to be the product of only one judge instead of the collegial product of the whole court.

The importance of oral argument is also illustrated by the fact that the tentative vote taken immediately after oral argument is seldom changed. After that vote is taken, the case is assigned to one of the justices who voted in the majority to write an opinion. It is usually weeks, or even months, later when that opinion is circulated and set for discussion at the court's regular, weekly opinion conference. Those justices who did not write the opinion will not remember the case in great detail and will tend to be persuaded by the views of the justice to whom the opinion was assigned. Thus, for practical purposes, the "tentative" vote taken immediately after oral argument, which is greatly influenced by the oral argument, generally decides the case.

In planning oral argument, it is important to know whether the court will be a "hot bench" or a "cold bench." A "hot bench" is one comprised of justices or judges who read the briefs prior to oral argument, and a "cold bench" is one comprised of those who do not. Many appellate judges feel that it is better not to read the briefs in advance of oral argument.

If the case is being presented to a "cold bench," the appellant who opens the case has a considerably heavier burden of stating the facts and the issues of the case in a clear, cogent manner. Even if the case is being presented to a "hot bench," it is safe to assume that few, if any, of the judges have had time to give really careful study to all the briefs. Moreover, to be on the safe side, counsel should assume that none of the judges has read the transcript of the record in advance of oral argument. Thus, the task of stating the case should be approached with the attitude that the attorney is trying to explain the facts and issues to legal peers who want to know and understand all they can about the matter.

Counsel should not read from briefs or other documents, except when short quotations will add emphasis or authority. For the nervous lawyer, it may be helpful to write out the first sentence or two of the oral argument, and perhaps the planned "closer" which emphatically summarizes the matter. Otherwise, concise notes or an outline should be relied upon, and there should be a maximum of both voice and eye contact so that there can be real communication of ideas.

A great appellate advocate, John W. Davis, suggested that the lawyer arguing an appeal should mentally change places with the judges on the bench. He should say to himself, "If you were up there and had a job to do deciding this case and wanted to do the best job you could, what would you want to hear from counsel?"

Counsel must choose the most persuasive points to raise. There is no need for reciting detailed citations unless one of the justices asks for them. Transcript and case citations should be available in the event a judge requests them. If not readily at hand, counsel should not spend time leafing through the brief, but should inform the court that they are in the brief and available by consulting the table of authorities.

Where counsel will rely on authorities not in the brief, they should be listed, filed with the clerk, and served on the opponent a day or two before the oral argument.

Before the argument, the attorney should visit the court and sit through the argument of another case. He should become familiar with the physical layout, especially with the space available on the podium for notes, files, and other records. If the podium is a modern one—adjustable in height—counsel should know how to operate it. The attorney should note the location of the clock or other timing device and find out how the court indicates time limits and warns when time is about to expire. Counsel must also know how to arrange to reserve part of the allocated time for rebuttal and how the court will signal when opening argument begins to encroach on rebuttal time.

Part of oral argument preparation is getting into the proper frame of mind. Counsel should be well-rested and alert, tense and sharp, quick rather than tranquilized or too relaxed. Oral argument can be an exciting and stimulating intellectual exercise, as well as one of the highest forms of the advocate's art.

Innovation and creativity are not confined to the trial level, but also may be most helpful on appeal. For example, demonstrative aids may be very persuasive in appellate argument. Thus, briefs should not attempt to explain or describe facts which can be illustrated by reproducing maps, blueprints, plans, photographs, or drawings. In a products liability case, photographs of the product, scale drawings, and photographs of the warning label involved or the part that allegedly failed can be very important. Since these items cannot be included in the brief or presented at oral argument unless they were admitted into evidence at the trial, the brief should refer to their exhibit numbers.

Even where not included in the brief, it may be helpful to display such demonstrative evidence exhibits to the court while arguing an appeal. For example, our court recently heard a criminal case in which the defense was mistaken identification. There had been a photo lineup in which the victim had been shown five photographs. Four depicted balding, middle-aged men, some with glasses. The other was of the rather young-looking defendant who had a full head of hair and no glasses. Such a demonstration is very persuasive to the appellate court. Similarly, an attorney should show the appellate court actual aerial photo blowups, mock-ups and models, as well as charts of accident scenes and other demonstrative evidence.

Every case is different, and each lawyer's style is individual. What works for one lawyer or one case may not work for all. But a few fundamental suggestions may be generally useful.

A straightforward, narrative style is probably the most useful to fit all that must be said into the brief time allotted. For example, an appellant who has twenty minutes to present his opening argument, with some additional time for rebuttal, should plan to state the case on the opening argument as if he were at the airport seeing off a lawyer friend whose plane leaves in twenty minutes. Given that twenty minutes to relate to the friend everything he wants him to know about this important case, how should the case be presented?

Unfair Tactics

Rebuttal time should be used for rebuttal. Many judges resent as unfair tactics the raising, in rebuttal time, of issues that were not discussed by the opponent and were not mentioned in the opening argument.

The side entitled to rebuttal should *always* reserve at least a few minutes for rebuttal. If no rebuttal is required, the time need not be used, and counsel will receive a "gold star" from the court for concluding the argument in less than the full time allotted. If no rebuttal time has been saved, however, and opposing counsel misstates the record or miscites a case, there is no opportunity to respond. If nothing else, reserving rebuttal time acts as a healthy deterrent to an opponent who otherwise might be tempted to stretch the record a bit in argument.

Timing the argument is extremely important. One must be sure to understand who keeps track of the time and what, if any, warnings about time are given. In our court, for example, each side is given thirty minutes in the typical case. There are three lights on the podium. A green light comes on when the lawyer begins his argument. After twenty minutes, a yellow light comes on to warn that only ten minutes remain. At the end of that time, a red light comes on. It has its usual meaning and is strictly enforced. One who wants to be informed when five minutes remain should make that request at the beginning of the argument.

A frequent tactical question is whether to divide one's precious allotment of oral argument time among two or more lawyers. In the typical case, dominated by a single major issue, this is probably not advisable, because it tends to diffuse concentration. In multiple issue cases, however, or those involving considerable public interest, different considerations may apply. For example, if an amicus curiae has been permitted to file a brief, and represents an important public interest group, it may be wise to grant the amicus some portion of your oral argument time. This adds not only persuasiveness to your case, but also importance to the case itself as viewed by the court.

One generally neglected weapon in the appellate advocate's armamentarium is the opinion written by the court below. It seems ironic that lawyers search far and wide for similar cases from which to quote judicial reasoning, yet almost never quote the often scholarly, well reasoned, and persuasive opinions of the trial court and the intermediate appellate court in the very case at issue. Mr. Justice Marshall has noted his Court's disappointment in counsel's common failure ''to use a beautiful opinion by the lower court, scholarly done, bursting with research.''

Our state has been blessed with an excellent court of appeals and many superb trial judges. Their work product in the form of opinions commands high respect in our court. Even a dissenting opinion in the intermediate appellate court can be most persuasive. In fact a well-written dissent is frequently determinative of our decision to grant certiorari. An attorney who fails to mention or quote from the dissent in that situation surely forfeits a real opportunity to persuade.

Just as there is a time to speak up, there is a time to be silent. If the trial judge whose decision you seek to uphold is highly regarded, surely he or she should be mentioned in your oral argument. In every state, however, there are a few trial judges whose decisions are as ''reversible'' as some jackets. Past experience with their work has taught appellate judges to scrutinize it with special care and to exercise less than the usual reluctance about reversing. If such a judge rendered the trial court decision in your favor, the less said about it the better.

He's Alive!

The question of questions is troublesome to some lawyers. How should counsel respond when oral argument is interrupted by questions from those stolid, black robes on the bench? The first response should be rejoicing! A question proves that at least one of the judges is awake. If perchance the question is relevant to the argument, it may even demonstrate that the interrogator is following the argument and you have captured his interest.

Most questions can be taken at face value and ought to be answered promptly and forthrightly. Evading an immediate, candid answer by putting off the question to be dealt with later not only irritates the judge who asked the question, but also may provide an opponent an opportunity to answer it on rebuttal.

Counsel should realize, however, that every question is not necessarily what it seems. Some appellate judges question counsel to persuade their colleagues on the bench. Such questions are really directed *through*, not *to*, counsel, and it is through the content of the judge's question, not the answer, that the interrogating judge intends to assist his slower-witted confreres to see the point of the case. The attorney must be "tuned in" to the question and its real purpose. If the questioner's attitude, and the sense of the question, seem favorable, a very brief, congenial response is appropriate. Above all, counsel should avoid becoming combative with a judge whose question is helping his cause. All too often an attorney bites the helping hand.

Some appellate judges succumb to the temptation to "play lawyer" at oral argument. Thus, counsel may be bombarded by probing questions as if he were a witness undergoing cross-examination. The victim of this form of lawyer abuse has no real remedy, except in the other judges' sense of fair play, but that remedy is usually sufficient.

The appellate lawyer must learn to deal with the "straw man" questions employed by some judges. Such a judge usually has made up his mind against the position being advocated on a particular issue. He steps into the argument with a question or a statement logically extending the argument to a ridiculous extreme, states an example in the form of a question, and tries to attribute the example to the lawyer by a statement such as, "Is that what you are arguing?" The lawyer must firmly—but as graciously as possible—state that he did not intend to make such a statement, then move quickly to another subject. He must not allow himself to be lured into wasting valuable time jousting with the straw man.

In planning oral argument, an important consideration is the *order* in which the issues will be discussed. Lawyers differ on whether the most important issue should be treated first, last, or somewhere in the middle. For several reasons, I advise discussing it at the outset. First, the court is freshest, most receptive, and most interested in the case at the beginning of your argument. Second, the principle of primacy teaches that the point first argued makes the deepest and most lasting impression. And, third, if the most important issue is reserved until last, the court's questions may use all the time allotted and there may never be a chance to discuss it.

Appellate advocacy requires that the lawyer be flexible and adaptable. One who mechanistically adheres to a previously plotted "game plan," in spite of unforeseen developments in the course of the argument, is not likely to communicate well. For example, when it is obvious from the court's questions that a majority have decided one issue in your favor, switch to other issues. There is always the danger of flaying a dead horse back to life with your tongue.

Leave Client Home

Lawyers differ on whether it is wise to bring the client to an appellate argument. Generally, that practice may influence one to engage in a more emotional, jury-type argument to impress the client. But it is not the client one needs to impress in oral argument. Nor are the justices likely to be swayed by the style that would sway the typical client. Therefore, for most cases, the better rule is probably to leave the client at home.

While not wishing to encourage emotionalism in oral argument, I must stress that the persuasive appellate advocate should communicate in bearing, tone of voice, and general attitude a strong feeling of the innate justice of the cause. Stated conversely, counsel must make the court feel a sense of injustice in what has happened to the client in the court below—or in what would happen to the client if that court were reversed. In short, a little restrained and tasteful righteous indignation will not hurt. Most judges who choose careers on appellate courts have given up highly lucrative pursuits to be there because they really care about justice. Thus it helps to "have a little justice on your side" and to be able to communicate that feeling. If you do not feel strongly a sense of the fairness of your case, and a sense of injustice in the opponent's position, perhaps it is a case someone else ought to argue.

Preparing for Appeal

by Steven F. Molo and Paul P. Biebel, Jr.

Reputation and experience mean little if you walk into court unprepared. A prominent government lawyer once learned this the hard way when arguing as an amicus curiae before the United States Supreme Court.

One of the justices asked about a significant case decided years earlier. The lawyer hesitated for a moment and then responded that the Court should overrule the earlier case. He could not understand why his colleagues at counsel's table broke into nervous whispers. After he sat down, he learned that he had urged the Court to overturn a 50-year-old precedent supporting his position.

Here is one approach to preparation for oral argument which is designed to prevent that sort of problem. It is based on our experience in handling a variety of appeals for a large government law office.

Bob Hanley says that, during the last 30 days before a trial, he enters into a state of complete and total misery. Hanley, *The Last Thirty Days*, 10 LITIGATION, No. 2 at 8 (Winter 1984). Notification that oral argument has been set often induces the same state.

Unlike the trial lawyer, the appellate lawyer does not have to orchestrate the testimony, exhibits, and arguments that must flow smoothly by a judge or jury. An appeal involves fewer human elements. But the appellate lawyer's job is just as tough.

The appellate advocate must take that trial and all its human elements, along with the two or three preceding years of litigation, and reduce the entire case to a coherent argument that will convince an appellate panel, in 30 minutes or less, that the result in the trial court was right or wrong.

Paul P. Biebel, Jr., formerly the First Assistant Attorney General of Illinois, is a partner in Winston & Strawn in Chicago. Steven F. Molo is an associate in the same firm.

The appellate lawyer *is* his case for those 30 minutes. He stands alone in the batter's box when the court throws a fastball, change-up, or curve. There are no walks or base hits. He either hits a home run or strikes out.

But he was not always alone while preparing for argument. He honed his arguments with the other lawyers who helped write the brief. They tried to anticipate every counterargument the other side might raise and every bizarre hypothetical question a judge might ask.

He tested his theories on anyone in the office who would listen and he consulted outside experts to make sure all the bases were covered. He subjected himself to the unflinching eye of a videotape camera and the critiques of his colleagues. He bored his wife, alienated his friends, and drove himself to the brink of insanity trying to reduce his case to its simplest terms.

So how does it all come together? The team approach works best, particularly if the case is complex or the advocate inexperienced. Yet even the most seasoned appellate lawyer with the simplest case can benefit from the assistance and insights of a legal Sancho Panza.

Working with a team has several advantages. First, it saves time by allowing you to delegate some tasks. Indexing the record, compiling photocopies of the important authorities, reviewing advance sheets, and going over the local appellate rules are necessary tasks, but the first-chair lawyer might not have time to do them all himself.

Do Not Duck Tough Questions

Second, the team approach gives you more knowledge to draw on. Working with people who are familiar with the case and the issues it presents can provide valuable insights and ensure that you are not ducking the tough questions.

Finally the team approach gives you perspective. Discussing your case with newcomers to the facts and the legal issues involved promotes clarity and simplicity.

So who should comprise your team? Of course, you will need the help of the lawyers who worked on the brief. If you did not handle the case in the lower court, rely too on the lawyers who did. As elementary as this sounds, in some large government offices an appellate lawyer might talk to the trial team only when preparing the brief, if at all. Remember, the case was once as much a part of your predecessor as it is now a part of you.

Our office consults with law professors and specialists in preparing for important arguments. We also have enlisted the help of former members of the Solicitor General's office and other experienced appellate lawyers. These people are eager to help in significant matters. If your case is simpler, rely on anyone in the office who has expertise in the area or experience with a similar issue.

Even if you are a sole practitioner, your secretary or spouse can help you with your phrasing and logic. Nonlawyers often have the uncanny

791

ability to see through the legal haze and ask the really tough questions about the practical effect of your positions. But do not rely on laymen alone; it is also a good idea to involve some lawyers who have had no prior exposure to the case.

Once you have selected your team, where do you start? First, get to know the battleground. Before you dig into the issues, take some time to learn about the court and the judges who will hear the appeal.

Study the Court

If you have not argued in the court before, become familiar with the court's rules. They vary significantly. For example, the rules in the Fifth Circuit are quite different from those in the Seventh Circuit. Learn the procedures for submitting new authority, supplementing the record, reserving time for rebuttal, requesting more time for argument, and checking in the day of argument. In short, be prepared for any procedural matter that might arise between the day the oral argument is set and the time the court renders an opinion.

Each of the federal circuits publishes a practitioner's handbook that sets forth the Federal Rules of Appellate Procedure, the local circuit rules, and the court's internal operating procedures. For Supreme Court advocacy, there is no better guide than R. Stern & E. Gressman, *Supreme Court Practice* (5th ed. 1978). Most state appellate courts publish their own rules. These sources often include both the rules and comments on oral argument.

The court's scheduling procedures may affect your approach. Some courts, like the United States Supreme Court, sit *en banc* and schedule arguments for intermittent five- or ten-day periods during which the court hears argument all day. If your case is before a court that schedules arguments that way, you might do well to spend a bit more time detailing the facts before you start your legal argument. Even if the court has read your brief and is familiar with the law, a thorough explanation of the case can help the judges to distinguish it from the other appeals on the calendar.

See if you can find out which judges will sit on the panel that will hear your appeal. Then learn something about the way those judges approach oral argument: Do they usually read the brief beforehand? Which judges ask the most questions?

Find out how the judges have decided similar issues. Will Justice Freemarket apply his economic analysis to your contract case? Will Judge Hardliner think that your client had a reasonable expectation of privacy in the bank satchels filled with the money he stole?

Talking to lawyers who regularly practice before the court is a good way to learn about how the judges think. LEXIS is another window to particular judges' views. It is also helpful to observe another argument before the same panel.

792

Now to the substance of your argument.

Remember that the brief and the oral argument serve different purposes. The brief gives the court the authorities and analysis supporting the result you seek. It also distinguishes the record excerpts, statutes, and cases cited by your opponent.

Oral argument gives you a chance to talk to the decision-makers. It is your opportunity to give life to the cold facts and authorities in your brief and to allay any doubts the judges have about your position.

Do not plan to argue every point in your brief. You simply will not have time. Besides, arguing too many points minimizes the impact of the ones that really count.

But how do you know which points really count? You do not know. Any lawyer who has not been an appellate judge is fooling himself if he thinks he does know. Even a former appellate judge can sometimes be surprised by what his former brethren seize on to reach a particular decision.

There are some things you can do, though, to keep on track. Decide what the case is really about. Reduce it to its simplest terms. Noted Chicago appellate lawyer Bill Harte calls this finding the "essence of the case."

Determine what you want the court to do and how that result will affect the law. What is the least the court must do to give you what you want? Can the holding you seek really be limited to the facts of your case? Will the result you seek conflict with precedent or with the decisions of other courts?

Isolate the most important reason for deciding in your favor. If the appeal were limited to one narrow issue, what would that be? Look at the big picture. If the appeal is discretionary rather than of right, ask yourself why the court decided to hear the case.

Consider these questions before rereading the brief. Think about the ultimate equities without immersing yourself in legal authorities or the record.

It helps to imagine how you would argue the appeal in ten minutes, then five minutes, then two minutes. What would you tell the court if you had only one minute to present your case? Imagine that your brief were limited to a one-page letter to the court. What would you write?

This will not always work. In *Illinois v. Gates*, our office had what we thought was a straightforward Fourth Amendment issue in an appeal before the Supreme Court. We wanted the Court to simplify the *Aquillar-Spinelli* test for reliability of anonymous informants used to obtain search warrants.

But the Court had other ideas about the case and wound up ordering additional briefing and argument on whether there should be a good-faith exception to the exclusionary rule. So sometimes there is no way short of clairvoyance to anticipate what will be important to the court.

793

Nonetheless, mortal appellate lawyers should do what they can to identify the important issues and focus their arguments accordingly.

Develop a theme. Keep it simple. It can be a sentence or phrase that sums up your case and that will recur throughout the argument. Like the theme of a successful summation or opening statement at trial, this is the glue that holds the whole argument together. A good theme makes for a smooth transition from point to point and provides a bridge back to your argument after you have responded to a bizarre hypothetical or confusing question.

A lawyer in our office recently handled an appeal concerning the use of documents that had been subject to a magistrate's protective orders. We were never a party to the suit in which the orders were entered, but we wanted to use the documents to expose a fraud that, we alleged, the appellant had perpetrated on another court in another case. The protective orders had been dissolved and reinstated several times in a series of inconsistent rulings that left the record in a procedural shambles.

The appellant charged that we had violated the protective orders when we obtained the documents from another lawyer. We said that we got the documents before any protective order had been issued, and that we were not bound by the orders in any event, because we were never a party to that lawsuit.

The appellant's lawyer began his argument by stating, "Let me first say what this case is not about." He then launched into an attack against our office, the district court, and the proceedings in which we wanted to use the documents.

Rather than tell the court why he was there, he began with a negative statement that failed to capture the essence of his case. He made a confusing appeal even more confusing and he never really told the court why it should decide in his favor. There was no cohesiveness. He lacked a theme.

Our lawyer did not dwell on the erratic procedural history or respond directly to the appellant's charges of misconduct on the part of our office. Instead, he focused the court's attention on the big picture. His theme was that the appellant "should not be allowed to use the Federal Rules of Civil Procedure to conceal a fraud that it perpetrated on another court."

It worked. Each time the argument came to an exchange on the rationale for the irrational orders, our lawyer brought the argument back to where he wanted it by returning to his theme.

Of course, incanting a theme should never substitute for answering a question from the bench. But a well-thought-out theme lets you redirect the court's attention to your main point after you answer a question that sidetracks you. This is particularly important when your case is complex or your opponent has led the court astray by strewing your path with red herrings.

Once you have found your theme, review the brief and decide which points *not* to argue. You have decided the case is about commercial speech, so why waste the little time you have talking about *res judicata*, unless the court asks about it? You think the admission of the co-conspirator's hearsay statements will be the most likely basis for reversing the judgment on the jury verdict, so why squander half your time arguing that your opponent's closing argument was improper?

Integrate your remaining points into a single argument drawn together by your theme. Think about how the argument should flow. Do not yet concern yourself with the fine points. Rather, establish the framework that you will fill in later.

Lead with your strongest punch. A well-known Chicago litigator once argued a complex commercial matter before the Illinois Supreme Court. His brief gave many reasons why the lower court's decision should be reversed. But he began his argument with one of the weaker points. The first question he drew within two minutes, was, ''Counsel, do you have something more substantial to say to us today?''

To avoid that embarrassment, leave the less important points in your brief out of your oral argument. Then rank the remaining points and cover them in order of decreasing importance.

As you decide what to include in your argument, remember that credibility is your most valuable but most fragile asset. In a case before the Illinois Appellate Court, a lawyer argued that his client's 30-year sentence for murder was excessive. He marshaled the mitigating circumstances and cited the appropriate rules of law, but he neglected to mention that the defendant had spent 11 years in prison on a previous murder conviction and was paroled only three months before he committed the second murder.

Whatever credibility the appellant's lawyer started out with was demolished when his opponent pointed out, in his opening remarks, the critical but previously unmentioned facts. As difficult as it sometimes may be, it is essential to maintain some degree of objectivity as you decide what you will argue to the court.

If your case involves multiple parties or an amicus curiae, you may have to decide whether to divide oral argument. This decision is best made after you have an idea of how your argument should flow. You will know then whether the issues can be painlessly divided between counsel. If before preliminarily structuring your argument you commit to dividing your time, you may discover during your preparation that your argument does not lend itself to division.

You will then be a likely victim of one of the three problems that commonly befall lawyers who divide argument time:

- The court questions lawyer A about the issues lawyer B will address.
- The court's questions take lawyer A past his allotted time, and law-

yer B makes a hurried, incomplete argument or never speaks.

- Lawyer A's thoughtful, well-prepared argument is cut short so that lawyer B can begin his abrasive, ill-prepared lecture to the court.

Do not divide your time, if possible.

If you must divide the argument, allocate discrete issues for each lawyer to address. Repetition bores the court and wastes your team's limited time. The less your issues overlap, the less likely it is that you will intentionally or inadvertently make your co-counsel's argument.

Now you are ready to get down to the business of learning the record and authorities. This may be drudgery, but it is essential. Even if you did not represent your client in the lower court, you must become the leading expert on the case.

Reread the cases and statutes cited in the briefs and prepare abstracts of the important ones. You should do this yourself, particularly if you were not the principal draftsman of your brief. This exercise forces you to become familiar with the pertinent authorities and to recognize the distinctions between your case and those that you and your opponent cite.

Arrange your abstracts and photocopies of the important authorities in an indexed, three-ring notebook. This will be a ready source of the relevant authorities for quick reference during your preparation and argument.

Use *Shepards*, advance sheets, session laws, and LEXIS to find any new statutes or cases on point. Do this during your initial review of the authorities, but check again periodically right up until the day before argument.

A few years ago, a lawyer from our office had an argument before the Supreme Court. The justices questioned him about another case that the Court had decided the day before. Fortunately, the second-chair lawyer had heard about the decision on the news, and he got a copy of the opinion from the clerk's office the morning of argument.

You must know the entire procedural history of the case right up until your appeal. A lawyer once had an appeal before the Illinois Appellate Court in a case that had been before the court previously on an interlocutory appeal. During oral argument, he unwittingly attempted to reargue a point that was decided against his client the first time the case was up on appeal.

After several minutes, one of the justices stopped him midsentence and asked if the court was not bound to follow its earlier decision, referring to the opinion on the interlocutory appeal. To the amusement of everyone in the courtroom, the uninformed advocate replied, ''But Your Honor, that case is distinguishable on its facts.''

Soliloquies Sound Stilted

Take notes on the important parts of the record and prepare an index. Use whatever format works best for you, but remember that an index is of value only if it provides a handy guide to the entire record.

You have selected a theme, sketched a framework, and reviewed the record and the authorities. Now you are ready to commit your argument to paper.

Working with the brief, your indexed record, and your notebook of authorities, prepare the first draft of your argument. Include all the details; worry about paring down your argument later.

Do not write a speech. If you have a full-blown text to read, you will be more interested in delivering your soliloquy than in answering the judges' questions. Also, a prepared address almost always sounds stilted.

Besides, it is unlikely that you will get through the text as you prepared it. Questions may make you lose your place and keep you from reaching important points. Lawyers with prepared texts also tend to give the off-putting nonanswer, "I'll get to that point in a minute," in response to a straightforward question.

So, how do you get your argument down on paper? Outline. Think in terms of the headlines rather than the whole story. You may have to jump from one section to another, depending on the questions the judges ask, and the more elementary your notes are, the easier this will be.

At the same time, carefully craft and write out a handful of key statements as you would like to say them to the court and integrate them into your outline. Because you will not be able to recite a whole prepared text, you should have a few sentences or phrases that capture your main points. Work on strong, affirmative phrasing in the active voice.

Some lawyers still feel the need to sound "lawyerly." Fancy, polysyllabic language obfuscates rather than elucidates.

Remember Strunk and White's admonition, "Omit needless words." Do not tell the court that "an incorrect standard was erroneously applied by the trier of fact when it considered and admitted the out-of-court statements offered for the truth of the matter asserted therein." Say "the trial court applied the wrong standard in admitting the hearsay statements."

Decide which points might need subtler phrasing. If you are prepared to concede a point, be sure not to give away your whole case. Sometimes a concession can enhance your credibility by making you appear reasonable. Yet the way you concede the point must be carefully planned.

We recently opposed a constitutional challenge to a state statute with a severability clause providing that, should a court find sections, words, or phrases of the act invalid, the remainder would nonetheless remain in effect. The trial court held that both of the operative sections of the act violated the due process clause.

Objectively, the constitutionality of each section was somewhat dubious. But we were not prepared to concede that. Addressing severability in our opening argument could have come across as such a concession.

797

We decided not to raise severability in our opening argument unless questioned about it but to address the issue on rebuttal if the court questioned our opponent on the point. Although you can never really plan your rebuttal, sometimes you can anticipate that an issue will be best addressed at that stage of the argument.

The strategy worked. During opening argument, our lawyer focused on the reasons for upholding both sections that the trial court had struck down. The question of severability arose during the appellee's argument, and our lawyer responded in rebuttal.

Coping in this way with a point that otherwise might have been perceived as a concession had several advantages. First, it allowed us in our first pitch to tell the court what we really wanted it to do—to uphold the entire statute. Second, it gave our lawyer a chance to listen to the court's questions about severability during his opponent's argument. Third, it provided our lawyer with an opportunity to address the court's concerns and rebut his opponent's analysis. Finally, arguing severability in rebuttal made the lawyer appear reasonable by tacitly conceding that there was another outcome we were willing to accept: the court could uphold one section of the act and find the other unconstitutional.

Bombarded with Questions

With your written outline to work from, you are ready to practice your argument. Prepare a version that uses about one-half to two-thirds of your allotted time if given without interruption. Run through this version alone to get your phrasing down.

Then present it to someone else and have him critique your argument's clarity, organization, style, and persuasiveness. Again, people who are unfamiliar with the case are often the best judges. If your argument is clear and persuasive to them, it should be clear and persuasive to the court. If you have access to videotape, now is a good time to use it.

Once you have your argument down and have satisfied yourself that it is intelligible and in basic working order, it is time to test it under fire. You are ready to present your argument to the lawyers most familiar with the case and the issues and have them bombard you with legal, factual, and hypothetical questions.

Do not worry about how long it takes to get through your argument the first few times you practice it with these people. The idea is to think on your feet and to deal with the tough questions.

Have your team members ask questions to disrupt your presentation and throw you off balance. Nothing is more disquieting than being asked about a point you intend to address last when you are only 30 seconds into your recitation of the facts. But that happens sometimes, and you should learn to roll with the punches while you are still sparring for the big match.

Learn to use questions to your advantage. John W. Davis's famous article, *The Argument of an Appeal*, 26 A.B.A.J. 895 (1940), says that the advocate should "rejoice when the court asks questions." Davis says that questions show that the court is interested in what you are saying, and they give you a chance to respond to the court's concerns.

Questions have another advantage. As you take note of the questions that come up during your practice arguments, you should be able to anticipate at least some of the major questions that the court will ask. Some issues are so significant that the court *must* ask you about them. Work the main points of your outline into the answers to these questions.

This serves two purposes. First it tells the court that you know your case, have thought about the important questions, and have logical (although not necessarily acceptable) answers. Second, it lets you make the most of your limited time by moving through your outline with the aid of, not despite, the court's questions.

Once our office had a case in the United States Court of Appeals for the Seventh Circuit involving a constitutional challenge to an Illinois law that resembled an Indiana law the court had struck down the year before. The difference between the two statutes was the heart of the case.

Our lawyer had intended to spend a great deal of time distinguishing the earlier case. During argument, he began by addressing the various reasons supporting the statute's constitutionality without mentioning the earlier case. When the court asked him about the case, he detailed the distinctions, answering the court's question and covering a major part of his outline at the same time.

As you practice with your team, anticipating questions and formulating answers, you refine continually. The entire process of preparation for oral argument is one of synthesis and clarification. It is helpful to put pen to paper to work over the rough spots even after you have gone through your argument with the people most familiar with the case and the issues.

Using flow charts or graphs while you prepare sometimes simplifies complicated points. Several years ago, a lawyer in our office had a Fourth Amendment case in the Supreme Court. In his brief, the respondent contended that the decision of our state court was based on an adequate and independent state ground and, therefore, that the Court lacked jurisdiction to hear the case.

The law governing that issue was confusing, and several recent opinions had discussed the issue without enunciating clear guidelines. Also, two justices seemed to have a special interest in the issue at the time, so it appeared likely that the issue would come up at oral argument.

Our lawyer feared that if the court got into a long dialogue on the procedural point, he might never reach his argument on the Fourth Amendment issue. He needed a quick but complete answer to a complex question.

He used a flow chart during his preparation to reduce the issue to its simplest terms. At the top, it said: "OK Counsel, don't we lack jurisdiction to hear this case since the decision below rests on adequate and independent state grounds?" Beneath that, it read: "There are three ways that this case is properly before the Court, Your Honor; count 'em." Each of the three grounds for jurisdiction was then summarized with the supporting law and facts diagrammed beneath it.

The lawyer was able to think through the issue by mapping out the problem and its solution on a 2-by-3-foot sheet of butcher paper. With this preparation, he was ready to give a satisfactory response to the first question the Court asked him, and he promptly moved on to the rest of his argument.

Except in the most extraordinary cases, charts and graphs should not be used during oral argument. Because your time is limited, you should avoid any distractions that might prevent you from making all your points. But charts and graphs can be a great aid in understanding the relationships between various facts or issues when you are preparing.

Once you feel confident in your ability to answer the hardest questions and get through your main points within your allotted time, you are ready to prepare your argument notebook.

There is no hard-and-fast format for your notebook. The only requirement is that it be arranged and tabbed so that it is easy to use at the podium. Unlike your authorities notebook, which contains all the statutory and case authority that you digested to formulate your argument, your argument notebook should contain no more than you think you will need during the argument.

The most important entry in your argument notebook will be your final outline. Like the notebook itself, the outline should be in whatever format allows for quick reference. Key words and phrases generally work best.

Jot down important record references or case names next to the major points. This way, the outline will be a handy guide to the record and authorities. It will let you find the citations you need without flipping through your notebook or fumbling with the other materials on the podium.

You may wish to use a different color ink to distinguish record references from the key words or phrases of your argument. Most people use some form of highlighting, underlining, or asterisks to call attention to the main points.

If you can, confine the outline to two 8½-by-11-inch facing pages in your argument notebook. With your outline containing key case names and record references in front of you, you may not need to turn a page during argument.

Along with your final outline, the argument notebook should include a brief index of the most important record entries. This will be more detailed than the notes on your outline but less detailed than the record index that you used in outlining your argument.

You may want an index to the major cases as well. Presumably, you will know the cases well enough not to need this, but it can be a comforting security blanket for the inexperienced lawyer.

Some people list alphabetically the 10 or 15 most important cases, with a one- or two-sentence summary of the holding and facts of each. Other lawyers group the cases according to the points they support. In any event, this list should not be more than a page or two to which you can turn if you get stumped during your argument.

Include photocopies of important statutory language, jury instructions, record excerpts, or anything else you are likely to refer to during argument. This section should be kept to a minimum, but it makes sense to have a copy of a contested statute or jury instruction at your fingertips if it is the basis of the appeal.

Finally, include brief outlines of the points that you do not intend to argue but that you covered in your brief. Despite your best efforts to anticipate the points that will most interest the court, the judges may want to hear about *res judicata*, even though you decided that the case is about commercial speech. Be ready just in case.

Mull Over the Case

If you have the time, it helps to run through one last practice argument after you have compiled your argument notebook. This final practice session will let you decide whether you are comfortable with the format of your notebook and whether you need to add or drop anything.

Leave yourself time to mull over the case as you prepare. We have set out some specific steps that can help you get ready. Yet preparation for oral argument means more than just completing a checklist of tasks. It includes random reflection, often at odd times, on the problems of your case. The essence of the case may come to you over early morning coffee or during your evening commute home.

At this point, you have done about all you can do, except for last-minute reviews of your notes and case abstracts. Your preparation has produced several tangible assets to aid you in court: your argument notebook with its outline and notes, your authorities notebook with its photocopies and abstracts, and your indexed record. But the most important thing your preparation has given you is intangible. It is the confidence you now have in your case and in your ability to present it succinctly and persuasively.

Winning on Appeal

by Daniel M. Friedman

This is a how-to-do-it piece. There is no adequate substitute in appellate advocacy for doing it. Thus this article will set forth practical considerations and suggestions based on a quarter century of my experience. This time was spent exclusively in appellate work, most of that in the Supreme Court of the United States but also in the United States courts of appeals.

First, a few general observations about appellate practice:

1. Perhaps the most important requirement—and one that many lawyers ignore—is to present your own affirmative case. A well-constructed and well-written brief should leave no doubt in the mind of the reader that the position is correct. It is not enough for the appellant to show that the lower court erred. That court's grounds for decision may be vulnerable, but even to invalidate that reasoning does not necessarily mean that the court's judgment will be reversed. The appellate court may discern other grounds on which the judgment should be upheld.

Similarly, to refute your opponent's argument does not ensure victory, since there may be other grounds for upholding his position. It is therefore essential to an effective brief that it affirmatively establish the party's case.

Of course, while establishing the affirmative case, the errors in the other side's position will be exposed. The appellant will also expose the errors committed by the lower court. Frequently, an effective presentation of one side's case will go a long way toward refuting the other side's and permit rather brief treatment of its arguments.

2. Do not simply reargue the case you presented in the lower court. A brief or oral argument that convinced a trial court may be unsuccessful

The author is a circuit judge on the United States Court of Appeals for the Federal Circuit.

before an appellate tribunal. The roles of the two courts are different. The trial court determines the facts and applies the law to those facts. The appellate court reviews the decision of the trial court to ascertain whether the latter committed reversible error. In the appellate court, the lawyer's function—depending on which side he represents—is to convince the tribunal that the lower court did or did not commit reversible error.

3. Avoid significant emotional involvement in your case. Under our adversary system, the function of the lawyer is to make the most effective presentation on behalf of his client. It is not his role to decide whether his client is right; that is the function of the court, not the lawyer.

Personal Attacks

An effective presentation of a case requires the lawyer to deal not only with its strengths, but with its weaknesses, as well as the strengths of the other side. To deal with them, you must be aware of them. If a lawyer becomes convinced that his client's position is totally correct and his opponent's case totally without merit, he loses the objectivity essential to effective advocacy.

A good brief must take account of the weaknesses as well as the strengths of both sides. If a lawyer becomes so convinced of the rectitude of his client's position that he can see no merit in anything the opponent argues, he will lose a substantial degree of effectiveness in representing his client.

In preparing his brief and oral argument, a lawyer inevitably becomes convinced of the soundness of his position, and there may be times when he finds it difficult to understand how the decision could go other than in his favor. A lawyer whose brief and oral argument do not carry the stamp of conviction and certainty is not an effective advocate. But every good advocate is aware of the weaknesses in his case and the strengths in his opponent's, and presents his case to reflect those considerations.

4. Do not make personal attacks upon your opponent, his lawyer, or the lower court that decided against you. Although such comments may give you and your client personal satisfaction, they will harm rather than aid his cause. They add nothing to the analysis of the case, they are likely to antagonize the court, and they may create sympathy for your opponent. If you are the recipient of a personal attack, whether on your skill or your integrity, it is best to ignore it and stick to arguing the case before the court.

5. In the United States Department of Justice, different lawyers usually handle a case on appeal. To some extent this reflects the huge volume of litigation the department handles and the increased efficiency that specialization permits. But the handling of appeals by lawyers not

803

involved in the trial of the case also reflects the judgment that other benefits result from the process.

By the time a case reaches the appellate court, the lawyer who has been involved in it from its inception usually has fixed views about its theories and presentation. If he handles the case on appeal, he probably will continue to urge the theories he argued—whether successfully or unsuccessfully—in the lower court. A new lawyer taking a fresh look at the case on appeal, however, may view it somewhat differently and use his fresh insight to shift the theories and approaches, at least in emphasis. This change in approach may avoid some of the pitfalls that led to a loss in the lower court or strengthen the grounds upon which an affirmance is sought.

Of course, the lawyer handling the case on appeal cannot function in a vacuum; he should work closely with the person who handled the case below and give him the opportunity to review the brief before it is filed. New or altered arguments that seem effective to the second lawyer may have to be dropped or changed because of factual problems or events at the trial level of which only the trial lawyer is aware. Moreover, for individual practitioners and small firms such a shift in responsibility may not be feasible. But where it is possible—in larger firms or in government agencies—the practice has substantial advantages.

A brief must be carefully and thoroughly organized before it is written. There is nothing worse than a rambling document that sounds as if it had been dictated off the cuff and filed virtually without change. That kind of brief is difficult to follow, frequently repetitious, often internally inconsistent, and always unpersuasive.

The basic organization of the brief should be developed at the outset. If the case is complicated and has a number of issues, an outline of the brief can be helpful in organizing the material and presenting it most effectively. Often the preparation of the outline discloses flaws in the tentative order or structure of the argument. That leads to changes that sharpen the presentation. If the facts are lengthy or complicated, an outline of them, broken down into subdivisions, either chronologically, by subject, or by a combination of the two, may be helpful in writing the statement portion of the brief.

Poor Writing

Good writing is the key to an effective brief. Good ideas are frequently lost or buried in poor writing.

Write simply and clearly. Avoid long and complicated sentences; short simple sentences are best. If necessary, break a complicated sentence into several separate sentences. A period followed by a new sentence is often better than an "and." Write in the active rather than the passive voice. "The court held" is both shorter and more effective than "It was held by the court."

1. *Facts*— The facts are often the most important part of a brief. If the court can be persuaded to take a particular view of the facts, the legal conclusions may follow almost automatically.

The facts must be stated with absolute accuracy. They cannot be over-stated. If the record shows that three people attended a meeting, do not say "a large number" or "many." Do not state as a fact something that is only an inference to be drawn from the facts. If the record shows only that three people were in Chicago, do not state that they met there. The latter conclusion is an inference that perhaps may be drawn from their presence in that city, but if the point is important, it should be made in the argument portion of the brief, not in the statement. The statement should be wholly objective, not argumentative.

The facts, accurately stated, should be organized to present the most effective case. They should be marshalled selectively. If there are adverse facts that the other side will stress, bring them out yourself, and explain them away or minimize their significance. That is better than to permit the other side to present them first and then accuse you of ignoring them. It also creates a good impression with the court, since the judges see before them a candid and forthright advocate.

State only the relevant facts. That the appellant is a New Jersey corporation, chartered in 1923 and with its principal place of business in Cleveland, may well be irrelevant to any issue in the case. Detailed dates may be unnecessary. It may be immaterial whether suit was filed on January 23 or January 29, 1961, or whether suit was filed in January or February, or whether it was filed in 1961 or 1962.

2. *Statutory materials*— If dealing with a statute, explain what it does and describe its various elements and requirements. If the statute is complicated, it should be summarized and thus simplified. Quote the critical language; it is ineffective merely to summarize in the text what the statutory provision does, and then append as a footnote a lengthy paragraph of statutory text. The reader is likely to ignore the footnote, and then be unable to follow the argument. If only a sentence or two of a lengthy statutory provision is involved, quote only those words; the entire provision may then be set forth in a footnote if it will be helpful to the reader.

In any case involving a statute, the starting point should be the statutory language. A brief that ignores or casually passes over the language of the statute and goes directly to the legislative history or statutory policy suggests that the language does not support the argument and therefore is being ignored. Although it is sometimes difficult to make the language support the argument, it is a rare case in which at least a plausible contention cannot be based on the language. If the language is so clear that there is not room for argument, the case will probably not be in court.

There naturally are exceptions: if the language unequivocally points in one direction but the legislative history is directly contrary, the language cannot be relied upon. But that situation should be explicitly stated at the outset.

3. *Captions*— Appropriate headings and subheadings increase clarity. They explain where the brief is going and provide signposts along the way. The captions should be as brief as possible, but sufficiently explicit to describe the point. Numbering of subpoints may also be helpful. That tells the reader that the brief is turning to a different but related aspect of the same subject.

4. *Underlining and other emphasis*— Effectiveness is lost by extensive capitalization, underlining, boldface type, or italics. These devices are helpful only if used on those rare occasions that emphasis dramatically drives a point home or draws an important contrast. But if every third sentence is underlined, there is no emphasis at all. The strength of an argument ultimately depends on its force, logic, vigor; a weak argument does not gain strength by undue emphasis of particular portions.

5. *Quotations*— Quotations from cases are effective only if used sparingly. Quoting at length from opinion after opinion is a lazy way of writing a brief, and the finished product is likely to be unconvincing. Long before the brief approaches its end, the reader has begun to skip over the quotations. If used with discretion, however, pertinent quotations from judicial opinions give a brief force and emphasis.

Quotations must be accurate and not taken out of context. Avoid the cropped quotation, with critical qualifications omitted, or an ellipsis of language that significantly alters or limits the language quoted. Not only will the other side point out the omission, but this technique also will likely destroy the court's confidence in the lawyer and make the court doubt other statements in the brief that are not similarly flawed.

6. *Unnecessary adjectives and adverbs*— Frequent use of colorful adjectives and adverbs does not make an argument more effective. The claim that a particular statutory provision covers the case does not gain strength by stating that it "clearly," "plainly," or "patently" does so. Nor is the phrase "the purpose of the rule" improved by inserting the word "plain" or "clear" before the word "purpose." Indeed, words like "patently" or "obviously" suggest that what follows is the *ipse dixit* of the writer, rather than a necessary conclusion.

7. *Weak arguments*— Do not make every argument possible. A poor argument is easily demolished. Its very presence suggests weakness, on the theory that the lawyer's case cannot be good if he is forced to rely upon unsound contentions.

8. *Technical material*— Technical material must be presented with sufficient clarity that someone not expert in the field can understand it. Too often, lawyers who work in specialized areas fail to realize that the judges to whom the arguments are made do not have a similar knowledge and expertise in the field. Avoid technical jargon. Simplify and ex-

plain complicated concepts in specialized areas. Explain them in terms that laymen can understand.

9. *Abbreviations*— The current practice of using initial letters of lengthy titles as a shorthand reference can become extremely confusing. Use of "NLRB" for the National Labor Relations Board presents no problems. But it is not unusual to read a sentence such as this in a brief:

> The Port Association of Freight Forwarders ("PAFF") entered into a Agreement Covering Loading Practices in the Inner Harbor ("ACLPIH") with the Seattle Chapter of the Union of Warehousemen and Stevedores ("SCUWS").
> Two pages later the following appears:
> Under the ACLPIH, SCUWS was required to consult with PAFF before taking that action.

This problem could be avoided if, instead of using these initials, the writer employed shorthand terms, such as "Association," "Agreement," and "Union." In place of the gibberish just quoted, the sentence would be fully comprehensible and succinct:

> Under the Agreement, the Union was required to consult with the Association before taking that action.

10. *Footnotes*— Footnotes have a place in a brief, but only a limited one. They may be used for citations, although it distracts the reader to shift his eye constantly from text to footnote. At some point, he is likely to stop reading the footnotes altogether. A large number of case citations ordinarily is unnecessary. The two or three pertinent cases cited for a proposition are more likely to be noticed if in the text.

Footnotes also may properly be used to block off areas of a case to note issues that the case does not involve. But the lengthy "talking" footnote, which runs on for paragraphs and even pages, should be avoided. Those footnotes usually involve either lengthy discussion of issues that are not in the case and therefore need not be discussed, or demonstrations by the author of the research he has done (which, unfortunately, has proven unnecessary) or his erudition. This type of footnote, although the staple of a scholarly law review article, has no place in an appellate brief. Busy judges, who must read a large number of briefs, are unlikely to read footnotes that are discursive and argumentative and contain intricate arguments.

11. *Anticipating the other side's arguments*— Often it is dangerous to anticipate the other side's arguments and answer them in the opening brief. Those arguments may be made better than the other side would state them. Or they may be made in a way that enables the other side to restate or refine the arguments so that they are more difficult to answer. Moreover, a well-presented affirmative case may remove all need to answer the other side's contentions in any detail.

Of course, there are some cases in which it is so clear that the other side will make certain arguments that they safely may be anticipated and answered. But generally the practice is not wise.

12. *Length*— The story of the lawyer who explained that he filed a 50-page brief because he did not have time to write a 25-page brief reflects the reality that tight writing is time-consuming. But it is so much more effective that it is worth the additional time and effort.

Briefs should be as brief as possible. Too many briefs are too long. Excessive length results from making unnecessary arguments, stating unnecessary factual detail, giving too many lengthy quotations, repeating needlessly, and failing to think the case through and organize it carefully before beginning to write. There are complicated and difficult cases that require lengthy exposition, but most briefs could be improved by tightening and sharpening. The shorter the brief, the more effective it will be.

There are lawyers who file a reply brief in every case. Those briefs usually merely restate, in shorter form, the arguments made in the opening brief. If the arguments have been fully and effectively presented in the opening brief, there is no reason to restate them in a reply brief.

There are situations, however, where a reply brief is necessary. If the other side makes strong arguments that were not anticipated or answered, or cites pertinent authorities not previously considered, a response is in order. Sometimes additional legislative history is presented for the first time in the case and must be dealt with. A reply brief also is useful in answering technical or detailed arguments—such as those involving complex mathematical calculations—that cannot effectively be dealt with in oral argument.

A reply brief should be short, punchy, and incisive. Do not file a reply brief, as some lawyers do, that is primarily concerned with correcting minor errors the other side has made. Such a brief is a sign of weakness: it suggests that you have no good answers on the merits, and therefore are nitpicking at the periphery.

In recent years, the Supreme Court has been flooded with amicus curiae briefs in most major cases involving important constitutional or statutory issues. Many of those briefs contribute nothing significant to the case, but merely repeat, in varying form, the arguments the parties already have made. Their major function seems to be to enable the organizations submitting them to gain publicity and to be able to advise their memberships after the decision that the Court adopted their views.

Sometimes an amicus curiae brief can make a real contribution to a case. If the amicus has important factual material that is not available to the parties, the brief is likely to aid the court in reaching a correct decision. Occasionally an amicus will develop a persuasive argument that the parties have overlooked. There are instances where the brief of one of the parties is inadequate and a good amicus curiae brief will clarify the issues. Generally, however, amicus curiae briefs contribute little or nothing to the decision of a case and require the court to do considerable unnecessary reading.

Oral Argument

The oral argument is the capstone of the appellate process. All that has gone before comes to a head in a brief period of spoken exposition and exploration. It is the only occasion that the court can question counsel, test his position to determine its strengths and weaknesses, and determine the implications and consequences of the arguments. It is the one chance the lawyer has to find out what is troubling the court and to assuage those doubts. It also is the single occasion when the opposing parties can be forced to face up to the difficulties in their positions. In the briefs the parties may pass each other without ever meeting, but at oral argument they can be forced to lock horns and determine which one must give way.

Virtually all judges who have written on the subject attest to the importance of oral argument. Although recently many courts have limited or eliminated oral argument in a substantial percentage of cases, they have done so not because of doubt about the desirability of oral argument, but because the step was necessary to deal with the great increase in appellate litigation.

An oral argument should not repeat the brief. It must focus upon the critical points in the case and expound them simply and effectively. A good oral argument should be a dialogue between the advocate and the court in which, through joint exploration of the case, the court gains information about the critical facts and issues and insight into the policy judgments that must illuminate and shape the decision.

A friend once suggested that the function of oral argument is to make the court want to decide in your favor, and that of the brief is to provide the court with the tools to do so. An effective oral argument will reflect this distinction.

Thorough preparation is the key to a good oral argument. Advocates have different methods of preparation, but all good ones know their case completely when they stand up in court.

The advocate must be completely conversant with the record. There is nothing worse than a lawyer who, when asked where something is in the record, fumbles around in the document, desperately turning the pages, and finally answers: ''I know it's there, but I can't put my finger on it.'' Similarly distressing is the lawyer who, when asked whether the record shows so-and-so, responds: ''I think it does, but I cannot cite you the page.'' Even worse, of course, is the lawyer who is forced to answer the question whether the record shows a particular fact with: ''I don't know.'' There is no excuse for an advocate not knowing what is in the record, and inability to answer questions about the record creates a bad impression with the court.

Knowledge of the record also is necessary to answer factual misstatements of the other side. Nothing is more effective than, after the other side has stated that the record contains no evidence on a particular point, his opponent can give a couple of record references to the evidence the other side has overlooked.

It is the rare lawyer who can know the record sufficiently well that he does not need some aids to help him quickly find critical portions. Some tab the record to identify various items. Others make a summary of significant portions, which can quickly furnish the necessary citations. Still others make notes of particular items they may want to have quickly available, such as important testimony or findings. Some use a combination of these techniques. Each advocate must find the devices most suitable for him, but some method of identification and recall is essential.

Methods of preparation also vary greatly. Some lawyers first read the record, then the briefs, then the cases, and only then prepare the actual argument. Others reverse the procedure. Hybrid methods are also used. Again, the proper procedure depends upon the needs of the particular lawyer.

Some lawyers have their colleagues conduct a moot court. Others talk the argument out, presenting it to the walls of the office. Going through the argument orally is helpful, because a presentation that seems fine on paper or in the mind may disclose flaws when spoken.

An important part of preparation is thinking through the implications of the position and developing answers to anticipated or possible questions from the bench. All too often a lawyer makes what sounds like a plausible contention, only to stand mute when a judge points out to him a difficulty that he apparently had not recognized and cannot answer.

Thorough preparation is also necessary to give the lawyer sufficient flexibility to be able to alter the order of presentation in response to questions. Early in the argument the court sometimes asks counsel to discuss a point he had planned to treat with later on. Only a well-prepared lawyer can quickly shift course and argue the point as effectively as he would have done if permitted to follow his original order of presentation.

Presentation of Content

To be effective, an oral argument must explain and argue the case simply and clearly. It may be necessary to oversimplify in order to make the issues and arguments easily comprehensible. Complicated issues are difficult to understand when presented orally. Figures are hard to follow when spoken; a string of percentages and dollar amounts quickly becomes meaningless to the court, no matter how convincing it may be after detailed study. If you must use figures, give one or two, not a large number.

At the beginning, tell the court in a few words what the case is about, what issues it must decide, and how the case reached it. If a statute is involved, read the critical language; do not just talk in generalities about the legislation. If the statute is complicated, with repeated cross-references between different sections, take it step-by-step, summing up at appropriate points to ensure that the court understands the legislation.

Do not try to cover every point in the case in oral argument. Select the two or three strongest points, and focus on them. If the court is concerned with other issues, it will ask about them. If a point is highly technical and difficult to expound orally, tell the court so and that it is fully covered in the brief. Again, if the court has questions about it, one of the judges will let you know.

In some cases it may facilitate presentation to use large maps, charts, or tables on an easel in the courtroom. If the route of a particular motor carrier is important, a map properly marked may explain the situation with greater clarity than any oral description. Instead of a large chart or map placed before the court, small copies of those documents may be distributed to the court before the argument, with the statement that counsel will refer to them.

An oral advocate must speak clearly, not too fast, and loudly enough to be heard. It is embarrassing when a judge asks a lawyer to speak louder. A staccato delivery in which arguments cascade from the advocate's mouth in an uninterrupted flow is difficult to follow and ineffective. Similarly, it is ineffective if a lawyer delivers his entire argument at a high pitch of passion; emphasis is telling only if used occasionally.

There are a few lawyers who can present an argument without any notes. That is the best technique, but unfortunately it is the rare advocate who has this skill. Notes, as detailed as necessary and with suitable underlining, are the best method of presentation. Key sentences and phrases may be written out when it is important to state a point exactly.

An argument should never be read. It sounds stilted, no matter how skilled the speaker. Contact between the court and lawyer is lost when the lawyer's eyes are glued to the page and do not face the court.

The facts are at least as important at oral argument as in the brief and probably more so. If they are properly shaped, the legal conclusions seem almost inevitable. Facts must be stated accurately and not overstated. If opposing counsel has misstated the facts, correction of his errors is likely to destroy his credibility with the court. Similarly, if you are inaccurate and the other side exposes the flaw, the court will lose confidence in you.

Do not discuss cases at length, or read copiously from them. The lawyer who drones on with a series of statements that ''In Smith vs. Brown, the court stated as follows,'' followed by a lengthy quotation, quickly loses the court's attention. If there are one or two controlling or pertinent authorities, discuss them briefly. But be familiar with the principal cases cited in the briefs, so that you can answer questions about them.

Cases often have serious problems and difficulties. If your case has them, it is better for you to bring them out and explain them away than for the other side or, even worse, the court, to raise them. The difficulties will not just go away if you ignore them. By bringing them out yourself, you can discuss them in the context and with the emphasis you want, and also take some of the wind out of the other side's sails.

If you are the appellee, a good opening is important. Sometimes the other side provides the opportunity. In answer to questions, or in the zeal of advocacy, a lawyer may overstate his case or exaggerate the breadth or reach of his opponent's position. Setting the case back on course often is an excellent way to begin.

Answering Questions

Questions from the bench usually put the advocate to his hardest test. Many lawyers dislike questions, on the theory that they interfere with a prepared presentation. Lawyers should welcome questions. It is the one opportunity to find out what is troubling the judges, and to answer them.

Although counsel engages in a lengthy colloquy with a single judge who seems hostile to his position and unconvinced by the answers, even that exercise may not be in vain. Other judges who have not said anything may have similar doubts, and the answers to their colleague may have satisfied them.

When a question is asked, answer it immediately. Do not say, "I'll get to it later." Often the lawyer never does get to it, and the problem that was bothering the judge continues to do so. Moreover, questions are most effectively dealt with when asked, not later on. If the question requires a detailed explanation that the lawyer was planning to give subsequently, the question may be answered briefly when asked, with the statement that it will be discussed in detail later.

If a question is embarrassing or exposes a weakness in the case, do not give an evasive answer. Answer it directly, with whatever explanation can best extricate you. Judges are quickly aware when counsel is evading a direct answer, and are likely to call him on it. Courts become irked and lose faith in a lawyer who tries to avoid answering difficult questions. Conversely, they respect a lawyer who faces up to difficult problems questions pose and answers the inquiries forthrightly and directly.

If a lawyer does not know the answer to a question, he should not try to bluff his way through it. He is likely to get caught and be seriously embarrassed. There is nothing wrong with saying "I don't know"—

provided you do not have to say it too often. If you are unclear about what the judge is asking, so indicate.

While a professor at Harvard Law School, Mr. Justice Frankfurter told his students that cases rarely were won in oral argument before the Supreme Court but often were lost. A case can be lost at oral argument if the lawyer is unable to give a satisfactory answer to a difficult question. Sometimes counsel makes a concession—indeed, perhaps, without being aware he is doing so—that gives his case away or make his position untenable.

Divided Arguments

Arguments in which more than one counsel appear generally are a mistake and sometimes are a disaster. Although the lawyers have arranged what appear to them to be a suitable division of the case, often the court questions the first lawyer about points the second is to cover, and vice versa. Unless each lawyer has fully prepared the entire case—including the portions he is not to argue—the result is confusing and usually they fail to make an effective presentation.

It is even worse when three or four lawyers argue a single case, popping up and down as one follows the other to the lectern. Barely has one gotten into his subject when he must yield to his colleague. When there are several parties, each represented by separate counsel, it may be difficult for all to agree to let one of them make the entire argument, but that is the best course. Some lawyers have solved the problem by retaining an outstanding person to make the oral argument for all of them, thereby insuring that no feathers are ruffled and no pride injured.

Rebuttal can be extremely useful, but it can also be dangerous. If there are effective answers to significant points the other side has made, make them. Rebuttal should be short and vigorous; do not waste time with correcting minor errors or making peripheral points. It can be extremely effective to show in rebuttal that the other side has misstated the record or important decisions.

The danger in rebuttal is that once the lawyer stands up, he is open to further questioning. That questioning can get him into trouble that he would have avoided had he remained silent. If, at the close of the appellee's case, the court appears sympathetic and unimpressed by the other side, there is no need to rebut. On the other hand, a good rebuttal can change the whole atmosphere of a case. One thing is certain; do not rebut unless you have something really important and telling to say, and unless you say it vigorously and effectively.

Protecting Your Record on Appeal

by Ellis J. Horvitz

Justice Frankfurter once characterized appellate courts as forums in which "[d]isappointed litigants and losing lawyers like to have another go at it." *Ferguson v. Moore-McCormack Lines*, 352 U. S. 521, 524 (1957). Ambrose Bierce in *The Devil's Dictionary* defined an appeal as putting "the dice into the box for another throw." But no litigant can simply have "another go at it" or "another throw" of the dice. The appellate process is both complex and bounded by rigid rules of review. Unless a lawyer is careful, he will find not only that he has lost his case at trial but also that his record reveals no errors for an appellate court to review.

An appeal differs fundamentally from a trial. At trial, a dispute is judged on its merits. On appeal the record below is reviewed to determine whether there was prejudicial error that probably affected the outcome of the case. The process is also different. At trial, the spoken word governs: witnesses testify, judges rule and instruct, attorneys examine, cross-examine and argue. By contrast, the written word dominates the appellate process: a written record of the proceedings below is prepared, written briefs are submitted based on the record, and the court ultimately submits a written opinion deciding the issues in dispute.

The starting point for any appeal is the written record. Unless the appellant can demonstrate prejudicial error in the record, his cause is lost. Since the record is merely a written transcription of what occurred in the trial court, an appellant's counsel must be sure that any error will be preserved in the record before the trial court and that it is then incorporated in the appellate record. For the winning party, protecting a record for

The author is a senior partner in Horvitz Levy & Amerain of Los Angeles. He is a past president of the California Academy of Appellate Lawyers and teaches appellate advocacy at the University of Southern California Law Center.

appeal means taking the necessary action in the trial court to deprive the other side of a legal issue that might be asserted as grounds for reversal on appeal.

Protecting the record on appeal can occur at every stage in the trial court from the initial pleading through a motion for new trial and other post-judgment motions. At the pleading stage demurrers, motions to dismiss, motions to strike and motions for summary judgment are all useful and often necessary procedural tools for raising and preserving an issue for appeal. For example, defenses based on a statute of limitations, lack of personal jurisdiction, improper venue, insufficiency of process or service, to name a few, may be waived and lost for appeal if not asserted in a motion or a responsive pleading.

Where a defect in a complaint or a defense may be correctable, conventional wisdom counsels against early identification to avoid educating the opponent to the defect in time to permit correction. Underlying this approach is the belief that the attorney who files a defective pleading can often be relied upon to prepare inadequately and to try the case poorly. A second reason why counsel frequently avoid summary testing of legal issues is that if the motion is successful all presumptions on appeal favor the losing side, thereby giving the opponent an appellate issue that might otherwise disappear if the case were tried on the merits.

New Varieties

In recent years, however, new varieties of cases have appeared where the conventional wisdom should not always apply. In most jurisdictions, new causes of action have arisen and old ones expanded, particularly in the law of torts. Additional parties, formerly immune, now find themselves subject to liability. Wronged parties are permitted to recover for new and previously unrecognized damages. These new appellate decisions expanding liability have a ripple effect in the trial courts like stones thrown into a pond. Following each such decision, the trial courts are flooded with new complaints, some designed to test the outer limits of the new rule.

In these cases, it may be helpful to both sides to test the new theory at the pleading stage. For the plaintiff, who frequently lacks financial resources, it may be far better to test the new theory on the basis of a carefully drafted complaint rather than incur the expense, delay and uncertainty of preparing for and participating in a complex trial. From the defendant's perspective, a successful motion bars the plaintiff from proceeding to trial and possibly stumbling upon a viable theory other than the one pleaded.

In jurisdictions where the pretrial conference is more than an occasion to set the trial date, it may offer an important opportunity to raise and preserve issues for appeal and at the same time bury an opponent's issues. Where the pretrial conference order governs the subsequent course of the case, it may be useful to obtain rulings on a variety of issues, including the availability of causes of action and defenses, appearance of witnesses, admissibility of evidence, and right to jury trial. All matters on which the court has ruled should appear in the pretrial order or be reflected elsewhere in the record. Without such care, the record may not present the omitted issue for appeal.

To preserve any issue concerning the oral proceedings at trial, there must be a transcript of the proceedings. Otherwise, it will do about as much good on appeal as taking a photograph with a camera that has no film in it. Counsel should therefore determine in advance if a reporter is routinely furnished and, if not, request one. This applies to every stage of trial, starting with voir dire examination of jurors, and including all testimony, conferences at the bench or in chambers, instructions, closing argument and argument on motion for new trial.

One of the easiest and most common ways to lose an issue for appeal is to fail to object before the trial court. Without an objection, the error is deemed waived. A close relative to waiver is the doctrine of invited error. A party cannot raise on appeal an error of his own making, such as challenging the admissibility of evidence he introduced, the correctness of an instruction he requested, or other error he caused. There is an exception to this rule where a party's error is simply a defensive tactic against a prior erroneous ruling. This may occur where a party is forced to offer evidence or request instructions on an irrelevant issue the trial court permitted the other side to raise over objection.

Limited Purpose

When he considers the introduction of evidence, a lawyer should be particularly careful in introducing evidence of limited admissibility. The record should show that the evidence was offered for a limited purpose only and that the jury was instructed accordingly.

Where a party is prevented from introducing evidence, it is critical that the record reflect an appropriate offer of proof. Counsel should state for the record precisely what evidence would have been forthcoming had the witness been permitted to testify. Without an offer of proof, it becomes virtually impossible to demonstrate prejudice as a result of the erroneous exclusion of evidence. There are two exceptions to this rule: (1) Where the question is asked of an adverse witness on cross-examination, many jurisdictions do not require an offer of proof, and (2) an offer of proof may be unnecessary where the substance of the disallowed evidence is apparent from the questions asked.

Where counsel seeks to exclude an opponent's offered evidence, a timely objection must be made along with a statement of the grounds for the objection. Where the question is answered before counsel has an opportunity to object, a prompt motion to strike will generally serve in lieu of an objection. Many able trial lawyers, to avoid antagonizing court and jury by repeated objections, allow opposing counsel to introduce harmless, inadmissible evidence. To avoid the need for repeated objections to a particular line of questioning, a lawyer may be able to make an early motion *in limine* or otherwise obtain a ruling that a single objection applies to the entire line of questioning.

Just as important as protecting your own record is suppressing the temptation to improve your adversary's record. All too often an essential element of the plaintiff's case in chief or the defendant's case is missing after direct examination, but the deficiency is then remedied by the meticulous cross-examination of opposing counsel. The message is clear: Never cross-examine adverse witnesses, particularly expert witnesses, merely to have them repeat their story. If you do not have a specific objective in mind and cannot think of any good reason to cross-examine an adverse witness, don't do it.

It frequently happens that significant conferences are held in chambers and are not reported. If rulings and stipulations are made that have a bearing on the case, the matter should be reflected in the record, either by having a reporter present in chambers or by repeating the ruling or stipulation for the record. Be certain that the record contains an adequate and accurate description of the ruling or stipulation.

In some courts, opening statement and closing argument to the jury are not reported unless specifically requested. If you anticipate the possibility of an appeal, request a reporter. Even if opposing counsel may not be guilty of misconduct, statements and arguments to the jury may contain valuable concessions.

Misconduct by counsel must be objected to at the time it occurs or it will be deemed waived. On the other hand, if objection is made and the court admonishes opposing counsel and instructs the jury not to consider the misconduct, thereby etching it even more deeply in the jurors' minds, it is deemed cured. Thus, in raising misconduct before the trial court, counsel is damned if he does and damned if he doesn't. On balance, it is more prudent to make the appropriate objection and take one's chances with the jury. If the verdict is unfavorable, counsel can move for a new trial before an appeal. Moreover, an unfavorable verdict may itself be some evidence of the prejudicial nature of counsel's misconduct. This is one of the many instantaneous judgment calls trial counsel must make, a burden that counsel on appeal is spared.

In the rare case where misconduct on the part of the trial judge occurs, even greater skill and judgment must be employed. If, for example, the judge has insulted or ridiculed counsel or a witness, or has indicated partiality toward one of the parties, counsel may take exception to the judge's remark and lodge an objection or motion for mistrial for the record. In some jurisdictions a motion for new trial based on misconduct may be required to preserve the issue for appeal.

817

Treasure Chest

Jury instructions are treasure chests of reversible error. Therefore, counsel should think carefully before requesting the court to give instructions of dubious validity or application. This is particularly true where a lawyer has a strong case and the instruction involved is not likely to have a significant impact on the jury's deliberations. Several experienced trial lawyers have told me that they withdraw questionable instructions when they feel their case has gone well.

There is also a danger in requesting too many instructions. You may find yourself the victim of the invited error doctrine. This rule not only prevents a party from complaining about an instruction that he himself has requested, it also prevents him from challenging an erroneous instruction given at the request of opposing counsel or on the court's own motion if the party has requested a substantially similar instruction.

Most jurisdictions provide for special verdicts, special findings or interrogatories to the jury in support of a general verdict. These informative aids have found increasing favor in the appellate courts, spurred in part by the adoption of comparative negligence rules in over half of the states. These procedural tools may be helpful or even vital to effective appellate review by enabling the appellate court to understand exactly what the jury's decision was on specific issues of fact.

Timely Objection

Where findings of fact and conclusions of law are prepared either by winning counsel or by the court, it may be necessary for the losing party to file timely objections and proposed counter-findings in order to preserve issues pertaining to the inadequacy of the findings. Conversely, the respondent will want to preserve victory by seeing to it that the findings and conclusions are properly drafted and support the judgment. Failure to make a factual finding on a material issue or other error in the findings or conclusions may be grounds for reversal.

A handful of jurisdictions require as a prerequisite to appellate review a motion for new trial which assigns as error the specific issues to be raised on appeal. Most jurisdictions have no such requirement. Nevertheless, in most jurisdictions it may be desirable to make a motion for new trial, particularly in a jury case. The trial court sits as a thirteenth juror and generally has far broader discretion than an appellate court to grant or deny a new trial.

If you are unfortunate enough to receive an adverse verdict, but fortunate enough to have the court grant you a new trial, be sure that the court's statement of reasons or grounds for granting the new trial are adequate. If the court order granting a new trial is defective in any respect, seek correction by the trial court, but do so with great care. If the trial judge will not accept your suggestion, you may have presented your opponent with an issue on appeal from the order granting the new trial.

After you have done everything necessary in the trial court to preserve your issues on appeal, those issues must be included in the record on appeal. This is done by designating for inclusion in the written record all court documents, exhibits and testimony of oral proceedings that may be relevant to the issues on appeal. You can make all the right moves in the trial court, but it is useless if you fail to designate the proper record on appeal. On the other hand, if you inadvertently create or inherit a deficient record on appeal, check the court rules carefully. If the omission can be corrected, most appellate courts will permit correction or augmentation on a proper showing.

To succeed on appeal, an appellant must demonstrate reversible error in the record on appeal. This is accomplished by making all the right moves in the trial court to preserve error, assuring that the error is properly recorded in written documents filed in the trial court or in the reporter's transcript of oral proceedings, and in designating all necessary materials for inclusion in the record on appeal. From this foundation, you can then take your best shot at "having another go at it."

Points on Appeal

by Arthur L. Alarcon

Using the language of the business world, it is the lawyer's job to sell or communicate the righteousness of his client's cause in the midst of many other earnest competitors for our attention. Those of you who practice in the federal courts are aware of our rising case loads. In the last two years, case participation per judge has increased from 184 to 286. At the same time, the number of cases filed in our court has increased by 19 percent. The result of our increased output, in response to an overpowering case load, is that we have less time to spend on your cases than did our predecessors.

Until you file fewer appeals, or we get more judges, all of us will have to accommodate ourselves to this reality—an increasing workload, given the same number of workers, means less time available per unit.

This condition, in turn, places a greater burden on appellate lawyers to produce briefs of the highest professional standards to assist judges in producing dispositions that are well-reasoned and correct. Because of our crowded argument calendars and mounting filings, you have an ever-increasing responsibility to your clients to write carefully, clearly, and briefly to gain our concurrence in the justice of your cause.

With the foregoing solemn sermon in mind, I will proceed to set forth some of my observations after five years of reading briefs and hearing oral argument as a circuit judge.

Make a Record

First, make a record. Justice Tobriner of the California Supreme Court once observed that trial judges spend their careers searching for the truth, while appellate judges look only for error. We simply cannot re-

The author is United States Circuit Judge in the Ninth Circuit Court of Appeals. This article also appeared in the June 1984 issue of ABTL REPORTS, *published by the Association of Business Trial Lawyers.*

verse a judgment unless error appears on the record.

Those of you who confine your labors to litigation exclusively and leave to others the handling of the appeal should be mindful that many errors can be disregarded by appellate judges if a proper objection is not made in the trial court. Let me set forth some examples of trial omissions we see frequently.

1. Affirmative defenses and matters in evidence such as immunity and res judicata must be pleaded and proved in the trial court. Failure to do so results in waiver. *See Santos v. Alaska Bar Ass'n*, 618 F.2d 575, 576–77 (9th Cir. 1980) (immunity and res judicata may not be raised for the first time on appeal).

2. Error in the admission or exclusion of evidence cannot be raised on appeal unless a timely objection or motion to strike appears on the record, stating the specific ground of objection, unless the ground is apparent from the record. FED. R. EVID. 103(a) (1). (Do not rely on your assessment that anything is apparent from the record—we may not agree with you.)

3. Evidence improperly received under one theory at trial may not be successfully defended on appeal on alternate grounds where a finding of the existence of requisite foundational facts must be made by the trial court before admission. *See Giordenello v. United States*, 357 U.S. 480, 488 (1957) (A party cannot support admissibility on a theory raised for the first time on appeal because it would unfairly deny the other side an adequate opportunity to cross-examine the government's witnesses or adduce rebuttal evidence). *See also Sims v. United States*, 405 F.2d 1381, 1383 (D.C. Cir. 1968). (Consideration of alternative bases for the admissibility of evidence received at trial refused because the argument was not presented to the trial court.)

4. Alleged attorney or judicial misconduct cannot be raised on appeal without a proper objection or motion unless it is so flagrant that the plain error rule applies (Again, I would not gamble that an appellate court will clean up behind you by holding that your silence is excused by the plain error rule).

5. Error in the giving or failure to give an instruction may not be raised on appeal unless a timely objection setting forth the specific grounds therefor has been made in the trial court. FED. R. CIV. P. 5.

Appellate courts are tolerant of the errors described above based on the theory that it is unfair to the trial judge and opposing counsel to sit back until an unfavorable judgment is rendered before raising issues that could have been cured by swift remedial action. If you fail to make a proper objection you risk an adverse ruling from an unsympathetic panel holding that had you done your job, the trial court would have ruled properly and your client would not have suffered.

821

Writing Briefs

Second, brief writing. My concerns about brief writing are not new. Unfortunately, the same problems continue to recur.

One. Use simple, clear language. Don't obfuscate or pettifog in setting forth your contentions in an effort to show your command of the English language. I may be too busy to look up a polysyllabic term you have used to impress us. (For example, don't use words like obfuscate, pettifog, or polysyllabic. Why not say "confuse" or "imprecise"?)

Two. Be blissfully brief. State your point concisely and once. Nothing is more irritating than to have the same question stated again and again in varying ways for forty-five sleep-inducing pages of redundancy. Let me add an incentive to the production of short and pertinent briefs. The longer you make your brief, the more likely that most of the preargument analysis of your case will be turned over to a law clerk who just finished the bar exam.

Three. Be accurate in summarizing the facts. A brief writer should summarize facts with scrupulous accuracy. If you slant the facts, or ignore evidence that hurts your position, you can be sure your opponent will highlight in outraged detail the facts you have distorted or omitted. Misstating the record can irretrievably damage your credibility with the court. You don't want to waste precious time at oral argument trying to rehabilitate yourself.

Another rule frequently overlooked is that which requires appellate courts to accept as true every fact that supports the judgment and to disregard contradicting evidence submitted by the losing party. We read many briefs that set forth only the evidence presented at trial by the appellant. We are then asked to reverse on the ground that the trier of fact erred in entering judgment for the appellee in the face of such overwhelming evidence. That type of brief lightens our workload. We must summarily affirm—although in the hands of competent counsel, reversible error might have been readily demonstrable.

Please don't misunderstand me. When you can demonstrate that error was committed, it is vitally necessary for you to present a fair summary of the evidence on *both* sides. If the evidence at trial was evenly balanced, then the impact of error in the admission of evidence, or the instructions on the theory of the case or the defense, or misconduct in closing argument may have been more damaging than in a case where the evidence in favor of the prevailing party was overwhelming.

In setting forth the facts, *always* refer to the page and line of the record where the testimony appears. If you fail to do so, you place the burden on the appellate court to search through the entire transcript to find some verification for your claim. That is not our job. We may fail to do it for you, or we may try and be unable to locate support for your position. Now let me hasten to add that most of us will in fact search the transcript for the facts you rely upon even if you do not refer us to the record. We do so, however, with some discontent and lingering doubts about your competency and the integrity of your arguments.

Four. In discussing the law that applies to your case, always cite and analyze those authorities that do not appear to support your position. You have an ethical duty to do so. Rule 3.3(a) (3) AMERICAN BAR ASSOCIATION, MODEL RULES OF PROFESSIONAL CONDUCT, Rule 3.3(a)(3); Section 6068(d), CAL. BUSINESS AND PROFESSIONS CODE § 6068d (West 1974). *See Shaeffer v. State Bar*, 26 Cal.2d 739, 747–48, 160 P. 2d 825, 829 (1945) (counsel must direct the court's attention to a decision that contains a decision contrary to his position).

If you fail to do it, you can be assured that your opponent will cite and discuss all the law that undermines your contention, with enthusiasm. If opposing counsel misses it, one of my law clerks will probably find it. If we discover these cases *after* argument, you have lost your opportunity to persuade us that these cases are either distinguishable, or should not be followed because of faulty reasoning, or that recent developments in the law support your position.

I have just finished working on a matter in which we were asked to adopt the law of another circuit. Counsel failed, however, to point out that the Ninth Circuit Court of Appeals had expressly rejected this precise suggestion four times in the last 12 years. Opposing counsel enjoyed the opportunity to expose this appalling and fairly obvious dereliction of duty. Counsel's lack of candor placed a great strain on our collective judicial temperament. We are, unfortunately, human.

Five. You should limit your issues on appeal. In every long trial, error is committed by one of the participants. With very few exceptions, only *prejudicial* error will result in a reversal. Use a scalpel and not a shotgun in shaping your appeal.

If, after combing the record, you find 37 errors that range in gravity from minimal to devastating, don't argue with equal vigor and passion that each one, standing alone, was prejudicial. You devalue your argument if you assert that error in overruling an objection to a compound or leading question compels reversal if you also argue that damaging hearsay evidence was admitted. (Has any court reversed because a trial judge erroneously permitted a witness to answer a leading or compound question?)

Try to limit your appeal to the three or four most serious issues in the case that you feel best demonstrate prejudicial error.

Present your strongest argument first. Don't hide it in the midst of a collection of your weakest points. If you put your best contention last, the court may lose confidence in your ability to recognize prejudicial error when you see it before they reach that issue.

Six. You waste your time giving us a long string of citations for relevant case authority that clearly supports your position. Just cite the earliest case in point and the most recent in order to demonstrate the continuing vitality of the principle you are espousing. Be sure that you read the cases you cite.

Recently, I read a brief that cited a case for a principle of law that was important to the writer's client. No jump citation was given to the page where the legal question was discussed by the court. In reading the case, I learned the reason. The favorable proposition appeared in a headnote but not in the text. Always refer the court to the exact page where your point is covered. Do not rely on us to read the entire case to ferret out the discussion that you believe supports your view.

Seven. In citing a case that you believe contains helpful language in a matter involving comparable facts, always give the court a brief statement of the facts. By so doing, you can state with accuracy and confidence that the law expressed in the cited case should be applied to your cause because the facts are analogous. Too often, counsel find themselves in the embarrassing position of being unable to answer the court's question, ''Counsel, what were the facts before the court in that case?'' A citation without some discussion of the treatment of the issue is not very helpful.

Eight. Avoid the use of footnotes. Avoid the temptation of parading the brilliance and depth of your research into related areas of the law by crowding your brief with footnotes. If the point advances your client's cause, put the discussion in the text. Do not bury it. If the discussion is not relevant, leave it out.

Footnotes force the reader to break his concentration on your discussion of an issue to chase after an often extraneous diversion. One of my colleagues has stated publicly that he never reads footnotes before oral argument. If you want our undivided attention, you should put your comment in the text.

Nine. Long quotations are exasperating and distracting. Further, they sometimes appear to be a lazy person's substitute for analysis. If you must quote, select the precise sentence that advances or supports your discussion of the law. If you use an ellipsis to show that you have omitted part of the quotation, do not cheat. If you leave out language that hurts you, we will find out. Whenever I see an ellipsis, I check to see what you have omitted. Your deliberate omission may emphasize what you may have tried to avoid.

Ten. If you are relying on a statute, rule, or regulation, include the relevant text in the body of your discussion. Do not assume that the judges have memorized 18 U.S.C. § 651(3)(c) or that they will enjoy being assigned the job of looking up the law and picking out the portion that advances your position. Make it easy for the judge to rule in your favor. Don't take the chance that a tired, aging judge may decide that your citation must not be too important or you would have set it out.

Remember also that most federal judges become generalists. Do not assume that we are as familiar with the buzz words or the numbers of the statutes or regulations that are commonplace in cocktail conversations among the experts in your specialty. (My wife has pointed out that it is not very charming for me to ask my California criminal defense lawyer friends in her presence if they are going to pursue their *Rost* motion and 995 before the 1368 hearing.) Do not do the same kind of thing to a judge who may not have heard of or visited a "scenes a faire" before your copyright case. Err on the side of explaining too much. We need your help in getting to the heart of your problem.

Eleven. The rules of our circuit require that you set forth the standard of review on appeal. 9TH CIR. R. 13(b)(2). On each calendar we have at least one lawyer who has no notion of the standard that limits our review of his appeal.

Twelve. Conclude your brief with a half-page summary of your argument and a clear statement of the precise relief you want from the court. If you want us to instruct the trial court to do something upon remand, suggest to us the precise direction we should give to serve your client's interests.

Thirteen. Do not duck any of your opponent's contentions or arguments. You may think it is so weak it deserves no answer. We may find it persuasive after a first reading. If you ignore it, we may be persuaded that it is irrefutable.

Oral Argument

Third, oral argument. After listening to oral arguments for many years, I have compiled the following list that I would try to follow if I were to return to the practice of the law.

1. Do not waive oral argument unless you have abandoned all hope or would be willing to guarantee reimbursement to your client if your confidence in the ultimate success of your position is wrong.
2. Do not waste time in summarizing the facts. The judges have read the briefs.
3. Start by advising the court you will be happy to address any questions before you proceed with your argument.
4. Begin your argument by outlining the dispositive issues you wish to address.
5. Do not argue every issue with equal fervor. Choose your sure winners. If you cannot tell, you are in trouble.
6. Be ready to concede that some of your contentions may not be as compelling for reversal or affirmance as the rest.
7. Do not get angry at the judge who attacks your position. He may be your best supporter on the appeal.
8. Respond to the court's questions. If you are caught by surprise—admit it and ask for the opportunity to file a letter brief. Do not wing it.

9. Speak up if you wish to be heard. We are getting older.
10. Make your argument as interesting as possible. Do not read and do not quote. Use your own words.
11. Quit if you sense you are ahead. You do not have to argue the allotted time.
12. Never argue credibility if you are the appellant. The court may view any contested facts or inferences in favor of your opponent.
13. Know your record and the exhibits. Be ready to cite exact pages and lines or exhibits by number to support your argument.
14. Be prepared to tell the court how you would like the dispositive paragraph to read if you could write the opinion.
15. Ask the court if there are further questions before you sit down. It is O.K. to thank the court for its courteous attention to your cause. Surprisingly, few lawyers do.

The Art of Brief Writing: What a Judge Wants to Read

by Albert Tate, Jr.

An appellate advocate wants his brief and argument to contribute to the success of his client's cause. My primary theme, however, is how the appellate brief can help the court, not the client. A court only uses briefs that help it make decisions. If counsel regards the appellate brief as more than a perfunctory, functionless tool, he therefore must prepare it primarily for the court. The judges may then rely on it as they prepare the decision. Win or lose, this always benefits the client, because *his* counsel has contributed to the decision making.

To help the judge, the brief need not be eloquent or even persuasive about the client's cause. It is sufficient that it furnish ready access to the record, the authorities, and the reasoning by which the lawyer's client is to prevail. If the client is to lose, the brief and oral argument should at least enable the judges to understand the authorities and reasoning that support the client's position. (Perhaps 50 percent of the briefs filed with our courts are so one-sided or superficial as to be essentially discarded after an initial skimming. From the point of view of both client and court, it is as if no brief at all had been filed.)

Before suggesting in more detail how briefs may perform this function most effectively, I should perhaps consider the appellate judge for whom the briefs are prepared.

As counsel writes the brief, he should visualize the judge, what he thinks he is trying to do in deciding the case, and how he will use the brief. He should keep in mind what the judge's approach may be to the problem, what will interest him, and what he may disregard as irrelevant or useless. The brief is not written to be fed into an impersonal,

Albert Tate, Jr., is a Senior United States Circuit Judge, United States Court of Appeals for the Fifth Circuit, and formerly an Associate Justice of the Supreme Court of Louisiana.

computerized justice machine, but to be read and studied and weighed by fellow human beings.

The present-day appellate judge performs in a milieu of ever-increasing appellate volume. In less than a decade, the law explosion has tripled the number of cases many appellate courts must decide each year. In my own court, for instance, each of the seven judges must participate in deciding nearly 2,000 appeals or supervisory writs during the year.

Yet the appellate judge today is essentially the same sort of man as his predecessor of two (or ten) decades ago. He shares the same central perception of his function and duty: in each case that comes before him, he accepts as his personal responsibility the duty of seeing that individual justice is done within the framework of the law.

The result that seems "just" for the present case must be a principled one that will afford just results in similar conflicts of interest. The brief, then, is addressed to a human judge, not an abstract legal technician. This judge has an initial human concern that the litigants receive commonsense justice, but he also realizes that the discipline of legal doctrine governs his determination of the cause.

High Volume

In writing for this judge, counsel must also keep in mind that the volume of cases exposes him to several hundred appeals a year. Consequently, he knows much law and has seen many approaches to appellate advocacy. He quickly recognizes sham and superfluous arguments. Each appeal in his burgeoning caseload competes for his interest and limited time. Considering all this, the appellate advocate will do well to concentrate on the strengths of his case, as concisely and lucidly as possible, if he wants to attract the judge's interest in and reliance upon his own brief.

In this era of high volume, the brief serves a function that is increasingly important: to obtain oral argument or, at least, an articulated opinion deciding the appeal.

Perhaps 80 percent of appeals present issues clearly destined to appellate rejection. They may involve the contested but correct application of settled law, or an attack upon a factual finding of the trier not clearly erroneous. They may even involve frivolous contentions or ones the appellate court has consistently rejected in the past. Since an articulated and published opinion will add nothing to the law or the parties' understanding of why the appeal resulted in an affirmance, some appellate courts have devised summary proceedings to eliminate full-scale consideration of such appeals and to provide for their disposition without opinion or oral argument. This helps to preserve more time to hear, study, and prepare opinions in appeals involving more substantial or uncertain issues.

In the summary instances, the appellant's brief is the primary basis upon which the screening is made. To assure a hearing beyond the brief, let alone to prevail, the appellant must strongly demonstrate the possibility of individual unfairness or of a truly arguable question of law, or its application, in need of articulated resolution. The appellee's brief, of course, should demonstrate the lack of merit to these contentions, if indeed there is none.

Although my suggestions primarily concern preparing a brief to help the court in deciding a case by an articulated opinion, after oral argument, the same considerations apply even more strongly where the appeal may be decided without oral argument or by summary affirmance or reversal.

I should not overemphasize the skills of advocacy in determining the result in the bulk of litigation. Although appellate advocates frequently disagree, most appellate judges feel that they might ultimately have blundered upon the correct result without the assistance of counsel. Litigation should be decided on the basis of the law and the facts, not on the technical skills of counsel. Most appeals are decided by the pleadings and evidence in the trial court and the law on the books, and not on the basis of appellate advocacy. This of course is as it should be.

On the whole, the effective appellate advocate's contribution will be to sharpen and hasten the decisional process while assuring full consideration of his client's position. Also, by his choice of issues and authorities, counsel may add important dimensions and perspectives to the rationale and future usefulness of the decision.

Generally speaking, the form and organization of a brief should serve two purposes. First, it should be so complete within itself that in writing the opinion the judge need not refer to extrinsic sources, except to confirm the accuracy of the presentation. Second, the brief should allow the court to understand it and obtain access to the record or authorities cited without spending any unnecessary effort.

Court rules about the form of the brief typically provide for (1) a ''preliminary statement,'' which states in one or two sentences the general nature of the action and the procedural history of the case; (2) a ''statement of the issues''—a succinct listing of the questions presented for decision; (3) a ''statement of facts''—a concise narrative summary of the material facts in the context of which the litigation arises; (4) the ''argument''—points of law or fact, discussed under appropriate point headings, with analysis of the legal problems on argument of law, and with presentation of the accurately cited evidence on argument of fact; and (5) the ''conclusion''—a succinct summarized reiteration of why the judgment should be reversed or affirmed, sometimes including a suggested decree. Whether the rule of court so provides or not, this format presents for ready comprehension by the judge the essential issues of law in their factual context.

829

The "preliminary statement" and the "conclusion" are self-explanatory. Before I note what I find helpful to the client's cause and to the court in a brief's statement of the issues, statement of the facts, and argument, I have some general observations applicable to the brief as a whole.

Be Concise, Lucid

Recognizing the mass of reading and research competing for the judge's time and attention, appellate counsel should revise to be concise and lucid. From the mass of materials available, he should repeatedly select and discard—*select* essential issues, facts, and authorities; *discard* and winnow others ruthlessly, along with excess words and repetitious argument.

Counsel's worry, of course, is that what he winnows as superfluous might, if left, somehow catch the court's eye. Hence, he errs unwisely on the side of inclusion. Unless there is particular reason to believe otherwise, however, a safe rule is to assume that appellate judges will have the same good sense as counsel in concluding that the winnowable issue or fact is indeed noncontributory. Part of the craft of counselling is the ability to balance the *possible* contribution of the issue or fact against the undoubted loss of impact and persuasion of a brief that wastes the court's time on side trails that lead nowhere.

Need I add that accuracy and candor should guide counsel's selection of the issues and statements of factual argument and of the arguable import of the authority relied upon? Inaccuracy in statement or misleading argument will obviously destroy the court's confidence in the brief.

For readability and easy comprehension, the brief should be coherently organized, with appropriate headings and subheadings to facilitate ready reference to topics of special interest. Short sentences and relatively short paragraphs allow immediate understanding. Italics should be sparingly used, exclamation points practically never, and capitalized boldface type not at all; rather, the emphasis should result from the content and arrangement of the thoughts. From reading several thousand briefs a year, a judge has learned that what is shouted and exclaimed could usually be whispered, if it needs mouthing at all.

Counsel should accurately note page numbers for facts in the record and have someone proofread for accuracy of doctrinal and decisional citations, including page numbers of quotations; case citations must be Shepardized to assure their current viability. Inaccurate citations will waste the court's time and subconsciously undermine confidence in the reliability of counsel's argument as well.

The brief is a companion of the judge from before the oral argument until after the rehearing is denied, and it will be referred to or reread as often as necessary. The judge to whom the decision is assigned will continually consult the effective appellate brief—issue by issue and fact by fact—in his research and as he drafts the proposed opinion. Primarily on the basis of the briefs, each other judge of the panel will decide to sign the proposed opinion or instead to dissent, concur, or suggest changes in it.

Even before the opinion is assigned and circulated, the participating judges all use primarily the briefs to prepare for oral argument and to reach a tentative conclusion for the opinion-assignment conference immediately following argument. After the opinion is issued, they again consult the briefs in deciding whether to grant a rehearing. At all stages, each participating judge relies largely upon the briefs when deciding whether to engage in independent research of the record or the law.

At the outset, the statement of the issues acquaints the court with the essence of the case. It should provide a concise statement of the controlling questions for decision. The statement of the issues is not the same as a statement of counsel's contentions; it is rather an attempt to state fairly to the court the crux of the case in terms of the precise legal issue to be decided and of the ultimate facts that gave rise to this issue. Ideally, the question should be stated so that the opponent must accept it. When the opposing parties frame an issue differently, the party who misstates what the court concludes to be the real issue loses much credibility.

Briefest Terms

The questions should be stated in the briefest and most general terms, without names, amounts, or details. The conciseness of what is expected is indicated by some court rules that provide that this statement should not ordinarily exceed fifteen printed lines and never more than a page. Of course, the statement of a central issue includes every subsidiary issue fairly comprised within it, which then may be developed more fully in subheadings of the argument proper.

In my experience, counsel often overlook the importance of the statement of the central issues and sometimes prepare it as an afterthought after having written the argument. The judge's initial reaction to the seriousness and merit of the appeal is often based upon this indication of what issues counsel considers to be vital to his case; in the light of this statement, and of the statement of facts, the judge tends unconsciously to screen the appeal as substantial or not, even though this impression may yield to later study. When the questions at issue are effectively stated, the judge is able to decide and to read and understand more quickly the argument that follows in the brief.

The questions should be one or few in number. Rare is the appeal with a great number of reversible errors; when a great number of questions are presented as serious issues, the judge's expectation that most or all of them are insubstantial is rarely disappointed. It has sometimes seemed to me that a great number of insubstantial issues raised might have been abandoned, and the argument section more tightly concentrated on the arguable issues, if counsel had attempted to articulate concisely the precise questions he wished the court to decide *before* writing his brief. I have never been able to understand the motives of counsel who raise a great number of issues they must realize the court will decide adversely to them: the few arguable issues raised by them tend to be regarded as nonmeritorious by association. It is like shooting with a blunderbuss crammed with eggshell, which will annoy and distract without affecting the outcome.

Selecting and characterizing the issues may determine the course of the appeal. Llewellyn once described an unsuccessful appeal, stated in terms of the duty of an "agent," and suggested that a contrary result would have been reached if the issue had been instead characterized as the duty owed by a "broker." In my own experience, an appeal—stated and briefed in terms of a subrogation issue—was nearly lost, until our court, after much study, discovered that the issue was one of indemnity. The issues stated should be selected not only in view of the facts and the state of the law, but also in the light of what will appeal to the particular reviewing court.

The most helpful statement of an issue is in terms of its facts, not as an abstract question of law. The statement should show the precise point of substantive law and its applicability to the facts at hand. Thus, "Was plaintiff guilty of contributory negligence?" does vaguely indicate the general issue; but how much more helpful to the court's concentration and understanding of the issue is: "Plaintiff's car struck the rear of a vehicle operated by the defendant, who had made an emergency stop without signalling. Where plaintiff admits that he could not have stopped his car within an assured clear distance ahead, is he chargeable with contributory negligence so as to bar his recovery?"

Do Not Argue Too Much

An overly argumentative statement of the issues turns me off. Self-evident, overtly self-serving, or overgeneralized statements are not helpful and may be misleading (and thus prejudicial to the court's appreciation of counsel's sincerity). Thus, the issue in a tax case, if stated as "Whether a man is taxable on income which his son receives?" is not indicative of the true issue: "Whether the owner of coupon bonds should include in his gross income the amount of coupons which he detached and gave to his son several months before maturity?" I should note that, if fairly stated, a formulation of the issue is not out of order when it subtly suggests the response desired by the litigant; as, for instance, in the tax collector's reformulation of the above issue to suggest the taxpayer's evasion of tax on income from property still owned by him: "The taxpayer owned coupon bonds. Several months prior to maturity of the interest coupons he detached them and gave them to his son, retaining the bonds themselves. Is he relieved of income tax with respect to such interest coupons?''

The statement of the facts is regarded by many advocates and judges as the most important part of the brief. In the first place, regardless of how much the judge knows about the legal issues beforehand, he does not know the facts until he reads this statement. Second, law and legal principles are designed to produce fair and socially useful results when applied to *facts*. This fundamental aim of law lurks always in the mind of the judge. If the application of the given legal principle produces a result deemed unfair by the judge, he will wish to study carefully whether indeed the given principle was truly intended to apply to the particular facts before him.

This initial statement of facts should not be confused with any argument about the facts to be advanced in the subsequent section of the brief. By this initial statement, counsel attempts to state accurately and with reasonable fairness the material facts, without failing to disclose those which are contested. The attempt is to summarize, without too much unnecessary detail, only those facts that are most cogent and persuasive, without omitting unfavorable circumstances, so that the court may understand the basic factual background of the legal issues. Accurate reference to the transcript or appendix should be provided to allow the court immediately to verify counsel's facts as stated. Counsel's selection, arrangement, and emphasis of these facts, if without sacrifice of accuracy, may readily suggest to the court how the legal issues presented should be decided.

John W. Davis and Frederick B. Wiener are numbered among America's greatest appellate advocates. Davis said:

> [I]t cannot be too often emphasized that in an appellate court the statement of the facts is not merely a part of the argument, it is more often than not the argument itself. . . . The court wants above all things to learn what are the facts which give rise to the call upon its energies; for in many, probably in most, cases when the facts are clear there is no great trouble about the law. Davis, *The Argument of an Appeal,* 28 A.B.A.J. 895, 896 (1940).

Wiener has said:

> The real importance of facts is that courts want to do substantial justice and that they are sensitive to the ''equities.'' Consequently the objective of the advocate must be so to write his statement that the court will want to decide the case his way after reading just that portion of the brief. Wiener, *Essentials of an Effective Appellate Brief,* 17 GEO. WASH. L. REV. 143, 145 (1949). *See also,* to the same effect, K. LLEWELLYN, THE COMMON LAW TRADITION: DECIDING APPEALS 238 (1960).

Judicial writers agree on the importance of the statement of facts, among them Justice Robert H. Jackson:

> It may sound paradoxical, but most contentions of law are won or lost on the facts. The facts often incline a judge to one side or the other. Jackson, *Advocacy Before the Supreme Court*, 37 A.B.A.J. 801, 803(1951).

Chief Judge Irving R. Kaufman of the Court of Appeal for the Second Circuit has said:

> Let the narrative of facts tell a compelling story. The facts are, almost without exception, the heart of the case on appeal. . . . The facts generate the force that impels the judge's will in your direction. "Appellate Advocacy in the Federal Courts," Address before Association of the Bar of the City of New York (April 21, 1977).

In the "argument" section of the brief, counsel is a partisan advocate urging the court to adopt his analysis of the legal authorities and his view of the facts. Here the points of law will be treated consecutively. Succinct headings and subheadings should indicate to the court the thrust of the argument on each point (e.g., "Appellant had notice of the defect and therefore is not a holder in due course"), following which counsel will analyze and argue the legal and factual data in support of each heading. If there are numerous points, a final summary may provide for the court a ready synthesizing review of the arguments covered that point toward counsel's position.

From the court's point of view, the principle of "select and discard" should here apply also. Only truly arguable points should be selected and relied upon; unessential or diversionary points rarely affect the result, and normally they should be discarded.

Generally, a point that goes to the very heart of the case should be argued first. An experienced judge will usually select the strongest issue for study first. But the judge initially may not know what is counsel's strongest issue, unless counsel, based on his knowledge of the facts and his legal research, so directs the court.

When the judge has decided on affirmance or reversal, he usually addresses the appellant's strongest premise first in drafting the opinion. If the judge accepts the premise and decides to reverse, often he need not research or address other points relied upon by the appellant. As a psychological matter, appellant's counsel should force the court early to face head-on his strongest argument; otherwise, the judicial impression of its forcefulness may be lessened, if its study is not reached until after the judge has half-decided on affirmance, having rejected counsel's previous arguments.

In many instances, of course, counsel cannot argue his strongest point first because of reasons of logical priority. He must then set forth his arguments in a logical step-by-step progression, relying upon placement, emphasis, and the "Statement of the Issues" to indicate the greater importance of a particular point. Also, the appellee's order of argument is normally directed by sequential response to the points raised by the appellant; if, however, the appellant has minimized some overriding argument in favor of affirmance, the appellee should likewise emphasize early the forcefulness of his strongest argument. An appellee may safely ignore an illogical sequence of insubstantial arguments, although he should explain why he does so, and he should explain at some point why the appellant's arguments lack merit, rather than ignore them.

The type of argument must of course vary with the type of case and the type of issue. However, counsel should prepare it, as he selected its points and the issues of his appeal, with some knowledge of the tribunal to which the brief is submitted. For example, a Louisiana intermediate court decides many workmen's compensation cases each year; detailed jurisprudential and statutory argument may unnecessarily burden a brief to that court, whereas it might enlighten the Supreme Court of Louisiana, which in this legal area only occasionally issues full-scale opinions. Similarly, there is no point in urging that a court overrule a prior decision if you know that court never overrules decisions. The same court may not be as reluctant to "distinguish" the same prior decision, with identical practical consequences. Some courts, or some panels of a court, are more oriented to technical issues of law or to innovative arguments than are others.

About citations: a lawyer should include as few as practical, mainly those of the leading or more recent cases. Also, where possible, citation should be made to decisions of the court that hears the appeal; the judges are more likely to be familiar with them and accept them without additional verifying research. If counsel intends to rely heavily on a particular decision, it is well for him to make the effort to summarize its facts, and to show that the cited case is applicable to the *facts* of the present case. Quotations from the case, if used at all, should be restricted to the relevant sentences. Opposing authorities should be distinguished, not ignored, lest the court feel that counsel cannot answer them.

Blind citation of precedent without functional analysis is of minimal assistance. As Justice Rutledge observed:

> What judges want to know is why this case, or line of cases, should apply to these facts rather than that other line on which the opponent relies with equal certitude, if not certainty. Too often the *why* is left out. Rutledge, *The Appellate Brief*, 28 A.B.A.J. 251, 253 (1942).

Further, to me, it is always useful and often persuasive to find counsel's position supported by an authoritative treatise or illuminated by law review commentaries and ALR annotations.

835

Arguments over facts are rarely persuasive if founded solely upon long excerpts of questions and answers from the transcript. The most useful and persuasive technique, if accurately done, is a concise summary of the factual evidence on the issue, including that opposed to counsel's position, with accurate reference to the pages in the transcript that verify these statements. Key phrases or statements, rather than entire dialogues, may usefully be quoted to give flavor and force if not done out of context. The strongest factual arguments emphasize the commonsense fairness of the client's position, or call into play the undoubted application of settled law; but it is important that, in so arguing, counsel does not distort or ignore contrary facts, however much he evades their forcefulness by explaining their context or supposed lack of weight.

For appropriate cases, such as where the court is essentially concerned with weighing policy values in the selection or creation of a rule with future consequences, I personally would like to see more nondecisional authority. Social statistics of which we may take judicial notice, for instance, sometimes afford data by which to evaluate practical implications of a proposed interpretation. Thus, in deciding whether a personal-injury lawyer violated ethical canons by his occasional advance of small loans to his impoverished client when the latter was beset by financial emergencies, we found to be of some aid the Bureau of Census reports concerning the population's poverty level. *Louisiana State Bar Ass'n v. Edwins*, 329 So.2d 437, 447 (La. 1976). In criminal cases the standard of fairness, or a better interpretation of our own procedural law, may often be formulated with the aid of studies and recommendations founded on both scholarship and practical experience, such as the American Bar Association Standards for Criminal Justice, the American Law Institute Model Code of Pre-Arraignment Procedure, or the National Conference of Commissioners on Uniform State Laws' Model Code of Criminal Procedure.

I have already mentioned the importance of headings and subheadings to clarity and immediate understanding. I should add that charts or tables may inform the judge at a glance of what he could similarly understand only with minutes of reading and of puzzling out words and figures. Complex machines or locales, such as unusual intersections, may likewise be quickly demonstrated or understood by a diagram, where it might take hours for counsel to write (and minutes for the court to read with understanding) words purporting to convey the same information.

Some Other Writings

Before concluding, I should note several publications that treat with much greater detail, with practical illustrations of effective and ineffective technique, effective appellate briefing: G. ROSSMAN, ed., ADVOCACY AND THE KING'S ENGLISH (1960); E. D. RE, BRIEF WRITING AND ORAL AR-

GUMENT (4th ed., 1977); and F. B. WIENER, EFFECTIVE APPELLATE ADVO-CACY (1950). *See also* Wiener, *Essentials of an Effective Appellate Brief,* 17 GEO. WASH. L. REV. 143 (1949).

In summary, the truly effective appellate brief, from the point of view of the court, is one quite similar to a superior law clerk's memorandum. It contains discussion and analysis and summary of all factual consider-ations and legal rationales necessary for the decision. Once the contents are verified, through the ready means furnished by accurate citation to the record and published material, the judge ideally should be able to dictate his opinion from the brief, including liberal paraphrasing or pla-giarizing of its concise and accurate wording. In serving through his brief as a valued research assistant to the court, counsel has certainly aided the administration of appellate justice, whether his client wins or loses.

I have emphasized my concept of the appellate brief as chiefly a vehi-cle to enable the judge to understand quickly the issues and facts, dis-puted or not, of the appeal, and for him most readily to grasp the argu-ment of counsel, in its strengths and weaknesses. I do not, however, imply that the brief's usefulness is negatived by its advocacy. By selec-tion, emphasis, and articulation, counsel properly attempts to persuade the court of the correctness of his client's position, although (if he wishes his brief to be useful to and used by the court) he must do so accu-rately and with candor about the factual and legal data applicable to the issues of the case. The more clear, concise, complete, and coherent is the brief furnished for the court's use, the more certainly will the brief afford the court access not only to the legal materials furnished by it for deci-sion, but also to counsel's persuasiveness in his brief's contention that the law and the facts demand that his client prevail.

Petitioning for Certiorari in the Big Case

by Charles G. Cole

Exxon Corp. v. United States was the classic Big Case. It lasted more than eight years and involved complex questions of federal energy law. The judgment entered against Exxon amounted to more than $2 billion. Five certiorari petitions, on behalf of 15 parties and supported by several amici, were filed in the United States Supreme Court.

Yet the Supreme Court disposed of the case in a single, crisp sentence: "The petitions for certiorari are denied." 474 U.S. 1105 (1986).

Exxon illustrated what most observers of the Court have known for some time—that big cases don't necessarily become Supreme Court cases.

There are several reasons for this: some obvious, others more subtle. First, the chances of obtaining a grant of certiorari from the Supreme Court are, in general, exceedingly slim. The Court hears an argument in only about four percent of the cases on its docket. Constitutional cases falling within the court's mandatory jurisdiction comprise some of these cases, so the prospects for the average petition for certiorari are even lower.

Ironically, the chances of obtaining certiorari in a big case are no better, and perhaps worse. Big cases often have many interconnected issues. The Court may be reluctant to review one issue because that may require accepting others and creating the risk that the Court will divide into several pluralities.

Second, big cases have big records. The Justices are scrupulous students of the record, but they cannot scrutinize extensive records in more than a handful of cases each Term.

The author is a partner in Steptoe & Johnson in Washington, D.C. He was a law clerk to Justice White during the 1977 Term.

Lastly, the attributes that make a case seem big to the litigants will not necessarily impress the Supreme Court. The number of parties, the dollars at stake, or the complexity or duration of the litigation will rarely affect the Court's decision whether to grant certiorari.

Instead, the Supreme Court has its own notion of a big case. The Court considers the nationwide impact of resolving the legal issue presented in the petition—not the size of the litigation in which the issue arises. The Court is concerned primarily with precedential impact. It wants to know how many other cases will be determined by the result in this one and whether doctrine will be affected. It evaluates these questions with an eye to the economic and social consequences for the nation as a whole.

In short, the Court often chooses small cases that present big issues over big cases with many smaller issues.

Of course, some big cases do have big issues that compel a grant of certiorari. For example, in *Sony Corp. v. Universal City Studios, Inc.*, 464 U.S. 417 (1984), the Supreme Court was asked to decide whether companies that sell home video cassette recorders to the public were responsible for copyright infringement. The eight-year-long litigation involved many corporate parties and hundreds of millions of dollars in potential royalties. The outcome of the case would affect the future of an important young industry, as well as the at-home activity of millions of Americans. *Sony* was a litigant's big case that also had every element of a big case from the Supreme Court's perspective.

But most cases—even big cases—do not. Usually a lawyer must work to persuade the Court that his case presents an issue whose resolution will affect many other cases and have practical consequences for the nation as a whole.

The first task is to identify the issue most likely to engage the Court.

The issue most intensively litigated in the lower courts often is not the most "certworthy" issue. Some secondary issues, such as a question of procedure or damages, may have greater appeal. Since the petitioner's overriding objective is to obtain a grant of certiorari, he must search for the best issue to hook the Court's attention.

The classic hook is an issue that has created a conflict between the lower courts. In fact, the Supreme Court identifies a conflict among the lower courts as the reason for granting certiorari in about one-third of its argued cases. Since the Court rarely explains its other reasons for granting certiorari, the conflicts rationale may be the easiest to identify, analyze, and invoke.

The Court's view of the role of conflicts in granting petitions for certiorari has changed dramatically over the last several decades. In preparing a petition using the conflicts rationale, it is important to understand the Court's current view.

At one time, the Court appeared to believe that it was obliged to ensure uniformity on matters of federal law. Under this theory, inconsistency on matters of federal law between two federal courts was itself an evil requiring prompt correction. Thus, a 1951 treatise on the Supreme Court declared that when two circuits reach decisions in direct conflict on a question of law, "the Supreme Court grants certiorari as of course, and irrespective of the importance of the question of law involved." R. ROBERTSON & F. KIRKHAM, JURISDICTION OF THE SUPREME COURT OF THE UNITED STATES § 322, at 629 (R. Wolfson and P. Kurland, 2d ed. 1951).

Recently many Justices have been following a different theory—what might be called the percolation theory of conflicts jurisdiction. Under this theory, a conflict is allowed to percolate in the lower courts until all theories and factual situations have been explored, and it is apparent that no consensus can be reached. When the conflict is widespread and recurring, the issue has "perked" and is ready for Supreme Court review.

Under the percolation theory, a conflict in the interpretation of federal law is not alone an adequate reason to grant review. Thus many petitions presenting conflicts are routinely denied review. Through his dissents from the denial of certiorari during the 1984 Term, Justice White identified 22 occasions when the Court refused to resolve a conflict during that Term. Apparently conflicts among the lower courts are no longer viewed as evils sufficient in themselves to require prompt correction, but only as evidence that particular issues may be difficult and ripe for review.

In view of this change in approach, what must the petitioner show to obtain a grant of certiorari based on the conflicts rationale?

First, that the conflict is a "true" conflict; second, that the conflict is recurring; and third, that it is important. Each of these criteria deserves attention in framing the question presented and in outlining the petition.

A true conflict is what Professor Felix Frankfurter called a "head-on collision" between two courts. Two decisions conflicting in dicta or even in principle are not enough. It must be clear that the *holdings* of two courts are in conflict—that Court A, if presented with the same facts as Court B, would decide that case differently. If there is any ambiguity in the doctrine of Court A that would permit it to reach the same result as Court B, the cases do not present a true conflict. The same is true if factual differences between the two cases justify different results. In these circumstances, the Justices' law clerks—who typically prepare the preliminary legal analysis of the petition—are apt to conclude that there is a "false" conflict.

A false conflict also may arise when the two decisions alleged to conflict are widely separated in time. The court from which review is sought may have considered recent developments in judicial doctrine, in the relevant body of statutes, or in the economy. The Supreme Court may conclude that the earlier court would have reached the same result had it been able to consider those developments. Thus, the reasoning goes, the alleged conflict is false.

A true conflict can exist between two federal circuits, between the highest courts of two states, or between a federal circuit and the highest court of a state. Generally, when a conflict involves only a federal circuit and a federal district court or intermediate state courts, the Supreme Court is not interested. Instead, the Court is prepared to let the issue percolate through the next level of review.

The petitioner cannot create a true conflict if none exists. But he can be artful in demonstrating the conflict.

Here some long-range planning can help. While the case is before the court of appeals, the litigant can create a record showing that the court of appeals was fully informed of the contrary views of its sister circuits but nevertheless refused to follow them. That will prepare the way for arguing that the conflict is a head-on collision.

Of course, precedents from other circuits are often included in appellate briefs to persuade the panel to adopt the litigant's position. But it is especially important to make the record for a certiorari petition after an adverse decision from the court of appeals. Then the litigant bound for the Supreme Court should file a petition for a rehearing, calling attention to the conflict between that decision and decisions in other circuits. Although this is unlikely to change the minds of any members of the original panel, it may cause the panel or another judge to acknowledge the conflict. Even if this does not happen, the petitioner still will be able to tell the Supreme Court that the court below was advised of the contrary position of another appellate court and refused to change its mind.

A word of warning. If the cases do not present a true conflict, do not try to manufacture one. Law clerks love to detect and highlight false conflicts in the memorandums they prepare for the Justices. Once the clerks uncover the false conflict, everyone is likely to lose interest in the petition. If the decisions below do not collide head-on, the litigant is better off designating the disagreements as conflicts "in principle" or as evidence of "confusion" in the lower courts.

Even if the petition demonstrates a true conflict, there is no guarantee of a grant. During the 1984 Term, for example, at least 80 percent of the cases in which the Court identified a conflict involved conflicts of three or more courts; half involved conflicts of four or more courts. For many Justices, once is not enough; the petition must show a recurring conflict.

The percolation theory suggests why. The lower courts may develop a consensus position as the issue percolates; if one court is out of step, it may be encouraged to fall back in line. In that way, the conflict may get resolved.

Alternatively, the lower courts may develop many different, competing legal theories from which the Supreme Court can choose. Also, the larger number of cases will allow the Court to see how the issue affects a wide variety of factual situations.

Finally, recurring conflicting opinions show a lively interest in the issue. Usually they are also a sign that no other institution—such as Congress or an administrative agency—is able to resolve the problem quickly.

The key to demonstrating a recurring conflict is to dig through the library for every case in which the issue has been decided. Once the petitioner demonstrates a true conflict among federal circuit courts or the highest state courts, other state cases and federal district court cases may be given weight. Such lesser authorities show the recurring nature of the issue and also may provide additional legal theories or factual situations.

Recent cases that have not yet been published are extremely important. Typically the most certworthy conflicts are those that have developed rapidly and recently because of new statutory, doctrinal, or economic developments. Decisions too recent to be published may signify such an emerging controversy. Of course, a case that has not been published at the direction of the deciding court is not as helpful because it lacks precedential impact.

The effort to demonstrate a recurring conflict presents one of the few occasions in which a lawyer will strengthen his position by presenting cases that support the opposition's legal position. This is because the petitioner aims primarily to show that the issue has arisen frequently, not that most courts have favored his position. Adverse precedent, even that not cited by the opponent below, helps because it is further proof of the conflict.

In attempting to demonstrate a recurring conflict, little is gained from mischaracterizing cases with only a marginal relationship to the conflict. The respondent or the law clerks will distinguish cases that are not really in conflict, and the petition will lose credibility. If these related cases are helpful in demonstrating that the problem is widespread and confusing—and such slightly off-point cases often are—then the best approach is to describe them as reflecting additional confusion on a related issue.

Also, in demonstrating a recurring conflict, the petitioner should avoid arguing that the decision he seeks to appeal conflicts with an earlier decision of the same court. This argument almost always backfires. The Supreme Court is likely to reason either that the court below was not aware of its prior decision—in which case the decision below is a "sport" unlikely to recur—or that the court below *was* aware of its prior decision—in which case the court below must have viewed the two decisions as harmonious. If the analysis the petitioner has invited shows that the earlier, supposedly conflicting decision remains good law in the circuit and the decision below simply represents an exception or a different application of the same legal standard, then the law in that circuit may be viewed as roughly consistent with the law in other circuits. In short, by stressing an internal circuit conflict, the litigant highlights a means of resolving the apparent intercircuit conflict.

Even if a petition has demonstrated a true and recurring conflict, the Justices may want something more. The petitioner also should show that the conflict is sufficiently important to warrant Supreme Court resolution. "Importance" as used in this context is hard to define, but it is best explained in practical, rather than doctrinal, terms. Who is affected by the conflict? In what way? How often? Can the person live with the conflict?

At one end of the spectrum of importance are conflicts about non-constitutional issues of procedure or evidence in the federal courts. An example is the long-standing conflict on the administration of the coconspirator exception to the hearsay rule, as Justice White pointed out in his dissent from the denial of certiorari in *Means v. United States*, 105 S. Ct. 541 (1984). Justice White cited conflicting opinions sufficient to show that the conflict was true and recurring, yet the Court had again refused to consider the issue. Perhaps because there is great procedural diversity in our federal system and because individual judges have wide discretion on evidentiary matters, the issues did not seem important enough for a grant of certiorari. Clearly, conflicts on such issues may percolate for a long time before the Supreme Court resolves them.

At the opposite end of the spectrum of importance are conflicts concerning rules of conduct for individuals or entities that must operate in more than one state. An example from the 1984 Term is *Pattern Makers' League of N. Am., AFL-CIO v. NLRB*, 473 U.S. 95 (1985), in which the Court upheld the NLRB's view that a union could not prevent its members from resigning from the union during a strike. The Court's opinion noted that "very few" unions had rules preventing resignations. *Id.* at 103 n.12. Yet the petitioning union did have such a provision in its national charter. The Seventh Circuit had held that a union could not restrict its members' right to resign, while the Ninth Circuit had held that it could. Thus, a national union's restriction on resignation might be unlawful in the Seventh Circuit, enforceable in the Ninth, and uncertain in the rest. The Court agreed to review the case even though the conflict consisted of only two decisions.

In the middle of the spectrum—where most of the cases lie—are cases raising issues about the appropriate secondary consequences of prohibited conduct. These cases typically address the rights of action or remedies for violations of federal civil and criminal statutes, not the conduct permitted or prohibited by those statutes. Such issues might include standing to sue under a federal statute or the applicable statute of limitations. In this middle range of cases, above all, a showing of the importance of the issue presented can affect the Court's decision about whether to grant certiorari.

843

How does a lawyer show the importance of the question presented?

First, quantify the problem. Tell how many similar cases are pending in the federal or state courts or how many incipient cases are moving through the pipeline of an administrative agency. Government reports are often good sources for such information. These include annual reports, budget statements, or rulemaking notices.

Private associations can help, too. Trade journals or other publications of industry trade associations are one source. Another is information collected by trade associations but not published. Third, the petitioner should consider putting a notice in an industry newsletter asking litigants or companies with similar problems to contact the trade association or the law firm drafting the certiorari petition.

If quantitative data is not available, the petition should discuss the practical consequences of the conflict for the petitioner. What economic opportunities has the litigant declined because of uncertainty about applicable law? Have there been additional litigation costs and delays because of the confusion created by the conflict? An accurate, detailed account of the quandary faced by the petitioner can often be as persuasive as numerical data.

Remember that the argument should focus on the problem created by the conflict—not simply on the undesirable effects of the adverse ruling below. Viewed individually, any one of the conflicting legal rules followed by the courts below may be workable, yet the uncertainty over the right rule may be hamstringing an industry or creating unnecessary litigation.

If a big case does not present a conflict, other strategies must be examined.

For example, Supreme Court Rule 17—which sets forth the criteria used by the Court in deciding whether to grant certiorari—refers to a category of cases in which ''a state court or a federal court of appeals has decided an important question of federal law which has not been, but should be settled by this Court. . . .'' This category permits the Court to initiate doctrinal advances (or halt them) in the absence of a conflict. Often the best sign that the Court is willing to consider such a case is a footnote in a recent opinion noting that a particular issue is unresolved.

Supreme Court Rule 17 also refers to cases involving the flip side of that situation, where the court below ''has decided a federal question in a way in conflict with applicable decisions of this Court.'' In reality, the Supreme Court rarely grants certiorari simply because a court has erred in applying a well-established Supreme Court opinion. The Supreme Court does not sit to correct individual errors. If there is already a clear opinion on point, the Supreme Court does not need to use its valuable time to restate the law.

More often, this category might be invoked if the court below has followed one strand of Supreme Court precedent and a different line of precedent seems more appropriate. Indeed, in most cases where the petitioner asserts that the decision below conflicts with Supreme Court precedent, the Court grants certiorari if it concludes that the issue presented involves a factual configuration that it has not addressed and that therefore requires clarification.

Whether a litigant proceeds on the basis of a "conflicts" strategy or another theory for seeking certiorari, the critical factor may well be the Justices' perception of the national importance of the issue. In every big case the petitioner should consider getting help from other sources to illustrate national importance.

First, the petitioner may seek support from amici curiae at the certiorari stage. Amici may be able to draw on their own experience to identify practical consequences of the decision below that are not apparent from the record. *See generally* Shapiro, *Amicus Briefs in the Supreme Court,* 10 LITIGATION, No. 3 at 21, 23 (Spring 1984). Of course, an amicus brief is most effective if the amici's position is not obviously compelled by self-interest. Thus, a brief from a regulated industry may carry great weight if it supports a regulation. Similarly, an amicus brief that argues for the prompt resolution of an issue but does not take a position on the merits could have substantial impact.

A second means of confirming the importance of a big case is to enlist the support of the Office of the Solicitor General in the U.S. Department of Justice. The Solicitor General has tremendous credibility with the Court, both because he represents the United States and because of his restraint in requesting a grant of certiorari. Even if the United States is not a party, the Solicitor General may file an amicus brief recommending a grant of certiorari. Moreover, after the petition and opposition have been considered by the Court, the Court frequently asks the Solicitor General for his views. The Solicitor General's answer can be decisive.

In seeking the Solicitor General's support, remember that the Solicitor General, like any other lawyer, perceives that his primary obligation is to his client, in this case the United States, and in particular the Executive Branch. The Solicitor General's office is not interested in correcting federal decisions simply because they are wrong, but it may respond to cogent arguments that the interests of the United States lie in reversal. Moreover, although the Office of the Solicitor General cannot be "lobbied" in the traditional sense, the clients of the Solicitor General can be. It is proper to seek support from the agencies or departments potentially interested in the case. The agencies then can talk to the Solicitor General, who has an obligation to listen to his client's views and, where appropriate, to follow them.

The structure of a certiorari petition in a big case should not be substantially different from that of any other petition. Two good articles about writing a certiorari petition are Randolph, *Certiorari Petitions in the*

Supreme Court, 4 Litigation, No. 2 at 21 (Winter 1978) and Baker, *A Practical Guide to Certiorari,* 33 Cath. U. L. Rev. 611 (1984). In drafting a petition in a big case, keep these guiding principles in mind.

First, resist the temptation to present a long series of questions reflecting the complexity of the litigation. All that will do is suggest to the Court that the petitioner does not have a great deal of confidence in the certworthiness of any one of the questions.

Second, do not quarrel with the court below over the facts. Any opinion deciding a case with a big record is bound to contain what are arguably factual errors. These factual disputes should not be highlighted and perhaps should not be mentioned at all. If it appears that the controversy turns on an assessment of the facts, the Court will be reluctant to take the case. The better approach is to emphasize that, even on the facts claimed by the respondent, the court below committed an error of law.

Sometimes, though, understanding a complex scientific or regulatory background is essential to appreciating the key legal issue. When this is true, provide the background information in clear terms at the outset of the petition. For example, in cases involving regulated industries, it is often useful to begin the Statement of the Case with a brief, neutral explanation of the governing statute so that the reader, often a law clerk with no prior experience in the regulatory scheme, can appreciate the significance of the facts presented in the litigation.

Lastly, avoid the "uniqueness" trap. Particularly in a big case, the petitioner may be tempted to assert that the factual background or litigation history makes the lawsuit the "first in history" or "one of a kind." From the Supreme Court's perspective, this makes the petition less, rather than more, enticing. A unique case will probably never recur. A decision on unique facts will not, in any event, have much precedential impact. Here again, unless the case is of extraordinary intrinsic importance, it is wiser to stress the ways in which the big case is similar to, rather than different from, other cases.

Finally, a word of encouragement. Small cases, too, can create good law. Even though the odds may seem daunting and your case may appear to be a small one, its issue may be certworthy. And once the Supreme Court has granted certiorari, any case becomes a Big Case.

Supreme Court Advocacy: Random Thoughts in a Day of Time Restrictions

by E. Barrett Prettyman, Jr.

I have previously ventured, however timorously, to give advice in law review journals about petitioning the Supreme Court of the United States for writs of certiorari, and about opposing such petitions when they are filed by one's adversaries. But I have curbed until now any tendency to counsel others about oral argument before our highest court. There are two reasons.

First, the subject has been brilliantly covered by a number of others, including John W. Davis and Mr. Justice Jackson. An ex-Solicitor General has written an article on advocacy before the Supreme Court, and a former member of the Solicitor General's staff has written a book that includes several sections on the same subject. Stern and Gressman, in their *Supreme Court Practice* (4th ed. 1969), p. 483 n.1, list thirteen judges who have counseled lawyers in print about arguing before appellate courts, including the United States Supreme Court. At first glance, this would not appear to be territory worth retrampling.

Second, oral argument is quite a different matter from petitions and briefs that are within the lawyer's exclusive control. In written submissions, what the lawyer chooses to say, he says, and what he chooses to leave out never faces judicial scrutiny. Advice about written submissions, therefore, goes directly to the substance and content of the attorney's argument and stands an appreciable chance of proving helpful. Oral argument—particularly before the Supreme Court—is another matter. An attorney frequently has very little choice over what he talks about, no matter how well he may have prepared himself in advance. The Justices can and frequently do take over the course of the discus-

The author, a partner in the Washington, D.C., firm of Hogan & Hartson, was law clerk to three Supreme Court justices, and practices regularly before the Supreme Court.

sion. Questions, the assertion of personalities, and conflicting legal viewpoints often combine to turn an advocate's well-rehearsed arguments into a shambles.

Despite all this, still more advice on Supreme Court advocacy may be in order. Most of the articles referred to above were written at a time when attorneys were granted an hour on each side to argue all or many of the cases heard by the Court. Today, the overriding fact of life in oral argument before the Supreme Court is that in every case (except those few granted special dispensation by the Court), the advocate is strictly limited to thirty minutes, including his answers to questions. This means that much of the prior advice about a coherent development of one's argument—stating the nature and history of the case, the facts and the applicable rules of law—may no longer apply in a practical sense, particularly when the Court is in a questioning mood.

Moreover, advocates before the Court are still making mistakes— often very bad ones. In fact, some arguments are so dreadfully dull that even a Justice sitting on his first cases would have trouble finding something of interest in them. This being so, some additional words of caution are perhaps in order.

In his famous article, "The Argument of an Appeal," 26 A.B.A.J. 895 (1940), Mr. Davis listed ten rules for the advocate to follow. I would add six more in light of the exigencies that face the lawyer before today's Court.

1. *If you are the petitioner, prepare two arguments.* The first should be about ten minutes, and the second about twenty, in length. The first argument presupposes that you are going to be bombarded with questions from the bench. If you are, you obviously must attempt to weave your main points into the answers to those questions. But the questions may be quite foreign to the main points you are seeking to make. Therefore, you should have notes that remind you of what it is you really want to get across in the brief time allowed.

The ten-minute argument will make you face up to something you should be deciding anyway, no matter how long you are allowed to argue: what, in your judgment, is the one main point that is most likely to win this case for you? No matter what questions are asked, no matter in what direction the discussion goes, you should make absolutely certain that this one overriding point in your favor is driven home to the Court at some time while you are on your feet.

In your brief, there may be any number of reasons for not placing your best point at the outset of your argument. For example, if you are making a constitutional argument, ordinarily it would not appear in fifth place in your brief on the theory that four other arguments are stronger. It would go first because otherwise the Court's reaction would be the same as any one else's: if a violation of constitutional proportions were really involved, it would not be brought to the Court's attention so late in the game.

But in a half hour's oral argument, you are not allowed the luxury of placing various points in sensible order. For one thing, if there are many questions you may have time to argue only *one* point before you sit down. For another, it may quickly become apparent that the Justices are interested in only one or two points, regardless of the ones you think should be capturing their attention. That is the reason you must "go for the jugular" in oral argument, as Mr. Davis and others have so often emphasized.

But what is the jugular? In *Hughes Tool Co. v. Trans World Airlines,* 409 U.S. 363 (1973), the Supreme Court reversed a judgment against petitioners in excess of $145 million on the ground that the challenged transactions were under the CAB's control and surveillance and thus immunized from antitrust attack. That point was number four in our brief for the petitioners and was not the first point made in oral argument. I say this not defensively, but merely to point out that even those presumably familiar with the Court cannot always judge just which argument has the best chance of prevailing. Certainly it is even a far more difficult task for those not used to the Court and who are approaching it for the first time. In any event, one must make the effort, and thus the ten-minute argument.

The reason for the twenty-minute argument, of course, is that you may not be asked so many questions, and yet you will want to reserve at least ten minutes for rebuttal. You should know within a few minutes after you have risen whether you will be forced to your ten-minute argument or whether you will be graced with the chance to give the longer version. Either way, the time flies like a sail in high wind, and your opportunity to convince at least five men to adopt your position slips all too quickly away.

In addition to the two arguments—one of which you actually plan to deliver—do not forget to map out notes, separately tabbed at the end of your notebook, covering points that you do not intend to bring up yourself but with which the Justices may confront you. These should relate not only to your own position, but to your opponent's.

I have repeatedly referred to notes. I do not agree with those who give blanket advice against standing up without notes, because on several occasions I have witnessed brilliant arguments when the podium was totally bereft of a scrap of paper. But I simply do not have the mind that allows people such as Charles Alan Wright or Anthony Amsterdam to do this; I need the crutch, if you will, of some written notes that will draw me back to sanity after a sharp exchange with the Court. I suspect that most persons reading this article will need the same crutch, whether they realize it or not.

When you prepare your two arguments, I agree wholeheartedly with those who advocate that you practice before a "moot court" of your partners or associates before the actual presentation to the Court. You should first give the argument you intend to make—not from a written speech but from key words or phrases that remind you of what you want to say. This should be done without interruption so that you can be judged on the quality and persuasiveness of your basic approach. Next, you should go through the exercise again, this time allowing your compatriots to interrupt you at will with pertinent, tough questions as well as with impertinent and wide-of-the-mark ones. The point is not only to prepare you but to dislodge you, upset you, throw you off balance, because this is precisely what may happen when you get to your feet in the real world of the courthouse.

I always put my notes on the right-hand pages of my notebook, and, even though these notes are themselves cryptic and truncated, I underline in red certain key words or quotes (which are kept to an absolute minimum). On the left-hand sheet facing each page of notes are the detailed citations to the record and to the key cases which support every statement I am making.

A number of advocates favor the use of tabs in the record to allow them to locate immediately any key sections of interest to the Court. This is satisfactory if the record is relatively small but becomes virtually unmanageable if the record is immense, and it often is in the complex cases before the Supreme Court. I favor an index of key words and phrases which I prepare myself. The index appears entirely on one page, if possible. Next to each word or phrase is the place in the record or the case citation relevant to the subject in question.

Thus, you have two ways of getting at the record or relevant cases very quickly. If you are asked about the very point you are discussing, the necessary references will appear on the left-hand page facing you, and you need not turn to any other source. If you are asked about a subject you are not then discussing, you can turn to the index in your notebook, catch the key word or phrase that brings that subject matter to mind, and again give the record or case citation without having to pick up and thumb through one or more volumes at counsel table.

It goes without saying that if you are going to prepare a ten-minute argument and a twenty-minute argument, not only must you restrict the points you wish to make to the one or two that you believe to be of crucial importance—no matter how many were discussed in your brief—but you also must stay totally away from obvious propositions of law, recitations of cases, string citations, virtually all quotations, and the like.

2. *Make a judgment about the intent and usefulness of each question asked.* I have read time and again that the questions from each Justice should be considered a golden opportunity because they reveal what is truly bothering him, and that the advocate should therefore solemnly address and fully answer each and every one of them. Of course you must answer questions—then and there. But not necessarily with the same degree of depth or precision. My own experience is that questions from the bench

are asked for a number of different reasons, not all of them of equal value or importance.

There is, indeed, the question that reveals what is truly troubling a Justice or one that he really needs answered to help him decide the case. Such a question most often seems to come from those Justices who very rarely ask questions. A second type of question is one that just happens to spring to the mind of the Justice and may or may not have very much to do with the case. He is simply inquisitive or curious; something occurred to him and so he asked about it.

A third type of question comes from the Justice who loves the battle of the courtroom, the jousting between lawyer and judge, the testing of wills and knowledge. He is having fun with you; he is enjoying himself. And the better you are, the more enjoyment he is getting. This type of questioning can be most misleading in the sense that it very seldom reveals what that Justice really feels about the case.

And finally, there is the question asked for the very simple reason that the Justice is bored. After all, he sits there day after day, week after week, year after year, listening to argument after argument. So much of it he has heard before. He has been referred again and again to the same cases (and even had some explained to him that he wrote himself). He has been told as if for the first time that due process does not allow the police to beat a confession out of a suspect, or that price fixing is a *per se* violation of the antitrust laws. One can hardly blame him if he breaks the monotony occasionally with a question, serious or silly, that simply helps him get through the day.

The point is that the advocate must decide on the spot which of these four types of questions is being asked. If the question is of the first variety—one that a Justice really needs answered—he may want to devote his entire argument to the answer, weaving his central points all through his reply. On the other hand, if the question really is not relevant or is being asked for one of the other reasons cited, the attorney must have the good sense to answer that question, with great respect, in an abbreviated fashion that will allow him to get on to more important matters. I have seen this done both very well and very badly.

One otherwise distinguished practitioner, I recall, used to throw a withering glance in the direction of the Justice who had asked what the attorney deemed to be a frivolous question, pause as if to say, ''I cannot believe you seriously intended to say what you just did,'' and then give an abrupt and cursory answer before returning to his main argument. This is obviously counterproductive, since it makes the questioning Justice feel like a fool—a very dangerous business indeed when every vote counts.

On the other hand, it is just as bad a mistake to take a question you very well know to be totally beside the point and treat it at great length simply because a Justice happened to ask it. Since you can never tell a

Justice that his question is irrelevant, the only guideline I can give is that counsel should answer such a question directly and courteously, but as quickly as possible. I must warn you, if you are a first-timer, that this is easier said than done in the case where the Justice is not aware of his question's irrelevance and fully intends to cling to your neck like a bulldog until he wrings an answer from you that satisfies him. I have seen as much as five precious minutes wasted in this kind of encounter.

3. *Assume that the Justices have at least a working knowledge of the case.* There has been a debate for years over which presumption you should make: that the Court knows nothing about the case when you take to the podium, or that each member has religiously reviewed the briefs and relevant parts of the record. My own view is that, for two reasons, your presumption should be somewhere in between. First, several Justices have recently said that all members of the Court review the briefs at least to some extent before argument. Second, it is almost never possible to tell the *whole* story in ten, twenty, or even thirty minutes. Therefore, your recitation of the facts and your argument itself should presume that each Justice has a general knowledge of what you are about. This allows for greater concentration on the points you hope will win the case.

4. *Be tougher with your own case than anyone else could, should or would.* Obviously, when first preparing your case, either in written or oral form, you must dream up and explore every possible argument that can be made on behalf of your client. The next step is to eliminate those which will not stand up and to give as much support as possible to those that appear to have merit. In my experience, too many lawyers stop there. I have mentioned above the usefulness of "moot court" sessions with associates, where they presumably will attack you with all of the weak points in your case. The able advocate, however, should not be satisfied with that. He should himself take the hardest look of all at what the case is really about. One method—a kind of extension of Mr. Davis' first rule—is to assume that you are a judge who for some reason (presumably legitimate) wants to hold against you. What possible grounds could he find for doing so? What possible facts could he rely upon? What possible theories could be used to destroy your own carefully laid plans for success? I am constantly amazed, during Supreme Court arguments, to hear an attorney virtually struck dumb by questions from the bench that anyone with any knowledge of the case should have anticipated. It is as if the attorney has become so imbued with the spirit of his cause that he has totally blinded himself to the legitimate concerns that someone else might have in adopting his position.

In this regard, many writers have advocated making concessions so as to impress the Court with one's fairness and faithfulness to the record. This is all very well when the concession does not in effect concede the outcome of the case, but there are a number of examples in which advocates have given everything away, apparently without realizing it at the time. *(See, e.g., Regional Rail Reorganization Act Cases,* 419 U.S. 102, 132-3 (1974); *Williams v. Georgia,* 349 U.S. 375, 381-2 (1955)). The trick is to make a concession only as to those points which you have carefully considered in advance and as to which you have a counterargument. Thus: "It is quite true that there is evidence in the record that could lead a jury to believe that X made those statements to Y, but I would remind the Court that the law in New York requires . . ."

The most dangerous mistake is to make a concession you have not thought out in advance and the natural repercussions of which you do not fully appreciate because of the tensions of the moment.

5. *Use your rebuttal time.* I know there are differences of opinion about rebuttal, with some judges and attorneys taking the position that you should not even make one except in the unusual case. My own view is that while rebuttals are more often than not mishandled —with attorneys attempting to answer virtually every point raised by their adversaries and cramming far too many facts, figures and arguments into a few moments' time—the carefully made rebuttal can be extremely helpful in leaving the Court with its focus not on the last words of your adversary but on the striking point that you believe to be most in your favor. The rebuttal should never be prepared in advance. You should make notes during the respondent's (or appellee's) argument, and then, just before he sits down, strike for discussion everything except the one or two points which are most helpful to your cause.

In a recent Supreme Court case, a lawyer representing a state felt called upon to defend the state's highest court for its delay in hearing an appeal from a trial judge's prior restraint on the press. He pointed out, quite accurately, that so many attorneys from around the state were scheduled to make arguments and had to make plans well in advance, it was virtually impossible for the state supreme court to expedite a matter involving a prior restraint. But this point, while sensitive to the problems of the state supreme court, was precisely the one opposing counsel had wanted to drive home. It was helpful during rebuttal to draw the Court's attention to the fact that what had in effect been conceded for the state—that it was a practical impossibility to obtain an immediate review of a prior restraint on the press—was equally true in most other states and in some federal courts, so that these orders, even if blatantly unconstitutional, could work their harm for prolonged periods.

6. *Be interesting.* By this, I obviously am not referring to theatrics or banging the podium or waving your arms or wandering back and forth, first in and then out of earshot of the microphone. What I am getting at is that too many of the arguments before the Court are simply dull. They are given in a kind of singsong voice, with very little intonation, as if the arguer himself is barely interested in his cause. Even several of the people who have argued a number of times before the Court are guilty of

mumbling or failing to change the tone of their voices by more than a few decibels.

Obviously, I cannot advise anyone to have personality. You either have it or you do not. But the fact is that to convince a court of your viewpoint—which is what advocacy is all about—you have to catch the Court's attention in the first place. If the Justices are writing, talking, or even thinking of other things, you might just as well have submitted your case on your briefs. So the answer is that, without flourish or bombast, without shouting or embarrassing mannerisms, you must make some effort to speak directly to each Justice, to catch his eye on occasion, to change the tone of your voice according to the nature or importance of the words you are speaking, to be interesting and agile even while you retain your own respect and proffer respect to the Court.

Mr. Justice Jackson said that "The most persuasive quality in the advocate is professional sincerity." I agree but would add that it should be a joy for the Court to hear you, not just its duty. Certainly it was always a joy for the Justices to hear Mr. Davis and then-Solicitor General Jackson, whether or not they were on the losing end of their causes.

Two examples of differing but effective styles appear in Richard Kluger's book, *Simple Justice*, the story of *Brown v. Board of Education*. In the first, John W. Davis argued to the Court on behalf of the State of South Carolina:

> . . . Who is going to disturb that situation? If they were to be reassorted or commingled, who knows how that would best be done?
>
> If it is done on the mathematical basis, with 30 children as a maximum . . . you would have 27 Negro children and three whites in one schoolroom. Would that make the children any happier? Would they learn any more quickly? Would their lives be more serene?
>
> Children of that age are not the most considerate animals in the world, as we all know. Would the terrible psychological disaster being wrought, according to some of these witnesses, to the colored child be removed if he had three white children sitting somewhere in the same schoolroom?
>
> Would white children be prevented from getting a distorted idea of racial relations if they sat with 27 Negro children? I have posed that question because it is the very one that cannot be denied.
>
> You say that is racism. Well, it is not racism. Recognize that for sixty centuries and more, humanity has been discussing questions of race and race tension, not racism. . . . [T]wenty-nine states have miscegenation statutes now in force which they believe are of beneficial protection to both races. Disraeli said, 'No man,' said he, 'will treat with indifference the principle of race. It is the key of history.'

The second example was the counterargument of Thurgood (now Mr. Justice) Marshall:

> . . . I got the feeling on hearing the discussion yesterday that when you put a white child in a school with a whole lot of colored children, the child would fall apart or something. Everybody knows that is not true.
>
> Those same kids in Virginia and South Carolina—and I have seen them do it—they play in the streets together, they play on their farms together, they go down the road together, they separate to go to school, they come out of school and play ball together. They have to be separated in school.
>
> There is some magic to it. You can have them voting together, you can have them not restricted because of law in the houses they live in. You can have them going to the same state university and the same college, but if they go to elementary and high school, the world will fall apart. . . .

The styles could not have been more different, but both arguments were interesting, logical, imaginative and arresting.

There are a few other points that have been made time and again in speeches and articles about the do's and don'ts of oral argument, particularly as they relate to the Supreme Court of the United States. A few bear repeating for the simple reason that they are so often ignored:

- It is a good idea for your notebook to contain brief abstracts of all cases both for and against you, particularly where a great many cases have been cited on both sides. The fact is that, unless you have one of those miracle memories, cases and their facts and holdings can become confused in your mind in the give-and-take of oral argument. You should prepare these abstracts yourself so that a brief glance at them can remind you of the information you need to know.

- I am opposed to putting a time schedule next to your notes, as proposed by some writers. The purpose is to clue you in as to where you ought to be, time-wise, at each section of your argument. The schedule starts at minute zero and is keyed to a watch which you take with you to the podium. The trouble is that in most instances the argument will not proceed according to your notes. You will be flipping back and forth between point 3 and point 1, or perhaps ignoring point 1 altogether. Any time schedule in your notes will simply confuse you once you have skipped a section or flipped back and forth from point to point.

- I agree with those who have recommended against the use of such confusing appellations as "plaintiff in error." But do not hesitate to use "petitioner," "respondent," "appellant," or "appellee" if those designations come easily to hand. Remember that the Court

855

has heard many arguments before yours, and your simple reference to "Mr. Jones" or to the "State Insurance Company" may not, particularly at the outset of the argument, inform the Justices that these are even parties to the case, much less which side they are on.

- I thoroughly agree with what has been said so many times about reading. Do not read your argument. Do not read from other cases. Do not read anything at all unless it is necessary and brief. A particular statutory provision may be so essential that it must be read and perhaps sections of it reread. The main point, however, is that you should not put everyone to sleep by pure recitation of the quotation of lengthy materials. A general rule of thumb is that quoting anything over two sentences should make your wary.

- Under no circumstances attack other judges, the litigants or opposing counsel, even when you feel justified in doing so. Insofar as other judges are concerned, their best friends or greatest admirers might be on the bench in front of you. As to a personal attack upon the parties or counsel, it is a demeaning practice and one that does not sit well with the Court. Far too often I have heard an attorney complain that his opposing number has distorted the record, misled the Court, manufactured facts not of record, and so forth. If opposing counsel has in fact been in error, the presumption on your part should be that he misspoke himself or that his lapse were inadvertent, even if you think you have reason to believe otherwise. Two officers of the Court do not attack each other. As for litigants, they are not there to speak for themselves, the Supreme Court podium is not the proper place to attack them, and it is simply bad advocacy to be anything but courteous in regard to them, just as you would always be courteous to the Court.

The point of all of this is to convince. And the balance may lie very close indeed, for even cases that are decided unanimously may have caused a great deal of difficulty for each individual justice. As my father related in his own discourse on this same subject (*Some Observations Concerning Appellate Advocacy*, 39 VA. L. REV. 285, 297 (1953)), one judge when worried about a particular outcome suggested to his brethren that they return the appellant's filing fee and tell him to take his case somewhere else.

The trouble with the Supreme Court is that there is nowhere else to go.

PART X

Settlement

Achieving Better Settlements

by Jim Sullivan

Law schools do not bother to stress the art of negotiating settlements. Yet, at least 92 percent of all civil cases filed in federal court settle before trial. So, somebody connected with the trial team needs to be a highly skilled negotiator.

Do not automatically assume that lead counsel should be the lead negotiator. Consider using someone else to negotiate and keep that first chair lawyer out on the battlefield and away from the peace conference. Placing him in the negotiating role could be a mistake for several reasons:

- A trial lawyer must be fired up about the case, and settlement talks bank that fire.
- Settlement talks can be protracted, but trial preparation must continue because trial is always possible.
- Preparation for successful settlement conferences requires techniques that are different from trial preparation.
- Most of the great trial lawyers are fighters, not peacemakers.
- An outside lawyer may not be sufficiently enthusiastic about a settlement that would terminate the need for his services.

The best bet for the role of chief negotiator often is the inside lawyer. The in-house lawyer can be invaluable in negotiating sessions. Since he continues to get paid after the case is over, he can be more objective. He also knows the client's people and what is acceptable industry behavior. He also may have better knowledge of the other side's inside lawyer, especially in a case involving competitors, customers, or suppliers.

Lawyers should take cues from negotiation methods used by diplo-

The author is a partner in the San Diego law firm of Sullivan, McWilliams, Lewin & Markham, and is a fellow of the American College of Trial Lawyers.

mats and other professional negotiators. If their techniques can turn enemy nations into friends and secure the freedom of hostages being held by maniacs, perhaps they can even be used to bring about rational compromises of commercial lawsuits.

Even experienced negotiators could benefit from books on negotiating techniques aimed primarily at nonlawyers, such as *You Can Negotiate Anything,* by Herb Cohen. Mr. Cohen and other masters of the art of negotiation teach that the first rule of successful negotiation is: you must project awesome power plus the will to use it. Nations as different from each other as Russia and Israel fully understand and follow this basic rule. America under Carter did not become militarily inferior to Russia, but friends and foes alike perceived this nation as reluctant to use its awesome might. Similarly, America has not suddenly become more powerful under Reagan, but its negotiating power is thought by many to be much greater simply because other nations perceive an increased willingness to use that power.

Many corporations have vast economic power, but only a few are viewed as willing to use that power in a competitive or legal dispute. Similarly, there are many large and powerful law firms. Each has highly competent lawyers who are experienced in discovery and motion practice. But there are only a few lawyers and law firms that regularly and convincingly project the will to try a business lawsuit. This may be because a large, highly publicized loss could damage a firm's reputation. There are many cases that should never be tried because the risk of loss is too great, but it is especially important in such a case to project a willingness to go to trial. The designated negotiator on the trial team should make certain that the correct image is being conveyed consistently to the other side.

Uncomfortable Enforcer

It is not enough for the lawyers to convey this image to each other. The client must understand the importance of projecting the correct image to the other side at the management level as well. A competent negotiator takes the other side's pulse constantly and looks for clues to answer one basic question: Is the other side serious about going to the mat?

Executives understand the importance of this image in business negotiations and will quickly grasp the importance of it in a lawsuit. Failure to explain this tactic adequately could be disastrous. For example, in a lawsuit involving an antitrust claim by one large company against another, a chance remark by an executive employed by the plaintiff indicating that his company feels uncomfortable in its role as an enforcer of the antitrust laws will result in that side leaving a bundle of cash on the table. Conversely, a well-prepared executive's remark to the effect that the company's honor is at stake and that the case will be presented (or defended) as a matter of principle sends exactly the right message. Also, be sure that all in-house lawyers, whether or not members of the trial team, observe these rules, since they may have contacts at the other company and unwittingly convey a weak image.

There are many ways the trial team can convince the other side that they are not only willing, but eager, to go to the mat. First, at the very start of the case, send the message to all outside and in-house lawyers that there is no possibility of settlement because an important principle is at stake. Second, make certain that the lawyer in the first chair loves to try lawsuits and that it shows. Most important, convince the other side that you are preparing for trial diligently and enthusiastically and have no interest in discussing settlement.

The last message sometimes is difficult to deliver in a believable way but it can be done. Try to convince the other side that they are dealing with a bunch of fanatics who insist on going to trial regardless of the cost or consequences. This can be done from the start if you write the last act first. Draft your closing argument and jury instructions first. If the other side receives a set of proposed jury instructions when the case is only a few weeks old, they will pay attention. A demand to videotape all depositions is also a clear signal that the case will be tried, since the primary value of the videotapes is at trial and they are somewhat expensive.

A few examples might be helpful. Suppose you represent a plaintiff with a weak case that is in whole or in part contingent. You must find a way to demonstrate the will to roll the dice. Assume an antitrust claim for $1,000,000 single damages, but that the best shot is realistically about $500,000, and the recovery range is $300,000–$500,000. The odds favor a defense verdict by about 3 to 1. Typically, the initial offer from the defendant will be nominal, perhaps $50,000. An appropriate plaintiffs response would be $1,500,000. This will prompt the other side to point to your weakest points and to try to convince you that your client cannot possibly win. An answer that increases the odds against a win ("Sure, it's a 5 to 1 shot but it will give our young lawyers a chance to hone their knives.") is disconcerting to the defendant's lawyers, especially if the aggressive young lawyers are pushed to the front while the partner moves to the third chair.

This technique also can work for defendants. For example, assume your client is charged with antitrust violations, that evidence of the violation is clear-cut and that the plaintiff has a credible damage study indicating possible single damages of $50 million. The odds are about 5 to 1 against a defense verdict and a loss would produce single damages of about $25 million. The plaintiff's trial team will be drooling over the case and will be enthusiastic in explaining their chances to the corporate client. Executives are not accustomed to dealing with fired-up and optimistic lawyers, so when outside and inside counsel give a written opinion that the company "should prevail" instead of "could" or some gloomier lawyer-like term, they are surprised. When the lawyers add that the victory would most likely result in a $25,000,000 recovery but the recovery could be as high as $50,000,000, they are astonished. They might even wonder if their lawyers are wrong, and that is a weakness the opposition must exploit.

Exude Optimism

Since the plaintiff's lawyers seem so sure they have a powerful case, its executives will expect an early settlement overture with a hefty opening figure. Obviously, members of the defense team must acknowledge that the exposure is heavy. But the defense team in this case *must* convince management to exude optimism consistently both inside and outside the company.

The trial team must also stay completely away from settlement negotiations. In a major business lawsuit there are usually premier trial lawyers on both sides. Therefore, the defense team's assessment of exposure will be fairly close to the plaintiff's. More important, the plaintiff's counsel will know that the defense team recognizes that their client really does not have a chance. It would be tactical suicide to use them to try to project willingness to use power to try a sure loser—they simply would not be credible.

Initial contacts regarding settlement should be made by one executive to another executive. Alternatively, the contact can be by an inside lawyer who is not primarily a trial lawyer to a similar lawyer on the other side, or between an executive and an inside lawyer.

The key to success is to exploit the prevalent executive doubts about lawyers. Do not take it personally. However, top corporate achievers find it difficult to put up with cautious and negative people, and lawyers who give business advice tend to be exactly that. Defendant's negotiator should not denigrate plaintiff's trial team, but merely project a very positive, confident hard line.

The crucial image of the will to use power can start with the cross-claim or counterclaim. There is almost always some basis for some such claim in business lawsuits. The initial settlement overture from the negotiator for the defendant and counterclaim plaintiff might well be an offer of a mutual release for the payment by the plaintiff of $15,000,000. If the plaintiff's negotiator is not very experienced, he may never recover from this unexpected shock.

The plaintiff's negotiator who is suddenly placed on the defensive often concludes that the other side sees something highly significant that his side has missed. Do they have a better expert? Are our lawyers misreading the law? How about the facts? How will my future be affected if I ride with our lawyers and we lose or get a marginal result? Can I force our lawyers to agree on a settlement sum that will minimize my career risk?

If this happens, the plaintiff's trial team is likely to be grilled by management representatives: Is everyone agreed that recovery is a virtual certainty? Is everyone agreed on the recovery range? Can we safely rule out any recovery by the other side? Can we all agree on a settlement sum that would be a good, if not a great, result? It is as if the defendant's skillful negotiator has turned the plaintiff's negotiator into an arbitrator.

The plaintiff's trial team will tell their negotiator that the whole thing is a giant bluff, that the defendant will not dare to run the risk of trial. "Just wait," they will say, "the defendant is sure to cave in." So the plaintiff's negotiator waits and watches. The defendant fights discovery battles as if preparing for a title bout. There is complete silence from the other side's negotiator. Why are they silent? Why are they obviously getting ready for trial? We seemed to have improved our position during discovery. They should recognize that. Why not take their pulse? The skillful defense negotiator will stand firm and continue to talk about receiving dollars from the plaintiff.

Awesome Power

This strategy usually results in reassessment of the defendant's bottom line. The most likely result will be a settlement for about $15,000,000. The defendant's representative has saved $60,000,000 of the estimated $75,000,000 in possible trebled damages. The plaintiff's directors will be pleased, and the plaintiff's negotiator will have a successful business career provided he stays away from any more negotiating roles. Plaintiff's trial team will shed the only tears, but they will not be too bitter and they will not last long. After all, they witnessed a classic example of a successful result derived from the use of Settlement Rule One: The projection of awesome power and the will to use it.

Settlement Rule Two, used by professional negotiators, recognizes the importance of saving face. We recognize this need in our personal lives. Business executives know this is very important, and so do diplomats.

In our example, a clever negotiator probably could have extracted a few extra million dollars from the defendant, and the defendant would have been happy to pay them if it saved face. Is anything really gained by crowing about victory? Is it necessary to rub the other side's nose in it? Probably not. If it will assist in achieving a better settlement, consider agreeing to a provision stating that neither side will claim victory nor reveal settlement terms unless it deems that a response to an inquiry should be made, and agree on a press release describing mutual releases and agreement on a "commercial solution." You could also structure the settlement as a commercial transaction that will result in lowering the plaintiff's future costs or increasing its profits by an agreed upon dollar amount.

The next rule used by skilled negotiators is to know your adversary and its representatives and the court. There are numerous ways to get to know the opposing company:

- Study its annual report and SEC filings.
- Check newspaper articles.
- Determine its cost for the product or service involved in the lawsuit.
- Find out whether it is considered scrappy.
- Does it care about its reputation?
- What are its fiscal condition and its future prospects?
- Who reports to whom and what are the limits of delegated authority?
- Who is the contact executive for each power center?
- What are the firm's short- and long-term goals?
- Has it established any deadlines?
- Has it ever gone through a big stakes trial or is it regarded as a settler?

Look for these clues about the other side's chief negotiator:
- Schools attended.
- Military service.
- What does "Who's Who" say?
- What is his employment history?
- What can be discovered about his personal life, including religion, hobbies, etc.?
- How is he regarded in the industry?
- Does he maintain a regular daily and weekly schedule? Work habits are extremely important, since timing is crucial in settlement negotiations.

Examine the opponent's trial lawyers. Start with the outside law firm in general:
- What percentage does business litigation work bear to the firm's total?
- Who runs the litigation section and what is he like?
- Who manages the firm?
- What is the firm's reputation and characteristics?
- Does the firm also handle any advisory work for its client? If so, does it do so regularly and does it rely on that client for a good deal of income?
- Is its fee contingent or on an hourly basis, regardless of the outcome?

Analyze their trial team:
- Where does the first chair lawyer stand in the firm's power structure—is he at the top or still on the way up?
- What about the lawyer's track record? Is he an experienced trial lawyer? Does he talk and act as if the case will be tried? Is he calling the strategic shots or is someone else? Does that lawyer have the case organized and have factual control? Is he from the old or new school of trial lawyers?
- What about the rest of the trial team? Are the people in the second

and third chairs jockeying for position and, if so, how can this be exploited? Do the paralegals act as if they expect the case to be tried? Is the trial team fired up or only going through the motions? Do any of the team members have trial experience?

Learn about the trial judge:

- Will the judge apply pressure to settle and even be an active participant in settlement conferences? If so, you must condition your client so that the executive who attends such conferences will not be surprised when the judge pokes holes in his case.

The last fundamental rule used by top negotiators recognizes the importance of timing. Japanese businessmen are masters of the art of timing and generally can outwait and thus out-negotiate Americans. Most successful American businessmen and lawyers operate on a tight schedule. It is important to remember that major decisions are never made until close to the end of scheduled meetings or conferences. If a one-hour negotiating session is scheduled, there will be 55 minutes of sparring. If three days are scheduled, not much will happen until the final hour of the last day.

So, find out about the other side's travel habits and plans and how much time they have set aside for the settlement conference. Spar and avoid making any commitments until the other side's negotiator is starting to worry about catching a plane or train. An inexperienced negotiator who is away from home will always do two things wrong:

- He will check out of the hotel in the morning of the last day of the meeting; and
- Bring his luggage to the meeting. This means that he intends to catch a plane and *nothing* will stop him.

Do not worry about your own schedule—it can be revised. If you are out of town, force yourself to leave your luggage in your room. Do *not* check out of the hotel. You must condition yourself to act like you have no deadline.

Trial teams must learn to apply modern settlement techniques. The stakes in modern business litigation and the size of the attorneys' fees involved are too high to settle cases without using the most persuasive methods. If you do not use them, you will find the opposition using them against you.

Settlement Negotiations

by Kenneth P. Nolan

Trial lawyers love to fight. Making witnesses squirm, the jury swoon, and the opposition grovel are all part of the thrill.

Trial lawyers are Clint Eastwoods in three-piece suits. Tough, macho, determined to win. Always ready for trial, always willing to take a verdict.

Rarely prepared to settle.

Yet, the reality is that 95 percent of all cases do settle. Despite this, no one takes the young associate aside and tells him that his 20-page pretrial brief may not be necessary. No one suggests that the lawyer should aim for a settlement now or explains how to get there.

Litigation sometimes gives lawyers tunnel vision, in which the light at the end is a verdict.

Plaintiffs' lawyers may forget that their primary objective is to get money to compensate the plaintiff for the injury. Defense lawyers forget that their goal is to minimize the defendant's financial loss.

With this in mind, a $10,000 settlement before filing suit may be a greater success than a $15,000 verdict three years later.

For one thing, both parties are likely to save money. The plaintiff's award is worth more money than the greater amount three years later, and the defendant will save money that would have been spent on attorneys' fees. The time and energy saved may be worth even more.

Consider the parties' emotions. How will a husband endure three years of anger waiting to face the doctor he thinks killed his wife? How will the doctor bear up under a charge that he caused the death of a patient? What if he is found liable?

Often the grinding pressure of litigation persuades parties to settle.

The author is an associate editor of LITIGATION *and a member of the New York City law firm of Speiser & Krause, P.C.*

Both parties, especially defendants, are relieved when a case is resolved.

It does not matter that the defendant has been told from the beginning, ''Don't worry, the plaintiff doesn't really expect $10 million for a broken ankle, despite what the complaint demands.''

Don't worry? Your client knows better. He has seen the complaint. He has read newspaper accounts of $10-million verdicts. In the back of his mind, he fears losing his home or business.

Settling soon also eliminates the risk that an unpredictable event will determine the outcome of the case. Between the time the claim is filed and the case is tried, witnesses can disappear or change their testimony, injuries can heal, and the law can change. Lawyers may find these changes exciting, but clients would just as soon be spared the drama.

Today defense counsel have an incentive to settle that they did not have 20 years ago. For most defendants, it is no longer realistic to believe that going to trial will result in a finding of no liability. Juries have become more sympathetic to plaintiffs. The law has changed to reflect a social policy that places the burden of loss and injury on those who profited from the product or business associated with the injury. Comparative negligence is the law in nearly every state.

One final point in favor of settlement.

Some lawyers may think that a willingness to settle is a sign of weakness. This is not true. In fact, sitting down and talking settlement in the early stages of litigation may take more guts and efficiency than proceeding mindlessly with litigation.

Success at early settlement involves early basic investigation. Settling early also involves an assessment that lawyers may not want to make: facing up to the weaknesses in your case.

In personal injury cases, initial evaluations of experienced lawyers are usually correct. Three years of battle does not change the outcome but merely delays it.

For these reasons, settlement should be considered as a successful resolution to every case.

Here are some rules that are helpful in settling personal injury cases. Some are basic rules of trial preparation; others are peculiar to settlement. All have proved useful to us in settling personal injury cases, primarily on behalf of plaintiffs but for defendants as well.

The first rule is to investigate early. Not when the case is on the trial calendar but as soon as you get the first telephone call.

If you are plaintiff's counsel, investigate before you file suit. Get the hospital records and have an expert review them to decide if that was malpractice. Take witnesses' statements. If the injury was caused by a machine, take photographs of the machine.

Take time to talk to the plaintiff and learn his history. It is amazing how many attorneys pigeonhole a case as ''a sprained back'' or ''a concussion'' without learning the idiosyncrasies of their client's sprained back. When you approach settlement, know exactly which vertebrae caused Mr. Smith to twist in bed with pain every night.

Before talking settlement, you should be confident that the plaintiff has a legitimate case and that you have discovered any likely sources of nasty surprises. The eve of trial is too late to get the hospital records and discover that "AOB" (Alcohol on Breath) is circled on every page and that your sainted client's admission of having been "polluted" while driving the car is recorded in the medical history. Your only choice then is to try the case and lose it or settle for far less than you or your client thought you could get.

Of course, if a prospective plaintiff is calling, and the case is a dog, you want to know that right away. Then you can call back quickly to say, "Sorry, but my busy schedule doesn't permit me to handle this one." Or better still, "Look, not everyone is injured because of someone else's negligence, despite what you read in the paper."

A rejection should also be in writing and hand delivered or sent by certified mail, return receipt requested. The appropriate statute of limitations should be cited. If you want to sleep well at night and keep your malpractice carrier happy, you will follow this rule strictly.

Defense counsel likewise will benefit from an early investigation of the case. If liability is as good as alleged, he must know. If there is a crucial witness whose testimony will not hold up, you should learn that quickly. Facing these weaknesses at the beginning is likely to save time, energy, and even money. Since the plaintiff may welcome a quick resolution of his case, he is likely to take less money than he would if he had to work for three years to get it.

Early investigation may include researching the law. If there are complex or new legal issues, open the law books. See whether the unfamiliar legal issue is decisive. There is nothing so impressive as a lawyer who cites a case to refute his adversary's argument in their first discussion. The message carries far. "If he is this well prepared now, imagine what he will be like at trial."

If the case does not settle early, continued thorough investigation is important. Do not rely on someone else's investigation. If the file lands on your desk with the investigation already "complete," be skeptical. You do not have to repeat every step. But talk to the critical witnesses, whether they are engineers, doctors, or truck drivers. Talk in person. In your office. Do the witnesses make a good appearance? Do their stories hold up? Will they withstand a strenuous deposition? The wrong answer to any of these questions may quickly tell you that settlement is not just the best resolution, it is the only one.

Once you have done a basic investigation of the facts and the law, you may be ready to evaluate the case and put a dollar figure on it. But you may need more. And if the case does not settle early, your evaluation will certainly include some additional steps.

Know your venue. Bronx County in New York City may border suburban Westchester County, but the counties are worlds apart. In the Bronx, the courthouse is in the South Bronx, and the jurors are angry at hospitals and corporations. It is plaintiffs' heaven. In Westchester, the juries are conservative suburbanites, and the plaintiff had better beware.

You may also want to know about jury verdicts and settlements in similar cases. Many such reports are available. Read them. If you are not sure what value a jury will place on the loss of an eye, these reports can guide you. If you think you know the value, read the reports anyway. You might be surprised.

Be sure to research similar actions in the locale where the case is being tried. Juries' attitudes are changing quickly, so learn about recent verdicts in the locale, either from published reports or from lawyers who practice there.

Learn about your adversary. You will, of course, learn some things firsthand as the case goes on. You can learn more by talking to other lawyers. Is he reasonable, or is everything hardball? If an insurance carrier is involved, what is its reputation?

Finally, talk to your partners, and also to your spouse and friends. Ask them informally for their thoughts. Lawyers often talk only to other lawyers. Sometimes it is your spouse who will show you that, despite your eloquent recitation of the facts and your intriguing legal defense, your client is likely to lose because what he did "just ain't fair."

After you put a dollar figure on the case, there is one more step before you can begin negotiations. You must talk to your client.

Tell your client how you evaluate the case and explain how you got there. Overvaluing the injuries to a plaintiff or minimizing the defendant's exposure may make a story that your client wants to hear. But it will be a difficult story to face as the case gets closer to trial.

"Mrs. Jones, great news! The defendant has thrown in the towel and offered $25,000 in settlement."

"Why should I accept $25,000? You promised me $100,000."

"When did I say that?"

"Two-and-one-half years ago, when we first met."

"Oh, yes. Well, er, what I meant was. . . ."

Whatever you say, do not promise too much. Clients are like elephants; they never forget.

After you have talked about the case with your client, get authority to settle. Your talk should be face to face, not on the telephone. And you should get settlement authority in writing.

In seeking authority, remember that you cannot predict with certainty what your opponent will offer. You are best off getting authority that protects against this risk.

Of course, there are times when reasonable talk about settlement will only make your client mad. If the plaintiff is set on revenge, little will be gained by exploring settlement. Likewise, the defendant may be intent on defending the integrity of his product or his reputation, and nothing short of vindication from a jury will be satisfactory. In these situations, settlement may be a topic best left unmentioned, at least until tempers cool or victory appears unrealistic.

Settlement talks are most likely to produce results after the parties know their strengths and weaknesses and before they begin intensive work on the case. Cases are most likely to settle before the complaint is filed, immediately after filing but before discovery, before final trial preparation, or on the proverbial courthouse steps.

Because the plaintiff is the one who has said he is entitled to be paid, the plaintiff must usually make the first demand.

If you are the plaintiff's lawyer, the first time to pick up the phone is before you file suit. Put down your cowboy hat, check your Colt .45 at the door, and call your opposing counsel. Talk to the defendant's lawyer and listen.

You may hear, ''There is no possibility that we will pay one cent on this claim.'' In that case you know what to do. Draft a complaint and get it served.

Instead the lawyer's reply may be, ''Sure, let's talk.'' Here is where your early investigation and evaluation can really pay off. Here is where you can show the lawyer how good your case is and how well you know it.

Offer to submit your client for a physical examination. You are not giving anything away—the defendant is entitled to an examination eventually—and an early examination may help you. Wounds heal and eventually the plaintiff will look and feel better. A physical soon after the injury will force the defendant's expert to admit, ''Yes, the plaintiff was on crutches when I examined her.'' Let the defendant's own doctor report to him: ''It's true; the injury is permanent.''

Find out what the defendant knows. With the present discovery rules, it is likely that each party will learn much of what is in the other party's files. Be brave. If the defendant's lawyer is missing the hospital records or police report, send them to him. If you have a witness statement that shows the weaknesses in his case, send that, too.

Wait until your adversary has all this information before discussing money. But negotiate with one eye on the statute of limitations. Beware of settlement discussions that drag on as the end of the limitation period gets closer. If there is any chance this will happen, file your complaint first and then talk.

When you start talking settlement, you enter a world of special communication and you had better learn the language fast. In settlement talks, the plaintiff's lawyer will always start by demanding more than the plaintiff will accept, while the defendant's lawyer will make an opening offer of less than he will pay. Settlement always involves negotiation, and negotiation always involves give and take.

Learn that rule quickly, for no one will believe you if you say, "My demand is $80,000, not a penny less. That is what it will take to settle the case." Lawyers have heard this before, and the cases have settled for less. Even if the defendant's lawyer has authority for $80,000, he will not meet this demand. "$80,000, are you nuts? The case is worth nuisance value, $7,500, maybe ten grand. That's it."

Demand more than you will accept. Offer less than you will pay. Yes, Virginia, there is a Santa Claus. But he delivers toys; he does not handle personal injury actions.

If you deviate from this rule, you will end up eating your own words. You may think, if I am reasonable in my demand, the defendant will snap it up, and I can avoid haggling. So you say, "I'm not going to give you a demand but a real bottom line. That number is $100,000."

In initial negotiations, there is no such thing as a real bottom line. Generally, if a case is going to settle, it is because of the facts and law not because of a "reasonable settlement demand."

Furthermore, the defendant will automatically assume that the plaintiff's demand is at least twice what he is willing to accept, whether or not it is reasonable. So after hearing about the $100,000 "bottom line number" from the plaintiff's lawyer, the defendant's lawyer is probably having the following conversation with his client or insurance carrier.

"The plaintiff has just demanded $100,000, so he is probably looking for $45,000 to $60,000. Give me authority for $60,000, and I'll try to save something on the case."

Because the plaintiff and defendant have misunderstood each other, this case is not likely to settle.

The plaintiff's lawyer would have been better off demanding $200,000 but keeping the door open to negotiate if the defendant made a reasonable offer. Then, if the defendant offered $50,000 or $60,000, the plaintiff should have understood that the defendant was signaling a willingness to approach the plaintiff's evaluation.

Defendants' lawyers make similar mistakes. Many times you hear defense counsel say, "I don't play games. I'll be frank; I'm authorized to offer $50,000."

Experienced plaintiffs' lawyers simply will not believe this. They will assume that the lawyer is offering 50 percent to 60 percent of his authority. If, instead, the defendant's lawyer is conveying his actual authority, he will be forced to request money in excess of his authority if he wants to continue settlement negotiations.

Making it through the first round of negotiations is just the beginning. Everyone has his own style of negotiating. But there are limits to any technique, and it always pays to be consistent. Do not rant and rave one day with a string of curses and then be the nicest guy on earth the next.

870

Trust has to be created, even if the foundation is shaky.

Be businesslike. Do not hang up the telephone when the offer is, ''The best I can do is $150,000.'' Try to be polite—even with a wise guy. Get your revenge by making him eat his words when he offers you $500,000 after he has said that $150,000 was his bottom line. When settlement is over, you can invite him for a drink and politely remind him of his ultimatum.

Skill at negotiating involves the same intuition it takes to pick a jury. If the juror smiles at you too much and has all the right answers, you know that something is wrong. You should have that same feeling if negotiations are too easy. Return to the file to see if you have overlooked something.

Use your common sense. If you do not know if you have any common sense, come to New York and take a ride on the IRT subway for an hour. If you survive, everything else in life is easy—even negotiating a settlement.

Consider various scenarios in advance. ''If I demand $500,000, and he offers $100,000, what should I say. . . . Maybe I should demand $350,000. . . . What if he offers $300,000? . . . .''

If you are unsure of whether to accept the offer, then wait. Give yourself time. Talk to your partners and your client. Then decide.

Before rejecting any offer, discuss it with your client. Malpractice rears its ugly head when you reject an offer your clients would accept, only to learn that the offer has been withdrawn. Now the case will have to be tried, and you cannot even think about losing.

When you start talking settlement, it is also important to know what not to say. Never minimize your case or advertise weaknesses. You are an advocate who should present your client's case in the most favorable light. Too many plaintiffs' attorneys have spoiled their clients' chances for settlement by saying, ''I'm sorry I took this lousy case but I have to get something for it.'' This self-flagellation does not help. No defendant has ever paid money to save his opponent from embarrassment.

Do not apologize for a weakness your opponent recognizes. Confront the weakness without alarm. You have thought your case through. Explain that you will counter the weakness with expert testimony, with a legal theory that avoids the weakness, or with a motion in limine that may eliminate it.

Do not tell your opponent that you think your client's evaluation of the case is unrealistic.

''My client thinks his machines are perfect, but we know they're not.'' ''The doctor may have goofed on this one.'' ''My client is looking to retire on this injury.''

Your adversary may have suspicions, but it is not your job to reinforce them.

Do not offer or demand two figures at the same time. ''We will settle this case for $40,000 to $50,000'' means that you have just demanded $40,000 to settle.

Do not be equivocal. "I am authorized to offer $75,000, and that's almost it." Why should the plaintiff settle for less than "it?"

"We'll pay $60,000, but that's getting close to my authority." The plaintiff's lawyer is not your pal; he wants to squeeze the last dollar out of you. Why should he accept this offer when you have signaled that you will pay more?

Do not bid against yourself. Every time a demand is lowered, the offer must be raised. If your demand is within reason, you should get an offer in response. Of course, you can dance around the verbal boxing ring bobbing and weaving to determine if there will be another offer. But if there is none, call an end to this round of negotiations. If you have been realistic, you should not let your opponent force you to negotiate with yourself.

But what if you have been unrealistic? Here is what happens.

"The demand is $2 million."

"What! Are you a comedian! I'm not going to bid against that demand."

"Are you telling me that you have no offer on this brain damage malpractice action?"

"No, I'm just telling you that your demand is out of reach."

Now you have only two choices. You can forget settlement and proceed to trial. Or you can reevaluate your demand and lower it knowing that the defendant will relish negotiating you down from the demand that you renegotiated with yourself.

By now you should have learned a lesson. Only make ultimatums that you intend to keep.

Never say, "Pay us $100,000, or the case will be tried," unless you will try the case even if the offer is $99,999.99. You destroy your credibility when the defendant offers $75,000 to your $100,000 ultimatum, and you gobble it up.

The other part of the lesson is this. Eventually you must give an ultimatum. And you must keep it.

Decide where you will make your stand and do not deviate from it. Your client must know the details of each step of negotiations. That way you may enforce the bottom line you have set together. With your client's approval, you may even try the case over a difference of $5,000.

For whether you convey your bottom line before bringing suit or at the eve of trial, you must really mean it.

Successful negotiators will always be testing to find their opponent's true bottom line. In this way, the parties will narrow the gap between the demands and reach a successful settlement.

To these general rules I will add two words of caution:

First, maintain records of settlement discussions. Negotiations heat up and cool down; lawyers may change; recollections may fail. Written records help keep settlement negotiations on track. Some lawyers make entries on a single settlement sheet; others write separate memos that they keep in a file. The method is not important. What is important is that you find a method and stick to it.

Second, a word of warning is in order about the person who may become a mediator for settlement: the judge. A judge can be crucial in bringing your unreasonable opponent to the bargaining table. But approach this three-way negotiation with caution, for the judge may want to drive a harder bargain than you are prepared to make. If this happens, keep this in mind: Even a judge can learn that, once you have an ultimatum, you really intend to keep it.

Once trial starts, settlement negotiations need not end. They may continue until the verdict is read and even through the appeal. Of course, you should be prepared to litigate and to try your case. But also be prepared to settle. Sometimes you will be happily surprised.

Settlement of Civil Cases: A View from the Bench

by Eugene F. Lynch

More than a hundred years ago, Ralph Waldo Emerson wrote, ''The people wish to be settled.'' Were he alive today he might have written: ''The people wish to litigate,'' for more than at any other time, people are turning today to the courts to help them solve their disputes. Our pluralistic, complex, and crowded society seems to breed lawsuits faster than pollution.

Every lawyer and judge, and virtually everyone for that matter, is aware that our courts are backed up with all types of litigation. As a result, people wait a long time to get into a courtroom after they file their lawsuit. This situation is so widely recognized and troublesome that it is difficult to read a newspaper, listen to the radio, or watch television without someone complaining that the courts are overloaded and in danger of coming to a halt.

Most civil master calendar judges now recognize that one of the most effective ways to keep the calendar current and to shorten the time between filing and the trial, is to use the mandatory settlement conference before a judge.

The formal settlement conference has had its ups and downs over the last twenty-five years. In the past, when the calendar of a particular court backed up suddenly, that court put great emphasis on the settlement conference; but as matters returned to normal, the use of the conference abated. Now, however, courts in most jurisdictions are putting continuing emphasis on the settlement conference. In California, for example, continuing education programs have begun to include lectures and demonstrations about the formal settlement conference.

A legitimate dispute exists between lawyers and judges about the best

---

The author is a Federal District Court Judge in San Francisco.

time to hold the formal settlement conference. The judges in San Francisco take a twofold approach. At the setting, or pretrial conference, some three months prior to the trial, the court fixes a date for the settlement conference. Optimally, that date is between two and four weeks before trial. The theory behind this is that the maximum opportunity for settling the case exists when all discovery has been accomplished and the trial date looms just ahead.

In addition, the presiding judge sets aside every Friday afternoon for stipulated settlement conferences, which are assigned to various judges. A case can get on this calendar at any time if all sides stipulate in writing that a conference would be helpful.

No doubt different judges and lawyers have different ideas about the proper time for the conference. However, enough time must have passed since the filing of the suit for discovery to have revealed to both sides the value and risks of the case.

Reasonable Success

Proper timing is only one of the requirements if the conference is to have reasonable success. Other minimal requirements are that:

1. Settlement conference statements (discussed below) must be filed with the judge at least three days before the conference.
2. Those present must include both the plaintiff and the defendant (or if the defendant is insured, a representative of the insurance company with sufficient authority to negotiate) as well as the lawyers who will try the case.

In some cases, the representative of the insurance company is quite a distance away, or the person with authority to permit the payment of large sums is in the home office in a different part of the country. In these situations, one representative with authority ought to be by the phone, regardless of the time or distance. In one instance, when the insurance representative with authority was testifying in a federal court in Montana, a call was placed to the judge handling that case. He adjourned his court for fifteen minutes to allow us to discuss settlement, and we were able to dispose of the case. In a number of instances, the court dealing with a local representative has telephoned a person with greater authority in the home office to give that person the firsthand benefit of the judge's appraisal. Often, this resulted in settlement, even where the parties were deadlocked, because home-office executives sometimes have difficulty appreciating the risks and problems of a case about which they have only read reports. Another problem occurs in malpractice cases where the insurance policy allows settlement only with the approval of the defendant. In these cases, the defendant must come to the conference to avoid wasting time in negotiating a settlement that the professional then refuses to approve.

The parties must have talked at least a week before the conference in an effort to explore settlement. At a minimum, the plaintiff must have made a demand, and the defendant should have made a counteroffer. Not only does this procedure often result in the parties settling the case themselves, but it is a waste of everyone's time when the defendants announce at the start of a conference that they cannot negotiate because they have just been given the first demand and they have had no time to consider it.

If the case settles before the conference, lawyers must not neglect to inform the judge so another conference may be substituted. Timely failure to notify of settlement is one of the court's biggest complaints.

Lawyers and judges know that proper evaluation of cases and good settlement techniques are skills that every trial lawyer must develop, since statistics show that over 90 percent of all civil cases settle prior to trial. However, while lawyers know these statistics, their clients often do not. Lawyers, therefore, must both inform their clients about the possibility of settlement and prepare them for it.

Lawyers should start this preparation from the time that they are first retained. Clients should be told that sometime during the case the issue of settlement is going to come up and they will have to consider making a demand offer. They should also be told that, at a minimum, the court is going to hold a formal conference at which both clients must be present and prepared to discuss seriously resolution of the case.

This preparation avoids the situation in which the client walks into the settlement conference only vaguely aware of its purpose, and feels most put upon to be asked then and there to make a decision regarding money. This experience not only hinders meaningful negotiations, but whether the matter is settled or not, it leaves the client with a bad impression of the process.

Unnerving Experience

In addition, most clients find coming into a courtroom an unnerving experience. The experience can be less jarring if counsel introduce their clients to the judge before the conference begins. This also gives the clients a sense of involvement in the process, so that when the judge and lawyers are negotiating (usually in the judge's chambers) the client in the courtroom does not feel left out.

In addition to preparing his client, plaintiff's counsel must also help the defense in the settlement effort by making available the information that insurance companies feel they must have, such as medical reports, verification of wages and copies of medical bills.

The rules of most courts require that each side present a settlement conference statement. Trial judges feel that many lawyers approach the preparation of this statement as a pro forma matter. In fact, lawyers should prepare the statement both as a tool to settle the case at a fair value and as a means of arguing their position to the court. In addition, the statement ought to give the court all the information it needs to act as a catalyst in bringing the parties together.

A good settlement conference statement is brief. Three pages should be the maximum in all but a few cases. In a catastrophe case, and other complex matters, you may want to prepare a booklet, complete with pictures, medical reports, highlights of expert testimony, diagrams, details of contract negotiations, photocopies of important pages of depositions, and so on.

If the case is a personal injury matter, the statement should include all medical reports obtained by the plaintiff or defendant, plus any expert reports. If there are no medical reports, the statement can involve a photocopy of a page of the hospital or doctor's record that gives the most information. It ought to include an accident or police report. If the case involves burns or scars, the statement should have pictures showing the past and present condition of the party. If it is a slip-and-fall injury, construction case, or product liability matter, the statement may have photos of the area or product. If it is a contract case, copies of the document should be included, with major parts underlined. If the document is too bulky, copies of the important sections can be attached. In any case, counsel should bring all medical records, business documents, and depositions to the conference so the judge can personally review this material if necessary.

The body of the statement should outline briefly, and without needless detail, what the case is about. When independent witnesses are crucial, the statement can briefly set forth their testimony.

In a personal injury case, the statement should describe the original injuries and their present status, and it should provide a list of all medical bills and match them with the names of the party or institution where they were incurred. It should also set out the amount of lost income and, if this is disputed, state the nature of the dispute.

Regardless of the type of case, if liability is effectively conceded for purposes of settlement, the statement should say so to allow the judge to focus his attention on the issues that are disputed.

The statement should also report all settlement discussions to date and the amounts of money or relief discussed. Because of this and because of all the other confidential information settlement conference statements contain, they should not be placed in the court's file; they should be returned to the trial attorney or destroyed.

The court's rules should provide that the settlement judge be different from the trial judge. The reasons for this are obvious; there is not only the possibility of actual bias, but the appearance of bias both to counsel and his or her client.

The art of negotiation, which is the essence of a settlement conference, is a very personal thing; what enables one judge to effect a settlement will not necessarily enable another to do the same.

Personally, I believe that the judge must evaluate the case on the basis of his overall experience and an analysis of the particular facts. He should not merely sound out the parties as to how much each side will pay and then try to bridge the difference. He must evaluate not only the facts, but the jury appeal of the case, and he must evaluate the impression each party will make as a witness. The judge may have to review parts of a deposition, medical reports or expert reports, or refer to cases cited to be able to arrive at an informed opinion about the value of the case.

During his lifetime, every judge works in a single community. He sees the same trial attorneys and the same insurance adjusters again and again. He thereby acquires a reputation regarding settlement. If his reputation is that of a judge who knows the value of cases and who works to appraise them properly, the attorneys and adjusters he sees will be more inclined to listen to his thoughts on settlement.

If attorneys prefer not to discuss the case at all with the other side present, they should express their feelings and the judge should accommodate them.

Since the primary role of the judge is that of a catalyst to help bring the parties together, the judge must *listen*. It is astonishing how much information a judge can pick up from the way the attorney and parties talk. Sometimes by the court's merely listening—by serving as a forum for the sides to meet and talk to each other about settlement—the case will settle with little persuasion or even discussion by the court. On the other hand, there is nothing wrong with the judge's taking a position and using arguments to back up his analysis.

Much more is accomplished by interviewing and talking to each side separately than both together. The judge may want to start out with both sides in chambers to get a better grasp of their positions, but it is when the parties are talking confidentially that the most is accomplished. It goes without saying that what is said in confidence must be kept that way unless counsel agrees that it may be told the other side. The court must use its intuition, based perhaps on its knowledge of the case from the settlement statement, to determine how the conference should begin. Sometimes I begin with all sides; sometimes with the plaintiff or the defendant alone; sometimes in multiple defense cases, with all the defendants together. Under all circumstances, counsel have a right to expect that the judge will give them an honest and well-considered opinion of the probable value of the suit.

During the conference, lawyers must bear in mind the time pressures on the court. The court cannot allow settlement conferences to interfere with its normal trial calendar; otherwise it has lost the rationale for the conference—expediting the calendar. Discussion and argument must be compressed; if time runs out and it appears that progress is being made, the conference can be continued to another date. In these situations, the continuation provides the benefit of a cooling-off period during which the parties can reassess their positions in light of the discussions.

Make Recommendations

The judge should talk to the individual plaintiff and make recommendations, but only if the plaintiff's lawyer asks him to. When I speak to plaintiffs, I say something like the following:

> This is your case, not mine, and in the final analysis you will have to make the decision; however, you should be guided by what your attorney says, since he is expert in these matters. I will also give you the advantage of my experience. The reason we have a settlement conference is to try to predict what the probable result will be in your case—that is, when the jury returns, what their verdict will be. If their verdict is for more money than you've been offered, you're ahead, but if it's for less, you're out tax-free dollars. Furthermore, the defendant insurance company or corporation is in a far better position to risk money than you are.
>
> I want to point out to you the problems and risks in your case from a jury standpoint and to analyze what is a fair value for your case and why this is so. This is not a game of chance, as juries are relatively predictable in terms of what they will do when they are given a certain set of facts.
>
> There are expenses in trying the case, and they will have to be deducted from the verdict. Therefore, a settlement at a certain figure is worth as much as a higher verdict obtained in court.

I then try to analyze the good points and the bad points about the case and how a jury will react to it. Experience shows that most clients—though not all—are impressed by what the judge says. Moreover, they feel that to a certain extent they have had their day in court and a chance to express their feelings. Often these clients go away with much better feelings about the legal system.

Settlement in a Personal Injury Case: The Imperfect Art

by e. robert (bob) wallach

There is not one of us who does not relish the role of courtroom advocate. Not only do we receive admiration and awe for our daily struggle with the intricacies of mind and artifice in the courtroom, but we may also associate ourselves with the tradition of noble advocates of the past, from Socrates through Sir Thomas More.

It is a comfortable notion with which to entertain our private selves. But in the reality of day-to-day practice, there is not one of us who does not acknowledge that the role of noble gladiator in a just cause is an illusion—at best, a momentary reality.

The fact is that there is no one currently engaged in personal injury litigation, for plaintiff or defendant, who does not settle 90 to 95 percent of the litigation. Settlement—not the brilliance of cross-examination or the eloquence of final argument—is our most often used technique. Yet the art of negotiation—an art that not only helps to preserve the rights of our clients, but continues to pay the overhead and send our children to school—is the least taught, most ignored, and often, most abused skill of the trial lawyer.

Despite recent advances in advocacy training in law schools, there is still a disdain for talking about the process of converting human pain and suffering or the consequences of death into dollars and cents. How difficult it is for the law professor to acknowledge that the vaunted preparation for the profession that fills the curricula of our law schools leads ultimately to the resolution of pecuniary rights in an arena populated by claims adjusters, claims committees, investigators, and lawyers who have traditionally occupied the bottom rung of prestige in the hierarchy of our elitist profession.

The author is a practicing trial lawyer in San Francisco and Washington, D.C. He is also Dean of the Hastings Center for Trial and Appellate Advocacy.

However, realizing that settlement is the art that we must strive to perfect if we are to fulfill the role of advocate and fulfill our obligation to represent competently our client, plaintiff or defendant, let us engage in the great American pastime of trying to formulate ''Black Letter'' rules—rules for the amorphous art of settlement.

We begin our discussion with the adage that has afflicted us since the first day we entered law school. Settlement discussions must not begin without the same preparation that any competent trial lawyer would bring to a trial.

In any confrontation of opposing views, it is essential to move dramatically and impressively at the outset. This is generally plaintiff's potential advantage, though plaintiffs often overlook it.

An increasing number of defense lawyers are beginning to realize that they do not have to wait for the overture of settlement from plaintiff's counsel. Often, it is in the interests of the defense, and certainly in the economic interest of the insurance industry, to initiate settlement discussions.

The quality of the settlement presentation by either side will be determined by its intimate understanding of the case, the witnesses, the parties, and the human intangibles.

The opening salvo is the preparation of a settlement brochure or an extensive settlement letter. The elements of either are essentially the same.

Flair of Persuasion

First, a statement of the facts is necessary. This should be carefully phrased, detailed not only with the evidentiary facts of the occurrence but also with the human factors that often determine the outcome of a personal injury case. It should be objective and not subject to the criticism that it has omitted salient facts that the opponent will be able to rely on at the same time; it should be phrased in a way that carefully carries the flair of persuasion for your client, much as a well-constructed opening statement would.

The fact statement is followed by a profile of the client (plaintiff or defendant). This element of persuasion, often overlooked entirely, should be advanced as early in the settlement negotiations as possible. It requires the lawyer to understand the client fully and to recognize the ways in which the injury or death has affected the lifestyle and future of that person. It requires more than a recitation of injuries or acknowledgement of the death. It requires knowing enough about the way the individual lived and the context of the individual's family, occupation, and interests or surviving family to personalize the consequences of the accident and its aftermath. It is often a good idea to include photographs that depict the plaintiff as he or she was before the injury, as the family was before the death—engaged in activities that were part of the joy of living.

Perhaps most important is to extract from depositions, medical records and statements of witnesses that have already been compiled during discovery, those observations that will be made from the witness stand and that will corroborate the terrible effects of this tragedy on your client.

While this human orientation is important in the evaluation of an individual personal injury matter, the core ingredient for most claims committees is the hard "specials"—the tangible economic loss as listed in medical bills and the wage loss, past and future. This is the most mechanical of the presentations, but the more skill you bring to it, the less likely it is to cause you harm and the more persuasive it will become. All medical bills should be carefully compiled, itemized, and their credibility checked. "Credibility" means that the bills must be unquestionably related to the event that is the subject of the action. While we are accustomed to thinking of this as primarily ground for an error by the plaintiff's lawyer, this maxim, like most others, is equally applicable to the defense attorney.

In a recent matter involving a young woman who had sustained a cardiac arrest and was in a coma following minor surgery, defense counsel undertook to determine exactly what it would cost on a monthly basis to maintain her in an adequate convalescent facility. He wanted to avoid the continuing extraordinary expense of an intensive care unit. While the defense lawyer expressed a good faith concern for the provision of adequate medical care to the comatose young mother, a check with the administrator of the convalescent hospital revealed that the figures defense counsel had provided were one-third of the actual expense projected for care considered essential.

Badly Shaken

One can accept the representations of defense counsel about his good faith and about an honest difference of opinion on the adequacy of medical care necessary to sustain life. However, his credibility was badly shaken in the eyes of counsel for plaintiff and in the eyes of the family by representations that proved to be inconsistent with everyone's expressed desire to care appropriately for this tragically ill woman.

Counsel may wish to include the estimates of an economist or an actuary, the projected cost of an annuity, a proposed evaluation of comparable, potential earning figures from other occupations, or a wide variety of data that appropriately fit into this section of "special damages." Such data provide the hard foundation for evaluation before proceeding to the more difficult and nebulous elements of general damages.

In an injury case, it is important to substantiate the injuries, and their ramifications, with as much reliance as possible upon medical evidence that will be admitted at trial. The inclusion of appropriate medical reports, excerpts from hospital records (including nurses' notes), consultative reports, and even extracts from medical articles that discuss the injury and its probable long-range effects, all accomplish the dual purpose of dramatically picturing the injury and corroborating the prognosis.

Include Photographs

The inclusion of appropriate photographs depicting the various stages of development of the injury, particularly in burn cases, is essential to demonstrate the various degrees of severity suffered by the plaintiff.

Defense counsel are no less able to create a formidable defense to the injury by presenting medical support data that contradicts, minimizes or, perhaps most importantly, recommends alternative lifestyles or methods of treatment that can alleviate the severity of the injury. There is, in the judgment of almost all conscientious defense counsel, a recognition of the obligation to provide expert medical consultation in the treatment of a severe or catastrophic injury. It is appropriate, not only to lessen the economic import of the injury, but to fulfill the humanitarian objective of assisting the plaintiff, to return to as normal a lifestyle as possible.

There are some adherents of the ''old school'' who would resist these suggestions on the theory that medical evidence should be withheld until trial. There is an element of risk for the trial advocate who exposes the totality of medical evidence at an early stage. However, if the testimony is valid and well-substantiated, the threat of destructive cross-examination is more theoretical than real.

At this stage of the presentation, the careful presentation of a mini-brief on the various legal issues presented continues to demonstrate the extent of your preparation. It may well disabuse opposing counsel, client or claims committee of any misplaced reliance they may have on either your lack of expertise or on legal arguments that they mistakenly thought were available to them.

The extent and complexity of the brief will vary with the issues and the magnitude of the case. Here, the advocate wrestles with a question of strategy and, for many, conscience. Should the mini-brief be so objective as to discuss at length potential arguments of the opponent? Is it necessary not only to discuss favorable theories but also seek to meet, by expressing them first, arguments our opponent will rely on? When I was in law school, the answer was simple. We were taught that it was not necessary to do our opponent's research. Many have questioned that philosophy, particularly in terms of presenting a memorandum to the court deciding the issue. Whatever the merits of that argument, settlement presents an equally perplexing decision. If the tenor of the settlement presentation is candor, is it possible for counsel to veer from that standard when the law is discussed?

Everyone must be guided by his or her own philosophy of practice. I personally choose the full exposition. The candid evaluation of a case for settlement is a thread that runs throughout the settlement presentation. If there are weaknesses in our legal position, we gain little by avoiding them; in my experience, defense counsel is as able as I am, if not more able. I find it better to deal with those arguments and attempt to find responses that will impress an opponent enough so that while the attorney may not agree, he or she at least understands and can communicate to the client the fact that the issue is not settled. It is no different from dealing with contested factual issues that a jury may decide either way and that counsel understand to have both strengths and weaknesses. Inherent in the ability to bring about a settlement is a complete understanding of both the strength and the frailty of our position.

Assume that you represent a severely brain-damaged young man who was struck while attending his disabled vehicle late at night on a well-lit freeway. The driver of the car that struck him left a bar fifteen or twenty minutes before, and after the accident is found to have blood alcohol of .015. Settlement with the driver and his carrier is quick, and you are left to seek the measurement of damages in a "dramshop" cause of action against the bar.

As is immediately apparent, the factual basis of this case is not nearly as strong as plaintiff's counsel would want in a traditional dramshop cause of action. But what of the law? Is it essential, in order to prove a case against the bar, that the bartenders be shown to have known, or in the exercise of reasonable conduct ought to have known, that the customer was "obviously intoxicated?" Is that the test? Is the sole standard to be applied a statutory basis, resting in the criminal sanction upon a bartender who serves an "obviously intoxicated person?" That will certainly be the position of defense counsel, and there is ample supporting law.

In this situation, everything argues for the preparation of an extensive memorandum that fully discloses the theory of plaintiff's case, founded on the substantive law that a bartender is held to the same standard of reasonable conduct as any other individual; that the test for a bartender, or the owner of a bar, is not "obvious intoxication," but the foreseeability of harm arising from the serving of alcoholic beverages in sufficient quantity to produce an .015 blood alcohol in an individual who must drive a vehicle when he leaves the bar.

Opposing counsel will evaluate a case differently if a jury will render a determination rather than a judge in response to a motion for summary judgment. Even as to the possibility of appeal, a carefully prepared legal brief presented during settlement negotiations may well diminish the enthusiasm of counsel and his client for appeal, if they must take seriously the prospect of making "bad law" in the process, together with the accumulation of interest during the appeal.

Both counsel for plaintiff and defendant have the same opportunities and rationale for the full presentation of the substantive law in a light that will educate opposing counsel and the client to the legal difficulties attending the case. Both sides should remember that, ironically, opposing counsel becomes an essential ally in the cause of the settlement. Only a complete, candid and reasonable settlement proposal will persuade your opponent that it is a sound basis for either consummation of settlement or beginning along that path. Unless opposing counsel is persuaded of its merits, he or she will not undertake the essential task of communicating the strengths of the settlement overture to the client in an effort to induce either the payment of substantial funds or the acceptance of an offer.

We are necessarily kept one step removed from the opposing party. That barrier, created by the sanctity of attorney-client privilege and the obligation to communicate with a client only through his or her representative, must be transformed into a bridge of communication by which our efforts toward settlement are effectively articulated and persuasively recommended by the client's own lawyer. To accomplish the metamorphosis of the opposing advocate into an ally in the interest of settlement requires not only the sort of presentation that we have discussed, but also an attitude of respect for the adversary.

The last portion of the presentation is the evaluation and demand for settlement, or the offer to be made. Most lawyers or claims representatives, upon receiving a settlement proposal, turn to this section before they begin to read any other. The ultimate test of the possibility of settlement rests in the reaction of trained counsel or claims personnel to the reasonableness of the figures suggested.

Here again, able lawyers will differ markedly as to the best approach. Many successful plaintiff's counsel believe firmly in the proposition that "You can always go down, but you can never go back up," and fix their demands accordingly. Equally able counsel for the defense or their clients adhere to the proposition that they should make every effort to "buy the case as cheaply as possible" and come up only in increments as the negotiations develop.

Time-Honored Waltz

Other lawyers have acquired for themselves an envied reputation for either placing a value on a case that commands immediate respect and acceptance, or for evaluating the case and offering an amount that plaintiff's counsel cannot refuse. The attitude we take in evaluating a case for ourselves may have to be very different from that which we can communicate to our opponent. However, there are circumstances in which we can feel confident that the individual or company has a history of candid and fair evaluations. An increasing minority subscribe to the philosophy that most settlement negotiations are a charade of meandering offers and counter-offers. The alternative is to abandon the time-honored waltz of settlement in favor of an efficient, firm evaluation based on realistic considerations.

We cannot assume that our offer or evaluation will be accepted without a history of relationships on which we have built our reputation. This does not mean that an evaluation should simply be an "opening shot" from which point "something will happen." There are at least two fundamental rules to be followed for the initial evaluation. From the plaintiff's standpoint, the demand must be a figure that is not so high that it removes from the defendant any potential threat that it will be achieved or exceeded by jury result. A demand beyond the range of the opponent's expectation about an ultimate jury verdict presents no reason for settlement. Why pay a figure that is, at best, the maximum jury verdict?

The principle can be put another way: a demand must be a figure in the range that will present the opponent a serious threat that it will be exceeded, and thus require that some explanation be offered after the result about why the demand was not accepted. No one likes to lose, but more importantly, no one likes to explain a loss that could have been avoided.

For defense counsel, the rule is the same in reverse: an offer must be made that is close to the jury verdict range. It must be a figure that will require plaintiff's counsel to explain to his or her client that while the figure may not be all that is desired, it is certainly within the realm of possibility that a jury will return less and not more, or not sufficiently more to warrant the risks and expenses of trial.

Major Stress

Either counsel makes the opponent's job easy when the evaluation is so far out of the "range of reason" that it removes the element of decision and choice. Especially for defense counsel, who usually presents a client on a continuing basis, undertaking a trial with knowledge that the demand prevented any real possibility of settlement relieves a major stress. Beyond this, each case must be evaluated on its own merits. Formulas are sometimes helpful (e.g., five times the specials). Increasingly, they seem less relevant than an individual presentation of the case and its effect upon the victim.

There is no way to bring computerlike accuracy to the evaluation of a personal-injury settlement. There is, however, the fact that a reputation for candor and fair dealing makes a figure submitted by either side initially more worthy of close consideration.

Recognizing that every case is different from every other, it is often possible to gain a range of values for a particular injury. With almost uncanny precision, juries will establish (in a given geographic area) a "value" for a broken leg or a cervical strain or the death of a housewife. Some years ago, two trials took place simultaneously in contiguous counties in northern California. Both involved the death of young women in childbirth following lengthy periods of labor. The theories of the cases were so similar and the circumstances so identical as to surprise both of the plaintiffs' counsel. Each case took approximately three weeks to try, and in each instance the jury returned a verdict for the plaintiff. The margin of difference in the verdicts was $5,000 even though neither jury knew of the other case. While this particular example may seem unique, experienced trial lawyers throughout the country will attest that there is, in fact, a range of values for injuries. While not certain, the range of values allows us to establish a "range of reason" within which our evaluation should fall.

Vigorous Denunciation

Recall the lawyer who estimated far too low the cost of convalescent care and so threatened his credibility in the settlement negotiations. Such conduct often breeds a response destructive to negotiations. In that case, one of the plaintiff's attorneys, who was intimately involved with the family tragedy and the efforts to try to sustain a home life for young children in the wake of the loss of their mother's presence, understandably responded to opposing counsel with a vigorous denunciation of counsel's motives and good faith. The letter was sent not only to the lawyer, but to co-plaintiff's counsel and to others legitimately interested in the settlement process. The response of defense counsel was immediate; settlement negotiations ended in his resentment of this attack on his professional integrity.

The most important lesson in this episode in this: the success of settlement negotiations of any type is interwoven with the regard the adversaries have from the integrity of each other. This is not limited to personal injury litigation, or indeed litigation. Norman Cousins, editor of the *Saturday Review,* recently disclosed an episode that took place during the Vietnam War. Hubert Humphrey, then Vice-President, was visiting in Japan and had grown disillusioned with America's role in Vietnam. Among Americans with him was a person who knew of a Japanese educator who had been a longtime personal friend of Ho Chi Minh, Premier of North Vietnam. Vice-President Humphrey met with the educator and implored him to go to Hanoi to persuade the North Vietnamese to meet with the Americans in secret in either Geneva or Poland in order that settlement—that is, peace—might be achieved. It was the time of the American suspension of its bombing of North Vietnam and President Johnson's expression of hope for peace. The educator went willingly and secured from Ho Chi Minh a willingness to meet. The representation was simple: "The Americans had demonstrated their credibility in truly seeking peace by their cessation of bombing. It is now time for Hanoi to respond in an equal overture of good faith by coming to the bargaining table." Humphrey returned, elated, to Washington and communicated this development to the Security Council and the President. One week later, President Johnson advised the American people, in a television address, that Hanoi had shown no willingness to negotiate settlement of the conflict and resumed the bombing. North Vietnam then launched its successful Tet Offensive. The Johnson administration repeatedly sent new overtures of negotiation through intermediaries. All were rejected with the response that there was no way in which America could be trusted again.

In our own enthusiasm to be advocates, we often treat our opposition as though they were somehow without merit or honor. Almost without exception, the contrary is the fact. Lawyers of great skill, dedication to their clients and high principle practice in all areas of litigation, including personal injury. Unless a lawyer or a principal has given unequivocal reason to believe otherwise, the conduct of settlement negotiations must reflect high regard for our opponent.

Everyone has problems in approaching settlement negotiations. Either plaintiff's or defendant's counsel may have a difficult client. Problems of excess insurance, pressures of trial schedules, and substantial outstanding debts of the plaintiff occasioned by the injury or death are but a few. While it may be difficult to qualify such elements, we know that these factors can and do influence the course of negotiations. It is imperative that we repeat to ourselves that this is a "human event" requiring not only calculation of the special damages but careful consideration of the intangibles.

Outside the context of violent combat or risk-filled adventure, we seldom think of courage as a quality in the art of advocacy. Yet, to be the faithful representative of a client requires the ability to stand firm despite the pressures of professional camaraderie, office overhead, ego satisfaction, or fear. Not one of us is free of the economic pressures that may press toward the settlement of a "good" case because the offer is "reasonable," although we may understand that it is not all the client deserves.

The pressures of ego also afflict us all. Plaintiff's counsel may want to "win the big one" despite the fairness of the offer. Defense counsel may see an opportunity to prevail over an opponent of high reputation, even though the demand is fair.

Our continuing relationship with those whom we admire may cause us to strive for an amicable settlement that is as much influenced by our knowledge that there will be future negotiations in other cases as by our sense of responsibility to this particular client.

Unnatural Act

There also abides within many trial lawyers a fear of the uncertainty of the courtroom. There is something not quite natural about the way trial lawyers submit themselves to regular and unpredictable battle with skilled adversaries. We regularly enter the joust with opponents who are capable of exposing our vulnerability in a way neither we nor others can avoid understanding. Small wonder that for more lawyers than we care to acknowledge, the prospect of trial works its silent pressures on the decision to settle.

Any of these pressures may cause us to change our original, dispassionate evaluation of the "range of reason" into which we believe our client's recovery should fall. For reasons of our standing with our colleagues, to say nothing of our own sense of self-respect, it is important that a final demarkation line be drawn—that point at which we know we will commence trial rather than compromise the client's interests any further.

For plaintiff's and defendant's counsel, courage is nowhere more apparent than in dealing with the "bad faith" case. In those instances in which we represent a client whose injuries or losses are so extreme, the available insurance coverage so limited, and the liability facts so postured that there is no alternative to a demand for the full policy limits, we can permit no other factors to enter our consideration as to value.

Bad Faith

For defense counsel, the task is no less difficult. The decision to reject a demand for bad faith when one fully understands that the consequence to the principal may be dire could easily be influenced by any number of rationalizations that would permit taking "the easy road."

In this situation, both lawyers ought to evaluate their clients' interests as quickly as possible, and if they must adhere to an inflexible position as a matter of conscience, respect that decision, recognize that the usual efforts at settlement are not available and proceed immediately to trial.

For decades, the law schools and the great deans of the trial bar have taught us that the role of the adversary is to prevail. What sweeter moment than the return of the jury and the announcement of victory over your opponent—the confirmation of the totality of your legal skills accepted by either judge or jury in full vindication of your client's rights?

But that is a limited definition of "victory." In these past two decades particularly, experienced trial lawyers first learned to accept and then to encourage the notion that an honorable settlement in the client's interest was as much skillful representation as the glamorous drama of the courtroom. Lawyers have learned to understand that overtures of settlement made by either side do not indicate weakness, but a mature understanding of the need to find an alternative to the uncertainties of trial whenever possible.

While others may phrase the need for settlement in terms of court congestion or the inadequate competence of counsel in trial, the true rationale is the knowledge that "there is nothing better for the client than a good settlement."

This means that the concept of the advocate requires redefinition. An advocate can, with genteelness and grace, deflect people from confrontations that may produce more emotional distress than any lawsuit can justify. An advocate can conclude litigation successfully without feeling a need to accomplish the ultimate subjugation of his or her rival, allowing all parties some dignity, some measure of fairness, allowing as many participants as possible to go on to future events without the pall of utter defeat. An advocate recognizes that victory need not be total to be complete, and that there is more to victory than conquest.

Traps in Multitortfeasor Settlements

by Joel A. Dewey

Your client is an unfortunate pedestrian injured in an auto accident caused by two drag racers. You sue both racers, alleging joint and several liability for the full extent of your client's grievous injuries. A lawyer for Racer$_1$ approaches you with a settlement proposal. After weeks of tense negotiations, you and your adversary agree on a settlement figure. You prepare a release based on one from your form file and settle down to plan your trial strategy against Racer$_2$.

Before you relax, consider this: You may just have committed malpractice. And if *you* did not, Racer$_1$'s lawyer almost certainly did.

What both of you forgot to consider is one of the great traps—and, potentially, one of the great opportunities—in litigation against joint tortfeasors ("JTs," for short): the effect of a release on claims by or against nonsettling JTs.

Historically—and in some states, even today—the common law rule was simple, inflexible, and drastic. The release of one JT released all others for the same claim. The rationale was that a plaintiff was entitled to only one compensation tor a wrong. Thus, as soon as even a single JT paid, the plaintiff's cause of action was satisfied. In addition, the settling JT was barred under common law principles of "unclean hands" from seeking any contribution from the nonsettlers.

To avoid the harsh effects of the common law rules, plaintiffs' lawyers avoided releases and developed an alternative: the covenant not to sue. In a covenant not to sue, a plaintiff does not give up his cause of action; he merely agrees not to enforce it against the other parties to the covenant. Because the covenant is a contract, the plaintiff breaches it if he sues, and he thereby becomes liable to the defendant for damages.

The author is an associate with Piper & Marbury in Baltimore.

Courts generally held that a covenant not to sue with one JT did not bar a plaintiff from recovering against others. But there were risks. Some courts held that a release by any other name was still a release, and they refused to let plaintiffs use covenants not to sue to evade the common law rule. Some defendants refused to sign such a covenant because, unlike a release, it gave them no repose. At common law, remember, a release automatically protected the defendant from any claim for contribution, since all other JTs were released. With a covenant not to sue, however, the plaintiff's claim is unextinguished and the settling defendant remains exposed to potential claims for contribution or indemnity from any nonsettling defendant against whom the plaintiff later recovers a judgment.

Enter the modern legislator.

In the past 50 years, statutes have modified the common law rule in most jurisdictions. These statutes provide guidelines for a plaintiff to release one JT without extinguishing his claim against nonsettling JTs. A plaintiff now can specify that he is willing to give up a portion of his claim in exchange for a stated consideration from the settling JT. In most situations, any future judgments for the plaintiff will be reduced by at least the amount the settling JT paid up front.

As a result, tortfeasor releases are fraught with uncertainty. At common law, the effect of a tortfeasor release was obvious on its face. Today, plaintiffs cannot always be sure what they are giving up in the way of future claims against other defendants, while settling JTs remain exposed to the possibility of future claims for contribution by their nonsettling brethren.

Because the rules vary, always check the law of the applicable jurisdiction. Some give a plaintiff more flexibility, some less. In some states, a release of one JT does not release others unless there is an express provision to that effect. Other jurisdictions apply the opposite presumption: For them a release of one JT does release all others unless there is an express reservation of the plaintiff's rights against remaining JTs. And a few jurisdictions still adhere to the old rule that a release completely extinguishes the plaintiff's claim, no matter what crafty limitations the plaintiff's lawyer has included in the release.

Of course, as plaintiffs gain flexibility, defendants lose repose. To the extent the plaintiff's claim remains alive, a settling JT remains exposed to potential claims for contribution by JTs against whom the plaintiff later recovers. To rectify this situation, the modern rule permits the parties to specify in a release that the plaintiff will give a settling JT a "joint tortfeasor credit" against any judgment the plaintiff ultimately wins. The credit is then applied against the judgment to reduce—or even eliminate—both the plaintiff's recovery on the judgment and the settling JT's liability for contribution to the judgment-debtor JT.

The nature and size of the joint tortfeasor credit define the battleground for negotiations over tortfeasor releases. The modern rules give a knowledgeable party a tremendous opportunity to structure a settlement to his advantage. The lawyer's obligation is to know the rules, identify the goals to be achieved through the release, and draft the necessary language.

As a plaintiff, you will want to:

- achieve a favorable resolution with the settling JT;
- make sure you have not barred any claims you may have against nonsettling JTs; and
- minimize joint tortfeasor credits that will reduce your future recoveries against nonsettling JTs.

As a defendant, you will want to:

- extinguish the plaintiff's claims against you in this lawsuit;
- extinguish any other claims the plaintiff might have against you; and
- make sure persons not a party to the settlement cannot recover contribution from you if the plaintiff later recovers against them.

Consider, first, the truly general release; it customarily contains language releasing "any other persons or firms who may be liable, become liable, or be claimed to be liable." Some plaintiffs' attorneys have been known to miss such language in a cursory once-over of the release, and agree.

But such a general release is an unconditional victory for the settling defendant. Virtually all states hold that it means what it says and that it will bar any future claim for the injury at issue. Thus, a general release achieves all of the defendant's goals and none of the plaintiff's—except in the unlikely event that the settlement was sufficiently generous to send the plaintiff home fully satisfied. (I have never met such a plaintiff.)

The moral is, defendants should always try for a general release. And plaintiffs should never agree to them.

Putting general releases aside, the parties sit down to haggle. In many states, the framework for multitortfeasor settlements is a version of either the Uniform Joint Tortfeasors Act or the Uniform Joint Obligations Act. Other states have adopted guidelines paralleling these acts through case law or statute. Always—it bears repeating—check the law of the applicable jurisdiction.

Generally, the rules governing contribution and joint tortfeasor credits apply if the following conditions are met: (1) a plaintiff must give a release (2) for a tort (3) to a joint tortfeasor (4) who is jointly and severally liable for the plaintiff's injuries and therefore faces a possible claim for contribution from at least one nonsettling party.

If all four of these conditions exist, joint tortfeasor rules usually will govern both the plaintiff's and the settling defendant's rights and obligations as against each other and as against nonsettling parties, including the nonsettlers' rights to contribution. Often, the parties to a settlement have a choice: They can structure the settlement either to fulfill or to avoid fulfilling one or more conditions. The choice will depend on the facts of the particular litigation.

First, a plaintiff must give a release and not some other document designed to end litigation with the settling defendant. The definition of a release varies from jurisdiction to jurisdiction. Most courts closely analyze an agreement such as a covenant not to sue to determine whether it triggers joint tortfeasor rules. As I noted above, some jurisdictions automatically treat such agreements as a release. Other courts flyspeck the covenant looking for indicia of at least a partial release. If there is any doubt, the document is regarded as a release. So, if the parties want to avoid joint tortfeasor rules with a covenant not to sue, they should make certain that the jurisdiction whose law governs the settlement will distinguish such agreements from a release.

A release will not do its job unless the parties to it are properly identified. The defendant especially should ensure that the terms "releasor" and "releasee" both include heirs, survivors, and personal representatives. That way, the defendant achieves the broadest possible protection from future suits. For similar reasons, if one or more parties are corporations, the corporation should be defined to include its employees, agents, servants, representatives, and subsidiaries.

Minor plaintiffs are a recurring problem in tortfeasor settlements, since at common law a minor was not bound by his contract. Almost all jurisdictions have adopted statutes specifying procedures for obtaining a release from a minor; examples are appointment of a guardian and best friend or a motion for approval by the court. The lawyer for a minor plaintiff should identify and follow applicable requirements.

Once you have established that your settlement involves a release and who the proper parties are, you should focus on the nature of the claim being released. The statutes governing multitortfeasor settlements apply only to claims in tort. That limitation is significant because many cases involve both tort and contract claims. For example, construction lawsuits frequently involve both a claim for breach of the construction contract and one for negligence in performing the work. Suits on covenants not to compete often allege alternative claims for breach of the covenant and for tortious interference with the plaintiff's client relationships. You can easily imagine other examples.

When a complaint sounds in both tort and contract, a release of one of several defendants generally should specify which counts are being released. Draftsmanship can be tricky here. Depending on the facts, you may or may not want joint tortfeasor rules to apply to the settlement.

Assume, for example, a two-count complaint. In count 1, Plaintiff sues A for breach of contract; in count 2, Plaintiff sues A and B for negligence. Plaintiff negotiates a lump-sum settlement with A that includes both counts.

894

Under the joint tortfeasor rules, it is in Plaintiff's interest to allocate as much of the settlement payment as possible to the contract claim in count 1; that minimizes the joint tortfeasor credit B can claim against any judgment plaintiff wins on the tort claim in count 2. But, conversely, it is in A's interest to allocate all or most of the settlement payment to the tort claim; that maximizes the potential joint tortfeasor credit and reduces the likelihood that A will have to pay any contribution to B.

In short, the side that knows the joint tortfeasor rules has an advantage.

One word of caution: Be especially careful when settling a claim for breach of warranty. Some jurisdictions classify warranty claims under tort; others treat them as contract actions. Make sure you know which way your jurisdiction leans.

Having established that you are settling a claim in tort, you must clarify whether the settling defendant is a JT. This may seem a trivial point, but overlooking it can undo all the rest of your cautious labors to protect your client. The problem arises because the settling defendant probably wants to be regarded as a JT so that he can take advantage of the rules allocating joint tortfeasor credits. At the same time, it is standard practice for a defendant to include language in a release expressly denying liability.

The result is an anomaly only a lawyer could dream up. Courts have held that a release that purports to be governed by joint tortfeasor rules but that contains a denial of liability by the defendant without any further qualification of his status as a JT, is not a joint tortfeasor release. The rationale is that the defendant cannot be a JT if he denies liability in the release, since there has been no finding of liability in tort. In other words, you cannot be a *joint* tortfeasor if you are not a tortfeasor at all.

The historical basis for this ruling is the doctrine that the release of one who is not negligent does not affect the liability of others who are. Thus, some courts have held that because the only evidence before them is the settling defendant's denial of liability in a release, that defendant cannot be a JT and must remain in the case so that it can be determined whether or not he is a tortfeasor and whether or not joint tortfeasor rules should apply. See, for example, *Swigert v. Welk*, 213 Md. 613, 133 A.2d 428 (1957).

Imagine the settling defendant's frustration. Having paid a settlement on the assumption that he was capping his litigation costs, he finds that he must remain in the case through trial just so that the court can determine his tortfeasor status. If that approach were routine, it would eliminate nuisance value as a basis for settlement, since the nuisance of litigation would not go away.

Luckily, neither the plaintiff nor the defendant has much incentive to encourage such a result. The settling defendant wants out of the case. The plaintiff presumably does not want the settling defendant to remain. Indeed, many plaintiffs settle with one defendant in order to focus their case at trial on the remaining malefactors.

The solution is to include specific language in the release to ensure that the settling defendant is treated as a JT for purposes of the joint tortfeasor rules. Here, again, draftsmanship is everything: Make sure that the release includes a proviso that the defendant, while denying liability, "shall be regarded as a joint tortfeasor for the purpose of allocating joint tortfeasor credits to the same extent as if a judgment had been rendered against it." Most courts will uphold such a clause, reasoning under familiar contract principles that it embodies the express intent of the parties to the release. And once the court is satisfied that joint tortfeasor rules apply to the settlement, it should have no reason not to send the settling defendant on his way. See, for example, *Jones v. Hurst*, 54 Md. App. 607, 459 A.2d 219 (1983).

But judges are not the only ones who may want to keep a settling defendant in the case. If the settler's release does not make it clear that he is a JT and that his settlement is governed by joint tortfeasor rules, nonsettling defendants may insist that he stay in, either through crossclaims or by impleader. The nonsettlers may want to prove at trial that he is a JT so that they can apply a joint tortfeasor credit to reduce the judgment against them.

In such a scenario, of course, one risk for the nonsettlers is that they will pay the costs to litigate against the settling defendant and lose. For obvious reasons, there can be no joint tortfeasor credit if the settling defendant is found not liable at trial. Another risk is disrupting potential cooperation among defendants to beat the plaintiff's claim altogether. And if you're a nonsettling defendant, you may *want* to let the settler get away without a fight so that, at trial, you can point to his empty chair and put the whole blame on the settler, who will not be there to defend himself.

So if you think your codefendant may settle, take an interest in the drafting of his release. If either he or the plaintiff will not let you participate, do a thorough cost/benefit analysis before determining how to proceed. Above all, remember that no matter what your goals in the case, you must evaluate how the joint tortfeasor rules can help or hurt you.

Once the parties have satisfied these initial prerequisites for invoking joint tortfeasor rules, they can focus on the critical issue: the amount of the joint tortfeasor credit.

Many releases used today simply recite the amount paid in consideration for settling and say nothing about the application of joint tortfeasor rules. Most jurisdictions will interpret such a release to give joint tortfeasor credit in an amount equal to the settlement consideration. (Of course, if you are in a jurisdiction that requires an express reservation of your rights against nonsettling defendants, there will be *no* joint tortfeasor credit unless you have included appropriate language protecting the claims, or parts of claims, you are not settling.)

Now what happens when the plaintiff goes on to win a judgment against a nonsettling defendant? The answer turns on the legal concept of "pro rata share."

Courts have not always agreed on what constitutes a JT's pro rata share of a judgment for plaintiff. Here, too, you must check the law of the applicable jurisdiction. In some cases in which the fact finder allocates fault—say, 40 percent to one JT, 60 percent to another—each JT's pro rata share will be a percentage of the total judgment equal to his percentage of fault. But in most cases and jurisdictions, the prorating involves simply dividing the total dollar amount of the plaintiff's judgment by the number of JTs.

Bear in mind that the number of JTs is not always identical to the number of defendants. For example, two of the defendants may be master and servant; they usually will be regarded as one JT for purposes of computing pro rata shares and joint tortfeasor credits. Thus, suppose Plaintiff sues Driver$_1$, Driver$_2$, and Driver$_2$'s employer. Because Driver$_2$ and his employer are counted as one share, not two, Driver$_1$'s pro rata share will be one half, not one third.

When a plaintiff and a JT settle, no one will know what each JT's pro rata share ultimately may be. That uncertainty can create contribution problems for a settling JT who thought his problems were over. Assume that Plaintiff sues JT$_1$ and JT$_2$. JT$_1$ settles before trial for $30,000; the release reserves Plaintiff's rights against JT$_2$ but says nothing about joint tortfeasor credits. Plaintiff later obtains a judgment against JT$_2$ for $100,000.

JT$_2$ gets a joint tortfeasor credit of $30,000—the amount JT$_1$ paid—but still must pay Plaintiff $70,000, which is $20,000 more than JT$_2$'s pro rata share of $50,000 ($100,000 total judgment, divided by 2). As a result, JT$_2$ has a $20,000 contribution claim against JT$_1$, who thought his troubles were over when he settled with Plaintiff.

JT$_1$'s attorney could have avoided this problem by addressing it in the release. All he had to do was to include a clause defining the joint tortfeasor credit created by the settlement as the *greater* of either (1) the amount JT$_1$ paid Plaintiff in settlement or (2) JT$_1$'s pro rata share of any ultimate judgment.

Such a provision protects the settling JT against the uncertainties of judgment awards. If the judgment turns out to be so high that the settler's pro rata share is more than he paid in settlement, the plaintiff has agreed to forgo the difference. If the settler's pro rata share turns out to be smaller than the settlement, he has already paid more than his share. Either way, he is protected against any future claims for contribution.

In the hypothetical above, when Plaintiff won the $100,000 judgment against JT$_2$, the court would examine the settlement with JT$_1$, compare

897

the $30,000 JT$_1$ paid with his pro rata share of $50,000, and reduce the judgment by the greater amount. The plaintiff would get a judgment against JT$_2$ for $50,000, and JT$_2$ would be barred from suing JT$_1$ for contribution. By settling before trial, JT$_1$ saved $20,000—and that is why people settle.

Note, however, that Plaintiff gave up part of his recovery. In this age of long delays before trial, Plaintiff may consider it a good deal to receive $30,000 now instead of $50,000 years down the line. But plaintiffs' counsel, beware. Carefully analyze your claims against the nonsettling defendants (and the law of your jurisdiction) before accepting a release that defines the tortfeasor credit as the settlement payment or the settling defendant's pro rata share, "whichever is greater." Make sure you know what you may be relinquishing.

Consider the following examples, both of them based on reported cases:

- Plaintiff sues Driver and the Manufacturer of Driver's automobile. In a settlement with Manufacturer, Plaintiff accepts a release reciting a settlement consideration of $10 and containing a "whichever is greater" definition of the joint tortfeasor credit. Plaintiff's real reason for settling with Manufacturer is Manufacturer's offer of technical assistance on the claim against Driver. At trial Plaintiff wins a judgment of $18,000. The court, recognizing that Manufacturer's pro rata share of the judgment—$9,000—is greater than the stated settlement consideration of $10, reduces the judgment by the larger amount and enters a judgment against Driver of $9,000. *See Jones v. Hurst,* 54 Md. App. 607, 459 A.2d 219 (1983).

- Plaintiff sues Doctor and Hospital for alleged malpractice during an operation. Plaintiff settles with Hospital for $725,000. Although Hospital's release provides that any judgment against Doctor shall be reduced by Hospital's pro rata share, the law of the jurisdiction reads a "whichever is greater" clause into every joint tortfeasor release. At trial Plaintiff wins a judgment against Doctor of $600,000. Since the settlement is greater than Hospital's pro rata share of $300,000, the court reduces plaintiff's judgment by the full settlement amount of $725,000. Plaintiff recovers nothing against Doctor. *See Martinez v. Lopez,* 300 Md. 91, 476 A.2d 197 (1984).

In each case, the plaintiff's attorney neglected to "play out the hand." The result (we may surmise) was an irate client.

There is an additional element to consider in structuring a joint tortfeasor release. Recall that the settling defendant must be "jointly and severally liable" for the joint tortfeasor rules to apply. If two distinct tortfeasors have committed two separate and independent torts, the release of one does not affect the other's liability.

The classic example is when Plaintiff is injured in a car accident caused by Driver's negligence and then sustains additional injuries from a negligent blood transfusion by Hospital. Most courts treat these injuries as separate torts. A settlement with Driver leaves the claim against Hospital unchanged. Similarly, if Plaintiff's building is destroyed through Superintendent's negligence, and Agency negligently failed to procure insurance on the building, Plaintiff has been injured by two discrete torts.

In analyzing a multitortfeasor case for possible settlement, you must determine whether the plaintiff alleges one tort or a series. Determining how many torts are claimed and which, if any, involve JTs will let you concede settlement issues that do not affect you. Then you can focus on the settlement terms that make a real difference.

For example, a plaintiff who concludes that he has alleged a separate tort against each defendant should be willing to include language in a release that would be favorable to the settling defendant if he were a JT (for example a "whichever is greater" clause for joint tortfeasor credit) but otherwise is meaningless. Similarly, a defendant who is not a JT can accept settlement terms (for example, a blanket denial of liability) that otherwise might increase the risk of a claim for contribution.

By the way, don't forget that releases often contain a choice of law clause—frequently a boilerplate recitation that the release will be governed by the laws of the lawyer's home state. If you have checked the laws of your state as they apply to settlements with JTs (and I stress again that you always should do so), you may want to specify a different jurisdiction, one where the law is more favorable to the settlement terms you want to include.

Do not forget as well that joint tortfeasor rules only allow a settling JT to protect himself against future claims for contribution of some portion of the plaintiff's claim. The rules do not apply to a nonsettler's claim for indemnity or full reimbursement of the plaintiff's judgment. Common law rules governing indemnity have survived the development of modern rules for JTs. Thus, unless a settling JT has obtained a general release extinguishing the plaintiff's claim forever, he may still find himself forced to remain in the case if a nonsettler has cross-claimed for indemnity as well as contribution.

Happily, genuine indemnity claims are rare birds in today's tort litigation. But if you think you may be exposed to one, try asking the plaintiff for an additional clause in your release providing that the plaintiff will dismiss any claim resulting in an indemnity action against your client. Some plaintiffs have been known to agree.

Finally, be alert to the impact of a satisfaction of judgment. Unlike a release, which surrenders the cause of action for consideration that may be inadequate, a satisfaction reflects that the plaintiff has accepted full compensation for the injury.

Suppose Plaintiff wins a judgment against JT_1 and settles for a lesser amount to avoid the expense of collecting the judgment. Suppose as well that Plaintiff gives JT_1 a release carefully drafted under the joint tortfeasor rules to preserve claims Plaintiff is contemplating against JT_2 and JT_3.

Having paid the settlement amount, JT_1 asks for an order of satisfaction of judgment, and the unsuspecting Plaintiff agrees. Under the traditional rule still followed in most jurisdictions, Plaintiff's claims against JT_2 and JT_3 are extinguished just as if Plaintiff had given a general release. The reasoning is the same: A party is entitled to only one satisfaction of a judgment.

So if you are a defendant, always ask for a satisfaction. And if you are a plaintiff, do not give it (unless you really are satisfied with what you already have).

A multitortfeasor settlement is like a baseball game: It ain't over till it's over. If you are lackadaisical in drafting your settlement papers, you may snatch defeat from the jaws of victory. But if you think and draft carefully, a good settlement will stay that way.

Settling Class Actions

by Donald G. Kempf, Jr. and Roger L. Taylor

While there are good reasons to settle most lawsuits, the incentives for settling class actions are especially strong. For defendants, the expense of litigation and the threat of a huge damages award are reasons enough to explore settlement. For plaintiffs, the opportunity for prompt relief can be equally attractive.

But class actions are not easy to settle. The issues are usually complex. Large classes often encompass claimants with divergent interests. And the lawyers negotiating the settlement must satisfy their clients, unnamed class members, and—not least—the judge.

Even if the parties come to a meeting of the minds, that is not the end. In most jurisdictions, the court must approve a class settlement, and that means there is plenty of work to be done after the parties agree on the terms.

In navigating the rocky shoals of class-action settlement procedure, begin with *The Manual for Complex Litigation 2d.* This recent comprehensive redraft brings the venerable *Manual* into the 1980s. It sets out useful guidelines and basic legal standards for settling federal class actions and getting settlements approved.

The *Manual* does not have all the answers, though. No formal guidelines can tell a lawyer what to say and do during settlement negotiations. Knowing that requires an intimate understanding of the issues and the case.

Lawyers should recognize that what they say during settlement discussions can be subject to both judicial scrutiny and discovery by interested parties, particularly objecting class members. A district court's re-

The authors are partners at Kirkland & Ellis in Chicago. Katherine C. Grady, a former associate at that firm, assisted them in writing this article.

fusal to allow class members to discover what was said during settlement negotiations has been held to be an abuse of discretion. *In re General Motors Engine Interchange Litigation*, 594 F.2d 1106, 1124 (7th Cir.), *cert. denied*, 444 U.S. 870 (1979). So it is advisable to proceed as if settlement negotiations were public events.

When considering how to approach settlement of a class action, remember that one topic is especially touchy: attorneys' fees. Since *Prandini v. National Tea Co.*, 557 F.2d 1015, 1020–21 (3d Cir. 1977), a number of courts have held that parties may not determine compensation for class counsel until they have settled on the merits. This strict rule arose from some courts' concern that agreeing about fees and class recovery at the same time might tempt counsel to trade the latter for the former.

Despite such concerns, the Supreme Court's recent decision in *Evans v. Jeff D.*, 475 U.S. 717 (1986), seems to establish that simultaneous merits and fees discussions are not prohibited. Nonetheless, lawyers negotiating class settlements should be aware of the potential conflict of interest. The safest course, at least in cases involving statutory fees awards, is still to defer any fees discussion until the merits settlement is wrapped up.

But deferral does not always work. In "common fund" fees cases, class counsel get paid from the class recovery. The court cannot intelligently approve the settlement without knowing what the attorneys will get. Even in statutory fees cases, deferral may be unacceptable. Defendants understandably want to know their total liability. A "good" $1 million settlement can quickly look bad if it triggers an unanticipated award of $500,000 or $1 million in fees.

When deferral is not practical, there are a number of choices. In common fund cases, the proposed fees award usually has to be discussed and agreed upon. To ensure that the settlement will pass muster with the court, a prudent class counsel will provide an explanation—in terms of hours and rates—of how the total fees were determined.

In statutory fees cases, intermediate measures may suffice. Plaintiffs can state what they will ask the court to award them; this will allow defendants to contest the request, but to know in advance what their maximum exposure is. Alternatively, plaintiffs' counsel can provide information on the time they have spent on the case and the rates they typically charge.

However you deal with the issue of fees, remember that the judge will probably scrutinize the request, and so may objecting class members. When you present a proposed class settlement to the court for approval, it is wise to reveal exactly what was, and was not, said about fees in the negotiations. An even safer procedure, especially if class members seem likely to object, is to ask the judge *during* the negotiations for permission to talk about fees.

In class actions, because the stakes are high and the issues complex, settlement talks often tend to go off course. One way to try to keep the negotiations on track is to start with a memorandum of agreement in principle. While a document of that sort may be legally unenforceable, the moral force of an agreement on general points can keep a discussion going when the parties might otherwise stall over minor differences.

An agreement in principle should recite that the parties wish to reach a settlement, if they can settle on a reasonable basis. It should describe generally any preliminary understandings that the parties have reached and should define the boundaries of further negotiations. To maximize its usefulness, a memorandum of agreement in principle should be signed by principals, not just lawyers.

A memorandum of agreement in principle can be especially useful when a government agency is a party to class litigation. Too often, lawyers who think they have an agreement with the government will be dismayed to hear opposing counsel try to up the ante by saying at the last moment, ''The Department won't approve the settlement unless. . . .'' A memorandum of agreement in principle should reduce that risk by compelling agency negotiators to obtain specific, advance guidance from officials with the authority to approve the settlement.

An agreement in principle can have another important benefit. By defining the subjects for future negotiations and reciting terms or concepts that have been agreed upon (subject to agreement on the remaining issues), it should help to move the parties toward a final settlement. Many plaintiffs' lawyers have found that once a corporate defendant *commits* itself—even in principle—to serious settlement negotiations, the focus of the corporation's bureaucracy is on settlement. The memorandum of agreement in principle can be used to reinforce and take advantage of that tendency.

Usually, the fuel that makes a settlement run is money. Unfortunately, sometimes the defendant will not or cannot meet the plaintiffs' monetary demands. In such situations, creative lawyers must come up with substitutes for more cash.

Often counsel can devise a form of relief whose value to the class members exceeds its cost to the defendant. For example, as a part of the settlement of a recent antitrust case against BAR/BRI, a bar exam preparation course, class members received their choice of a coupon for a $25 discount on a BAR/BRI course or a discount on the purchase of books published by the parent company of BAR/BRI. *Phemister v. Harcourt Brace Jovanovich, Inc.*, 77-C-39, SLIP. OP. (N. D. Ill. Sept. 14, 1984). In another case, the court approved the offer of a 50 percent discount on selected kitchenware products manufactured by the defendant, up to a maximum discount of $100 per class member. *In re Cuisinart Litigation*, 1983-2 Trade Cas. (CCH) ¶ 65,860 (D. Conn. 1978).

In cases involving products or services, defense counsel should enlist the assistance of the defendant's sales or marketing staff. They can help structure settlements involving coupons, reduced prices, or other devices that will bring customers to the defendant and reduce the actual cost of the settlement. *See Abrams v. Household International*, 74-C-2244, SLIP. OP. (N.D. Ill. 1983) (coupons for reduced car rental rates used to settle securities class action).

Employment discrimination class actions provide many opportunities to use cash substitutes. Preferential hiring and promotion lists and restructuring of seniority lists are good examples. Commitments to career counseling and training courses can also be noncash incentives to settle. The cost of such programs can be absorbed as an expense of the employer's ongoing personnel activities. From the employer's standpoint, that kind of settlement may even be cost-free. After all, a class member hired off a preferential list fills a vacancy that would have been filled by someone in any event.

Noncash settlement consideration is also common in securities cases. A corporate defendant can offer warrants, stock dividends, or other classes of securities instead of—or along with—cash. *See, e.g., Zipkin v. Genesco, Inc.* [1980] Fed. Sec. L. Rep. ¶ 97,594 (CCH) (S.D.N.Y. 1980) (settlement consisting of $250,000 in cash and $750,000 in warrants). Even though each class member receives a marketable security that he can readily convert to cash, the real cost to the company is usually lower than a cash payment equal to the face value of the security.

Noncash settlement devices have their risks. You have to be careful in reporting the value to the class of noncash relief. To assess the fairness of the settlement, the judge may want to know what the noncash items are worth, but the issue can be tricky.

The parties can use expert witnesses to appraise the value of a noncash settlement. *See, e.g., Bennett v. Behring Corp.*, 96 F.R.D. 343, 347 (S.D. Fla. 1982); *Blank v. Talley Industries, Inc.*, 64 F.R.D. 125, 130 (S.D.N.Y. 1974). But such experts' opinions are far less certain—and far more vulnerable to attack by disgruntled class members—than is the value of cash. To limit the risk that the settlement will be disapproved, lawyers should take a conservative view of the value of noncash consideration.

Valuing noncash consideration can also drive a wedge between the parties in cases where plaintiffs' counsel are entitled to a statutory fees award. In such situations, class counsel may plan to argue that they should get a large fees award in part because they achieved an exceptionally valuable settlement. So they may try to assign a very high money value to the noncash portion of the settlement. Defense counsel, who might otherwise welcome a generous valuation to get the settlement approved, will be understandably reluctant to characterize the settlement as extraordinary.

A head-on confrontation is best avoided by keeping the defendant out of the process and letting the plaintiff alone advocate specific values. The defendant can say that the settlement's value is "significant" or "appropriate," and, if necessary, can disclaim the specific valuation the plaintiffs advance. That way, the parties can save the fees fight for another day. *See EEOC v. Burlington Northern*, 618 F. Supp. 1046 (N. D. Ill. 1985).

Even with all the ingenuity, coupons, and merchandise discounts in the world, some class actions are hard to settle. The parties may have sharply differing views of the defendant's potential exposure. In class actions, such differences often arise from fundamental disagreement over how many people are really in the class, or how many class members deserve relief. When this happens, the lawyers should search for a solution that allows the opposing parties to put their money where their mouths are.

Suppose, for example, the lawyers for the class believe that 10,000 victims of the defendant's conduct will prosecute claims, but the defendant thinks there are only 1,000 likely claimants. If both sides will risk testing their beliefs, they should agree on a settlement that includes a fund not to exceed a certain cash amount. This can be accompanied by a proviso that if the plaintiff is right (and more claimants show up), the fund will be paid out completely; but if the defendant is right (and fewer claimants come forward), all unclaimed money will revert to the defendant.

A reversionary settlement must address claims procedures and standards for eligibility. Unfortunately, those procedures can create later problems. They may be expensive for both sides. Defendants, who want to retain as much of the settlement fund as possible, may fight every claim. What was supposed to be a settlement may turn out to be just a new front in the same war.

There is another, related, risk in fashioning a class-action settlement. Even if both sides agree on money and the number of class members, they may not agree on—or even know—how much each class member should get. The defendant may not care. But the allocation of class settlement funds is a problem that must be solved.

The defendant may be tempted to leave allocation and distribution up to class counsel. In statutory fees cases—where class counsel can get fees awards for settlement administration—that can be an unfortunate choice. It can take a lot of time to devise an allocation system and, as all lawyers know, time is money. A defendant who has finally settled a prolonged class action may be disappointed to receive a $75,000 fees bill for work done after the case was settled. To avoid such unpleasant surprises, try to include in the settlement a simple, almost self-executing formula or set of standards to determine who gets what. That should minimize post-settlement attorney time.

A similar allocation problem is unique to class actions. How much should the named plaintiffs get? Often they get significantly more than the average unnamed class member. The larger recovery is typically said to be compensation for the named plaintiffs' commitment and support

905

throughout the litigation. It is they who institute the case and, often, bear the brunt of defense discovery.

Skeptical courts and disgruntled class members may see disproportionate payments to named plaintiffs almost as bribes for giving up vigorous prosecution of the case brought on behalf of all class members. *See, e.g., Holmes v. Continental Can Co.,* 706 F.2d 1144 (11th Cir. 1983); *Plummer v. Chemical Bank,* 91 F.R.D. 434 (S.D.N.Y. 1981), *aff'd & remanded,* 668 F.2d 654 (2d Cir. 1982). But that is not a universal view. Disproportionate payments have been approved, sometimes to reward service to the class or because of the arguably disproportionate strength of the named plaintiffs' individual claims. *See Roberts v. Magnetic Metals Co.,* No. 78-0023 (D.N.J. 1982); *Kyriazi v. Western Elec. Co.,* 527 F. Supp. 18 (D.N.J. 1981).

The fact is that extra compensation for named plaintiffs is common, much more common than are cases approving the practice. Good sense should be used. If the named plaintiffs get a lot, most class members' recoveries had better be significant. If most class members get nominal awards, the named plaintiffs' recoveries should not exceed a few thousand dollars.

With ample effort, ingenuity, and care, lawyers in a class suit may reach agreement. But that does not mean it is time to relax. Half the battle has yet to be fought.

In most jurisdictions, the court must approve a class settlement after notice to the class and an opportunity for objecting class members to be heard. This process—often a gauntlet of expense, delay, and frustrations—is mandatory in federal courts. *See* FED. R. CIV. P. 23(e). Most of the distinctive difficulties of settling class actions arise at this stage.

Some wily lawyers have tried to avoid the burdens of Rule 23(e) by settling *before* a class is certified. If the defendant believes that the named plaintiffs are likely to be the only people who will sue, it may be willing to settle with them alone, even though it will not enjoy the protection of a binding classwide settlement. If a class has not been certified, the parties may reason, Rule 23(e) does not apply, notice—which might stir up litigants—need not be given, and the class allegations can be dismissed without prejudice.

It is not always so simple. Some courts are sensitive to the danger that class allegations may be used for bargaining leverage. They may also be concerned that alleged class members have refrained from filing their own suits, perhaps even letting the statute of limitations run, in reliance on the pendency of the class action.

Such courts may follow the requirements of Rule 23(e), even though no class has been certified. *See Lyon v. State of Arizona,* 80 F.R.D. 665, 669 (D. Ariz. 1978). They will insist on notice to prospective class members, advising them of the case, their right to sue, and the running of the statute of limitations. The *Manual for Complex Litigation 2d* suggests this as well. Unfortunately, it is exactly what the parties usually do *not* want. So it is important to know how your court is likely to handle this issue.

Other courts will not insist on notice and the other Rule 23(e) procedures. *See, e.g., McGann v. Mungo*, 578 F. Supp. 1413, 1415 (D.S.C. 1982); *Bantolina v. Aloha Motors*, 75 F.R.D. 26 (D. Hawaii 1977). Where there is doubt, it may be advisable jointly to ask the judge if the notice requirement can be avoided through precertification settlement.

If a case is settled before class certification, a court sanctioned confidentiality agreement should be part of the bargain. The plaintiff does not want other potential claimants to attack his individual settlement. The defendant wants to avoid publicity that might prompt others to bring cases of their own. The solution is an order that seals both the court file and the parties' lips.

Despite its occasional allure, precertification settlement has drawbacks: It is risky, it can prejudice putative class members, and it offers the defendant only limited protection. To solve these problems, lawyers have devised an equally controversial device: the tentative or temporary settlement class.

The parties simply agree on what the class is. The defendant agrees not to challenge certification if the judge approves the settlement. The members of the temporary class are simultaneously notified of the pending suit, the class certification, and the settlement. All loose ends are tied up. Everything is approved, and everyone lives happily ever after.

Not quite. This short-circuiting of the normally lengthy class certification process, and the collapsing of settlement and certification, have provoked a good deal of controversy.

Critics argue that the elaborate criteria for certification provide important safeguards—some of constitutional dimensions—for class members. They also contend that the abbreviated procedure hampers the court's ability to get objective information on the fairness of the settlement and the propriety of the class. They fear that the parties may collude and sell out the class.

Reflecting such concerns, the previous version of the *Manual* could scarcely have been more hostile to the temporary settlement class: "There is, to say the least, serious doubt that this practice is authorized by Rule 23." Settlement classes "should not be formed." *Manual for Complex Litigation* § 1.46. The new *Manual* is somewhat more restrained, but it says that courts should be "wary" and use "great caution" in this area. *Manual for Complex Litigation 2d* § 30.45.

Despite such reservations, stipulated classes have been used and approved. *See, e.g., Weinberger v. Kendrick*, 698 F.2d 61 (2d Cir. 1982), *cert. denied*, 464 U.S. 818 (1983); *In re Beef Industry Antitrust Litigation*, 607 F.2d 167 (5th Cir. 1979), *cert. denied*, 452 U.S. 905 (1981). As with the question of payments to named plaintiffs, practice and theory seem to diverge.

907

Most lawyers and many judges recognize that use of a settlement class is often the only way to avoid a trial; defendants often settle as much to avoid the expense of a certification battle and class-wide discovery as they do out of fear of a loss on the merits.

As the current *Manual* observes, some of the money that might otherwise be spent on certification trench warfare can be used to find a litigation peace treaty. A settlement premised on an agreed class need not be unfair and is usually not collusive. In short, use of a settlement class often is the best choice. If it makes sense, do it. But remember that you may be subject to extra scrutiny. The use of a settlement class requires an unusually detailed, objective, and forthcoming presentation to the court on the substance of the settlement and the scope of the class.

Once you have a settlement, how do you get the court's approval? What do you have to show? Rule 23(e) is little help. It merely requires court approval. But, guided by earlier versions of the *Manual for Complex Litigation,* courts have adopted what amounts to a three-step process.

The first step is a preliminary fairness hearing. Its purpose is to determine whether there is any reason not to notify class members of the proposed settlement and to proceed with a full-scale fairness hearing.

At the preliminary hearing, counsel jointly present the settlement agreement to the judge, describe it, and explain why it is appropriate. In such a nonadversary setting, the judge is in a position simply to determine whether there is some obvious defect in the proposed arrangement. While a preliminary hearing is not mandatory in many jurisdictions, it is generally advisable. Giving notice to the class—an expensive process—and conducting a full-blown fairness hearing would be futile gestures if the court finds some of the settlement terms unacceptable at the outset.

A preliminary hearing is not always a cursory event. There may be something troubling in the agreement. In *Liebman v. J. W. Peterson Coal & Oil Co.,* 73 F.R.D. 531 (N.D. Ill. 1973), for example, the judge refused to give even preliminary approval to an antitrust class-action settlement because he thought the apparent facts justified a higher settlement offer. There is always the risk that the court just will not buy what you are trying to sell.

After getting preliminary approval, the next step is notifying the class of the proposed settlement. Federal Rule 23(e) requires such notice, but says little else. The details of the notice—its content, timing, and method of service—are left to the discretion of the court, subject only to the limits of due process and good sense.

At minimum, a settlement notice should contain a description of the case; a summary of the proposed settlement and what it means from a class member's perspective; an explanation of the upcoming fairness hearing, including its purpose, date, time, and place; instructions on where to get more information (usually from class counsel), and on how and by when to object. The *Manual* covers these points and others and includes a sample notice. Consult it.

It is wise to include in the notice a statement IN LARGE LETTERS that class members who do not object need do nothing, except perhaps to send in a claim form. That admonition will reduce the number of telephone calls and letters to counsel from class members who just want to be sure they get their share of the settlement. It may also minimize the number of objectors who come forward to oppose the settlement.

Drafting a settlement notice can present problems. The notice is the *court's* notice, but judges usually rely on the parties to present a proposed text, which they often adopt verbatim. The parties, though, may disagree on what the notice should say.

The defendant may think the case description tars it with a black exaggeration of unproven claims. If unclaimed settlement funds are to revert to the defendant, it may want to dampen any "come and get money" message in the notice.

For their part, class counsel sometimes think the defendants' proposed verbiage is unnecessarily forbidding; what should be an informative notice in plain English reads like a writ of attachment. Sometimes these differences cannot be resolved. As indecorous as it may seem, the only solution is for otherwise settling parties to submit competing draft notices and let the judge decide.

The final step in getting a class-action settlement approved is a fairness hearing. In this proceeding, the court considers the parties' justification of the settlement, along with objecting class members' criticisms. The level of scrutiny varies with the court.

A judge may ask some or all of the following questions: Have the parties conducted enough discovery to understand the case? Are the negotiating lawyers reputable and experienced, and did they engage in arm's-length discussions? Does the history of the negotiations or do the terms of the agreement suggest collusion? In light of the strengths and weaknesses of the case, does the settlement seem fair? Are the named plaintiffs getting too much, or any segments of the class too little? Is there anything to the objectors' criticisms?

Counsel's submissions should respond to these concerns. It is a good idea for the two sides to submit separate briefs to avoid any appearance of collusion. The briefs should summarize the extent of discovery, the lawyers' credentials, the course of the negotiations, and the settlement itself. Supporting affidavits are usually helpful.

Two issues addressed in the supporting memoranda often cause difficulties. The first has to do with justifying the settlement in terms of the merits of the dispute. At best, this requires the parties to engage in argumentative backflips.

The defendant, which the week before had staunchly denied any exposure, is forced to explain why it has agreed to pay a lot of money. The plaintiffs, who had previously insisted on the defendant's undeniable and unlimited liability, must explain why they have settled for 30 cents on the dollar. Courts are familiar with these about-faces and are generally tolerant.

But the parties face a greater risk than just inconsistency. They must consider what happens if the settlement is not approved. If the litigation then lurches forward, their statements and evidence at the fairness hearing may undercut their litigation positions. The result of all this is that the briefs in support of a class settlement are often written in a cramped and qualified way. This, too, is something most courts know about.

There is a final occasional difficulty in the parties' attempts to justify a settlement. In statutory fees cases, the defendant may discover that the plaintiffs' submission is a springboard to a big fees request. The description of the litigation may read like an heroic epic; plaintiffs may describe the massive battles they fought, the enormous odds they faced, and the rich prizes they won.

If that happens, the defendant should do something. Because a fairness hearing is no time for a pitched battle, defense counsel's best course is simply to note disagreement with the hyperbole and observe that fees questions should be saved for another day.

At the fairness hearing, two things happen. First, counsel for the parties speak on behalf of the settlement. The second and most significant part of the hearing is when unhappy class members present their objections.

Any class member who has not opted out can object. Usually, objectors are required to file written objections with the court beforehand. They can then appear in person or through counsel at the fairness hearing. But the judge may accept late-filed objections or hear from class members at the fairness hearing even if they have failed to file written objections at all. In fact, most judges will hear from all reasonable objectors. This limits the chances of reversal and has a therapeutic effect.

The defendant should not attempt to limit objectors' testimony. Instead, the parties should be prepared to show why the objections are ill-founded; this is a key reason for insisting on prior submission of objections in writing. If there are written objections, class counsel can also contact objectors and attempt to persuade them that their objections are based on misconceptions or are otherwise without merit.

After hearing from all interested parties, the judge will approve or disapprove the settlement. Technically, those are the judge's only options. He does not have the power to modify the terms of the settlement or rewrite the agreement. Practically speaking, though, if the judge rejects the settlement, he will usually suggest changes that, if implemented, will secure its approval.

Once the district court approves a settlement, the drama is usually over. All that is left is implementation. But there is one final risk: an appeal.

Approval of a class-action settlement covering the entire class is an appealable final order. But not every class member may appeal. Unless a class member has followed the procedures for objecting to the settlement in the trial court, he has waived his right to appeal.

Because approval of a class-action settlement depends mostly on factual determinations, it can be reversed only for abuse of discretion. So much depends on knowing the facts and the history of the case that an appellate court will usually not disturb the decision of the trial judge, who is intimately familiar with the litigation. This circumstance is normally an advantage for the proponents of a settlement, but not always.

The appellate court's distance from the facts can sometimes present a problem. There are some settlements that, divorced from an intimate knowledge of the facts, seem strange or suspect. The named plaintiffs may be getting half of the money. Class counsel may be getting twice as much as the class. Some such arrangements *are* odd, but many make good sense to those— like the district judge—who have lived with a case for years and know the personalities and issues involved.

The best antidote for the appellate court's distance from the facts is a good record below. At a minimum, the record should contain ample evidence of arm's-length negotiations, an evaluation of the strengths of each side's case, an account of discovery proceedings, an analysis of the complexity and expense of further litigation, evidence of the reactions of class members to the settlement offer, and the plan for dealing with attorneys' fees. And, long before an appeal, the negotiating lawyers ought to consider whether anything in the bargain they have struck may puzzle outsiders. If so, they should make sure the factual record deals directly and explicitly with the otherwise puzzling features of the settlement.

Another way to deal with an appeal from a settlement order is to settle. Just as the concerns of objectors can often be assuaged, appellant class members can frequently be persuaded to settle. This is particularly true if the appeal is not an attack on attorneys' fees, and class counsel, with the court's approval, has some discretion over the allocation of settlement funds. Such a settlement should, of course, be presented to the district court for approval.

In the end, and throughout, settling a class action—and keeping it settled—depend on a few key skills: ingenuity, energy, negotiating ability, and a sound knowledge of the ins and outs of Rule 23.

Paying Tomorrow's Claims with Tomorrow's Dollars

by Perry L. Fuller

A California case of a 9-year old girl severely brain damaged by alleged medical malpractice received much attention because of a $26-million settlement reported by the press. Actually, the settlement was bought by payments of less than a million dollars, and the case dramatically illustrates how using tomorrow's dollars for tomorrow's damages can provide for economical settlement of big-money claims.

Nowadays it is much easier for lawyers to settle cases with future dollars than for juries to use this technique in litigated cases. However, some changes in the tax laws and in litigation rules and procedures—as well as in the way we think about the traditional lump-sum method of awarding damages—could encourage a widespread use of tomorrow's dollars, with results that might satisfy party litigants, their lawyers, and society in general.

In the California case, the little girl was going to require extensive medical care for the rest of her life, whatever that eventually proved to be. The settlement—which in fact would total $26 million only if the girl survived to age 74 (the 65 years predicted in life-expectancy tables)—was achieved through payments totaling $820,000 on the following terms:

- Two defendants' liability insurance carriers paid out $150,000 in cash.
- For a single premium of $430,000, the defendants purchased an annuity from a life insurance company, which agreed to underwrite the risk of paying $16,000 a year for the special care the parties agreed would be necessary to maintain the girl. This contained a built-in inflationary increase of 7.75 per cent a year and also provided that if either parent survived the child he or she would receive $100,000.

The author is a Chicago lawyer.

- The defendants bought another annuity for $240,000 to pay the plaintiffs' attorneys' contingent fee of $30,000 a year over a ten-year period. The agreed upon fee, according to one report, was computed as one-third of the smallest probable jury award estimated by anyone associated with the case.

Had the case gone to trial, the plaintiffs might have convinced the jury, through expert testimony, that there was a reasonable likelihood that the girl would survive to age 74 and that the expense of maintaining her to that age would be increased by inflation at a compound rate in excess of 10 percent a year. The projections, however, do not indicate she will actually live that long, and the life insurance company, relying upon its experience in the field of annuities, was willing to assume this risk. It knows its obligation ends upon death.

Awards similar to this settlement could also be made by juries in cases where the parties are unable to agree on liability or on critical elements of the damage award. As the example demonstrates, once it is determined by a fact finder or by agreement what the amount of damages is for the next year and that the loss is a continuing one, the question remains: when will the defendant's obligation cease? Use of the annuity makes it immaterial whether the claimant's contentions about life expectancy are exaggerated. The fact of death will determine that. (A life expectancy of, say, 40 years simply means that the person statistically has a 50 percent chance of living that long.)

Changes Required

The tradition of awarding all a plaintiffs damage in a single lawsuit, however, can probably only be changed by statute—or, in some instances, by court rule. Within its special medical malpractice legislation, California has taken such a step. Section 667.7(a) of the CALIFORNIA CODE OF CIVIL PROCEDURE now provides:

(a) In any action for injury or damages against a provider of health care services, a superior court shall, at the request of either party, enter a judgment ordering that money damages or its equivalent for future damages of the judgment creditor be paid in whole or in part by periodic payments rather than by a lump-sum payment if the award equals or exceeds fifty thousand dollars ($50,000) in future damages. In entering a judgment ordering the payment of future damages by periodic payments, the court shall make a specific finding as to the dollar amount of periodic payments which will compensate the judgment creditor for such future damages. As a condition to authorizing periodic payments of future damages, the court shall require the judgment debtor who is not adequately insured to post security adequate to assure full payment of such damages awarded by the judgment. Upon termination of periodic payments of future damages, the court shall order the return of this security, or so much as remains to the judgment debtor.

Special Findings

Before juries could award damages in this fashion, jury instructions would need to be revised to provide for use of special findings. Special interrogatories to the jury would elicit necessary findings on such things as the amount of the monthly or yearly loss of income or profit, monthly or yearly expenses to be incurred and the duration of each particular loss or expense. Also, an inflation percentage could be built into the calculation, either by jury finding or by legislation. For example, future payments could be tied to a cost of living index that could fluctuate either way (although this could complicate the actuarial computations for buying the annuity).

On the other hand, it would no longer be necessary for the jury to determine an appropriate interest rate to discount an award to its present value. The defendant or insurer would invest the sums as it saw fit and long, sometimes convoluted instructions on reduction to present value could be eliminated.

In states that allow subjective awards for pain and suffering, disability or disfigurement, the fact finder would have to set some unit value for these elements. This approach, however, will trouble those who believe plaintiff's counsel should be forbidden to argue that awards should be based on a mathematical formula that allows a certain number of dollars for a unit of time.

Modifying or abolishing the collateral source rule should also be considered. California chose to do away with it for medical malpractice claims. If the periodic payments are to conform to reality and the plaintiff is to be put back in pocket, then those collateral sources really should be taken into account.

It has been argued that the tortfeasor should not benefit from the plaintiff's precaution to protect himself against expenses or lost wages or the largesse of the plaintiff's employer. It is accepted, however, that the plaintiff should enjoy the benefits of the defendant's precaution in procuring liability insurance which often far exceeds what would be available if the defendant were uninsured.

The equitable solution may be to allow a setoff where both parties have exercised good sense and provided for the payment of compensable obligations. First-party obligations of health and accident coverage, workmen's compensation benefits, social security, and life insurance proceeds could be declared the primary source, and proceeds available from third party liability coverage would be a secondary source to satisfy the balance of the award.

The impact of tax laws and regulations now favorable to the claimant should be carefully considered. The Internal Revenue Code now excludes from gross income any damages received by ''suit or settlement'' on account of personal injuries or sickness. INT. REV. CODE, 1954, § 104(a)(2). If the claimant receives a lump-sum settlement or award and puts it in an interest-bearing account, the interest is included in his gross income for tax purposes.

If a settlement is made on an annuity basis, segmenting the payment does not affect the claimant's right to exclude the amount from his gross income for tax purposes. Any tax on the increment would be charged to the stakeholder.

Paying the plaintiff's attorney's fees raises still another problem. The lawyers for the nine-year-old California girl were to be paid $30,000 a year over a ten-year period. It would encourage this kind of settlement for the I.R.S. to recognize this arrangement and allow the lawyers to treat the payments as income received in each year a payment is made. Under present tax law, a lawyer may not defer his fee to a later year if it is earned pursuant to a conventional contingent fee contract. Upon settlement, he has performed his services and earned his fee. He has constructive control of the fee and it therefore must all be included in his gross income for the tax year in which it is earned.

One partial way to solve this problem may be for the attorney to amend his back returns for the years in which services were actually performed. The lawyer also may assure equitable tax treatment for himself under present law if he is willing to commit himself to a deferred fee when he contracts with his client. The I.R.S. recognizes a taxpayer's agreement to accept deferred payment if the agreement is made unconditionally before the service is to be performed. But if the lawyer retains the right to choose afterward, he must include the whole fee in his gross income for the year in which it is first received.

Whatever way one underwrites the obligation for periodic payments, this does not change the amount to be received by the claimant or vary the terms of the settlement or award. The only one who stands to gain or lose as the future becomes history is the stakeholder. If the events that are to begin or end payments occur in a manner favorable to the stakeholder, he may salvage a sum from the single premium and profit from the undertaking. If future events occur in a manner that requires him to pay over a longer period than estimated, he loses from it.

Several options are available to the defendant, or his insurer, when called upon to make periodic payments. One that has much to commend it is the annuity type, as in the California example. The company undertaking the obligation will undoubtedly be a life insurance company with considerable information in the field. It will accept a single premium from the defendant and invest it. Its assumed risk will be spread among all of its annuitants. It will be an established company with sufficient capital and assets to offer adequate security to the claimant.

Another alternative is to establish a trust fund. A trustee will invest the money, collect the income and, subject to the contingency requirements of the settlement or award, guarantee the periodic payment. If the contingency that ends the obligation occurs earlier than estimated and a balance remains in the account, this is returned to the defendant or his insurer. However, if the estimate of the trust's requirement is too low, the defendant or his insurer must deposit additional funds with the trustee. Without some mechanism to make sure this occurs automatically, this complication is one the claimant would probably choose to avoid.

A third choice is an extended claims settlement device now in use by some casualty insurers. Under this system, the casualty insurer (and not a separate life insurance company) is the stakeholder and in effect buys an annuity from itself to guarantee payments of the future sums. However, under their charters casualty companies cannot ordinarily engage in the sale of annuities. Therefore these settlements are treated as a lump-sum payment of the present value of the amount necessary to meet the future obligations.

This is set aside in a special account from which the payments to the claimant are made. If the estimate of the period for payments works in the insurance company's favor, any unpaid portion may be returned to the company's capital account. If the company is stable and well-managed, with adequate assets and a good history, there should be no reason to refuse to permit it to underwrite the obligation.

When periodic payments are agreed to by way of settlement, the parties can establish terms and conditions that will serve the best interests of the particular claimant. His own and his family's future needs may not be protected by the traditional form of award, including the periodic payments provided under most workmen's compensation statutes.

For example, a totally disabled claimant may have planned a college education for his children. This ambition can be fulfilled by providing an agreed upon amount for each child, either a lump sum or periodically, when he reaches a certain age. This amount would be available for the child's use in college whether the claimant survived or not.

Additionally, the need for future medical care is many times speculative and a specified sum can be set aside and available for use by the claimant as the need arises. If he dies before the fund is exhausted, the balance will revert to the defendant or his insurer and not become a stranger's windfall.

Unlimited Options

The options for contingencies are unlimited. A settlement can be tailor-made for the particular needs of the claimant. In meeting these needs, the periodic payment approach provides a form of money management that the average person recovering damages for substantial future losses badly needs. Like the lottery winner, the claimant whose future damages have been paid in advance may not be able to manage that fund to achieve the goals for which it was paid. Thus, periodic payments may have a social value that goes beyond achieving greater fairness in measuring awards.

The adversary system cannot survive if it is perceived generally as unjust or unworkable. Both lawyers and laymen are becoming aware of the economic impact of the proliferation of claims and the dramatic increase in the size of awards by courts and juries. The medical profession is frantically trying to solve the threat of professional liability judgments. Manufacturers are studying alternatives to submitting product liability claims to a jury. Accountants, lawyers, brokers, and businessmen are reacting to class actions that seek to impose obligations for ill-defined and speculative damages alleged to result from securities law violations. Corporate executives shiver at the prospect of antitrust treble damage claims.

The speculation, guess, and conjecture about future damages that the courts have authorized and encouraged are a result of the concern of judges to protect from the future's uncertainties someone who has suffered substantial loss. The alternative suggested in this article should satisfy the courts and restore confidence in the adversary system. If each wrong deserves a remedy and if that remedy must be an adequate award, let us borrow from the wealth of experience gained in the fields of pensions and annuities and award only the amount needed, only at the time it is needed, and only to the person entitled to receive it.

Drafting Settlement Agreements in Commercial Litigation

by Palmer Brown Madden

Since more than ninety percent of commercial litigation is settled, litigators who work on commercial matters spend much of their time negotiating settlements. The typical result in business litigation is not a jury verdict but a settlement agreement. Therefore, familiarity with the law of settlements is an important skill in a litigator's repertoire.

Settlement agreements in commercial cases typically receive extended attention from all of the parties. While this extended examination may ferret out ambiguities, the compromises necessary to achieve agreement often produce a document that lacks clarity. The lack of clarity may be ascribed to several causes. Primarily, the parties have a fundamental disagreement and have usually gone to considerable cost to achieve their goals. As a result, the parties usually approach each other with suspicion. Since each party is concerned about a potential concealed trap in every agreement draft, the prose is sometimes so convoluted that it is almost unintelligible. A second source of difficulty is drafting by committee. By the time four or five people, or more, have worked over a document, it may well be impossible to produce a crisp statement. Finally, it is sometimes the case that the parties are unable to resolve their dispute entirely, and they purposely leave ambiguities in the settlement agreement and hope that if it is necessary to enforce the agreement, the ambiguity will be resolved in their favor. Faced with such problems, one can understand why some settlements read with no more clarity than an 18th century indenture agreement. Notwithstanding these problems, clarity is achievable by counsel who are familiar with the settlement process, and who know the applicable law.

The focus of this article is not on settlement agreements in general, but

The author is associated with the firm of McCutchen, Doyle, Brown & Emerson in Walnut Creek, California.

on certain problems that are common in settlements of commercial litigation. First, there are the applicable legal standards. Second, there are the questions of: ''What is the scope of the release; who is granting the release; and who is being released?'' Third, there are certain provisions that should be avoided in settlement agreements.

During negotiations, litigation counsel should seek as early as possible the advice of tax counsel about the tax impact of the proposed settlement. There is a potential for important tax advantages if proper planning and documentation are undertaken. One will also want to seek the advice of other legal specialists to insure that the settlement is proper. For example, settling one matter may only invite subsequent litigation because it appears that the settlement is part and parcel of an ongoing antitrust conspiracy. *See, Settling Complex Commercial Litigation,* PLI No. 186 (1978).

Three stages

Typically, drafting occurs in three stages. First, the general outline of a possible agreement is reached. This general outline often consists of no more than a conversation between counsel wherein each sketches the terms to be recommended to their respective clients. In the second step the parties reach a more detailed, written understanding that lists the elements of the settlement but does not reduce these elements to legal terms. Finally, a complete written agreement is produced.

During this drafting process, counsel should appreciate that there is no special law of settlements. Settlements are contracts and are governed by contract law. *Shriver v. Kuchel,* 113 Cal. App. 2d 421, 248 P.2d 35 (1952). Note, however, that personal injury settlements have spawned a series of peculiar rules that an unsophisticated court might apply in a commercial context. This is particularly true about the admissibility of parol evidence to explain the intent of the parties. Because there may be rules peculiar to settlement contracts in the applicable jurisdiction, it is prudent to review the existing general case law before you begin preparing a settlement.

When undertaking settlement, counsel must be careful that the scope of the commitment is carefully delineated so that if no final agreement is reached, no harm will come to his or her client. There is plenty of room during the course of settlement discussions for misunderstandings about whether a binding settlement agreement has been reached.

The potential for misunderstanding is enhanced because it is the common rule that a settlement agreement need not be in writing, *see, e.g., Hammond Lumber Co. v. Cravens,* 82 Cal. App. 685, 256 P. 428 (1927), unless by its terms it violates the Statute of Frauds. *Hall v. Puente Oil Co.,* 47 Cal. App. 6II, 191 P. 39 (1920). Furthermore, where the parties have reached an oral agreement on all the settlement terms and conditions with the intention that it be binding, the fact that the parties are unable subsequently to agree upon a written statement of their understanding will not invalidate the agreement. *McKenzie v. Boorhem*, 117 F. Supp. 433 (W.D. Ark. I954); *Dominguez Estate Co. v. Los Angeles Turf Club, Inc.*, 119 Cal. App. 2d 530, 259 P.2d 962 (1953). However, an oral settlement is not enforceable when it is reached on the understanding that it will not be valid until it is reduced to writing. *Las Palmas Winery and Distillery v. Garrett & Co.*, 167 Cal. 397, 139 P. 1077 (1914). In light of these general principles, at the beginning of the settlement negotiations, counsel should reduce to writing an understanding that no discussion is to be binding until it is in writing and signed by all the parties.

Statements Made

Counsel also must be concerned with another matter. Statements made during a negotiation toward settlement typically are protected and cannot be used in subsequent litigation. *See, e.g.*, California Evidence Code, §§ 1152 & 1154. However, it has been held that statements unconnected with any attempt at compromise and made during the course of a settlement negotiation are not excluded in subsequent litigation. *San Francisco Iron & Metal Co. v. American Milling Industrial Co.*, 115 Cal. App. 238, 1 P.2d 1008 (1931); *see* Annot., 80 A.L.R. 919 (1932). Of more practical concern is that once a statement or concession has been made, it can never be taken back. One must carefully avoid unintended revelations engendered by the camaraderie that often accompanies a settlement negotiation. Not only can such statements be used out of court during subsequent negotiations, but they also may come back to haunt your client in the litigation if the settlement is not completed.

Most formal settlement agreements begin with a recitation of introductory material. This recitation is often viewed by counsel as mere boiler plate. Actually, introductory recitals offer counsel an opportunity to clarify the parties' intent. One strives for clarity in a settlement agreement to take advantage of the general rule that an unambiguous provision manifesting the intent of the parties precludes the introduction of parol evidence. However, if you will look through the decisions on settlements, you will find many cases where successful attacks have been made on the parol evidence rule. In these cases the language of the written instrument is reduced to mere evidence that is to be weighed against other evidence on the intent of the parties.

In some jurisdictions counsel will have the benefit of statutory provisions similar to California Evidence Code, § 622, providing: ''the facts recited in a written instrument are conclusively presumed to be true as between the parties thereto, or their successors in interest; but this rule does not apply to the recital of a consideration.'' Under this and similar rules and statutes, by fixing the intent in writing you make it a fact that is conclusively presumed, and the court need not guess about the intent of the parties.

Two Problems

Two problems plaguing commercial settlement agreements concern the proper parties to the agreement: who is granting the release and who is to be released? Where your client expects that the settlement will dispose of all problems concerning the given issue, you must identify all who may have a claim and include all such potential claimants in the settlement. You must also be certain that the party granting the settlement agreement has the authority to settle. Thus, with a corporation it is wise to provide a representation in the settlement agreement that the person who signs is authorized to sign for the corporation.

Similar problems arise about the parties to be released. Under traditional, common law notions, the release of one joint tortfeasor automatically releases all joint tortfeasors. *Riley v. Dun & Bradstreet, Inc.*, 195 F.2d 812 (1952). To circumvent this rule, there developed the practice of using a covenant not to sue, which did not extinguish a cause of action and therefore did not release joint tortfeasors. *See, e.g., Holtz v. United Plumbing & Heating Co.*, 49 Cal. 2d 501, 319 P.2d 617 (1957). By statute, some jurisdictions have recognized that this formalistic distinction is of no utility and have provided an integrated law about settlements with joint tortfeasors. *See, e.g.*, California Code of Civil Procedure, § 877.

You also will want to be aware that it is possible to have a defendant who is not contributing to the settlement participate in the agreement and get the protection of the judgment or the release. *Glicken v. Bradford*, 35 F.R.D. 144 (S.D.N.Y. 1964). Along this line, you should consider *Stella v. Kaiser*, 218 F.2d 64 (2d Cir. I954), concerning the protection that may be extended to parties by a release in a derivative suit.

The next problem, perhaps the most difficult one to be addressed in any settlement, is the scope of the agreement. The parties should make every effort to delineate those matters they intend to release. To the extent that matters are known to exist between the parties, specific language can be prepared that will delineate the scope of the release. Unsophisticated parties, however, could well release a matter they did not intend to release. For example, the dismissal of a counterclaim with prejudice may well bar any compulsory counterclaim that was available even though it had not been asserted.

The black letter law is that a compromise settles only such matters as the parties intend to settle. Matters that existed at the time, but were not intended to be part of the settlement, are excluded. *Richmond v. Tidewell*, 234 F.2d 361 (9th Cir.), *cert. denied*, 352 U.S. 1002 (1957).

The modern trend recognizes that it is acceptable in a commercial context for a party to release unknown claims by proper language in an agreement. *See Larsen v. Johannes*, 7 Cal. App. 3d 491, 86 Cal. Rptr. 744 (1970). But it may be possible for the releasor to reform the agreement because of a mutual mistake. Reformation may also be based on a unilat-

921

eral mistake where the releasee's conduct is unconscionable because it knew of the claim and knew that the releasor did not know of it. *Lucio v. Curran,* 2 N.Y.2d 157, 139 N.E.2d 133 (1956). The issue is whether the parties took into account the possibilities of unknown claims when they made the settlement. *Houston v. Trower,* 297 F. 558 (8th Cir. 1924). Not all of the case law has favored plaintiffs. For example, it has been held that a general release failing to mention antitrust claims nevertheless would release all antitrust claims. *Three Rivers Motors Co. v. Ford Motor Co.,* 522 F.2d 885 (3rd Cir. 1975).

Counsel must appreciate that the language of the release cannot be relied upon to establish intent conclusively, and that a court may permit the introduction of additional evidence on the parties' intent when they signed the settlement agreement. Among the factors that a court will consider in determining whether to uphold a release of unknown injuries are the amount of consideration compared to the risk of the existence of unknown injury; the presence of negotiations and bargaining leading to the settlement; the closeness of the issue of liability; and the reasonableness of the contention that the injury was actually unknown at the time the release was executed. *E.g., Casey v. Proctor,* 59 Cal. 2d 97, 28 Cal. Rptr. 307, 378 P.2d 579 (1963).

When the person obtaining the release is aware of facts unknown to the person granting the release, it is prudent to consider the effect of cases like *Chattanooga Ry. & Light Co. v. Glaze,* 146 Tenn. 49, 239 S.W. 394 (1922), holding that a misrepresentation made to obtain a release will invalidate the release. Moreover, there are also decisions like *Palmquist v. Mercer,* 43 Cal. 2d 92, 272 P.2d 26 (1954), and *Creson v. Carmody,* 310 Ky. 861, 222 S.W.2d 935 (1949), holding that a failure to disclose material facts affecting the essence of a release may constitute actual fraud that will invalidate the release.

Where a subsequent development arises from a known fact, the question is whether the fact was one the parties assumed to be the basis upon which they entered into their contract. RESTATEMENT OF CONTRACTS § 502; RESTATEMENT OF CONTRACTS (SECOND) § 294 (Tent. Draft No. 10, 1975). If the fact was not the basis of the bargain, it is collateral and does not affect the obligation of the parties. There are cases voiding an agreement because the consideration was so inadequate as to shock the conscience, where a release was granted and later developments show that the release was for a very small amount in light of the actual damages, *see Carr v. Sacramento Clay Products Co.,* 35 Cal. App. 439, 107 P. 446 (1917); and some cases hold that such gross inadequacy is the result of a mutual mistake and the release is invalid. *Touhy v. Owl Drug Co.,* 6 Cal. App. 2d 64, 44 P.2d 405 (1935).

To release unknown claims, you should incorporate into the agreement language that will show a court that the person signing the waiver had full knowledge of its importance. Where the party granting the release is an individual, it may be prudent to require counsel to sign a separate document declaring that counsel explained to the client the importance of this language.

Multiple Defendants

Where there are multiple defendants, and a plaintiff settles with one of them, questions arise about how the settlement should be set off against any damages that plaintiff obtains against the other defendants. The general rule is that a party who settles with one joint tortfeasor can recover from the other joint tortfeasors only so much of the damages that have not already been paid. *Cseri v. D'Amore*, 232 Cal. App. 2d 622, 43 Cal. Rptr. 36 (1965).

Where there are multiple parties to litigation or there is the possibility of subsequent litigation, one of the parties to a settlement often wants to keep the agreement confidential. This may be to the advantage of a plaintiff where the plaintiff believes that the amount of settlement will be used as a bargaining counter by other defendants. For example, in litigation that will last for many years, a well-recognized strategy of many plaintiffs is to settle early with a few defendants for amounts smaller than plaintiffs will seek from the remaining defendants. The plaintiff hopes to use the early settlements to carry the cost of litigation, and this strategy provides a substantial incentive to defendants to settle early. However, if the amount of the settlement were disclosed, attorneys for similarly situated defendants could argue that they are unable to persuade their clients to pay more than one of the earlier defendants.

A defendant may also choose to have the amount of settlement made confidential because it may fear that the amount will induce other plaintiffs or potential plaintiffs to form a line at the corporate cash register and take advantage of corporate willingness to settle. As a result, the parties in commercial litigation commonly seek to protect the confidentiality of the settlement agreement. However, nonsettling parties may be able to discover the terms of the settlement agreement.

Several courts have considered this problem. The starting place is the rule found in most jurisdictions that ''[p]romising to accept a valuable consideration . . . to compromise a claim which was disputed . . . is not admissible to prove liability. . . .'' FED. R. EVID. 408. It can be argued that since the amount of the settlement is not even admissible in evidence, it also should not be discoverable. However, in many jurisdictions, as in the federal jurisdiction, a matter is discoverable even if it is not admissible if the information sought appears calculated to lead to the discovery of admissible evidence or, as with insurance coverage, if the discovery will facilitate settlement.

To date [Fall 1987], I have discovered the following reported cases that consider this issue. In *Uinta Oil Refining Co. v. Continental Oil Co.*, 226 F. Supp. 495 (D. Utah 1964), the court held that the plaintiff had to answer an interrogatory propounded by a defendant seeking information on the terms of a settlement between the plaintiff and the other defendants; in *Rohlfing v. Cat's Paw Rubber Co.*, 17 F.R.D. 426 (N.D. Ill. 1954), the court held that a defendant was entitled to discover the terms of a settlement between the plaintiff and the other defendants; in *Walling v. R.L. McGinley Co.*, 4 F.R.D. 149 (E.D. Tenn. 1943), the court granted the government's motion under the Fair Labor Standards Act for production of certain settlement agreements; in *Maule Industries, Inc. v. Roundtree*, 264 So. 2d 445 (Dist. Ct. App. Fla. 1972), the court held that a defendant was entitled to pretrial discovery of a "Mary Carter" agreement between the plaintiff and other defendants; and in *Cseri v. D'Amore*, 232 Cal. App. 2d 622, 43 Cal. Rptr. 36 (1965), the court held that where the amount of a settlement would reduce pro *tanto* the amount of another defendant's liability, the fact of the settlement may be properly made known to the jury so the jury may deduct the settlement amount from the total damages sustained by the plaintiff.

A review of the above cases reveals that the parties have been very imaginative in developing plausible legal theories justifying the discovery of settlement agreements. Consider also the following additional arguments: (1) One of the major purposes of discovery is to facilitate out-of-court settlements. Knowledge of the amount of the settlement with other defendants facilitates such settlements. *See, e.g., Holliman v. Redman Development Corp.*, 61 F.R.D. 488, 491–92 (D.S.C. 1973); 4 MOORE's FED. PRAC. ¶26.02[2] (1976 Ed.); (2) a party can also argue that it is entitled to discover the amount of a settlement when any person who will testify in the trial will come from one of the settling defendants, citing those cases holding that a jury is entitled to know, as a factor affecting credibility, if a witness has a stake in the settlement, *see* Annot., 161 A.L.R. 395 (1946); (3) A defendant can argue, in those jurisdictions that retain the traditional rule distinguishing between the effect of a release and a covenant not to sue, that defendant is entitled to discover the terms of the settlement agreement to ascertain whether the release by plaintiff of one defendant has released all the defendants; (4) a plaintiff can point to those courts permitting the introduction of a prior settlement as evidence of negligence and can argue from such decisions that the amount of the settlement may be used to support plaintiff's claim, *see* Annot., 20 A.L.R.2d 304 (1951); (5) a creative defendant could argue that the settlement between the plaintiff and the settling defendants is part of an ongoing antitrust conspiracy, and that the amount and terms of the settlement should be discoverable to ascertain whether an antitrust counterclaim is warranted, *see, e.g., Bass v. Gulf Oil Corp.*, 304 F. Supp. 1041 (S.D. Miss. 1969) (action taken by antitrust defendant after the complaint is filed may be proper subject for discovery if relevant); *Jack Winter Inc. v. Koratron Co. Inc.*, 375 F. Supp. 1, 54 (N.D. Cal. 1974) (the fact that a settlement between competitors is secret does not prove an antitrust violation, but it may be evidence of an intent to violate the antitrust laws); and (6) a defendant can argue that the settlement amount is relevant to the damages question in matters like antitrust cases where the losing defendant is entitled to deduct from the damages assessed the amount that a plaintiff has received from other settling defendants. *Flintkote Co. v. Lysfjord*, 246 F.2d 368, 397–98 (9th Cir.) *cert. denied*, 355 U.S. 835 (1957).

Unethical Agreement

There are certain matters that should not be a part of any settlement agreement. For example, Disciplinary Rule 2-108(b) and Informal Opinion 1039 (1968) indicate that it is unethical to solicit an agreement that the plaintiff's lawyer will not represent other potential plaintiffs in similar litigation against the defendant. The rationale seems to be that such an agreement deprives other potential clients of their choice of a lawyer, or deprives the plaintiff's lawyer of employment and is thus a restraint of trade. It has also been held that an agreement providing for venue in subsequent litigation is void as against public policy. *Johnson v. United States Industries, Inc.*, 469 S.W.2d 652 (Tex. Civ. App. 1971). A party's attempt to secure a release from future negligence is also void as against public policy. *Tunkl v. Regents of the University of California*, 60 Cal.2d 92, 32 Cal. Rptr. 33, 383 P.2d 441 (1963). It has been similarly held that a release from future antitrust liability is void. *Redel's, Inc. v. General Electric Company*, 498 F.2d 95 (5th Cir. 1974); *Fox Mid-West Theaters, Inc. v. Means*, 221 F.2d 173 (8th Cir. 1955); *Westmoreland Asbestos Co. v. Johns-Manville Corp.*, 39 F. Supp 117 (S.D.N.Y. 1941).

The keys to a well-drafted settlement agreement are the identification of the problem areas; legal and factual research in these areas; and clear expression of the parties' intent. It is also necessary to consider as early as possible the consequences of other laws, such as tax and antitrust. A careful attorney who follows these principles will help all the parties prepare a good settlement.

PART XI

Special Problems of the Criminal Case

What to Do 'Til the Plumber Comes

by Jill Wine-Banks and Carl S. Nadler

Sometimes there is no way out.

You know all the reasons against it. Criminal law is a genuine specialization. The criminal jungle is not just in the streets. It is in the station houses and courts as well. One false step, and a simple case becomes a nightmare. Statements are made, objections waived, procedural protections vanish—all because a civil lawyer becomes involved in a criminal case. And the prospect of trying to save such a case on appeal by making the claim of very real incompetent representation at trial is not a happy one.

So you know what to tell your client: Call a criminal lawyer, or let me call one for you.

Only sometimes there is no way out.

It is 10:00 P.M., Friday night. Your best client is on the telephone. She is very upset. The police have arrested her son. The only criminal lawyer she knows is out of town until Monday. She wants your help, and you cannot refuse. But you practice civil law. You have never handled a criminal case in your life. You do not even know where the jail is.

What do you do?

First, you find out everything your client knows about the arrest. What is her son's name? When, where, and why was he arrested? Where was he taken? Then arrange to meet your client at the police station as soon as possible.

Next, call the son. If the police deny that he is at the station, ask to speak to the highest ranking officer present. Get the officers' names and identification numbers. *See* Wolfson & Cutrone, *The Attorney-Client Rela-*

Ms. Wine-Banks is Executive Vice President and Chief Operating Officer of the American Bar Association. Mr. Nadler is an associate with Jenner & Block in Washington, D.C. The views expressed are those of the authors.

tionship in IICLE, ILLINOIS CRIMINAL PRACTICE 1–13 (1980). If the son is there but the police will not bring him to the telephone, give them your name and number so that he can call you. If the son does not know your name, tell the police that you are his mother's lawyer, she has asked you to represent him, and you plan to do so if he wants it.

The accused has a statutory right in many states to make a reasonable number of phone calls. Applicable statutes are listed in ALI, A MODEL CODE OF PRE-ARRAIGNMENT PROCEDURE. Appendix V, at 633 (Proposed Official Draft 1975). The right to call an attorney, moreover, is constitutionally protected. *See Miranda v. Arizona*, 384 U.S. 436 (1966). And telling the police you are the mother's lawyer and have been asked to represent the son can be important. A confession may be invalid if it is given after the police deny a minor access to an attorney retained by his mother, even if the minor did not ask to see a lawyer. *People v. Nemke*, 23 Ill.2d 591, 179 N.E.2d 825 (1962).

When you reach the son, tell him that his mother called you and asked you to get involved in the case. Tell him that if he agrees, you will come to the police station immediately to represent him.

He may want to talk to you about the case right then on the telephone. Do not let him. Never discuss the facts of the case with your client on the telephone. The police may be listening on the line or they may overhear your client speaking.

Although you should not let your new client tell you anything on the phone, there is some advice you should give him in this initial call. First, advise him to say nothing. Not a word to the police, government attorneys, cellmates, reporters, or anyone else. Tell him as clearly and as firmly as you can, and in as many ways as you can think of, that he must refuse to say anything until you have arrived. It is not enough to advise him not to make a "statement." He may interpret "statement" to mean only a formal, written confession. *See* A. AMSTERDAM, B. SEGAL & M. MILLER, TRIAL MANUAL FOR THE DEFENSE OF CRIMINAL CASES, 2–21 (2d ed. 1971). (This is a particularly useful book with a number of sound suggestions.) Tell him not to answer any questions, to refuse interrogation, and not even to talk to the friendly guard or to cellmates.

This advice is critical. If your client makes a statement, the prosecutor may use it as direct evidence of his guilt, or to impeach his testimony at trial. Even if the police have not given him proper *Miranda* warnings, or if they interrogate him after he has said he wants his lawyer present but before you arrive, any statement he gives may be admissible to impeach his testimony at trial. *Harris v. New York*, 401 U.S. 222 (1971). But if you convince him to say nothing, his silence cannot be used against him. *Doyle v. Ohio*, 426 U.S. 610 (1976).

There is a second piece of advice you should give your client in the first phone call: Tell him to refuse to participate in lineups or other identification procedures until you arrive, but not to resist such a procedure physically. Advise him to refuse any physical examination, inspection of his body, or other test, including a lie detector, until you arrive. Again, tell him not to resist physically.

The legal standards police must meet to conduct these tests vary significantly. Procedures that invade the body, such as blood sampling, stomach pumping, or the surgical extraction of evidence, may require the police to: (1) use reasonable methods; (2) have probable cause to believe evidence will be discovered; and (3) obtain a search warrant or have emergency circumstances justifying their failure to obtain one. *See Schmerber v. California,* 384 U.S. 757 (1966) (blood sampling) and *Rochin v. California,* 342 U.S. 165 (1952) (stomach pumping). A good general source book is 2 W.LAFAVE, SEARCH & SEIZURE (1978).

On the other hand, to conduct non-intrusive procedures such as fingerprinting, the police need only legal custody of the defendant.

The standards required for other tests, such as taking hair samples, swabbing or scraping parts of the body or obtaining urine samples, vary widely. Some jurisdictions only require police to have lawful custody to perform these tests. Others may require probable cause or a warrant.

Whatever the standard, all of these rights will be waived if your client consents to the test. It is up to you to make him understand that he must refuse to take any tests.

Next, tell your client to remain calm if news reporters try to photograph or interview him. Tell him not to duck, hide his face, or make faces. If the newspapers or television show him that way, it could give prospective jurors a bad impression and make him look bad in his own community.

Finally, before ending this first phone call with your new client, ask him if he has been mistreated in any way, and if he knows of police plans to move him to another location.

Your next call should be to the police officer responsible for your client's case. Find out all of the charges that have been filed or are being considered. Ask the officer if bail has been set or, if not, what he thinks it will be. Find out if the police plan to move your client and, if so, to what location. Tell the officer that you have instructed your client to refuse interrogation, lineups, identification procedures, and physical tests until you have arrived. Be sure you get the officer's name and identification number. Keep careful notes of what you tell the police and what they tell you.

Before you leave for the police station, get copies of the statutes your client is charged with violating and the rules of criminal procedure as well. Take them with you. Also, before leaving for the police station, determine whether the mother can post bail or whether you need a bail bondsman. If you do, look in the yellow pages, call the bail bondsman, and make the necessary arrangements before leaving for the station.

When you arrive at the station, identify yourself at the station house desk. At the station, you can often obtain complaint or arrest papers that will identify the charges against your client. Do not skip this step. These documents may show some defect in the charges or procedures that led to your client's arrest.

The next step is meeting your new client. The first interview with a criminal defendant is a delicate matter. Unless you already know him, a detailed interview is probably inappropriate. Having his mother present may keep him from being entirely candid with you about the facts. Worse, her presence may waive the protection of the attorney-client privilege. So it may be better to wait until you have gained your new client's confidence before asking for detailed responses about the charges. Nevertheless, you must cover some important points at your first meeting with the son:

- Learn the most basic facts of the events. In particular, determine if there are places you must see or objects you must preserve immediately.
- Ask about the circumstances of the arrest. Was a search made? Was anything found? Did the police have a search or arrest warrant? Were others arrested with your client?
- Were there witnesses to the alleged crime? If there were, you must locate them before they move or become impossible to locate.
- What has happened since the arrest? Has your client been abused? Was he advised of his rights? When? Have the police interrogated him or conducted identification procedures or tests? If so, what are the results?
- Finally, get the facts you will need to have your client released on bail. You may wish to put these facts in an affidavit for your client to sign which then can be attached to any necessary pretrial release motions.

You should normally defer any decision about defense strategy pending a full investigation. *See* Sullivan & Warren, *White Collar Crime*, NAT'L L.J., June 20, 1983, at 22, col. 1. There is at least one exception to this rule. It is when your client admits his guilt, or the government has clear evidence of it, the other participants are represented by separate counsel, and the prosecution needs a participant-witness in their case. Then full investigation may be less important than speed in contacting the prosecutor's office. The first participant to offer the government his cooperation will probably receive the best deal. If you choose to negotiate, keep a few rules in mind:

- Before contacting the prosecutor, do enough investigation so you can give the prosecutor an accurate summary of your client's expected testimony. If your version of the facts varies from what the prosecutor already knows, the prosecutor may not want to deal.
- Negotiate with the prosecutor, not the police. The police are often unable to make binding agreements. The Federal Rules of Evidence,

931

moreover, provide a privilege for statements made by a defendant in plea negotiations with the prosecutor. This privilege does not extend to negotiations with the police. FED. R. EVID. 410(4).

- You—not your client—should do the negotiating. Your client will have a natural tendency to minimize his involvement in the alleged criminal activity when talking to a prosecutor. Even after giving you an accurate account of his involvement, he may be less candid with the prosecutor, and a misstatement may be fatal to the negotiations. If the prosecutor insists on interviewing your client, prepare him for the interview as you would for his trial testimony, to prevent misstatements or understatements.
- Finally, in deciding whether your client should cooperate with the government, you must consider his safety after testifying. You may wish to discuss witness protection or relocation with the prosecutors.

Back to the station house. You told your client to refuse any identification procedures until you arrived. Now you are there, and the police want to proceed with a lineup. What do you do?

The police may not let you attend the lineup. Your client has a Sixth Amendment right to assistance of counsel at a lineup only after adversary criminal proceedings have been instituted. *Moore v. Illinois*, 434 U.S. 220 (1977). If your client is in federal custody, he may not have a right to your presence at a lineup shortly after his arrest. *See Kirby v. Illinois*, 406 U.S. 682 (1972).

Several states, however, require counsel at all pretrial identification procedures. *See generally* F. MILLER, R. DAWSON, C. DIX & R. PARNAS, CRIMINAL JUSTICE ADMINISTRATION 524–25 (1982). So check the state law before going to the police station to determine whether your client has a right to your presence at the lineup.

If you are permitted to attend the lineup, your role is generally limited to observing the procedure to ensure that the police conduct it fairly. ALI, A MODEL CODE OF PREARRAIGNMENT PROCEDURE, 428–33 (Proposed Official Draft 1975). Your client has protection under the due process clause against lineups that are "unnecessarily suggestive and conducive to irreparable mistaken identification . . ." *Stovall v. Denno*, 388 U.S. 293, 302 (1967). So at the lineup, do everything you can to prevent suggestive procedures and to preserve your client's rights. You should tell the officer in charge about any problems you see. If they are not corrected, make a careful record.

Watch for:

- The date, time and lighting conditions of the lineup, and the distance of your client from the person who is identifying possible subjects in the lineup.
- How many individuals are in the lineup and their appearance as compared to your client. If possible, get the names, addresses, mug

shot numbers, and photos of everyone in the lineup.
- How many witnesses view the lineup and what is said between the witnesses and the police.
- The names and description of the police officers who are present.

If you cannot attend the lineup, tell your client to observe these things.

Having talked with your client and attended whatever tests or procedures are necessary, you are ready to leave. Before you do, repeat every one of the warnings you gave your client in your initial telephone conversation with him. Speak to the investigating officer and ask him to tell you what he knows about the case. He may say nothing, but it is worth asking. After talking to the officer, tell him again that your client is not to be interrogated or tested in your absence. Finally, see if the complaining witness or other eyewitnesses to the alleged crime are still present at the police station. If they are, try to interview them.

One task remains. Your client's main concern is likely to be getting out of jail immediately and staying out pending trial. Getting him out of jail should be a major concern of yours as well. The sooner your client is released, the less chance there is that he will make a damaging statement to the police. The quicker he is out of jail, the more opportunity he will have to help his defense by finding witnesses and other evidence, and by just talking to you without the constraints of the jailhouse.

In almost every jurisdiction, an accused has a right to pretrial release on bail or other conditions in noncapital cases. R. CIPES, CRIMINAL DEFENSE TECHNIQUES § 1.02[1], at 1–25 (1983). Traditionally, pretrial release in this country has been conditioned on the defendant's deposit of monetary bail with the court. In the last two decades, however, legislatures and courts have placed greater emphasis on alternate conditions of release.

The best example of this change is the Federal Bail Reform Act of 1966, 18 U.S.C. § 3146 (1976). The Bail Reform Act provides that in setting bail, the judicial officer shall consider: (1) the nature and circumstances of the offense charged; (2) the weight of evidence against the accused; and (3) the accused's family ties, employment, financial resources, character, mental condition, length of residence in the community, record of convictions, and record of appearances or failure to appear on previous court proceedings. These factors tell you the information you will need from your client so you can make a persuasive argument for his release without bail.

In non-capital cases, the Bail Reform Act provides that a defendant should ordinarily be released pending trial on his own recognizance or on his execution of an unsecured bond. 18 U.S.C. § 3146(a). The court may impose additional conditions of release only after a finding that the conditions are necessary to secure the defendant's appearance. After making such a finding, however, the court may impose various conditions, ranging from release into someone's custody to a traditional cash bond.

You must determine at which point your jurisdiction sets these conditions of release. In federal proceedings, a defendant's conditions of release are established at his first appearance before a judicial officer. This is usually the arraignment. But state procedures vary. In some states, the court issuing the warrant will endorse on the warrant the amount of bail required. In others, the police are authorized to release a defendant on bail according to an approved schedule keyed to the nature of the charge.

If your client is not released through one of these methods, bail will be set at an "initial appearance" before a judicial officer. Almost all states have statutes requiring that the defendant's initial appearance occur "without unnecessary delay," "immediately," or within a specified time, usually 24 to 48 hours. *See* ALI, A MODEL CODE OF PRE-ARRAIGNMENT PROCEDURE. Appendix I, at 626–27 (Proposed Official Draft 1975).

The actual timing of the initial appearance, however, will depend on when a judicial officer is first available to set bail after your client's arrest. Some jurisdictions have night court or bail commissioner systems to ensure that conditions of release can be established promptly even for defendants arrested at night or on the weekend. Defendants in other jurisdictions are not so fortunate. In about half our cities, no weekend court is conducted to set bail. If you live in one of these cities, you may have trouble finding a judicial officer before Monday morning.

But no matter what the procedure, if your client cannot establish acceptable conditions of release at his initial appearance, he may appeal the bail decision or challenge the conditions of release through habeas corpus.

You have now taken your client through the first stages of his case, including his pretrial release. You have significantly helped him in all the proceedings that will follow. Finally you can return home to what is left of your weekend.

On Monday, thinking back over the spectacular job you did on the weekend, you may be tempted to handle the entire case yourself.

Resist.

Remember that effective criminal practice requires experience. Bring in an attorney with that experience.

Heading Off an Indictment

by Andrew J. Levander

"Another opening, another show" would be an appropriate theme song for many criminal defense lawyers. Most defense counsel thrive on trial work; they revel in the art and drama of the courtroom.

No doubt, as far as professional experiences go, there are few things as exhilarating as a crisp cross-examination or a scintillating summation before a packed courtroom in a criminal jury trial. During a break at a recent criminal trial in New Orleans, an experienced practitioner from Chicago told me: "Cross-examination is my life."

The courtroom also seems to furnish defense attorneys with a kind of bonding experience. In my observation, criminal lawyers uniquely appreciate, if not exult in, the successes of their comrades-at-arms (albeit, perhaps, with varying degrees of wistful jealousy). Certainly, the courtroom is the primary source of our war stories and folklore. In fact, if autobiographies like *Gunning for Justice* and *My Life in Court* are any gauge of the defense bar's collective psyche, trials are the only aspect of criminal defense work worth talking about.

I too enjoy the thrill of trial work. Often, though, defense counsel's first duty and primary task is to avoid trial. Particularly in the area of white collar defense work, the indictment of your client is a disaster, even if he is later acquitted. Politicians, executives, licensed professionals, fiduciaries, and others simply cannot withstand the opprobrium of indictment, much less the scrutiny, tension, and stress that they and their families must endure during a public criminal trial.

Ask former automobile magnate John DeLorean, former national security advisor Thomas Reed, or former Arthur Andersen partner Warren Essner whether acquittal at trial restored their careers. I do not deni-

The author is a partner in Shereff, Friedman, Hoffman & Goodman in New York City.

grate the skill of the trial lawyers who represented them; to the contrary, their results speak for themselves. Nor do I suggest that the lawyers in those cases did not ably attempt to head off the indictment at the pass. But the fact remains that a publicized indictment and trial almost inevitably sully a person's reputation and close off career paths, despite a jury's verdict of not guilty.

So the skillful criminal lawyer's repertoire necessarily includes the art of disposing of criminal matters before indictment and trial. This less publicized role of defense counsel involves a variety of strategies and techniques quite different from courtroom skills. If you are going to represent defendants in criminal cases, you should be familiar with the techniques that have been used to convince prosecutors not to indict.

First, some words of caution: Sometimes the prosecutor will indict regardless of the defense lawyer's skills. And each case is unique, requiring careful evaluation of all the facts and circumstances and difficult judgment calls that are subject to second-guessing. Even the same case may require different approaches at different times.

Equally important, different lawyers would handle the same case in very different ways, and each approach may well be sound. During my days as a federal prosecutor, I was repeatedly impressed by the effectiveness of strikingly dissimilar approaches taken by different defense counsel in the same white collar case. In short, the strategies discussed in this article are neither exhaustive nor fail-safe.

The sooner a lawyer gets started, the better. Unfortunately, the timing is usually beyond his control. Whenever you are retained, though, the first step should be an in-depth investigation of your client's situation.

Ordinarily, the investigation begins with *thorough debriefings* of the client. Although some defense counsel believe that, at least in some cases, it is better not to know the full story from the client, the attorney is usually best prepared to serve his client if he knows all the facts, good and bad.

Despite lawyers' best efforts to explain that to their clients, and despite the attorney-client privilege, clients are often reluctant to confide in their lawyers. Perhaps because of embarrassment, fear, or mistrust, most clients tend initially to sugar-coat or even dissemble the events under investigation. A client may also labor under the misapprehension that the lawyer will not work as hard if he thinks his client is less than angelic.

Through hard work and patience, these barriers can usually be overcome. It is necessary to remind a client often about the attorney-client privilege and to resort to homilies such as, "A doctor cannot treat a patient properly if the patient won't tell him the symptoms." Or, as a partner of mine tells his clients, "You can tell me now, when I can help you, or you will tell me later, when I may not be able to help you." With enough encouragement, most clients will tell you most of the facts. Almost always this process takes time and persistence.

At the same time, counsel should consider what other sources of information are available. If a case involves documents, the attorney should review them carefully. That is necessary for trial anyway, and the earlier you digest the "hard" evidence, the better informed your early and often critical decisions will be. You may also need to hire an expert, like an accountant, to help evaluate the documents. To preserve the privilege, it is essential that the lawyer and not the client retain the expert. *See United States v. Kovel,* 296 F.2d 918, 922 (2d Cir. 1961).

In some cases, you may also be able to interview other witnesses. But be careful not to disclose the fact of the government's investigation to witnesses who are not already aware of it. As the municipal corruption investigations in New York have vividly demonstrated, the publicity surrounding an investigation can be as ruinous to your client's reputation (and health) as an indictment or conviction. If the fact of the investigation is not already public, you may decide to skip certain interviews altogether, rather than risk potentially disastrous leaks to the press. In addition, since defense counsel's interviews are discoverable, consider whether an interview would risk tipping your hand for the prosecutor to see.

If you decide to conduct interviews—for example, with your client's key employees or associates who are already aware of the investigation, or with potential alibi or other defense witnesses—bring someone with you, such as a paralegal or a private investigator. In some cases, you may decide not to participate at all, and instead rely entirely on a trusted investigator.

You may wish to avoid a face-to-face interview if the defense of the case rests on demonstrating that the witness is lying or that he despises your client. In still other cases, only the lawyer will be able to interview the witness, such as the chief executive officer of a major company.

Generally, it is better to conduct interviews without your client. Occasionally, though, a witness, such as a spouse, may refuse to talk to you in the absence of your client. If the witness is inclined to help your client, say that, to best serve your client's interests, you need to understand exactly what happened. It is also good practice, if the witness is a corporate officer or employee, to tell him that you represent your particular client and not the witness.

Other lawyers in the same case may also be a source of information. Defense counsel's willingness to share facts depends on their professional relationship as well as their clients' relationship. Generally, the lawyers should communicate, rather than allowing their clients to talk about the case.

Discussions among counsel are ordinarily covered by the joint-defense and work-product privileges, while conversations among clients are not privileged. To avoid any incriminating statements or claims of obstruction, instruct the client not to discuss the investigation with anyone.

937

Even counsel for witnesses adverse to your client may be willing to talk to you. Sure, a lawyer for a hostile witness is not going to give you devastating impeachment material. But most witnesses are reluctant to testify, and the other lawyer may decide to give you a summary of the witness's testimony to encourage your client to plead guilty. Also, even if a witness's testimony would hurt your client, the witness may still be sympathetic enough to let you interview him or to provide information through his counsel.

The prosecutor, too, may provide important information. Most prosecutors will at least disclose the general nature of the investigation and tell you whether your client is a subject or a target. If the government lawyers are confident of their case, they may tell you much more than that before they indict.

Also, when the government wants a quick guilty plea or your client's cooperation, you can often get the prosecutor to talk. When I was on the other side of the fence, I regularly invited defense counsel to review documentary evidence or to listen to tape recordings early in the investigation. That kind of disclosure depends largely on the chemistry between the lawyers. So, while keeping in mind that the prosecutor is not your client's friend, it may be important to tone down the adversarial nature of your initial dealings with him.

As you seek information from the government, you begin to form impressions of the prosecutor and of where the investigation is likely to go. Is the government intent on making a case, and, if so, against whom? Is your client a major target or a peripheral figure? At what stage is the investigation? Will the prosecutor listen to your presentation fairly and with an open mind? Especially if you have not dealt with the particular government lawyer handling the case, it is certainly worth getting your colleagues' views of the person who will largely determine your client's fate.

Armed with as much information as possible about the prosecutor, the investigation, and the client, you must devise the best strategy for avoiding indictment.

If your client is an important target and the violations are serious and obvious, there may be few alternatives. In some cases, there may be no choice but to wait out the investigation in the hope that the prosecutor will be unable to make a case or that, with a change in government personnel or priorities, the case will slip between the cracks. If, as usual, this tactic fails and the client is about to be indicted, the only options are plea bargaining, limited motion practice, or trial.

In most cases, though, defense counsel should not simply await the indictment. Rather, develop a plan of attack to beat the charges before they are brought. Although this is an uphill battle, it is usually worth fighting.

First consider whether your client is a candidate for immunity. If he played only a minor role in the events under investigation, the government will probably grant immunity. Even if the client's role was significant, sympathetic circumstances such as old age or poor health may commend the exercise of prosecutorial discretion.

Perhaps even more important to the prosecutor is the impact of your client's potential testimony on the investigation. "Who can your guy give up?" or "Can your guy testify against Mr. X?" are questions frequently heard in the prosecutor's office.

More than once, a prosecutor has granted immunity to a former lover or a longtime subordinate of the main target despite that person's involvement in serious offenses over a long period of time. According to published reports, the key witness against former Undersecretary of Defense and LTV chairman Paul Thayer was his girlfriend, Sandra Ryno. Ms. Ryno was granted immunity despite her participation in an insider trading scheme, her apparent participation in the initial stages of a cover-up before the SEC, and her personal profits from the fraud of more than $150,000. Thayer was sentenced to four years in prison.

Timing is critical in the immunity game. It is sound courthouse wisdom that the first one in gets the best deal.

The recent municipal corruption scandal in New York City vividly illustrates this point. Ordinarily, a federal prosecutor relishes the opportunity to go after a corrupt lawyer. In the early stages of the New York City investigation, though, the U.S. Attorney's Office granted immunity to a lawyer who had paid cash to one or more city officials, but who was in a position to testify against a powerful politician.

When I was a prosecutor, a lawyer who represented a middle-level conspirator in a securities fraud case came to my office to volunteer a "proffer"—a hypothetical recitation of his client's testimony. After he made a detailed proffer (without names) regarding the fraud, I consulted all relevant agencies to confirm that the government was unaware of the scheme.

Satisfied that serious crimes might otherwise go unpunished, I reluctantly recommended immunity in exchange for cooperation and complete restitution. The very day after the immunity agreement was signed, the victims of the scheme came to my office to report the crime. To this day, the defense counsel in that case reminds me of his good timing whenever we see each other.

Although early requests for immunity are usually more successful, sometimes a prosecutor will be compelled to give immunity late in an investigation because of lack of evidence or other problems with the case. If, after exhausting all other leads, a prosecutor needs a critical piece of proof or feels uncomfortable with a largely circumstantial case, he may immunize someone he would otherwise indict. Occasionally, even a murderer or a drug dealer is the beneficiary of this circumstance. Although luck may play a part in who gets immunity, a defense lawyer serves his client well by keeping track of the investigation as it unfolds, so that he can go for immunity, if circumstances warrant it, at the most propitious moment.

Of course, before attempting to arrange immunity, a lawyer must consult with his client. Sometimes a client will not want to cooperate—the price tag may be unacceptable—even if immunity is available. Fear, business realities, or loyalties to family or friends may outweigh immediate self-interest.

The lawyer must carefully explain all the consequences of and alternatives to the decision to go for immunity. In particular, it is the defense attorney's obligation to explore with his client any possibility of violent retaliation; the practical impact on the client's life, including loss of livelihood; and the likelihood that the client will be prosecuted, convicted, and sent to jail if he does not cooperate. Ultimately, of course, it is the client's decision whether to seek immunity and to cooperate if immunity is offered.

It is especially important that the client understand that immunity ordinarily results in the disclosure of all criminal problems, not just the facts of the particular violations under investigation. So, if the client has other skeletons in the closet, cooperation may be out of the question, even though his role in the events being investigated was minor.

The Importance of Candor

Emphasize that in talking with the prosecutor your client must be completely candid and accurate, and that any attempts to cover up can only lead to disaster. Partial cooperation will result in damaging admissions and preclude an effective defense. Prosecutors are understandably hard on "cooperators" who fail to tell the whole truth, and judges are notoriously unsympathetic to defendants who blow their immunity agreement by lying to the prosecutor or the grand jury.

If, after full consultation, the client elects to seek immunity, do everything you can to get it for him. Since timing may be critical, a prompt visit to the prosecutor's office is in order.

In almost all cases, the prosecutor will want at least an oral proffer spelling out the testimony your client will give. You should agree to make a proffer only after the prosecutor agrees to treat it as a hypothetical recitation that he will not use directly against your client if you do not get together on an immunity agreement. In my experience, all prosecutors accept such limited-use proffers. But be sure to make your agreement explicit.

Generally, the fewer details that the proffer divulges, the better. If immunity is not granted, too many details could provide the prosecutor with leads that he can follow up without violating the letter of your limited-use agreement. The resulting turn in the investigation could lead the government right back to your client.

Also, a witness's recollection of events often varies upon retelling, and you do not want to be in the position of having to explain discrepancies between your proffer and your client's actual statements to the prosecutor. For similar reasons, written proffers are to be avoided.

But it is equally dangerous to say too little. If the grant of immunity is based on a proffer that omits material facts of your client's involvement in the events under investigation or of his other crimes, the immunity agreement may be voided. Or the prosecutor may insist on a guilty plea to the crimes that were not disclosed. In either event, you will lose your credibility with both the prosecutor's office and your client, and your client will lose much more than credibility.

In some cases, the prosecutor will request a proffer that comes right from the client's mouth. That poses tremendous risks.

With your client present to tell his own story and to answer the prosecutor's questions, the prosecutor learns about your defense case and, if you do not get together on an immunity agreement, he can use what he learns to shape the investigation and to avoid surprises at trial. Your client will also undoubtedly make damaging admissions in the course of the proffer.

By getting the prosecutor to agree in writing to the limited use of the proffer, defense counsel can control some of these risks. Nevertheless, a proffer by the client inevitably locks in his story and divulges leads, wrinkles, and avenues for cross-examination that the prosecutor can often use to demolish the defense case and, with it, your client's future if you do not get the immunity you wanted.

So, if the prosecutor insists that the proffer come directly from your client, carefully weigh the risks against the likelihood of obtaining immunity. Particularly if you suspect that the prosecutor is not acting in good faith or is unlikely to be sympathetic to your client, you should usually decline to bring your client in to make his own proffer. Some defense lawyers flatly refuse to submit their clients for in-person proffers under any circumstance, and most prosecutors will not insist on a direct proffer.

If the prosecutor is willing to grant immunity, the next question is what form of immunity best serves your client's interests. Federal and most state prosecutors can provide either transactional or testimonial immunity.

Transactional immunity offers complete protection against any criminal liability relating to the specified transactions. But transactional immunity covers only the events described in the immunity agreement.

Because transactional immunity is generally governed by contract, it binds only the government authority that enters into the agreement. So a transactional immunity agreement with one federal prosecutor does not preclude the local prosecutor or even a federal prosecutor in another district from indicting your client.

Although the prosecutor granting immunity can usually convince the prosecutor in the other jurisdiction to honor the immunity agreement, it is imprudent to rely on their good relations. Turf battles among law enforcement authorities are neither rare nor gentlemanly. To protect your client, arrange for immunity agreements with each authority investigating the case.

Testimonial or statutory immunity, which in the federal system requires both a court order and approval from the Department of Justice, bars any direct or indirect use of the immunized testimony. *See* 18 U.S.C. §§ 6001 *et seq.* Technically, though, a prosecutor remains free to indict so long as he can demonstrate that his proof is wholly independent of the immunized testimony. *See Kastigar v. United States,* 406 U.S. 441 (1972). Because "taint" or *Kastigar* hearings are so burdensome and because they require pretrial disclosure of the government's entire case, as a practical matter testimonial immunity ordinarily precludes prosecution of your client.

Particularly when only one prosecutor's office is investigating or likely to investigate a matter, transactional immunity is generally your best bet. Some clients nonetheless prefer testimonial immunity because they can tell their associates that they did not voluntarily cooperate but did do so only under compulsion of court order. Also, unlike transactional immunity, testimonial immunity is binding on all federal, state, and local prosecutors. But testimonial immunity cannot bind foreign prosecutors. *See Zicarelli v. New Jersey,* 406 U.S. 472 (1972).

Testimonial immunity may also have one other advantage. Experienced defense lawyers know that, despite their repeated admonitions to tell the truth and their client's insistence that they *are* telling the truth, some clients still lie. In the case of transactional immunity, such falsehoods breach the agreement and subject the client to prosecution for all offenses, including the underlying crimes plus perjury.

In contrast, a mendacious witness who testifies pursuant to a grant of testimonial immunity probably cannot be charged with the underlying crimes, although he can be prosecuted for perjury, false statements to a grand jury, and obstruction of justice. This distinction may be small comfort, though, for the client who opts for testimonial immunity and gets caught lying. Under federal law, perjury is punishable by up to five years in jail and a $10,000 fine.

Suppose immunity is not a viable alternative. Say your client is the prime target of the investigation. Or your client is a highly visible figure, a politician, a lawyer, or chairman of the board. What then?

First, you can resort to familiar damage-control measures: Prepare potential witnesses (keeping in mind that, if they are not your clients, your preparation sessions will be discoverable) or advise them to retain counsel and to have their counsel prepare them; make sure that all witnesses are advised by counsel of their rights, including the right to remain silent; review all documents before your client produces them and take vigorous good-faith positions on the attorney-client and other applicable privileges; and take steps to limit the scope of any subpoenas served on your client.

A target of an investigation may also go to court to protect his rights. Lawyers have had mixed success recently in challenging grand jury subpoenas *duces tecum* on Fifth Amendment grounds. In rarer circumstances, Fourth Amendment claims of unlawful searches and seizures may be litigated prior to indictment. *See* FED. R. CRIM. P. 41.

Other issues that may be litigated at the preindictment stage involve the attorney-client and spousal privileges, grand jury abuses, and violations of the rules governing parallel criminal and civil investigations. When the investigation concerns foreign banking records or other documents maintained abroad, potential defendants often succeed in invoking bank secrecy and foreign blocking statutes in litigation both here and in foreign countries to bar, limit, or delay production of incriminating records.

If successful, preindictment litigation may result in suppression of evidence or may even derail an investigation. And, whether or not it is successful, litigation at this stage may compel the government to make helpful disclosures about its activities. The government may also decide to abandon certain aspects of the investigation because of the delay and expense involved in litigating complicated issues. Especially if the statute of limitations is about to expire, the prosecution will be unable to await an appellate ruling on a complicated privilege or treaty question.

Balance the Psychological Impact

Against the possibility of winning usually limited victories through preindictment litigation, balance the psychological impact it is likely to have on the prosecutor. When faced with a series of witnesses invoking the Fifth Amendment and fighting document production, he will inevitably conclude that somebody has something to hide. If he already appears to be dead set on putting your client in the slammer, you have little to lose by throwing up every barrier you can get your hands on. But if you still hope to convince the prosecutor that there has been no crime or that whatever technical violation there has been does not warrant criminal sanctions, you cannot simultaneously engage the government in guerilla warfare.

Before you decide which way to play it, consider the nonconfrontational alternatives.

At some point in the investigation, many defense lawyers make a pitch to get the prosecutor not to indict. Although anyone who regularly throws strikes in this league is an all-star, the game is very often worth a try. If nothing else, in the course of the dialogue, the prosecutor may reveal the government's theories or its evidence. Also, even if your pre-

943

sentation does not convince the prosecutor to abandon the investigation, you may lay the groundwork for a favorable plea bargain. And, in some cases, prosecutors do change their minds.

The presentation should be orderly and low-key. There is no percentage in yelling at the person in charge of the investigation, and a rambling presentation is as ineffective as a rambling opening or summation. Even if histrionics are your style, save them for the courtroom.

Think through in advance what your pitch should be. What issues are really worth discussing with the prosecutor? What are the investigators' concerns? Why shouldn't the government go forward with its case? Keep in mind that, in the prosecutor's office, the target is presumed guilty until proven innocent, no matter what the judge charges a jury.

It is often effective to let the prosecutor know right off that you have considered his position, that you realize that the government has invested considerable time and effort in the investigation, but that you are confident he will fairly consider what you have to say. Most prosecutors are responsible people with a sense of fair play and some degree of rationality. Many are inexperienced. Appeal to the prosecutor's better instincts, but avoid talking down to him, even if you are 20 years his senior. And be careful not to overstate or overplay your hand. Any inaccuracies will undermine your credibility with an already skeptical audience.

What you say will, of course, vary from case to case. The most effective presentations generally focus on two or three major points.

Reasons to sympathize with the client, including poor health and old age, are favorite themes—so much so that, during my years as a prosecutor, I began to wonder why every potential defendant has a dying relative and is either old and decrepit or a young, naive victim of some older Svengali. Aside from reacting to such arguments with a certain degree of cynicism, prosecutors often respond that those considerations are appropriate for the sentencing judge. Nonetheless, personal circumstances that favor your client should not be ignored. Remarkably, most prosecutors are human.

You may also be able to argue that criminal sanctions are unnecessary. Defense counsel often contend that the client has suffered enough—through restitution, loss of license or business, other professional sanctions, public opprobrium, and the like—and will not repeat the mistake. It is sometimes appropriate to suggest that criminal sanctions would be disproportionate to the alleged misconduct.

In a close case, it may be possible to convince a prosecutor that civil sanctions, such as an SEC injunction, are sufficient, and that a criminal prosecution would destroy the career of a generally upstanding citizen. Although these points are worth making, they rarely save the day.

Another common tactic is to emphasize the weaknesses in the government's case. Nobody likes to lose. More than that, with the government's scarce resources, a responsible prosecutor may agree to drop a marginal case, particularly if your client is not a bad guy or a recidivist. But to be persuasive, you must be able to point to major flaws in the government's case. Mere aspersions against the informant, for example, are unlikely to have any impact on the prosecutor unless the case is a one-on-one swearing contest and there is independent evidence to corroborate your client's version.

Also, the prosecutor may be sensitive to claims of serious government misconduct. Depending on the nature of the problem, he may choose to drop the case rather than to expose the government's dirty deeds.

After the recent arrest in New York of an assistant U.S. attorney on charges of stealing drugs and money from the prosecutor's safe, the government dismissed cases that the same assistant U.S. attorney had been handling. Likewise, prosecutors occasionally abandon cases in which law enforcement agents have committed egregious Fourth or Fifth Amendment violations.

Sometimes, defense counsel try to convince the prosecutor that he lacks jurisdiction or that the incident in question is really "civil" in nature and not a crime. These arguments, bordering on the metaphysical, are most likely to be effective in technical cases involving tax, securities, or similar matters, or in any case where intent is a critical issue. Sometimes it is possible to argue that what is at issue is a controversial technique, such as a tax "straddle," the illegality of which has not been clearly established, and that the target acted on the advice of counsel or other experts.

Besides just making oral presentations, experienced defense counsel often give the prosecutor a brief presenting the applicable law and marshalling the relevant facts. Of course, a written submission has its risks. The prosecutor may go after additional proof, revise his instructions to the grand jury, or restructure the charges to get around the problems that the defendant's lawyer has raised. Still, a good brief submitted to a fair-minded prosecutor sometimes heads off the indictment. So, at least when the indictment would be devastating to the client and the prosecutor has an open mind, submitting a brief is often a good idea.

Sometimes defense lawyers go one step further: They give the prosecutor a preview of their client's case. In essence, the defense tries its case in the prosecutor's office to avoid an indictment and the publicity that comes with it.

The risks of this tactic are great. If the prosecutor is not persuaded to drop the case, the government can redirect or extend its investigation, revise the charges, pursue new leads, and prepare a response to the defense, including a rebuttal case. In short, the defense gives up the element of surprise.

Since the "testimony" of the target is ordinarily the centerpiece of this kind of presentation, this approach also locks in the defense, supplies the prosecutor with damaging admissions, and gives him a unique opportunity to prepare the most devastating cross-examination possible. No wonder many defense counsel *never* take this approach. Certainly in most cases, it is far too risky.

There are special situations, though, in which defense counsel should consider rolling the dice and bringing the client in to talk to the prosecutor. Too often, prosecutors forget that their target is a human being with feelings, hardships, and a reasonable explanation for his behavior. An effective face-to-face interview can restore the human element, which, in some cases, might tip the balance in your client's favor.

Recently, a prosecutor told me that she had decided to drop an investigation because the target turned out to be so much more impressive and credible than her informant. Although hardly commonplace reactions like these are not unique.

In the difficult calculation of whether to expose the defense case before the indictment, a critical factor is the prosecutor. Is he fair minded? Will he listen, or is an indictment inevitable?

Have a chat with the prosecutor about the possibility of laying your cards on the table. Although few people admit to having closed minds, the nuances you pick up and the impressions you form at a face-to-face meeting are invaluable guides. A prosecutor's general reputation among defense lawyers is another useful barometer. Let's face it: There are some law enforcement officials who probably cannot be trusted to come to a reasoned conclusion under any circumstance. In a particularly important case, you might also consider making a presentation to a panel of prosecutors.

An equally important factor is your best objective evaluation of your client and his story. Does the defense seem probable? Is there any corroboration for your client's version of what happened? Will your client be a credible witness and make a good impression? Unfortunately some people appear to be lying even when they are telling the truth.

Give your presentation a dry run in front of a colleague who is not closely familiar with the case. If your colleague does not believe the defendant, neither will a cynical, mistrusting prosecutor.

Some defense lawyers give their clients a lie detector test before taking them to the prosecutor's office. Although the results of these tests are usually inadmissible as evidence in court, a test administered by a reputable operator is useful for several reasons.

First, a favorable polygraph report increases the likelihood that your client will be credible and that you will have confidence in his presentation. Second, a lie detector examination is a useful form of corroboration in the prosecutor's office, even if it is not admissible in court, and a positive result may be decisive in a close case, particularly if it comes down to your client's word against that of an informant or other witness. Third, when the client has passed a reliable private examination, his lawyer should be eager to allow a government operator to conduct a second polygraph examination—something that prosecutors often request in any event.

Lie detector or no lie detector, in deciding whether to submit your client for an interview with the prosecutor, the fundamental question is whether the presentation is likely to persuade him to stop the investigation. If the government's evidence is unambiguous, not even Abraham Lincoln could talk his way out of an indictment. It makes sense to try your defense in the prosecutor's office only if the case is a close one. Also, the presentation is most likely to be effective if the case turns on your client's knowledge, intent, or some other credibility issue.

Say your client, a licensed stockbroker, is about to be indicted on insider trading charges because of his suspicious pattern of securities transactions and his close relationship with someone who had access to confidential information. If your client can credibly deny receiving confidential information and also offer another believable explanation for his investment pattern—particularly one that someone else can corroborate—the risk of bringing him in to talk to the prosecutor may well be worth taking.

Once you decide to make a presentation, you need to consider when and how to do it.

It is usually inadvisable to make a full-scale presentation to the prosecutor early in the investigation. He will ordinarily not be in a position to make a final judgment, and he will be able to steer his investigation around any obstacles you present. Later in the investigation, you can get a better read on the prosecutor's strengths, attitude, and goals, and you can better judge whether a presentation might be effective.

By delaying the presentation, you run the risk that the prosecutor will so harden his position over the course of a lengthy investigation that no presentation, however brilliant, will shake his resolve to indict. In my view, though, it is unlikely that a prosecutor would reach a different conclusion following a thorough investigation after a presentation. And you can always approach the prosecutor early on to plant seeds of doubt and to let him know that, later in the investigation, you would be willing to consider bringing your client in to discuss the case.

As usual, though, there are no absolute rules. If you believe that an investigation is really off the mark and the allegations are frivolous, you may wish to put your ace on the table early in the game. But you will rarely have that good a hand.

Before the actual presentation, establish the ground rules, put them in writing, and arrange for both lawyers and the client to sign. The prosecutor ordinarily agrees not to use anything the client says as part of his direct case. Defense counsel in turn should be prepared to let the prosecutor use the presentation for leads. The prosecutor should also be free to take notes at the meeting, but not to tape-record it, mainly because

947

recording equipment increases the tension and formality of an already stressful event.

The difficult question is whether to permit the prosecutor to use the client's statements on cross-examination or in the government's rebuttal case if the client is indicted and he testifies at trial. Although this issue is worth negotiating, I would not let it become a sticking point.

Presumably, you have decided to try your case before the prosecutor only after satisfying yourself that your client is telling the truth and is not likely to change his testimony. The statements your client makes to the prosecutor will only become significant at trial if he changes his story. And, by refusing to allow his statements to be used for cross-examination, you may subliminally communicate a lack of confidence in your client's story.

In preparing the presentation, take the same pains that you would in preparing a client to testify at trial. Several preparation sessions may be required.

Aside from thoroughly going over the facts and any documents, brief your client on the prosecutor's concerns and attitude and take him through all the tough questions that the prosecutor might ask. Make the client understand that he must be completely accurate and forthright in his answers and that, if he does not comprehend what he is being asked, he should get the investigators to repeat or explain their questions. Although repeated conferences between attorney and client during the presentation will make a bad impression, I always instruct my client to consult with me privately if he feels the need.

Get Some Feedback

In the prosecutor's office, I ask for a break whenever my client seems tired or starts to flounder. Try to get some feedback from the investigators early in the meeting. If you sense that the prosecutor and the law enforcement agents utterly disbelieve your client, cut your losses and call it a day. If the conversation has become a one-way street, do not let them exploit the opportunity for discovery they otherwise would not get.

You may want to present other evidence to the prosecutor as well. I would be inclined to bring in any powerful corroborating or exculpatory proof you have. Do not waste the prosecutor's time with character witnesses or other incidental matters. But consider whether to save one or two little surprises for the courtroom in case the presentation fails.

Occasionally, the prosecutor will encourage the target to testify before the grand jury. More often, your client will want to tell the grand jury everything in order to clear his name now.

Resist these temptations. A defendant's testimony before the grand jury is given under oath, subject to the penalties of perjury, and can be used in the government's direct case. Besides, in the federal system, counsel is not allowed into the grand jury room. Even in those states where counsel may be present during a client's testimony, the prosecutor almost always controls the proceedings. So, if the presentation in the prosecutor's office has not convinced him to drop the investigation, an appearance before the grand jury is usually a suicide mission.

If the prosecutor decides to indict despite your presentation, consider a preindictment appeal. In most jurisdictions, counsel can arrange to meet with at least a supervisory level prosecutor, if not with the chief prosecutor. Beyond that, in certain federal cases, including tax and RICO prosecutions, you can appeal to the Department of Justice. Usually, the national office is more conservative about bringing prosecutions than are the local United States attorneys. To maintain good relations with the prosecutor handling the case, politely ask him to arrange the appeal, rather than just going above his head.

Experienced defense lawyers recognize that a preindictment appeal is rarely productive, and usually not worth pursuing. If you appeal every time a prosecutor decides to indict your client, you will quickly lose all credibility with the senior authorities. But, by picking your shots, your few most deserving cases will get more serious attention. Investigations involving serious legal problems, circumstantial proof, or government misconduct are usually the best candidates for review. The chief prosecutor is simply too busy to review credibility determinations or other run-of-the-mill prosecutorial decisions of the staff.

And, of course, when all these strategies fail, strap your six-guns back on and get ready for the showdown at your old favorite corral—the courtroom.

The Grand Jury: An Overview

by James M. Kramon

It is by now commonplace to hear it said that grand juries no longer serve their historic function of protecting citizens against arbitrary or even malicious prosecutions. Indeed, while it is clear from the history of grand juries, both in England and in the United States, that the right to be tried for serious offenses only after presentment of a bill of indictment was conceived of as a basic form of protection for the accused, somewhere between Blackstone and Holmes the conception of the grand jury changed radically.

Today no one casually familiar with the work of grand juries would seriously defend their existence on protective grounds. The grand jury is, as every lawyer with any prosecutorial experience knows, an instrument of the prosecution, and because it emerged in the Anglo-American criminal law system clothed in a different garb, it is a particularly insidious instrument.

So that my position will be clear, I state at the outset that I am offended by the preservation of the fiction of the protective grand jury and by the unbridled power the grand jury system confers upon prosecutors, some of whom have sound judgment and some of whom do not. For my own part, I would abolish grand juries.

A salient aspect of grand jury proceedings is that they are almost totally *ex parte* and unreviewed. Counsel for witnesses, who may be potential unindicted co-conspirators or even defendants, are not permitted to enter the grand jury room. In fact, under federal and many state procedural rules, the presence of anyone other than the grand jurors, the reporter, if any, the prosecutor or prosecutors and the witness, renders the hearing unlawful.

The author is a member of the Baltimore firm of Kramon and Graham.

Since the grand jury does not generally have its business reviewed, it is not in any meaningful way bound by limitations on the subject matter of its inquiry. The scope of admissible evidence is broad—to say the least—and, even in the unusual case where the evidence presented comes up for review, hearsay, multiple hearsay, not-the-best evidence, tainted evidence and other forms of evidence the admission of which would clearly be precluded in any other judicial proceeding suffices to satisfy the government's burden.

The great bulk of indictments returned are based solely upon hearsay since the only witness who presents himself is the government agent or police officer who has investigated the offense. Since that person is clearly present to persuade the grand jury to indict, most presentations do not include facts that would, in the mind of someone not disposed to indict, raise a question as to the existence of probable cause.

Unfettered Discretion

Even the burden of proof, to the extent that there is one, is largely established by the prosecutor since he alone is available to reinterpret for the grand jury the meaning of the probable cause requirement. In essence, then, the prosecutor runs the grand jury in his almost unfettered discretion, deciding what to investigate, how to investigate it, what evidence to produce, what procedures to use and what standard must be met for it to act.

"Special" grand juries are from time to time empaneled expressly to investigate particular offenses or categories of offenses such as "racketeering," "organized crime," or "narcotics," but the great bulk of grand juries in federal and state courts are general grand juries with a mandate to investigate all offenses indictable in the courts by which they are empaneled. Occasionally certain functions with respect to reviewing public agencies and issuing reports are assigned to grand juries in some state court systems; however, these represent a very minor portion of total grand jury efforts.

While the formalities of empaneling grand juries vary somewhat, certain similarities transcend all such procedures. At the outset, grand jurors are selected in the same general fashion as petit jurors, usually from voter lists, from which the clerk of the empaneling court composes the grand jury. In the absence of motions or requests by the government to strike particular individuals, usually after they have found their way onto a grand jury panel, the procedure will necessarily take place without any equivalent of peremptory strikes or strikes for cause.

At its first session a judge or lesser judicial officer will advise the grand jury of the offenses it is to investigate and, in the case of a special grand jury, of the limited role it will enjoy.

Grand juries are empaneled for particular terms, such as twelve

951

months, but they may be extended for a variety of reasons with the consent of the court.

The primary function of a grand jury is to determine whether there is probable cause to believe that crimes have been committed and that particular individuals have committed them. The proof necessary to meet the elusive probable cause standard is not entirely clear. Upon its empanelment each grand jury is advised about what constitutes probable cause.

The advice is first given by the grand jury judge, then explicated by either a senior prosecutor or the prosecutor who will be in charge of the grand jury. As problems arise over the interpretation of probable cause, it is the person who is seeking to use the grand jury to obtain an indictment who interprets the meaning of that standard. There is general agreement among persons who have worked with grand juries that probable cause is at best not very much cause and at worst none whatsoever.

In one not-so-funny experiment, a federal grand jury was asked to indict an individual upon a proffer by a special agent of the Secret Service that contained no evidence whatsoever. In effect, the special agent told the grand jury that he was fairly convinced the individual had committed the offense for which he was being presented or, the agent suggested, some other similar offense at some time. The indictment received the requisite number of votes and the foreman affixed his signature to it in the normal course of business.

The probable cause requirement may, however, be utilized in certain artful ways by skillful defense counsel. For example, it is well established that probable cause must be found for each element of an offense charged. If one dissects a statutory or common-law crime to isolate its constituent elements, it may appear unlikely that any evidence tending to show the existence of one element, or more, was presented to the grand jury.

Useful Procedure

In such a case, the prosecution may be required by appropriate motion to proffer to the court the evidence that was presented regarding the element or elements, failing which the indictment would be dismissed. While dismissal is unlikely, the procedure is particularly useful where the requisite proof of a particular element of an offense is in question. In such cases it may be utilized to determine at an early stage what the court interprets to be the requirements for proving the offense, since the court must necessarily define the elements to interpret the proffer meaningfully.

The court's definition, if it is more restrictive than the government would like it to be, may afterward be used to limit the range of proof upon which a conviction could be sustained at trial. In effect, such a motion is a useful adjunct to normal discovery motions or those to require a bill of particulars.

Once the grand jury is empaneled, its scope of inquiry defined for it and the burden of proof necessary to indict set out, it begins its business of hearing evidence. Whether transcripts of its hearings are prepared is determined largely by custom. In some federal districts and states all grand jury proceedings are transcribed; in others, none are. In some, the prosecutor may choose to have certain proceedings, but not others, transcribed.

One common form of differentiation is to transcribe the testimony of outside witnesses, especially before special grand juries, but not that of government agents or employees. In all instances, the prosecutor reserves the right to speak "off the record" and does so simply by indicating to the court reporter that his remarks are not to be transcribed.

A Big Obstacle

Obviously, the unavailability of grand jury transcripts has presented a substantial obstacle when alleged infirmities in the proceeding are sought to be challenged. While there is little definitive authority, many lawyers familiar with grand jury procedures feel that judicial requirements of plenary, or at least non-selective, grand jury transcription are on the horizon.

In districts or states where grand jury proceedings are transcribed as a matter of course, or in instances where a proceeding is transcribed at the behest of the prosecutor, review of grand jury proceedings before trial will, when required by a defense motion, frequently be conducted *in camera*. When a witness who testifies at trial against a defendant has previously testified before a grand jury and that testimony has been transcribed, it will be provided to defense counsel pursuant to the federal Jencks Act, 18 U.S.C. § 3500, (requiring the production of the testimony of a government witness after the conclusion of his direct testimony at trial) or an analogous state statute.

As noted, the decision concerning what evidence is presented to a grand jury is strictly within the prosecutor's control. He may present all of the evidence about a violation being scrutinized or only some of it. He may present the inculpatory evidence without presenting the exculpatory evidence. He may permit a witness who wishes to testify to do so or he may not. Although grand juries do occasionally "ask" for certain evidence, experience teaches that aside from very infrequent "runaway" grand juries, most such requests coincide nicely with the prosecutor's objectives.

Many prosecutors, mindful of the responsibility that attends their ability to exercise unfettered discretion, devise rules for their own personal conduct before the grand jury. For example, a number of prosecutors will not, simply because they deem it offensive to use the power of the grand jury in that fashion, require parents to testify against their children or children against their parents or brothers and sisters against one another.

Many prosecutors will invite a potential defendant to testify if he or she wishes to do so and will also present the same opportunity to a third-party witness who believes he can provide exculpatory information. As a matter of prosecutorial ethics, the Standards of the American Bar Association require a prosecutor to decline to call a witness before a grand jury if the purpose is simply to cause him to invoke his constitutional privilege not to testify about matters that may tend to incriminate him.

Some prosecutors go beyond this and advise each potential "target" defendant of his status as such when it becomes clear; they also advise him that he will be entitled to appear before the grand jury if he wishes, but will not be required to do so. A number of prosecutors tell witnesses who may be in precarious positions that they are in need of counsel and that their attendance will be postponed until they obtain a lawyer.

Since the requirements respecting admonitions to vulnerable witnesses are less stringent before grand juries than in other forums (in general, *Miranda* warnings need to be given only to a "putative" defendant), these self-imposed standards are particularly commendable. In my own experience I have found that one hallmark of a responsible and fair-minded prosecutor is the extent to which he goes beyond the requirements of law in an effort to use the grand jury in a manner consistent with generally accepted standards of fair play and decency.

Take Counsel Along

Every witness before a federal or state grand jury is entitled to counsel and in some courts there are provisions for the appointment of counsel for an indigent witness. As a general rule, even if a witness's appearance before a grand jury is purely a formality, he is very foolish to attend without counsel. Although counsel is not permitted to enter the room, a witness is permitted to leave after as many questions as he wishes—even after every question—to confer with his counsel about the appropriate answer.

Representing witnesses before the grand jury requires considerably more than customary legal skill. First, counsel must be aware of the manner in which the grand jury is being used, the scope of its inquiry, and the way in which his client fits into the matter under investigation. He must determine whether his client is vulnerable to prosecution—not in the mind of the fairest, most evenhanded person, but in the mind of a prosecutor and a grand jury, most of whose members will have become more than a little cynical as their term progresses. If the witness is vulnerable, counsel must understand the nature of that vulnerability and the options available for dealing with it.

Sometimes the prosecutor may be prepared to make certain commitments to a grand jury witness. Such a commitment may take the form of a limited or total immunity from prosecution and may range from a statutory, self-actualizing immunity from all offenses about which a witness will speak to the most limited of use and, perhaps, derivative use immunities. To judge how to proceed in such circumstances, counsel for a grand jury witness must know exactly what kind of immunity is being considered, how complete that immunity will be with respect to his client's situation, and what choices the attorney may present his client at each juncture in the proceeding.

Obviously, there are some occasions when a lawyer will advise his client that he as his attorney should tell the prosecutor his client will invoke his privilege not to testify about a matter that may tend to incriminate him. This should be done in writing to preserve a record. If the client is nevertheless called, he should state his name and invoke the privilege in response to the very first substantive question. No knowledgeable attorney would ever advise his client to invoke selectively a privilege against self-incrimination before the grand jury. The risks of unintended waiver always outweigh any possible benefits of such a choice.

On other occasions an attorney will advise his client, quite properly, to go beyond the questions asked and provide particular information to the grand jury even if it is not specifically sought. One might do this, for example, in representing a federal grand jury witness who has been immunized pursuant to the federal witness immunity statute, 18 U.S.C. § 6002, upheld in *Kastigar v. United States*, 406 U.S. 441 (1972). Since use immunity encompasses in most instances derivative use immunity as well, defense counsel will wish to foreclose other avenues by which the government could, if it chose, establish a case against his client by independent evidence.

Where immunity is pursued, counsel should also be aware of the doctrine of *Murphy v. Waterfront Commission*, 378 U.S. 52 (1964), that immunity in state proceedings presumptively carries over to federal proceedings absent a clear showing of independent source. The *Murphy* doctrine is a two-edged sword. On the one hand it renders largely futile an effort to withhold information over a proffered immunity on the basis that there is a residual fear of prosecution by the other sovereign. On the other, it accommodates the interest of an immunized witness by erecting a substantial hurdle in the path of a prosecution by the nonimmunizing sovereign. There is at least one possible exception to this, where the immunity conferring sovereign is cooperating with the other, but in that situation the possibilities of the latter sovereign proving independent source are so small as to make it especially attractive not to assert the self-incrimination privilege before the former.

Write It Down

Whenever counsel elects to permit his client to testify pursuant to some form of offer of immunity that is not conferred in a recorded judicial proceeding in the presence of counsel, he should commemorate the conferral of immunity in an explicit letter, hand-delivered to the prosecutor himself in advance of any relevant grand jury session.

The privileges available to witnesses before grand juries are essentially the same as those available in judicial proceedings generally. While the available privileges differ among states and between the federal government and various states, all assertions of privilege take the two generally acknowledged forms of vicarious and personal assertions of privilege. Into the vicarious class fall privileges such as those of husband-wife, attorney-client, physician-patient, accountant-client, and priest-penitent. A grand jury witness who invokes one of these privileges will be doing so on behalf of the absent privilege-holder. The other form of privilege is the personal privilege against self-incrimination. In that instance, of course, the witness invokes the privilege for himself.

It is difficult to say anything general about privileges other than that most attorneys experienced in grand jury work agree that, when in doubt, a privilege should be invoked. There is little to be gained and much to be lost by voluntarily providing information that might otherwise be withheld from a grand jury. Almost surely if an indictment is sought against the witness or a third person, it will be returned with or without the possibly withheld evidence and, when that occurs, the only party to the ensuing case that will benefit from the statements before the grand jury is the state. Almost never does a witness before a grand jury vindicate himself or someone else.

In complex cases the acquisition of massive documentation by grand juries has presented problems. The grand jury is no doubt entitled to demand and receive copious quantities of original documents if they are available. On the other hand, copies are often received in lieu of originals, particularly from cooperating witnesses. Any counsel representing a client from whom voluminous documents are subpoenaed should devise some agreeable procedure for maintaining a complete record of his client's documents.

If the documents to be supplied are too voluminous to copy, some agreement with the prosecutor should be reached about access to them. If not, a duplicate set should be prepared so that the attorney will have one available to him at all times. Where counsel is familiar with grand jury procedures and with how to deal with prosecutors, a mutually satisfactory arrangement is generally possible. Occasionally, however, courts have had to pass specific orders controlling how documents will be delivered, copied and stored.

Where the necessity for producing testimony or documents is disputed, the generally accepted method for bringing the matter before the court is a motion to quash the subpoena, which should be filed sufficiently in advance of the return date. Since the procedure is usually somewhat rushed, it is customary to deliver a copy of the motion directly to the grand jury judge. In appropriate instances the motion to quash should be accompanied by a motion to seal. In all instances it should include an explanation of the basis for the motion, a brief statement of the authorities relied upon and, if the disposition of the motion requires the court to notice facts, a proffer, perhaps supported by one or more affidavits. In courts that require it, a hearing should specifically be requested.

Obviously grand juries acquire substantial information that would be useful in a variety of contexts other than the criminal cases growing out of their indictments. As a result, procedures have evolved by which government agencies in particular may obtain access to information acquired by a grand jury and use it in other proceedings. All of these procedures have the common element of required judicial approval.

In federal practice Rule 6(e) of the Federal Rules of Criminal Procedure is construed to provide, upon order of court, for the transfer of information gathered by a grand jury. In some instances, such an order may be sought to transfer information from one grand jury to its successor. In others, such as criminal investigations in which information having civil tax implications is found, the information may be ordered to be made available to an entirely different arm of the government. In state grand jury practice, information is at times made available to professional licensing associations and other state regulatory agencies.

Counsel for a client who has provided information to a grand jury, and who has a reason for not wanting that information transferred, will generally be given the opportunity to address the court before a determination is made about a request to transfer. Very few courts will ever approve a transfer of information other than to a government agency that has demonstrated a proper purpose for having the information. Even in those instances, a compelling showing of a reason not to transfer the information may be successful. In all instances, the matter is largely discretionary, and any hope of overturning the decision of the deciding judge, who is usually the supervising grand jury judge, is very small.

Delegated to Prosecutor

In recent years, as increasingly complex cases have been presented to grand juries, a trend has developed toward delegating the functions of the grand jury to the prosecutor and his investigative agents and assistants. In many situations the subpoena power is delegated to the prosecutor, who then issues and serves the subpoenas and subpoenas *duces tecum* in the name of the grand jury. Prior approval of the grand jury for each subpoena may or may not be sought.

Where the case is particularly complex, the delegation may go one step further: The prosecutor may ask the grand jury's permission to forgo bringing before it all of the evidence acquired. For example, in a

957

case where extremely copious documentation is sought, the prosecutor may designate certain government agents or accountants to review the evidence for the grand jury and to summarize their findings for it at some future time. As this procedure progresses, additional steps are omitted so that it is not uncommon for the documents never to appear in the grand jury room nor for any real summarization of them to take place.

Occasionally an overzealous prosecutor may overstep the wide limits of permissible delegation and, for example, require evidence to be delivered to him pursuant to a subpoena duces tecum on a day when the grand jury is not even in the courthouse. If defense counsel can find such a clear violation of the prosecutor's authority, it may sustain a motion to dismiss the indictment. Where a dismissal even with the certainty of reindictment might yield a tactical benefit, it is well worth defense counsel's time to review the technical aspects of the grand jury proceedings, including days of convening, presence of a quorum and concurrences of the requisite number of grand jurors in the true bill vote.

Most lawyers who have had experience with grand juries believe that there is a trend toward greater scrutiny of their conduct, largely because of increasing concerns about their legitimacy. This trend is reflected in one way by the nascent concept that the presentation of different evidence to different members of the grand jury is a denial of due process, since that procedure fails to insure that any particular member of the grand jury has considered all of the evidence upon which the ultimate indictment is based and, therefore, undermines the requirement of a quorum and a certain number of concurrences.

Perhaps the most delicate of all grand-jury-related lawyering is the bargaining that takes place between defense counsel and prosecutors outside of the grand jury room. Here the first rule is for defense counsel to learn exactly what the prosecutor thinks his client has done and is able to say to the grand jury if he chooses to speak.

Next, counsel must learn the prosecutor's objective—whether he wishes to have the client indicted, to make him an unindicted co-conspirator or simply to use him as a witness. Even if the last is the prosecutor's objective, there is still much for counsel to do.

For many clients the way in which their testimony is to be used in subsequent trials is of particular concern, since their relationships with other people may be very much affected by this and since the publicity that may attend their testimony in court may be nearly as damaging as the use of their name in an indictment. Therefore, whatever the prosecutor's objective, it must be understood and the client advised in accordance with that understanding. If there is doubt about the objective, either the doubt must be resolved or the client advised to invoke all available privileges and to resist questioning in every lawful way.

The sparring between the prosecutor and counsel for a grand jury witness who is vulnerable to prosecution is a sophisticated form of cat-and-mouse. On the one hand, the prosecutor does not usually wish to tell counsel for such a witness exactly what he knows and what he suspects. On the other hand, counsel for the witness does not under any circumstance want to highlight the area of vulnerability by raising questions concerning it unless and until he can be certain that the exposure of his client's knowledge is in the interest of his client.

Only One Course

If it is clear that one's client is a target of a grand jury investigation and that the prosecutor will, under no circumstances, abandon his intention to seek the indictment of that client, then there is but one undisputed course of action to follow: absolutely no information whatsoever should be provided to the grand jury (or to the prosecutor in any other fashion).

Counsel in this instance should write to the prosecutor, advising him that he represents the individual, that if called before the grand jury his client will invoke his constitutional privilege not to testify about matters that may tend to incriminate him, and that he expects the prosecutor, having been so advised, not to call that individual to testify. If the witness's subpoena is a subpoena duces tecum, an alternative method for delivery of the requested items, assuming that they are unprivileged, should be sought.

If the possibilities are less clear, however, and if counsel believes the prosecutor can be persuaded to entertain various alternatives for his client, then head-on dealing becomes essential. The negotiation usually takes the following form: Counsel for the witness will ask the prosecutor how he envisions the role of his client in the matter under investigation. In doing this, he will seek to elicit some reasonably clear understanding of the prosecutor's objectives regarding his client.

Some prosecutors will candidly tell counsel for a grand jury witness that the possibilities are "witness or defendant." In other situations a full knowledge of the possibilities may require a number of carefully conducted sessions and, in a few situations, the prosecutor himself may be uncertain of all the possibilities. If the possibilities include that of non-indictment, counsel should also determine whether his client may still become an unindicted co-conspirator or be placed in a position where the testimony he will be required to give may badly damage him in civil or collateral matters.

Once it is clear that the client may escape indictment, defense counsel must obviously determine how that can be accomplished. The prosecutor will generally inform defense counsel that if, arguendo, certain information were forthcoming from his client, he would be assured of not being indicted in the investigation. The assurance might take the form of a letter of immunity, a statutorily authorized judicial conferral of immunity, or some other vehicle.

Hypothetical Disclosure

Whichever is the case, the prosecutor will want to know, before he agrees to immunity, that the witness will say the things he hopes he will say. At this point defense counsel should offer to make "hypothetical disclosure," a disclosure in which counsel for a witness, with the witness not present, presents in generalities what his client would, if an agreement were reached, agree to testify.

Usually by the time a hypothetical disclosure takes place defense counsel already knows that a particular scenario will bring about the desired results. Astute defense counsel will, in the same manner as is often done in plea bargaining, tailor his client's knowledge to the prosecution's needs.

As the prosecutor becomes more definite in his undertaking, the hypothetical disclosure becomes more specific. Later, when the agreement is ultimately reached and made concrete, the actual interrogation of the client may also take place outside the presence of the grand jury.

In those instances where the immunity is one that flows from the use of the grand jury and the discussions are to take place outside its presence, it is particularly important to make certain that all discussions are expressly agreed to be pursuant to the mechanism by which immunity is to be conferred and that judicial approval for that procedure is, if necessary, obtained.

For a variety of reasons, both sides often prefer to work outside the grand jury room where counsel for a witness (who may now be doing all he can to assist the government's investigation) may be present and where the prosecutor may explore certain avenues without the risk of commemorating what may turn out to be exculpatory testimony.

Of all of the difficulties besetting modern grand juries, the problem of secrecy is perhaps the greatest. Grand jury investigations, especially those with political or public interest overtones, rarely can be conducted with total secrecy. As a result, many persons often are unfairly embarrassed simply by having their names associated with a process suggestive of wrongdoing.

Witnesses Often Talk

As a general rule the prosecutor, all persons under his supervision, the reporter and the grand jurors themselves are subject to strict rules forbidding them to divulge information that comes to them in the grand jury sessions. Witnesses, however, are not generally burdened by such limitations, and they frequently discuss quite openly their testimony and their general feelings about the matter. Furthermore, in any major grand jury investigation there is always a good deal of collateral investigating outside the grand jury, and in most instances the line between the two becomes somewhat blurred.

Experienced counsel almost always advise clients who appear before a grand jury not to discuss their testimony because the risk of such conduct far outweighs any potential benefit. Prosecutors become quite unhappy when their grand jury proceedings are publicized and, if they learn the source of such publicity, they may respond unfavorably to it. There is also a quality inherent in the entire criminal process that often makes persons find themselves wishing they were able to put words they have spoken back into their mouths. If the witness has testified in a certain fashion, he may by speaking publicly, perhaps not wholly consistently with his testimony, be raising a suggestion of per jurious testimony that otherwise would never have been present. Perhaps the best reason for not discussing one's testimony before a grand jury is that a great many witnesses who are called before grand juries are vulnerable as a result of their association with the matter under investigation and the less attention such a person draws to himself the better off he may be.

Whatever its shortcomings the grand jury system survives as one of the chief investigative tools of prosecutors in all state and federal courts. The implications of its use are many and varied as are the procedures available to counsel who must deal with it. There are very few aspects of the practice of law where the risks of incomplete knowledge or ill-considered action are greater.

Preparing Grand Jury Witnesses: Some Practical and Legal Points

by Stephen H. Sachs and Robert B. Levin

"Rabbi," asks the pious villager in *Fiddler on the Roof*, ". . . is there a blessing for the Tsar?"

"A blessing for the Tsar?" responds the rabbi, his scholarship sorely taxed. "Of course. May God bless and keep the Tsar—far away from us!"

A similar benediction for the grand jury should be offered by every witness called before it. For, at best, a grand jury subpoena generally means an enormous intrusion into daily routine. At worst it may announce the peril of criminal prosecution. In any case, it is very rarely an invitation to be sought.

Despite the traditional image of the grand jury as a "shield" for the accused, it is the grand jury's role as a sword wielded by the prosecution that has become its preeminent, if not exclusive, function. It is the purpose of this article to offer some practical guides to counsel in preparing a witness for a grand jury appearance and to review current legal issues concerning the grand jury's operation.

The grand jury's development into a cutting investigative edge for prosecutors is a natural outgrowth of its procedural and institutional framework, rather than a sinister distortion of its purposes. In most federal and state investigations a grand jury subpoena is the only process by which pretrial testimony can be compelled and the grand jury is the only forum for receipt of statutorily immunized testimony. Given these facts, there can be little wonder why prosecutors perceive the grand jury as an indispensable investigative resource.

The utility of the grand jury to the prosecutor is heightened by the mi-

Mr. Sachs is a member of the Washington, D.C., firm of Wilmer Cutler & Pickering. Mr. Levin is a member of the Baltimore firm of Frank, Bernstein, Conaway & Goldman.

lieu in which it operates. The proceedings are secret. There are few limitations on the scope of questioning. Witnesses have no right to the presence of counsel in the grand jury room. Evidence that would be inadmissible in an adversary proceeding on the merits is routinely adduced from the grand jury witness. Questioning is conducted by a trained prosecutor who has only a slight duty, if any, to inform either the witness or his counsel what the investigation has previously developed. The inquiry takes place in a setting where the threat of a perjury indictment or a contempt proceeding is a brooding omnipresence for the witness perceived to be untruthful or recalcitrant.

In addition, only the naive would place great reliance upon the members of the grand jury as substantial checks on the exercise of prosecutorial discretion. In form, the prosecutor is no more than the legal adviser to the grand jury, and both process and indictments issue in the name of that body. In substance, however, the prosecutor leads the grand jury in the direction he believes it should go. Again, this is not a malign mutation of the grand jury's role but a corollary of the fact that grand jurors typically are average citizens who generally participate in the investigation only when they are called upon to hear witnesses. They rarely participate in the ongoing strategy of the investigation and only know what the prosecutor tells them concerning witness interviews and other investigatory steps conducted by the prosecutor and his agents between grand jury sessions. The decision to investigate, the selection of witnesses to be called, the choice of documents to be sought, and myriad other investigatory steps, though done in the name of the jury, are prosecutorial decisions on which the grand jurors usually have little or no impact.

Knowledge, Power

To be sure, individual jurors may question witnesses, although this is likely to be perfunctory at best. Moreover, the "runaway" grand jury is not an unheard-of phenomenon. In the vast majority of cases, however, the witness called before the grand jury is questioned behind closed doors by a prosecutor who combines broad knowledge of facts, enormous power to conduct the investigation, and almost unfettered discretion in using that power. The client who tells you that he or she has received a grand jury subpoena is potentially calling upon you for advice in a context where the lawyer's knowledge and judgment may make the critical difference between mere inconvenience and utter ruin.

Counsel's first task when confronted with a subpoenaed client is to determine whether the client is a target of the investigation. The only source of this information is the prosecutor and a preliminary discussion with him is indispensable—if he is willing to discuss the matter. Counsel should try to find out the nature and scope of the investigation and, more specifically, how the prosecution perceives the client. The best

963

news is that the client is simply a source of factual data, indisputable or at least benign in character, where disclosure involves no risk to the client. This may sometimes be all that is involved, particularly if the witness is simply asked to produce records for which he or she is the custodian.

Try for Immunity

If the client is an active or potential target of the investigation or if the information in the client's possession is potentially incriminating, counsel should try to convince the prosecutor that the witness's testimony is available only in return for a grant of immunity, either by an exchange of letters or by a formal grant of statutory immunity such as that contained in 18 U.S.C. § 6002. Without an immunity grant, and absent extraordinary circumstances occasionally encountered in white collar investigations, the witness should be advised to invoke his Fifth Amendment privilege against compulsory self-incrimination. Many witnesses, particularly in white collar investigations, find "taking the Fifth" a humiliating, degrading experience and one of counsel's most difficult tasks may be to convince a client that exercising his constitutional rights is perfectly permissible and may be necessary. Counsel would be well-advised to furnish his client with a written statement invoking the privilege, which could be read in the grand jury room. The language need not be elegant; it may be blunt. Most importantly, the client should be instructed to assert the privilege at the outset of the questioning after giving only his name and address, to avoid the danger of waiving the right entirely.

As a practical matter, however, the privilege is not always a realistic alternative. Some clients simply will not endure the perceived humiliation, especially if the episode may some day become public. And in some circumstances invoking the privilege is inconsistent with the client's assertion of total innocence; its very assertion may raise suspicions that encourage a prosecutor to seek an indictment based on allegations that the witness has refused to explain away.

Counsel may therefore be called upon to prepare his client to appear and testify before the grand jury even though legal instinct and training call for invocation of the privilege against compulsory self-incrimination. Thorough preparation of the witness is plainly essential. It should range from explaining to the client such apparent trivia as the physical arrangement of the grand jury room, the presence of a stenographer, and the personality of the prosecutor to a thorough drill of all expected questions including as rigorous a cross-examination as counsel can imagine. It is often helpful to have another lawyer play the role of cross-examiner.

How effective counsel can be depends both on the information he has been able to obtain concerning the scope of the inquiry and his skill in preparing his client. Counsel may not be able to exorcise unpleasant facts, but if his client gains a mastery of the relevant material counsel will have made an invaluable contribution to the impression his client makes on the prosecutor and jurors. "He didn't ask me anything we haven't gone over a thousand times" is probably the highest praise a lawyer can receive from his client after the grand jury appearance is over.

At the conclusion of a grand jury appearance, the client should immediately record all he can recall of the questions and answers. The debriefing by counsel is essential, for unless the client is subsequently charged, counsel will normally not receive a copy of the secret grand jury transcript. Yet, in preparing for possible subsequent testimony, evaluating his client's continued "exposure" and dealing with the prosecutor in the days ahead, an intimate knowledge of the client's testimony and the prosecutor's questions is essential.

Protections Possible

Despite the enormous power of the grand jury and prosecutor, courts have at least left open the possibility of certain protections for the witness even if they have not uniformly required their use. In *U.S. v. Washington*, 431 U.S. 181 (1977), the Supreme Court left open the question of whether grand jury witnesses must receive *Miranda*-type warnings, but it held that grand jury testimony will only be suppressed upon a showing of actual compulsion of answers by the prosecutor. 431 U.S. at 187. In *U.S. v. Mandujano*, 425 U.S. 564 (1976) and in *U.S. v. Wong*, 431 U.S. 174 (1977), the Supreme Court found that the failure to give *Miranda* warnings to a grand jury witness would not protect him from a subsequent prosecution for false statements to the grand jury. The concerns that animate the plurality opinions in *Mandujano* and *Wong*, and that may indicate the Court's current view of the grand jury, are that it is an historic shield against arbitrary or malicious prosecution, and that the public, through the grand jury, has a right to every man's evidence. All of the Justices who participated in the cases agreed that a witness could not assert any possible violation of his rights as a defense to a perjury prosecution; the plurality opinion in *Mandujano*, however, went on to state that *Miranda* warnings have no place before a grand jury.

A grand jury witness may be able to resist answering certain questions even without asserting his Fifth Amendment privilege. While a grand jury witness may not normally refuse to answer questions on the ground that they are based on illegally seized evidence, U.S. v. *Calandra*, 414 U.S. 338 (1974), the Supreme Court has held that a witness may lawfully refuse to answer questions derived from or based upon material acquired from illegal wiretapping. *Gelbard v. United States*, 408 U.S. 41 (1972). Under *Alderman v. U.S.*, 394 U.S. 165 (1969), the witness may be entitled to an adversary hearing before the court to decide whether illegal wiretap evidence has been used. A witness may also be able to assert, on the basis of certain dicta in *Branzburg v. Hayes*, 408 U.S. 665 (1972), that he is not required to answer questions that might chill the right of association protected by the First Amendment.

The client's subpoena frequently will call for the production of documents, particularly in the investigation of alleged business crimes. In that case, besides the housekeeping steps of retaining copies of each document produced and obtaining a receipt for their production, counsel may be able to limit production on Fifth Amendment grounds despite the discouraging language of *Fisher v. United States*, 425 U.S. 391 (1976). *Boyd v. United States*, 116 U.S. 616 (1886) had long been thought to hold that the Fifth Amendment prevents the compelled production of documents belonging to the witness that incriminate him. But in *Fisher* the Supreme Court held that several pronouncements in *Boyd* had not "stood the test of time." The Court declared:

> [T]he Fifth Amendment does not independently proscribe the compelled production of every sort of incriminating evidence but applies only when the accused is compelled to make a *testimonial* communication that is incriminating. 425 U.S. at 408.

Substantial Compulsion

The Court acknowledged that a subpoena served on a taxpayer to produce an accountant's work papers in his possession involves substantial compulsion. But the Court noted that such production does not compel any testimony. The work papers were presumably written voluntarily and the compelled act of producing them is not "testimony." Therefore, the Fifth Amendment, according to *Fisher*, is not violated when the documents—even though incriminating—are required to be produced.

In light of *Fisher*, a subpoena *duces tecum* can still be challenged on the grounds that the mere production of the incriminating documents involves communicative aspects that are protected by the Fifth Amendment. As *Fisher* noted, compliance with the subpoena "tacitly concedes" the existence of the papers and their possession or control by the client. Depending on the specificity of the subpoena, some subjective selective process may be involved in responding to the subpoena. Further, if the client produces fewer documents than the prosecutor expects, an inference of destruction may arise. The client in effect is compelled to testify that he may have destroyed documents relevant to the criminal investigation.

The Supreme Court was aware of the Fifth Amendment problems that arise when compelled document production has communicative overtones, such as conceding the documents' existence or nonexistence, authenticating or otherwise vouching for them. As Mr. Justice White noted:

[T]he more difficult issues are whether the tacit averments of the taxpayer are both 'testimonial' and 'incriminating' for purposes of applying the Fifth Amendment. These questions perhaps do not lend themselves to categorical answer; their resolution may instead depend on the facts and circumstances of particular cases or classes thereof. 425 U.S. at 410.

What emerges from *Fisher* is the suggestion to defense counsel in a grand jury investigation at least to investigate whether compliance with the grand jury subpoena *duces tecum* would involve testimonial incrimination. In this context, Judge Friendly's reasoning in *United States v. Beattie*, 522 F.2d 267 (2d Cir. 1975), *vacated*, 425 U.S. 967 (1976) could be pursued. In that case, the Court reasoned that compelled production of a witness's own documents may be an admission that the documents belong to the witness and thus may constitute a form of testimonial compulsion. For a detailed discussion of this problem and the related one of the strategy to employ for subpoenaed third-party documents, see Brodsky, *Self-Incrimination in White-Collar Fraud Investigations: A Practical Approach for Lawyers*, 12 CRIM. L. BULL. 125 (1976).

Despite the Supreme Court's apparent endorsement of the grand jury as a major weapon in the prosecutor's arsenal in *Mandujano* and *Calandra*, serious and well-motivated criticism persists. The Section of Criminal Justice of the American Bar Association, for example, is now considering new criminal justice standards that would alter drastically existing grand jury practices. Richard Kuh, former District Attorney for New York County, succinctly stated the policy underlying these proposed reforms: "The grand jury should not be a Star Chamber where the prosecutor is king and to hell with the defendant." The proposed new standards, set forth in 4 *Criminal Justice*, No. 3 (Fall, 1976), include the following:

    a. Witnesses in grand jury proceedings should have the right to have an attorney present with them during the grand jury appearance. The attorney would not be allowed to address the grand jury.

    b. The court should provide an attorney to counsel a witness at grand jury proceedings, if the witness cannot retain one.

    c. Failure of a grand jury or prosecutor to afford a witness the opportunity for grand jury counsel should immunize that witness from any prosecution, including perjury or contempt, utilizing that witness's testimony or any of its fruits, insofar as that testimony was responsive to questions propounded.

    d. Before any person is indicted by a grand jury, that person should have the right to appear before the grand jury as a witness in his own behalf.

    e. A defendant or person against whom a criminal charge is being or is about to be brought in a grand jury proceeding should have the right to request the grand jury, either orally or in writing, to call a person designated by him as a witness. The grand jury should have discretion to grant or deny such a request.

f. Motions to quash or modify subpoenas should be returnable in the locality where the witness lives, where the documents are being kept, or where the grand jury sits.

g. A reasonable period before trial, the defendants should be given the testimony of all witnesses to be called at trial.

h. A prosecutor should present to the grand jury only evidence that he believes admissible at trial.

i. The prosecutor should not compel the appearance of a witness who indicates in advance that he will exercise his constitutional rights.

These reforms will not come quickly. Most of them probably will not come at all. And so counsel and clients should continue to offer up the fervent prayer to keep the grand jury "far away from us." If there is a more reverent blessing for that venerable institution only prosecutors know it.

Representing the Grand Jury Witness

by Howard E. O'Leary, Jr.

Rarely does a lawyer feel more ineffective than as he paces the halls outside the grand jury room. Like the expectant father of a less participatory age, he can only hope that no complications arise during the delivery of his client's testimony in the next room.

Since the grand jury's mission is to determine whether there is probable cause to believe that a crime has been committed and to indict those responsible, the client is there because the prosecutor believes he possesses relevant information. Inside the grand jury room, the prosecutor poses questions to the client in the presence of a panel of citizens. The citizens are there to find the facts. The panel varies between 16 and 23 members in different places.

A reporter transcribes what is said. No judicial officer is present to protect the client against a prosecutor's transgressions. The lawyer waits outside, hoping the client will not find the situation so intimidating that he forgets to ask for advice. Most witnesses—while entitled to confer with their lawyers in the hall—fear that to step outside suggests they have something to hide.

The unusual nature of this tribunal means the lawyer must employ unusual tactics to protect his client appearing before it. I am assuming that the client has waived the Fifth Amendment's privilege against self-incrimination or has been compelled to testify by a grant of use immunity. If so, you must deal with three things that separate the grand jury appearance from an ordinary civil deposition:

1. The exclusion of the lawyer from the proceeding. Not only can the lawyer not see and judge for himself, but the client cannot communicate easily with his lawyer, because the lawyer has to stay outside.

The author is a member of Dykema Gossett in Washington, D.C.

2. The client testifies before a live audience that is supposed to be finding the facts, so he naturally seeks to talk to them.
3. After the witness testifies, you will not know what he said, because he usually cannot have a transcript of his testimony. Even more important, he will not have an opportunity to correct what he has said.

If the prosecutor—generally an assistant United States attorney—includes the client's name in a proposed indictment, he will be indicted. It is as simple as that. Perhaps, somewhere, sometime, a witness's winning smile and earnest demeanor persuaded the grand jurors not to indict him, but it is doubtful.

Consequently, you may safely advise the witness to ignore the presence of the grand jurors. To represent him effectively, you must advise him to interrupt the proceedings frequently, causing the grand jurors considerable inconvenience. Unless the witness keeps the lawyer informed of the nature of the questions, the client is merely paying for the dubious comfort of knowing that his lawyer is in the next room. It will be difficult for the witness to turn his back on them and walk out, but he has to do it.

Logistics alone are enough to deny the client effective representation. The witness will find it embarrassing to ask to be excused to consult with his lawyer. The witness must exit the grand jury room feeling responsible for leaving between 18 and 25 people hanging on an unanswered question. He must then take time to summarize the current line of questioning, describe where he thinks the prosecutor is headed, and relate the significance of the pending question.

That is too much for most mortals. The client typically rushes outside, blurts out a garbled version of what has occurred, forgets the pending question in the process, and then—anxious because he has kept the grand jurors waiting so long—rushes back inside before he and his lawyer have had a chance to discuss why he emerged.

Representing a witness is much easier if you train him to ignore the grand jurors. Clients invariably mistrust such advice. After all, who can resist playing to a live audience? Moreover, witnesses find it hard to believe that the august body of citizens hearing their testimony really has no useful function. Drive it home. The witness has to learn to listen carefully and report to the lawyer so he can take advice.

Probably every lawyer doing federal criminal work has experienced the frustration of attempting to piece together hours of a client's grand jury testimony. The problem is greatest in grand jury investigations of complex commercial crimes, where the witness may be examined about an endless succession of documents.

Some witnesses, of course, are blessed with excellent recall, and can recreate the questions and answers in reasonable detail. For others, even many of superior intellect, the task is almost hopeless.

This tedious exercise is best carried out immediately after the witness's appearance, when his recollection is fresh. It is the last thing a client feels like doing after a long day in the grand jury room. Generally, the higher the witness's station in life, the less amenable he is to participating in these mental calisthenics after his appearance.

Yet the exercise is necessary. The busy executive who escapes debriefing is inevitably the one summoned to reappear months later.

The lawyer must assume that the witness will not have the right to see his testimony when he prepares and debriefs his client. Consequently, the witness must be prepared for his appearance with a view to making his debriefing easier.

Clients should enter the grand jury room with a blank yellow pad. Typically, the prosecutor reacts by demanding that any notes be left in the grand jury room or by asserting that no notes may be taken. I know of no authority that prohibits a grand jury witness from taking notes. Grand jurors take notes, so why shouldn't the witness?

This technique is most useful when you think the client will be shown many documents. Instruct the witness to list each document and to tell you about the list after a certain number of documents have been shown to him.

If the prosecutor objects, instruct the witness to consult with you after the prosecutor shows each document to him. Faced with this alternative, most assistant United States attorneys will agree to a procedure that smooths their examination and accommodates the defense lawyer.

A list of documents will provide a road map of the witness's testimony and make debriefing considerably easier. If documents are not used to interrogate the witness, your task is more difficult. Some witnesses are capable of making a simple outline, or a list of the subjects they are asked about. The danger is that the witness may become so preoccupied with his list that he fails to concentrate on the questions and answers.

In any event, the lawyer should list those subjects beforehand about which he expects questions. During breaks in his client's testimony, the lawyer can check off the items covered. When a question is posed that requires consultation with counsel, the witness should ask the reporter to read back the question and write it down before asking to be excused.

Representation would obviously be more effective if the lawyer could take notes during his client's testimony and the witness could obtain a transcript. After indictment, a defendant is entitled to inspect and copy a transcript of his own grand jury testimony. A corporate defendant is entitled to inspect and copy the testimony of those employees capable of legally binding the company to the conduct constituting the alleged offense. FED. R. CRIM. P. 16(a)(1).

A defendant may also obtain the grand jury testimony of others on a showing ''that grounds may exist for a motion to dismiss the indictment because of matters occurring before the grand jury.'' FED. R. CRIM. P.

6(2)(c)(ii). Non-defendants—grand jury witnesses and third parties—may have access to grand jury testimony only "when so directed by a court preliminarily to or in connection with a judicial proceeding" FED. R. CRIM. P. 6(e)(C)(i).

Most courts reject a witness's petition to inspect and copy a transcript of his testimony. They hold that the required showing of "particularized need" has not been made. *Bast v. United States,* 542 F.2d 893, 894–96 (4th Cir. 1976); *United States v. Fitch,* 472 F.2d 548, 549–50 (9th Cir.), *cert. denied,* 412 U.S. 954 (1973); *In Re Bottari,* 453 F.2d 370, 371–72 (1st Cir. 1972); *Valenti v. United States,* 503 F. Supp. 230, 234 (E. D. La. 1980); *In Re Grand Jury Witness Subpoenas,* 370 F. Supp. 1282, 1285–86 (S.D. Fla. 1974); *In Re Alvarez,* 351 F. Supp. 1089, 1090–91 (S.D. Cal. 1972). In these cases, the witnesses generally sought access as a matter of right, rather than particularized need.

A few courts have granted witnesses access to their testimony while the grand jury investigation was still in progress. *Bursey v. United States,* 466 F.2d 1059, 1079–80 (9th Cir. 1972); *In Re Braniff Airways,* 390 F. Supp. 344, 345–57 (W.D. Tex. 1975); *In Re Russo,* 53 F.R.D. 564, 569–72 (C.D. Cal. 1971); *In Re Craven,* 13 Crim. L. Rep. 2100 (1973).

The *Bursey* and *Russo* cases both held that a grand jury witness is not required to make a showing of particularized need. The "particularized need" test was formulated by the Supreme Court in *United States v. Proctor & Gamble Co.,* 356 U.S. 677 (1958). In that case, the government brought civil suit following a federal grand jury investigation of criminal antitrust matters. The grand jury returned no indictments.

Single Grand Juror

The trial court granted the company's motion to discover the entire grand jury transcript. The Supreme Court reversed, holding that the company had not shown sufficient "compelling necessity" or "particularized need" to overcome the "indispensable secrecy of grand jury proceedings."

The Supreme Court has endorsed the particularized need test for requests by third parties for grand jury testimony. *Douglas Oil v. Petrol Stops Northwest,* 441 U.S. 211 (1979). That case involved the request of private antitrust plaintiffs to obtain the testimony of the defendants' employees before a grand jury that had concluded its investigation. The defendants had been indicted, and pled nolo contendere, and had already obtained transcripts of their employees' grand jury testimony. The Supreme Court held that the plaintiffs had made a showing of particularized need that outweighed any interest in continued grand jury secrecy.

The Supreme Court summarized the reasons for grand jury secrecy with the following quotation from *United States v. Rose,* 215 F.2d 617, 628–29 (3rd Cir. 1954):

972

(1) To prevent the escape of those whose indictment may be contemplated; (2) to ensure the utmost freedom to the grand jury in its deliberations, and to prevent persons subject to indictment or their friends from importuning the grand jurors; (3) to prevent subornation of perjury or tampering with the witnesses who may testify before the grand jury and later appear at the trial of those indicted by it; (4) to encourage free and untrammeled disclosures by persons who have information with respect to the commission of crimes; (5) to protect innocent accused who is exonerated from disclosure of the fact that he has been under investigation, and from the expense of standing trial where there was no probability of guilt.

Since a grand jury witness may dispense with secrecy by talking about his testimony, the reasoning of the courts about transcripts is a mystery. Under Rule 6 of the Federal Rules of Criminal Procedure, the witness may disclose his recollection to anyone—including the target of the investigation. Logic suggests that the witness should either be barred from divulging what took place to anyone but his lawyer, or he should be permitted to have a transcript.

The use of a United States magistrate as a one-man grand jury would be far more efficient and probably less expensive than the traditional grand jury. More important, when the grand jury is used to investigate, the witness's counsel could be present without fear that the proceedings would be disrupted. The magistrate's presence would also help prevent abuses by the prosecutors. Regrettably, a one-man grand jury in the person of a federal magistrate may be so different from the institution envisioned by the founding fathers that the Constitution might require amending to implement this proposal.

In our federal criminal system, the grand jury performs two functions. One is to return indictments after an enforcement agency such as the Federal Bureau of Investigation has completed its work. The other is to assist in the investigation by issuing subpoenas for documents and receiving testimony.

Since the Constitution requires that felony charges be presented to a grand jury, the first function predominates. Most criminal investigations are conducted by law enforcement agencies, not grand juries. Matters are usually presented to the grand jury after the investigation has been completed and the United States attorney believes that the evidence against the accused is sufficient to prove guilt beyond a reasonable doubt.

Typically, the agent who conducted the investigation appears before the grand jury and testifies about the evidence. The prosecutors seek an indictment. Thus, in the overwhelming number of instances, the grand jury crowns the enforcement agency's investigation with an indictment.

973

The grand jury is also used to investigate, particularly when compulsory process is needed. Investigations of complex commercial crimes, for example, often require grand jury subpoenas to compel production of documents. After the prosecutors review the documents, the grand jury may subpoena live witnesses to describe how business is conducted, interpret certain documents, and answer questions about specific transactions.

The traditional grand jury does not perform either function—indictment or investigation—efficiently. The grand jury cannot transact business unless a quorum is present, generally begins after 9:30 A.M. never completes lunch in an hour, always finishes before 4 P.M., and recesses at least once during both the morning and afternoon sessions. It is, in short, a cumbersome institution.

The rule excluding lawyers reduces the grand jury's slow movement. After allowing for the witness's entrances and exits to confer with his lawyer, the grand jury is fortunate to be in session for four hours during a working day.

Perhaps grand jury service is so uplifting for our citizenry that the institution should be retained despite its frailties. My guess, admittedly skeptical, is that grand jurors sense that their usefulness is questionable at best. If any Congressional committees conduct hearings on reform legislation, they might consider testimony from former grand jurors on the value of their service.

A magistrate sitting as a one-man grand jury could conduct business more efficiently and at less public expense. As a lawyer and an experienced judicial officer, the magistrate is better equipped to ferret out the rare instance in which something is wrong in the government's investigation. The only serious objection to having a magistrate preside is that this small reform perpetuates an institution that has long survived any usefulness. Even in England, the source of the grand jury, the institution was abolished in 1933.

The Justice Department objects that the presence of lawyers in the grand jury will destroy the spontaneity of the witness's testimony. That objection harkens back to the scene that occurs during congressional hearings, where the witness and his lawyer—sitting side by side—confer in hushed tones before answering each question. In 1981, the Department of Justice wrote the Senate Judiciary Committee as follows:

> If a witness had counsel at his side and counsel was permitted to consult him before answering questions, in our view, the fact-finding process would be severely impaired because of the tendency for the witness to become dependent upon, and to repeat or parrot responses discussed with the lawyer, rather than to testify fully and frankly in his own words.

No one suggests that a witness testifying during a trial parrots his lawyer's words because the lawyer is present in the courtroom. Congress can require the grand jury witness to testify from the witness stand. He does not have to sit beside his lawyer. The magistrate, as a judicial officer, can also make it clear that the grand jury is interested in receiving the witness's testimony, not his lawyer's.

The assumption that the witness will not testify frankly because his lawyer is present is unwarranted. It is far more reasonable to assume that the lawyer has advised the witness either to assert the privilege against self-incrimination or to tell the truth. The lawyer has almost certainly told the witness that the maximum penalty for perjury is five years in jail and a $5,000 fine. For all practical purposes, it is impossible for the Department of Justice to dispute a witness's assertion of the Fifth Amendment privilege. If the prosecutors remove the privilege through a grant of use immunity, the lawyer will surely advise his client that the only safe course is to tell the truth.

The magistrate's presence eliminates the objection that a lawyer's presence will transform the witness's appearance into an adversary proceeding. This objection only makes sense in the context of the traditional person grand jury, where no judicial officer controls the proceedings. The magistrate sitting as a one-man grand jury would presumably have the same contempt powers as the judge conducting a trial. With these he could control both the prosecutor and the lawyer representing the witness.

The important question is not whether the proceedings take on a more adversarial tone, but whether the magistrate would be a more effective grand jury. A magistrate would hardly be more soft on crime than the current grand jury. A skillful magistrate may actually enhance the grand jury's ability to investigate by improving on the prosecutor's examination and suggesting additional leads.

Transcripts Important

The one-man grand jury would transfer some control over the proceedings from the prosecutor to the magistrate. While the magistrate might misuse his power, the presence of the witness's lawyer should offset the potential for abuse.

An alternative would be to permit the witness's lawyer to be present without disrupting the proceedings, but retains the traditional grand jury with a magistrate presiding at the witness's request. This would avoid any question of a constitutional amendment.

This approach would perpetuate the illusion that the traditional grand jury protects the innocent from wrongful prosecution. Actually, the legal standard applied by the grand jury, proof of probable cause, is so easily met that virtually anyone can be indicted.

The innocent man's protection lies in the legal standard applied by the petit jury, proof of guilt beyond a reasonable doubt. Perhaps our real protection lies in having institutions that ensure that United States attorneys and law-enforcement agents are honest and competent professionals who recognize that their interests are served only when justice is done.

While the lawyer's presence in the grand-jury room reduces the need for a transcript, the witness should have an opportunity to review his testimony. Grand-jury witnesses and court reporters are no less prone to error than anyone else. The ability to correct a mistake or clarify an answer should help the search for truth. The dishonest witness may have an opportunity to alter his testimony, but the government will have notice that such a man is willing to risk prosecution for perjury and contempt to obstruct justice.

Some of the decisions denying witnesses their testimony say that release of the transcripts might impair the grand jury's ability to obtain information by subjecting the witness to retaliation. The answer, of course, is that the witness who fears retaliation need not apply for a transcript. The court might also restrict the witness to an inspection in camera by only the witness and his lawyer. The court could even deny a request for inspection.

No good reason justifies a general rule that denies the witness a transcript of his testimony. The grand jury's investigation will be compromised—if at all—by the witness's freedom to disclose, not by a transcript. As Judge Wyzanski put it: "The horse is out of the stable and all that we are considering is whether to lock the barn door so that the horse may not carry its master's correct colors."

Basic Strategy in Federal Criminal Defense Litigation

by George J. Cotsirilos and Robert M. Stephenson

In your reception area sits a person staring starkly at the wall. His face is ash gray and drawn, reflecting his recent sleepless nights. Life suddenly seems hopeless to him. His appearance is surprising. He is an executive vice president at a major bank, a person of means with a lovely family, who lives on a tree-lined street in an affluent suburb.

This peaceful existence was shattered a week ago, when a federal grand jury returned a 20-count indictment, charging him with violations of the federal mail fraud statute and the Racketeer Influenced and Corrupt Organizations chapter of the Organized Crime Control Act. If convicted, he faces a maximum jail term of 115 years, a maximum fine of $44,000, and the prospects of a ruined reputation and a broken family.

Scenes like this, where human liberty is at stake, are familiar to the criminal defense lawyer. Criminal defense work is the most romantic in the law. Our democratic processes are dedicated to protecting individual freedoms and dignity. There is no nobler undertaking than representing defendants threatened with the loss of their liberty. With this task comes a heavy burden—the obligation to provide effective assistance of counsel. Here are some ways to provide that assistance.

The first client interview is the most important meeting you will ever have with the client. Gain the confidence and trust of the distraught client; deal with the psychological trauma he is experiencing. Always allow sufficient time for the interview. First impressions leave an indelible mark. A crisply conducted interview, with no opportunity for the client to express his thoughts, spells doom for your later relationship. At the

Messrs. Cotsirilos and Stephenson are members of Cotsirilos, Crowley, Stephenson, Tighe & Streicker, Ltd. in Chicago.

outset what you say is less important than having an understanding and listening ear.

If possible, your work should have begun before this interview. If the client already has been indicted, obtain a copy of the indictment. Become thoroughly familiar with the factual allegations of each count and the statutes involved. In addition, contact the prosecutor who is assigned to the case. Explain that you may be representing a defendant in the case and that background information would help your first client meeting. In most instances, the prosecutor will cooperate. If the prosecutor does not yet know much about the case, ask for permission to speak to the investigating agent.

If the client has not been indicted before your first meeting, you should still speak with the government. Discover the scope of the investigation and your client's role in it. If the case involves multiple defendants or subjects, talk to the lawyers representing them. They may provide you with a reservoir of knowledge about the case. This kind of preparation enhances a client's confidence in his lawyer.

Suicidal Impulses

When the client arrives for the first interview, he is often frightened and bewildered. He sees his life crumbling into oblivion and may even have suicidal impulses. Your first task is to ease the client's tension. If you do not already know the client, introduce yourself and describe the nature of your practice. Discuss the lawyer's role in the case. Assure the client that you represent him, that his interests are paramount to all others, that you owe him total loyalty, and that you will do everything within the bounds of propriety to protect his rights.

Explain the attorney-client privilege and the work product doctrine in laymen's terms. It is important for the client to understand that communications between lawyer and client are confidential and are protected from disclosure except in very rare circumstances. Encourage the client to talk freely. Impress upon him the importance of his participation throughout the case. He should talk to you about the case and also about any problems that confront him or his family. In turn, tell the client you are willing to deal with whatever arises.

Then ask the client whether there are any problems he wants to discuss with you such as jeopardy of professional licenses, related civil actions, and bond in the event of a conviction. Explain to the client that your representation is complete and genuine.

Next, review the indictment generally. If the client is not yet under indictment, discuss the subject matter and scope of the investigation. Let the client know that you have prepared beforehand. Tell him about your discussions with the prosecutor or the investigating agent. The client is entitled to know the obstacles that confront him.

Probe the client's background—his employment history, education, family, military record and past contacts with authorities. Listen to him. Here is your first opportunity to know whether you have succeeded in gaining his trust and confidence.

Complete Candor

Only then are you ready to focus on the client's version of the specific charges in the indictment or the investigation. This is also the time to respond to any additional problems, personal or otherwise, the client has raised. Emphasize the need for complete candor. Compare yourself to a doctor treating a patient. Without the correct information, you cannot diagnose the disease or recommend treatment. Avoid extensive note-taking during this stage of the interview. Nothing is served by placing things in concrete—especially at this time in the proceedings. Recollections change as they are refreshed.

In some cases it may not be wise to discuss the client's version of the events at the initial interview. It may be best to await the results of your independent investigation. Then, after thoroughly reviewing your information with the client, you can ask about the client's version. If you believe that the client does not have total confidence in you, or has a faulty or confused memory, then defer discussion of the client's version until a later date.

The client's fee arrangement must be discussed at the initial interview. To avoid any misunderstandings, make certain that you have a written fee agreement. Generally, charge a retainer against which you will bill hours spent on the case. When the retainer is exhausted, either bill subsequent services on an hourly basis or charge an additional retainer, with the same conditions. Meticulously record your hours, describing the actual work performed for each hour. At the end of each month, give the client a monthly status report describing the work done and the status of the retainer. He is entitled to no less.

Before the initial interview ends, tell the client not to speak to anyone else about the case. If he is contacted by anyone, he should politely decline comment and say that he is following your advice. If the questioner persists, he should be referred to you. In any case, the client should advise you immediately of the contact.

Avoid appraising the case at the initial interview. Early predictions are rarely correct and often return to haunt the predictor. However, a client who has an unrealistic view of his problem should be brought back to reality. If possible, tell the client generally about his chances of success, or in the event of failure, the likely punishment. As investigation and preparation proceed, the lawyer can be more specific in assessing the case.

When the initial interview ends, tell the client that you will begin work on his case immediately and that you will keep him informed about your progress. Encourage him to communicate with you again when he feels

979

the urge. When the client leaves your office, he should feel at least a little better than the distraught person who first sought your help.

Once you begin your defense of a criminal case, a vigorous motion practice is essential. Study the indictment and the manner in which the grand jury investigation was conducted. Instead of assuming that things have been done properly, scrutinize every move of the prosecutor and investigating agent and every paragraph of the indictment.

There are some objections that must be made before trial or else they will be waived. *See* FED. R. CRIM. P. 12(b). Many of these pretrial motions also help to define the issues at trial. A motion for a bill of particulars, a motion to suppress unconstitutionally seized evidence, a motion to exclude evidence, such as evidence of prior convictions, or a motion for severance based on improper or prejudicial joinder each limits the boundaries of admissible proof against the client. A favorable ruling on one of these motions often deprives a prosecutor of such a key to his case that it may even result in a dismissal of the action.

These motions may also force the prosecution to disclose information that otherwise would have remained hidden in the normal discovery available in criminal litigation. *See* FED. R. CRIM. P. 16. Finally, pretrial motions may place before the court mitigating circumstances that serve to explain the client's conduct, even if they do not constitute a legal defense.

For example, in a bid rigging conspiracy case brought under the federal antitrust and mail fraud laws, the defendant moved for leave to present state of mind evidence to show that he had acted as he did because he feared economic reprisals from a dominating labor union. Although the trial court ultimately rejected the proffer because it was not evidence of a legal defense, the information proved very helpful when the court had to decide how to sentence the defendant.

The other virtue of filing legitimate pretrial motions, even if they are denied, is that they prolong the proceedings. Buying time often increases the likelihood of a favorable turn of events in a criminal case. Exculpatory evidence may turn up; recollections may change; prosecutorial misconduct may surface. At the very least, a vigorous use of properly available motions creates obstacles to the prosecution that may improve your bargaining position for a more acceptable disposition of the charge. Remember: delay never serves the prosecution. More than likely, it will benefit the defense.

Thorough Investigation

Most criminal cases ultimately turn on the facts, rather than the law. A successful defense depends on a thorough investigation. Your efforts should exceed the prosecutor's, rather than pale by comparison. Employ independent investigators for much of this work. Good ones always are available and often come from the ranks of former government agents. The investigator's fee will be less than you would have to charge the client for this work, and your time will be freed for other tasks. Because of their expertise, training and contacts, good investigators have access to people and information that are difficult for lawyers to uncover. Finally, investigators can testify to establish a key point of the defense or to impeach a prosecution witness.

The nature of the case dictates the type of investigator. In a tax case, hire a former intelligence agent from the Internal Revenue Service or a reputable accounting firm. Other financial crime cases may require a former FBI agent or a postal inspector who is familiar with the kind of business involved in the case.

Do everything possible to preserve work product protection for the investigator's activities. You, not the client, should hire him. Draft an employment agreement, carefully stating that the investigator acts as your agent. Require him to surrender his work to you upon request, and make him notify you first before responding to any subpoena. Instruct the investigator not to tape interviews, or memorialize them verbatim in any form. Instead, the investigator should discuss with you his impressions of the information derived from the interviews.

Finally, always keep the lines of communication open with the prosecutor. Any information you receive as a result of these communications is part of a thorough defense investigation. Immunity or some other favorable disposition may become possible. Always be ready to listen. To foreclose this avenue of investigation only hurts the client. Also work closely with other defense counsel. If there are common defenses, the attorney-client privilege protects communications among counsel and their respective clients. Of course, if the defenses are antagonistic, you must go it alone. Even then, do not sever all lines of communication. There is validity to the timeworn phrase, ''United we stand, divided we fall.''

After completing your investigation, meet with the client to review the results, including your discussions with the prosecutor, to discuss the client's version of the events, and to evaluate his position. Based on this meeting, you will decide either to prepare for trial or to recommend withdrawing the not guilty plea. If this meeting occurs before the client has been indicted, the client must decide whether to seek immunity.

When you review the case with the client, be frank and open. Do not paint any false pictures, but do not be a false prophet of doom. The final decision about how to proceed rests with the client, but he will seek your advice. Give it. The client hired you for that purpose.

If an indictment has been returned, the number one priority is keeping the client out of jail. If that result can be attained only through trying the case, then prepare for trial. However, if the prosecution is willing to accept a guilty plea in return for no jail, consider the offer seriously. It would be intolerable for the client to reject the offer and then be sentenced to jail after a protracted trial.

If prison is an inevitable result, either with or without a trial, the next priority is to obtain the least restrictive sentence available, such as a sentence to a work release program. Sometimes trying the case may achieve this goal by bringing out mitigating factors to convince the court that the conduct charged in the indictment is not as heinous as it first appeared. Other times a negotiated plea can reduce the incarceration period.

It is vital to know the sentencing habits of the judge. Before some judges, it is very dangerous to plead guilty without either some limit on the potential maximum period of prison or an agreement on the exact sentence to be imposed. Finally, if your client is the object of a grand jury probe but has not yet been indicted, the first priority is to avoid indictment. Explore the possibility of obtaining immunity, either by court order or by letter agreement, in exchange for your client's cooperation with the grand jury.

If your client decides to go to trial and you expect it to be a protracted one, make certain the client understands the costs—especially if there is little hope of success. Make certain the client knows all the consequences of a guilty plea. Explore the possibilities that the client may lose his professional license or face private civil damage suits. These consequences may be as important as the risk of jail, and the client may prefer to "go the course."

If the client decides to go to trial, begin your preparation immediately. There are some key commandments that apply in every case.

- Know the documentary exhibits. Generally, the prosecutor will give you copies of the prosecution exhibits prior to trial. Study them. Commit them to memory. Prepare an exhibit list for those exhibits as well as for your exhibits.
- Review the prior statements of the prosecution's witnesses. In our district, the prosecutor generally discloses those statements before trial. To a great extent, your cross-examination of these witnesses will be shaped by their prior statements and other valuable impeachment material.
- Prepare an outline of your closing argument before the trial. Although this outline will change to match the evidence, your defense investigation should enable you to develop a theory of defense that will shape the argument. If it does not, you are not ready for trial.
- Outline your cross-examination of the prosecution witnesses. Elicit only information that supports the defense theory and forget about everything else. Many a defense lawyer has proved the prosecution's case during his cross-examinations. Do not join that long gray line of barristers.
- Plan as though the defendant will testify, but try the case on the assumption that the defendant will not testify. Too often, the defendant is his own worst witness. If the defendant is nervous, arrogant, timid, or there is some other reason why he will not be a good wit-

ness, keep him off the stand. Build your defense around disinterested witnesses and cross-examination of the prosecution's witnesses. At times, properly instructed juries do acquit without hearing from the defendant. Conversely, a jury that has doubt about guilt will convict after hearing from a defendant whose testimony is basically weak or who is badly impeached.

- Prepare the defendant before he testifies. This preparation should begin as early as possible, even during the investigative stages. Go through mock cross-examinations with the client; ask him the hard questions. Continue this process until that fateful day when you decide that the client must testify. Then, Godspeed!

Unfortunately, despite your best efforts, the trier of fact may convict your client. This does not end your work. Indeed, the services that you render the client at the time of sentencing may be the most meaningful of all.

Most districts have qualified probation offices that submit presentencing reports. Do not rely on this report. Prepare a written sentencing brochure introducing the client to the judge and relating his family and employment history. Tell the judge about the client's military record, his philanthropic efforts, and the state of his health. Submit character references from people who know the client best. Have the client's children or spouse write on his behalf.

The defendant in white collar crime cases usually has a wealth of material that will help persuade the court to give a more lenient sentence. Too often, lawyers forget that our primary task is to make it as difficult as possible for the court to sentence the client to jail.

Opening Statement for the Defense in Criminal Cases

by Richard J. Crawford

A trial is like a football game. The opening statement is the only time during a criminal trial when there is light between the defense and the goal line. The defense attorney must use the opportunity to put points on the board while he can. But points are not enough—the game must be put out of reach of the prosecution so that it will be left with playing unsuccessful catch-up ball for the rest of the trial. If the defense attorney does not take advantage of this opportunity, the game will be lost, for from that time forward, the format and momentum belong to the state. Opening statement is a time to score.

There are several ways to justify my strong position. The defense attorney who gives his opening statement immediately following the prosecution has the advantage of giving the last speech until the closing argument. The speech can hover over the entire trial affecting the perceptions of all jurors throughout the trial. It gives the defense a psychological-persuasion advantage—the *only* one the system offers to the defense.

The opening statement also gives the defense attorney a chance to gain credibility from the jury. This is critical because jurors relate to, identify with, and are persuaded by lawyers they like and respect. A well-done, effectively delivered statement sends a message to the jury— ''that lawyer is competent, has direction and purpose, is confident and highly skilled.'' This opportunity to make a favorable impression on the jury is enhanced by the fact that most prosecutors do not prepare effective opening statements.

The third reason why the opening statement is so important is that

---

Professor Crawford is professor of communications at the University of Northern Colorado in Greeley, Colorado, and a forensic communications consultant.

jurors usually make up their minds long before the trial is over. The Chicago Project in the 1960s suggested that 80 percent of jurors do not change their minds following opening statements; my own judgment is that it is probably higher than that. Real persuasion in a trial therefore comes *before* the presentation of evidence.

We also know from numerous studies that jurors do not deliberate in the traditional sense of that word. The jurors take a first ballot and then they wait. The process is essentially a matter of the majority saying to the minority, ''We've got you; now how long are you going to hold out?'' Thus, if the defense can convince seven or eight jurors during his opening statement, the majority will take care of the rest in the deliberation room. On the other hand, if the prosecutor gets a majority, a conviction may be assured.

From what I have said, it is obvious that you must give your opening statement early. You simply cannot afford to allow jurors to start down the prosecution track since you will likely never get them back.

Set the Lenses

There is another reason for the early presentation. Psychologically, what you are trying to do is set the lenses through which the jury will see the trial. The jurors' perception of the actual trial and evidence will be determined by how the opening statements grind the lenses. If you wait to give your opening statement the jury will see and hear a different trial than if you give an early statement.

Your opening statement also gives you an early opportunity to explain the evidence. As you describe what your witnesses will say, jurors accept the evidence as having been presented. They also understand it better through your presentation. If you are clear and effective, you will give your witnesses' testimony more effective punch.

You must also focus the jury on the weaknesses and vulnerabilities of the state's case. Your goal is to contaminate the prosecutor's case so that it will never impact the jury. You must show the frailty of their witnesses *before* they testify so as to nullify their direct testimony.

An example involves a killing that occurred a few years back in my county on a dance floor with roughly 50 people present. The single eyewitness to the shooting was named Lucy. The victim was her father-in-law, with whom she was living at the time and with whom she had come to the dance. The defense attorney's opening statement focused primarily on Lucy's character, especially the fact that she was living with her father-in-law.

The drama of the trial came as the defense sat down from opening statement and the state called Lucy as its first witness. As she walked through the courtroom to take her seat in the witness box, the jury gave her a long, cold, small-town stare. She had been fatally contaminated by the defense attorney. Of course, the defense attorney could have waited and hurt her during cross-examination. But then she would have testified for an hour under direct testimony as a pristine bereaved lady and the impact would have probably made a lasting impression on the jury. Because the defense gave its opening statement early, Lucy's direct testimony was viewed with suspicion at best. The jury saw and heard a different state case than if the opening statement had been held for later presentation. The defense ground the glasses for the jurors and influenced what they saw.

The final reason for giving your opening statement early is that a relatively weak but unchallenged opening statement becomes strong. The state speech takes on an aura of authenticity as it hangs over the courtroom without refutation. It provides a positive setting for the prosecution witnesses.

Any audience, including a jury, will listen with deep intensity for a minute or two to any speaker regardless of how bad the cause or how poor the presentation. After that point, attention falls for even skilled speakers. This can be translated into a simple persuasion strategy. Always take your best shot in the first few minutes of your opening statement when you are most likely to form an imprint on the minds of the jury.

Unfortunately, most lawyers refuse to follow this advice. Consider the traditional opening statement introduction:

> Ladies and gentlemen: This is the part of the trial called opening statement. What I say during this speech and what my colleague, Mr. Smith the prosecutor, says during his speech, is not evidence. This is merely an outline of what the trial is about from our points of view. You will hear the evidence presented later and you must remember that what you are going to hear now is not evidence of any sort.

Grocery List

In addition to throwing away your "prime time," what else does this introduction say to the jury? It says that you do not think the speech is important and that the jury might as well work on a grocery list or think about something else until the speech is over. The lawyer is also saying that it is only because it is a required part of the trial that he is speaking at all.

There are unlimited ways to fire your silver bullets in the beginning minute to hit the target. Here is a possibility in a self-defense case:

> Ladies and gentlemen: Johnny and I have been waiting a long time to have this chance to show how Johnny tried to defend himself and his family on the night of January 16. You see, we know that a man in this country has a right to protect himself and his family and we also know that you as Johnny's neighbors know it too. You

are going to hear clear evidence that Johnny did not commit murder, is not a killer, and does not belong in this courtroom.

This type of introduction does more than state the theory of the case. You tell the jury that you intend to win, that you are sure you will win, and that your client is clearly not guilty of murder. This crisp, direct, and confident stance should greet the jury as you begin your first and most important direct contact with them. Their attention to you and your case is at its highest intensity and you need to burn into their minds an imprint of what is critical, not what is ritualistic filler.

Another introduction can include a theme, a metaphor, or an analogy. Such approaches may be dangerous in closing argument since they can be turned against you by a clever rebuttal speaker. But you are reasonably safe in the opening statement. Here is an example:

Ladies and gentlemen: You know, I always marvel at the mysteries of Mother Nature and the animal instinct in all living things. An animal when it is cornered and in fear of its life or the lives of its young will act in ways which seem to defy understanding. It will rush to its death, perhaps attack an animal which will mean certain death or behave in other ways which cannot be explained except by instinct. That's really what this case is about today, for you will learn that Johnny experienced such terror that his reason seemed to leave him as he was dominated by instinct. Yes, he fired the fatal bullet to survive, but he ran, not because he had done something wrong, but because his instinctive drive was triggered by tremendous terror.

The recency effect applies not only to the opening statement as the last speech in a series, but also during the final words inside a single message. Thus, at the conclusion of opening statement, you should take your best shot again, in different but carefully prepared words. The opening statement in Johnny's self-defense case might end as follows:

So, ladies and gentlemen, that's why Johnny is here—to show you how he acted to protect his own life and the lives of his wife, Marsha, and his baby, Diane. He has chosen a jury from his own community because he is sure you will listen and understand. He knew before the tragic accident of January 16 and he knows today that defending yourself is not murder. Indeed, it is not a crime at all; it is only a part of the normal human instinct to survive and protect. That's what this case is about.

Here again, there is confidence and directness. The goal of the opening statement throughout is not merely to set things in motion. Rather, it is to predispose the jury to give you an acquittal. That commitment is necessary if the defense expects to win.

The body of the speech itself must focus on the theory of the case, repeating that theory in a manner that maximizes whatever evidence and arguments you have to support your thesis. If a point cannot tie to your thesis, it is not useful. Nor are small or scattered arguments going in every direction effective. Your statement must be focused and simple. Consider the following example:

> So, how will the evidence in this case prove how Johnny acted in self-defense? There are three independent pieces of evidence which we think will show you it was not murder and exactly what happened. First, Johnny did not run after the tragedy. That will become critical to you as you understand that he did not run because he knew he had done nothing wrong. But that's not all. You will hear Johnny's wife, Marsha, tell you about the incident and you will understand the self-defense evidence which will prove our case clearly. You will also hear Johnny tell what happened precisely as he told the police on that tragic day in January. You will know it was self defense just as surely as Johnny knew it then and knows it now.

Well-Told Story

The approach is positive, upbeat, and confident. The evidence is grouped around the thesis so that it can be repeated over and over again.

Nothing so captures us as a well-told story. The opening statement is perfect for such an approach. The defendant's story, told from his vantage point, can burn an indelible mark on the psyche of each juror. The device has no equal if the narrative is meticulously thought through and even more meticulously worded to include every detail and nuance.

Narrative statements are best used when the defendant is going to testify. Only then can you tell the story through his eyes and be able later to validate your narrative as "evidence." Below is an edited opening statement given in a first-degree murder case by Craig L. Truman, Chief Deputy Public Defender for the State of Colorado.

> Ladies and gentlemen: It was a cool day in Ft. Lupton on December 9, 1978. A recent snowfall had packed the roads and streetways with snow. About 2:00 P.M. Lino Gonzales, the man charged with murder here, went to visit his nephew in Ft. Lupton—Juan Benavidez—nicknamed "Gordo." They had a beer, talked as do relatives and friends. They then decided to go have some other drinks in some saloons in Ft. Lupton.
>
> They went to a place called the Silver Moon, and then they went to a place called the Town Tavern. It's around six o'clock that Saturday. Gordo, Juan Benavidez, didn't have any money, and his uncle, Lino, lent him five dollars. There was a discussion about, "Now you've got my five dollars, why don't you buy me a beer?" Gordo said he didn't want to. There was some argument back and

forth, and Gordo, a huge man at 240 pounds, turned around and blasted Lino, knocking him to the floor of the Town Tavern. Gordo was on top of Lino. Lino will tell you he doesn't remember exactly what happened, but that when the fight was broken up by patrons in the bar, he had a cut on the bridge of his nose, a swollen eye, and he'd been kicked in the ribs and groin area. There were threats exchanged back and forth before Lino left the bar.

After that, Lino went home, as did Gordo, and they both talked with their respective spouses about what had happened. Lino changed his blood covered shirt and left with his wife to go down to Brighton to a place called the GAO. They were there awhile and went over to a place call Efrem's and, make no mistake, Lino was still upset about this incident. He had been beaten, he was sore, he had been bloodied; and he talked with other relatives that he ran into. Lino and his wife got home around midnight, and Lino asked Maria Perez, the baby-sitter of his three children, if she would stay and have some supper. She said, ''No, I have to get home.''

Lino decided to go find Gordo and make up. This wasn't the first time they had fought. In fact, they had had a fight the previous Tuesday, with Gordo beating Lino up while they were both drinking. Then, of course, they got back together. They were family, friends, and they buried the hatchet and got their relationship back where it had been. So this time Lino decided, ''I'm going to go see Gordo and make it right.''

Earlier, in the Town Tavern where they had the fight, Gordo had said, ''I'm gonna kill you.'' Lino remembered this and decided he had better take a rifle with him for protection just in case Gordo was still drinking and didn't want to make up. Lino goes to Gordo's house. Gordo's car and Gordo's pickup truck aren't there. He drives around, looking for Gordo for awhile; finally he sees Gordo coming home from the bars in Brighton, follows him home to his street.

Gordo gets out of the pickup truck. Lino stops in the middle of the street, opens the door, is going to talk to Gordo, and sees he's been drinking, sees the look in his eyes. Gordo asks Lino, ''What in the hell do you want?'' Lino says, realizing it's not any use to talk to this man, ''Get in the house.'' Gordo starts advancing on him again, saying, ''What in the hell do you want?'' Lino says, ''Are you going to beat me up? Are you trying to beat me up again?'' And Gordo says, ''Do you want me to beat you up again?,'' and advances toward him. Lino, afraid of this man who has beaten him up twice in the past, afraid of this fellow who's told him six hours earlier, he's gonna kill him and is big enough to get the job done, takes out the 30.06. Now it's a 30.06, with a scope; it's a hunting rifle; it's a deer-killing rifle. It's a big gun. He pointed it at Gordo; he doesn't aim the gun, he points it at hip level. Gordo keeps coming; Lino pulls the trigger; Gordo goes down.

Lino, frightened, puts the gun in the car and goes home, puts the gun away, lays down and begins to pray, hoping that Gordo will make it. An hour or so later the police come; they come into Lino's cooperative; Lino tells them here's where the gun is; here's where the bullets are; take this scientific test from my hands. He goes down to the Ft. Lupton police department, where about four in the morning, he says, "I don't know anything about this." At eight o'clock in the morning, 8:25 exactly, a Sergeant Armejo and the Chief of Police come to talk to Lino, and Lino tells them all about it. Lino gives him a tape-recorded statement that tells exactly what happened that night. I believe that tape-recorded statement will be played for you.

I can tell you this is not a whodunit; this is a question of what really happened. When you're through seeing our evidence, if you feel the fear that Lino Gonzales had, when this mountain of a man, who had beaten him twice, who had threatened to kill him, came toward him, you'll see why this happened. You will find Lino Gonzales acted in self-defense.

Detail and Vividness

Note how the details of the case from the defense view come alive in story form. The critical part of the speech centers around the description of the seconds just before and after the shooting. The detail and vividness of the description may win or lose the jury. The story structure gives the defense the best possible opportunity to highlight such significant seconds allowing the jurors to relate to and remember them all the way into the deliberation room.

The narrative statement discussed above drew no objections from the prosecution, although some of it seems clearly to be argument and might have been challenged. The first rule in avoiding objections is to know your opponent and his tendency toward being a "strict interpretationist" of the guidelines about being argumentative. You may choose to give the prosecutor a little extra latitude during his statement as a form of insurance against interference in yours.

You can also avoid objections by sprinkling little phrases, "We will show that," and "The evidence will reveal" throughout your speech. Using such phrases, you can make your argument almost as if it were closing argument. Of course, you must leave out the adjectives and adverbs. Your vivid description of the facts of the case from the defendant's perspective will allow the jury to fill in the adjectives—probably stronger ones than you would have offered in the first place.

Inflame the Jury

The third rule for avoiding objections is a restrained delivery. It is amusing to note that the same words delivered forcefully will cause an objection but if delivered softly will not. Ironically, the soft delivery will scream far more loudly than the raised voice could ever do. You should never draw an objection during your opening statement if you are careful and well prepared. This is true although your goal is to argue your case and even inflame the jury.

If you were Daniel Webster in Salem, Massachusetts, in 1830, and you were prosecuting a murder case, you might say:

> Truly, here is a new lesson for painters and poets. Whoever shall hereafter draw the portrait of murder, if he will show it as it has been exhibited, where such example was last to have been looked for, in the very bosom of our New England society, let him not give it the grim visage of Moloch, the brow knitted by revenge, the face black with settled hate, and the blood-shot eye emitting livid fires of malice. Let him draw, rather, a decorous, smooth-faced, blood-less demon; a picture in repose, rather than in action; not so much an example of human nature in its depravity, and in its paroxysms of crime, as an infernal being, a fiend, in the ordinary display and development of his character.

There was a time for such oratory, but that time is gone.

"Eloquence," however, in the sense of careful and precise language is still crucial. The word choice must be simple, clear, direct, and appropriate to the case and the jury. Your delivery must likewise be appropriate, varied, interesting, often very conversational and always direct and communicative. Sincere and direct word choice and delivery represent modern eloquence.

Finally, remember that "good art conceals itself." In one sense, you must become invisible to the jury; your message must dominate the perceptions of the jury totally, and you must become only a messenger. You should not use notes. Neither should the statement be memorized word for word. Outline your statement and practice it—if possible with video-tape and before an audience. Revise it and above all know and feel what you will say. Your effort will pay off in the impact your statement makes on the jury.

Witness for the Prosecution

by Frank Oliver

In August 1983, Frank Oliver of the Chicago bar defended a client against a federal prosecution that hinged on the testimony of one criminal informant. The defense centered on one question: Could the jury believe the testimony of a paid government informant who was a self-acknowledged murderer, arsonist, and thief?

Oliver's client, Anthony Giacomino, was accused of mail fraud and conspiracy in connection with the bombing of a discotheque called Bump City. The informant, a 44-year-old Chicagoan named Frank Cullotta, had made a career of petty and brutal crime and had been arrested in Las Vegas for stealing a washing machine and a toaster. He appeared as a government witness.

The following are excerpts from the opening, cross-examination, and closing argument by Mr. Oliver. Mark S. Prosperi and John L. Burley were the lawyers for the government.

Opening Statement

OLIVER: Members of the jury: What I want to do is . . . to impart to you a kind of point of view from which you can look at this case and evaluate the witnesses in the case.

Now, it appears to me from what I'm able to learn about this case that the testimony against Mr. Giacomino, whom I represent, is probably pretty much boiled to the statements made by this man whom Mr. Volpe has described to you as a human being, a description that I would personally reject because I'm a human being and I don't want to believe that this creature is the same species as I am. What the evidence is going to portray about this man is evil.

Now most of you have not had the kind of exposure to certain features

This argument and cross-examination is adapted from an article that appeared in The Chicago Lawyer *in October 1983.*

of this world that will give you a ready sense of evil. But you are all, each and every one of you, laden with some kind of a religious commitment, and that is what you must use to evaluate the evil that you are going to encounter. . . .

He is going to tell you that he has done everything from stealing hubcaps to stealing a lady's washing machine and I guess her electric toaster. He is a sometime part-time pimp. He's a petty dope seller. He portrays himself as a master criminal.

Now, why any human being who is a human being would want to do that is beyond me. And let me add this: He's going to testify that he has committed all kinds of crimes, and I don't even believe him and won't believe him as to his own criminality. You just won't be able to tell when you can believe him and when you can't because he is a self-described sink of immorality, dishonesty, disloyalty, malevolence, jealousy. Name any sin. He will agree that he has committed it. Think of any trait of character that is bad. He will concede that he has it.

Now, the government has a problem in this witness. Somehow they have got to come before you later in this case and say to you jurors, ''You can reach down into this slimy cesspool of evil and pick something pure out of it that we call the truth, something so pure that you can find another man guilty based upon his truth, guilty beyond a reasonable doubt.'' I don't think they are going to be able to do it. Proof beyond a reasonable doubt is the kind of proof that would overcome any tendency on the part of prudent people.

PROSPERI: I object, your Honor.

THE COURT: Yes, objection sustained. Ladies and gentlemen, the court will instruct the jury on the law at the proper time.

OLIVER: I was about to speak about law, and I really mustn't. That is the judge's job, thank God, and not mine.

Nevertheless, I am entitled to say that they must prove guilt beyond a reasonable doubt, and I will urge throughout and at the conclusion of these proceedings that you folks cannot as decent and conscientious people determine something beyond a reasonable doubt from a source as polluted as this man who will be testifying.

PROSPERI: I object to the argument, Judge.

THE COURT: Yes, that is more properly closing argument than an opening statement, Mr. Oliver.

OLIVER: I am going to sit down before I get in trouble here.

Cross-Examination

The cross-examination was preceded by the government's direct examination in which Cullotta claimed to have committed or participated in four or five murders, roughly a half dozen arsons and bombings, 300 or 400 burglaries, and about 200 armed robberies. In committing one murder, the witness had hunted his victim through a house—employing 12 bullets, which required re-

loading a pistol, in what appeared to have been slow butchery. Oliver developed these and other details in examining other witnesses preceding the cross-examination.

Q: The first thing that happened to you when you came to this courtroom, this trial, was to have an oath administered to you. That is right, isn't it?

A: Yes, sir.

Q: His Honor put his hand up and you put up your hand, is that right?

A: That's correct.

Q: And his Honor asked you if you would tell the truth, the whole truth, and nothing but the truth, so help you God. Correct?

A: That's correct.

Q: And you understood from that oath that you were swearing to tell the truth not only so far as the court was concerned, but that you were swearing unto your God to speak truthfully. You understood that, didn't you?

A: That's correct.

Q: Now, this same God unto whom you have sworn to tell the truth is the very God whose laws and commandments you have violated repeatedly over the course of your entire lifetime. Is that right?

PROSPERI: Objection, your Honor, to getting into his religious aspects here.

Q: He is the one that swore to God.

THE COURT: Overruled. He may answer. You may answer.

A: To tell the truth in this courtroom.

Q: You swore to your God to tell the truth.

A: That's correct.

Q: And that is the same God whose laws and commandments you have violated from the time you were a little boy. That's true, isn't it?

A: I'm telling the truth in this courtroom and in any other courtroom I testify in.

Q: You swear to God.

A: I swear to God. That's what I've done.

Q: You know that God tells us, "Thou shalt not kill," don't you?

A: Yes, sir.

Q: And you have borne false witness against your neighbor, haven't you?

A: No, sir.

Q: You never bore false witness against, for example, this boy Mastro?

[*Cullotta had sought to have Mastro convicted of murder to shield Cullotta's partner in crime from the accusation.*]

A: Yes, sir.

Q: So you violated that commandment of God, didn't you?

A: Yes, sir.

Q: When you took that oath before this jury, you intended that the jury should believe that the oath had the same seriousness to you that it would to a human being. Isn't that right?

A: Yes, sir.

Q: You intended they should understand your oath to have the same deep significance to you that their oaths, to judge your words honestly and fairly, should have to them. That is true, isn't it?

A: Yes.

Q: So that so far as the oath that you have taken is concerned, you put yourself on a pedestal with these jurors who have taken an oath, isn't that true?

A: I guess. I don't know if it's the same pedestal.

Q: Your recitation entails an admission that you have committed crime after crime after crime of all descriptions, isn't that right?

A: Yes, sir.

Q: Do you have any idea how many kinds of crimes you have committed?

A: No, sir.

Q: Do you know of any crime whatever that a man could commit that is beneath you morally?

A: I don't know.

Q: There isn't one, is there?

A: I don't know.

Q: You cannot think of a crime that would be below you, can you?

A: I imagine there is, but I don't know.

Q: You have never heard of it. Right?

A: I don't know.

Q: And that is because you will commit any crime, isn't that true?

A: I don't know about that.

Q: Do you think there might be some crime you might not commit?

A: It's possible.

Q: Some time ago, someone acting on your behalf worked out some kind of a deal whereby you would go unwhipped of justice in exchange for testimony. Isn't that right?

A: I don't know about going unwhipped. I received time.

Q: You got time?

A: Yes, sir.

Q: How much time is that? Eight years?

A: And five years' probation.

Q: And five years' probation?

A: That's correct.

Q: In serving that time thus far, you have spent mighty little of it behind bars in a cage. Isn't that true?

A: That's not true.

Q: You have spent some of it behind bars in a cage. Right?

A: It's a jail.

OLIVER: And you expect to get out or go before the Parole Board when? In 20 months or something like that?

A: I believe 25 or 26 months.

Q: At that time, you expect a grateful government acting through its agents and prosecutors to commend your services to the sympathy of the parole board. Isn't that right?

A: Yes, sir.

Q: So that you will be discharged from the rigors of punishment?

A: Yes, sir.

Q: So that you will be restored to the company of the citizenry to go about your business. Is that right?

A: Yes, sir.

Q: And it is your understanding that the government will supply you with a new identity. Is that right?

A: Yes, sir.

Q: The purpose of supplying you with that new identity is so that people won't know who you are. Right?

A: That's correct.

Q: The understanding that you have is, is it not, that you will take that identity and go to a place where you are not now known. Correct?

A: That's correct.

Q: A place where your reputation is not known. Is that right?

A: Yes, sir.

Q: So that the government proposes to assist you in settling down in a community of decent citizens who have no knowledge of what you were and what you are. Is that right?

A: Yes, sir.

Q: So that out there some place, some small town, some little city, sits a group of honest, decent, law-abiding, hard-working, dedicated, peaceable citizens who will suddenly find you as part of their community. Right?

A: That's correct.

Q: At which time, what you are and who you are will be concealed from them. Right?

A: Yes, sir.

Q: So that you will then be free to prey upon them committing every kind of criminal depredation that occurs to you against an innocent and unwarned community. That's what they have in mind for you, isn't it?

A: No, sir.

Q: Well, the reason you say ''No, sir,'' is because you have reformed, haven't you?

996

A: That's correct.

Q: Together with the deal that was concocted by unwise and probably too youthful men in your behalf, at that time, you experienced some sort of spiritual rejuvenation. Is that right?

A: Rejuvenation. I don't know about spiritual.

Q: Well, spiritual awakening whence you came to perceive the difference between good and evil. Is that what you're telling us?

A: Yes.

Q: So that whatever happened the day before, you were crawling evil, and then with this awakening, became a paragon of decency. Is that it?

A: Yes.

Q: That must have struck you as a remarkable day in your life, didn't it?

A: Yes.

Q: Did a light flood your soul?

A: No.

Q: You laugh?

A: Yes.

Q: You laugh because what I say is amusing, isn't it?

A: Yes.

Q: Because you cannot perceive of such a thing as a light of decency, isn't that right?

A: I can see decency, but I don't know about no light striking me or anything like that.

Q: You can see decency?

A: That's correct.

Q: Well, let's see. You said that there might be some crimes that you would not commit. Right?

A: That's correct.

Q: Rape is not one of those crimes that you would not commit, is it?

A: I don't ever remember doing it.

Q: You don't remember whether you committed a rape or not?

A: That's correct.

Q: Is it something that just kind of could have happened and slipped out of your mind?

A: I never raped nobody, if that makes you happy.

Q: What causes you to suppose that anything you could possibly say would make me happy?

A: I have no idea.

Q: Let's talk about the Widow Polito. She was a woman of unsound mind, wasn't she, and you so testified, didn't you?

A: She was a little off, yes.

Q: A little off. Right?

A: That's correct.

Q: She was crazy, wasn't she?

A: A little bit.

Q: A little bit crazy. And her deceased husband, Philly Polito, was a man that you claimed was your friend. Right?

A: Yes, sir.

PROSPERI: Objection to this line of questioning, I just don't think it is relevant.

THE COURT: The objection is overruled. You may proceed.

Q: And before your friend's body was lowered into his grave, you carnally knew and violated his widow, isn't that true?

A: No, sir.

Q: After his body was lowered into his grave?

A: Yes, sir, but not violated.

Q: Did you not have carnal connection with the Widow Polito?

A: I had sex with her, if that is what you are referring to, yes.

Q: This crazy woman?

A: A little off, yes.

Q: Who was incapable of giving you consent, isn't that right?

A: No, that's ridiculous.

Q: Now, your vile sexual lusts weren't confined to such as the poor, mentally insecure Widow Polito, were they?

A: My vile trust, is that what you said?

Q: Lusts.

A: Lusts. That confuses me, that question.

Q: Well, you were in the Illinois State Penitentiary, weren't you?

A: That's correct.

Q: And you were there for some time, weren't you?

A: Yes, sir.

Q: And during that period of time, you had men around you. Correct?

A: That's correct.

Q: And one of those men was an innocent young man by the name of Linderman. Isn't that right?

A: I don't even know who he is.

Q: Well, perhaps you forgot. Did you not commit a violent homosexual assault upon the body of a young man by the name of Linderman while you were incarcerated in the Illinois State Penitentiary?

A: No, sir.

• • •

Q: Some time back in February of this year in proceedings in this building, you testified, did you not, that one of your lines of criminal activity took the form of muscling joints. Is that true?

A: Yes, sir.

Q: And when asked by the prosecution what you meant by "muscling joints," you explained that it was obtaining money from

998

joints in order that they should be permitted to stay open. Right?

A: Yes.

Q: And the joint that you named as the one joint that you muscled was the place known as The Bitter End. Right?

A: Yes.

Q: At that time, you said nothing about having been engaged in blowing up The Bitter End, did you?

A: No, sir. I don't recall. I don't believe I did.

Q: Well, you do recall being told then or taking an oath then to tell the truth, the whole truth, and nothing but the truth. Isn't that right?

A: Yes, sir.

Q: And if you didn't tell about The Bitter End being blown up by you at that time, you failed to tell the whole truth. Right?

A: I don't know if I was asked it. I don't recall.

Q: Well, you don't have to be asked to tell the whole truth, do you?

A: If I'm asked a question, I will tell it. If I'm not asked, I can't volunteer.

Q: You will keep it a secret, won't you? Well, when you came in here and testified about this thing, you claimed, did you not, that your activities with respect to The Bitter End consisted of blowing it up with Mike Swiatek. Right?

A: That's correct.

Q: And you said that Mike Swiatek came to you and said he wanted to blow up The Bitter End. Right?

A: That's correct.

Q: The reason he wanted to blow up The Bitter End had to do with his girlfriend. Right?

A: That's correct.

Q: His girlfriend that worked there?

A: Correct.

Q: What was her name?

A: Lucy Cantalupo.

Q: Lucy Cantalupo?

A: That's correct.

Q: Mike Swiatek wanted Lucy Cantalupo to give up her job at The Bitter End. Right?

A: That's correct.

Q: That is what you testified to. Right?

A: Yes, sir.

Q: And she refused?

A: That's correct.

• • •

Q: And your story is that, because Swiatek's girlfriend wouldn't give up her job and because her bosses wouldn't fire her because she was doing a good job, that Swiatek blew the place a mile into the air. Right?

999

A: Correct.

Q: And came to you before he did so. True?

A: He came to me.

Q: Right.

A: Yes.

Q: And he told you that he planned to blow it up? Right?

A: He wanted to, yes.

Q: And that made perfectly good sense to you, didn't it?

A: Yes, sir.

Q: And you thought it was perfectly sensible. The man's girlfriend wouldn't quit her job and her employers wouldn't fire her because she was doing a good job, so you thought it made perfectly good sense to blow the place up. Right?

A: Right.

Q: Back to you. It struck you as being a perfectly sane, plausible, realistic way of going about solving a problem, right?

A: That was his way, yes.

Q: And your way?

A: Yes.

Q: And as you look at it now, it seems to have been a perfectly sound judgment on your part, doesn't it?

A: Yes.

Q: The very kind of sound judgment that we can expect from you when we greet you as a fellow citizen courtesy of the prosecution. Right?

A: I guess.

Q: Yes. And these men are going to write letters on your behalf?

A: Yes, sir.

Q: Do you know if they have told the victims of any of your crimes that they have given you immunity and are going to write letters on your behalf? Do you suppose they have told any of the victims that?

A: I have no idea.

Q: What do you think the victims would say?

PROSPERI: Objection, Judge.

THE COURT: Objection sustained.

Q: Well, you claim to have seen the light. I suppose that you regret all of those terrible things that you have done. Right?

A: Yes, sir.

Q: You have a sense of shame about them?

A: Yes, sir.

Q: Remorse. True?

A: That's correct.

Q: Contrition. Right?

A: Yes, sir.

Q: Have you ever told that to anyone?

A: I may have. I don't recall.

Q: Well, you testified yesterday to having hunted a man down in his own house with a pistol. Right?

A: That's correct.

Q: The man was the father of a little boy?

A: That's correct.

Q: A wife?

A: That's correct.

Q: You hunted him down while he begged for his life?

A: That's correct.

Q: He implored you not take his life away from him?

A: Yes, sir.

Q: You showed him no remorse and no pity, did you?

A: No, sir.

Q: But now, you are contrite and remorseful. Correct?

A: That's correct.

Q: Well, have you expressed that to the widow, or have you done anything for this little child that your criminality has orphaned?

A: I can't see her.

Q: How about the other victims of your atrocities? Have you sought forgiveness of any of them?

A: Yes, sir.

Q: Name them.

A: Name the victims?

Q: Yes, from whom you have sought forgiveness.

A: I can't reach out and talk to anybody. I can name the victims that I feel bad for: McCarthy's wife.

Q: McCarthy's wife, you feel bad for. That was the McCarthy . . . let's see, that McCarthy, yeah. McCarthy. He was a thief, wasn't he?

A: That's correct.

Q: And you would go out and steal with McCarthy from time to time, wouldn't you?

A: That's correct.

Q: The reason that you set him up was to really separate yourself as much as possible in the minds of resentful people. Isn't that right?

A: I don't believe that's correct.

Q: He was a torturer, wasn't he?

A: A torturer?

Q: Yes, that's the same William McCarthy who would pull a man's teeth out one by one while getting the combination to the safe, or throw a bucket of gasoline over a man's child and wave a match and threaten to light the child unless he came up with his money. Isn't that right? That is that McCarthy, isn't it?

1001

A: That's news to me. I don't know.

Q: You don't know about that?

A: No, sir.

Q: In any event, this was the man whom you regarded as your friend. Right?

A: Yes.

• • •

Q: We were discussing one William McCarthy whose slaughter you arranged. Do you recall that?

A: Yes, sir.

Q: You claimed to have been his friend. Correct?

A: Yes, sir.

Q: And so far as you knew he thought of you as a friend. Right?

A: That's correct.

Q: And so you telephoned him, didn't you?

A: Yes, sir.

Q: And spoke to him as a friend. Correct?

A: That's correct

Q: And he spoke to you as a friend. Right?

A: That's correct.

Q: And as his friend you sought to arrange for his appearance at a certain time and at a certain place. That's true, isn't it?

A: That's correct.

Q: And portraying yourself to him as his friend, you encouraged him to go there at that time. That is true, isn't it?

A: That's true.

Q: At the time that you did that you had in your mind a secret motive. Isn't that right?

A: No, sir.

Q: Well, you knew that when he met that appointment he was meeting an appointment with death, didn't you?

A: I wasn't sure.

Q: But you reassured him that everything was all right, didn't you?

A: Yes, sir.

• • •

Q: So that what you did in arranging for his presence at that time and place was to betray your friend. Is that right?

A: Yes, sir.

Q: You were a latter-day Judas Iscariot to your friend. Is that right?

A: I guess so.

Q: Have you ever asked a Power that is greater than yourself for forgiveness?

A: Yes.

Q: You have fallen on your knees and said, "My God, my God, why dost Thou look so fierce upon me?"

A: Not like that, Mr. Oliver. (Laughter.)

Q: You have never fallen on your knees and prayed for forgiveness, have you?

PROSPERI: Objection, Judge.

THE COURT: Objection sustained.

Q: Have you ever done anything in your entire life that we could regard as decent and humane and honest and honorable and good and caring?

A: I probably have.

Q: But you can't think of any such event, can you?

A: If I had the time, I probably could.

Q: Can you think of anything about your character as we now have come to know it that can cause us as decent human beings to believe one word out of your mouth?

A: I don't see why they shouldn't believe me.

Q: Why should we believe you?

A: I have no reason to lie. I could only be charged with perjury.

Q: You have no reason to lie?

A: That's correct.

Q: Well, how about this for a reason for lying? As long as you sit on a witness stand and swear to tell the truth, you can say anything whatever, and the government will take care of you. How's that for a reason for lying?

A: It's ridiculous.

Q: That's ridiculous?

A: That certainly is.

Q: Since you have been a federal witness, the pride of the United States Government, isn't it true that you tried to get another prisoner to falsify an accusation against a man by the name of Newman with a suggestion to that other prisoner that, ''You could make lots of money from the federal government by accusing him falsely?''

A: That's a lie.

• • •

Q: Now, I asked you if you had been given a psychological test after you became a government witness, or agreed to become one.

A: No, sir.

Q: So that for all we know, you may be the kind of human being, if you are a human being, that is called a psychopath, which is a man totally incapable of telling the truth. Is that right?

A: I don't know that.

Q: And as far as you know, the Government has made no effort of any kind to make that determination. Is that right?

PROSPERI: Asked and answered, Judge.

THE COURT: Sustained.

OLIVER: Well, I think. I'm about now boring everybody, Judge. If you will give me just a couple of minutes to confer.

THE COURT: Two minutes? By all means.

OLIVER: They have threatened to never speak to me again if I continue, your Honor. (Laughter.)

THE COURT: Thank you, Mr. Oliver.

Closing Argument

I am here to warn you. I didn't know when I came into this case that that thankless task would fall upon me. And I know what happens to those whose mission it becomes to sound a warning.

Folks say I'm old-fashioned. All right, I'll be very old-fashioned today. I'm going to be 3,000 years old and tell you first about Cassandra, whose mission it was to warn, and what her fate was. She promised to bed the god Apollo if he would give her the power of prophecy, which he did, and then she spurned his further advances. So the god Apollo spit into her mouth; and while she retained the gift of prophecy, no one believed her. And the city of Troy was destroyed just about 3,000 years ago.

Nevertheless, I will accept, more or less unwillingly, this kind of mission, because I think you ought to be warned.

When we started this case, I knew something about this fellow Cullotta, and I have been reluctant even to say his name because I have been trying to build in my own mind some notion of what "that" is we are looking at. And I insist we are not looking at a person. We aren't looking at a "him." We are looking at some kind of a "thing," some sort of ugly, distasteful thing. It is not enough to call him names. I shan't bother to call him names. To call him names truly, I think, misses the point.

Now, somehow or other, I want you to perceive what I mean when I say what we have perceived before us is a personification, an apotheosis, of evil. That was evil. That was unadulterated evil that you saw there.

How I wish you were all 90 years old. I'm glad that there is one grey-beard in your panel. Older people have a very different comprehension of evil from that accorded to younger people. Possibly it's that premonition that life isn't going to go on forever, a tendency to look back on one's life and to consider what was good and what was evil and what was the nature of evil. Old folks do have a better perception of it.

You see, I'm not talking about something that is just bad. We've all been bad; we've all done things that we wish we hadn't done. I don't care who it is in the courtroom. Let us take his Honor, Judge Bua, as the paragon of virtue. I'm willing to do that unquestioningly.

THE COURT: You're too kind, Mr. Oliver. You're much too kind. (Laughter.)

OLIVER: Pardon?

THE COURT: I say you're much too kind. (Laughter.)

OLIVER: Well, hang on a minute. (Laughter.)

Even a man of such stature, if brought to it, will think of something in the quiet of his chamber that can cause his cheeks to flame with regret at something he has done at some time in the past. It's true. You, and you, and you, and you, and I, a thousand times over. I make no pretense of superior virtue. We've all been bad. But we are not evil. There is something in us that is susceptible to some kind of redemption.

When you were being qualified as jurors, I was anxious that we have people that have some sort of religious comprehension on this jury, and my reason was this: I'm not a minister; I'm not what you would call a religious man. I'm deeply respectful of religion, but I'm not out there dropping money in the plate every Sunday and getting to the confessional, although that would not be appropriate for me anyway. That isn't the church to which I belong, I am none of those things, and I expect most of you are not.

But the fact that we have had that religious training at least assures us that, when we speak of evil, we are speaking of something as to which we have some common ground for discussion. When the violin repeats what the piano has just said, the sounds will be different. The chords won't be the same, but we will recognize the logic of the two events and observe the similarity such that we can say, "They are the same music."

What language, what experience in human history, is available to us to examine into the nature of evil? Science doesn't help us. Science deals with what we can weigh, what we can measure. We can't weigh evil. We can't measure evil.

Is there something that can tell us about evil? Yes, there is if we will look at it. If we look at certain ancient literature that used to discuss such things as evil, we can start to get some comprehension of that.

For the last week I have been sitting over there, mostly reading morality plays from the fifteenth century, looking again at Dante's *Inferno*—that was written in about 1320, something like that—because those men were deeply interested in this subject. They had a profound comprehension of what evil is, and what it is all about, and what we can do with it, and what we must not do with it. One thing we must not do with it is to use it.

You cannot use evil to achieve anything good. No, not even if you are a federal prosecutor. Doctor Faustus tried that. He made his compact with Lucifer, or Satan, through Satan's agent, Mephistopheles, just as the government represented by young men such as these young men here have made a compact with evil. They think they can employ evil to do something good. I tell you you may not touch evil. To touch evil is to become evil. To use evil is to be evil.

[Facing the prosecutors:] Young men, I implore you to consider the profound wisdom of the words of Alexander Pope, when he said to such as you and me:

Vice is a monster of such hideous mien,
As to be hated needs but to be seen;
Yet seen too oft, familiar with her face,
We first endure, then pity, then embrace.

It is precisely what has taken place here. These young government agents have looked upon the face of evil. It has disgusted them. They could barely endure it. They commenced to pity it. And they ended up embracing it by entering into a compact with a manslayer, a burner, a rapist, a drug seller. They are going to enter into a compact with pure evil, and they expect to accomplish something good with it. No. [To a juror:] Grandfather, tell these people that cannot be done. That is impossible.

I even looked to see if I couldn't find a description some place that would perhaps awaken something in you so that you can realize the foulness of what you are asked to weigh. You are asked to weigh evil. How can you weigh evil? How can you touch evil? You are asked to weigh something that emerged from evil. Evil doesn't have weight. You must ignore it. There are only two ways to deal with evil, by the way. And your older people on your jury will tell you this. You must either fight it or stay totally away from it. You can't handle it and deal with it. It's as though you made a compact with evil yourselves.

Now, I'm not a superstitious man. I'm not talking about demons flying around here and there. But when the ancients spoke of demons and evil spirits, they had in mind such things as we might as well say invaded the body of this—possibly—former man. I can't admit that he's human. I'm human. I will not accept the proposition that anything like that can be of my species. It is unacceptable to me.

Let's see if we have anything of description that will help. Here's poor Dante. He wants to enter Hell in the company of the poet Virgil, and he can do so, I guess, with a grant of immunity. Guarding the portals of Hell is this She-Wolf of Incontinence. Let's get a description of this monster:

And down his track, a She-Wolf drove
    upon me, a starved horror
    ravening and wasted
    beyond all belief.
She seemed a rack for avarice, gaunt
    and craving.
Oh many the souls she has brought to
    endless grief!
And then the poet Virgil tries to describe her a little better for the traveler, and says:
That mad beast that flees before
    you there, suffers no man to pass.
She tracks down all, kills all, and

knows no glut, but, feeding, she
    grows hungrier than she was.
She mates with any beast, and will
    mate with more.

It is that kind of foul object that the government has brought before you with the hope and expectation that you will accept anything from that source. I tell you if he tells me he committed a crime, I don't even believe that, because he is likely to say that he committed any crime if he can say somebody else committed it with him. And so, here, government, is another fresh head.

• • •

You know, he can get on the stand all day long and talk about his rehabilitation and his moral rejuvenation, but I don't see any of it and neither do you. What you see is a man who is shameless, totally lacking in remorse. He has no grief for the grief he has caused. He does no penance and expects to do no atonement. Has he sought absolution from the victims of his offenses? He has bragged about them.

The government—this is so appalling—the government literally has forgiven conduct that the ancients, who thought a great deal about evil, claim that God Himself will not forgive. Do you remember that ghastly scene? Here is a man in his own house being hunted like an animal through this house by this thing with a pistol in his paw. By the way, can you imagine meeting him and letting him shake your hand even? But he is chasing him through the house with his pistol, and the man is begging for mercy. That was the testimony. He begged for mercy. He begged for his life.

There is one lost soul that God will not redeem, according to the ancients. It is him who is without pity. It is him who is without mercy. When I asked him,
    "Did you have pity?"
    "None."
    "Did he beg you for mercy?"
    "Yes."
    "Did you show him mercy?"
    "No."
In Everyman, God sends his messengers out. His messenger is Death, and Death goes to Everyman, and tells him that he must appear before the Throne of the Great Lord, Adonai, and there make his accounting for his life. Everyman visits his friend Good Fellowship, his Kindred, his Goods. They all say, "No."
    "Whether ye have loved me or no, by Saint John, I will not go."
They won't accompany him to his death. Yet he has got to appear before his Maker, and he has got to give his accounting.

And, finally, he learns that all he is able to take that means anything are his Good Deeds, of which he has, as most of us have, all too few.

This man, if he is a man, could not think—and I asked him, "Can you tell us one decent, honorable, caring, humane, good thing you have done in your entire lifetime?"—and he thought he might be able to, if I gave him time enough. Just as, "Can you think of any act, any crime, that is morally beneath you?" Well, he was sure he could think of one of those, given enough time.

This is what the government asks you to believe, this man without pity, without mercy. We learn from Everyman of the condemnation of such a one who lacks pity or mercy, because as the author says when he appears before the Throne:

God Almighty saith:

Ite maledicti in ignem eternum.

Depart ye accursed to everlasting flame.

This pitiless, this merciless, unregenerate man is what the government wants you to believe. That is what they have forgiven, the very creature that the ancients tell us God Almighty cannot forgive.

Now, I warn you. One fine day, young men such as these and these among them will be writing letters to parole boards:

Dear Parole Board:

We have known Frank Cullotta for three years. We find him of good moral character, whatever he has been. He has been of great value to the Government, and we commend him to your merciful hands.

Yours truly,
THE PROSECUTOR

I hope, when these young men sign such letters, they will realize they are signing the death warrant of some innocent person. He is a manslayer. He will slay again. They are sending him out there without anything from which anyone can be warned of the desperate nature of his character.

• • •

This manslayer is going to be placed out in some honest, decent, law-abiding, hard-working community, among people like yourselves, and he will slay again. He has robbed, and he will rob again. He has burned, and he will burn again. And when he does, I'll tell you what will happen, because these folks when they entered into a compact with evil took on a much longer contract than they thought they were going to take on. Because the first time he gets accused of a crime, he's going to be on the telephone to some federal agent, saying, "You'd better come and help me." And the federal agent will say, "Why should we come and help you?" And the answer will be, "Well, if you don't come and help me, I'm going to start telling everybody that I lied in every one of the cases in which I was a witness, and that you told me to do it." And he is going to extort further protection from men such as this.

[To the prosecutors:] Oh, please, don't let this happen to you. Don't you know that when you sow the wind, you reap the whirlwind?

I'm sorry that I have this sad commitment. I think I wouldn't have it if our law were as civilized as it was 200 years ago, but we have gotten all so smart in our modern thinking. We are just so much smarter than anyone that lived before us. Why, it's just a pity that those men back there couldn't have been as bright as we are. I mean, after all, we have television and all the advantages of a modern education.

Let me tell you something. Newton, the great Sir Isaac Newton, said, when he was commended for his tremendous scientific work, "I stood on the shoulders of giants."

Ladies and gentlemen, civilization today did not make itself in the last 20 minutes, or just since you were born, or since you both [to the prosecutors] were graduated from law school. We are standing on the shoulders of our ancestors, and we are in many cases standing upon the shoulders of giants.

Now, I may not argue law. But I may argue history. And let me tell you what the history of witnesses such as this has been.

THE COURT: You have four minutes left, Mr. Oliver.

Q: Well, it won't be much of a history lesson, will it? (Laughter.)

On the subject of witnesses, that last of our legal sages, Sir William Blackstone, had the following to say of a slightly older legal sage:

> Sir Matthew Hale observes that more mischief hath arisen to good men by these kinds of approvements upon false and malicious accusations of desperate villains than benefit to the public by the discovery and conviction of real offenders. And, therefore, in the times when such appeals were more frequently admitted, great strictness and nicety were held therein.

We don't do it with any great strictness and nicety now. We're too smart for that. We do it carelessly. We used to do it with judicial supervision. Now, we just let it be done any way any prosecutor anywhere wants to do it. And it is dangerous. I warn you. I warn you not for your sake. I warn you for your children's sakes. I warn you for your grandchildren's sakes. I can be utterly unselfish. It isn't something for me. It isn't something for mine. I have no "mine." Please do it for yourselves.

Find these men not guilty because to do otherwise requires you to attempt to use evil to accomplish good. And the older persons on this jury are going to tell you . . .

THE COURT: You have run past your time, Mr. Oliver.

Q: Thank you, your Honor.

. . . you cannot accomplish anything good by the employment of evil.

After closing arguments, the judge charged the jury with the case. The jury acquitted Mr. Oliver's client.

Making Criminals Credible

by Nathaniel H. Akerman

Jimmy ("The Weasel") Fratianno was initiated into the brotherhood known as *La Cosa Nostra*—the Mafia—in 1948. Thirty years later, Fratianno, then 65 years old, turned state's evidence and became a government witness.

His past was filled with things to attack. Fratianno was convicted in 1978 for obstruction of justice and murder, in 1971 for conspiracy to commit extortion, in 1970 for conspiracy to violate the California public utilities laws, and in 1968 for making false statements. In addition, he admitted to being involved in nine murders between 1947 and 1953 for which he had never been charged.

In ten different criminal prosecutions, defense lawyers hammered away at Fratianno's criminal past, trying to persuade juries not to believe him. Even so, seven of the ten juries believed at least some of Fratianno's testimony, convicting nineteen of the twenty-five defendants.

Accomplice witnesses reach the prosecutor through various paths. Typically, when a law enforcement agency investigates organized crime, they decide who are the most important targets in the criminal group and approach their underlings to testify against the targets. It is also common for a witness, particularly one in prison, to approach the authorities with testimony about illegal activities they may not be aware of.

But Fratianno was different. The FBI approached him. He was having problems with the other Mafia leaders. It became so serious that the top echelon of his "family" decided to have him killed. When the FBI heard this, they used it to persuade him to turn against his former friends in exchange for anonymity under the Justice Department's Witness Pro-

The author is a member of the New York City firm of Pryor, Cashman, Sherman & Flynn.

tection Program. Fratianno had two choices: fend for himself and risk becoming the victim of another Mafia hit, or get protection from the government and testify.

Fratianno had been under investigation for years. He had been indicted for murder in Ohio and racketeering in California, but the prosecutions' cases were weak. Fratianno knew it, and believed he would never go to jail on either of the charges. So his motive was an exception to the general rule that witnesses with criminal backgrounds cooperate so they can stay out of prison. But Fratianno's decision to cooperate was consistent with another general rule about accomplice witnesses. None are motivated out of good citizenship.

The most important decision for the prosecution in using an accomplice witness is how to get his testimony. What the prosecution does makes a difference in what they get and how it is viewed by the jury.

Freedom for the witness is the prosecutor's biggest carrot. The prosecutor has the power to grant the witness immunity from his crimes, ensuring he will not go to jail. There are two kinds of immunity, transactional immunity and use immunity. Transactional immunity protects the witness from prosecution on whatever offenses the grant of immunity specifies. With transactional immunity, the witness cannot be prosecuted on those transactions and therefore cannot refuse to answer questions about them on the basis of his privilege against self-incrimination.

Use immunity is more limited. Whatever a witness testifies to cannot be used against him in a criminal prosecution, so he cannot claim his Fifth Amendment privilege. Use immunity is what the federal government employs now in dealing with accomplice witnesses. Theoretically, use immunity will not stop the government from trying the witness for his crimes, but the prosecution must meet a "heavy burden" to show that none of its proof came directly or indirectly from the immunized testimony. As a practical matter, immunity witnesses are rarely prosecuted.

If the witness is cooperative, immunity can be granted through an agreement. Since the agreement will be admitted into evidence, attacked by defense counsel, and examined by a jury, it is essential that it be in writing.

It does not have to be a cooperative venture. If the witness is hostile, immunity can be obtained by court order, and the witness can be compelled to testify. As a matter of trial strategy, a court order helps even when there is a voluntary agreement. It protects against the charge that the prosecution is coddling the accomplice, and lets the prosecutor argue to the jury that it is forced to take its witnesses where it finds them.

Even so, there are problems with immunity witnesses. Immunity generates the defense charge that the witness is fabricating his testimony, shaping it to fit the prosecution's version of events, and that the reward for this creativity is staying out of jail. It leaves a bad taste with a jury who must ask themselves whether they can convict one accomplice when the prosecution has chosen to let another go free.

These are legitimate concerns. Usually the best way to overcome them is an agreement in which the accomplice pleads guilty to some of the charges. The prosecutor has wide discretion in fashioning plea bargains, which can range from a lesser offense to all of the witness's crimes. From the prosecution's standpoint in arguing to the jury, the accomplice's plea and chance for a prison sentence should be appropriate for his crime, particularly in relation to the defendants he will be testifying against.

Sentencing should be delayed until after the witness testifies. This does two things. First, it helps the witness, who wants to paint a picture of cooperation to his sentencing judge. Second, it helps the prosecutor, who wants to maintain an incentive for the witness's cooperation. But there is a price for this protection. The defense will inevitably stress the witness's desire for a lighter sentence and the prosecution's hold over the witness.

Immunity agreements should explain what will happen if the witness lies. In the case of a formal grant of immunity, the witness can be charged with perjury if his testimony is not truthful. Court orders granting immunity usually state this explicitly. A letter agreement with the prosecution can go further and add that if the witness lies, his deal is cancelled, and he can be prosecuted for whatever crimes he has revealed to the prosecutor during the negotiations. These qualifications let the prosecutor argue that the motive of the accomplice is to give truthful testimony. The obvious response is that the prosecution decides whether the witness is speaking the truth.

Fratianno's agreement with the prosecuting authorities fit the traditional mold with two significant differences:

First, Fratianno entered into agreements with two jurisdictions, the United States (through the Justice Department's Strike Force in Los Angeles) and the State of Ohio.

Second, his cooperation was not limited to the jurisdictions with whom he made his agreements. He promised to testify anywhere in the United States where he had knowledge of criminal activities. Fratianno was a particularly valuable witness because his associations brought him in contact with the Mafia leaders across the country, especially in New York, Illinois, and Ohio.

In return for his cooperation, the Strike Force in Los Angeles agreed to accept a guilty plea to obstruction of justice for Fratianno's role in a murder plot to kill a California Mafia leader suspected of being an FBI informant, and the State of Ohio accepted a guilty plea to aggravated murder for Fratianno's role in introducing a hit man to a Cleveland Mafia family who used his services. Both agreements provided that Fratianno's maximum jail sentence would be only five years.

Although Fratianno was sentenced to the full five years, this extraordinarily short sentence brought the response by defense lawyers that a murderer was given virtual immunity for testifying. This was troublesome when Fratianno testified against defendants who were charged with nonviolent crimes. Then the prosecutor was hard pressed to argue that the defendant was worse than the witness. When Fratianno testified against defendants charged with murder, the leniency of his deal had less impact. And when Fratianno was testifying against crime figures higher up than he, it lent some justification to his treatment. In a sense Fratianno's criminal background supported his credibility. What better man for the defendants to recruit for a murder plot than an experienced murderer?

But that is just the start. Independent proof is an essential ingredient of showing that an accomplice is telling the truth. Once the immunity deal is struck, the next stop is to get that proof.

The most effective corroborating evidence is the testimony of an unbiased eyewitness or an admission by the defendant. Unbiased eyewitness testimony is rare in immunity cases. If the prosecutor has it, there is usually no need to grant immunity in the first place. Admissions by the defendant are more common. They can come from tape recordings from consensual or court authorized eavesdropping, or through the testimony of a second accomplice.

If the cooperating witness is still friendly with the potential defendant, the prosecutor can have the accomplice (wearing a hidden tape recorder) meet with the suspect. Nothing makes an accomplice witness more believable than tape-recorded admissions by the defendant.

This kind of corroboration is not always available. Fratianno was marked for death, and was certainly not going to try to make any recordings. But in one of the cases there had been court-authorized interceptions of conversations with details that supported Fratianno's testimony, and in at least three of the other cases, there were other cooperating accomplices who backed up what he said.

Circumstantial corroboration is different. It includes documents such as memoranda, cancelled checks, correspondence, notes, and phone records; scientific tests such as fingerprints and handwriting analysis; and witnesses who testify to supporting facts. Once a deal has been made with the accomplice, his testimony should be checked against the available circumstantial evidence.

For example, Fratianno testified against Russell Bufalino, a Mafia boss in Pennsylvania. Fratianno testified that Bufalino had recruited him and Michael Rizzitello to murder Jack Napoli, a witness in the Justice Department's Witness Protection Program. Napoli was scheduled to testify against Bufalino in a loan shark case. Shortly after Fratianno claimed that he and Rizzitello had met with Bufalino to discuss the murder of

Napoli, Rizzitello was arrested on unrelated charges. The police found a piece of paper in his wallet. On it was Napoli's name, the city where he had been relocated by the Witness Protection Program, and his new line of business. There was no innocent explanation for Rizzitello having this information. It was circumstantial evidence, but it was great corroboration.

The opening statement is the prosecution's first opportunity to present its version of the case. That is when to start dealing with the problem of the immunity witness. The prosecutor's goal should be to diffuse the impact of using an admitted criminal as a witness. Rather than letting the jury learn first from defense counsel that the case against his client is built on the testimony of a "crook," the prosecutor should tell the jury at the beginning that the main witness against the defendant will be an accomplice who participated in the defendant's crimes. Any other criminal background should also be disclosed. The prosecutor should use the word "accomplice" (a term likely to be used by the court in its charge) so it does not appear that he is being presented as anything other than what he is. At the same time, the prosecutor should emphasize that the jury will be hearing from an insider who was in position to tell them what actually happened.

The prosecution should talk about the immunity deal during the opening statement. The details, including the written agreement, will come out in the evidence. The court, however, may not admit the agreement into evidence until the accomplice has been cross-examined. *See United States v. Arroyo-Angulo*, 580 F.2d 1137, 1146-7 (2d Cir. 1978), *cert. denied*, 439 U.S. 913 (1978).

The opening statement should concentrate on the most important question about the accomplice, not whether he is a bad person, but whether he is telling the truth. The prosecutor should invite the jury to check the accomplice's testimony by keeping track of the other evidence in the trial that supports it.

In keeping with the tone of this opening, the accomplice must be prepared to expose all of his blemishes when he takes the witness stand. He must admit all of his wrongdoing, his convictions, his past and present financial situation, even any false statements he may have made on previous income tax returns. He must admit to any prior inconsistent statements, whether made to friends, law enforcement officials, or on a transcribed record. The way to deal with this kind of information is to bring it out on direct.

And direct examination of the witness is also the best time to use the corroborating evidence. The idea is to support the evidence as you go along, not wait until later. For example, in a white-collar fraud prosecution, there is usually a trail of documents that can be identified by the accomplice. His testimony can be interspersed with the documents so the independent proof shows he is telling the truth.

In the prosecution against Mafia boss Frank Tieri, Fratianno testified to a meeting with Tieri in May 1978. Immediately after this testimony, while Fratianno was still on the stand, the prosecutor played a tape-recorded telephone call in which Fratianno told a co-conspirator that he was going to meet with the ''old man''—a nickname for Tieri. Standing alone, the tape recording meant little. Intertwined with Fratianno's testimony, it backed up what he said.

It also helps to show the bond between the accomplice and the defendant. This can be done with photographs of the accomplice and the defendant at social occasions, office diaries showing how often they met, and telephone toll records showing frequent calls they made to each other. All of this sets up the argument that the witness is not testifying because he is a friend of the prosecution, but because he was a friend of the defendant.

Then comes cross-examination, and the accomplice must be ready for it. He should be prepared for cross-examination like any other witness, with three additional warnings:

One, he must be prepared to acknowledge that his acts were wrong. Nothing hurts a prosecution more than a witness who tries to rationalize his crimes. A jury will not convict a defendant on the basis of testimony by a witness who is not truthful about himself.

Two, the witness must be prepared to answer questions about his immunity. He must understand every aspect of his agreement, since his motive for testifying will hinge on what he expects to receive as a result of his cooperation. He must be ready to admit that he entered into the agreement so he would spend less time in jail, not out of a desire to be a good citizen.

Three, the witness should be ready to handle compound questions, confusing questions, or questions that shade or misstate the facts. He should be able to do this himself, without the help of the prosecutor. Suppose the witness is asked ''How many days did you rehearse your testimony with the prosecutor?'' The witness must understand that if he spent a total of four hours over three separate days talking to the prosecutor, he should answer ''four hours,'' not ''three days.'' Furthermore, the witness should not accept the cross-examiner's characterization of these four hours as a ''rehearsal.''

The prosecutor should make as few objections as possible during the cross-examination. He does not want it to seem that he is trying to protect the witness. He wants the jury to view the accomplice as a witness whose testimony is so truthful that it can withstand the test of cross-examination without outside assistance.

At the end of the trial, the prosecutor usually has two summations: the principal argument and rebuttal. Most of the arguments supporting the accomplice should be saved for rebuttal, after the defense has made its attack and has no further reply. In the principal argument, the prosecutor should focus once more on whether the accomplice was telling the truth, not on whether he is a bad person. But the bulk of the summation should be the story told by the evidence. It should assume the accomplice is believable and weave the corroborating evidence into the basic story.

Although every case is different, the defense summation will somehow ask the jury to disbelieve the accomplice because of his criminal background. There are a number of general lines of rebuttal that can be tailored to each case.

First, the defense will probably attack the law enforcement authorities for using a witness with such a sordid past. The most effective response is to ask the jury what responsible law enforcement officials who have cornered a criminal like the accomplice should do. Should they refuse to listen to what crimes have been committed because of the witness's background? Or should they listen skeptically and see if the other evidence supports what he says?

Another response is the importance of having an accomplice testify, especially in a conspiracy case. By its nature, any criminal conspiracy is a secretive group with ringleaders who are insulated by underlings. The only way law enforcement authorities can bring the leaders to justice is through the testimony of their associates. The prosecutor can argue that he would have preferred to have had the testimony of a respectable citizen, like a bank president or a school principal, but honest citizens are not the type of person a criminal deals with.

Second, the defense will argue that the immunity witness is motivated to produce results for the prosecution. In the Tieri case, the defense argued that Fratianno invented Tieri's involvement in a murder plot and a bankruptcy fraud so Fratianno would have someone to deliver to the government. There are good responses to this argument, and they all work in similar cases.

One, the agreement motivated Fratianno to tell the truth. If he lied, he could be prosecuted for perjury as well as all of his other crimes—including the murders. Would Fratianno take such an enormous risk and lie? Note that it is important for the prosecutor to present this argument without personally vouching for the accomplice's credibility, which is an improper argument. See *United States v. Arroyo-Angulo*, 580 F.2d 1137, 1147 (2d Cir. 1978), *cert.denied*, 439 U.S. 913 (1978).

Two, Fratianno had no motive to single out Tieri. The evidence did not show any animosity between the two. They were members of the same organization, the Mafia.

Three, if Fratianno were lying, he would have invented a better case against Tieri. This was a telling point because Fratianno's testimony against Tieri was brief, its most incriminating part simply described two short meetings.

In rebuttal, the prosecutor can often use the defense's cross-examination in arguing the accomplice's credibility. In most instances, defense counsel makes little or no headway in shaking the accomplice on the substance of his testimony. The argument is that in cross-examination, the real test of truth, the defense did not dent the witness's testimony.

Finally, the defense lawyer probably asked the accomplice some questions on cross-examination that do not make much sense at the end of the case. This is usually because the defense was unable to develop other evidence to connect with this dangling information. For example, a series of questions about the description of the defendant's clothing on a particular day may make no sense if his clothing turns out to have nothing to do with the case. This last argument is that the defense asked meaningless questions on cross-examination because he had nothing else to ask in his futile attempt to discredit the accomplice's testimony.

Expert Testimony in Criminal Trials

by Paul S. Meyer

An unattended child fell down the stairs at home. He died. An unusually severe consequence, perhaps, of an all-too-common accident. A tragedy for the child's mother and stepfather, to be sure. But hardly a matter of concern for the district attorney. Yet, by using a battery of experts to reconstruct what actually killed that child, the prosecution recently persuaded a jury to convict the stepfather of first degree murder. *People v. Dellinger*, Orange County Superior Court, No. C-45768.

The *Dellinger* case illustrates the increasingly innovative use of expert testimony in criminal cases. The prosecution and defense still rely heavily on expert testimony in traditional areas such as fingerprinting, handwriting comparison, and ballistics. But, as recent appellate cases show, a new wave of expert testimony is also engulfing criminal trials.

This new wave of expertise encompasses five areas:
- credibility expertise, such as lie detector tests, psychiatric opinions on credibility, and truth serum tests;
- comparison tests of items such as bite marks, tool impressions, and blood;
- forensic dynamics, reconstructing movements, mechanics, and pathology from the resultant evidence;
- expertise involving mental processes, including hypnosis and psychiatric opinion on a person's mental state; and
- analysis of circumstances, such as expert testimony on the battered child syndrome and gang culture.

Some of these new forms of expert testimony are admitted routinely in

Mr. Meyer is in private practice in Orange County, California. He serves on the California Police Officers Standards and Training Commission and is an instructor in criminal trial practice for Western States School of Law.

criminal cases, others are usually rejected, and others meet an uncertain fate.

Courts generally refuse to allow experts to testify about their opinion of another witness's credibility. For example, lie detector test results are usually inadmissible because courts find the tests inherently unreliable. In California, lie detector test results cannot even be used on collateral motions. *In re Joaquin S.*, 88 Cal. App. 3d 80, 83–84, 151 Cal. Rptr. 508 (1979). Indeed, in California it is reversible error to ask a witness whether he has taken a lie detector test and whether charges against him were thereafter dropped. *People v. Andrews*, 14 Cal. App. 3d 40, 45, 92 Cal. Rptr. 49 (1970).

Most courts allow expert testimony concerning a medical condition, emotional disturbance, or psychological abnormality that impaired a witness's ability to perceive, recollect, or relate the facts. *See* Juviler, *Psychiatric Opinions as to Credibility of Witnesses: A Suggested Approach*, 48 CALIF. L. REV. 648 (1960).

Psychiatric Expertise

But, despite recent studies showing that psychiatric expertise can provide important insights into the credibility of "normal" witnesses, *see* LOFTUS, EYEWITNESS TESTIMONY (Harv. Univ. Press, 1980), most courts refuse to allow such testimony. Affirming the trial court's exclusion of a psychologist's testimony "dealing with the ability of witnesses accurately to perceive, recall and relate and with the distorting effects of excitement and fear on perception and recollection," the court in *People v. Johnson*, 38 Cal. App. 3d 1, 7, 112 Cal. Rptr. 834 (1974) stated:

> The present occurrence [armed robbery of a liquor store] was frightening but hardly deranging. There is no evidence or claim of emotional disturbance or psychological "abnormality" of any of the prosecution witnesses. [Citations.] In rejecting defendants' offer of the psychologist's expert testimony, the trial court declared in effect that the testimony would take over the jury's task of determining the weight and credibility of the witness' testimony. The ruling was well within the range of discretion.

Interviews conducted by an expert with a witness under the influence of sodium amytal or some other "truth serum" are generally inadmissible because such interviews have not been proven scientifically reliable. *People v. Johnson*, 32 Cal. App. 3d 988, 1000–1002, 109 Cal. Rptr. 118 (1973). Some resourceful attorneys have managed to sneak truth serum interview results into the record by having an expert witness testify that he has relied on the test results as one basis for his expert opinion on some closely related issue. Even in those cases, though, courts have excluded videotapes of the interviews. *People v. Hiser*, 267 Cal. App. 2d 47, 61–62, 72 Cal. Rptr. 906 (1968).

As tempting as it may be to try to give the jury an expert answer to the most difficult issue in any trial—the credibility of witnesses—the odds against admission of expert testimony on that subject are sufficiently high to deter most practitioners from attempting to introduce such evidence.

Comparison Testing

Comparison testing of physical evidence has taken great strides in recent years. Virtually every physical characteristic of a criminal defendant, from his feet to his head, now can be analyzed and compared to traces left at the scene of the crime. Expert testimony concerning such analyses and comparisons is routinely admitted because it does not preempt the jury's traditional role. Instead, the jury can follow along with the expert and reach its own conclusion.

In *People v. Barker*, 113 Cal. App. 3d 743, 170 Cal. Rptr. 69 (1980), a physical anthropologist was allowed to testify about her comparison of plaster casts of shoeprints found outside the victims' homes with the shoes the defendant was wearing when he was arrested. The witness admitted that footprint and shoeprint analysis did not have the same degree of scientific acceptance as fingerprint analysis; indeed, she said she was the only person then working on her concept of the ''unique shoeprint.'' Nevertheless, the trial court admitted her testimony, and the court of appeal affirmed, reasoning:

> Voiceprints, and similar scientific tests such as lie detector tests, require scientific assumptions and hypotheses which cannot be proven in the courtroom and which lie beyond the knowledge of the average juror. The shoeprint testimony in the instant case was based on a comparison of photographs and plaster castings with actual shoes. The jurors could see the photographs, the castings and the shoes. They could follow the testimony of Dr. Robbins and either accept or reject it. Likewise, they could do the same with the testimony of the defense experts. Accordingly, the testimony was properly received.

113 Cal. App. 3d at 769. *See also People v. Guillebeau*, 10 Cal. App. 3d 322, 343–45, 162 Cal. Rptr. 897, *vacated*, 107 Cal. App. 3d 531, 166 Cal. Rptr. 45 (1980) (affirming admission of a shoeprint test).

Another recent California case upholding shoeprint analysis, *People v. Daniels*, 116 Cal. App. 3d 851, 861–64, 172 Cal. Rptr. 353 (1981), illustrates the imaginative use of such expert testimony and suggests how persuasive it may be, particularly when suitably supplemented by demonstrative evidence:

> Officers recovered from the victim's home a man's shoe which the assailant had dropped in flight. Ms. Hartnett, the county criminologist, performed a comparison study of the insole of that shoe, an

innersole from a shoe worn by appellant after his arrest, an inked impression of appellant's bare foot, and a cast of the upper portion of his foot. These items were presented to the jury, along with a photographic display of the first three. Using a grid system, Ms. Hartnett had compared some 50 different features of the items. Ten of these were diagrammed on the photographic display.

Ms. Hartnett testified that there were no inconsistencies between appellant's known foot impressions and the foot impressions found in the suspect's shoe. She opined that there was a "good probability" that appellant's foot had made the impression inside the shoe recovered from the crime scene.

(Footnote omitted) 116 Cal. App. 3d at 861–62. Daniels was convicted of forcible rape and burglary.

Comparison analysis of shoeprints and foot impressions has become so accepted in California that it is now referred to by the facetious, trade jargon term, "Cinderella analysis." *See People v. Puluti*, 120 Cal. App. 3d 337, 348–351, 174 Cal. Rptr. 597 (1981).

Bite mark comparisons have also met with judicial favor for the same reason: the jury can follow along with the expert as he draws to their attention aspects of the physical evidence that they otherwise might not have noticed. In a recent and particularly gruesome murder case, three dentists testified for the prosecution about comparisons they had made between bite marks on the corpse's leg, plaster casts of the defendant's teeth, and teeth from a large number of other persons. *People v. Slone*, 76 Cal. App. 3d 611, 619–625, 143 Cal. Rptr. 61 (1978). Similarly, in *People v. Marx*, 54 Cal. App. 3d 100, 111, 126 Cal. Rptr. 350 (1975), the court of appeal upheld admission of bite mark comparisons, reasoning:

What is significantly different about the evidence in this case is this: the trier of fact, here the court, was shown models, photographs, X-rays and dozens of slides of the victim's wounds and defendant's teeth. It could see what we have seen in reviewing the exhibits to determine the admissibility of the evidence. First, for example, the extent to which the appearance of the wounds changed between the time that the autopsy was performed and the time that the body was exhumed in Dallas. Second, the extent to which the purported bite marks appear to conform generally to obvious irregularities in defendant's teeth. Thus the basic data on which the experts based their conclusions were verifiable by the court. Further, in making their painstaking comparisons and reaching their conclusions, the experts did not rely on untested methods, unproven hypotheses, intuition or revelation. Rather, they applied scientifically and professionally established techniques—X-rays, models, microscopy, photography—to the solution of a particular problem which, though novel, was well within the capability of those techniques. In short, in admitting the evidence, the court did not have to sacrifice its independence and common sense in evaluating it. (Footnotes omitted.)

Teeth are not the only things that leave marks on a victim's body. In a recent murder trial, the prosecution successfully introduced expert testimony comparing a pair of vice grips found in the defendant's possession with unusual ridged impressions left in the skin of the murdered child. The jury sentenced the defendant to death.

Comparison tests can also be run on a wide variety of other types of physical evidence, including soil samples and tire tracks. Even the weathering characteristics of important materials have been grist for the criminologist's mill. The key to admission of comparison tests, and the key to convincing jurors by such evidence, is a painstaking, step-by-step description by the expert of what he did to compare one physical object with another. Correctly presented, such testimony can be particularly compelling because it involves the jurors in the same Sherlock Holmesian search for clues that the expert performed. When the jurors arrive by the same process at the same conclusion the expert did, they will be convinced the expert is right.

Blood Analysis

One old, but still developing type of comparison testing, blood analysis, does not permit jury participation to the same extent as other comparison tests. Advanced microscopic, spectroscopic, and electrophoretic methods of blood analysis cannot be replicated in the courtroom, and the scientific principles that underlie those methods are difficult to explain to most jurors.

Nevertheless, particularly with the recent development of human leukocyte antigen (HLA) tests, blood analysis has become a highly effective identification tool. *See Joint AMA-ABA Guidelines.—The Present Status of Serological Testing in Problems of Disputed Parentage*, 10 FAM. L.Q. 247, 257–58 (1976). An increasing majority of states now admits blood tests not only to prove that the defendant could *not* be the criminal, but also to prove his guilt. *People v. Lindsey*, 84 Cal. App. 3d 851, 863–66, 149 Cal. Rptr. 47 (1978). *See also Cramer v. Morrison*, 88 Cal. App. 3d 873, 153 Cal. Rptr. 865 (1979).

Where comparison testing uses physical clues to establish identity, forensic dynamics uses similar physical evidence to reconstruct how people or things moved. The courts have long allowed experts to testify to their reconstructions of events from the pattern of blood spattered on the victim and his surroundings. In *People v. Carter*, 48 Cal. 2d 737, 749–751, 312 P.2d 665 (1957), for example, an expert was allowed to state his opinion, based on his analysis of blood spatters, concerning where the assailant stood and what weapon he used to beat the victim. This type of evidence is now routinely admitted.

Biomechanical Engineering

Many more sophisticated techniques are now available to prove that only one movement of the human body is consistent with the physical evidence in a case. The biomechanical engineering that underlies some of these new techniques has gained increasing acceptance in both civil and criminal courts. When jockey Alvaro Pineda died, his heirs sued the racetrack claiming he died when his head struck a portion of the metal starting gate that the racetrack had negligently left unguarded. The racetrack was allowed to present expert testimony from a biomechanical engineer who had studied videotapes of the accident, photographs of the jockey's helmet and silks, and the autopsy report, and who had concluded that Pineda's mount jerked its head up with such force that it dealt a death blow to Pineda's skull. *Pineda v. Los Angeles Turf Club, Inc.,* 112 Cal. App. 3d 53, 169 Cal. Rptr. 66 (1980).

This type of biomechanical expertise helped the prosecution obtain a guilty verdict in *People v. Dellinger,* the case mentioned in the first paragraph of this article. When the incident was first reported, it appeared to be an unfortunate accident. But the autopsy revealed cocaine in the two-year-old victim's blood. That finding touched off an extraordinary scientific investigation.

Two forensic pathologists first reviewed photographs of the scene and x-rays of the child. Then they visited the scene, using a lifelike manikin, supplied by the Department of Motor Vehicles, to test whether the child, whose weight and height closely matched the manikin's, could have fallen and sustained the fatal injuries. Next, using precise measurements of the child's skull, the pathologists ran a computer analysis to determine how hard the child had to be hit before his skull would fracture as it had. Finally, the pathologists reviewed scientific literature on the subject and consulted other experts in the field to check their results. Their conclusion: to fracture the child's skull, it had to be hit with four times the force it would have received in the worst possible fall down the stairs.

Both the conclusion and the investigative work that supported it were allowed in evidence after a hotly contested hearing on their admissibility. The jury's conviction of the stepfather for first degree murder attests to the persuasive impact of good expert testimony even in cases in which no eyewitnesses and no direct physical evidence exist.

Expert psychiatric or psychological testimony concerning the defendant's mental state is, by now, commonplace in criminal trials. Recently, the prosecution has attempted to use such experts in new ways: to judge the reasonableness of a victim's resistance and to enhance witnesses' memories through hypnosis.

1023

In *People v. Guthreau*, 102 Cal. App. 3d 436, 441–42, 162 Cal. Rptr. 376 (1980), and *People v. Clark*, 109 Cal. App. 3d 88, 167 Cal. Rptr. 51 (1980), the prosecutor had been allowed to present at trial a "police expert on rape" who testified that the degree of resistance displayed by the victim was entirely reasonable under the circumstances. In both cases, the appellate court held that admission of this expert testimony was error, but only because the testimony addressed the wrong issue. In a rape case, the relevant question is not whether the victim's resistance was reasonable, but whether her resistance was sufficient to manifest reasonably to the defendant that she did not consent to intercourse with him. Because the "rape experts" opined only about the victim's conduct and not its effect on the defendant, their testimony was irrelevant and should have been excluded.

Time Running Out

The narrowness of the holding in *Guthreau* and *Clark* suggests that we soon will see experts testifying in rape cases about whether a person in the defendant's position would have formed a bona fide belief, based on the victim's statements and actions, that she did consent to intercourse.

On the other hand, time may be running out on the use of hypnotic interviews to enhance witnesses' recollections. Though many courts and experts have cautioned that "investigatory use of hypnosis on persons who may later be called upon to testify in court carries a dangerous potential for abuse," *United States v. Adams*, 581 F.2d 193, 198 (9th Cir.), *cert. denied*, 439 U.S. 1006 (1978), in the past, most courts have held that hypnotic enhancement of testimony affects the credibility of the witness's testimony, not its admissibility. *Id.*

Recently, though, a number of courts have found that a poorly administered hypnotic interview so alters a witness's recollection that his testimony becomes unreliable, but unassailable by cross-examination. During hypnosis, inaccurate information can be supplied to fill gaps in the witness's memory, and the witness may accept that information as his own true recollection. Because the witness will sincerely believe in the truth of his reconstructed "recollection," his testimony may become unshakable by cross-examination.

These concerns led the Arizona Supreme Court to hold that it was error, but not grounds for reversal, to have allowed a victim to testify after her memory had been reconstructed by hypnosis. *State v. La Mountain*, 125 Ariz. 547, 611 P.2d 551, 555 (1980). The Minnesota Supreme Court agreed that such testimony should not be admitted, pointing out that there is no way to tell which parts of the witness's post-hypnotic memory are accurate, which are fanciful, and which are lies. *State v. Mack*, 292 N.W.2d 764, 768–69 (Minn. 1980). The Minnesota court was particularly concerned that after hypnosis the witness would be convinced of the absolute truth of the reconstructed memory regardless of its actual veracity. *Id.* Other states, however, continue to allow testimony from witnesses whose memories have been enhanced by hypnosis, at least when the hypnotic session has been conducted carefully, using appropriate safeguards. *State v. Hurd,* 173 N.J. Super. 333, 414 A.2d 291, 305–306 (1980) (dicta), aff'd, 86 N.J. 525, 432 A.2d 86 (1981). *See also* Feldman, *Look Me in the Eyes and Tell Me That's Admissible,* 8 BARRISTER 4 (Spring 1981).

Given the uncertainty of the law in this area, attorneys who decide to use hypnosis to enhance a witness's memory should be extremely careful to select the right hypnotist and assure that the hypnotist follows appropriate procedures. The hypnotist should be fully qualified, with sufficient credentials to impress the court and with the ability to testify clearly and persuasively. To avoid any contention that the hypnotist has consciously or unconsciously suggested answers to the witness, the hypnotist should be told as little as possible about the case before the hypnotic session. Furthermore, the hypnotic session should be recorded, preferably on videotape.

Even with these precautions, however, the witness may not be allowed to testify after his memory is jogged by hypnosis. Consequently, it is safest to obtain a thorough statement from the witness under oath before the hypnotic session. The statement itself might be admitted under an appropriate exception to the hearsay rule, or at least it will show the court what portion of the witness's testimony is hypnotic reconstruction and what was remembered independently so that the court might permit testimony concerning the facts the witness independently remembers.

Analysis of Circumstances

Until recently, the inferences the jury should draw from circumstantial evidence were generally addressed only in closing arguments. Now, however, many lawyers are attempting to address the question earlier and more persuasively by having an expert witness fit the pieces of circumstantial evidence together for the jury. Such an expert can place the particular facts in their social context, thus explaining apparent ambiguities.

In child abuse cases, for example, doctors are permitted to testify that a pattern of repeated injuries of particular types over a period of time is symptomatic of the "battered child syndrome" and is inconsistent with the defendant's usual claim that the injuries were accidental. *People v. Ewing,* 72 Cal. App. 3d 714, 717, 140 Cal. Rptr. 299 (1977); *People v. Jackson,* 18 Cal. App. 3d 504, 506–508, 95 Cal. Rptr. 919 (1971). Such expert testimony often is the crucial evidence in child abuse cases, connecting the defendant with a larger pattern of violent injury.

Somewhat further afield was the "gang expert," a policeman assigned for more than six years to the street gang detail in south central

Los Angeles, who testified in a recent murder trial about the sociology and psychology of gangs. *People v. McDaniels,* 107 Cal. App. 3d 898, 902–905, 166 Cal. Rptr. 12 (1980). The officer was found to be properly qualified as an expert on gangs, and his testimony was appropriately based on hearsay and other inadmissible matters he had learned about gangs. More important, he was allowed to opine that by crossing into another gang's territory, the defendant's gang exhibited, according to youth gang custom, an intention to inflict serious bodily injury on a member of the rival gang. According to the expert, if the gang had merely desired a fistfight, as the defense contended, the gang would have engaged its rival on neutral turf.

Expert analysis of circumstantial evidence can go too far, though, when the expert draws a conclusion crucial to the case which the jury is equally well equipped to draw itself. In *People v. Brown,* 116 Cal App. 3d 820, 827–29, 172 Cal. Rptr. 221 (1981), a police officer was permitted to testify as an expert on narcotics traffic. His testimony was perfectly proper when he defined the special "street meanings" of various terms, including *runner.* But he strayed beyond the permissible when he said that in his opinion the facts proven at trial showed the defendant was a *runner.* Under the court's instructions, a *runner,* as defined by the officer, was necessarily guilty of selling heroin; therefore, the expert's opinion was tantamount to saying the defendant was guilty. Furthermore, having the evidence and the officer's definition of *runner* before it, the jury was as able as the officer to determine whether the facts fit the definition.

So long as care is taken to avoid having an expert opine on matters the jury is equally capable of deciding, attorneys should have little difficulty securing the admission of expert testimony analyzing circumstantial evidence in the case.

As experts are used more frequently, particularly by the prosecution, it has become increasingly important for the defense to find and adopt strategies to block admission of that testimony or to diminish its impact whenever possible. In many instances, the expert testimony will enter no matter what the defense does, but in other areas there is still a fighting chance to exclude the opposing expert.

Under the law of most American jurisdictions, great leeway is given the trial court in determining when a challenge to admission of an expert's testimony should be heard. FED. R. EVID. 104(c); CAL. EVID. CODE § 402. The opponent of expert testimony should use this flexibility to his advantage.

In many cases, the opponent of expert testimony should question its admissibility by a motion *in limine* before the jury is selected. More time is then available for careful consideration of the challenge; no jury is waiting impatiently in the wings; and the judge may also be less inclined to think that the jury he has not seen will accord little weight to questionably admissible testimony. The issue can be approached calmly and unemotionally before the prosecution has been able to color the controversy with an impassioned opening statement and a series of emotional fact witnesses all setting the stage for the expert's testimony. Before the jury is selected, the case is in a vacuum, passions are not aroused, and a sleepy motion *in limine* hearing may be the perfect forum in which to dispose of the expert.

The prejury-selection hearing is dangerous for defendants, however. Jeopardy does not attach until the jury is empaneled and sworn. *Serfass v. United States,* 420 U.S. 377, 388 (1975). If the prosecution loses a motion *in limine* before jury selection, it may be able to appeal from the ruling or seek an extraordinary writ from an appellate court to review the trial court's decision. Alternatively, the prosecution might dismiss the action and, assuming the statute of limitations has not run, refile the action to try its luck before another judge.

For this reason, the defense may wish to postpone its motion *in limine* until after the jury has been sworn, but before opening statements. At that time, jeopardy will have attached, but the prosecution will not yet have injected emotion into the case. Nor will the prosecution have been able to mention to the jury what expert testimony it anticipates presenting, thus titillating the jury's curiosity even if the evidence is eventually excluded. The judge may be especially receptive to an *in limine* motion at that time, wishing to give the jury a breather atter lengthy jury-selection proceedings.

Best of all, the defense may parley such a motion *in limine* into two chances by seeking at this early stage simply to keep the prosecution from mentioning the expert testimony in opening statements, while reserving for a later time—when the objection can be more finely tuned and more extensively briefed—the objection to admission of the testimony itself.

In any event, every effort should be made to have the admissibility of an expert's testimony determined before the expert takes the stand. Once the jury sees an expert, its curiosity is aroused and the opponent's case is damaged—even though the expert is never allowed to say more than his name.

Apart from timing considerations, efforts to exclude expert testimony involve close strategy questions. Even if there is no real likelihood that an expert will be kept from testifying, a *voir dire* examination on a motion to exclude the expert's testimony may provide the opponent with valuable insights for later cross-examination. On the other hand, the *voir dire* examination may be equally or more effective in educating the expert about potential lines of attack, causing him to prepare more carefully and testify more convincingly when he eventually appears before the jury.

Expert testimony in criminal cases provides a rich source of material to prove the defendant's guilt or innocence. Though courts have set a few boundaries around the use of expert testimony, in most areas, the attorney's imagination is the only limit on the types of expert evidence that can be presented. Attorneys opposing experts in criminal cases, therefore, must be extremely careful in timing and framing their attacks on what may prove to be the most persuasive witnesses against their client.

Settling Criminal Cases

by James Douglas Welch

Settlement by plea bargain is the most common mode of disposition of criminal cases in virtually all jurisdictions. Yet for many lawyers not regularly engaged in criminal work, plea bargaining retains a slightly malodorous quality. They associate the practice with furtive hallway conversations between members of the courthouse in-crowd who appear to be brokering defendants' rights like chips in a poker game. This negative view is rooted in the murky history of plea bargaining, which, although widespread, was for the most part conducted *sub rosa* in the federal system until the 1974 amendments to the criminal rules. Before then it was commonplace for prosecutors and defense counsel to be seen exchanging promises outside the courtroom and minutes later denying on the record the existence of any inducements leading to the entry of the agreed-upon plea.

An understood part of this system was for clients to be instructed (putting it kindly) to mislead the court when asked whether the tendered plea was freely given and not based on promises. Most attorneys involved in criminal litigation practice before the rule change have witnessed at one time or another the charade that took place when a defendant got his lines wrong and, in response to inquiry from the bench, described his plea bargain—whereupon the plea was declined and the matter continued to the end of that day's calendar, when the players reappeared to run through the newly rehearsed exercise. This time the defendant usually denied that he was induced to plead by promises from the prosecution, and the court entered sentence on the plea. One cannot overestimate the naturally corrosive effect of this low drama on the atti-

The author is a partner in the Washington office of the Minneapolis-based firm of Popham, Haik, Schnobrich & Kaufman.

1029

tude of the persons convicted, and on the public in general, toward the workings of our criminal courts.

Despite the unsavory connotations and controversy that surround the process, negotiated termination of cases without trial is an absolutely essential part of our criminal justice system. It offers many legitimate benefits to defendants, prosecutors, and the public. A bargain allows an accused to have his case decided quickly and without the expense and risk associated with trial. As a consequence of his plea, some of the charges against him may be dismissed or he may receive a favorable sentence recommendation from the prosecutor. These concessions are made by the government because it, too, benefits from the speed, certainty, and reduced cost of a bargained-for disposition. In many cases a plea agreement is the only way the government can obtain cooperation essential to other important prosecutions. And, from a public policy standpoint, a fairly negotiated settlement is often the fastest, surest, and cheapest way to satisfy the goals of the criminal justice system.

Always With Us

But there are even more basic reasons why—like them or not—plea bargains will always be with us. As long as prosecutors have discretion to file and to withdraw charges, they will be subject to the entreaties of resourceful defense counsel, and many will be willing to condition the exercise of their discretion. Furthermore, as a practical matter our court system would be crushed by the case load if negotiated dispositions not requiring a trial were eliminated. Last year, 85 percent of all criminal cases in the federal courts were ended by entry of a plea of guilty or *nolo contendere*. Accordingly, if a mere 5 percent fewer criminal matters were concluded by plea bargain, the criminal trial load faced by judges and U.S. Attorneys would increase by 33 percent (from 15 percent of all cases to 20 percent). Existing court calendar backlogs and prosecutors' and public defenders' case loads make the social costs of an even larger number of trials unacceptable, especially in view of the longer delays in civil dockets that would also inevitably result.

There is, then, no present prospect that plea bargaining will disappear. Its status as a matter of law was secured when the Supreme Court eliminated any lingering doubts about the constitutionality of properly handled plea negotiations in *Santobello v. New York*, 404 U.S. 257 (1971). More recently, in *Bordenkircher v. Hayes*, 434 U.S. 357 (1978), the Court recognized the constitutional legitimacy of the pressure that bargaining places on a defendant by forcing him to weigh the risk of a harsher sentence after losing at trial against the certainty of a deal.

The Court's general view of the contours of proper plea bargaining is best seen in the 1974 amendments to the Federal Rules of Criminal Procedure. Rule 11(e) finally brings plea negotiations into the open in the federal courts by authorizing bargaining between the prosecution and defense and by establishing a procedure for presenting the terms of an agreement to the district court for its approval.

The role of the court is limited. Judges may not participate in the bargaining process, and they are not required to accept pleas negotiated by the parties. Indeed, some federal judges maintain an announced policy of rejecting *all* plea agreements as a matter of course, with no regard for their merit. Such a *per se* ban on settlements is contrary to the expressed views of the Supreme Court (in its opinions and in the rules), of the Congress (in its adoption of the rules), of the American Law Institute (MODEL CODE OF PRE-ARRAIGNMENT PROCEDURES § 350.3(1)), and of the National Conference of Commissioners of Uniform State Laws (UNIFORM RULES OF CRIMINAL PROCEDURES 443(a)). But since the Rule contains no standard by which a judge must evaluate a plea agreement, arbitrary rejection of all bargains is probably unassailable legally, notwithstanding the public policy favoring settlements.

Rule 11 describes three things that can be offered in exchange for the defendant's plea of guilty or *nolo*—the prosecutor can dismiss other charges (11(e)(1)(A)); he can agree to make a certain sentence recommendation or not to oppose a request by the defendant for a particular sentence (11(e)(1)(B)); or he can agree that a given sentence is the appropriate disposition of the case (11(e)(1)(C))—In practice, numerous other promises are commonly exchanged. Where a *nolo* plea is entered by agreement in a white collar crime case, for example, defendants often are enjoined from making any public statement inconsistent with the plea (this would have prohibited former Vice-President Agnew's protestations of innocence on the steps of the Baltimore courthouse minutes after his "no contest" plea was accepted, and for this reason is often referred to as a "Spiro Agnew clause"). Frequently, the defendant will be required to provide continuing cooperation in other government prosecutions. From the defense side, if an accused agrees to plead to one of several offenses on the understanding that other charges will not be brought, he may, as a part of the settlement, obtain a promise that the offenses dropped will never be reprosecuted. Some bargains benefit parties other than the defendant—officers and employees of an indicted corporation have achieved protection against prosecution in deals made by their employer.

A judge who accepts a proffered plea agreement must "inform the defendant that [the court] will embody in the judgment and sentence the disposition provided for. . . ." (11(e)(3)). Acceptance of an 11(e)(1)(C) (type C) bargain, therefore, is equivalent to a binding promise by the judge to sentence in accord with the specific disposition set forth in the agreement. Should the court reject the bargain, the rule gives the defendant an opportunity to withdraw his plea after being advised that if he pleads anyway the outcome may be "less favorable" than the one proposed.

1031

This warning requirement has in the past had special significance in connection with a "type B" (recommended sentence) agreement. Although the rule stated that a bargained-for recommendation was not binding on the court, it nevertheless was interpreted to prevent imposition of any sentence harsher than that requested. The legislative history and case law that gave rise to this reading stemmed from the unfair confusion that was said to result because the warning of a possible less favorable outcome was not given at the time the "type B" agreement was accepted. Defendants were not the only ones confused—the *United States Attorneys' Manual* suggested that since many judges labored "under the misimpression that they may accept a subparagraph (B) agreement and yet impose a more onerous sentence," they should be advised to the contrary by the prosecutor.

This problem was addressed, albeit obliquely, in a Rule 11(e)(2) amendment that became effective August 1, 1979. The new provision requires the court to advise the defendant "that if the court does not accept the recommendation or request the defendant nevertheless has no right to withdraw his plea." It surely can be argued that this language puts the accused on notice that a "type B" agreement is merely a recommendation, and that a court is free to accept the plea and still impose a harsher sentence. On the other hand, if that is the meaning of the amendment, it seems fair to ask why the court did not simply track the "less favorable outcome" wording of Rule 11(e)(4), which underpinned the contrary reading of the prior provision.

In most circuits, plea bargains are enforced like contracts, but there is a growing body of "plea bargain law" from which new concepts are emerging. In *United States v. Cooper*, 594 F.2d 12 (4th Cir. 1979), the Fourth Circuit concluded that the governing principle is a defendant's constitutional right to be treated with "fairness." In *Cooper*, application of rules drawn strictly from contract law gave the defendant no right to relief. The court said that the government's obligation in a plea bargain situation is not so limited, and granted the accused rights that go beyond Corbin where necessary to do justice. The Ninth Circuit has taken a similar position, enforcing plea agreements based on reasonable, good faith reliance by the defendant rather than engaging in a doctrinaire application of traditional contract law. *United States v. Goodrich*, 493 F.2d 390 (9th Cir. 1974).

These developments should speak loudly to the lawyer engaged in negotiating a criminal settlement: You must maintain an accurate, written record of all communications with the prosecutors. Especially important are memos of representations made by the government about its conduct at sentence allocution or statements about the penalty the judge actually will impose. It is good advice generally to bargain with the lawyer in charge of the prosecuting team, but under *Santobello* all government attorneys are held responsible for what they say in plea negotiations.

Hence, any conversation with any member of the prosecution staff should be noted. (On this point, the *U.S. Attorneys' Manual* advises against "indiscriminate" statements to opposing counsel and likewise suggests the need to keep an accurate record of all contacts with the defense.)

Plea Agreement

If at all possible, the final plea agreement should be embodied in a document signed by the attorneys for both sides and by the defendant. This will eliminate later controversy with the client or the prosecutors about the substance of the understanding, and it facilitates presentation of the agreement to the court for approval. The argument is usually in the form of a letter, which can be filed as an exhibit to a joint motion seeking acceptance of the agreement under Rule 11(e)(3).

Many less formal kinds of settlements fall outside the ambit of Rule 11 and need not be submitted for court approval. A timely assessment of the evidence may suggest an approach to the prosecutor with a request for immunity while the investigation is still underway. If the attempt fails and charges are brought in any event, early efforts to cooperate are solid grist for an argument that a lesser offense is the appropriate charge. The Antitrust Division has an announced policy of "giving serious consideration to leniency" for the first company in a conspiracy to come forward with information about an otherwise undetected Sherman Act violation (there are important caveats to this policy that should be investigated before disclosure is made). Even in these less formal settings, any agreement reached should be reduced to writing. A surprising amount of the "plea bargain law" now on the books arises in cases where the pivotal issue is whether an agreement was ever made.

The course to be followed in actually negotiating a plea bargain defies written analysis. A host of subjective variables are involved—the past relationships of the actors, their personalities and experience, the policies of the prosecutor's office, the temperament and sentencing history of the judge, the nature of the crime, and the involvement of the victim in prosecutorial decision making are all factors that have a potentially significant influence on the outcome of the discussions. The best bargaining strategy for any particular case is as much a matter of instinct as anything else. Notwithstanding the futility of attempting to develop fixed guides on how to achieve good results, the following tips may prove useful.

First: Thorough discussion of the matter with the client is essential to define the bounds of counsel's negotiating authority. Apart from establishing clear objectives, there must be a common understanding of minimally acceptable results. It is the lawyer's job to conceive the strategy of bargaining, but there should be a shared comprehension of these tactics. The attorney must evaluate for the defendant the impact of sentence alternatives offered by the government. Some estimate—and it must be clearly identified as no more than an estimate—of the probability of success at trial and of the likely sentence in the event of a guilty verdict is a necessary ingredient to these conversations. As appropriate, the collateral consequences of conviction should also be reviewed. Where the defendant holds a licensed job that would be jeopardized, or where he might be deported, these ancillary factors could be dispositive.

Second: Negotiations do not substitute for homework. The defense attorney must become the complete master of the ins and outs of his client's situation. Successful bargaining requires a command of the factual and legal defenses available as well as the mitigating factors that will influence the sentence or that indicate the peculiar desirability of certain sentence alternatives (e.g., only through a work release program can the defendant maintain his employment). Without a clear understanding of the facts, the lawyer deals in the dark, possibly making crucial concessions to achieve goals of no consequence to his client. Moreover, credibility with the prosecution is always vital in negotiations and it cannot be maintained in the absence of a solid grasp of the case.

Third: The defense's strategic posture must be continually reassessed to gain maximum advantage from bargaining initiatives. In complex, white-collar cases this means staying abreast of present as well as anticipated document production and grand jury testimony. An offer to plead before damaging material has been disclosed will naturally be more effective than one made after the handwriting is on the wall. In more straightforward prosecutions, substantial benefits can flow from timing plea proposals in light of court calendar and prosecutorial work load schedules. For instance, if Judge Jones is known to give harsh sentences in the type of case at hand but will be on vacation during a certain period, consideration should be given to ordering the plea bargaining process so that the plea will be entered (and the judge assigned) during that interval.

Fourth: Never forget whom you represent. The client is not the court system, which institutionally thrives on dispositions without trial and which encourages judges to place inordinate pressure on defense lawyers and clients to tender pleas. Nor is it the attorney himself, whose continuing good relationship with the prosecutors may benefit from "playing ball" in a particular case. In the final analysis, the decision to plead remains the province of the defendant, and the lawyer's job is simply to provide guidance. As negotiations move forward, you must remember that the goal is not to reach any agreement, but to reach agreement only on those terms that confer maximum benefit on the defendant. Intransigence may frequently be the only available course, even though in some cases it may lead to trial, and even though a loss at trial generally means a harsher sentence than would be imposed on a plea. This is perhaps the most difficult aspect of plea bargaining, because once discussions are initiated, psychologically, the bargain tends to become an end in itself, consuming the lawyer in the search for a middle ground.

Staying Clean

by Donald H. Beskind and David S. Rudolf

If you can't try the case—try the cops.
> The last resort for the criminal defense lawyer.

If you can't get the defendant—get his lawyer.
> The prosecutor's version.

Going after the defendant's lawyer is an increasingly popular tactic. But unlike the defense strategy of trying the police, it is not a last resort. Neither is it aimed only at criminal practitioners. Most white-collar criminal defendants once had civil lawyers representing them. The result is that some lawyers who think they are working on civil cases find that the government has a different view of the case—and of them.

The increase in investigations of lawyers is partly the result of broader theories of criminal responsibility under the conspiracy statutes and the prosecutor's new favorite—the Racketeer Influenced and Corrupt Organizations Act.

To be sure, some lawyers knowingly violate these or other laws, and the government has the duty to investigate and prosecute them. But all too often, prosecutors investigate attorneys whose only crime has been aggressive representation of their clients' legitimate best interests. And, it seems, the more prominent and newsworthy the lawyer, the better.

Even if the lawyer is not the target of such a prosecutor, he may find himself and his records subpoenaed in an investigation of his clients. You must understand that your files are not exempt from the government's reach. The attorney client privilege generally does not protect information such as a client's identity, the amount and source of fees, and the manner in which the fees have been paid. *See In re Michaelson*, 511 F.2d 882 (9th Cir.), *cert. denied*, 421 U.S. 978 (1975). Nor will the privilege

---

The authors are partners in the Durham, North Carolina, firm of Beskind and Rudolf.

protect documents transferred to the lawyer that would not have been privileged if they had been in the hands of the client. *Fisher v. United States*, 425 U.S. 391, 401–05 (1976).

In recent years the government increasingly has used subpoenas and even search warrants to seek leads and incriminating evidence from lawyers' files. When that happens, the evidence may cast suspicion on the lawyer as well as the client.

So how does an honest attorney minimize the chance of learning criminal law the hard way—from the inside out? Adopting some practices widely accepted by experienced criminal defense lawyers will help.

If you represent criminal defendants, do not:

- socialize with clients;
- do business *with* clients;
- do business *for* clients;
- provide civil legal advice to clients;
- represent more than one witness or party in any one case;
- take the client's property as fees; or
- take fees from someone other than clients or their families.

Civil practitioners may be surprised by some of the rules, particularly the first. In civil practice, business development is important, and socializing with clients is an excellent way of getting new business. It is understandable that civil practitioners may choose not to follow these stringent rules. But understanding why criminal defense lawyers follow them may help civil lawyers avoid a grand jury subpoena, search warrant, or indictment.

To appreciate the risks of socializing with clients, consider the criminal defense lawyer who meets his client in the Caribbean and then uses the client's yacht for a sail from Eleuthera to Miami. A customs search in Miami reveals that the yacht is carrying cocaine. Will anyone, especially a United States Attorney, believe the criminal defense lawyer who claims not to know the client was smuggling drugs? After all, he would not need your services if he were not involved in criminal activities. And you are close enough to be a guest on his boat. Add one crewman who thinks he heard an incriminating conversation, and a conspiracy is born.

Criminal defense lawyers should know that any time they are in business *with* one of their clients, they are at risk. If it turns out that the business is illegal, it will be virtually impossible for the lawyer to claim surprise. Nor should criminal defense lawyers ask clients to invest in lawyer's projects.

Criminal defense lawyers also should avoid doing business *for* their clients. They should not buy or sell property for their clients. Nor should they let clients run businesses out of their law offices. Criminal defense lawyers should say ''no'' whenever they are asked to do anything for a client that does not relate to the criminal case they are handling. They should not even take business messages for a client.

Do you doubt this?

Consider the lawyer who received a seemingly innocuous telephone call. A client's friend said he had tried to call the client and had been unsuccessful. The lawyer agreed to contact the client with the friend's message, "I'll be in town tomorrow." He passed the message on. The next day the client was arrested with the friend and a kilo of cocaine. When the friend turned out to be an informant, the lawyer was subjected to a lengthy and anxiety-provoking investigation of his "participation" in a conspiracy to import drugs by helping set up the delivery.

Criminal defense lawyers should also avoid advising their clients on civil matters. The obvious risk is that you will give the wrong advice in a field in which you do not regularly practice. But even if you give your clients the right answers, the government may be interested in why you gave any answers at all.

For example, one lawyer advised a client who was charged with running a successful smuggling ring on how the government keeps track of the movement of cash through Cash Transaction Reports, 31 C.F.R. §§ 103.22 *et seq.* He explained only what the law said: that all cash transactions over $10,000 had to be reported by the bank that received the cash. Unknown to the lawyer, the client never again deposited more than $9,000 at one time. Perfectly legal? Perhaps not. At least one lawyer has been indicted for avoiding the statutory reporting requirement by splitting up his cash fees to make sure that $10,000 was never deposited at any one time.

A less obvious example is the lawyer who advised a client charged with RICO violations on how to set up certain kinds of trusts. While this advice may be perfectly proper for civil clients seeking to avoid estate taxation, the government may think the attorney is assisting in an attempt to obstruct the forfeiture provisions of RICO, 18 U.S.C. § 1963 (c).

It may also be risky to represent more than one witness or client in a case. Even if your clients do not object, the government may. When the government moves to disqualify you, you may lose all of your clients in the case. Much worse, the government may indict you. The theory will be that your representation of Client A was part of a conspiracy to obstruct justice for Client B by keeping Client A from cooperating with the prosecution against Client B.

Finally, there are two questions on fees: what to take as fees and who should pay them? First, criminal defense attorneys should not take clients' property as fees. The automobile or house that you take as a fee may have been used in illegal activities. It is then subject to forfeiture under various laws such as RICO. What was once a large fee turns out to be a large nightmare. That is not all. Because your name is in the chain of title, the government may think your involvement is less than innocent.

Second, do not take fees from anyone other than clients or their families. One lawyer's former client received a grand jury subpoena. He asked the lawyer to represent him again. With him was a "friend" who was willing to pay the retainer that the client could not afford. The attorney took the money. He vigorously opposed the subpoena and angered the prosecutor. The prosecutor began to think that the legal services had been provided to the client as a part of the cover-up of the original conspiracy. The lawyer received a grand jury subpoena and was faced with answering the question, "Who paid your fees?" or going to jail. No privilege—and not a happy choice.

Even if you take the advice offered so far, and are entirely circumspect and honest in your dealings with clients, the investigation may still focus on you. Generally, this means a subpoena for your records.

What do you do?

Assume the worst and take the matter seriously. At the least, the prosecutor has put you in the unenviable position of having to explain to your client why certain matters that he always assumed were protected by the attorney-client privilege may be disclosed, such as the amount of money he paid you for your legal advice. At worst, the subpoena may mean that the prosecutor has zeroed in on *you* as a target of the grand jury's investigation. Underestimating the seriousness of this situation may prove disastrous.

The subpoena may force you to risk contempt. Until you are held in contempt for refusing to comply, you cannot appeal a denial of your claim of attorney-client privilege. *Cf. United States v. Dionisio*, 410 U.S. 1 (1973). The prospect of being cited for contempt is unpleasant and anxiety-provoking, even if imprisonment is extremely unlikely.

You should do what you would advise any client to do: call another lawyer with experience in this area. It is important to get a second opinion from someone who can be objective and has dealt with such subpoenas before. Such a person may be able to tell, just from looking at what the subpoena requests, whether the government views you as a suspect or just a witness. Even if this is not possible, it is often easier for that person to call the prosecutor and explain your concerns about being subpoenaed to provide information regarding your clients. At the same time, your lawyer can find out what is going on.

In addition to getting independent and objective advice yourself, notify your client of the subpoena. Tell your client to get the advice of an independent lawyer on whether he wishes you to assert the attorney-client privilege. Why should you do that? The chances are that asserting the attorney-client privilege is exactly what your client should do. Why does he need a second lawyer just to tell him that? Because if you are being investigated, the prosecutor may view your advice that your client assert the attorney-client privilege as an attempt to obstruct the investigation and protect yourself.

If your client wants to assert the privilege, it is your ethical duty to protect his confidences. On the other hand, the judge may order you to disclose the information. To avoid this dilemma, the client, through another lawyer, should move to intervene in your subpoena. The client has an absolute right to do this to protect his privilege. *See* FED. R. CIV. P. 24 (a)(2); *cf. Gravel v. United States*, 408 U.S. 606 (1972). Once intervention is granted, a court order requiring compliance with the subpoena is immediately appealable without the necessity of a contempt citation for the attorney. *In re Grand Jury Proceedings* (Katz), 623 F.2d 122 (2d Cir. 1980). Finally, it is not enough to get the objective advice of another experienced attorney. *Listen* to the advice. Your natural inclination will be to cooperate—to show the prosecutor that you have nothing to hide. But cooperation, if it means giving up records over your client's claim of privilege, may violate your ethical obligations. Also, it may be against your own interest to cooperate without a grant of immunity. If you are a target, it may be necessary to assert your Fifth Amendment privilege, even if you believe there is nothing to hide. The line between an innocent act and a criminal one will be drawn by the prosecutor—not by you. If the prosecutor has decided to indict you, what you say *will* be used against you.

Then silence is golden.

These suggestions are intended to make it less likely that the government will try to get you if they cannot get your client. But no matter what you do, all that stands between you and a subpoena, or even an indictment, is a prosecutor who acts in good faith and exercises good judgment. If he does not, you may join the growing list of attorneys who have learned that the term ''criminal lawyer'' has two meanings—depending on where the prosecutor puts the emphasis.

Defending Government Contractors in Criminal Cases

by Milton Eisenberg

Whether your client makes a $2 socket wrench or a $25 million jet fighter, government contracting suddenly has become a risky business.

Defense contractor billing practices have become front-page news events. The result has been to focus unprecedented attention and resources on alleged government contractor fraud. Recent indictments have involved such firms as General Dynamics, General Electric, Rockwell, GTE, and a score of lesser known companies.

Unlike other criminal cases—even white-collar crimes—defending the government contractor is a different ball game. The government has one important trump card: it punishes your client *before* trial. Before the criminal trial, the government can simply suspend all business with the contractor. It costs your client a valuable, and sometimes its only, customer.

Because of this threat, the pervasive influence of the government suspension and debarment regulations underly all your strategies.

The government's power to suspend business summarily with your client cannot be overcome by a bond or by posting bail. Instead, it requires prompt and difficult choices, often including the waiver of protections against self-incrimination to lift (or at least limit) the suspension order.

The suspension and debarment regulations, which are in the federal Acquisition Regulation (FAR), 48 C.F.R. § 9.400–9.407-5 (1985), generally provide that federal agencies may not solicit offers from, award contracts to, or consent to subcontracts with, any company or individual who has been suspended or debarred.

Suspension is a temporary prohibition pending the completion of the

---

The author is a partner in the Washington, D.C., office of Fried, Frank, Harris, Shriver & Jacobson.

investigation or legal proceedings at issue. Debarment is a prohibition for a specified period of time, usually not more than three years. The regulations provide that an indictment for a criminal offense in connection with obtaining, attempting to obtain, or performing a public contract or subcontract is adequate evidence for suspension. Conviction is grounds for debarment.

To understand the impact of a suspension on an indicted government contractor, consider what the situation would be without a suspension:

The defendant could be told that despite the indictment, it is entitled to a presumption of innocence. The court will instruct the jury that the indictment is not evidence and may not be considered as any proof of guilt.

The defendant could be told that the burden of proof is on the government and that it is a heavy burden. The government must present evidence that convinces the jury beyond a reasonable doubt as to each element of the offense charged.

The defendant could be told that it is not required or expected to assist the prosecutor in any way. If the defendant is an individual, he cannot be called as a witness or be required to disclose any of his documents. Even if the defendant is a corporation, it does not have to cooperate with the government. While a corporation does not have a Fifth Amendment privilege against self-incrimination, once an indictment has been returned, the government cannot use grand jury process to obtain trial testimony or documents from an indicted corporation. Of course, both the government and the defendant can subpoena documents, but they need not be produced until the trial unless the court directs otherwise.

For better or worse, all of these limitations (and many others) are firmly in place. Some are rooted in express commands of the Constitution, while others are implied in the due process clause. All have as their purpose a system of criminal justice which deals fairly with persons accused of wrongdoing and which safeguards against the conviction and punishment of defendants who may be innocent despite their indictment by the state.

But that is not what happens when a government contractor has been indicted.

First, forget about the indictment not being evidence, the presumption of innocence, and the government's burden of proof.

The suspension and debarment regulations draw on a different tradition. Under the express provisions of the regulations, when a government contractor is indicted for any of the offenses designated in the suspension and debarment regulations, that indictment—without anything else—is enough evidence for suspension.

This does not mean that the contractor must be suspended after indictment. The regulations say that suspensions are discretionary by using the word "may" instead of "shall" before the list of causes for suspension. In addition, the regulations require a determination ''that immediate action is necessary to protect the government's interest'' before a suspension is imposed. Nevertheless, it is a rare case in which the government's exercise of discretion results in a decision not to suspend an indicted contractor pending trial.

If the contractor does nothing after a notice of suspension, the suspension will remain in effect until the indictment is dismissed or the criminal proceedings are concluded. In other words, the burden shifts to the defendant. The contractor must act to challenge the suspension, rather than wait for the government to prove its case.

This means the contractor must submit in person, in writing, or through a representative information and argument in opposition to the suspension. It does not mean, however, that the contractor has an opportunity to examine either the government's evidence or its witnesses. But in most cases it does mean that the contractor must make a full disclosure of its evidence on the merits and any matters in mitigation.

So the defense lawyer has a critical choice.

Does he challenge the suspension and thereby compromise or surrender his client's rights in the criminal proceeding, or does he accept the suspension and defend the criminal case with all his client's rights intact?

The answer is crucial and one of the most difficult any defense lawyer will ever face. There are no safe assumptions or presumptions. While each case must turn on its own facts, there are some factors to consider.

First, you must recognize that the official imposing the suspension has already decided that the suspension is justified. His decision may have been based solely on the indictment, or on a broader review of all of the factors. In either case, the suspending official has exercised his discretion and made a judgment in your client's case that suspension was necessary to protect the government's interest.

In most cases this means that the defendant must convince that very same official to change his mind. While this has actually been known to happen, the burden on the contractor is enormous.

Realistically, you cannot expect a suspending official—who has acted on the basis of an indictment—to reverse himself as long as the United States attorney is continuing the prosecution. He is likely to say that you are entitled to your day in court, and if you are right, your client will be acquitted. If your client is acquitted, the suspension will be lifted.

This will not be much solace to your client. Months and sometimes years may go by before the case goes to trial and there is a final judgment.

Also recognize that there is nothing in the regulations to keep the prosecutor from obtaining the evidence you presented in opposition to the suspension and using it in the criminal trial against your client. In fact, any affidavits or statements submitted in the suspension proceeding may become the basis for additional counts or allegations against your client.

There is a theoretical balance to this. The law permits you to use any evidence the government presented in the suspension proceedings when you are defending the criminal case. The difficulty is that the government is not required to produce any evidence in the suspension proceedings because the entire burden is on the contractor.

Another problem is a possible conflict in the objectives of the corporate defendant and the individual defendants, typically the corporate officers and employees involved in the alleged misconduct. A corporation can only be subjected to monetary penalties, but people can face possible jail terms. The lawyer for the individuals may be less willing than the corporation's lawyer to jeopardize the individuals' defense by cooperating in a pretrial suspension proceeding.

This conflict may be intensified because the individuals are likely to be on administrative leave with pay while the charges are pending, and therefore do not share the financial pressures on the corporation. Without the cooperation of the charged officers and employees, the corporation's ability to contest the suspension is seriously impeded.

Your Client's Survival

These are obvious drawbacks to any challenge to a suspension. But you cannot stop your analysis here. Consider some economic issues which, in practice, are often compelling:

How important is your client's survival to the government? Until very recently, if a contractor was big enough, it would not face suspension and debarment. Many of the largest corporations in the United States have been indicted and even convicted for offenses included in the suspension and debarment regulations. But they were not added to the government's blacklist because their services were considered essential to the government.

This led to a serious public relations problem, since it implied that the Pentagon was tougher on small companies than on the giants of the defense industry. The Department of Defense finally yielded to this criticism and in the past year suspended a number of major contractors. Obviously these suspensions did not last very long or were quickly limited in impact, so the public relations problem continues. There is still a world of difference in how you represent one of these industrial giants caught up in a suspension and how you represent a run-of-the-mill company with lots of competitors for its products.

Size is important. You may be able to limit the suspension if the company is big enough to be organized into several divisions for different business lines and if only one division is involved in the indictment.

Convincing the agency to limit the scope of the suspension may require your client to terminate—or at least place on administrative leave—

any officers or employees charged in the indictment. It may also require your client to implement a number of extraordinary internal and external controls over its operations. And it helps if the government happens to want or need some of your client's products.

There is an additional problem in the regulations that affects attempts to limit the scope of a suspension. The regulations impute conduct to associated individuals and affiliates. Generally speaking, imputation works up, down, and sideways. Any conduct charged against any officer, employee, or other individual associated with a contractor may be imputed to the contractor if the conduct occurred in connection with the individual's performance of his duties for the contractor or with the contractor's knowledge or approval. In addition, any conduct charged against the contractor may be imputed to any officer, employee, or other individual associated with the contractor who participated in, knew of, or had reason to know of the contractor's conduct.

The regulations also provide that unless the suspension is limited by its terms to specific divisions, organizational elements, or commodities, the suspension includes all divisions or other organizational elements of the contractor and in addition, any affiliates of the contractor specifically named in the notice. These provisions go beyond even the liberal tests of the criminal law for imputing an employee's wrongdoing to his corporate employer. As a result, you may find that the suspension includes individuals and even companies not charged in the indictment. And observe: If these individuals and companies are in fact independent of the defendants, they may not share any of the defendant's concerns about compromising their rights to a fair trial.

The viewpoint behind these rules is easy to understand. They are motivated first by a desire that no one tainted by the defendant's wrongdoing continue to do business with the government. Second, there is an assumption that wrongdoing does not occur at any level of a corporation if senior management is doing its job of instilling proper ethical attitudes among the company's employees.

Of course, there are many situations in which the corporation cannot be separated from the wrongdoing or the wrongdoer. Then the imputation regulations make sense. But in many other cases, it is hard to justify a system in which the act of one employee or a small group of employees is allowed to jeopardize the jobs of thousands of innocent workers and the investment of thousands of innocent shareholders.

The attempt to justify such harsh results in the name of corporate responsibility is nonsense. No one would suggest putting the CIA, the FBI, or the IRS out of business because one of its agents or employees is charged with a crime. Even in the private sector, rarely will an investment banking firm or accounting firm be threatened with a suspension of the right to continue to do business because one or more of its employees is charged with committing a criminal offense in the course of their employment. But if your client is a government contractor, this is what you must face.

When we couple the imputation rules with the government-wide application of suspensions, it is apparent why suspension of a government contractor will in many cases put the business in mortal danger. When that happens, you will not have to ponder your choices for very long. You will be forced by economic necessity to do whatever you can, as quickly as you can, to terminate or limit the suspension. Whatever concerns you may have about preserving the company's right to a fair trial will pale against the spectre of imminent ruination if you do not capitulate.

In these circumstances, the defendant's number one priority will be to bring the criminal proceedings to an early end. This almost always requires some kind of plea bargain.

(There is nothing defense counsel likes less than a plea negotiation involving a contractor under suspension. At this point, the company's due process rights are the least of your problems. It is possible extortion that confronts you. Capitulation in these cases often requires not only that the company accept as true every charge made against it in the indictment, but also that it turn out every officer or employee named as a defendant before any evidence has been presented in any judicial forum. And there is little you can do about it if the company's survival depends on resolving the criminal proceedings.)

But now you have to recognize that even total capitulation will not end the company's woes.

For one thing, the company cannot simply plead guilty. That will just take it from a suspension to a debarment, since convictions are to debarments what indictments are to suspensions.

A Global Settlement

Your company cannot plead nolo contendere, even with the court's consent. At common law a nolo plea was a plea of no contest that allowed sentence to be imposed without an admission of guilt. Under the Federal Rules of Evidence, a nolo plea is not admissible as evidence against the defendant in any civil or criminal proceeding. But under the suspension and debarment regulations, a nolo plea has exactly the same significance as a plea of guilty or a conviction after a full trial.

If the company cannot plead guilty or nolo contendere, what can it do to bring the criminal proceedings to an early end?

Negotiate what is called a Global Settlement. It is an overall agreement for the disposition of the criminal case and all related civil and administrative issues, including suspension and debarment.

Given a choice between facing criminal charges and paying even exorbitant money damages, most individuals are more likely to pay rather than to risk even the remote possibility of a conviction and jail time—

regardless of the merits of the case. Because of the possibility of coercion and a denial of due process in this situation, for many years the Department of Justice would not settle civil cases while related criminal charges were unresolved. But that policy has changed, and global settlements are now viewed with favor by prosecutors and defense counsel alike.

In the case of defense counsel, however, a global settlement is more a matter of necessity than desire. Necessity stemming from simple economics. Suspension and debarment—whatever their theoretical basis—may be more severe punishments than any penalty against corporations found in the criminal code. The company's concern with having a principal (and in many cases, exclusive) source of business cut off or curtailed will often overshadow any concern about the stigma of a criminal conviction or the amount of damages.

Global settlements are not easy. The bureaucratic obstacles are enormous because of the dispersal of responsibility and the refusal (or inability) of the Department of Justice or any other one agency to assert control.

Political considerations also make fair settlements harder. The government officials with whom you have to deal find themselves in the forefront of the administration's effort to outdo its most strident congressional critics in the crusade against fraud, waste, and abuse. This atmosphere encourages normally reasonable officials to hold out for the toughest possible sanctions regardless of the merits of the case. Since prosecutors also are aware of the economic pressures on the contractor to settle, they do not have the usual incentives to sift through the facts and evidence in complex or marginal cases.

The result is that global settlements tend to be costly. Contractors sometimes make payments out of all proportion to the merits of the offenses alleged just to avoid debarment.

And what if you cannot settle?

The criminal justice system should operate as a safeguard. A number of cases that have gone to trial have resulted in acquittals. Even in the present atmosphere, the only way to keep your client from being pushed around unfairly is to make it clear to the prosecutor that you will go to trial rather than submit to any unjustified or unreasonable demands.

You can take this position only if your client is willing and able to suffer the economic consequences of a continued suspension during the period required for trial. Despite the Speedy Trial Act, this sometimes can be a long time because of the complexity of many contractor fraud cases and many exclusions from the prescribed 70 days between indictment and trial. Your client's suspension may be helpful, however, in convincing the court to expedite the proceedings.

To take advantage of this, do not let suspension inhibit trial preparation. The government sometimes investigates contractor fraud cases for a year or more before an indictment is returned. If the defense has done no trial preparation during this time, it may not be in a position to press for expedited proceedings without jeopardizing the case. Moreover, unless the prosecutor senses that you are actually ready for trial, your threat to put the government's case to the test will not be credible. And that is a problem for which there is only one cure—preparation.

White Collar Crime: The Defendant's Side

by Boris Kostelanetz

The white collar defendant is usually a first offender, sympathetic in character, pleasant in appearance. This business or professional client does not have the profile of petty thief or forger, and his alleged offenses hardly ever are caused by poverty. Indeed, the defendant may have too much money, or at least more than he shows on his tax return.

The crimes with which he is charged—women are rarely accused in these cases, for reasons that may be left to another paper—encompass substantial controversies and complex facts and law. Tax evasion, stock manipulation, bank fraud, insider trading, antitrust, and the like invariably involve complicated books and records, economic and financial statements, and even scientific formulas and computer technology.

White collar trials are almost always time-intensive, and are preceded by months, sometimes years, of investigation. In the preindictment stage, squads of state or federal specialists have scoured banks, brokerage houses, present and former customers and creditors, and even neighbors to produce the hundreds of facts necessary to prosecute. In fact, the white collar defendant usually is well aware that the government is scrutinizing his conduct over many years and in many transactions. He may be disappointed when he sees the written charges, but he will hardly be surprised.

Whether retained before or after indictment, the lawyer for the white collar defendant must take charge from the start. So start with the fee.

Over and above the initial—and substantial—retainer, the defendant must be prepared to pay for what in an ordinary criminal case might be termed unnecessary luxuries.

For example, daily transcripts of the testimony should be ordered and

---

Boris Kostelanetz is a founding partner of Kostelanetz, Ritholz, Tique & Fink, in New York City.

available for close analysis. One or two associate attorneys, a legal assistant, an accountant, an investigator, a chemist, and a computer technician may be vital to the case. Certainly, three professionals sitting at the defendant's table ordinarily will not outnumber the prosecutor's team.

Also, the lawyer should not be required to play banker. Except for public corporations or wealthy defendants with impeccable credit, the client should commit to refreshing the retainer as needed and should understand that there is no discount defense. Alternately, a guarantee of a sum certain or an open letter of credit will relieve the lawyer of any concern about having a creditor-debtor relationship with his client.

Although aspects of white collar litigation are almost indistinguishable from civil litigation, in many ways the lawyer's approach is substantially different. Some strategies that would constitute improper conduct in civil litigation may be required and approved in defense of the criminal.

Guilt or innocence is not decided by counsel, but by courts and juries in adversary proceedings. Absent a private confession of guilt, a lawyer should presume, as does the common law, that his client is innocent. Even where guilt is privately confessed, a lawyer still is obligated to determine his client's defenses with the knowledge that his client, within sanctioned rules, may not necessarily be proved guilty of the charge. Unless the lawyer takes this approach, he is not performing his function. The client can find his way to jail all by himself.

Trial preparation demands creative thinking and sophisticated techniques. The lawyer cannot rely on his genius for persuasion or his self-conceived talent for shattering the opponent's case. Instead, the lawyer should concentrate on these tasks:

First, develop alternative and flexible theories for the client's defense. At trial, the lawyer must be able to shift his thinking as the emerging evidence requires. Obviously, you will attempt vigorously to pry from the prosecution all the details of the charges. However, alternative theories of defense will help you overcome surprises. Also, your theories will vary, depending on whether the client will testify in his own behalf—a decision that may be made and remade during the course of the trial.

Second, scout the judge. Obviously, any competent attorney knows something about the judge he is appearing before. But the defendant's offensive strategies require having a complete book on the judge. You will have enough problems handling hostile witnesses and a stressed-out client without wondering why the judge's eyes have glazed over during your cross-examination. Likewise, know your opponents' background, attitudes, and favorite procedural ploys. This kind of personal knowledge will give you a better chance of anticipating the prosecution's plans.

Third, consider interviewing all witnesses, including those hostile to the client, and even the outright informers. In dealing with hostile witnesses, adopt the precaution used by government investigators: have at least two interrogators present who can testify about what was said. This procedure ensures accuracy and obviates claims of improper pressure or undue influence.

Fourth, advance your timetable for trial preparation, so that tasks you would ordinarily handle during a trial are completed well beforehand. Assemble memoranda of law anticipating questions that may arise during trial. Draft alternative sets of proposed jury instructions, paying close attention to changing nuances that flow from your alternative theories of defense. Be sure to comb the judicial opinions on the usual legal propositions for language more favorable to defendants than the standard instruction offered by the prosecutor. Remember that the defendant is entitled to instructions on any theory of defense for which there is evidentiary foundation.

Reproduce all materials, exhibits, and charts that you intend to distribute to the jury and court. Draw up and refine lists of questions for each witness. Repeat your review of discovery materials and analyze anew your reactions and responses.

The defendant's case is not likely to fly without the aid of an expert. The expert—an accountant, for example—must satisfy three criteria. First, he must be an active planner in the defense strategy. Second, he must help prepare the cross-examination of the prosecutor's expert. Third, he—or another expert—must totally support the defendant's contentions, particularly in the opinions he testifies to in court.

Obviously, the accountant who testifies will not be the one regularly employed by the client. He has given statements to the prosecution, and would face devastating cross-examination. Nor should the witness be the accountant hired to develop the case and whose work product falls within the attorney-client privilege. That accountant has learned a great deal about the case's strong points—and also its weak ones. Under cross-examination, he may be compelled to disgorge secrets revealing that the client's case is a little short of perfect.

In gathering opinion evidence, be prepared to retain an accountant whose personality and qualifications may differ greatly from those of the experts upon whom the client and you have relied up to then. An expert accountant, no matter how vast his substantive knowledge, will be ineffective if he cannot relate that knowlebge—and himself personally—to the jury.

Accountants as a group are not noted for their expressive articulation, but those who have had both professional and teaching experience generally make the best expert witnesses. That background combines technical experience with the ability to explain and simplify difficult concepts and jargon. So, go to the universities. Find a professor noted for his ability to communicate to students. The ability to clarify the complex will work equally effectively in the courtroom. At the same time, the professional title will enhance the expert's credibility.

Ordinarily, the defendant may choose between trial by court or trial by jury. In federal criminal cases, a jury may be waived with the prosecutor's consent.

I believe that the defendant should never waive a jury; well, almost never. If the judge appears to be predisposed to the defense, then the defendant might as well stand trial by the court alone. Otherwise, remember that our forefathers had something in mind when they provided for juries in criminal cases.

The task of picking a jury differs significantly in state and federal courts. The personal rapport that a lawyer tries to establish with prospective jurors during voir dire—sacred in many state courts—is almost impossible to obtain in most federal courts, where a judge asks the questions. Still, federal judges should ask prospective jurors questions about specific areas, and the information obtained may give cause for challenge.

In tax cases, the government inevitably asks the court to inquire about the prospective jurors' experience in audits of their own returns and similar matters. The defendant may request questions about prospective jurors' knowledge of bookkeeping, accounting, and the preparation of tax returns.

In a case that turned on the testimony of a hostile certified public accountant who had formerly prepared the defendant's tax returns, inquiry by the court disclosed that four prospective jurors were bookkeepers. The defense did not challenge them, reasoning that persons who are supervised generally do not like their supervisors. Neither, for some reason, did the government challenge. As might be expected, in coming to a not-guilty verdict each bookkeeper undoubtedly contributed a nail to the coffin of the prosecution's case.

The opening statement can be a trap for defense counsel. In courts that permit you to reserve the opening statement until the prosecution completes its case, do so. An opening statement by the defense before the government adduces any proof is, in effect, a contradiction to the presumption of innocence; presumably the defendant is not obligated to prove—or say—anything.

In courts that compel the defendant's lawyer to follow the prosecutor's opening statement, be aware of the danger posed by the hundreds of facts in this type of case. Why is this a problem? Because every fact you recite in the opening statement can be used as a test of the defendant's credibility. If you do not prove each statement you offer, you will be in trouble. Here is how the prosecutor's closing statement will sound.

In his opening statement, Mr. Smithers represented to you that his client was in Buffalo on the key date, November 19th. That is what he said [prosecutor reads from transcript]. Now, Mr. Smithers is an honorable person. I'm sure he truly believed that his client was in Buffalo on that date. But, members of the jury, we have been sitting here for three months, and we have not heard a single word about where the defendant was on November 19th—not one word. Why is that? The answer is that someone must have lied to Mr. Smithers. Who do you think would lie to him about something so critical?

You can guess the jurors' answer to that question.

Some litigators are fond of recounting how they got their clients acquitted on the basis of their detailed opening statements. Since pretrial discovery is so limited in criminal cases, I think a detailed opening statement usually is unwise. There are only three, rather rare situations in which I use a full opening statement.

First, in a case that is being retried. Whether the new trial is prompted by a mistrial, a hung jury, or a reversal, the lawyer has a record of sworn testimony. The summation in the first trial can serve as a basis for the opening statement.

Second, there is the unusual situation in which critical adverse facts are indisputable. If the only issue left is whether the defendant acted willfully (or had the requisite mens rea), the defense may want to concede some of the factual issues. The emotional impact of the harmful facts is diffused. Instead of listening to time-consuming testimony about the facts, the jury's attention is directed to the issue of willfulness.

The third situation deals with a denunciation of evidence to be offered by the prosecution. Thus, if it is clear that the prosecution will call the complainant-informer and if the facts fit the image, an elaborate and detailed discussion of the informant's uncontradictably bad conduct and scurrilous character may well be in order.

But absent these exceptions, it is better to explain to the jury that the defendant need not prove anything. Say that the defendant's plea of not guilty is a denial of the charges, that the jurors should keep an open mind until the case is concluded, and that in so doing they will be enforcing the law of this Republic. Say this in different ways for five minutes and then sit down.

Of course, everyone likes to enforce the law, and it may be news to jurors that law enforcement, in an appropriate setting, means favoring the defendant instead of the prosecution. So remind the jury at this point and later that when, based on the evidence and the court's instructions, they vote for the defendant, they are rightly enforcing the law.

White collar defense tactics during the course of the prosecution's case are not much different from those in any criminal trial. In addition to stipulating away part of the government's case in an opening statement, concessions may also be stated for the record when a prosecution witness takes the stand. A prosecutor who tries to prove facts already conceded may succeed only in boring the jury.

A celebrated former governor of Georgia reportedly told the state prison association: "There will never be genuine prison reform in Georgia until we have a better class of prisoners." His remark brings to mind a special cross-examination opportunity unique to white collar cases. Often, the informer government-witness who has received immunity qualifies as one of the "better class:" Depending on his character (which you must assess accurately), the informer may be embarrassed to be in the position of having to tell all. Through a careful and frequently time-consuming cross-examination, defense counsel may be able to exploit the witness's discomfort. An appeal to the informer's ego and his natural desire to please the people listening to him, coupled with the fact that he is all alone on cross, may well change the impact of his statements.

Several times I have been able to cajole the informer into saying that what he did and intended to do while engaging in the conduct now alleged to be illicit was actually law-abiding, honest, and decent—just as he is. Depending on the facts, this testimony can dissolve the prosecution's prima facie case. At a minimum, such kind words will somehow, in measure large or small, tend to favor the defendant.

During a case with complicated facts, it does not pay to be too polite in registering objections. The defense lawyer never knows for certain when a properly-asserted objection will preclude the prosecution from proving some essential part of its case. You should meet every doubtful evidentiary proffer with whatever technical objections are available, particularly if the prosecutor seems poorly prepared or ignorant of the fine points of the rules of evidence.

In the midst of being so "objectionable," you must not forget to preserve your record for appeal by pressing for a decisive ruling from the bench. I have discovered, fortunately only rarely, that the appellate lawyer's view of your record is invariably rich with afterthoughts. Well do I remember a particular judge, now long gone, who would repeatedly say to each side, "Now I will hear you," then listen at length and say, "Proceed," without ever making the actual ruling. The objection without a ruling presents the appellate court with a presumption that the failure to press for a ruling was a withdrawal of the objection.

Equally important to appellate review are your decisive motions to strike items of evidence and to make offers of proof. Without these, the appellate court will be hard put to find an error in admitting evidence or refusing to accept it.

Also, do not worry about the effect of your frequent objections and bench conferences on the jury. In civil trials, objections can be overdone. But in white collar defense, proper objections and correct rulings are the beginning of a good offense. Which reminds me of one particular defense.

A few years ago, after days of trial, a co-defendant called me aside during a recess and confidentially inquired, "Boris, who is this guy Wagmore?" I said, "Wagmore? What do you mean?" He said, "He is all over this case. Every time you say something is the law to this judge, the prosecutor gets up and says that Wagmore said exactly the opposite. So I am beginning to notice that this judge wonders who to believe, Kostelanetz or Wagmore, and every time he believes Wagmore." Displaying the kind of thinking that had got him where he was that day, the co-defendant added, "Anyone can see this Wagmore has a real 'in' with the judge."

Often the prosecution's expert witness will use charts, tables, summaries, or models that purport to represent and summarize certain evidence. These visual aids are usually blown up to seemingly life-size models. They develop their own personality, which often is prejudicial to the defense. You can counter this prosecution tactic on two fronts.

First, apply the computer principle of "garbage in, garbage out" to the evidence underlying the charts. Argue that the visual aids must accurately reflect only credible, reliable, and admissible evidence in every detail. Any omission or deviation should be used to disqualify the proffered evidence from the courtroom or, at least, in the minds of the jurors.

Second, remind the jury whenever possible that the visual aids are not evidence in and of themselves, but only a representation of what the prosecution contends is evidence. The snazziest flowchart or model can be flawed by the nagging of a persistent defense counsel, so that the prosecutor wishes he had never heard of demonstrative evidence.

I like to use charts that can be prepared on individual pages and distributed to each of the jurors. Everyone has seen jurors who sleep through explanations or large charts, particularly when they are presented one after the other by a sonorous declaimer. When the same charts are distributed individually to jurors, peer pressure requires them to look at the papers in their hands, turn them over, and follow the expert when he says, "Please look at column 3, line 12" Similarly, you should make copies for each juror of relatively complicated exhibits (such as work papers) that each juror can follow as the witness talks.

Finally, the prosecution's case may present defense counsel with a chance to develop the defendant's contentions from witnesses whose credibility the prosecution has inferentially vouched for. By structuring the defense on cross-examination, you may, by way of maximum result, be able to move for judgment, at least on some counts, before presenting the defendant's case or, even better, to rest his case.

The most desirable defense is that the defendant did not know about the facts claimed to form the charge against him. An alibi defense, though rare in white collar cases, also is possible.

In an antitrust case celebrated in the late 1950s as the electrical industry conspiracy, we were able to demonstrate that the executive vice-president of one of the country's great companies was innocent because he could not possibly have received pertinent knowledge of the conspiracy at the time and place stated, much less have had the opportunity to act on it. When the records of my client's company showed exactly where he and the other company employees (his accusers) were at the time and place charged in the indictment, it was as if the alleged illicit meeting had never happened. The prosecutor declined to proceed with the suit.

Showing a lack of knowledge may involve placing the blame for knowledge and responsibility on others. Or it may involve a showing of plain stupidity, which reminds me of a trial held in Arizona before a jury of farmers. The defendant was an emigre from New York. On direct examination the defendant's lawyer said to his client, "It says in this here indictment that in 1957 you knew the adjusted gross." The defendant replied, "In 1957, Justin Gross I didn't know. I knew Morris Gross." The Arizona jury acquitted this New Yorker.

The defenses related to willfulness vary, depending on the facts. I will only highlight those that crop up most often:

- The questioned conduct that allegedly violated a statute requiring specific intent was motivated by totally lawful or minimally defensible acts. For example, what appeared to be falsification of records or concealment of income may not be connected with the offense charged, but rather motivated solely by an unpleasant relationship with an ex-spouse.
- The defendant's reliance, under proper circumstances, on competent but incorrect advice from experts, sought and received in good faith, is a complete defense.
- Zealous prosecutors may characterize as a criminal sham a business transaction that can be shown to be a lawful scheme of tax avoidance. The defense lawyer should distinguish between the lawful objective of the business deals and the alleged unlawful methods.
- Restitution, either before or after the indictment, is generally no defense. Given special circumstances, however, some courts permit evidence of restitution to show a lack of intent. Certainly courts hearing criminal tax evasion cases have received this kind of evidence.
- The conduct of a defendant when the allegedly fraudulent papers were officially filed with authorities can negate the charge of willfulness. If a problem is openly stated and apparent from supporting documents, no jury is going to believe that the document was willfully falsified. For example, in *Lucien T. Wilcox*, a holding of the Board of Tax Appeals (predecessor of the tax court almost half a century ago), taxpayer Wilcox found himself charged with civil fraud. On March 15, 1933, the date returns were due in the old days,

Wilcox appeared at the office of the collector, picked up a blank income tax return, wrote his name and address on it, and attached to it a check for $10 and a letter. The letter stated in substance that Wilcox was attaching a check for $10 as evidence that he was not trying to evade payments. It recited that he was about to go to Nevada to seek a divorce and, if successful, he would make an amended return. Wilcox added, "Otherwise I will continue to prefer federal to domestic incarceration." Said the Board of Tax Appeals, no fraud. He had a real problem and he revealed it to the collector.

In the same spirit, a defendant's conduct attributable to negligence, even gross negligence, should not be considered equal to the evil conduct that criminal statutes requiring mens rea prescribe. Negligence and fraud are mutually exclusive.

Still another defense is mental illness or incompetence. The difficulty is that ordinarily the defendant is an active and successful doctor, lawyer, stockbroker, or executive who does not fit the image of the mentally ill or portray any lack of competence. Given proper facts, however, this defense can raise viable issues negating criminal responsibility.

Should the defendant testify? Every defense lawyer has a theory about the value of the defendant's testimony. It is very easy for a lawyer to say, "I will let them put in their case, then I'll put my client on the stand. If the jury doesn't believe him, it is his fault not mine."

I believe that generally a white collar defendant should not testify. His activity covers years and years. He has written letters. He has done things he cannot possibly remember and, since his testimony is so critical, it must be letter perfect. If it is not, he simply will not be believed.

The defendant's testimony may be further discredited by the manner in which the court instructs the jury about how to test the credibility of witnesses. After the judge describes bias and interest as disqualifying and tarnishing factors, a lawyer may feel ashamed that he has called his client to the stand.

Usually the lawyer should prepare his case on the assumption that his client will not testify. Then he should prepare alternative theories in case the client does testify, and leave any final decision to be made during the course of the trial.

Naturally, these observations about the hazards of the defendant's testifying do not apply to street crimes, which generally are single occurrences. But white collar defendants should take them seriously. I prosecuted white collar crimes for nine years and never lost a case—not because of my brilliance, but because the defendants insisted on removing any reasonable doubt about their guilt by testifying.

The closing argument is the most critical and potentially valuable part of white collar defense. The jury must be told again and again that they will be fulfilling their function in upholding and enforcing the law if, considering the evidence and the presumptions about which they were charged, they acquit the defendant. The jury should be told in every way possible that no one can be convicted on the basis of suspicion, bias, guesswork, or attractive charts.

Throughout the trial, the closing argument should be taking shape in your mind and on paper. Jot down telling points as they occur to you. Project an image of the defendant as you would like the jury to see him. Was he foolish, greedy, pompous—but not a criminal? Did he simply slip up? Does your client deserve to go through the rest of his life known as Dr. Grandfellow or as Grandfellow the felon? The prosecutor has his own version of the defendant. Yours must be more compelling and believable. Particularly if you have access to current minutes and you are able to point to page numbers from the record for your assertions of fact, you can aid your own credibility and be in full control of your case.

In a tax prosecution, if you can convince the jury that the case really belongs in the tax court where tax questions and deficiencies are resolved by experts, then you have won a great point. Similarly, you can argue that a business dispute can be better resolved in civil court where, after all, only money is at stake. Be sure to point out to the jury that a criminal court cannot grant the prosecution a nickel in a criminal trial. Looking ahead, the chances of acquittal on concededly inexact statistics are about one in three, a percentage much more favorable to the defense than the percentage for run-of-the-mill criminal charges.

Likewise, punishment for those found guilty is not necessarily harsh, except when a prosecutor feels compelled to seek vindication of the public's demand that the rascal be given his due.

Whatever the outcome, trials for white collar offenses will stay in the lawyer's memory with startling detail as rewarding challenges that call for optimal professional effort and skill.

Defending a Drunk Driver

by Nancy Hollander

It's 2:15 A.M. when the phone rings, jarring you awake. You listen to an old friend and long-time client stammer that he has been stopped by a cop for careless driving and—more ominously—for driving while intoxicated. He wants to know whether he should submit to a blood-alcohol test. Standing just outside his phone booth is a policeman, tapping his foot and telling your client that he has about two minutes to make this decision.

There is no time to research the law, and you have never handled a criminal case. What do you do?

The safest course would be to give him the name of a criminal defense lawyer and go back to sleep. DWI's are serious business. No longer can you trot over to the courthouse and wing it, as you might with a simple traffic offense.

County jails are filled to capacity with DWI offenders. Your respectable business client could be on his way to thirty days in jail and the loss of his driver's license. If he has previously been convicted of DWI, he may face a year in jail and a substantial fine. Should you find yourself in this situation and decide to represent your friend, here are a few things you should keep in mind.

Return to the initial dilemma—should he take a blood-alcohol test and if so, which one? The answer is not easy. In most jurisdictions, anyone whose blood-alcohol level registers 10 percent or above is presumed to be driving while intoxicated. A tenth of a percent is one thousandth of a part alcohol. This percentage represents the "impairment standard" in most jurisdictions, although some set the standard as low as .05 percent. The impairment standard means that the state presumes that one's

The author is a partner in Freedman, Boyd & Daniels, P.A., of Albuquerque, New Mexico.

judgment and ability to drive a car safely is impaired when one part in a thousand of one's blood is alcohol.

There are two major considerations that influence the rate of absorption of alcohol and the resulting concentration of alcohol in the blood. The first is the presence of food in the stomach, and the second is the concentration of the alcoholic beverage consumed. For these reasons, it is impossible to tell your client with any reasonable certainty what the test will show. If your client drank only two or three beers during the hour before his arrest (and a like amount in the hours before that), a chemical test will register considerably below any definition of driving while intoxicated and he should take the test. If, however, he drank much more than that, he might consider refusing any test. Refusal may cost him his license for a year, but it may also destroy the only solid evidence against him on the criminal charge.

If your client was involved in an accident and anyone was injured, has died, or is in danger of dying, he may face a felony charge of vehicular manslaughter. A homicide resulting from a vehicle accident may be either a felony or a misdemeanor. The distinction often turns on whether the defendant was driving while intoxicated. If he refuses the test, your client will lose the only evidence that he was *not* intoxicated. On the other hand, losing his license for a year is preferable to creating evidence that he was driving while intoxicated. The choice is difficult.

Whether your client has the choice of a direct blood test or a breath test depends on the jurisdiction. The policeman may not be required to offer this choice. The policeman may also not be required to tell him of his right to an additional test at his own expense.

In most cases, an additional test only adds incriminating evidence. A direct blood test will probably register 10 percent higher than a breath test. The only reason to take a second test is to cast doubt on the first test. If your client registered .10 percent on the breath test, a blood test of .11 percent will not help your case.

Both breath and blood tests are blood-alcohol tests. Through a mathematical formula, one can compute the percentage of alcohol in the bloodstream after determining the percentage of alcohol in a sample of alveolar breath. If your client has taken and flunked a field sobriety test (which is police lingo that actually means a test for drunkenness at the place of arrest), smells of alcohol, was weaving between lanes, was driving too slowly, was in an accident, or failed to turn his headlights on at night, the state may have sufficient evidence regardless of the test results. If so, your client should take the test to save his license—at least for a while.

Your next concern is to secure your client's release from jail, if necessary. The jurisdiction might compel him to remain in jail until he is sober (usually about four hours). Bond on a DWI should be relatively low, but a bondsman must be found or someone must bring cash to the jail.

The booking desk at the jail will tell you the amount of the bond. These are usually "station house bonds" that are the same for everyone, barring unusual circumstances. The booking-desk policemen will also tell you whether they accept checks for bond. Most do not, but they may accept checks drawn on a lawyer's trust account.

Once your client is out of jail, sober, and has had a good night's rest, discuss the incident with him. Avoid talking with him in jail, if possible. A jail experience, no matter how brief, makes everybody a little crazy. Give him a day or two to return to normal. There is a second reason to delay this discussion. The police reports should be obtained before the interview. These will help in establishing the legal issues.

Your client must tell you any prior criminal record, including DWI convictions and other traffic offenses, as well as unrelated felonies and misdemeanors. The prosecution may use these offenses if your client testifies, or they may later influence sentencing. Moreover, in most jurisdictions, those convicted of a first DWI may attend a DWI school. You must learn if your client has ever attended the school. Someone charged with a second or third DWI may be eligible to attend school if he has never done so.

Loss of driving privileges for a year usually accompanies a DWI conviction. Completion of the DWI school, in most jurisdictions, has the advantage of saving your client's driver's license, unless he refused to take a blood-alcohol test and subjected himself to the penalties of the implied consent laws. If so, he will lose his license for a year even if he is ultimately acquitted of the DWI.

Ask to see your client's driver's license. The license itself should show on its face whether it is a limited or special license. It may also show, by its color or other markings, any prior DWI. Ask your client to describe his car. Are there any peculiarities about the car that would cause it to weave or be otherwise difficult to control, such as an alignment problem, or faulty brakes? If this is the case, have the car repaired and save the receipt as evidence.

Decide whether your client made any admissions to the police. Ask him to recount both his and the policeman's exact words. In most cases, the policeman asked him if he had anything to drink and if so, how much. Since the police rarely include this information in their reports, learning what your client told the policeman who arrested him is extremely important. Find out whether the policeman gave your client any *Miranda* warnings before the policeman asked these questions.

The process is usually this: The policeman stops someone, demands to see his license, smells alcohol on his breath, and asks, "Have you had anything to drink?" You would be surprised at the number of people who will answer, "I only had two beers." They mistakenly believe that this is exculpatory. Be sure your client understands that these words constitute an inculpatory admission. You must know exactly what he has said.

In most cases, the police will have asked your client to perform field sobriety tests. These tests usually include a request that your client walk heel to toe for ten spaces, that he attempt to pick up some coins from the ground or, with his eyes closed, his head tilted back, and his arms outstretched, touch each index finger to his nose. He might also have been asked to count backwards or to recite the alphabet. The details of the tests administered, as well as the policeman's evaluation of your client's performance, should be in the police report. But the report will not give the location at which the field tests were performed, whether the terrain was rough, smooth, hilly, or flat, or what kind of shoes your client was wearing. Any of these facts may have had a bearing on his performance.

Ask your client if he has any physical problems that might have influenced his performance. Ask if he was taking any prescription drugs. In some jurisdictions, the police videotape the field sobriety tests. If so, you should examine the videotape and evaluate whether your client failed the test.

The police report may also state that your client had a strong odor of alcohol on his breath. Find out how long before being stopped he had taken his last drink. A drink taken too recently to have entered the bloodstream, and thus too recently to cause impairment, could still cause a strong odor. The odor of alcohol on your client's breath, under these circumstances, would be irrelevant.

Ask your client how long it was from the time he was stopped until he took the blood-alcohol test. The policeman should wait at least 15 or 20 minutes before administering the test. You can determine this by comparing the time on the blood-test result card with the time of the initial stop.

Your client's clothing and what he had been doing just before being stopped are important. If it appeared to the policeman that your client had been sleeping in his clothes, this appearance will bolster the evidence that he had been drinking for a long time. Perhaps your client, like Clarence Darrow, always sleeps in his clothes. Find out. In a close case, this kind of evidence can be crucial in convincing a judge or jury that the prosecutor has no circumstantial evidence that your client had been drinking.

Find out if your client has a drinking problem and whether he has ever been in an alcohol treatment program. You must know if he would be willing to undergo such treatment. If so, the treatment program should begin immediately. If he ultimately appears before the judge for sentencing he can demonstrate his sincere interest in rehabilitation. Many alcohol treatment programs are available. The probation office is a good source of information about these programs. So is Alcoholics Anonymous or any hospital or mental health clinic.

Ask your client if he is employed and whether he has any dependents. Working people are less likely to go to jail than those not working. Even if the judge sentences him to jail, he might be eligible for a work-release program.

Learn everything you can about the type of blood-alcohol test, and if he was given a choice of tests or requested a second test. Blood-alcohol levels are tested by a variety of machines into which the suspect blows air, or by the drawing and analyzing of an actual blood sample. Find out when and where he took the test, and, if it was a breath test, what kind of machine the police used. If he did not take a test, find out the reason.

Determine whether any witnesses exist. If any passengers were in the car, interview each and ask how long he was with your client, what (if anything) he saw your client drink, and how he was acting. Learn how much each witness drank.

If your client was in an accident, ask him if the policeman actually saw him driving or if the police have any proof that he was the driver of the car. After an accident, if the passengers are outside the vehicle, the policeman's first question when he approaches will be, "Who was driving?" Find out what your client and the witnesses said.

Finally, ask your client if the policeman who arrested him was in uniform and in a marked police car. Many jurisdictions require that traffic stops be made only by uniformed policemen in marked cars.

Next, review the court file. It will probably contain the complaint and copies of the tickets your client received. Examine the tickets to find out what, if anything, your client is charged with in addition to DWI. Check the date and time of the arrest and the make of the automobile described. Then determine whether these tickets apply to your client. The tickets may also contain information that is inconsistent with a policeman's later version of what happened. That information may lead to fruitful material for cross-examination.

For example, if the ticket describes the car as a green Buick and your client was driving a blue Pontiac, it shows that the policeman does not pay attention to detail. Perhaps his description of your client's conduct is equally sloppy. Depending on your jurisdiction, the file may contain the result of any blood-alcohol test. Examine the report to determine whether it appears valid on its face. Check the date, the time, the date the equipment was last calibrated, and the name of the technician.

The court file should also contain a print-out from the motor vehicle department that shows your client's complete driving history. If not, you may have to request this information from the motor vehicle department, the district attorney's office, or the arresting agency. A long history of moving violations, even if unrelated to DWI, may affect the amenability of the prosecution to compromise.

Obtain all police reports, including any accident reports from either the district attorney's office or from the arresting agency, depending on your jurisdiction. A copy of your entry of appearance or a signed authorization may be needed to secure the information from the arresting agency.

Perhaps the most important part of your pretrial discovery will be a careful review of the police reports. Look for the following information:

1. Any statements of admissions of your client. Determine when, if at all, the policeman gave *Miranda* warnings to your client. The report may include a box that states, "The driver admitted consuming intoxicating liquor. Yes or No." This may be the only clue that your client made a statement.

2. The result of the blood-alcohol test. If it is high or the police report shows your client to have been greatly impaired, you can assert that no admission was voluntary.

3. Indicia of driving behavior inconsistent with impairment. For example, if the officer followed your client for some distance and found that he was speeding, but maintaining a proper lane, this may constitute evidence that he was *not* impaired. Any other indications of rational, sober thinking, such as cooperating with the officer, speaking coherently, or making decisions about what should be done with his car can help the defense.

4. Make sure your client was actually driving. If he was passed out at the wheel on the side of the road with the engine off, he may not be within a statute making it illegal for a person to drive a vehicle under the influence of intoxicating liquor or drugs. Some statutes, however, include the phrase "to drive or *be in physical control* of any vehicle" within the definition of a punishable DWI offense. That language will probably include anyone in the driver's seat.

5. Whether probable cause justified stopping your client. If the policeman did not give him a ticket for anything other than DWI, you should question why he stopped your client in the first place. If the policeman lacked probable cause, the stop was illegal and any subsequent evidence, including the results of a blood-alcohol test, should be suppressed.

6. Consider any other fruitful suppression issues. For example, if the police gave your client a blood-alcohol test, check your jurisdiction to determine if the test must be preserved for independent analysis. Some jurisdictions require the preservation of direct blood tests but not the breath tests. Other jurisdictions do not require any preservation. Still others insist that the results of all tests be preserved. Some breath-test machines are equipped with a device that will preserve the sample of alcohol for future independent testing.

7. Finally, call the policeman to determine what he remembers without his having reviewed his police report. The best time is 15 minutes before his shift begins or 15 minutes after his shift ends. Most policemen are willing to discuss the case if enough background is provided to help remember your client. Of course, your investiga-

tor should actually interview the policeman, not you, because you yourself cannot testify to impeach the policeman if he testifies differently at trial.

The next task is to prepare pretrial motions and subpoena witnesses for the motion hearing. If you are preparing a DWI case for the first time, talk to experienced lawyers for advice. The motions you should consider in any DWI case include:

1. A motion to suppress evidence seized as the result of an arrest made without probable cause.
2. The policeman must have probable cause to stop the car, although this may be unrelated to the DWI. The problem arises when there is no justification for the stop. If your client it not charged with anything other than DWI, or charged with something spurious, such as driving 57 miles an hour in a 55 mile-per-hour zone, you should compel the state to prove the legality of the stop.

Because an arrest is a Fourth Amendment seizure, the court must suppress the fruits of any search or seizure that results from stopping a vehicle without probable cause, barring some independent intervening probable cause.

3. A motion to suppress statements on the ground that the police took them without *Miranda* warnings. Establish that your client was in custody. Ask the policeman to provide the background: Why did he stop your client? When did he first suspect the client was driving while intoxicated? Why? Once you have established that something about the defendant's driving or the smell of alcohol on his breath alerted the policeman to the possibility of a DWI, you ask: Now, had my client said to you that he no longer wished to remain parked next to your car and that he was ready to leave, you would not have let him go, would you?

If the policeman says: "Of course I would have let him drive away," he is lying. If he replies that he would not have let your client leave, your client was in custody and the police should have given him *Miranda* warnings.

The argument that your client was entitled to the *Miranda* warnings may be double-edged. If the policeman admits that your client was not free to leave when he made the statements, or your client testifies that he did not believe he was free to leave, you argue that he was in custody and should not have been asked any questions before the *Miranda* warnings. If, on the other hand, the policeman says that your client was free to leave, you argue that he was not under arrest and therefore should not have been required to take a blood-alcohol test. Consult the local law to determine how the courts in your jurisdiction have viewed similar facts.

4. A motion to suppress statements on the ground that they were in-

voluntary because the defendant was too drunk to make a voluntary statement.

The question of the voluntariness of the statement is distinct from the question of a statement given in violation of *Miranda v. Arizona*. A statement may be involuntary even if the policeman told the defendant his rights under the *Miranda* case. You argue that your client was so drunk, he could not possibly have understood his rights or voluntarily waived them. A statement suppressed because it is involuntary cannot be used even if the defendant testifies, but a statement made after violation of the *Miranda* case can be used for impeachment.

The problem with this motion is obvious—you are admitting your client's intoxication. It is only to be used if your client's statements were the only proof of his driving, that is to say, if the policeman arrives at the accident and asks, ''Who was driving?'' and your client mumbles, ''I guess I was.'' Later, when sober, he remembers that he was too drunk to drive and someone else was driving. The driver left after the accident and before the police arrived.

5. A motion to suppress the results of the blood-alcohol test on the ground that the police did not preserve the sample for independent analysis, or that the police did not inform your client of his right to a second test (if required in your jurisdiction). The success of this motion will require some knowledge of the testing apparatus and a thorough research of the case law in your jurisdiction.

6. A motion to dismiss the case because of failure to provide a lawyer at a critical stage.

Some jurisdictions have held recently that if a defendant requests a lawyer before deciding whether to take a blood-alcohol test, that is a critical stage of the prosecution entitling him to a lawyer. Evidence that might be exculpatory, such as the results of an independent blood test, will be lost forever if the defendant does not receive the advice he seeks. Your client must have specifically requested a lawyer before agreeing or refusing to take a blood-alcohol test.

7. A motion to dismiss on the ground that the statute is vague. Many states have recently passed legislation making DWI a strict liability crime.

This legislation takes the form of a statute making it illegal per se to drive with a blood alcohol level of .10 percent or above. Impairment is no longer an issue. There have been some challenges to these statutes on the ground that they offend due process because they do not provide the required notice. How is one to know when he has reached the magic level? It is too soon to know what direction this litigation will take. Try it if appropriate.

You have completed your motion hearing and lost, or at least, you have not obtained a dismissal or a good plea—now you are going to trial.

If a trial is inevitable, consult a criminal defense lawyer or treatises that explain the examination of policemen, chemists, and witnesses in DWI cases. Depending on your jurisdiction, your client may be entitled to a jury (in places, jury trial only occurs for a second or subsequent DWI charge). If you are entitled to a jury, use it. Judges are practically immune to DWI defenses, but you might raise a doubt before a jury.

Let's assume a marginal blood alcohol result—.10 percent or .11 percent, a presentable client, and a field sobriety test open to interpretation. (Your client stood on one foot until the count of eight, picked up two of the three coins before falling, and only missed one letter in the alphabet.) If the issue is impairment, you have a triable case. If your client is charged under a per se statute, all you have to work with is the chemistry.

Read everything you can get your hands on about the blood-alcohol test administered to your client. Call the manufacturer of the breath test machine and ask him to send you the descriptive brochures about the machines. If the manufacturer's brochures and your chemist contend that the machine is accurate only within a certain range of the percentage it shows, argue that the state cannot prove beyond a reasonable doubt that your client was over the presumptive level.

Next, check the chain of custody. Did the policeman note the name of the technician on his report? If not, can the technician remember this particular test? Can the test be tied sufficiently to your client?

Pick apart the field sobriety test. The police report could say, "Subject failed the test." Or the report might detail the test results: "Subject was only able to pick up two coins and walk eight steps before stumbling." Turn it around.

Q: My client picked up two coins without any difficulty, did he not?

Q: My client walked eight spaces just like you told him to, did he not?

Q: When you say he flunked the test, you are really saying he didn't do everything perfectly, isn't that correct?

Q: In other words, he didn't make an A+?

Whether your client should testify will depend on the defense you choose, the state's evidence, and, of course, what your client has told you. As in every criminal case, your client can be your greatest asset or your worst liability. What he says and how he says it may make all the difference to a jury. Weigh the options with him, give him the benefit of your knowledge and judgment, but remember, it is his decision.

The case is tried and lost, or your client has admitted guilt. Now for sentencing.

If this is either your client's first DWI conviction or he has not attended a DWI school as a result of a previous conviction, he may avoid losing his license by attending a school. DWI school may be a one-day course or a course consisting of four to six one-hour sessions. Successful completion of the course (attending each session and passing a written test similar to a driving test) should result in dismissal of the charges and retention of his driver's license.

Although DWI school is a good option in a bad case, it should never preclude a thorough investigation and aggressive defense. Someday your client may be charged with another DWI. If you can obtain an acquittal, that is your duty. All too frequently, lawyers unfamiliar with the criminal process see nothing wrong with a quick plea to a first DWI because the consequences appear slight: six weeks of school and a month of probation.

That is shortsighted. The consequences of a first DWI cannot be overlooked. Your client may be charged with another DWI and face a mandatory jail sentence. If your client fails to attend the DWI school, he may be held in contempt, be back before the judge, and receive jail time or a substantial fine in addition to losing his license.

If your client has enrolled in an alcohol treatment program or is willing to do so now, the judge might consider sentencing him to that program or deferring sentencing while he attends the program. (In some instances, the judge might agree to defer the entire case pending successful treatment. Six months down the road your client may appear to the judge as a reformed alcoholic, rather than a crazy drunken driver.)

Your client should, of course, plead not guilty or nolo contendere if an accident occurred. Never plead guilty to an accident. If your client does not wish to go through a full trial to avoid collateral use of a guilty plea, consider submitting the case to the judge on stipulated testimony. This will avoid an admission in any future civil lawsuit.

If, despite your best efforts, your client is going to jail, you can still request that he be placed in a work-release program or that he serve his sentence on weekends.

Finally, assuming your client is working and carries liability insurance, you can help him obtain a permit to drive to and from work. That is a civil procedure and the district court clerk can explain the local rules.

As the outcry against drunken driving mounts in volume, so will the number of those arrested. The lawyer who accepts a DWI case must be familiar with the law, the procedure, and the policies of the local police and the courts. Remember that your client may indeed be blameless.

Prescription for Drug Cases

by Edward A. Mallett

Illicit drug use has been part of our culture for so long that it has become an institution. Movies and popular music constantly remind us that drugs are fun, everybody uses them, and the police rarely hear about it. For example, the movie "The Big Chill" showed use of pot, cocaine, methamphetamines, and Quaaludes to an extent punishable by life in the Texas Department of Corrections. That renders every family in America liable to drug prosecution.

When America's finest families receive that call from jail, they turn to you for counsel. The following suggestions are directed to civil lawyers, so they can help provide their clients the best possible defense for the child, relative, employee, friend, or neighbor. The best possible defense requires that the family's lawyer help with the defense.

The civil lawyer can help in the following ways:
1. Place the event into an emotionally acceptable perspective.
2. Hire the best criminal lawyer.
3. Negotiate the legal fees.
4. Obtain pretrial release.
5. Communicate the defense strategy to the client.

In addition, the civil lawyer can help the criminal lawyer get paid, help preserve the defendant's confidences, and confirm for the client that the disposition of the case—if not a dismissal or acquittal—is the best that could be accomplished. In short, all parties benefit if the civil lawyer keeps an active interest in the defense.

Your participation will include human relations as well as legal counselling. Your client's responses will have an emotional content absent from your ordinary commercial communications: you are dealing with a

---

The author is a partner in the firm of Mallett, Trichter & Brann in Houston.

mom and dad, and their attention will focus on what the drug arrest says about their family. That this could happen to their child often seems incredible. Some people can understand that their child might be a thief more easily than that junior and his fraternity brothers smoke pot and snort cocaine.

The "simple possession" arrest will rarely ruin a child's life. Overreaction from parents can be more damaging than the result of a routine case. Even those accused of distribution for profit (drug dealing) are increasingly treated as economic criminals, people who make a tax-free living without working very hard. Assure mom and dad that society needs to extract something less than the death penalty for junior's participation in a national pastime, then go visit junior.

The family's first concern is for the physical welfare of their child. They fear violence in the jail, or at the hands of the police. Someone must go to the jail. Immediately. Even in the middle of the night, and even though you may be advised by telephone that the accused is being "processed" or is involved with ill-defined "booking procedures" that may take hours. It is better if the visit is by a lawyer. Late-night jail visits should be in the job description of every new associate.

Tell the police making the arrest not to interview their suspect in the absence of counsel. Order the child to keep quiet, and reassure him that help is on the way. Report to the jailer any difficulties with incarceration, including medical problems or threats from other prisoners, and address him politely but with persistence. Visit any others arrested to verify that they have been granted right of access to counsel. You may run into other lawyers, and you can compare notes about the case.

This visit has some points you will not immediately realize. You may preserve any potential for joint defense strategy by reducing the probability the accused or a co-defendant will immediately roll over and confess. If he does that, he waives any objections to the legality of the search by providing a confession or other independent source of evidence. Your presence will also encourage the jailers to insure that the accused suffers no physical harm during confinement. Although you cannot be certain that the visiting area for lawyer and client is not bugged—probably not—you can learn about the seriousness of the case.

Ask the accused, "Tell me what the police will say about the amount of dope and how you were arrested." An informal, respectful conversation with the arresting policeman may yield valuable information and create a foundation for later efforts to reach a satisfactory disposition of the case. After all, in any serious case, the prosecution will review his recommended plea agreement with the policeman in charge.

On the other hand, do not disclose your theory of the case. The criminal lawyer can find his hands tied later by free discovery or concessions of fact made by well-intentioned civil counsel unfamiliar with the practice of policemen and prosecutors of keeping notes of all conversations.

1069

Tell your client that there will be an arraignment shortly after the arrest, no later than the next business day and often in the middle of the night. This arraignment is to ascertain that the accused understands his *Miranda* rights and has had a phone call. Bail may be set, but no plea will be taken. Days later, after there has been an opportunity to consult with a lawyer, a more formal arraignment will be held. Then the charges will be read and a plea taken.

What to Tell the Judge

Do not assert that personal relationships at the courthouse or in law enforcement will materially affect the outcome. Discourage the idea that money or influence will cause a quick, favorable result. Influence peddling is more useful to lawyers obsessed with collecting fees than committed to providing the best defense.

A credible civil lawyer, however, can persuade a judge to deviate from routine criteria for pretrial release. Judges know that the criminal defense lawyer is a hired gun. You may lend credibility to the case as a witness, formally or informally. For example, "Judge, this boy's father is my best client. Of course he'll come to court: the family will back him 100 percent." Partly out of professional courtesy, but more from the knowledge that people who have invested in good lawyers rarely run, your client's pocketbook may get a break.

If you can, determine whether the defendant's personal history includes any symptoms of a genuine disorder, possibly indicated by a history of arson, shoplifting, or truancy. If you discover that background, the child may have a serious problem. Drug use can exacerbate other problems like gasoline on a fire. The criminal lawyer knows when drug rehabilitation is indicated and which programs will have credibility with the courts, if needed at sentencing.

Do not seek to educate your client about the law in any significant detail during the hours shortly following the loved one's arrest. You will only add to the inevitable confusion. Every narcotics squad will have its own personality—for being tough on out-of-towners, or hard on sales cases, or willing to decline to prosecute in exchange for cooperation, and so on. The personality of the individual prosecutor and judge will vary with each case.

Even the time of year is important. Do not expect to get lenient treatment in a narcotics case just before election time, unless the judge is retiring. Do not debate whether marijuana or cocaine is a narcotic with cops or judges.

Nine times out of ten, a child defendant will say, "They never read me my rights." So what? It does not matter, unless junior confessed, in which case the officers will always report and offer to testify that their suspect was fully warned. In 14 years, I have never seen a drug case dismissed for a *Miranda* violation.

In short, drug-law enforcement is a looking-glass world. Values and expectations are often the reverse of the client's impressions. Just let the client know you are ready to help.

After these preliminary steps, direct mom and dad to a criminal lawyer. If the drug arrest occurs in a distant jurisdiction, there are several reliable resources for locating a good defense lawyer, including the National Association of Criminal Defense Lawyers (202-872-8688) and the National Organization for the Reform of Marijuana Laws (202-331-7363), both in Washington, D.C. There is Barry Tarlow's NATIONAL DIRECTORY OF CRIMINAL LAWYERS (2d ed. Darby 1983). Many states issue certificates of special competency and publish lists of specialists. For example, the State Bar of Texas maintains a board of legal specialization in Austin. Also, a criminal defense lawyer in your town can probably suggest how to find a good lawyer in another jurisdiction.

It may be difficult to locate the best lawyer, but it is easy to know who to avoid. In THE BEST DEFENSE (Random House 1982), Alan M. Dershowitz of Harvard Law School describes the best and worst criminal lawyers. The worst will include lawyers who:

- Associate themselves with the financial success of underworld clients (several lawyers are indicted each year).
- Call the attention of the press to a case for self promotion, with little regard for whether the client desires publicity or if publicity will improve the result.
- Are still prosecutors at heart: they prefer to represent informants and cooperating defendants, never seriously contest a case or challenge the prosecution or the police, and often hold a hidden ambition for a judicial appointment or other means to return to public employment after a short period as a private lawyer.
- Are the integrity lawyers, who place their reputation for developing the truth, for moderation, and for statesmanship over the possibility that a result in a particular case can be gained through artifice or intimidation, or simply by asserting the citizen's Fifth Amendment rights.
- Place causes before clients.
- Are overzealous or underzealous on behalf of their clients, particularly when dealing with the courts.
- Claim or imply that by bribery or other improper influence they can get to the judge, the prosecutor, or the witnesses.

Dershowitz holds that the best lawyer is only concerned with his client's interest. This lawyer's arsenal will be diverse. At a minimum, it will include credibility with his adversaries and the courts as a bargainer, competence as a trial lawyer, and the ability to preserve judicial error for appellate review.

A drug-law specialist can protect the client from exorbitant costs in obtaining pretrial release. Bail bondsmen consider themselves legitimate businessmen. Largely self-regulating, the potential for abuse is great. The bondsman guarantees that the full amount of bail will be promptly paid, if the accused absconds and the government makes a demand. For obtaining a release, the bondsman charges a negotiable, non-refundable fee of five to twenty-five percent of the bail set by the system— sometimes by a judge, but more often by a magistrate or clerk (representing a judge). The latter two will rubber-stamp the amount recommended by the prosecution or the police. Bondsmen want judges to set the highest affordable bail, hence they are heavy campaign contributors.

The criminal lawyer can request a bond reduction or junior's release on "personal recognizance," which is the accused's promise to appear. The lawyer knows from experience what reduction or modification can realistically be expected in any jurisdiction.

The federal system favors release on the least onerous conditions. Consequently, the lawyer can save the client hundreds, even thousands of dollars by modifying the original bond.

On the other hand, if the family is frustrated by delays in obtaining pretrial release or in what appears to be excessive cost, the well-informed civil lawyer can be constructive by counselling patience. Sadly, our pretrial release practices all too often suggest that a presumption of guilt attaches with any accusation.

To illustrate: Prosecutors in the Western District of Texas favor prosecution of large numbers of people in conspiracy indictments. Bail, impossible to afford, is set when arrest warrants issue. Any motion to modify must be in writing and filed with a magistrate. The government has three working days to respond. Then the magistrate holds a hearing. He then issues a written finding, generally adopting the government's position. The defendants can appeal to a district judge. The government will be permitted to answer the defense objections to the magistrate's findings. The district judge will not grant relief without a hearing.

When to Cooperate

Three things follow: First, virtually all defendants in criminal cases in the Western District of Texas serve a lengthy jail term as a consequence of being accused. Second, many lawyers are fired because defendants stay in jail for an unreasonable period. Third, many defendants agree to cooperate, because cutting a deal is the fastest way to escape jail.

A second illustration: In many jurisdictions, narcotics officers typically choose to execute arrest and search warrants on Friday afternoons. Everyone on the premises where contraband is found is usually arrested. After defendants have been through three to four hours of drug laboratory testing and booking procedures, bail is set by clerks based upon a recommendation from the police or a prosecutor. As a practical matter, no judge may be available to reconsider the initial bail until Monday, which is the busiest trial day.

Thus, unless money is no obstacle, a person arrested Friday for anything more than a low-grade routine offense must remain in jail until the following Monday evening. The civil lawyer can help the family accept those and other unfortunate obstacles.

Cooperation with police agencies is a delicate topic. The police often offer to speak to the prosecutor or judge, if the defendant will help them make cases by informing on other violators. Some lawyers refuse to represent defendants who become informants. Others rarely have any defense strategy other than full cooperation. Most consider cooperation simply one of many options.

The decision to cooperate has complex ethical and practical considerations. The United States Supreme Court has blessed the punishing of defendants for refusal to cooperate. *United States v. Roberts,* 445 U.S. 552 (1980). Dissenting, Justice Marshall reminds us that the American people have not unanimously and without reservation admired those who inform on others, as demonstrated by the common terms "stool pigeon," "snitch," "squealer," and "tattletale." Some judges reward informants with reduced sentences, but others do not.

Assure your client that the lawyer knows who can make an enforceable trade of leniency for cooperation. Generally, it is only safe to negotiate with the prosecutor. When the police make a deal at the station during the shock of arrest, they always get the better end of the bargain. Indeed, the prosecutor may not feel bound to honor an agreement made with the police.

The criminal defense lawyer will almost certainly charge a fixed fee. The amount of the fee will vary with your client's ability to pay, with the law and facts of the case, with the lawyer's assessment of the work likely to be required, and with other considerations. You can help the client avoid unreasonable demands by speaking directly with the lawyer, by obtaining more than one opinion, and by speaking with other criminal lawyers. You can hold the fee down by insisting that you want no referral fee—that you will be paid by the client or not at all.

Reach a clear understanding with the attorney-in-charge about your role in the case. Offer, without insisting on daily updates, to mediate information for the family. Your greatest service may occur in persuading the family to accept the result. If there is a dismissal, everything will be fine, except that your client may grouse that it was too expensive. If there is an acquittal, they will feel they got what they paid for. For a conviction followed by a stiff sentence, you will know what contribution each party made to the decision to go to trial. But if there is a plea bargain, which is the final disposition in more than 95 percent of all cases, you will be asked your opinion of the specialist's work.

When there is a strong resistance to accept the plea bargain recommended by the specialist, there are usually three reasons: one of the lawyers has exaggerated the prospect for a better result, the child or his family is not prepared to accept the inevitable, or the law or facts did not develop as hoped.

You may assure your clients that no one is more unhappy than the criminal defense lawyer when his client is dissatisfied. Respect the specialist's opinion. No one knows better than the experienced and expert lawyer that judges really do charge rent for the use of the courtroom. They measure the rent in extra years of confinement for those who put their cause to the jury and lose.

And when, the day before trial, the child finds a lawyer who will substitute into the case and, for a big fee, promises victory because he has never lost, check it out. The criminal defense lawyer who has never lost a case has certainly not tried many.

PART XII

Special Problems in Civil Litigation

Defending the Multi-Party Civil Conspiracy Case

by W. Donald McSweeney and Michael L. Brody

Why conspiracy codefendants should work together is simple: most of the time, they are more likely to mount an effective defense together than alone or working at cross-purposes. There are exceptions. Occasionally a conspiracy defendant may end-run a coordinated defense and succeed where others have failed, but that is rare. Usually all defendants will stand or fall together. At least three considerations common to most conspiracy suits favor cooperation.

First, if knowledge is power in litigation, then shared knowledge is power multiplied. Even a moderately complex civil conspiracy case involves an extensive cast of characters interacting for a long time in a variety of transactions. The result is at least a small mountain of correspondence, memorandums, computer runs, and invoices. By cooperating, conspiracy codefendants get to look at more documents sooner and to look with each other as friendly guides.

Second, codefendants can often make better use of nonparty witnesses, who may be friendly with some of them but hostile or indifferent to others.

Third, they may benefit from their collective memory and their broader view of the litigation.

Consider this case.

A discount electronics store sells a manufacturer's goods at 15 percent below the price charged by his competitors. The competitors complain to the manufacturer. So do retail customers, who dislike the discounter's high-pressure sales tactics and his incompetent and uncooperative service department. Ultimately, the manufacturer terminates the discounter's dealership. The discounter sues the manufacturer and com-

Mr. McSweeney and Mr. Brody are partners at Schiff Hardin & Waite in Chicago.

peting dealers, alleging that they have entered into a resale price maintenance agreement in violation of the Sherman Act.

How can these defendants help each other?

Working together, they can, in a short time, assemble a more complete record of pricing, sales, and promotions for all electronics brands in the plaintiff's market than any one of them could alone. Their joint recollection is likely to generate a more comprehensive account of the relevant sales meetings and promotional events than any single defendant could construct.

They can learn more from nonparty witnesses than any defendant could learn alone. For instance, another electronics manufacturer with useful information about the market will be hesitant to talk to the defendant-manufacturer but happy to cooperate with a defendant-dealer who carries his brand. Similarly, a defendant-dealer's former sales manager is more likely to talk to the company he left on good terms than to the manufacturer with whose line he now competes.

More important, though, the events leading up to the dealer's termination may look very different to the defendant-manufacturer than to the defendant-dealers. The manufacturer will see a conflict between the discounter's way of doing business and the manufacturer's nationwide strategy of seeking a premium price by maintaining the product line's high reputation for quality and courteous service. The local dealer will focus on the difficulties of maintaining a highly skilled sales force and service department despite the pressure the discounter has put on his profit margin. Putting these perspectives together makes a stronger defense than is possible from either perspective alone, because it provides a broader range of evidence that more persuasively explains why each defendant did what he did.

Now consider a second case.

A pension trustee is accused of masterminding a fraudulent scheme to siphon off pension-fund assets for his own benefit. The trustee is charged with investing in a series of shell corporations that transfer funds back to the trustee's own business. When a local newspaper exposes the scheme, the beneficiaries of the pension bring a class action against the trustee, his company, his cotrustees, and the plan's independent accountants, alleging violations of the Racketeer Influenced Corrupt Organizations Act.

This kind of case is usually brought as a class action or as an individual case by an unsophisticated plaintiff. Either way, the moving force is likely to be a lawyer. The plaintiff typically begins with the facts in the newspaper article that sparked the suit and then uses his own money to finance further investigation. Inevitably, the plaintiff relies partly on inference and conjecture to hold his case together. As discovery proceeds, he plays catch-up. He never assembles the comprehensive record that a coordinated defense team has from the start; yet he must examine the defense witnesses who have been prepared for their depositions on the basis of a comprehensive record and a unified theory of the case.

When the case comes to trial, a coordinated defense can offer the jury a theory that accounts for the complex relations between the various groups and subgroups of defendants: trustees, accountants, and the various corporations that are allegedly part of the scheme. The defendants may have a host of concerns that innocently explain their cooperation. But to prove the conspiracy, the plaintiff must argue that the diverse conduct, actors, and motives are part of a unified scheme with a single goal to loot the pension plan. The richer the description of events that cooperating codefendants offer the jury, the starker the contrast to the plaintiff's one-dimensional interpretation of the facts.

The most important benefit of this cooperation is a unified defense. This is important in every complex commercial case. The case is tried to an unsophisticated jury that may be bored and even confused. That jury will form its own understanding of what happened. It is dangerous for defendants to present a hodgepodge of fragmentary theories based on each defendant's parochial view of the events. Absent cooperation, the defendants speak with a babble of voices that gives a jury no alternative but to accept the only version of the case that makes sense to them—the plaintiffs'.

Sometimes the plaintiffs are in disharmony. This can happen, for example, when several opt-out cases follow a class action suit. Then the defendants can turn the tables on the plaintiffs by picking apart the plaintiffs' uncoordinated description of events. But once again, the defendants need to stick together to take advantage of the plaintiffs' disunity.

Finally, cooperation among codefendants forces the plaintiff to prove his case. Assuming equally solvent defendants, the plaintiff usually does not care who is caught in the conspiracy net, so long as somebody is. The plaintiff's fondest hope is that he will face an uncoordinated defense, with defendants blaming each other for an undisputed wrong. With the defendants proving the plaintiff's case, the issue no longer is whether someone will pay, but who and how much.

Given these advantages, cooperation among codefendants would seem inevitable. In fact, it is not. Achieving a unified defense creates challenges throughout litigation.

Sometimes the crush of events will force civil defendants to establish a working relationship quickly. A classic example is a civil case following the compressed proceedings in injunction hearings or criminal trials (or not at all).

When there is no emergency, defendants have a chance to find formal ways to ensure their cooperation. A good way to begin is to negotiate a sharing agreement.

A sharing agreement is any arrangement among codefendants allocating their responsibilities. Ideally, the agreement should be a formal written document, and ideally it should divide up all the principal responsibilities.

The most important purpose of the sharing agreement is to determine responsibility for an adverse judgment, including the responsibility of defendants who settle. If the defendants can agree on this at the outset, they have resolved the issue that is most likely to threaten their ability to work together. Cooperation does not come easily. It is particularly difficult when some defendants are more likely to be found liable than others.

The defendant who is peripheral to the conspiracy and whose risk of liability is comparatively small may be tempted to turn on the other defendants and go it alone. Take the pension case, for example. Suppose the outside auditor of the plan is named as a defendant for having failed to uncover an ongoing fraud allegedly masterminded by one of the trustees.

The auditor may want to defend himself by asserting that the fraud was so thorough that nothing could have uncovered it including the rigorous examination he says he conducted. The risk to this argument is that the jury may not believe the auditor did not know what was happening. By confirming there was a fraud, the auditor has created a problem he did not contemplate. Once the auditor defects, nothing will stop the other defendants from attacking the turncoat and arguing that the auditor knew everything there was to know. If the auditor failed to make the appropriate disclosures, he is just as much to blame as anyone else. But despite these risks, the centrifugal force pulling the peripheral defendant away from cooperation may be strong.

For the defendant at the center of the alleged conspiracy, the incentive to abandon the coordinated defense comes from a different quarter. In any multidefendant case, the plaintiff will try to settle with one defendant at a comparatively low figure. The point is to cause panic among the remaining defendants for fear they will be held responsible for more than their fair share of the liability. The defendant whose risk of liability is high—like the mastermind in the pension case—is tempted to get out cheaply. But there are risks here, too.

For one thing, the plaintiff and the defendant may disagree about what is a cheap settlement. Because negotiations have a way of leaking out, the injury to continued cooperation among the defendants can be substantial, as is the incentive for other defendants to leave the failed settler out on a limb by making deals of their own. Further, if contribution or indemnity actions are available—antitrust is a notable instance where they are not—a cheap settlement may ultimately be undone by a later suit holding the settling defendant liable to its ''coconspirators.'' Although such a settlement just postpones the inevitable, when the exposure is high, the temptation to settle and get out is strong.

1079

Deciding to allocate responsibility for an adverse judgment is not easy. Indeed, if one or more defendants decides from the outset that long-term cooperation is not in its best interest, agreement will be impossible.

Still, if the defendants share a genuine initial commitment to cooperation, some circumstances may ease such an arrangement. In particular, if contribution will be available down the road, failure to enter a sharing agreement may merely postpone a future battle over degree of responsibility. Moreover, since an early agreement strengthens the defense alliance, it also minimizes the defendants' view of their potential joint liability. They will find it earlier to allocate this sum if they think about the larger amount that would come from an adverse verdict following an uncoordinated defense. The odds of reaching agreement will also increase if the risk of exposure is similar for all the defendants or if there is an objective way to measure their risk (as in an antitrust price-fixing case where exposure is based on market share or dollar volume of sales).

Even if the defendants cannot agree on how to share liability, a formal agreement can still be valuable. The defendants may be able to allocate responsibility for many common expenses. The sharing agreement should specify the principal expenses covered, such as fees for jointly retained experts, rent for a central office, and the expenses of joint data processing.

The sticking point is apt to be how to figure each defendant's share. Large defendants will favor a per capita rule. Small defendants will want a rule weighted toward size. Everyone will take offense at a rule based on relative fault. Once again, the most promising approach is a neutral standard based on an objective determination of the parties' relative exposure such as market share.

Once the sharing agreement is negotiated, the second step is creating a coordinating committee. This committee defines joint defense tasks and policies, assigns responsibilities, and coordinates and oversees joint defense activities. Typically, the committee members represent the defendants with the greatest exposure, since they are most willing to commit the necessary resources. If the court has not already appointed a liaison for the defendants, the committee should do so. This lawyer can distribute communications from the court and circulate the defendants' shared work product. The coordinating committee should also establish any other committees needed to deal with common problems.

A typical example is a joint experts committee. While each defendant could present its own expert testimony—and many will have special needs for expert help—the expert testimony on joint issues should be provided by jointly retained and prepared witnesses. Otherwise the defendants risk providing the jury with conflicting testimony. Besides, too many experts may overwhelm the jury with an avalanche of mind-numbing discussions of downward-sloping demand curves and chi-square tests, leading the jurors to fall asleep or even suspect they are being bamboozled.

Finally, defendants should think about establishing a central office. It will help to have it located near the courthouse. Before trial, this office provides a central document and deposition depository, a centralized computer, an office for specially retained joint staff, and a workspace for out-of-town counsel.

Once this central office and the committees are in place, the key to using them effectively is to have regular, well-organized meetings. The defendants will need to identify and assign responsibility for researching legal issues, drafting motions, interviewing witnesses, and handling depositions. The coordinating committee must decide how to handle depositions of hostile witnesses without foreclosing anybody from asking questions. Computerizing the discovery record should be a joint project. As individual defendants settle out, their tasks will need to be reallocated. Finally, the results of all of this work need to be shared, reviewed, and criticized.

One typical result of these meetings is that each defendant becomes responsible for its own employees as witnesses. If former employees have left on good terms, the defendant employer is responsible for them as well. If there is hostility, other defendants will need to step in. Developing other third-party witnesses will depend on the abilities or circumstances of each defendant and its lawyers. Thus, the lawyers should recognize and use a client's special relationship with a third party, or an attorney's unusual sophistication in a particular area.

While the desire to create a united front is central in these efforts, inevitably one or more defendants cannot agree about something. The goal is unity, but not at the price of straightjacketing the nonconforming defendant. Small disputes can mushroom into charges of bad faith and recalcitrance, harming cooperation. Regular and candid communication is the only antidote.

In planning for trial, the principal tasks are allocating responsibilities for primary direct and cross-examination and sequencing the presentation of testimony and the order in which the codefendants participate.

Responsibility for the witnesses will largely parallel the assignments made during discovery, with adjustments made to accommodate last-minute settlements. A joint strategy should cover which witnesses to display prominently, which ones to sandwich in, and which to omit. These decisions, and decisions about the order of witnesses, must be based on agreement about how to present the most comprehensible and persuasive narrative of events and how to explain the overarching policy and economic issues.

The defendants must also decide when each attorney will participate. Should opening and closing statements be sequenced to reflect counsels' rhetorical skills or the significance of their clients? Should the attorney who opens first and closes last also be prominent during cross-examination of the plaintiffs principal expert? Instead, should an attorney with greater analytic skills be featured? Who should argue motions that concern all defendants, such as the unavoidable dispute about the admissibility of coconspirators' admissions? The answers depend on the lawyers' strengths and weaknesses. The subject is touchy, and the coordinating committee must take care to avoid a clash of egos.

During trial, as during discovery, the key to cooperation is communication. Lawyers should use the central office to eat lunch together, so they can discuss problems that came up during the morning session, finish plans for the afternoon, and assign tasks to be performed out of court. The group should meet at the end of the trial day, too. Besides being a site for these joint meetings, the central office should be the workspace for trial counsel and their staffs, where everyone has access to the computer and document depository and to each other.

A unified defense is not a guarantee of success, but failing to unify comes close to insuring failure. Given the odds, the effort is worth it.

Simple Lessons from a Complex Case

by Norman J. Wiener

Big, complex cases usually do not teach useful lawyering skills. The huge securities and antitrust suits that live for years in some unfortunate courts are just too unusual to teach much of general benefit. You may know the standards for multidistrict consolidation by heart, but will you ever use them again? You may be the world's greatest expert on the treatment of discovery "waves" in the *Manual for Complex Litigation.* So what? Young lawyers in big firms often avoid big cases. Their aversion shows great wisdom.

There are times, however, when even a big case reveals important truths. If this happens, pay attention. If a lesson fights its way through the tangle and clutter of multidistrict, multiyear litigation, it must be very hardy.

This article describes some of those hardy truths, from the perspective of a defense lawyer involved in one of the more unusual parts of one of the most complex proceedings ever: the "opt-out trial" in *In re Corrugated Container Antitrust Litigation,* 756 F. 2d 411 (5th Cir. 1985).

Corrugated, like many antitrust cases, began as a criminal proceeding. In 1975, a Texas grand jury started an investigation into the pricing practices of the corrugated box industry in the United States. Three years later, price-fixing indictments were returned against 14 manufacturers and 26 individuals. Some of the defendants pleaded nolo contendere and were fined. Those that went to trial were acquitted in April 1979.

Plaintiffs' antitrust lawyers can detect big money grand jury proceedings a thousand miles away. The *Corrugated* grand jury investigation was no exception. Even before indictments were handed out, civil suits

Norman J. Wiener is a partner in the Portland, Oregon, law firm of Miller, Nash, Wiener, Hager & Carlsen. He represented one of the defendants, Willamette Industries, Inc., in all stages of the Corrugated Container litigation.

sprouted nationwide. There were ultimately 55 treble-damage class action suits aimed at 37 corrugated box manufacturers. All were consolidated for pretrial proceedings and trial in the Southern District of Texas. All were assigned to Judge John Singleton, who also presided over the criminal price-fixing action. In late 1978, Judge Singleton certified a nationwide class under Rule 23(b)(3) of the Federal Rules of Civil Procedure.

The *Corrugated* class action was massive in every way. There were 200,000 class members. Scores of lawyers represented the class and its subclasses. They were grouped into committees rivaling the organization chart of a major corporation. There were 39 pretrial hearings, 205 pretrial orders, and 15 appeals. Millions of pages of documents were copied. Hundreds of depositions were taken.

The scope of *Corrugated* made a ruinous judgment a troubling possibility, even for manufacturers certain that their actions had been proper. This risk increased when the class was certified. There was a chance that, if the jury concluded some defendants had violated the law, it would find that all the defendants were part of a large, ill-defined conspiracy. This concern was heightened for some of the largest defendants that—at about the same time the *Corrugated* class was certified—were found liable in a separate case for conspiring to fix prices in the plywood market.

Settlements inevitably followed. By manipulation, selection, and timing, the capable plaintiffs' lawyers achieved settlements in 1979 and 1980 with all but three of the defendants. These settlements totaled almost $400 million. The three remaining defendants went to trial in June 1980. Two settled before a verdict. One—Mead Corporation—went through three and one-half months of trial, only to be found in a jury special verdict to have taken part in a price-fixing conspiracy with 18 other manufacturers. Thirteen companies were found in the special verdict *not* to have violated the law.

After many lengthy, expensive skirmishes, including legislative efforts, Mead also settled for $45 million, before judgment was entered on the special verdict. All that remained was to distribute the settlement money, which had accumulated to $550 million, and to award plaintiffs' counsel attorneys' fees, which were more than $40 million. By the end of 1983, the great *Corrugated* class action was over.

But *Corrugated* was not yet dead. Because the *Corrugated* class was certified under Rule 23(b)(3), class members could opt out of the action and pursue their own lawsuits. Nineteen of the largest purchasers of corrugated containers—companies like Pillsbury, Kraft, and Armour Foods—did just that. Eleven of the 19 lawsuits they filed settled before trial, but eight proceeded on. Thus, after extensive criminal and civil litigation, the question of whether there was a price-fixing conspiracy in the corrugated container industry was to be litigated again—not once, but in eight different lawsuits. Despite all that had gone before, more massive discovery occurred. More than 500 new depositions were taken. Hundreds of thousands of pages of documents were produced—some for the second or third time.

The eight opt-out cases were not identical. Not all the five remaining defendants were named in each case. Despite these differences, all eight opt-out cases were consolidated for one trial before a single jury. Judge Singleton presided again.

The opt-out trial began in October 1982. Plaintiffs' cases lasted two and one-half months. Defendants' evidence took another month. After seven hours of closing arguments, the jury retired. In less than a day and a half, it returned with dispositive answers to the first two questions on the special-verdict form: *Yes*, there had been a national price-fixing conspiracy, but *no*, none of the plaintiffs had been damaged by it. These answers meant the jury never had to answer whether any of the defendants had been part of the conspiracy. Plaintiffs' posttrial motions and appeals were unsuccessful. This defense victory was sustained at all levels. By April 1985, the *Corrugated* opt-out litigation was over.

Cases as complex, interwoven, and overlapping as those in *Corrugated* produce one novel dilemma after another. Procedural complications, scheduling conflicts, and discovery disputes never seem to end. These are all tough problems. They were important to the litigation. But they are the stuff of law reviews: abstract, complicated, and sometimes unique. This is not surprising. As hard cases make bad law, complicated cases make odd law. What *is* surprising, though, is that even the *Corrugated* litigation—and especially the opt-out trial—taught some bigger lessons. A few of those follow.

One of the clearest lessons is that juries like people, not paper. To an unusual extent, the parties in the opt-out trial learned how jurors think. Judge Singleton permitted interviews of the alternate jurors while the regular jury was deliberating; the jury itself was interviewed after it reached a verdict.

These discussions with jurors suggest that what is evidence to lawyers is not to jurors. In two and one-half months of evidence, the unsuccessful plaintiffs presented 142 witnesses, but only six were flesh and blood. The remaining 136 were deposition transcripts, read into the record. Of these, 55 were from people who took the Fifth Amendment and refused to testify. Only one employee of any plaintiff corporation testified.

Defendants, by contrast, put on 28 live witnesses, along with 35 depositions. Representatives of most of the defendant companies testified.

Jurors Want Real People

The jury's preference was obvious. They were bored by the reading of depositions. They wondered why so few representatives of the plaintiff companies had the fortitude to testify. They were unimpressed by readings of the Fifth Amendment. It is one thing to see a witness—perhaps visibly nervous, perhaps arrogant—refuse to answer. Among other things, this can prompt memories of organized-crime hearings. It is quite another thing to hear someone's lawyer read the invocation of the Fifth Amendment 55 times. That has no impact.

Jurors expect, and want to see, real people. They expect human interest and drama, even in the most complex case. They cannot evaluate transcripts, and what they cannot evaluate they will discard.

Apart from the sheer dullness of listening to depositions, and apart from the jury's desire to see human beings, the opt-out trial also suggests that people speak on behalf of corporations better than paper does. Lawyers representing corporations before juries must try to humanize their clients. It can be easy for a jury to believe a large, faceless corporation took part in a vague, formless conspiracy. Conversely, it is hard for jurors to have sympathy for a company that appears only through deposition transcripts. But jurors can sympathize with people. They may find it harder to believe that the pleasant, articulate man or woman who spoke to them could do anything illegal.

A word of warning: though juries like people, even the driest transcript is better than a dumb, evasive, weak, or unprepared witness. In fact, almost the only virtue of transcripts is that they neutralize such human failings, burying them under pages of faceless ink and paper. A stenotype machine does not record hesitation, tone of voice, or nerves. So, if certain facts can be proved only through one person, and he is a clod, read in the deposition, if possible. But remember, in its own way, the jury may think the presence of a deposition and the absence of a person mean something is being hidden.

Although jurors prefer human witnesses, they do not like expert witnesses very much. In complex litigation, experts are inevitable: damages must be proved, markets defined, and economics explained. Very often, however, experts are just the kind of witnesses who—when possible—should appear in writing and not in person. Abstractions, complexity, and even pedantry punctuate much expert testimony. Jurors—and judges—do not like any of it.

The *Corrugated* opt-out trials illustrate the perils of basing a complex case on expert testimony. Both sides had experts. The plaintiffs had two, but since they had only six live witnesses in all, expert testimony was a major human element of their case. A much higher proportion of the defense case was fact testimony and not expert opinion. Worse yet for the plaintiffs, the testimony of their experts was complex and inconsistent. One thought price fixing had added as much as 10 percent to container prices, the other 26.1 percent. One relied on multiple regression techniques, the other on something he called "contribution" data.

All this left the jury skeptical and bored stiff. The substance of the testimony had no intrinsic interest. The spectacle of obvious disagreement in approach and result by experts on the same side of the case was not compelling. This was compounded by the virtual failure of any plaintiff-employee to testify in commonsense terms about the injury his company suffered. And, of course, many jurors believed that an expert would say anything he was hired to say.

Not all of these problems could be avoided. Experts are an intrinsic element of complicated cases, especially antitrust litigation. But they should not be a major element of such litigation. An important lesson of the opt-out trial was this: Use experts as little as possible. Above all, do not use experts as first-line witnesses or—worse yet—as spokesmen for your client. If possible, have employees explain in everyday terms how their company was hurt, where it sells or buys, what it does, and the like. Experts should fill in the gaps only, and the gaps should be small.

Once the jury has heard live witnesses, it should be able to record its conclusions on a special-verdict form. In *Corrugated,* the use and design of a special-verdict form played a major role in the defendants' opt-out trial success. Few lawyers—especially defense lawyers—should fail to use such a form in a complex case. Some of the reasons are familiar and help both sides: A special-verdict helps organize the jury's thinking. It lets you know what you have when the case is over; you can tell what facts were found and what were not. It helps focus any appeal. It permits different treatment for different defendants.

For defendants, there is another, less noble, but important, reason for using a special-verdict: It can give a defendant a lot of chances to win. Usually a special-verdict form asks a yes-or-know question for each of the facts related to each element of the cause of action. To win, a plaintiff usually needs to get all "yeses." A defendant only needs one "no." Relying on a general verdict is much less desirable from a defense standpoint; jurors who simply dislike a defendant may find for the plaintiff even though they could not honestly answer yes to every question on a special-verdict form.

When using a special-verdict form, pay careful attention to the organization and number of the questions. A defendant will want some of the earliest inquiries to be knockout questions: if the jury can answer "no" to the question, then it need not proceed to any others. In the *Corrugated* opt-out trial, the organization of the form meant the jury had to answer only two questions—"Was there a conspiracy?" and "Were the plaintiffs damaged?"—instead of the 300-plus questions on the 17 pages that followed. Had the jury been asked a series of relatively innocuous questions at the beginning of the form and had they answered them "yes," the psychological momentum for affirmative answers might have been irresistible.

Order Is Important

The arrangement of particular questions on a special-verdict form can also be important, and was in the opt-out trial. There, as noted, the order of initial questions was basically this: 1) existence of conspiracy; 2) damage to plaintiffs; 3) involvement of defendants in the conspiracy. Because the jury answered "no" to the second question, they did not need to answer the third. Had the second and third questions been reversed, the defendants' position might not have been strong. The jury might have found some were conspirators. Minimally, this would have been embarrassing. Worse, it would have produced a less favorable setting for appeals and postjudgment motions. And it might have caused later battles over the collateral estoppel effect of the verdict.

Along with controlling the formalities of proof—witnesses, verdicts, and the like—*Corrugated* shows it is important to give attention to more informal attempts to gain an evidentiary advantage. In particular, lawyers in complex litigation must try to control references to related cases.

By the time the opt-out cases were tried, the alleged corrugated container price conspiracy already had been litigated twice. The opt-out plaintiffs may have left the *Corrugated* class and may have had no direct involvement in either previous action, but they nonetheless referred to those proceedings repeatedly in the opt-out trial. Particularly common were references to some of the defendants' indictments and to the fact that employees of some of the defendants had invoked the Fifth Amendment in earlier testimony. The plaintiffs also sometimes mentioned evidence in the class litigation that put other manufacturers—not parties in the opt-out trial—in a bad light. These seemed to be efforts to prove guilt by association. The plaintiffs apparently believed that, by referring to criminal matters and refusals to testify, they would give the jury a generally poor impression of the defendants.

Such innuendoes are a threat in any case that is part of a pattern of overlapping lawsuits. Parties—particularly defendants—should be alert to it. The problem, however, is easier to describe than it is to solve. The *Corrugated* opt-out defendants tried a bit of everything: motions in limine, arguments at pretrial conferences, and objections during trial. Unfortunately, none of these was completely effective. Judge Singleton—perhaps because of conclusions he reached during the criminal or class proceedings—was unwilling to take a hard line on the problem. In fact, although the judge allowed the references to indictments and invoking the Fifth Amendment, he barred defense attempts to point out that some defendants had *not* been indicted and that some had been found *not* to be involved in a conspiracy during the *Mead* trial.

All a party faced with this related-case problem can do is to raise it early, often, and forcefully and hope for the best. Be careful, however: try to restrict these arguments to the pretrial stage of the case. Unless very artful, trial objections about references to other cases may at best seem picky to the jury and could suggest there is something to hide.

More troubling than references to related cases was the use of testimony from those earlier cases as evidence in the opt-out trial. By the time the opt-out cases were tried, earlier incarnations of the *Corrugated* case had produced mountains of testimony. Not all of the opt-out defendants had been present—or even parties—when such testimony was given. This created a host of problems: Transcripts of testimony in the *Mead* trial, to which few of the defendants had been parties, were introduced against them in the opt-out case. Testimony of persons taking the Fifth Amendment in depositions was introduced against defendants who did not employ those witnesses and had not been indicted by the grand jury.

Of course, depositions can sometimes properly be used as trial evidence. Rule 32 of the Federal Rules of Civil Procedure provides for it in appropriate circumstances. But using depositions and trial transcripts against a party that had no opportunity for cross-examination should not be countenanced. This is particularly true in a consolidated proceeding before a jury that may not be able to remember or determine which strand of evidence pertains to which party. It is doubly true when one of the previous proceedings is a criminal case. Again, the remedies are clear but not certain: motions in limine, objections, and the like. Again, success depends on the disposition of the trial judge.

For all their reliance on the fallout from related cases, the opt-out plaintiffs that went to trial lost. Careful examination of this result may explain why—except possibly in employment discrimination litigation—opt-out trials are uncommon: Opting out can hurt plaintiffs on the merits.

There are many reasons why staying in the *Corrugated* class should have made sense. The plaintiffs' essential allegation in *Corrugated* was that a nationwide price-fixing conspiracy had injured most purchasers of corrugated containers. The case was thus an effort by a large group of alleged victims to redress wrongs committed by a large group of alleged conspirators. The nature of the litigation almost inherently suggests a class. It may be easier for a trier to grasp the theory of a multiparty dispute when most of those parties are in the case. In this way, a procedural step—class certification—can reinforce the substance of the case.

There is another psychological advantage to having a class. Juries may well believe that class counsel is a "private attorney general" protecting the common good. They are more likely to think those representing a few companies are motivated by narrower—mostly monetary—corporate interests.

There are also more practical reasons why nationwide price-fixing cases can benefit from class treatment. Often, a defense tactic in antitrust conspiracy matters is to chip away at the case, party by party, to argue that *this* defendant could not have been involved in a conspiracy or *that* plaintiff could not have been harmed. In a class trial, there is often little patience with this splintering. There are simply too many individual situations for an efficient trial. Few judges will abide the clutter. In fact, there is a respectable view that a class trial is meant to deal only with common class-wide matters. In this view, individual questions are relegated to a second, relief stage. For most defendants, that is cold comfort. No one wants to be in a fight about who will pay a multimillion-dollar judgment.

Finally, a class action can provide unintended proof advantages for antitrust plaintiffs. It is, bluntly, a very good setting for proving guilt by association. The law on the admissibility of evidence against co-conspirators is complex. Lots of defendant parties can be confusing. Evidence on three or four bad actors may stain ten or fifteen much less involved codefendants. Even the most attentive jury or intelligent judge will have trouble keeping the evidence straight. What they will often remember is the bad news—the smoking guns—not the good. A class proceeding is a major opportunity for this bad news to be spread uncritically. With a broad brush, class plaintiffs can make a big smear.

Despite all these potential advantages, the *Corrugated* opt-out plaintiffs went their own ways. They may have had sound reasons. They probably thought they could make more money on their own. Nonetheless, at trial the absence of a class seemed to hurt them. The opt-out defendants tried to focus the evidence on the purchasing practices of individual plaintiffs, in an attempt to disconnect them from any of the defendants and from any conspiracy. This approach was successful. Though it found a conspiracy, the jury concluded that none of the plaintiffs had been harmed by it. This would have been far less likely if a class comprising every purchaser had been the plaintiff group.

There are sometimes good reasons for opting out of a plaintiff class. The *Corrugated* plaintiffs may still believe they did the right thing: they were, after all, able to negotiate $60 million in pretrial settlements with some of the opt-out defendants. Even after expenses, their settlement share in the class proceeding might not have been as large. In other cases, there are even better reasons for opting out: A class member, on principle, may not support the suit. A class member may not have confidence in class counsel. It may dislike the named plaintiffs. There may be an unbridgeable strategic gap between class counsel and counsel for the class member. Intervention can sometimes solve such problems, but not always. Opting out may be the proper choice. But before taking such a step, a class member should always analyze how procedure could affect the merits.

Corrugated is a paradigm example of the wasteful, needless consequences of opt-out litigation. Litigation costs simply for the *Corrugated* opt-out suits exceeded $8 million. If a case like *Corrugated* is to be litigated at all, every effort should be made to achieve maximum efficiency. Given the limited resources of the courts and the expense of discovery and trial, it makes no sense to litigate the same allegations more than once. Quite apart from the criminal proceeding, the *Corrugated* class action produced mountains of paper. Because the opt-out proceeding involved theoretically—but not really—different cases, much of that discovery had to be done all over again. In fact, there was so much to do that depositions were taken while the trial was underway. None of that makes sense. No rational system should permit such unnecessary repetition.

Repetition was not the only flaw in the *Corrugated* opt-out litigation. Multiple litigation of the same questions created layer on layer of testimony on the same points. Though they left the class case, plaintiffs were, as noted earlier, unfortunately allowed to use testimony from it and from grand jury proceedings, in the opt-out trial. The defendants thus not only had to spend time and money on repetitive discovery and testimony, they also had to defend against material generated in proceedings of which some of them were not a part. That is not simply nonsense. It is unfair.

Of course, the opt-out provisions of Rule 23 are not whimsical. The draftsmen of the rule had reasons for what they did. They thought class members locked into class actions—like some of those certified under subsection (b)(3)—in which class members' interests varied might be denied due process. Such rights are fundamental. They must be protected. But surely such protection need not take the form of an automatic right to opt out and to create duplicate litigation. Even in a (b)(3) proceeding, if only common issues are tried, if class counsel are capable (as certification is supposed to signify), and if there are no issue conflicts between class members and named plaintiffs, then there seems little danger of violating due process. This is particularly true since class members are entitled to intervene as parties in (b)(3) actions. Given the need to conserve resources and make big cases manageable, Rule 23 should be changed to give courts discretion to permit, bar, or condition opting out. In such situations, a class member ought to have the burden of showing why it needs to opt out. Such a flexible approach is more efficient, and no less fair, than the automatic opt-out right now contained in the rule. If *Corrugated* teaches anything, it demonstrates that there must be a better way.

Thinking About Class Actions

by Christopher Lutz

Class actions have a peculiar fascination for lawyers. They may be the most confused, abused, overpraised, and overanalyzed aspect of procedure. But—despite all the scrutiny—class actions are never boring. They evoke strong reactions. This is partly because the existence of a class increases the stakes; it multiplies the risks and rewards. However, the lure of class actions is also that they seem so different; they go beyond the parties immediately in court, affecting the rights of hundreds or thousands. The effect is almost magical.

Unfortunately, the special quality of class litigation too often produces only emotion and reaction, but not much thought. Some in the plaintiffs' bar seem to add class allegations to every complaint they file, while some defense counsel would not sit in the same room with a copy of Rule 23. Neither response is sensible.

The first thing to consider is whether you really want a class action at all. If you represent a plaintiff, should you file a class complaint? If you are defense counsel answering a class complaint or motion, should you adamantly oppose any class whatsoever? If you think either answer is simple, you probably have not thought enough.

For plaintiffs' counsel, careful thought is an absolute necessity. Blithely filing a class complaint can be a bad mistake. You may find you do not know what to do or do not have the resources to do it. You may find yourself with the wrong plaintiffs. You may not have enough time, or your interest may wane. In short, if you do not think before you begin, you may find yourself overwhelmed by the endeavor, wanting to return to the simple world of individual plaintiffs. *But*—and this is a critical point—once you begin a class action, you cannot just switch it off.

The author is editor-in-chief of LITIGATION *and a partner in Steptoe & Johnson in Washington, D.C.*

Even voluntary abandonment of class allegations may require court approval. Once you have filed a class suit, you may well have to live with it. Think first.

The most obvious question for prospective class counsel is whether the suit has real substantive potential as a class action. Groups of people rarely form a class and then find a lawyer. Rather, lawyers deal with individuals who have their own personal problems in mind and not those of a whole group.

How do you decide whether you should move from representing the client sitting in your office to a whole class? Think about his complaint. Can it be generalized? Is your client complaining about a problem that concerns him or her alone or about actions that affected many others in about the same way? Is she complaining about a slur from a particular supervisor or instead an employment test that she—and many others— failed? If you cannot generalize, if your client is not talking about a course of conduct that affected many others in about the same way, hesitate to suggest a class action.

If you have a client whose problem seems to be one that many might have, you next need to determine if you have the right plaintiff. Class representatives have a fiduciary duty to a lot of class members: fellow employees, security holders, or businessmen. Especially during the certification battle, they will be subject to considerable uncomfortable scrutiny. Your opponent will depose them, possibly more than once, and may try to depict them as unaware, unprincipled, poor, or otherwise defective. Class plaintiffs will be asked what they know about the law and the facts and whether they will pay "thousands of dollars" in court costs if the class loses. In light of all this, class representatives need to have a degree of commitment and fortitude. Pursuing a class suit will undoubtedly delay ultimate resolution of their own individual claims; a person whose claims could have been tried to judgment in one year may have to wait five times that long if he represents a class. Explain these things to your client.

The facts behind your plaintiff's claim are as important as his personal qualities. Even though a brokerage house may have consciously misrepresented a stock, a plaintiff who purchased on the brokers' oral advice will have difficulty securing a class, while one who relied on a written representation is more likely to succeed. In an employment discrimination case, for example, a plaintiff who assails generally applied educational requirements for promotion but who has a history of discipline and absence problems may have a hard time qualifying as a class representative. Be sure there is nothing so unique, peculiar, or personal in your client's claims that it overwhelms the general. In addition, it always helps if your client's personal story is one that will engage the court's sympathy. Since the judge may hear in person only from a few class members, how he reacts to their concerns will certainly affect his attitude toward the class.

If you want to be class counsel, the third thing you should think about is yourself. Can you prosecute a class action? Obviously, you should know Rule 23 and the substantive law you will sue under; a judge considering certification will require that as a minimum.

But there is more.

Have you ever participated in a class suit? Do you know how to manage one? Do you want to be a fiduciary for hundreds or thousands of class members? Are you ready for their phone calls at home? Where will you get the support staff to deal with discovery, with notice and the like? Think about how big the case will be: If you seek a nationwide class, can you manage nationwide discovery?

Think about your practice: Successful class action attorneys can make lots of money in court-awarded fees, but they usually are rarely paid on a monthly basis. Will your banker support you? Can you pay the expenses you will incur? If the class does not win or settle, and you get nothing, can other cases in the office maintain you? You have to think about what the case might require and what you can handle before you start.

All this may seem like an ordeal of self-examination from which no class suit will ever emerge. That is not so. If you have the right plaintiff with the right claims, if you know what will be required, and if you can handle and want a class suit, forge ahead. But think first.

After being served with a thick class complaint, the defense lawyer's analysis need not be as involved as that of prospective class counsel. But it must be done. Unfortunately, many defense lawyers scarcely think at all. They—and their clients—simply react. Many defense counsel approach a proposed class much like they would a proposed case of smallpox.

That kind of reaction can be counterproductive. It is true that even thoughtful defense counsel end up opposing class allegations. But opposition should not be automatic. Occasionally, a class may offer long-term protection instead of risk. Are your defenses strong? Is the putative class counsel less than skillful? Do you think you have a good chance of winning? Are there likely to be other, more formidable attempts at a class suit in less attractive forums if this one is not certified? Could your client be nibbled to death by a series of individual suits? If these things might happen, you and your client should consider accepting a class.

Why?

Because, if there is a class and if you win, the whole class loses. Everyone will be barred from litigating about the supposed securities fraud, price fixing, or unconstitutionality that produced the suit. The case will be over.

The advantages for the defendant are not always so great. Normally, there will be little reason to fear future individual suits. Few individuals have the resources to mount another class, or even individual, action.

Besides, the sheer cost of defending a class suit may exceed the cost of repeated individual defenses. In addition a class judgment may not provide protection against such subsequent litigation.

In employment discrimination cases—the single most fertile source of class actions—the Supreme Court's decision in *Cooper v. Federal Reserve Bank of Richmond*, 467 U.S. 867 (1984), seems to eliminate most class judgment protection against individual suits. And, of course, if you accept a class you might lose on the merits. Accepting a class as alleged is a high-stakes gamble. The combative, conservative nature of most lawyers leads them to take up the fight and avoid the gamble. That is very often the right decision, but be sure you reach it for the right reasons.

Defense counsel should also ask themselves a second question: Is no class at all the only alternative to the class alleged? This is a more difficult and more important inquiry. In some cases, a fair-minded look at the facts and Rule 23 will strongly suggest that a class is going to be certified. Often it also will indicate that the class the plaintiffs want is insupportably broad. This happens most often in employment discrimination actions; a plaintiff whose claim could justify a class within a single department or facility seeks to represent all of the defendant's comparable employees, nationwide. In cases like this, you face a tough question: Should you deny the propriety of any class or suggest a smaller class than the one the plaintiffs want?

The answer depends as much on litigation style as on logic. Some attorneys believe in taking extreme positions to get intermediate results and that any concession signals weakness. Others take aggressive but reasonable positions, because they believe that doing otherwise risks losing the court's goodwill and attention.

Whatever your basic approach, suggesting a reduced class can be good strategy for a number of reasons. It may simply be right. It often has the advantage of novelty. Judges who daily read one virulent class opposition after another may be shocked to greater attention by a less extreme approach. In addition, carving a class down to a more appropriate size may also mean you have carved unfavorable facts out of the case.

After thinking whether to have a class, you next need to determine *where* the class should be. It is not so much a question of detailed venue rules which have to be considered—but rather the more basic question of whether to file in federal court or state court.

To most lawyers, this may seem pointless inquiry. Class actions are almost always federal actions based on federal laws. A few states do not even have class action rules, and others have restrictive rules. Federal discovery is not as geographically confined as state discovery.

Federal judges may be somewhat more comfortable and familiar with class practice than state judges. And if you file in federal court, you can be sure a federal court can extend jurisdiction over class members in

1095

other states. That question is unsettled for state class actions.

But, once again, thought should precede reflex. If you think you can file a diversity-based class action in federal court, think again: To satisfy the jurisdiction requirements, *every* class member must have a $10,000 claim; that is rare. Besides, some state court judges—those in California, for example—are quite familiar with class actions. And some states, such as Pennsylvania, have liberal class action rules. Most important, a variety of important class-based causes of action—such as suits by the beneficiaries of a trust or victims of nuisance—are almost entirely matters of state law. Therefore, before you rush into United States District Court, be certain state court is not a better destination.

The final major topic for careful thought is how you convince the judge you are right. Certainly, you always need to think about the best way to make your points. In class action battles, this preliminary thought is doubly important. Class action motions and oppositions have a deadening sameness. Usually too long and too shrill, they often merely consist of fracturing Rule 23 into its subparts, quoting them, asserting they are or are not met, and attaching a string of citations. To avoid such problems, consider a few points, which apply equally to plaintiffs and defendants.

First, some ground rules. Some courts have time limits for filing class motions ranging from 30 to 90 days. The court may deny certifying a class simply because you missed the time limit. And even if the court is lenient, you will always erode your claim to be an "adequate" class attorney. Even absent such time limits, Rule 23 requires that class questions be decided "as soon as practicable." This admonition should lead both sides to focus discovery mostly (if not exclusively) on class matters. Depose class representatives fairly early on—both sides should prepare for that.

Finally, especially if you are plaintiffs' counsel, even at an early stage, remember the overall case record. Even if you have a class certified and you win at trial, you might still have the whole thing torn apart on appeal because the record is barren of class findings and evidence. Most circuits encourage a class hearing, and you should seriously consider proposing one. If there is not a class hearing, be sure affidavits, discovery excerpts, and the like are introduced with the class papers. This can be time-consuming but is a valuable insurance policy.

Having considered such preliminary matters, plaintiffs' and defense counsel can think about the themes they want to emphasize in seeking or opposing a class. I begin with a heretical observation: Do *not* be guided very much by the text of Rule 23 or comparable state rules. The rules themselves provide little guidance. Class action arguments relying only on what the rules say can get bogged down in extended, academic, semantic debates:

- Rule 23(a) requires the claims of named plaintiffs to be "typical" of those of class members, but how are "typical" and "atypical" claims distinguished?

- In (b) 3 actions, common claims must "predominate." Is that judgment made by counting claims or weighing them, or by some other process?

Of course, volumes of case commentary try to answer these questions, and you will have to discuss and meet the rule's requirements. Nonetheless, large parts of the class action rules are, by themselves, simply not prescriptive. They grow out of but do not illuminate a variety of practical concerns. They are built on but do not explain years of equity practice and experience under joinder and intervention rules. Because their operative language is slippery—"adequate," "typical," "common," "superior," "predominate"—they normally do not provide a basis for compelling argument.

A more effective approach is to talk about concerns and policies underlying Rule 23. Rather than simply asserting that common claims do not predominate, explain what the lack of predominance will lead to in your case and facts. Instead of merely saying the class representative is inadequate, show how his inadequacy will affect prosecution of the case. By tying facts to policies, you should be able to avoid the semantic hairsplitting that plagues many class action papers.

What are the concerns underlying Rule 23? Judges considering whether to certify a class seem mainly concerned with four questions: First, does a "class" *really* exist here? Second, will class litigation in this case lead to the efficiencies Rule 23 is meant to achieve? Third, is it fair to bind class members by the actions of the lawyers and named plaintiffs? Fourth, if certified, is this case likely to spin off into an unmanageable snarl? Each of these concerns finds expression in Rule 23's various subparts, but relying solely on the text of the rule will not allow you to explain them in your case.

The first question—does a class really exist?—may seem silly. After all, defining the characteristics of a class is what Rule 23 is meant to do. The existence of common questions, typical claims, and the like are what Rule 23 and classes are all about. Nonetheless, I have more than once seen a judge after he has listened to an hour of rarified discourse on Rule 23(a) and (b) lean over the bench and ask, "But does a class *really* exist?"

There is more at work here than the technical fine points of Rule 23. Most judges want to have a deeper sense, based on evidence, that there exists a definable group of people, tied together by common concerns, experiences, or claims. The court usually wants to know whether the class is a unified group. So, if you want a class, try to show that you represent people who have suffered the same harm and experienced the same facts and who share important unifying characteristics. Try to show that the group is sharply defined: You can tell who is in and who is not; you can determine roughly how many class members there are.

1097

Defense counsel, on the other hand, will want to try to convince the court that the class is not defined at all, that it is possibly limitless and has no sharp boundaries (for example, "all Americans affected by air pollution"). Defense lawyers should also try to show that the plaintiffs' class definition ties people into a class by accident or sleight of hand. No one would expect an antitrust class to be certified consisting of those who purchased from two separate companies. Marketing policies of a single corporation in various regions may make it equally inappropriate to include all the company's purchasers in the same group. The goal is to point to differences in the class that will *make* a difference; distinctions that will make litigation about the named plaintiffs' claims inapplicable to the class as a whole. All of these points should surely be clothed in the trappings of Rule 23, because the rule requires it and has meaning. But never forget the court's basic concern: Is there *really* a class?

The second concern—efficiency—is more straightforward. One of the aims of Rule 23 is to provide a means for resolving, once and for all, factual and legal questions affecting many people. This prevents similarly situated people from experiencing different results in court. Properly applied, it also means that only one court needs to decide the common questions.

The rules'—and courts'—concerns for efficiency mean you will help yourself to become class counsel if you can convince the judge that certifying a class and trying its claims will prevent him and other judges from hearing the same kinds of claims, case after case. The "commonality" and "typicality" sections of Rule 23 touch on this issue. You should talk about them. But it is even better if you can show concretely that there are many suits or administrative complaints pending which could be resolved in one class suit. If you are suing about a well-publicized occurrence likely to spawn lawsuits—a spectacular corporate failure, an antitrust violation prosecuted by the government, or (possibly) a widely known disaster—say so.

Defense counsel, on the other hand, want to demonstrate that no real efficiencies would come from a class suit. You should show—relying (if appropriate) on the rule's predominance standard—that the questions common to the class are not central to the problems of the individual class members. Later suits would be required to decide significant, individual questions. A related approach is to demonstrate that the facts affecting class members vary so much that follow-up suits would be needed to determine how the results of a class action should apply to the individual class members. Finally, if you decide to argue that a class suit will be an ungovernable mess, argue that the protraction and complexity of class litigation will be far more costly and time-consuming than all the individual suits.

There is one "anti-efficiency" argument defense counsel should *not* make. It may be tempting to say that the courts will not be burdened by individual litigation because the cost of litigation exceeds what is at stake on an individual basis. This might be the case in an antitrust suit challenging relatively modest overcharges or an action attacking imposition of a few percentage points of excess interest. But such an argument would be a mistake. There is a very respectable view that class actions are designed in part to make the righting of such wrongs feasible. Arguing that economics make an inefficient proliferation of individual cases unlikely may very well convince a judge that a class suit is the only efficient way to right the wrongs alleged.

The third point of argument about certification—fairness to class members—is probably the most important. I have never encountered a judge who was not acutely concerned about the proper treatment of class members. This concern exceeds any solicitude for named plaintiffs, defendants, and attorneys. Most courts want to be sure that, by certifying a class, they will not be doing a disservice to hundreds or thousands who will not be present in court to protect their rights.

If you have filed a class motion, your job in regard to fairness is clear. Relying on the rule's "adequacy" standard, show the judge you know what you are doing. Prove you are a capable attorney, well-versed in the substantive law and familiar with class actions. Show that your individual clients are committed and aware of the burdens they might face. Here is where thinking before filing will pay off: If you have the right plaintiff, you should have an adequate class representative. If you have thought about the burdens you may face as class counsel, you should be able to satisfy the court during a class certification hearing.

Defense counsel should think doubly hard before arguing that class members may be inadequately represented. Professional attacks on opposing counsel and personal attacks on their clients can backfire. In extreme cases, however, such tactics may be proper. If your opponent has been suspended from practice or has frequently mishandled class suits, you can plausibly argue he is a dubious fiduciary for the class. The same is true if the proposed named plaintiff in a securities suit has been convicted of stock fraud.

A defense argument about inadequate representation need not always involve personal attacks, however. In some ways, Rule 23's "typicality" requirement guarantees fairness. It embodies the principle that a true class representative will litigate in a way that matches the concerns of the class as a whole. For example, in a discrimination suit, a class of rejected applicants with claims about testing or educational requirements might not have their interests well represented by a person who was rejected in part because he got into a fight with a hiring officer. A class suit directed by such a person might tend to focus more on his personal vendetta than on the interests of the class. So if you perceive an odd or unusual plaintiff—perhaps one who says he is interested only in money and not injunctive relief—or you see that his claims arise out of unusual facts, consider a fairness argument.

The last concern of Rule 23 is manageability. While manageability is explicitly a requirement only in classes certified under Rule 23(b) (3), it is a real concern for many courts in *any* class suit. The reason is simple. No judge wants a class albatross that will live on his docket for four or five years. So, if you are prospective class counsel, show the court that class issues can be proved relatively simply, without scores of individual anecdotes. Demonstrate that you know how to use mailing firms, statistical sampling, and other techniques that simplify case management and proof. In general, show that you will be in control of your part of the case.

The agenda for defense lawyers is obvious. Discovery will take years; there will be thousands of motions and scores of intervenors. The trial—if it ever comes—will never end. If all this is likely and can be shown crisply, do it.

But beware the perils of sameness. Judges hear bone-chilling manageability arguments from defense lawyers almost every week. If you write the usual ten-page "parade of horribles" on manageability, the court will very quickly resort to reading only the topic sentences of your paragraphs, if that much. Be short, specific, and concrete. If your opponent flubbed a past suit into a protracted mess, say so. If discovery suggests that 500 witnesses will be called, say so. Whatever you say on manageability, remember that the judge has heard most of it before. Novelty is critical. Remember also that saying a case is unmanageable comes close to saying your judge will not have the skill to manage it. Be careful.

That ends my list of things to think about, but some qualifications are in order. Rule 23 does, of course, matter. It is a highly structured, complicated set of requirements. Understand it. You need to satisfy the rule or show it cannot be met. Because Rule 23 treats specific kinds of class suits differently, not all of my observations apply with equal force in all cases. The important point is this: The rule's surface complexity hides years of common law and statutory history, volumes of case commentary, and many important practical considerations. To deal with class suits successfully, you need to understand the themes that run through that background, using them in an effective, specific way.

Most of all, you need to *think*.

Checkmate—Takeover Litigation Strategy

by Jonathan J. Lerner

In the frenetic world of high-stakes corporate takeovers, litigation is the legal equivalent of a championship chess tournament played at ultrasonic speed for megabuck prizes. Masters of strategy confront each other (often flanked by cadres of kibitzers), while knights of all shades—white, black, and grey—maneuver to checkmate the target and capture its crown jewels. As the rapidly unfolding events are featured daily in the financial press, trial counsel for the target of the hostile takeover and for the acquiring company (sometimes pejoratively called the "raider") must coordinate and manage a host of simultaneous proceedings. These often involve federal and state actions as well as administrative proceedings—and virtually all include demands for emergency injunctive relief.

As a general rule, the acquiring company has the white pieces and moves first. Until that opening move, all information concerning the prospective takeover strategy is secret. The bidder must be cautious because any breach in the confidentiality concerning a planned takeover—such as premature disclosure of the identity of the target company—could result in the misuse of inside information to trade in the target's stock.

Once the acquirer picks its target, it may choose a conventional opening and announce a "formal" tender offer. Or it may select a different gambit, such as obtaining enough stock through open-market purchases and block trades to gain control of the target.

Which opening move the acquirer plays depends on a number of factors, including its budget. Unless a formal tender offer is commenced for all the target's stock at a preemptively high price, the target's reaction is

The author is a member of Skadden, Arps, Slate, Meagher & Flom in New York City.

likely to be hostile. So usually the acquirer must assume that litigation will be one of the target's defenses.

As in any chess game, the target's litigation moves will be governed by the kind of acquisition threat it faces. One common takeover strategy is to acquire a large stock position in the target (sometimes exceeding 20 percent of the target's voting stock) in open-market and privately negotiated purchases. By this method—sometimes called a "creeping tender offer"—an acquirer may accumulate enough shares to block (or at least deter) other companies from competing for control, gain representation on the target's board of directors, or even get control over the entire board in a proxy fight.

Confronted with this threat, targets often resort to the courts. Most often, the case is brought in federal court and attacks the adequacy of the acquirer's disclosure of information that is required by Section 13(d) of the Securities Exchange Act of 1934, as well as the legality of the open-market and block purchases. Section 13(d) requires any person who acquires five percent of any class of shares of an issuer to file a Schedule 13D within ten days after reaching that level of ownership. The information required includes the number of shares owned by the acquirer and anyone acting in concert with him, the purpose of purchases, and the identity of persons who "control" the acquirer.

Despite these disclosure requirements, it is possible that an acquirer intent on controlling a target may try to obscure its purpose, especially if it wants to buy additional shares of the target's stock without paying the increased price that might come from word of a possible takeover. The result is that compliance with the disclosure obligations of Section 13(d) has been a popular subject of litigation. But even though hundreds of actions have been filed under Section 13(d), the results have been mixed. Only a handful of targets have gotten any injunctive relief beyond correcting the acquirer's Schedule 13D disclosure.

To be sure, litigation under Section 13(d) can be a formidable weapon with a severe bite, as demonstrated by the action brought by General Steel Industries against Walco National Corporation and its founder, former Congressman Frederick W. Richmond. General Steel not only succeeded in obtaining an order requiring Walco to *rescind* the sale of all the shares acquired after its Schedule 13D was filed but also got an injunction halting Walco's tender offer for additional General Steel stock until divestiture of the unlawfully acquired shares.

Walco's attempt to control General Steel began on a promising note when Walco acquired a 25 percent block of General Steel shares. With an additional four percent that Walco had already surreptitiously purchased, Walco now owned nearly 30 percent of General Steel's outstanding stock.

Walco's Schedule 13D stated that this substantial position was "purchased for investment." Walco, however, kept buying General Steel stock and acquired an additional four percent. Walco filed several amendments to its Schedule 13D; each stated that the purchases were made purely for "investment" and disclaimed any present intention to acquire control. On November 2, 1981, Walco abruptly commenced a formal tender offer to acquire an additional 17 percent of General Steel's stock. If successful, Walco would own more than 50 percent of General Steel's stock and control the company.

General Steel filed suit in the Eastern District of Missouri, where its headquarters were located, claiming that Walco's Schedule 13D and amendments were false and misleading. Chief Judge Kenneth Wangelin ordered expedited discovery to begin on November 11, 1981. Under the provisions of the Williams Act, which regulates tender offers, the right of General Steel shareholders to withdraw any shares they had tendered to Walco in its tender offer expired on November 24. Unless an injunction was obtained by that time, Walco could have bought enough shares to control General Steel. A hearing on General Steel's preliminary injunction application was scheduled for November 23, only hours before the deadline. Thus, even under the expedited schedule, General Steel had less than two weeks to prove its case.

Walco's strategy was to delay discovery so as to capitalize on the limited time available to General Steel. Consequently, Walco moved to adjourn discovery until November 16, which would have left General Steel only one week to review documents, conduct depositions, and prepare its moving papers. Walco's plan backfired when the court not only granted its requested adjournment but also extended the withdrawal date of Walco's tender offer for five business days. Before General Steel's lawyers could breathe a sigh of relief at this short reprieve, the Court of Appeals for the Eighth Circuit vacated the portion of the order extending the withdrawal date because no hearing had been held.

One week before the withdrawal deadline, discovery finally started. Smoking guns are rare, but Walco's document production literally radiated heat. On the same day that Walco had stated in an amendment to its Schedule 13D that its purchases were for "investment" and that it had no intention of seeking control, Walco's controlling shareholder and former chairman, (then Congressman) Richmond, had written a memorandum to the company's chief executive officer unequivocally admitting that "our aim is to own 51 percent of the company." *General Steel Indus., Inc. v. Walco Nat'l Corp.*, [1981-82 Transfer Binder] Fed. Sec. L. Rep. (CCH) Sec. 98, 402 at 92,413 (E.D. Mo. 1981).

On November 23, the court determined that Walco had willfully violated Section 13(d). The Court issued an order requiring Walco to rescind its unlawful purchases and also enjoined it from further purchases of General Steel stock pending rescission "to deter future violations of law and to prohibit Walco from taking advantage of a position it has illegally obtained." *Id.* at 92,418.

Where the threat is a tender offer and where the target's directors decide to resist a takeover, the target often turns to Section 14(e) of the 1934 Act. The challenge is to the disclosures made in the bidder's Offer to Purchase. This broad antifraud provision applies to all tender offers, whether or not the target's shares are publicly traded. Section 14(e) requires the offeror to disclose to the target's shareholders information material to the tender offer.

Usually an injunction under Section 14(e) in a tender offer case is likely to be temporary—lasting only until corrective disclosures can be made. For a permanent injunction against a tender offer, a target must generally look to the antitrust laws, specifically Section 7 of the Clayton Act, or find a violation of some regulatory statute. But increased disclosure under Section 14(e) can still have value. In addition, even a brief extension under Section 14(e) may be enough for the target to find another bidder willing to pay a higher price—a "white knight"—or to take some other defensive action.

Although the relief obtained by a target under Section 14(e) can be limited, the information about a bidder that a court may deem "material" can be wide-ranging. This means, from the acquirer's standpoint, the litigation issues must be identified and evaluated before—not after—the offer becomes public.

This rule—evaluate before the offer is public—is illustrated by General Steel's complaint attacking Walco's tender offer under Section 14(e). In addition to its holding that Walco had violated Section 13(d), the court made a preliminary finding that General Steel had shown a probability of success in demonstrating that Walco's largest shareholder, Congressman Richmond, had:

- diverted Walco's corporate funds to satisfy obligations by the Richmond Foundation (his personal foundation) and to benefit himself politically;
- regularly received secret and substantial subsidies from Walco for his use of an apartment in New York City;
- caused Walco to make "charitable" contributions in Richmond's name (rather than Walco's) for his political aggrandizement.

General Steel Indus., Inc. v. Walco Nat'l Corp., supra, at 92,417.

Apart from the adverse publicity created by these preliminary factual findings, a federal grand jury began a criminal investigation into Richmond's activities. Even though Walco finally abandoned its effort to control General Steel and sold its shares to General Steel's white knight, the damage to Richmond was more lasting. After an investigation by the United States Attorney's Office, he pleaded guilty to tax evasion stemming from the failure to report benefits that Walco had provided as taxable income. The case demonstrates that any skeletons a bidder has in the closet may be exposed by litigation and that the consequences can transcend the particular transaction.

The *General Steel* case was decided on extraordinary facts, and the relief awarded under Section 13(d) was unusual. More typical was Ludlow's unsuccessful case seeking to enjoin Tyco under Section 13(d) from purchasing any more of its stock.

Tyco had first tried to control Ludlow through a tender offer for 100 percent of the company. Immediately after this offer was aborted, Tyco acquired approximately 10 percent of Ludlow's stock, which it held passively—in the beginning.

Then, two years after its takeover attempt failed, Tyco began to accumulate additional Ludlow shares and soon owned 28 percent of Ludlow's stock. According to the amendments Tyco filed to its Schedule 13D, these purchases of Ludlow stock were for the purpose of "investment." After its share ownership exceeded 28 percent, however, Tyco amended its Schedule 13D to disclose that it was considering the possibility of acquiring control of Ludlow.

Ludlow sued Tyco in the District of Massachusetts, where Ludlow's executive offices were located, claiming that Tyco's series of "investment" amendments were false and asking for an injunction against further purchases by Tyco as well as an order directing Tyco to offer to rescind its open-market and block purchases.

Ludlow's immediate objective—stopping Tyco from buying more of its shares—was successful. The district court granted Ludlow a temporary restraining order and ordered expedited discovery, holding that "the large volume of purchases involved here over a relatively short period of time, the past history of tender offers on the part of Tyco, and the current position of Tyco as the largest stockholder of Ludlow raises sufficient question as to the accuracy of the 13D filing and sufficient likelihood of success on the merits to warrant further inquiry into the defendants' purpose in purchasing large amounts of Ludlow stock." *Ludlow Corp. v. Tyco Laboratories, Inc.* [1981-82 Transfer Binder] Fed. Sec. L. Rep. (CCH) Sec. 98,382 at 92,302-03 (D. Mass. 1981).

But Ludlow's victory was short-lived. After a preliminary injunction hearing, District Judge Rya W. Zobel ruled that Ludlow was not entitled to a permanent injunction because of what happened in the interim. Tyco had made a detailed public proposal to acquire all Ludlow's stock, "curing" any prior omissions. As the court said, "Whatever ambiguity or confusion may have been created by Tyco's [earlier] Schedule 13Ds was dispelled by its recent filings. . . ." *Ludlow Corp. v. Tyco Laboratories, Inc.*, 529 F.Supp. 62, 66 (D. Mass 1981). In reaching this conclusion, Judge Zobel followed other courts that have denied rescission or other injunctive relief beyond insuring that misleading statements are corrected. The Tyco theory is that the interests to be protected "are fully satisfied when the shareholders receive the information required to be filed."

Given the difficulty in getting an injunction, a target must maximize its chances for success should it choose to sue. Picking the most receptive forum is critical. One possibility is the target's own headquarters. For the target's executives, this may be the most convenient court in which to testify. In addition, the target may draw a judge who is familiar with the company and its operations—and who may be more sensitive to the target's argument that a takeover would be disruptive. Not surprisingly, home court is a favorite choice for a target. Virtually every case in which rescission has been granted as a remedy for a violation of Section 13(d) has been tried in the target's home court.

On the other hand, a target that makes a mad dash into the local federal courthouse may find that it has rushed into the wrong one. There may be adverse case law in the circuit relating to the available relief or other key issues. For example, the Williams Act, 15 U.S.C. Sec. 78n(e), does not contain a specific provision conferring a private right of action, and the Supreme Court has not specifically decided that a target may use it to obtain injunctive relief. Although the vast majority of lower courts that have considered the issue have ruled that a target has standing to seek injunctive relief under both Sections 13(d) and 14(e), the Court of Appeals for the Eleventh Circuit has concluded that there is not standing under either section. *Liberty Nat'l Ins. Holding Co. v. Charter Co.*, 734 F.2d 545 (11th Cir. 1984).

The art of selecting the most favorable forum is not simple. While it may not be difficult to choose the most favorable forum in which to challenge the bidder's conduct, and while one need not be a rocket scientist to determine whether standing to sue will be sustained in that jurisdiction, a choice of forum based solely on these criteria may yield the right answer to the wrong question. Although these factors may point to the best court for the target *to sue* an acquirer, that forum may not be the most favorable place for the target to *be sued*, should its own defensive actions become the subject of litigation by the bidder. The target must think like a potential defendant as well as a plaintiff in picking the right forum.

Traditionally, litigation has been considered primarily a weapon in the target's arsenal. But the conventional wisdom is fading with the advent of diverse corporate defensive actions by targets, which may or may not be protected by the "business judgment" rule. These defenses, sometimes characterized as "scorched earth" tactics, may involve any number of corporate actions by the target. The target may attempt to make itself less attractive to a hostile bidder by selling a key asset or "crown jewel," or it may try to keep the bidder from proceeding by acquiring a competitor of the bidder to create an antitrust obstacle, just to name two techniques.

So before selecting a forum, the target should evaluate how the judges view "defensive" corporate tactics as well. There can be significant differences in evaluating these transactions, and the target may argue that any subsequent claim by the bidder against a defensive maneuver by the target is a compulsory counterclaim and must be brought in the forum selected by the target to challenge the bidder's conduct.

The Sixth Circuit, for instance, differs sharply from other courts in evaluating the legality of "lock-up" options given by a target to induce a "white knight" to bid higher. A "lock-up" option gives a third party an option to purchase shares directly from the target company. Similarly, the target may give the third party the right to acquire some of the target's key assets if its offer fails. In *Mobil Corp. v. Marathon Oil Co.*, 669 F.2d 366 (6th Cir. 1981), the Court of Appeals for the Sixth Circuit held that certain "lock-up" options were unlawful "manipulative acts" under Section 14(e), even though it accepted the district court's conclusion that the Marathon directors acted loyally and in good faith.

In contrast, courts outside the Sixth Circuit have concluded that Section 14(e) is strictly a disclosure statute, that such transactions do not constitute "manipulative acts or practices," and that the legality of "lock-ups" will be tested under the business judgment rule. *See, e.g., Buffalo Forge Co. v. Ogden Corp.*, 717 F.2d 757 (2d Cir.), *cert. denied*, 464 U.S. 1018 (1983).

In addition, there also may be differences among those courts that test certain "defensive" transactions under the business judgment rule. Under the internal affairs doctrine, the application of the business judgment rule generally has been based on interpretation of the law of the jurisdiction in which the target is organized. This doctrine may be undergoing erosion, however, especially in states whose statutes apply provisions of that state's corporation law to corporations doing business there, even though incorporated elsewhere.

Such a statute made the difference in the recent case of *Norlin Corp. v. Rooney, Pace Inc.*, 744 F.2d 255 (2d Cir. 1984), a case that shows that even the best strategy sometimes will not work. When Norlin became aware that large blocks of its stock were being acquired by Rooney, Pace, it rushed into the United States District Court for the Southern District of New York, claiming that the rapid accumulation of more than 30 percent of its shares was an unlawful "creeping tender offer." After its applications for a temporary restraining order and expedited discovery were denied by District Judge David N. Edelstein, Norlin unleashed its doomsday defense.

Norlin issued nearly a million shares of voting-preferred stock to a wholly owned subsidiary and to an employee stock option plan. These transactions would have effectively diluted the acquirer's holdings from almost 45 percent to 27 percent and would have allowed Norlin's management to vote nearly 49 percent of all outstanding shares and perpetuate itself forever.

Although voting of shares issued to a wholly owned subsidiary is barred by the laws of virtually every state in the United States, Norlin tried to sustain defense by relying on the law of Panama, under which it was incorporated. Panama corporate law requires that shareholders adopt a resolution before a derivative action for breach of duty can be brought against the directors. Panama also permits (under limited circumstances) a subsidiary to vote shares that it holds of its own parent. Norlin hoped to avoid the New York corporation law and public policy by using these quirks of Panamanian law.

Norlin's reliance on Panama law was strained, especially since its headquarters were in New York and its stock was listed on the New York Stock Exchange. So the district court refused to follow Panama law, and it enjoined Norlin from voting the new shares. The second circuit affirmed.

While a target contemplating litigation must think like a possible defendant as well as a plaintiff in picking the best forum, it is the bidder who may be in a position to preempt the choice of forum. Where a formal tender offer is made, it is a ritual for the bidder's first move to start a suit in every state that has a state takeover statute that might apply to its tender offer, seeking to enjoin enforcement on constitutional grounds. Since the Supreme Court decision in *Edgar v. Mite Corp.*, 457 U.S. 624 (1982), these actions have routinely resulted in injunctive relief against enforcement of state takeover statutes, although the Eighth Circuit recently upheld a Minnesota statute enacted after the *Mite* case. *Cardiff Acquisitions, Inc. v. Hatch* [Current] Fed. Sec. L. Rep. (CCH) Sec. 91,854 (8th Cir. 1984).

Some bidders have attempted to use these state statute actions (so far unsuccessfully) to contend that a target's subsequent challenges to the actual tender offer must take the form of compulsory counterclaims to the bidder's action and therefore must be asserted in the bidder's chosen forum. *See, e.g., General Steel v. Walco*, 527 F.Supp. 305 (E.D. Mo. 1981).

In other cases, a bidder has forced any challenge to its tender offer to be made in a court it selects. A bidder does this by suing first, before suit is brought against it by the target corporation. Usually the claim is based on press releases prematurely issued by the target, which comment on the tender offer. In such cases, the acquirer has immediately started suit in the forum it prefers, attacking the press releases as false and misleading and has claimed that any later action by the target under the securities or antitrust laws must be brought as counterclaims in the same action. *See, e.g., H. K. Porter Co. v. Fansteel, Inc.*, [1975-1976 Transfer Binder] Fed. Sec. L. Rep. (CCH), Sec. 95,546 (S.D.N.Y. 1976) (enjoining subsequent action). Given the current split on the right of targets to sue under the Williams Act, a bidder that succeeds in forcing a target to maintain its securities claims in an Eleventh Circuit court might preclude any viable challenge by the target to its disclosures.

Even where a target succeeds in enjoining a tender offer from proceeding, an acquirer may countermove to attempt to stalemate the target, thereby neutralizing its victory. A few courts have granted requests by bidders that have been enjoined to maintain the status quo for *both sides* by keeping the target from engaging in any defensive transaction while an injunction is pending. *Muskegon Piston & Ring Co. v. Gulf & Western Indus.*, 328 F.2d 830 (6th Cir. 1964); *Dan River, Inc. v. Icahn*, Civ. Action No. 82-2014 (W.D. Va. 1983), *rev'd on other grounds*, 701 F.2d 278 (4th Cir. 1983).

So far nearly everything we have discussed has taken place in federal court. In takeover litigation, state courts play a peripheral, but sometimes important, role. Where targets are engaged in heavily regulated businesses such as insurance, the application of the relevant statutes is often thrashed out in state courts. Similarly, battles over the application and constitutionality of state takeover statutes, especially when they are invoked in the context of creeping tender offers, have been fought in state courts. Bidders would rather challenge state statutes in the federal courts, but, if they do not sue early, they may be forced to litigate in the state courts preferred by state officials and target companies.

The state forums may play an increasingly important role in litigation over the validity of defensive transactions in cases where diversity of citizenship does not provide an independent basis for federal jurisdiction. The recent spate of state laws regulating hostile takeovers as well as the Supreme Court's decision in *Schreiber v. Burlington Northern, Inc.*, 472 U.S. 1 (1985) (to violate Section 14(e), misrepresentation of nondisclosure must be involved), may force a bidder challenging such a transaction into state court. And, absent an independent basis for federal jurisdiction or a basis of pendent jurisdiction, the bidder may be limited to a state court action. *See Data Probe, Inc. v. CRC Information Sys.*, N.Y.L.J., at 7, Col. 2 (Dec. 28, 1984).

Finally, selecting an appropriate forum is only the opening gambit. Whether a takeover ends in a checkmate or a stalemate will depend on any number of additional factors, including the skill, planning, and master strategy developed by the players throughout the match.

Patent Litigation

by Laurence H. Pretty

The image of the patent lawyer is a preoccupied guy with a green eye-shade and sleeve garters, a slide rule on his belt and a calculator in his pocket. He almost never goes to court, and, when he does, no one understands him except other patent lawyers. But all that is changing. Trial lawyers are trying more patent cases, and patent lawyers are learning more litigation skills. The strengthening climate of patents makes businesses less inclined to tolerate infringement of their products and more eager to protect their competitive positions.

A patent lawsuit is nearly always a major undertaking. The size of the economic interests necessary to justify suit, the variety of defenses requiring discovery, the numerous documents, and the often widespread separation of the parties and witnesses add up to serious business. The climate alone can cause classic mistakes. Too often litigators file first and worry about the facts when they get into discovery. Dangerous in any practice, it is taboo in patent litigation. Before you file, you need to study your client's position meticulously for any weaknesses. Do not waste your client's time and money by a premature complaint. A recklessly filed patent lawsuit can expose the patent owner to an adverse award of the defendant's attorney fees and, in extreme circumstances, even to an antitrust claim. *Zenith Radio Corp. v. Hazeltine Research, Inc.*, 395 U.S. 100 (1969).

Many patent suits begin like this: Your client, Cucamonga Gadget, comes into your office screaming with anger that his prime competitor, Pocatello Widget, has just knocked off a copy of Cucamonga's hottest-selling new product. After calming your client down with sympathetic outrage, your first step is to get a sample of Pocatello's product (or what-

---

The author is a member of the law firm of Pretty, Schroeder, Brueggemann & Clark in Los Angeles.

ever other information is available) and make a comparison with the patent claims to determine whether there is an infringement. In addition, your patent owner, Cucamonga, should investigate the prior art, its own files, and available witnesses to find whether the patent has any incurable defects that would cause a court to hold it invalid or unenforceable.

If there are other patent infringers (unrelated to Pocatello), you have to make some early choices: Whom do you sue first? Do you go against more than one simultaneously? These are important questions in any kind of case. But in patent litigation, they are crucial because of collateral estoppel.

Why?

If your first lawsuit results in the patent being held invalid, the patent is also invalid in any later cases. *Blonder-Tongue Laboratories, Inc. v. University of Ill. Found.*, 402 U.S. 313 (1971). So it is important to bring the first case against the infringer that offers the best prospects for a win. Winning the first case does not legally insulate the patent from further attack, but it helps. If the patent is once sustained, it improves the chances for getting favorable settlements from the other infringers or a favorable outcome in later trials.

Now the question is where to try the case. And the stream of commerce can provide the plaintiff with an expansive choice of places to file the patent enforcement action, despite the narrowness of the patent venue statute. Rather than file the case against Pocatello Widget at their home in Idaho, you can file at your home base in Los Angeles, where Pocatello has a sales office and has sold the offending product. If the infringer is a foreign national or company, your choice of venue is even broader, and you can sue in any district that meets the "minimum contacts test." *Brunette Mach. Works, Ltd. v. Kockum Indus., Inc.*, 406 U.S. 706 (1972).

Often it is tempting to save your client expensive litigation fees by merely sending Pocatello Widget a form demand letter.

But be careful.

That demand letter can backfire. Instead of rolling over and giving up the product that infringes on your patent, Pocatello Widget may seize the initiative, and, in its home court in Idaho, file a declaratory judgment action to determine that your patent is invalid and not infringed, 28 U.S.C. Sec. 2201.

Your demand letter can also haunt you later on in litigation. Often the letter is a demand that Pocatello cease infringement, turn over its entire inventory, and account to your client for the damages suffered. Do not be surprised if your opponent waves that letter in front of the jury to make you look ruthless and overbearing. So if you send a demand letter, word it carefully to cast your patent owner as one who has been provoked to the last resort of litigation by the infringer's theft of the owner's invention.

Where you file your suit includes what court. While patent infringement is exclusively the jurisdiction of the federal district courts, 28 U.S.C. Sec. 1338(a), other cases involving patents (such as an action to quiet title to a patent or a suit for patent license royalties) may need to be brought in the state court. An action for compensation for unauthorized use of a patent by the United States government can only be brought in the U.S. claims court, 28 U.S.C. Sec. 1498. No separate action lies against the government's supplier in the district courts, *Western Elec. Co. v. Hammond*, 135 F.2d 283 (1st Cir. 1943).

Where you file your patent suit can often determine victory under the axiom, "Better your home court than his." The special venue statute, 28 U.S.C. Sec. 1400(b), is narrower than the "doing business" or "minimum contacts" tests familiar in other types of civil lawsuits. You can only sue a patent infringer in the district where it resides (for a corporation, its state of incorporation) or, alternatively, where it has a "regular and established place of business" *and* has committed an act of infringement.

While this would often require you to file your case in a distant court (increasing the cost of your client's litigation), our increasingly interdependent economy has provided more flexibility in choosing your forum. An infringing item often passes in a chain from a manufacturer or importer through distributors to retailers to ultimate purchasers—each transaction creating an additional venue possibility.

Once you have filed your patent complaint and learned the identity of the judge, you must decide whether to ask for a jury. Historically, patent lawyers have avoided juries. But increasingly, patent owners are demanding that their cases be tried by a jury.

How do you decide whether to do that, too?

Your trial judge's record on patent validity is the key factor. The data base may be skimpy. There are a few federal judges who have invalidated all, or virtually all, patents brought before them over a broad enough sample to make chance a lame explanation. There are, of course, other factors that are no different than those in any other suit, such as big company versus little and outsider against local enterprise.

If you choose a jury, can it handle the case?

My own experience has been that jurors are extremely conscientious and quite well able to understand issues of technology if they are explained clearly enough.

Discovery in patent cases can be expensive and time-consuming. The patent's national reach leads to disputes between litigants separated by great distances. Making an invention frequently involves many people, from conception through development to marketing. On the infringer's side, there can be a chain of people from copying to sales. There can be years between the acts surrounding the making of an invention and the time of trial. The documentation, created by many people in different places over a long period of time, is frequently extensive and hard to track down. So you must be imaginative, persistent, and economical in using the tools of discovery to develop the evidence needed for trial.

And discovery may have its own rewards—totally aside from the case itself. You learn many interesting things in discovery for patent lawsuits. I have retraced the history of the first aluminum beer can to the discovery of a still surviving beer-filled can from the first-ever production run in this country in 1959.

I have visited the last field of ramie—a tall, Asian hemp—growing in the United States, surviving in Florida nearly 40 years after several of America's largest corporations walked away from their multimillion-dollar attempts to commercialize nature's strongest natural textile fiber. Anyone who thinks patent litigation lacks human interest has no appreciation for the fascinating human endeavors into which it reaches.

Confidentiality is key in patent lawsuits. Discovery can reach technical and business information that each side wants to shield from its opponent and the eyes of other competitors. This concern is accommodated in most patent cases by a protective order under Rule 26, Fed. R. Civ. P., often by stipulation. The order may provide, for example, that discovery information will not be used by the receiving party for purposes other than the lawsuit and is to be kept in confidence and that any confidential information filed with the court shall be under seal.

Sometimes an order may be necessary to protect the privacy of witnesses, particularly when medical inventions are involved. Recently I had to depose nine women concerning breast-implant operations. Under a carefully drafted protective order, the depositions were taken in a way that got the key information for the case while assuring the patients anonymity and lack of embarrassment.

The length, range, and frictions of discovery in patent cases often can be eased by trying liability and damages separately. Unless there has been a demand for a jury (which would cause the plaintiff and the court to resist bifurcation), the parties may be able to stipulate to an order under Rule 42(b), Fed. R. Civ. P., that infringement and validity will be tried first and damages will be left to a second trial if liability is established.

A problem can remain even after bifurcation, if the patent owner intends to prove commercial success at the liability trial to support its position that the patented invention was not obvious. That will require discovery of the extent of the patent owner's sales of the patented product and the infringer's sales of its version.

Sometimes it is not the product but the way of making it that is patented. Those are method patent cases in which it can be helpful to obtain an order for an entry on land under Rule 34, Fed. R. Civ. P. The purpose is to inspect the details of the defendant's manufacturing process. If you do, take along a photographer and your expert witness so that you can gather enough evidence for trial. The expert can be very valuable in a plant inspection. Some years ago, in a case involving a food manufacturing process, my sharp-eyed expert saw that some of the pipe joints in the defendant's plant were suspiciously bright and shiny. That led to the discovery that the pipe runs had been changed around to a noninfringing arrangement for the day of inspection.

When the patent owner has sued a number of unrelated infringers in different judicial districts, there is an opportunity to avoid duplication on common issues by a petition to the judicial Panel on Multidistrict Litigation under 28 U.S.C. Sec. 1407. If the petition is granted, discovery is consolidated in one court on issues common to all cases, typically patent validity. At the end of discovery on the consolidated issues, the cases are returned to their originating districts. If there are not enough defendants for this procedure, an alternative may be to press the litigation in a targeted forum and move to stay the other lawsuits until the target suit has been tried and decided.

Like any complex case, organizing information for a patent trial can be a nightmare. It is, perhaps, a more serious problem in patent cases because of the unusually wide variety of defenses. I have been able to use a microcomputer effectively to keep track of discovery information and sort it to the issues of patent litigation in chronological format. L. Pretty, "Harnessing a Personal Computer to Win Cases," 69 ABA J. 1438 (1983).

As the case develops in discovery, you will start to learn your adversary's defensive strategy, drawn from the wide range of defenses in patent cases.

- The defendant of course will deny infringement, asserting that its product or process does not come within any patent claim.
- Usually the defendant will claim that your patent fails to meet the statute's requirements for patentability. For example, the defendant may claim that, under 35 U.S.C. Sec. 101, the patent is invalid because it is for subject matter outside the classes of patentable subject matter or that the invention is not useful (which usually means that, as disclosed in the patent, it would not work).
- Other invalidity defenses arise under 35 U.S.C. Sections 102 and 103 based on "prior art," a term used to denote earlier relevant devices, products, or processes.
- The defendant also may assert that the invention was anticipated by a previous device or that the invention would have been obvious by combining features from different items of prior art.
- Other invalidity defenses (known as "statutory bar" defenses) invalidate the patent if the invention was placed in public use or on sale in this country more than a year before the application for the patent was filed.

There are equitable defenses, too. One type is known as the "fraud on the patent office." That is when the patent should be invalidated because the patent owner concealed or misrepresented facts to the Patent and Trademark Office to secure the patent. Another line of equitable defenses, known as "patent misuse," is based on the theory that the court should withhold enforcement of the patent because the patent owner has acted in some improper manner in its commercial activities involving the patent, such as tying, price fixing, or package licensing. Laches and equitable estoppel are further defenses in this area.

Then there are technical defenses. The plaintiff's title to the patent may be defective, or an indispensable party—such as the exclusive licensor or licensee—may have been omitted. The defendant may assert that the patent is inadequate because it does not sufficiently teach how to practice the invention or that its patent claims are not definite enough to enable the public to understand what the patent covers. Other defenses go by such shorthand names as double patenting, misjoinder or nonjoinder of inventorship, and foreign filing without a license. You have to anticipate them all.

As trial approaches, the patent lawyer puts down his green eyeshade and begins to grapple with how to present complex questions of fact, rambling expert testimony, and myriads of blueprints, diagrams, computer printouts, and the like to a jury composed of truck drivers, housewives, shopkeepers, and—maybe, if he is lucky—a high school physics teacher.

Advanced technology is not the sole preserve of patent lawsuits, and there are patent cases that involve technology well within a layman's general knowledge. Nonetheless, many patent cases do involve inventions beyond the level of technical knowledge possessed by laymen. Few federal judges have a scientific or engineering background. Understandably, many of them approach patent cases with less confidence than they do more familiar matters.

That means the patent trial lawyer has a delicate task. He must educate the judge or jurors well enough so they feel comfortable with the technical principles necessary to find infringement and validity. Yet he must do so without creating a false light of simplicity that blurs the distinction between the invention and the prior act.

There is a subjective character to the core issues in a patent trial of 1) obviousness of the patented invention and 2) equivalency of the infringing product to the patent claims. The relative persuasiveness and credibility of each party's witnesses can determine the outcome of many patent cases in which closely balanced facts on these issues would let the case go either way. For the patent owner, testimony on these issues often can be most effectively provided by the inventor. Because of the inherent interest of his role, he is well placed to explain the technology, describe the evolution of his invention, show how it differs from what existed before, and point out how the defendant's product embodies his patented invention.

Unfortunately, a common problem for the patent owner's lawyer is the inventor who is unable to carry this central role because of unavailability, poor ability to express himself, or other failings as a witness. The central role must then be shifted to a technical expert witness. In choosing a technical expert in an advanced field, I use an expert who has significant "hands-on" experience in the industrial application of the relevant technology rather than a pure theoretical. Finding the expert should start early. A good expert can help early in discovery in analyzing technical issues affecting infringement and the prior art and in making suggestions.

The patent law expert is another type of special witness. His testimony goes to the significance of actions taken in the examination of the application for the patent, the training of patent examiners, the search facilities available to them, and other fact issues bearing on the patent. A patent expert is usually needed in a jury trial, if only to guide the jurors through the patent file. In a trial before a judge who is experienced in patent cases, it is sometimes better to dispense with a patent expert. Some judges view a patent expert as no more than a talking brief for the side that calls him.

A third type is the accounting expert, who may be needed to testify about lost profits or reasonable royalties.

Choosing a defense expert is no easier. If the designer of the accused device worked without knowing of the patented device, he may be the best one to explain that the product was nothing more than what was obvious to those in the field. But when there was some actual copying, choose a less-tainted, outside expert witness, such as a university professor.

Patent cases are tailor-made for interesting exhibits. Large, colorful graphics can literally decide your case before a tired jury. I like—

- 40-by-60-inch photo-enlargements of the drawings of the patent-in-suit, mounted on foam board and colored by hand.
- Drawings of principal items of the prior art.
- Retyped versions of the patent claims in issue.
- Drawings or photographs of the defendant's product.
- Diagrams of the steps of defendant's process.
- Time charts showing important dates in sequence.
- Educational exhibits that illustrate technical subjects that would be hard to grasp from oral testimony alone.

Overhead projectors, using transparencies made by electrostatic copying machines, are very helpful for displaying exhibits that are not of sufficient importance to justify the expense of enlargements.

Physical exhibits can include prototypes of the invention and its current commercial embodiments. The contrast between the homemade nature of an inventor's first devices and the commercial version on the market brings home the extent of his achievement. Other physical exhibits usually will include the infringing product and, when they help, machines and products from the prior art. If the infringer has made a look-alike copy of the patent owner's product, showing it helps to convince a jury that the inventor has been wronged.

There must, inevitably, be documentary exhibits. Usually they will include the patent itself, the patent office file, the inventor's notebooks, the infringer's project memoranda and drawings, summaries showing the commercial success of the patented invention, and documentation of the infringer's sales.

Do not overdocument the trial and lose the excitement and pace of your plaintiff's case in a morass of paper.

Another serious problem is allowing the judge or jury to decipher the way patents are written—which to most lay people is less understandable than Sanskrit. The patent office requires precise and technical claim wording in the patent to distinguish the invention from the prior art. Courts, on the other hand, tend to cut through the fine distinctions of claim language to the judge's perception of ''the invention.'' The language technicalities are also a frequent problem for witnesses, particularly those inventors who are not articulate.

A further problem can flow from too much breadth of language in claim terminology. A patent claim may, for example, refer to a brush as a ''rotating cleaning means.'' This attempt to obtain broad claim coverage in drafting the patent can backfire at trial. The broad language gives rise to the argument that your patent reaches some earlier device and is therefore invalid.

One approach to overcoming the difficulties presented by patent claims is to provide a shorthand redefinition of the invention, keyed to its novel results, which is easier to understand than the claims yet highlights the differences that set the invention apart from what had gone before. But this may help a defendant argue the patent owner has conceded the weakness of its claims by abandoning them for the shorthand definition. So I prefer to stick with the skeleton of the broadcast patent claim, reworded into simple language. If this can be done with enough clarity, the defendant's concentration upon precise claim terminology will appear to be mere wordplay to camouflage that the defendant had taken the substance of the patented invention.

Another unique problem for the patent owner's lawyer is overcoming the insidious effect of hindsight on the issue of obviousness. The patent statute, 35 U.S.C. Sec. 103, requires that obviousness be resolved by the test of what would have been obvious to a person of ordinary skill in the art at the time that the invention was made. A judge at trial has had the solution to a technical problem made obvious to him by reading the answer provided by the inventor's patent. He may not recognize the difficulty in appreciating why others, with their eyes unopened by hindsight, did not find it obvious to make the invention when the inventor did years before the trial.

To offset the power of hindsight, the patent owner's lawyer must bring the state of technology as it was five, ten, or fifteen years ago back to life in the courtroom. The inventor's early models and tools; the inventor's false starts, insights, and eventual success; his wife's account of the help she provided in his tests and experiments; faded newspapers or trade journals of the time describing reaction to the invention in its field; the testimony of elderly men who remember the impact that the inventor's contribution had on their trade at the time; experts who said his invention would never work—these are the tools of a powerful trial presentation.

Understand that these unique aspects of a patent trial are challenges, not barriers. Imagination, drama, and America's fascination with the efforts of its inventors throughout its history provide strong emotional hooks for the successful trial of a patent owner's claim.

Pick up your calculator and green eyeshade, and join the fray.

Planning Fees Fights

by Christopher T. Lutz

If a contest were held to determine the kind of lawsuit that puts the parties in the sourest frames of mind, attorneys' fees litigation would come in first. It is easy to understand why.

If you are a defense lawyer, there are few things more difficult than telling your client that, for the privilege of losing or reaching a grudging settlement, he must pay the very lawyers who have been a source of irritation for years. Plaintiffs' counsel, for their part, see fees litigation as an indignity and sometimes an insult. For them, a fees battle delays already delayed compensation and creates a gauntlet of criticism and second-guessing that few defense lawyers face.

These attitudes can make fees litigation bitter. A defendant who was temperate toward the plaintiffs in the merits litigation may want to take off the gloves with the plaintiffs' lawyers. Plaintiffs' counsel may conduct fees litigation like a full-scale crusade. Parties who settle the merits sometimes litigate fees for years.

Emotion can be a good thing in litigation. Small amounts of anger can give arguments a punch they would otherwise lack. But emotion by the bucketful—a standard dose in fees fights—can be harmful. It blocks clear thinking. Too much emotional engagement in attorneys' fees litigation keeps the participants from soundly planning their course in the controversy.

Careful thinking is especially important in conducting discovery in fees fights. Fees discovery has features and pitfalls different from those usually encountered in merits discovery.

In planning the parry and thrust of a fees duel, first get your bearings. Think about what the merits litigation was like. Was it a bitter fight or

The author is editor-in-chief of LITIGATION and a partner in Steptoe & Johnson in Washington, D.C.

relatively decorous? Was it a civil rights case or a commercial litigation? The tone and the substance of a case are important clues to the course of a fees battle.

If defense conduct was tough, even obstreperous, or if plaintiffs' lawyers have vindicated fundamental rights of thousands, dogged, detailed resistance to a fees request may be unwise. On the other hand, if the suit was a purely commercial battle between two corporations, plaintiffs' counsel should expect steely-eyed scrutiny of their request.

As important as the nature of the case is the nature of the judge. Normally, lawyers do far too much handicapping and psychoanalysis of judges. These efforts are usually a waste of time or, worse, highly misleading. But it is useful to review your judge's past fees opinions and other evidence of his attitude toward fee awards. The reason is that most people—judges particularly—have strong feelings about fees litigation.

Many judges' feelings about fees litigation seem like the sentiments of Justice Brennan in a related context: They view such disputes as ''one of the least socially productive types of litigation imaginable.'' *Hensley v. Eckerhart*, 461 U.S. 424, 442 (1983). It is not hard to understand why. Fully occupied in deciding pressing criminal and civil matters, the last thing most judges want is a battle between lawyers about how much plaintiffs' counsel should be paid. If you think you have been pressured to settle in lawsuits on the merits, wait until you try fees litigation.

But not all judges share this blend of impatience and hostility toward fees litigation. Some seem to like it. These are the judges you want to know about in advance. Such enthusiasts fall into two polar groups. Some react to fees petitions in the manner of an accountant who feels stiffed by his own lawyers. They, or their clerks, review page upon page of time and expense records with a jeweler's eye. They ferret out vague time descriptions, duplicate efforts, and unreasonable copying charges. That kind of scrutiny seems motivated by a belief that petitioning lawyers—either in general or in a particular case—invariably pad their records and requests.

Far different are those judges who wade hip-deep into fees litigation because of a concern that plaintiffs' lawyers may be underpaid. These judges believe, often deeply, in the policies underlying antitrust, securities, and antidiscrimination laws, and they think that plaintiffs' counsel, who act as private attorneys general, should be very well paid to enforce those laws. Such attitudes usually result in less quibbling about details, a greater inclination to grant a substantial award, and impatience with anything, including discovery, that might delay petitioning counsels' pay day.

After reviewing the nature of the case and sizing up the judge, consider the stakes. If you have represented the plaintiffs, you should already know what you are going to ask for. If you are defense counsel, the plaintiffs may have already told you what they expect. If not, look at your own bills to your client. They are a very rough guide to what your opponent may seek.

As in most disputes, the size of the likely request is a good measure of the intensity of the fight and the resources you should expect to commit to it. If the request is less than $50,000, settle. If the request is under $100,000, settle almost all the time. It is simply not worth anyone's time to wage full-scale war over such sums. Even if you think such litigation is time well spent, the court will not.

All rules have exceptions, and these observations on settlement are themselves no exception. If you represent a defendant, there are a few circumstances in which you should vigorously resist the fees' application: (1) when plaintiffs' counsel want to be paid even though they lost, or got almost nothing; (2) when the requested fees, though small, exceed the money recovery by a factor of two or more; (3) when your client wants to fight on principle and there are good-faith grounds for doing so; and (4) when the petitioning lawyers have sued your client in other cases in which fees might be awarded. In the latter circumstance, your fight over a small fee request will inevitably affect rates and other issues in the larger battle.

A special comment may be in order about fee requests that significantly exceed the underlying money recovery. The Supreme Court has recently held that, so long as the hours compensated and rates awarded are reasonable, a fee award may be proper even though it dwarfs the money recovery. *City of Riverside v. Rivera,* 477 U.S. 561 (1986). This may be especially true in civil rights cases, where much of the value of the relief lies in injunctive remedies. Nonetheless, disproportionate fee requests can be red flags for two reasons. First, they will surely inflame the defendant. Second, and more significantly, their size may be a symptom of unreasonable rates, padded time claims, and similar defects.

If a fee request is large, and will likely lead to extended litigation, what next? If you are a defense lawyer, have a heart-to-heart talk with your client. The news will not be good, but your life will be easier later if you deliver it now: The fees litigation could take months, maybe years. It will likely require discovery, principally document requests and depositions. There could be a long hearing.

The whole thing will cost money. The client will have to pay your fees, whether he wins or loses the fees battle. If resistance to the fee request proves unsuccessful, your client will have to pay not only the fees sought, but also the fees incurred by plaintiffs' counsel in conducting the fees litigation.

Fees on Fees

The "fees on fees" potential of attorneys' fees litigation cannot be overemphasized. It affects most strategic considerations, and it complicates settlement analysis. The defendant's potential liability, and therefore the appropriate settlement level, can become ever receding horizons. No matter how fast and long the parties run, they never approach the end of the road. It is like owing money to a loan shark: The longer you take to pay, the more you owe, until you owe more interest—or fees on fees—than principal.

Both sides have one more decision before embarking on discovery. Should they retain special counsel for the fees litigation? Ninety-five percent of the time, from a defense perspective, the answer is no. The lawyers who litigated the merits will understand the suit—and the efforts of plaintiffs' counsel—in a way outside counsel cannot without a lot of catching up, which would be expensive and time-consuming.

But there are certain cases in which defendants should consider retaining fees counsel. Ask yourself these questions: Has the defendant's lawyer so botched the litigation that he has lost his client's confidence? Has he done a good, tough job, but, in the process, utterly alienated the judge? Will the fees battle be so complex that special expertise in fees law might be required? If the answer to any of these questions is yes, and the fees request is likely to be large, a defendant should consider hiring new lawyers.

For the petitioning lawyers, retention of separate counsel is more common, though far from universal. Aside from the adage that the lawyer who represents himself has a fool for a client, there are often other sound reasons to get new counsel.

Petitioning counsel usually have to testify—live or by affidavit—in support of a fees petition. In this situation, the canons of ethics may require separate representation. There is also a practical consideration: An argument for big fees often involves lavish praise of plaintiffs' counsel and their litigation handiwork. It is often more comfortable—and seems less vain—to have someone else deliver the panegyric.

Two caveats for plaintiffs' counsel contemplating a new fees lawyer: First, not all judges will view another lawyer as a reasonable expense, especially if the amount in dispute is small. If you win, you can probably get the defendant to pay your lawyer, but that is not guaranteed.

Second, and more importantly, be absolutely certain the lawyer you pick, aside from knowing fees law, knows something about litigation under the law that produced the merits dispute. The tone and approach of securities litigation, antitrust disputes, and employment discrimination cases differ. These differences are reflected in the fees disputes that grow out of each. If your fees lawyer does not appreciate the distinctions, he may try to sell the wrong thing in the wrong way.

Before diving into discovery, think again about settlement. By now, you should know the stakes. Plaintiffs' counsel have probably filed their petition, and, even if they have not, they have probably announced what they will seek. Now is the time to try to resolve the dispute. It really is only money. Rarely should it be a matter of principle.

Even if you do not want to talk settlement, the court will probably force you to. Most judges do not want to hold a fees hearing, and the pressure to force a settlement can be intense.

Here is a favorite technique: The court calls a chambers conference on fees matters. He looks at the parties and says: "Don't come back until you settle." He then issues an order that no fees discovery may be conducted until the parties have had a reasonable time to discuss settlement. This may last for months. Especially for plaintiffs' counsel, a little delay can sharply focus the mind on compromise.

Even if a complete settlement is impossible, try to settle pieces of the problem. Fees litigation is usually susceptible to piecemeal resolution. Fees requests are based on several discrete elements: expenses incurred; hours worked; hourly rates claimed; and a multiplier. In theory, any of these elements can be settled without compromising anybody's position on the others. If your real dispute is over hourly rates, try not to spend a lot of time fighting about copying charges or time-sheet legibility. By settling in pieces, you can focus the dispute on the real points of conflict.

Not all fees differences can be amicably resolved, though. If settlement is impossible, how do you plan for discovery? First, consider whether you *can* conduct discovery.

Judges who do not like fees litigation like fees discovery even less. They can do many things to restrict it. An order suspending discovery to allow settlement talks is just one restriction you may face. Another approach the judge may take is to set a hearing or final briefing date 30 or 60 days after the formal fees petition is filed. In that little time, not much discovery is possible. Finally, courts often sustain objections to especially probing inquiries. You can try to conduct discovery, but you may not get anything in the face of resistance.

But why worry about discovery? Who needs it? If a petition with supporting documentation is filed, what more does the defendant need? And why would the plaintiffs ever need discovery from the defendant?

For a defendant, the answer is that a petition is often uninformative. While a petition should be intelligible and contain sufficient supporting detail, some counsel unfortunately take a notice-pleading approach to fees requests: Expenses may be uncategorized and reduced to a single figure. Attorneys' hours may be cumulated, and not broken down by either lawyer or activity. In such cases, a defendant has three choices: accept the request on faith; resist it as facially insufficient; or conduct discovery to see if the conclusory demand can be supported by a detailed accounting.

Few defendants choose the first course, and none should. An uninformative fees petition is very often a sign that detailed supporting documentation is not available. Time and expenses may have been reconstructed or invented. Hourly rates may have been plucked from the air. You need to ask to know.

Defendants rarely take the second course—attacking the petition on its face—because that is a big risk. You may think the petition is unsatisfactory, but the court may disagree. If this happens, and you have had no discovery, you are stuck.

Even with very detailed petitions, there are usually good reasons for a defendant to conduct discovery. For example, petitioning counsel may intend to present witnesses or affidavits to show what great lawyers they are. Who are the witnesses? What will they say?

The petition may say that $225 is an appropriate rate for lawyers' services. What is that based on? Counsel may want the court to double their usual hourly rate to reward them for the great result they say they got. Will they present any evidence to show that this multiplier is justified? What will it be? None of these questions can be answered very well without discovery.

There are also reasons for petitioning counsel to conduct fees-related discovery. Defendants may present rebuttal witnesses, affidavits, or other evidence. Plaintiffs will often need discovery into this material. And plaintiffs' counsel can use requests for admissions to narrow the points in dispute if the defendant unreasonably wants to fight everything.

Another kind of discovery that plaintiffs sometimes seek in fees litigation is more controversial. It might be called reciprocal discovery. It might also be called embarrassment discovery.

Suppose you represent a defendant opposing a $1 million fees request as excessive. You open your mail. Out drops a set of interrogatories from plaintiffs' counsel asking your client for detailed information on all fees and expenses paid in defense of the underlying suit. Through a fog of disbelief, you see the envelope also contains a document request demanding that you produce copies of all your bills.

Most defense lawyers' reaction is predictable: outrage. Such discovery, they think, pries into the minute details of the financial relationship between them and their clients. It seems to compromise the attorney-client relationship. And their first instincts tell them that the information plaintiffs are after is irrelevant to boot.

But petitioning counsel have an argument for the discoverability of such material: If the question is what level of fees is reasonable for handling a lawsuit, what better measure is there than the amount that the defendant invested in the case? Surely, plaintiffs would say, how much the defendant spent to litigate the same facts and issues is highly germane. How can $1 million be too much if the defendant spent $4 million?

Despite defense outrage, such arguments sometimes win the day. The propriety of reciprocal discovery varies depending on the component of a fees request that it concerns. The important point is that such counter-punching is possible. A similar risk exists in almost any kind of dispute, but, in fees battles, boomerang discovery can seek out especially sensitive information: what defense counsel charge, what they collect, what they make, and the like. If you are a defense lawyer planning a no-holds-barred discovery program, do not forget the kinds of questions you and your client might have to answer in return.

The specific pattern of discovery in a fees battle depends on the contested issues. Remember that fee requests are made of four main elements: expenses, lawyer and paralegal hours, hourly rates, and a multiplier. Each of these elements can be the subject of discovery.

Take expenses first. Litigating about the costs and expenses incurred by plaintiffs' counsel is one of the duller things a human being can do. Reviewing messenger charges, plane tickets, and copying slips is no fun. More important, from a defense standpoint, it is often uneconomic: If you spend five paralegal hours (at $40 per hour) finding, and one attorney hour (at $100 per hour) writing about, a dubious $250 copying bill, your client has lost money.

For a defendant, a gradual approach to getting expense information is advisable. First, look at the petition. Add up all the expense items. Compare the total to the expenses your client incurred. If plaintiffs ask for what your clients spent or less, it is unlikely you will be able to chip much off the request. Extensive discovery probably will not make sense. As a check, look at the categories of expenses claimed. If plaintiffs want to be paid for the same kinds of things your client paid for, again extensive reduction of the expense bill is unlikely.

A defendant seeking expense information now has a hard question to answer: How much further should he go?

At least go far enough to be sure there is documentary support for the expenses claimed and that no individual items are scandalously high. You may be able to do much of this with the petition itself. A competently assembled petition will often include attachments listing expenses item-by-item. If the petition lacks such information and it is not produced voluntarily, a defendant should go after it through discovery.

But what discovery device do you use? The logical answer would seem to be interrogatories or requests for production of documents, but Rules 33(a) and 34(a) provide that those discovery devices may be directed only to parties. Are the petitioning lawyers—who almost certainly have the information you need —"parties"? As a technical matter, probably not, even though the fees petition is really their request.

In statutory fees cases, the relevant statutory language usually provides reasonable fees and costs to "prevailing parties" in the underlying litigation. But, like it or not, petitioning counsel *are* the parties for all practical purposes in a fees litigation. Whatever the statutory fiction, it is usually *not* the case that the award goes to the plaintiff, who passes it along to the lawyers. This blurring of who the real party is has caused courts some concern. *See, e.g., Rainsbarger v. Columbia Glass and Window Co.*, 600 F. Supp. 299, 301 (W.D. Mo. 1984). In practice, though, fees petitions are routinely filed by the lawyers themselves, with little or no reference to their clients.

So what does the uncertainty over whether petitioning lawyers are "parties" mean in the conduct of fees discovery? A defense lawyer who wants expense details and records and who wants to be technically correct has a choice: Either serve a Rule 45 subpoena *duces tecum* on the lawyers or direct a document request or interrogatories to the plaintiffs. The first approach will work, but it is cumbersome, unless it prompts voluntary production. The second route—service on the plaintiff—should also work, and also often leads to voluntary production.

Unfortunately, occasionally the plaintiff's response to a Rule 34 document request will be, "I don't know the answers to your questions and I don't have the stuff you want. Maybe my lawyer knows." Again, the defendant has two alternatives: Serve a Rule 45 subpoena on the lawyers, or, sometimes better still, get the court involved, by way of a motion to compel or to strike the plaintiffs' request for expenses (if that is what the discovery concerned). Such a motion can be a good way to show the judge that petitioning counsel are playing games. Plaintiffs' counsel decidedly do not want the judge to see them in that light. As a result, if there really are expense records to produce, the game playing usually stops short of a court order.

The compelling practical incentives for petitioning counsel to provide back-up information mean that defense counsel rarely have to worry about who the "parties" are in planning discovery. But that issue can be important when *petitioning* counsel want to conduct discovery.

Defendants and their lawyers do not have to be as concerned about whether their discovery positions bother the judge. Because many judges are skeptical of attempts to secure fees information from defense counsel, objections to discovery of defendants' expenses are often sustained. So petitioning counsel should remember that the defendant is a party but its lawyers are not. The form of discovery must vary depending on who the target is.

Having decided on what form of discovery to use, you need to figure out what information to go after. If you represent a defendant, the first step is to ask for an itemized breakdown of expenses and the supporting invoices and other original documents. If you get a list, you can scan it to determine what underlying material you want to examine. Often, though, there will not be a list. Having described expenses in broad categories, petitioning counsel will rely on Rule 30(b)(6), or its equivalent, and invite you to examine the records.

If you get such an invitation, what you do depends on the number and location of the documents. If the expenses claimed are small and the records are few and nearby, have a paralegal spend an hour or two examining them. But if there are thousands of expense records, do not spend weeks with them. Sample instead. Look at every third or sixth item, and look particularly at records supporting very big expenditures.

If the records seem to be in order, stop. If you have grounds for contesting significant expense claims, you will know it by now. There may be a dubious charge lurking in the mountain of paper, but it will likely cost more to find it than you will save.

Expense discovery by petitioning counsel is far less common. It is most likely to occur when the defendant has argued that the plaintiff's expenses in general were too high, or that the plaintiff spent too much on certain projects. If the defendant bridles at paying 15 cents per page for copying, for example, plaintiff may want to know what defense counsel's firm charges.

Such reciprocal discovery ordinarily produces a flurry of objections. Besides snorts of indignation and claims of privilege and confidentiality, the defendant's main argument will be based on relevance considerations. Defendants and plaintiffs do different things, they say; there is no necessary relationship between the amounts that the two sides spend. And, some defendants may argue, what defendants and their attorneys voluntarily decide to spend may be more than the "reasonable" expenses an adverse party can be forced to reimburse.

Such arguments have met with mixed success. Whether discovery of the defendant's expenses is allowed will depend less on the law than on the judge's attitude toward fees litigation.

After disbursements, the next major element of a fees petition is the number of hours that the lawyers and paralegals spent on the case. Petitioning counsel will say the time spent was reasonable. Defendants will look for inefficiency, duplication, excess, and invented time.

Like disputes over costs, arguing about time claims can be dull and expensive. Settlement is usually advisable. When the parties cannot get together on the time that plaintiffs' lawyers reasonably spent on the case, the battle over hours is usually hard fought. And, once the fighting gets going, truces are less common on this front.

Judges tend to get more deeply involved in reviewing the reasonableness of hours claimed. The subject is slightly more interesting than the propriety of a $57 messenger charge. Judges often have strong feelings about what lawyers ought to do and how much time it should take them to do it. For their part, petitioning counsel often have a strong personal interest in justifying the reasonableness of work they have done.

Because of the parties' stronger feelings and the judge's greater interest, the parties usually exchange a considerable amount of information on hours claimed. For defense counsel, the task is much as it is with expenses.

Begin with the petition. See if it gives you enough detail to make judgments about the kind of work performed and the efficiency of plaintiffs' staffing. Compare the hours and tasks listed to what you did.

Use Rule 45 subpoenas, if necessary, to get a more detailed breakdown of lawyers' and paralegals' hours. Try to get the original time sheets, so you can sample them and satisfy yourself that they exist and appear to be contemporaneous. As always, how much discovery the defendant conducts has to be sensibly related to how much is at stake and how plausible the hours claimed seem to be.

The issue of hours claimed can be usefully explored in depositions of petitioning counsel. If the time records look fishy—showing, for example, a single 30-hour entry for three days of work, or 50 hours of undifferentiated legal research or client consultation—it may be useful to quiz petitioning counsel about how they kept their time records. If they testify that they "reconstructed" or estimated their time, probing examination is the only effective way to understand how they did it, if that *can* be understood at all.

If you want to conduct a deposition of petitioning counsel, remember these points: First, use a Rule 45 subpoena. Second, remember that deposing a lawyer can be frustrating—he will know the case as well as you do, is likely to be well schooled in the techniques of deposition testimony, and may raise a cloud of privilege objections. Before you conduct a deposition, reflect on whether you are likely to get much. Do not do it simply for the pleasure of grilling—or yelling at—your adversary.

Finally, and most importantly, judges can be very impatient with fees depositions of lawyers. They may quash Rule 45 subpoenas and sustain privilege or work-product objections. Judges sometimes give aid and comfort to plaintiffs' lawyers, it seems, not because plaintiffs' objections are analytically sound, but because of a general feeling that, at some point, enough is enough.

Petitioning counsel frequently attempt discovery related to time claims. Sometimes they get it. The logic of such discovery is much as it was for expenses. If the defendant complains that the 600 hours that plaintiffs' counsel says he spent on the case is too much, for example, it might be relevant to determine whether defendant's lawyers spent 2,000 hours defending the same suit. Some courts have agreed with this logic. *See, e.g., Blower v. Lawyers Coop. Publishing Co.*, 526 F. Supp. 1324, 1326 (W.D.N.Y. 1981).

Other courts may reach the contrary conclusion, reasoning that defendants and plaintiffs do different things, and so even the time spent on similar work may properly be quite disparate. For example, most plaintiffs invest less time drafting interrogatories than defendants do answering them. *See Ohio Sealy Mattress Mfr. Co. v. Ohio Sealy Inc.*, 776 F.2d 646, 659 (7th Cir. 1985); *Johnson v. University College of the Univ. of Ala.*, 706 F.2d 1205, 1208 (11th Cir.), *cert. denied*, 464 U.S. 994 (1983).

Also, some courts, rightly or wrongly, seem to regard discovery of defendants' counsel's time records as harassment and excess. They believe they can judge the efficiency of plaintiffs' efforts based on the petition and what they know about the litigation. As a result, defense objections on grounds of the work product rule, the attorney-client privilege, and irrelevance, though sometimes just barely plausible, may be sustained.

Discovery on the question of hourly rates is more often sought and allowed, though there are limits. Usually, petitioning counsel just state a series of hourly rates for lawyers and legal assistants. There is normally little or no explanation. Among other things, defense counsel will want to know: How were the rates selected? How do they compare with what petitioning counsel charge, or collect from, other clients? What evidence will counsel present to show that the rates are appropriate charges in the market? What is the relevant market?

The need for defense discovery on such points is obvious. Usually it is permitted. The first step is easy: See if there are reported decisions on fees awards to your adversaries. If the cases are old, be sure to adjust the rates for inflation.

Next, a good way to begin formal discovery on rates—providing opposing counsel do not quibble—is with interrogatories. At minimum, ask who will testify, by affidavit or in person, that the rates claimed are appropriate. Think about deposing those witnesses, but remember that, because they may qualify as experts, you may have to dance the procedural minuet required by Rule 26(b)(4). Remember also that, because rate witnesses are often prominent local lawyers, they may be frustrating to question. Try to find out if petitioning counsel expect to rely on a survey of prevailing rates in the market; if they do, request a copy and consider deposing whoever did the survey. If plaintiffs' counsel themselves will be the only sources of rate testimony, consider deposing them on that topic (as well as hours claimed).

Attempting discovery of further information on the rates that plaintiffs' lawyers have requested can lead to extended battles, because that information usually concerns the internal finances and management of their law firm. Say plaintiffs want $150 per hour for a particular lawyer's time, but you think he normally bills only $110. Can you ask for copies of bills to other clients? If you got them, would that be enough? Not all lawyers collect what they bill. Can you ask for canceled checks from clients? The list of documents and other information requested could be extended almost indefinitely and ever deeper into the recesses of law firm management.

The only reliable answers to the questions about how much defendants can poke around behind petitioning counsel's claimed hourly rates are: *Yes,* you can ask for such information; *yes,* it is all sufficiently relevant to be discoverable; but *no,* a court will not compel answers to all such questions if petitioning counsel resist. At some point, the judge will conclude that, though the material is somewhat relevant, he can determine a proper rate without further scrutiny of otherwise private financial matters. How far a defense lawyer should test the judge's tolerance in this area depends on the stakes and the tenor of the dispute.

What about discovery of hourly rate information from defense counsel? This can be an especially touchy question. Some courts simply bar it. *See, e.g., Samuel v. University of Pittsburgh*, 80 F.R.D. 293 (W.D. Pa. 1978). But others permit it, at least to a limited extent.

The argument for such discovery is by now familiar. If the defendant paid $175 per hour to a lawyer with ten years of experience to defend the case, why should the defendant not pay the same rate to comparably experienced plaintiffs' counsel?

Whether such information is discoverable will depend mostly on how much information petitioning counsel want and where defense counsel are located. If all that is sought is a list of rates, that discovery may be permitted. If petitioning counsel have demanded copies of defendant's bills, records of payments, or depositions of defense counsel, discovery will probably not be compelled. And if the court and petitioning counsel are in Dallas, but defense counsel are in New York City, it will be hard to convince the judge that what the defendants paid their lawyers has any bearing on the rate prevailing in Dallas. Overarching all these points is the court's attitude. Some judges believe they can decide an appropriate rate for plaintiffs' counsel without knowing anything about what defense counsel charge.

The final topic for fees discovery—and always the most disputed—is the multiplier. A few words of background are needed on this point.

The Multiplier

Instead of simply seeking the product of rates times hours, most petitions multiply that product—the "lodestar"—by a number larger than one. A 1.25 multiplier thus produces a 25 percent premium over market rates. A 3.0 multiplier—and some have been sanctioned, though rarely—awards a 200 percent premium to plaintiffs counsel. It is multipliers that produce awards of $300 to $600 per hour worked. Though the Supreme Court has held that multipliers should be reserved for "rare" and "exceptional" cases, *Pennsylvania v. Delaware Valley Citizens' Council for Clean Air*, 478 U.S. 546 (1986), *rev'd on reh'g*, 107 S. Ct. 3078 (1987), they are routinely sought.

Discovery on multipliers usually revolves around the two justifications most often given for their appropriateness. One of those justifications—which the Supreme Court has now recognized as valid—is the result. *See Blum v. Stenson*, 465 U.S. 886 (1984). If a lawyer achieves a very special result —"exceptional" relief in the Court's words—perhaps accomplishing more than a lawyer at his hourly rate level might be expected to achieve, a bonus may be appropriate.

A second, and more hotly debated, ground for a multiplier is risk. Plaintiffs' counsel advocate a risk-based multiplier because, when they lose, they receive no fees. They say that the laws require that they receive the same average income as defense counsel, who assertedly are paid in every case, win or lose. To prevent plaintiffs' work from being less attractive economically than defense practice, say the advocates of risk-based premiums, there has to be an enhancement of fee awards to account for the time spent on unsuccessful cases where plaintiffs' counsel receive nothing.

Though many defendants believe such reasoning is oversimplified and has legal shortcomings, it has been accepted in some form by a number of courts. The Supreme Court itself has split over the issue. Upon rehearing in *Delaware*, 107 S. Ct. 3078 (1987), a majority (four dissenting justices and Justice O'Connor who concurred in the judgment but wrote a separate opinion) supported the principle of multipliers, while four justices argued that most fee-shifting statutes do not allow multipliers. But Justice O'Connor supported the plurality's reversal of the district court's use of a multiplier because she did not believe that a multiplier was justified on the facts of this case, making the precedential value of the case unclear.

In discovery on multipliers, a defendant's first task is to determine why plaintiffs believe their lawyers are entitled to any premium at all. If this is not spelled out in a brief accompanying the petition (and usually it will be), the rationale can be discovered through interrogatories and, rarely, depositions of petitioning counsel. Almost always, you will quickly learn that plaintiffs' counsel think that both risk and relief achieved justify a multiplier. Typically, other factors—such as delay in payment and preclusion of other work—will also be mentioned.

Discovery on the success justification for enhancement is fairly simple. Besides generously praising their own work and deprecating results in past cases, petitioning counsel will likely rely on just a few kinds of evidence: their own testimony; testimonials from other lawyers and experts; and, occasionally, testimony from economists about the economic value of the injunctive portions of the relief.

If defense lawyers believe that evidence like this might justify a multiplier, the answer is depositions. Serve a Rule 45 subpoena on petitioning counsel and find out why they think the result is exceptional. How does it compare with the results in other specific cases? What unusual legal hurdles did lead counsel face?

Notice the depositions of noneconomist experts (after complying with Rule 26(b)(4)) and probe their familiarity with the details of the case. Determine how much they know about the issues, the evidence, and the plaintiffs' strengths and weaknesses. Find out what they think "exceptional" means, and determine whether—especially if they are plaintiffs' counsel themselves—their testimony has been shaped by their economic self-interest.

Deposing economists who purport to value nonmonetary relief can be entertaining. Plaintiffs' lawyers—especially those who handle civil rights litigation—present such testimony because they fear some judges

1131

may give them insufficient credit for securing complex injunctive relief, and may look exclusively at the money payout. Some judges have been impressed by such appraisal evidence. *See, e.g., Arenson v. Board of Trade*, 372 F. Supp. 1349 (N.D. Ill. 1974). Others have not. *See, e.g., EEOC v. Burlington Northern Inc.*, 618 F. Supp. 1046, 1059–60 (N.D. Ill. 1985) *aff'd in part, rev'd in part, sub nom, In re Burlington Northern, Inc. Employment Practices Litigation*, 810 F.2d 601 (7th Civ. 1986), *cert. denied*, 108 S. Ct. 82 (1987). The main aim in deposing relief appraisal experts is, not surprisingly, to determine how the appraisal was done and what assumptions it is based on.

Besides trying to find errors and illogic, the goal of such a deposition should be to show that the expert's analysis is alien to the subject of the suit. This may be difficult in antitrust and securities suits, which are awash in economic analysis. But it can be productive in civil rights suits.

In a recent large employment discrimination class action, for example, plaintiffs' money valuation of hiring quotas in a consent decree depended on how many people the defendant would hire in the coming years. The parties differed sharply about this issue. Plaintiffs presented an expert who had constructed an econometric model to predict hiring over the course of six years and to value the settlement.

The expert's prediction for the first year exceeded the actual hiring by 1,000 percent. This inaccuracy did not faze the expert. He insisted that his model was as good as anything the defendant itself had to say about its future hiring needs. He said at the deposition he could meaningfully forecast hiring without knowing anything about the defendant's business. In fact, he testified, he needed to know only two things to forecast hiring for the particular defendant: the year and the Gross National Product. When asked how he could account for all the variables affecting the defendant's industry and business, he said basically just this: "Add a quadratic term to the equation."

The judge, who was used to thinking of hiring levels in terms of people and business needs, seemed unimpressed. He gave no weight to a valuation exercise based on hiring predictions based on the year, the GNP, and a "quadratic term."

Discovery concerning the risk justification for a multiplier can be complex, far-reaching, and controversial. The first thing for a defendant to do is to determine whether plaintiffs' lawyers will present an expert— who again would probably be an economist or a lawyer with economic training—to talk about risk. If so, depose that person; discover the logic of his analysis and the depth of his knowledge of the case.

There are other kinds of risk-related discovery that a defendant can consider. If the plaintiffs claim that there was a high risk of loss, try to find out—by interrogatories or possibly depositions—what their success rate has been in comparable cases. Be sure not to focus solely on victory after trial. Most cases are not tried, and settlement is an outcome that often should be treated as success for fees purposes, because attorneys who settle may be awarded fees. *Maher v. Gagne,* 448 U.S. 122 (1980).

If petitioning counsel have won or settled 80 percent of their past cases—not an implausible figure—but have typically received a 1.5 multiplier, they have been overcompensated, at least if the multiplier has been based solely on risk factors. Very often courts will allow discovery of ''past experience'' evidence, if only because it is relevant to questions of counsel's experience and qualifications, which themselves bear on the proper hourly rate.

Even though the multiplier is usually a hotly contested issue, there is rarely any occasion for plaintiffs' counsel to conduct discovery on this issue. There just is not much to ask. Neither the defendant nor its lawyers will have much useful information about the degree of success achieved. If you ask them, they will probably say that any settlement was ''appropriate'' and will simply observe that they disagree with the propriety of any judgment they resisted. On risk, there is equally little that plaintiffs can expect to get from the defendant or its lawyers.

Because there is little benefit to discovery by petitioning counsel on the issue of the multiplier to be applied, they should almost never conduct such discovery. In fact, petitioning counsel will have their hands—and minds—full with the developing case law, which seems to pose ever-higher barriers to the use of multipliers for any reason. *See Delaware Valley Citizens' Council, supra; Blum v. Stenson, supra.*

A final thought: Discussing the planning of fees litigation discovery does not mean that I necessarily endorse extensive fees discovery in all cases. Justice Brennan had it right when he observed that many aspects of attorneys' fees litigation are not very ''socially productive.'' Discovery is no exception.

If you can settle the controversy, or if you can litigate it without discovery, do so. There will, however, be occasions when discovery, sometimes extended, is unavoidable. If you encounter such a case, do everything you can to make discovery crisp, efficient, and quick. Target your inquiries. And don't let your frustration, or your client's bitterness, get the upper hand. As in all kinds of litigation, control is essential. If you do not impose it in fees litigation, the court will.

Representing a Victim of Employment Discrimination

by Barry L. Goldstein

You earned your stripes in litigation combat five years ago. Your career is a litany of litigation's varieties: the claims and defenses of two dozen businesses, your share of consumers' complaints, and a trio of contested divorces. You followed some of these cases on to the state supreme court and your federal circuit court, winning and losing along the way.

But this morning brings a case the likes of which you have only heard: the claim of a young black worker who was fired and did not get a promotion he thinks he deserved. More than likely, the case comes to you by way of a very Senior Partner who received a call from his old law school buddy, now a federal judge. The pro se plaintiff came before the judge, and the judge knew there was a better way.

This client's story stirs a sense of justice in you, and you think the story will appeal to a judge and jury.

The question right now is not the character or appeal of the case, but whether you can succeed in a complex and intricate legal arena unknown to you. There is no doubt that your experience as a litigator will benefit your client. It is also true that as a result of fee provisions in the fair employment laws, you may well turn a profit for the firm, with or without payment from the client.

My advice as a regular and enthusiastic practitioner in employment discrimination is: Go For It.

You can count on the support of your litigation experience and considerably broaden and deepen the quality, if not the satisfaction, of it by taking up what the Supreme Court has called the mantle of the "private attorney general." *Newman v. Piggie Park Enterprises, Inc.*, 390 U.S. 400 (1968).

There is no doubt that this litigation arena requires decision making

The author is assistant counsel for the NAACP Legal Defense & Educational Fund, Inc., in Washington, D.C.

each step along the way, and requires matching preceding steps and decisions with succeeding steps and decisions.

It requires an intricate and subtle dance.

The federal employment laws, such as Title VII of the Civil Rights Act of 1964, 42 U.S.C. § 2000e *et seq.*, and the Civil Rights Act of 1866, 42 U.S.C. § 1981, are "separate, distinct and independent." *Johnson v. Railway Express Agency, Inc.*, 421 U.S. 454 (1975). They run parallel to each other: they do not dovetail, but sometimes overlap, and you can move them in harness for the benefit of your client. You will not necessarily sacrifice one cause of action by electing another. Your client may allege many causes of action and an aggregate of potential remedies sufficient to raise the stakes and force the boss to defend on different fronts. To get the benefit of those overlapping remedies, you must meet precise procedural and timeliness requirements for each cause or remedy. Tolling or other equitable arguments will not fill this bill.

The fair employment laws provide a potential plaintiff with a collection of claims. The best first step is to create an inventory of them, noting the following by each:

1. Procedural and time requirements;
2. Standard of proof;
3. Potential forums; and
4. Available remedies.

As the positive thinkers say, visualize the case on a long-term basis, from the pleading possibilities through strategy, on toward realization of the remedy and its satisfaction.

I am going to hold up in front of you each component of an employment discrimination suit, and then attach each part to other interrelated parts, like the blind man investigating different parts of the elephant. In this case, however, you will be able to remove your blindfold and see the case from beginning to end, trunk to tail.

First, you must deal with the administrative agency and overcome initial procedural hurdles. A plaintiff must file administrative charges with the existing state or local fair employment agency and with the Equal Employment Opportunity Commission (EEOC) before bringing a federal action under Title VII (for job discrimination based on race, color, gender, national origin, or religion); under the Age Discrimination in Employment Act (for job discrimination against people over 40); or the Equal Pay Act (which bars paying women less than men for performing substantially the same work). To insure that the local and federal filing requirements are met, the plaintiff should personally file with both the local fair employment agency and the EEOC.

The EEOC charge must be filed within a certain period—for example, under Title VII—180 days from the alleged illegal act. By filing first with a state or local government fair employment agency, the period for filing with the EEOC may be extended to 300 days.

Once the charge is filed with the EEOC, the plaintiff is required to wait at least 180 days before bringing a lawsuit. This allows the agency to investigate, determine, and attempt to resolve the charge. After the expiration of the waiting period, the plaintiff requests a "right to sue" letter from the EEOC. Having filed a charge and waited the required period, your client has an absolute right to file the lawsuit even if the EEOC or the state agency did not investigate or process the charge, or if the agency found that there was no "reasonable cause" to believe that the law has been violated.

Some practitioners ignore the administrative process, thinking that their representation will truly commence with the filing of a complaint. This is a serious mistake. The administrative stage provides the best opportunity to avoid the procedural wrangles that profit defendants and delay the plaintiffs day in court—or deny it altogether.

The charge should include a broad statement of all employment practices your client may want to litigate. For example, it should include not just the discharge that brought the client to you, but also the denial of a promotion or the harassment before the client was fired. If appropriate, assert that your client was not alone in suffering the discrimination, that instead what happened was not an isolated incident, but part of a continuing pattern. In *Bazemore v. Friday*, 478 U.S. 385, 395 (1986), the Supreme Court stated, "[e]ach week's pay check that delivers less to a black than to a similarly situated white is a wrong." Your client may recover under Title VII even though the discriminatory pattern began years before a charge or suit was filed, even before Title VII became law.

A broad, clear charge warns of potential and significant relief through a possible class action, and denies the defense argument that a court should limit the federal action because the claims raised are not "like or related to" those presented to the administrative agency.

You must monitor the administrative process to prevent the officer from paring your charge down. Because more than 70,000 charges are filed with the EEOC each year, there is a strong bureaucratic tendency to push charges to resolution quickly. The philosophy is: the more narrow the charge, the less work—and the more likely a voluntary settlement. Unfortunately, the settlement often will have only nuisance value.

If the boss wants to settle, do not get excited yet. His desire does not have much to do with the quality of the case or your stature as a lawyer.

The truth is that there is a bias toward settlement, and it principally works to the benefit of the employer.

The people who run the system—whether union or company, whether grievance negotiators or administrative agency officers—will pressure you and your client to settle early. The perceptive defense lawyer will make an offer at the "going rate" for a minimal settlement early in the process to thwart development of an effective class action or jury trial lawsuit. Recognize the speedy resolution bias of the process and how the defendant's attorney takes advantage of the bias, and advise your client accordingly.

The investigation will need your spurring. Commonly, there is only "desk investigation," which means that stock questions are asked and stock answers are given. Yet, private counsel can prod some investigators to prepare penetrating questions, request detailed documentation, and, at the "fact-finding" conference attended by both parties, permit the plaintiff's attorney to question the company's managers. Since a charging party has access to the investigation record before filing suit, the administrative process offers inexpensive discovery and an opportunity to preview the merits of the lawsuit.

Under Title VII, a plaintiff may receive back pay covering the two-year period before the administrative charge is filed. Note that the filing of a Title VII charge does not toll the running of the statute of limitations for a claim brought under another act such as 42 U.S.C. § 1981, one of the Reconstruction Civil Rights Acts, which the Supreme Court has interpreted as prohibiting racial discrimination in employment. The applicable statute of limitations for a § 1981 case is determined by state law. Many state statutes provide more than a two-year recovery period and, accordingly, if a plaintiff waits to file his § 1981 lawsuit until after the completion of the Title VII administrative process, the recovery period for back pay may be reduced. Therefore, consider filing a federal lawsuit under § 1981 when the Title VII administrative charge is filed and perhaps, as suggested by the Supreme Court in *Johnson v. Railway Express Agency, Inc.*, request the court to stay the suit until the administrative process is completed.

There are two principal standards of proof for fair employment laws. Under the "disparate treatment" standard, the plaintiff proves discriminatory motive, that is, that the employer purposefully denied the promotion to the black because of his race. You may show discriminatory purpose by indirect or circumstantial evidence, for example, by a difference in the application of rules or by statistical proof.

Under the "disparate impact" standard, the plaintiff demonstrates that an employment selection procedure, such as a written or physical test or a height or educational requirement, excludes a disproportionate percentage of the protected group. If you show this disproportionate impact, the burden of proof shifts to the employer using the selection procedure. He must show that the practice is "job related" or, in other words, that the procedure produces better job performance.

A plaintiff may establish a Title VII violation under either the treatment or the impact theory. But, your client often receives no greater remedy when malicious intent is proved than when an inadvertent impact claim is shown. Title VII gives broad discretion to the district court to impose affirmative and injunctive relief to end discrimination practices and to remedy the consequences of these practices.

Title VII is well designed to give prospective relief for practices that unjustifiably limit job opportunities for minorities or women, yet it often provides paltry relief for the individual victim. Monetary relief is limited to lost "back pay," which may include all actual earnings lost, like pension, vacation benefits, and interest, for the two years before the charge was filed. As a general rule, injunctive relief is restricted by the so-called "rightful place" principle, because the courts have decided that it is improper to "bump" white job incumbents even if they hold those jobs as a result of racial discrimination. This means that a discrimination victim is not entitled to immediate reinstatement, but must wait until a vacancy occurs.

Finding the Forum

There are alternative or additional claims to Title VII that give the victim of employment discrimination remedies somewhat comparable to successful tort or contract claims. The Federal Equal Pay Act and Age Discrimination in Employment Act provide for a limited amount of liquidated damages. The reliance on § 1981 or pendent state claims may provide an effective jurisdictional basis for claiming significant sums, including compensatory and punitive damages. To establish a violation of § 1981 or a state claim for compensatory damages, however, you must prove "disparate treatment."

By choosing to expand beyond a straight Title VII claim, you may change forums or triers of fact from federal to state and from judge to jury. It is a decision that requires looking ahead carefully.

Traditionally, civil rights lawyers have steered away from juries and toward the federal court because of that court's role in the history of civil rights enforcement. However, that is not a hard-and-fast approach anymore. Analyze this case as you would a case in your regular practice, selecting the forum and trier of fact best suited for the client.

If you decide to stick with tradition and choose the federal judge, then proceed under Title VII. (A Title VII case is tried only before a judge because the courts have determined that back pay falls under equitable restitution, not legal damages, and gives no right to a jury.) If you add any other federal claims, request only equitable relief.

Alternatively, you may take a flier: request compensatory and punitive damages under 42 U.S.C. § 1981. If the defendants do not make a timely request for a jury, you have the forum, trier of fact, and remedy package you want. The defense bar does not fall asleep often, but it might this time.

A combination of factors has led some lawyers to file fair employment cases before juries or in state courts, or both.

First, the potential for extensive legal damages available under federal or state causes of action other than Title VII is a strong incentive to put your money on a jury.

Second, fair employment plaintiffs have had some notable successes before juries, and not just before predominantly black juries. If the plaintiff is an elderly worker and age discrimination is a factor, take advantage of the truth that we all grow old. Juries may respond favorably to a story of a big company or a union unfairly treating a struggling worker, whether the worker is black, Hispanic, or female.

Third, not every federal judge is receptive to civil rights claims. Recently, a colleague who has practiced law for years in the South tried an individual race discrimination case before a jury. The jury awarded more than $100,000. The lawyer says that he has never won a race case before that presiding federal judge, and he believes that he would not have won this case either without a jury.

For similar reasons, some lawyers have brought cases in state court. In some jurisdictions, the staff jury panels or judges are more sympathetic to plaintiffs' civil rights cases than are the area's federal panels or judges. Moreover, federal appellate courts are increasingly reversing favorable lower court judgments for civil rights plaintiffs. Consider the track record of the area's federal and state appellate courts in choosing your forum.

Of course, other considerations not particularly related to fair employment cases, such as docket congestion or availability of discovery, may influence your choice of forum.

It is true that a Title VII action tried to a court can end discriminatory practices and vastly improve the lives of minorities or women. But it is less likely to produce real and needed bucks for the individual victim of discrimination. That comes in an action permitting damage claims tried to a jury.

Tie your discovery plan to trial or settlement strategy as tightly as you can. In fair employment cases, the boss controls the relevant records and thus the objective proof. At the same time, he will raise cries that your demands are unduly burdensome or irrelevant.

You can expose defense protestations for the smoke screens that they are through efforts that start at the beginning of your representation. By using the administrative process to get copies of company documents, attending interviews of company managers, and exploring different channels of possible discovery, you can lay the groundwork for justifying more extensive discovery.

You have the opportunity to get the first jump in discovery; take it. Consider filing carefully focused interrogatories or a request for production of documents with the complaint. A broad set of first interrogatories regarding all relevant employment selections is less useful than a request for company documents (including those kept in computer-readable form); examples of each type of document; and a description or copies, if written, of all the company's relevant employment policies. If the documents are not self-explanatory after the initial request, follow with a deposition limited to obtaining a description of the documents, what the codes mean, how the information is recorded, and how it is used.

This approach reaps genuine benefits. First, you are not depending on interrogatory answers prepared by the defense lawyer, nor are you faced with reviewing an unnecessarily large mass of paper in a window-less room pursuant to Fed. R. Civ. P. 33(c). When defense protests sound, you can show the court that you are proceeding along the least burdensome route for gathering the relevant information.

Often you will discover one document or computer file that has significant information and substantially reduces the time and cost of obtaining and analyzing information.

The human drama and harm caused by discrimination is submerged at a trial focused on statistics, job patterns, and document fights. Confusion and complexity will work against your client and may convince the judge to avoid any involvement in this mud wrestle. Develop discovery in a manner that simplifies the trial and moves it quickly past detailed explanations of job structure and employment patterns directly to the critical issues.

A thorough analysis of the company's documents and careful interviews with your client and other workers will prepare you to depose company personnel managers, supervisors, and others. The documents and the depositions spawn requests for admission of facts or stipulations that put your case in sharp focus, and perhaps establish a prima facie case.

You should know the relevant operation of the employer's workplace better than his witnesses or his attorney's advisors. This is not hard to do.

The personnel manager relies on the contract or policy manual and what supervisors tell him; usually he is not familiar with the personnel records or the "common law" of how the shop runs. Learn how the shop works from the perspective of the worker, the supervisor, the personnel manager, the personnel documents—and most important—from the contract or manual that says how it should work. This knowledge will provide opportunities during trial to demonstrate that the system operates inconsistently and unfairly, and that the managers do not know what really occurs on the shop floor.

It is critical to discover the nondiscriminatory reason the company will use. The Supreme Court emphasized in *Texas Dept. of Community Affairs v. Burdine*, 450 U.S. 248 (1981), that, although substantial relevant evidence is controlled by the defendant, the "liberal discovery rules" should permit "the plaintiff meriting relief to demonstrate intentional discrimination." Use this rationale to lock the defendant into its justification. The company can easily use a legitimate reason for a selection decision: not enough education, not the right kind of experience. But it is just as easy for you to undercut the company's stated reason by using factual examples. An affirmative answer (which you ensure by having a copy of the relevant personnel record) to the question, "Isn't it true that your supervisor selected Joe Jones for the same position two years ago, even though Jones had less experience than the plaintiff?" devastates a defense based on the plaintiff's lack of experience.

Your case also may depend on expert testimony. A labor economist determines the availability of qualified black workers in the labor market, an industrial psychologist analyzes whether a selection procedure that disproportionately excludes blacks is used appropriately, and a statistician calculates and describes the significance of employment patterns. Consider whether an expert is required early in the case and, if so, consult experts as soon as possible. Frequently, if an expert is retained late in the process, you will discover (when there is little time to change direction) that the wrong emphasis or theory has been developed or that you have failed to uncover important information.

For example, a statistician's testimony that the average black employee's salary is significantly lower than the average white employee's salary may support a discrimination claim until the employer presents evidence, which the plaintiff neither discovered nor scrutinized before trial, that the salary disparity is due to differences in relevant job experience.

Many defendants depose the plaintiff immediately after the complaint is filed. That deposition will be the most crucial event of the litigation. By striking early, defendants often catch the plaintiff unprepared. Begin preparing your client for this deposition at the first interview, well before the filing.

The Supreme Court has issued six opinions on the burden and order of proof in fair employment cases brought by an individual. A thread running through them is that the plaintiff may establish a prima facie case of intentional discrimination by inferential or circumstantial evidence, since overt evidence is unlikely. Therefore, "the burden of establishing a prima facie case of disparate treatment is not onerous," the Court wrote in *Texas Dept. of Community Affairs v. Burdine*, 450 U.S. 248 (1981).

A Prima Facie Case

The Court indicated in *McDonnell Douglas Corp. v. Green*, 411 U.S. 792 (1973), its first opinion on the issue, that a plaintiff establishes a prima facie case when he proves four points:

1. that he belongs to a racial minority;
2. that he applied and was qualified for a job for which the employer was seeking workers;
3. that he was rejected for employment; and
4. that, after his rejection, the position remained open and the em-

ployer continued to seek applicants from persons with his qualifications.

The Supreme Court's use of circumstantial evidence is a guide for establishing a prima facie case, not a mold into which the factual circumstances of every case must fit. You should also convey to the judge or jury why the Court established this minimal standard for the prima facie case. Given the prevalence of racial discrimination and Congress's determination to end it with a broad fair employment law, the Court deemed that a plaintiff had established a prima facie case once he had demonstrated at least that his rejection did not result from the two most common legitimate reasons, lack of a job vacancy or lack of the necessary job qualifications.

When the prima facie case is established in a disparate impact case, the defendant has the burden to produce evidence that "articulates" a "legitimate nondiscriminatory reason" for rejecting the plaintiff, according to *Texas Dept. of Community Affairs*. You may then present evidence showing that the reason is a pretext for discrimination. The plaintiff may show pretext by establishing that the employer's proffered reason was not the real reason or the entire reason for the employment decision.

The burden of proof never shifts in an individual disparate treatment case. Once all the evidence is submitted, the question for the trier of fact is whether the employer intentionally discriminated.

Add "Something Else"

What this means to your trial strategy is that your prima facie case is easy to establish, but it is very fragile. Build into the trial strategy the prima facie case plus "something else." The something else can be evidence of historical discriminatory practices that have ceased in name but not effect, incidents of racial insensitivity or hostility, or statistical evidence showing marked disparity between the promotion of blacks and whites.

The prima facie case will get the merits to the judge or jury, but the something else will convince the trier of fact to rule for the plaintiff. In one particular case, a white city employee testified that he had overheard a supervisor state to another employee, "I finally got accomplished what I've been trying to do a long time. We fired the nigger." The jury ruled for the plaintiff, but the district court entered a judgment notwithstanding the verdict because the employer had introduced evidence that the plaintiff had wrongfully used city equipment to improve his home. In reversing and reinstating the jury verdict, the appellate court expressly relied upon the testimony about the supervisor's candid comment. *Abasiekong v. City of Shelby*, 744 F.2d 1055 (4th Cir. 1984).

Of course, the critical evidence often is less dramatic. Supervisors sometimes embellish their testimony with factual assertions that careful discovery may show to be wrong or misleading. In one case, a supervisor asserted that he had expressly directed that social workers not take files home. In a civil service proceeding held several years earlier, however, the same supervisor had testified that social workers were not prohibited from taking files home in order to catch up on their work. The inconsistency in this testimony, which was not essential to the employer's case, discredited the supervisor, undercut the proffered nondiscriminatory reason, and led to a jury verdict for the plaintiff.

Testimony brings cold figures to life and the order of witnesses puts that life into perspective.

Follow the bumbling presentation of a company supervisor with an earnest, well-spoken plaintiff or a black employee who works in a similar situation. The search for this juxtaposition of evidence should commence early in the case preparation.

Almost always, the question, addressed to a group of black workers, as to who is the "dumbest" supervisor will engender a lively and enlightening discussion. The "dumb" white supervisor is worth his weight in gold to a plaintiff.

The testimony of a black worker and white supervisor about the operation of the seniority system in a foundry is a good example. The black worker had learned the machinist trade in the army, worked as a supervisor in installations throughout the Pacific, and had received an army certification as a machinist. In returning to the plant, he was placed in a job category that did not allow for promotion to machinist positions. The white supervisor entered the plant straight from high school as a trainee with no previous machinist experience. During his training, the black worker showed him many of the tricks of the trade. The seniority system permitted the white worker, but not the black worker, to advance as he learned the job. The contrasting careers of the two workers showed the irrationality of the system and led the court to conclude that the seniority system was created and maintained with an intent to discriminate.

Let us assume you have tried the fair employment case and won. Now you file an application for attorneys' fees. You should have considered fees from the start of the representation, for attorneys' fees are recovered for work performed during the administrative agency process.

If you are to recover fair and reasonable fees, keep careful records of your time and the work performed. Many attorneys, especially those who work on a contingency basis, are not in the record-keeping habit and find their compensable hours substantially reduced because they lack record proof. In fact, the *Manual for Complex Litigation 2d* states simply that "[t]he award of attorney's fees must be based upon . . . records and not upon estimates." An attorney who fails to keep contemporaneous records risks losing a significant amount of his entitlement to fees.

Litigating Cases Before Administrative Law Judges

by Lawrence P. Postol

For many attorneys, knowledge of the administrative process starts and ends with a law school course that touches lightly on the Administrative Procedure Act, 5 U.S.C. § 551 *et seq.*, and surveys the few landmark cases setting out the powers of administrative agencies. Many others have even less knowledge of the administrative process. As the administrative process invades more aspects of everyday life, more litigators will need to know as much about administrative adjudication as they know about litigating in traditional courts.

Whether your clients are pensioners or multinational corporations, an active litigator today needs to know how to conduct proceedings before an administrative law judge. To handle this litigation, you must know about the rules, practices, and customs used by administrative law judges. The variety of administrative agencies seems almost endless, ranging from local school boards to massive federal departments. And even though the rules and practices vary from agency to agency, and indeed from judge to judge, certain principles are universal and must be understood.

The Administrative Procedure Act is the starting point. It sets the outer limits for administrative law judges. Agency rules give further shape to practice before administrative law judges, and custom and tradition regulate the inner core of the proceedings. Also, most states have their own versions of the Administrative Procedure Act, many of which are patterned after the federal act. Thus, practitioners who have dealt with state agencies already may have some familiarity with the basics.

Matters get before an administrative law judge in one of three ways.

The author is a member of the national law firm Seyforth, Shaw, Fairweather & Geraldson; his office is in Washington, D.C.

When an agency denies a benefit—such as a license, permit, or a welfare benefit—the action can be appealed to an administrative law judge within the agency. Second, numerous agencies have power to regulate individual conduct, but can do so only after notice and hearing before an administrative law judge. Finally, agencies must give notice and conduct hearings before administrative law judges as part of rule making.

Interested parties can participate in and can even initiate the rule making. They must be given notice of hearings and an opportunity to present evidence and arguments. 5 U.S.C. § 554(b) and (c). Administrative law judges may exclude ''irrelevant, immaterial, or unduly repetitive evidence,'' and decisions must be based on the evidence in the record, which must be ''reliable, probative and substantive.'' 5 U.S.C. § 556(d). The proponent of an order has the burden of proof. 5 U.S.C. § 556(d).

The agency may review and change the decision of the administrative law judge, although in some instances statutes and regulations impose a substantial evidence test as the standard of review. 5 U.S.C. § 557(b). On appeal, an agency's decision must be upheld by the reviewing court if it is based on substantial evidence in the record; is not arbitrary, capricious, or an abuse of discretion; and accords with the statutory mandate. 5 U.S.C. § 706.

Judging the Judge

An administrative law judge must be disinterested and impartial. 5 U.S.C. § 556. In cases where the agency acts as the prosecutor, such as enforcement proceedings under the Occupational Safety and Health Act or before the Federal Trade Commission, there is an inherent conflict between the administrative law judge's role as an employee of the federal agency and his role as a judge. Defenders of the system argue that the judge's association with the agency and his familiarity with the cases coming before him provide a level of expertise that far outweighs the possible prejudice. Of course, such conflicts should not arise when the judge rules on a dispute between two private parties, such as in workers' compensation claims.

Nevertheless, in cases where the agency is a party, an argument can be made for having a pool of administrative law judges with no loyalty to any particular agency, and some states have adopted such a system. In my view, the inherent conflict is never a real factor and is far outweighed by the benefit of the administrative law judge's expertise.

Knowing the limits set by the Administrative Procedure Act is important, but the act tells very little about how a particular administrative law judge will act or rule in a case.

Will the judge follow the Federal Rules of Evidence? Will he sequester witnesses? What type and form of discovery will he allow? Often the answers are found in the agency's enabling statute and regulations.

The enabling statute determines how the administrative law judge will rule on the merits of the substantive issues. For example, the National Labor Relations Act determines what conduct constitutes an unfair labor practice before the National Labor Relations Board. Enabling statutes may even regulate some procedural questions, such as who is an interested party and the agency's standard for reviewing the judge's decision. More than likely, however, the agency will have promulgated regulations governing most procedures. Enabling statutes are found in the United States Code, and regulations in the Code of Federal Regulations.

Unfortunately, some lawyers appear before administrative law judges without becoming familiar with the statute and regulations. Such omissions lead not only to procedural failures, but also to situations where the judge and the client lose confidence in the lawyer. Administrative law judges, like traditional judges, are human—they distrust lawyers who are not well prepared. If you do not know the law and regulations, administrative law judges may well assume that your substantive legal and factual arguments are weak, too.

Knowing the substantive statute is especially important when practicing before an administrative law judge specializing in cases governed by that statute. He knows the statute intimately. He easily detects the lawyer's errors, is reluctant to excuse mistakes, and may well be insulted if it seems that the lawyer has not taken the time to read the statute. Examples of such blunders are endless—they range from mistakenly informing the judge that the other party has the burden of proof, to misciting the judge's jurisdictional limits. If you do not read the statute, you do not know where, when, or how you will falter. If a case is worth trying, it is worth a cover-to-cover review of the statute and regulations.

While agency regulations are not uniform, they generally adhere to a central core of principles and rules. In discovery, regulations are often relaxed versions of the Federal Rules of Civil Procedure. Almost all federal agencies provide for using subpoenas and depositions. About half have the full arsenal of discovery tools, including interrogatories, requests for production of documents, and requests for admissions.

No Fishing Expeditions

The administrative proceeding is supposed to be a streamlined adjudication process. Discovery should only take months, not years. Administrative law judges do not tolerate fishing expeditions. Thus, discovery requests should be specific and precise. Administrative law judges are less tolerant of requests that "may eventually lead to relevant evidence" or that deal with collateral issues. The judges tend to require that discovery seek only relevant, admissible evidence, or that it at least clearly lead to such evidence.

Lawyers should limit the number of interrogatories to fewer than 30 and request only specifically identified documents. Broad-based, shotgun-type requests are not well received.

The same is true for depositions. Do not try to depose every conceivable witness in the case; rather, limit yourself to the main actors. Limit formal discovery by using informal discovery first. Where possible, witnesses first should be interviewed instead of deposed, and documents should be requested through voluntary channels.

Most administrative cases turn on facts, not law. Indeed, the primary purpose of having an administrative law judge is for him to gather facts and to produce a record for the reviewing agency or board, which established the policy (the law) that must be applied to the facts of the case. Yet, many practitioners try a case before an administrative law judge without researching agency case law until preparing the post-hearing brief.

This foolish practice can be costly. You must know the pertinent case law in order to know what facts are relevant and how they should be presented. You should not discover the precedent "on all fours" after the record has been made. This will not impress the judge.

I have seen an administrative law judge interrupt an otherwise fine opening statement because the lawyer's argument was based on a case that had been reversed. I could not see the client's expression, but I am sure the client was no more impressed with his attorney than was the judge.

Obviously, you must know relevant case law before trying a court or administrative case; yet the administrative process presents additional hazards to the unprepared lawyer. First, for reasons that are not completely clear, many lawyers take administrative proceedings too lightly. The same lawyer who spends hours researching the case law before going before a district court judge may somehow feel comfortable doing no research prior to appearing before an administrative law judge.

Second, the administrative proceeding may involve unusual legal doctrines, and the agency precedent is hard to find and digest. Finally, since administrative law judges specialize in one field of law, they are more likely to know the relevant case law than will a district court judge. For example, an administrative law judge in a National Labor Relations Board case understands the difference between an economic strike and an unfair labor practice strike, and knows that fights, picketing, and tire slashing often accompany strikes. Keep the judge's expertise in mind if you contemplate trying to "wing it."

Except for decisions reviewed by a court of appeals, administrative cases are not published in the West system. Some agency decisions, however, are published in well-known private services, some in more obscure ones. A call to the agency's library usually will locate the publisher.

Often it is also important to know if the agency maintains an index or digest of cases that are not published by private services. The administrative law judge will know about such decisions, and many law firms practicing before a particular agency collect all agency opinions, including administrative law judge opinions. You do not want to be the only participant in a case who does not know about a critical agency decision. Indeed, the cost of collecting and analyzing agency decisions is one of the main reasons that practitioners often specialize in handling cases before only one agency. Still, agency libraries may be open to the public, which gives you access to all the decisions available to the most experienced practitioners.

Often it helps to read several opinions written by the administrative law judge assigned to your case: get a feel for the type of evidence he considers relevant, and for the way he analyzes the facts and the law. The wise attorney then tailors his case to the pattern the judge has accepted before.

Most administrative law judges are extremely informal about motions. They usually have no prescribed form, often accepting letters as motions. Similarly, they usually will rule on motions without a hearing, or will hold hearings by telephone. If you have a question about the judge's procedures and practices, call his secretary or law clerk.

Administrative law judges usually are more interested in the facts and the equities of discovery disputes than in case citations. They often allow broad discovery in terms of relevance, as long as the requests are specific and not overly burdensome. But they are sensitive about the need to avoid building an unmanageable record, especially since they have to read the record: under the Administrative Procedure Act, the judge must issue a written opinion discussing all the evidence in the record.

For that reason, many judges do not tolerate attorneys who use the "dump and run" technique—offering piles of paper into evidence and letting the judge figure out what the case is about and which documents are relevant. Rather, when faced with a stack of documents, the judge may make the lawyers go through the stack, eliminating the irrelevant documents and marking the ones they want the judge to consider in making his findings of fact.

Many problems that arise in civil litigation appear in practice before the administrative law judge, but in a different context. First, discovery disputes will be decided on the papers or after a telephone conference call. Administrative law judges do not have a motions day; rather, the administrative case usually involves only one hearing—the trial.

How does a lawyer deal with these limitations? To begin with, since the judge may rule on the pleadings, make sure that your motion papers are complete. Any documents necessary to rule on the motion, such as interrogatories, should be attached to the motion papers.

Taking the initiative also helps. If you want an oral argument, call the judge's law clerk offering to set up a telephone conference with the judge and opposing counsel. Government operators are difficult to deal with, and most administrative law judges are happy when the lawyer offers to set up the conference call. Also, try to limit discovery motions, and try to be the first to file. Finally, offer to draft a proposed order, a step that makes the judge's life easier since his secretarial help may be limited.

Administrative law judges are quite liberal about receiving evidence, but are careful not to let the record become too large and not to violate principles of due process. Since there is no jury, the judge does not have to worry about jurors being confused by irrelevant information or swayed by prejudicial evidence of limited relevance.

Judges do, however, become bored or tired, particularly at the end of the day. Relevancy objections are more likely to be sustained then, although the judge may merely suggest that the lawyer move on to a more relevant area.

Always follow that advice unless the evidence is critical. Except to preserve the point for appeal, there is no sense in continuing if the judge thinks the evidence is not relevant.

Unless their regulations provide otherwise, administrative law judges are not bound by technical rules of evidence. Documents usually will be admitted without proof of authenticity, even though technically they are hearsay. Nevertheless, administrative law judges follow the central requirements of due process on which the Federal Rules of Evidence are based.

Administrative law judges almost always protect the right of cross-examination. However, they will effectively shift the burden of proof on evidentiary objections. For example, they may ask the objecting party to prove that the offered document is not authentic, instead of making the offering party prove admissibility.

Yet some judges sustain hearsay objections, particularly when the offering party controls the person who made the original statement. These judges reason that if the witness can easily be produced at the hearing, it is unfair to admit a hearsay statement and make the opposing party chase after the witness to exercise his cross-examination rights. If you do not know the judge's view about this, you should have the witness available to testify if needed.

In using leading questions on direct examination, most administrative law judges allow more latitude than a district court judge would. For example, many judges allow using leading questions on direct examination of an expert witness whose opinion already is in a report. But when a lay witness's testimony is at the heart of a party's case, leading questions will not be allowed.

Even if you think you will be allowed to lead your witness, you should prepare the witness so that you do not need to ask leading questions if they are not permitted. Properly phrased leading questions produce a clear, concise transcript which then can be liberally quoted in the post-hearing brief; but be careful of overdoing the technique.

The difference between administrative and court proceedings can easily be seen by looking at the results. Testimony in district court usually is designed for a jury, while the administrative process is designed to create a hearing transcript that the judge reads and evaluates before issuing a decision. Thus, most administrative law judges will exercise broad discretion in helping produce a record that is organized, complete, and fair.

If a party produces a surprise witness or document, an administrative law judge usually will allow the other party an opportunity to offer rebuttal evidence, even if the lawyer did not make the proper discovery request to require disclosure of the witness or document before the hearing. Since a decision is not rendered at the hearing, many judges will keep the record open for a post-hearing deposition in place of live testimony. On the other hand, some judges do not like post-hearing evidentiary submissions, since they may prejudice the opposing party. Because preferences differ, counsel must know what this judge allows. Finally, most judges appreciate an organized set of exhibits and like the testimony to be presented logically and clearly.

Most judges allow the parties great latitude in compiling the record. Opposing counsel should work together to agree on certain evidentiary issues such as authenticity of documents, and the use of pre-hearing or post-hearing depositions. Indeed, in ruling on most motions or requests, the judge usually begins by asking if the other party opposes the request. If not, the judge usually grants any reasonable request.

You may be confused about whether to treat the administrative law judge like a jury or as a district court judge. An administrative law judge is neither.

Remember these simple principles that not only reflect the administrative law judge's role as the trier of fact, but also recognize that he has the job of deciding legal questions and resolving discovery disputes.

First, treat the judge with respect. Too many lawyers think they can treat the judge like just "one of the boys" or worse. No matter how friendly the judge, no matter how informal the hearing room and surroundings, never forget the judge is just that: a judge.

Of course, this does not mean that you must knuckle under. If you disagree with the judge, do not be afraid to say so; just be polite about it.

Another way of showing respect is by making the judge's life easier—be cooperative and provide whatever information or case law the judge needs to rule in your favor. For example, if you cite to cases or statutes that the judge may not have nearby, provide him with a copy. (While many agencies have access to their own decisions, they do not have standard references such as Federal Supplement and the U.S. Code Annotated.)

Since many lawyers take administrative law judges for granted, the judges are especially sensitive to improper behavior. Be as polite as possible to opposing counsel, be fair in your arguments, and never, never mischaracterize a fact to the judge.

One of the prime advantages of trying a case before an administrative law judge is the judge's expertise—after a judge has tried 100 black lung cases, he has learned a lot about lungs. Federal Trade Commission judges know more about economics than many economics students. Keep this in mind when formulating your evidence. Confront hard questions and try answering them; the administrative law judge will not overlook them. Where appropriate, expert witnesses, at least the good ones, can be particularly effective. Since the judge usually will understand the field, he will appreciate a truly impressive expert witness. University professors often make the best witnesses because of their uncontroverted expertise and their lack of bias. Administrative law judges who have heard and seen many experts in a particular field are better equipped than a lay jury to distinguish a good expert from a bad one.

Although administrative law judges are educated specialists, they are still human. If they dislike an attorney, they will find a way to make him pay the price. If you make the judge's life hard, he will return the favor.

Most important, the judge wants to "do justice." Too often, attorneys plead "the law" to the judge. Rather, the lawyer first should convince the judge that justice requires his client to win. Once the "justice" question has been addressed, you can argue "the law" and present the judge with tools for ruling for your client.

Starting with your opening statement, and ending with your post-hearing brief, give your evidence in a clear, logical order, demonstrating that your client has acted fairly and properly, and that the other side is the villain, the liar, or the cheat. Naturally, you should tie the evidence together with legal principles the judge already knows. Juries get legal instructions at the end of the case, but administrative law judges know the law right away. Once the evidence is set out and the judge is convinced that you should win, you can show him the way the law requires ruling in your favor. If the judge believes you should lose as a matter of fairness, the law usually allows him sufficient leeway to reach that result.

Smoothing the Road

Administrative law judges often have heavy case loads. Like all of us, if they are set traveling a road that is smooth and easy, they will follow that path and not be swayed. Do everything in your power to make the judge's trip easy. Beginning with discovery disputes, offer to arrange a telephone conference call and provide the judge with the relevant pleadings (which often are lost in the agency bureaucracy). In your opening statement, show the judge the clear path to follow, and provide him with sufficient information so that he will understand the testimony. Documents should be legible and logically organized. Finally, the post-hearing brief should be a fully annotated guide for the judge.

The post-hearing brief is to an administrative law judge what the closing argument is to the jury, only much more so. Many judges do not listen closely to testimony during the hearing, knowing that they can rely on the hearing transcript. However, in many cases the record is massive. The post-hearing brief is your final chance to convince the judge that your client is right and to make it easy for him to rule in your favor. Go over the evidence fairly, as if the judge will write the decision from your brief. Discuss both sides of the evidence—note why your evidence is persuasive and the other party's evidence is not. Give the judge the reasons for making credibility determinations in your favor—point out the inconsistencies in the other side's testimony, explain why your expert is the better expert, and why your client acted fairly.

Finally, make the judge's life easy. Do not just cite a page in the record, forcing the judge to pull the record out. Quote the record liberally in your brief. In fact, if the judge indicates he would not be offended by a proposed decision and order, draft one. Otherwise, draft your brief in a form from which the judge can easily write his opinion—perhaps taking whole sections from your brief.

The administrative law judge is the trier of fact, but his decision may be appealed within the agency. There are two possible standards for agency review of administrative law judges' decisions. Many agencies use the usual substantial evidence test that many civil appellate courts adhere to. Some agencies, however, provide for a de novo review on the record created by the administrative law judge. If the agency's standard of review is substantial evidence, then the agency must affirm the administrative law judge's decision if there are no errors of law and there is substantial evidence in the record to support the judge's decision. That the agency might have weighed the evidence differently is not a ground for reversal. If the agency does not follow the substantial evidence test, then the agency can reweigh the evidence, although it is bound by the record created by the judge. The agency normally cannot accept new evidence on appeal.

The standard of review may be part of the agency's statute or set out in regulations. After review, the next level is to the United States court of appeals, normally on a substantial evidence test.

Administrative law judges provide the expertise to handle administrative adjudications in a fair and efficient manner. However, to get the most out of the system, the lawyer must know and follow the rules, regulations, practices, and customs of the administrative law judges. In many ways, a trial before an administrative law judge is tougher than one before a district court judge, since the lawyer must cope with strange agency rules and customs, as well as the peculiarities of the particular administrative law judge he is appearing before. The judge is the trier of fact, and all dealings with him, beginning with discovery disputes, must bear that reality in mind. While agency case law is difficult to find, it is imperative that counsel know the applicable precedent as well as the evidentiary rules and customs the judge follows.

Finally, written skills can be as important as oral skills, since a post-hearing brief can be the key to winning a case before an administrative law judge. Instead of taking administrative proceedings for granted, trial counsel must be totally prepared when appearing before an administrative law judge.

Representing Witnesses in SEC Formal Investigations

by Robert H. Winter

Representing a witness testifying in a "formal investigative proceeding" ordered by the Securities and Exchange Commission (SEC) is a serious matter. The investigation can result in an administrative proceeding for remedial sanctions, in an injunctive proceeding in Federal District Court, or in a reference to the Department of Justice for criminal prosecution. Whether an investigation will result in Commission action, and the nature of the action, depend in major part upon the information developed by the Commission's staff through testimony taken during the investigation. Representing a witness in such a proceeding is similar to representing a deponent in a deposition under the Federal Rules of Civil Procedure. There are, however, significant differences.

Formal investigative proceedings are governed by special Rules Relating to Investigations, 17 C.F.R. §§ 203.1, *et seq.* The Federal Rules of Civil Procedure do not apply. Similarly, except where specifically provided otherwise, the Commission's General Rules of Practice governing adjudicative or rulemaking proceedings do not apply. Rules 4 through 8 of the Rules Relating to Investigations apply directly to witnesses. They deal with the commencement and nature of the proceedings (Rules 4 and 5), the availability of transcripts (Rule 6), the rights of witnesses (Rule 7) and the service of subpoenas to testify or produce documents (Rule 8). Before representing a witness in any proceeding, counsel should be thoroughly familiar with these rules as well as with the Administrative Procedure Act, 5 U.S.C. §§ 551, *et seq.*, which also applies to Commission proceedings.

A formal investigation begins with the Commission's entry of an order of investigation directing that the investigation be held and autho-

The author is a member of Arnold & Porter in Washington, D.C.

rizing designated individuals in the appropriate divisions or regional offices to take testimony. It is nonpublic unless otherwise ordered by the Commission (Rule 5). It may, but need not, follow a preliminary or informal investigation in which no process is issued or testimony compelled. If an informal investigation is conducted, by the time an order of investigation is issued, the staff may have gone far in developing information, and its views may be quite fixed.

Even in instances where there has been an informal investigation, counsel may be contacted by the staff and requested to present his client for examination on short notice. In view of the severe civil and criminal sanctions that may result from an investigation, counsel should not agree readily to a date that does not permit adequate preparation. Some formal investigations are conducted on an expedited basis. More, however, tend to be time-consuming affairs and it is generally possible to negotiate a reasonable accommodation with the staff.

Not Like Complaint

Adequate preparation may nevertheless prove difficult. An order of investigation is not like a complaint under the Federal Rules of Civil Procedure. It generally recites only the name of the company or companies involved; that the staff has reported information that tends to show false or misleading filings with the Commission, untrue public statements, stock market manipulation or similar conduct; and that the Commission deems such conduct, if true, to be possible violations of specific sections of the statutes it administers. An order of investigation is not required to set forth the facts or legal theories relied upon by the staff. It is conclusory rather than reasoned. Even where fraud is suspected, the order does not have to meet a particularity requirement comparable to Federal Rule of Civil Procedure 9(b). Moreover, there is no equivalent in the Rules Relating to Investigations to a motion for a more definite statement.

While the order may indicate the subject matter being investigated, it often does so only in a very general way; for example, that a company's financial statements did not adequately reflect contingent liabilities resulting from violations of federal labor laws, or that a proxy statement did not adequately disclose the ''nature, extent, purpose and effect'' of transactions between a company and its affiliates. Particularly in the case of testimony taken at an early stage in a proceeding, counsel and the witness may have only a limited idea of the facts or theories that the staff is relying upon, or the potential charges that the staff may bring. Counsel's task is obviously difficult in such circumstances.

A witness has the unqualified right, upon request, to read the order of investigation (Rule 7(a)). The examiner usually tenders a copy of the order to the witness and counsel for their review at the start of the examination. Although the order of investigation is only a limited guide to the scope of the investigation, counsel should always examine the order and make notes of the material portions. The staff does not furnish copies of the order to the witness or his counsel to retain without the express approval of a regional administrator or a director, associate director or assistant director of the division supervising the investigation. The staff has discretion to refuse a request for a copy of the order if they believe production would impede the investigation or interfere with the privacy of persons involved in the investigation (Rule 7(a)). Even if counsel has made notes of the text of the order, he should formally request a copy of the order from the appropriate regional administrator or division director.

The Commission's regulations provide that upon request the staff has discretion to advise persons involved in a formal investigation "of the general nature of the investigation, including the indicated violations as they pertain to them." 17 C.F.R. § 202.5(c). There is rarely a reason why such a request should not be made before the witness appears. In preparing a witness, information about the staff's theory of the case, its sources of information and the likely focus of its examination can be critical. The staff itself often will be a principal source of information about an investigation. While the practices of the staff vary, persistent attempts to glean information about the status and scope of an investigation are usually successful—at least partially.

Even when counsel has learned the staff's present view of the case, adequate preparation for a particular examination remains difficult. The intended scope of an investigation is often only a limited guide to the questions that may be asked or the charges that ultimately may be brought. It is not extraordinary for an investigation to result in charges unrelated to the original focus of the inquiry. For example, an investigation that begins with allegations of improper accounting for inventory may lead to charges about foreign payments discovered during the course of the investigation.

Other Problems

It is important for counsel to consider not only the intended scope of the examination, but also other problem areas involving the witness. This is often a troublesome assignment. A witness's time and concentration span are both limited. It is easier to prepare a witness on one subject rather than many. Nevertheless, it can be a major mistake if counsel ignores the possibility of questions on potentially dangerous subjects that are tangential to the primary focus of the investigation. Subjects that counsel should normally consider, even if not within a literal reading of the order of investigation, include issues raised by documents produced under subpoena or otherwise; issues that may have been brought to the attention of the staff by informers or other witnesses or targets; and current fashion issues of the day, such as political contributions, foreign payments or management perquisites.

An additional reason why adequate preparation for testimony may be difficult is that entities and witnesses who were once represented by a single counsel are often, in formal investigations, represented separately. It is not unusual for a target company, and all or some of its directors, officers, employees and former employees to be represented separately. One consequence of this practice is that many counsel are new to the matter under investigation and have little familiarity either with their client or the target company. Separate representation may also result in counsel having only limited or indirect access to other witnesses who would ordinarily be represented by the same counsel.

Separate Representation

Before appearing with a witness, counsel representing more than one entity in the proceeding should always consider, and discuss with the witness well in advance of his testimony, whether separate representation is necessary or appropriate. In view of the difficulties separate representation may impose upon counsel, it is not surprising that the staff often appears to encourage the practice. During the examination, the staff may ask counsel representing more than one party, such as a corporation and one of its officers, in what capacity he is representing the witness, whether as counsel for the company or the individual. It should be made clear that the representation is on behalf of the individual. The staff may also ask counsel if he has considered potential conflicts of interest or imply that the witness should be separately represented. Indeed, Rule 7(b) apparently attempts to require representation of witnesses by separate counsel. It provides "that all witnesses shall be sequestered, and unless permitted in the discretion of the officer conducting the investigation no witness or the counsel accompanying any such witness shall be permitted to be present during the examination of any other witness called in such proceeding." However, the right to counsel in formal investigations has been interpreted to mean counsel of one's choice and it appears that the courts will reject attempts by the Commission to stop a witness from selecting counsel also representing other witnesses, particularly where the interests of the witnesses are common and the practical effect of sequestration of counsel may be to deprive the witness of effective representation. *See SEC v. Csapo*, 533 F.2d 7 (D.C. Cir. 1976); *SEC v. Higashi*, 359 F.2d 550 (9th Cir. 1966).

Counsel to other witnesses may provide an important source of information in preparing a witness for testimony. Those counsel should be asked about the scope of the investigation, the focus and manner of prior examinations, the areas of likely interest to the staff, the identity of other possible witnesses, the documents produced to the staff by other parties, and similar matters. In the absence of special circumstances, counsel should not allow his own witness to discuss with previous or potential witnesses the scope of their testimony or anything else relating to the case. It is a common practice for the staff to ask a witness if he has spoken to other persons involved in the proceeding and to inquire in detail about those discussions.

Conversations among witnesses are not privileged, while conversations between a witness and his counsel are privileged even when counsel relays to the witness information learned from counsel to other parties. In addition, conversations among witnesses about testimony to be given may call into question the witness's credibility or even raise issues of obstruction of justice. While there doubtless have been instances where a witness has had helpful discussions with other witnesses, this is one area where the risks—and they are real—far outweigh the likely rewards.

Overall Strategy

As in any legal proceeding, before appearing with a witness, counsel should have in mind an overall strategy. Although an overall strategy is sometimes difficult to develop, particularly in an investigation where the staff has the initiative and the information available to counsel is limited, it is nonetheless important. Testimony once given is a matter of record, and it will have a major impact upon the final outcome of the investigation and any related proceedings.

Whether to testify at all is the most basic, important decision. The Fifth Amendment privilege is available in any proceeding where a witness is asked questions and the answers may tend to incriminate him. Testimony by a witness in a formal investigation constitutes a waiver of the Fifth Amendment privilege and can lay the basis for a subsequent criminal prosecution, as well as provide a transcript for use against him. If it appears that a criminal reference is a possibility, counsel must consider in advance whether the better course would be for the witness to assert the privilege and refuse to testify at all.

Counsel may approach an investigation or a particular witness's testimony with a number of goals in mind: to avoid a criminal reference; to avoid an administrative proceeding or an injunctive action; to avoid a particular party or claim being included in an enforcement action; to position the case for settlement; to minimize the possible effect upon related private litigation, to name only a few. These goals need not be mutually exclusive. It may prove difficult, however, to accommodate them all. For example, a witness's waiver of the attorney-client privilege may be helpful if the primary goal is to avoid an enforcement recommendation, yet at the same time it may exacerbate the problems in related private litigation. One measure of counsel's skill is whether the witness has been prepared so that his testimony helps achieve all of the intended goals.

A witness may find it helpful if he has some understanding of counsel's strategy: It is nevertheless usually a mistake for the witness to attempt to establish his case affirmatively through his testimony. There are instances where testimony can be used to "educate" the staff to the witness's side of the story, particularly in investigations where the examining officer has little familiarity with the industry under investigation. However, instances where this tactic is successful are atypical. The witness is usually better advised to leave the "education" function to counsel's conversations with the staff and written submissions to the staff or to the Commission. Counsel should advise the witness to keep his answers succinct, not to be argumentative and, unless previously discussed with counsel, to resist the temptation to amplify his answers to include information that he thinks will be helpful, but that the question does not require.

Unpleasant Experience

As part of his preparation, counsel should review with the witness in general terms the type of examination to expect. Investigations can and should be conducted civilly. Nevertheless, it is not a pleasant experience to be the subject of an investigation. Even to someone who has been a witness in private litigation, it may be unsettling to have a federal officer state or imply that he doubts the witness's credibility or that he has "facts" that contradict the witness. An attorney should tell his witness that the examination will take place before the staff of the Commission and that there is no neutral judge, magistrate or similar official present. The witness should also be told that the reporter will accept instruction to go off the record only from the staff and that statements made off the record may nevertheless be remembered and testified to and have impact.

An attorney should also prepare the witness for the litany of warnings that will be given, even if the witness is not a "target" of the investigation. The customary warnings include advice that the investigation is being conducted to determine whether there have been violations of the federal securities laws; that facts developed in the investigation could constitute violations of other federal or state criminal or civil statutes; that any evidence given or stated or materials provided may be used against the witness in any civil, criminal or administrative proceeding by the Commission or any other agency; that the witness may refuse to answer questions that may tend to incriminate him or subject him to a fine, forfeiture or penalty; that § 1001 of Title 18, United States Code, provides criminal sanctions for a person who knowingly and willfully makes a false statement, conceals or covers up by any trick, scheme or device a material fact, or makes or uses any false writing or document in connection with an investigation conducted by an agency in the United States; that § 1621 of Title 18 provides criminal sanctions for a person who willfully states or subscribes under oath to any material matter that he does not believe to be true to an officer of the United States Government and that the examiner is considered to be an officer of the Commission.

The officer conducting the investigation also advises the witness of the possible impact of the Freedom of Information Act, 5 U.S.C. § 552, and the Privacy Act of 1974, 5 U.S.C. § 552a. Commission subpoenas are accompanied by statements dealing with the Privacy Act, the Freedom of Information Act and the routine uses that can be made of the testimony. Counsel should review these attachments and the relevant statutes and should be aware of the circumstances in which testimony given in private proceedings may be made public. The witness should be aware in advance of the possible uses of the testimony he is giving.

There are many difficult issues relevant to the possible use of testimony taken in a formal investigation. It is almost always better practice to err on the side of excessive discussion of these matters with the witness. It can be extremely unfortunate to a lawyer's relationship with his client if the client's testimony is used in a way the client did not understand was possible when the testimony was given.

Securities Act Release 5571, February 21, 1975, sets forth the procedures for requesting confidential treatment of testimony. The request, directed to the director of the division of enforcement, must be in writing and state the specific testimony that is considered to be confidential and the legal or factual basis upon which the claim is made. If a request for confidential treatment is to be made, it is useful to note that fact for the record at the commencement of the testimony.

Counsel's Role

Counsel should also review with the witness the role counsel is likely to play during the examination. Rule 7(c) provides that in a formal investigation the right to be represented by counsel means the right to have counsel present during the proceeding and to have counsel advise the witness before, during and after the conclusion of the examination, question the witness briefly at the conclusion of the examination to clarify any answers the witness has given, and make summary notes during the examination for the use of the witness. There is no provision in the Rules Relating to Investigations for objecting to questions or evidence or for refusing to answer any question. This is in marked contrast to the Commission's rules of practice governing depositions and interrogatories in noninvestigatory proceedings. *Compare* 17 C.F.R. § 201.15(c). As a practical matter, however, counsel will usually have little difficulty in going well beyond the role specified in Rule 7(c). It would be a mistake for him to try to take over the examination, to object continuously or comment upon questions to the point that it obstructs the examination. Unnecessary intervention by counsel is generally counterproductive. It prolongs the examination, which may ultimately cause a more thorough examination. On the other hand, counsel should not sit by and permit the witness to answer material questions that are ambiguous, misleading or otherwise subject to serious defect. Counsel should note the problem with the question or request the examiner to restate the question. Counsel can also suggest an alternative formulation of the question that may prove acceptable to the examiner.

If an examination turns to areas outside the scope of the order of investigation, counsel can direct the witness not to respond. An attorney should give that instruction only if he is satisfied, after careful consideration, that it is important to his case. There is little point in objecting to harmless questions or giving hypertechnical interpretations of the language of the order. It inevitably increases the suspicions of the staff and, while that is not itself a sufficient reason to avoid the instruction, the staff may seek court action to compel an answer or to have the order of investigation amended to increase its scope. In the case of subpoenas issued under certain statutes administered by the Commission, a person may be found guilty of a misdemeanor if he fails, without just cause, to answer a lawful inquiry. However, the staff may also let the matter drop for any one of a variety of reasons, including the need to complete the investigation.

Brief Questions

There is usually little to be gained by examining the witness after the staff has completed its examination. However, if it appears that the transcript will be confusing or that the witness has misunderstood a question or misstated an answer, a few brief questions may prove helpful. In such circumstances, it is generally better to take corrective action at the time of the occurrence, rather than wait until the staff's examination is concluded.

The Commission's regulations provide that a person involved in a formal investigation may, upon his own initiative, submit a written statement to the Commission setting forth his position on the subject matter of the investigation. In the event the staff recommends commencement of enforcement proceedings, the submission—a so-called Wells submission, named after a former Chairman of the Commission—is forwarded to the Commission with the staff's memorandum. *See* 17 C.F.R. § 202.5(c) and Securities Act Release 5310, September 27, 1972. A Wells submission frequently presents a question of timing. It is not useful to make the submission at too early a date while the investigation is proceeding and the issues and facts are still developing; on the other hand, the submission is of little use if it is presented too late. Moreover, the purpose of the submission may be as much to convince the staff not to recommend an action, or to limit the scope of the action recommended, as to have an impact on the Commission itself. The Wells submission may be the only opportunity for counsel to present his case in writing before action is taken that can seriously harm his client. It appears that the courts will not set aside Commission action if the staff fails to advise a witness that he is a target and counsel therefore does not make a timely submission. *SEC v. National Student Marketing Corp.*, 538 F.2d 404 (1976), *cert. denied*, 429 U.S. 1073 (1977). The regulations provide, however, that the staff upon request may advise the witness of the amount of time that may be available for preparing and submitting a statement before the staff makes its presentation to the Commission. 17 C.F.R. § 202.5(c). When the testimony starts, counsel should always make a request on the record that if the staff intends to make a recommendation that the Commission take any action, counsel be given an opportunity to make a submission under Release No. 5310.

A witness has the unqualified right to inspect the official transcript of his own testimony. Although a witness is entitled upon written request to obtain a transcript of his testimony, that request may be denied by the Commission "for good cause" (Rule 6). *See Commercial Capital Corp. v. SEC*, 360 F.2d 856 (7th Cir. 1966). While as a general matter the witness should request a copy of the transcript, there are circumstances when that may be inadvisable. Once requested, a transcript of testimony in a formal investigation is not privileged and can be ordered produced in discovery in private litigation. *LaMorte v. Mansfield*, 438 F.2d 448 (2d Cir. 1971). If a copy of the transcript is not requested, or the request is denied, the official transcript should be inspected so that counsel can decide whether the transcript was garbled by the reporter or if any action to correct the transcript is advisable.

A final note of caution: The Commission's enforcement staff is often quite young, with little experience compared to members of the private bar involved in significant investigations. It can be both tempting and a serious mistake to assume an attitude of superiority toward the staff or to grandstand to impress a client. It inevitably offends the staff, which has a large measure of discretion about the actions they will recommend to the Commission. The client only loses if his lawyer gives the staff an additional incentive to make a recommendation for enforcement action. Equally important, it is unprofessional to offend an adversary unnecessarily, and it is foolish to underestimate an opponent.

What to Do When a Defendant Goes Bankrupt

by Martin L. Grayson and Douglas D. Dodd

Tactics

Answer 1: Consider suicide.

Answer 2: Ignore it.

Answer 3: File a proof of claim and then ignore it.

Ask an experienced trial lawyer how to deal with a bankrupt debtor who is a defendant or codefendant in litigation. His answer, probably one of the above, will reflect despair. Even Answer 3, a course of action that at least registers the claim in the bankruptcy court record, is one of resignation rather than hope.

But one can do more than merely file a proof of claim and notice of representation in the bankruptcy court (see A Primer on the Law, page 1167) and then await a fate unquestioned and unchallenged by most litigants.

You might think that it would be an exercise in futility to press a claim against a party when the return might amount to ten cents on the dollar. But not always. Consider the potential benefits for plaintiffs and codefendants who must deal with a bankrupt defendant:

1. For the plaintiff, getting the debtor into court eliminates the "empty chair." Other defendants will not be able to point a finger at the missing party and attempt to place all liability there at your client's expense. On the other hand, when liability is based on the conduct of the debtor (as with an indemnitor or surety) the codefendant might want to take the lead in getting the debtor to respond because the plaintiff will be more than willing to lay blame on the empty chair.

Martin L. Grayson is an associate editor of LITIGATION *and an associate with Johnson & McAlpine in New Orleans. Douglas D. Dodd is a partner with Stone, Pigman, Walther, Wittmann & Hutchinson in New Orleans.*

2. Getting the debtor into court may result in a judgment. A judgment might improve your client's prospects for recovery in bankruptcy—a real consideration if large sums are involved and even a small percentage return would be worth the chase. At the very least, a judgment will liquidate the claim and defuse any later attempt to dispute it or the amount in question.

3. A litigant's time, effort, and energy, and the client's money, often will be better served by pursuing a debtor in a civil action rather than in bankruptcy proceedings. If, for example, a debtor avoids civil litigation, in bankruptcy another adversarial procedure might be required to determine liabilities. Another time-consuming alternative would be to require the bankruptcy court to make a complete, independent evaluation of the estimated claim. (See A Primer on the Law, page 1167.)

4. Getting the debtor into court may prompt his insurer to answer and defend the action.

Perhaps the last item is the real bargain. For many causes of action, the bankrupt party may have insurance coverage that would answer your demand. Major casualty cases, almost all maritime filings, and many corporate actions involve claims for which an insurer stands behind the bankrupt party.

What a comforting thought. Especially because the major hurdle to clear in the bankruptcy court is convincing the judge to lift the automatic stay. This stay goes into effect whenever a person or company files for bankruptcy. The stay bans all pending and prospective litigation, collection attempts, amicable demands, and other actions against the debtor. Judgments already recorded against a debtor are still valid. However, execution of judgment is halted.

The court will look more favorably on a motion for relief from the automatic stay that names an insurance company, rather than the bankrupt, as the real party in interest, because the debtor's assets available to satisfy his creditors will not be depleted. On the other hand, if the debtor has no insurance coverage or only a limited amount and claims are substantial, the bankruptcy court might wish to supervise the distribution of insurance proceeds. If it does not, then proceeds might quickly be exhausted by one set of claims, requiring a subsequent claim to be paid from the assets that otherwise would have been available to satisfy creditors. Supervision by the bankruptcy court means maintaining the stay of the action in the court in which the suit is pending and bringing the dispute (or the part of the dispute that involves the debtor) to bankruptcy court.

Finding out if a party is insured and the name of the insurer is usually not very difficult. The bankruptcy court record will reveal the name of the debtor's counsel or trustee, and one phone call will often produce the necessary information. In fact, if schedules (see A Primer on the

Law, page 1167.) have already been filed, insurance premiums may be listed as outstanding items, and the name of the insurer would be in the record. One can also contact the creditor's committee, usually comprised of major creditors who know a good deal about the debtor or are in the process of learning fast. With the name of the insurer available, you can move the court for relief from the automatic stay to allow you to name the bankrupt party in an attempt to bring the insurer to the debtor's defense.

In direct action states (Louisiana and Wisconsin), finding the name of the insurer is all that you require to draft or amend your complaint to name the insurer rather than the bankrupt. In other states, the route is a bit circuitous, but the result should be the same.

If the insurer is not readily identifiable, then you may have to back up a step. Rather than petitioning the bankruptcy court to lift the automatic stay so you can sue the debtor (and its insurer), you must move the court to lift the stay to allow discovery against the debtor concerning its insurer. Such a request should not be burdensome for the debtor. Because the court may be suspicious that discovery might proceed into areas that address the claim itself or even the bankrupt's capacity to respond directly, you should be careful to draft a specific motion and supporting memorandum seeking only the identity of the insurer and insurance limits and coverage.

Once you learn the availability of insurance, you may then proceed with a second motion to lift the stay for the purpose of bringing suit. Assuring the debtor has insurance, what arguments and points of law should you advance to convince a bankruptcy court to lift the automatic stay?

The motion may request a lifting of the stay to proceed with a suit against the debtor, to enter judgment against the debtor, or even to allow an execution of judgment, although this last request would almost certainly be denied. Whatever the purpose of seeking to lift the stay, however, courts have found the following arguments to be persuasive.

First, material harm to the litigants, and perhaps other creditors, may result from delay. The failure to institute or proceed with the suit in a timely fashion might result in the invocation of coverage defenses by insurers. You should submit to the court copies of the relevant insurance policies with limiting language. Alert the court to the potential of an added burden on the debtor's bankruptcy estate if the policy defenses stand and insurers are released from their obligation to indemnify the debtor. At the same time, full redress may be denied innocent claimants. Also, if the debtor emerges from bankruptcy or for some reason is unable to avoid a judgment, the debtor may be forced to defend the suit and satisfy a judgment alone, without benefit of insurance. Such a result would hinder any attempt at economic recovery by the debtor already in difficult financial straits and deprive him of the benefit of his insurance.

Second, you can argue to the court that there may be insurance coverage adequate to satisfy any judgment. In other words, you should stress that the assets of the debtor, if any, would not be at risk. This argument should be soothing to the bankruptcy court, trustees, debtors, creditors, and others whose primary concern is the conservation of the assets of the struggling, or moribund, bankrupt. So long as the bankruptcy estate of the debtor will not be invaded, there should be no viable objection to allowing suit to proceed against the debtor.

Third, you must point out that the rights and interests of plaintiffs, codefendants, or third parties, who might seek indemnity, contribution, or recovery against the bankrupt and its insurers, are also entitled to some consideration and protection. Those rights and interests cannot be protected except by timely institution or completion of suit against the debtor. This is an argument based in equity rather than a strict reading of the Bankruptcy Code, but it would be cynical to assume it must fall on deaf ears.

Finally, in some cases you can argue that the stay should be liked because of special circumstances. For example, the Code does not prohibit the filing and prosecution of suit against a debtor on claims that arise from activity undertaken before a filing for reorganization under Chapter 11 of the Bankruptcy Code. For example, say a small oil exploration company files for Chapter 11 protection. While the company continues its operations, one of its dredges strikes and bursts an oil pipeline causing extensive pollution and loss of product. Because the incident occurred *after* the bankruptcy court had approved the activity resulting in the loss-the debtor should not be permitted to interpose the automatic stay as a shield against suit. The court allowed the company's business to proceed with the understanding that obligations thus incurred, whether in tort or contract, would have to be discharged in full.

You should also remind the bankruptcy court that lifting the stay for the purpose of allowing a claim to be liquidated is different from allowing a judgment to be executed. The court automatically stays execution of judgment. However, if the court allows a suit to proceed to judgment, the creditor-adversary would have a liquidated claim to bring to the bankruptcy court. No harm to the bankrupt, a bit of equity for the injured adversary, economy for the courts.

There are probably other ways to lever the automatic bankruptcy stay off your client's claim to allow that claim to be heard. Those noted above can give you a start without the expenditure of a lot of time. The results may be surprising and gratifying.

Now, what about those folks we dismissed earlier? The ones with the suit on open account? Definitely file a proof of claim in the bankruptcy action. Waiting a long time and lowering expectations is also a perspicacious approach. Answer number 1 (Consider suicide.) is always available.

A Primer On the Law

As soon as trial counsel learns that an opposing party has sought refuge under the bankruptcy laws, he should consult members of his firm who are familiar with the Bankruptcy Code and Bankruptcy Rules.

But even if the firm has no attorney familiar with the bankruptcy laws and rules, there are several simple steps that trial counsel should take to protect his client's interests. These steps will cost the client little and will protect the client from prejudice in the bankruptcy proceedings. Although the advice applies to claims generally, it is more directly relevant to holders of unsecured claims.

1. *Prepare and File a Proof of Claim.* Clerks at bankruptcy court and legal stationers have preprinted proof-of-claim forms, or one can retype the appropriate Official Bankruptcy Form (i.e., 19, 20, and 21) with the necessary insertions. A properly executed and filed proof of claim is prima facie evidence of the validity and amount of a claim under Rule 3001(f). Bankruptcy Rule 3002(a) states that unsecured creditors must file a proof of claim for their claims to be allowed, except as otherwise provided in Rules 3003-3005. In "no asset" Chapter 7 cases, consult Rule 2002(e).

Regardless of whether your client's claim is scheduled (See 5. *Review the Schedules.*) or your belief that there will be no distribution of bankruptcy estate assets to unsecured creditors, you *always* should file a proof of claim on behalf of your client. This is inexpensive insurance that the client will participate in distribution and receive notice of other aspects of a bankruptcy case.

2. *Estimation of Claims.* Under Section 502(c) of the Bankruptcy Code, the bankruptcy court must estimate for the purpose of allowance any contingent or unliquidated claim when the precise fixing or liquidation of that claim would unduly delay the administration of the case. The court also must estimate any right to payment from an award of an equitable remedy for breach of performance. Your proof of claim should reflect clearly that it is your own estimate of the amount owed your client, including the fact that the claim may be contingent on another event (such as, if you are codefendant, the granting of your third-party demand or cross-claim against the debtor). The bankruptcy court makes the ultimate estimate. Consult Section 502(e) for the treatment of claims of co-debtors.

3. *Time for Filing.* In cases under Chapter 7 (liquidation) and Chapter 13 (reorganization of personal finances), Bankruptcy Rule 3002(c) provides that a proof of claim usually must be filed within 90 days after the first meeting of creditors. Such a meeting usually takes place within 45 days of the filing for relief. In the more common Chapter 11 (corporate reorganization) cases, the rules require the court to fix a date within which claims must be filed. Check the record for orders establishing claim bar dates.

4. *File a Notice of Representation.* This should insure that you receive all notices distributed by the clerk. There is no particular form for this document. In some cases, local practice will permit counsel to indicate on the rear of the proof-of-claim form information about your claim that is not indicated elsewhere. This could include an appearance as counsel of record on behalf of the claimant. When in doubt, check with the bankruptcy court clerk about the need for filing a formal notice. It is prudent to notify the debtor's counsel of your appearance apart from filing a notice with the clerk.

5. *Review the Schedules.* Either you or your client can do this. The Bankruptcy Code requires the debtor to file schedules listing all assets and liabilities, including debts. Rule 3003(b)(1) states that the schedules filed in Chapter 9 and 11 cases are prima facie evidence of the validity and amount of the claim, *unless* the claim is scheduled as disputed, contingent, or unliquidated. Because by their very nature, claims involving litigation are contingent, unliquidated, or disputed, trial counsel should *never* rely on a listing in the debtors' schedules. A proof-of-claim should always be filed. If the case is converted to one under Chapter 7, creditors must file a claim anyway. The consequences of improperly relying on the schedules that reflect your client's claim as contingent, unliquidated, or disputed are severe: under Rule 3003(c)(2), a creditor whose claim is scheduled as contingent, unliquidated, or disputed is not entitled to treatment as a creditor for purposes of voting or distribution.

The schedules, if properly prepared, are full of information that you and your client will need to evaluate the desirability of becoming more active in the bankruptcy or of obtaining relief from the stay proceedings in the trial court. The cost of obtaining copies of the schedules and statement of financial affairs, in all but the largest and most complex bankruptcies, is worth the investment. Contact the clerk to obtain information on copying.

6. *Review the Bankruptcy Court Record.* Aside from the schedules, there are other documents filed by a debtor that may enable you to determine its financial health and the wisdom of pursuing your client's claim. Moreover, there may be documents that reveal the existence and identity of insurance carriers available to respond to your demands. Also, there may be orders pertaining to the constitution and appointment of a committee of creditors. Depending on the size of your client's claim, trial counsel or the client may wish to serve on that committee.

7. *Always Attend the First Meeting of Creditors.* There must be a meeting of creditors within a reasonable time after the order for relief in a bankruptcy case. Rule 2002(a) provides that creditors who are listed in the schedules or have filed proofs of claim must receive 20 days' notice of the meeting. Section 343 of the Code requires the debtor to appear and submit to examination under oath. Bankruptcy Rule 2004(b) governs the scope of the examination, which is broad, although not without limit: it

may relate "only to the acts, conduct, or property or to the liabilities and financial condition of the debtor, or to any matter which may affect the administration of the debtor's estate, or to the debtor's right to a discharge." In Chapter 13 and most Chapter 11 cases, the examination may also inquire into the "continued operation of and desirability of continuance of any business" and other topics including "any other matter relevant to the case or to the formulation of a plan." You may also use the meeting to determine the debtor's attitude toward your claim. In rare cases, the debtor may admit the validity and amount of your claim.

To maximize the value of the first meeting of creditors as a source of information, counsel (or the client, if the client will attend the meeting) should review the bankruptcy schedules well before the meeting.

The meeting of creditors and the information set forth in the schedules should enable you and your client to decide whether it is worth the time and expense of more aggressive action to pursue the client's claim within the bankruptcy. Alternatives include the possibility of obtaining bankruptcy counsel or seeking relief from the automatic stay to continue the nonbankruptcy litigation.

These simple and relatively inexpensive steps, some of which can be undertaken by the client rather than trial counsel, describe the basic moves to protect a litigant's interests should an opponent file for relief under the Bankruptcy Code. They also will help you and your client decide how best to proceed to recovery.

Collecting a Judgment

by James J. Brown

You win the big one: a $5 million judgment. With it comes rave reviews from clients, colleagues, friends, and relatives. You have the judgment framed and hang it on your wall.

But wait a second. "Where's the money?" the managing partner asks. The real world rears its ugly head. It dawns on you that the defendant isn't going to stroll into your office with a certified check for five million bucks.

You close your door, take the judgment off your wall, and replace it with the certificate you got for coaching your daughter's little league team. You stop taking phone calls and start looking for the rules on collecting judgments.

Begin with Federal Rule of Civil Procedure 69. It says that procedures for enforcing judgments follow state law, except when a federal statute specifically governs.

Under state law, the first step is to record the judgment in the county where the debtor resides or owns property. A federal judgment may be recorded in the same manner as a state judgment in any locality within the federal district where the judgment was entered. File a certified copy of the judgment in the county land records, usually at the registry of deeds or county recorder's office, and pay the filing fee. The judgment becomes a lien on the debtor's property in the county where you record it 28 U.S.C. §1962.

Say you have a federal judgment from the United States District Court for the District of Maryland at Baltimore. If the debtor owns property in Howard County, Maryland (which does not encompass Baltimore, but

The author, who is now with the firm Weinberg and Green in Baltimore, was Deputy Chief of the Judgment Enforcement Unit, U.S. Department of Justice, Washington, D.C.

is in the same federal district), you would record the judgment by filing a certified copy with the appropriate office of Howard County. The judgment will then be a lien against the debtor's Howard County property.

You can encumber property in other jurisdictions as well. Before the judgment can be recorded in another jurisdiction it must be properly enrolled on the court docket there.

If you know the debtor has property in other counties in the same state but outside the federal district where the judgment was entered, follow the state procedures for registering the judgment there. Registering the judgment means enrolling it on the court docket. Then record the judgment in the new county so it becomes a lien on any real property the debtor owns there.

Judgments obtained in a federal district court may also be registered in other federal districts once they become final by appeal or otherwise. 28 U.S.C. § 1963. In addition, there are statutory procedures for registering judgments of the Court of International Trade and the United States Claims Court in the district courts. 28 U.S.C. §§ 1963A, 2508.

Judgments registered in a new jurisdiction have the same effect as in the original jurisdiction, and are treated the same way. *Stanford v. Utley*, 341 F.2d 265 (8th Cir. 1965). *United States v. Palmer* 609 F. Supp. 544, 547 (E.D. Tenn. 1985). So once you register the judgment in another district, you can record it and get the resulting lien against the debtor's property in any county within the registering district.

As a practical matter, some court clerks do not understand that, once a judgment has been registered, you do not need to follow state law procedures for enforcing "foreign" judgments. If you have trouble with the clerk on this point, talk to the chief clerk and walk him through the pertinent cases and statutes, giving him copies for comfort.

Now you have liens on the debtor's property in various places. That is a good start, because it will establish your priority interest in that property if you get into a scuffle with creditors who come along later. But how do you get your money?

If the debtor has property in the jurisdiction where the judgment was entered or registered, have the court clerk issue a writ of execution against the property (sometimes called an attachment writ or a garnishment writ). Then present the writ to the U.S. marshal, who will attach the property to satisfy your judgment. Federal Civil Procedure Rule 69 says that the procedure on execution follows the state practice.

You should describe the property to the marshal as specifically as possible. If there are different kinds of property, request different writs from the clerk. For example, in the federal district courts, there are usually separate forms of writs for: Attachment on Judgment (personal property, goods, chattels); Attachment on Judgment (credits); and Attachment on Judgment (garnishment of wages, earnings, salary, commissions and pensions). Consult the clerk on what writs should be issued.

If the debtor's property is in the hands of a third party such as a bank, proceed in accordance with state law (unless a particular federal statute applies) to attach (or garnish) those credits and have them applied against your judgment. (You should check applicable state and federal law on exemptions, especially when garnishing wages.) Writs of attachment on a judgment may be obtained from each court where your judgment is registered, and the process can be repeated until your judgment is satisfied.

Federal administrative agencies have a way around registering a judgment in other districts. A writ of execution obtained for the use of the United States may be executed in any state or territory, or in the District of Columbia. 28 U.S.C. § 2413; *see United States v. Thornton*, 672 F.2d 101 (D.C. Cir. 1982).

This procedure, commonly called long-arm execution, is a very effective collection device. Although it is normally available only to the agencies of the United States, there are exceptions. In some situations, a private party can use long-arm execution if the basic cause of action is in the United States and the judgment is "for the use of" both parties. *See United States ex rel. Marcus v. Lord Elec. Co.*, 43 F. Supp. 12, 13 (W.D. Pa. 1942); *United States v. Palmer, supra*, 609 F.2d at 547.

If the debtor owns personal property, recording the judgment in the county courthouse or registry of deeds may not be enough. For example, if the property is an aircraft, the U.S. marshal should attach it in accordance with state law, but the attachment and levy should be recorded with the Federal Aviation Administration Aircraft Registry Division in Oklahoma City, Oklahoma, following the procedures of the Federal Aviation Act (49 U.S.C. § 1403).

To attach a ship, follow admiralty law and procedure. (These procedures are contained in Rules B and C of Supplemental Rules for Certain Admiralty and Maritime Claims.) If, in settling a judgment, the debtor gives your client a ship's mortgage on a vessel weighing more than 21 tons, follow the procedures set out in the Ship's Mortgage Act (46 U.S.C. § 921), and record the ship's mortgage at the home port of the vessel with the Collector of Customs or U.S. Coast Guard Vessel Documentation Office.

Be sure you instruct the U.S. marshal on the proper method of attaching and levying on each item of the debtor's property, researching any special procedures that might apply to anything big or unusual. Once the marshal has attached and levied on the property, he will auction the property, sell it, and apply the sale proceeds, after expenses, to the judgment. Any excess proceeds are distributed to other lienholders in the order of their priorities, and, if there is anything left, to the debtor. (In many cases, you should consult a creditor's rights lawyer to assist you in sorting out priorities and handling related problems.)

To find the debtor's assets, you may use the same discovery devices available in prejudgment litigation, and more. Federal Civil Procedure Rule 69 entitles a judgment creditor to use the discovery procedures found in Rules 26 through 37. In addition, you may use applicable state discovery procedures and state supplementary proceedings. As usual, the timing and sequence of discovery is your choice. An examination of the judgment debtor in supplementary proceedings is an excellent way to begin post-judgment discovery.

To start the process, file a petition for supplementary proceedings. In that petition, recite the facts concerning your judgment, and include a request to examine the judgment debtor and have him bring documents. Along with the petition, file an order authorizing the procedures you want to use. If the debtor is a business, you should normally request at least these documents:

- All documents relating to any leasehold or freehold interest of the debtor in real property and tangible or intangible personal property, including any options to purchase and any property that the debtor owns or leases as a member of a partnership or with any other person or business entity.
- All canceled checks, check stabs, bank statements, ledgers, and correspondence showing disbursements and receipts over the last five years.
- Copies of all federal and state tax returns for the last five years.
- All records relating to any transfer to others of title to or any other interest whatsoever in any real or personal property within the last five years.
- All documents relating to any cause of action pending against debtor, or any loans or advances of money to the debtor.
- Master payroll file.
- All documents relating to the funds, other assets, liabilities, ownership, capitalization, and incorporation of the debtor.

The list can be expanded or contracted depending on what information you already have and whether the debtor is an individual, a partnership, or a corporation. If the debtor is a publicly held company, your request should call for quarterly and annual reports filed with the Securities and Exchange Commission. If the debtor is required to file other disclosure documents with local, state, or federal agencies, get those too.

In post-judgment discovery, more than one examination of the debtor is often necessary, and you may have to move for sanctions under Rule 37 to get all the necessary documents from a recalcitrant debtor. You should also go after other sources of information about the debtor and his finances.

If the debtor has an accountant, subpoena the accountant and his records concerning the debtor. In cases applying federal privilege law, such as bankruptcy cases, there is no accountant-client privilege, even though there may be such a privilege under state law. *See* FED. R. EVID. 501; *United States v. Arthur Young & Co.*, 465 U.S. 805 (1984).

Even if the debtor has "lost" his financial statements or tax returns you will find them in the accountant's files. If the debtor does not have an accountant, and still has not produced tax returns, move the court for an order requiring the debtor to give you written authorization to obtain copies of his returns from the Internal Revenue Service.

In some cases, you may suspect that the debtor has not produced all his bank records. When that happens, go right to the source. If you know where the debtor banks, subpoena the records from the bank.

A few years ago, I was involved in enforcing a judgment against a corporation. I subpoenaed records from the bank where the corporation maintained a checking account. The documents that the bank turned over demonstrated that, at the time the corporation was indebted to my client, it had repaid certain debts due its president by an unusual and circuitous method, and had made transfers to related corporations, violating my creditor's priority. Without the bank records, I would have been unaware of the potential claim my client had against the corporation's president and the other corporations.

Armed with the information I got from the bank, I filed a new action in federal court to recover fraudulent transfers and pierce the corporate veils of the related companies to satisfy my judgment. I eventually recovered about two-thirds of the judgment debt by settling the action against the company's president and the related companies.

Credit card records are another source of information about the debtor and his activities. In cases where the debtor has little personal income, but is employed by a corporation he controls, you may find that he uses corporate credit cards to maintain his life-style.

Some debtors use corporate credit cards to pay for such "business expenses" as suits, socks, microwave ovens, tennis rackets, panty hose, and stereo sets. Credit card account statements are clues to the debtor's spending patterns, and they can help you trace exactly where he was on a given day. The records might show that the debtor stopped at a marina for food and gas, using a boat you did not realize that he or his alter ego corporation owned. Such items are usually obvious personal expenses, which may demonstrate that the debtor uses the corporation as his alter ego.

Judges find it hard to stomach that kind of corporate abuse and will usually allow you to pierce the corporate veil when the corporation is merely a shell to protect the debtor's personal assets from creditors. Or the court may give you a monthly payment order on your judgment based on the debtor's noncash "income" from the corporation.

The debtor's family members are also good sources of information. Sometimes apparently uncollectible judgments become collectible when you uncover fraudulent transfers of valuable assets to the debtor's close friends or relatives without adequate consideration.

The biggest debtor I ever went after (he was six-feet-two and weighed about 350 pounds) was a poultry farmer. In reviewing documents I had subpoenaed from a bank, I discovered that, before the judgment, the debtor had transferred his liquid assets to a trust "for his children." It was amazing how his children's trust paid for his home mortgages, his car, and other personal expenses. Subsequent fraudulent-transfer litigation resulted in my client's recovery of almost all the debt, which was over $100,000. That's a lot of chickens, even for a big poultry farmer.

During post-judgment litigation, you can often get injunctions or writs to freeze or attach assets that the debtor has transferred to others. This will prevent the assets from being further dissipated while your post judgment litigation proceeds.

In a recent case, we got an injunction preventing the transfer of several hospital buildings, a mortgage note, and bank accounts. At the same time, we proceeded to litigate whether a successor corporation was the alter ego of three corporations against which we had obtained a $1.4 million judgment. We knew the three companies were mere shells, without assets.

After two years of discovery, the case was finally tried. We won the alter ego suit, getting a judgment for about $1.3 million against the successor corporation. Because the property had been frozen during the litigation, our client was able to satisfy its judgment from the assets still in the hands of the successor corporation.

You should consider restraining asset transfers during a postjudgment appeal by invoking Federal Civil Procedure Rule 62. If the debtor is unable to post a supersedeas bond, you can move the court to set other conditions for securing the judgment pending appeal. *Trans World Airlines, Inc. v. Hughes*, 314 F. Supp. 94 (S.D.N.Y. 1970). This will make it easier to collect the judgment if the debtor's appeal is unsuccessful. If the debtor does post a bond, the judgment can be satisfied against the bond.

A few years ago, I was enforcing a $38 million judgment against an oil refinery company and its president. The company owned various properties in four different states. The president owned a cattle ranch and livestock in another state. The judgment debtors were unable to post a bond for such a large judgment amount.

I moved the federal district court under Rule 62 to set other conditions to secure the judgment pending appeal. The court ordered that all corporate stock was to be escrowed at a national bank; the creditor was to be given security interests in all oil refinery and ranch properties; the creditor could file its judgment as a lien against the refinery's real property, and could file deeds of trust or notices of interest in real property against various parcels of land that the corporation and its president owned in several other states; the creditor was to be given periodic access to the books and records of the refinery and the ranch; the salaries of corporate officers and ranch managers would be fixed at an agreed rate of compensation during the appeal; the corporation and its president were prohibited from paying notes, debts, or other obligations to one another, or incurring any debts except in the ordinary course of business; and the corporation and the ranch were prohibited from making any major capital improvements or additions.

After the debtors lost their appeal, I filed in the federal district court for the appointment of a receiver for the refinery and the ranch. Under certain state and federal laws, receiverships may be established to administer the affairs and conserve the assets of financially troubled companies. More often than not, bankruptcy is the preferred method of administering and reorganizing insolvent companies. In our case, we proceeded under federal receivership statutes, 28 U.S.C. §§ 754 and 959, to give us quick access to the debtor's business and to prevent further dissipation of assets.

Later, the individual debtor filed a bankruptcy petition, claiming the ranch and the corporate stock of the refinery as his individual assets. During the following three years, we fought a battle that included nine post-judgment appeals and a jurisdictional struggle between a bankruptcy judge and a chief district judge. *See In re Dalton*, 733 F.2d 710 (10th Cir. 1984), *cert. dismissed*, 469 U.S. 1185 (1985). Throughout the skirmishing, it was a great comfort to have the security of the stringent conditions set pending the initial appeal. The case illustrates that a judgment does not end the litigation, and may be just the beginning of longer and more complex proceedings.

The postjudgment litigation may be lengthy and expensive. There is no easy way at the beginning to assure your client that the money he spends in post-judgment discovery and litigation will produce an even bigger recovery. Usually the preliminary post-judgment discovery, if done properly, will tell you how much of the judgment you can collect. In other cases, further litigation against third parties may be necessary.

Epilogue

Interview with Edward Bennett Williams

by Priscilla Anne Schwab

Editor's Note: *Edward Bennett Williams was acknowledged to be one of America's finest trial lawyers. He was also a warm and humorous person, a friend, and teacher for numerous other lawyers. He died on August 13, 1988. This article orginally appeared in the Winter, 1986 issue of* Litigation..

Edward Bennett Williams. The name rolls off the tongue like a drill sergeant's cadence count. The man has marched through his legal career almost as precisely, with only occasional stumbles to remind him—and those around him—that winning may be everything, but you do not always win. Edward Bennett Williams almost always did—and still does. From those whose batting average is less than near perfect, the question is how—how did he do it? That is more easily answered than why.

Today Williams heads an 85-plus lawyer firm in Washington, D.C. Williams and Connolly specializes in litigation, civil and criminal, and is known for its name clients such as promoter Don King, the *National Enquirer,* John Hinckley, Bobby Baker, John Connally, William F. Buckley, Jr., and *The Washington Post.*

A successful person in any field of endeavor can tell you how he or she reached the pinnacle. Most can articulate why, when, and through whom. Williams is no exception. But he starts from the premise that either you've got it, or you don't. If you don't, you're going nowhere. If you do, you find out how much you've got. Then you learn to cultivate what you've got and succeed without what you don't got. Got it? Good.

Williams began that process on May 31, 1920, in Hartford, Connecti-

The author is an associate editor of LITIGATION *and an attorney in the Employee Benefits Division of the Solicitor's Office, Department of Labor, Washington, D.C. The article is based on two interviews with Mr. Williams and includes substantial excerpts from* Edward Bennett Williams for the Defense *by Robert I. Pack (Harper & Row, 1983) and a chapter written by Mr. Williams for* Listen to Leaders in Law *(Tupper & Love, 1963).*

cut, where his father was a buyer and floorwalker at the Brown Thomson department store. His middle name, comes from his mother, Mary Bennett, who was one of four daughters. Both parents were devout Roman Catholics, and their son shares that legacy.

The biographical details are interesting but unsurprising. You would expect Williams to achieve nearly straight A's in grammar school. Of course his boyhood passion was baseball, which he played on a pickup basis and watched—minor league Hartford Senators—on an over-the-fence basis.

As is true of most top litigators, his goal was set early. ''Ed always wanted to be a lawyer, there was never anything else in his mind, says his high school friend, Muriel (Jerry) Waterhouse. Similarly, his athletic prowess was confined more to observation than to participation. He ran the mile in high school but was no threat to any record. In his sophomore year at Bulkeley High School, he reported on sports for the school newspaper, the *Torch*, and there he found a base from which to shine. He initiated ''Inside Stuff,'' a weekly column heavy on school gossip and adolescent humor, and became co-editor in his senior year, immediately endowing the paper with the masthead motto, ''New England's Snappiest Scholastic Weekly.''

Williams's introduction to Journalism might have detoured him from the law. Like lawyers, most top journalists begin their obsession early. The irony is that, today, Edward Bennett Williams has few words for the media, although his friendships with individual editors, such as Benjamin Bradlee of *The Washington Post*, remain unblemished.

Naturally, Williams graduated near the top of his class in 1937, was voted most popular, and won a scholarship to Holy Cross. As in high school, his scholarship was exemplary—he was summa cum laude, voted ''most learned,'' and graduated number one in 1941. By then, two character traits were obvious: Williams was a committed perfectionist, and he had a natural ability to learn rapidly—the classic ''quick study.'' These qualities, plus the four strenuous years of mental gymnastics the Jesuits call a liberal arts education, helped Williams master Georgetown Law School.

His legal education was interrupted by the war. He joined the Army Air Corps for the ''romance'' of getting his wings, but his fly-boy career was stillborn—soloing, he had to crashland and flipped upside down in his single-engine trainer. The resultant back injury got him discharged from the Army and has bothered him all his life. That brush with mortality left Willliams ''unsettled,'' but he held his course through property, procedure, and probate to graduate in 1944.

Sound advice to those who make it through the rigors of legal training is threefold: find a firm, pass the bar, and choose a mentor. Williams did that in rapid-fire fashion.

He had planned to return to Hartford and earn his place in the legal and political hierarchy of the late Thomas Spellacy. An unexpected offer from the then smallish firm of Hogan and Hartson in Washington, D.C., changed all that. Naturally Williams was "in the right place at the right time," according to one of his professors, who introduced him to Howard Boyd, the head of the firm's still tiny trial department. After passing the D.C. bar, Williams started defending Washington's streetcar company in personal injury cases.

His mentor was, of course, Howard Boyd, whom Williams credits for most of his development as a litigator. Mr. Boyd, who left the firm in 1952 to take over the El Paso Gas Company in Houston, Texas, knew early on he was teaching one of the great ones. "It was perfectly apparent he was going to be a leader. . . . He is the most able trial lawyer in the United States today and has been such for many years."

Some may quarrel with that ranking, but none can legitimately question Williams's genius in criminal defense. Where did it come from? When did it begin?

MR. WILLIAMS: It's been said a thousand times—the secret of great trial work is preparation, really tedious, really intense preparation. I've always said I could go on doing trial work until I was 89 years old, if I didn't have to prepare the case with this terrible, torturous physical and psychic discipline you have to impose upon yourself.

It's like an old fighter. Fighters don't quit because they hate to fight. They quit because they hate to train. And that's the way it is with old trial lawyers. They don't want to do that awful training anymore—they dread it—yet they don't want to quit the courtroom, either.

MS. SCHWAB: How does a trial lawyer go into training? Most lawyers think they spend enormous amounts of time preparing, yet a good many get into court and discover that, one, they did not prepare nearly enough; two, their characterization of the case is completely unconvincing to anyone; three, facts about which they had no idea undermine their legal theory; or, four, they end up with a jury with which they know they will have no rapport. What went wrong before the trial actually began?

MR. WILLIAMS: Any lawyer surprised by facts at a trial has failed in the preparation. It's that simple.

MS. SCHWAB: How do you avoid it?

MR. WILLIAMS: First, you or those working with you have to interview every single person who has any even remotely relevant information concerning the case. You have to read every document that is remotely relevant. That may mean that you read seven times more documents and interview seven times more witnesses than will ever be used. But what you're doing is obviating the possibility of surprise. Nothing should happen factually for which you are not ready. You must know more about the case than anyone else involved.

If you know all the facts, the documents, and the testimony that can possibly be offered, then you have prepared your case as effectively and cogently as it can be. After that, the next step is to prepare your defendant and the witnesses equally as thoroughly. Much too often, defendants are put on the stand without thorough preparation.

MS. SCHWAB: Sometimes they won't sit still for it.

MR. WILLIAMS: Well, they will if they want me to defend them.

MS. SCHWAB: It's not a matter of two or three hours the day before trial?

MR. WILLIAMS: Uh, uh. If it's a big case, with complex facts, it may be a matter of two or three weeks. Daily meetings, repetitive briefings. You have to ask the defendant all the questions that can be asked, particularly stressing those that can weaken his case.

MS. SCHWAB: Isn't there a danger of too much prepping? Putting words in the defendant's mouth just gives him a chance to forget his lines and get lost in improvisation.

MR. WILLIAMS: I don't put words in my clients mouth. The purpose of the preparation is to show him *how* to say what he has to say. For example, it is relevant where the defendant, John Smith, was on the night of January 6. Almost certainly he will be asked that question. John Smith, unprepared goes on the stand:

> PROSECUTOR: Where were you, Mr. Smith, on the night of January 6, 1958?
>
> Smith looks at the prosecutor and says, "I don't remember."

This answer certainly does not create any positive impression in the minds of the jurors. At best, it is neutral. And it may be negative. On the other hand, the question answered in another way gives a totally different effect:

> PROSECUTOR: Where were you, Mr. Smith, on the night of January 6, 1958?
>
> MR. SMITH: Mr. Prosecutor, I thought you were going to ask me that question, and I have racked my brain trying to remember where I was on the night of January 6, 1958, because I want to answer all these questions. But for the life of me, I just can't remember where I was on that night.

In both answers, the defendant has given, as far as actual facts are concerned, the same answer: He does not remember. But the second form of his answer may have made a positive impression, it may even have evoked sympathy for him, because he has shown to the jury that he is trying to cooperate.

That is why I say that a trial lawyer has to teach a witness how to testify. When he does, things that otherwise might not be fruitful can make a tremendously positive impact on the jury.

You must unmistakably differentiate between how to testify as I have just indicated—and what to testify. You can legitimately influence the "how," but the "what" is always determined by the facts.

In preparing a witness, you can never tamper with the facts. However, within the exacting demands of truth, there is a great variance of impact on the minds and on the emotions of the jury. Positive impact is possible in every action in the trial, every question, every answer, for the benefit of the defendant. Always within the limits of the truth. Always.

Ms. Schwab: How do you force a high-powered client like John Connally to go through this learning process?

Mr. Williams: I have three 99.9 percent unbreakable rules: One, I demand and keep absolute control of the case. Two, I demand complete candor and honesty from the client—no holding back. Three, I demand and get economic compensation that makes sense for the client.

Ms. Schwab: What do you mean by total control? I know you turned down some clients because they wouldn't put themselves in your hands completely. You turned down Senator McCarthy once. . . .

Mr. Williams: Well, he didn't want me to be his lawyer. He wanted me to be there with him at the Army hearings, as sort of counselor. He wasn't going to let me run his show. When the censure case came along later, he agreed to give me total control, but he reneged on the deal. I controlled what went on inside the hearing room, but I couldn't control him outside the hearing room, and he made all these wild and reckless statements to the press.

Ultimately, we lost the case on account of what he said to the press. We won on all the charges for which he was brought to congressional trial. But he would go out and excoriate Senator Watkins, who was a lovely, nice old man who was trying to be fair. Called him some terrible names.

Ms. Schwab: How do you explain to a client that you will have total control?

Mr. Williams: I don't explain it. I tell the client that I have to have it, that I can't work without it. I give a bad analogy. I say, look, if you want me to take your appendix out, I have to have absolute control of the operation. You can't put your hand on the scalpel, not if you want to survive. If you don't have absolute confidence in my ability, as a lawyer, then find somebody—one person—in whom you do have confidence.

Ms. Schwab: As a trial attorney, you don't work with banks of lawyers?

Mr. Williams: I do have two or three attorneys working, but they are all subordinate to me. They have to take direction. I'm the captain, and I'm in control. I have to be, or I don't try it. But I do have help. Other lawyers do legal research, prepare witnesses, draft motions, but I do all the oral work.

Ms. Schwab: So second chairs just sit?

Mr. Williams: I was brought up in a school of practice in which one person tried a case and tried it in toto. Even with some help, in the courtroom there was only one voice. And I like that.

Ms. Schwab: What about a complex case, say, an antitrust action with thousands of pages of documents, hundreds of witnesses. How can you handle that in a courtroom single-handedly? With total control?

Mr. Williams: My impression of that so-called "big document" case is that 95 percent of the documents are worthless. Just piles of paper to impress the jury. One of the great tragedies of litigation today is these paper wars. The whole profession gains nothing but disrepute when one of these big firms puts 21 lawyers on a case, and they start multiplying documents, paper times paper.

Now obviously in a few cases, the issues are so complex that there are, maybe, thousands of documents. But my experience has been that law firms multiply paper unnecessarily. They make litigation more prolific than necessary. They don't have an instinct for the jugular. They don't isolate the major issues of the case and simplify them into comprehensibility. And they engage in massive overkill in discovery.

Ms. Schwab: But there always seems to be a need for more discovery. You say yourself you must uncover every fact, however remotely relevant.

Mr. Williams: True, but discovery today is not used primarily to uncover facts. It's used to delay, to obfuscate, and, too often, to replace real investigation.

Ms. Schwab: Is the discovery hassle the reason you take mostly criminal cases?

Mr. Williams: We don't. The criminal cases get a lot of the attention, but our practice is more heavily civil than criminal. The civil doesn't get the attention of the press.

Ms. Schwab: Speaking of the press, is it true that you won't be quoted on the cases you are handling, that you say "no comment' to every question?

Mr. Williams: Listen, trial by newspaper is a real problem in this country, especially in criminal trials. So often, newspapers will generate a lot of publicity around a trial. They will print stories, confessions, past records, and this, almost always, is adverse to the defense.

I do not think that the newspapers should be blamed for this or that anything should be done to curb them from printing anything to which they can get access. I do not advocate adopting the English system which holds a newspaper in contempt for printing pretrial information that might influence a possible juror.

However, we would eliminate a large part of this prejudicial publicity if we would only enforce the canons of ethics that now exist. I do not think that any lawyer, whether defense or prosecution, should ever make a comment to the press evaluating his case or any evidence.

Second, I do not think that he should state to the press what he is going to prove. He should never say what he intends to show at any future time in court, whether that time is one hour later or three days later.

I believe, too, that nobody on the defense side should ever give this kind of information or this evaluation to the press.

Also, the defendant should never talk to the media. *Never.*

On the prosecutor's side, I think that we should not have statements coming from the police that are damaging and prejudicial to the defense.

I am also dedicated to keeping television cameras out of the courtroom. There are many reasons for this. One is that the networks would never show the full trial. They would leave out the boring parts, showing only the sensational and overlooking the fact that sometimes the least exciting part of a case is really the most significant. They would also manage to give a story treatment to the trial, thereby creating a completely wrong impression of the administration of justice.

The search for truth in a courtroom is difficult enough without putting it on stage. Let a witness realize that he is in front of a camera, and he may become more concerned with his histrionics than with his oath. This applies not only to witnesses, but also to judges and jurors and lawyers, all primping and nudging to get on camera and stay there as long as they can.

Ms. SCHWAB: How can you tell if a client is completely candid with you? How do you ferret out the whole truth?

MR. WILLIAMS: You certainly don't get all the facts in the first interview. The whole truth comes only from the exacting preparation I've described. You literally leave no stone unturned. You compare every fact, however seemingly insignificant, with every other fact. You look for the shading, the slight inconsistency—you hammer away at any you find until they are all smoothed out. You grill the client more exactingly than any prosecutor will do. You explain over and over that you must know every detail of the case, no matter how remote. You do the same with your witnesses, even if they are only for character.

If I put a witness on the stand, I know him, know his background, know his character, know how to handle him. I have already taken into account whether he is smart or dull, reticent or voluble.

I will also have gone over his testimony with him, every shred of it, and gone over it with him again, and still again. He knows each question I will propose, and I know each answer. If, by chance, I get an answer that is different from the one I expected, it will mean that he has changed his mind after he took the stand.

Ms. SCHWAB: How can you tell if your client—or a witness—is lying?

MR. WILLIAMS: There's an odor of mendacity. You will know when a person is covering up. If you have mastered all the facts and have thought through the significance of each one, and you're trying to elicit an acknowledgment of those facts from someone who doesn't want to admit them, you can usually tell when the person is veering from the truth. I can't recall being deceived by a witness. I've been surprised but not deceived.

Ms. SCHWAB: What do you do if you know a witness is lying? Just keep pressing?

MR. WILLIAMS: Not if you're getting nowhere. Some people you can't crack. It's like running into an eggbeater. You'll get whipped. Some people are just brazen enough to lie under oath. You have to prove through extrinsic evidence that they were lying for you will not get the truth from their mouths.

Life is not like Perry Mason. There the witnesses always crack and confess, but it's not like that. Sometimes you can chip away at a witness so that the inconsistencies, evasions, and statements that do not add up become apparent to the jury. But be sure not to chip away so much that you generate sympathy for the poor witness.

Ms. SCHWAB: But you've had a few Perry Mason scenes in the courtroom, haven't you?

MR. WILLIAMS: Well, of course. Once I was defending a streetcar company against a woman who claimed she had been injured when the bus collided with another. Although doctors could find nothing wrong with her she did have a mysterious fever. I studied her charts thoroughly, and the same sequence of events kept leaping out: During her hospitalization, she had requested a hot-water bottle about a half-hour before her temperature was to be taken. This pattern had been repeated about 50 times. The conclusion was obvious, and as I cross-examined her, I kept asking about the hot-water bottle, the thermometer, and the relationship between the two. Finally, she burst into tears. "You think I put the thermometer on the hot water bottle, don't you?" she said. "Well, how else could I make them know how sick I was?"

Case dismissed.

Ms. SCHWAB: One thing most lawyers never talk about except to their clients is their fees. How much do you charge an hour?

MR. WILLIAMS: If you had asked me that a few decades ago, I might have told you. Now I don't have a charge for my own time, because I sometimes am able to do things in half an hour as a result of 37 years' experience that might take six months for someone else to do.

I don't want to work on a clock. I want to work with other factors weighed in—the result, the experience I've had. I keep a record of how much time I put in, but we don't bill for my time. After a job is completed, I decide how much it should be worth to the client, depending primarily on the outcome and only secondarily on how long I spent on the case.

Ms. SCHWAB: You are reported to be a master of the art of cross-examination. It's said that's how you got John Connally off.

MR. WILLIAMS: Well, that's not right. I didn't get him off. The government's whole case was based almost entirely on the testimony of a man indicted for fraud and perjury. How could the jury believe him?

Ms. Schwab: Your cross-examination certainly destroyed any credibility Jake Jacobsen could have had.

Mr. Wllliams: It illustrated the detailed preparation. A less careful lawyer might have noted the fact that gloves were allegedly used by John Connally in counting the money. But it wasn't just gloves; was it one or two; were they rubber or cloth; what color were they?

Ms. Schwab: I think the point is best illustrated by the trial transcript. Let's run through it.

Williams: You told us . . . that Mr. Connally and you had a meeting in his office alone, that he excused himself, left his office for ten minutes, and came back with a cigar box and a rubber glove or rubber gloves on top of a pile of money in the cigar box, is that right?

Jacobsen: Well, it was something like that.

Williams: No, tell me what it was, Mr. Jacobsen, not whether it was something like that or not. . . . You tell us exactly how it was, Mr. Jacobsen.

Jacobsen: I believe the rubber glove was on the side of the money in the cigar box. The rubber glove or gloves was on the side of the money.

Williams: I'm sorry?

Jacobsen: I say the rubber glove or gloves was on the side of the money not on top of the money.

Williams: Now, when you told Mr. Tuerkheimer (the prosecutor) in your interview with him back last year about this episode, you told him it was a rubber glove, did you not?

Jacobsen: Yes.

Williams: And when you testified before the grand jury on March 23, you told the grand jury it was a rubber glove, did you not?

Jacobsen: Yes, sir.

Williams: But when you testified on Thursday here in this courtroom before His Honor and this jury, you said it was a rubber glove or gloves: Is that correct?

Jacobsen: Yes sir.

Williams: When did you decide it might have been a glove or gloves?

Jacobsen: Between the time I testified before the grand jury and the time I testified here.

Williams: What was it that changed your recollection from it being a glove to it being a glove or gloves?

Jacobsen: Just the logic of it being gloves instead of glove.

Williams: It was the logic of it, is that right?

Jacobsen: Yes.

Williams: Was that because, Mr. Jacobsen, the prosecutors

pointed out to you that nobody could count money with one glove on one hand and a big pile?

Jacobsen: No, sir.

Williams: Well, what was the logic of it that changed your mind . . . and caused you to testify on Thursday that it was a glove or gloves?

Jacobsen: Well, the fact that you couldn't hardly handle money with one glove.

Williams: Well, that was what I asked you, Mr. Jacobsen.

Mr. Williams: I took an apparently minor point and showed the jurors that Jacobsen would tailor his testimony to ''logic'' or—presumably—to anything. Then I pressed him about the color of the gloves. Jacobsen said, ''I'm not sure about the color. It was either that light beige or yellow, one or the other, I'm not sure.''

Williams: It was either beige or yellow, but you are not sure?

Jacobsen: I'm not sure.

Williams: Could it have been black?

Jacobsen: I don't believe so.

Williams: Or white?

Jacobsen: It could have been. It was a light color.

Ms. Schwab: How do you learn that kind of detailed cross-examination?

Mr. Williams: You sure don't learn it by reading about it. Cross-examination is the most difficult part of trial work, because you can only learn by doing. Very tough art form. Very few have mastered it.

Ms. Schwab: Why?

Mr. Williams: Why? Because today you have truth seekers—they just shake the Christmas tree and hope something good falls off. Usually, of course, more bad stuff comes off than good. That's because the lawyer doesn't know where he's going, let alone how to get there.

You have to plan how to control the witness who is out to damage you. The most effective cross-examination is so tightly reined that the witness never has a chance to go his own way. The bridle is so taut on the witness that all he can do is follow your lead, answering your questions, yes or no.

There are some basic rules in cross-examination, and the first is you never ask a question to which you do not know the answer. This may seem difficult in cross-examination, and it is. But only a very foolish lawyer asks a question, whether in direct or cross-examination, when he does not know the exact answer.

Second, you never ask an adverse witness why he did something. Why! You never ask him why. Ask a man why he did something, and he can talk for 20 minutes. He can give all his motivations. He can make a speech, every bit of it unfavorable to you.

Let me give you an illustration. I once tried a case involving a man who had been killed by a streetcar in Washington. There was some suggestion that he might have been drinking before he was hit, but there was no proof. He did have a tendency to drink too much, but there was no evidence that he had had a drink when he was hit by the streetcar.

I put the man's son on the stand. Although he had not witnessed the accident, he had come upon the scene shortly thereafter.

When the defense lawyer took him over on cross-examination, he said to him, "You went out in the street, didn't you? Your father was lying there, wasn't he?"

The boy answered, "Yes."

The lawyer said, "You went out and leaned over him, didn't you.

"Yes."

"As a matter of fact, you put your face right down close to him, didn't you?"

"Yes."

The lawyer said, "You were sniffling for alcohol, weren't you? Looking for a bottle, weren't you?"

"No, sir."

"Did you smell alcohol on him?"

"No, sir."

"Weren't you bending over looking in his pockets, trying to get a bottle out of his pocket?"

"No, sir."

"Well, witnesses have testified that you leaned over him, lying on the road. Why did you lean over him?"

The boy said, "Because he was my father, and he was dying, and I leaned over and kissed him."

There was no recovery from that. There could be no recovery. Why? The lawyer found out why, all right. You don't have to ask whether he lost the case.

Ms. SCHWAB: That was devastating. Couldn't he see the danger?

MR. WILLIAMS: Probably not. He hadn't thought through the questions he wanted to ask, what the various answers might be, and what each of those answers might mean. He knew he wanted to show negligence by getting the witness to testify that he smelled alcohol on his father's breath. But the lawyer had no plan to make that happen. He tried to throw a haymaker at the witness instead of leading him, and he got knocked cold.

If you do not know what is ahead and do not know where you are going, then don't start. It is better to have no cross-examination at all than to have a bad one.

An adverse witness, like an unbroken horse, is going to try to break away and take you where you don't want to go. But you know exactly where you intend to go, and the idea is to bring the witness, however reluctant, down that course to where you want him.

Never give him a chance to break away. Hold him on the course that you have been over again and again while preparing the case, knowing every dip, every bend, every inch of it. You may ask him a question and get an answer different from the one you expected, but this can mean only that his answer is different from the truth, from what he should have answered.

If he gives conflicting statements, you just tighten your grip on him, holding him steady no matter how hard he tries to break loose. He may be trying to trick you or give you a shock, but don't let him. You must keep asking him what you know, and you move him from your A to your B and on to your C wherever it is you intend to take him.

To ask "why" is foolish. To ask a question when you do not know the answer is foolish. To ask an extra question is just plain silly. There can be no reason for it and no possible good in it.

Ms. Schwab: Everyone who teaches trial techniques warns against asking the one question too many. How do you know before you ask it that your next question is the one too many?

Mr. Williams: You have to be certain of what you want each question to accomplish. For example, the classic story is the man charged with mayhem for biting off the ear of his opponent.

So the case went to trial. A witness was on the stand, and the defense lawyer took him over on cross-examination. "Now, you saw this fight, did you?' "Well," he said, "I didn't see all of it."

"As a matter of fact, you didn't see very much of it, did you?"

"I didn't see very much of it, no."

The lawyer said, "As a matter of fact, you never saw the defendant bite the complainant's ear, did you?"

And the witness said, "No, I didn't."

Okay, That's it. All the lawyer has to do is quit. He's proved this witness didn't see the fight. But the lawyer doesn't quit, does he? He asks the next question.

"But you testified that he bit it off, didn't you?"

"Yes."

"Well, how did you know that the defendant bit the complainant's ear off?"

"Because I saw him spit it out."

After this, there could be only one verdict, and the defense lawyer had brought it on himself.

Ms. Schwab: But how do you *know* not to ask the next question? It's natural curiosity.

Mr. Williams: Because you should know. You're sitting in the catbird seat. You've proved what you wanted to prove, which is that he didn't see it. That's all you want to do. You don't want to know why he didn't see it.

I don't ever ask questions that begin with the word why, unless I know the answer. Why people do things, I mean, some people could go on for days. And when you try to cut the witness off, the judge will say, well, you asked him, so let him answer. "How" is the other word. You don't need to know how from a witness, find out how beforehand.

Ms. Schwab: Some attorneys don't seem to have any sense of where they are when they are trying cases. They treat the courtroom as some kind of strange place they have found themselves in.

Mr. Williams: So many cases are tried with no conceptual thinking about what the defense is. It becomes sort of shotgun—scattered all over the place, instead of a clear concept of putting the best face on the facts and then making every question count to persuade the jurors that it is the truth.

Ms. Schwab: But some attorneys think they don't need a theory of the defense. They only have to blunt the offense. A sort of George Allen approach.

Mr. Williams: Well, maybe that will turn out okay. George did win a few games. But you ought to have a well-conceived defense. You have to have it. If you just try to batter away at the offense, you'll be running into windmills. You have to have something to take the wind out of the prosecutor's case, something which the jury can believe, besides the theory that the other side's case is no good. The jury has to have something positive to believe about the defendant.

I used to do a survey years ago, but I stopped because the results were so overwhelming. How many defendants in this country are acquitted who don't say anything in their own defense. That covers a lot of situations, but overwhelmingly 95 percent of the people who say nothing are convicted. If the defendant offers no explanation, he's probably going to be convicted.

Ms. Schwab: You're not saying every defendant has to take the stand? The lawyer can come up with a defense theory.

Mr. Williams: No, I'm saying that if the defendant doesn't take the stand, he is in tremendous peril of being convicted. We talk about presumption of innocence in this country, and it's become a tremendous part of the judge's charge, but all that does is to try to countervail the presumption of guilt that exists in the minds of the public with respect to defendants who are brought into the criminal courtroom.

Ms. Schwab: So it's a myth? People don't really believe in the presumption of innocence?

Mr. Williams: All it does is neutralize the presumption of guilt. In certain situations, anyone who says the defendant is presumed to be innocent is talking Alice in Wonderland. The often-convicted shoplifter up on yet another shoplifting charge is not presumed to be innocent by anybody. The defendant is presumed to be guilty. And you as the defense lawyer had better do something to explode that presumption.

Ms. Schwab: But if criminal defendants who say nothing in their own defense are convicted 95 percent of the time, what do you do with a defendant who is a bad one? How do you explode the presumption with a convicted felon?

Mr. Williams: That's a tremendous handicap. If you have a defendant with a criminal record, he's in big trouble. Most likely, he will be convicted again, unless he has a real defense.

Ms. Schwab: What about the defendant who is not a criminal? Say Bobby Baker. He was not a good witness for himself. That was the consensus. What do you do with a witness whom you know will not do well for himself on the stand? How do you minimize the damage?

Mr. Williams: One of the greatest paradoxes of the trial is that, oftentimes, you are at your peak of achieving acquittal as far as the jury is concerned when the government rests. And when you put on the defense, you go downhill. I've seen that happen so many times. Yet, if you put on no defense, the defendant will probably be convicted.

Ms. Schwab: That leaves the defense attorney in the classic Catch-22 situation.

Mr. Williams: That's right. I have felt in some of my own cases that I had effectively bombarded the government's case, and the jury was 100 percent on my side, yet they still wanted to hear from me. They were disgusted with the government's case, perhaps, but they were still waiting to hear from the defense. And when they heard from me, I may have eroded the defendant's case. The trick is not to lose too much ground with the jury. Not to lose what you have gained with cross-examination and not to lose all your defendant's credibility.

If you stand on the government's case, statistics show that you're not going to be successful too often. It's a daring gamble to take, because one of the jurors, you can be certain, will say: "Well, if he's so innocent, why in hell didn't he get on the stand?"

That's the other side of the phrase, "No inference may be drawn from the defendant's silence." Another one of those legal fetishes that has survived the mythology of our Anglo-Saxon jurisprudence. And it's a devastating question. You cannot lay your defendant open to it. Better to have him get on the stand and tell his story and get shot at by the government. So he looks like a piece of Swiss cheese after cross-examination. But at least he's told his story, and maybe somebody is going to believe it.

Ms. Schwab: So you have to take that chance?

Mr. Williams: I think it's risky business not to put the defendant on. He's got to be prepared, of course. What about DeLorean? I was surprised at the verdict. The government had apparently mucked the case up badly.

Ms. Schwab: Well, they got caught in the shoals of entrapment.

Mr. Williams: Sure. A real mire.

Ms. Schwab: Appearance and presence in the courtroom. It's been compared to the live stage or to a one-ring circus. But most trial attorneys don't have a commanding presence. They don't think of themselves as a stage manager for the leading actor, the defendant, and they probably couldn't carry it off if they tried to. How do you make your presence effective? By the way, are you nervous when you go into the courtroom? I know we all are, but are you?

MR. WILLIAMS: If you stop being nervous, you should quit, because then you don't care anymore. Anytime you go into a courtroom, there are high stakes. A person's freedom. There has to be tension. And if you don't have tension, you're not effective, I think.

Basically, you have to be yourself. You can't take a wimp and give him some dramatic presence that's suddenly going to arrest the attention of the jury. So he's just got to do the best he can.

MS. SCHWAB: Can you get a jury to like a wimp?

MR. WILLIAMS: Sometimes, by tuning your handicap around. You can make your lack of presence a plus instead of a minus, by saying, hey, look at me. I'm not a great orator. I can't mesmerize you. I'm nothing. Focus the jury's attention on the defendant or on the dramatics of the prosecutor.

Terribly dramatic lawyers are the easiest kind to do this with, the show-boats. You say, look, we're not here for an exhibition of histrionics, we are here in a search for the truth. You don't necessarily find the truth by flashing around the courtroom arguing to a high decibel count. I think flamboyancy went out with high-button shoes—William Jennings Bryan and his type. I don't raise my voice very often. The jurors can always hear me, even if they are not sure what I'm saying.

MS. SCHWAB: But you have a commanding presence in the courtroom. How does any defendant upstage you?

MR. WILLIAMS: Look, the principal actor in every trial is the defendant himself. People often talk about the trial lawyer taking the center of the stage. This he does occasionally, for even in the great plays the subordinate actors sometimes take the stage. But the truly fine lawyer will rarely take the spotlight from the defendant, certainly not for long, since the defendant must always be the star of the show.

If the lawyer for the defense really does his job, the jurors at the end of the trial will like the defendant or at least feel sympathy for him, no matter how unfortunate the role in which he may have been cast.

I believe the practice of trial law is perhaps the most creative art extant. One time I had an argument about this with Robert Rossen. He, to the motion-picture industry, is what a triple threat man used to be in the old days of football. He is a writer. He is a director. He is a producer. He once wrote, directed, and produced a picture which won the Academy Award in all three departments. It was called ''All the King's Men.''

One night we began talking of law and I said that the trial of a major criminal case required more creative talent than the production of a great motion picture. He disputed this.

The reasons I gave him, which finally convinced him, were these:

When a lawyer is in the trial of a major criminal case, he is staging a production that is designed to create an impression on the jury, and he has no opportunity for retakes. One mistake, and he may be through.

Secondly, he has no backdrop, no lighting, no effects to create illusions. He is working on a bare stage.

Third, he is not dealing with fiction. He has only the facts, and he must always confine himself within their limits. There is no chance for fabrication, no way to extricate himself by breaking the bonds of truth.

Fourth, he is working to create an impression not on seven out of twelve, or ten out of twelve, but *twelve* out of twelve. He must win everybody to get an acquittal, whereas a playwright, or a movie producer, who gets ten critics out of twelve on his side has done a great job.

Lastly, of course, he is working for the highest stakes for which a man can compete. He is working for human liberty and, in some cases, for human life.

Ms. SCHWAB: Courtroom tactics against opposing attorneys: What do you do?

MR. WILLIAMS: It depends on how he or she is being perceived by the jury. If they perceive him as a nice, fumbling incompetent, you don't do anything to dispel that image. If he's a mean, hostile sort, you kind of play along with him, show him up for what he is.

Ms. SCHWAB: Do you prepare a profile of the opposing attorney? His mannerisms, style?

MR. WILLIAMS: No, I don't do that. I don't think any of that side play is any good unless it's spontaneous. Better to put full time and attention on what you're trying to present. The peripheral stuff will take care of itself. I don't like to get into personal stuff with other lawyers. I do it only when I'm outraged.

Ms. SCHWAB: It's said that character witnesses are your trademark.

MR. WILLIAMS: I don't use them too often. I used them very effectively in the Connally case. You have to have someone as clean as the driven snow. Plenty of people out there don't have any arrests or blots in their copybooks. If this is your defendants first encounter with the law, you can usually put on a pretty good parade of character witnesses. It's a powerful weapon, because you are entitled to very good instructions. I try to get intelligent, respectable people who will be highly articulate to deliver a message about the defendant. The ones in Connally's case did a good job.

Ms. SCHWAB: How did you persuade former Representative Barbara Jordan to speak for Mr. Connally?

MR. WILLIAMS: She's a very good woman. Barbara has high ideals, and she didn't particularly like Connally, but she couldn't believe that he would take money. His reputation was excellent as far as his integrity and discharge of his duties as a public servant. She didn't agree with him politically, of course. She was a good witness.

But Billy Graham was the best. He was a good friend of Johns. Spoke very highly of him, I asked Mr. Graham what his occupation was. He said, "I teach the gospel of Jesus Christ across the face of the earth." I was right next to the jury box, and I heard a juror say softly, "Amen." I thought that was a good sign.

Ms. SCHWAB: How would you describe the art of advocacy?

MR. WILLIAMS: A lot of lawyers think that advocacy is practiced in a courtroom. A judge sitting on the bench, and 12 jurors sitting in the box. And that's where it starts, and that's where it stops. I think trial practice is a continuing process of advocacy. When you're talking to a prosecutor and he's trying to decide whether to make a certain settlement, you're an advocate. When you're taking to your client, when you're talking to witnesses, you're trying to persuade them to a course of conduct. You don't necessarily win the case in the courtroom talking to the jury. You win the case out there talking to the principals—the client, the witnesses, the investigators, the prosecutors. It seems to me that advocacy is a never-ending process, a small fragment of which takes place in the courtroom.

Ms. SCHWAB: It seems an impossible task to remember the thousand or so facts needed for just an average trial, relate them each to the other, and somehow recognize the combination that will ensure the prosecution falls short of beyond a reasonable doubt. How do you cram all that knowledge and strategy into yourself?

MR. WILLIAMS: You must have crammed for law school tests or the bar exam. Why do you think the professors load on the reading assignments? Several years ago, I tried a case in Washington involving a bank merger. My clients were stockholders in a smaller bank which was merging with one of the big banks in Washington, and they were resisting the merger.

I knew nothing about bank mergers, absolutely nothing. So I found the man widely heralded as the outstanding authority in the United States on bank mergers and I took a course from him. For one week we worked 16, maybe 18, hours a day, an intensively concentrated, one-week study of the direct area that would confront me.

When I emerged from this course, I knew as much about this narrow area as some people who had been in the field all their lives.

The result was that when adverse witnesses got on the stand and began to paint with a broad brush, I could button them down. They quickly realized, from my questions, that I knew what I was talking about. This flustered some of the witnesses quite badly. People who consider themselves wiser in some particular field than anybody else do not like to be questioned by someone as knowledgeable in that narrow area as they are. It confuses them, and they often show their confusion and sometimes their anger. This produces an adverse effect on the jury and a favorable effect for the lawyer who is doing the questioning.

So for this immediate month in trial practice, there may be a bank merger. Next month it may be a ruptured intervertebral disc, then a manipulation of the stock market. So it goes, month after month, always shifting as you move from trial to trial.

You wonder how you can possibly learn enough to try all these technical cases. This is the way it works. Perhaps you had the experience of getting behind in a course, then staying up for two nights and pounding the subject into yourself, getting ready for a big exam. You pass the exam, but a week later you do not know any more about the subject than before you crammed. I do not know anything about bank mergers anymore, but I knew an immense amount for the life of the trial.

This takes a certain kind of mind able to endure intensive concentration and capable of absorbing innumerable details. It also requires an unusual memory not only for immediate details but also for the background and the history of the subject at issue. Such memory is tremendously important, both in the preparation of a case and in the actual trial itself. You must remember everything.

Ms. SCHWAB: That's why I said it seems impossible. How do you train your mind?

MR. WILLIAMS: I think teaching helped me a lot. I taught at Georgetown and at Yale and for one semester in Europe. Teaching gives you experience in making things comprehensible. I probably wasn't a good teacher in the sense of crossing new frontiers of legal thought; I operated on the socialistic intellectual premise of getting everybody to pass. I was reaching for the lowest common denominator so that I could instill the maximum amount of knowledge on the subject and excite the maximum amount of curiosity in all the students. Stimulate and challenge everyone in the class, rather than just a few intellectual aristocrats.

That kind of teaching taxes your ability to make things comprehensible. I got a lot of benefit out of teaching. Probably one of the most enjoyable things I have done in the law.

Ms. SCHWAB: Did questions from the students clarify the issues?

MR. WILLIAMS: Yes, a lot. The selection process got better in the schools, and the student body got better, and it was really challenging. Probably every trial lawyer should have some teaching experience. That and debate.

Ms. SCHWAB: Why is debate helpful to would-be trial attomeys?

MR. WILLIAMS: It teaches you to think on your feet and spontaneous thinking is one of the necessities of trial work. I did debate the last two years at Holy Cross. At that time, debate attracted almost as much interest as intercollegiate sports. Our debating team travelled to colleges in the East and even out West. And 2,000 people would turn out to hear a debate. It was a big thing debating Harvard or Boston College. I mean, it was a big thing, and an excellent foundation for trial practice.

You had to know all sides of an issue, because the side you took depended on the flip of a coin. The same is true in preparing the legal strategy of a case. Developing every possible legal question that might be involved in the case sometimes requires the preparation of perhaps 50 questions of law, though only two of them may arise later in the trial.

It is like preparing a football team. The coach practices defenses against 50 or 60 combinations of plays, and maybe only one is used. When he stops the play cold, everybody says, "What a brilliant defense. What an inspired genius that coach is to have foreseen that they were going to use that offensive weapon against him."

It is not inspired genius at all. It is brains, sweat, and toil. It is going over every single possible play that could be used against him and working out his defense. Then, when one of them comes, he is ready for it.

So it is in preparing for a trial. A lawyer must be prepared for every question of law that might arise against him. He dare not omit one.

I believe that a lawyer should always have the devil's advocate. In my office, the devil's advocate researches each of our cases as we prepare it, persistently finding the holes and forcing us to prepare specifically against each of them. Whenever I go into court, I have completely prepared both sides of the case.

Some trial lawyers do not want to do this. They say, "My opponent is skillful. He will find all the law on his side. I am going to prepare only my side." But I don't like it that way, and I don't think it can be done that way.

I believe a lawyer must prepare both sides so that he will not be surprised by whatever may be hurled at him. After he is prepared in this way, even if his opponent does come up with some detail that may have escaped him, it cannot be so far from the facts already known that it will completely surprise him or put him at a total disadvantage.

This kind of preparation can give you some interesting experiences in a courtroom. Sometimes I wondered at the way my opponent had not prepared his case. It can be worrisome to sit in a courtroom and see justice affected by the lack of industry on the part of an opponent.

Ms. SCHWAB: What about when justice is affected by the type of jury a trial lawyer gets? You seem to establish rapport with a jury easily.

Mr. WILLIAMS: I think I do understand people well, and I can bring that to bear injury selection. I rely on my own instinct, as I have done over the years. I trust that more than some scientific selection process by some psychology major from Bryn Mawr.

Ms. SCHWAB: Ben Bradlee says the things he values most about you are your guts and instincts. But trial lawyers just starting out may not have much instinct. Should they still rely on their instincts, undeveloped as they may be?

MR. WILLIAMS: I think so. You have to feel you are right when you select a jury and have confidence in yourself and not be indecisive. If you make a mistake, don't regret it. Just try not to make it again. That's all.

Juries have to like you. They have to identify with you, enjoy your successes. Grieve with you when you fail. You can't be aloof if you want to sway a jury.

MS. SCHWAB: You're not saying just take the first 12 people who are called?

MR. WILLIAMS: Not at all. I go through a careful voir dire, tailored to the facts of the case. But I have never taken more than one day to get a jury, even in those cases that attracted tremendous public attention. I don't think it's ever necessary to spend more than one day selecting a jury. I watched the Profumo trial at the Old Bailey in London, with Christine Keeler, Mandy Rice Davis, and Stephen Ward. Fleet Street and the rest of the world press in full cry. They picked the jury in half an hour. Remarkable.

MS. SCHWAB: Well, what about four months of jury selection, then?

MR. WILLIAMS: I think it's the worst disgrace in the whole system. When I was teaching at Yale, they were trying the Bobby Seale case in New Haven. From the time I started my course at Yale in September until it finished in January, they were selecting the jury in that case. Everybody says, what kind of justice is this? It's just crazy. The Manson case went the same way. Just madness.

The trial lawyers are just trying to forestall the inevitable. Better to be going through the selection process than getting a guilty verdict. But it makes a travesty of our system. Something can always happen. It's like a train in a railway yard. The train comes down the track, and anything the defense attorney can do to derail the train on the way to the terminal is beneficial to his client.

MS. SCHWAB: Why don't they use all that effort to make a case for the defendant?

MR. WILLIAMS: They should. It's almost an obstruction of justice to take that length of time to select a jury. It's outrageous to try to psychoanalyze jurors, to probe into their most intimate private lives. You're looking for 12 clean test tubes, that's all. With no residue from predilection or publicity. If you can get 12 clean test tubes, that's all you're entitled to. And you can determine that with fairly simple questions. The jurors, after all, are not on trial. Most people are honest. They come to the court, wanting to perform a service, wanting to do well. They grumble a bit. They don't conceal their prejudices. I think, unfortunately, too many people invent prejudices to get off the jury.

MS. SCHWAB: And you have to be able to spot those who are concealing prejudices or who are closed-minded?

MR. WILLIAMS: Well, there are certain elementary things. You don't want a labor leader in an antitrust case. You don't want a business owner in an employee dispute. Or a policeman in a narcotics case. There are some ethnic things you might look for. In my experience, people with a Scandinavian background are very tough jurors. In criminal cases, anyway. Jewish and Irish jurors seem much more compassionate. And, of course, there are all kinds of exceptions to all my general observations about jurors.

Ms. SCHWAB: How do you get jurors to like you?

Mr. WILLIAMS: You know. You can tell whether you're establishing any rapport with a juror. It's like chemistry.

Ms. SCHWAB: Do you strike a juror because your instinct says you'll be talking to a wall?

Mr. WILLIAMS: Well, sometimes you just realize that there is no chance you are going to be able to communicate successfully with a juror. You can tell while asking the questions. But now, you're at the mercy of the judges. A lot of federal judges insist on taking the voir dire. If you don't have any dialogue with the jurors, you can only judge by observation, which is not the best way to do it. You should try to persuade the judge to let you ask at least some questions. I don't like to rely on observation.

Ms. SCHWAB: Would you agree that in complicated cases, there should be special juries, rather than just 12 "peers"?

Mr. WILLIAMS: Well, some factual patterns are so esoteric that it's really expecting too much of a jury of 12 average people to be able to understand. I don't know how juries are educated to understand highly technical cases involving computers and advanced scientific principles. It's very difficult, I agree.

You have to start with the premise that if you cannot explain to a reasonably intelligent person the subject that you have to know for trial, then you really haven't mastered the subject at all. And you won't be able to explain so that a jury will understand. You don't know enough about the case yourself if you can't explain it to a person who knows nothing about it.

First you have to persuade the jurors that they want to know about your theory—your complicated subject. Then you have to explain it so they will understand it and remember it. Even then, they may not believe it.

Ms. SCHWAB: You didn't seem to communicate very well with the Bobby Baker jury, although your closing argument on Baker's behalf was rated "masterful."

Mr. WILLIAMS: That's a good example of how you can't win 'em all. Baker himself has said the defense theory was "too complicated." It was a bitter experience for me; it was well prepared, well tried, but bitter.

Ms. SCHWAB: Baker seemed inclined to blame the intelligence level of the jury—they didn't understand what was going on.

Mr. WILLIAMS: Mike Tigar [a former partner and Williams's assistant at Baker's trial] has a story about that. It's probably apocryphal. He recalls that after a witness had testified about capital gains, the marshal [assigned to care for jurors] reported the next morning that one juror turned to another and said, "Who's that Captain Gains that they were talking about today?" And the other one said, "Oh, he's going to testify tomorrow."

Ms. SCHWAB: How do you keep the jury's attention focused on your case even though the testimony is repetitive or the witness is mumbling or the air conditioning has failed?

MR. WILLIAMS: Obviously, you can't have the jury at fever pitch throughout the trial. Sometimes, it's worth the candle to let a little boredom set in, because you're setting up the testimony you'll use later for a terrific final argument. I'll take half a day of tedium if I'm collecting nuclear weapons to use at the end of the case.

For example, I tried a case some years back involving the Reconstruction Finance Corporation in the Truman administration. A lawyer in Washington was charged with perjury in front of the grand jury investigating the RFC, by denying that he had ever given anything of value to anyone employed at the RFC. Subsequently, it developed that he had given a television set to one of the employees a few years before at Christmas.

His defense was that he had forgotten about it at the time the question was asked and that he had later remembered the incident and had wanted to tell the grand jury, but it had gone out of session.

At the trial, one of the lawyers who had worked on the case as an investigator was on the stand. In cross-examination, I asked him an almost irrelevant question. It was so irrelevant that the opposing lawyer, who was a very able man, did not object because he did not figure it could possibly hurt him. I asked: "Now who were the other lawyers from the Department of Justice who worked with you on this investigation for the grand jury?"

He said, "Mr. Smith. Mr. Brown. Mr. Black. Mr. Blue. And Mr. Johnson."

"Now you worked on this investigation for a whole year, and those are the only lawyers who worked with you?"

"That's all. Those are the ones. There were six of us."

So later in the defense, I called Mr. Smith, and under the guise of simply testing the accuracy of the transcription of some testimony, I asked a couple of questions that appeared meaningless and boring. Then I asked him one even more meaningless and boring. "Who were the other lawyers who worked with you on this?"

And Mr. Smith said, "well, there was Mr. Brown. Mr. Black. Mr. Blue. Mr. Jones,"—then he named the man who had testified earlier—"and Mr. Murphy."

And nobody—of course these questions were buried in a melange of hundreds of pages of testimony—but nobody in that courtroom had any concept of the significance of what had happened. And I did not tell them! I just put it away in the icebox.

In the summing up, I said, "Now here we have the Department of Justice asking that you return a verdict of guilty beyond a reasonable doubt against this man whose reputation to this point has been unsullied. They are unwilling to accord him the benefit of a mistake in recollection, and yet the very lawyers who got the indictment all have mistaken recollections about the very same grand jury that indicted him. All six of them have mistaken recollections about a transaction of one year ago. Yet they are asking you to convict this man whose recollection failed about a matter three years ago."

Well, you know, this was a belly shot. It created a tremendous impact on the jury.

Now if in cross-examination on that first day, I had said, "But you forgot Mr. Jones, didn't you?"

"Oh, yes, I forgot Mr. Jones."

Then, right away, all of them would have gotten together and prepared themselves. From then on, they would all be right, and I would have lost the impression that was rightfully ours and lost its favorable impact on the jury.

Ms. SCHWAB: Speaking of closing arguments, how do you make a two- or three-hour final statement without a note and without histrionics and without juror somnambulance?

Mr. WILLIAMS: I think the first impression you make on the jury is crucial—you start with voir dire, if you have it. Then you make an opening statement. I don't remember ever passing up that opportunity. And whatever you say in your opening statement, you had better be prepared to prove. Make sure you're absolutely right on the law and the facts. Don't expose your flanks to any of the gray areas in opening. Your aim is to present the best first impression of your case and your client as possible. Opening statements serve that purpose, and then the purpose is dissipated. You get to the evidence and the legal maneuvering.

Nothing remains the same from the start of a case to the finish. Everything changes. You have to be amenable to the changes and use them. So what might be effective with one jury would do the opposite with another. You stay with your theme of the case, your factual concepts, so the jury hears it over and over again. The major portion of a good defense is attacking the evidence. A minor portion is stating the affirmative case for your client.

Ms. SCHWAB: And then you bring it all together.

Mr. WILLIAMS: I know what I'm going to say. I know the broad areas I'm going to cover, and I'm used to talking, I've done it all my life. And I can talk. The closing isn't unstructured, a stream-of-consciousness-type thing. I know precisely where I'm going. I've mapped it out before, on paper and in my mind. I know where I'm beginning, how I'm going to build it, and how I'm going to end it. It's better not to use any notes. It's not always possible. If you can avoid using notes, it's more interesting. The jurors watch you and listen to you all the time.

MR. SCHWAB: How do you learn to do it? Just by doing it? The trial-and-error technique?

MR. WILLIAMS: I do believe trial practice is learned only through long and tough experience. There is no substitute. In a trial, a lawyer makes mistakes, and he finds out why and where he made them. He can be told the do's and don'ts. He can read all the books written on trial techniques. But he learns the craft only in actual courtroom combat, not from lectures or observation. You see, I started practicing law with Hogan and Hartson, and at that time, they had the streetcar company in Washington, D.C., as a client. That company had 2,000 cases or so a year, mostly personal injury. I was in court from October through June for five years, just trying case after case. Day after day. And I had an excellent teacher, a superb trial lawyer named Howard Boyd. He tried a case for the El Paso Natural Gas Company, and they offered him the presidency, and he went to Texas to live happily ever after.

Ms. SCHWAB: But there's a palpable distinction between good trial lawyers and not-so-good ones. How do you get to be the former by just learning from your mistakes, the number of which could be legion?

MR. WILLIAMS: You show me a trial lawyer who has never lost a case, and I will show you a trial lawyer who has never tried more than two.

There is a tremendous delusion about the effectiveness of trial counsel. In actual fact, the area of efficacy for a trial lawyer is very narrow. Suppose we take 100 cases, any 100 cases. The best trial lawyer in America might win 60 and lose 40. The most incompetent will win 40 and lose 60. Yet people think that they can go into the office of a great trial lawyer, and he can win the case for them no matter what the facts are, no matter what the merits of the case. It is impossible to win an impossible case. But I'm addicted to contest living. Almost everything I do is in the area of confrontation—in the courtroom or in the stadium. Everything winds up on the scoreboard as a win or a loss. It's probably the most exacting way in the world to live.

Ms. SCHWAB: So what is the measure of success—the mark of greatness?

MR. WILLIAMS: There's no real answer to that. There is only the method. It's like the drunk draped around a lamppost. He asked a man in black tie and tails, who was hurrying by with a cello case: "How do you get to Carnegie Hall?" And the musician replied: "Practice, practice, practice."

How to Try a Jury Case: A Lawyer's View

by Richard "Racehorse" Haynes

Q: Do you try many jury cases?

A: When I started practicing I set out to try one jury case a month, and I've pretty much held to that for the last twenty years. In the last year or two, I've fallen back from that program some. The cases have been getting longer, and I'm not kicking the ball quite as hard.

Q: What are you trying to do when you select a jury?

A: When you get ready to select a jury you need to understand what your case is all about and what the other side's case is all about. If the lawyer has done his homework, he ought to have some idea of what kind of jury he wants for the kind of a result he's looking for. In criminal cases you don't always try to find a jury that's going to resolve the issue of guilt or innocence in favor of the accused, because a lot of times the issue cannot be resolved in any way except against the accused. The facts are that the accused is guilty. Then the question becomes, can they prove it? If that question is answered affirmatively, then the issue is: what is an appropriate punishment? So lawyers make an error when they take a case where the state has got thirty-five 8" x 10" color photos with circles and arrows, a confession, four eyewitnesses including a priest and a Baptist preacher, and then go before the jury and pound on the table and claim the prosecution doesn't have any evidence. You can't pull the wool over the jury's eyes. Period. They know.

The Biased Juror

Q: How do you ferret out the biased juror in voir dire?

Mr. Haynes is a partner in the Dallas firm of Haynes and Boone. This article is based on an interview with Mr. Haynes by William Pannill, a former editor-in-chief of LITIGATION.

A: Most people, if you put them on their honor as human beings, eye to eye, to tell what's in their mind or their heart that's likely to affect their resolution of issues, not on the basis of evidence but on the basis of preconceived notion or bias or prejudice, they'll tell you. But I've noticed lawyers who, when they get the opportunity to start selecting a jury, immediately come up to the rail that separates the lawyer from the prospective jurors and encroach on the juror's territory. You can see the jurors crossing their arms and rejecting the lawyer and see the jurors thinking, "You're not going to make a fool out of me, lawyer, in front of all these people—I know about lawyers. You're trying to trick me into saying something, and I'm not going to." You can watch the resentment build up just by the simple failure to obtain from the prospective jurors permission to come over and talk to them on a one-on-one basis.

Q: How do you gain permission?

A: I talk to them first from the lectern or from way back as part of a group, to let them know what it is that I am about—that there's going to be no sleight of hand, no wizardry, no magic, no rabbits out of the hat, no perry Mason, and if you came here thinking that's what you're going to see, I'll tell you now, you're not going to see that.

Q: Do you just say to them, literally, "I wish you'd open up and tell me if there is anything that would reflect on your fitness to serve?"

A: Almost that way, just dead on. You've got some standard things. It's a gross mistake in a criminal case to accept anyone as a juror in a case who is a reserve police officer of any sort, or a relative of a police officer or any member of the constabulary, and it's a tragic mistake to accept a prison guard. That's ludicrous, but I've seen that happen. A prison guard got a chance to serve on a jury, and the case involved one of Texas's most able lawyers. The lawyer didn't ferret out that facet of the man's background because the question was too narrow, and he lost the case.

I don't like as jurors people who have a job that calls for them to have to say "No" to people who are in need. You take a bank officer—a loan officer—that person has to sit over there in his office, eight hours a day, and folks come before him for help. Their houses are burned; their wives have cancer; their sons have been killed in Vietnam; and they want to borrow $750. But they don't have any collateral, so the bank officer has to say, "No." So he develops a callousness.

Q: What other kinds of people do you strike?

A: Some sorts of engineers and accountants. Not all. But engineers look for mathematical precision in resolving issues. Facts aren't susceptible to resolution with mathematical precision.

Q: What do you ask jurors in general?

1203

A: I like to find out something about where they live. I need to know something about their education. I like to find out what their reading habits are. If you read something more than the paper, it tells me a little something about your intellect, your curiosity. I like to know the kinds of things you read—if you read history, science fiction, best sellers. If you read the *New Yorker,* that lets me know a little something about you.

Q: Do you get many jurors who read the *New Yorker?*

A. I try to.

Q: How do you inquire into a juror's reading habits?

A: They may be the kind of folks who always carry a book with them and are reading all the time. Those are generally not bad prospective jurors.

In state courts where you get an opportunity to go one-on-one, you can just ask: "May I ask you please if you would mind telling me what your reading habits are when you have time for it? Do you subscribe to any magazines? If so, would you mind telling me what they are?" You have to be careful that you don't embarrass a juror who doesn't read anything in front of other prospective jurors. You can tell sometimes because you have folks who will say, "Well, I read the Reader's Digest," because they can think of that.

Lawyers can learn a lot hanging around a barber shop. Watch folks come in, see what they pick up from the magazine rack. Is it going to be sports? Can you guess in advance what they're going to pick up? I sometimes will take magazines to the barber shop so they'll have whole collections of them, just so I can watch. I get my hair cut in different parts of town for that very reason. When I go out in my area of town, it's mostly professional people. They pick up different kinds of magazines than folks in the part of town where I grew up. But you'll find occasionally that people from a blue-collar area will pick up *Fortune* or *Newsweek.*

Intellectually Interested

Q: What does that tell you?

A: They're interested, intellectually, outside the sphere of their activities. And when I spot that, I like to go and strike up a conversation, just to see how they feel.

Q: How does that help you, when you're looking at those twelve people in the box, after you've gotten them all selected?

A: It helps me not to be afraid of people. One of the things that I think lawyers are afraid of, and I've experienced that same fear, is that we will put our foot in our lawyer mouth in front of the jury. And so we comfort ourselves in court in a stereotyped, rigid way—ever on guard, lest we say something under three syllables and reveal that we're not super-intellects. I think juries like to see the lawyers as human beings, who care, who are interested in what they're doing, who are serious about what they're doing. But who may stumble on a word, may malaprop, you know, may put the legal foot in the legal mouth and then come right out and say, "I'm sorry." Because we all make mistakes. I was reading the other day that at one time there were only two-cars in the state of Massachusetts, back at the turn of the century, and they ran into each other.

Q: Do you use intuition developed over the years in selecting a jury?

A: Intuition, plus a lot of concentration, and every kind of observation of people. For example, I try to be there very early so that when the panel itself comes down, they can see me as long as they can and as often as they can in contact with the client. The object of the exercise is to cause the jury to see the client as a human being, not as a subject or a number or a defendant. The jurors will be more inclined to analyze sharply if they're sitting in judgment on a real person. The other part of getting there early is to watch the jurors come in. I can see who limps, who doesn't, who talks to whom, if they're selective in how they pick their seats. I make notes as to whether they deem the occasion solemn enough to wear a necktie and shirt, marking them as potential foremen. That gives you a chance to look for the things they might carry—badges on their lapels, rings of keys on their belt loops, or four or five pencils in the top pocket.

Q: What would a ring of keys on a belt show you?

A: Often the ring of keys is kind of a badge of authority. The guy with the ring of keys is a guy in charge, who supervises other people or who is in charge of property.

Q: Why would anybody carry four or five pencils in their top pocket?

A: Lawyers do. I carry two pens, one a ballpoint and one a fountain pen; one's for signing my name on official documents, the other one's for taking notes. Part of my job is to take notes—it's part of the tools that I use. Now suppose you've got a juror whose job does not call for him to have his tools, pencils, in the top pocket? Question: has he brought those pencils to court with him specially for that day? Does he wear those pencils all the time? Does he have one of those little plastic things that protect your top pocket from wear and tear from the pencils? That could indicate that he carries them all the time. I'm trying to figure why. Does he work crossword puzzles? Does he fancy himself a lawyer? Has he come equipped to render service as a juror with all the tools that he has in the house? Pencil, pad, books on the law? It is not unusual to see prospective jurors reading books that relate to lawsuits.

1205

Twelve Angry Men

Q. Would you strike that juror?

A: He may be interested in the system. I really believe that most people believe in their own minds and their own hearts that they could be lawyers—trial lawyers. You gather many responses from people who say, "I took a half-year of law at New Mexico Body and Fender." Everybody at one time fancies that he or she could be a trial lawyer.

Did you see Henry Fonda in *Twelve Angry Men*? For several months after that movie is on TV each jury will have somebody on the panel or on the jury who saw the movie on the late show. They become Henry Fondas. You couldn't get a better juror. So, the guy with the multiple pencils in his pocket, is he Henry Fonda? Is he the type of fellow who's going to relate to authority, who's going to accept the prosecutorial role?

Q: Do the jurors really vote on the lawyers and not on the clients?

A: Well, I've heard that. I know that there have been cases when they voted against the lawyer and adversely affected the client. I'm not too sure that they would vote in favor of the lawyer. In a close case, it could make a difference. I know some good lawyers think it's appropriate to be abrasive in court. This was more prevalent during the unrest of the 1960s. But to me, that's counterproductive. So I've always thought that the best way to handle that was to be courteous to the court, to the jury, to counsel—a gentleman and a protector so that you can't be faulted. It's hard to get down on a guy who's a good straight shooter like that in court.

Q: What about your personal appearance or dress?

A: I try to dress appropriately. I'm not going to go there in bermuda shorts. I've got to let the jury know that I think it's a solemn occasion. So I suppose I wear a uniform.

Q: Is there a particular uniform that you pick?

A: I like the dark blues and grays and the pinstripes, the solemn colors. Those who think about it argue that the prosecutors ought to wear the dark blues and the pin stripes and the grays, and counsel for the accused ought to be wearing the earth tones, but I disagree with that. My courtroom suits are all pretty much the same—in fact I must have a dozen or so and you can hardly tell them apart. Those who argue in favor of the earth tones, the browns, the tans, say that those colors will cause the jury to see you as one of the fellows. I disagree. When I'm in the courtroom, I want the jury to know that I am as much an officer of that court as the prosecutor is. It's not his court; it's not my court—it's the jury's court and the litigants' court. I'm simply an officer of that court, and I want to be as official-looking in my dress as I can.

Q: Is there anything particular that you tell clients to wear?

A: Oh, I try. If they are accused of being a big-time cocaine dealer, I don't want them to come in there looking like they were just sent down from central casting as a bigtime cocaine dealer. I want them dressed for the occasion. It's like a funeral; it's like a wedding; it's like church.

Q: Do you remember any specific juries?

A: I've heard lawyers say that one of the best things that can happen to a trial lawyer is to have a juror wink at him. What's even better than that is to have the jury applaud. When I concluded a cross-examination one time, it was one of those lucky things where the witness was high and dry. He'd been very neatly boxed and trapped and caught on the line, and he had to admit that lie. When I said, "No further questions," the jury applauded. Of course, that jury was not out very long before they returned a verdict of not guilty.

One time I was arguing in federal court, and I had my hand on the rail and was arguing on the basis of some charts. I felt a hand pat me on the forearm. It was a juror. I obviously didn't want to offend the juror, who thought enough of what I was saying at that point to be reassuring to me. Those jurors I remember.

I have people come up to me all the time and say, "I served on your jury, I was on your panel."

Q: Do you develop a feeling for your former jurors?

A: Yes, sure you do. These people have worked with you and lived with you. You have a feeling for them. One of the things I work on, right from the beginning, is learning who they are and what they are. Their marriage, their religious preference, where they work, the kind of work, how many kids they have, how old they are, you know, all the things that you get from voir dire examination. I put all that information into a chart on the first page of my trial book, so that I'm watching them in the box while the prosecution is putting on its case. I'm thinking about them as individuals, as people, so at the conclusion of the trial, I kind of know them.

Q: Do you analyze the jury as a group—as well as the individuals?

A: Sure. One of the things that always concerns a trial lawyer is whether the jury will take the same seats. Juries traditionally take the same seats, day after day. When we decide on a seat, that's our seat on the jury. And it's always interesting when you find a jury that doesn't take the same seats. You begin to wonder. Then the question is, how long will it be in terms of this trial before they take a regular seat and stay there? It's very few juries, but I can recall some that never took the same seats at all.

Q: What does that tell you?

A: That this is an independent jury.

Q: Do you think it really makes a difference how you present yourself to the jury?

A: Oh, there is no question about it. I think it's true, not just from my own personal experience, but from talking to lawyers and from talking to jurors. When I get an opportunity after a case that some other lawyer has tried, if I find any citizen who tells me he served on a jury, at parties, at social events, or church, or wherever, I ask: "How about the lawyers, what'd you think, what did they do right, what did they do wrong—did they do what you expected?"

I remember one time we had two crackerjack lawyers who prosecuted against us. Both of them wore crew cuts, and they were good-sized guys. I had read an article years before that the tobacco industry spent a lot of money wondering why cigar sales were so poor. They found that people equated the fat cigar with the crooked politician, the gambler, the Mafia, the hood, and the B-movie villain. In addition to finding about the fat cigars, they also found out that when females go to the store to buy a pipe for their boyfriends, they always buy a curved pipe. When the male goes, he buys a straight pipe, but a curved pipe reminds women of a kindly old professor, the old philosopher, old granddad, solidarity, understanding, that kind of thing.

So in cases where the court permits smoking in the courtroom, Haynes has the curved pipe. For those two fellows who prosecuted cases against me, I would go to the counter in the morning and I would buy fat cigars and I would give them to those two guys. And they would sit in the courtroom, smoking Al Capone cigars and prosecuting my client, represented by a kindly old professor with a curved pipe. They never won and I never told them.

Now, whether or not that had impact on the jury by itself, I don't know. But I talked to the jurors afterwards, and they just didn't like those prosecutors. They were mean, they were overbearing, they overreached their office, they weren't being fair. They were really not all that way. They were vigorous, they were big and beefy and aggressive, but with that added dimension of a fat cigar, they looked villainous. As a consequence, they lost. Over and over.

Second Nature

Q. Isn't this all second nature to you now?

A: No. I think you make a mistake trying a lawsuit or flying an airplane if you don't have a checklist. No matter how many times you have done it, if you don't have a checklist, you might not put the flaps down, you might land too hot, or you might be distracted and omit something.

When I go to the courthouse to try a case, I have a Xerox in the file of the statutory provision. I have the cases copied and in my file. I've got a checklist of the things I want to cover with the prospective jurors. I've got a checklist of the things I want to develop from the witnesses who will be called by the prosecution against me; I've got a list of what I want to develop on cross that I think hurts their case as opposed to helping my case. I've got a plan that I've already worked out that is the way I think the prosecution will call its case and the take-offs on that game plan that they might use so that I can be prepared. When they call witness Jones, I've got the information I need to have before me about witness Jones there and I've already looked at it and I'm thinking about what I want to do.

I'm a firm believer in the checklist and I think that is true even if you have tried cases to juries, as I have, several hundred times. I don't want to rely on my ability to remember all the things I need to know, because if I inadvertently leave out one thing, that could be the nail that cost me the horse, that cost me the battle, that cost me the war, and I don't need that.

Q: When you stand up to communicate with this jury that you speak about so much, what do you do? Is it like being an actor? Is it Laurence Olivier or Henry Fonda addressing this jury?

A: I think every lawyer takes from the other lawyers that he meets, associates with, watches, tries cases against—the things that you admire. We have a mental picture of the lawyer we would like to be. What I have concluded is this: You have to be yourself as much as you can. I admit that of the lawyers I have seen and admired— the real lawyers—I have incorporated into my program things that they do and the ways they do them. I learn from watching other lawyers, and if I get a day over in the courtroom where I'm waiting to go to trial and there is some lawyer putting on his case, I go watch him, because I take from that lawyer. By watching that lawyer, I see how I would do it. You don't get to see yourself that much, although we use videotape. I'll get up and do a blither into the videotape. And then I'll play it back and look at it. Is that the best I can do? Am I communicating with my body, verbally, intellectually? Am I really communicating? And I go back and do it again, and then do it again.

I have a tape recorder in my car and I'll grab the thing and make an argument in the car and then play it back. Wow, it's terrible, and I'll do it again.

I've concluded that I can't be Percy Foreman or Edward Bennett Williams. I'm me. I may have some of the things that all these people do in my program, but I've got to recognize when the jury might perceive that that's not me. They've got to see the real guy there. The real lawyer doing it. They've got to see him.

1209

Q: But why do they have to see him?

A: It gives you more credibility. If the jury perceives that you are being artificial or acting, then how can what you say have credibility. They might as well go to a movie. This is not a movie; this is real. We are here with real people—a real cause. What you do is real.

Q: Whenever I read about these immensely long cases, I wonder how the jury pays attention? How can the jury possibly decide with that mass of material before them?

A: I think we've been guilty of underestimating the intelligence of the jury. Properly selected, those twelve people really possess a cumulative I.Q. of 1200 or more with greater recall than a computer and more ability than a computer. So it falls back to the lawyer—the lawyer on both sides—to keep the jury's attention focused on issues.

PARALLEL TABLE

The articles in this book were originally published in the following issues of LITIGATION:

1. Initiating Suit

2. Discovery

3. Depositions

8. Evidence Issues

9. Appeal

10. Settlement

11. Special Problems of the Criminal Case

12. Special Problems in Civil Litigation

Epilogue